CUBA IN TRANSITION

Volume 8

Papers and Proceedings of the

Eighth Annual Meeting
of the
Association for the Study of the Cuban Economy (ASCE)

Miami, Florida
August 6-8, 1998

(ISBN 0-9649082-7-1)

Cuba in Transition volumes may be ordered from:

Association for the Study of the Cuban Economy
José F. Alonso—ASCE Books
2000 Osborn Drive
Silver Spring, MD 20910-1319
Tel. 301/587-1664
Fax 301/587-1664
E-mail: jalonso@erols.com

PREFACE

The papers published as part of the proceedings of ASCE's Eighth Annual Meeting are a testimony to the commitment of its members to the serious study of the Cuban economy and society. The papers cover a wide area of topics including the implications of the economic and political experiences of Latin America for Cuba; the role of enterprises in the second economy of Cuba; an analysis of the recent CEPAL report on the Cuban economy; macroeconomic and transition issues; issues on specific sectors such tourism, agriculture and the external sector in general; social and economic indicators; the environment; investment topics; legal issues; an analysis of the effects of the U.S. embargo on health and nutrition in Cuba; and the culture of the opposition. The papers generated lively discussions when they were presented at the meeting but always in an environment of openness and respect for the opinions of others, something that is badly needed on discussions regarding Cuba. ASCE members can only hope that in a not-too-distant future, this type of meetings can be held on Cuban soil in an atmosphere that permits the free discussion of ideas.

This volume of the proceedings of the Eighth Annual Meetings is dedicated to Dr. José D. Acosta, a member of the Board of Directors of ASCE, who passed away in November 1998 in Miami, in recognition of the valuable contributions he made to ASCE. Acosta (our dear Pepucho) had a Doctorate of Law from the Universidad de la Habana and pursued graduate studies in economics at the Universidad de Villanueva (in La Habana) and the George Washington University (Washington). He had a distinguished career at the Organization of American States (OAS), where he was both a tax policy economist and a legal advisor. He retired from the OAS in 1989 after serving as Director of the Department of General Legal Services of the Secretariat of Legal Affairs. In ASCE, Pepucho was an active participant in the annual meeting and in the sessions of the Board of Directors. He played a key role in the development of the new by-laws of the association in 1997.

On behalf of the Board of Directors of ASCE, I want to take this opportunity to thank our past president, Jorge Pérez-López, and José Alonso for all the work that they have put into preparing this publication. ASCE also wants to express its gratitude to the co-sponsors of the Eighth Annual Meeting, the Business School and the School of International Studies of the University of Miami, and to several other corporate sponsors who contributed financially to the meeting.

Lorenzo L. Pérez
ASCE President

TABLE OF CONTENTS

ASSOCIATION FOR THE STUDY
OF THE CUBAN ECONOMY (ASCE)

Eighth Annual Meeting
Biltmore Hotel, Coral Gables, Florida
August 6-8, 1998

Conference Program

Panel Discussion: The Current Situation

Carmelo Mesa-Lago, University of Pittsburgh

Marifeli Pérez-Stable, SUNY at Old Westbury

Grupo de Trabajo de la Disidencia Interna para el Estudio de la Situación Socio-Económica Cubana (La Habana), read by Ricardo Puerta

Frank Calzón, Center for a Free Cuba

Implications for Cuba of Latin American Economic and Political Experiences

Perspectives from Latin American Economic Developments and Implications from Cuba

> Claudio Loser, International Monetary Fund

Discussant: Jorge Sanguinetty, DevTech Systems

Cuba: The Latin American Political Context

> Mauricio Font, Queens College

Discussant: Alfred Cuzán, University of West Florida

Tourism

Back to the Future: Cuban Tourism in the Year 2007

> Nicolás Crespo, Cuban Society of Tourism Professionals

Cuba's Tourist Industry: Sol Meliá and Varadero as Case Studies

> Félix Godínez, Case Western Reserve University

Promoting Place Through Architectural Heritage: Restoration and Preservation
of Twentieth Century Architectural Design in Miramar

> Artimus Keiffer and Sarah K. Wagner, Indiana University Purdue University at Indianapolis

Discussants: María Dolores Espino, Economatrix, Inc., and Evaldo Cabarrouy, University of Puerto Rico

Legal Issues

The Rush to Register: U.S.-Cuba Intellectual Property Rights and Foreign Policy

> Pamela Falk, City University of New York School of Law

Discussant: Steven Escobar, U.S. Department of Commerce

Investment

Panel Discussion: A Critical Analysis of the Effects of the U.S. Embargo on Health and Nutrition in Cuba

Social and Economic Indicators

Culture of Opposition in Cuba I

Macroeconomics

Ernesto Hernández-Catá, International Monetary Fund

Discussant: Manuel Lasaga, StratInfo

La crisis del peso mexicano y lecciones para Cuba

Roberto Orro, Universidad de Guanajuato

Discussant: Armando Linde, International Monetary Fund

Culture of Opposition in Cuba II

Lecciones de la paz en Centroamérica: Un intento de aplicación a Cuba

Nelson Amaro, Universidad del Valle de Guatemala

Public Opinion Dynamics and Building a Civil Society

Ernesto Betancourt, International Development and Finance

Political Culture and Democracy in Cuba: Comparative Reflections

Mauricio Solaún, University of Illinois

Political Disaffection: Cuba's Revolution and Exodus

Silvia Pedraza, University of Michigan

Discussant: Benigno Aguirre, Texas A&M University

External Sector

Are There Interrelated Implications for Agriculture of Cuba's Efforts to Integrate into the Global Economy and Trends Toward Expanded Caribbean Integration

William Messina, University of Florida

Discussant: Antonio Gayoso, World Council of Credit Unions

The Cuban Economic Crisis of the 1990s and the External Sector

Jorge Pérez-López, U.S. Department of Labor

Discussant: Eric Baklanoff, University of Alabama

The Cuban Cigar Industry and the International Cigar Market

Joseph Perry, Louis A. Woods and Stephen Shapiro, University of North Florida

Discussant: José Alvarez, University of Florida

Agriculture and Technological Change

Experiencias agriclimatológicas de República Dominicana y el Caribe adaptables a Cuba

Hipólito Mejía, Agrocentro, C. por A.

Discussant: Raúl Fernández, Inter-American Development Bank—Retired

El sector agropecuario cubano bajo el capitalismo de estado

Manuel Sánchez Herrero and Arnaldo Ramos Lauzurique, Grupo de Trabajo de la Disidencia Interna, La Habana (read by Ricardo Puerta)

Discussant: Antonio Gayoso, World Council of Credit Unions

Overinvestment and Technological Change in Cuba

Manuel Madrid-Aris, University of Southern California

Discussant: Luis Locay, University of Miami

Panel Discussion: Pope John Paul II's Visit to Cuba

La visita del Papa a Cuba: Reunión y Reconciliación

Silvia Pedraza, University of Michigan

Lo que fue y no fue: La visita del Papa a Cuba

José Manuel Hernández, Georgetown University—Emeritus

Impressions from the Pope's Visit to Cuba

María C. Werlau, Orbis International

Transition Issues

Panel Discussion: Opposition in Cuba—Current Realities and Alternatives

THE CUBAN ECONOMY IN 1997-98: PERFORMANCE AND POLICIES

Carmelo Mesa-Lago

The timid, oscillating and tightly-regulated market-oriented reform has been halted since March 1996, when Raúl Castro strongly criticized the negative effects of the reform, followed by the purge of some academic reformists. That halt was ratified by the Economic Resolution approved by the Fifth Communist Party Congress held in October 1997. Rather than turning back the reform (an unfeasible option) or moving ahead (as the purged reformists recommended), the Party maintained the status quo, because a further opening of the economy and expansion of the non-state sector could have threaten the regime's control. Political logic, therefore, prevailed over economic logic, i.e., the limited but positive effects of the reform. This paper analyzes performance in 1997 and preliminarily until mid-1998, as well as policies (and targets) set by the Economic Resolution of the Party Congress and Castro's speech at the National Assembly held in July 1998.

ECONOMIC PERFORMANCE

Table 1 summarizes Cuba's major economic and social indicators, as reported by key government institutions and the U.N. Economic Commission for Latin America and the Caribbean (ECLAC) based on official data. The series start in 1989, the year before the crisis began, show their worst point in 1993, and sluggish recovery in 1994-97. A few targets are shown for 1998, and a comparison of performance in 1997 versus 1989 is presented in the last column. All these indicators are scrutinized below (for a more detailed analysis of the 1989-96 period see Mesa-Lago 1998; for 1996-97 see Pérez-López 1997).

Domestic Macroeconomic Indicators

Policies prior to the halt of the reform, although modest and with reversals, in general produced fair economic results, but there has been a significant slowdown since 1997. The GDP growth target for that year was initially set at 4% to 5% but actually was 2.5% (2% per capita); official reasons given for the poor performance were: the failure of the sugar harvest planned to be 5 million tons but that actually reached only 4.2 million tons; restrictions on external credit due to the Helms-Burton Act; paralysis/delays in two-thirds of the supply of inputs for the sugar harvest; the heavy burden of debt service; the hurricane of 1996 that caused an estimated loss of US$800 million; bad weather in the winter of 1996-97; and pests in 1997 that harmed agriculture. The annual average GDP per capita growth rate in 1995-97 was 3.6%; even at that rate, it would take 15 years to recover the GDP per capita level that Cuba had in 1985, which was a meager one to begin with.

The GDP growth target initially set for 1998 was from 2.5% to 3% but, in May of that year, the lower figure was projected. The main reason for the downgrading was, again, the failure of the sugar harvest, originally set at 4.5 million tons but with actual output officially reported to be "less than 3.3 million tons" (unofficial estimates range from 2.8 to 3.2 million tons, the latter conservative figure has been selected for Tables 1 and 2). Lage ("Palabras..." 1997) claimed that the planned growth rate for 1998 still will be achieved through increases in the nickel and tourism industries, but world prices of nickel de-

Table 1.   Selected Economic Indicators for Cuba: 1989-1998

Indicators	1989	1993	1994	1995	1996	1997	1998 (targets)	1997/1989 (%)
A. Macroeconomic (%)								
GDP growth absolute rate[a]	1.2	-14.8	0.7	2.5	7.8	2.5	2.5[j]	
GDP growth per capita rate[a]	0.2	-15.1	0.0	1.9	7.1	1.9	2.0[j]	
Gross domestic investment/GDP[a]	26.7	5.4	5.7	8.8	9.0	9.4		-74
Inflation rate[b]	n.a.	19.7	25.7	11.2	0.5	2.9		-85
Monetary liquidity/GDP[c]	21.6	73.2	51.8	42.6	40.6	39.7		+84
Fiscal balance/GDP[c]	-7.2	-33.5	-7.4	-3.5	-2.4	-3.1[g]	-3.0[j]	-58
B. External (billion US $)								
Exports (goods)	5.4	1.1	1.3	1.5	1.8	1.9	2.1	-65
Imports (goods)	8.1	2.0	2.1	2.8	3.6	4.3	4.5	-47
Trade balance (goods)	-2.7	-0.9	-0.8	-1.3	-1.6	-2.4	-2.5	-11
Terms of trade (1989=100)	100.0	57.5	79.7	70.5	61.0	60.0		-40
External debt (hard currency)	6.2	8.8	9.1	10.5	10.5	10.5		+69
Foreign investment	n.a.	n.a.	n.a.	2.1	n.a.	n.a.	2.2[j]	
Exchange rate (pesos per 1 US$)[d]	7	78	95	32	19	23		+228
Tourism gross revenue (millions)[e]	168	720	850	1,100	1,380	1,500	1,830	+793
Tourism net revenue (millions)[e]	101	240	280	363	455	495		+390
C. Physical output (thousand metric tons)								
Sugar	8,121	4,280	4,000	3,300	4,450	4,252	3,200[k]	-48
Nickel	47	30	27	43	54	62		+32
Citrus	1,016	644	505	564	662	808		-20
Fish catch	192	94	94	106	120	137	149	-29
Cigars	308	208	n.a.	181	189	n.a.		-39
Oil	718	1,107	1,299	1,471	1,500[h]	1,500[h]		+100
Electricity (billions Kwh)	16	11	12	12	13	14	14	-12
Cement	3,759	1,061	1,067	1,400	1,485	1,700		-55
Rice	532	177	226	223	239	325		-39
Milk	1,131	585	622	608	640	571		-50
Eggs	2,673	1,512	1,561	1,415	1,282	1,460		-45
Employed (thousands)	4,356	4,313	4,195	4,131	4,106	4,183		-4
Open Unemployment (% EAP)	7.9	6.2	6.7	7.9	7.6[i]	6.9[i]		-13
Real Wages (1989=100)	100.0	81.8	63.4	58.5	61.2	n.a.		-39
Infant mortality (per 1000)	11.1	9.4	9.9	9.4	9.0	7.2		-35
University enrollment (thousands)	242	166	141	122	112	n.a.		-54

[a] Constant 1981 prices. [b] GDP deflator. [c] Based on current prices. [d] Unoffical rate, annual average. [e] Gross revenue includes costs of inputs; net revenue deducts costs of inputs (author's estimate). [f] Author's estimate based on ECLAC wages, and inflation rates based on Mesa-Lago 1998. [g] Ministerio 1998; ECLAC 1998 gives -2%. [h] Rounded. [i] ECLAC 1997 gives 6.8% for 1996 but ECLAC 1998 raises it to 7.6% and gives 6.9% for 1997. [j] The official target is from 2.5% to 3.5% (2% to 3% per capita); ECLAC 1998 shows a projected GDP growth rate of 0.7% in current prices (Table 27). [k] Actual output; estimates range from 3 to "less than 3.3" million. [l] Actual figure released by Osvaldo Martínez, Director del CIEM, EFE, Havana, May 17, 1998.

Source: BNC 1995, 1996; ECLAC 1997, 1998; Mesa-Lago 1998; Ministerio de Economía y Planificación 1998.

clined in 1998 and tourism faces high costs of imported inputs (as Cuba has been unable to produce them domestically). The projected value of sugar and nickel exports, as well as revenue from tourism (*gross* or including costs of imported inputs, and *net* excluding them) for 1997-98 are exhibited in Table 2: if the gross tourist revenue for 1998 is chosen, its combined value with nickel exports is $148 million less than in 1997, while if the net revenue is used, the result is $248 million less; these estimates rebut Lage's assertion. ECLAC's (1998) report on the Cuban

economy for 1997 shows (bottom of Table 27, p. 41) the GDP in current prices for that year (23,500 million pesos) and the projected figure for 1998 (23,667 million pesos), for a growth rate of 0.7% (0.2% per capita); these and other data to be analyzed latter suggest that GDP per capita will either stagnate or have a low growth rate in 1998.

Gross domestic investment as a percentage of GDP shrunk from 26.3% to 5.4% in 1989-93, but rose since 1995, reaching 9.4% in 1997, still 74% below

Table 2. Estimates of the Dollar Value of Cuban Sugar and Nickel Exports and Tourism Revenue: 1997-1998

Revenue	1997	1998
Sugar		
Output (thousand tons)	4,252	3,280[d]
Exports (thousand tons)[a]	3,552	2,630
World Market price (U.S. cents/pound)[b]	11.16	10.70
Revenue (million US $)	853	620
Nickel		
Output (thousand tons)	61.5	64.0[e]
Exports (thousand tons)[a]	61.0	63.0
World Market price (U.S. cents/pound)[b]	314.3	264.7
Revenue (million US $)	423	368
Tourism (million U.S. $)		
Gross revenue	1,500	1,650[f]
Net revenue [c]	495	545
Sub-totals (million US $)		
1. Sugar	873	630
2. Nickel and tourism (gross)	1,923	2,018
3. Nickel and tourism (net)	918	913
Totals (millions U.S. $)		
1 + 2	2,796	2,648
1 + 3	1,791	1,543
Difference 1998 over 1997 (million U.S. $)		
1 + 2		-148
1 + 3		-248

[a]Based on previous years' ratio of exports/output. [b]Annual average in 1997, January-June average in 1998. [c]Based on ratio net/gross in 1990-96. [d]High estimate; others are as low as 3 million tons. [e]Author's projection based on installed capacity. [f]Author's projection based on 1996-97 growth.

Source: 1997 sugar and nickel output and tourism revenue from Table 1; 1998 are author's estimates. World Market price 1997 from World Bank, *Pink Sheet* 1998, and 1998 from *Wall Street Journal,* January-June 1998.

the 1989 level. Lage ("Palabras..." 1997) told the V Party Congress that investment had been "almost totally interrupted" before, but had "begun again" in 1997, and the Economic Resolution stated that new investment projects should not be started unless a previous feasibility study is done.

The inflation rate decreased from a peak of 25.7% in 1994 to reportedly 0.5% in 1996 (a questionable figure) but increased to 2.9% in 1997. The monetary liquidity was reduced from 11 to 9.2 billion pesos in 1994-95 (from 73.2% to 40.6% of GDP), but increased again in 1996 (to 9.5 billion pesos) and decreased in 1997 (9.3 billion pesos and 39.4% of GDP), still twice the 1989 level (an intriguing question is how come there was virtually no inflation in 1996 when the monetary liquidity rose). The fiscal deficit was cut from 33.5% to 2.4% in 1993-96; there are contradictory figures for 1997: 3.1% according to the Ministerio de Economía (1998) but 2% based on ECLAC (1998).

External Sector

After its dramatic decline of 79% in 1989-93, the value of exports increased by 73% in 1993-97 (still 65% below the 1989 level); imports dropped 75% and rose 105%, respectively (still 47% under the 1989 level). As imports expanded faster than exports (mainly due to the decline in sugar output and exports), the trade deficit per capita jumped three-fold in 1993-97 and became close to that of 1989. There was a significant steady deterioration in the terms of trade in 1989-97 (-40 percentage points) as the world prices of sugar and nickel dwindled. The world price of oil also fell, helping to reduce the share of oil in total imports from 35.4% to 26.4% in 1994-97. Export concentration on sugar decreased from 72.7% to 51.4% of total export value in 1993-96, mainly a result of the fall in sugar export volume and value, and yet although all other export shares increased, their actual value shrunk (ECLAC 1998; Mesa-Lago 1998). In 1998, Cuba was granted observer status in the Lomé Agreement and moved towards admission into CARICOM, a more political than economic triumph as Cuba has little to export to countries in both regional groups.

The hard-currency external debt jumped from $6.2 to $10.5 billion in 1989-95 and has been stagnant since then; as of August of 1998 there has not been an agreement with the Club of Paris on that debt, the cause for Cuba not receiving new loans. (The debt with Russia has significantly decreased in dollar terms but Cuba has neither paid any part of it nor reached an agreement on the sum to be repaid, an irritant in trade relations between the two countries.) Access to external credit is extremely limited: new one-year loans from foreign banks were received in 1996-97 to finance the sugar harvests of 1997 and 1998 (from $200 to 300 million each year), but the cost was quite high (14% to 16% interest), and the net gain was lower that the amount of the loan and interest because of low sugar production. Lage and the Resolution acknowledged the financial difficulties caused by the crop failure of 1997 including less foreign credit available for 1998.

Cumulative foreign investment since 1990 was officially reported at $2.1 billion in 1995 and $2.2 billion in August 1998, almost stagnant over three years. Furthermore it appears that only one-third of it has been disbursed.

Gross revenue from tourism steadily rose from 168 million pesos in 1989 to 1.5 billion pesos in 1997 (about eight-fold); but the net revenue was about one-third of the gross, due to the high cost of inputs, and rose from 101 to 495 million pesos in the same period (about four-fold). Although occupancy of the growing number of tourist rooms has been climbing since 1993 (44%), it was only 57% in 1997 (ECLAC 1998), raising the question of how the added rooms will be filled. My estimate of all Cuban hard currency earnings in 1997 (combining exports, tourist net revenue, foreign investment or aid, and external remittances) shows it was 70% less than in 1989.

The exchange rate of pesos to one U.S. dollar in the black market deteriorated from 78 to 95 in 1993-94, steadily appreciated to 19 in 1996, and deteriorated again to 23 in 1997 (state exchange houses established in 1995 pay about one peso less than the black market).

Physical Output

Except for nickel, production for export was significantly lower in 1997 than in 1989. We have referred already to the poor performance of the sugar sector: output in 1993-97 averaged one-half of the 1982-89 average. Citrus production sharply decreased in 1989-93 and increased in 1994-97, but was still 20% below the 1989 level; similar trends occurred in fish catch and cigars: their output in 1996-97 being 29% and 39% below 1989, respectively. Nickel production decreased 43% in 1989-94 but, with the help of Canadian investment, surpassed the previous peak in 1996 and kept climbing in 1997 (output level that year was 32% above 1989). Canadian investment, however, has focused on the former U.S. plants, not in the new plants built with CMEA aid (Punta Gor-

da and the not completed one in Las Camariocas) due to their obsolete technology. Hence, there are questions about increases in output in the near future absent significant new investment and technology transfer.

Oil extraction reached almost one million tons in 1986, declined by 44% in 1987-91, and steadily rose in 1992-95 to reach 1.5 million tons (a 109% jump over 1989 but 60% over 1986); extraction was virtually stagnant in 1996-97 and the contribution of domestic output to total supply shrank from 20% to 17.8% in 1995-97 (while oil imports increased). Manufacturing output generally decreased in 1989-93 and rose thereafter but in 1997 was still below the 1989 level, e.g., lower by 55% for cement and 12% for electricity (in per capita terms the gap was bigger).

The 1998 sugar harvest has been the lowest under the Revolution and in the last 55 years: production in 1943 was 2.8 million tons and in 1998 about 3.2 million tons; in per capita terms, the former (0.60 tons) was more than twice the latter (0.29).

The non-sugar agricultural sector has had a poor performance and its recovery has been sluggish and unsteady, thus in 1997 output was well below the 1989 level, e.g, -50% in milk, -45% in eggs, -39% in rice (the same trend was observed in the output of fruits-other-than-citrus, tubers, green vegetables, poultry, beef and pork). The number of heads of cattle and the production of beans were stagnant. The only crops that in 1997 reportedly had a higher output than in 1989 were corn and plantains (ECLAC 1998). The major problem in the whole agricultural sector is the inefficiency of the new cooperatives created in 1994 (UBPCs), which are highly dependent on the state which in practice directs production and buys virtually all of it at prices set below the market price, hence, creating severe disincentives. As a result, in 1997, the UBPCs' share of cultivated land was 57.6% but their share of total sales in the free agricultural markets was 3.6%; conversely the private sector's shares were respectively 16.9% and 72.7%, while the state farms' shares were 25.5% and 23.7%. Furthermore, total cultivated agricultural land decreased by 15% in 1990-96. UBPCs' yields in the

1998 harvest sank, which forced an increase in state subsidies (ECLAC 1998).

Social Indicators

According to ECLAC (1998) figures, the open unemployment rate decreased from 7.9% in 1989 to 6.2% in 1993, then rose to 7.9% in 1995, but fell to 7.6% in 1996 and 6.9% in 1997; this trend contradicts that of the employed labor force which steadily declined in 1989-96 with a small increase in 1997. In this year, the employed labor force was 4% below that of 1989 but the open unemployment rate was one percentage point lower. ECLAC (1997) has also estimated that the "equivalent unemployment rate" (open unemployment and displaced workers receiving unemployment compensation) peaked at 35.2% in 1993 but decreased to 27% in 1996 (no estimates are available for 1997). The cost of unemployment compensation of surplus workers is a heavy fiscal burden, and led to the announcement of the dismissal of 500,000 to 800,000 unneeded workers in the state sector in 1995. Three years later such dismissals have not taken place, due to the lack of jobs in the private sector, in turn caused by the government's resistance to allow its expansion. The increase in the cost of licenses (300%) and fees (650%) imposed on the self-employed in 1996 led to a drop of 18.5% in the number legally registered at the end of that year: from 208,500 to 170,000, although there was an increase to 175,267 towards the end of 1997 (ECLAC 1997, 1998). Urban mean real wages (based on 1989 levels) steadily shrank to 58.5% in 1996 and slightly rose to 61.2% in 1997, 38.8 percentage points below the year base. The cost of social security (basically pensions) rose again in 1997 and took 7.1% of GDP.

The infant mortality rate reportedly decreased from 11.1 (per 1,000 born alive) in 1989 to 9 in 1996 (with an increase to 9.9 in 1994) but fell dramatically to 7.2 in 1997, almost two percentage points in one year (Ministerio 1998, reproduced by ECLAC 1998); this rapid drop in infant mortality is unusual, particularly in a country as Cuba with already such a low rate, and the 1997 figure is seriously questioned also in view of the overall deterioration in health standards.

University enrollment dropped by one-half in 1989-96 due to the lack of incentives for university graduates, who are unable to find jobs in the state sector and prohibited from practicing their professions as self-employed.

I have estimated that, in 1995, the ratio of extreme income inequality was 800:1 *vis-a-vis* 4.5:1 in 1987 (Mesa-Lago 1998), while figures released by Castro (1998) suggest a ratio of 143:1 between the salary of a teacher and the income of a restaurant operator. Rationing has been extended to all consumer goods but ceased to be a significant equalizer because the monthly rations cover less than two weeks of the minimum food requirements; the rest has to be bought in state dollar shops or the agricultural and black markets, at very high prices affordable only to those who earn or receive hard currency from abroad.

ECONOMIC POLICIES

The V Party Economic Resolution and the 1998 National Assembly

The V Party Congress took place in October 1997 but its Economic Resolution was not published until February 1998 ("Resolución..." 1998). It maintained and strengthened the current system, neither endorsing new reforms nor setting a date for the implementation of those pending. According to the Resolution, the reforms are geared to maintaining the predominance of state property, which shall continue to be an intrinsic element of the socialist system, and its efficiency increased above other property forms such as cooperative and private. The transition from "excessively centralized planning" to another form (not defined, but based on financial balances) is still in process, but planning will continue to play a fundamental role and the state will keep the direction of the economy. Although some space has been opened to the market, the latter will be kept under strict state control and regulation, and the government will correct any distortions created by it and impede unjustifiable profits. Enterprises managed by the armed forces shall be extended to other economic branches, and state enterprises should be profitable, except in cases of national or social interest, when they will be subsidized.

The majority of UBPCs suffer from inefficiency and must correct their problems and increase output, but within the current system. The partial reform of the banking system approved in May 1997 (it relegated Cuba's National Bank to commercial functions, transferred its central bank functions to a newly created Cuban Central Bank, and established a legal framework for commercial banks and financial institutions under the latter's supervision) was briefly mentioned by the Resolution but without specifying when the full banking reform will take place. There was no reference to the needed price reform, but the Resolution ratified that prices should be centrally set, although avoiding monopoly prices (an oxymoron). The Congress stressed the need to move gradually toward a more realistic and adequate foreign exchange rate, but without setting a timetable, and declared that the peso should be strengthened by increasing the nation's output but without a concrete plan.

There will be an adequate balance between economic and moral incentives — the Resolution stated — and voluntary labor will be re-asserted. Self-employment will continue under current regulations and control, despite the decline in the number legally registered. A draft law granting Cuban citizens the right to manage small and medium businesses, circulating for almost three years, was not mentioned in the Resolution (Lage explained that it was not a government priority and would have to wait), and it did not say anything either on authorizing university graduates to practice their professions as self-employed. Concern was expressed on the existing labor surplus (without alluding to the 500,000 to 800,000 state workers scheduled for dismissal in 1995), as well as on open unemployment-underemployment and the need to create jobs, but this was said to be a relatively small problem compared with other Latin American countries, and no concrete program was suggested (the Congress ignored ECLAC's estimate of 27% "equivalent unemployment," as well as its recommendations to expand the private sector to create jobs).

The Resolution acknowledged that social security is a heavy fiscal burden and that the 1994 tax law had mandated (although postponed) the imposition of a payroll tax on the workers, but did not stipulate the date of implementation (Lage said it would have to wait until "proper conditions" were present); the Resolution did not even mention the wage tax, also included in the 1994 law. The new regulations introduced in May 1997, establishing the right to rent rooms to citizens or foreigners, albeit requiring a permit and paying a tax, were equally overlooked. Finally the Resolution stated that once "the worst disequilibria are attenuated," but certainly not solved, a new stage will begin with emphasis on export diversification, rising labor productivity and enterprise profitability, achieving food self-sufficiency, etc. but, in the short run, current restrictions will continue.

In his closing address to the Party Congress, President Castro made clear that he opposes any type of privatization of state enterprises as the Chinese have done, and the Party Secretary in Havana declared that Cuba could not follow China's path because of different conditions and the adverse effects it would cause on social services (Rohter 1997). At his speech to the National Assembly, on July 22, 1998, Castro expressed his disgust about the negative social effects of the reform: "The more contact I have with capitalism, the more revulsion it causes me." He then criticized the legal operation of small restaurants and house renting because of their high earnings, saying that the amount of money owners have is causing much harm. Castro warned that the state will not sell cars and other durable consumer goods to those "Creole" millionaires and may increase their taxes even more (Castro 1998).

Short and Medium-Term Targets and their Feasibility

The cut in the 1998 GDP target and its unfeasibleness have been analyzed already. Equally unrealistic, in view of the decline in sugar output, low world prices of sugar and nickel, and poor performance of agriculture, are the 1998 targets to expand exports by 10.7% (contrasted with a 0.6% increase in 1997) and reduce the expansion of imports to 4.7% (compared with a jump of 20% in 1997); even if those unfeasible targets were to materialize, the merchandise trade deficit would slightly rise. Another unrealistic goal for 1998 is the swell of occupancy in tourist rooms by 7 percentage points (from 57% to 64%), despite a projected increase in the number of such rooms and an expansion of the occupancy rate of only 1.1 percentage points in 1997 (1998 targets from ECLAC 1998).

The Congress set very ambitious targets for the medium term (apparently for 1998-2002), but failed to come up with concrete, detailed policies to achieve them (the following targets come from Table 1; "Resolución..." 1998; and ECLAC 1998): (i) GDP will grow at an annual rate of 4% to 6% (compared with 2.5% in 1997, possibly less than 1% in 1998, and an average of less than 3% in 1994-98); (ii) sugar output will increase to 7 million tons, contrasted with 3.2 million in 1998 and an average of 3.9 million in 1993-98 (mechanization and fertilizer use should be limited, and replaced by manual work, animal traction and natural fertilizers); (iii) nickel output will reach 100,000 tons (a 61% leap over the 1997 level), tobacco 50,000 tons (a 100% jump over 1995 level), and the level of fish caught "sustained" (but an 8.8% increase is planned for 1998); (iv) 2 million tourists and a gross revenue of $2.6 billion will be reached (a 100% vault over 1997); (v) oil needs shall be met with increasing domestic production, savings, cut in population consumption and in use by public transportation mainly through bikes (the domestic contribution to total oil supply in 1995-97 decreased down to 17.8%); (vi) 50,000 dwellings will be built annually, particularly in the countryside (difficult to achieve because of the low domestic production of cement, part of which is earmarked for exports); (vii) health care should continue to partly rely on traditional and herbal medicine (a palliative but not a solution to the current problem); (viii) state pensions should be supplemented with individual savings accounts and life insurance (the question is how many people can save a significant amount to finance such supplemental pensions); and (ix) inequalities will be curtailed through taxes (but these would lead to less incentives in the non-state sector).

The possibility of achieving these unrealistic goals, particularly on agricultural production, is seriously put into question by the severe drought that the five eastern provinces of Cuba (Holguín, Santiago, Guantánamo, Las Tunas and Granma), and to a lesser extent the central provinces, have been suffering in 1998, attributed to *El Niño* and reportedly the worst since 1941. In July it was estimated by an international mission of the U.N. World Food Program (together with FAO, UNDP and UNICEF) that the drought would reduce food output by 42% in those provinces (from 609,648 to 259,000 metric tons) due to partial or total loss of thousands of hectares planted with beans, yucca, plantain, green vegetables and rice, as well as thousands of heads of cattle dead or transferred to other areas, which has led to a decline in milk output; poultry and egg production also have been harmed. The drought is likely to affect both the 1999 sugar harvest and the grandiose target of 7 million tons for 2002: it is calculated that as much as 14% of the sugar cane sown in 1997 has been lost, and significant delays have occurred in the sowing of new cane for the 2000 harvest (only one half of the planned target has been achieved, and most of the afflicted provinces are in the central part of the island, not in the east: Villa Clara, Ciego de Avila, Camagüey and Las Tunas). About 539,000 people have been adversely affected by the drought through lack of water and food, and decline in income, and $7 million in relief has been granted by international agencies. In August 1998, the decline in food output began to push up prices in Havana and the western provinces, which should lead to an increase in inflation in the rest of 1998 (*Juventud Rebelde*, July 12, 1998; EFE, La Habana, July 26, 1998; *Miami Herald*, July 31, 1998; and *El Nuevo Herald*, August 9 and 10, 1998).

Cuban authorities should leave aside their ideological resistance in order to: further open up the economy; facilitate the expansion of the private sector; transform the UBPCs into real cooperatives, which are autonomous and have more incentives to increase production and profitability; allow university graduates to practice their professions as self-employed; and authorize Cuban citizens and groups of workers to manage small and medium businesses, hence, creating enough jobs in the non-state sector to permit the dismissal of non-needed workers in the state sector; complete the banking reform and implement a comprehensive price reform; create a domestic capital market; allow foreign enterprises and joint ventures to hire, promote and pay their employees directly; establish a truly convertible peso; introduce a progressive income tax and workers' contributions to social security and reform the pension scheme; and devise a social safety net to protect the most vulnerable groups of the population. The decisions taken in the V Party Congress do no augur that such urgently needed reforms will be implemented in the near future. Therefore, the probability of a strong, steady recovery in Cuba appears to be very low, particularly after the poor performance of 1997-98.

REFERENCES

Banco Nacional de Cuba (BNC). 1995. *Informe económico 1994*. La Habana.

_____. 1996. *Economic Report*. La Habana.

Castro, Fidel. 1998. Speech at the National Assembly. *El Nuevo Herald* (July 25), p. 6.

Economic Commission for Latin America and the Caribbean (ECLAC). 1997. *La economía cubana: Reformas estructurales y desempeño en los noventa*. México: Fondo de Cultura Económica.

_____. 1998. *Cuba: Evolución económica durante 1997*. México: LC/MEX/L.35, July 15.

Mesa-Lago, Carmelo. 1998. "Assessing Economic and Social Performance in the Cuban Transition of the 1990s." *World Development* 26:5 (May): 857-876.

Ministerio de Economía y Planificación. 1998. *Informe económico año 1997*. La Habana.

"Palabras de Carlos Lage ante el Congreso..." 1997. *Granma* (October 10).

Pérez-López, Jorge. 1997. "The Cuban Economy in Mid-1997." *Cuba in Transition—Volume 7*. Washington: Association for the Study of the Cuban Economy.

"Resolución Económica del V Congreso del Partido Comunista de Cuba." 1998. *Granma International* (February 22).

Rohter, Larry. 1997. "Cuba's Party Peers Ahead, Chooses to March in Place." *The New York Times* (October 12), p. 6.

1997: RESUMEN ECONÓMICO DE UN AÑO

Manuel Sánchez Herrero y Arnaldo Ramos Lauzurique[1]

La economía cubana creció en 2.5% en 1997, según informes oficiales. Sin embargo, en casi todos los sectores de la economía nacional, no se cumplieron con las metas de producción, productividad e inversión.

En Cuba, como en muchos países de economía abierta, el crecimiento económico esta asociado fundamentalmente con el incremento de las exportaciones, y en el caso cubano, aún más por las características que tiene el mercado interno, mientras que la extrema escasez de recursos financieros externos hace en estos momentos más necesario generar superavit comerciales. Lo necesario no se logró en 1997.

Excepto en algunos sectores o productos del area dolarizada de la economía—turismo, tabaco, níquel y algunos segmentos de las empresas mixtas de orientación externa—sigue sin relacionarse el esfuerzo del trabajador y la remuneración que recibe, o sea, entre trabajo y salario.

En las publicaciones oficiales siguen las quejas de los dirigentes por la falta de disciplina laboral y baja productividad en el trabajo, mientras que se continúa explicando la crisis y la falta de desarrollo del país en base al bloqueo, la introducción de plagas desde el exterior y hechos naturales adversos. Todos ellos factores externos incontrolables por la gestión pública según la actual dirigencia cubana.

A nivel estructural, continúan vigentes las varias economías: la financiera del Comandante; la dual dolarizada y no dolarizada; extranjera y estatal vs. la cuentapropista reprimida; la negra de la informalidad; la roja de la corrupción y los privilegios de sectores de la nomenklatura.

En Cuba no hay tendencias ni cambios. Es un sistema represivo, monolítico y totalitario. La represión aumenta cada día. El gobierno cubano, cediendo a presiones internacionales, ha cambiado sus medios de represión al igual que ha hecho muchas veces en el pasado, pero continúa el hostigamiento ostensible y peligroso, y no hay cambios—ni esperanza de los mismos.

ANALISIS GLOBAL DE LA ECONOMIA

De acuerdo con la CEPAL, el desempeño económico de Cuba del 1991 al 1996 fue el peor de América Latina y el Caribe, incluyendo Haití, registrando en ese período una tasa promedio acumulativa anual del -4.8%. No obstante, el Gobierno le ha pedido a sus economistas que digan que la economía mantiene un crecimiento irreversible y de ahí el entretenimiento si ya tocó fondo o no. Entre los que han tratado de cumplir esta consigna estan José Luis Rodríguez, Ministro de Economía y Planificación, y Osvaldo Martínez, Presidente de Asuntos Económicos de la Asamblea Nacional.

Considerando la fuerte correlación que existe entre los valores de las exportaciones y los del Producto Interno Bruto (PIB), se llevó a cabo un análisis de re-

---

1. Basado principalmente en el trabajo "Recuento de un año," publicado en el Boletín No. 8 del Grupo de Trabajo de la Disidencia Interna para el Análisis Socioeconómico de la Situación Cubana (Diciembre 1997). El resumen fue elaborado y leído en la reunión de ASCE por Ricardo A. Puerta.

gresión lineal con una serie de datos, el cual dio como resultado una discrepancia entre la tasa de crecimiento informada por el régimen para el PIB en 1997 (2.5%; el plan era llegar al 4.0%) y la obtenida mediante los cálculos realizados (0.1%, o sea, practicamente sin crecimiento). Por eso se duda del 2.5% de crecimiento en 1997.

De todas maneras, no olvidemos lo escrito por Carmelo Mesa-Lago en 1995. En caso de que la (supuesta) recuperación se mantuviera al 4% anual habría que esperar hasta el 2,009 para tener el mismo PIB per cápita de 1985.

COMPORTAMIENTO POR SECTORES Y PRODUCTOS ESPECIFICOS

Los sectores y productos que crecieron en 1997 incluyen el turismo, la producción industrial, y la producción de níquel y de tabaco. Los que disminuyeron incluyen el sector agropecuario y del azúcar. Hay dudas con respecto a la producción de arroz y leche. Específicamente, hay informes contradictorios sobre las producción de leche y de arroz, si se tiene en cuenta lo reportado a la Asamblea Nacional por José Luis Rodríguez (crecieron ambas) y lo reportado por el *Boletín de Estadísticas Seleccionadas de Cuba 1996* de la Oficina Nacional de Estadísticas, p. 6 (ambas declinaron).

Sector agropecuario

La producción del sector agropecuario en 1997 decreció en 2.8% con relación al año anterior. En la producción de alimentos, en 1997 no se ha podido recuperar los decrecimientos arrastrados desde 1989, en cuanto a volumen físico de la producción agropecuaria, volumen físico de cultivos agrícolas y volumen físico de la producción pecuaria.

En la zafra 1996-97 se esperaba lograr un nivel algo superior a las 4.446 millones de toneladas (lo logrado en la zafra 1995-96) y se reportó 4.252 (96%, o sea 194 mil toneladas menos que en la zafra anterior).[2]

Diez de las 13 provincias azucareras incumplieron su plan.

Por razones técnicas[3] la zafra 1996-97 no pudo alcanzar los 4 millones de toneladas y la cifra que se informó (por el Gobierno) tiene el propósito de no dar la verdadera dimensión del desastre de la última zafra, y de paso hacer creible el crecimiento anunciado de 2.5% en el PIB, mientras disminuye en forma alarmante la principal producción del país. En 1997 los ingresos azucareros (estimados) registraron un descenso de un 12.5% con relación al año anterior.

A pesar de esto, el régimen es bastante optimista sobre el sector agropecuario. Espera que en 1998 crezca entre 6.5 y 7.5%, un objetivo dificil de alcanzar en vista del estancamiento, desaceleración o dismininución de la producción sufridos por muchos de sus productos en períodos anteriores, a lo cual se agregaría en 1998 el descenso de la producción cañera.

Exportaciones y balanza de pagos

En 1997 se incumple el plan de exportaciones en un 10.2%. Las exportaciones se vieron afectadas por la disminución en volumen y precio del azúcar y el descenso del precio del níquel. En realidad, el descenso tendencial de los precios de los productos básicos en los mercados internacionales impide realizar una elemental planeación de los ingresos por exportación. Ahora el desenvolvimiento de la economía cubana—dependiente en grado extremo del comercio exterior—esta condicionado fundamentalmente a los resultados de fuerzas y fenómenos económicos internacionales sobre los cuales la dirección nacional no puede ejercer gran influencia. Es una situación bastante desventajosa, pues los pocos créditos que puede obtener el país son en condiciones muy onerosas.

Con el bajo crecimiento de las exportaciones (0.6%) y el incremento de las importaciones (casi 20%), Cuba registró en 1997 uno de los mayores saldos adversos en la balanza de pagos de los últimos años, estimado en más de 400 millones de pesos, a pesar del

---

2. Informe de José Luis Rodríguez a la Asamblea Nacional, en *Trabajadores* (15 de diciembre de 1997).

3. Ver Arnaldo Ramos Lauzurique y Manuel Sánchez Herrero, "¿Cuál es la realidad de la zafra 1996-97?" Boletín No. 8 del Grupo de Trabajo de la Disidencia Interna para el Analisis Socioeconómico de la Situación Cubana (Diciembre 1997).

aumento de los ingresos del turismo internacional y de las remesas familiares.

Industria

Según el reporte de José Luis Rodríguez a la Asamblea Nacional, la actividad industrial creció en un 7.8%; de 21 ramas industriales, crecieron 15. Y eso ocurrió, añadimos nosotros, a pesar de la sustancial reducción de la producción de azúcar.

Las producciones industriales que más crecieron—con relación a 1996—fueron generación de electricidad, acero, cemento, tobaco torcido y jabón de tocador. Pero estos aumentos de producción tuvieron un efecto menor en la actividad económica que el de la producción azucarera.

Dos comentarios sobre el jabón de tocador y el tabaco torcido:

- Casi toda la producción de jabor de tocador se destinó al turismo y al mercado en divisas y poco a través del mercado racionado. Es decir, que las personas que no entraron en 1997 en el porciento con acceso a divisas (49.5%) pasaron grandes apuros para asearse.

- La producción de tabaco torcido en 1997 (250 millones de unidades) superó en más del 30% los niveles de 1995 y 1996 (181.4 y 189.1 millones de unidades, respectivamente), pero quedó por debajo del nivel de 1957 (340 millones) y más aún de los que se elaboraron en 1920 (563 millones, el máximo), en 1947 (400 millones) y en 1952 (403 millones).[4]

En el mercado local, se acentuaron las carencias en casi todos los productos manufacturados de consumo directo.

Minería y petróleo nacional

Las estadísticas oficiales sólo reportan el níquel, de lo cual se infiere que los otros renglones de la producción minera—cromo refractario, cobre concentrado, etc.—siguen en crisis.

Cuba esta considerado el primer país en reservas absolutas de níquel en el mundo y ocupaba antes de la crisis minera, el quinto lugar como productor. La producción de níquel en 1997 aumentó en 16.8% con relación al año anterior. Aunque se incumplió el estimado de producción para ese año de 67.0 miles de toneladas, la cifra alcanzada de 62.6 miles de toneladas rompe records anteriores. El metal tuvo un descenso en su precio en el mercado mundial en 1997.

La producción petrolera en 1997 declinó ligeramente con relación al año anterior. Ya entre 1995 y 1996, el incremento fue de sólo 0.3%, pasando de 1470.9 miles de toneladas a 1475.9 miles de toneladas. Según un especialista del Ministerio de la Industria Básica, la mayoría de los pozos de petróleo, con excepción de los de Varadero, han llegado a su límite productivo y será necesario poner en explotación nuevos pozos para lograr nuevos incrementos de producción.

Turismo

En los últimos tres años, los ingresos brutos por turismo sobrepasaron los de las zafras. Esto ocurrió en parte porque el ingreso por turismo aumentó y el de la zafra disminuyó. Los ingresos totales generados por el turismo crecieron en 1997 en más del 12% (con 1,180,000 visitantes) con respecto al año anterior, aunque se incumplió la meta en un 5.3%. Los ingresos por turista disminuyeron entre 1995 y 1997 en un 13.4%. Para 1998 se prevee un aumento en ingresos totales del 22%, con 1.4 millones de visitantes.

Presupuesto

El déficit presupuestario alcanzó el 2% del PIB, estimándose entre 450 y 470 millones, según el Ministro de Finanzas y Precios, dentro de los parámetros planificados. La principal medida para reducir el déficit fue el aumento del impuesto de circulación, un impuesto de tipo indirecto, es decir, de los que paga el contribuyente, sin saberlo, al comprar bienes y servicios. Este impuesto no ha sido establecido por la crisis económica; en 1989 el impuesto de circulación representó casi el 20% del Producto Social Bruto (PSB) y el 26% del Producto Interno Bruto (PIB). El Ministro de Finanzas y Precios estima que las pérdi-

---

4. *Estadísticas Seleccionadas de Cuba* (abril de 1997), p.5 y *Anuario Estadístico de Cuba 1957*, p. 177.

das de las empresas estatales en 1997 excedieron en 200 millones al subsidio asignado para cubrirlas. Para 1998 se prevee un ligero incremento del déficit fiscal, situándose a un nivel del 2.9% del PIB.

Liquidez monetaria

La liquidez en manos de la población, medida en moneda nacional, disminuyó de 9,634 millones de pesos al cierre de 1996 a una cifra estimada entre 9,334 y 9,384 millones de pesos en 1997. Sin embargo, todavía es algo más que el doble que la existente en 1989 (4,163 millones de pesos). En realidad, el exceso de liquidez no es un fenómeno nuevo y propio de la crisis, pero si agrabado por la misma. La escasez de bienes y servicios ha estado enraizada en nuestro país desde los inicios de la década de los años 60, manifestándose su efecto, en mayor o menor medida, sobre la circulación monetaria y dando lugar a la aparición, desarrollo y permanencia de la bolsa negra y ahora de la roja. Para 1998, se predice que la liquidez se reducirá en 200 millones por aumento de los impuestos, el incremento de una oferta estatal más diversificada y el alza de los precios al consumidor.

Inversiones

Financiar el plan económico sigue siendo la misión imposible para los asesores económicos del gobierno. Las fuentes se mantienen escasas, y las que hay, a veces se cierran por el incumplimiento de adeudos anteriores.

Sin embargo se sigue soñando. Si durante 1997 las inversiones crecieron en 7.6% frente al 10% planificado, ¿cómo es posible que para 1998 se prevea una aceleración del proceso inversionista con un incremento del 22%?, cuando el reajuste que conllevará la reducción de la zafra por debajo de los 4 millones de toneladas determinará nuevas estrecheces de carácter financiero. El sector externo se le hace cada vez más difícil al régimen, pues el saldo del balance en cuenta corriente es cada año más adverso.

Indicadores de eficiencia

En 1997, la productividad del trabajo alcanzó un discreto crecimiento del 0.6%, resultando comparativamente desfavorable con relación al salario medio, que creció 3.3%. Esta cuestión no es nueva en la economía cubana. La política de empleo continúa erosionando la productividad del trabajo. Se sigue absorbiendo en forma generalizada e improductiva el desempleo, aplicando criterios estrictamente sociales (evitando efectos políticos, como los del Malecón en agosto de 1994). Desde fines de la década del 70, la CEPAL viene señalando los efectos nocivos de dicha política.

El índice físico de consumo energético, como de costumbre, sigue creciendo por encima del crecimiento del PIB. Antes de la crisis (1985-90) también crecía (1.2% anual), aún cuando en ese mismo período el PIB decreció al 0.81% como promedio anual.

PROBLEMAS RELACIONADOS DIRECTAMENTE CON LA POBLACION

La creciente brecha entre la demanda solvente de la población y la oferta estatal de bienes y servicios durante la crisis sigue alimentando la espiral inflacionaria. La apertura de los mercados agropecuarios desflacionó en algo los precios de la economía sumergida (bolsa negra). Pero parmanecen altos en ese mercado, en el de los productos industriales y en la gastronomía privada y estatal. En 1997 el salario medio mensual pasó de 207 a 214 pesos. Sin embargo este aumento se reconoce como insignificante frente a la inflación.

Aumentó el consumo de la población en los mercados regulados o que venden en divisas y el consumo en el mercado racionado se mantiene a niveles de 1996. Comparando los precios en el mercado paralelo estatal de 1986 con el agropecuario de 1997 los aumentos en 1997 fluctúan entre 233% y 1,400% para artículos como el arroz, frijoles negros, carnero, cerdo, tomate de ensalada y aguacate.

Cuba ha pasado de ser un país de remitentes de remesas (españoles y chinos) a receptor de remesas. Estudios independientes estiman que por lo menos el 35% de la población recibe remesas del extranjero, principalmente de Estados Unidos. Los cubanos en el exilio son "los nuevos españoles y chinos" para el régimen de La Habana. Un estudio de la CEPAL fija las remesas familiares en 800 millones anuales (confirmando estimados dados en reuniones de ASCE) de los cuales 620 millones (casi un 80%) son captados por el régimen a través de sus cadenas de establecimientos en divisas. Ello posibilita que el régimen aumente sus ingresos en moneda libremente convertible, esperando en 1998 un aumento del 17.8% en las venta de mercancías y servicios en divisas convertibles.

En este sentido, los gusanos y apátridas siguen ayudando a subsistir a una buena parte del pueblo cubano. El 25% de la población recibe remesas y el 49.2% de los ciudadanos forma parte del "nivel de tenencia de divisas."

Los productos con dificultad de encontrar en 1997 incluyen el combustible doméstico y el aceite. El sector de peor desempeño es la vivienda. En 1994 el 46% del fondo de viviendas era considerado en el mal estado en La Habana. Lo construído en 1997 por los sectores estatal y cooperativo cumple con el 89% de lo que se pensaba construir y no cubre el deterioro anual.

En resúmen, ¿qué es lo que le propone el régimen al pueblo cubano como metas futuras? Sencillamente, niveles de producción que ya fueron alcanzados o sobrepasados en décadas pasadas. En 1925, por ejemplo, se registraron producciones de azúcar y tabaco torcido superiores a las cifras previstas para 1998, con la gran diferencia que en 1925 Cuba tenía una masa demográfica que no sobrepasaba en mucho a los 3 millones de habitantes (3,415,216), mientras que en 1998 tendrá más de 11 millones.

Y mientras tanto ... más Período Especial. Que según el jefe del régimen, "no importa si dura toda la vida."[5]

---

5. Fidel Castro, en *Trabajadores* (13 de octubre de 1997), p. 4.

ECONOMIC REFORM IN
LATIN AMERICA AND THE CARIBBEAN AND POSSIBLE
IMPLICATIONS FOR CUBA

Claudio Loser

Thank you for the opportunity to join you in Miami today and participate in your stimulating discussions on the Cuban economy. The main focus of my remarks will be a broad overview of the recent reform effort in Latin America and the Caribbean.

Some may say that the differences between Cuba and the rest of the region are so large that this experience is of little relevance for Cuba. But I submit that in spite of some very obvious differences, there is significant common ground, and that Cuba can draw important lessons from the experience of other countries of the region. More specifically, I believe that in the early 1980s Latin America and the Caribbean faced a sudden reversal in its external circumstances that is in many ways similar to that faced by Cuba in the 1990s: economies that were relatively closed and heavily regulated had to cope with an abrupt deterioration in their terms of trade and a sudden drying up of external finance. This led to a period of protracted financial instability and weak economic growth that many have labeled as "the lost decade" for Latin America and the Caribbean.

There is, however, a more positive angle to these developments. I believe that the debt crisis provided the region with a "wake up call" that highlighted the shortcomings of the region's traditional approach to economic policy: its reliance on heavy state intervention to reach objectives that proved to be ever elusive. This new awareness prompted most countries in the region to implement deep, extensive reforms that

have increased the region's potential output and raised income growth in the region and—what may even be more meaningful—have put it in a position to better withstand new kinds of adverse external shocks such as the Mexican crisis of 1994-95 and the current financial crisis in East Asia.

THE DEBT CRISIS OF THE EARLY 1980s

But let me first recall briefly the Latin American debt crisis of the early 1980s. As I mentioned earlier, it resulted from both domestic and external factors. You will remember the external context: after an era of rapidly rising oil and other commodity prices and seemingly unlimited financing at relatively low interest rates in the 1970s, Latin America's key export prices declined markedly in 1981-82 while international interest rates rose sharply, both contributing to a marked widening in the region's current account deficit (from 2-3 percent of GDP in the late 1970s to 5½ percent in 1982). At the same time, there was a drying up of financing (the well known recycling of dollars by oil exporters came to an end), and eventually a sharp contraction in foreign capital flows to the region (from a record US$52 billion in 1981 to less than US$8 billion a year over 1983-89).

But these external developments also unmasked profound imbalances in the region's economies themselves. These imbalances were reflected on a sharp increase in *foreign borrowing*, the mirror image of the lending I just discussed, with the region's foreign debt quadrupling in barely seven years (from US$74 billion, or 19 percent of GDP, in 1975, to close to US$300 billion, or 43 percent of GDP, in 1982). These imbalances also reflected was the pursuit of *inconsistent and unsustainable macroeconomic policies*, including in particular the combination of fixed or heavily managed exchange rate regimes with overly lax fiscal policies (the region's fiscal deficit grew from an average of 2 percent of GDP in 1975-79 to 4.5 percent in 1982); as a result, many currencies became seriously overvalued in the early 1980s—for instance, between 1979 and 1981 the Chilean peso appreciated by 37 percent in real effective terms, the Mexican peso by 27 percent, and the Argentine peso by 19 percent. And in the structural area, most of the economies of the region had for decades followed *a misguided development model based on import-substitution, pervasive state intervention and ownership, extensive price and other quantitative controls, and extremely high tariff protection.* As a result, exports accounted for barely 10 percent of GDP in the early 1980s, compared to about 15 percent for OECD countries and 30 percent for Asia. Relative prices were highly rigid and productivity growth was low. Such heavily regulated, distorted and overheated economies were clearly in no position to respond to a rapidly changing external environment without major economic disruptions.

The economic impact of the 1980s debt crisis was particularly severe: output growth and investment dropped following the onset of the crisis, in some countries by very large amounts, and were generally slow to recover. Inflation surged to unprecedented levels, and exchange rates fluctuated wildly, generating considerable strains on domestic financial institutions, which in many countries had to be intervened and restructured. Such financial instability undermined investors' confidence and often contributed to a vicious circle of ever lower investment and growth. In all, by the end of the "lost decade," average output per capita in Latin America and the Caribbean was still below that registered ten years earlier.

THE REFORMS OF THE LATE 1980s

What was the policy response to the crisis? There was of course *no common policy reaction* across all countries. Some countries embarked on an ambitious re-

form path early on, while others tried to deny the profound nature of the external changes that had occurred and treated them as temporary; still others reacted by initially stepping up direct intervention in markets. The scope of reform, and its sequencing from one policy area to another, also differed markedly across countries.

Eventually, however, a common strategy did emerge—one that represented *a radical turnaround in the region's approach to economic policy, from one based on heavy government intervention to one that relies on market forces.* Sooner or later in the aftermath of the debt crisis, most governments in the region opted for leaving behind the old views that sought to maintain the public sector as the engine of inward-looking economic growth, and embraced an outward-looking, market-based economic agenda, rooted in the conviction that freer markets make it possible to use productive resources more efficiently and lead to faster, more equitable output and income growth. A key objective of economic policy has thus come to be a widening in the scope of markets and improvements in how they function, instead of curbing their development and distorting their operation. This is a remarkable departure from decades of state intervention, with far-reaching consequences in all areas of economic policy.

If we look more closely at specific reform policies, we can identify four basic areas of action: fiscal reform; improved monetary discipline and a radical change in the way monetary policy is conducted and financial savings allocated in the economy; trade liberalization; and privatization.

- Let me start with *fiscal policy*, possibly one of the most important areas of reform. For the region as a whole, the overall fiscal balance improved from a deficit of 4-5 percent in the late 1980s to about 2 percent in the past few years. Of the 32 developing countries of the region, about 20 countries have improved their fiscal balance between 1989 and 1997, often by a sizable amount. In many cases, this has required an overhaul of the tax system, significant reductions in government expenditure, extensive institutional reform, including through the complete or partial overhaul of social security systems, and the restructuring or privatization of public enterprises and public financial institutions to eliminate their operating losses. Such measures are not easy to take, particularly in a context of weak economic growth and large social demands for government programs. But I cannot overemphasize the critical contribution that this fiscal consolidation has made for the stabilization of the economies of the region. And it is also important to remember that a sounder fiscal sector helps improve the efficiency of the economy, as it allows scarce financial resources to be dedicated to productive, income-generating investment.

- A second key element was *improved monetary discipline and changes in the conduct of monetary policy*. The shift in monetary policy was of course facilitated to a large extent by the improvements in the public finances. At the same time, direct credit controls were abandoned in most countries, bank reserve requirements were lowered substantially, and interest rates were deregulated and allowed to reach positive levels in real terms. As a result, money growth slowed sharply in most countries, and inflation went down from an average of 900 percent at the end of 1990 to less than 11 percent at end 1997, the lowest level in 30 years. So that in this region once known for stratospheric rates of inflation, in many cases close to hyperinflation, by the end of 1997 only two countries had inflation rates over 30 percent. At the same time, significant institutional changes were introduced to the region's financial sectors, including the modernization of banking regulations and the establishment of more demanding prudential standards.

- In the area of *trade*, tariffs were reduced and unified, falling from a regional average of over 40 percent in the mid 1980s to less than 14 percent at present; the once pervasive import permits and other quantitative restrictions on trade were for the most part eliminated, with their coverage falling from 36 to less than 6 percent of imports. And finally, the multiple exchange rate regimes that had become common in the aftermath of

the debt crisis were also dismantled, and they are now the exception—in fact, most of the Latin American and Caribbean region now subscribes to the Article VIII of the IMF's Charter, which means that they maintain no restrictions on their current external transactions. Restrictions on capital transactions were also eliminated or at least significantly softened.

With this change in external policies, external trade of the developing countries of the region has increased markedly. It is particularly interesting to note that exports have grown to about 12 percent of the region's GDP. And with the reduction of controls on capital *outflows*, capital *inflows* to the region have increased over tenfold, from some US$8 billion a year in the early 1980s to about US$40 billion in the early 1990s and US$90 billion in 1997. Importantly, reflecting regained invertors' confidence, private, long-term investment flows now account for the lion's share of this total.

- Finally, the scope of *privatization*—another highly visible component of reform—has been remarkable. Over 800 enterprises have been privatized since 1988, many of them in the utilities sector, which traditionally was closed to private sector participation and where the potential for productivity and efficiency gains is ample. There have also been significant sales in the financial and banking sectors, thereby bolstering financial sector reform. More generally, many markets have been deregulated, and many restrictions to the development of private enterprise eliminated.

As I said earlier, the specific scope and pace of each of these reforms has varied significantly among countries. But the drive to implement them has been bold and comprehensive in the whole region. In fact, many analysts have now come to emphasize that in the area of structural reforms, most Latin American and Caribbean countries have advanced farther in a decade than many European or Asian countries have in over 30 or even 50 years.

THE IMPACT OF THE CRISIS IN ASIA AND THE POLICY RESPONSE

I would like to discuss how this shift in policies has strengthened the economies of the region and enabled them to recover quickly from the Mexican crisis of 1994-95. But time is short and I will jump to the current situation where the preliminary conclusion that one can draw point in a similar direction. The story of the crisis in Asia is far from fully told at this point, but it clearly has been affecting Latin America and the Caribbean through the same two major channels as the debt crisis: a sharp contraction in foreign financing coupled with a significant terms-of-trade loss.

- *Medium- and long-term capital inflows* to the region, which had been averaging US$8 billion a month through the first ten months of 1997, fell to an average of US$3.5 billion a month from November 1997 through February 1998. There was also a notable decline in stock prices: a regional composite index of stock prices fell by 30 percent from its level in September 1997 (in U.S. dollar terms), in some cases reflecting a fall in domestic asset prices compounded by currency depreciation. I want to point out that neither of these factors—lower asset prices and currency devaluation—has led to a major banking collapse, as it had in many cases the early 1980s. Moreover, capital inflows were quick to rebound when there was at least a temporary respite in the crisis situation—inflows went back to US$7 billion a month in March-May 1998—although there are indications that they subsequently weakened again.

- At the same time, *external markets turned very sluggish under the impact of a decline in import demand from Asia and a sharp drop in the world prices of oil and other key commodities*. The average price of the main commodity exports from Latin America and the Caribbean fell by over 30 percent between October 1997 and June 1998. Nonetheless, and partly reflecting the impact of trade liberalization on export diversification, other exports, mainly manufactured goods, were broadly unaffected.

In stark contrast to the experience of the early 1980s, the policy response of countries in our region to the Asian crisis was fast and unequivocal. In most cases, the authorities have expressed swiftly and clearly their commitment to macroeconomic stability. They have tightened credit policy and taken additional and often painful fiscal adjustment measures to stabilize their currencies and restore market confidence. So far, they have been relatively successful in their attempts, partly because of the swiftness of their policy response, and partly because of the stronger and more resilient economies they now manage, themselves the fruit of previous reform efforts. Banking reform, for instance, has enabled the authorities to significantly tighten credit policy without compromising banking soundness. Output growth is expected to slow, but remain at a respectable 3 percent (from 5 percent in 1997). Encompassing privatization and market deregulation have attracted large foreign direct investment (FDI) flows, thus reducing the region's vulnerability to more volatile short-term inflows. And close to one year after the onset of the crisis, most Latin American and Caribbean countries have maintained their external credit ratings and their access to voluntary private financing, as evidenced by several recent successful bond issues—albeit at higher spreads.

Important risks and challenges remain, however, and it would certainly not be prudent to claim that the region is on safe ground. There is the risk of policy slippages, particularly in the monetary and fiscal areas. Many governments of the region are facing or preparing to face electoral contests, and there is the temptation to ignore external developments or to resort to populist financial policies or misguided policy responses such as the reintroduction of trade barriers. In my recent visits to countries of the region, however, I have been encouraged by the authorities' awareness of these risks, and by the efforts they are making to gain political support for measures that can help defend their economies from further negative shocks and sustain their ability to grow.

What should be the focus of these measures? First, furthering reforms in areas where they have often stopped short, such as fiscal reform, improvements in the targeting of social programs, particularly in the areas of education and health, and the strengthening of banking practices and banking supervision. And second, broadening the reform effort to address new, in many cases unchartered areas such as labor market reform, competition policies and governance, whose importance for effective economic performance on today's global markets have been clearly evidenced by the Asian crisis.

CONCLUDING REMARKS: POTENTIAL LESSONS FOR CUBA

In the end, what are the lessons from the Latin American and Caribbean experience that are relevant for Cuba? I am no expert on the Cuban economy so I will leave to others the task of drawing concrete conclusions on this subject. However, I think that two general policy lessons can be drawn that can be of use for Cuba as for other economies transiting to market-based principles. The first is that stabilization must be an immediate, unrelenting objective; the second is that the strategy of structural reform must be boldly comprehensive, and encompass at the same time price and market liberalization, public sector reform, and the development of a modern legal and financial infrastructure.

First, **steadfast stabilization is the key to any successful economic reform strategy.** The initial stages of liberalization are likely to be associated with a surge in prices, especially when price and other quantitative controls were pervasive. The removal of price controls and of direct or hidden subsidies, as well as trade liberalization, will lead to an increase in the price of many goods, particularly tradables, from their previously low, subsidized level; it will also release a previously pent-up demand for foreign goods. In this context, traditional stabilization policies, through monetary and credit restraint and fiscal austerity, must be at the top of the economic agenda.

The Latin American and Caribbean experience shows, however, that inflation may only respond with a lag to financial restraint, because of a number of factors such as unexpected fluctuations in the velocity of or demand for money, inflationary expectations and uncertainty with respect to the future macroeconomic stance, and the ability of other agents—

i.e., local governments or public enterprises—to offset monetary restraint through informal credit or payment arrears. In those cases, the authorities' determination to resist demand pressures and keep tight financial policies until inflation effectively subsides has been a major element in ensuring the eventual success of reform. Supporting policy measures that clearly signal the authorities' commitment to reform and stabilization also have been used to facilitate the disinflation process by enhancing credibility and confidence in the currency. These include wage restraint, the maintenance of positive rates of return on domestic monetary assets, and steadfast advances in the structural area, including through privatization. Some Latin American countries, most notably Argentina, also have used a fixed exchange rate to help stabilize their economies; however, policy makers should remember that the use of an exchange rate peg does require a strong commitment to supporting adjustment measures, particularly fiscal restraint, while the experience of several other countries has shown that a peg is not necessary for the achievement of stabilization objectives.

The crucial importance of stabilizing quickly, and of maintaining sound financial policies thereafter, has gained new relevance in today's global goods and capital markets, because there is even less room for policy inconsistencies or complacency. In the global environment, market anxieties can spread quickly from one country to another, rapidly exposing underlying weaknesses. Misguided policies can then have more abrupt and pronounced consequences than in the past; and sound, prudent macroeconomic policies are even more important, because markets are not forgiving—much less forgiving, I must say, than official financial institutions like the IMF. Polcy makers must stand ready to react quickly to signs of emerging imbalances, before market pressures build up. As I said earlier, in the aftermath of the Asian crisis the prompt policy response of the authorities in the Latin American and Caribbean region was key to maintaining financial stability. Such a capacity for swift response is becoming an even more central element of sound macroeconomic management, and policy makers should ensure that they are able to address underlying weaknesses rapidly and decisively.

Second, **the accompanying effort at structural reform must be comprehensive.** The agenda is very wide, but three elements appear as effective cornerstones:

- the *steadfast liberalization of prices and the deregulation of goods and labor markets*; this includes the liberalization of all foreign transactions, including trade, foreign exchange operations, and foreign investment. These are key elements to prompt the required shifts in labor and other resources and elicit a quick supply response, thus minimizing the length and costs of the adjustment period, and which has had a clear positive impact in the region;

- there is a need for *a deep reform of the public sector, both at the level of the government and at the level of public enterprises.* Overall, its size must be reduced, and its efficiency increased. For the government, an encompassing tax reform must be designed together with efforts to control and redirect spending to its most efficient use, including through a means-tested social safety net. Public enterprises should be privatized quickly, and if delays are encountered in this process, they should be immediately reformed to respond to market signals, with subsidies or credits eliminated or severely curtailed; and

- the authorities should develop a *modern legal and financial infrastructure*, including a sound banking and payments system, properly regulated, as well as a set of laws and institutions suited to a market economy, such as enforceable property rights and bankruptcy laws. Simultaneous, complementary advances in each of these three fronts are required to foster the development and smooth, efficient functioning of markets.

The importance of many of these issues has been clearly underscored by the recent crisis in East Asia, as now they have come to the forefront of any reform agenda, including in industrial countries. What we see is an environment where countries, without consideration for ideology, need to make a hard but inevitable decision to integrate with the world economy. Such choice would help create the conditions for sustained economic growth with stability, that would be required to survive as viable economic, social and political entities.

COMMENTS ON

"Economic Reform in Latin America and the Caribbean and Possible Implications for Cuba" by Loser

Jorge A. Sanguinetty

It is a privilege to be invited to discuss a paper written by Claudio Loser. I must say that Dr. Loser has written a short but excellent paper that carries a very important lesson for the future of the Cuban economy. That lesson is, in Dr. Loser's own words, "Cuba can draw important lessons from the experience of other countries in the region." There are many who believe that Cuba is so special that it has to find its own solutions. That is true, but does not invalidate the fact worth repeating that "Cuba can draw important lessons from the experience of other countries in the region." As a matter of fact, I would add, that Cuba would also have to take into account the experience of other ex-socialist economies in their road towards a market economy or in their reluctance to do so.

As I agree with practically everything Dr. Loser submits in this paper, I would address my comments to discuss, very briefly, how the differences between the countries of the region and Cuba will influence, not the general principles that Dr. Loser proposes, but the specific ways in which those same principles will have to be implemented in Cuba when the opportunity arises. In this discussion I will follow the same order of the "four basic areas of action" that Dr. Loser uses.

FISCAL REFORM

We will divide the discussion of this area into the two traditional areas: (a) taxation; and (b) expenditures.

On taxation. Until recently, the payment of taxes in Cuba was virtually non-existent. More recently, some Cubans working as self-employed have been forced to pay taxes. In the future, an entirely new tax structure and administration system will have to be built almost from scratch, and Cubans will have to be educated on paying their corresponding taxes, a challenge that can be expected to be greater than in any other Latin American country given Cuba's recent past.

On expenditures. Cubans have been made to believe that the state can afford to pay for services in the so-called social sector (education, health and retirement pensions) without regard for the economy's capacity to generate the corresponding revenues. Even today, there is little understanding that the past extravagant behavior of the Cuban government regarding education and health was only made possible by significant Soviet subsidies. Even though the current crisis in Cuban education and health systems will help understand the imbalances created in the past and the need to adjust social expenditures to a "hard budget constraint," a transition government committed to fiscal reform is bound to find considerable opposition to any austerity program, unless it prepares the ground for fiscal reform with a public education and information campaign explaining the need to have a stable fiscal system. The same applies for the reforms necessary on the taxation side of the fiscal reform. Increasing public understanding on these matters will not do the work by itself, of course. But the transition government and, especially, its fiscal authorities must avoid the traditional approach of formulating and implementing a reform program without consideration for the public, an unacceptable strategy in a country that will be struggling to reestablish a democratic system as it endeavors for the establishment of a market economy.

MONETARY REFORM

Monetary discipline will be indispensable for the economic reconstruction of Cuba. In fact, it will be an important complement of fiscal stabilization. A rapid economic reconstruction of Cuba requires the injection of massive volumes of foreign direct resources to create new productive capacities, increase levels of output and generate sufficient employment. Inflation, uncertainties in exchange and interest rates, and in general, incoherent monetary and fiscal policies will discourage foreign investments in Cuba. At the same time, the adequacy of discretionary monetary policies, whether we like it or not, will depend on the quality and integrity of the individuals in charge of monetary policy. We do not know if the "right" type of individuals will be available in Cuba to be in charge of discretionary policies. A system of "rules" versus "discretion" might be more advisable for Cuba during the first few years of a transition to a market economy. This is why Cuba, unlike its Latin American counterparts, might prefer to continue for a while with the current system of monetary dualism in which the U.S. dollar is already playing the role of a stabilizing instrument, while the devaluated peso represents the obsolete economic system inherited from socialism. This system, of course, depends on the stability of the U.S. dollar, but we have no reasons to believe that the current U.S. policy of almost zero inflation cum low interest rates is about to change.

TRADE LIBERALIZATION

This will require much more than simple "shock therapy" or "big bang" types of approach. In Cuba, full trade liberalization can not be achieved without profound changes in the institutional and organizational structure of the country. For the last four decades, trade—domestic and international, retail and wholesale—has been almost completely dominated by state monopolies. The only private trade that existed was in black markets, heavily persecuted by the government, though at times tolerated de facto as a result of its size and predominance. Today, there is some level of legal private trade at the retail level which will serve as the basis for a trade liberalization policy. Nevertheless, the institutional and organizational changes referred to above require widespread actions to provide new entrepreneurs with the means necessary to freely exercise the commerce function. This means that privatization, in its many forms, will have to take place at the same time that other reforms are implemented.

Liberalization of imports will be easier to achieve as the government allows private entrepreneurs to freely import all kinds of goods and services. But even in this area, things are not going to happen as quickly as desired, since the ability to pay for imports will be severely constrained, as export industries are not similarly liberalized and put to work into full capacity. Also, the limited existence of a commercial banking system (there is something in Cuba already, serving the capitalistic sector of the economy managed directly by Fidel Castro and the foreign business community) may have to develop much further throughout the entire territory before a full expansion of import trade takes place.

Another important point to be made here is the interdependence between the fiscal reform and trade liberalization. For trade liberalization we need a system of low tariffs. The government, on the other hand, will be under heavy pressure to finance expensive social programs with a bankrupt economy and a concomitant narrow tax base. Besides, it may be difficult to collect other taxes from the population, due to lack of tradition, etc. In such a case, the government may be tempted to rely heavily on customs taxation, including export taxes, to cover revenue requirements. This would be devastating for Cuba's prospects of a fast recovery, and represents another important argument why increasing public understanding of these issues is essential in any Cuban economic transition.

PRIVATIZATION

In Cuba, privatization means, essentially, returning confiscated property to their previous owners, but exceptions will have to be made. One exception refers to real estate in the forms of housing that is occupied today by individuals and entire families that do not have alternatives but to stay where they currently live, albeit creating a major social crisis of unacceptable political dimensions. The rights of the corresponding owners will have to be recognized by different means, possibly by compensation.

Returning other properties to their previous owners or their heirs may not be easy, since not all claims can be established as rapidly as it would be desirable. Privatizing by selling to the highest bidder may not be as expedite as returning properties to previous owners from the point of view of a rapid recovery of production levels. Nevertheless, it is not clear whether former owners or their heirs have the wherewithal to put their former enterprises to work at full speed. Many, if not most of such enterprises, will need significant investments to overhaul machinery and equipment that has been subjected to mismanagement, neglect of maintenance, or sheer obsolescence.

Another point that establish a significant difference between Cuba and other Latin American countries with regard to privatization requirements is that the traditional public enterprise in Latin America had to operate in economic systems that had a strong presence of market economics, even if highly imperfect and monopolistic. Latin American public enterprises, even when suffering chronic deficits, never abandoned their accounting systems and the notion of profitability and the need for accounting and a minimum of financial management. Cuban public enterprises will come from a much farther distance to market economics than the Latin American enterprises. Privatization, in its many different ways, will have to take place with restructuring efforts such as: changing the management system and culture, learning to operate under the concept of profit, learning to operate autonomously and not under the direct orders of a planning authority, learning to market and to compete, etc.

In any case, despite these differences, Dr. Loser's remarks are to be taken as the compass by which we should guide Cuba's steps into a modern economy. This is why I recommend to all serious reformers, in Latin America, Cuba and the rest of the world, to read Claudio Loser's paper thoroughly and repeatedly, no matter how we might think each country differs from the rest. The general principles stated in this paper are universally valid, until the contrary is proven.

CUBA AND LATIN AMERICA: THE POLITICAL DIMENSION

Mauricio A. Font

The peculiar situation of the Cuban economy in the 1990s has brought to central stage the island's role in world society.[1] The severe crisis induced by the collapse of communist regimes in Eastern Europe and the old Soviet Union left Cuba's state socialism facing the challenge of reintegration into a largely-capitalist world society. But the international context of the 1990s differs from that Cuba might have expected in earlier decades in at least three major dimensions—the massive shift toward democracy since the 1970s, the consolidation of global capitalism, and the new momentum in integration processes. This paper explores this conjuncture and notes Cuba's response to it. It probes in particular the significance of Latin America, as it explores Cuba's international strategy and search for a new role in the world economy.[2]

CUBA'S NEW INTERNATIONALISM

The post-1989 collapse of state socialism in Eastern Europe led to a severe contraction in the Cuban economy and with it the need to either refine the state-centered development model or find new support from the international community.[3] Significant forms of change followed, including expanding the tourist sector in partnership with foreign private capital, the legalization of dollar holdings, and the limited liberalization of food and crafts production and

sale. The response to the crisis was essentially a new outward strategy that sought to minimize reforms in the internal economy. The main policies were largely oriented to attract dollars to stabilize the Cuban currency and trade accounts and concentrate resources in a segmented part of the economy linked to the outside. While part of the economy's external sector has grown, the critically important sugar sector and much of the non-external sector remained stagnant. By most accounts, the country has a segmented economy and has yet to define a viable new development strategy.

The official response to the crisis can be partly explained by the institutional characteristics of Cuban state socialism—centralization, collectivization, moral/ideological orientation, charismatic authoritarian, and a high degree of non-market external support (Font 1996). Cuban state socialism was shaped by a peculiar international context that made possible heavy outside sponsorship of Cuba's extreme form of state socialism. Soviet and Council for Mutual Economic Assistance (CMEA) support during the 1970s and 1980s allowed Cuba's socialism to develop in relative isolation from the difficult market forces that drove much of Latin America into a structural crisis in the 1980s followed by a major era of reform in the 1990s. Cuba's outward strategy before 1989 had in-

---

1. This essay draws from and extends the analysis presented in M. Font, "Advancing Democracy in Cuba: The International Context," in P. Alamos et al. (1998).

2. A set of statements bearing on the relationship between Latin America and Cuba can be found in P. Alamos, et al. (1998). The processes of integration and globalization have received widespread attention. The "third wave" of democracy, the processes of democratization since the 1970s, has been studied by Samuel Huntington and others.

3. The essays in Centeno and Font (1996) discuss various aspects of Cuba's post-1990 crisis.

deed been quite successful in mobilizing international resources to the island and left as legacy a high international profile, including a large and effective foreign service. Through the second half of the 1990s Cuban leaders continued to deny the need for substantial market reforms, proclaiming the viability of the state socialist model and the notion that it represented the only legitimate option for the Cuban nation.

Cuba's new internationalism in the second half of the 1990s sought to find a mode of international insertion through which the island could hope to make up for the loss of markets, aid, and resources since 1990. The search has led to significant progress in the development of bilateral relationships. Compared to the pre-1990s pattern, the rate at which it has developed diplomatic and commercial relations with Latin American and the Caribbean has been almost phenomenal. But Cuba's new internationalism of the 1990s also faced an acceleration of processes of regional integration and globalization, including a policy-making context driven by major market-oriented reforms. In this rapidly changing context, Cuba's process of international "re-insertion" faces the difficult task of developing institutions and policies to gain admission into the major trading or economic blocs in formation in the Western Hemisphere—particularly the emergent Free Trade Area of the Americas (FTAA) and MERCOSUR, but also CARICOM and the Central American Common Market (CACM). (See the Appendix for more information on Western Hemisphere organizations.)

The broad challenge for Cuba is to forge development-oriented international coalitions and institutionalized multilateral economic relations to obtain credits and investment, grants and technical assistance, access to markets, and the like. Having largely exhausted its capacity to mobilize internal investment resources, the country badly needs credits and fresh investment to modernize its eroded capital stock and infrastructure—a figure hard to estimate

but that probably exceeds 20 billion dollars at a minimum. Canada, Mexico and Spain have emerged as key partners in this regard. But the bilateral relationships with these countries is unlikely to yield by themselves the full developmental coalitions able to meet the country's needs. With relations with Europe, Asia and Africa also having ceilings in the current context, the Latin American and Caribbean region is of considerable importance to the island.

In the evolving context of the late 1990s, processes of integration in the region figure prominently in this regard.[4] In principle, Cuba could hope for membership in MERCOSUR or even NAFTA-FTAA, the two largest blocs in the hemisphere. Membership in CARICOM emerged as another possibility (Erisman 1997). A diplomatic Cuban offensive in this regard seemed poised for success in mid-1998. But, even if it fully materializes, the value of this membership would be more symbolic than real, since the Caribbean is just too small, competitive with the Cuban economy, and relatively poor to provide the kind of partnership Cuba needs. Something comparable can be said about the CACM, while the potential of the newly forming Association of Caribbean States will take many years to bear fruit, given the diversity of cultures, political dynamics, and previous disinterest in the countries making up the Caribbean Basin.

Cuba's outward strategy forces its leaders to face economic and political conditions defined by the regional organizations and processes of integration to which it hopes to join. The larger regional blocs have "democratic clauses" which a country has to meet in order to gain or maintain membership. Major political and institutional obstacles related to Cuba's authoritarianism top the list of impediments to a rapid breakthrough in the country's ability to join the main international organizations and integration processes. Though the precise terms of admission Cuba could expect are not yet fully clear, what is less uncertain meanwhile is that the current crisis of the island deprives it of the ability to set these terms. With the

---

4. Besides FTA's, other possible options are Customs Unions, Common Markets, and Full Economic Unions. Cuba's bilateral relationships have failed to produce bilateral free trade agreements with industrial nations and are unlikely to do so in the near future.

end of the Cold War, Cuba went from an era of substantial international leverage to one in which it finds itself with little and probably decreasing influence in world affairs as well as enhanced external dependence. It hence seems unlikely that the country could hope for full membership in the main economic blocs without engaging in a serious process of institutional change and even democratization.

Cuban policymakers therefore face a dilemma with regard to participation in regional integration and cooperation. If they fail to adopt reforms to conform to the regnant liberalization paradigm, Cuba will probably continue to play a marginal role in the main forms of economic and political cooperation governing the turn of the century in the region. A meaningful program of reform will on the other hand be likely to accelerate and deepen the economy's ability to join the processes of integration, but at the cost of fundamental changes in Cuba's state socialism.

The year 1999 will bring important tests in this regard. That year will see Cuba host the Ibero-American Summit. Before that, it would also like to take part in the summit between the European Union and the Rio Group. Cuba has approached and will continue to approach the Rio Group and MERCOSUR. The 1998 deepening of negotiations regarding MERCOSUR and FTAA has added pressure. Unless it joins the talks surrounding the FTAA, it will be left out of a critical axis of cooperation in the hemisphere.

LATIN AMERICA AND CUBA

The New Consensus on Democracy in Latin America

From a broad perspective, Latin America's special significance to Cuba goes beyond the current phase of economic integration. It also derives from the region's experiences with democracy and transitions to democracy—a process which actually shapes the Latin American approach to integration. Still unfolding,

these processes define the main political developments in the region. The experiences with democratization are also a reservoir of practical and theoretical knowledge that could help Cuba's own search for a modernized political system. Latin American democratization is also important because it defines the political and institutional framework governing the region's relations with Cuba. Given the new emphasis on democracy (with all its problems, at no other point in history has Latin America been so uniformly engaged in the construction of democracy), the marked inclination is to go beyond the preference for deeper relations with other democratic countries toward the explicit promotion of democracy.[5]

This trend toward democracy is in fact a key underlying historical process facilitating regional integration. To Latin American policymakers, the latter would be inconceivable without basic consensus on forms of governance and the bonds linking current democratic leaders in the continent. While the processes of democratic transition in Latin America have been rooted in local conditions, there are many signs of effective cooperation. In the case of Brazilians and Chileans, there is a unique bond, as many of the leaders of the Brazilian democratic movement of the last two decades developed close personal and institutional relationships and networks during exile in Chile in the 1960s.[6] Perhaps more importantly, political parties of the left have generally embraced democracy. This includes the Workers Party of Brazil, the PS and PPD of Chile, MAS in Venezuela, and the PRD in Mexico. In Chile, this movement made possible a very strong coalition, Concertación, with the Christian Democratic Party (PDC), a historically centrist political organization whose intellectuals also have very strong links with democratizing movements in the region. Democratic socialist and social-democratic currents in Latin America have in fact played key roles in processes of democratic transition and consolidation. At the same time, conservative

---

5. For instance, the Rio Group has maneuvered repeatedly to prevent the return of authoritarianism in Paraguay.

6. Brazilian exiles in Chile during the 1960s include current President Fernando Henrique Cardoso as well as such prominent figures in his government as José Serra (past Minister of Planning), Francisco Weffort (Minister of Culture), Paulo Renato Souza (Minister of Education), and several others. Several leaders of other parties, including the Workers Party, also lived in Chile in the 1960s.

forces in the region have experienced processes of re-newal which have taken them to reaffirm democracy. The movement of Latin American society to reaffirm and deepen democracy as the only legitimate political organization is hence both broad and deep.

The rich research and debate generated by processes of democratic transition and consolidation in the re-gion has implications for the Cuban case. They have yielded and continue to yield major results and im-plications for the understanding of political change (for recent reviews see Brachet-Márquez 1997, Sø-rensen 1993, Remmer 1995). The task of extrapolat-ing these experiences to the Cuban case is fraught with great perils. Yet, there would seem to be plenty of illuminating lessons.

The Latin American experiences made a large num-ber of scholars favor actor-centered, strategic models of democratization over those emphasizing structural prerequisites. Few such prerequisites could be found to predict short-term advances or failures of democ-ratization in the region. Rather than viewing Latin American democracy as the natural result of econom-ic development, education, or value systems, much of the emphasis has come to be placed on political ac-tors making decisions. In this context, transitions take place in the context of divisions in the authori-tarian regime often prompted by economic crisis, new patterns of mobilization, the death of autocratic leader, military defeat, foreign pressure, or some combination of these factors. Those who start politi-cal reforms see themselves surviving in the new re-gime.

In this perspective, there is no single path to democ-racy, as the actions and interactions toward democra-cy cannot be easily predicted. Paths differ in terms of speed, elite continuity, nature of elite settlements, role of the masses, and the relative role of internal and external forces.

The Latin American experiences tend to confirm the view of transitions as path-dependent phenomena in which institutional and structural frameworks con-strain choice, even if they in turn are re-shaped by them. The nature of the pre-existing constrains rever-berate through time, creating conditions for continu-

ity. Democracy is partly contingent on ideological shifts and institutional developments. The new con-sensus in the region is that it requires active care and defense.

The discussion of democratization in Latin America has centered on the paths of the Southern Cone and Brazil, including decisions "from above" and peace-ful negotiation. Even if such experiences as Nicara-gua and Mexico represent differentiated transitions that have not been fully theorized, strategic interac-tions by consequential actors have been identified as critical in all cases in the region.

The "strategic interaction" approach justifies opti-mism about the prospects of installing or maintain-ing democracy even when prerequisites may not seem to be present. But certain strands of the "pre-requisites" school can also lead to optimism in Latin America and even Cuba. Latin America made deci-sions largely as a result of the strengthening of the democratic impulse within, in the context of long struggles for democracy as well as ideological shifts. And, as recognized in Samuel Huntington's recent reaffirmations of culture and political culture, Latin America as a whole should be seen as part of the tra-dition of Western civilization.

Cuba is not really an exception in this regard. Like Latin America in previous decades, it accompanied the ebb and flow of political liberalism since at least the turn of the century. The Cuban revolution itself began as a reflection of a long-sustained struggle for democracy. Through four decades of Marxism-Le-ninism, important segments of the Cuban popula-tion have probably remained wedded to the basic val-ues and institutional organization conforming Western civilization. And, as noted, Cuba is desper-ately seeking incorporation into regional and interna-tional blocs dominated by the liberal or liberalizing democracies of the West, including Canada and Spain. There are hence grounds to surmise that Cu-bans might eventually adopt or reaffirm the kind of institutional and political profile found throughout the West and much of Latin America.

The Latin American experiences with democratiza-tion tend to confirm some of the lessons from the

Eastern European transitions, including the role of outside factors. Distillates of the literature based on Eastern European cases often favor a policy of assertive engagement with such features as:

- sensitiveness to the need for balance between economic and political reforms;

- providing outside support and understanding to construct a political order based on pluralism, rule of law and respect for human rights, free media, free markets, and the like;

- offering outside technical assistance in designing and maintaining safety nets;

- helping to build civil society, including the creation of a non-profit sector of national and international non-governmental organizations; and

- encouragement of incorporation into the post-Cold War system of international security.

The Western Hemisphere too has taken significant steps toward an engagement policy in support of democracy and democratization.[7] The Ibero-American summits, the Summit of the Americas, and Mercour/ Rio Group have converged on an assertive stance in this regard. The new willingness and ability of Latin Americans to engage in joint action to support democracy and peace has included the leadership of the Rio Group and the Contadora group.

In the early 1990s the OAS began to reflect the new sentiment.[8] The General Assembly meeting in Santiago de Chile in June 1991 adopted a strong endorsement of democracy in "The Santiago Commitment to Democracy and the Renewal of the Inter-American System," calling for "the creation of efficacious, timely, and expeditious procedures to ensure the promotion and defense of democracy." More broadly,

the United States and Latin American governments are collaborating with counterparts in Europe, Asia and the hemisphere to create "a vast interlocking array of organizations, mechanisms, and programs" to promote human rights and democracy (Millet 1994). A growing list of examples shows how the above array of organizations are supporting regional cooperation in favor of democratic development—monitoring elections, reforming electoral laws and proceedings, training police forces, improving democratic administration and legislatures, strengthening the courts, and the like (in Nicaragua, Dominican Republic, Guatemala, Haiti, Paraguay, Guyana, Ecuador, Panama, and even Mexico).

The Cuban case presents a challenges for the region. Cuban state socialism still elicits considerable sympathy among some sectors, including the perception of it as a rare case of successful standing up to U.S. hegemony and interventionism. Moreover, while engagement with Cuba over this issue risks complicating relations with either that country or the United States, the odds of success seem low. Nevertheless, countries playing exemplary or leading roles in the region—including Chile and Brazil—have opted to tackle the difficult regional dilemmas and political costs associated with the international promotion of human rights and democracy.[9]

One of the issues in need of clarification is how to gauge the character of political trends and dynamics in Cuba, including the regime's claim to have already embraced a distinctive form of democracy billed as superior to others in the region in terms of social policies. The Sixth Ibero-American Summit in fact emphasized the idea of multiple paths toward democracy in the region. In the process, it left open to interpretation important aspects of democratic devel-

---

7. Millet (1994) provides a useful overview.

8. Within the OAS, some early steps include the formation of a Unit for Promotion of Democracy in 1990.

9. For Chile, see "Cuba no va a ser invitada a la Cumbre," an interview with the Chilean Foreign Minister (*La Epoca*, May 25, 1997, pp. 12-13). Chile has emerged as a leader in the hemisphere. It has completed the most mature and consolidated economic and political reforms in Latin America, has experienced sustained economic growth for more than a decade, has hosted a number of important international gatherings (including the 6th Ibero-American Summit and the upcoming Summit of the Americas). It is next in line to join the NAFTA countries into an expanded free trade area in the Americas and in that role will serve as a link between that body and MERCO-SUR. Chile has been a member of the UN's Human Rights Commission.

opment and precisely where the Cuban case stands in that regard.

Latin American Integration and Democracy

This section explores in more depth how the regional processes of cooperation and integration accelerating since the late 1980s shape Latin American policy toward Cuba. Progressively in the 1990s, the Rio Group, MERCOSUR, the Ibero-American Summits, and the Summit of the Americas jelled or peaked in political importance, in the context of the consolidation of democratizing and liberalizing reforms in the largest and most influential countries in the region. In Central America and the Caribbean, previous efforts of the Contadora Group, the G3 (Mexico, Colombia and Venezuela) led to the creation of the Association of Caribbean States. In part, this broad movement meant the loss of function by the Washington-based Organization of American States, though some see a subsequent process of invigoration of the OAS. In counterpoint with these processes, the official U.S. agenda for the Americas still called for turning NAFTA into a free trade agreement for the entire hemisphere by the year 2005, to be known as the Free Trade Agreement of the Americas.[10]

Throughout the 1980s and the first half of the 1990s, Latin America countries focused on democratization, economic policy to arrest a lingering crisis, and peace-making efforts. Multilateral efforts had a narrow sub-regional focus. For instance, the Rio Group emerged as the main political forum in the region, focusing on processes of democratization in Brazil, the Southern Cone, and other countries in South America. This consultative body went on to focus on economic liberalization and economic integration, paving the way for MERCOSUR.

Through mid-1996, Latin American statements about advancing democracy in Cuba remained vague and did not really articulate a coherent alternative approach linking Cuba's international reintegration to

a process of democratization. The importance of the Sixth Ibero-American Summit[11] in this context is that it took a major step in this direction.

Latin American countries generally pursue an approach to Cuba likewise marked by independence and distance from Washington's official line. The early September, 1996 meeting of the Rio Group, for instance, strongly condemned the Helms-Burton law. The Rio Group, an organization of eleven Latin American countries representing 300 million people (Brazil, Mexico, Argentina, Chile, Venezuela, Colombia, Peru, Ecuador, Bolivia, Paraguay and Panama), was formed in 1986 to promote democracy and economic integration in the region. It is the main political forum in the region. It has a strong democratic clause. The vote against U.S. policy toward Cuba came out in spite of direct pleas by Madeleine Albright, the current Secretary of State and then U.S. envoy to the United Nations. Earlier that year, the Inter-American Juridical Committee, an agency of the Organization of American States, declared the Helms-Burton legislation "not in conformity with international law."

The Sixth Ibero-American Summit: The Sixth Ibero-American Summit confirmed the anti-embargo position of Latin America, passing a resolution against Helms-Burton and other clauses decrying obstacles to free trade. But its focus on the consolidation of democracy in the region led to a more general call for democracy. The twenty-one signatories of the Summit's Viña del Mar Agreement, a list which included Cuban President Fidel Castro Ruz, endorsed the region's commitment to democracy (and the latter's superiority over authoritarianism and totalitarianism), political pluralism, and the primacy of human and civil rights.

Like the governments of Mexico and Canada, Latin American leaders clearly advocate the incorporation of Cuba into the region's multilateral bodies, seeing this as a better way to promote changes in the island.

---

10. French-Davis (1995) notes at least 25 bilateral and multilateral trade agreements between 1989 and 1995 (see also Byron 1997, p. 3).

11. The Declaration of Viña del Mar is discussed in Barzelatto and Font (1997).

But they are evolving toward a more assertive position with regard to calling for democratization.

The Sixth Ibero-American Summit did not directly assess the claim in Castro's presentation to the twenty-one delegations that Cuba already has a system of direct grassroots participation that is better than "representative democracy." In fact, the Summit emphasized the role of "national traditions" and other factors in determining the "means, instruments, and mechanisms most suitable" to define a road toward democracy. That way, it endorsed the idea of diverse forms and approaches to democracy.

However, several major statements during the Summit demanded the return of democracy to Cuba. Shortly before the event, the Chilean Congress passed a resolution urging full democratization in Cuba. During the summit, Chilean President Eduardo Frei dismissed the idea that the Cuban polity was democratic, emphasizing that the only legitimate democracy is one built on respect for human rights and one which "makes decisions according to majorities expressed in honest elections." Spanish Prime Minister José Maria Aznar was even more blunt, directly pressing Castro for democratic reforms and hinting that European aid was conditional upon such moves. The Spaniards pointed out that the continuation of Cuba's single-party system and Castro thirty-seven year rule contradicted Castro's very signing of the Summit's final resolution.

It is noteworthy that during stay in Castro, that country's Socialist Party organized a luncheon for him in which prominent party figures, including Hortensia Bussi de Allende, Salvador Allende's widow, made dramatic pleas for democracy in Cuba. This seems to reflect a broad consensus in that country on the need for socialism to unambiguously embrace democracy.

Much of Latin America was hence moving toward a distinctive third position in relation to the positions of the United States or those of Canada-Mexico. While Latin America opposes the Helms-Burton law and is sympathetic to the idea of Cuba's integration into the region's economy and multilateral organizations, the Ibero-American Summit indicated that it was evolving toward a form of assertive cooperation and diplomatic pressure to help the Cuban people move toward democracy after nearly four decades of authoritarian rule by one party, one leader, one regime, and one model of social organization.

The II Summit of the Americas and the Negotiation of the Free Trade Area of the Americas: The debate about the relationship between integration and democracy and the implications regarding Cuba's inclusion are also present in the movement toward the creation of the FTAA. From the perspective of the United States, the idea behind the FTAA is to extend NAFTA to the rest of the hemisphere. Ironically, NAFTA did not contain a democratic clause. In fact, the United States and Canada ignored the authoritarian characteristics of the Mexican political system. When the I Summit of the Americas (Miami, 1994) placed the FTAA on the hemispheric agenda, it justified Cuba's exclusion with strong argument by the United States, the host county, about the absence of democracy in the island. But it did not advance a formal democratic clause.

The II Summit of the Americas, which convened in April 1998 in Santiago de Chile, did take major steps toward formalizing a democratic clause. As it opened the negotiations for an eventual FTAA, some of the lobbying surrounding this event came from a hemispheric "leadership council" that included several past Latin American presidents and Richard Feinberg, a high-level Latin American policy-maker in the first Clinton administration. Such a clause was defended on the grounds of preventing attempts at destabilizing democracy in the region as well as providing an incentive in the Cuban case.[12] The final accords of the II Summit of the Americas had strong language in favor of preserving and strengthening democracy and human rights. It emphasized such areas as a strong and independent judiciary, enhanced educational opportunities, deepening of civil society,

---

12. "Proponen establecer cláusula democrática en Acuerdo del ALCA," *El Mercurio* (17 de abril de 1998), p. C4.

protection of human rights, the modernization of the state, and the battle against corruption, crime, and terrorism.

Though the political climate in Santiago de Chile in 1998 differed greatly from that of Miami in 1994, Cuba was not invited and hence was not part of the official agenda. But Cuba was extensively discussed informally. As President Clinton discussed the agenda with his counterparts in the hemisphere, newspapers and various interest groups pressed for more open discussion of the Cuban case. With journalists asking persistently about Cuba's absence, it dominated the formal press conference closing the Summit. This time it was Brazilian President Fernando Henrique Cardoso who stole some headlines with an inspired statement acknowledging social achievements in Cuba but also asking why democracy was not given to Cuban society. This was a historic moment in that it symbolized, at the same time, Latin America's independence from Washington and its demand for democracy.[13]

Throughout the Summit, Latin American countries had tried to mediate the differences between the United States and Cuba, asking both that the United States revise its policy toward Cuba and that Cuba begin a process of democratization. Chile's Foreign Minister, for instance, acknowledging that Cuba was being discussed in informal conversations, lamented Cuba's absence but argued that NAFTA negotiations were only for countries that met prerequisites in terms of democracy—i.e., Cuba needed to take steps toward democracy if it hoped to join the process of regional integration.[14] Caribbean countries asked for Cuba's inclusion in the FTAA process. Even Argentina's Carlos Menem and Peru's Alberto Fujimori pronounced themselves in favor of that notion, as did

Canada's prime minister Jean Chrétien—who made public plans for an imminent trip to Havana.

The MERCOSUR Summit of 1998: The question of democracy re-emerged shortly after in the 14th MERCOSUR presidential summit of July 1998. The six Latin American presidents meeting in the southern Argentine city of Ushuaia, in Tierra del Fuego, signed a protocol in defense of democracy. The statement holds that "respect for democratic principles is an essential element of the process of integration."

The 1998 MERCOSUR summit provided a test of the strength of the Latin American commitment to integration and democracy. This summit dealt with a difficult trade integration agenda, including differences with respect to the auto industry, canned goods (the threat of flooding the Brazilian market with canned products originating in countries outside MERCOSUR), and sugar (Argentine tariffs but also Brazilian subsidies). The presidents did not reach agreement on the economic agenda. But it was clear that their governments maintained a diplomatic thrust in support of the further development of the accord. The agreements in the political area took the limelight. The "democratic clause" adopted foresees the possibility of sanction against any member state that experiences an institutional rupture. The summit also generated a strong statement in the area of national and regional security, declaring MERCOSUR a "peace zone." The clause is an important step toward formalizing the notion of MERCOSUR as a region free of nuclear weapons. It invokes sanctions against countries participating in wars. The document reinforces other documents about regional security and cooperation in the battle against illegal drug and weapons trade and terrorism.[15] This is a major step that takes member countries beyond

---

13. Brazil paid a price for this role. In the aftermath, a visit to Cuba by the Brazilian Foreign Minister largely failed in further improving relations between the two countries.

14. E.g., "Cuba debe dar señal para reintegrarse a Hemisferio," *El Mercurio* (19 de abril de 1998), p. C2.

15. See Monica Yanakiew and Isabel Braga, "Presidentes tornam Mercosul uma zona de paz," *O Estado de São Paulo* (July 24, 1998), www.estado.com.br/edicao/pano/98/07/24. Assessments of the 14th MERCOSUR Summit can be found in "Mercosul, devagar e sempre," *Folha de São Paulo* (July 26, 1998), www.uol.com.br/fsp/opiniao, and in Gilson Schwartz "Economia dificulta aliança no Mercosul," *Folha de São Paulo* (July 26, 1998), www.uol.com.br. The MERCOSUR website is at www.rau.edu.uy/mercosur.

"concertación política" and toward political integration.

Once again, Cuba ended up receiving more coverage than anticipated at this MERCOSUR gathering. South African president Nelson Mandela, a special guest, gave an interview in which he defended Cuba and stated that democracy with hunger and illiteracy was an "empty shell." Brazilian President Cardoso rapidly replied that in this country the shell was not empty and that in any case democracy was the best way "to fill the shell."[16]

Latin America's regional gatherings (in the context of the Ibero-American Summits, FTAA, the Rio Group, MERCOSUR and the like) will no doubt continue to debate the defense of democracy and its relationship to integration. The forms of democracy being consolidated or deepened in Latin America are still imperfect and in some cases in danger of reversal. Structural, institutional and cultural realities and practices impose limitations on the development of democracy in the region. Deepening is hence neither guaranteed nor is it likely to occur without political effort. It is precisely the realization what drives Latin American leaders to emphasize the active defense of democracy. The link between democracy and integration is a political choice that conditions enhanced forms of economic cooperation to the embrace of democracy. The hope is that the formalization of democratic clauses will help prevent reversals to authoritarianism and provide incentives for democratic development.

With democracy a long-term goal of regional multilateral organizations, the turn of the century will probably see efforts to define the specific patterns of cooperation and "conditionalities" deemed effective in the development of democracy in members or prospective members, including Cuba. While Latin American countries will give top priority to trade and integration issues in the context of the proposed Free Trade Area of the Americas, the Cuban question will continue to draw attention.

With Canada and much of Latin America and the Caribbean in support of that notion, the United States will have a difficult time keeping Cuba out of the third FTAA summit to be held in Canada in 2001. But effective membership in this process seems remote at this point, given Cuba's official policy. After all, trade and economic liberalization is one of the central premises of the new integration process in the hemisphere. Likewise, Cuba would have to make major liberalizing reforms to hope to join MERCOSUR one day.

If Cuba's evolving relationship to Latin America will hence need to take into consideration the region's economic re-alignment process favoring regional economic units, the chief underlying issue is really Cuba's readiness to embrace the region's prevailing economic and political trends. With Cuban authorities on record as dismissing Latin American democracy and arguing that Cuba has the best democracy in the hemisphere, there are few grounds for optimism that the Castro regime will decide to organize a democratic transition in Cuba. In fact, in the framework of the analysis advanced here and Font (1997, 1998), what can be expected is a sustained international offensive by the Cuban authorities oriented to obtaining external support and resources to minimize the need for internal change. In a speech on July 26, 1998—as this essay was being readied for distribution—Cuba's President Fidel Castro announced a series of trips for the rest of the year that would take him to several countries in the Caribbean, Portugal and South Africa. Earlier, Cuban authorities had announced a major international conference on globalization to take place in Havana in January 1999.

In the light of previous statements, it might be surmised that the regime is preparing itself for the tough debates ahead in the context of Ibero-American summits and the advancing regional negotiations about integration. Cuba's president will participate in the Ibero-American Summit of 1998 (Portugal) and will host the Ibero-American Summit in 1999. The issue of democracy will surface at these gatherings, as

---

16. "Democracia só vale sem fome, diz Mandela," *O Estado de São Paulo* (July 24, 1998), www.estado.com.br.

heads of state in still democratizing societies ask the Cuban delegation about the commitments which it signed in the 1996 Summit of the Americas in Santiago.

The very internationalization of the debate about the promotion of democracy in Cuba will draw from the three approaches to the subject found in the region. Two alternatives to U.S. policy hence can be discerned in the Latin American and hemispheric debate about Cuban democratization. That represented by the traditional positions of Mexico—a country that had a political system diagnosed as authoritarian as it signed an integration agreement with the two paramount democracies in the hemisphere—maintains that economic contact with little or no pressure is the best way to handle Cuba. This position has many points in common with that of Canada, with whom Mexico shares deepening economic interests in Cuba. The rest of Latin America seems to be moving toward a position emphasizing assertive cooperation to enhance the prospects for political development.

IMPLICATIONS

If Cuba's process of re-insertion into the changing Western Hemisphere and world economy can be expected to have profound implications for internal political and economic dynamics, the precise impact of this process on the development of Cuban democracy hinges on Cuba's willingness and capacity to engage in substantive reforms. The Cuban state retains a pronounced anti-market, ideological, and authoritarian institutional form. Cuban state socialism has adopted limited market measures reluctantly, cautiously, and with a sharp eye to maintaining itself. It has seemed to prefer antagonism to rapprochement with the United States and on the grounds that proximity would endanger political unity. At least on the short term, a reinsertion process that did not challenge these premises would tend to reinforce the pre-established response.

It seems reasonable to expect that changes in Cuba's institutional framework will take time and effort. One plausible scenario for the institutional-ideological factor to change is an extended period of "social learning" driven by poor performance and crises. The regime either believes that state socialism can survive or so fears the consequences of economic liberalization and democratization that it will not embrace either or, much less, both. Either way, the end result is a decision to maintain reforms to a minimum and retain control.

If—as many believe—Cuba does not have the size or other conditions to successfully maintain such a policy, then crisis or a prolonged period of stagnation in the socialist sector of the economy will be the result. Such a prolonged crisis would lead to change probably in the medium or long term, possibly in the course of changes in the top leadership. If such a pattern of change could take a relatively long time to occur, the resulting "transition" might be likely characterized by political and social turmoil. It is hence possible that reforms might come "too little, too late" to make a substantial difference to most Cubans. It seems worrisome in this regard that so few policymakers in Cuba acknowledge that insufficient interim reforms will delay substantially an eventual process of full recovery.

Meanwhile, it is certain that Cuba will continue to place in high and even increasing priority its relationship to the international system. The island's new internationalism cannot but deepen. The above discussion has emphasized external influences on the island. However, apparently there is enough fluidity in the international system to continue to justify among some Cuban decision-makers the notion of a process of re-insertion that minimizes or even reduces the need for change. This enhanced outward strategy can be expected to include tactical innovations and eventful foreign relations in the near future.[17] Relations with the Caribbean and Latin America are of special strategic significance in terms of member-

---

17. The visit of Pope John Paul II to Cuba in early 1998 confirms this prospective analysis written in early 1997. By the same logic, other events will take place after full assimilation of the Pope's visit.

ship in larger economic units in formation and the process of gaining international leverage.

It follows from the line of analysis sketched above that major internal reforms will probably await the results of these campaigns, as Cuban policy-makers will need to have exhausted all possibilities in the international arena before they adopt massive internal reforms. Meanwhile, a policy shift in the United States—added to the acceleration of regional and global multilateralism (or "globalization")—might indeed help bring about conditions that alter the dynamics and terms of Cuba's reinsertion. As noted above, critics of the current U.S. policy claim that it is counterproductive to democratization on various grounds, including the fact that the Castro regime uses it to justify its rule. The embargo failed to induce change in Cuba for nearly four decades and clashes with notions of sovereignty.[18] Unilateral interventions have generally failed to promote democracy. Castro's longevity in power owes in part to his ability to play to the worst fears of Cuban nationalists and convince Cubans that the United States is bent on intervening in the island to gain unfair advantages. The Helms-Burton law gives support to those skeptical of U.S. intervention in Cuban affairs.

In this context, it seems likely in the short run that enough Cubans will distrust U.S. policies and oppose any form of rapprochement that does not respect the principle of Cuban sovereignty. If so, the Helms-Burton law will not succeed in either overthrowing the current regime or creating conditions conducive to democracy. In addition, the Helms-Burton law might be a significant impediment to political stability and democracy in a post-Castro Cuba, since governments coming to power under its rule will tend to be seen as lacking legitimacy by vast sectors of the Cuban population.

The toughened embargo policy toward Cuba is being challenged in the United States as well as throughout the Western Hemisphere and Europe, where it is seen as clashing with important international principles and trade policies endorsed by the United States. President Clinton inherited from George Bush a vision of trade integration partly as a way of shifting from the regime of development aid which had guided policy making since the late 1940s. Enthusiasm for NAFTA and trade integration cooled down considerably in response to labor opposition as well as the Mexican crisis of 1994-95. However, though support for a Free Trade Area of the Americas, originally proposed by the U.S. President in 1994, was also receding in the United States, liberalized trade and economic relations continue to be pillars of the foreign policy of the United States. The growing perception is that the Helms-Burton law neglects to take fully into account the interests and views of with other nations in the hemisphere as well as important lessons from transitions in various parts of the world. This aggressive legislation, not present even in the depths of the Cold War, will fuel intensified international opposition in the context of trade and economic liberalization and integration. In this context, it is indeed conceivable that U.S. policy toward Cuba will experience significant revision in the not too distant future. If so, hardliners in Cuba will not be able to claim that the island's authoritarianism and poor economic performance are explained or justified by U.S. aggressiveness.

CONCLUSION

Several implications follow from the above discussion. First, to the extent that democracy and the promotion of democracy have emerged as international norms, particularly in the context of Latin American and European integration, it seems likely that inter-

---

18. Indeed, Cuban nationalism has been wounded by U.S. policies well before Castro came to power. The very rise of the United States to world power entailed costs to Cuba. Most Cubans believe that the Spanish-American War (1898) took victory away from the hands of Cuban insurgents and led to a humiliating intervention (lasting until 1902, but later repeated) and the much-resented Platt Amendment imposed to the Cuban constitution, giving the United States government constitutional rights to intervene in the island's affairs. Cuban nationalism, fueled by fears and resentments about U.S. designs on the island, simmered throughout the ensuing decades of the 20th century and was no doubt a major factor in defining the course of the Cuban revolution of 1959. Cuban nationalists base their arguments on a two-century history that began with George Washington's efforts to buy the island of Cuba from Spain and includes the Manifest Destiny and the rise of annexionist currents in the United States and Cuba.

national actors will play a key role in Cuba's dynamics of transformation compared to other democratizing transitions. A word of caution, however, is necessary. Powerful economic actors have apparently decided to lobby against any law or policy that links or subordinates trade to political goals. Much will depend on how politicians and policymakers in the region interpret their roles in the process of globalization and integration.

Second, Latin America provides an important framework to help orient actors in the critical decisions shaping Cuba's inevitable long-term path toward integration and democracy. The integration process in Latin America and the Caribbean (MERCOSUR, CARICOM, and CACM) is a key stage in which to define Cuba's new role in the world economy. But, as noted, this influence is not unambiguous. Policymakers and policy-oriented fora in the region have yet to fully probe the mutual relevance between the Cuban dynamics of transformation and the processes of regional integration and change. If negotiations about Cuba's participation in regional integration processes can advance the dynamics and prospects of democratization in the island, an immediate task is to develop channels of discussion and assertive cooperation that bring key players together to address the difficult predicament of the Cuban nation and the role of Latin America and the Caribbean in the search for constructive solutions. The Ibero-American summits, one of the few regional fora in which Cuba participates, can be important in this regard.

Third, broader negotiations for an expanded Free Trade Area of the Americas are a critical factor in structuring new patterns of cooperation in the hemisphere. This process brings together all nations in the hemisphere, except Cuba. In fact, Cuba is not part of any of the key regional organizations in the Western Hemisphere—the Organization of American States, the Inter-American Development Bank, NAFTA, and the like. Obviously, this situation will need to come to an end at some point. Other things being equal, it is best that this happen sooner rather later. Cuban society will be damaged for a long time to come if it plays a marginal role in the formative stages of this process. It is primarily up to the Cuban authorities to respond to this challenge. Nevertheless, debate on a policy toward Cuba and its hemispheric integration may perhaps make such an adequate response more likely, while beginning to forge the context governing the island's incorporation into the regional integration and cooperation schemes. Again, the first challenge in this wider context is to specify the conditions and processes under which Cuban society could have access to the changing Inter-American system. Beyond that, the task is to construct an effective framework to engage all actors. Discussion in the context of the European Union will be central in defining the conditions of Cuba's access to other forms of international cooperation and integration.

Lastly, if the United States, which has a key role in the process of global liberalization and cooperation, also adopts a fresh approach toward Cuba, the island might face an international context so clearly favorable to overall liberalization that it would be a decisive test of the readiness of the current Cuban regime and society to change and embrace democracy.

Appendix
ORGANIZATIONS IN THE WESTERN HEMISPHERE

ACS: Association of Caribbean States. In 1992 the leaders of the Central American Common Market decided to begin to negotiate with CARICOM the formation of a broad regional organization including the two. Mexico, Colombia and Venezuela joined the deliberations. Collectively, member countries have a population of 202 million inhabitants and income of more than $500 billion dollars in mid-1990s. [See Byron (1997), Ceara-Hatton (1997), Erisman (1997).]

CACM: Central American Common Market. Signed in 1960 by Costa Rica, El Salvador, Guatemala, Honduras and Nicaragua. [See Erisman (1997).]

Andean Pact: Initially called the Andean Subregional Integration Agreement, its purpose was to promote economic integration by the progressive elimination of tariffs and coordinated industrial development. Original agreement signed by Bolivia, Chile, Colombia, Ecuador, and Peru in 1969. Venezuela joined in 1973, but Chile withdrew in 1977. Bolivia, Ecuador, and Peru have suspended membership for brief periods, responding to bilateral conflicts with other member countries. After 1992, the Andean Pact aimed at the creation of a free-trade zone and then an integrated common market by 1995, but its limited success has been overshadowed by the rise of MERCOSUR.

CARICOM: Caribbean Community and Common Market. Created in 1973, taking the place of the Caribbean Free Trade Association of 1965. Its purpose is to promote trade and development within the region. Governed by a Council made up of Ministers of Government. The Secretariat is in Georgetown, Guyana. Current 14 members: Antigua and Barbuda, Bahamas, Barbados, Belize, Dominica, Grenada, Guyana, Suriname, Jamaica, Montserrat, St Kitts-Nevis, St Lucia, St Vincent and the Grenadines, and Trinidad and Tobago. It also has 2 Associate Members and 9 Observers. [See Ceara-Hatton (1997), Erisman (1997): 20-23.]

FTAA (ALCA): Free Trade Area of the Americas (Acuerdo de Libre Comercio de las Américas). Concept articulated in I Summit of the Americas (Miami, December, 1994) and further developed by Ministerial and lower level meetings (e.g., Ministers of Trade Meeting, Belo Horizonte, Brazil, May 1997) as well as Business Fora. The II Summit of the Americas (Santiago de Chile, April 1998) formalized the start of multilateral negotiations for the establishment of the FTAA. [See Ceara Hatton (1997).]

Group of Three (G-3): Informal association between Mexico, Venezuela, and Colombia, the three largest countries/economies in the Caribbean basin.

LAIA: Latin American Integration Association. Established in 1980. Latin America Free Trade Area (LAFTA) came into existence in 1961 with the goal to promote trade and became LAIA in 1980, with the limited purpose of protecting existing intra-regional trade.

MERCOSUR: Decision to form it made in 1991 by the presidents of Argentina, Brazil, Paraguay, and Uruguay. Trade liberalization started in December 1994. Grew out of bilateral accords. With population of 200 million and a combined GNP of $420 billion. Bolivia and Chile joined as associate members in 1996. Cuba would like to join, but MERCOSUR is likely to remain a South American phenomenon for some time. Its headquarters are in Montevideo.

NAFTA: Following an earlier accord between the United States and Canada, in 1992 Mexico initiated discussions to form a free trade agreement among the three countries. Came into existence on January 1, 1994. Trading bloc of 320 million people.

OAS: Organization of American States.

The Rio Group: The Rio Group is an organization of eleven Latin American countries representing 300 million people (Brazil, Mexico, Argentina, Chile, Venezuela, Colombia, Peru, Ecuador, Bolivia, Paraguay and Panama) formed in 1986 to promote democracy and, later, trade and economic integration in the region. Cuba and the Dominican Republic have expressed interest in joining, but the Rio Group has repeatedly declined.

SELA: Sistema Económico de América Latina (Latin American Economic System). Founded in 1975. Regional organization of Latin American countries, excluding the United States and including Cuba, to promote economic cooperation and development. Emphasizes study and discussion. Has 26 members. Decisions are made at annual conferences held in Caracas, where SELA's secretariat is located. It has had a limited impact on public debate and policy.

BIBLIOGRAPHY

Alamos, Pilar, Mauricio A. Font, José Augusto Guilhon Albuquerque and Francisco León, editors (1998). *Integración económica y democratización: América Latina y Cuba.* Santiago de Chile: Instituto de Estudios Internacionales.

Baloyra, Enrique (1987). "Democratic Transition in Comparative Perspective," in E. Baloyra ed. *Comparing New Democracies: Transition and Consolidation in Mediterranean Europe and the Southern Cone.* Boulder: Westview Press.

Barzelatto, Elba and Mauricio A. Font (1997). *Cuban Affairs/Asuntos Cubanos.*

Brachet-Márquez, Viviane (1997). "Democratic Transition and Consolidation in Latin America: Steps Toward a New Theory of Democratization." Paper presented at LASA, April 17-19, Mexico.

Bryan, A., ed. (1995). *The Caribbean: New Dynamics in Trade and Political Economy.* Coral Gables, FL: University of Miami, North-South Center.

Byron, Jessica (1997). "The Association of Caribbean States: New Regional Interlocutor for the Caribbean Basin?" Paper presented at LASA, April 17-19, Mexico.

Calvert, Peter (1994). *The International Politics of Latin America.* Manchester and New York: Manchester University Press.

Campbell, John. (1995). "State Building and Postcommunist Budget Deficits." *American Behavioral Scientist* 38 (5, March/April): 760-787.

Campbell, John. (1993). "Institutional Theory and the Influence of Foreign Actors on Reform in Capitalist and Post-Socialist Societies," in J. Hausner, B. Jessop and K. Nielsen, eds. *Institutional Frameworks of Markets Economies.* Aldershot, England: Avebury.

Cardoso, Fernando Henrique (1986-87). "Democracy in Latin America." *Politics and Society* 15 (1) 23-41.

Carothers, Thomas (1997). "Democracy Without Illusions." *Foreign Affairs* 16 (1, Jan/Feb), 85-100.

Ceara Hatton, Miguel (1997). "The Island Caribbean in the Dynamics of Hemispheric Integration." Paper presented at Fifth Conference of the Association of Caribbean Economists, Havana, Cuba, November 30-December 2.

Centeno, Miguel (1994). "Between Rocky Democracies and Hard Markets: Dilemmas of the Double Transition." *Annual Review of Sociology.*

Central Intelligence Agency (1997) Cuba: *Handbook of Trade Statistics.* Springfield, VA: National Technical Information Service.

Centeno, Miguel Angel and Mauricio A. Font eds. (1996). *Toward a New Cuba?* Boulder: Lynn Rienner.

Cuban Communist Party. (1996). *Report of the Cuban Communist Party Politburo approved at the fifth PCC Central Committee plenum in Havana on 24 March, read by Army General Raúl Castro.* FBIS-translated text.

Di Palma, Giuseppe (1990). *To Craft Democracies.* Berkeley: University of California Press.

Domínguez, Jorge (1993). "The Transition to Somewhere: Cuba in the 1990s," in The Cuban Research Institute, ed. *Transition in Cuba: New Challenges for U.S. Policy.* Florida International University.

Eckstein, Susan Eva. (1994). *Back From the Future: Cuba Under Castro.* Princeton, N.J.: Princeton University Press.

Eguizábal, Cristina, ed. (1988). *América Latina y la crisis centroamericana. En busca de una solución regional.* Buenos Aires: Gel.

Erisman, H. Michael. (1995). "Cuba's Evolving CARICOM Connection," in A.R.M. Ritter and J.M. Kirk, eds. *Cuba in the International System: Normalization and Integration.* London: MacMillan Press.

Erisman, H. Michael (1997). "Beyond Political/Economic Diversification: Cuba's Coalition-Building Activities." Paper presented at LASA, Mexico, April 17-19.

Feinsilver, Julie. 1995. "Cuba's Current Integration into the International and Hemispheric Systems," in A.R.M. Ritter and J.M. Kirk, eds. *Cuba in the International System: Normalization and Integration.* London: MacMillan Press.

Faucett, L. and A. Hurrell, eds. (1995). *Regionalism in World Politics: Regional Organization and World Order.* Oxford, U.K.: Oxford University Press.

Ffrench-Davis, Ricardo (1995). In J.J.Teunissen ed. *Regionalism and the Global Economy: The Case of Latin America and the Caribbean.* The Hague: FONDAD, pp. 90-118.

Font, Mauricio A. (1998). "Cuba Policy in the United States: Toward a New Chapter?" Paper presented at I Academic Colloquium of the Americas, March 1998, Costa Rica.

Font, Mauricio A. (1996). "Cuba: Crisis and Reform," in M.A. Centeno and M.A. Font eds. *Toward a New Cuba? Legacies of a Revolution* (Boulder: Lynn Rienner).

Frohmann, Alicia (1996). "Cooperación política e integración latinoamericana en los '90." Santiago, Chile: FLACSO. Nueva Serie Flacso.

Frohmann, Alicia (1994). "Regional Initiatives for Peace and Democracy: The Collective Diplomacy of the Rio Group." In C. Kaysen, R.A. Pastor and L. Reed, eds. *Collective Responses to Regional Problems: The Case of Latin America and the Caribbean.* Cambridge, MA: American Academy of Arts and Sciences.

Grabendorff, Wolf (1993-94). "Germany and Latin America: A Complex Relationship." *Journal of Interamerican Studies and World Affairs* 35 (4, Winter): 43-100.

Hausner, Jerzy, Bob Jessop and Klaus Nielsen. (1993). "Post-Socialism, the Negotiated Economy and other Western Models," in J. Hausner, B. Jessop and K. Nielsen, eds. *Institutional Frameworks of Markets Economies.* Aldershot, England: Avebury.

Held, David. (1991). "Democracy, the Nation-State and the Global System," in David Held ed. *Political Theory Today.* Stanford, California: Stanford University Press.

Higley, John, Judith Kullberg and Jan Pakulski. (1996). "The Persistence of Postcommunist Elites." *Journal of Democracy* 7 (2): 133-147.

Hurrell, A. (1995). "Explaining the Resurgence of Regionalism in World Politics." *Review of International Studies* 21 (4, October): 331-358.

Inter-American Dialogue (1994). *Advancing Democracy and Human Rights in the Americas: What Role for the OAS?* Washington: Inter-American Dialogue.

Jessop, Bob. (1995). "Regional Economic Blocs, Cross-Border Cooperation, and Local Economic Strategies in Postsocialism." *American Behavioral Scientist* 38 (5, March/April): 674-715.

Kaplowitz, Donna Rich, ed. (1993). *Cuba's Ties to a Changing World.* Boulder Colorado: Lynne Rienner Publishers.

Karl, Terry L. (1990) "Dilemmas of Democratization in Latin America." *Comparative Politics* 23 (1).

Karl, Terry L. and Philippe Schmitter (1991). "Modes of Transition in Latin America, Southern and Eastern Europe." *International Social Science Journal* 128 (May).

León, Francisco. (1995). "The International Reinsertion of Cuba: Emerging Scenarios," in A.R.M. Ritter and J.M. Kirk, eds. *Cuba in the International System: Normalization and Integration.* London: MacMillan Press.

Lowenthal, Abraham F. ed. (1991). *Exporting Democracy.* Baltimore: Johns Hopkins University Press.

Millet, Richard (1994). "Beyond Sovereignty: International Efforts to Support Latin American Democracy." *Journal of Interamerican Studies* 36 (3).

Ministerio de Relaciones Internacionales de Chile (1994). *Grupo de Rio: Documentos oficiales del principal foro político de América Latina y el Caribe*. Santiago de Chile: BAT.

Muñoz, Heraldo and V.P. Vaky (1993). *The Future of the Organization of American States.* New York: Twentieth Century Fund.

Muñoz García, Humberto, ed. (1993). *Las transiciones a la democracia.* México: Cambio 21.

O'Donnell, Guillermo (1989). "Transition to Democracy: Some Navigational Instruments," in Robert Pastor, ed., *Democracy in the Americas: Stopping the Pendulum.* New York: Holmes and Meier.

O'Donnell, Guillermo. (1993). "On the State, Democratization, and Some Conceptual Problems: A Latin American View with Glances at Some Postcommunist Countries." *World Development* 21 (8): 1355-1369.

Pastor, Robert (1993). "Forward to the Beginning: Widening the Scope for Global Collective Action," in Reed and Kaysen, eds., *Emerging Norms of Justified Intervention.* Cambridge, MA: American Academy of Arts and Sciences.

Poitras, Guy (1997). "Regionalism after NAFTA: Muddling Through, Widening or Deepening?" Paper presented at LASA, April 17-19, Mexico.

Przeworski, Adam (1988). "Democracy as a Contingent Outcome of Conflicts," in John D. Elster and P. Slagstad eds *Constitutionalism and Democracy.* Cambridge: Cambridge University Press.

Przeworski, Adam (1991). *Democracy and the Market: Political and Economic Reforms in Eastern Europe and Latin America.* Cambridge: Cambridge University Press.

Reed, Laura W. And Carl Kaysen, eds. (1993). *Emerging Norms of Justified Intervention.* Cambridge, MA: American Academy of Arts and Sciences.

Remmer, Karen (1995). "New Theoretical Perspectives on Democratization." *Comparative Politics* 23 (4).

Ritter, A.R.M. (1996). "Consequences for Canada of Prospective Cuba-United States Relations: From the "Helms-Burton" Bill to Rapprochement." Developing Studies Working Paper 15, The Norman Paterson School of International Affairs, Carleton University, Ottawa, Canada

Schmitter, Philippe (1994). "Dangers and Dilemmas of Democracy." *Journal of Democracy* 5:2 (April):61-62.

Schumpeter, Joseph (1950). *Capitalism, Socialism and Democracy.* New York: Harper and Row.

Smaldone, William. (1996). "Observations on the Cuban Revolution." *Monthly Review* 47 (11, April): 20-32.

Sørensen, Georg (1993). *Democracy and Democratization.* Boulder: Westview Press.

Teunissen, J.J. ed. (1995). *Regionalism and the Global Economy: The Case of Latin America and the Caribbean.* The Hague: FONDAD.

COMMENTS ON

"Cuba and Latin America: The Political Dimension," by Font

Alfred G. Cuzán

Professor Font's paper offers an analysis of both the expected and, what is not the same thing, the hoped-for impacts of Latin America's democratization and economic liberalization and integration on the Castro regime as the latter, having survived the Soviet collapse, seeks economic and political re-insertion into the region.

Over the last two decades, Latin America has shed military dictatorships and statist approaches to economic development in favor of democracy and markets. The region's economies are becoming integrated through international trade agreements, and these usually include democratic clauses requiring member countries to respect human rights and political liberties. This sea-change in the political economy of Latin America has taken place at a time when the Castro regime, its project for revolutionary internationalism having failed, is pursuing a foreign strategy designed to attract desperately needed capital and acquire or augment diplomatic support against the U.S. embargo, especially the Helms-Burton law. Re-establishing economic relations with Latin America and the Caribbean is part and parcel of this strategy. However, Cuba's bid for membership in trade agreements is blocked by the democratic clauses the regime is required to meet.

Professor Font explicitly lays out the dilemma faced by the Castro regime: either (a) democratize and hence risk losing political control in order to gain admission to Latin America's trading blocs or (b) keep a tight grip on political life, but at the risk of regional

marginalization and prolonged economic crisis eventually leading to political collapse.

In analyzing this dilemma, the author seems to be of two minds. He is realistic enough to expect "a sustained international offensive by the Cuban authorities oriented to obtaining external support and resources to minimize the need for internal change." In other words, far from democratizing in order to meet external conditions for support, the regime will attempt to coax international support in order to avoid having to give up any power at home.

At the same time, the author is not without a certain naivete. In an ambiguous passage which I may be misinterpreting, and which I call on him to clarify, he appears to advocate admitting Cuba into regional organizations such as the OAS, the Inter-American Development Bank, NAFTA, etc., and "[t]he sooner, the better." He seems to think that a mere *debate* on a policy toward Cuba and its hemispheric integration" will increase the likelihood that the regime will "respond to the [political] challenge" to democratize [emphasis added].

In fairness to him, Font does say that "the first challenge in this wider context is to specify the conditions and processes under which Cuban society could have access to the changing Inter-American system." But aren't "the conditions and processes" already specified in the democratic clauses attached to international trade agreements? What if the regime continues to "claim to have already embraced a distinctive form of democracy billed as superior to others in the region in terms of social policies"? What then?

Even less realistic is the author's hope that if only the United States were to adopt "a fresh approach toward Cuba," i.e., lift the embargo, "the island might face an international context so clearly favorable to overall liberalization that it would be a decisive test of the readiness of the current Cuban regime and society to change and embrace democracy." As if "embracing democracy" did not involve a fundamental change in the very nature of the regime, a transformation that, if the transitions in Eastern Europe and Latin America are a guide, would, at a minimum, result in the removal of the Castro brothers and their subalterns from power, the release of political prisoners, the freeing of the press, and the carrying out of investigations that would expose the truth, long repressed and covered up with lies, of four decades of crimes, corruption, and sheer waste of resources.

If the Castro regime faces a dilemma, so do the Latin American democracies. They want to admit Cuba to the developing inter-American community of democracy and trade, but the very nature of the regime, i.e., a centralized autocracy practicing an "extreme form of state socialism" fails to qualify for admission. So, the democracies either (a) require the regime to comply with the democratic clauses, which it won't, therefore risking having to exclude Cuba from the region and being accused of subordinating their foreign policy to that of the United States or (b) admit the regime as is and hazard undermining their own commitment to democracy, a dangerous precedent in light of the region's history of military dictatorships.

In the face of this dilemma, the Latin American democracies have opted to pursue a rather tortuous course, calling on the regime to democratize while in fact tolerating it and, while not granting it formal admission to regional markets, nevertheless carrying on bilateral trade agreements with it. In fact, the 1999 Ibero-American Summit will take place in Cuba, the only country in the group ruled by a non-democratic regime.

As the passages quoted above appear to imply, the author seemingly advocates taking this strategy still further, settling for minimalist or even cosmetic reforms in exchange for some sort of participation in trading blocs in the hope that Cuba's insertion into on-going processes of economic integration will eventually cause the regime to undergo real democratization. As I acknowledged earlier, given the ambiguity of key passages, I may be misinterpreting him, so again I call on Professor Font to make his meaning clear.

The author makes references to processes of democratization in Latin America and Eastern Europe, but does not analyze them in a systematic manner. All he offers is a list of "lessons" on how to promote the process of transition *once it has begun*. But these lessons do not help us analyze the likelihood of regime change in Cuba in light of the new political economy of Latin America. Part of the problem is that the author does not always consistently or clearly distinguish between *regime* and country, or rulers and ruled. In a democracy, where the government is the product of competitive elections and subject to public opinion, this is not a serious failing. But when dealing with a non-democratic regime, losing sight of this distinction is fatal for analytic integrity.

In estimating the likelihood that the Castro regime will democratize, it is helpful to review the Latin American record on transitions. From the 1980s to the 1990s, dictatorship gave way to democracy, in part or in full, in 14 Ibero-American countries: Mexico, Guatemala, Honduras, El Salvador, Nicaragua, Panama, Ecuador, Peru, Bolivia, Paraguay, Brazil, Chile, Argentina, and Uruguay. All transitions were prompted by some sort of regime failure, political (loss of popular referendum, breakdown of elite consensus), economic (hyperinflation, default on international debts), or international (Argentina's defeat in the Falklands/Malvinas war). Nevertheless, some regimes undertook to democratize more or less voluntarily while others had to be compelled to do so by force of arms, either civil war or external intervention (U.S. capture of Noriega in Panama).

In seeking to understand why some dictatorships gave way voluntarily and others in the face of violence, it is instructive to distinguish between two types of dictatorial regimes: one-man dictatorship, or tyranny, and oligarchy. Tyranny is an autocracy identified with and dominated by one man for an extended period, say around ten years or more. An oligarchy, by contrast, is a dictatorship with collective or rotating leadership in which no one man dominates for any length of time.

Table 1. Mode of Transition by Type of Dictatorship in Latin America, 1980s-1990s

Mode of Transition	Regime Type	
	Tyrannies	Oligarchies
More or less voluntary	Chile	Argentina
		Boliva
		Brazil
		Ecuador
		Honduras
		Mexica
		Peru
		Uruguay
Involuntary	Nicaragua	El Salvador
	Panama	Guatemala
	Paraguay	Nicaragua (Sandinistas)

Table 1 displays the tabular relationship between type of dictatorship and mode of transition in Latin America from the 1980s to the 1990s. Note that, by a better than a 2:1 margin, oligarchies transitioned to democracy more or less voluntarily whereas only one of four tyrannies did so. (When Pinochet stepped down from the presidency, he once again illustrated Chile's political exceptionalism in Latin America.)

If this distribution is representative, it appears that, almost always, a tyrant clings to power at all costs, and it takes power to dislodge him. It could be that, psychologically, returning to private life is more difficult for a tyrant, who towers above all others, than for members of an oligarchy, accustomed as they are to exercise a smaller share of political power and for a shorter time. Knowing no equal in the state, a tyrant acquires habits of arrogance, insolence, and holding all opinions but his own in contempt. Once ousted, his usual fate is exile, for if he cannot abide loss of power, neither does the public feel safe with a former tyrant in their midst.

If they cannot oust him by force, which is normally the only way he will go while alive, the people's other option is to wait for death to take him. Although no Latin American tyrant died in office during this period, it may be noted that, a decade earlier, two Iberian tyrants—Franco of Spain and Salazar of Portugal—did die in office, and it was their deaths that paved the way for the restoration of democracy in those two countries, rather directly in Spain and in Portugal only after the Caetano interregnum and the military regime that overthrew it. An even earlier example comes from Venezuela. In 1935, General Juan Vicente Gómez, the legendary "tyrant of the Andes," died, and was succeeded by a military oligarchy which within a decade gave way to the first—if short-lived—democratic government in that country's history.

Now in his early seventies, Fidel Castro could live another decade, and may yet break the world's record for a tyrant's tenure (on January 1, 1999, he will mark four decades in power). At his death it is very possible that his brother Raúl will attempt to seize the reins. How long he can hang on is an imponderable. Before his chances are summarily dismissed, one must note that in North Korea Kim Il Sung's son has managed to keep the succession in the family, as did "Baby" Doc Duvalier in Haiti, who after "Papa" Doc died ruled for some fifteen years before his ouster. However, it is unlikely that Raúl will be able to rule like a tyrant. Once Fidel dies, even if Raúl succeeds him as head, the regime will begin to resemble an oligarchy. At that time, both the probability of democratization and, more to the point, that of a *coup*, will jump.

In conclusion, trade or no trade, embargo or no embargo, the likelihood that the Castro regime will "embrace democracy" is nil. Tyrants are not prone to give up power voluntarily and Fidel Castro, being more tyrannical than most, is even less likely to do so, no matter how many carrots are offered by potential trade agreements. Only the stick can do the job. There being no chance of outside intervention, the only realistic hope for democratization before Fidel Castro's death rests with the military. Such are the parameters of Cuba's political dimension.

BACK TO THE FUTURE: CUBAN TOURISM IN THE YEAR 2007

Nicolás Crespo

At last year's ASCE meetings we presented a paper comparing the future of the Cuban tourism industry and its economic impact under two scenarios. We accepted the Ministry of Tourism's figures projected through the year 2000 and formulated our own estimate of a ten-year projection through the year 2007. We chose to project ten years into the future and avoided consideration of the variables, issues, theories, predictions and suggestions regarding changes in the political system in Cuba. In this manner, we did not cloud the purpose and methodology of our study with political issues.

The two scenarios were defined as follows:

First Scenario: Assumes the continuation through the year 2007 of the current political and economic system, perhaps with minor changes having a minimal impact.

Second Scenario: Assumes the complete elimination of political and economic barriers, both internal and external. We also assumed a free capitalistic economy, where American citizens and residents, as well as Cuban citizens, are able to invest in, operate, visit and enjoy any of Cuba's tourism facilities; to develop any enterprise to support the tourism industry; and to satisfy the growing consumer demand for better products and services.

Table 1 summarizes our estimated tourism statistics under both scenarios, for the year 2007.

Table 2 shows the economic impact of tourism in Cuba in 2007 estimated on the basis of Puerto Rico's multipliers. Please refer to Appendix II for the em-

ployment, production and income multipliers used for the table.

On the basis of Puerto Rico's employment and production multipliers, Cuba's tourism will annually be forfeiting the opportunity to generate $7.575 billion in economic impact.

Measured in terms of income, the government of Cuba will not receive annually from $4.162 billion to $9.262 billion (depending on the use of Type I or Type II multipliers) because it continues with the present political, social and economic models.

The above annual losses expressed on a daily basis indicate that every day of the year 2007, Cuba will be forfeiting from $20.8 million to $25.4 million.

We estimate that Cuba is currently losing between $4.6 and $5.7 million of economic impact per day.

The extraordinary effort made by Cuban authorities to develop the tourism industry is only partially effective because of its poor economic performance. Should Cuban citizens be allowed to actively participate and benefit from the ripple effect of the economic multipliers that tourism activity would generate, Cuba might have solved the problem of the Soviet Union's discontinuance of subsidies to the island. Thus, it could be argued, the so-called "special period" would have ended by now.

Some of the comments and feedback received from colleagues, friends and critics included the suggestion of comparing the Cuban experience with that of another tourism area similar to the island. This would

Table 1. Cuba's Estimated Tourism Statistics, Year 2007

	First Scenario	Second Scenario	Increase In Units	Percentage Increase
Rooms	69,000	69,000	-	-
Annual Visitors	4 million	5 million	1 million	25
Tourism Revenue	$7.50 billion	$11.25 billion	$3.75 billion	50
Annual Room-Nights Available	25.185 million	25,185 million	-	-
Annual Room-Nights Occupied	16.798 million	21,004 million	4,206 million	25
Annual Occupancy	66.7%	83.4%	16.7%	25
Average Number of days of stay	4.2 days	4.2 days	-	-
Expenditure per Visitor	$1,875	$2,250	$375	20
Daily Expenditure per Visitor	$446	$536	$90	20
Direct Number of Employees	138,000	103,500	-34,500	-25
Indirect Number of Employees	130,000	180,000	50,000	39
Total Number of Employees	268,000	283,500	15,500	6

Source: Cuban Society of Tourism Professionals

Table 2. Economic Impact of Tourism in Cuba for 2007, Estimated on the Basis of Puerto Rico's Multipliers (Billion U.S. dollars except number of employees)

	First Scenario	Second Scenario	Difference
Employment Multipliers			
Gross Revenue	$7.500	$11.250	$3.750
Direct Employment	114,225	171,337	57,112
Indirect Employment	203,320	304,979	101,659
Induced Employment	239,700	359,550	119,850
Production Multipliers			
Gross Revenue	$7.500	$11.250	$3.750
Production Generated in the Rest of the Economy	$7.650	$11.475	$3.825
Income Multipliers			
Type I	$8.325	$12.487	$4.162
Type II	$18.525	$27.787	$9.262

support our claim that the Cuban Government is shortchanging itself and its citizens.

SEARCH FOR A COMPARABLE EXAMPLE

After an exhaustive search we identified Cancún, in the State of Quintana Roo, Mexico, and the development of a tourism corridor that begins with Cancún and continues south down the coastal areas. The development of Cancún is the successful result of a strategic alliance among the Mexican government, Mexico's private sector, and the international hospitality industry.

Mexico, unlike many other countries in the world, developed important tourism centers by creating master-planned destination resorts. Several Federal agencies built the first hotel properties and infrastructure and soon were followed by private investors who acquired land from those agencies to build new

hotels. These developers acquired the land ready with utilities and urban infrastructure.

How the Mexico and Cancun Story Began

The enormous development of the tourism industry in Mexico originates with the governmental support to the industry throughout the last 24 years. The Secretariat of Tourism (SECTUR) and other governmental agencies, including the National Trust Fund for the Development of Tourism (FONATUR) pioneered the "polo turístico" concept of "destination resorts" in the country, resulting in a major success for the industry. The five fully integrated tourism centers—Cancún, Ixtapa, Los Cabos, Loreto, and the Bays of Huatulco—are products of an alliance between the government and the private sector.

Just 27 years ago, Cancún was a sleepy fishing village near archeological treasures surrounded by beautiful

Table 3.   Hotel and Tourism Statistics for Cancún, Q.R., Mexico, 1980-97

Year	Number Of Rooms	Average Occy.	Number of Visitors		Total Visitors	% Change Prior Year
			National	Foreign		
1980	3,930	65.7%	218,400	241,600	460,000	16.2%
1981	5,225	64.4%	264,000	276,800	540,800	17.6%
1982	5,258	63.8%	307,400	336,400	643,800	19.0%
1983	5,709	80.8%	244,500	510,200	754,700	17.2%
1984	6,106	72.3%	214,300	499,600	713,900	-5.4%
1985	6,591	72.1%	226,900	503,000	729,900	2.2%
1986	7,028	81.1%	227,400	641,900	869,300	19.1%
1987	8,910	83.5%	200,100	760,500	960,600	10.4%
1988	11,891	55.8%	180,700	657,500	838,200	-12.7%
1989	15,310	57.0%	296,500	857,100	1,153,600	37.6%
1990	17,470	68.0%	395,200	1,180,500	1,575,706	36.6%
1991	17,971	69.4%	479,700	1,432,400	1,912,100	21.3%
1992	18,376	75.0%	488,100	1,584,400	2,046,500	29.9%
1993	18,913	72.0%	487,000	1,492,400	1,979,400	-3.3%
1994	19,998	69.0%	515,500	1,446,300	1,963,800	-0.8%
1995	20,278	75.6%	492,244	1,671,985	2,164,229	10.0%
1996	21,097	77.9%	475,648	1,835,992	2,311.640	6.8%
1997	21,683	81.0%	551,987	2,069,281	2,621,268	13.4%
Compound Annual % Change	11.5%		3.9%	15,3%	11.7%	

Source: SECTUR, Asociacion de Hoteles de Quintana Roo, Phoenix Hospitality and Consulting Corp.

Caribbean beaches. Today, it is one of the most visited tourist destinations in the country, and the world. The number of visitors in 1997 reached 2.6 million, with 79 percent being foreign visitors.

FONATUR has provided, during its first 24 years of existence, more than US$1.7 billion in loans for new tourism projects and renovation of existing ones, adding more than 180,000 rooms to Mexico's inventory. FONATUR has also acted as a catalyst, bringing together resources from public and private sectors in Mexico and attracting foreign investment to the tourism sector. Cumulative foreign direct investment in Mexico's tourist sector amounted to US$5.4 billion between 1989 and 1997; meanwhile, domestic investment in this sector exceeded US$2.0 billion. Funding from the World Bank and the Inter-American Development Bank to FONATUR was used mainly for infrastructure improvements and tourism centers. Commercial banks have been the vehicles to channel funding for tourism projects. In addition, commercial banks are permitted to act as developers and promoters and assemble deals for projects ranging from a single hotel property to mixed-use destination resorts.

The role of commercial banks in the development of tourism in Mexico has been significant, even in the period when banks were "nationalized." The portfolio of hotels and other tourism assets has fluctuated, following the ups and downs in the market. Because Mexico is still in the process of becoming a totally-free-economy, actions by the government's finance authorities impact on the tourism industry, often beneficially.

As a result of the implementation of the North American Free Trade Agreement (NAFTA), both sides of the border began an intensive exchange of acquisitions, joint ventures, and other forms of trade and business arrangements. These activities caused an improvement in the confidence level regarding the investment opportunities that were offered on both sides.

At the last Acapulco Tiangis (an annual tourism meeting) a number of U.S. hotel chains announced development programs in Mexico by joint ventures, management contracts, and franchising. These plans are still active, in spite of the economic crisis of 1994-95, a period that provided an education for foreign entrepreneurs on the management of inflation and devaluation in Mexico.

Cancún, like any other tourism destination in Mexico, may be affected by the ups and downs of the Mexican economy. History, however, has proven that Cancún has been able to protect itself from situations related to currency devaluation faster than other Mexican destinations because of the practice of pegging room rates and cost of packages to the U.S. dollar. This is due to the fact that the bulk of the demand for this destination is from foreign sources. Because payments in foreign currency precede chronologically the payments of expenses in pesos, the industry benefits and technically is protected from the effects of devaluation. As we know, the wise practice of operating in foreign currency is paramount in the Cuban tourism activity.

In order to appreciate the growth of tourism in Cancun, Table 3 presents Cancún's tourism statistics from 1980 to 1997.

CANCUN AND CUBA

The Mexican Caribbean, including Cancún, compares with Cuba in as many ways as they differ. Table 4 summarizes those similarities and differences that show how each tourism dollar of revenue behaves so differently under the two political-economic regimes.

It is interesting to note that the average expenditure per day per person has increased in Cuba while it has decreased in Cancún. This is due in part to the increase in new all-inclusive properties in the Cancun market, which generally cater to a price sensitive client, and to better marketing on the part of the Cuban tourism authorities. Sales of Cuban cigars for resale and for own consumption account for $24 of the average expenditure per person per day in the island.

This comparison of selected tourism issues tells only part of the story. In order to understand the ramifications of the tourism activity, its necessary to estimate the economic ripple effect that tourism causes in each of the two cases in their respective economic systems: Cuba, a socialist economy, and Cancún, Mexico, a free market, capitalist economy.

In Table 5 we provide such a comparison. The comparison is based on the methodology followed in the Year 2007 exercise described at the beginning of this report. Due to the absence of data from the island, the author made assumptions in several of the variables.

CONCLUSION

Cuba in 1997 received $1.500 billion in gross revenue from tourism. On a daily basis, this represents $4.1 million per day.

However, on the basis of employment and production multipliers, Cuba's tourism industry in 1997 forfeited the chance to generate $913 million in economic impact.

Measured in terms of income multipliers, the government of Cuba failed to receive in 1997 between $738 million to $1.857 billion (depending on whether Type I or Type II multipliers are used) because it continues with the present political, social and economic model.

The above annual estimated losses expressed on a daily basis indicate that every day of 1997 Cuba forfeited from $2.5 million to $5.1 million.

Table 4.   Comparison of the Tourism Industry in Cuba and Cancun Today

Issues	Cuba	Cancún
Development Issue		
Government initiative and participation in development	Only the government.	Government agency FONATUR provides development of infrastructure and creates master plan.
Real Estate Issues		
Participation of private sector	Yes, only foreign entities or persons under leases, joint ventures or contracts to exploit tourism under special rights.	Yes, FONATUR sells sites with infrastructure and public utilities. Buyers are local, foreign or mixed entities.
Ownership transfer from the government to a buyer	No. There is a system that allows foreign entities the right to use land under certain conditions such as loans, advances, etc.	Yes, all sites are sold under the regime of trusteeship. May be sold to locals or foreigners.
Resale of property to a third party	No. With government approval the rights may be transferred to another foreign entity.	Yes, to any Mexican or foreign entity.
Marketing Issues		
Market demand	The destination resorts are mostly marketed as All-inclusive hotels or prepaid package plan. Habana and other major cities offer European Plan service since they also cater to individuals often on business.	In this resort destination there are both European Plan hotels and All-inclusive hotels. Generally the first group are in the Gran Turismo and Deluxe categories. The All-inclusive hotel market is growing at a faster rate.
Marketing resources	The government hotel chains and their official agencies abroad promote and sell the destinations. Partnerships with wholesalers and other demand suppliers.	The government has a support role in promoting the destination. Hotels are encouraged to participate in the joint promotions. Hotels, hotel chains and representatives perform sales and marketing functions.
Origin of demand	Mostly Europe and Canada. U.S. demand is limited due to legal restrictions.	Mostly North America and Europe followed by South and Central America, Asia
Principal market competitors	Dominican Republic, Isla Margarita, Cancún, Panama, Costa Rica.	All the Mexican coastal area resorts. In the low end of the All-inclusive market segment, Dominican Republic, Margarita, Costa Rica and Cuba.
Number of rooms	27,394. It is reported that 59% are in the four and five-star categories.	21,683 at the end of 1997. This figure does not include condos or time-sharing non-hotel properties.
Number of rooms planned for the year 2000	49,558. Estimated by the Ministry of Tourism in 1997.Reported under construction: Hoteles Taino 1,3,and 4 in Varadero; Hotel Covarrubia in Las Tunas; Hotel Río Oro in Holguín; Hotel Parque Central and Hotel Habana in Havana; and Hotel Gregorio in Cayo Coco. Also the "polo turístico" of Trinidad.	43,500. It includes the new "polos turísticos" Riviera Maya and Mundo Maya. There are 6,500 rooms under construction scheduled to open within 18 months.
National tourism	Normally, Cubans are not permitted to use foreign tourists' facilities. The rationale given is to expedite economic recovery during the "special period." Hotels for Cubans are available.	Yes. Mexicans represent 19 to 21 percent of all visitors to Cancún. **Note:** 50,000 Mexican families own timeshare units in Cancún.
Average Days of Stay	6.8 days	5.1 days
Occupancy percentage	63.9	81.0
Total Revenue 1997	US$1.500 billion	US$1.952 billion
Average Expenditure per Visitor per Stay	US$1,280.96	US$744.92
Number of Visitors 1997	1,155,000	2,621,000
Average Expenditure per Person per Day	US$188	US$146

Table 5. Table 5: Economic Impact of Tourism in Cuba and Cancún for 1997
(billion U.S. dollars except number of employees)

	First Scenario Cuba	Second Scenario Cancún	Difference
Employment Multipliers			
Gross Revenue	$1.500	$1.952	$0.452
Direct Employment	22,845	29,728	6,883
Indirect Employment	31,755	52,920	21,165
Induced Employment	34,613	62,500	27,887
Production Multipliers			
Gross Revenue	$1.500	$1.952	$0.452
Production Generated in the Rest of the Economy	$1.530	$1.991	$0.461
Income Multipliers			
Type I	$1.430	$2,168	$0.738
Type II	$2.962	$4,819	$1,857

Appendix I
IMPACT OF CUBAN TOURISM
DEVELOPMENT IN THE CARIBBEAN

Cuba continues its accelerated growth in number of rooms, visitors and revenue from tourism.

Cuban statistics indicate its fast growth from practically zero to today's maturing hospitality industry. This tempo continues while competitors in the Caribbean prepare to satisfy the increase in demand for destination resorts and other lodging facilities in the area.

Number of Visitors in Cuba and the Caribbean

Appendix III demonstrates the growth in the number of visitors to a selected group of countries in the Caribbean in 1997. You will notice that Cuba and the Dominican Republic lead the pack with 25% increase in the number of visitors, followed by Puerto Rico with 19.9%. However, in terms of market share

of the total visitors to the Caribbean, Puerto Rico is the leader with 22.8%, followed by Dominican Republic at 15.1% and Bahamas at 10.9%

Cuba attained 7.9% of the total visitors to the Caribbean a substantial jump from the 4.4% it had in 1990.

Tourism Receipts in Cuba and in the Caribbean

Appendix IV presents the growth in terms of dollars received from the tourism activity by a selected group of countries in the Caribbean in from 1993-97.

The leader is Cuba, with an average annual increase of its tourism revenue at 20.4% followed by Dominican Republic at 14.0% and the emerging Guadeloupe at 11.9%.

Appendix II
PUERTO RICO'S EMPLOYMENT, PRODUCTION AND
INCOME MULTIPLIERS FOR TOURISM HOTELS
ACCORDING TO THE 1982 INPUT-OUTPUT TABLE

Employment Coefficients of:

Direct Employment requirements	15.23
Direct and Indirect requirements	42.34
Type I multiplier: (Direct and Indirect)	2.78
Type II multiplier: (Direct, Indirect, and Induced)	4.88

Production and Income:

Production Multiplier:	2.02
Coefficient of:	
Direct Income requirements	0.19
Direct and Indirect Income requirements:	0.41
Type I income multiplier	2.11
Coefficient of:	
Direct, Indirect and Induced income requirements:	0.67
Type II Income multiplier	3.47

Basic Definitions:

• **Production Multiplier:** Indicates how much production (defined as intermediate plus final

sales) is needed to satisfy one dollar of final demand concerning any industry included in the Input-Output Matrix.

• **Employment Multiplier:** Shows the direct and indirect employment generated in the economy for each direct employment created in a particular sector or industry.

• **Income Multiplier:** Shows the direct and indirect income generated by unit of final demand required from a particular sector.

Our thanks to Mr. Santos Negrón Díaz, a distinguished Economist from Puerto Rico, for his valuable input in economic matters.

Appendix III
MARKET SHARE OF TOURIST ARRIVALS (OVERNIGHT VISITORS) SELECTED CARIBBEAN DESTINATIONS

Country	1993	Market Share	1997	Market Share	Increase 1993-1997	%Total Increase
Cuba	544	4.4%	1,152	7.9%	608	25.3%
Antigua & Barbuda	240	2.0%	231	1.6%	(9)	-0.4%
Aruba	562	4.6%	650	4.4%	88	3.7%
Bahamas	1,489	12.2%	1,592	10.9%	103	4.3%
Barbados	396	3.2%	472	3.2%	76	3.2%
Bermuda	413	3.4%	380	2.6%	(33)	-1.4%
British Virgin Islands	200	1.6%	251	1.7%	51	2.1%
Curacao	223	1.8%	210	1.4%	(13)	-0.5%
Dominican Republic	1,609	13.1%	2,211	15.1%	602	25.1%
Guadeloupe[a]	453	3.7%	660	4.5%	207	8.6%
Jamaica	1,105	9.0%	1,192	8.1%	87	3.6%
Martinique	366	3.0%	514	3.5%	148	6.2%
Puerto Rico	2,854	23.3%	3,332	22.8%	478	19.9%
Saint Lucia	194	1.6%	248	1.7%	54	2.3%
Saint Maarten	503	4.1%	425	2.9%	(78)	-3.3%
Trinidad and Tobago	249	2.0%	324	2.2%	75	3.1%
U.S. Virgin Islands	550	4.5%	411	2.8%	(139)	-5.8%
Total	12,237	100.0%	14,636	100.0%	2,399	100.0%

Source: Resort Development Consultants, Inc., Phoenix Hospitality and Consulting Corp., World Tourism Organization

a. Includes French St. Martin

Appendix IV
INTERNATIONAL TOURISM RECEIPTS
(US$ MILLION) SELECTED CARIBBEAN DESTINATIONS

Country	1993	1994	1995	1996	1997	Annual % Change	Receipt/ Tourist
Cuba	636	763	977	1,231	1,338	20.4%	$1,161
Antigua & Barbuda	277	293	247	257	260	-1.6%	$1,126
Aruba	467	453	517	553	570	5.1%	$ 877
Bahamas	1,304	1,333	1,346	1,450	1,510	3.7%	$ 948
Barbados	528	598	662	685	717	7.9%	$1,519
Bermuda	505	525	488	472	474	-1.6%	$1,247
British Virgin Islands	196	198	205	268	270	8.3%	$1,076
Cayman Islands	271	334	376	368	369	8.0%	$ 969
Curacao	195	183	175	186	187	-1.0%	$ 890
Dominican Republic	1,246	1,428	1,576	1,842	2,106	14.0%	$ 953
Jamaica	942	973	1,069	1,092	1,131	4.7%	$ 949
Guadeloupe[a]	318	389	458	496	499	11.9%	$ 756
Martinique	332	379	384	382	383	3.6%	$ 745
Puerto Rico	1,628	1,728	1,828	1,898	1,996	5.2%	$ 599
Saint Lucia	221	224	268	269	270	5.1%	$1,089
Saint Maarten	390	420	349	325	327	-4.3%	$ 769
Trinidad ^ Tobago	81	87	73	107	108	7.5%	$ 333
U.S. Virgin Islands	902	919	822	688	601	-9.7%	$1,462
Total	10,439	11,227	11,820	12,569	13,116	5.9%	$ 896

Source: Resort Development Consultants, Inc. Phoenix Hospitality and Consultants Corp., World Tourism Organization

a. Includes French St. Martin

CUBA'S TOURISM INDUSTRY: SOL MELIÁ AS A CASE STUDY

Félix Blanco Godínez[1]

When assessing Cuba's ability to overcome the socio-economic crisis which resulted from the disintegration of the USSR and the Eastern European communist bloc, the Cuban tourism industry is of vital importance for two reasons. Firstly, the progressively critical condition and poor yields of Cuba's traditional main economic sector, the sugar industry, with receipts of only US$971 million in 1996,[2] in contrast to the rapid development and growth of tourism, have placed the latter as Cuba's main source of foreign currency revenues. Secondly, the tourism industry has proved to be a useful instrument for bringing about much needed change into Cuba by: (i) introducing non-orthodox-socialist concepts through tourist contacts with the Cuban people; (ii) encouraging the regime to adopt socioeconomic and legal reforms; and (iii) drawing the attention of the international community, thus eventually influencing both Cuban internal politics, and U.S. foreign policy towards Cuba.[3]

Moreover, as an emerging sector, tourism can ideally play a strategic triple role as a hard currency generator, a technology transfer instrument (both for marketing and management skills) and a development catalyst for infrastructure.[4] Since 1990, gross revenues in hard currency from tourism have grown over six fold, reaching US$1.54 billion in 1997, of which 50% was generated in related economic activities.[5] Thus, the tourism industry has considerably energized other sectors; for instance, in 1997 airline travel[6] earned US$160 million, entertainment and culture US$23 million,[7] and retail sales of national goods a reported US$150 million.[8] Hence when evaluating Cuban tourism profitability, one should consider that unlike other Caribbean countries, Cuba includes revenues from other sectors in the tourism industry. Although lack of information has prevented analysts from making an accurate assessment of the

---

1. The author would like to thank Lawrence Whitehead, Carmelo Mesa-Lago, Jorge Pérez-López, and Nicolás Crespo for their comments and suggestions, and Sol Meliá for providing Annual Financial Reports and documents. This paper presents the author's personal opinion. Comments and suggestions are very welcome.

2. In fact, sugar exports were second to nickel with a total US$1.350 billion in 1996, compared to US$971 million, both on an fob basis (EIU Country Report 1st quarter 1998, p. 6).

3. Not in any order of importance.

4. Françoise. L. Simon, "Tourism Development in Transition Economies: The Cuban Case," *The Columbia Journal of World Business*, Vol. 30, No. 1 (Spring 1995), p. 27.

5. Sectors not directly associated with tourism. Growth, however, has been based on a large import component.

6. In 1997, 99% of passengers from international flights, and 31% of all domestic travelers were tourists.

7. Of which 92% was in hard currency.

8. Iraida Calzadilla Rodríguez, "El turismo es el corazón de la economía," *Granma* (28 February 1998), p. 3.

net revenues, the net income is estimated to be about 33% of the reported gross figure.[9]

The relative high rate of growth, considerable revenues and strategic economic advantages maintained by the tourism industry within the last eight years has recently led government economic strategists to consider this industry as "the heart of the economy."[10] In February 1998, Dr. Carlos Lage, Vice President of the Council of State of the Republic of Cuba and overall economic spokesperson for the government, said that the sector was, and would remain in the future, the country's largest source of U.S. dollars, generator of new employment opportunities and financial resources, and a vast market for domestically-produced products and services.[11]

By comparison, in 1990, the tourism sector had gross revenues of only US$250 million. In 1988, fewer than 300,000 tourists visited Cuba. In 1987, the island accounted for 3% of the tourists visiting Caribbean area countries. In contrast, in 1997, Cuba accounted for 7% of the tourists visiting the Caribbean.[12] According to Vice President Lage, the tourism sector in Cuba grew at an annual rate of 19.3% from 1990 through 1997, compared with 4.3% for the Caribbean area countries as a group.

As of March 1998, there are 21 joint ventures in tourism, with over US$600 millions in capital. Nineteen of those are hotel companies which will eventually manage 10,900 rooms. Of those, 2,500 rooms are fully operational and the rest in the design or construction stages.[13] Cuba currently has 181 hotels of varying quality with 28,000 rooms, most of which are two-star and three-star, and 23 joint ventures in this sector.[14] The tourism sector within Cuba directly employs approximately 71,000 workers or about 1.6% of the total national workforce of approximately 4,500,000.[15]

By the year 2010, Cuba officially expects to receive 10 million tourists, generating gross profits and tax revenues of US$5 billion, which would be twice the hard currency generated by the entire economy in 1997.[16]

As the largest corporation in the industry and the pioneer of large scale projects in a semi-socialist economic and political regime and an unknown market, Sol Meliá's performance substantially affects the initiatives of competing corporations. While its success may create an incentive for potential investors, any substantial failure may discourage both potential investors and companies operating on the island. As discussed in the latter part of this paper, an empirical analysis shows that the island has been consistently Sol Meliá's most profitable market during the last years, and this giant company has proved to be Cuba's most influential strategic asset in the tourism industry.

SOL MELIÁ AS A CASE STUDY

This analysis of Sol Meliá, the leading foreign corporation in the Cuban tourism industry, has been restricted due to lack of available data specifically covering Cuba, and the reluctance of managers to be interviewed because of the tense political and economic

9. Simon, "Tourism Development," p. 30. Cuban officials recently reported that 38% of gross revenue in 1997 was net profit. Reuters News Report (11 May 1998).

10. Minister C. Lage, stated: "*Yo no diría que el turismo es uno de los sectores más importantes, el turismo es el corazón de la economía.*" See Calzadilla Rodríguez, "El turismo," p. 3.

11. *Economic Eye on Cuba*, (23 February-1 March 1998).

12. Notice that Cuba's 1.17 million tourists in 1997 do not represent a very sizeable percentage of the total 18 million visitors to the Caribbean during that year; however, comparatively, it is a substantial achievement for a crippled economy developing its tourism industry during the last 6 years.

13. EIU Country Report, 1st quarter 1998, p. 22.

14. *Economic Eye on Cuba* (23 February-1 March 1998).

15. Ibid.

16. More realistic estimates foresee a more conservative figure.

climate between the United States and Cuba.[17] Sufficient information, however, has permitted the formulation of two meaningful conclusions. First, even though 1997 was a disappointing year, particularly for the region of Varadero, overall Cuba has been one of the most profitable divisions for the Spanish corporation in the 1990s, and certainly the leader in the Caribbean in terms of revenues generated by management fees.[18] And second, given the high levels of profitability, the comparative market advantages which the corporation enjoys in Cuba and its vast investment commitments, Sol Meliá is likely to continue to be the leading joint venture partner and the most important catalyst of foreign capital inflow into the Cuban tourism industry.[19]

General Global Profile

As early as 1976, the top twenty hotel companies in the world accounted for 67% of the rooms in the *Service World International*'s top 100 largest chains. The economies of scale afforded by pooled marketing efforts and shared computer reservation system has allowed the leading hotel chains to effectively dominate the market. This rapid growth has been made possible through a flexible ownership and management control system. As in the case of Cuba and its joint ventures, management contracts have become an increasingly popular form of operation since they allow the chains to expand with minimal capital investment, while the owners have the advantages of being part of a larger, standardized, and well-organised chain. Accordingly, the absence of an entrepreneurial class, foreign exchange and skilled labour in the developing world has led to the rapid intrusion of

large-scale foreign capital and management in the lodging industry.[20] It is in this context that Sol Meliá should be primarily studied.

At present, Sol Meliá is ranked 14th in the world international hotel companies.[21] Operating 205 buildings with 53,000 rooms (100,000 beds) in 25 countries of four continents, Sol Meliá is the largest hotel corporation in Spain and the third largest in Europe. Over 19 million persons annually stay at hotels. In 1997 the company reported a competitive room occupancy of 71%.

Sol Meliá, founded in 1956 by Gabriel Escarrer, its current president, has 21,000 employees and a presence in Europe, America, the Mediterranean Basin and Asian Pacific, through its eight brands: Gran Meliá, Meliá, Meliá Comfort, Sol Ilite, Sol Club, Sol, Sol Inn and Paradisus, covering the different market segments. The company is structured in five independent business areas which have a general management status: European Urban Hotels, European Resort Hotels, America, Cuba and Asian Pacific. Management is organised under five main areas of activity: Economic-Financial, Marketing, Human Resources, Consulting and Systems, and Maintenance.[22] Sol Meliá is also a pioneer in the hotel sector incorporating advanced sales and marketing systems, launching the first loyalty programme in the sector (the Mas card) and signing strategic alliances with other leading companies such as Iberia, Avis and American Express.

Total net profits after tax for 1997 were reported to be US$37.2 million,[23] an increase of 20.04% over

---

17. To insure the safety and security of individuals, the names of employees are not disclosed in this essay.

18. Sol Meliá 1996 Management Report, p. 76.

19. The Spanish corporation maintains that its present operation and expansion in Cuba do not contravene the U.S. Helms-Burton law, which seeks to punish foreign companies investing in property confiscated after the 1959 revolution. See "Spain's Sol Meliá Expanding Hotel Chain in Cuba," Reuters, Havana, (April 9, 1998), http://www.netpoint.net/~CubaNet.

20. See Keith G Debbage, "Oligopoly and the Resort Cycle in the Bahamas," *Annals of Tourism Research* (1990), pp. 513-527.

21. According to U.S. magazine *Hotels*. See Luz Marina Fornieles, "The Privilege of Being Pioneers," *Cuban Foreign Trade*, No.2 (1997), p. 5.

22. Sol Meliá was founding member of the Quality Management Club and received the 1993 Principe Felipe Prize for Business Excellence. At the European level, it was the first hotel company to obtain ISO 9002 Certification for hotel management services in its eight brands and, at the national level, the Meliá Lebreros in Seville was the first hotel to receive the ISO 9000 Quality Certificate.

23. 5,723 million pesetas (US$1=153.8 pta).

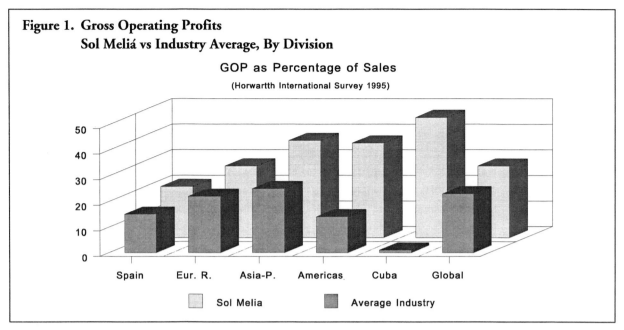

**Figure 1. Gross Operating Profits
Sol Meliá vs Industry Average, By Division**

GOP as Percentage of Sales

(Horwartth International Survey 1995)

the previous year. Income for management services in 1997 reached US$86.9 million,[24] an increase of 16.4% over 1996. Sol Meliá, which was the first Spanish hotel company to be quoted on the stock exchange, saw its share value increase by 42% in 1997.[25]

Latin America: The Latin American region has the second highest estimated growth potential for tourism from 1997 to 2007 according to the World Travel and Tourism Council. The region is a key market for Sol Meliá in terms of fee contribution (around 21% of total fees for 1997), brand recognition, language and culture, and hotel owner relations. It is also the most profitable Division in the Sol Meliá portfolio in terms of GOP[26] margins at the hotel level, in fees obtained per hotel or available room, in occupancy-average daily rate (ADR) mix and finally in profitability from investment in minority stakes.

According to Oscar Ruiz, Chief Financial Officer, in recent years Sol Meliá has found very attractive ac-

quisition opportunities in Latin America that have not been fully exploited due to the company's policy not to purchase real estate assets, save for certain minority stakes in hotels. The desire to capitalise on these opportunities is the main reason for the creation of MIA, a subsidiary that will build or acquire hotels that are as profitable as others managed by the corporation.

Current Profile in Cuba

Of the 340 joint ventures currently operating within the island, Sol Meliá manages the largest in the tourism industry and channels substantial foreign capital into Cuba. Although Cubanacán is its largest partner in Cuba, the company also manages three hotels with the Cuban State Gaviota Group.[27] In 1997, 56% of Sol Meliá's hotels in Cuba were located in Varadero, 20% in Holguín, and 24% in Havana. *Meliá Cohiba*, located in the capital was the most profitable, while *Meliá Varadero* was the least in 1997.

Ownership Structure of Sol Meliá-Managed Hotels
CIHSA, a Spain-based corporation, has a 50% share

24. 13,370 million pesetas.

25. See Sol Meliá, *Annual Report 1996* and "Sol Meliá: Profile as a World Leader," (April, 1998). See www.solMeliá.es.

26. Gross Operating Profits.

27. *Sol Río de Mares*, in Holguín with 238 rooms; *Sol Club Río de Luna* also in Holguín with 218 rooms, and *Sol Club Las Sirenas* in Varadero with 250 rooms.

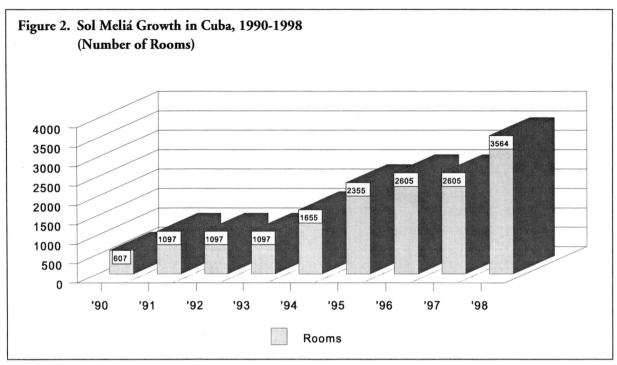

Figure 2. Sol Meliá Growth in Cuba, 1990-1998 (Number of Rooms)

in the *Meliá Varadero*, a 50% share in the *Sol Club Palmeras*, and a 50% share in the *Meliá Las Américas*, all of which are located in Varadero. The remaining 50% share in the three hotels is held by Cuban government-operated Cubanacán S.A.. The ownership of CIHSA is as follows: Sol Meliá S.A. (33.5%), Mr. Enrique Martinón, a Spain-based investor (50.5%), and a Barcelona-based corporation controlled by two individuals (16%). The Barcelona-based corporation, however, is seeking to sell its 16% share of CIHSA for US$7 million, stating that the purchaser can expect a minimum annual rate of return of 15% on the investment.[28]

Operational Expansion in Cuba and Elsewhere

In April of 1998, Sol Meliá announced that it was expanding its hotel chain in Cuba to 11 by the end of 1988 from the then-current 8 hotels. Company sources have confirmed that three new hotels, with a total of nearly 1,000 rooms, would open later this year (1998) in Havana, the eastern province of

Holguín, and Cayo Coco key, off Cuba's northern coast. The two new hotels outside Havana are to be run on management contracts, while Sol Meliá is investing an unspecified amount in the Havana unit.[29] The new resort *Meliá Comfort Habana*, located in the city's most elegant and exclusive area of Miramar, adding 409 rooms, should be completed in August 1998; *Meliá Cayo Coco*, with 250 rooms is scheduled to open in November, as well as *Meliá Río de Oro*, with 300 rooms, located on the coast of the northern province of Holguín.[30] In the next 10 years, Sol Meliá is likely to operate another 14 hotels that are expected to be built on the island.[31]

Cuba's new resorts in 1998, are significant in absolute terms, but small within Sol Meliá's rapid expansion plans world wide. The investments made throughout 1997 in the *Meliá Tulum* (Mexico), the 667 rooms/apartments *Gran Meliá Caracas* complex and the *Meliá Sancti Petri* amount to 2,324 million pesetas, each of them with an expected rate of return

---

28. See *Economic Eye on Cuba* (9-15 February 1998).

29. "Spain's Sol Meliá Expanding Hotel Chain in Cuba," Reuters, Havana (April 9, 1998), www.netpoint.net/~CubaNet.

30. Prensa Latina, La Habana (8 April 1998), www.sol Meliá.es.

31. Emily Valere, "Cuba Sees Tourism Doubling by 2000," Bloomberg, Port-of-Spain, Trinidad. (13 May 1998).

of more than 20%. Of strategic importance has been the management contract signed for the *Meliá Bruselas* (Brussels), which represents a further step towards the expansion objectives in the main cities of Europe. In the Dominican Republic, the incorporation of the *Meliá Santo Domingo* and the *Meliá Juan Dolio* has positioned the company as leader in this important tourist destination.[32] In total, the company added 27 hotels globally in 1997, and signed agreements with 12 hotels which are to be added before the end of the year 1998. There are 34 additional signed agreements for hotels to be added in the next three years, and 35 in an advanced stage of negotiation. For 1998, the company believes that general conditions remain positive for the European Resort and City Divisions.

According to Carlos Pareda, Sol Meliá director of the Cuban Division in 1994,[33] the island's safety environment for tourists is a key competitive advantage vis-a-vis its Caribbean neighbors.[34] It is important to highlight the significant disparity between street crime and burglary. While Sol Meliá hotels, and most tourist areas, are heavily patrolled by police forces, once the tourist leaves the resorts the danger increases.[35] Sol Meliá's initiative to enter the Cuban market despite the structural problems and the threat of U.S. measures against company interests dwells also and mainly on Cuba's current situation: absence of U.S. competitors and the potential for profitability which Cuba is expected to offer once economic and political relations with the United States are improved.[36]

The deficiencies of the basic product (lack of differentiation, segmentation and specialization) have re-sulted in a very low repeat rate, not only for Sol Meliá, but for all major hotel joint ventures. While Sol Meliá's repeat rate ranges between 8% and 10%, LTI's all-inclusive type resorts have reported 12%.[37] Shifts in marketing strategy have borne little improvements in the return rates. Consequently, the main strategy continues to be basically expansionary and quantitative in number of tourists rather than qualitative in terms of tourist expenditure. This market oriented policy has been adopted based on the present limitations and potential for improvement in the future. Additional resorts in 1998 may even reduce further Sol Meliá's occupancy levels in Varadero. For example, *Sol Palmeras'* 33.71% occupancy rate from 1 September to 30 November 1997, could decline to 28% for the same period in 1998.[38]

Comparative Analysis: The Cuba Division vs All Others, 1996-1997

Using data from the latest Company Official Report available (1996), the performance of the Cuban Division of Sol Meliá can be compared with the other four Divisions (European Urban Hotels, European Resort Hotels, America, and Asian Pacific). Despite some fluctuations in total net revenues and low repeat rates, the Cuban Division has been a very profitable market for Sol Meliá. From 1992 to 1995, the overall results of the Cuban resorts were comparatively higher than during the 1996-1997 period. In 1995, the Cuban Division generated 8.1% of all revenues with less than 3% of the company's facilities. The following year, 1996, the Cuban Division accounted for 9.8% of total revenues with only 3.9% of the global holdings, due mainly to a 33% increase from the previous year in management fees. As the

32. Sol Meliá, letter from the Chief Financial Officer, 1997.

33. Currently, Gabriel Canaves Picornell is the Director of the Cuban Division. Sol Meliá, *1996 Annual Report.*

34. Simon, "Tourism Development," p. 35.

35. Most crimes committed against tourists, however, are property thefts committed when the tourists leave their items unattended. Cuban authorities have recently created a Special Unit for Crimes Committed Against the Tourist. Source: Author's interviews with policemen on the island in 1996 and 1997.

36. Source: Author's interview with 3 middle-level managers in Varadero, 1997 and 1998.

37. Simon, "Tourism Development." p. 37.

38. *Sol Palmeras Varadero:* Occupancy rate in September 48.89%, October 27.85%, November 24.39%. Source: Sol Palmeras' *Booking Mensual Cristalizado,* September-November, 1997 (unpublished).

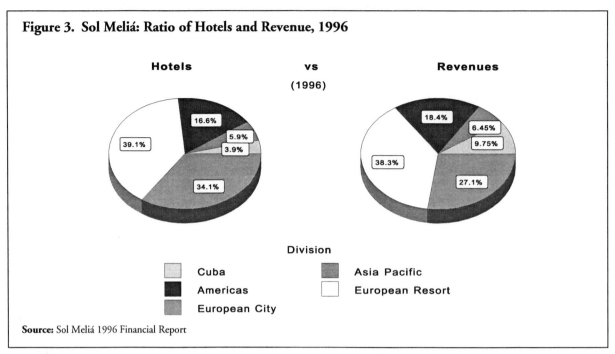

Figure 3. Sol Meliá: Ratio of Hotels and Revenue, 1996

Source: Sol Meliá 1996 Financial Report

figure below shows, no other Division came close to this level of profitability. In 1996, the eight hotels included in the Division registered an average occupancy rate of 75.7% and an average daily rate (ADR) of 7,842 pesetas, generating revenues of 833 million pesetas for Sol Meliá in management services.[39] Whether it can be sustained as in other Divisions is a different issue.

Profit levels in first three quarters of 1997 were lower in the Cuban Division that in the others mainly due to a low occupancy rate and the negative effect of the rising dollar on the demand for Cuba from European visitors. Instability and uncertainty in profitability levels due to European currency exchange fluctuations vis-a-vis the U.S. dollar may not continue to hinder demand from European visitors after January 1999 when the Euro is expected to replace 11 European currencies. Despite the low returns of the Cuban Divisions in 1997, better results are expected for 1998 as the winter season in the Cuban Division is promising according to the bookings and contracts made to date. To put this into context, the following

analysis of the company's five Divisions may prove helpful.

In terms of price, in 1997 Sol Meliá hotels in the Dominican Republic (DR) and Cuba were very similar within the hotel quality rating system. Tour operators in Madrid, for example, sold a 14 night package at the *Meliá Varadero* (five star) for 199,000 pesetas (US$1259 approximately) for the low-season month of May. The same package at the *Meliá Bavaro* in the DR cost 194,200 pesetas (US$1229). *Meliá Cancún* in Mexico, however, was more expensive—352.600 pesetas (US$2231), almost twice the price for similar services.[40]

The good performance of the European Resort Division together with the consolidation of leisure and convention activity in several cities in the European City Division have compensated the under-performance of the Cuban and Asian hotels in 1997. According to a company report, the newly added *Meliá Las Sirenas* and the contribution of *Meliá Cohiba* have also offset the lagging resorts in Varadero. The negative effect of the rising dollar on the demand for

---

39. Sol Meliá *1996 Annual Report*, pp.15-16. See the Appendix for full data.

40. See *Unidad* Magazine, Servicios Integrales de Turismo, S.A., 1997.

Cuba from European visitors has affected the occupancy rate of the Cuban Division[41] which has nevertheless experienced an increase in management fees of nearly 22%.

According to company reports, prospects for 1998 also look positive for the European Resort Division in light of the contracts negotiated with tour operators for the coming year, with average increases in prices of 4-5% and greater presence in all feeder markets. The favorable conditions initiated in the second quarter of 1997 in the European City Division seem to be holding for 1998, driven by the buoyant Spanish economy.

The economic environment in Asia has affected the performance of this Division, which in spite of this has benefited from an increase in management fees of 46% thanks to the contribution of the *Gran Meliá Jakarta*, added in the second half of 1996, and the *Meliá Bali*, which was closed the first three months of 1996 for refurbishment. Although the impact of the financial crisis in Asia was not very detrimental in terms of fee generation until the fourth quarter of 1997, such effects in 1998 must be closely followed.

The performance of the Americas Division has been considered satisfactory by the company's standards, with an increase in fees of 30% helped by the prosperity of the Latin American economies and the effect of the management contracts added in 1996 and 1997 in this Division, about 39% of the total. The Americas Division's prospects are very promising not only from an operational point of view but also from an expansionary point of view thanks to MIA, although the effects will not be fully evident until the year 1999. Sol Meliá, together with Inmotel Inversiones and the Escarrer family, has recently founded a company whose main activities are centred on the ownership of hotels in Latin America and the Caribbean (not including Cuba). The management contracts that this new structure will provide Sol Meliá are intended to be as profitable as the first 15 most profitable management contracts in the company's portfolio.

Cubanacán: Sol Meliá's Main Joint Venture Partner

Sol Meliá's alliance with Cuba's Cubanacán is not a unique condition of the Cuban Division, as it is often thought given the legal constrains and peculiarities of the Cuban market. Sol Meliá's business strategy relies often on strategic alliances and joint ventures with other market leading companies. Globally the company has formed alliances with suppliers, tour operators, travel agencies, hotel owners, financial institutions, real estate developers and other hotel companies, whenever mutual benefits can be obtained from synergy and the globalization of the activities. For example, of the 41 hotels that joined Sol Meliá in 1996, 26 arrived through management agreements, 14 through franchise agreements and 1 through a commercial alliance; 17 of these 41 were in the form of joint ventures.

Cubanacán was formed after the Cuban government dismantled the Instituto Nacional del Turismo (INTUR), the monolithic, inefficient, bureaucratic state organization which was in charge of the island's tourism since 1959. Grupo Cubanacán is an entrepreneurial holding company in the field of tourism and trade. Some of its facilities are marketed through joint ventures and other trading companies. It employs over 20,000 workers in the hotel industry, trade and services to tourists, while Sol Meliá employed 21,000 (December 1996).

Grupo Cubanacán has set up nine branch offices in various European and American countries, and eighteen companies which operate the following facilities:[42]

- 51 hotels (three, four and five-star) located at beaches, cities and countryside areas;

- 52 restaurants and coffee shops at beaches and cities in Cuba;

---

41. In 1997 the occupancy rate fell to 69.2% from 75% in 1996; however revenue per available room (REVPAR) and ADR increased substantially. See the Appendix.

42. Cuban Ministry of Tourism; Cubanacán website, www.Cubanacan.cu.

- a chain of shops;

- 3 marinas, 13 scuba diving centres and various nautical sites at beaches throughout the country;

- 38 health centres and hotels specialized in health tourism;

- a tour agency to guarantee full services to tourists;

- a transport agency which offers transfers, car rental and taxi cabs; and

- a Conference Center at Varadero beach.

Cubanacán's strong position has allowed the development of another sector which is increasingly strengthening in the Caribbean: businesses and financing facilities to other economic sectors in Cuba and abroad. In pursuing this objective, the Group has set up nine business associations with important foreign enterprises. The Cuban Ministry of Tourism expects growth for this Group to reach a total of 5,500 rooms by the year 2000, of which over 2000 rooms will be located in Havana and around 1300 rooms at Varadero Beach. Such growth will further strengthen the role of Grupo Cubanacán as leader in the field of tourism in Cuba.[43] Even though Sol Meliá has recently signed additional management agreements with Gaviota and other Cuban government tourism entities, Cubanacán's dominance of most of the island's four and five-star hotels will constrain the Spanish giant to limit the scope of joint venture agreements.

CONCLUSION

A few significant conclusions may be drawn from this analysis. Despite general structural and sectorial deficiencies, Sol Meliá's financial reports indicate that the company has been relatively successful in obtaining substantial profits from management fees in Cuba. Sol Meliá's financial success in Cuba, its considerable consistency in channelling investment into

the industry, and the recent increase in management contracts with its Cuban counterparts—reaching 11 in 1998—have shown the potential of the island for investment in the tourist sector. Due to the adverse, current political externalities, this potential seems limited to large multinationals which can manoeuvre the financial and commercial obstacles created by U.S. foreign policy towards Cuba.

The island has been able to benefit from an experienced management company. Sol Meliá's regional operational success from 1990 to 1996 was due mainly to lack of competition in the market, which is guaranteed by the structural and operational inability of the Cuban Ministry of Tourism to create competing enterprises on the island. Similarly, these characteristics have been a major incentive for Sol Meliá and other companies to become pioneers in an uncertain and unknown market, handicapped by macroeconomic inefficiencies and socialist management policies.

While Cuba has been relatively successful in attracting a large low-budget segment of European tourists, the island has become increasingly vulnerable to the strength of the U.S. dollar. This problem, however, is also reflected in the other Caribbean destination that are direct Cuban competitors (e.g., Isla Margarita and Dominican Republic).[44] This trend in Cuba was clearly illustrated by the poor performance of Sol Meliá's hotels in Varadero in 1997. Joint efforts between the Cuban Ministry of Tourism and Sol Meliá's marketing strategy to increase demand from Canada and Latin America may produce more favorable results in 1998 and subsequent years. Despite these drawbacks, the company has the ability to compensate from more stable markets in other parts of the island. Hence, aided by consistent increases in revenue from management fees, Sol Meliá continues to profit from its operation on the island.

---

43. Id.

44. In March 1998, for example, there were independent hotels in the East and South coasts of the Dominican Republic selling all inclusive packages at $18-$25 per day. The independent hotels (not chain affiliated) are the first to suffer when the dollar strengthens in Europe.

Appendix

Table 1. Sol Meliá: Basic and Incentive Fees by Division 1996-1997

Management Fees, Revenue by Division Fees Revenue (million pta.)		1997	Increase 96/97	1996
European Resort	Basic	2.341	10.34%	2.122
	Incentive	1.212	5.00%	1.153
	Total	3.552	8.46%	3.275
European City	Basic	1.773	0.00%	1.773
	Incentive	669	23.42%	5.42
	Total	2.442	5.48%	2.315
America	Basic	895	36.66%	655
	Incentive	1.148	25.18%	917
	Total	2.043	29.96%	1.572
Asia-Pacific	Basic	405	41.49%	286
	Incentive	399	50.55%	265
	Total	804	45.85%	551
Cuba	Basic	704	25.22%	562
	Incentive	311	14.62%	271
	Total	1.014	21.77%	833
Total Basic		**6.118**	**13.34%**	**5.398**
Total Incentive		**3.737**	**18.71%**	**3.148**
Grand Total		**9.855**	**15.32%**	**8.546**

Note: Basic fees include franchise fees.

Table 2. Sol Meliá: Hotel Statistics by Division 1996-1997

		Occupancy (%)	Revenue/ room	Average Daily Rate
European Resort	1997	80.41%	4.905	6.100
	%1996	1.88%	7.87%	5.88%
	1996	78.93%	4.547	5.781
European City	1997	63.14%	5.724	9.065
	%1996	3.38%	4.25%	0.84%
	1996	61.08%	5.491	8.990
America	1997	65.77%	9.318	14.168
	%1996	-0.43%	24.27%	24.80%
	1996	66.05%	7.498	11.353
Asia	1997	57.97%	4.009	6.967
	%1996	-11.16%	-17.25%	-6.85%
	1996	65.26%	4.881	7.480
Cuba	1997	69.02%	7.276	10.542
	%1996	-8.87%	22.50%	34.43%
	1996	75.74%	5.940	7.842
Total	1997	70.36%	5.732	8.147
	%1996	-0.73%	7.83%	8.63%
	1996	70.88%	5.316	7.500

Source: Sol Meliá *1997 Financial Report.*

PROMOTING PLACE THROUGH ARCHITECTURAL HERITAGE: RESTORATION AND PRESERVATION OF TWENTIETH CENTURY ARCHITECTURAL DESIGN IN MIRAMAR, HABANA, CUBA

Artimus Keiffer and Sarah K. Wagner[1]

Habana Vieja was designated a World Heritage Site by UNESCO in 1982. It is, in a sense, a living museum, its visible landscape almost identical to accounts given in travel guides and journals published over the last hundred and fifty years. As a result, the Cuban government has injected money and resources to preserve and maintain this historic part of Habana. Large tour buses crawl through the narrow streets giving passengers a controlled, glimpse of life in a colonial city, the 80,000 or so residents adding realism as they go about their day to day activities.

Tourism, which has become Cuba's number one industry, is the catalyst for major historic preservation and renovation projects in this part of the city. Most of the architectural design is based on European models; an eclectic landscape featuring Spanish, Moorish, Greek and Roman architectural elements meets the eye. Old Habana, however, is only a small part of the city. Other urban areas deserve more attention as well to reveal their potential economic worth for preservation based on architectural style and land use.

One of the most conspicuous residuals of American influence in the built landscape in Habana is the presence of a large block of former single-family housing stock in both Vedado and Miramar. The development of the western fringe of Habana between the years of 1902 and 1959 utilized architectural design influenced by both European and American models. As a result, many large homes were constructed with local materials and imported trimmings in the Neo-Classical, Spanish Baroque, Art Deco and International styles. The number of Art Deco styles, for instance, rivals the famous South Beach area in Miami and has been referred to as some of the best examples in the Caribbean (Scarpaci 1996).

This paper will present an observational study done in June 1998 by faculty and students from the Geography Department at Indiana University Purdue University at Indianapolis classifying the architectural design in a specific area in Miramar as well as former and current uses of the structures. The data was recorded by direct observation and mapped using GIS software. This paper examines the potential to promote place through architectural heritage by stabilizing and preserving the area so it can be utilized by tourists, tourism facilities, embassies, and offices of foreign firms.

As the tourism market in the Caribbean continues to grow, should more effort be put into restoring available "National Treasures" for tourist consumption or promote continued entrepreneurial and international

---

1. This paper is only a part of on-going research on the architecture and land use in La Habana.

development in these restorations? Will this constitute sound economic planning, save energy and resources, and capitalize on extant culture, or will it create a new economic enclave of social stratification? Although these issues are beyond the scope of this paper, continued research and observation can reveal the long-term effects of current urban design policies.

HISTORICAL ARCHITECTURE

Spanning nearly 500 years, the architecture of Cuba is one of its most precious cultural attributes. Many cities in Cuba are veritable "living museums," several having been declared World Heritage Sites by the United Nations. In most of Cuba, and exemplified in Habana, there are three distinct periods of architectural development: the Colonial (1512-1898), the Republican (1898-1959), and the Revolutionary (1959-present). Not only do these three periods roughly indicate the political and economic ideologies of the time, they also reflect the geographic resources and technologies available. Moreover, in residential structures, the types of building materials, along with the interior layout, speak to economic status, family size, and the perception of what the proper house should look like and how its spaces should function.

The three periods, influenced for the most part by European models, represent vast differences in architectural styles, although somewhat modified for the tropical climate. The Colonial period was influenced by European urban layouts and features colonnaded overhangs to help protect against the tropical sun and sporadic downpours and create shade to keep the buildings cool. High ceilings and corresponding massive doors and windows allow breezes to pass through the structures while wooden shutters protect against cold spells and violent storms. The red tiled roofs, common to Mediterranean climates, also permit rainwater to be funneled into underground cisterns. The remaining colonial architecture is located in Old Habana and around the inlet area, mostly within the old, walled city of the 18th and 19th centuries and concentrated on narrow, sometimes winding streets following the shallow contours around the harbor.

The Republican period resembles urban planning designs incorporated in United States cities in the early 1900s. A grid system of streets crossing at right angles, created rectangular blocks that were divided into lots. Curved streets were straightened and widened to accommodate the automobile. Neo-classical, Bauhaus and Mediterranean styles from Europe as well as Art Deco and Moderne styles from the United States dominated single-family residences, complete with front yards and garages. Builders used concrete, stucco and brick, and windows featured screens to keep out the insects and closed tightly to keep out the cold. Pastel colors, decreed by the early Spanish in their building codes to help keep buildings cooler, gave a tropical look to this period of architectural design. Many examples of these architectural types are located in Vedado and Miramar.

The Revolutionary period contributed another European concept, that of pre-stressed concrete used in multi-level designs and sometimes referred to as the International style. These high-density designs allowed quick construction and were used to in-fill many vacant lots around the city after the revolution. The major housing projects outside the city, although advanced for their day, show their age and have contributed to a change in the perception of high-density residential areas. Today, new urban design strategies in Habana incorporate low-density housing, green spaces and accessibility (interview with Mayda Pérez Alvarez, Subdirector, Grupo Para el Desarrollo Integral de la Capital, Habana, July 1998).

The mix of these three periods, however, gives the city its charm. Given the economic problems that have prevented maintenance of the buildings, the older buildings continue, for the most part, to survive the lack of paint, plumbing and electrical supplies. Walking around parts of Habana today is not much different than walking around Habana 40 years ago, or even 400 years ago. Economic investment at different periods of Cuban history has left its mark on the urban landscape. As historic preservationist Rachel Carley put it, "this remarkable built legacy has been preserved largely through benign neglect, and so the island today serves as a rare archive of Caribbean architectural history waiting to be rediscovered" (Carley 1997).

HISTORY OF MIRAMAR

The development of Miramar was greatly influenced by the American presence after Cuba's war for independence. The location of a military base to the west of the city during the American occupation from 1898 to 1902 had a profound affect on the location of Habana suburbs. Geographically, it made sense. The spacious harbor inlet limited movement to the coastal areas east of Habana. It was much easier to push westward, towards Marianao, an area where affluent habaneros had places of summer residence. U.S. occupation forces also found this area much to their liking and General Fitzhugh Lee, military governor of the island's western end, located his headquarters there (Schwartz 1997). The magnificent architecture and tropical canopy in Miramar today are no accident. It was the potential of this heretofore undeveloped parcel that attracted the attention of land speculators.

The flock of tourists to the island early in the twentieth century, as detailed by Rosalie Schwartz in her book *Pleasure Island: Tourism and Temptation in Cuba,* increased during the boom years of global tourism. In the mid-1920s, the Almendares River was bridged allowing automobile traffic to flow unrestricted to areas west of the city, where many North American visitors found the country club, the racetrack, casino and beaches irresistible (Schwartz 1997). Many of the tourists bought homes and President Machado authorized Carlos Manuel de Céspedes, the Public Works Secretary, to construct a broad avenue from the Almendares to Marianao. The result was a broad east-west avenue known as La Quinta Avenida. At the junction of Fifth Avenue and the river, Céspedes built a sizable green stucco house (which was later burned by angry habaneros [Schwartz 1997]) replete with a $200,000 mosaic shrine from India. He recognized the demand for housing in western Habana and not only supervised the construction of the grand thoroughfare through Miramar, but with banker and developer Claudio G. Mendoza, bought much of the land that would soon be developed into the western suburb of Miramar. Mendoza developed the subdivision and financed the homes while Céspedes oversaw the building of streets and highways to make those homes convenient to

downtown Habana. Miramar became a neighborhood of sumptuous homes and lush gardens (Schwartz 1997).

By the early 1950s, the Malecón had been extended some 8 kilometers to the Almendares and in 1957, a tunnel joined Vedado and Miramar, cutting automobile travel time from downtown to 20 minutes (Scarpaci 1996). By the late 1950s, Miramar was known for its modest to palatial housing and upper middle-class residents, many of whom fled to Florida after the revolution. In the early 1960s, the revolutionary government divided many of these houses into apartments, schools, government offices and boarding houses (Segre, Coyula, and Scarpaci 1997). During the 70s and 80s, many of the elitist structures were occupied by government ministries, foreign embassies and Communist Party officials (Scarpaci 1996).

All of this changed in the early 1990s, however, as space was needed for offices for foreign investors, due in part to the "special period" of the Cuban economy. Miramar was the perfect place. It was well planned, easily accessed and had the amenities that were needed for storefronts, offices and hotel development. As a result, many of the old structures, which were modified for revolutionary uses, are now being refurbished with hard currency. "Land use in Miramar still includes the presence of embassies, housing for foreigners, and Cuban government officials. However, there is an unprecedented surge in retail outlets for Cuban and foreign shoppers with hard currency...as well as new joint-venture offices" (Segre, Coyula, and Scarpaci 1997, 132-133). From its stark beginnings as a planned grid, Miramar has matured into a tropical, eclectic neighborhood, changing its primary land use from single-family to high-density residential, and then to mixed residential/office/retail. "In this regard, Miramar has become the Habana neighborhood with the greatest change since the triumph of the revolution" (Segre, Coyula, and Scarpaci 1997, 133).

In 1998, the neighborhood continues to change, especially at its western-most end. Several new hotels, condo suites and shopping areas are either under construction or completed. Further east, towards the Almendares, Fifth Avenue, is called "Embassy Row."

The wide fig-tree-lined boulevard is flanked by mansions that have been restored to an earlier grandeur, while the Ministry of the Interior's police kiosks sit side by side with bright, colorful retail signs (Baker 1997).

CONCLUSION

In Miramar it is obvious that historic preservation has a different meaning than the one used in Habana Vieja. It is not the tourist that is being attracted, it is the foreign-owned businesses renting properties, restoring facades and upgrading systems. Habana Vieja is over 400 years old. Miramar is only 70. Spatially, the old part of the city can be seen on foot. Miramar cannot. Hard currency for restoration in Habana Vieja is generated by a non-government organization (NGO) with governmental authorization. In Miramar, private investors and government agencies are furnishing capital to finance restorations. Some observers have suggested that Miramar is becoming more socially stratified than the rest of the city due to the influx of tourist and investment dollars. Those dollars do not contribute to continued restorations as in Habana Vieja. As a result of the actual land use, very few tourists actually see Miramar as a tourist destination even though much of the tourist economy and related facilities actually reside there.

With continued corporate and government restoration, however, the suburb will continue to demand high rents from foreign occupants. Most businesses and embassies appear to locate on the main east-west thoroughfares, as opposed to the smaller side streets. But a recent survey done in June 1998 by students from Indiana University Purdue University Indianapolis found that a higher concentration of new retail business and offices are starting to become more dispersed throughout the neighborhood. The displacement of residents appears to be increasing as former apartment houses and single-family homes are converted to new uses.

Even though the motivation for preservation in Miramar is focused on attracting foreign businesses, there is still a considerable amount of historic preservation taking place. The preservation and refurbishing of this neighborhood may, in the end, lead to increased tourist development. Although most of the palatial architecture is not located by the water, there are still a number of waterfront properties that can be developed as tourist accommodations. The focus of historic preservation must also examined. A house cannot simply be renovated and considered historic. The history of an area makes a structure significant in the neighborhood. No plaques relating to the history of the development of Miramar were noted. It is historical, but few know the history.

There are notable examples of specific architectural styling such as turned columns and embellishments on massive Spanish Baroque houses, various styles of Art Deco (including Tropical, Pueblo and Streamlined) and monumental Neo-classical designs that have utilized imported decorative detailing in their construction materials (granite and marble). Originally, many of these houses were designed by famous European and American architects for use as single-family homes. Today, many carry a mixed-use label and the change in function has caused severe neglect and decay.

Socialist economic policies play a large part in the deterioration of many of Miramar's and Habana's outstanding architectural examples. Former large private residences have been subdivided into apartments as a solution to housing shortages. This has led to neighborhood deterioration, under capitalistic definitions. Regentrification, common in U.S. urban areas, has restored a sense of place to older neighborhoods, but at the price of displacing former residents due to higher property taxes. The continued development of Miramar into a neighborhood of foreign investment could facilitate a capitalistic fate for the residents as the government forces them to relocate to other areas inside or outside the city. On the other hand, this does promote the restoration and preservation of Miramar's architectural heritage. This also constitutes sound economic planning, saves energy and resources, and capitalizes on extant culture. But the question remains, should local residents have a voice in neighborhood development or should the government continue its quest to stimulate foreign investment in capitalistic enterprises in Miramar?

REFERENCES

Baker, C. 1997. *Cuba Handbook*. Chico, California: Moon Publications, Inc.

Carley, R. 1997. *Cuba: 400 Years of Architectural Heritage*. New York: BPI Communications, Inc.

Scarpaci, J. 1996. "Back to the Future: The Sociopolitical Dynamics of Miramar's Real-Estate Market," in *Cuba in Transition-Volume 6*. Washington: Association for the Study of the Cuban Economy.

Schwartz, R. 1997. *Pleasure Island: Tourism and Temptation in Cuba*. Lincoln, Nebraska: University of Nebraska Press.

Segre, R., M. Coyula, and J. Scarpaci. 1997. *Havana: Two Faces of the Antillean Metropolis*. West Sussex, England: John Wiley and Sons, Ltd.

CUBAN IMMIGRATION: CHALLENGES AND OPPORTUNITIES

Matías F. Travieso-Díaz[1]

Immigration is one of the fundamental issues that policy makers in both the United States and Cuba will have to address early on during Cuba's transition to democracy and a free-market economy. Recent history suggests that countries which have made successful free-market transitions have been helped along by the inflow of foreign investment, the privatization of state-owned enterprises and, in general, by the free flow of goods and people across national borders. In order for Cuba to follow this model, it will need to design and implement an open and efficient immigration policy that allows workers, investors and visitors to move with relative freedom in and out of Cuba. Indeed, as a practical matter, "moving goods and services in international commerce also involves moving the people who trade in those goods and services."[2] Accordingly, Cuba must develop an immigration policy that opens the country's doors to those who can make a positive contribution to its economic recovery.

Given the large Cuban population in the United States and the close proximity of Cuba to U.S. borders, the United States also has a significant interest in Cuban immigration issues. On the one hand a strong, free Cuba will provide new opportunities to investors and offer U.S. businesses new markets and a potential source of skilled workers. On the other hand, there is a significant risk of a mass exodus of

Cubans to the United States if economic conditions take a turn for the worse, as has happened in many countries during the early phases of their free-market transitions. U.S. immigration policy towards Cuba should therefore be designed to allow Cubans meeting certain criteria to work temporarily in the United States, yet keeping control over the entry of legal and illegal permanent immigrants. Thus, in addition to lifting the trade embargo and developing new economic relationships with Cuba, the United States will also have to craft a new immigration policy towards Cuba that implements these potentially conflicting objectives.

This paper seeks to present some suggestions as to what the respective immigration policies of the United States and Cuba should be during Cuba's free-market transition. The programs suggested here are offered in the hope that current immigration policies will be changed as soon as practicable once the transition gets under way, so that the existing confrontational approach can swiftly give way to cooperation in achieving both countries' common objectives in this important area.

POST-REVOLUTION IMMIGRATION TRENDS AND POLICIES

Throughout the first half century of Cuba's independence (1902-1959), there was no separate U.S. im-

1. This paper is a condensed version of the one presented at the Eighth Annual Meeting of the Association for the Study of the Cuban Economy in Miami, Florida, on August 6, 1998. The author gratefully acknowledges the assistance of John Barton and Pablo Yacub in the preparation of this paper.

2. Gene McNary, *Moving Goods and People in International Commerce: Remarks of the Honorable Gene McNary*, 2 Duke J. Comp. & Int'l L. 247 (1992).

migration policy towards Cuba. Cuban immigration was part of the overall U.S. immigration apparatus. Cuba was not a problem country from the immigration standpoint, because the flow of Cubans to the United States was relatively small and there was little illegal immigration.[3] Thus, it was not until after the Cuban Revolution in 1959 that the United States had the need and the incentive to establish a distinct immigration policy towards Cuba. Likewise, the relatively small number of Cubans seeking to leave the island for the United States did not warrant Cuba's formulation of a policy towards those of its citizens who migrated.

This situation changed drastically following the triumph of the Cuban Revolution in 1959, which led to a dramatic emigration process that continues to this day. While the Cuban exodus is relatively recent and well documented,[4] it is important to understand how it developed and how it led to the current immigration regime between Cuba and the United States, since some variation of the present framework is likely to be in place at the time the free-market transition gets underway in Cuba.

Shortly after the new revolutionary regime came to power, Cuban nationals started to leave the island at a growing pace. The driving forces behind the exodus were sometimes political and others economic, although in many cases both factors were present. The vast majority of the Cuban émigrés came to the United States.

The first stages of the migration saw Cubans being driven out of their country by the radical policies of the revolutionary regime.[5] Since 1980, however, economic necessity has become the predominant factor motivating Cubans to emigrate. Faced with a deteriorating standard of living, Cubans have sought to come to the United States in hope of a better life.[6]

The social composition of the immigrants also changed with time. In the early stages, many of those who immigrated to the United States were members of the economic and intellectual elite, or members of the middle class who were discontent with or fearful of the new regime.[7] By comparison, the Cubans who have come to the United States in the post-1980 stages of the exodus typically belong to the lower social and economic classes, although such terms have relatively little meaning in Cuba's current society.[8]

The evolution of U.S. immigration policy towards Cuban nationals parallels to some degree the shift in the socio-economic makeup of the Cuban immigrants and their motivation for coming to the United States. The United States encouraged the influx of Cuban immigrants for over three decades when to do so was consistent with the country's international political objectives. Since the end of the Cold War, there has been less of a need for an open door policy towards refugees from Communism, and increased public opposition to allowing foreigners to burden the national and local economies.[9] Accordingly, following the disintegration of the Soviet Bloc and the trend towards economic-driven immigration from Cuba, the United States has erected new barriers against large-scale Cuban immigration.

---

3. Of the one million Cubans presently in the United States, less than 70,000 immigrated before the Cuban Revolution in 1959. U.S. 1990 Census, as reported in Silvia Pedraza, *Cuba's Refugees: Manifold Migrations,"* in CUBA IN TRANSITION—VOLUME 5, ASSOCIATION FOR THE STUDY OF THE CUBAN ECONOMY 311, 315 (1995) [hereinafter PEDRAZA].

4. The reader interested in a history the Cuban emigration since the Revolution came to power in 1959 is referred to the paper by Pedraza, *supra* note 3, and to Miguel González-Pando, *Development Stages of the Cuban Exile Country*, CUBA IN TRANSITION—VOLUME 7, ASSOCIATION FOR THE STUDY OF THE CUBAN ECONOMY 50 (August 1997) [hereinafter GONZALEZ-PANDO].

5. PEDRAZA, *supra* note 3, at 312-13.

6. Id.

7. GONZALEZ-PANDO, *supra* note 4, at 51.

8. PEDRAZA, *supra* note 3, at 312-13.

9. These issues are further discussed *infra*.

U.S. Policies from 1959 to 1964

It was the policy of the United States from 1959 to 1994 to allow relatively free entry of Cuban nationals into the country, regardless of whether the individuals seeking entry would qualify for admission under existing immigration standards. Once the two nations severed diplomatic relations in 1961, Cubans were allowed to come to the United States on a parole basis, without the need to obtain visas, and were admitted as refugees even if they came illegally. No attempts were made by the U.S. Coast Guard to intercept or turn back to Cuba those traveling from Cuba in rafts or small vessels.[10]

Once in the United States, arriving Cubans did not experience some of the hardships suffered by other immigrant groups. They were given financial assistance under a special program enacted by Congress for their benefit.[11] In addition, the many Cubans who entered the country as parolees were given preferential treatment in attaining legal immigrant status: in 1966, Congress passed the Cuban Refugee Adjustment Act, which allowed Cubans to adjust their status to that of permanent U.S. residents, without leaving the country, one year after arriving in the United States.[12] Unlike other asylum seekers, Cubans could adjust their status to that of permanent residents without showing a well-founded fear of persecution on account of race, religion, nationality, membership in particular social group, or political opinion.[13] This preferential treatment eased the integration of the Cuban exile population into the United States.

These favorable policies led to the settlement of over 750,000 first-generation immigrants from Cuba into the United States in the thirty year period 1959-1990.[14] The flow of these Cuban immigrants came in spurts, in response to intermittent changes in Cuba's willingness to allow those discontent with political and economic conditions in the country to emigrate.

The downfall of communism in the Eastern Bloc in the early 1990s had severe consequences for the Cuban economy. Starting in the 1960s, Cuba had become increasingly dependent on trade with, and economic subsidies from, its Eastern Bloc allies, particularly the USSR.[15] With the fall of communism, Cuba was left with an enfeebled economy, resulting in ever increasing privations for the Cuban people.[16]

By 1994, the economic crisis had reached its most critical point. As conditions worsened, discontent mounted, and a growing number of people began to risk their lives and fled from Cuba in boats or rafts. One group seeking to escape hijacked a ferry boat, which was immediately sunk by the Cuban Coast Guard, eliciting international condemnation over the

---

10. Kathryn M. Bockley, *A Historical Overview of Refugee Legislation: The Deception of Foreign Policy in the Land of Promise*, 21 N.C. J. Int'l L. & Comm. Reg. 253, 269 (1995).

11. Migration and Refugee Assistance Act, Act of June 28, 1962, Pub. L. No. 87-510, 76 Stat. 121 (1962).

12. Cuban Refugee Adjustment Act, Pub. L. No. 89-732, 80 Stat. 1161, 8 USC §1255 note (1966).

13. The Cuban Refugee Adjustment Act eliminated the need to individually screen Cubans, many of whom entered the United States illegally by boat, to determine whether they feared persecution if they were returned to Cuba. Congress in effect decided that because Cuba under Castro was Communist, in general no Cuban should be deported. The nationals of no other country had at the time the same screening exemptions. *The U.S. Humanitarian Entry Program Lacks Coherence,* Testimony of American Federation for Immigration Reform, submitted for the record of a Feb. 24, 1998 Congressional hearing on the U.S. refugee program.

14. 1990 U.S. Census, *as reprinted in* PEDRAZA, *supra* note 3, at 317.

15. With the fall of the Soviet Union, "Cuba lost socialist economic aid of more than $6 billion annually." Carmelo Mesa-Lago, *Cuba's Economic Policies and Strategies for the 1990s,* in CUBAN COMMUNISM 1959-1995 (Irving Louis Horowitz ed., 1995) 187.

16. *See generally,* Carmelo Mesa-Lago, *The Economic Effects on Cuba of the Downfall of Socialism in the USSR and Eastern Europe,* in CUBA AFTER THE COLD WAR (Carmelo Mesa-Lago ed.,1993) 133-188. Concomitant with the weakening of its economy, Cuba started to incrementally reduce the age limit for those allowed to emigrate legally. Since 1992, all Cubans over 20 years old have been eligible to apply for exit visas. *See* AMNESTY INTERNATIONAL, UNITED STATES/CUBA: CUBAN "RAFTERS"—PAWNS OF TWO GOVERNMENTS, AI Doc. No. AMR 51/86/94 (1994) [hereinafter "AMNESTY"].

attendant loss of life.[17] The sinking also provoked anti-government demonstrations.[18] In response to the growing unrest, on August 6, 1994, Fidel Castro announced the end of government efforts to prevent people from leaving the country by sea.[19]

The removal of exit restrictions resulted in an immediate rush of large numbers of Cubans to the high seas towards the United States.[20] President Clinton responded to the crisis by ending the open-arms policy that for decades had granted automatic asylum to Cubans who arrived in the United States. On August 19, 1994, Clinton announced that the United States would henceforth bar entry into the United States of Cuban *balseros* (rafters). Instead of allowing them to enter the country, the U.S. Coast Guard was ordered to capture the *balseros* at sea and transport them to the Guantanamo Bay Naval Base or other U.S. refugee camps for eventual repatriation to Cuba.[21]

In the following weeks, the immigration crisis intensified as *balseros* continued to flee Cuba in inadequate rafts in shark-infested waters, despite President Clinton's announcement that all Cubans intercepted at sea would be sent indefinitely to refugee camps.[22] Meanwhile, U.S. and Cuban representatives met to discuss an agreement that would curb the flow of *balseros* and admit a greater number of Cubans legally into the United States.[23]

The crisis was not resolved until September 9, 1994, when the United States and Cuba entered into the Cuban Migration Agreement. In what both countries publicized as an agreement aimed at saving human lives, Cuba and the United States agreed to measures to encourage legal immigration.[24] The United States promised to admit at least 20,000 Cuban immigrants

---

17. The Cuban government claimed that the sinking of the ferry boat was accidental. However, survivors claim that the boat was pummeled by the water cannons from three of the government's tugs and then rammed by one of the vessels. The boat sank, and 37 of its passengers drowned. In the three weeks following this incident, three other passenger ferries were hijacked, along with an airplane and a military vessel. Geoffrey W. Hymans, *Outlawing the Use of Refugees as Tools of Foreign Policy*, 3 ILSA J. Int'l & Comp. L. 149, 152 (1996) [hereinafter "HYMANS"].

18. On August 5, 1994, rumors that a ferry boat was going to be hijacked to Florida drew more than 500 people to Havana docks, and the most serious anti-government riot since Castro assumed power occurred. *Id.* at 153.

19. Castro answered the riot by declaring, through the government news agency Prensa Latina, that "we will stop blocking the departure of those who want to leave the country" and that "we cannot continue to guard the coasts of the United States." *Id.*

20. Sonia Mikolic-Torreira, *The Cuban Migration Agreement: Implications of the Clinton-Castro Immigration Policy*, 8 Geo. Immigr. L. J. 667(1994) [hereinafter "MIKOLIC-TORREIRA"].

21. *See generally*, GAO, CUBA - U.S. RESPONSE TO 1994 CUBAN MIGRATION CRISIS, GAO/NSIAD 95-211 (Sep. 1995); David Gavilan, *¿Y Qué Pasó? ("And then what Happened?"): The Plight of Cuban Detainees at Guantanamo Bay*, 4 Card. J. Int'l & Comp. L. 451 (1996) [hereinafter "GAVIILAN"].

22. By August 24, 1994, rafters were departing from the Havana *Malecon* (waterfront) "in full view of government office buildings and large crowds of onlookers." HYMANS, *supra* note 17, at 153. Indeed, the departures appeared to be occurring with the cooperation of the Cuban authorities. Robert Suro, *Havana Giving Tacit Approval to Rising Tide of Rafters*, WASHINGTON POST, Aug. 24, 1994 at A24.

23. Cuba may have had as its agenda to force discussion of the U.S. embargo. As one observer noted:

Castro [used] the exodus in the way that the Kim dynasty in North Korea used its program to build atom bombs as a lever to prod the United States to open wide-ranging talks. But U.S. negotiators have refused to discuss Cuba's loudest demand— easing of the American trade embargo.

D. Williams, *Cuban Response to U.S. Immigration Offer Outlandish*, WASHINGTON POST, Sep. 5, 1994, at A14. However, at the end, the United States succeeded in limiting the discussion in that and subsequent meetings (of which there have been nine rounds since 1994) to the terms of the immigration accord and their implementation. U.S. Dep't of State, Press Statement, Jun. 25, 1998; Nicole Winfield, *U.S., Cuba Talk Migration Issues*, ASSOCIATED PRESS, Jun. 29, 1998.

24. For a discussion of the terms of the Immigration Agreement, *see* MIKOLIC-TORREIRA, *supra* note 20; U.S.-Cuba Joint Communique on Migration, Sept. 9, 1994, 5 U.S. Dep't State Dispatch 37 (1994).

annually.[25] In exchange, Cuba agreed to take effective measures to deter unsafe departures. With Cuba clamping down on departures by sea, the number of *balseros* declined dramatically and the exodus came to an end by December of 1994.[26]

Changes in U.S. Immigration Policy After the "Balsero" Crisis

The stated basis for the end of the U.S. open door policy towards Cuban illegal immigration was a desire to avoid the loss of human lives.[27] However, there were other reasons for the U.S. reversal of its Cuban immigration policy. For instance, allowing Cubans to immigrate to the United States ceased to have major foreign policy implications after the fall of the Soviet Union.[28] During the Cold War, granting political asylum to a person fleeing a communist country served to highlight the negative aspects of Socialism and underscore the advantages of the American way of life. However, with the fall of the Soviet Union, the incentive of granting political asylum to Cubans disappeared.

In addition, the Clinton Administration apparently saw the stemming of the immigration tide as way to force Cubans on the island to work towards bringing about a democratic transition. In a June 1995 speech, the President defended his policies as follows:

> We simply cannot admit all Cubans who seek to come here. We cannot let people risk their lives on open seas in unseaworthy rafts.... Regularizing Cuba migration also helps our efforts to promote a peaceful transition to democracy on the island.... For too long, Castro has used the threat of uncontrolled migration to distract us from this fundamental objective. With the steps we've taken, we will be able to devote ourselves fully to our real long-term goal. [29]

Another important factor in the equation was the growing anti-immigrant bias that developed in the United States at about the same time the *balsero* crisis was unfolding. California led the way in the anti-immigrant sentiment, which was reflected in the passage by the State's voters in the November 1994 election of Proposition 187, which barred undocumented immigrants from public education, social services

---

25. This promise to establish a 20,000 visa floor was a broadening of the previously-existing immigration agreement between the United States and Cuba, under which there was a *ceiling* of 20,000 visas to be issued to Cuban nationals. Joint Communique Between the United States of America and Cuba, Dec. 14, 1984, U.S. - Cuba, T.I.A.S. No. 11,057. While that ceiling was increased in 1990 to 27,845, in reality, the neither figure was ever reached; in 1993/1994, prior to the crisis, only 2,700 visas were granted to Cubans. AMNESTY, *supra* note 16; Patrick Costello, *Cuba: Reforms, Migration and International Reforms*, WRITENET COUNTRY PAPERS, Nov. 1995, Section 3.4 (no page citations available).

26. David Hancock, *Influx of Cuban Rafters Ends; Zero in December*, MIAMI HERALD, Jan. 9, 1995, at 1B. In all, approximately 32,000 Cubans were picked up at sea by the U.S. Coast Guard during the crisis and confined in the Guantanamo Bay Naval Base and a U.S. military base in Panama. GAVILAN, *supra* note 21, at 452-53.

27. MIKOLIC-TORREIRA, *supra* note 20, at 668.

28. As an analyst put it:

> Immigration and particularly asylum policy were viewed as part of the overall foreign policy efforts against the Soviet Union and its sphere of influence. Emigration on one side and granting political asylum was encouraged. Indeed, the arrival of each political refugee from the Soviet Bloc was viewed as reaffirmation of the validity of our own system. Similarly, the Freedom Flotilla was viewed as a blight on the Cuban revolution and a validation of our foreign policy. In addition, for the Cuban refugees, their journey was a logical extension of their unhappiness with the revolution.

Boswell, Richard, *Throwing Away the Key: Limits on the Plenary Power?*, 18 Mich. J. Int'l L. 689, 695-96 (1997).

29. Speech by President Clinton directed to Cuban-Americans, ASSOCIATED PRESS, Jun. 27, 1995. *See also,* John Lantigua, *Clinton Defends Policy*, MIAMI HERALD, Jun. 28, 1995, at 1B.

and non-emergency health care.[30] The anti-immigrant backlash was also an important campaign issue in Florida, where the images of destitute *balseros* arriving on the State's shores prompted concerns about their impact on the local economy.[31] Florida's incumbent Governor, Lawton Chiles, made an issue in his 1994 re-election campaign the opposition to allowing mass immigration from Cuba and, when President Clinton announced in November 1994 that he would allow the entry of 10,000 of the Cubans interned at the Guantanamo Bay Naval Base and in Panama on humanitarian grounds, Governor Chiles filed a suit for nearly $1 billion against the United States, claiming that the federal government should pay the State's cost of admitting illegal immigrants because they failed to prevent illegal immigration.[32] Even though the suit was dismissed, Chiles claimed that the "lawsuit was successful in that it raised awareness of the extraordinary impact of illegal immigration on border states like Florida."[33]

Implementation of the U.S.-Cuba Immigration Agreement

The United States ultimately did not make good on its threat to return to Cuba the *balseros* it seized in 1994. Instead, in May 1995, after holding secret meetings with Cuba, the Clinton Administration reversed its Cuban immigration policy by announcing that the United States would admit the 21,000 refugees still being held at the Guantanamo Bay Naval Base, but would in the future send back to Cuba all "illegal immigrants" found at sea.[34] In so doing, the United States created a remarkable disparity of treatment between the Cubans who are intercepted at sea—who are almost invariably returned to Cuba—and those who manage to touch American soil, who in most instances are given asylum in accordance

---

30. *See* Tanya Broder and Clara Luz Navarro, *A Street Without an Exit: Excerpts from the Lives of Latinas in Post-187 California,* 7 Hastings Women's L.J. 275, 277 (1996) [hereinafter "STREET"]. Sponsors of Proposition 187 knew that certain provisions would probably be deemed unconstitutional, such as denying elementary and secondary education to undocumented children, which appeared to be inconsistent with the U.S. Supreme Court's decision in Plyer v. Doe, 457 U.S. 202 (1982), which required that K-12 education be available to all children, notwithstanding their immigration status. *Id.* Similarly, Proposition 187 appeared to violate the Omnibus Reconciliation Act of 1986, which mandated that undocumented immigrants be given "emergency health care, including pregnancy services, under the Medicaid program." Jonathan C. Dunlap, *The Absent Federal Partner,* SPECTRUM, January 1, 1994 [hereinafter "DUNLAP"] (no page citations available).

31. A 1996 report by the Center for Immigration Studies appeared to lend support to many of the economic concerns raised by Florida's anti-immigrant forces. Some of the report's findings were summarized in the press as follows:

> By the year 2020, Florida's population will jump 57 percent to 22 million. The state's public schools will be crowded with an additional 750,000 students, and its roads clogged with nightmarish traffic. … And a 30 percent growth in foreign immigration will be to blame for much of the problem afflicting the state. … By 2020, whites will make up 58 percent of Florida's population, down from 73 percent in 1990.

Report: State has Immigrant Problem the Study says that by the 2020 the Schools will be Jammed and the Roads will be Clogged, ORLANDO SENTINEL, Jan. 19, 1996, at D4. Whether or not the report's findings are given credence, they served to fuel the anti-immigration sentiment in Florida.

32. Florida was one of several states to file suit against the United States. Other states with a high immigrant populations, such as California, Arizona, New Jersey, New York and Texas, also sued the federal government separately. One article depicts the suits as governors' courting the anti-immigrant vote in those states:

> Accompanied by a blaze of publicity, the states filed separate suits in 1994 arguing they should be reimbursed for the costs of illegal immigrants. At the time, the state's governors were running for re-election and polls showed widespread public resentment of illegal immigration.

M. Puente, *Court Rejects Florida case on Illegal Aliens, State Sought Federal Funds,* USA TODAY, May 14, 1996, at A5.

33. Id.

34. Daniel Williams and Ann Devroy, *Serious Alarm Bells led to Talks with Cuba,* WASHINGTON POST, May 5, 1995, at A4; The White House, Joint U.S.-Cuba Statement, May 2, 1995; Ann Devroy and Daniel Williams, *In Reversal, U.S. to Accept Cubans Held at Navy Base,* WASHINGTON POST, May 3, 1995 at 1A.

with the Migration and Refugee Act of 1962, which remains in effect.[35]

The new policy was described as being prompted by many factors, including the high cost of keeping the refugees detained in Guantanamo, the recurring threat of riots among the detainees, and the sense that the majority of the population supported curbing illegal immigration.[36] Indeed, while the change in immigration policy was received with indignation by many in the Cuban-American community, a poll taken in Miami shortly after the new policy was announced found that "[a]n overwhelming majority of Dade [County] residents, including a significant number of Cuban-Americans, believe the time has come to sharply limit immigration from Cuba."[37]

Virtually all the over 30,000 rafters that were interned in 1994 were eventually admitted into the United States, although the process was not completed until January of 1996.[38] The United States has also kept its promise under the 1994 Cuban Migration Agreement to admit 20,000 Cuban immigrants annually, in addition to those Cuban nationals admitted through the visa processing system as the next of kin to United States citizens.[39] Visas are granted to people with close relatives in the United States, people who qualify for political asylum, people qualifying for visas as relatives forming part of the same household as others granted visas, and other immigrants to be selected by lottery.[40]

The State Department needed to make certain changes in its practices in order to increase the number of Cubans legally entering the United States. Among the changes made, the State Department loosened the criteria for granting asylum to Cubans,

---

35. Thus, since its May 1995 agreement with Cuba, the United States has returned over one thousand refugees captured at sea to Cuba. *U.S. Returns Over 1,000 Cubans Since 1995,* REUTERS, Jun. 17, 1998. At least some of the returned refugees are reported to have faced harassment upon their return to Cuba. *2 Cubans Report Harassment,* FT. LAUDERDALE SUN SENTINEL, May 27, 1995 at 12A. By contrast, every year an increasing number (which thus far in 1998 already exceeds 300) of Cubans—many of them smuggled by third parties—make it to land in the United States and, in most instances, are granted political asylum. John Nordheimer, *Those Reaching Shore Gain Legal Advantage,* NY TIMES, Aug. 27, 1994; Andres Viglucci, *Cubans who Reach U.S. May get to Stay,* MIAMI HERALD, May 5, 1995 at A1; Andres Viglucci, *U.S. Eases up on Refugee Detentions,* MIAMI HERALD, DEC. 11, 1995 at 1B; Manny Garcia, *Cubans Land on Beaches to Open Arms,* MIAMI HERALD, Sep. 24, 1996 at 1A; Deborah Ramirez, *Smuggling Operations on Rise From Cuba,* FT. LAUDERDALE SUN-SENTINEL, Jun. 18, 1998; Angus Mc.Swan, *Summer Brings Waves of "Boat People" to Florida,* REUTERS, Jun. 17, 1998; Andres Viglucci, *Smuggling Seen in Refugee Rise 2 Arrested; Boat Seized,* MIAMI HERALD, Jun. 25, 1998 at 1A; *but see,* Liz Balmaseda, *Rescue not a Happy Ending,* MIAMI HERALD, Jun. 24, 1998 at 1B.

36. *See* Steven Greenhouse, *U.S. Will Return Refugees to Cuba in Policy Switch,* NY TIMES, May 3, 1995 at A1; Tom Fiedler and Alfonso Chardy, *Goal of 'No More Mariels' Led to Clinton's Painful Choice,* MIAMI HERALD, May 3, 1995 at 15A. The point was driven by a subtle change in semantics. The Cubans seeking shelter in the United States, who for over thirty years had been described as "exiles," "refugees," "freedom seekers," and other terms with positive connotations, became in official U.S. government parlance "migrants" and "illegal immigrants." *See, e.g.,* Testimony of Doris Meissner, Commissioner U.S. Immigration and Naturalization Service before a May 18, 1995 Hearing of the House Subcommittee on Western Hemisphere on the U.S. Cuban migration policy; *U.S. Will Return Refugees to Cuba in Policy Switch, supra.* These terms had previously been applied to justify the return of undocumented aliens (such as Haitians) seeking to enter the United States by boat to their country of origin, *see* Executive Order 12807, Interdiction of Illegal Aliens, 57 Fed. Reg. 23133 (May 24, 1992); Elizabeth Harris, *Economic Refugees: Unprotected in the United States by Virtue of an Inaccurate Label,* 9 Am.U.J. Int'l L. & Pol'y 269, 280 & n.73 (1993). Before 1994, the term had apparently not been applied to Cuban rafters.

37. John Lantigua and Stephen Doig, *Limit Cuba Immigration? Yes, Most in Survey Agree,* MIAMI HERALD, May 15, 1995 at 1A.

38. John Lantigua, *Guantanamo: Mission Accomplished,* MIAMI HERALD, Jan. 19, 1996 at 1B.

39. *U.S. Fulfills Migration Pact with Cuba,* REUTERS, Aug. 22, 1995; Carol Rosenberg, *New Visa Lottery Will Help Cubans Migrate to U.S.,* MIAMI HERALD, Jun. 6, 1998 [hereinafter "ROSENBERG"].

40. Mimi Whitefield, *New Rules on Cuban Immigration Released,* MIAMI HERALD, Oct. 13, 1994, at 21A. This is not to say, however, that everyone who is granted a visa actually emigrates to the United States. Thousands of the people granted visas are ultimately prevented from leaving the country by the high exit fees charged by the Cuban government ($500 per adult, $400 per child, payable in dollars only), the costs of transportation, and other hurdles. Andres Viglucci, *Costly Exit Fees Keep Some Cubans From Using Visas,* MIAMI HERALD, Aug. 9, 1998, at 1A [hereinafter "FEES"].

broadened its parole powers, and increased the number of Cuban immigrant visas selected by lottery.[41]

Attorney General Janet used her emergency powers to raise the number of Cubans admitted each year beyond the legal ceiling. Immigration law permits the Attorney General to grant parole in cases of emergency or in the public interest. In the past, the Attorney General limited the use of the parole power to situations in which an individual needed the services or protection of the United States, such as a cancer victim needing a bone marrow transplant. Reno expanded the use of the parole power of her office to increase the number of Cubans allowed to reach the United States.

The United States also broadened its asylum guidelines. The eligibility requirements for Cubans seeking asylum were loosened to include certain people that did not meet that well-founded fear of persecution required by U.S. immigration law. According to the new guidelines, Cubans were eligible for asylum if they had been human-rights activists, had experienced religious discrimination, had been consigned to work camps in the period from 1965 to 1968, or had the exercise of their vocations curbed as a result of their perceived or actual political beliefs.[42]

Additionally, through the immigration lottery and the increased number of lottery visas to Cuban nationals, the United States kept its vow to take an active course in promoting legal Cuban immigration while effectively tackling many concerns about illegal aliens. The increased number of lottery visas allowed many Cubans to legally immigrate to the United States although they may not have otherwise qualified.[43] This opened the door to the United States to those in Cuba who lacked an immediate relative with legal status in the United States and did not suffer sufficient persecution to qualify for political asylum. On the other hand, the lottery requirements served as a filter of the Cubans admitted to the United States. By requiring lottery applicants to have completed high school, have a minimum of three years work experience, have passed a medical screening, and have relatives in this country, the United States took precautions to exclude criminals and possible welfare recipients.[44] Although these restrictions limited the pool of Cubans able to qualify for lottery visas, more than enough visa applications were submitted to enable the United States to fulfill its promise of granting more than 20,000 visas to Cuban nationals.[45]

Current Status of Cuba-to-U.S. Immigration

The U.S. government's handling of the *balsero* crisis sent a clear message that the United States would no longer provide an unlimited safe haven for discontent Cubans. Many, therefore, expected that the U.S. government's policy would become more restrictive with time, and that it would become more difficult for Cubans to enter the United States and for those in the United States to adjust their status. The anticipated hardening of the U.S. stance concerning Cuban immigration, however, has not taken place. Cubans still enjoy the preferential treatment that began when President Johnson established an open-door policy to Cuban immigrants.[46] There are sound legal and political reasons why such treatment should con-

---

41. MIKOLIC-TORREIRA, *supra* note 20, at 668.

42. Id.

43. In 1994, the United States granted 8,400 visas to Cuban nationals seeking to immigrate to the United States. Since 1994, nearly 29,000 Cubans were granted U.S. visas under the lottery system. ROSENBERG, *supra* note 39. The total number of immigrant visas granted to Cubans since 1994 exceeds 42,000. FEES, *supra* note 40.

44. Andres Viglucci, *2nd Lottery Will Open U.S. Door to Cubans,* MIAMI HERALD, Mar. 12, 1996, at 1B; PR NEWSWIRE, *INS Announces Details of Special Cuban Migration Program,* Nov. 4, 1994.

45. 189,000 Cubans applied for the first lottery in 1994, and 435,000 applied for the second one in 1996. ROSENBERG, *supra* note 39.

46. In fact, the number of Cuban refugees adjusting their status to permanent U.S. residents nearly doubled the first year the new immigration policy went into effect, from 12,355 in 1995 to 22,542 in 1996. U.S. Immigration and Naturalization Services Web Page Statistics, Immigrants Admitted by Major Category of Admissions and Region and Selected Country of Birth: Fiscal Year 1996 and 1995, Table 6.

tinue, at least as long as the current regime retains its repressive policies against those who seek to escape the country.[47]

Those seeking to immigrate to the United States from other countries have not received the same reception given to Cubans. In recent years, Congress has attacked illegal immigration through the Anti-Terrorism and Effective Death Penalty Act of 1996 ("Anti-Terrorism Act")[48] and the Illegal Immigration Reform and Immigrant Responsibility Act of 1996 ("IIRIRA").[49] The Anti-Terrorism Act tightens admissibility standards by means such as expanding the term "aggravated felony" to include conduct that in the past would not have barred an alien from legally immigrating to the United States. For its part, contrary to previous law, the IIRIRA makes an alien inadmissible if he entered the United States without having been admitted or paroled. Thus, both acts create new obstacles for aliens seeking legal immigrant status in the United States.

Cubans have not been adversely affected by the latest tightening of the U.S. borders to immigrants. Instead, Cubans have had a much different experience. For instance, in April of 1996, when moves were made to repeal the Cuban Refugee Adjustment Act, the Senate voted to retain the legislation in place until a democratic government is in place in Havana, and legislation to that effect was enacted.[50] This indefinite retention of the Cuban Refugee Adjustment Act preserves the preferential treatment of Cuban nationals in the United States, at least until the end of the communist rule.

Moreover, as part of the District of Columbia Appropriation Act of 1998, Congress recently passed the Nicaragua Adjustment and Central American Relief Act ("NACARA"),[51] which extends immigration privileges to Cuban nationals. The new law requires a Cuban national seeking to adjust his status to that of a permanent resident to have resided in the United States since December 1, 1995, rather than the former one year requirement set under the Cuban Refugee Adjustment Act. On the other hand, applicants for status adjustment under NACARA are not subject to the provisions of section 245(c) of the INA, which bars aliens from adjusting if, *inter alia*, they worked in the United States without authorization or remained in the United States beyond their authorized stay. Also, Cuban nationals that entered illegally are eligible for amnesty under NACARA.[52] Such amnesty is not available to nationals of other countries.

THE CHALLENGES AND OPPORTUNITIES OF A POST-TRANSITION IMMIGRATION REGIME BETWEEN CUBA AND THE UNITED STATES

Although one cannot predict with certainty the reaction of the U.S. government to the start of Cuba's democratic transition, its immigration policy towards Cuba is unlikely to remain the same once the process gets under way. For over three decades, the United States has accepted hundreds of thousands of Cubans without applying to them the standard rules for granting asylum or admitting aliens as permanent residents. The preferential treatment given to Cuban immigrants will almost certainly cease with the end of Communism in Cuba, unless the political condi-

---

47. Because of founded fears of persecution should they return to the island, obtaining political asylum in the United States remains critical for Cuban citizens who leave their native country to escape political persecution. Andrew Bonavia, *United States v. Rodriguez-Roman: Prosecuting the Persecuted*, 22 N.C. J. Int'l L. & Com. Reg. 1039, 1040 (1997) [hereinafter "BONAVIA"]. U.S. courts have upheld the Cuban exiles' claim to political asylum based on fear of reprisal for abandoning their country. *See* IRodriguez v. INS, 98 F.3d 416 (9th Cir. 1996).

48. Pub. L. 104-132 (Apr. 24, 1996).

49. Pub. L. 104-208, 110 Stat. 3009 (Sep. 30, 1996).

50. Pub. L. 104-208, Title VI, § 606, 110 Stat. 3009-695, 8 USC § 1255 note (Sep. 30, 1996).

51. Pub. L. 105-100, 111 Stat. 2160 (Nov. 19, 1997).

52. *See* Adjustment of Status for Certain Nationals of Nicaragua and Cuba, 63 Fed. Reg. 27823 (May 21, 1998).

tions in the island remain unstable and warrant continuation of some program for the handling of refugees. The Cuban Refugee Adjustment Act, for example, is scheduled to be repealed upon the establishment of a democratic government in Cuba.[53] Therefore, after Cuba's democratization, Cuban nationals may well find themselves facing the same barriers that citizens from other countries presently experience in seeking to migrate to the United States, since the immigration policy of this country is to provide uniform treatment to aliens seeking admission, regardless of their country of origin.

Nevertheless, because of the unique relationship between the two countries, special legislation will likely be enacted (together with an eventual treaty) to properly address the interests and concerns of both the United States and Cuba in the area of immigration as Cuba undergoes its transition to democracy. The terms of that legislation and treaty will be dictated by several factors.

First, U.S. policy toward Cuba in the last forty years has been motivated exclusively by the interest of the United States in fighting Communism and replacing the current Cuban government with a democratic regime. During the transition, immigration policy will be driven primarily by economic rather than political factors. Accordingly, travel restrictions will be liberalized and preferential treatment programs will be re-examined and probably phased out.

Second, immigration is a politically explosive issue in the United States, particularly in those states in which most immigrants have traditionally settled. Any new immigration proposals relating to Cuba are likely to be surrounded by substantial controversy. Legislators are therefore bound to consider Cuban immigration proposals both on their merits and in light of their political ramifications.

Third, although both countries will be working toward similar goals, the challenges they will confront are very different. Whereas Cuba's main objective will be to attract new investors and specialized workers, the United States will focus primarily on balancing its need to facilitate Cuba's transition through open immigration policies, with the somewhat conflicting goal of limiting Cuba-based immigration to manageable amounts.

Finally, immigration in the United States is already governed by a comprehensive policy that, with a few minor exceptions, applies equally to all countries: even Mexico and Canada are given few special immigration privileges despite their participation in the NAFTA.[54] Thus, while immigration from Cuba may be the subject of special provisions, those provisions will have to be of limited duration and will need to be consistent with existing U.S. immigration policy.

Cuba, for its part, must develop an immigration strategy which fosters the movement of goods, ideas and people across its borders during the transition. Once it becomes apparent that Cuba intends to liberalize its economy and commit to a democratic form of government, foreign investors and Cuban expatriates will seek to visit Cuba in substantial numbers. During the transition, it is essential that Cuba encourage such visits by developing and open and efficient immigration policy.

A Potential U.S. Approach to Cuban Post-Transition Immigration

It is probably not in the national interest of either country to continue fostering permanent migration of Cuban nationals into the United States, even for a limited time, during the transition. Rather, given the need to rebuild Cuba, U.S. policy should encourage the temporary, business-oriented movement of Cubans in and out of the United States. Programs

---

53. As noted earlier, *see* note 50, *supra* and associated text, the Cuban Refugee Adjustment Act has been repealed prospectively; the repeal will be effective upon a determination by the President under Section 203 (c)(3) of the LIBERTAD Act (22 USC §6063(c)(3)) that a democratically-elected government in Cuba is in power.

54. See Kevin Johnson, *Free Trade and Closed Borders: NAFTA and Mexican Immigration to the United States*, 27 U.C. Davis L. Rev. 937, 940-941 (1994) [hereinafter "JOHNSON"] ("[W]hile NAFTA provides for a reduction of restraints on trade with the hopes of increasing commerce between the three nations, it for the most part does not deal with the flow of people between those same nations.")

should be instituted to allow the free movement of business travelers and to allow Cubans to work in the United States long enough to gain technical and administrative skills necessary to succeed in the restructured Cuban economy.

Under this approach, the current refugee programs would be eliminated, and concentration of the immigration policies would shift from political to economic goals. Congress would establish new visa and immigration policies which would allow Cubans to travel and work in the United States for limited periods of time, without issuing them permanent immigrant visas. This approach would result in no net increase in the number of Cubans migrating permanently to the United States, and may actually result in a reduction of the number of permanent Cuban immigrants from what it would be if the approach were not implemented, because some Cubans who might qualify for permanent visas may opt for temporary visas instead. The elements of this approach are described below.

The Mexican Model: Although the situations of Mexico and Cuba are very different and likely to remain so, the relations between both countries and the United States raise many of the same immigration issues. Both have weak economies relative to that of the United States, both are located at or close to U.S. borders, and both have been the source of large numbers of legal and illegal immigrants to the United States. As a consequence, it is logical to assume that once the Castro regime no longer commands special treatment, U.S. policy makers will approach immigration from Cuba much like they have dealt with Mexican immigration.[55] Thus, if nothing else, U.S.-Mexican immigration policy provides some guidance as to what boundaries policy makers should stay within given the political climate in the United States.

Despite its seemingly natural link to free trade, immigration was not addressed in any meaningful manner by the NAFTA.[56] Consequently, "many commentators maintain that the NAFTA was not designed with the intention of creating a freedom-of-movement-of-person regime. On the contrary, it is an agreement specifically encouraging the freedom of movement of goods, capital, and services, and which in conspicuous silence excludes persons from its regime."[57] Thus, with a few exceptions,[58] Mexicans are not given preferential immigration treatment. The limited immigration scope of the NAFTA "reflects the tension between the goals of preserving national autonomy, border security, and protecting the permanent employment of each Party's domestic labor force on the one hand, and encouraging the liberalization of trade on the other."[59] Although somewhat contradictory, the U.S. Mexican immigration policy is designed to encourage free and open trade across a relatively closed border.

The issues are virtually identical for Cuba. On the one hand, the United States has an important national interest in facilitating the transition to a strong free-market Cuba. An economically strong Cuba would consolidate what will most likely be a new democratic regime that would offer new markets in which U.S. businesses can operate. Perhaps more importantly, a strong Cuba would eliminate the need of Cubans to seek work abroad, and thereby mitigate the labor, security and cultural problems that many perceive immigration to cause. An immigrant policy that promotes the free movement of skilled workers

---

55. See The North American Free Trade Agreement, Dec. 17, 1992, U.S.-Can.-Mex., 32 I.L.M. 296-456, 612-799, 33 I.L.M. 649-57, 663-64, 671, 80 (1994) (hereinafter "NAFTA").

56. See Johnson, *supra* note 54.

57. Noemi Gal-Or, *Labor Mobility Under NAFTA: Regulatory Policy Spearheading the Social Supplement to the International Trade Regime*, 15 Ariz. J. Int'l & Comp. Law 365, 366 (1998).

58. NAFTA creates a special category of temporary "TN" visas for which only Mexican and Canadian workers are eligible. Mexicans are limited to only 5,500 TN visas annually, so this program does not significantly affect U.S.-Mexican immigration trends. See Chapter 16 of the NAFTA and Appendix 1603.D; 8 CFR § 214.6(c).

59. Ellen G. Yost, *NAFTA: Temporary Entry Provisions—Immigration Dimensions*, 22 CAN.-U.S. L. J. 211 (1996).

between the United States and Cuba has the potential for helping advance these interests. Nonetheless, as long as immigration policy continues to be evaluated primarily as a political rather than economic matter, the United States is unlikely to view the immigration issues presented by a free Cuba much differently than it did those presented by NAFTA. Any proposal addressing immigration during the transition that stands a chance of generating the requisite political support will therefore have to be consistent with the existing immigration policy of the United States toward Mexico and the rest of the world.

Permanent Immigration of Cubans into the United States: The permanent immigration policy of the United States is relatively inflexible and very unlikely to be modified to cater to Cuba's needs during the transition. Moreover, to the extent that the goal of both the United States and Cuba is to allow Cubans to gain training, experience and new skills that they can later use to rebuild Cuba, permanent immigration should be discouraged. Nonetheless, because many Cubans will still be eligible to immigrate permanently into the United States, it is important to briefly examine how the global U.S. immigration policy will apply to Cubans during the transition.

U.S. immigration policy is driven primarily by four principles: family unification, harboring of refugees, cultural diversity and employment. Of the roughly 800,000 permanent immigrants that enter the United States each year, the vast majority enter through a program based upon one of these principles.[60] Although a few special programs are tailored to address the needs of specific ethnic groups or nationalities,

for the most part the policy applies equally to all countries.

Family unification, currently accounting for over 62% of all new immigrants, is clearly the cornerstone of the permanent immigration system.[61] Of those 62%, over half enter as spouses, children or parents of U.S. citizens. There are unlimited visas available to these close relatives of U.S. citizens.[62]

The remainder of the 62% is comprised of immigrants sponsored by either U.S. residents or by more distantly related U.S. citizens. Despite the issuance of approximately 200,000 visas to applicants falling in the latter category, some family members can expect to wait up to thirty years before they can legally enter the United States.[63] Nonetheless, in both family unification categories, the large number of Cubans already residing in the United States will allow Cubans to benefit substantially from family-oriented visa programs. There is no reason to believe this trend will change during the transition.

Around 16% of current permanent immigrants arrive as refugees, many of whom originate in Cuba.[64] If we accept the premise which is the basis for this paper, i.e., that during its transition Cuba will observe democratic principles, few Cubans are likely to qualify as refugees.

In an effort to promote diversity from countries which have not traditionally supplied many immigrants to the United States, Congress has provided for 55,000 visas to be issued by lottery.[65] However, given that nearly 6.5 million people are competing for these "diversity" visas, few Cubans are likely to gain entry into the United States under this pro-

---

60. *See* Prepared Testimony of Susan Martin, Executive Director U.S. Commission on Immigration Reform Before the Judiciary Committee Subcommittee on Immigration and Claims, U.S. House of Representatives, Federal News Service (May 17, 1995).

61. Id.

62. Id.

63. *Id.* The amount of time an applicant can expect to wait depends largely upon which country he/she is from. Quotas are assigned to each country, and certain countries' limits are quickly reached each year.

64. Prepared Statement of Alan Reynolds, Director of Economic Research, Hudson Institute, Before the Judiciary Committee Subcommittee on Immigration and Claims, U.S. House of Representatives, Federal News Service (April 21, 1998).

65. Id.

gram.[66] Moreover, because Cuba is not an "undersubscribed" country, its citizens will probably not receive any preferential treatment from the United States in the interest of cultural diversity.

Finally, and most relevant to this discussion, 140,000 permanent visas are granted each year through employment-based programs, all of which are subject to limitations which protect the U.S. labor market.[67] Most of these visas are granted to applicants who are among the best in their fields, who are able to make substantial contributions to society in the United States, or who are high-level executives in international companies. If none of these criteria are met, applicants must show that they intend to fill a position for which there are no qualified U.S. workers available.[68] Additional programs are also available for applicants intending to invest money in or otherwise benefit the U.S. economy in some way.

Although there are limitations on the number of such visas, the limits are rarely exceeded, for the eligibility criteria are stringent enough to effectively curtail permanent immigration for employment reasons from any country. Nevertheless, any Cuban that meets the substantive requirements of the employment-based programs will be eligible for permanent admission into the United States.

Categories of Non-Immigrant Visas Allowing Work in the United States: A noted earlier, U.S. policy should focus primarily upon providing opportunities for Cubans to work or study in the United States for limited periods of time.[69] This strategy is appropriate for several reasons:

1. It does not permanently drain Cuba of skilled workers who would otherwise be able to make significant contributions to the consolidation of a democratic free-market Cuba. Rather, it allows those workers to acquire additional technical and administrative skills and experiences in the United States over a period of years that they can subsequently use to benefit Cuba;

2. It temporarily relieves the burden on what will likely be a fragile democratic regime to provide the Cuban population with benefits and jobs. Moreover, Cubans working in the United States will be able to send money home to support relatives in Cuba during the transition;

3. It is much easier to gain political support for temporary work and study programs than for policies promoting permanent immigration.

The discussion that follows examines some of the temporary work categories that could be used advantageously by Cubans during the transition period.

Professional Worker Visas: The most useful vehicle for Cubans to enter and work in the United States during the early years of the transition could be the "H-1B" visa.[70] H-1B visas would be available to professional workers from Cuba who have at least a bachelors degree, or equivalent work experience. The main obstacles to Cubans obtaining H-1B visas are: (1) The prevailing wage requirement mandates that an employer pay any foreign national at least the "prevailing wage" for a given type of work.[71] To the extent that these wages are set too high, U.S. companies may lack an incentive to hire workers from Cuba; (2) The H-1B applicant must already have a job lined up in the United States. This should not be overly burdensome, for it is to be expected that skilled Cuban workers will be in demand in the

---

66. Id.

67. *Id. See also,* American Immigration Lawyers Association (ALIA), 1 1998-99 IMMIGRATION & NATIONALITY LAW HANDBOOK 278-296 (1998) [hereinafter "HANDBOOK"].

68. HANDBOOK, *supra* note 67, at 296.

69. Temporary non-immigrant visas are provided for in the Immigration and Naturalization Act of 1952.

70. INA §§ 101(a)(15)(H), 212(n), 8 USC § 1101(a)(15)(H); 8 CFR § 214(h).

71. Employers must file a Labor Condition Application with the U.S. Department of Labor attesting that it intends to pay the H-1B workers at least the "prevailing wage" in the geographical area of employment for the position that worker is expected to fill. HANDBOOK, *supra* note 67, at 171; INA § 212(n)(1)(A), 8 USC § 1182(n)(1)(A); 20 CFR § 655.730(b)(3).

United States, especially given the large number of potential Cuban-American employers in the United States and Cuba's geographic proximity; and (3) there is a limit on H-1B visas—no more than 65,000 may be issued in any one given year.[72] In 1997, for the government fiscal year ending on October 1, the cap was reached by mid-August.[73] In 1998, all 65,000 visas had been issued by early May.[74]

Intra-Company Transferees: A second type of non-immigrant work visa (the "L-1" visa) is available for Intra-Company Transferees.[75] Employees of a U.S. company or affiliate who have worked abroad for one continuous year in the preceding three years in an executive, managerial or specialized knowledge capacity, are eligible to be transferred to the United States to work in a similar capacity for an affiliate of that same company.[76] These L-1 visas are likely to become increasingly important as the economies of Cuba and the United States become more intertwined. As more foreign investment enters Cuba, more Cuban employees will become eligible to work in the United States. Conversely, as more workers return to Cuba with newly-developed skills and work experience, more foreign investors will be willing to invest in Cuba. The primary advantages of this visa over the H-1B visa is that it is not limited by either quotas or prevailing wage requirements.

The main drawback of the L visas is that they will not be available during the early stages of the transition, because U.S. companies will not have been established in Cuba long enough for their Cuban staff to satisfy the one year employment requirement. On the other hand, the eventual availability of these visas should provide an incentive to U.S. employers to hire capable Cuban employees early and give them management responsibilities right away, so they can be available for transfer, if desired, to the company's facilities in the United States.

Treaty Traders and Investors: A class of non-immigrant visas ("E visas") is available to Treaty Traders and Investors.[77] Applicants must demonstrate intent and capacity either to engage in substantial trade and commerce in the United States, or to invest in and develop a new and substantial enterprise that would benefit the U.S. economy. Treaty investors and traders must also be from a country with whom the United States has a treaty of commerce and navigation, a free trade agreement or a bi-lateral investment treaty.

The basic concept behind the E visas is that they should be granted to those who generate significant trade or invest in the U.S. economy, and either directly or indirectly create jobs. Assuming the United States and Cuba enter into some type of trade agreement, this visa category may apply.[78] While this program has the potential to increase the aggregate number of Cubans working in the United States, the portion of the program that gives immigration benefits to investors serves U.S. interests largely at the cost of Cuba's development. Since the money of Cuban investors could be better spent in Cuba, the E-class visa program would not be helpful to facilitate Cuba's transition. Also, as a practical matter, it would be some time before Cuban entrepreneurs developed with the means to qualify as investors. On the other hand, the trader portion of the E-visa category is arguably beneficial to both countries and generates jobs in both, so it should as a matter of policy be encouraged.

---

72. HANDBOOK, *supra* note 67, at 174.

73. Id.

74. Immigration and Naturalization Service May 11, 1998 Notice: Fiscal Year 1998 Numerical Limitation Reached for H-1B Non-immigrants, 63 Fed. Reg. 25870-71 (1998).

75. INA § 101(a)(15)(L); 8 CFR § 214.2(l) (as amended by 56 Fed. Reg. 61117-37 (Dec. 2, 1991)).

76. HANDBOOK, *supra* note 67, at 202.

77. INA § 101(a)(15)(E), 8 USC § 1101(a)(15)(E); 8 CFR § 214.2(e).

78. It would be important to Cuba's economic recovery that it negotiate a trade agreement with the United States as early in the transition as possible. *See* MATIAS F. TRAVIESO-DIAZ, THE LAWS AND LEGAL SYSTEM OF A FREE-MARKET CUBA—A PROSPECTUS FOR BUSINESS 183-84 (1996).

Other Visa Categories Allowing Cubans to Work in the United States: The U.S. government may determine that the national interest of the United States is best served by allowing more Cubans to temporarily enter and work in this country during the transition than would be possible under the existing immigration system. If such a decision is reached, Congress may implement several measures, including the following:

- Increase the H-1B quota to allow the issuance of more visas to skilled or professionally-trained Cuban workers.

- Establish a TN-like visa category for Cubans. This would allow Cubans to enter the United States independently of whether the H-1B numerical limit has been reached. Although Congress can legally provide for as many special TN-like visas as it deems appropriate, it may be faced with strong protests from Mexico if the number of visas set aside for Cubans is set at or above Mexico's limit of 5,500.

- Develop special visa programs for those foreign visitors with special knowledge or ability. Generally, "O" visas allow scientists, athletes or artists of extraordinary ability to work in the United States.[79] O visas may prove useful to talented Cubans who do not qualify for E, H or L visas, but who might benefit from working temporarily in the United States. Also, in addition to the O visas, other programs may be developed to encourage the immigration of former government employees who may possess valuable or sensitive information deriving from Cuba's relationship with the former Soviet Union. To the extent that the United States has an interest in obtaining or protecting such information, it may consider al-lowing those officials to enter the United States under "O"-type visas.[80]

All of the above initiatives have the potential to help both Cuba and the United States. They provide a means for Cubans to work in the United States, but only to the extent that those workers are needed by U.S. companies. As a result, they should be less controversial than other immigration issues in that they should not deprive U.S. workers of jobs and would be consistent with the interests of the U.S. economy.

Other Categories of Temporary Visas: If Cuba is to make a successful transition, it is essential that Cuban business people be able to travel unimpeded to the United States. Whether it be to attract foreign investors, negotiate with U.S. businesses or recruit skilled workers, Cubans need to be able to enter and exit the United States with relative ease to conduct business. These needs should be adequately met by the existing B-1 visa program, which allows travelers to temporarily enter the United States to engage in business if they comply with certain procedural requirements. As long as consular officers do not find that potential travelers have the intent to settle in the United States, B-1 visas should be routinely granted to all Cubans having legitimate business to conduct in the United States.[81]

In order to help meet Cuba's immediate need for trained professionals during the transition, the United States might establish a special type of education-related visa that Cubans working or studying in certain fields could obtain. A program could be created which would allow Cuban workers and students to temporarily enter the United States to acquire skills and experience determined to be lacking in Cuba. Cubans who fell into one of the categories on the "skills list" would be eligible for a "J" type of visa as

---

79. INA § 101(a)(15)(O), 8 USC §1101(a)(15)(O); 8 CFR § 214.2(o).

80. A similar program was implemented following the collapse of the Soviet Union, under which an immigration category was established to allow scientists or government officials of the former Soviet Union or Eastern Europe who had "expertise in a high-technology field" to more easily enter the United States. *See* 8 CFR § 204.10.

81. Visitors traveling with a B-1 visa cannot intend to work or settle in the United States. INA § 101(a)(15)(B), 8 USC § 1101(a)(15)(B); 8 CFR § 214.2(b).

long as they were sponsored by a U.S. citizen, lacked intent to abandon their residence abroad, and agreed to leave the United States for at least two years following the expiration of their visa.[82] (These requirements are designed to increase the probability that foreign workers will use their newly acquired skills in their home countries.) The broad guidelines for granting J visas provide ample leeway to tailor a program specifically to meet the needs of a free-market Cuba.[83]

Handling of Illegal Immigrants: U.S. immigration policy will also have to address the fact that a free and open Cuba will give rise to increased illegal immigration. The U.S. is currently negotiating with Mexico about ways to strengthen border security and decrease illegal immigration. However, the problem that exists with Mexico (and potentially with Cuba) is that the interests of the United States and Mexico are directly opposed in this area. Mexico has neither the money nor the interest to curb the illegal immigration of workers (generally of lower socio-economic classes) for which it cannot provide jobs.

A similar situation is likely to arise in Cuba. Indeed, with the large population of Cuban-Americans and Cuban immigrants in the United States, the opportunities for Cuban visitors to stay in this country after the expiration of their visas are likely to be large,

potentially undercutting other programs intended to provide an orderly flow of temporary visitors. This is a problem that will need to be faced through increased enforcement action by the U.S. immigration authorities.

Legislative Approach: Immigration is currently an extremely explosive issue in the United States, especially in the states, like Florida, in which most immigrants tend to settle. Regardless of the economic rationale for allowing Cuban workers in the United States, Congress is certain to have difficulty generating support for any legislation or agreement which substantially increases the number Cubans that qualify for visas and which appears to threaten U.S. jobs. The best strategy may be to link the expanded temporary work visa provisions with strong entry controls and anti-illegal immigration policies. Such a strategy would allow all sides of the immigration dispute to feel they have accomplished their aims, and might result in the enactment of useful legislation.

Cuba's Immigration Policy in a Post-Transition Environment

Since the first wave of Cubans immigrants arrived in the United States, a desire to return to their native country has nested in the hearts of most Cubans in exile.[84] Many Cuban-Americans perceive this dream to be impossible of realization while the Castro regime is in power; however, there has been movement on the Cuban side to facilitate short term visits to the

---

82. Currently, immigration laws define a "J-1" category of exchange visitor, who is an alien: having a residence in a foreign country which he has not intention of abandoning; who is a bona fide student, scholar, trainee, teacher, professor, research assistant, specialist, or leader in a field of specialized knowledge or skill; or other person of similar description, who is coming temporarily to the United States as a participant in a program designated by the Director of the United States Information Agency, for the purpose of teaching, instructing or lecturing, studying, observing, conducting research, consulting, demonstrating special skills, or receiving training. INA § 101(a)(15)(J), 8 USC § 1101(a)(15)(J).

83. Examples of J-1 programs currently in existence include: (1) Students may enter the United States to complete up to 24 months of post-secondary study and 18 months of practical training work authorization upon completion of their studies. Post-doctoral training is permitted for 36 months after the degree is awarded; (2) Professors, researchers and international and government visitors may be granted a J-1 visa to participate in conferences, workshops, etc.; (3) Alien physicians may take a residency of up to 7 years; (4) Camp counselors, teachers, specialists and au pairs may work temporarily in the United States. 22 CFR § 514.

84. In a survey conducted by a Spanish-language television station in Miami, "one in five Cubans in the metropolitan area said they would return home, although the results are regarded ... more as coming from the heart than the head." Laura Parker, *Radio Marti Director Ousted as Exiles Discuss Returning to Cuba,* WASHINGTON POST, Mar. 13, 1990, at A3. In economic terms, Cuban-Americans contribute hundreds of millions of dollars annually in remittances to their impoverished relatives in the island. U.S. Department of State, BACKGROUND NOTES: CUBA 5 (Apr. 1998).

country by Cubans residing abroad.[85] In late 1978, the policy towards Cuban exiles experienced a turn for the better when Cuba lifted restrictions on émigré travel to Cuba.[86] In 1994, additional assurances were given that no action would be taken against those Cubans who returned after attempting to immigrate illegally.[87] However, those who have left Cuba illegally still have reason to fear reprisal and imprisonment from the Cuban government despite its agreement to cease such punishment. Cuba's "illegal exit" and "illegal entry" laws remain in effect and the government's assurances of non-punishment are insufficient to ensure the safety of exiles upon their return to Cuba.

Upon its transition to democratic rule, Cuba is expected to repeal most if not all the existing travel restrictions and allow Cuban exiles to return freely to the island.[88] Once the travel restrictions on Cuban exiles seeking to return to their native country are lifted by both the United States and Cuba, the de-

mand for opportunities to travel to Cuba is likely to be enormous, and such travel is likely to be limited only by the physical ability to transport and accommodate the visitors in Cuba.[89] Such a massive reverse exodus raises important policy questions for a future transition government. We examine some of these questions next.

Cuban Policy Regarding Permanent Immigration of Cuban Expatriates: The mass return of Cuban exiles to the island on a permanent basis is likely to be fraught with difficulties. One obstacle to the repatriation of the Cuban exiles is their legal status upon returning to Cuba. Presently, the Cuban Constitution provides that Cuban citizenship is lost by becoming a citizen of a foreign country, and holding a dual citizenship is not allowed.[90] Thus, unless the new constitution or other transition period statute provides otherwise, those Cuban émigrés who have become naturalized citizens of other countries, including the United States, will have to renounce the other coun-

---

85. The United States, however, continues to impose restrictions on travel to Cuba by exiles. The Cuban Asset Control Regulations ("Regulations"), promulgated by the Office of Foreign Assets Control ("OFAC") of the U.S. Department of the Treasury, implement the U.S. trade embargo against Cuba. Cubans who have become U.S. citizens or permanent residents are prohibited under current U.S. law from traveling to Cuba without obtaining a license from OFAC. According to the Regulations, licenses are only granted to journalists, official government travelers, members of an international organization of which the United States is also a member, and persons traveling once a year to visit close relatives in Cuba. *See* U.S. Code of Federal Regulations, Title 31, Section 515.

86. GONZALEZ-PANDO, *supra* note 4, at 56.

87. BONAVIA, *supra* note 47, at 1040.

88. On November 6, 1995, Cuba loosened travel restrictions by allowing Cuban émigrés to remain in Cuba indefinitely or travel back and forth as many times as they want as long as they renew their visitors permit every two years. Exiles living in the United States cannot take advantage of these relaxed Cuban regulations because U.S. law permits them to travel to Cuba only once a year without obtaining a specific license from OFAC. Eaton, *Cuban Exiles win Right to Return Home*, NEW ORLEANS TIMES-PICAYUNE, Nov. 7, 1995, at F11.

89. Cuban exiles are eager to return to the island for various reasons, which include reuniting with relatives, revisiting their birthplace, and contributing to its political and economic growth. Achy Obejas, *Miami, Havana: Jealous Rivals Pope's Visit Pushes Resentments to Fore*, CHICAGO TRIBUNE, Jan. 19, 1998.

90. Under Cuba's constitutions, both pre- and post-revolution, a Cuban citizen who becomes a citizen of another country loses his Cuban citizenship. CONSTITUCION DE LA REPUBLICA DE CUBA (1940) [CONSTITUTION], art. 15 (CUBA), reprinted in 1 **Constitutions of Nations** 610 (Amos J. Peaslee ed. & trans., 2d ed.); *see* CONSTITUCION DE LA REPUBLICA DE CUBA (1992) art. 32 (Cuba), *published in* Gaceta Oficial (Aug. 1, 1992). *See also Reglamento de Ciudadanía* ("Citizenship Regulations"), Gaceta Oficial (Mar. 3, 1944), Art. 33 [hereinafter REGLAMENTO].

try's citizenship and apply for reinstatement of their Cuban citizenship.[91]

Whether as reinstated Cuban citizens or as resident aliens, a large number of Cuban expatriates, mainly Cuban-Americans, are likely to want to settle permanently on the island. This raises the question of whether the Cuban economy will be able to accommodate a mass return of expatriates. In the post-transition period of Nicaragua, for example, the president voiced concerns over repatriation and the inability of its country's fragile economy to support a mass return of exiles.[92] Cuba's economy is also likely to be in severe distress at the time of the transition. However, unlike other groups of returning émigrés, Cuban-Americans have largely achieved a high standard of living and are unlikely to become a burden on Cuba's economy should they choose to return permanently to the island, but to the contrary will be capable of bringing with them capital to invest in Cuba.[93] Nonetheless, a transition Cuban government will need to impose admission criteria based on absence of criminal record and financial self-sufficiency before allowing Cuban-Americans or other foreign nationals to settle permanently in the island.[94]

Cuban Policy Towards Non-Immigrants: Cuba must develop an immigration policy which will promote the movement of goods, ideas and people across its borders during the transition. Once it becomes apparent that Cuba intends to liberalize its economy and to commit to a more democratic form of government, foreign investors and Cuban expatriates will seek to visit Cuba in substantial numbers. During the transition, it is essential that Cuba encourage such visits by developing and open and efficient immigration policy. That policy should include among others the following features:

---

91. It has been argued, based on the presumed continued vitality of Cuba's 1940 Constitution (which in Art. 15(a) states that those Cubans who acquire another country's citizenship lose their status as Cubans) that the automatic loss of citizenship provided by Art. 15(a) should not apply to Cuban exiles who have opted to become citizens of their country of residence because to do so would bar the exiles from "participating in the Cuban political process." José D. Acosta, *El Marco Jurídico-Institucional de un Gobierno Provisional de Unidad Nacional en Cuba,* in CUBA IN TRANSITION—VOLUME 2, ASSOCIATION FOR THE STUDY OF THE CUBAN ECONOMY 61, 82 (1992). However, the opposite argument appears more persuasive: it is precisely to protect the Cuban political process from undue influence by those who have sworn allegiance to a foreign country that the automatic loss of Cuban citizenship provision for those who opt to become citizens of another country should remain in effect. In this context, it is instructive to recall that the process for regaining Cuban citizenship that was in place before 1959 was anything but automatic. It required a formal re-application for citizenship, followed by one year of continuous residence in Cuba, followed by another formal appearance before a public official, in order for the reinstatement of citizenship to become effective. REGLAMENTO, *supra* note 90, Art. 35.

92. With an estimated per capita income of $465, Nicaragua is the second poorest country in the Western Hemisphere. U.S. Department of State, NICARAGUA COUNTRY REPORT ON HUMAN RIGHTS PRACTICES FOR 1997, *released by* the Bureau of Democracy, Human Rights, and Labor, January 30, 1998. After the Sandinistas were removed from power, the Nicaraguan government reacted to its economic dilemma by pleading for hundreds and thousands of exiles to return and rebuild the country: on December 16, 1996, "President-elect Arnoldo Aleman... invited hundred of thousands of Nicaraguans abroad to return to their country and said they would be allowed to bring back their money and belongings tax-free." REUTERS, *Nicaraguan Exiles Told to Return, Bring Assets,* FT. LAUDERDALE SUN-SENTINEL, Dec. 17, 1996 at A16. Nevertheless, the Nicaraguan government realized that its weak economy could not support a mass return of its exiles, even with the economic assistance that was given by the U.S. Therefore, Nicaraguan President Aleman extended a plea to the United States, calling for the "U.S. government not to begin a mass deportation of Nicaraguans living illegally in the United States," and cautioned that the exile return must be gradual. Tracy Wilkinson, *Central American Leaders Fear Mass Return to Their Nations,* LA TIMES, Nov. 26, 1994.

93. The poverty rate for people of Hispanic origin was 30.3% in 1995 and 29.4% in 1996. Source: U.S. Census Bureau, March Current Population Survey, Poverty 1996. In contrast, only 16.5% of all Cuban immigrants fall below the poverty line. *See* PEDRAZA, *supra* note 3, at 323.

94. While it may be argued that Cuba may not deny admission into the country to those of its nationals residing abroad, it would appear that, at least with respect to those who have lost their Cuban citizenship, Cuba has the right to impose and apply immigration standards to keep unfit persons from settling in the country. Indeed, before the Revolution, Cuba denied the right to acquire its citizenship to individuals who had been convicted of a felony, those of "dubious morality," and those who advocated doctrines or principles "incompatible with the current organization of the Cuban state or with its democratic regime and form of government." REGLAMENTO, *supra* note 90, Art. 25, 29.

Cuban expatriates who are citizens of other countries should be treated as "foreign investors," so they are eligible for any special benefits given to such investors.[95] Even though granting Cuban expatriate investors privileges unavailable to resident nationals could lead to resentment from people on the island, this is a necessary consequence of the likely treatment as aliens of those who have lost their Cuban citizens by becoming citizens of other countries.

Foreign investors should have the ability to employ foreign personnel, particularly for key positions.[96] The Cuban government should therefore refrain from unduly limiting the number of foreign personnel a company can bring into the country, or imposing unreasonable time limits on their visas. It is likely that there will be an acute shortage of skilled management personnel in Cuba during the transition to a market economy, so foreign managers will be necessary to operate foreign investors' enterprises until the local population acquires the requisite management and business skills.[97] Allowing foreign managers to enter and work in Cuba serves a dual purpose. *First*, it introduces Cuban workers to modern work practices that they need to compete in the global marketplace. *Second*, it assures foreign investors that they will have the personnel they need to effectively operate their businesses.

The visa structure should be open and simple to administer. In contrast to the United States, Cuba will not be affected by large scale migrations of uneducated or impoverished workers, at least not from the United States. As a result, Cuba should eliminate all visa requirements for short-term pleasure or business trips originating in the United States and other developed countries.[98] Doing away with the need for visas avoids expending scarce resources in the administration of the immigration program, and allows foreign investors easy access to the island. While Cuba should seek reciprocal arrangements with the United States and other countries, the importance of foreign investment to Cuba is such that Cuba should unilaterally eliminate visa requirements even if reciprocal treatment is not granted by the United States and other developed countries.[99]

The Cuban visa structure should not establish special visa categories for particular classes of foreign investors. An example of a special type of visa is the "alien entrepreneur" visa program in the United States, which reserves a certain number of immigrant visas for investors "who establish new commercial enterprises in the United States, invest at least $1,000,000 . . . and employ at least ten Americans."[100] This type of special incentive is warranted only if a restrictive business visa structure is in place, which should not be the case in Cuba during the transition to a market economy; both large and small investors should be allowed easy access to the island.

CONCLUSIONS

For the last forty years, the United States and Cuba have used immigration as a foreign policy weapon. For most of that period, the interests of both countries, although diametrically opposed, coincided in encouraging large numbers of disaffected Cubans to leave the island and come to the United States. The arriving Cubans, whether they followed the legal procedures set by both countries or came without ob-

---

95. *See* Matías F. Travieso-Díaz and Steven R. Escobar, *Cuba's Transition to a Free-Market Democracy: A Survey of Required Changes to Laws and Legal Institutions,* 5 Duke J. Comp. & Int'l L. 379, 414-15 (1995).

96. *See* IBRAHIM F. I. SHIHATA, LEGAL TREATMENT OF FOREIGN INVESTMENT: THE WORLD BANK GUIDELINES 155, 159 (1993).

97. Matías F. Travieso-Díaz & Alejandro Ferraté, *Recommended Features of a Foreign Investment Code for Cuba's Free Market Transition,* 21 N.C.J. Int'l Law & Com. Reg. 511, 557 (1996).

98. There are several countries in close proximity to Cuba having large impoverished populations. Unskilled migrants from those countries, under favorable conditions, may seek to relocate in Cuba. For that reason, some sort of visa structure must be retained to control the entry of immigrants who may become public charges.

99. *See Opening the Door for Business Travel to a Free-Market Cuba,* 1 FREE MARKET CUBA BUS. J. 8, Shaw, Pittman, Potts & Trowbridge (Spring/Summer 1992).

100. INA § 203(b)(5), 8 USC § 1153(b)(5) (1990).

serving legal formalities, were received in the United States with open arms and were helped along in becoming part of the American society.

After 1994, the interests of both Cuba and the United States changed and, even though still opposed, again coincided in their approach to immigration: neither country had any longer an interest in fostering a mass exodus of Cubans to the United States. Thus, the current arrangement was reached. It contemplates a limited, orderly migration of Cubans towards the United States under established visa procedures, with only relatively infrequent instances of "illegal immigrants" attempting (and in some cases successfully making) an unauthorized escape towards the U.S. shores.

While the current situation is stable, there is no guarantee that this stability will endure. As has already happened repeatedly, events in Cuba could at any moment upset the delicate balance that has been achieved. For, as long as there is an impoverished population in Cuba and a government that uses emigration as an escape valve to rid itself of malcontents, there is always the possibility that another Camarioca or another Mariel will take place, testing the resolve and the moral principles of whoever is running the U.S. government at the time.

When Cuba makes the long-awaited transition to a free-market, democratic society, the governments of both countries will have the opportunity to develop, for the first time in half a century, immigration policies that are not dictated by political considerations but by the desire to contribute to Cuba's economic reconstruction. At that moment, and for a period whose duration will be determined by the length of the transition, the United States should put in place special programs such as those described in this paper, to allow qualified Cubans to enter the United States on a temporary basis, make an economic contribution here, and at the same time prepare themselves for taking their newly developed skills and economic resources back to the island. This form of assistance to Cuba's transition will be perhaps as important and considerably less costly than the economic aid programs that have already been promised and will undoubtedly be made available to Cuba by the United States and other international donors.[101]

Cuba must help the process along by establishing an open and efficient immigration policy that provides the greatest possible ease of transit in and out of the country to business people, consistent with maintaining public order and security. No artificial limitations should be placed on the numbers of people who travel from the United States to Cuba, on the lengths of their stay, or on the activities they are allowed to conduct in the island, including the hiring of domestic and foreign personnel. The legal status of Cuban-Americans who seek to return to Cuba should also be addressed, but whatever solution is given to this thorny issue should not discourage the flow of people, goods and ideas from the Cuban-American community to their brothers in the island. Specific measures should be taken to stimulate foreign investors from all over the world to travel to Cuba to investigate business prospects and establish operations. In short, Cuba should take all reasonable steps to ensure that immigration does not become another obstacle in what is likely to be a difficult road to democracy and economic stability.

---

101. President of the United States, SUPPORT FOR A DEMOCRATIC TRANSITION IN CUBA, Jan. 28, 1997; Title II of the Cuban Liberty and Democratic Solidarity (LIBERTAD) Act, 22 USC § 6062 *et. seq.*

PROMOTING AND FINANCING THE DEVELOPMENT OF AN ENVIRONMENTAL INFRASTRUCTURE IN A POST-CASTRO CUBA

Aldo M. Leiva

Among the many challenges a post-Castro Cuba will face is the environmental condition of the island after four decades of environmental neglect and mismanagement. Besides creating a new political and socioeconomic framework, Cuba's new leaders will have to ensure that economic development does not occur at the expense of environmental and human health concerns, an unfortunately common condition in many developing countries.

This article addresses the Cuban environmental crisis and the legal and economic factors involved in the resolution of this crisis through development of an adequate environmental infrastructure. The goal is to present recommendations to promote the development of such an infrastructure, which today is essentially non-existent. The article will summarize and critique present environmental laws, followed by an analysis of economic factors at play in a post-Castro, transition Cuba, including a review of the sources of funding available for environmental infrastructure projects. Lastly, recommendations of legal, economic, and policy reforms intended to promote infrastructure development are provided.

THE CUBAN ENVIRONMENTAL CRISIS
The Cuban Environment:
A Priority for a Free Cuba

The enormity of tasks and issues awaiting a transitional post-Castro government is evident in the volume of scholarly analysis devoted to the subject. Although the majority of this research focuses on the political, economic, and social "environments" in which Cubans will live, another key consideration is the actual physical environment in which Cubans will develop their new society. A Cuban citizen's newfound political and economic freedom will be incomplete without adequate safeguards for the land, waters, and air of the island, especially in an economy where tourism will comprise a major source of revenue. For these reasons, the environment must always remain an integral component to the national agenda of Cuba.

Cuba's future leadership must avoid the all-too-common debate of "economy versus environment." Such a debate is essentially meaningless in Cuba, where, by virtue of the moral, aesthetic and economic value of its geography and natural resources (and their limits), a healthy environment will actually contribute to a healthy economy. A Cuban environmental infrastructure, besides being a much-needed investment for its people, will serve as a positive investment in its economy, not a drain. Clean beaches, safe and sanitary drinking water, clean air, protected forest reserves and arable soil, free of contaminants, will be essential in promoting an enhanced quality of life for Cubans, as well as in the development of a tourism industry.

Unfortunately, the Castro regime's policies, especially in the midst of the economic chaos brought about by the collapse of the Soviet Union, have been wholesale environmental destruction in exchange for foreign currency.[1] In fact, the current regime's view of the environment has alternated between disregard and cynicism, destroying it at times in the name of socialist progress while claiming a keen interest in environmental protection, albeit in the hopes of receiving international grant monies.[2]

Current Environmental Conditions in Cuba

Soil: Cuban soils are negatively impacted by a combination of factors, the great majority of which are directly due to official government practices and policies. For example, the official agricultural model followed by the Castro regime involves the clearing of low-quality soils that are prone to erosion.[3] In fact, erosion remains one of the most serious problems facing Cuba, as indicated by the estimate that 50% of the arable soil in Cuba is eroded.[4] Another contributing factor to soil erosion is Cuba's high rate of deforestation.[5]

Salinization of soils is also a serious problem,[6] as is pollution by toxic metals associated with strip mining.[7] Lastly, soils are also polluted by the many dumpsites dotting the Cuban landscape, the majority of which are illegal.[8]

Deforestation and Loss of Habitat/Biodiversity: Cuba's Special Period, with its lack of fuels, has triggered an increased demand for firewood, which has in turn elevated rates of deforestation.[9] In fact, based on official reports of the Cuban government, forests constituted 26.8% of Cuban land area in 1993[10] but had decreased to 21% by 1996.[11] Most importantly, 75% of deforestation is occurring in old-growth forests, where the majority of endemic species dwell, contributing to extinctions.[12]

In fact, loss of natural habitats, on land and in the sea, has led to the loss or disappearance of native species, as has introduction of non-native species.[13] On land, accelerated deforestation, poaching, and collection for sale are among the factors causing extinctions.[14] In Cuban waters, pollution of bays and rivers, both from agricultural runoff and toxic waste, has resulted in the loss of coral reef habitats.[15] Coral reefs are also being extracted from the sea, to use calcium carbonate in nickel processing operations.[16]

Waters: Among the environmental problems identified in Cuban waters are: (1) accelerated rate of extraction from aquifers; (2) intrusion of salt water into aquifers due to accelerated extraction; (3) contamination of rivers, streams, estuaries, coastal zones, and

1. Carlos Wotzkow, *Natumaleza Cubana* (Miami: Ediciones Universal, 1998).

2. Id.

3. Sergio Díaz-Briquets and Jorge F. Pérez-López, "The Environment and the Cuban Transition," in *Cuba in Transition—Volume 7* (Washington: Association for the Study of the Cuban Economy, 1997).

4. Agencia Ambiental Entorno Cubano (AAMEC), *Situación Ambiental de Cuba*, Informe Anual de la AAMEC (1997).

5. Sergio Díaz-Briquets and Jorge F. Pérez-López, "The Special Period and the Environment," in *Cuba in Transition—Volume 5* (Washington: Association for the Study of the Cuban Economy, 1995).

6. Id.

7. Díaz-Briquets and Pérez-López, "The Environment and the Cuban Transition."

8. Id.

9. Id.

10. AAMEC, *Situación Ambiental de Cuba*.

11. Id.

12. Id.

13. Díaz-Briquets and Pérez-López, "The Environment and the Cuban Transition."

14. AAMEC, "Desaparecen Especies de la Avifauna Cubana," *CUBAECO* # 1 (October 1997).

15. Díaz-Briquets and Pérez-López, "The Environment and the Cuban Transition."

16. Id.

bays by industrial waste, chemical runoff, and sugar industry wastes.[17]

Contamination with pollutants is reported in a wide range of locations on the island. Urban rivers are polluted with raw sewage, solid waste, and such industrial waste as waste oils, cement, greases, and detergents.[18] In rural locations, rivers are contaminated with coffee bean husks and waste, and industrial waste.[19] Rivers in rural areas are also contaminated with waste from sugar mills, many of which lack industrial waste treatment equipment (estimated by some authorities as 70%), and thereby pollute rivers with hydrocarbons, acids, and grease.[20] Coastal zones and bays, primarily Havana Bay, are contaminated as well with hydrochloric acid, lead, oils and greases, fertilizers, and industrial wastes.[21]

Pedraplenes, or causeways, built to link the Cuban mainland with small keys for the purposes of promoting tourism wreak havoc on stream systems and harbor environments,[22] closing them off from the ocean and resulting in concentration of toxic pollutants in those waters.

Oil spills also occur, causing extensive damage to marine life and seabirds[23] and polluting waters with heavy metals, oil, and toxic wastes.[24] Marine exploitation of sand and coral mud also deteriorates the marine ecosystem and degrades beaches.[25]

Air: Although the Special Period has resulted in an overall decrease in industrial production,[26] air pollution continues to be problem in Cuba. Cuban cement factories, often with little or no filtration technology, emit smoke and dust into the atmosphere.[27] Mining, especially for nickel, also results in production of mercury, arsenic, smoke, and nitric and sulfuric acid wastes.[28]

The Cuban government's reliance on cheap imported low-quality oil has also generated dense clouds of smog over La Habana and near power plants.[29] Domestic oil is also generally of a low-quality, and likewise produces high amounts of contaminants upon combustion.[30]

CAUSES FOR THE LACK OF A CUBAN ENVIRONMENTAL INFRASTRUCTURE

The key contributing cause of the Cuban environmental crisis is the lack of an adequate environmental infrastructure under the existing system of government. As in other socialist countries, Cuba's central planning has led to environmental abuse.[31] As the owner of virtually all property and industry, the Castro regime is the major source of pollution on the is-

17. Sergio Díaz-Briquets and Jorge F. Pérez-López, "Water, Development, and Environment in Cuba: A First Look," in *Cuba in Transition—Volume 3* (Washington: Association for the Study of the Cuban Economy, 1993).

18. AAMEC, *Situación Ambiental de Cuba*.

19. Id.

20. Id.

21. Id.

22. José R. Oro, *The Poisoning of Paradise: The Environmental Crisis in Cuba* (Miami: Endowment for Cuban American Studies, 1992), p. 11.

23. Id., at 57.

24. Id., at 58.

25. Id., at 52-53.

26. Id., at 48.

27. Id., at 49.

28. Id., at 51-52.

29. Díaz-Briquets and Pérez-López, "The Special Period and the Environment."

30. Id.

31. Díaz-Briquets and Pérez-López, "Water, Development, and Environment in Cuba: A First Look," citing Feshbach and Friendly, *Ecocide in the USSR* (New York: Basic Books, 1992).

land.[32] Likewise, as the sole determiner of environmental policy, the regime has exclusive power and discretion over the Cuban environmental infrastructure. In this capacity, the regime has engaged in central planning, focusing on the quantity, rather than the quality, of output and favoring heavy industrialization.[33] Lastly, there is a complete lack of public participation in environmental decision-making.[34]

Further, as will be discussed below, Cuba's environmental laws are relatively young, and authorities are relatively inexperienced in applying such laws. In most cases, authorities are simply unwilling or unable to apply them due to official state policy and limited financial resources. Considering Cuba's competing economic priorities, such as increasing industrial development and output, and lobbying efforts designed attract foreign investment, it is not surprising that environmental enforcement is sacrificed. In addition, current Cuban statutes do not mandate the aggressive development of a comprehensive environmental infrastructure. Thus, the leading causes of the lack of an infrastructure are essentially a combination of legal, practical, and economic factors.

Existing Environmental Law

The key Cuban environmental law is Law No. 33, also called the "Law on Environmental Protection and the Rational Use of Natural Resources."[35] The law is a brief document, only 25 pages long, and is intended to "establish the basic principles to conserve, protect, improve and transform the environment and the rational use of natural resources, in accordance with the integral development policies" of the Cuban government.[36] The Law consists of four chapters: (1) general provisions; (2) specific areas of environmental protection and the use of natural resources; (3) organization of administrative and enforcement agencies/entities; and (4) enforcement procedures.

Unfortunately, rather than creating an effective procedural and substantive legal framework, the Law provides only a broad policy statement, with undefined and vague terms.[37] For example, the Law requires "proper treatment" of wastes before release into the environment, but does not define and clarify the term "proper treatment" nor does it define "wastes." The law also fails to set standards and contamination limits,[38] making it virtually unenforceable. Like the rest of the statute, the Chapter setting out fines is vague and ill-defined.[39]

Perhaps responding to its critics, the Cuban government has stated that the Law does not include clear definitions of management categories, since such regulations should be promulgated by the legislature.[40] However, to date, none have been created.[41] Similarly, enforcement provisions remain inoperative and are not applied.[42] In fact, as will be discussed below, in practice, environmental laws are seldom applied and are not considered in policy-making decisions.[43]

In 1997, the Cuban government promulgated Law No. 81, which focuses on pollution control. Like its

---

32. See, e.g. AAMEC, "Fuentes Contaminantes del Ambiente en Cuba," *CUBAECO* # 2 (October 1997).

33. Díaz-Briquets and Pérez-López, "The Environment and the Cuban Transition."

34. Id.

35. Wotzkow, *Natumaleza Cubana.*

36. B. Ralph Barba and Amparo E. Avella, "Cuba's Environmental Law," in *Cuba in Transition—Volume 5* (Washington: Association for the Study of the Cuban Economy, 1995).

37. Id.

38. Id.

39. Id

40. Wotzkow, *Natumaleza Cubana*, p. 71.

41. Id.

42. Id.

43. Barba and Avella, "Cuba's Environmental Law."

predecessor, the law is overly broad and ill-defined, but sets out enforcement guidelines, sanctions, and violations. Its effectiveness remains to be seen, as authorities have not yet fully initiated implementation of the law.

Also, Cuba's law focuses primarily on current compliance rather than on cleaning up past contamination. Because no law exists addressing pre-existing contamination, there is no impetus for state-owned industry or foreign investors to address these problems, thus acting as a disincentive to the development of an infrastructure to address past contamination.

There are also no general requirements for treatment of wastes prior to disposal. In the absence of such requirements, parties seeking to comply with the spirit of the law have no guidance and compliance efforts are thereby negatively affected.

Environmental Regulatory Entities

Following promulgation of Law 33, the Commission for the Environment and Natural Resources (CO-MARNA) was created for the stated purposes of preventing environmental damage, public education regarding the environment, development of a system of environmental control, and establishment of penalties for violations of the law.[44] However, those laws proposed by COMARNA, and approved by the National Assembly of the People's Power, are never or poorly enforced.[45] Another flaw is the absence of standards or concentrations for pollutants.[46] In addition, although the laws provide for fines, license revocations, bonds, prosecution and imprisonment, the vagueness and lack of standards hamper the law's effectiveness.[47]

Currently, all environmental policy continues to be developed by COMARNA.[48] However, because CO-MARNA's goals are deemed inconsistent with competing goals of industrialization and development, other Cuban ministries have actually worked to slow the implementation of new environmental policies. Thus, inter-agency conflicts frustrate goal-setting and environmental infrastructure planning.

For example, on the local level, regional Commissions for the Environment fall under the authority of the Ministry of Agriculture (MINAGRI), which is designed to promote development of resources, rather than protection of the environment.[49] Other supposedly environmental authorities, such as the National Enterprise for the Protection for Flora and Fauna, a subministry of MINAGRI, have the overriding mission to exploit natural resources by exporting indigenous species.[50] Likewise, the Ministry of the Fishing Industry (MIP) and the Institute for Ecology and Systems (IES), adopt official central policy objectives and actually promote intensification of sugar agriculture, building of pedraplenes, damming of rivers, and hotel plans.[51] In sum, COMARNA is subject to the jurisdiction of other government entities with competing agendas.

As a result of the shifting of these responsibilities, there has been no institutional or political continuity in environmental protection, making environmental policy itself both transitory and inconsistent. In the absence of consistent policy, the setting of priorities with respect to infrastructure development in particular, is precluded.

---

44. Oro, *The Poisoning of Paradise*, p. 8.

45. Id., pp. 9-10.

46. Id., p.10.

47. Id., p. 10.

48. Wotzkow, *Natumaleza Cubana*, p. 41.

49. Id., p. 42.

50. Id.

51. Id., p. 43.

Practical and Legal Reasons for Lack of Enforcement in Present-Day Cuba

As seen above, the legal structure and institutions of the Castro regime have inherent flaws that prevent serious enforcement of environmental law. First and foremost, as a totalitarian dictatorship, centered on the whims of a caudillo, the concept of a rule of law in Cuba is non-existent. The Cuban Communist Party is the sole controlling political entity and as such has exclusive control over all branches of power. Despite an extensive code of laws and regulations, all are applied selectively and arbitrarily by government functionaries, who place party objectives above the law.

In addition, the law itself includes broad language and suffers from vagueness, to allow government authorities the maximum flexibility in pursuing the Party's directives. For this reason, laws in present-day Cuba are often broad statements of policy, bereft of any detail, transparency, or consistency.

Other factors inhibiting environmental protection in Cuba include:[52] (1) economic inefficiency of the communist economic model; (2) loss of subsidies following the economic and political collapse of the Soviet Union; (3) official policy favors economic development over environmental protection; (4) lack of environmental considerations in Cuba's nuclear energy and research program; (5) over-centralized decision-making process; (6) lack of access by COMARNA specialists to adequate scientific instruments and materials; (7) subservience of COMARNA to other more powerful ministries; and (8) top-down decision-making, with COMARNA at the end of the decision-making pipeline.

Another reason for the lack of enforcement is the absence within the existing totalitarian regime for any true form of public role or pressure in promoting enforcement. Although a few small civic environmental organizations exist, there have been no major non-governmental organizations to protest against government projects with a negative environmental impact.[53] Such groups, if they oppose an official policy decision, are often deemed political dissidents.[54]

In sum, for the reasons outlined above, Cuban environmental laws are not enforced and the Cuban environmental regulatory entities are neither adequately funded nor staffed, resulting in the present environmental crisis.

In the coming years, any transition[55] government will face this crisis in the midst of potential chaos and uncertainty, as Cuba shifts its political system, values, culture, economy, and institution from totalitarianism to a free-market democratic republic. The remaining portion of this paper will address the economic, practical and legal factors that will affect the promotion and financing of an environmental infrastructure in a transition-era Cuba.

POTENTIAL FUNDING SOURCES FOR ENVIRONMENTAL INFRASTRUCTURE IN A POST-CASTRO CUBA

In addition to the many legal and practical issues that will be at play, economics will have the most important role in developing Cuba's environmental infrastructure. Under the Castro regime, the state, as the sole controller and manager of the Cuban economy, has been the primary funding source for infrastructure development. In a post-Castro, free-market Cuba, public financing would undoubtedly be transformed and would be comparable to that in other newly-developing countries, such as direct government expenditure of funds, general-obligation bonds, subsidization, and concessions to state-owned enter-

---

52. Oro, *The Poisoning of Paradise*, p. 11-13.

53. Wotzkow, *Natumaleza Cubana*, p. 15.

54. Id., p. 45.

55. Note: For the purposes of this discussion, transition government will refer to any government seeking to establish a democratic republic in Cuba, following the death or removal from power of Fidel Castro and the present ruling elite of Cuba.

prises.[56] However, relying on public financing has significant limitations, such as required generation of public approval to issue bonds, revenue and debt limits, economic deficiencies, and poor financial management.[57] For these reasons, Cuba, like many developing countries, will probably opt for foreign capital as a source for funding infrastructure development.[58]

Domestic Sources of Funding in a Post-Castro Cuba

Public Funding: A post-Castro Cuba will have several options in funding environmental infrastructure projects, such as disbursing funds obtained from international organizations, foreign governments, or those held by the Cuban government itself. As in Mexico, these funds may be loaned to private commercial banks that would in turn make loans to the private or public sector.[59]

However, several factors may inhibit the creation of such loans during or after a transition to a free Cuba. In a newly developing Cuban economy, with the probability of high interest rates, commercial banks and businesses may be discouraged from approaching such entities for loans. Further, unless a the Cuban government guarantees its loans, intermediate lenders may be held responsible in the event a borrower defaults.

The Cuban government may also administer World Bank funds to support environmental infrastructure development.[60] Such funds may be re-lent to local municipalities to address environmental needs. A drawback to this option is that poor communities will probably not be able to afford to borrow funds from either the government or from commercial banks with lower interest rates.

Another potential funding source is the use of bonds. Of course, this will depend on the creation of laws authorizing provinces/municipalities to issue tax-exempt bonds in domestic capital markets to fund public improvements. Cuban law may also permit provinces/municipalities to borrow directly from foreign creditors, encouraging foreign investors to enter into such loan agreements. In sum, provinces and municipalities may be able to develop their own funding sources for infrastructure development, thereby reducing or eliminating financial dependence on a central national government. Independence from a central government may also allow provinces and local communities to gain much-needed experience in planning, developing, and managing public works projects.

Private Sources: Cuban banks may provide another source of financing. Unfortunately, in light of the foreseeable problems and uncertainties in a newly-emergent Cuban economy, the role of Cuban banks as a funding source remains questionable. First, newly-established Cuban banks will lack experience in financing environmental infrastructure development. Second, assuming that the banks will charge high interest rates, all but the largest corporations will be precluded from financing infrastructure projects. Considering these conditions, it is unlikely, at least initially, that Cuban banks will be able to provide the massive amounts of capital necessary for the development of an environmental infrastructure.

International Public Programs

The World Bank: The World Bank assists in the development of its member-state's territories, promoting and supplementing private foreign investment, and facilitating international trade.[61] To accomplish these goals, the bank lends directly to member-states,

---

56. Christopher J. Sozzi, "Project finance and facilitating telecommunications infrastructure development in newly-industrializing countries, 12 *Santa Clara Computer & High Technology Law Journal*, 435, 438 (1996).

57. Id.

58. Id.

59. National Law Center for Inter-American Free Trade, *Disparities between law and practice in the management of hazardous waste in North America* (1995), p. 93.

60. "The U.S.-Mexican Border Region: Binational solutions to environmental problems," *Government Finance Review* 13:1 (1997).

61. Sozzi, "Project finance and facilitating telecommunications infrastructure development," 435, 438.

and guarantees loans.[62] In order for countries to qualify for such loan assistance their economic policies must conform with World Bank standards, such as privatization, elimination of domestic subsidies, and balanced budgets.[63]

Although the World Bank has traditionally focused on stabilizing economies rather than addressing environmental issues,[64] a new trend appears to have arisen in recent years, with the creation of National Environment Action Plans in Latin America, and an increased funding of environmental projects.[65]

In order to apply for such funds, Cuba will have to become a member of the World Bank, an important step which will help secure funding for other purposes as well. However, in light of its overwhelming international debt, a new Cuban government may have an aversion to taking out such loans, especially with the recent experience of the 1980's debt crisis in Latin America.[66]

Inter-American Development Bank (IADB): Like other regional multilateral financial institutions, the IADB lends funds to the public sector of developing countries for infrastructure development.[67] Although such programs have been effective, inefficient planning and disorganization have led to duplication in funding and unreliability.[68] Like the World Bank, the lending terms of IADB are also not highly con-

cessional, and may thus fuel the search for funds from alternative sources.[69]

U.S. Programs

The U.S. Agency for International Development (USAID), along with other development assistance programs, may be a source of funding, but this is uncertain. USAID's purpose it to address "basic human needs" and, considering that it has refused to issue loans for basic infrastructure projects such as roads and telecommunications,[70] it is uncertain whether environmental infrastructure would be considered a "basic human need."

Another possible funding source is the U.S. Export-Import Bank, which provides financing for exports of U.S. goods and services through export credit insurance, loan guarantees, and loans.[71] The Bank also supports U.S. exports of environmental goods and services through a special environmental exports program.[72] The ability of Cuba to rely on the Ex-Im Bank will largely be determined by agreements between both governments, as well as the status of the Cuban economy at the time.

Lastly, the Overseas Private Investment Corporation (OPIC) provides financing and political risk insurance to U.S. companies investing in developing countries.[73] The agency offers financing in the form of loans or loan guarantees, provides investment

---

62. Id., 435, 438-439.

63. Id. , 35, 439.

64. National Law Center for Inter-American Free Trade, *Disparities between law and practice*, p. 94.

65. William Partridge, "Latin America and the Caribbean Regional Enforcement Division," World Bank, Latin America and the Caribbean Region, internet article.

66. Stephen Zamora, "The Americanization of Mexican Law: Non-trade issues in the North American Free Trade Agreement," *Law and Policy in International Business* 4:2 (1993).

67. Sozzi, "Project finance and facilitating telecommunications infrastructure development," 435, 439-440.

68. Id., 435, 440.

69. Zamora, "The Americanization of Mexican Law."

70. Sozzi, "Project finance and facilitating telecommunications infrastructure development," 435, 440.

71. Jill A. Kotvis, "Environmental issues in international project finance, 745 *PLI/Comm* 243, 281 (1996).

72. Id.

73. Id., 243, 290.

guaranties against a wide variety of political risks, and also issues grants to fund feasibility studies.[74]

Multilateral Trade Institutions

If a hemispheric trade agreement indeed comes to pass in the Americas, and Cuba chooses to become a party to the agreement, Cuba may receive further assistance, depending on the degree to which the environment will be taken into account in any such agreement. If a hemispheric Environmental Side Agreement is created, Cuba could collaborate with other parties to address environmental needs.

Private Sources of Funding from Abroad (Foreign Investment)

Another alternative funding source which developing countries have been approaching with increasing frequency is private funding, in the form of foreign investment.[75] However, relying on this form of financing necessitates not only that the nation seeking funding "approve" of the investor, but also that the foreign investor find suitable conditions for investment. With respect to a post-Castro Cuba, foreign investment on the island will be radically altered from its present form, especially with the entry of the United States into the Cuban market. Cuba's new leadership will have to measure the practical need for foreign investment and the conditions under which it occurs against domestic political consideration and a need to create Cuban national industries. This is especially true in light of current foreign investment practices on the island whereby Cuban citizens are exploited through unsafe working conditions and payment in the form of the almost-worthless peso.

Most foreign investors seeking to enter the foreign markets prefer transparency, which refers to a clear, open and fair set of investment policies.[76] In other words, transparent policies clearly establish and publish all relevant rules applying to foreign investors,[77] thereby providing them with the necessary information with which to make informed investment decisions. For this reason, it is absolutely essential that Cuba's new legal and investment structure have transparency.

Possibilities for Foreign Investment in a Post-Castro Cuba: As a funding source for the Cuban environmental infrastructure, direct foreign investment provides several benefits to both Cuba and the investor. First, by its very nature, direct investment creates a long-term commitment to the domestic business. Also, because it is more difficult to pull out the investment, such investors are more likely to stay and weather difficult times. Lastly, direct investors can directly manage the business and thus better protect their interests. Thus, direct investment in Cuban infrastructure will provide Cuba with the dual advantages of capital and technological support, while allowing foreign investors to retain greater management control over operations.[78]

In addition to the theoretical advantages of foreign investment in the Cuban environmental infrastructure, various incentives and disincentives will impact foreign investment in a free Cuba. In the U.S., several sectors of the environmental technology industry, particularly the hazardous waste industry, are struggling.[79] In fact, the only areas for growth in the industry are in foreign markets,[80] including a free market Cuba. The sale of environmental goods and services in Latin America grew to $7 billion in 1995, and is predicted to grow to twice that level in the

---

74. Id., 243, 281.

75. Sozzi, "Project finance and facilitating telecommunications infrastructure development," 435.

76. National Law Center for Inter-American Free Trade, *Disparities between law and practice*, PP. 111-112.

77. Id., p. 112.

78. Sozzi, "Project finance and facilitating telecommunications infrastructure development," 435, 443.

79. "U.S. experiences net loss in 1995 of hazwaste treatment facilities," *Air/Water Pollution Report's Environment Week*, 34:13 (March 22, 1996).

80. Id.

next five years.[81] Due to these expected demands, the U.S. Department of Commerce has initiated the Latin American Environmental Initiative to promote environmental technology exports to Latin America.[82]

Such a program may play an important role in an emergent Cuba, where many of the largest potential Cuban customers may include public sector agencies, such as environmental and energy authorities. Potential opportunities may also be found in the private sector, especially among major multinational corporations which follow corporate environmental standards.[83] The largest part of the market may involve the provision of environmental equipment and services to petroleum, chemical, and petrochemical industries, including the processing, collection, transportation, and recycling of waste.[84]

Business opportunities based on Cuba's many unmet environmental needs will also include: (1) treatment of solvents, oils, and paints; (2) treatment of heavy metals, acids, resins, adhesives, silicon and plastics; (3) waste confinement technology; (4) recycling hazardous and non-hazardous waste; and (5) waste collection/transportation. Other options could include the recycling of hazardous wastes in nascent Cuban industries, assuming that the proper technical, marketing, economic, environmental, and regulatory factors would be in place.

In sum, an enhanced environmental infrastructure may actually be aggressively pursued by foreign corporations and governments, because Cuba, and Latin America in general, present a potentially lucrative market for environmental products and services.[85]

Despite the potential incentives for foreign investors to pursue business in the Cuban environmental market, however, the previously-described uncertainties inherent during or after a transition period may be problematic. Because foreign investment will be entering a Cuban free market for the first time since the 1950s, there will be few indicators to predict how foreign investors will fare in a new, potentially volatile, Cuban market. As previously stated, a key factor affecting such investment will be transparency.

Other potential economic disincentives impeding foreign investment may include: (1) limited public sector financing in a post-transition period; (2) insufficiently developed capital markets; (3) potential lack of long term financing in the local and international markets; (4) potential lack of adequate mechanisms to cover political, financial and legal risks of investment in Cuba, at least initially; (5) reliability of demand and revenue forecasts; and (6) inadequate funding for feasibility studies and preliminary design and engineering.[86]

Additional disincentives may also exist within Cuba, such as the problematic history of foreign investment in Cuba, contributing to a potential mistrust of foreign investors, as evidence by the public perception in Cuba that some foreign investors have degraded the Cuban environment by taking advantage of Cuba's lax enforcement of environmental laws.[87]

The quality of environmental technology being introduced into Cuba may also be at issue. In other nations, such imports have been criticized by experts as technology that is "end of pipe" technology, designed to deal with already-generated waste.[88] The United

---

81. Id.

82. "Latin American market momentum opens region to ET," *Business America*, 117:4 (April 1, 1996).

83. Id.

84. Id.

85. "Pressures to protect environment and promote sustainable development policies in Latin America grow," *NotiSur-Latin American Political Affairs* (October 18, 1996).

86. Derived from National Law Center for Inter-American Free Trade, *Disparities between law and practice*, p. 92, citing Jerry M. Keys, "The Impact of NAFTA on Border Environmental Issues," p. 38.

87. Díaz-Briquets and Pérez-López, "The Special Period and the Environment."

88. National Law Center for Inter-American Free Trade, *Disparities between law and practice*, p. 83 (1995).

States in particular has exported older and outdated technologies, no longer appropriate for the U.S. market, to foreign countries.[89] While such technology aids in the treatment of existing waste, it does nothing to reduce generation of such wastes. For this reason, critics point out that imported environmental technology should instead be centered on waste minimization technology, which is better suited to an country in the process of industrialization.[90] All combined, these factors may inhibit sourcing funds from foreign investors.

RECOMMENDATIONS TOWARD FACILITATING THE DEVELOPMENT OF A CUBAN ENVIRONMENTAL INFRASTRUCTURE

As described above, the factors determining development of a Cuban environmental infrastructure will be legal, practical, and economic. Having identified these obstacles, there are a number of measures which may be adopted to either minimize or perhaps eliminate such obstacles.

Legal Factors

Because all of the legal factors inhibiting development of environmental infrastructure are a product of Cuban law, the key actor in this area will be a new post-transition Cuban government. However, because new Cuban environmental laws will be developed in a foreseeably nationalistic period by a newly-created democratic body, the issue will ultimately involve the reality of Cuban sovereignty. In fact, attempts by the U.S. to take a direct approach in forcing a certain environmental/legal framework upon Cuba will likely face substantial resistance in Cuba, especially in the face of a new Constitutional Convention. Thus, the forms and degrees to which any legal recommendations are made must, at their center, acknowledge and respect sovereignty concerns of a new Cuban democratic republic.

In the area of environmental law, however, it is clear that Cuba requires the creation of a comprehensive environmental legal framework, with clear standards, transparency, and elimination of official corruption. In the spirit of assisting transition and post-transition-era Cuba, the following recommendations are offered for consideration.

First, Cuba should establish a clear jurisdictional framework for environmental law, such as clearly specifying the degree to which local action is precluded by a national government. Such a step will assure both Cuban business entities and future investors of transparency, and greater ease in complying with the law.

Another aid in clarifying the law would be to avoid broad and ambiguous language, as seen in the present version of Cuban environmental law. Such definitions will be required to help promote a market for confinement/treatment sites and treatment infrastructure. Such regulations may include a list of hazardous waste substances and approved treatment/disposal methods and container requirements. Cuban officials may also develop comprehensive standards for thermal treatment of wastes, also intended to promote investment.

In addition to more detail, however, Cuban officials should consider filling in the gaps in the law, such as the aforementioned lack of specific requirements and treatment modalities. Another major gap which also needs to be filled is the absence of a statute like the Comprehensive Environmental Response, Compensation and Liability Act (CERCLA) to provide for existing hazardous waste sites in Cuba, many of which have been polluted by foreign joint ventures that currently operate in the island. Also, high technology standards and waste minimization requirements for Cuban industry should be adopted. Of course, generating new laws in these areas will require additional enforcement, which, as discussed below, will create additional resource allocation problems for officials. Nonetheless, such legislation may create new incentives for industry and investors.

---

89. Id.

90. Id.

Perhaps a more practical approach is to re-analyze existing law to create such incentives. For example, one such possibility may be to allow for hazardous waste exports to other nations for proper treatment, at least until Cuba develops such facilities. Also, mobile treatment systems based in the U.S., and already used in Mexico, may be shipped to Cuba for on-site treatment. Such a proposal is feasible, however, only after satisfactory demonstration of existing infrastructure. To address this problem, the Cuban government may use tax incentives or perhaps direct assistance, as well as set a specific date for lifting of the export requirement, thereby guaranteeing investors that a market is forthcoming.

Lastly, in addition to establishment of an environmental legal infrastructure, a new Foreign Investment Law must be established, elaborating on the types of environmental technology imports that will be acceptable in Cuba while providing greater transparency to foreign investors. Considering the many benefits of direct investment in the form of environmental infrastructure development, such measures may benefit Cuba both environmentally and economically.

Practical Factors

Cuban Authorities: Practically speaking, a post-Castro Cuba will need to provide adequate funding for its environmental enforcement efforts. Unfortunately, as discussed elsewhere in this paper, such funding is directly linked to the status of the Cuban economy. Under the foreseeable need for an aggressive economic recovery plan, budget cuts, not increases, may be required for Cuba's conversion into a free market economy.

Stronger enforcement of the law and increased use of sanctions will be the best means of creating incentives for infrastructure development. The environ-mental technology market is different from other markets in that market demand is driven by such government action as environmental legislation, regulations, standard-setting, and enforcement.[91] In developing countries in particular, limited enforcement will deter increased demand for environmental technologies.[92] Domestic industries in such nations may not comply with environmental laws or may choose to pay fines, rather than invest in environmental technology.[93]

A free Cuba's environmental market, like that of the United States environmental market thirty years ago, will evolve into a sophisticated and competitive market only after environmental regulations are developed and enforced. To reach this goal, Cuba must avoid the mistakes of other developing countries, such as Mexico's decision, due to lack of funds, to take several steps away from a command-and-control approach.[94]

In light of Cuba's foreseeable lack of funds to aggressively enforce its laws, Cuban authorities should begin to consider alternative means of enforcement. For example, Cuba may study a successful Indonesian program which has cut pollution in that nation by half.[95] In the Indonesian system, pollution data are collected and then ranked and published, which generates public pressure, with the worst polluters rapidly taking corrective action.

Cuban Industry: Cuba's future private industrial sector should also take steps to promote environmental infrastructure development. First, it may voluntarily establish well-defined compliance policies, as has been done among large multinational corporations. Such policies will demonstrate a commitment to obeying the law and adopting ecologically-responsible management practices. Self-policing would also

---

91. Richard Sousane, "Overview of environmental technologies," *Business America*, 117:4 (April 1, 1996).

92. Id.

93. Id.

94. John Nagel, "Mexican official describes 'Environmental regulation revolution,'" *BNA International Environment Daily* (August 19, 1995).

95. "Indonesia public information system may help poor countries cut pollution," *Hazardous Waste News*, (September 16, 1996).

create an alternative to more frequent government inspections.

Second, larger entities should establish services for smaller entities, such as collecting wastes from small generators of waste and in turn recycling them for use or for sale to third parties. For example, in a future Cuban cement industry, large companies may collect waste oils from small companies for sale as fuel to cement kilns. Such practices would address pollution among smaller entities while generating additional income for collectors of such waste.

Economic Factors

Cuban Authorities: Ideally, Cuba should demonstrate its commitment to protecting its environment by increasing funding for enforcement. However, as stated previously, Cuba's ability to generate adequate such funds may be problematic due to its economic troubles. In addition, the question of how such limited resources should be allocated is troublesome, especially since Cuba will face a wide variety of environmental issues and will need to prioritize them in an effective manner. For example, gastrointestinal disease is a leading Cuban public health problem, a result of a lack of clean drinking water and inadequate sewage treatment facilities. In the face of such basic public health issues, more-abstract issues, such as cancer-causing industrial wastes, may not be considered a top priority.[96]

Nonetheless, Cuba should adopt measures to promote the generation of such funds. Some of these have been described above as suggested legal reforms. Ultimately, the question is one of political will; if the environmental protection is to be adequately funded, the Cuban people, and their elected representatives, will have to commit to reach such goals.

In addition to adequate funding, the Cuban government should adopt incentives, both positive and negative, to promote the development of a Cuban environmental infrastructure. Among the negative incentives are increased enforcement, imposition of fines, penalties, and administrative arrests. Such command and control modalities have been effective in the U.S. and, as previously discussed, should create a demand for environmental services.

Positive incentives should also be adopted. For example, a Cuban government agency may create a list of environmental products that may be given tariff-free import status to boost both trade and environmental cleanup. Domestic consumers of such technologies should also be offered incentives, such as tax incentives or subsidies, to establish consistent and monitorable environmental management techniques.

A new Cuban government should also consider setting a liberal bond policy at the local level, allowing local officials to raise funds independent of the national government, and applying them where they are most needed. Thus, a heavily industrialized province or municipality would have an alternative source of funding for infrastructure development.

Further, despite the foreseeable difficulties in a new Cuban economy, any national financing entity should keep its interest rates low. Lowering of such rates may have the dual benefit of increasing financing options for local investors as well as triggering the lowering of rates among Cuban commercial banks.

Lastly, as stated above, creation of a new foreign investment law and resolution of jurisdictional issues are among the legal reforms which may be adopted to further encourage funding from foreign investors.

International, U.S.-Based, and Bilateral Institutions: Foreign public lending sources should re-examine lending policies and interest rates, since such factors inhibit the use of such funds by developing countries for infrastructure needs.[97] Re-evaluating such policies will not only provide Cuba with more viable funding options, but will ultimately serve the goals of promoting international trade, in that Cuba will be able to purchase environmental goods and services from other nations.

---

96. Zamora, "The Americanization of Mexican Law."

97. Id.

International, U.S.-based, and bilateral public funding sources should adopt development policies to further encourage environmental infrastructure development in Cuba. Such policies will be consistent with international goals of facilitating free trade, since facilitating foreign investment in the Cuban environmental infrastructure will undoubtedly benefit the economies of environmental products exporters.

USAID may also consider clarifying whether environmental infrastructure falls within the scope of "basic human needs," since these are the needs that USAID programs are intended to fund.[98] Such basic human needs as health and adequate living conditions are undoubtedly linked with the need for adequate management and treatment of pollutants.

As Cuba's largest trading partner and neighbor, the U.S. in general will need to promote and facilitate investment in Cuban environmental infrastructure. As evidenced by the Department of Commerce's efforts in this area,[99] such development ultimately benefits both nations. Such efforts should serve as a blueprint for similar policies by different U.S. agencies.

Foreign Investors: As discussed in previous sections, Cuba may be wary of some forms of foreign investment. Coupled with immoral and abusive practices by other investors during the Castro regime, foreign investors will have to prove to the Cuban people that such investment will benefit Cuba, rather than drain its resources. Based on this history, foreign investors seeking to participate in Cuba's nascent environmental industry should also develop several policies to further promote investment.

First, investors seeking to establish operations in populated areas should encourage extensive participation by Cuban communities in any permitting processes. A key part of any investor's entry into the Cuban market should be public education and participation. Essentially, the investor must involve the local community and demonstrate the benefits, both economic and health-wise, of the proposed operation. In this

way, local concerns can be addressed in the early stages, before a substantial investment is made, thereby hopefully avoiding a loss to both parties.

With respect to hazardous waste cleanup, foreign investors should establish operations at pre-existing sites, volunteering to clean up the polluted site in exchange for permit guarantees. Considering the history of rampant illegal and indiscriminate dumping in Cuba, many illicit landfills sites exist in Cuba. Future investors should therefore establish treatment sites at pre-existing dumps, but only those which satisfy landfill requirements (i.e. safety from floods, runoff, etc.) Coupled with an effective public information program, such investors will demonstrate a specific benefit of commencing operations at the once-illegal site. With the establishment of enough such facilities, cleanup operations of illegal sites which fail to meet landfill requirements may commence.

Foreign investors in hazardous waste treatment and disposal should also promote waste recycling. For example, some types of hazardous wastes may be used as fuel for cement kilns, and kiln operators often may be willing to pay for such fuels. Thus, in addition to treating and disposing waste, investors may invest directly into such recycling services, thereby cleaning up the environment and returning a profit. Recycling will also cut down on the amount of space required to dispose of waste, allowing landfills to operate for longer periods of time.

Lastly, another step foreign investors can take is to rely on higher technology standards and on the best available treatment modalities. Resorting to outdated technology to address Cuba's environmental technology needs is counterproductive for several reasons. First, such measures have been established to be ineffective or inefficient in treating toxic wastes in more developed countries, suggesting that such technologies will ultimately provide a lower standard of protection for the Cuban environment and Cuban citizens. Second, use of such technologies may also give rise to community opposition and challenges from

---

98. Sozzi, "Project finance and facilitating telecommunications infrastructure development," 435, 440.

99. "Latin American market momentum opens region to ET."

environmental activists. Lastly, it will also result in the high costs of retrofitting aging equipment. In sum, technology used in Cuba should be as modern and effective as that used in other Western nations.

CONCLUSION

Clearly, Cuba faces a huge challenge in adequately addressing its environmental crisis. Legal, practical, and, most significantly, economic factors will determine the success of efforts to solve this problem. Ultimately, political will and capital are the transforming factors that will solve the problem; admittedly, however, in light of a transition-era Cuba's other pressing needs, such will and capital may be in short supply.

Nonetheless, several actors will be committed to changing this reality. On the one hand, Cuban officials of the New Republic, who, aware that economic development does not mandate environmental deg-

radation, will develop new policies and laws that actually seek to promote both environmental protection and economic growth. These two societal goals need not compete with each other and, as seen in the U.S., may be attained concurrently. Cuban private industry must also adopt this view and seek to invest in environmental infrastructure development for this purpose. Outside Cuba, international funding bodies should modify their lending practices to promote such development. Lastly, foreign investors, as evidenced by their efforts in other Latin American countries, will be interested in developing an environmental technology/treatment market in Cuba. These actors should consult each other, since they ultimately share similar goals in this area. The recommendations listed above are but a beginning step in expanding this dialogue and in recognizing the valuable contributions that each can make in solving Cuba's environmental crisis.

COMMENTS ON

"Cuba's New Entrepreneurs: Five Years of Small-Scale Capitalism" by Philip Peters and Joseph L. Scarpaci

José M. Ruisánchez

The authors are commended for having accomplished a mission impossible: they have written a paper on small-scale enterprise which is informative, readable and most interesting.[1] This is due mainly to an abundance of snapshots and summaries of specific businesses where the entrepreneurs voice their own challenges and ways of overcoming them. These mini-cases and the accompanying analysis convey the flavor and reality of what it is and what it takes to be self-employed in socialist Cuba today. Hopefully, the authors' perceptive and original work on small-scale business in Cuba will continue and expand in the future.

These comments cover three main areas: the size of the enterprises; their employment numbers; and their potential.

Regarding business size, the paper focuses on Cuba's self-employed or "cuentapropistas" (CPs). These are businesses which, except for restaurants (where family members are allowed to work with the proprietor), consist of one owner-employee who cannot employ others. Hence Cuba's CPs are much closer to what in the rest of Latin America and the Caribbean are generally known as microentrepreneurs (i.e., up to 5 employees) than to small-size enterprises, which are often defined as having up to 500 employees.

Aside from size, the main similarity between a Cuban CP, as presented in the paper, and a Latin American microentrepreneur is that both are led to self-employment mainly because of the absence of formal employment which can provide a living income. These are no Bill Gates pursuing a high-tech dream of growth and profits as they start a business from the family's garage, nor an artisan who learns and furthers the family's traditional craft. Rather, unless the CP employs himself or herself, the family does not eat (or not as well).

On the other hand, there are a number of radical differences that render the business life of the CP in sharp contrast to that of a typical microentrepreneur in other countries of Latin America. For example:

- Informality is essential to microenterprise, whereas Cuba's CPs require a permit and are subject to regulations in order to be self-employed.

- Anyone can perform any economic activity as a microentrepreneur, but in Cuba a university graduate is forbidden to be self-employed in his or her career.

- Governments generally welcome microenterprise as a source of employment and contribution to the economy and to social development, whereas

---

1. The paper by Peters and Scarpaci is not included in this volume. It is available in the internet at http://www.adti.net/html_files. Ed.

in Cuba CPs are permitted to exist as a sort of necessary evil which conflicts with the state's Marxist dogma (e.g., unemployment does not exist).

- Employees and partners are commonly found in microenterprises, yet they are forbidden in Cuba.

- Microenterprise almost never pays income tax, while Cuba's CPs pay up to half of revenues in income taxes. Most probably this makes CPs the most highly taxed microentrepreneurs in the world.

- The frequency of the government's inspections and the magnitude of the fines which accost CPs is the exception rather than the rule among Latin America's microentrepreneurs.

One gets the sense that the Peruvian microentrepreneurs who gave Hernando de Soto the raw materials for his *El Otro Sendero* had an easier life than Cuba's CPs.

Concerning employment numbers, the authors estimate that CPs account for some 3% of Cuba's labor force. This is in sharp contrast with microenterprises in Latin American countries which provide employment for up to 50% of the labor force. With Cuba suffering from economic hardship and a dearth of well-remunerated jobs, one wonders whether the low numbers of CPs are due to restrictions in the issuance of licenses or inaccuracy in official statistics.

Regarding potential, the reader is impressed by the "initiative and ingenuity of individual Cubans" as portrayed by the authors in their summaries of some of the individual interviews they had with 152 CPs. No doubt these and other CPs could make a major contribution to Cuba's economy if they were allowed to work free from the many obstacles and encumbrances that are documented in the paper. This potential could become the focus of new research which the authors might consider in the future.

SECOND ECONOMY, SECOND SOCIETY, AND POLITICAL CONTROL IN CUBA: PERSPECTIVES FROM NETWORK AND INSTITUTIONAL ECONOMICS

Mario A. Rivera

While economic liberalization movements in Latin America have much in common, national policies often take distinctive forms. Even Cuba has found it necessary to take a number of market-oriented steps to address the economic crisis ushered in by the loss of Soviet economic support after 1989. At issue in this regard are patterns of interaction among market liberalization policies, along with specification of the institutional sources and effects of policy. On the basis of network economics, it will be suggested that incipient institutional change may be found in the development of entrepreneurial, managerial, and interorganizational networks.

Cuba's *sui generis* liberalization policies are tentative, opportunistic, and tactical in nature, consistent with earlier market experiments. Economic policy is conditioned by an overriding propensity toward political control. Cuba's response to the end of Soviet subsidies is one instance, involving stricter rationing of food and consumer goods to curtail demand, diversification and expansion of exports, expansion of tourism, and strategic efforts to bolster the nation's international relations.

Notwithstanding these efforts, during the first three years of the so-called "special period" there was a 40 percent drop in the gross domestic product, 70 percent drop in industrial and agricultural capacity, and 60 percent decline in domestic consumption. Beginning in 1993, the government undertook additional liberalization measures, legalizing certain kinds of

foreign investment and private microenterprise as well as legalizing the dollar. It thus sought to balance diverse aims on a fulcrum of political control: to create demand abroad for Cuban products, and generally to obtain hard currency, while attending to growing domestic demand that far outstrips rationing. Cuba has thus approached market liberalization in the nineties as it did in the early eighties, with contingent policies always subject to modification for political reasons.

CUBA'S SECOND ECONOMY

Cuba's distribution system for foodstuffs and essential consumer goods consists of the old rationing system complemented by alternative markets (farmers' markets and government-run "parallel" markets) and a fast-growing "informal" sector which accounts for a rapidly increasing share of domestic production and consumption (Betancourt, 1992). In addition to the state-run "first economy" and the newly-established, market-based "second" economy (joint ventures, foreign investment), there is a partially legalized informal economy. There is therefore significant development of market mechanisms and incentive structures (Pastor and Zimbalist, 1995).

As Jorge Pérez-López argues, participation in informal or second economy activities has come to the fore during the post-Soviet transition (Pérez-López, 1995b). He describes the difficult balancing act that the legalization of private or "own account" economic activities represents for citizens and the government alike. Own-account activities range from the most common type, services—cook, taxi driver, mechanic, electrician, produce seller, small restaurateur (running small restaurants out of private homes)—to production, of beef, agricultural products, and small-scale manufactures. Restrictions include requirements for vendor registration and an often-flouted prohibition against hiring salaried employees who are not close relatives. Other strictures affect university-trained professionals, who were at first totally excluded from selling services but more recently have been allowed to do so if these lie outside their area of university training. Still excluded from self-employment are public officials, members of the armed forces, judges, prosecutors, and others holding a public charge. A related issue is the deprofessionalization of traditional professions as state compensation falls far behind remuneration in private commerce. And while new registration and taxation requirements seem onerous to Cubans, the number engaged in private economic activity of all kinds exceeds a million.

Ironically, the coupling of limited liberalization with efforts at close regulation has only underscored the institutional limits of state control. Mesa-Lago raises the issue rhetorically:

> . . . Is the state capable of executing the legal dispositions and regulations that have been approved? Can the government really act against the hundreds of thousands who work on their own without registering? How many inspectors would be needed to control the hundreds of thousands of mini-businesses which very often do not have a fixed locale but operate as temporary mobile vendors? How can the hiring of salaried employees who are not family members be avoided? What exactly constitute "excessive" earnings and prices? To what extent is the vagueness of these formulations a weapon that the government is ready to use against own-account work, in case the process escapes its control? The answer given by a Cuban economist to all these queries was: the leadership knows that the law is unenforceable; these restrictions are established for ideological reasons, to give the impression that the State is still in control of the economy and to let those who are excluded from own-account work that these activities occur within a severely limited framework and that those operating

there are obligated to turn over a part of their profits to society (Mesa-Lago, 1995, p. 69).

Service workers in tourist resorts—whose names are drawn from Party lists—are closely monitored to ensure they turn over at least 40 percent of dollar tips to management for pesos, an often futile effort at surveillance. Under current law (decree No. 50), the government contracts with joint ventures to hire workers at an average monthly remuneration of U.S. $400 in hard currency. This goes to the state, which in turn pays workers an average of 250 pesos per month—U.S. $20 at current exchange rates of twenty pesos per dollar. Many justify underreporting of earnings by recalling these confiscatory policies, involving retention by government of some nine-tenths of wages in the tourism/foreign investment sector.

One concern about the informal sector found in the empirical literature is that the greater level of illegal activity, the more people are prone to combine legal with illegal forms of activity, so that flouting of law becomes ubiquitous, undermining civil society (Wolfsfeld, et al., 1994). Likewise, Mesa-Lago (1995) suggests that in Cuba significant informal sector growth arising from looser regulation would prompt more illegal activity, as economic linkages proliferate and incentives for theft from the state multiply. Kummels (1995) describes patronage networks in the Cuban economy and the way they come to involve almost everyone:

> Despite the external differences between defenders of socialism and of capitalism, in daily life … there is a close cooperation between [them] . . . Those who are not socialists depend on the cooperation of Party militants to obtain lucrative jobs in meat or sausage plants, in the tourist network or in diplomatic circles. These positions are advantageous because of the possibility of access to hard currency, beef, rum, or other goods, which can later sustain black market activity. Furthermore, the non-socialists need the protection of the militants for their illegal businesses. Only with their help can they obtain and produce the goods which the central administration cannot make available to the public, at least in sufficient quantities. For their part, the declared socialists need these tradespeople in order to be able to enjoy illegally-acquired goods with clean hands . . . [I]n daily life, cooperation

between socialists and non-socialists is assured above all by way of family solidarity and the understanding that without the tradespeople the planned economy would long ago have come to an end (p. 136).

Most Cubans, therefore, find it necessary to buy from or sell in the parallel economy, access to which depends on cross-cutting familial and social networks that span political boundaries. This reality helps explain government's reluctance to police the second economy: The often-revised decrees that regulate it may be little more than a *paean* to revolutionary principles and an effort to mollify those who are unhappy with the turn toward capitalism.

THE IMPLICATIONS OF INDEPENDENT ECONOMIC ACTIVITY

The implications of independent economic activity are not all salutary for the state. While there could be dramatic productivity growth in an expanded private sector, with growing incomes reducing fiscal pressures on the socialist welfare state, the pluralization of economic activity is seen as an ideological and practical threat in Cuba. Although the informal economy typically serves as an economic outlet and social buffer, in Cuba it acts more as an irritant for a population closely attuned to economic inequalities.

The dollarization of the economy, overvalued peso and scarce consumer goods, unprofitable operation of state enterprises, and orientation of joint ventures toward export, tourism, or other hard-currency-generating activities rather than to domestic needs, combine to make for repressed inflation in the state-run economy and sharply rising prices in the second economy. These tendencies also play into ideological conflicts: A recognition of the problems associated with monetary and pricing policies led during the first years of 1989-93 "special period" to a rift between two factions: technocrats in several ministries with significant peso holdings, who proposed decontrolling prices, ending subsidies, and imposing new taxes, and a losing "populist" faction which wanted the issuance of a new currency under conditions unfavorable for those with peso savings or profits, notably farmers and merchants in the second economy (Valdés, 1995, p.2). In a similar vein, wrangling between *dirigist* and reformist factions has led to the re-

shuffling and renaming of ministries in the guise of restructuring (Mesa-Lago, 1995). While there may be elite consensus about the need for economic change, there is little agreement concerning *means*.

In Cuba as elsewhere, *dollarization* has been in part a response to high inflation, an effort at fixing prices (Melvin and Peiers, 1996), but also a way of releasing hoarded dollars into the economy and encouraging exile remittances, which have consistently exceeded U.S. $600 million a year. The divergence of prices in the first and second economies shuts out of the parallel economy anyone without dollars, which are typically obtained through remittances from relatives abroad or by access to the tourist industry. Only 15 percent of the population, mostly concentrated in Havana, receives dollar remittances, and relatively few have access to hard-currency generating activities, so that the vast majority of the population is excluded from the dollar economy. This is a situation in which public policy places "a fiscal constraint on a government that follows long-term inflationary macroeconomic policies" (Melvin and Peiers, 1996, p. 10). This occurs in Cuba with the rationing system, radically redistributive pricing and social policies, and the systemic protection of an inconvertible peso. The risk of dollarization, according to Melvin and Peiers (1996, p. 11), is that "the domestic currency will lose its role in providing the major functions of money." In Cuba, the peso is becoming a political currency for price-controlled goods and subsidized services, while the dollar becomes the marketplace alternative.

Thoroughgoing liberalization of the Cuban economy—which would likely presuppose internal political change and the lifting of the U.S. trade embargo—would mean a natural realignment of Cuban trade toward the United States. As much as 80 percent of Cuban exports and imports would shift away from current partners, especially Canada and Japan but also Spain, Germany, and other European countries (Montenegro and Soto, 1996). The Cuban elite does not relish the prospect of a cultural or political repenetration of the country by the United States in the wake of economic *rapprochement*. Contrariwise, were it to relinquish some of its control over the economy, a growing domestic market would foster Cuba's integration with the world economy as a whole, not just with the United States.

The Cuban government has just begun to permit producers' associations, consumer cooperatives, and quasi-contractual private associations that create small service enterprises. There is also tentative movement toward allowing own-account workers to pool their resources in partnerships, for example to provide services such as auto repair (Valdés, p. 16). Castañeda and Montalván (1994) suggest that it is because of ingrained collectivism and centralism that such microeconomic relations are lacking, while, collaterally, the government is incapable of managing them; as far as foreign investment is concerned, Cuba has moved haltingly and inconsistently, in ways that "avoid and postpone unavoidable and necessary changes" in the structure of economic relations (p. 6)."

INSTITUTION-BUILDING

Economic reforms introduced in the 1990s may be significant in the Cuban context but are modest in comparison to those instituted by other countries in Latin America, Asia, and Eastern Europe. In Latin America (for example, Peru) the creation of trade associations and pressure groups, along with small-scale financial institutions, has given "informals" significant political leverage and facilitated various kinds of economic integration, notably subcontracting. The Cuban government has looked to China and Vietnam as models of centrally-controlled political and economic change, but it has been unwilling to go as far as these nations in instituting legal and institutional reforms of property relations and contracts. Without settled policies and laws that protect private property and the freedom to contract, entrepreneurial activity and technical innovation in the economy will be stunted. Organizational innovation in the economy—the development of institutional structures that correspond to market demand—will likewise lag, leaving Cuba behind in competitive global markets.

Kelley (1994) finds that it is principally the lack of formal sector employment that generates informal activity, which affects the capital- and labor-intensity of the economy and complicates distributional issues when demand, productivity, and incomes in the formal and informal sectors diverge. His findings are consistent with the situation in Cuba, where so-called factor productivity—efficiency in the use of financial, technical, and labor inputs—is *higher* in the informal sector than in the economy as a whole, contrary to what is known of informal economies in general. For instance, state-run factories, are grossly overmanned, and either idle or functioning well below capacity (Valdés, 1995, p. 18).

Mead and Morrison (1996) find an inverse relationship between a nation's level of politico-economic institutional development and the scope and type of its informal economic activity, so that large are seen as a sign of institutional insufficiency. Morrison et al. (1994) similarly examine the institutional links of informal enterprises with the suppliers and consumers of goods and services, and they conclude that regulatory constraints and insufficient financing make for diminished institutional capacity as well as fiscal evasion. This underscores the need for public policies that support banking and commercial credit for ordinary citizens and small enterprises. In Cuba, there has been debate about reform of the banking system in this direction, but with great reluctance about reform: One issue has been whether foreign banks should be restricted to dollar (rather than peso) accounts for Cuban nationals (Mesa-Lago, 1995, p. 76).

In a comparative East Asian study, Ranis and Stewart (1994) focus on the relation of economic informality to: (1) the viability and productivity of the agricultural sector; (2) the nature of economic linkages and institutions in the urban formal sector; and (3) type of governmental intervention. They contrast instances of policy success when, as in Taiwan, there is a moderately-sized urban informal sector with significant production and consumption links to the modern economy (such as subcontracting and various forms of vertical integration), along with adequate labor absorption, to instances of policy failure such as the Philippines, where urban informal and traditional subsectors and agriculture have grown in isolation from modernizing elements of the economy. There, inadequate financing mechanisms and inflationary monetary policies make for excessive labor mobility and a labor surplus.

In Cuba, direct state intervention in the agricultural sector is decreasing, and the quantity and quality of output correspondingly increasing, in newly-established forms of private and cooperative farming, though inputs like chemical fertilizers, fuel, and irrigation equipment are in short supply. In the 1980s, Cuba had institutional mechanisms for centralized administration in agriculture under the System of Management and Planning of the Economy (Meurs, 1992). The creation of cooperatives (Basic Units of Cooperative Production) in former state farms as a substitute mechanism is part of a stated policy of switching to low-input and self-reliant farming. However, the simultaneous creation of military Agricultural Districts may signal the *militarization* of the agricultural sector (Rosset, 1997). In October 1977, the military added to its control of ministerial posts at the head of Communications, Transport, Ports and Merchant Marine, Fishing, Civil Aeronautics, State Reserves, Justice, and Higher Education the portfolio of Sugar Minister (with the appointment of first deputy Armed Forces Minister Rosales del Toro, Raúl Castro's second-in-command and a Politburo member). Some attribute the military's key role in the economy, through top appointments and control of commercial enterprises, to a relatively high level of professionalism and institutional strength. It has also capably conducted policy experiments, with limited tests of initiatives such as the Agricultural District farms before full implementation.

There are over 200 farmers' markets in Cuban cities (more than 30 in Havana alone), providing a fourth of all of the foodstuffs the population consumes. The development of an agricultural economy in which both private and state enterprises (and the military) operate is far more advanced than counterpart markets for small-scale manufactures, craft products, and services in the second economy; in fact, it is the agriculture is making for the "generalization of monetary-mercantile relations" across Cuba Valdés (1995, p. 15). The centrality of this sector has implications for institutional development, as Betancourt (1991)

suggests: (1) because those active at the commercial end of Cuban agriculture tend to have "experience in participation in market exchanges" (p. 15) and are thus poised to adapt to changes in agricultural organization and commerce; and (2) because this sector lends itself to privatization, possibly beginning with provisional grants of secure property rights to farmers and operators of parallel markets, which would allow for continuity in food distribution together with new forms of agricultural enterprise. However, there is still no sign of the kind of market innovation and institutional integration in agriculture that should drive relations between it and other sectors of the economy. What is apparent instead is what economic theory calls *disarticulation*, or weak linkages between economic sectors, and production disparities limiting the growth of markets (Wickrama and Mulford, 1996, p. 378).

With regard to governmental reform or restructuring, Valdés (1995, p. 17) stresses the way that the "State, progressively, has stopped being employer," no longer accounting for 95 percent of all employment, as it did in 1990, but for 80 percent or less for the economically active population of 3.6 million; government rhetoric is no longer concerned with "unemployment" as such but with the "rationalization" of work and "reordering" of the labor force (p. 18), which may simply amount to a tacit acceptance of unemployment. It would not seem too large a step, in light of the regime's apparent willingness to reconsider programmatic positions, to address changes in property rights and the creation of a contract law system in a revised constitutional framework. Following the arguments of Betancourt (1991) and of Alvarez and Puerta (1994), however, such steps would entail fundamental institutional as well as ideological change. Political and economic reforms, according to Pérez-López (1995a), are instead tentative and self-limiting:

> Cuba's reforms—legalization and liberalization of self-employment, changes in the agricultural sector that converted state farms into cooperatives, reauthorization of farmers' free markets and artisan markets, some managerial reforms, encouragement of incoming foreign investment—bear a strong resemblance to the (Soviet Union's) *perestroika* program, although

the Cuban reforms fail to include measures that stimulate a domestic private sector, such as those embodied in the Soviet Law on Cooperatives, and [fail to] grant state enterprises freedom to manage their own affairs.[Unlike China] Cuba has not undertaken meaningful price reforms and has not created free economic zones to attract investors (pp. 15-16).

CIVIL SOCIETY OR SECOND SOCIETY: PROSPECTS FOR POLITICAL CHANGE

Today, Latin American political thought stresses the idea of civil society, with emphasis on deliberate institutional change and reform. The argument is that the state should not unduly limit institutional autonomy, nor any options for the creation of a multiplicity of social and economic associations capable of acting in the public arena (Trinidade et al., 1988). Poland, Hungary, and Czechoslovakia "experienced the emergence of [such a] second society even within the framework of authoritarianism," while in Romania, Bulgaria, and Albania, "where neither economic reforms nor a second, or civil, society quite jelled, the ruling Communist parties [was nonetheless capable of calling] elections amid the regional revolutionary wave of 1989-90 (Pérez-Stable, 1995, p. 1)." The development of a more pluralistic political culture in Cuba, even to these standards, would require fundamental and widespread acceptance of democratic rules, greater respect for differing interests, values, and political views, and a greater trust in the basic fairness and trustworthiness of political and economic institutions. Instead, as Castañeda and Montalván (1994) argue, "[Cuban] civil society is very poorly developed, providing almost no organized counterweight to the pervasive and weighty influence of the state. ... There is no space or tolerance of open (or public) debate, dissent or even disagreement, because the leadership is extremely hostile to public criticism...(p.9)."

John Hall (1995) suggests that the ability of a nation such as Cuba to manage a transition from communism is determined by the state's ability to cooperate with as well as coordinate society—to organize society without resort to despotism—so that in postcommunist transitions "more rather than less democracy is needed," in the sense of incorporation of excluded actors and greater political participation.

Rather than ideological positions favoring either the state or the market, the public and private sectors should be regarded as having unique and complementary capabilities. Master (1997) cautions, however, that *incomplete* and *inconsistent* market reform creates political and economic difficulties beyond the responsive and absorptive capacity of existing institutions.

The Swedish economist Stefan de Vylder (1991), in a study of Cuba, Chile, Nicaragua, and Peru, finds that avowedly progressive social policies, though aimed at combating inequality and mobilizing popular participation, have often worsened income and resource disparities and promoted various forms of corruption. These policies exhibit complex causation: overspending based on "exaggerated optimism" engenders shortages and deficits along with excess demand and a lack of financial and monetary discipline, while an overvaluation of central planning, price controls, subsidies, and redistributive policies, perpetuates demand for government largess and in effect, therefore, strengthens the institutional mechanisms of political control in the economy. In Cuba, the pattern of excess demand and consumer good shortages already noted has led to "spiraling black market prices in spite of widespread price controls and severe rationing of most goods and services" (Castañeda and Montalván, 1994, p. 7). Castañeda and Montalván argue that, rather than satisfy basic needs, the ration system has "stimulate[d] administrative corruption because [of the] widening gap between official prices and market prices" (p. 7).

There is a theoretical countercurrent that rejects the "civil society" thesis in the Cuban case, despite the endemic problems of socialism. Valdés dismisses the argument that a civil society *in opposition* to Cuba's political, economic, and social system should or could appear there. Neither the appearance of dissident groups nor the creation of institutional spaces for independent thought and action (e.g., among academics and research scientists), nor even the reduction in "number and functions of state organizations" and "lateralization" of state power, translate into the creation of a civic space in the liberal sense (p. 4). For Valdés, 1993 is the watershed year in a transition from a statist and dual economy to a "progressively mixed economy where new sectors are opened, but gradually . . . [a] process which has come to be called the *new socialist market economy*" (p. 6). Progression toward less state control of the economy and more "self-management" ("autogestión") at the level of the firm, enterprise, or microenterprise, is affecting the state-economy but not the state-society relation. Market forces and values are ever more pervasive, but there is no radical transformation of the revolutionary state in prospect.

That the Cuban leadership seems little concerned with the establishment of reliable procedural and substantive rules for either politics or commerce is consistent with the thesis that a liberal reconstitution is unlikely in Cuba. If nothing else, rectification policies and the fear and uncertainty they create militate against liberalization and liberal-democratic values.

As suggested earlier, in Cuba government restructuring has meant the downsizing and consolidation of certain ministries. The Communist Party has been implementing reductions in personnel in state agencies since 1991, and the loss of what are pejoratively called "functionaries" has resulted in delegation of authority to lower levels of the Party and provincial and municipal governments. Also making for shifts in administrative authority is friction between "new professionals" and Party cadres whose careers owed principally to political considerations. This conflict, which surfaced during the 1986 rectification, is one which the younger officials should win, if only by attrition. It is still often the case, however, that "political credentials govern managerial appointments," making for "widespread dissatisfaction [among] middle-managers and technicians and demoralization among younger professionals" (Castañeda and Montalván, 1994, p. 10).

Andrej (1996) argues that under "conditions of institutional uncertainty," what he *calls articulatory managerial networks* can play an important compensatory role. These entail "parallel processes" in the development of managerial and organizational capabilities, and they can serve as the "scaffolding" on which new ideas, outlooks, and behaviors become institutionalized (Gilmore and Krantz, 1991). Network ap-

proaches to institutional analysis suggest that the introduction of multiple, decentralized, interlinked centers of administrative control can create functional substitutes, and potentially the foundations, for new institutions.

Barring a violent transition in Cuba, the enabling condition for the development of administrative capability and organizational autonomy will be the creation of countervailing institutions, or institutional "countercontrol" (Lamal, p. 84). This took place in the Soviet Union by means of new political parties, multicandidate free elections, labor strikes, and public demonstrations led by dissident groups immediately prior to the collapse of the political system. These very undesirable results have strengthened Fidel Castro's distrust of *perestroika* and rejection of anything like it for Cuba.

NETWORKS AS INCIPIENT INSITUTIONS

It was suggested earlier that the overweening exercise of political control in Cuba has tended to thwart the full development of market structures such as commercial and property law, even to the limited extent that these have taken shape in China and Vietnam. Coupled with American sanctions, this creates a climate of uncertainty that deters investment and entrepreneurial activity. Network analysis is gaining prominence in economics on the premise that it is precisely in circumstances of fundamental uncertainty that enterprises seek strategic alliances, conducting business cooperatively as well as competitively in pursuit of common goals, operating at the conjunction of the organizational and the personal. Such alliances are functionally interdependent, basing their operations on the control of activities, resources, and knowledge. Networks are defined structurally by actual and latent relations, and by their positioning, whether horizontally across firms or vertically. Government can engage in coproduction activities with and otherwise support such networks, if it affords them enough autonomy. The development of autonomous networks in commerce is tantamount to the institutional development of markets.

In a similar vein, managerial networks can develop as managers' interactions within or across sectors (e.g., tourism, trade, and shipping) settle into predictable, social-exchange forms of governance or coordination, which gain structural "embeddedness" in the course of complex exchanges under conditions of uncertainty. Network structures are characterized by an institutionality of process rather than hierarchy, particularly in a society and economy of Cuba's scale, where there is little difference between managerial or inter-firm relations and interpersonal relations. Cuba's is a relational rather than individualistic culture (Earp, 1996) so that entrepreneurial and managerial nets consist mainly of interpersonal ties and reciprocal exchanges even when the institutions involved are well-developed. Network structures involve an identity-type of relation, i.e., relationships where social status predominates, whether based on school or family ties, social class or political standing, or provenance (e.g., coming from the same town or neighborhood, an important consideration in Cuba). The earlier analysis of Cuba's second economy similarly found that it is based on cross-cutting family and social networks.

The argument of the network literature is that institutional development based on the increasing embeddedness of process (of social resources and production and commercial transactions) is salutary, on the assumption that network ties reduce transaction costs, noise, friction, and uncertainty in economic activity. Moreover, they do so without resorting to hierarchy or bureaucratic rules, so that process supersedes structure—as tends to be the case with informal economies. Social and human capital then become a function of brokerage activities, as key individuals (managers, entrepreneurs, and other *boundary-spanners*) facilitate transactions on the basis of interpersonal ties, obligations, and tactical alliances. The economic value of networks is a function of their requisite complexity along with traits like flexibility and maneuverability. Networks depend on the ability of some individuals to span institutional gaps (or "holes") and to connect with other critically-situated individuals in common courses of action.

There are some early signs of the development of more autonomous management practices outside of the state ministries in Cuba, particularly in the liberalization and decentralization of trade relations by

parastatal agencies, and it is here that one might look for prospective managerial networks. While imports and exports were until recently entirely a matter of state control, now any manager of an enterprise producing for export may arrange commercial transactions directly. During a roughly ten-year period (begun with the mid-eighties rectification program) Cuba undertook an intensive process of managerial development, beginning with a three-year collaboration with the United Nations Development Program through an agency called the Unified System for the Selection, Development and Training of State Managers (Brandwayn, 1993). From the ranks of over 14,000 administrators trained during this period, and hundreds of others trained more recently in England, Spain, and elsewhere, have come the managers of the many new types of hybrid enterprise, including the import-export arms of state agencies, joint ventures in tourism, "mixed enterprises" (a foreign partner and a parastatal agency forming a mercantile society), and "risk contract" partnerships—foreign and Cuban investors retaining separate legal identities and assuming risk individually, an arrangement that is becoming common in mining and petroleum (Valdés, 1995, p. 7). In these new kinds of public-private enterprise, managers act as entrepreneurs, avidly seeking commercial associates and investors in Cuba and abroad.

The State Committee for Economic Collaboration (Comité Estatal de Colaboración Económica) assumed major responsibility for foreign investment in 1991 and to that end formed a "Central Negotiating Group" which works with counterpart trading groups in most state ministries (Monreal and Rúa del Llano, 1995, p. 156). Despite the reluctance to abandon centralism that its very existence betrays, this trade and investment mechanism allows managers unprecedented access to the marketing and distribution networks of foreign companies and to "marketing agreements, joint-production agreements and other types of strategic alliance between state enterprises and transnational corporations" (Brandwayn, 1993, p. 368). It is in these defining elements of domestic and international market integration that one might find the basis for institutional development in commerce and trade, following Andrej. Here managers directly experience the world of commerce with a rare measure of independence, in a setting where productive initiative is rewarded.

Again, however, the development of social and economic institutions of this kind in Cuba is limited by the exercise of state control. There is pendular movement toward and away from the codification of rules, control of information, and political repression. The institutional base for changes in economic and commercial practices is lacking, and a sustaining foundation for essential legal institutions such as contract or property law is missing. As a consequence it is found that the rapid move toward international joint ventures and foreign direct investment has meant improvised rules essentially detached from Cuban civil law.

Nonetheless, new institutional linkages and developments are evident everywhere in Cuba today, notably in trade and commerce, as the following instances in the area of trade and services suggest: (a) there is a rapidly growing transportation and logistical infrastructure, warehousing, and distribution system in Cuba, including maritime facilities and import-export and insurance services; (b) corresponding to the growth of cargo transportation and logistics systems has come growth in customs law and regulation, along with the introduction of tariffs and income taxes (U.S. prohibitions under the trade embargo dictating that vessels docking in Cuban ports may not enter U.S. waters for 180 days already double the cost of shipping, so that taxation seems all the more burdensome to those concerned); (c) free trade zones (FTZs), found throughout Latin America, have come to Cuba on a limited scale, notably with the Villa de Berroa FTZ in Havana and the Santiago de Cuba FTZ; and (d) mining (under Minister of Basic Industry Marcos Portal) has seen the development of 52 risk-contract partnerships with foreign investors, in concert with hundreds of foreign consultants; Cuba produces 10 percent of the world's cobalt, is the third largest nickel producer, and its National Geological Service has made geological mapping along with specialized technical services available to potential investors. Petroleum has recently established 40 joint ventures, including land exploration contracts and offshore risk contract partnerships.

The island's telecommunications system, which until 1993 was a state monopoly under the Ministry of Communications, has been broken up into a series of hybrid enterprises: the national telephone company, EMTELCUBA, found a foreign partner in Grupo Domos, a Mexican holding company, while the CU-BACEL cellular telephone company paired with other Mexican investors and Japanese suppliers; notwithstanding the Cuban Democracy Act and the tightening of the U.S. embargo, beginning in 1995 trilateral negotiations among the American and Cuban governments and AT&T resulted in the reactivation of the undersea cable to Cuba and expansion of long-distance service, MCI was licensed to provide direct-dial service via satellite, and other services and companies moved to provide service, among them IDB WorldCom (for telex and telegraph), LDDS Communications (long distance service), WilTel International (construction of fiber-optic lines from Florida), and ItalCable (for a satellite earth station linking Cuban resorts with Ital-Rome). Several of these joint ventures provide for conjoint operations networks among foreign managers and Cuban counterparts.

Negotiations over the expansion of telecommunications and liberalization of access by U.S. and European providers have been the most intensive, sustained, and effective of bilateral talks, engaging both sides in commercial policy determinations apparently unaffected by the United States trade embargo. In this case, it may have been the pragmatic, technical collaboration of a transnational elite network that bridged the great divide of U.S.-Cuba relations.

CONCLUSION: ALTERNATIVE PROSPECTS AND THEORECTICAL IMPLICATIONS

The prevalent view of Cuban-American students of the Cuban transition might be the one voiced by economist Antonio Villamil (1993), who argues that, whether through modest or radical change, Cuba will have to move toward a free-market or mixed economy and also toward democracy. Doing so would enable it to involve the United States, Latin America, Europe, and international financial institutions (the World Bank, the Interamerican Development Bank, and the International Monetary Fund in particular) in national reconstruction. Villamil's argument is that a liberal civic culture is inherently and necessarily prone to generate institutional diversity, autonomy, and capacity, and economic dynamism.

Pérez-Stable (1995) suggests that the overwhelming presence of Fidel Castro has prevented the effective institutionalization of even one-party politics. A measure of the weakness of the Communist Party of Cuba is its inability to "call and win [at least] a first round of elections," as did corresponding parties in countries of Eastern and Central Europe—which, however, could claim a modicum of autonomy in civil society. Pérez-Stable claims to detect the emergence of civil (or what she calls "second") society in Cuba, but not yet its institutional "articulation" or integration (p. 2). In sum, Cuba is lacking today, as much as it ever has under the Revolution, in the political and institutional preconditions for transition to a democratic society.

If there is a general lack of independent institutions in Cuba, there is also an absence of intermediary institutions capable of mediating citizenry relations with the state. Centeno (1995) contends that "the capacity for order will rest on the ability of the FAR [Revolutionary Armed Forces] to maintain some institutional coherence (p. 5)," since the Communist Party cannot be relied upon to maintain the "organizational infrastructure of the state (p. 6)," and since there is neither "organized and institutionalized politics" nor "the symbolic or institutional slack needed to manage the delicate balance of imposing neo-liberal policies while maintaining legitimacy and control (p. 7)." In short, for Centeno and other observers, it might be a Hobson's choice between institutions of state control and some unimaginable domestic crisis or intervention engendering a transition. That "the level of collectivization or socialization of economic activity was more extensive in Cuba than in Eastern Europe" represents an obstacle to a liberal transition, and the "divisions stemming from access to dollars or to nomenklatura privileges" may also represent a significant obstacle (p. 9).

The Cuban nationalist view, which Nelson Valdés (1995) may exemplify, is that the current transition will be worked out in unique Cuban terms on the is-

land, in basic continuity with the Revolution; Valdés believes that even the most spontaneous change, such as the aforementioned appearance of small, informal groups of scientific and academic researchers involved in international collaborative networks, is occurring within revolutionary bounds. The fits and starts of policy initiative and rectification characterizing recent liberalization policies have simply been manifestations of the conflicting imperatives of political reform and control. In Valdes' view, therefore, the cyclical nature of economic policymaking in Cuba is not cause for concern so much as a corollary of pluralism—of a plurality of intersecting and competing interests within the confines of a socialist civil society. The creation of mixed enterprises, joint ventures, and other hybrid forms of commerce, and the rise of managerial, entrepreneurial, and other social networks in the economy, is an indication of a potential for the development of capable institutions, both public and private, in a democratic direction.

What are the theoretical implications of this overview of Cuba's transition? It may be argued that neo-classical economic models are of little value in assessing new institutional forms such as own-account work and hybrid joint ventures. Unlike classical economics, network theory stresses sociocultural issues, like those found in the reorientation of entrepreneurship and management toward the market in Cuba. There, exchange and patronage networks once served to consolidate the institutions of the Revolution, mainly through the incorporation of critics (Linger, 1993). One might now look for so-called *venture-support* networks, mechanisms (common to socialist transitions) which surmount political and institutional barriers, engaging entrepreneurial "outsiders" with political insiders who offer resources and provide logistical support and protection (recall Kummels 1995).

What is suggested is a research agenda focused on institutional transitions toward the market and emerging proto-institutional networks in Cuba. Network brokers and innovators are interstitial actors poised between existing and emerging institutions, and between present and future sociopolitical and economic systems. Once again, the point at issue is what these realities and changes portend for Cuba's political transition. The operative assumption is that institutional change and development in the economy in a liberal direction will have corresponding political effects in Cuba.

REFERENCES

Alvarez, J. and Puerta, R. A. (1994). "State intervention in Cuban agriculture: Impact on organization and performance." *World Development, 22,* 1663-1675.

Andrej, R. (1996). "Access and mobilization—Dual character of social capital: Managerial networks and privatization in Eastern Europe." American Sociological Association Paper, Columbia University.

Betancourt, R. R. (1991). "The New Institutional Economics and the Study of the Cuban Economy," in *Cuba in Transition.* Miami: Florida International University.

Betancourt, R. R. (1992). "The Distribution Sector in a CPE: Cuba," in *Cuba in Transition—Volume 2.* Washington: Association for the Study of the Cuban Economy.

Brandwayn, S. (1993). "Cuba's economic and management policy response to the changing global environment." *Public Administration and Development, 13,* 361-375.

Castañeda, R. H. and Montalván, G. P. (1994). "Cuba 1990-1992: Political intransigence *versus* economic reform," in *Cuba in Transition—Volume 4.* Washington: Association for the Study of the Cuban Economy.

Centeno, M. A. (1995). "Domination, contract and trust in the Cuban transition." Draft study, 12 pages. Available: http://www.princeton.edu/~sociolog/papers/cuba/html.

de Vylder, S. (1991). "How progressive are progressive economic policies? A note on Latin America's 'Catch 22.'" *Economic and Industrial Democracy, 12,* 19-29.

Earp, F. (1996). "Transactions, circuits, and identity: Proposing a conceptual network." *Journal of Economic Issues 30:* 407-412.

Gilmore, T. N. and Krantz, J. (1991). "Innovation in the public sector: Dilemmas in the use of ad hoc processes." *Journal of Policy Analysis and Management, 10:* 455-68.

Hall, J. A. (1995). "After the vacuum: Post-Communism in the light of Tocqueville," in B. Crawford (Ed.), *Markets, States, and Democracy: The political economy of post-Communist transformation.* Boulder: Westview.

Kelley, B. (1994). "The informal sector and the macroeconomy: A computable general equilibrium approach for Peru." *World Development, 22,* 1393-1411.

Kummels, I. (1995). "La cotidianidad difícil: Consideraciones de una etnónologa sobre la crisis y la cultura popular," in B. Hoffman (Ed.), *Cuba: Apertura y Reforma Econónica—Perfil de un Debate* (pp. 131-143). Caracas: Nueva Sociedad.

Lamal, P. A. (1991). "Aspects of some contingencies and metacontingencies in the Soviet Union," in P. A. Lamal (Ed.), *Behavioral Analysis of Societies and Cultural Practices.* New York: Hemisphere Publishing.

Linger, E. (1993). "Networks and the institutionalization of the Cuban Revolution, 1960-1990." American Sociological Association paper, New School for Social Research.

Master, G. (1997). "Red reform." *The International Economy 11,* 56-60.

Mead, D. C. and Morrison, C. (1996). "The informal sector elephant." *World Development, 24,* 1611-1619.

Melvin, M. and Peiers, B. (1996). "Dollarization in developing countries: Rational remedy or domestic dilemma?" *Contemporary Economic Policy, 14,* 30-40.

Mesa-Lago, C. (1995). "Evaluación y perspectivas de la reforma económica cubana," in B. Hoffmann (Ed.), *Cuba: Apertura y Reforma Económica—Perfil de un debate* (pp. 59-89). Caracas: Nueva Sociedad.

Meurs, M. (1992). "Popular participation and central planning in Cuban socialism: The experience of agriculture in the 1980s." *World Development, 20,* 229-240.

Monreal, P. and Rúa del Llano, M. (1995). "Hacia una transición: Apertura y reforma de la economía (1990-1993)," in B. Hoffmann (Ed.), *Cuba: Apertura y Reforma Económica—Perfil de un debate* (pp. 147-166). Caracas: Nueva Sociedad.

Montenegro, C. E., and Soto, R. (1996). "How distorted is Cuba's trade? Evidence and predictions from a gravity model." *Journal of International Trade and Economic Development 5,* 45-70.

Morrison, C., Barnard, H., Lecompte, S., and Oudin, X. (1994). *Micro-enterprises and the Institutional Framework in Developing Countries.* Paris: Organization for Economic Cooperation and Development.

Nichols, J. S., and Torres, A. M. (1998). "Telecommunications in Cuba." Available: http://www.ctr. columbia.edu/vii/papers/cuba.html.

Pastor, M., Jr., and Zimbalist, A. (1995). "Waiting for change: Adjustment and reform in Cuba." *World Development, 23,* 705-20.

Pérez-López, J. F. (1995a). "Coveting Beijing, but imitating Moscow: Cuba's economic reforms in a comparative perspective," in *Cuba in Transition—Volume 5.* Washington: Association for the Study of the Cuban Economy.

Pérez-López, J. F. (1995b). *Cuba's Second Economy: From behind the scenes to center stage.* New Brunswick, N.J.: Transaction Publishers.

Pérez-Stable, M. (1998). "The invisible crisis: The exhaustion of politics in 1990s Cuba," in M. A. Centeno and M. Font (Eds.), *Toward a New Cuba?* Boulder: Lynne Rienner.

Ranis, G., and Stewart, F. (1994). "V-goods and the role of the urban informal sector in development." *Yale Economic Growth Center Discussion Paper 724.*

Rosset, P. M. (1997). "Alternative agriculture and crisis in Cuba." *IEEE Technology and Society Magazine, 16,* 19.

Thurston, C. W. (1996a). "Cuban logistics improve as capitalism evolves." *Distribution, 95,* (September) 28.

Thurston, C. W. (1996b). "FTZs: Gateways to Latin America." *Distribution, 95,* (December) 44-46.

Trindade, H., Noll, M. I. and Salazar, G. J. (1988). "Crisis y modernidad en Brasil." *Revista Mexicana de Sociología 50,* 3-10.

Valdés, N. P. (1995). "El estado y la transición real: Creando nuevos espacios en Cuba." Unpublished paper, Latin America Data Base, the University of New Mexico.

Villamil, A. (1993). "The impact of global economic, investment, and commerical trends on post-Castro Cuba." *North-South, 2,* 29-32.

Wickrama, K. A., and Mulford, C. (1996). "Political democracy, economic development, disarticulation, and social well-being in developing countries." *The Sociological Quarterly, 37,* 375-390.

Wolfsfeld, G., Opp, K. D., Dietz, H. A., and Green, J. D. (1994). *Social Science Quarterly, 75* 98-114.

APRECIACIÓN Y ANALISIS DE LOS ACIERTOS Y LOS MITOS DEL ESTUDIO DE LA CEPAL

Rolando Castañeda[1]

"...de un país en desgracia, pobre, solitario y "socialista" (p. 70)..."

"Socialismo o Muerte, valga la redundancia" (p. 20)

— Zoé Valdés, *La Hija del Embajador.*

El estudio de la CEPAL (en adelante ESCEPAL)[2] es el más amplio y completo estadísticamente sobre la economía cubana desde 1989; no obstante, acepta sin mayores salvedades las estadísticas de un país socialista, excepto que comenta que "adolecen de imprecisiones" (p. 8),[3] cuando se ha comprobado que las mismas han resultado poco confiables. Hoy está claramente establecido que la Unión Soviética y los países socialistas europeos sobreestimaron muchos datos por razones de prestigio y relaciones públicas.[4] Cuba no debe ser una excepción, especialmente cuando publica escasas series estadísticas, no tiene cifras confiables de inflación[5] y provee números engañosos sobre variables importantes como la inversión extranjera. También las series históricas sobre el producto han sido puestas en duda por investigadores especializados.[6]

ESCEPAL muestra la precaria y decadente situación de Cuba (ver Cuadro 1) y hace dramáticas advertencias a las autoridades cubanas. Sin embargo, tiene importantes sesgos y errores en cuanto a las causas, condicionantes y diagnósticos de los problemas existentes, que constituyen falsas premisas para las prescripciones, algunas inconsistencias de análisis, y omisiones cruciales. Además, el tratamiento de los principales temas es descriptivo a veces y analítico en otras ocasiones. Por lo tanto, no es de extrañar que llegue a apreciaciones y recomendaciones erróneas sobre algunos problemas fundamentales de la economía y sus perspectivas futuras.

El propósito de estos comentarios es analizar algunos temas macroeconómicos centrales cubiertos por ESCEPAL. La sección que sigue presenta observaciones de tipo general sobre las falencias básicas de ESCEPAL referentes a los mencionados sesgos, errores,

---

1. El autor agradece los comentarios de Francisco León. Las opiniones aquí expresadas son de su exclusiva responsabilidad y no reflejan sus vínculos institucionales. Se dedica este ensayo a Félix Antonio Bonné Carcassés, René Gómez Manzano, Vladimiro Roca Antúnez y Marta Beatriz Roque Cabello, quienes están encarcelados arbitrariamente y sin ser sometidos a un debido proceso legal desde junio de 1997 por el "delito de opinión."

2. Comisión Económica para América Latina y el Caribe, *La economía cubana: Reformas estructurales y desempeño en los noventa.* México: Fondo de Cultura Económica, 1997.

3. Todas las citas y referencias a cuadros son de ESCEPAL, excepto el Cuadro 1 que es de estos comentarios, pero se basa en ESCEPAL.

4. Ver por ejemplo, Easterley y Fischer (1994).

5. Por ejemplo, el deflactor implícito del PIB muestra cifras negativas para 1991, año en que la tasa de cambio de mercado negro pasó de CU$7 a CU$20 (ver Cuadro 1).

6. Ver Mesa-Lago y Pérez-López (1985).

omisiones e inconsistencias de sus apreciaciones, interpretaciones y análisis. La próxima hace un análisis crítico sobre algunos eventos históricos claves a que el estudio hace referencia y que están detrás de la precaria situación por la que atraviesa la economía cubana. La tercera sección discute el tratamiento del sector externo. Las siguientes secciones comentan sobre los recientes procesos de estabilización, reformas económicas y otros temas vinculados al desempeño y resultados macroeconómicos tratados en ESCEPAL, respectivamente. La última sección presenta conclusiones diferentes que induzcan a opciones distintas y a facilitar decisiones más apropiadas y responsables sobre el desarrollo del país que las recomendadas o sugeridas por ESCEPAL.

LAS FALENCIAS BÁSICAS DEL ESTUDIO

ESCEPAL señala fehacientemente algunos de los serios problemas existentes, en especial los de empobrecimiento en forma de remuneraciones reales, nivel de empleo y su calidad, y el deterioro de los servicios sociales y de la seguridad social. Cuba tiene malos índices de inversión, ahorro nacional, exportaciones, deuda externa, estabilidad económica, posibilidades de crecimiento y de deterioro de sus logros sociales (ver Cuadro 1), así como una institucionalidad insostenible en el largo plazo. ESCEPAL destaca la ausencia de programas integrados para superar dicha situación y advierte que "el proceso de reformas no podría detenerse sin consecuencias al parecer graves" (p. 20) y que "reprimir...la ¨segunda economía¨... podría provocar el surgimiento de estallidos sociales, expresados en mercados negros y corrupción generalizada" (p. 20). No obstante, mantiene una visión apologética de las deficientes reformas recientes en los capítulos 1 y 2 sobre temas generales, que está en contraposición con lo que sostiene posteriormente en mayor detalle en los capítulos 3 y 4 sobre temas sectoriales específicos, así como con la posición reciente de la CEPAL sobre el desarrollo económico de la región (CEPAL, 1992, Ramos, 1997 y Ocampo, 1998).

ESCEPAL tiene algunas consideraciones económicas que más que heterodoxas son erróneas. A continuación se destacan cuatro:

- Señala que la profundidad de la crisis fuerza segmentaciones (financieras, cambiarias, laborales,

etc.) en la economía (p. 14). Es lo contrario, son las segmentaciones impuestas por los erróneos diseños de políticas y gestiones públicas, los que crean y agudizan la crisis sistémica, generalizada, prolongada y de mayor magnitud a la que indica ESCEPAL, y que impiden superarla al crear distorsiones y efectos negativos en toda la economía.

- Indica que las **políticas cambiarias empleadas de marcada dualidad e ingeniería de controles y asignaciones de divisas** son "políticas modernizadoras adaptativas" (p. 14). Es lo contrario, estas políticas han agudizado los problemas preexistentes a la crisis en vez de superarlos, al desalentar la producción de los bienes transables en el contexto de una severa escasez de divisas y un entorno internacional de creciente competencia.

- Presenta **diagnósticos (causas y condicionantes) de los problemas con un énfasis desproporcionado en el origen externo de los mismos**, pero ignora que muchos se generaron internamente por el diseño de malas políticas e instituciones, que se han arrastrado año tras año y que en su conjunto han creado nefastos efectos acumulativos. Específicamente, ESCEPAL desconoce que la severidad conque la crisis ha afectado a Cuba, en forma de costos adicionales, ha dependido en gran medida del incompetente y postergado ajuste que las autoridades adoptaron frente a ésta (demora e insuficiente intensidad de las medidas tomadas).

- El análisis sobre **los efectos distributivos del ajuste** es incorrecto, tanto estática como dinámicamente, ya que ignora que los frutos del mismo se han concentrado y se están consolidando en sectores reducidos de la población y que no existen tendencias para mejorar la igualdad de oportunidades y opciones a largo plazo. Las políticas aplicadas han creado grandes diferencias a través de las remuneraciones segmentadas que se traducen en marcadas desigualdades de ingreso, "Más de un millón de trabajadores reciben estímulos pecuniarios, conforme a distintos regímenes" (p. 19) ESCEPAL no analiza la exclusión que se de-

Cuadro 1. Algunos Indicadores Seleccionados de ESCEPAL sobre la Economía Cubana, 1989-1996

Indicadores	1989	1990	1991	1992	1993	1994	1995	1996
1. Deflactor implícito del PIB a/	1.8	3.4	-7.1	3.6	17.3	23.1	12.0	-0.8
2. Importaciones de bienes y servicios como % del PIB b/	41.4	38.4	26.8	16,7	14,3	11,7	13.5	17.7
3. Importaciones de bienes de capital como % de las importaciones totales g/	22.6	26.5	21.7	8.0	3.8	3.2	6.0	nd
4. Exportaciones de bienes y servicios como % del PIB b/	28.8	28.5	20.3	15.4	12.0	10.7	11.4	13.4
5. Déficit de cuenta corriente como % del PIB (Partidas 2-4, no incluye transferencias)	12.6	9.9	6.5	1.3	2.3	1.0	2.1	4.3
6. Producción de azúcar, millones toneladas j/	7.6	8.4	7.2	7.2	4.2	4.0	4.3	3.3
7. Deuda bruta como % del PIB a/	29.3	32.6	37.0	39.1	52.9	44.2	44.5	49.6
8. Inversión bruta interna como % del PIB b/	24.3	23.3	13.0	6.0	5.8	5.0	6.4	7.5
9. Ahorro nacional bruto como % del PIB c/	9.9	11.1	4.7	3.4	3.5	3.9	4.2	5.5
10. Ahorro nacional bruto como % inversión interna bruta (Partidas 9/8)	40.7	47.6	36.2	56.7	60.3	78.0	65.6	73.3
11. Déficit fiscal como % del PIB d/	6.7	9.4	21.4	29.7	30.4	7.9	3.2	2.3
12. Liquidez monetaria como % del PIB e/	20.0	23.9	38.0	51.0	66.5	48.4	39.2	37.8
13. Tasa de desempleo equivalente i/	7.9	10.8	19.2	25.6	35.2	33.5	31.5	27.3
14. Salario medio mensual (1990=100) a/	103.8	100.0	96.4	86.2	77.2	59.5	56.1	58.6
15. Tipo de cambio extraoficial a fin de año f/	5	7	20	45	100	60	25	19
16. Gasto social primario, millones de pesos de 1981 h/	3295	3174	3186	2926	2588	2088	1974	2168
17. Gasto social primario como % del PIB h/	15.7	15.6	17.3	17.6	18.1	14.5	13.4	13.6
18. Gasto en educación, millones de pesos de 1981 h/	1664	1578	1578	1445	1195	936	851	903
19. Gasto en educación como % del PIB h/	7.9	7.8	8.6	8.7	8.3	6.5	5.8	5.7
20. Gasto en salud, millones de pesos de 1981 h/	912	914	970	950	929	744	694	764
21. Gasto en salud como % del PIB h/	4.3	4.5	5.3	5.7	6.5	5.2	4.7	4.8

Fuente: ESCEPAL. a/ Cuadro A.1, b/ Cuadro A.3, c/ Cuadro A.4, d/ Cuadro a.8, e/ Cuadro A.12, f/ Cuadro III.12, g/ Cuadro A.19, h/ Cuadro A.60, i/ Cuadro III.2 y j/ Cuadro IV.15 y estimados de otras fuentes para 1996 y 1997.

riva de estas políticas, ni si las oportunidades y opciones para los ciudadanos están mejorando o empeorando a través del tiempo, ni si todo ello es compatible o contradictorio con el sostenimiento de un alto ritmo de crecimiento, que permita mejorar las remuneraciones de todos los trabajadores y resolver los problemas urgentes de la pobreza. Se volverá sobre estos cuatro temas más adelante.

ESCEPAL tiene omisiones cruciales en lo referente a los derechos humanos básicos, libertades económicas fundamentales, la sana gobernabilidad, la transparencia de la gestión y políticas públicas, la falta de incentivos privados positivos, y los conflictos de intereses privados y públicos que afectan muy negativamente la calidad de vida del cubano. Cuba es uno de los pocos países a nivel mundial que no ha firmado ni ratificado los Pactos Internacionales de Derechos Civiles y Políticos (1966) y de Derechos Económicos, Sociales y Culturales (1966), los cuales reciben tanta atención en los estudios sobre el Desarrollo Humano del

Programa para el Desarrollo de las Naciones Unidas (PNUD, 1998). También ESCEPAL omite el trascendental tema ambiental y la creciente emigración.

ESCEPAL tiene marcadas inconsistencias internas y evidentes contradicciones respecto a la situación existente y los resultados alcanzados. El estudio destaca varias veces que Cuba ha logrado: (1) estabilizar su economía, pero también indica que el excedente monetario le impide hacer algunos ajustes en la economía y (2) proveer servicios sociales por arriba del que disfrutan economías de similar y aún mayor nivel de ingreso, pero a la vez señala que estos niveles son insostenibles. Adicionalmente, hay abundantes inconsistencias respecto a cómo resolver los problemas existentes. Por ejemplo considera "limitar los procesos de liberalización de la 'segunda economía' por sus efectos segmentadores en la sociedad o en la dispersión del poder político" (p. 22), "no se dispone en Cuba de muchos márgenes de maniobra, ni se pueden tomar riesgos mayores" (p. 23), pero "lo anterior no niega la necesidad de cancelar de manera progresiva distorsiones económicas flagrantes" (p. 25), "legalizar y liberalizar la formación de pequeñas empresas familiares" (p. 381) y "alentar ese clima libertario de reconstrucción de valores sería tarea insoslayable del gobierno" (p. 382).

Las prescripciones de ESCEPAL son incompletas, inadecuadas e inconsistentes porque mientras señala que hay realizar cambios fundamentales sólo apoya cambios parciales e insuficientes. El énfasis de ESCEPAL es en mantener el sistema socialista y la distribución del ingreso más que en superar la crisis económica fundamental y sistémica. Tampoco ESCEPAL hace el caso por la imperiosa necesidad de una estrategia económico y social que simultáneamente aborde y asegure un crecimiento estable de la economía, con creación de empleo de calidad, mejoras en la productividad y los salarios reales, políticas públicas que permitan una mejor calidad de vida en sentido pleno, así como oportunidades y opciones a toda la población. Ya en 1992, la CEPAL planteaba la necesidad de un enfoque integrado que privilegiara las políticas conducentes tanto al crecimiento como a la equidad social (CEPAL, 1992).

Los análisis y las soluciones de ESCEPAL son parte esencial de los problemas, atacan los efectos, pero no sus verdaderas causas y condicionantes. Para enfrentar el futuro hay que saber en dónde se está, cómo y por qué se llegó a esta situación. Adicionalmente, se requiere creatividad, audacia y tener una visión de un desarrollo integral y sustentable del país. El cubano requiere un nivel de bienestar y calidad de vida mejores y ESCEPAL contribuye poco al respecto.

LA RESEÑA HISTÓRICA-INSTITUCIONAL: UNA VISIÓN SESGADA DE LA HISTORIA ECONÓMICA DE CUBA EN LA SEGUNDA MITAD DEL SIGLO XX

La apreciación y análisis de esta sección se basa en algunos temas cubiertos en el Capítulo 2 de ESCEPAL que difieren mucho del propósito de "situar en un contexto apropiado la crisis desencadenada en 1989 y las estrategias de acomodo y ajuste implantadas" (p. 7), lo cual es muy pertinente.

Los Problemas Estructurales Principales que Enfrentaba la Economía en los Años 50

ESCEPAL señala que, a comienzos del período socialista (1960), Cuba presentaba rezagos tecnológicos e insuficiente desarrollo industrial, bajo dinamismo de la producción y la inversión, marcada concentración de la distribución del ingreso (p. 28). Sin embargo, no señala igualmente que el período socialista ha agudizado la mayoría de los problemas estructurales mencionados y que si bien mejoró la distribución del ingreso, lo hizo sobre una base económica artificial e insostenible que se está deteriorando con rapidez, como el propio estudio establece en los Capítulos 3, Sección E y 4, Sección D.

Un análisis detallado de la situación económica general de Cuba muestra que el país estaba en una mejor situación para enfrentar el crecimiento económico, orientado al exterior, con equidad social en la década de los 50 de lo que está actualmente, tanto en términos absolutos como en términos relativos a los otros países de la región.

Según el Informe de Desarrollo Humano de 1998 (PNUD, 1998), Cuba tenía un índice de desarrollo humano de 0.729 en 1995, y ocupaba el lugar 85 en el mundo entre los 174 países considerados. En la región este índice es inferior a los de Barbados (.909), Chile, Bahamas, Costa Rica, Argentina, Uruguay, Trinidad y Tobago, Panamá, Venezuela, México, Colombia, Brasil, Belice, Ecuador y Jamaica (.735). Cuba tiene un índice mayor al que le correspondería considerando sólo su producto real per capita, medido por la paridad de poder adquisitivo (US$3,100), el cual también es inferior a los de Perú (US$3,940), República Dominicana, Paraguay, Guyana (US$3,205) y Guatemala. Cuba sólo tiene mayor nivel de producto real per capita en la región que El Salvador, Bolivia, Honduras, Nicaragua y Haití (PNUD, 1998, p. 21 y 138).

Las Deficiencias del Sistema de Dirección y Planificación de la Economía

El análisis de ESCEPAL del período 1975-1985 (pp. 37-38), conocido como Sistema de Dirección y Planificación de la Economía (SDPE), período inmediatamente anterior al proceso de contrarreforma iniciado en 1986, es simplista. Sólo destaca varias de las dificultades de funcionamiento y las deficiencias de desempeño del SDPE (actitud paternalista hacia las entidades productivas, excesivo tutelaje corporativo, presupuestos blandos, poca relación entre incentivos materiales y resultados, inventarios excesivos, etc.), que son intrínsecas al sistema del socialismo real y que ameritaban, al menos, una mayor utilización de los mecanismos de mercado y de los incentivos económicos para enfrentarlas, tal como hicieron China y Vietnam. En cambio, no señala los elevados costos, ni el descuido de los equilibrios macroeconómicos (fiscales, monetarios y del sector externo) del radical proceso de contrareforma de 1986-1993, que eliminó los escasos mecanismos de mercado y los incentivos materiales existentes hasta 1986. Por lo contrario, menciona los "resultados en general favorables a los logros en materia social" (p. 360) del nefasto proceso de contrareforma, aunque señala que "la rigideces de la planificación y la excesiva centralización en la distribución de los recursos dañaron la gestión y la eficiencia de las empresas" (p. 38).

Fue paradójicamente el período 1975-1985, el de mayor prosperidad económica en la época socialista (ver gráfica III-1, p. 60), ya que disminuyó el desempleo, aumentó el nivel de vida y de bienestar, mejoraron los servicios sociales, y se caracterizó por reformas parciales e insuficientes muy similares, pero en algunas áreas más amplias y profundas, a las recientes, que ESCEPAL considera transformaciones estructurales de envergadura, por ejemplo el autofinanciamiento y la descentralización de las empresas. Además, la segunda parte del SDPE (1981-1985), "puso acento en la productividad y la eficiencia" (p. 30). En los años 80 hasta 1986 Cuba era un país socialista que experimentaba con decisión en los procesos de liberalización económica.

Cabe preguntarse si Cuba hubiese sufrido el estancamiento del período 1986-1989, la severidad de la crisis de 1990-1993 y los problemas posteriores de no haber eliminado el SDPE al comenzar con el Proceso de Rectificación de Errores y Tendencias Negativas en 1986. Este fue el penúltimo, pero no el primero, de reversión de procesos de liberalización económica y de reafirmación del socialismo real. Al respecto, el propio ESCEPAL indica que "el producto interno bruto registró magros crecimientos a finales de los años ochenta, retrocediendo su relación por habitante (1989) a las cifras de cinco años atrás" (p. 41).

La Desaparición de la URSS y el Campo Socialista

El énfasis de ESCEPAL en el capítulo 2 es que Cuba se ha visto muy afectada por "la pérdida en los términos de intercambio" y del comercio con la desaparecida URSS y los antiguos países de Europa oriental. Sin embargo, ESCEPAL minimiza que los precios subsidiados para el azúcar, el níquel y petróleo, así como que el comercio preferencial no tenían fundamentos económicos y ocultaban la marcada debilidad de la capacidad competitiva y el retraso tecnológico de la economía. O sea, no fueron algo coyuntural, sino que representaban elementos estructurales; por ello, es que Cuba enfrenta un tremendo desafío para enfrentarse al dinámico mundo globalizado y competitivo de finales del milenio. La medición y el análisis de los términos de intercambio de Cuba debería ser realizado a precios mundiales y no a los precios subsidiados de la URSS.

Es evidente que la desaparición de la URSS y del campo socialista han sido cruciales en explicar parte de los problemas que ha sufrido la economía cubana a partir de 1991. Sin embargo, un análisis de las cifras muestra que dichas situaciones simplemente desnudaron las falencias que venía exhibiendo la economía, exceso de gastos respecto al producto o, lo que es lo mismo, crecientes déficits en cuenta corriente (ver Cuadro 1), que reflejaban la enfermedad holandesa resultado de las elevadas transferencias de la URSS y eran insostenibles. Las autoridades consideraron que se podía continuar sin requerir de un ajuste en el gasto o en la tasa de cambio real, pero los problemas que llegaron de la URSS aceleraron un destape que más temprano que tarde debería llegar y se tradujeron en costos significativos. Si bien dicho ajuste era inevitable, aún sin la desaparición de la URSS, es indudable que ésta aceleró el punto de quiebre. Con políticas más lúcidas que las empleadas, el aterrizaje pudo haber sido más suave y la salida de la crisis con pie más firme. Así no todos los costos de la crisis derivada del "shock" eran inevitables; hubo costos adicionales determinados por el recesivo ajuste utilizado y costos debidos a la tardanza de la puesta en marcha del ajuste ("costos de oportunidad del ajuste tardío," que hicieron la situación inicial más difícil y compleja por sus efectos acumulados en términos de contraer la producción, alto desempleo y reducción en los salarios reales). Ambos tipos de costos, aunque evidentes, no son mencionados en ninguno de los dos capítulos generales.

ESCEPAL considera semejante la caída de la producción de los países socialistas europeos y de Cuba en la década de los 90, pero ambas son diferentes, aunque tengan algunos condicionantes similares referentes al colapso del comercio artificial del Consejo de Ayuda Mutua Económica (CAME). En los primeros se han producido marcados cambios estructurales en la producción, eliminando bienes y servicios no rentables (reestructuración y mejoramiento de la capacidad productiva) y están en vías de superar problemas de transformación vinculados con la sana gobernabilidad e institucionalidad de sus economías que tienen que ver con el desarrollo a largo plazo y con aspectos de microeconomía y normativos, que aún no se han comenzado a realizar en Cuba (restructuración y mejoramiento institucional y normativo). Además, en esos países hay una producción de bienes y servicios de pequeñas y medianas empresas que aún no se registra adecuadamente en la contabilidad nacional, mucho mayor que en Cuba donde estas empresas son clandestinas.

El Período Especial y las Reformas desde 1989

Como se indicó, ESCEPAL no comenta la tardanza y limitación del proceso de ajuste en 1989-1993, que profundizó y amplió los efectos negativos de la crisis y el rechazo por las autoridades de las propuestas aperturistas sometidas por las bases en ocasión del IV Congreso del partido comunista de Cuba de octubre de 1991, que anticiparon las reformas posteriores. En contraste, ESCEPAL destaca que Cuba superó los problemas de estabilización e inició el ajuste estructural "en condiciones singularmente desfavorables" (p. 13). El manejo macroeconómico inicial dificultó el ajuste y las medidas adoptadas después han sido de insuficiente intensidad. Los equilibrios logrados son frágiles e insostenibles, ya que se basan en la inflación reprimida y la excesiva liquidez; la dualidad y el marcado diferencial cambiario; un déficit en cuenta co-

rriente del orden del 4.3%, sin mayor financiamiento externo de largo plazo; y niveles de inversión bruta y ahorro nacional de un dígito. También, las reformas estructurales adoptadas son tímidas e incompletas para lograr la reinserción internacional, un crecimiento alto y sostenido, y mantener los logros sociales, ya que el crecimiento es un requerimiento esencial para el desarrollo social (CEPAL, 1992 y ESCEPAL, p. 381) y Cuba tiene en la actualidad inéditos bajos niveles de ahorro, inversión y de comercio internacional. Cuba perdió la oportunidad de utilizar el dinamismo de la economía mundial en los 90 para impulsar un proceso de reformas estructurales.

El problema de Cuba es principalmente de cantidad y calidad de oferta exportadora, producir más y más eficiente, lo cual no se ha enfrentado aún en forma adecuada e integral. Algunos cambios realizados, tal como señala ESCEPAL, son resultados forzados por las nuevas circunstancias (desmonopolización del comercio exterior, promoción de la inversión extranjera y el establecimiento de las cooperativas agrícolas) más que por el convencimiento de las autoridades, todavía ancladas al pasado y a la reafirmación socialista, lo que explica la limitación, incoherencia y cautela en la aplicación de reformas. Aún no se han adoptado las políticas económicas requeridas: privatización de actividades para pequeñas y medianas empresas nacionales, mayor utilización de los mecanismos de mercado y del sistema de libre determinación de precios, y lograr y consolidar los equilibrios macroeconómicos, que contribuyan a las perspectivas de crecimiento económico de mediano plazo y a compensar los cambios adversos recientes en la economía mundial (1997-1998).

Perspectivas: La Contradicción Esencial

ESCEPAL es inconsistente en cuanto a las perspectivas de la economía. Por una parte, considera que, debido a que los problemas existentes son mayores, Cuba tiene que adoptar reformas fundamentales para insertarse adecuadamente en la economía internacional, lograr una tasa de crecimiento alta y sostenida, conservar sus avances sociales y hacer viable una seguridad social digna. Por otra parte, no reconoce apropiadamente la amplitud y profundidad de esos problemas ni cómo se desarrollaron; confunde los objetivos prioritarios del país en la situación actual al poner un tenaz énfasis en mantener el sistema socialista y la distribución del ingreso existente y no en la modernización institucional y de gestión, ni en el crecimiento alto y sostenido para la superación de la pobreza generalizada. Cuba no aprovechó la expansión del comercio mundial en los 90 y no está preparada para enfrentar los efectos de la crisis asiática y rusa. Cuba está prácticamente excluida del proceso de modernización de finales del milenio. En el mejor de los escenarios las perspectivas son muy difíciles mientras mantenga el socialismo real sin ningún tipo de renovación.

EL SECTOR EXTERNO

La Política Cambiaria y la Crisis del Sector Externo

En la sección inicial del capítulo 3 ESCEPAL señala la elevada magnitud de los subsidios y transferencias externas estimados en 28% del PIB (p. 63) y que la inversión nacional se financiaba en un 69% con ahorro externo (recuadro p. 68), lo que es sinónimo de déficit en cuenta corriente y de falta de competitividad externa. De hecho, Cuba ha experimentado un déficit permanente y creciente en el sector externo en el período socialista (p. 31 y 33) y tiene un bajo índice de apertura externa (exportaciones en relación al PIB, ver Cuadro 1). Dada esta debilidad y vulnerabilidad estructural, Cuba sufrió un fuerte "shock" externo por la abrupta eliminación de las transferencias y de los mercados protegidos de la URSS y Europa del este y necesita "perfeccionar su autonomía productiva, recobrando la capacidad de acrecentar exportaciones" (p. 33). Las exportaciones de bienes y servicios en 1996 sólo eran el 56.4% de las de 1989, mientras que las importaciones de bienes y servicios en 1996 sólo eran el 51.8% de las de 1989 (Cuadro A.3).

El diagnóstico de esta sección de ESCEPAL es uno de los que presenta un tratamiento más realista en cuanto a la visión general de la crisis y sus condicionantes en un sector fundamental. Sin embargo, es incompleto, debido a que no trata en detalle algunos temas estratégicos—por ejemplo el financiamiento externo y las remesas del exterior—que pudieran contribuir con celeridad y en forma decisiva a superar

la crisis y echa la responsabilidad del déficit creciente, que es insostenible, al embargo (p. 34). Cuba es un país pobre y altamente endeudado que podría beneficiarse de las iniciativas internacionales para condonarle la mayoría de su deuda externa y podría utilizar mucho mejor las remesas externas.

Cuba continúa especializada en productos tradicionales (azúcar, tabaco, níquel y turismo) con instalaciones "obsoletas y sus estándares de calidad no corresponden a las exigencias de los mercados actuales" (p. 36). Las "exigencias de eficiencia demandan alta flexibilidad y capacidad de adaptación" (p. 36) al mundo de la competencia e innovación tecnológica. Los enclaves de las actividades tradicionales orientadas al exterior son utilizados para mantener un socialismo decadente e ineficiente en el resto de la economía. Esto es en realidad lo que determina fuertes segmentaciones en la economía (mercados cambiario, laboral, real) con sus consecuentes distorsiones en el uso y asignación de recursos y en las incertidumbres de cómo se van a corregir. En el Capítulo 3, p. 64, ESCEPAL indica que Cuba "tiene que salir del patrón neotradicional de inserción en el comercio mundial", pero el gobierno está anquilosado y le falta voluntad para actuar en consonancia con la gravedad de los problemas económicos, sociales y previsionales. Cuba con un régimen de comercio muy distorsionado y mercados no competitivos, tiene mucho que ganar a través del tiempo con la liberación del comercio y la reducción de prácticas no competitivas. Estas ganancias van mucho más allá de las ventajas tradicionales de la especialización que permite el comercio internacional, incluyen también ganancias de eficiencia a través del acceso a mejores insumos y la presión para innovar que se deriva de la competencia.

Las erróneas políticas empleadas de una marcada dualidad cambiaria (tasa de cambio oficial CU$1=US$1 y tasa de cambio de mercado CU$22=US$1 en 1996, ver Cuadro 1), así como de ingeniería social con controles y asignaciones de divisas, han agudizado los problemas preexistentes a la crisis en vez de superarlos, ya que no apoyan la apertura económica ni la inserción internacional, pues no constituyen un marco propicio para estimular las exportaciones. ESCEPAL defiende dichas políticas a corto plazo por razones distributivas "se intenta distribuir las cargas de la crisis y sostener las redes de protección social" (p. 51); no obstante, reconoce que es necesario una política cambiaria más flexible para estimular los bienes transables, así como que la paridad oficial antes de 1989 guardaba "poca relación con la competitividad del aparato productivo" (p. 35).

De hecho el peso oficial ha estado atado al valor internacional del dólar y como el dólar ha subido fuertemente respecto de casi todas las monedas en el período post Unión Soviética, y especialmente después de comenzada la llamada crisis asiática en julio de 1997, el peso oficial lo ha hecho junto con él. Esto ha sido una decisión errada de política económica y los hechos posteriores lo están demostrando con altas tasas de desempleo y contracción económica que están complicando innecesariamente los efectos de la crisis y han hecho la economía más vulnerable a la creciente volatilidad externa. Un tipo de cambio real mayor y unificado hubiera permitido ajustar la competitividad.

Un país no puede tener la expansión monetaria que Cuba experimentó en 1989-1993 con un índice de liquidez monetaria que aumentó del 20% en 1989 al 65% en 1993 (ver Cuadro 1) y mantener fija su tasa de cambio. Cuba está condenada a un círculo pernicioso. Ante una política de cambio fijo, es sabido que la variable más importante de ajuste pasa a ser el gasto público. La única forma de resolver los problemas planteados sería reducir el gasto fiscal en una magnitud de tal importancia que generara respuestas y expectativas de que ya no sería necesario producir una devaluación para ajustar la economía y recuperar la competitividad externa y la estabilidad en el futuro. A la larga tasas de desempleo elevadas son tan insostenibles como la devaluación; son dos caras de la misma moneda a mediano plazo. Una política de tasa de cambio más realista y flexible, como la que utiliza la República Dominicana actualmente, lograría el doble propósito de contraer la demanda agregada y de estimular la oferta agregada, alentando la reestructuración y mejoramiento de la capacidad productiva y la corrección de la eficiencia y competitividad internacional, pospuestas por tanto tiempo.

El Uso de las Remesas: Parte de los Costos Innecesarios del Ajuste a la Crisis

Como se señaló antes, el ajuste a la crisis ha sido innecesariamente recesivo y severo debido a que las autoridades no han permitido un uso más amplio de los recursos disponibles, entre ellos las remesas. Las remesas por su magnitud (unos US$800 millones anuales recientemente) han facilitado enfrentar la crisis. No obstante, la ayuda familiar recibida sólo ha tenido efectos temporales y de corto plazo, que son insostenibles, debido a las políticas vigentes. Estas políticas han impedido que los que reciben las remesas puedan emplearlas para hacer inversiones y desarrollar actividades económicas permanentes para superar la precaria situación existente y posiblemente han desalentado remesas de muchos expatriados que estarían dispuestos a invertir en Cuba para sus familiares o para ellos mismos en áreas como viviendas y pequeñas y medianas empresas.

Los Efectos del Embargo Norteamericano

ESCEPAL menciona posibles efectos negativos del embargo varias veces en el estudio, pero sólo cita una fuente cubana para medir dichos efectos sin especificar en qué consisten ni cómo llegó al elevado estimado (recuadro p. 64). En este tema ESCEPAL no ha sido riguroso en la exactitud de los hechos ni en la independencia y confiabilidad de la fuente, así perdió una gran oportunidad de analizar independientemente el tema y señalar por qué la mayoría de los países de la región consideran que el embargo no es la forma de producir los cambios deseados en Cuba. Más aún, ESCEPAL señala que para superar la crítica situación del país hay que levantar el embargo "la velocidad e incluso la dirección de algunos cambios están relacionadas con la posibilidad de relajar las condiciones externas que mantienen al país al margen de los mercados financieros y de muchas corrientes de comercio" (p. 43). Esto es sencillamente incorrecto. Es posible superar la situación del país aún con el embargo, tal cual lo hizo Vietnam a principios de los 90, con la implementación de políticas adecuadas.

Durante la reciente Cumbre Hemisférica de Santiago de abril de 1998, como generalmente sucede en los foros regionales, se debatió el tema de la exclusión de Cuba de esas reuniones y que su aislamiento y embargo comercial no son propicios para lograr los cambios en el sistema político y económico del país que la comunidad internacional apoya. Este debate se hace generalmente por razones de principios del derecho internacional y hay pocas referencias a los severos daños que causan las políticas económicas vigentes que agudizan y magnifican los efectos del embargo externo, o sea, lo que los opositores al régimen llaman el embargo interno. O lo que el Papa Juan Pablo II calificó como que "Cuba se abra al mundo."

Los cambios sistémicos, tipo transformaciones, que se produjeron en Europa oriental y la antigua Unión Soviética, y los cambios tipo transición que se están realizando en Vietnam y China fueron por el convencimiento de los gobiernos de estos países de cómo enfrentar mejor el tercer milenio y no por respuesta a las presiones internacionales. En tanto, actualmente existe en Cuba una inercia perversa de achacar todos los problemas económicos del país al "bloqueo" y a las presiones externas y ninguno a un sistema, el socialismo real, que ha sido progresiva y casi totalmente descartado a nivel internacional por su marcada ineficiencia para permitir a los países enfrentarse al reto de la modernización y la competitiva globalización.

EL PROCESO DE AJUSTE Y LA ESTABILIZACIÓN

Síntesis de los Temas Macroeconómicos Tratados

La síntesis del Capítulo 3 destaca que, partiendo de rigideces estructurales, entre 1993 y 1996, el déficit fiscal y la liquidez monetaria se redujeron, las exportaciones y las importaciones se recuperaron y el peso "libre" o de "mercado negro" se apreció (ver Cuadro 1). Sin embargo, no destaca igualmente que persisten problemas macroeconómicos de bajos niveles de inversión y ahorro nacional, alto endeudamiento externo, bajo nivel de reservas internacionales y, que en consecuencia, por problemas de liquidez y solvencia internacional hay elevados "spreads" por los préstamos externos de corto plazo con sus implicaciones fiscales y de balanza de pagos, y que se está a merced de los inversionistas y financistas internacionales. Tampoco en esta parte del estudio señala que hay problemas significativos de desempleo y subempleo, caídas del nivel de salarios reales y de los gastos reales en servicios sociales, y que los servicios sociales y la

seguridad social ofrecidos exceden la capacidad de la economía.

El análisis de ESCEPAL no señala que el ajuste interno requerido no ha tenido la intensidad necesaria para atender los problemas existentes y comenzar una recuperación sustentable, ni que ha sido innecesariamente tardío y recesivo, lo que tiene en sí el germen de la generación de la pobreza, en la medida que la economía va quedando progresivamente rezagada en el plano internacional. Más bien indica lo contrario, que fue la "única vía accesible" (p. 12).

Esta visión del presente y el simplismo del análisis subyacente ("el costo de la política de estabilización resultó relativamente bajo y su distribución más equitativa en comparación con otras economías latinoamericanas," p. 66) es contradictoria, ya que pone énfasis en algunos resultados parciales de corto plazo, que son frágiles e insostenibles, y no en las reformas estructurales de mediano y largo plazo que están pendientes y que hay que emprender decididamente. El propio ESCEPAL reconoce que hay que tener mayor coherencia entre los ajustes interno y externo. Adicionalmente, como destaca Ocampo (1998), muchos países latinoamericanos han realizado considerables reformas estructurales que han mejorado significativamente sus condiciones económicas fundamentales—han aumentado la tasa de crecimiento del producto, de la inversión, de las exportaciones y del gasto social—y han puesto a estos países en mejores condiciones que Cuba para lograr el crecimiento económico con equidad en el tercer milenio.

El Proceso de Estabilización

"... pienso en la gente de allá, en la libreta, en las colas, en el pan de boniato, en las desgracias diarias..." (p. 195)

"...la corrupción no llegaba al grado de la que existe en la actualidad..." (p. 139)

— Zoé Valdés, *Café Nostalgia*

ESCEPAL considera incorrectamente que el proceso de estabilización ha sido superado ("ha sido en gran medida exitoso," p. 12; "Resuelta la fase estabilizadora del 'período especial,'" p. 21; y "se ataca a fondo el problema de la inflación y de los desajustes comerciales externos," p. 43); sin embargo, también anota que no se puede "considerar que dicho proceso se hubiese finiquitado por completo" (p. 12), así como que los precios garantizados por la libreta de abastecimiento y las colas se utilizan "con todos sus inconvenientes de mediano y largo plazo en la asignación de recursos y en la eficiencia" (p. 133). En Cuba hay inflación reprimida, escaseces y robos a las empresas que menciona en otras secciones, por ejemplo "hay, en consecuencia, inflación reprimida que se manifiesta en validar el racionamiento y en las colas de consumidores" (p. 195). La cobertura de ESCEPAL del tema del excedente monetario y el no cubierto de la marcada dualidad cambiaria muestran la fragilidad e insostenibilidad de la estabilización, que aún no se ha resuelto, es crucial y constituye un problema serio. Por ejemplo el estudio indica que la extensiva liquidez monetaria ha impedido implantar una corrección general de salarios.

Por ello si Cuba ha logrado una situación de equilibrio, ésta es frágil e insostenible, ya que pretende atacar parcialmente el problema por el lado del control administrativo de la demanda agregada y no por el lado de estimular la oferta agregada donde realmente radica, y en la forma como lo están resolviendo China y Vietnam, por un lado, y los países de Europa oriental, por otro lado.

El racionamiento, que cubre menos de dos semanas de abastecimiento básico al mes, agrava la marginación social de los que no poseen los medios para adquirir los bienes en el mercado negro. Estos precios están fuera del alcance del ingreso de la mayoría de la población, fomentan el tráfico de influencias, conflictos básicos de intereses y corrompen a las autoridades por las altas ganancias o rentas que genera el creciente diferencial en los precios oficiales y los del mercado negro, y obligan a realizar actividades asociales (robos a las empresas) o caer en la delincuencia. La eliminación del racionamiento por alza de precios, simultáneamente a la concentración de los subsidios en los más vulnerables, aumentaría la producción y eventualmente reduciría los precios. La solución tiene que venir por liberalizar e imprimir mayor grado de transparencia a los mercados, fomentar una sana competencia, y brindar incentivos que otorguen señales para

mayor iniciativa y esfuerzo a los productores, nacionales o extranjeros.

En esta sección ESCEPAL indica que el ajuste fue tardío, aspecto que no menciona en los capítulos 1 y 2, así como que el ajuste debe ser gradual, pero fundamenta erróneamente el por qué de la gradualidad "las soluciones han de ser graduales por cuanto la dualidad monetaria y de mercados ha creado válvulas valiosas de escape" (p. 115).

LA INSUFICIENTE INTENSIDAD Y LA TARDANZA DEL PROCESO DE REFORMAS ESTRUCTURALES

Los Cambios Institucionales o Estructurales Recientes: ¿Son Transformaciones Suficientes?

El énfasis de ESCEPAL en el capítulo 2 es que Cuba ha comenzado un importante proceso de reformas ("se incorporaron cambios institucionales de envergadura, p. 42), tales como: el nuevo estatuto de inversión extranjera, "adelgazó" el estado, "desincorporó" el grueso de las tierras estatales, "restructuró" el sistema financiero) y de políticas de estabilización que permitirán superar los problemas socioeconómicos fundamentales del país. Sin embargo, el análisis más detallado de los temas, que presenta en los capítulos 3 y 4, establece lo contrario. O sea, que las transformaciones realizadas, aunque significativas por el extremo sistema socialista real, son incompletas e insuficientes para resolver los problemas socioeconómicos fundamentales del país ("las fallas estructurales internas," p. 9; el "lento desarrollo de las capacidades competitivas," p. 10; y las "deformaciones en la estructura económica e institucional que se expresan en baja eficiencia y entorpecen el desarrollo," p. 40). La recuperación lograda también es insostenible, ya que ni siquiera existe una expansión neta de los equipos e instalaciones productivas. La inversión, como señala ESCEPAL y la CEPAL en otros estudios (CEPAL 1996, p. 200), no alcanzan para reponer la capacidad productiva existente "la economía sufrió un proceso de desinversión neto (estimado en más de 3000 millones de pesos en el período 1989-1996), que afectó tanto la capacidad productiva nacional, como la disponibilidad y calidad de vivienda" (Recuadro, p. 68). El nivel de inversión bruta y de ahorro nacional respecto del PIB son de sólo un dígito desde 1992 (ver Cuadro 1).

Las reformas específicas no han tenido los resultados esperados o enfrentan fuertes limitaciones. Así, ES-CEPAL indica que la inversión extranjera suscrita sólo ha ascendido a US$1,000 millones, ha creado 60,000 empleos, que la ley sigue siendo casuística, los trabajadores son contratados a través de empresas del estado y que se requieren convenios comerciales de protección mutua con los países de los inversionistas (p. 44-45). ESCEPAL no menciona que la ley de trabajo para estas empresas elimina un conjunto de derechos laborales básicos. En lo referente a los cambios agrícolas, señala que no hay experiencia gerencial y que la nueva forma de propiedad cooperativa (UBPC), que tiene responsabilidad, pero no autoridad para tomar ciertas decisiones, "alientan imperfectamente la reinversión, la innovación tecnológica o el cuidado de los recursos naturales" (p. 50). La sección sobre planificación económica y amplia intervención del estado en la economía es, en general, muy positiva sobre lo que ha hecho y planea hacer; no obstante, termina con esta expresión "la exigencia específica de rehacer la división del trabajo en Cuba con el exterior, configuran restricciones reales a las que difícilmente escapan los países, singularmente las naciones en desarrollo" (p. 58).

No hay un proceso de reorganización económica seria, mientras persistan los niveles de ahorro nacional, inversión y de comercio internacional. ESCEPAL identifica la asignación eficiente de los recursos entre los temas aún pendientes (p. 72). No hay fundamentos para la excepcionalidad del éxito del socialismo real en el caso cubano. Cuba requiere fortalecer y modernizar su economía rápida y adecuadamente. La llegada de la crisis asiática, recientemente acentuada por la crisis rusa y las turbulencias externas, que afectan en especial a los países en desarrollo, vino a agravar un panorama ya complicado sin la presencia de éstas, que parecen ser mayores y cuyos efectos contagio difícilmente serán de corto plazo.

El Saneamiento Fiscal

El énfasis de ESCEPAL es que se eliminó el déficit fiscal mediante mayores impuestos y que se necesita un sistema impositivo más eficiente (p. 19). El tema fiscal no sólo es de mayores tributos para lograr el equilibrio como sugiere el estudio, sino de racionalización, reducción, monitoreo y evaluación del gasto público, así como de un nivel y distribución de la tributación que no desaliente o paralice la producción, ya que es la capacidad productiva del país la que determina en última instancia el nivel de los gastos públicos y no lo contrario. El gasto público, que es excesivo, se contrajo menos que la reducción en la producción en 1990-1993, originando un insostenible déficit fiscal del orden del 30.4% del PIB (ver Cuadro 1) y puso presión sobre el déficit en cuenta corriente y la competitividad externa. El ajuste a la crisis ha recaído esencialmente en el aumento de los impuestos y los precios, en vez de en reducir el gasto público y estimular la oferta agregada. Es evidente que el peso del ajuste no debe descansar sobre los impuestos y los precios, sino también emplear la corrección de la tasa de cambio para fomentar las exportaciones, estimular la oferta agregada—liberando la capacidad productiva nacional mediante los pequeños agricultores y los cuentapropistas—y reducir y racionalizar el excesivo gasto público. La evidencia internacional muestra que mientras más alto es el gasto público improductivo, menor es el crecimiento (Barro, 1996).

La llamada reforma del estado que menciona ESCE-PAL ha consistido en un reajuste del aparato público de tipo operativo táctico ante las nuevas realidades internacionales, pero no incluye la incorporación de mecanismos modernos de administración ni incentivos—tales como criterios para asignación de recursos e incentivos económicos de acuerdo a resultados y desempeño. Es sólo un cambio cosmético y no un cambio organizativo ni administrativo de fondo por la importancia relativa interna del estado y el mercado. Las nuevas Unidades Básicas de Producción Cooperativa (UBPC) son en realidad empresas estatales parcialmente descentralizadas con serios problemas de gestión, más que verdaderas cooperativas agrícolas. Por ello, el pretender la reducción del déficit de las empresas estatales agrícolas convirtiéndolas en UBPC, no resuelve el problema de fondo, como lo han demostrado fehacientemente los pobres desempeño y resultados de la producción azucarera en los últimos años (ver Cuadro 1), lo que es semejante a la experiencia china cuando utilizaba una forma semejante de cooperativas antes de las reformas que inició a finales de los años 70.

ESCEPAL ignora el efecto del aumento de impuestos, especialmente en los cuentapropistas, y el nivel inadecuado de las remuneraciones salariales de los que trabajan, que determinan efectos distorsionantes y negativos sobre la asignación de recursos y fomentan conductas especulativas. El problema de Cuba, con muy bajos salarios reales, no es elevar el nivel de impuestos orientado en última instancia a financiar un abultado estado con elevados gastos. Más bien hay que motivar el trabajo y el esfuerzo para superar la situación de pobreza generalizada.

La Reforma Financiera

ESCEPAL pone énfasis en las nuevas instituciones financieras creadas. Sin embargo, en el contexto del nivel y el desarrollo de los mercados existentes en Cuba, donde no existen siquiera la pequeña y mediana empresa legalmente, dichas instituciones son prácticamente irrelevantes porque no se relacionan directamente con el funcionamiento de la economía, salvo para prestar servicios al sector enclave, y no tienen mayor relevancia para alentar una mayor producción, fomentar el ahorro y la inversión, y facilitar una mayor actividad económica.

OTROS TEMAS MACROECONÓMICOS: LOS RESULTADOS DE CUATRO DÉCADAS DE SOCIALISMO REAL

El Retroceso y No Sustentabilidad de los Avances Sociales

Según ESCEPAL, a mediados de los años ochenta "se habían eliminado la pobreza y la indigencia tanto en las zonas urbanas como rurales" (p. 37). Es probable que se eliminara la indigencia; sin embargo, definitivamente no se eliminó la pobreza, ya que la situación actual de la población es de bajos ingresos aún en el contexto latinoamericano en el cual Cuba ocupa una de las más bajas posiciones (ver sección anterior, lo referente al Estudio de Desarrollo Humano de 1998).

En la sección IV.D, ESCEPAL destaca retrocesos significativos y la precariedad de los avances sociales logrados hasta 1991, que "comienzan a reflejarse de manera muy desfavorable en los servicios" (p. 369). Concretamente, cabe destacar, entre otros:

- La disminución de la calidad de los servicios sociales prestados (menor gasto real social, deterioro de las instalaciones y los equipos, escasez de insumos y materiales básicos, sueldos reales más bajos del personal). El gasto social primario real disminuyó en un 29.3% en 1989-1997, de $3,295 millones (a precios de 1981) o el 18.1% del PIB en 1989 a $2,330 millones o el 14.1% del PIB en 1997 (ver cuadro IV.23, p. 379).

- El "hacinamiento y deterioro" (p. 360) de la vivienda "donde se resienten déficit y atrasos significativos" (p. 360). Ya en 1987, antes de la crisis, la construcción de nuevas viviendas no alcanzaba a satisfacer la reposición de viviendas (p. 372).

- El aumento del desempleo disfrazado y abierto hasta el 35% de la población económicamente activa en 1993 (ver Cuadro 1), con su consecuente marginalización.

- La marcada disminución de la matrícula secundaria y universitaria y el retraso del nivel educacional. Los estudiantes matriculados en escuelas medias (en miles) disminuyeron de 1,703.1 en 1989 a 710.6 en 1996 y los estudiantes matriculados en escuelas superiores (en miles) de 242.4 en 1989 a 111.6 en 1996 (ver Cuadro A.59).

- El deterioro en los servicios básicos de agua potable y alcantarillado por falta de mantención y repuestos con sus implicaciones para la salud y la calidad de vida, temas que no se mencionan en ESCEPAL, pero que son destacados por los visitantes a Cuba.

- ESCEPAL considera que los gastos sociales y el sistema de previsión social se han convertido en una carga y exceden "la capacidad de la economía nacional" para sostenerlos (p. 59).

El Mercado Laboral, los Incentivos Materiales y la Seguridad Social

"... llevamos añales tratando de largárnos de este cabrón país..." (p. 15)

—Zoé Valdés, *Café Nostalgia*

ESCEPAL señala que hay "una dificultad para generar empleo productivo como resultado de una importante restricción externa complicada por los problemas para insertarse en la economía internacional, tanto en la esfera comercial como financiera" (p. 181), cuando realmente son la organización productiva interna y las políticas adoptadas (p. e. la política cambiaria y el manejo de la deuda externa y de las remesas) las que generan la restricción externa y complican la inserción.

ESCEPAL muestra con un índice simple que la productividad por trabajador media cayó en un 22% entre 1989 y 1996. Asimismo, calcula un nivel de desempleo equivalente al 27.3% en 1996, debido al desempleo abierto, la caída en productividad y la menor participación en la PEA (ver Cuadro 1).

ESCEPAL identifica las siguientes políticas de ajuste relevantes al problema del desempleo: el trabajo por cuenta propia, otorgar pequeños terrenos para cultivos y la inversión extranjera, pero no destaca las amplias limitaciones conque se han aplicado y que han impedido mayores efectos de las mismas. Al respecto, ESCEPAL señala que la inversión extranjera carece del dinamismo para resolver el problema de empleo en el país (p. 192), pero no indica que esto se debe a errores de diseño de la política respectiva y al riesgo país de Cuba con verdaderos problemas de solvencia y liquidez internacional, aunque en el capítulo 2 menciona las muchas limitaciones de la política utilizada. Además, los empleados "por cuenta propia no pueden contratar personal asalariado y en la práctica se encuentran marginados del crédito bancario" (p. 53), por lo que cabría alentar más decididamente la expansión del mercado de trabajo y de las empresas de la "segunda economía" aún a sabiendas de aceptar cierta polarización en la distribución del ingreso.

ESCEPAL estima la caída del salario real entre un 81% al 44% entre 1989 y 1995 (p.194). En 1996 el salario mensual real era el 58.6% de 1990, lo cual junto a una política de incentivos al trabajo o remuneraciones arbitraria, que sólo beneficia a un tercio de la población, han creado fuertes efectos distorsionantes sobre los hábitos y la motivación al trabajo (p. 197).

En cuanto al tema de la seguridad social, ESCEPAL indica que el nivel "en el producto no es sinónimo de alivio permanente a la pobreza" (p. 203). Para ello hay que "ligar en forma transparente beneficios y financiamiento (p. 205). En el caso de Cuba "toda vez que los beneficios son independientes de las recaudaciones (p. 206), no se conoce "si son atribuíbles a una previsión social mal diseñada o una política excesivamente generosa" (p. 206). En nuestra opinión ambas son ciertas.

Descenso de la Industria Azucarera

ESCEPAL indica en el capítulo 4 que parte del marcado descenso de la industria azucarera (ver Cuadro 1) se debe a "problemas de organización". En realidad por años se descuidaron la productividad y la tecnología moderna (se utilizaron "tecnologías atrasadas y dispendiosas de energía", p. 9).

La Omisión del Tema Ambiental

El tema ambiental tan crucial en el concepto moderno e integral del desarrollo, ha sido prácticamente omitido en ESCEPAL, a pesar del marcado deterioro de las aguas y las tierras, lo cual subestima en forma considerable los efectos negativos del régimen socialista en Cuba.[7]

RESUMEN, COMENTARIOS FINALES Y CONCLUSIONES

"...quien así habla no conoce Cuba, no sabe del hambre y el terror que sufren los cubanos, quien así habla sólo conoce los hoteles de lujo o las casas de protocolo...." (p. 129).

— Zoé Valdés, *La nada cotidiana*

ESCEPAL es muy rico en información estadística y en la descripción de algunos deplorables problemas existentes y hace importantes advertencias a las autoridades sobre algunos temas centrales. Sin embargo, es sesgado y erróneo en sus apreciaciones y análisis sobre eventos y situaciones históricas claves, así como sobre el diseño, manejo y gestión de algunas políticas económicas fundamentales (p.e. del sector externo),

---

7. Ver Sección "Current Environmental Condition in Cuba" en Leiva, 1998.

así como sobre el avance y los resultados logrados en los procesos de estabilización y de reformas estructurales.

Las consideraciones económicas sobre las segmentaciones, la política cambiaria, el origen externo de los problemas y los efectos del ajuste sobre la distribución del ingreso son erradas y parecen más dirigidas a complacer a las autoridades nacionales que a mostrar sus costos para la economía cubana y sus amplias y profundas ineficiencias y deficiencias. Así los análisis de ESCEPAL son erróneos en cuanto a la relación causal entre las segmentaciones y los problemas existentes, así como los efectos distorsionantes del diferencial cambiario y de la asignación de divisas. También en el énfasis sobre el origen externo de la crisis, que realmente fue el detonante, no señala de igual forma los abundantes y repetidos errores estratégicos y tácticos de diseño, manejo y gestión de política económica e institucional que fueron la carga. Tampoco indica los costos innecesarios del ajuste sobre la distribución del ingreso y tiene una visión estática y cortoplacista sobre la misma.

ESCEPAL muestra que la economía está empobrecida y presenta problemas difíciles y complejos, como nunca antes en su historia republicana, con un deficiente desempeño y con un riesgo latente de una verdadera debacle, lo cual ha debilitado al país en su negociación con la requerida inversión directa extranjera y los financistas internacionales. Cuba tiene índices malos de inversión, ahorro nacional, solvencia y liquidez internacional (o sea el riesgo país), estabilidad económica, posibilidades de crecimiento y de deterioro de sus logros sociales, lo que es resultado de la crisis y de las medidas de ajuste para enfrentarla, innecesariamente recesivas y tardías. El remedio es la reforma estructural y sistémica, no sólo levantar el embargo norteamericano.

Las autoridades mantienen, a pesar de las críticas internas—tanto de disidentes como de opositores—y externas, una política macroeconómica e instituciones inadecuadas a la crisis que pospone las reformas en vez de fomentarlas, que se refleja en la debilidad

estructural, tecnológica, organizativa, institucional y normativa del sector productivo, y que es acentuada por el entorno de creciente globalización, dinamismo y competitividad internacional. Si bien, como señala ESCEPAL, se iniciaron algunos cambios acertados y en la dirección correcta a partir de 1993, el margen estrecho de los cambios, la fragilidad de los progresos alcanzados, la lenta marcha—prácticamente paralizada a partir de 1996—y la dirección vacilante hacia las correcciones imprescindibles, determinan que las reformas aún no se hayan consolidado y que estén afectando el desarrollo del país y el nivel de bienestar y calidad de vida del cubano en términos de remuneraciones, nivel de empleo y calidad del mismo. Tampoco hay credibilidad ni confianza en los planes de reformas de las autoridades nacionales, pues éstos ni siquiera han sido completamente esbozados, ni han habido señales de que el proceso va a continuar con firmeza. Existe una sensación de inseguridad, avalada por los hechos y por las continuas declaraciones de reafirmación socialista. Este entorno genera y es propicio a conductas rentistas y orientadas a la especulación de los agentes económicos, tanto internos como externos.

El libro de Maurizio Giuliano *El caso CEA: Intelectuales e inquisidores en Cuba* ilustra el daño que ESCEPAL es muy probable haya causado y aún esté causando en el país, al debilitar la posición de los economistas cubanos independientes y aún de los centros dependientes y asesores del partido comunista, por ejemplo el caso del Centro de Estudios sobre Améerica (CEA), quienes han planteado la necesidad de adoptar cambios significativos de políticas y reformas institucionales para la gobernabilidad económica, aún dentro del socialismo, y superar así los problemas existentes. De hecho, algunos economistas del propio CEA propusieron una alternativa concreta a las políticas económicas y reformas institucionales y normativas oficiales,[8] lo cual incomodó notablemente al gobierno, q siquiera de los intelectuales del partido comunista, según consta en las actas de las reuniones efectuadas en el CEA resumidas en el libro de Giuliano. Así el gobierno desató una severa repre-

---

8. Ver Carranza, Gutierréz y Monreal (1997).

sión contra estos economistas en 1997, simultáneamente a los preparativos de la visita del Papa Juan Pablo II a Cuba. Dicha represión incluyó, entre otras medidas, una solicitud formal de autocrítica, una fuerte amonestación para que no continuaran analizando la economía cubana, y su traslado a otros centros de trabajo.

ESCEPAL contribuye al ambiente enrarecido al respaldar el discurso socialista y redistribuidor, que lleva a la vacilación y el "corcoveo" con lo cual queda muy poco por corregir. Resulta extraordinariamente grave abandonar el desarrollo y la modernización como objetivos nacionales que deben ser abordados decididamente para superar la pobreza generalizada en esta generación y en el actual entorno internacional. ESCEPAL debió apoyar nuevos avances liberalizadores y de correcciones positivas, como lo hicieron en su oportunidad el Informe Solchaga y la propuesta de los economistas del CEA. Especialmente cuando hay una amenaza latente de volver a viejas políticas que han fracasado no sólo en Cuba sino en el mundo entero.

Las instituciones internacionales tiene una obligación ética de presentar información y análisis correctos sobre la situación de los países y alertar sobre la misma para impedir acciones irresponsables de los gobiernos y para facilitar acciones apropiadas por los agentes privados y públicos, nacionales e internacionales, que, en última instancia, las financian. De lo contrario, están contribuyendo a que dichos agentes actúen incorrectamente o aumenten sus riesgos innecesariamente. ESCEPAL puede convencer a los partidarios, confundir al público, pero difícilmente a los analistas especializados.

En la precaria situación de Cuba es indispensable realizar diagnósticos, apreciaciones y análisis serios,

completos y coherentes para establecer las bases de un proceso de transformación hacia una sociedad que restaure y sea respetuosa de las libertades y derechos fundamentales de los ciudadanos, con un sistema judicial independiente y donde prevalezca la legalidad y el estado de derecho. Para así, mediante una organización institucional y normativa capaz y adecuada, que provea incentivos que alienten el esfuerzo y la productividad, y políticas desarrollistas basadas en los mercados y la libertad económica, enfrentar exitosamente el dinámico proceso de globalización y competencia internacional, emprendiendo un desarrollo propio, genuino y pleno. De esta forma se evitará la inminente catástrofe derivada de la pretensión de entrar al tercer milenio con el socialismo real, una organización económica, social y política probadamente fracasada, disfuncional y anacrónica, que desconfía de los ciudadanos y es incompatible con la complejidad de la organización económica mundial, la naturaleza de las innovaciones y los intereses del país. Un modelo con muchas deformaciones y muy excluyente para Cuba como país, y que incuba condiciones para estallidos de impredecibles consecuencias.

El problema no es tanto de mantener la distribución del ingreso lograda ni mucho menos mantener el socialismo real mundialmente fracasado sino de alcanzar un desarrollo sustentable y equitativo viable que elimine la pobreza generalizada y la inequidad en un entorno internacional de creciente y difícil competencia. Cuba no ha alcanzado una meta sino por el contrario tiene que comenzar vigorosa y decididamente un proceso de transformación institucional, modernización y reinserción internacional. Urge actuar pronto para evitar más perjuicios innecesarios e importantes.

REFERENCIAS

R. Barro, "Institutions and Growth: Introductory Essay" en *Journal of Economic Growth*, I, 1996, pp. 145-148.

J. Carranza, L. Gutiérrez y P. Monreal, *Cuba: La Restructuración de la economía* (segunda edición).

Santiago: Alerce Talleres Gráficos, S.A., abril de 1997.

Comisión Económica para América Latina y el Caribe (CEPAL), *Equidad y Transformación Productiva: Un Enfoque Integrado*, Santiago de Chile: CEPAL, 1992.

Comisión Económica para América Latina y el Caribe (CEPAL), *Estudio Económico de América Latina y el Caribe 1995-1996*, Santiago de Chile: CEPAL, 1996.

W. Easterly y Stanley Fischer, *The Soviet Economic Decline Historical and Republican Data*, NBER Working Paper 4735, mayo de 1994.

A. Leiva, "Promoting and Financing the Development of Environmental Infrastructure in a Post-Castro Cuba," en este volumen.

C. Mesa-Lago y J. Pérez-López, *A Study of Cuba's Material Product System, Its Conversion to the System of National Accounts, and Estimation of Gross Domestic Product Per Capita and Growth Rates*, Staff Working Paper 770, Washington: World Bank, 1985.

J. A. Ocampo, "Charla Magistral sobre 'Modelos de Desarrollo: La Economía Latinoamericana 1950-1997'" en ocasión de la inauguración de la Quinta Promoción del Magister de Gestión y Políticas Públicas de la Universidad de Chile, el 3 de agosto de 1998.

Programa de Naciones Unidas para el Desarrollo (PNUD), *Informe de Desarrollo Humano 1998*, Madrid, España: Mundi-Prensa Libros, S.A. 1998.

J. Ramos, "La Política de Desarrollo Productivo en Economías Abiertas" en W. Pérez (coordinador), *Políticas de Competitividad Industrial*, México: Siglo Veintiuno Editores, 1997, p. 289-307.

J. Ritter, "Internal Obstacles to Cuba's Reinsertion in the Latin American Economy" en P. Alamos, M. Font, J.A.G. Albuquerque y F. León, *Integración Económica y Democratización: América Latina y Cuba*, Santiago: Instituto de Estudios Internacionales, mayo de 1998.

ECLAC'S REPORT ON THE CUBAN ECONOMY IN THE 1990's

Carmelo Mesa-Lago

This is a brief analysis of some issues in the U.N. Economic Commission for Latin America and the Caribbean (ECLAC) book *La economía cubana: Reformas estructurales y desempeño en los noventa*. A more comprehensive review of this book (dealing with different topics), is forthcoming in an issue of *Cuban Studies* to be published in 1999. I regret that a representative from ECLAC was not able to attend this session of the ASCE meetings and respond to my comments, but hope that an answer will be published in future proceedings.

POSITIVE ASPECTS OF THE BOOK

This is a very important book for at least four reasons. First, it fills a serious gap in Cuban statistics resulting from the halting of publication of the *Anuario Estadístico de Cuba* (*AEC*, the official statistical yearbook) after 1989. The Cuban National Bank (BNC) published, in 1995 and 1996, annual economic reports with statistics, but they have a small fraction of the data that appeared in the *AEC*; furthermore, the 1997 issue has been unavailable, perhaps due to the May 1997 bank reform that relegated the BNC to a secondary role and created Cuba's Central Bank. The Ministry of Economics and Planning published a report in 1998 which, in turn, is considerably smaller than the BNC reports. ECLAC's book provides 128 statistical tables and 35 graphs which constitute the most extensive collection of data available on Cuba for the 1990-96 period (a few include 1997). Although many of these tables are questionable (methodologically or factually), the same can be said of Cuban official statistics, a problem that has not impeded scholars to study, scrutinize and cautiously use them for four decades.

Second, the book is not limited to publishing official data and includes ECLAC's valuable estimates, never available before, in several important areas, e.g., on the labor force, open unemployment and underemployment, the cost of unemployment compensation, and so forth. Those of us that have worked on Cuba's labor sector for many years faced the enormous vacuum of data on the EAP (which led to gross estimates with wide variations among them) and the estimates in the book are of great value although obviously will be the subject of future analysis.

Third, a good part of the data and views in the book are favorable to Cuba (particularly after 1993), but many others show critical problems, for instance, the sharp decline in production in 1989-93 (and, in many areas, output levels in 1996-97 well below those of 1989), the deterioration in the caloric intake, the cut in half of the higher education enrollment in 1989-96, the enormous size of "equivalent unemployment" (i.e., open unemployment plus displaced workers receiving unemployment compensation) and so forth.

Fourth, Cuba is a member of the United Nations and also affiliated with ECLAC, hence, the language of the book had to be much more diplomatic than that normally used by scholars. Furthermore, in my opinion, one objective of the book was to push the economic reform further in Cuba (a goal that has obviously failed, at least until August 1998) and, in order to do that, tried not to alienate the island's authorities (which could have blocked the publication of the original report). But a careful reading of the

Table 1.   Official and ECLAC's Series on GDP of Cuba 1985-1997
(in million constant pesos of 1981, index 1985=100)

Years	BNC — ONE			ECLAC		
	Pesos (millions)	Rate (%)	Index	Pesos (millions)	Rate (%)	Index
1985	20,369		100.0	20,352		100.0
1986	18,998	-6.7	93.3	20,385	0.2	100.2
1987	18,489	-2.7	90.8	19,934	-2.2	97.9
1988	19,351	4.7	95.0	20,644	3.6	101.4
1989	19,586	1.2	96.2	20,960	1.5	103.0
1990	19,008	-3.0	93.3	20,349	-2.9	100.0
1991	16,976	-10.7	83.3	18,415	-9.5	90.5
1992	15,010	-11.6	73.7	16,591	-9.9	81.5
1993	12,777	-14.8	62.7	14,332	-13.6	70.4
1994	12,868	0.7	63.2	14,421	0.6	70.8
1995	13,185	2.5	64.7	14,783	2.5	72.6
1996	14,218	7.8	69.8	15,908	7.6	78.1
1997	14,574	2.5	71.5	17,117	2.5	84.1

Source: Mesa-Lago 1998, updated with Ministerio de Economía 1998; ECLAC 1997 and 1998.

book reveals many criticisms of current flaws and recommendations to correct them.

SOME OF THE FLAWS
NOTED IN THE BOOK

I do agree with many of Rolando Castañeda's specific criticisms detailed in his comments (although not in his overall evaluation) and add herein others.

First, the report was written by a team of experts and, obviously, was not carefully checked by a skilled editor, thus resulting in contradictions. Some examples follow: (a) "in 1989 Cuba had virtually full employment" (p. 53), but the unemployment rate was "less than 4% in 1989" (p. 36), and 7.9% in the same year (Table III-20); (b) the daily per capita caloric intake was 2833 in 1992 (Table IV-22), but one year later suddenly dropped to 1863 (Table A.59); (c) the illiteracy rate was 4% in 1981 (p. 36) but 6% in the 1990s (Table A.58), and "currently [1997] is 4%" (p. 371); and (d) the infant mortality rate was 60% in 1958 (p. 36) but the *AEC 1972* (p. 22) gave it as 33% for the same year.

Second, there are some significant gaps in the book or analysis which is factually incorrect. Two examples should suffice. The most glaring omission is the anti-market Rectification Process launched by Fidel Castro in 1986-90, which reversed the previous approach (the SDPE in 1975-85); there is an absolute lack of analysis of this serious economic error which

makes it difficult to understand the recession caused by it. Exogenous factors, particularly the U.S. economic embargo, are blamed for the bad performance in this stage, but the embargo was not tightened until the Torricelli Law was enacted at the end of 1992 and, mainly, by the Helms-Burton Act of 1996.

Third, the rest of this comment is devoted to analyze a significant incongruence between Cuba macroeconomic data and that published in the book, as well as differences between the latter and the most recent ECLAC study *Cuba: Evolución económica durante 1997* (thereafter abbreviated as ECLAC 1998). Table 1 reproduces in its first column the official Cuban statistical series of GDP at constant (1981) pesos for 1985-97, based on the BNC, the Oficina Nacional de Estadística (ONE) and the Ministerio de Economía y Planificación (the rates and the index are my calculations). The second half of Table 1 reproduces the corresponding series from ECLAC, based on the book and estimates for the year 1997 from the growth rate published in the *Balance Preliminar de la Economía de América Latina y el Caribe 1997* (I estimated the index).

Until 1994, and with the exception of the year 1988, the ECLAC series shows higher growth rates than Cuba's series; as a result, GDP in 1997 according to the former was 17.4% higher than the latter (17.1 vis-a-vis 14.6 billion pesos), and the respective indices for 1997 were 84.1 and 71.5, which means that

Table 2.   Fiscal Deficit and GDP Deflator in Cuba: 1989-1996

	Cuban Data and Author's Estimates					ECLAC Estimates			
	Budget Deficit (million current pesos)	Deficit as % of GDP in current pesos	GDP (million current pesos)	GDP (million constant pesos)	Implicit GDP deflator (%)	Deficit as % of GDP in current pesos	GDP (million current pesos)	GDP (million constant pesos)	Implicit GDP deflator (%)
	(1)	(2)	(3)	(4)	(5)	(6)	(7)	(8)	(9)
1989	-1,403	7.3	19,273	19,586	n.a.	6.7	20,795	20,960	n.a.
1990	-1,958	10.0	19,630	19,008	4.9	9.4	20,880	20,349	3.4
1991	-3,765	23.1	16,245	16,976	-7.0	21.4	17,554	18,415	-7.1
1992	-4,869	32.7	14,877	15,010	3.2	29.7	16,382	16,591	3.6
1993	-5,051	33.5	15,076	12,777	19.1	30.4	16,606	14,332	17.3
1994	-1,421	7.4	19,196	12,868	26.3	6.9	20,561	14,421	23.1
1995	-766	3.5	21,737	13,185	10.5	3.2	23,613	14,783	12.0
1996	-572	2.4	23,500	14,218	0.2	2.2	25,197	15,908	-0.8

Notes: Columns 1, 2 and 4 are offical data; column 3 is estimated multiplying column 1 by 100 and dividing it by column 2; column 5 is estimated by

the formula $\dfrac{X_t Current}{X_t Cons\tan t} = IPD_t; \left[\dfrac{IPD_t + 1}{IPD_t}\right] - 1(100)$; columns 6 to 9 are from ECLAC's book.

Source: Mesa-Lago 1998; ECLAC 1997, 1998.

the economic recovery in relation to the year base 1985 was 12.6 percentage points better according to ECLAC than Cuba. In spite of this significant difference, the book lacks a methodological explanation on how the ECLAC estimates of GDP were done, a most relevant issue because we totally ignore how Cuba did the conversion from GSP (material product system) to GDP (system of national accounts) for 1985-93 when both series are available. Furthermore, there are many unanswered questions on whether or not Cuba can accurately estimate GDP in view of the important informal sector of the economy. Finally, in spite of the long scholarly debate (ignored by the book) on the use of an abnormal year as a base for the series in constant prices (1981, faulty due to its high inflation and the way Cubans calculated it), and on its continued use for 17 years, ECLAC develops an apparent new series but keeps the dubious year base.

Complicating this problem further, the ECLAC 1998 report on the Cuban economy reproduces not the book GDP series but the Cuban series for the entire period 1989-97. This puzzle raises even more questions: if a new methodology was indeed developed in the book to revise the official series, why then did ECLAC retrogress to the latter in its most recent publication? If a new methodology was not developed, why do the book series exhibit a much

better economic performance than reported by Cuba, and how can such a difference be explained?

Since 1988 Cuba has not published the GDP deflator, which is crucial to assess its economic growth in constant pesos. Table 2 presents my estimates of the implicit deflator (based on official data) and compares them with the implicit deflator calculated in the book, both for 1990-96. In addition, Table 2 contrasts the official and series contained in the book on the fiscal deficit as a percentage of GDP for 1989-96, showing that the latter percentages are systematically lower than the former. Hence, ECLAC once again shows better economic performance than the Cuban data. This is an statistical illusion, however, the result of ECLAC using the same budget deficit in absolute figures as Cuba, but estimating GDP in current pesos considerably higher than Cuba (an annual average of 8% higher); as in other cases, the book lacks any explanation for such a difference. Furthermore, ECLAC 1998 reproduces the official fiscal deficit percentages, instead of those in the book, thus raising the same questions as before when we discussed GDP growth in constant pesos.

The comparison of the implicit GDP deflator for 1990-96 shows that in five of the years the deflator in the book was lower than Cuba's, in one year it was the same, and in two years it was higher, once again indicating a better performance based on the ECLAC series than on the official series. A good part of the explanation is that both GDP in constant and current pesos are higher in the book than in the official series, but the relationship between the two is important also. Particularly troublesome is the year 1996, when my estimated deflator is 0.2% but the book is a negative 0.8%. Finally, ECLAC 1998 publishes, for the first time, *inflation* rates which are abnormally mismatched with the GDP deflator from the book, as follows: 12% and -11% (yes, it is negative!) in 1995 and 0.8% and -5% in 1996.

The above analysis and questions are examples of those that scholars who work on the Cuban economy will be raising concerning the ECLAC book. Hopefully some of the presented puzzles and queries will be answered by ECLAC officials and contribute to a deeper analysis of the Cuban economy and more refined data to assess it.

REFERENCES

Economic Commission for Latin America and the Caribbean (ECLAC). 1997. *La economía cubana: Reformas estructurales y desempeño en los noventa*. México: Fondo de Cultura Económica.

_____. 1998. *Cuba: Evolución económica durante 1997*. México: LC/MEX/L.352, July 15.

Mesa-Lago, Carmelo. 1998. "Assessing Economic and Social Performance in the Cuban Transition of the 1990s." *World Development* 26:5 (May): 857-876.

A PROJECT FOR FACULTY DEVELOPMENT IN A TRANSITIONAL CUBA

Jorge Luis Romeu

"Enseñar puede cualquiera; educar, tan solo quien sea un evangelio vivo."

— Don José de la Luz y Caballero.

Education is one of the most important infrastructure investments any nation can make. And, on this count, Cuba has always been among the leaders in Latin America. For example, in the half century elapsed between 1899 and 1953, adult literacy rate went up from 10 to 73 percent—one of the highest in Latin America, at its time—public secondary schools (institutes) increased from 6 to 21, and scores of private ones appeared throughout the island (Cuban Censuses, 1899 and 1953).

The university system in Cuba also grew very rapidly. It was founded in Havana in 1728 as Seminario de San Carlos, later becoming the University of Havana (U.H.). By 1956, it had three public, autonomous, institutions at Havana (U.H.), Santa Clara (Central) and Santiago (Oriente). In the late 1940s and early 1950s, several smaller and private universities were created, the most important being Santo Tomás de Villanueva, in Havana.

The present Cuban dictatorial regime, organized in the wake of the 1959 revolution, has also done much in education, during its nearly forty years in power. For example, literacy rate went up to over 95 percent after intensive government campaigns, during its first five years—but other countries such as Costa Rica have also achieved similar literacy levels without such high political costs (Romeu, 1995) and without literacy handbooks doubling up as propaganda and in-

doctrination material, that helped consolidate the new system. Finally, all levels of education became free, highly politicized and widely available—especially in the countryside and remote villages, where they had traditionally been neglected—after all private and religious schools were taken over by the government in 1961.

After 1959, universities also became highly politicized and lost their traditional autonomy. Among other major changes, several new universities were created in the provinces; the U.H. was divided into one smaller university and several specialized institutes (e.g. Pedagógico E. J. Varona, Polytechnic J. A. Echevarría, de Ciencias Médicas, Ciencias Agropecuarias, etc.) and the Ministry of Higher Education was created to control and supervise them. Finally, and most important, the selection of students and professors (and their expulsion when necessary) as well as that of texts and curriculum, became based on political considerations. In short, the entire (higher) education system became part of the machinery that consolidated and kept the regime in power, acquiring the dual function of educating as well as indoctrinating its students.

However, many excellent students and professors endured this governmental and political pressure. And much good teaching and research has occurred, in spite of this. It is necessary not to throw away the baby with the bath water, once the inevitable process of transition to pluralism starts. At the risk of starting some controversy, we need to separate the good from the bad—save the good and foster more of it. Much is solid and should stay, for education is one of the two main achievements of Cuba's 40 years of dictatorial regime. In addition, public education will be one of the main pillars to get the country back on the road to recovery.

OBJECTIVE AND ORGANIZATION

The objective of the present paper is: (1) to take a serious look at ways to provide much needed faculty development aid to Cuban higher education, in the forthcoming post-Castro era; and (2) to propose a project to undertake this effort. Our work is based on our experiences as students and professionals in the Cuban higher education system, as students and faculty in U.S. and several Iberoamerican universities, and as developers and coordinators of faculty development projects in the United States, Latin America and Spain.

Everything stated and proposed in this paper intends to improve and redress the current state of higher education in Cuba, and in particular in the University of Havana, our beloved Alma Mater. At the outset, we recognize the need for all Cubans, inside and in exile, to work together on this project. Unfortunately, at this time, those inside the island are not in a position to actively contribute to this project, which requires immediate attention. Therefore, the pressing need to start thinking and planning about these problems forces us to start without them—but with the certainty that they will become an intrinsic part of it as soon as it is possible. Finally, this is neither a partisan nor political proposal.

This paper is organized as follows. To obtain a better grasp of the problem, we first compare the features of the present *versus* the previous higher education organization in Cuba; then we discuss the student and faculty development needs during the transition. This is followed by an overview of some of our past efforts working in faculty development projects and discuss ways of adapting them to the forthcoming Cuban transition. Finally, we propose and discuss in detail a project for faculty development in Cuba, during and after the transition, to develop a sounder higher education system where students (1) are taught without political discrimination and (2) can

grow, not only technically, but also intellectually and humanly.

CUBAN UNIVERSITIES BEFORE AND AFTER 1960

There are qualitative as well as quantitative differences between education in Cuba before and after the rise to power of the present regime. Qualitative, because before 1959, education was considered a tool for the improvement of the individual, and after 1959 it acquired an additional political function. Quantitative, because before 1959, Cuban public education had a relatively small budget, provided by a poorly organized and endowed state and had to compete with private schools. And after 1959, public education (the only one left) received substantially larger resources provided by a rich, strong and well organized government that had taken over the entire economic private sector.

In broad terms, before 1959 the Cuban university system consisted of three public, autonomous universities that were nearly tuition free and (at least on paper) open to all citizens independent of religion, race, social or economic class or place of residence. These university centers were ideologically and politically pluralistic, specialized and emphasized humanistic careers such as philosophy, law, education and social sciences, but still maintained high quality and internationally recognized faculty and programs in medicine, sciences and engineering.

In addition the Cuban university, as an institution, fulfilled a second, very important function: to provide leadership in the political life of the nation. It was literally the cradle of ideas and national leaders. The revolutions of 1933 and 1959 came out of university ranks. And most of our political, social an economic ideas were first conceived by university faculty and students. Just to name a few top national figures, Enrique José Varona, Ramón Grau San Martín, Eduardo Chibás, Carlos Prío Socarrás and also Fidel Castro, were all faculty or student leaders.

After 1959, the number of universities, technical institutes and research centers increased by an order of magnitude, as did the number of university students (1953 and 1981 Cuban Censuses). The new university also became primarily technically oriented, providing large resources for the engineering and science curriculums. In turn, access to the largely diminished humanistic careers (law, journalism, philosophy) was now based on ideology and tightly controlled. For example, Catholic students and faculty were first expelled (in the early 1960s) and later quietly but systematically discriminated against (by not allowing them to register for engineering, education, medicine, economics, etc.). Government allegiance became the litmus test for faculty and student selection, as also did ideology, for curriculum and textbooks. For example, Marxism became a required subject during the 1970s in the School of Mathematics.

This author, for example, was expelled together with hundreds of others from the Engineering School in the Spring of 1965 for active, but peaceful, dissent against government policies. Public "purification" or expulsion meetings frequently carried a special motion that the person be sent (as additional punishment) to the Military Service, to work in the UMAP (Unidades Militares de Apoyo a la Producción) forced labor camps.

The result of forty years of such educational policies is that Cuba's current university system has produced thousands of qualified doctors, engineers and other professionals—but no leaders of national stature. It is relevant, though, that dissent still starts at the university, in spite of government control. For example, Félix Bonné, one of the four drafters of the document La Patria es de Todos, was among many U.H. faculty who signed a petition in 1993, and were subsequently expelled from for it. Martha B. Roque, Ricardo Bofill, Elizardo Sánchez and many other dissident leaders have also been U.H. faculty.

On the other hand, it is also true that before 1959, it was difficult for many students with scant means, or who lived far away from Havana, Santa Clara or Santiago, the provincial capitals where the existing universities functioned, to receive a university education. For, in spite of the low tuition, they had to absorb income loss (studying instead of working) and pay for room, board and textbooks. After 1959, when several university centers were created in other provinces, textbooks became free and student scholarships in government provided housing units was free and easily available for those students who were accepted into the politically controlled university system, such situation improved significantly.

This background constitutes the basic building blocks for the understanding of the current situation (how we got there and how we may be able to move on). We need to recognize them if we are attempting to work in and for the reconstruction of the Cuban universities, with any hope of success.

NEED FOR AID TO UNIVERSITIES DURING AND AFTER TRANSITION

Health and education have been the two most widely publicized achievements of the forty years of Fidel Castro's dictatorial regime. Maintaining them, once a transition to political and economic pluralism is achieved in Cuba, is of utmost importance. Failure to do so will contribute to justify (1) the crude existence of the present dictatorial regime and (2) its lack of will to undergo a transition to pluralism. The latter is an important consideration.

Therefore, the first need for the proposed faculty development aid project is simply to maintain the service at its present level. But better yet, such aid could easily help to upgrade and update Cuban higher education by introducing new technology (computers, labs, etc.), new teaching methods and better books, as well as updating the curriculum.

In addition, it is crucial to help *redefine* the institutional *goals of education*, from also being a political arm of the government ideology to that of strictly furnishing the knowledge that provides a better quality of life. This will change the university both qualitatively and quantitatively. Once this change is effected, anyone, regardless of political, religious or ideological views may register in any curriculum, if he or she meets the intellectual and educational requirements. It is, therefore, necessary to help faculty and staff to draft the new procedures to run the university without the current political constrains, as well as to train them in their application.

In addition, faculty also need more technical skills. They need to master how to use new technology in support of education, in research and in their daily work. They need to master the use of new hardware and software, in conjunction with the Internet, to enhance their teaching and scholarly activities and to develop faculty relations between Cuban and foreign institutions.

Cuban faculty must also develop new organizations and publications based on professional needs and purposes instead of mainly political ones. They must learn how to use them, to support faculty development and international exchanges. Finally, they should receive also training in grantsmanship so they can seek and obtain funds for research and education, both from national and international organizations, as is now-a-days customary in any open society.

Students, as well as faculty, have long been subjected to the current political constraints that the Cuban regime imposes. The disappearance of fear, mistrust, reliance on political (rather than intellectual) merit, as means of advancement, will require some rethinking. The new rules of the game have to be clearly laid out and explained, so all can equally benefit from them. There will be some resentment from those who profit under the present rules, and are unwilling to accept the change. But this is a challenge that will have to be faced across the board, during the transition, from all corners of Cuban society.

Students, in turn, need to master the new economic opportunities that a market economy (as opposed to a statist one) offers them. They need to learn about the roles, responsibilities and activities of contractors and entrepreneurs, as opposed to those of mere employees and functionaries (which is what the Cuban universities have produced in the past 30 years). Students need to pick up how to network among themselves, with their new professional organizations, and also with international student and professional organizations. Students must learn the benefits of continuing education, via periodic short courses, professional meetings and publications—as opposed to perceiving the end of their learning cycle once they leave the university. Finally, students should also master the art of grantsmanship, to obtain funds from external sources. For, within a short period of

time, they will be also be full fledged professionals, requesting funds for research and development.

SOME PAST EXPERIENCES IN FACULTY DEVELOPMENT

This author has learned much about faculty development from the literature, but also from several very interesting first hand experiences in international education. For more details of all these projects, see Romeu (1998).

We are an alumnus of the Fulbright Program, having served as Senior Lecturer in Mexico in 1994. There we learned about the advantages and the problems involved in faculty exchanges. We also gained experience in faculty development by teaching several short, specialized statistics courses in regional institutions.

Upon our return from Mexico, we created and have since developed, the State University of New York (SUNY)-Mexico faculty and student exchange project (Romeu, 1997). Through it a dozen Mexican faculty have attended SUNY professional meetings with full scholarships and other types of support. We have also arranged the donation of many boxes of science and mathematics books to several Mexican regional institutions. And we maintain an Internet list of Mexican faculty, who remain linked and periodically exchange education information.

We have also privately developed a network of Spanish universities where we have taught specialized, short and intensive simulation courses. This has taught us the advantages and problems involved in developing privately supported faculty development work—as opposed to that which is government and internationally supported.

We have participated, with an international team of five faculty, in the development of the Masters-level curriculum in Operations Research for the University of Comahue, in Argentina. We worked entirely through the Internet, meeting only "in virtual space." Nevertheless, the task was successfully accomplished, on time and yielding a quality product.

We have developed a novel "internship" program with the University Rómulo Gallegos, in Venezuela, serving as education consultant in programs funded through Fundayacucho by the World Bank. This "internship" experience consists in inviting a faculty member to our university in the United States to spend several weeks working with us. The visitor learns our teaching methods and advances in technology and the way American institutions operate. The "intern" then works as "resource" in developing teaching materials in his/her native language, in exchange for room and board. And the "intern's" institution pays for the air fare. There must be a total commitment by the inviting faculty who, in addition to mentoring, shares office and all other personal facilities with the "intern."

We have developed extensive collaborative research programs with Mexico. As Principal Investigators, we have submitted two proposals ranked as finalists to the National Science Foundation (NSF), to conduct joint ecological research with universities in Mexico City and Guadalajara. We have also been Co-Principal Investigators in a joint proposal, submitted to the Fund for the Improvement of Post-Secondary Education (FIPSE , part of the U.S. Department of Education) in 1997, whereby four institutions in Veracruz, Mexico, two universities in Canada and three in the U.S. proposed to place several dozen Mexican, American and Canadian students for a full year across their borders to study ecological problems in one of the other two countries.

Finally, we submitted a proposal to NSF to move twenty students from SUNY to Mexico, teaching them several bilingual science and mathematics courses in SUNY and completing the sequence at the Universidad Veracruzana

SOME PRACTICAL METHODS IN INTERNATIONAL EDUCATION

From the previous section we can extract several very important lessons in the area of international education that could be applied to a Cuban faculty development project. It would appear that many of these activities could begin now, at least from the U.S. side.

First, this author relies heavily in Email, the Internet and computers to undertake international education work. This is not only much faster, but much less expensive. And money (or lack thereof) is one of the crucial problems we have found in our work.

A very important, component of international education is the personal commitment and mentoring relationship. This can also be done via the Internet. Cuban faculty working in the United States and elsewhere can form "partnerships" with faculty working in Cuba, and serve as mentors and personal advisors to them, giving help in the many activities discussed above.

Another important component in faculty development is faculty exchange. There are short, medium and long stages, according to the different goals and needs. For intensive courses, conference participation, seminars, etc., short exchanges are best suited; these can often be accomplished during short (Spring, Winter) breaks and vacations. Medium exchanges can be organized during the Summer periods, when longer, more effectively paced courses can be taught, field practice conducted and research contacts established. Finally, long exchanges (of a semester or more) can be used for receiving training in special topics, postgraduate (Masters or Ph.D.) degrees, collaborative research projects, etc.

Many (if not all) of these projects can be initiated and even partially conducted via the Internet and the World Wide Web. In addition, these media can be used in conjunction with mail, phone, FAX, television, CD-ROM's, tapes and books, in Distance Learning (DL) education. DL keeps the education project content very current and makes it very accessible once the initial expenditure for DL installations are accomplished. DL provides a larger impact, making the project available to a wider and more geographically scattered audience. Finally, due to the required installation investments that make DL possible, the development of permanent links between delivering and receiving institutions are fostered.

These links, which are essential for the sustainability of any faculty exchange project, can be of different types and work at different levels:

- First, there is, the faculty-faculty link. This is particularly easy to implement in the Cuban case, given the natural relationships between Cuban exiles, family, friends and former colleagues. It can be quickly reestablished and easily maintained via Email and FAX.

- Second, there is the university-university (or in general institution-institution) link. Many of us Cuban exiles work today in, and have many contacts with, institutions of higher learning and research, in the United States and other countries. It should be possible for some of us to raise to these institutions the importance that links with Cuba could have for Cuban development and to aid the transition.

- Third, the present Cuban government has created a strong higher education structure (Ministerio de la Educación Superior, Academia de Ciencias, Centro Nacional de Investigaciones Científicas, etc.). In the United States, FIPSE, NSF, USAID and other similar governmental institutions exist, as they also exist in Mexico, Venezuela, Spain and other Iberoamerican countries. It is only logical to build upon them, by establishing further and stronger links that help in the restructuring of Cuban higher education.

- Fourth, student organizations in Cuba and abroad can also provide links. These can prove especially helpful in finding scholarships and providing mentorship to students and in enhancing mutual understanding of the different realities that have existed throughout these years, and in ways to effect their positive evolution.

- Fifth, professional organizations, especially Cuban-American organizations, can provide a substantially strong link. This author knows of (and belongs to) the professional associations in exile dealing with engineering, economics and education. We also know of several others, in exile and inside Cuba, who could join in this effort. In addition, American, Iberoamerican and worldwide organizations (for example the American Statistical Association, the Asociación Mexicana de Estadística and the International Statistical Institute, in our main area of expertise) can join in through the auspices of its Cuban-American members and associates.

- Finally, Cuban civil society and exiled organizations can also contribute to the effort of linking its members and institutions inside Cuba and in the Cuban diaspora. In our mind, establishing the first contacts is crucial; the rest would happen naturally and much easier.

All of these links can help obtain individual and institutional funds and other types of aid for Cuban higher education institutions, during the transition. Links can also contribute to obtain aid and funds from international organizations such as Inter-American Development Bank (IDB), the International Monetary Fund (IMF) and the World Bank (WB), who are currently providing such type of help to other Iberoamerican countries.

A CUBAN FACULTY DEVELOPMENT PROJECT PROPOSAL

Taken by themselves, all of the above are of small practical value. In order to achieve something positive, an organization that provides unified, consistent direction and purpose must be created. Such an organization would also provide the continuity to sustain the initial efforts, once the aura and spell of the first moments of a Cuban transition have passed. It would also provide the overall vision to comprehensive aid that benefits all Cuban institutions, no matter how new or how far from Havana they might be.

Such an organization would also help in avoiding effort duplication, waste, budget over-runs and needless delays. It can help in establishing contacts between Cuban faculty in the island and abroad, and between all Cubans and non-Cubans willing to cooperate in this effort. It can help in avoiding misunderstandings and in quickly redressing them, if and when they occur. It can avoid or prevent loose ends in the project. And most important, such an organization can provide follow-up and follow-through, so that a faculty development project actually fulfills the sustainable needs of all Cuban institutions of higher learning during and after a transition to pluralism in Cuba.

We think of such project organization as a sort of *Clearinghouse* that would operate, first and foremost, a central data base (DB). The DB would contain lists of all Cuban institutions of higher learning and research, of all individual faculty in the island interested in working on this project, and of those outside Cuba willing to cooperate. The Clearinghouse's first task would be to put them all in contact and help in establishing, enhancing and maintaining such initial contacts. This could be started now.

The Clearinghouse DB should also have a list of project topics and ideas that must have been thought through and developed prior to the start of the transition. Once the transition is underway, these projects can be refined and expanded, through discussions with Cuban faculty and institutions. Such projects should be comprehensive and should pursue a general development policy—rather than being a collection of patch-work ideas. Some of these projects can already be under development, at least in broad lines, when the transition starts—if we start now. We cannot afford to start thinking about the projects at the crucial time when the transition is already ongoing.

The Clearinghouse DB should also have is a list of potential donors and a preliminary operations budget. With some initial commitments from potential donors, as well as some preliminary mechanisms, this project could also start now.

There are many more functions that a Faculty Development Project requires. But the three mentioned are extremely important and also ones that ASCE, perhaps in conjunction with others and the support of some funding organization, can start working on immediately. Long-range planning requires lots of good thinking—and definitely some financial support.

DISCUSSION

Many friends and colleagues have provided input and encouragement to this work. I would like to acknowledge Uva Clavijo's comments as discussant at the ASCE session as well as Stuart Lippe's careful commentary. They form the basis for the discussion in this section. I will briefly touch on three issues: (1)

there has been an improvement in conditions inside Cuba; (2) there already exist a number of "similar" programs to the one proposed in this paper; and (3) whether this project could be started now.

It is true that, recently, the political climate has changed in Cuba. There is less indoctrination, political pressure and religious discrimination in the universities today than we suffered as students 25 years ago. But it still exists and, relaxed as it may be, the problem cannot be ignored. It is also true that today there are more contacts among Cuban and foreign faculty than before. However, it is still scarce and limited to a reduced group of faculty. And it is not always open to all those faculty interested—but to a select group of faculty members.

This author has interacted with Cuban faculty at international professional meetings and via Internet. He still finds them isolated, both scientifically and professionally, and cautious. And the use of a figure of 5 or 6 Internet messages per day as an indicator of Cuban Email transactions volume, when there are dozens of universities and research centers and thousands of faculty and researchers in Cuba, is simply not acceptable.

Actually, the strength of the project presented in this paper is, precisely, that it deals with the above problem and with the discussant's argument that similar programs already exist between Cuban and U.S. and other foreign institutions. Programs do exist that interact with—and reward—the top elements in the highly pyramidal Cuban university structure. Those are the Deans, Center Directors, etc., in today's Cuba. Under the current arrangements, when the transition occurs, these functionaries will continue to benefit from existing programs—at the expense of those who may have been slighted due to current government selection.

Our proposed project, by creating an open DB process, where anyone may be included—irrespective of ideology, rank, etc.—provides selection opportunity based on merit: equal opportunity. This, in the mind of this author, is the strongest argument in favor of this proposal.

Finally, yes, the time has come. The project should be started now.

CONCLUSIONS

Throughout this paper we have discussed the background to current problems and needs of Cuban universities. This topic is not only very close to us, but also one where we have had long and first hand experience. This author studied five years in the University of Havana, graduating in 1973. His mother taught there for fourteen years, before 1959 and all his siblings and both parents also graduated from the same institution many years ago.

There is an unquestionable need to help renew the Cuban institutions of higher learning, once the unavoidable transition gets started. The infrastructure among Cuban exiles to assist already exists: professional organizations, faculty members, international organization functionaries, researchers, professionals, entrepreneurs. It is just a matter of organizing such rich and varied infrastructure and using it for this worthwhile purpose.

Finally, potential donors do exist—even if they may be difficult to find. The United States and the Iberoamerican countries are all interested in a transition in Cuba, as may also be such international organizations as the IDB, IMF and WB. However, they will only be in a position to cooperate when there is a government in Cuba they can deal with (i.e., a government willing to undertake such a transition).

However, there are some U.S. non-profit organizations that can be tapped. This author has already approached the Ford, Rockefeller, ARCA and John D. and Catherine T. MacArthur foundations as well as government organizations such as the National Security Education Program (NSEP) and FIPSE. Some have already expressed an interest—even if their charters may not allow them to fund this effort. And there are always the universities and the Cuban American professional associations.

There is hope.

REFERENCES

Cuban Censuses (1899; 1953, 1970, 1981).

Romeu, J. L. "Experiences in Iberoamerican International Collaboration." *Proceedings of III CIBEM: Third Iberoamerican Conference in the Teaching of Mathematics*. Caracas, Venezuela (July 1998).

Romeu, J. L. "The Internet in Education Across Borders." *Proceedings of the CIT98: Conference of Instructional Technologies*. SUNY-Cortland (May 1998), pp. 111-113.

Romeu, J. L. "Technology and International Education." *Proceedings of the CIT97; Conference on Instructional Technologies*. SUNY-Brockport (May 1997), pp. 98-100.

Romeu, J. L. "More on the Statistical Comparison of Cuban Socioeconomic Development." *Cuba in Transition—Volume 5*. Washington: Association for the Study of the Cuban Economy, 1995, pp. 293-301.

RAINFALL IN LITTLE HAVANA

Diego R. Roqué

The work presented here is divided into two major parts. The first part gives an abreviated and informal discussion of the theoretical framework underpinning the methodology that is to be applied in the second part. It is based on material put together in Roqué (1996) which in turn was based on material incidentally derived in Roqué (1982). The topic is time-varying Markov chains for which there is not an extensive amount of literature. The reader is refered to the classical and very important work of Hajnal (1956, 1958). There is also a very good treatment of the subject matter in Howard (1971). The topic on non time-varying Markov chains, on the other hand, has generated an overwhelming amount of literature and it is treated by almost every major contemporary author. Among these, some of the best are Ross (1983, 1985), Çinlar (1975), and Karlin and Taylor (1975).

All Markov chains, time-varying or not, have in common that they satisfy the Markov property. A Stochastic Process is a collection of random variables indexed by time and a discrete time Stochastic Process $\{X_n : n = 0, 1, 2, ...\}$ defined on a discrete state space E is a Markov chain if :

$$P(X_{n+1} = j \mid X_0, X_1, ...X_n)$$
$$= P(X_{n+1} = j \mid X_n = i)$$

for all i and j in E and all times $n \geq 0$.

This property simply states that whatever state the process will move into depends only on where the process currently is and not on any prior history. If the state space E is finite, the Markov chain is also called finite. Our attention in this paper is restricted to finite Markov chains. If the cardinality of the set E is the integer v, and if the transition probabilities (as in equation (1)) do not vary with time, then the finite Markov chain has a well defined stochastic square matrix of dimension (v x v) which is usually labeled P and is called the matrix of transition probabilities. This matrix contains an orderly arrangement of the transition probabilities and the entries in each row must add up to one.

The second part uses the theory described in the first part to update the very successful work of Gabriel and Newmann (1957, 1962) in predicting rain probabilities and analyzing weather cycles in Israel. Their work was amply documented in Cox and Miller (1968) under the title "Rainfall in Tel Aviv." They used the state space E = {0, 1}, where the two states represented "wet day" or "dry day." The 2 x 2 transition matrix was estimated using 27 years of accumulated data on daily rainfall for the months of the rainy season. Their Markov chain was not time varying. It was used to predict the probability of wet and dry days and to analyze weather cycles during the months of the rainy season. They obtained probability distributions for the duration of both dry and wet spells. Here one will emulate their effort using instead a time-varying Markov chain that will permit estimating year round probabilities for both the Wet and the Dry seasons for both the short and the long terms.

ERGODICITY

Given the Stochastic Process $\{X_n : n = 0, 1, 2, ...\}$ (here a finite Markov chain), then its ergodic properties are those that relate information derived from one realization of the process (usually a time average) to information derived from the entire ensemble of realizations (usually in the form of an expected value). One may borrow and adapt the discussion in Gross and Harris (1974) to illustrate the concept of ergodicity. If one assumes the following limits exist for all k integer, $k \geq 1$:

(a) $limit_{n \to \infty} \frac{1}{n} \sum_{i=1}^{n} X_i^k = a(k) < \infty$

(b) $limit_{n \to \infty} E(X_n^k) = b(k) < \infty$

(c) $limit_{n \to \infty} \frac{1}{n} \sum_{i=1}^{n} E(X_i^k) = c(k) < \infty$

Then the process is ergodic with respect to all its moments (i.e., ergodic in distribution function) if a(k) = b (k) = c(k) for all k integer, $k \geq 1$.

These processes, when ergodic, become independent of time and possess a stationary or steady state probability distribution. It can be shown they also become independent of any initial distribution. In short, any one realization of the process yields all relevant information about the process behavior in the long run. The time varying process discussed here, however, will only exhibit weak ergodicity in distribution, that is, it is only the case that a(k) = c(k) for all k integer, $k \geq 1$.

The reason the limit b(k) does not figure in the definition of weak ergodicity in the distribution function is because the time varying process will not always possess a steady state distribution. Instead, there will exist a unique finite length stationary cycle of probability distributions (vectors) that becomes independent of time and independent of any initial distribution. Any one realization will still yield all relevant information about the long-run behavior of the process. The process becomes independent of any initial distribution and except for the repetitive nature of the cycle, completely independent of time as well.

Let $\Pi((k))$, k = 1, 2, ...,N be such a stationary cycle of probability distributions (vectors), then the following proposition becomes relevant:

Proposition: For the repeating stationary cycle, there exists a Cesaro sum convergence (coordinate wise) vector, Π'', which itself forms a probability distribution.

The proof of this proposition is very simple and is omitted here.

THE PROCESS

The time varying Markov chain considered here is defined in the state space E = {0, 1}. According to Cox & Miller (1968), this is the smallest non-trivial state space. Any pair of ergodic (i.e., regular) non time varying Markov chains defined on this state space will suffice to construct the time varying process. The two Markov chains will be represented by the two 2 x 2 transition matrices P(1) and P(2). Matrix P(1) will have eigenvalues 1 and α, and steady state distribution (vector) Π (1). The second matrix P(2) will have eigenvalues 1 and β, and steady state distribution (vector) Π (2). Regularity requires both $|\alpha| < 1$ and $|\beta| < 1$. One may then define a cyclic process with each repeating cycle of constant length (n + m) time epochs. In every cycle, as it repeats itself, transitions are governed by the chain P(1) during the first n epochs, inmediately followed by m time epochs where transitions are governed by the chain P(2). Hence transitions are varying in time as a consequence of alternating the two transition probability matrices.

Fortunately, for 2 x 2 stochastic matrices, the property of regularity is closed under matrix multiplication. One has a process here that easily overcomes the objections outlined in Hajnal (1958). The time varying process will also continue to satisfy the Markov property and the Markov chain process may be denoted $\{Y_n : n = 0, 1, 2, ...\}$.

Showing weak ergodicity in distribution function for this process in the binary state space gets even easier if one makes the following observations: First, all moments for this process are identical, second, all sums of the indexed Y random variables count the number of transitions into state 1 and hence Cesaro sums represent proportion of time (or of transitions) in (or into) state 1, and finally, all expected values of the indexed Y random variables simply recover the probability of being in state 1.

The key to showing weak ergodicity in distribution requires borrowing and adapting some concepts from the theory of Simulation (see Law & Kelton (1982)). One must assume the time index has gotten very large and stationarity has set in. At some point after stationarity has set in, one begins looking at the sample paths of the chain. Alternatively, one may conceive of a process that simply starts at cyclic stationarity. From the theory of Simulation then, the end of each cycle is a Regeneration Point (actually all epochs in the cycle may be viewed as Regeneration Points). This simply means the process probabilistically restarts itself at the end of each cycle for the one realization being observed.

A simple thought experiment should convince the reader of this. Assume one has a countable infinity of probabilists. Each probabilist arrives at the process sequentially one at a time just before the next cycle begins. Each probabilist is given information on the state probability distribution at the beginning of the cycle, the two chains, and the rules of the process. Each probabilist, aided by the Markov property, is asked to derive the probability distributions of all finite trajectories of the sample paths of the chain from that moment on. Clearly, all probabilists, possessing identical information, will derive identical results.

One may then define for the jth cycle

$$s_j = \sum_{i=1}^{n+m} Y_1$$

It is then possible to treat $S_1, S_2, ...$, etc. as independent, identically distributed (i.i.d.) random variables.

Since the cycle length is completely deterministic and given by the constant $(n + m)$, one may then let for the jth cycle

$$Z_j = \frac{S_j}{n+m}$$

Then $Z_1, Z_2, ...$, etc. are also i.i.d. random variables. Now, one may note that for any cycle, say the jth one, $0 \le Z_j \le 1$ which implies $E(Z_j) = p$ for some p in the interval $[0, 1]$. It is then the case that

$$E(Z_j) = \frac{1}{n+m} \sum_{i=1}^{n+m} E(Y_1) = p$$

and appealing to the Strong Law of Large Numbers (SLLN) it is the case that

$$\frac{Z_1 + Z_2 + ... + Z_n}{N} \xrightarrow[N \to \infty]{} p \ \ w.p. \ 1$$

which is clearly the same as

$$\frac{S_1 + S_2 + ... + S_n}{(n+m)N} \xrightarrow[N \to \infty]{} p \ \ w.p. \ 1$$

and hence one has weak ergodicity in distribution function. This argument can easily be implemented for larger state spaces as well. Here one has a process, then, that in the limit converges to regeneration epochs ($(n + m)$ of them).

EXISTENCE THEOREM

The following theorem is crucial for it shows the existence of one such stationary cycle of probability distributions (vectors) and of the weak ergodicity in distribution limits.

Theorem: For the process considered here let $\alpha'' = \alpha^n$ and $\beta'' = \beta^m$. Then the stationary cycle is given by

$$\Pi((k)) = \Pi(1) + \Gamma(k)(\Pi(2) - \Pi(1))$$
$for \ k = 1, 2, ..., n$

and

$$\Pi((k)) = \Pi(2) + \Delta(k)(\Pi(1) - \Pi(2))$$
$for \ k = n+1, n+2, ..., n+m$

where

$$\Gamma(k) = \frac{\alpha^k(1-\beta'')}{(1-\alpha''\beta'')} \ \& \ \Delta(k) = \frac{\beta^{k-n}(1-\alpha'')}{(1-\alpha''\beta'')}$$

When $\alpha \& \beta$ are both greater than zero, it is obvious the entire cycle are convex combinations of $\Pi(1)$ &

$\Pi(2)$. In all cases the entire cycle are probability distributions. This is guaranteed by the contruction. It is also worth noticing that in the limit the time varying process becomes disoriented in the sense that it does not matter which non time varying chain begins the cycle. The theorem continues as follows: The Cesaro sum limit of this process is given by

$$\Pi'' = \frac{n}{n+m}\Pi(1) + \frac{m}{n+m}\Pi(2)$$
$$+ \frac{K}{n+m}(\Pi(2) - \Pi(1))$$

where

$$K = \frac{(1-\beta'')(1-\alpha'')(\alpha-\beta)}{(1-\beta)(1-\alpha)(1-\alpha''\beta'')}.$$

From this theorem, the following results are also obtained:

Corollary 1: If $\alpha = \beta$, then

$$\Pi'' = \frac{n}{n+m}\Pi(1) + \frac{m}{n+m}\Pi(2).$$

Corollary 2: If $\Pi(1) = \Pi(2)$, then Π'' is a stationary or steady state solution of the time varying process, where $\Pi'' = \Pi(1) = \Pi(2)$.

Corollary 3: As $(n+m)$ gets large, it is the case that

$$\Pi''---- \rightarrow \frac{n}{n+m}\Pi(1) + \frac{m}{n+m}\Pi(2).$$

The proof of the theorem and its corollaries may be found in Roqué (1982). A stronger, far more general version of corollary 2 may be found in Hajnal (1956).

EXTENSIONS

In order to extend these results to larger state spaces, some repeating sequence of factors in an infinite product of matrices is a requirement. Even if all matrices are regular, if they go on forever in the infinite product with no discernible pattern and with different steady state vectors, obviously the sequence of transient responses will go on indefinitely and the process will not cycle. The work in Howard (1971) strongly supports this conjecture. A repeating sequence under the right conditions as evidenced in the cases considered here insures cyclic behavior.

The case of 2 x 2 regular matrices is the only exception to the objections outlined in Hajnal (1958) to the approach using characteristic roots. The objection is simply that the product of two regular matrices may not be regular. Obviously, for larger state spaces some kind of restriction may be necessary. One that comes to mind right away is due to Hajnal (1958) and may be called "The Hajnal Qualification." This qualification would require that one consider only repeating sequences of factor matrices that always begin with the same "scrambling" matrix. (See Hajnal (1958) to insure regularity throughout the infinite product of matrices.) A scrambling matrix is any regular stochastic matrix such that for any two of its rows there always is at least one column with non-zero entries for both rows. If the repeating pattern of factors in the infinite product of matrices is set for almost all matrices except, say the first one, then it may be possible to start the infinite product with an arbitrary starting scrambling matrix. The transient effect due to this starting matrix should vanish in the long-run and regularity would be ensured throughout the entire product.

To show that scrambling matrices are not necessary for ergodicity and hence weak ergodicity, simply alternate any non-scrambling regular matrix with the identity matrix.

It should be noted that the two state processes considered here meet the criterion for weak ergodicity given by Hajnal (1956, 1958), but Hajnal's criterion does not imply Cesaro sums convergence (see Hajnal (1956)). This convergence, on the other hand, is a requirement for weak ergodicity in distribution function. So the requirements for weak ergodicity in distribution are in fact more restrictive. One of the restrictions may very well be cyclic structure and behavior.

Another conjecture one may make is that the cycling processes, that in the limit may be exhibiting a new kind of stationarity, have autocovariance functions that are strictly a function of within cycle position and between cycle lags.

It is worth mentioning that the processes described here exhibit all kinds of peculiar new behavior. For example, there may be stochastically induced completely deterministic oscillation between two states (0 and 1). If one begins to shrink the time interval, at some point the oscillating entity will appear to be in both states simultaneously. Would a particle oscillating in such a fashion thru time exhibit wave-like characteristics? The same phenomenom shows there is a way in and out of absorption into a state and in fact this is what generates the oscillation. All of this generated by alternating a pair of distinct regular Markov chains without any absorbing state in them. Their behavior, and the oscillation, become independent of time and independent of initial conditions.

In more specific terms, this oscillation occurs when one lets n = 1 and m = 1 in the cycle, and the product of the two distinct alternating 2 x 2 regular matrices, in whichever order multiplied, yields a regular 2 x 2 matrix with one absorbing state in it.

The oscillation or periodic phenomenom can easily be extended to larger state spaces. It requires three matrices products for the 3 x 3 case, four matrices products for the 4 x 4 case, etc. The columns of the respective identity matrices alternate as the stationary cycle of probability distributions. As such, this constitutes a special class of time varying Markov chains. To show this all that is needed is the work in Howard (1971). An example of the 2 x 2 case (period = 2) is:

$$\begin{bmatrix} 0 & 1 \\ x & x \end{bmatrix} \begin{bmatrix} x & x \\ 1 & 0 \end{bmatrix}$$

An example of the 3 x 3 case (period = 3) is given by:

$$\begin{bmatrix} 0 & 1 & 0 \\ x & x & x \\ x & x & x \end{bmatrix} \begin{bmatrix} x & x & x \\ 0 & 0 & 1 \\ x & x & x \end{bmatrix} \begin{bmatrix} x & x & x \\ x & x & x \\ 1 & 0 & 0 \end{bmatrix}$$

Although one can learn and infer from this oscillatory finite Markov chains, nevertheless no matter how small the transition interval selected, it is possible to select a smaller observation interval and observe the actual state. The Quantum problem is just the oppo-

site; no matter how small one makes the observation interval, the transition interval can and will become even smaller making it impossible to observe the actual state. Obviously continuous time analogs to these models and perhaps even continuous state spaces are necessary.

For this oscillatory class of processes, if the periodicity is v, then the 1 x v frequency vector Π'' has every component equal to (1/v). As v gets larger, this vector approaches an infinite size column vector whose every component is equal to zero.

This large class of finite time varying Markov chains also has the property that the processes can start with the highest levels of entropy as initial conditions and terminate at cyclic stationarity with absolute zero entropy. One wonders if neural pathways, for example, process information this way.

THE APPLICATION

The theory thus far described can now be put to work in reviving and bringing up to date the work of Gabriel and Newmann (1957, 1962). These authors were very successful in studying weather cycles and generating rain probabilities during the rainy (or wet) season in Tel Aviv. Here the analysis will be conducted for the City of Miami which encompasses Little Havana. The author is indebted to William R. E. Locke of the National Weather Service and to Father Pedro Cartaya, S. J., of the Belen Jesuit Prep. School Observatory who were instrumental in obtaining the data for this study.

The states of nature for the purpose of this analysis are only two. State 0 represents a dry day, that is, a day for which no rain (or only a trace amount) was recorded and state 1 represents a wet day, that is, a day for which at least .01 inches of rain was recorded. The recording station was the weather station at Miami International Airport. Amounts of rain on any given day less than .01 inches are considered a trace amount and are labeled as such by the recording station. Such days are considered dry days in this study.

The data consisted of 10 years of daily rainfall records comprising the years 1984 thru 1993, a total of 3653 days. The year was divided into a Dry season comprising the 181 days from November 1 to April

30 and a Wet season comprising the 184 days from May 1 to October 31. The data consisted then of 1813 Dry season days and 1840 Wet season days.

There were 429 wet days and 1384 dry days in the Dry season and there were 879 wet days and 961 dry days in the Wet season. This data yielded the following inmediate information: It rains an average of 42.9 days in the Dry season with an average downfall per season of 15.01 inches. The average downfall per day of precipitation in the Dry season was .35 inches with a standard deviation of .69 inches. For the Wet season, it rains an average of 87.9 days per season with an average downfall of 41.31 inches per season. The average downfall per day of precipitation in the Wet season was .47 inches with a standard deviation of .69 inches. The average total yearly precipitation was then 56.32 inches of rain.

To construct the time varying Stochastic Process, two Markov chain transition probability matrices were estimated using relative frequencies (Maximum Likelyhood Estimators). The data results for the Dry season were the following:

Dry Season		Actual Day		
		Dry	Wet	Total
	Dry	1125	259	1384
Preceeding Day				
	Wet	261	168	429

This data yielded the first part of the Stochastic Process cycle:

$$P(1) = \begin{bmatrix} .813 & .187 \\ .608 & .392 \end{bmatrix}, \Pi(1) = \begin{bmatrix} .765 \\ .235 \end{bmatrix}$$

where $\alpha = .205$, n = 181, and $\alpha'' \approx 0$.

The steady state or long term probability of rain on any given day of the Dry season was .235, that is, it tends to rain on slightly less than one fourth of the days. Similarly, the data results for the Wet season were the following:

Wet Season		Actual Day		
		Dry	Wet	Total
	Dry	622	339	961
Preceeding Day				
	Wet	337	542	879

This data yielded the second part of the Stochastic Process cycle:

$$P(2) = \begin{bmatrix} .647 & .353 \\ .383 & .617 \end{bmatrix}, \Pi(2) = \begin{bmatrix} .520 \\ .480 \end{bmatrix}$$

where $\beta = .264$, m = 184, and $\beta'' \approx 0$.

The steady state or long term probability of rain on any given day of the Wet season was .480, that is, it tends to rain on approximately one half of the days.

The Markov chains can be used to generate probabilities outright. For example, if on any given day of the Dry season there is an estimate of a 50% chance of rain, then the probability that it rains the following day can be obtained from the following product:

$$(.50 \ .50)\begin{bmatrix} .813 & .187 \\ .608 & .392 \end{bmatrix} = (.71 \ .29)$$

It yields a subsequent probability of rain of .29 (and .71 of a dry day).

One can use the Markov chains to analyze the weather cycles within each season (see Cox & Miller (1968)). Let the duration of a Dry season dry spell (in days) be denoted by the random variable DSDS. Then the probability of a dry spell during the Dry season lasting j days is given by:

$$P(DSDS = j) = (.813)^{j-1}(.187), j = 1, 2, \ldots$$

The mean of this geometric distribution is $1/(.187)$, yielding an average duration of a Dry season dry spell of 5.35 days. The variance is $(.813)/(.187)^2$, which yields a standard deviation of 4.82 days. Similarly, the duration of a Dry season wet spell in days as a random variable denoted DSWS has the following probability distribution:

$$P(DSDWS = j) = (.392)^{j-1}(.608), j = 1, 2, \ldots$$

As in Gabriel & Newmann (1957), one can define a Dry season weather cycle (DSWC) as a dry spell followed by a wet spell. They showed the pertinent random variables may be assumed statistically independent. Then,

$$DSWC = DSDS + DSWS$$

The weather cycle random variable is the convolution of two distinct and independent geometric random variables.

One can repeat this analysis for the Wet season by defining the random variables Wet season dry spell (WSDS), Wet season wet spell (WSWS), and Wet season weather cycle (WSWC), in which case:

$$P(WSDS = j) = (.647)^{j-1}(.353), j = 1, 2, \ldots$$

$$P(WSWS = j) = (.617)^{j-1}(.383), j = 1, 2, \ldots$$

and

$$WSWC = WSDS + WSWS.$$

Tables 1 and 2 summarize basic information concerning all the weather cycle random variables. They give the mean and standard deviation of all pertinent random variables.

Table 1.   Average duration (in days) of weather cycles

Season Type	Dry Spell Days	Wet Spell Days	Weather Cycle Days
Dry	5.35	1.64	6.99
Wet	2.83	2.61	5.44

Table 2.   Standard Deviation (in days) of weather cycle random variables

Season Type	Dry Spell Days	Wet Spell Days	Weather Cycle Days
Dry	4.82	1.03	4.92
Wet	2.27	2.05	3.06

Finally, one can obtain the results for the time varying Stochastic Process. The stationary or long term probability of rain for the jth day of the Dry season is given by:

$$\Pi_1((j)) = .235 + (.205)^j(.245)$$
$$j = 1, 2, \ldots, 181$$

The stationary or long term probability of rain for the kth day of the Wet season is given by:

$$\Pi_1((k)) = .480 + (.264)^k(.245)$$
$$k = 1, 2, \ldots, 184$$

Both probabilities settle down very quickly to the respective steady state values for each season but one can identify the boundary interaction between the alternating seasons as a stationary residual transient response that somewhat smooths out the change of seasons. During the first few days of the Dry season, the probabilities of rain are slightly higher than the normal tendency for the season and during the first few days of the Wet season the probabilities of rain are slightly lower than the normal tendency for the season.

Tables 3 and 4 summarize the stationary probabilities for the respective seasons.

Table 3.   Stationary probabilities of rain for days of the Dry season

Date	Day No.	Probability
November 1	1	.285
November 2	2	.245
November 3	3	.237
November 4	4	.235
November 5	5	.235
April 29	180	.235
April 30	181	.235

Table 4.   Stationary probabilities of rain for days of the Wet season

Date	Day No.	Probability
May 1	1	.415
May 2	2	.463
May 3	3	.475
May 4	4	.479
May 5	5	.480
October 30	183	.480
October 31	184	.480

Since it tends to rain slightly less than one fourth of the days during the Dry season and approximately one half of the days during the Wet season and since both seasons last approximately the same, it stands to reason that it should rain slightly over one third of the days throughout the years. This can be confirmed by calculating Π_1'':

$$\Pi_1'' = \frac{181}{365}(.235) + \frac{184}{365}(.480) - 0.00007$$
$$= .358$$

CONCLUSION

The methodology of Gabriel and Newmann yields a wealth of information on year round climatic conditions. This information should prove of value to planners in both the agricultural and tourism sectors of the local economy. It should prove useful to the researchers of the Mobile Irrigation Laboratory and to the agronomists of the Homestead Agricultural Center. Even though the data reflects values calculated for the City of Miami, results should not be too dissimilar for regions throughout Miami Dade County. At the very worst, the methodology may be re-implemented on other regions.

The methodology implemented here is applicable in any country of the world that is subject to a subtropical climate with well defined Dry and Wet seasons. Cuba and Puerto Rico, for example, are two such nations.

REFERENCES

Çinlar, E., (1975), *Introduction to Stochastic Processes,* Prentice Hall, New Jersey.

Cox, D. R. & Miller, H. D., (1968), *The Theory of Stochastic Processes,* John Wiley, New York.

Gabriel, K. B. & Newmann, J., (1957), "On a Distribution of Weather Cycles by Length," *Quart. J. R.. Met. Soc.* 83, 375-80

Gabriel, K. B. & Newmann, J., (1962), "A Markov Chain Model for Daily Rainfall Occurrence at Tel Aviv," *Quart. J. R. met. Soc.* 88, 90-5

Gross, D. & Harris, C., (1974), *Fundamentals of Queueing Theory,* John Wiley, New York.

Hajnal, J., (1956), "The Ergodic Properties of Non-Homogeneous Finite Markov Chains," *Proc. Camb. phil. Soc.* 52, 67-77

Hajnal, J., (1958), "Weak Ergodicity in Non-Homogeneous Markov Chains," *Proc. Camb. Phil. Soc.* 54, 233-46

Howard, R. A., (1971), *Dynamic Probabilistic Systems,* vol. 1, John Wiley, New York.

Karlin, S. & Taylor, H. M., (1975), *A First Course in Stochastic Processes,* Academic Press, New York.

Law, A. & Kelton, D.W., (1982), *Simulation Modeling & Analysis,* McGraw-Hill, New York.

Roqué, D. R., (1982), "Queueing Networks Structured Via Interacting Overflow Lines," Doctoral Dissertation, George Washington Univ., University Microfilms # 8302633, Ann Arbor, Michigan.

Roqué, D. R., (1996), "On the Stationarity of Some Time Varying Markov Chains," Departmental Seminar, Dept. of Mathematics, (April 9), Barry University, Miami Shores, Fl.

Ross, S.M., (1983), *Stochastic Processes,* John Wiley, New York.

Ross, S. M., (1985), *Introduction to Probability Models,* Academic Press, Orlando, Fl.

COMMENTS ON

"Rainfall in Little Havana" by Roqué

Jorge Luis Romeu

It is with much professional satisfaction that we discuss Dr. Diego Roqué's Markov model, implemented in his paper "Rainfall in Little Havana." For, as we have stated in previous ASCE papers (Romeu, 1996) there is much need for review, update and implementation of quantitative modeling methods in our analyses of the Cuban situation.

Roqué's paper is a clear, clean and useful example of the use of Markov Chains in forecasting. It can be easily implemented with Cuban data, in the same manner Roqué has done in the Little Havana example. This work could even be broken down by provinces, or by geographical regions, and used in agriculture, construction and other outdoor activities that are substantially affected by rain, with obvious benefits for the Cuban economy.

However, Markov modeling can go much further. In addition to forecasting, such models can be used in the study and control of many time dependent processes, including socioeconomic and political processes. And it is in this direction that we would like to discuss and expand Roqué's paper, in lieu of commenting on his neat math derivation.

Implementation of Markov Chains require the definition of: (i) two or more states; (ii) a transition mechanism defined by a (TPM) matrix of probabilities of change from one state to another; and (iii) a time domain with fixed increments (e.g., the system is observed by hours, days, weeks, months, etc.). In such case we obtain a "memoryless" process, where the future is dependent on the past only by way of

the present. This model allows the description of a process as a "black box" and provides, among other important performance measures: (i) the probability of being in a given state, at a given time in the future; (ii) the mean time to reach a given state; (iii) the probabilities (or mean times) of sojourning in each of the steady states; and (iv) the time to reach the system steady state. All of this Dr. Roqué has illustrated with states "rain" and "dry" in his "Rainfall in Little Havana" paper.

However, we could attempt to implement Markov models in socioeconomic contexts closer to the activities of ASCE. For example, we could define two states: one "unstable" (say dictatorial or revolutionary) and another "stable" (say democratic) for a country (say the Cuban republic during the XX Century). If we could also estimate the transition probabilities from one state to another, then we could, as Roqué did, use a Markov Chain approach. Then, we could forecast say, the probability of being in a given state on a given year (e.g., arriving at a democratic state in 2000) when starting in another given state (say, under a dictatorial regime) at some previous time (e.g., in Cuba, in 1990).

The main problem with modeling socioeconomic problems is, precisely, obtaining the data to estimate the transition (TPM) matrix. As seen from Roqué's work, there are several years of daily rain data that allow the estimation of his TPM matrix. However, we usually do not find enough state transitions, in our mentioned socioeconomic context, to do likewise.

One alternative would be to pool data from similar countries. For example, we could assume that certain Latin American countries that share the same history and socioeconomic conditions, could be modeled in a single process by pooling their data. Unfortunately, if we pool too many countries together, however, their dissimilarities will introduce variability into the process, and the (TPM) transition estimations will suffer. Finally, we can refine this model by considering the time T, to the next transition, as a (second random exponential) variable, as opposed to the fixed daily, monthly, etc., time increments. This refined model is now an Embedded Markov Chain.

SOME USEFUL MODEL EXTENSIONS

Following the nomenclature and approach in Kalbfleisch and Prentice (1980), let us now consider T, the continuous and positive random variable "time to failure or transition." We will denote its associated Survivor Function $P\{T>t\}$ as $F(t)$; its density function as $f(t)$ and its instantaneous failure or transition rate, at time $T=t$ (also called Hazard Function) as $\lambda(t)$. We can see that: $\lambda(t) = f(t)/F(t)$.

The Hazard Function $\lambda(t)$, which depends on the time $T=t$, can also be characterized as minus the derivative of the natural logarithm of the Survivor Function. This characterization makes the Hazard Function the centerpiece in the definition of both, the Survivor and the density functions of T. Therefore, we can now transfer our modeling efforts of variable "time to failure" T, into modeling its Hazard Function $\lambda(t)$.

First, notice that $\lambda(t)$ can be an increasing, decreasing or mixture (bathtub curve) function. In industrial reliability studies, for example, an increasing hazard occurs when failures tend to become more frequent as the (device or) process ages. Decreasing Hazard Functions occur when process failures become less frequent over time. Finally, the bathtub Hazard Function characterizes the entire process life cycle. It occurs because failures tend initially to be more frequent (infant mortality) then stabilize at a low level (useful life) and finally rapidly increase again (during the aging period).

Let us adapt this to a socioeconomic context, like the one in our Cuban example. An increasing Hazard Function can be justified in a new, revolutionary regime, whose emerging authority is initially challenged by many and can lose power. On the other hand, a decreasing hazard may be justified in a personal regime, legitimized by time and a well defined succession structure (e.g., monarchy), where authority is stable and widely accepted with passing time.

Finally, the well known and mathematically convenient constant hazard rate is obtained, in industrial applications, by curtailing the process life cycle—and hence modifying the bathtub curve. First, screen testing (weeding out infant mortality items) and then the implementation of an efficient replacement policy (items are taken out of service before they reach their aging process) leaves only the "useful life" period.

In the socioeconomic context, such bathtub hazard helps explain the entire political life cycle of a successfully consolidated dictatorship. At the onset, such regime faces strong opposition, which can bring it down, inducing a large hazard. With time, it entrenches itself (through force) crushing most of the opposition and stabilizes in power (lower, constant hazard). Finally, the hazard increases again as the dictator ages, the regime demoralizes, its traditional leaders either die or become incapacitated by old age, and a younger, better prepared generation of technocrats challenges the old guard to make changes.

Such life cycle system behavior can be currently observed in Mexico and in China. It was also characteristic of the military dictatorships of Salazar in Portugal, Porfirio Díaz in Mexico, and Stroessner in Paraguay. And it is also likely also occur in Cuba, with Castro.

Finally, political stability (constant hazard) in socioeconomic contexts results from preventing abrupt government changes, such as revolutions and military coups, as well as prolonged personal governments. It plays the same role as screening for infant mortality and good replacement policies for aging problems in the industrial setting.

In either of these two contexts (socioeconomic or industrial) constant hazard rate is what allows the application of Markov Models (which require constant transition rates to guarantee the "memoryless" property). A functional example of such processes is the Exponential model, which exhibits the classical constant Hazard Function (or failure rate).

Finally, the Two Parameter Weibull (λ, p) Model, constitutes a generalization of the Exponential. The Weibull Hazard Function is:

$$\lambda(t) = \lambda p (\lambda t)^{(p-1)}$$

If p = 1, the hazard $\lambda(t)$ is constant and the model reduces to the Exponential. However, if p > 1 the Hazard Function is increasing and if p < 1 it is decreasing in t.

REGRESSION MODELS

Let us now "open the Black Box" in the following way. Let $z = (z_1, \ldots z_p)$ be a vector of p "covariates" or process explanatory variables, and let the Hazard Function $\lambda(z)$ be:

$$\lambda(t; z) = \lambda(t) c(zb)$$

where b is also a vector, of p coefficients (i.e., weights) and the function c(zb) either linear, inverse linear or exponential (i.e., c(zb) = 1+ zb or $(1+ zb)^{-1}$ or exp(zb)).

Now we have a Hazard Function $\lambda(t; z)$ that depends not only on the time t to failure (through $\lambda(t)$) but also on a set of device or process characteristics, defined by the vector of (explanatory) covariates z, weighted by the coefficients b. In the socioeconomic context, this would mean that T (i.e. time to transition) is now associated with a set of problem covariates that describe particular characteristics of the different countries included in the analysis, such as population, GDP, unemployment, etc.

The crux of the problem now becomes modeling this new relationship, akin to the problem of determining the parameters of a regression model. We usually select, for modeling convenience, the functional form:

$$\lambda(t; z) = \lambda(t) \exp\{zb\}$$

As a result, the conditional density function f(t) of T (time to transition) is now:

$$f(t; z) = \lambda \exp\{zb\} \exp[-\lambda t \exp\{zb\}]$$

Using the transformation Y = Log (T), we can eventually arrive to the following model, that expresses the log failure rate as a linear function of covariates z:

$$Y = - Log (\lambda) - zb + W$$

where W is a random variable (specifically, having extreme value distribution).

Skipping the mathematical details (that the reader can find in the reference given above) this result provides a regression model on covariates z, with coefficients b, which leads to the development of the Proportional Hazards Model (Cox, 1972).

PROPORTIONAL HAZARDS MODEL IN CUBAN SOCIOECONOMIC STUDIES

This model has been successfully and widely used in cancer studies, where it has served two very important goals. First, it has allowed the inclusion, in the model, of many different patients, with many different medical and physical conditions, thus increasing the pool of available data and leading to better estimates of the transition rates and the times to remission, to death, etc. Second, it has allowed the establishment of "risk factors," parameters that affect (increase or decrease) the Hazard Function and consequently also the time to failure in the process (sometimes positively, other times negatively). These risk factor estimations provide (i) a relative weight for each factor analyzed and (ii) their statistical significance (or lack of significance). The latter, has proven useful in determining what are the prime (and the secondary) factors affecting the cancer process, providing a better understanding of it and ultimately some degree of control over its course.

In the Cuban socioeconomic context, we propose using this approach to study and understand the factors and subprocesses associated with the current Cuban situation. We can apply this modeling approach with certain economic and social factors known to effect the political stability. Then, we can analyze and quantify their contribution, sign and statistical significance, as described above, and use them to help redress the state of the nation.

To find enough data to implement this approach we first need to define a subset of appropriate Latin American countries. Then, a set of covariates such as GDP, inflation rate, unemployment, current account, etc. would be defined. Then, we also need to define the set of states (e.g., democracy, dictatorship) we are interested in studying, with the transition modes to go from one to the other (e.g., revolution, coup, foreign intervention, election). We then collect, from the countries selected, for the historical period included in the analysis, the time to state change (say in years or months) and the corresponding values of the covariates. Finally, we use the Proportional Hazards model with the above defined times and covariates and obtain estimates of their values, signs and statistical significance.

There is yet another statistical alternative to the above mentioned approach. It is also of the regression class, though not related to reliability modeling. It consists in implementing a Discriminant Analysis.

It may be possible to divide the Latin American countries into three groups. One group will be comprised of those countries considered unambiguously as "positive." A second group is comprised of those considered unambiguously as "negative." Finally, there is a third group composed of those countries for which we do not have a clear cut position or evaluation. We can again measure specific factors or variables (say, size, GDP, inflation, unemployment, etc.) and implement a Discriminant Analysis using them. Such approach would also yield the degree of influence, sign and statistical significance of the factors sought. But this is material for a future, separate paper for ASCE.

To conclude, we believe that Dr. Roqué, with his well developed example of the use of Markov Chains to study environmental problems, has provided an opportunity for ASCE researchers to review the wealth and potential of the Markov, Reliability and Proportional Hazards models, in the study of Cuban socioeconomic problems.

REFERENCES

Cox, D. R. (1972). "Regression Models and Life Tables (with discussion)." *Journal of the Royal Statistical Society*, Series B. Vol. 34, pp. 187-220.

Kalbfleisch, J. and R. Prentice (1980). *Statistical Analysis of Failure Time Data*. New York: Wiley.

Romeu, J. L. (1996). "Comments on the Future Phases of the Cuban Economy." *Cuba in Transition—Volume 6*, pp. 317-319. Washington: Association for the Study of the Cuban Economy.

SOCIALISM AND ENVIRONMENTAL DISRUPTION: IMPLICATIONS FOR CUBA

Sergio Díaz-Briquets and Jorge Pérez-López

All societies and economic systems—industrialized or developing, market economy or socialist—must deal with environmental disruption. In market economies, environmental disruption has been the subject of considerable economic analysis. Environmental disruption is associated with "failure" of the market mechanism in the face of externalities and public goods. Much less attention has been paid to environmental disruption under socialism, in part because of theoretical arguments that environmental disruption would not arise in socialist societies. A former Soviet Minister of Public Health found environmental disruption in market economies perfectly understandable: "The capitalist system by its very essence is incapable of taking radical measures to ensure the efficient conservation of nature (Goldman 1970, p. 37)." The implication is that the Soviet Union and other socialist countries could take, and had taken, such measures.

The environmental devastation in Eastern Europe and the former Soviet Union that became evident upon the fall of socialism and the lifting of the information curtain enveloping these countries, makes it clear that the theoretical arguments about the incompatibility between socialism and environmental disruption had very little to do with reality. We fear that the environmental situation in Cuba, an eager implementer of the socialist economic model, may be similar in many respects to that which prevailed in Eastern Europe and the former Soviet Union.

This paper reviews the literature on the theory and practice of environmental disruption under social-

ism. It discusses specific features of centrally planned economies that make these economies prone to environmental disruption, with special emphasis on the socialist model of agricultural development. The paper concludes with a discussion of some of the features of socialism in Cuba that have shaped the island's environmental situation and prospects.

SOCIALIST ECONOMIES AND THE ENVIRONMENT

Advocates of socialism argued, on theoretical grounds, that environmental disruption could not occur in a socialist society. Environmental disruption occurs in market economies, they argued, because economic decisions are made by individuals whose own interests—rather than those of society—are paramount. In centrally planned economies, decisions are centralized and the objective function for the economy that is maximized by central planners includes environmental quality. Under socialist organization, therefore, there can be no environmental externalities since environmental issues are not external to decisionmaking by central planners (Gregory and Stuart 1974, p. 407). The following quote from a Soviet economic journal captures the essence of the perceived superiority of socialism:

> The effective management of the economy is incompatible with the capitalist system. This is manifested most clearly by the vast amount of environmental degradation in most capitalist countries. It is clear that within the framework of a capitalist economy there is no point in even raising the question of management of the environment on a nationwide scale.

But such a formulation is logical and necessary in conditions of a planned socialist economy (Kramer 1974, p. 886).

The argument for the superiority of socialism over market economies with respect to environmental quality has also been posed in terms of property rights. Public ownership of the means of production under socialism eliminates the structural cause of excessive pollution that exists in market economies arising from private ownership of capital and land. The incomplete specification of property rights in market economies permits an important share of the costs of production and consumption to fall on individuals external to realized market transactions. In a socialist economy, where all productive assets are owned by "society," property rights are fully assigned and correctly specified; external costs by definition do not exist, and every economic decisionmaker has direct material reasons to recognize the full economic costs of his or her actions (McIntyre and Thornton 1978, p. 187).

Several other theoretical arguments regarding the compatibility of socialism with environmental quality have also been put forward. Oskar Lange, for instance, argued that socialist central planners would place a high value upon a clean environment, ensuring that economic growth is accompanied by environmental quality. In Lange's view, a socialist economy would be better able to construct the set of remedial taxes to internalize external costs because it would not be confronted by the political difficulties and managerial resistance that result from the incomplete specification of property rights in market economies (McIntyre and Thornton 1978, p. 188). Maurice Dobb suggested that in the real world, central planners might have some difficulty in obtaining and processing information; nevertheless they would make economic decisions with maximum global vision and keeping in mind their environmental impact. Jan Tinbergen endorsed the notion that, in general, decisions made at the higher possible levels minimize the problem of externalities (Gregory and Stuart 1974, p. 408).

Finally, the case has been made (McIntyre and Thornton 1978, pp. 189-190) that decisionmakers in a Soviet-type centrally planned economy have an advantage over a market-type economy in obtaining the required information to make meaningful analyses of the benefits and costs of pollution abatement systems. Due to their position, central planners have access to three types of information that are critical for cost-benefit analyses: (1) the specific production processes used by enterprises; (2) the locational circumstances of enterprises; and (3) the relative merits of centralized or decentralized abatement strategies. That is, should Soviet political decisionmakers at the highest party and government levels embrace a commitment to environmental quality, planners would have access to the technical information required to make efficient environmental choices (McIntyre and Thornton 1981, p. 147).

The Reality of Environmental Disruption Under Socialism

However, "many of the theoretical advantages that a socialist society would seem to have for coping with the problem [of environmental disruption] have proven to be illusory in practice" (Goldman 1972, p. 326). The reality of environmental disruption in socialist countries—amply demonstrated by the severe environmental degradation observed in the former Soviet Union and socialist countries of Eastern Europe—contradicts the theoretical propositions:

> One of the ironies of the former centrally planned economies, we have come to learn, is how little they cared about protecting their environments. Such rapacious behavior should not be so prevalent in societies whose purported objectives were defined in terms of the social rather than the private good. Nevertheless, virtually every one of the countries of Central and Eastern Europe is confronting a Herculean task in slowing down the rate of pollution and cleaning up decades of environmental neglect (Bohi 1994, p. vii).

It was well known to Western scholars that by the 1960s and 1970s, the Soviet Union and the former socialist countries of Eastern Europe already faced serious environmental problems (e.g., Bush 1972, 1974; Goldman 1970, 1972, 1973; Volgyes 1974). Industrial pollution threatening pristine Lake Baikal, a fire in the Iset River in Sverdslok, the gradual disappearance of the Aral and Caspian Seas because of the diversion of the rivers that fed them, smog and polluted air in Central Europe from low-quality coal, had all been documented in the literature.

Nevertheless, the lack of official statistics and reports made it difficult to appreciate the breadth and depth of environmental disruption in socialist countries. The information barriers began to break down in the late 1980s with the implementation by the Soviet Union of a policy of openness ("glasnost") that brought about the publication in 1989 of the first-ever official reports on the state of the environment (Altshuler and Golubchikov 1990; Yablokov 1990).

The magnitude of the environmental disaster in the Soviet Union and the Eastern European socialist countries that became apparent upon the fall of socialism surpassed the expectations of even the most pessimistic observers. As Feshbach and Friendly (1992, p. 1) put it with regard to the Soviet Union:

> When historians finally conduct an autopsy of the Soviet Union and Soviet Communism, they may reach the verdict of death by ecocide. ... No other great industrial civilization so systematically and so long poisoned its land, air, water, and people. None so loudly proclaiming its efforts to improve public health and protect nature so degraded both. And no advanced society faced such a bleak political and economic reckoning with so few resources to invest toward recovery.

The situation in Eastern Europe, and the diagnosis of its cause, were very similar:

> The legacy of our polluted continent [Europe] can partly be blamed on the policies adopted by the socialist Communist states over the last four decades. The Eastern bloc countries never admitted to pollution problems during the first two decades of the post Second World War era. In spite of Stalinist and post-Stalinist heavy industrialization policies, pollution of any kind was, according to their propaganda, only to be found in the West where capitalist profit motive was the cause of their environmental degradation problems. Hindsight has now proved the fallacy of such claims, but does not solve the way forward in these countries (Carter and Turnock 1993, p. 189).

The recent literature on the "environmental disaster" in the former Soviet Union and the socialist countries of Central and Eastern Europe is vast. Some of the most salient examples of environmental disruption in the former Soviet Union and the socialist countries of Eastern Europe include:

Air: The industrial sector was the most important source of air pollution in the former Soviet Union. Coal-fired power and heating plants, steelworks, and chemical plants emitting high levels of pollutants were located across the nation. Emissions of air pollutants exceeded established health norms in all industrial areas. In 103 industrial cities—with combined population of over 50 million people—emissions exceeded normal standards by ten-fold or more; during 1988, pollution reached 50 times the standard in 16 cities. Heavy air pollution was responsible for a high incidence of lung disease in several areas of the country and also for forest die-back in Lithuania, the Urals, the Ukraine, and Siberia (Satre Ahlander 1994, pp. 7-9).

Eastern Europe suffered from more severe air pollution problems than the former Soviet Union (Ziegler 1991, p. 89). Air pollution arose primarily from the heavy reliance on lignite, or brown coal, as an energy source: over three-quarters of Poland's energy consumption and two-thirds of Czechoslovakia's and the former East Germany. Coal's noxious fumes damaged many buildings and forests and caused serious health problems throughout the region (Carter and Turnock 1993, p. 189).

Water: Highly polluted surface waters—those with concentrations of pollutants about 10 times the permitted maximum—in the former Soviet Union included the Western Bug, the Dnestr, Danube, and Don rivers, and the rivers of Sakhalin Island; the Volga and the Irtysh and the Amur river basins also had high levels of pollutants and impurities (Feshbach 1991, p. 231). In some areas, the main culprits of such pollution were the pulp and paper industries, steelworks, and the chemical industry. In others, agriculture was the main source of water pollution because of the intensive use of mineral fertilizers and pesticides (Satre Ahlander 1994, p. 14). In 1988, the Soviet Union was able to treat only 30 percent of its sewage to meet established sanitary norms; 50 percent of the sewage was improperly treated, while the remaining 20 percent was dumped into the water untreated (Satre Ahlander 1994, p. 15).

One of the most poignant examples of environmental disaster in the former Soviet Union was the desiccation of the Aral Sea. An ill-conceived plan initiated in the 1950s to increase cotton acreage in Central Asia by massive irrigation of marginal lands and intensive use of fertilizers diverted water that normally fed the Aral Sea; in 1989, only one-eighth as much water as in 1960 reached the Aral Sea from its two main feeders, the Syr Darya and the Amu Darya (Feshbach 1992, pp. 73-75). The Aral Sea itself, formerly the fourth largest inland sea in the world, has lost over one-third of its area, the surface level has dropped by 13 meters, and the volume reduced by 790 cubic kilometers. Moreover, whatever water reached the Aral was heavily contaminated with phosphates, ammonia, nitrites, nitrates, and chlorinated hydrocarbons from agricultural runoff. Major storms of dust, salt, and toxic residues from the exposed seabed of the Aral have contaminated the surrounding region, turning once-fertile pastures into a desert and severely affecting the health of the population. Ironically, it is estimated that over one-half of the water drawn off from the Aral Sea Basin is wasted because of highly inefficient irrigation systems, evaporation, and carelessness and incompetence. Excessive application of water to crops coupled with inadequate drainage have turned large tracts of land into saline swamps (Akiner 1993, pp. 256-257).

Direct and indirect pollution of surface water resulted in the poisoning of lakes and rivers in Eastern Europe through acid deposition from refineries, mining operations, and other industrial activities. In Poland, both the Vistula and Oder rivers are virtually ecologically dead as a result of pollution from mining operations in Silesia. The Baltic Sea is heavily polluted with waterborne sewage, industrial effluents, and agricultural chemical waste. The Black Sea is on the verge of a catastrophe because of extremely high pollution levels, with some reports suggesting that all life could disappear from the Black Sea; much of the pollution entering the Black Sea is carried by the Danube, along whose banks are located paper mills, iron and steelworks, petroleum and sugar refineries,

chemical plants, cement plants, coal and minerals-processing plants, breweries, and canneries (Carter and Turnock 1993, pp. 191-192).

Land/Vegetation: There is a large literature that documents the adverse results on the environment of the implementation of the Soviet agricultural model, which relied heavily on large-scale farming, chemical inputs and mechanization. According to official sources, 58 percent of total agricultural land of the former Soviet Union was affected by salinization, erosion, acidity, or waterlogging. Despite a ban, DDT continued to be used. A survey conducted in 1989 of 841 farms producing grain, rice, wine, tea, fruit, and vegetables found DDT in 35.5 percent of 250 agricultural products; 16.6 percent of the soil had been polluted by DDT (Feshbach 1991, pp. 229-230). In 1988, one-fifth of the Soviet population lived in regions where the ecological situation was deemed to be unsatisfactory; agricultural lands affected by overgrazing, intensive cultivation, deforestation, changed chemical composition of the soil, wind erosion, desertification, and compacting of the topsoil, accounted for a significant share of these lands deemed unsatisfactory (Satre Ahlander 1994, p. 6).

Farming, although itself suffering from air pollution, was one of the main polluters of land in Eastern Europe. Tillable land suffered also from open air mining methods and deposition of municipal and industrial waste. Further, poor agricultural practices led to water and wind erosion and soil degradation (Satre Ahlander 1993, p. 193).

One of the most visible signs of environmental disruption in the region is the destruction of forests; vegetation, especially from forests, suffers from raised contamination by industrial waste emissions and other pollutants. Damage to forests in the former Czechoslovakia has been attributed to emissions from the Polish copper refining town of Legnica in Silesia. The region from Cracow in southern Poland to the Tatra Mountains in the former Czechoslovakia is covered by a semi-permanent pall of sulphur, nitrogen, and other pollutants emitted from negligent enterprises in both countries (Carter and Turnock 1993, p. 194).

Nuclear contamination: The April 1986 accident at the Chernobyl Nuclear Power Plant in the Ukraine is without parallel as a technological disaster. It exposed 400 million persons to radiation and caused 31 directly attributable deaths, as many as 28,000 delayed cancer fatalities, evacuation of 116,000 people, and polluted ground water deposits throughout Europe (Lofstedt and White 1990, p. 2).

Nuclear radioactivity in the former Soviet Union is a much broader environmental hazard, however. The magnitude of the network of "atomic cities" (atomgrad) that carried out the development and production of nuclear weapons in the former Soviet Union is still not known with certainty, but as many as 90 locations have been identified; not known with certainty either are the level of radioactive contamination of the areas, the stocks of nuclear materials that are stored, or the condition of the storage facilities. The same is true for nuclear waste dumps in the Barents, Kara, and White Seas of the Arctic, the Sea of Japan, and locations in the Far East. It was revealed in 1992 that in the city of Moscow alone there were 636 radioactive toxic waste sites, 1,500 in St. Petersburg, 1,000 in Penza, and 200 in Omsk (Feshbach 1993, pp. 233-234).

The use of nuclear power for commercial power generation in the former Soviet Union and Eastern Europe has been a source of radioactive contamination and has the potential for a nuclear catastrophe. Antiquated methods of uranium mining in the former Czechoslovakia and processing in Bulgaria have affected local health; disposal of nuclear wastes accumulated in power plants is problematic for Eastern European nations given that the former Soviet Union no longer takes back spent fuel rods and reprocessing service costs in the open market are very high (Carter and Turnock 1993, p. 196). In the Soviet Union, a radiation leak occurred at the nuclear power plant at Sosnovy Bor in March 1992 and a radiation explosion at the Tomsk-7 reactor in April 1993 (Greenblatt 1993, p. 245).

The safety of the 58 Soviet-designed commercial power reactors in operation in the former Soviet Union and Eastern European nations is a matter of serious concern. Experts agree that these reactors do not meet international safety standards and pose significant safety risks because of deficiencies in their design and in their operation by plant managers and personnel who lack adequate training in many of the safety procedures practiced by operators in Western Europe, Japan, and the United States. Twenty-five of the reactors—including 15 of the model that was involved in the Chernobyl accident—are considered to be the least safe because of the lack of a containment structure and other inherent design deficiencies and cannot be economically upgraded (U.S. General Accounting Office 1994, pp. 1-3).

Explanations of Environmental Disruption Under Socialism

Three general explanations of environmental disruption in the Soviet Union have been presented in the literature. These three explanations, which are also applicable to environmental disruption in Cuba and other centrally planned economies (CPEs), are: (1) failure of the system; (2) conscious neglect; and (3) central planning implementation problems.

System Failure: The thrust of this line of argument is that environmental disruption occurs in CPEs because the economic organizational model in fact does not incorporate the environment into the planning process. The central planning mechanism fails to generate appropriate resource valuations, including the costs of environmental disruption and of the use of natural resources. Unaware of appropriate resource valuations, planners cannot allocate resources rationally even if they wished to do so (Gregory and Stuart 1974, p. 411).

In reality, allocation of environmental expenditures in CPEs tends to be made by the central authorities on the basis of the "branch principle," whereby resources are distributed through the hierarchy of ministries rather than directly to regions or cities where environmental protection expenditures could be most effective. Ministries, in turn, assign such resources to their own priorities, not necessarily the ones that would be best for the environment on a national scale. The emphasis in CPEs on quantity information and direct commands—rather than on the flow of price information among economic agents—in resource allocation decisions have given rise to situations in which harmful, yet potentially useful, waste products of an enterprise may have been discarded into convenient waterways rather than used as an input into a complementary production process, even where enterprises were located physically close to each other (Satre Ahlander 1994, p. 26).

The valuation problem is further complicated by Marxist theory, which is prejudiced against charging for natural resources (Gregory and Stuart 1974, p. 411). Central planners tended to use natural resources as free goods or assign them a very low valuation, thereby creating an incentive for the extensive use of natural resources. An example related to the mining sector is instructive:

> ... after a Soviet mine operator has extracted the richest ore, his marginal costs and average variable costs begin to rise. As it takes more units of labor and machinery to extract one unit of ore or oil, the mine director begins to look for another, more easily exploited mine or oil deposit. This is a natural reaction since in the slang of the economist, "bygones are bygones," that is the mine operator does not have to worry about recovering his old fixed costs (Goldman 1972, p. 315).

Moreover, enterprise managers tended to be rewarded on the basis of fulfillment of output goals, rather than prudent use of resources (Satre Ahlander 1994, p. 27).

Finally, fines imposed on enterprises that violated environmental rules were insignificant compared to bonuses for overfulfillment of production plans (Goldman 1972, p. 322).

Conscious Neglect: Another general explanation of environmental disruption in the former Soviet Union is that environmental concerns were consciously discarded, as they were considered as one of the costs of rapid economic growth and industrialization. Czarist Russia was a backward, developing country at the turn of the century. Although not the highest priority, conservation of the environment was important during Lenin's tenure at the helm of the Soviet Union, at least in terms of legislation adopted. However, even before Lenin's death, rapid economic growth and industrialization became para-

mount and other economic objectives, including conservation, set aside (Goldman 1973, p. 57).

The policy of rapid economic growth and industrialization pursued by the Soviet Union since the rise of Stalin emphasized the development of gigantic heavy industry enterprises. These enterprises used huge amounts of natural resources and generated vast amounts of pollution. Another element of this policy was to increase output in the short run, neglecting "non-productive" activities such as pollution abatement. During this period, then, the Soviet leadership deliberately traded off environmental protection for short-term rapid growth; it did not recognize the real costs of growth and postponed some of the costs (e.g., environmental clean up) by letting them accumulate in the form of a stock of pollution (Gregory and Stuart 1974, p. 410).

Implementation of Central Planning: Perhaps the most powerful explanation of environmental disruption in the Soviet Union and other CPEs is that the perfectly-centralized system of decisionmaking foreseen in the socialist economic model has not proven to be practical in the real world (Gregory and Stuart 1974, p. 411). First, contrary to central planning myth, most crucial economic decisions are not made by a small group of planners at the apex of the planning hierarchy with a broad view of the economy. In reality, they are made by ministerial and regional authorities and by plant managers none of whom can—or cares to—see the entire economy and the effects of a given decision on different aspects of the economy (Gregory and Stuart 1974, p. 411).

Second, ministries and other organizations with decisionmaking power in charge of managing a given industry and promoting its growth also have responsibility for preventing environmental damage by that industry (Kelley 1972, p. 571). Opponents of projects find themselves in the awkward position of having to lobby against national ministries or regional organizations on projects they believe create environmental disruption; these same organizations, in theory, are responsible for preventing environmental disruption (Gregory and Stuart 1974, pp. 411-412). According to Kramer (1974, p. 887), the reality of the Soviet system differs substantially from the theory of a centrally-planned monolith state that pursues the true interests of society. Instead, "government bureaucracies in the Soviet Union appear to be the functional equivalent of the capitalist entrepreneur who greedily pursues his private gains to society's detriment."

Third, central planning has relied almost exclusively on fulfilling output goals. Less quantifiable goals—such as cost reductions, innovations, and environmental quality—have played a very limited role in decisionmaking (Gregory and Stuart 1974, p. 411).

And fourth, investment planning has tended to favor industrialization through the creation of new production capacities rather than through retrofitting of existing ones. Investment policies promoted the building of new plants rather than modernizing existing heavy industry enterprises—gigantic plants that were technologically obsolete and generated large amounts of pollution. The emphasis on quantitative targets meant that older plants were kept in production as long as they met output plans, without regard to the pollution they generated (Satre Ahlander 1994, pp. 30-31).

SYSTEMIC REASONS FOR ENVIRONMENTAL DISRUPTION UNDER SOCIALISM

There are certain characteristics of CPEs—mostly arising from the pervasive role of government in the economy—that generate pressures resulting in environmental disruption. According to an analyst,

> It is possible, at one extreme, to inflict great damage [to the environment] whilst generating very little economic welfare; on the other hand, it is possible to generate significantly more welfare with relatively little environmental disruption. It is now clear that the communist economic and political systems are the worst embodiment of the former extreme. The East European countries, currently in transition from communism, are incomparably less prosperous, while being more environmentally damaged, than the industrialized Western nations. A cynic might say that industrial effluent and atmospheric pollution per unit of national product was the only field where the ... [Eastern Europe] ... has secured a decisive lead over the Western nations (Sobell 1990, p. 47).

Some of these systemic characteristics—what Goldman (1970, p. 41) calls "incentives to pollute under socialism"—have been mentioned earlier, but they are discussed briefly below for the sake of providing a fuller presentation.

Marxist theory of value and pricing of natural resources: Unless some specific exception is made, resources under the Marxist labor theory of value are treated as free goods. For many years, the Soviet Union treated natural resources in this fashion in its planning system. Thus, whenever mine operators or oil drillers had exploited the most accessible ore or oil deposits, they moved to a new site where average variable costs were lower, wasting valuable ores and multiplying environmental disruption (Goldman 1970, p. 41). In the 1970s, resource valuation was raised to a priority economic task because of rising extraction costs for a number of mineral and other natural resources, and low rates of nominal rate of return to capital in extractive industries (Thornton 1978). Despite these efforts, the proper valuation of natural resources continues to be an intractable problem for socialist economies.

Central planning's emphasis on quantitative goals: Managers and state officials in CPEs were judged almost entirely on the extent to which they fulfilled quantitative production goals (Goldman 1970, p. 41). Given this virtually single evaluation criterion, there is no incentive for managers or state officials to divert productive resources from output-generating applications in order to preserve the environment.

Unbalanced growth: The emphasis on economic growth through industrialization created an industrial structure in CPEs biased toward heavy industry. Heavy industries tended to be prominent users of energy and raw materials; CPEs consumed about twice as much energy (and even more raw materials) to produce one unit of gross domestic product than the advanced capitalist countries, and they used less efficient and more ecologically offensive fuels such as coal and lignites in doing so (Sobell 1970, p. 47). The priority assigned to heavy industry, a major contributor to pollution, coupled with the low level of environmental technology, explains why industrial pollution of the atmosphere was substantial in the former Soviet Union and Eastern and Central European socialist nations (Satre Ahlander 1994, p. 7).

Another example of unbalanced growth and its impact on the environment is the experience of the chemical industry of the Soviet Union. In the early 1960s, Khrushchev ordered that the Soviet Union should have a large chemical industry, and in response, numerous plants sprung up throughout the country. The decision to enlarge the chemical industry, and its implementation, were so sudden, that there was not sufficient time to consider the environmental disruption that would be caused (Goldman 1970, p. 41).

Failure to use potential economies of scale arising from state ownership of resources: In the Soviet Union and other CPEs, economies of scale were used against the environment: "rather than mobilizing resources to protect the environment, they were mobilized to combat the environment and change it in order to facilitate the fulfillment of politically determined production targets" (Satre Ahlander 1994, p. 21). Contrary to what was argued on theoretical grounds by supporters of socialism, state-owned companies have been no different from privately owned companies in the extent to which they have damaged the environment (Dahmén 1971, pp. 44-45). The lack of private property in CPEs means that these economies are also unable to measure private costs, as there are no private property owners to complain about decisions that affect their holdings or estimates of the value of the damage (Goldman 1970, p. 41).

Land tenure and extensive agricultural cultivation techniques: In most CPEs, land was in the hands of the state, typically organized in large enterprises and relying heavily on tractors and other mechanized equipment. Increases in production were based on bringing additional land under cultivation or introducing additional productive inputs (extensive cultivation). This agricultural production model was very disruptive of the environment: the pressure for additional agricultural land required massive irrigation projects and threatened water resources, heavy tractors compacted the soil and added to erosion prob-

lems, generous application of fertilizers and pesticides polluted water resources and affected the quality of food and public health (Satre Ahlander 1994, pp. 18-19). Agriculture was the heaviest polluter of water and soils in the former Soviet Union (Danilov-Danilian 1993, p. 33).

More broadly, collectivization created serious problems related to the stewardship of natural resources, which was most evident in the agricultural sector. Agricultural workers, who did not own the land they farmed, had little incentive to conserve resources. Relatively simple soil conservation techniques, such as crop rotation, were abandoned in the Soviet Union as input-intensive agriculture was embraced. This was less of a problem in other CPEs—such as Poland—where a significant portion of agricultural land remained in private hands.

Ineffective regulation: In theory, CPEs are a regulator's paradise: nearly all productive resources are owned by the state and the central plan, with its very detailed input and output targets, provides a very powerful instrument for regulators to influence production processes. The reality is very different. Hungarian economist Kornai (1992, pp. 140-145) has observed that enterprises in CPEs operate under a "soft budget constraint," meaning that if they overspend their financial plan, they can turn to the state for additional financial resources. Losses are financed by the state because drastic actions such as insolvency, bankruptcy, and plant closure create worker dislocations and are avoided at all costs.

Monetary penalties (fines) for violations of environmental standards, one of the strongest instruments available to regulators, are meaningless in the presence of soft budget constraints and do not create incentives for managers to comply. When they are used, fines tend to be very low in comparison with environmental disruption being done or alternative ways to remedy it. Goldman (1970, p. 39) relates the case of paper and pulp mills operating near Lake Baikal and threatening its ecosystem. A technological solution to the effluent problem caused by the mills was to build a sewage conduit to transport the effluents to another location where they could be properly disposed. Construction of the bypass was estimated to cost $40 million, while the mills were assessed fines of $55 for each violation. This disparity may be responsible for what Goldman calls the "lack of enthusiasm" on the part of mill managers to pursue the technological solution. Because fines are paid out of enterprise funds, this is tantamount to the state paying itself, and guilty managers in practice suffer no effective penalty when rules designed to stop pollution are ignored (Nove 1980, p. 79).

Fragmentation of decisionmaking: The ministerial system of economic decisionmaking that prevails in CPEs creates coordination problems and barriers to the efficient use of resources. The problems associated with the ministerial system of economic decisionmaking, and its ability to generate environmental disruptions, are most evident in large projects and in instances where the sequencing of activities is critical. Because responsibility in large projects is shared by several agencies, it is easy to shift blame to another organization and no one is answerable for environmental disruption. For example, eight different departments or ministries had responsibility for the development of a timber complex in Siberia where the potential for environmental damage was considerable (Nove 1980, p. 80). Different ministries have responsibility for the extraction of various types of minerals, wasting valuable natural resources and harming the promoting environment:

> ... many ores in nature appear in complex compounds intermingled with other minerals. Thus iron ore may also contain copper and lead and apatite may be combined with nepheline, a valuable mineral used in the production of aluminum. Unfortunately, the Ministry of Ferrous Metallurgy is usually unauthorized to process non-ferrous metals, and has no funds to handle such materials. As a result, it frequently happens that the spoils that are discarded are more valuable than the basic product that is extracted (Goldman 1973, p. 63).

The bureaucratic fragmentation of administrative responsibility has a more direct effect on the environment since each ministry or organization is responsible for setting standards for the area of the economy over which it exerts responsibility. The bureaucratic fragmentation for setting pollution standards and en-

forcing them leads to confusion and raises potential conflicts between regulatory agencies and the industries and municipalities they regulate. Environmental control is next to impossible when there are numerous ministries involved and each is charged with regulating its own particular sector. The multiplicity of agencies and ministries with some control means that ultimately no single agency is assigned overall responsibility (Goldman 1973, p. 59).

Lack of central environmental authorities: CPEs traditionally charged sectoral ministries with the simultaneous use and protection of natural resources. Each ministry established environmental standards with regard to the sector under its competence, made administrative decisions that affected the use of resources and protection of the environment, and received complaints from the public regarding environmental disruption. Agencies charged with using natural resources tend to be less than forceful in enforcing environmental mandates (Kelley 1976, p. 571).

Scarcity of capital: Pursuit of rapid growth and industrialization created a chronic shortage of capital in the Soviet Union. One of the strategies pursued by the government to deal with this shortage was to stretch available capital as far as possible. Inevitably, this meant that expenditures for non-productive construction and equipment (e.g., electrostatic precipitators for air treatment, water treatment systems, tertiary treatment plants for sewage control) were systematically dropped from investment projects in order to permit the financing of other projects that increased production (Goldman 1973, p. 58).

Lack of political accountability: The absence of political accountability in CPEs aggravated their inability to respond effectively to signals of environmental distress. Political and economic power rested with the communist party, which granted freedom to economic sectors to pursue their activities—including the freedom to pollute—so long as they produced the goods (Kabala 1992, p. 10).

Weak environmental movement: Environmental citizen lobbies in CPEs tended to be weak, and their ability to influence government actions was very limited. In the Soviet Union, environmental citizen lobbies, whether semi-official public conservation organizations or informal coalitions of environmentalists formed on certain key issues (such as the preservation of Lake Baikal), lacked extensive organizational base and the direct links with important party and state agencies that characterized their opponents in industry (Kelley 1976, p. 578). The weakness of environmental citizen lobbies in the former Soviet Union is consistent with the "atomization" of society that characterizes CPEs (Rev 1993, p. 12). Officials who make decisions that affect the environment in CPEs are not politically accountable; they typically "do not have to face a voting constituency which might reflect the conservation point of view, such as the League of Women Voters or the Sierra Club" in the United States (Goldman 1970, p. 41).

Control of information: One of the reasons for the weakness of environmental movements in CPEs was the control of information by the central government. The very limited amount of information that was disseminated placed the public at a disadvantage in challenging government action. In particular, "access to information on pollution—the principal weapon of citizens' groups in any country—was frustrated by the predilection toward secrecy in communist systems. For a long time, secrecy limited the degree of public pressure that could be brought to bear on the government to force environmental quality" (Kabala 1992, p. 11).

THE SOCIALIST AGRICULTURAL DEVELOPMENT MODEL

While the specific features of the socialist agricultural development model embraced by socialist countries varied from place to place according to political, cultural and national circumstances, the basic blueprint was inspired by the Soviet Union's historical experience. The features of this model are central to a study of the Cuban environmental situation and prospects given Cuba's predominant agricultural character and the fervor with which the ruling socialist elite replicated it in the island.

The essential characteristics of the agricultural organizational model that emerged in the former Soviet Union and was later adopted by other socialist countries were: 1) large-scale production units; 2) extensive cultivation; 3) mechanization; 4) technological interventions; and 5) heavy use of agricultural inputs such as chemical fertilizers and pesticides. They shaped Soviet agricultural policies and practices, and resulted in chronic agricultural shortages and environmental degradation. In the 1960s and 1970s, Cuba adopted the Soviet agricultural organizational model and, not surprisingly, replicated that country's negative record on agricultural production and preservation of the environment.

One of the first actions of the Bolshevik regime in 1917 was to confiscate large estates and to distribute land among the peasants. This change in land tenure meant that Russian peasants were no longer obligated to deliver a predetermined share of their output to landlords (as rental fees) or to the state (as taxes or principal payments) and for the first time had the freedom to make decisions regarding production of agricultural output and its marketing. A year later, as part of the regime of war communism, the Bolshevik leadership under Lenin introduced a system of requisitioning of agricultural surpluses from peasants, with the police serving as enforcers. However, the New Economic Policy (NEP) that began to be implemented in 1921 reversed the latter policy and allowed peasants to retain control over their land. It has been estimated that in the late 1920s, individual peasants farmed over 95 percent of the land; the Soviet government's role in agriculture during this period was primarily as a purchaser of grain from individual producers (Pryor 1992, p. 15).

In 1929, the Communist Party under Stalin's leadership began a ruthless drive to collectivize agriculture. By the mid-1930s, the collectivization process was essentially completed. It has been estimated that in 1938, 93.5 percent of peasant households were in collective farms (Gregory and Stuart 1974, pp. 106-107). In the late 1920s, Stalin argued on a number of occasions that simply combining farms would lead to increases in agricultural production; a further economic rationale for collectivization he often used was that small peasant farming produces the smallest marketable surplus, intimating that large-scale production units would benefit from economies of scale (Pryor 1992, p. 46).

The predominant form of collective production organization in the former Soviet Union was the collective farm or *kolkhoz*, in theory a cooperative organization in which the peasants voluntarily joined to till the soil using means of production contributed initially by those who joined. Another important form of collective organization was the state farm or *sovkhoz*, essentially "a factory in the countryside" (Gregory and Stuart 1974, pp. 232-233) owned by the government where workers were wage earners. Although ideologically the state farm was considered a superior type of economic organization—or a higher type of "socialist property"—than the collective farm, the two forms of organization coexisted in the Soviet Union. State farms gained in importance in the 1940s and 1950s, however, as collective farms were consolidated into larger state farms and new lands brought under cultivation were organized as state farms (Gregory and Stuart 1974, p. 244; Volin 1962, pp. 252-253).

Large-scale production units: Farm size is a function of many variables, including population density, quality of the soil, climatic conditions, kind of crop grown or animals raised, etc. Even after accounting for differences in these variables, farming units in the Soviet Union tended to be very large. Among the economic reasons that have been given in the literature for large farm sizes in the Soviet Union are (Thiesenhusen 1995, p. 32):

- modern production techniques can be introduced much more quickly in large-scale farming than in family farms because of centralized management—instead of training millions of individual farmers only some thousand have to be trained;

- large-scale farming is more efficient because full advantage can be taken of mechanization;

- capital and credit are more accessible at more favorable terms;

- marketing and quality control can be achieved more efficiently; and

- planning can be executed more skillfully.

In Nove's view, the economic arguments in favor of large farm units in the Soviet Union can be reduced to one: administrative convenience (Nove 1965, p. 3).

In addition to economic reasons for large-scale agricultural production units, the ruling ideology also justified such pattern of land concentration. Volin (1962, p. 254) identifies "farm giantism" as a distinctive trait of Soviet agricultural organization. He states:

> The cult of bigness, a feature of Soviet policy, has its ideological roots ... in the orthodox Marxist doctrine of economic concentration, which stresses the similarity, as far as large-scale methods of production are concerned, between agriculture and manufacturing. This doctrine, which makes no distinction between the large and the optimum size of an enterprise, was further reinforced by the unbounded enthusiasm of Lenin and his disciples for farm mechanization, modeled on the American pattern. It was one of the motivating forces in the collectivization of small peasant agriculture and establishment of huge state farms.

The Soviet proclivity toward large-scale operations in industry has also been referred to as "gigantomania" (Gregory and Stuart 1974, 246). According to Laird (1965, p. 149):

> From the beginning of Bolshevik rule, traditional Russian gigantomania, arising largely out of a sense of the vastness of the land, was wedded to the Marxist-Leninist conviction that large industrial enterprises are superior organization forms. Therefore it has almost always been assumed that the larger Soviet farms are better.

Nove (1965, p. 2-3) reports that the average size of a Soviet *kolkhoz* increased five-fold between 1949 and 1961; the average size of *sovkhozes* increased as well, although at a slower pace.

Extensive cultivation: Another feature of the Soviet agricultural model was extensive cultivation. With no rent charged for land, it was sound economic decisionmaking by farm managers to increase production by expanding the size of the farm units rather than by more intensive cultivation of existing units (Raup 1990, p. 101).

For example, to address the chronic problem of shortfalls in agricultural production—especially of grains—the Soviet Union under Khrushchev engaged in a campaign to expand cultivation to lands that theretofore had not been used for agricultural purposes. The so-called "virgin lands program," which began in 1954, brought large tracts of land in Siberia and Kazakhstan under cultivation. By 1960, 42 million hectares of land had been reclaimed and seeded, roughly 20 percent of all sown land in that year (Gregory and Stuart, 1974, p. 243). Between 1953 and 1961, total cropland expanded by 30 percent in the Soviet Union as a whole (Zoerb 1965, p. 29).

Although the virgin lands program was a great success in terms of land brought under cultivation, and agricultural output rose in the short term, long-term results were poor. Allocations of agricultural machinery to the virgin lands program were large and were made at the expense of other agricultural areas. Much of the new virgin lands brought under cultivation were marginal in terms of quality of the soil and, more important, subject to hazardous climate—dry, hot winds that blew into the virgin lands from the Central Asian deserts coupled with Arctic winds that brought snow as early as August, and uneven rainfall (Willett 1962, p. 101).

Massive crop failures in the 1960s ushered changes in farming methods and agricultural management aimed at overcoming inefficiencies. The emphasis of these changes was on more intensive exploitation of areas already under cultivation instead of further extension of the sown areas (Novak-Decker 1965, p. 193). Nearly two decades later, increases in agricultural productivity through intensification of farming on existing agricultural farmland was one of the objectives of Gorbachev's *perestroika* in the agricultural sector (Laird and Laird 1990, pp. 109-110).

Mechanization: As noted above, Lenin's "unbounded enthusiasm" for American-style farm mechanization was instrumental in shaping the Soviet Union's collectivist agricultural model. Volin (1962, p. 250) writes:

> In developing agriculture along new collectivist lines, the Communist rulers were guided by the Marxist orthodox doctrine of the absolute superiority of large-scale production in agriculture as in industry. Lenin added to this doctrine the enthusiasm for that American invention, the tractor, as a vehicle for collectivist transformation of small peasant agriculture. As far back as 1918 he thought that if the Russian peasants were given 100,000 tractors and supplies needed to operate them, they would plump for communism, which he recognized was merely a fantasy in those days.

To make agricultural mechanization services available to small peasant farmers too poor to afford their own machinery, the Soviet authorities created state machine tractor stations (MTS). These were special units that brought together tractors, combines and other large farm machinery together with facilities for operating machinery and repairing and supervising personnel. After collectivization, farm sizes increased greatly and the importance of mechanization rose: "he who controlled the tractor—the new form of farm power—controlled agriculture" (Volin 1962, p. 258). Since collective farms were not allowed to own machinery, MTS wielded enormous power and decisions made by MTS managers had tremendous impact on agricultural output. The MTS were scrapped in 1958 and henceforth collective farms were allowed to own and operate agricultural machinery.

The drive toward more intensive and efficient agricultural exploitation undertaken in the late 1950s and early 1960s relied heavily on mechanization. A very large share of investment in the agricultural sector was devoted to the procurement of agricultural machinery and equipment, assigned mainly to state farms, but also to collective enterprises. Despite the large investments in agricultural machinery and equipment, mechanization imbalances were commonplace: some operations, like harvesting grain, were highly mechanized, while others, such as cleaning and drying grain, were still largely carried out inefficiently by hand labor (Volin 1962, p. 269).

Technological interventions: Soviet authorities had a proclivity to rely on "campaigns" from above to try to resolve the chronic agricultural problems of the country. These campaigns often involved grandiose schemes that relied on scientific and technological solutions to bottlenecks arising from limitations on cultivable land resources. The view that science and technology could conquer the problems of soil quality and unsuitable climate spread the myth of the unlimited agricultural resources of the Soviet Union and diverted attention from the management and incentives problems that were at the center of the agricultural production quagmire.

Among the best documented of these agricultural campaigns based on technological interventions are:

- The so-called "Stalin Plan for the Transformation of Nature," introduced in the 1940s, and consisting of: 1) a plan for planting shelter belts and reforestation; 2) a plan for introducing crop rotations with perennial grasses; and 3) a plan for building ponds and other reservoirs for storing water from local sources for the purpose of limited irrigation and water supply (Timoshenko 1953, p. 254).

- A massive project to turn semi-arid lands of several Central Asian republics into a cotton producing area. This required technological intervention in the form of a massive irrigation scheme in the Aral Sea basin that drew water from the Syr Darya and Amu Darya rivers, two of the main feeders of the Aral Sea (Akiner 1993, p. 256).

As Nove (1980, pp. 131-132) has said about these campaigns:

> Some [of the campaigns] were built around much-publicized projects, or methods. The list is a long one. The introduction of an alleged rubber-substitute plant, *kok-sagyz*, occupied space in the press in the thirties, as did the raising of rabbits, and the *travopolye* (ley grass) crop rotation scheme. Then after the war came Stalin's "plan for the transformation of nature." ... More recently, under Khrushchev, there was a whole series of campaigns: the ploughing up of virgin and fallow lands, expansion of acreage under

maize, "overtake America in the production of meat and milk," reduction in the area under sown grasses, the introduction of two-stage harvesting, the use of "peat-compost pods" (*torfo-peregnoynyye gorshochki*).

At another level, the "campaign" mentality had perverse impacts on agricultural production. For example, sowing had to be completed and reported to the central authorities by a certain date whether or not the soil and climate conditions called for such activity; often, the method of sowing (e.g., sowing corn in squares rather than rows) was dictated by the central authorities as part of a campaign. The same held for harvesting. In the Soviet Union in the 1950s, the Party prescribed a campaign to engage in "two-stage" harvesting of grain, where the grain was cut at one date and it was picked up for threshing at another, regardless of the ripeness of the grain and whether the delay in threshing would affect yields and quality of the grain. The priority of the local authorities was to report fulfillment of plans related to the use of the "advanced" two-stage harvesting method rather than grain output (Nove 1965, pp. 10-11).

Use of agricultural inputs: Faced with stagnation of production by the agricultural sector, Khrushchev coined a new version of Lenin's slogan by declaring that "Communism is Soviet rule, plus electrification of the whole country, plus 'chemicalization' of the economy" (Novak-Decker, 1965, p. 193).

Demand for fertilizers and pesticides grew rapidly in the 1950s as a result of the expansion of land under cultivation pursuant to the virgin lands program. Chemical fertilizer production increased rapidly as well, with the expansion of chemical plants and facilities to mine large deposits. The drive to cultivate land more intensively and efficiently resulted in even higher usage of fertilizers and pesticides in collective and state farms.

Poland, where agriculture remained largely in private hands during the socialist period, provides an interesting contrast to the Soviet agricultural model with regard to use of fertilizers and pesticides. Cook (1988, pp. 136-137) makes the point that fertilizer use in Poland declined in the 1980s and that Poland ranked near the bottom in Europe in the use of plant protection chemicals, such as herbicides and pesticides.

THE ENVIRONMENT AND SOCIALISM IN CUBA: INSTITUTIONS AND PRACTICE

In the early 1960s, the Cuban government adopted socialism and began to replicate in the island the institutions and practices that (mis)managed the economy in the Soviet Union and Eastern Europe. As was the case in the latter countries, socialism in Cuba engendered environmental degradation. Specific instances of such environmental degradation have been documented in numerous official publications (e.g., Ministerio de Ciencia, Tecnología y Medio Ambiente 1995, 1997) and unofficial sources (e.g., Oro 1992; Wotzkow 1998). Rather than covering this same ground, this section of the paper describes selected features of socialism in Cuba that illustrate how closely it paralleled institutions and practice in the former Soviet Union and Eastern Europe and raise concern about the environmental implications for the island.

Centralized decision making: As in other socialist countries, political and economic decision making in Cuba is invested in the Communist Party. All government officials in leadership positions are also members of the Communist Party. In practice, key political and economic decision making rests within a small group of Communist Party officials dominated by President Fidel Castro. Alternative political parties to the Cuban Communist Party are not allowed and public expressions of dissidence from Party views are severely punished. Popular elections for the top leadership positions have not been held in the island for the nearly 40 years that the Castro regime has been in power.

Collectivization: Although data to make precise comparisons of the degree of collectivization across socialist countries are not available, fragmentary information suggest that at the end of the 1980s, state ownership of the means of production in Cuba was as significant, if not more so, than state ownership in other socialist countries. In the late 1980s, Cuba was among the socialist states with the highest percentage of agricultural land in state farms. Similarly, the share of national output generated by the state sector in

Cuba in 1989 (96 percent) was comparable to East Germany's and higher than the share produced by the state sector in Hungary, Poland, and Vietnam (Pérez-López 1995, pp. 38-44). Structural changes made in the 1990s, for example the break-up of state farms and the creation of Basic Units of Cooperative Production (*Unidades Básicas de Producción Cooperativa*, UBPCs) as well as the promotion of joint ventures with foreign investors, have reduced somewhat the share of the state's ownership of productive resources, but it remains very high.

Central planning: By the 1970s, Cuba had adopted full fledged physical central planning mechanisms to manage its economy. These mechanisms paralleled very closely those in place in the Soviet Union and Eastern Europe and were established with technical assistance from the latter countries. Cuban government planners drew up very detailed annual plans which covered imports, investments, domestic production, exports, and so on. Once adopted by the Communist Party/government, these plans carried the force of law. Cuban planners also developed longer-term plans, typically five-year plans, which were coordinated with other socialist countries. As in the Soviet Union, there were many instances in which central directives were implemented within the framework of national campaigns; the best known instance was the national mobilization to produce a ten million-ton sugar harvest in 1970.

Industrialization: Imbued by industrial prowess of the socialist countries, the Cuban leadership embarked in the 1960s on a rapid industrialization path that foresaw the establishment of heavy industries in the island. Plans called for the construction of integrated steel mills, metalworking complexes, and even automobile production plants. These plans were set aside when it became apparent that Cuba did not have the natural resource base to support these industries, but the fascination with industrial gigantism remained. Manifestations of industrial gigantism are the very large plant to produce sugarcane combines in Holguín and the incredibly ambitious nuclear power program conceived in the 1970s that would have built three nuclear power plant complexes—with as many as 12 nuclear reactors—across the island. Industrial plants imported from the Soviet Union and Eastern Europe—to refine metals, to manufacture chemicals, cement, and paper products—embodied the same environmentally unfriendly technology that caused environmental damage in these countries.

Large-scale agriculture: In 1963, the Cuban government redefined its development strategy to give agriculture—and sugar in particular—a central role. The new agricultural strategy, inspired by the Soviet agricultural model of gigantism and extensive agricultural production, included significant expansion in the area devoted to sugarcane cultivation, increase in the use of chemical inputs, intensive use of irrigation, and mechanization of sugarcane cultivation and harvesting. Sugar cane lands that had been nationalized and turned into cooperatives were converted into large state farms to reap economies of scale in mechanization, irrigation, fertilizer application, etc. Progressively, private farmers were coopted to give up their land and to turn it over to the state to increase the size of state farms and other forms of collective farming. Large-scale farming in state-owned land was the predominant form of agricultural production in Cuban until the 1990s, when UBPCs were established.

Institutions: To manage its socialist economy, Cuba built institutions that mirrored very closely those in the Soviet Union and Eastern Europe. This was, in part, a practical necessity: as Cuba deepened its ties with the socialist community and domestic organizations had to be created to interact with foreign counterparts. Cuba's central planning institutions resembled very closely those of other socialist countries; they were built with technical assistance from the socialist countries, and these countries provided classroom and hands-on training for key personnel.

One form of institutional development inspired by the Soviet Union and Eastern Europe that had an adverse impact on the Cuban environment was the creation of industry-specific ministries which had responsibilities for both industry promotion as well as pollution control and conservation of resources. Examples are the Ministry of the Sugar Industry (*Ministerio de la Industria Azucarera*), the Ministry of

the Steelworking Industry (*Ministerio de la Industria Sidero-Mecánica*), and the Ministry of the Construction Industry (*Ministerio de la Industria de la Construcción*). Environmental protection agencies were empowered to investigate violations of environmental laws and regulations by state enterprises, but enforcement was reserved for the corresponding Ministry responsible for the industry.

Environmental information: Socialist Cuba has emulated the Soviet Union and the socialist countries of Eastern Europe with regard to the lack of public access to environmental information. The Cuban government controls all forms of media and exercises very strict controls over the form and amount of environmental information made available to the public. On occasion, specific instances of environmental degradation (e.g., environmental damage caused by open pit mining, garbage that pollutes beaches, wastes dumped illegally in streams and rivers) is featured in the official media, but generally with a political purpose, such as building support for a government-led economic initiative or singling out officials who may become victims in power struggles within the Communist Party. Statistical yearbooks and other official sources do not provide time series data on environmental indicators.

Lack of environmental NGOs: Cuba has the dubious achievement among socialist countries of not permitting independent environmental non-governmental organizations (NGOs) to operate openly. This is so despite the fact that the Cuban Constitution of 1976 recognizes the freedom of Cuban citizens to associate freely and allows the formation of mass and social organizations; the Constitution also guarantees the right of mass organizations to exist and to own property. In 1988, the Cuban government dissolved the Life Naturist Association (*Asociación Naturista Vida*), an organization established in the 1930s that brought together individuals interested in environmental matters (Alfonso 1991); it also arrested the leaders of the Green Path Ecopacifist Movement (*Movimiento Ecopacifista Sendero Verde*), a group created in 1998 with the objective of restructuring the Cuban political system to enhance ecological principles and spoused returning land to farmers and using solar rather than nuclear energy for electricity generation (Santana 1992).

SUMMARY AND IMPLICATIONS

The environmental devastation in the former Soviet Union and in Eastern Europe that became evident upon the fall of socialism in 1989-90 and the lifting of the information curtain enveloping these countries makes it abundantly clear that the theoretical arguments about the compatibility between socialism and environmental preservation had very little to do with reality. In fact, the breadth and depth of environmental disruption in these countries surpassed the expectations of even the most pessimistic observers. Environmental degradation was generalized, affecting air, water, and land/vegetation.

Certain characteristics of centrally planned economies—mostly arising from the pervasive role of government in the economy—make them prone to environmental disruption. These characteristics include the emphasis of central planning on quantitative goals, unbalanced growth that favored the heavy industry sector, lack of political accountability, weak environmental movement, close control over information, land tenure and extensive agricultural techniques, ineffective regulations, etc.

In the early 1960s, Cuba embraced political and economic relations with the Soviet Union and the socialist countries of Eastern Europe. These countries became Cuba's principal economic partners, purchasing the bulk of Cuba's exports and providing most of the island's imports, including its industrial plant and equipment. Industrial plants imported from the Soviet Union and Eastern Europe embodied the same environmentally unfriendly technology that caused significant environmental damage in these countries.

Over nearly four decades, Cuba has been an avid practitioner of socialism, replicating the range of institutions and policies implemented in the Soviet Union and the Eastern European socialist countries. Unfortunately for Cuba, it would not be surprising if the legacy of socialism in Cuba is environmental disruption in the island mirroring that experienced by the Soviet Union and Eastern Europe.

REFERENCES

Akiner, Shirin. 1993. "Environmental Degradation in Central Asia." In *Economic Development in Cooperation Partner Countries from a Sectoral Perspective*, pp. 255-263. Brussels: NATO Economics Directorate.

Alfonso, Pablo. 1991. "Ecopacifistas abogan por armonía en la isla." *El Nuevo Herald* (March 25):1A, 4A.

Altshuler, Igor I., and Iurii N. Golubchikov. 1990. "Ecological Semi-Glasnost." *Environmental Policy Review* 4:2 (July):1-12.

Bohi, Douglas R. 1994. "Foreword." In Michael A. Toman, editor, *Pollution Abatement Strategies in Central and Eastern Europe*, pp. ii-viii. Washington: Resources for the Future.

Bush, Keith. 1974. "The Soviet Response to Environmental Disruption." In Ivan Volgyes, editor, *Environmental Deterioration in the Soviet Union and Eastern Europe*, pp. 8-36. New York: Praeger Publishers.

Bush, Keith. 1972. "Environmental Problems in the USSR." *Problems of Communism* 21:4 (July-August):21-31.

Carter, F.W., and D. Turnock. 1993. "Problems of the Pollution Scenario." In F.W. Carter and D. Turnock, editors, *Environmental Problems in Eastern Europe*. London: Routledge, 1993.

Cook, Edward. 1988. "Prospects for Polish Agriculture in the 1980s," in Joseph C. Brada and Karl-Eugen Wadekin, editors, *Socialist Agriculture in*

169

Transition, pp. 131-145. Boulder: Westview Press.

Dahmén, Erik. 1971. "Environmental Control and Economic Systems." In Peter Bohm and Allen V. Kneese. Editors. *The Economics of Environment*, pp. 44-52. London: Macmillan.

Danilov-Danilian, Victor. 1993. "Problemas ecológicos en la Federación Rusa." *Cuadernos del Este* 10:33-40.

Feshbach, Murray. 1995. *Ecological Disaster: Cleaning Up the Hidden Legacy of the Soviet Regime.* New York: Twentieth Century Fund.

Feshbach, Murray. 1993. "Environment: Improved Knowledge, Expanded Concern." In *Economic Development in Cooperation Partner Countries from a Sectoral Perspective*, pp. 233-240. Brussels: NATO Economics Directorate.

Feshbach, Murray. 1991. "Economics of Environment: Costs, Needs and Realities." In *The Soviet Economy Under Gorbachev*, pp. 223-246. Brussels: NATO Economics Directorate.

Feshbach, Murray and Alfred Friendly, Jr. 1992. *Ecocide in the USSR.* New York: Basic Books.

Goldman, Marshall I. 1979. "The Convergence of Environmental Disruption." *Science* 170 (October 2):37-42.

Goldman, Marshall I. 1972. "Externalities and the Race for Economic Growth in the USSR: Will the Environment Ever Win?" *Journal of Political Economy* 80:2 (March/April):314-327.

Goldman, Marshall I. 1973. "Pollution Comes to the U.S.S.R." In Joint Economic Committee, *Soviet Economic Prospects for the Seventies*, 56-70. Washington: U.S. Government Printing Office.

Greenblat, Sara Reva. 1993. "Internal and External Perspectives of Energy Security Issues in Eastern Europe and the Former Soviet Union." In *Economic Development in Cooperation Partner Countries from a Sectoral Perspective*, pp. 245-254. Brussels: NATO Economics Directorate.

Gregory, Paul R., and Robert C. Stuart. *Soviet Economic Structure and Performance.* New York: Harper & Row, 1974.

Kabala, Stanley J. 1992. *Environment and Development in the New Eastern Europe.* Occasional Paper No. 3. Middlebury, Vermont: Geonomics Institute.

Kelley, Donald R. 1976. "Environmental Policy-Making in the USSR: The Role of Industrial and Environmental Interest Groups." *Soviet Studies* 28:4 (October):570-589.

Kornai, János. 1992. *The Socialist System: The Political Economy of Communism.* Princeton: Princeton University Press.

Kramer, John M. 1974. "Environmental Problems in the USSR: The Divergence of Theory and Practice." *The Journal of Politics* 36:4 (November):886-899.

Laird, Roy D. 1965. "The Politics of Soviet Agriculture," in Roy D. Laird and Edward L. Crowley, editors, *Soviet Agriculture: The Permanent Crisis*, pp. 147-158. New York: Praeger Publishers.

Laird, Roy D., and Betty A. Laird. 1990. "Perestroika in Agriculture: Gorbachev's Rural Revolution,'" in Karl-Eugen Wadekin, editor, *Communist Agriculture*, pp. 107-119. London: Routledge.

Lofstedt, Ragnar E., and Allen L. White. 1990. "Chernobyl: Four Years Later, the Repercussions Continue." *Environment* 32:3 (April):2-5.

McIntyre, Robert J., and James R. Thornton. 1978. "On the Environmental Efficiency of Economic Systems." *Soviet Studies* 30:2 (April):173-192.

McIntyre, Robert J., and James R. Thornton. 1981. "Environmental Policy Formulation and Current Soviet Management." *Soviet Studies* 33:1 (January):146-149.

Ministerio de Ciencia, Tecnología y Medio Ambiente. 1997. *Estrategia Ambiental Nacional.* La Habana.

Ministerio de Ciencia, Tecnología y Medio Ambiente. 1995. *Cuba: Medio Ambiente y Desarrollo*. La Habana.

Novak-Decker, Nikolai. 1965. "Soviet Efforts to Introduce Intensive Farming," in Roy D. Laird and Edward L. Crowley, editors, *Soviet Agriculture: The Permanent Crisis*, pp. 193-199. New York: Praeger Publishers.

Nove, Alec. 1965. "Some Thoughts on Soviet Agricultural Administration," in Roy D. Laird and Edward L. Crowley, editors, *Soviet Agriculture: The Permanent Crisis*, pp. 1-13. New York: Praeger Publishers.

Nove, Alec. 1980. *The Soviet Economy*. Second Edition. London: George, Allen & Unwin.

Oro, José R. 1992. *The Poisoning of Paradise: The Environmental Crisis in Cuba*. Miami: The Endowment for Cuban American Studies.

Pérez-López, Jorge F. 1995. *Cuba's Second Economy: From Behind the Scenes to Center Stage*. New Brunswick: Transaction Publishers.

Pryor, Frederic L. 1992. *The Red and the Green: The Rise and Fall of Collectivized Agriculture in Marxist Regimes*. Princeton: Princeton University Press.

Raup, Philip M. 1990. "Structural Contrasts and Convergences in Socialist and Capitalist Agriculture," in Karl-Eugen Wadekin, editor, *Communist Agriculture*, pp. 90-104. London: Routledge.

Rev, Istvan. 1993. "La naturaleza antiecológica de la centralización." *Cuadernos del Este* 10:9-17.

Santana, Maydel. 1992. "Grupo ecologista anuncia 'plan de erosión de emergencia.'" *El Nuevo Herald* (May 23):3B.

Satre Ahlander, Ann-Mari. 1994. *Environmental Problems in the Shortage Economy*. Aldershot, England: Edward Elgard.

Sobell, Vlad. 1990. "The Systemic Roots of the East European Ecological Crisis." *Environmental Policy Review* 4(1):47-52.

Thiesenhusen, William C. 1995. "Landed Property in Capitalist and Socialist Countries: The Russian Transition." In Gene Wunderlich, editor, *Agricultural Landownership in Transitional Economies*, pp. 27-53. Lanham: University Press of America.

Thornton, Judith A. 1978. "Soviet Methodology for the Valuation of Natural Resources." *Journal of Comparative Economics* 2(4):321-333.

Timoshenko, V.P. 1953. "Agricultural Resources," in Abram Bergson, editor, *Soviet Economic Growth*, pp. 246-271. Evanston: Row, Peterson and Company.

Turner, R. Kerry, David Pearce, and Ian Bateman. 1993. *Environmental Economics: An Elementary Introduction*. Baltimore: The Johns Hopkins University Press.

U.S. General Accounting Office. 1994. *International Assistance Efforts to Make Soviet-Designed Reactors Safer*. GAO/RCED-94-234. Washington: U.S. General Accounting Office.

Vedensky, George. 1965. "The Soviet Chemical Fertilizer Industry," in Roy D. Laird and Edward L. Crowley, editors, *Soviet Agriculture: The Permanent Crisis*, pp. 180-192. New York: Praeger Publishers.

Volgyes, Ivan. 1974. "Politics and Pollution in Western and Communist Societies." In Ivan Volgyes, editor, *Environmental Deterioration in the Soviet Union and Eastern Europe*, pp. 1-7. New York: Praeger Publishers.

Volin, Lazar. 1962. "Agricultural Policy of the Soviet Union." In Morris Bornstein and Daniel Fusfeld, editors, *The Soviet Economy: A Book of Readings*, pp. 243-276. Homewood, Illinois: Richard D. Irwin.

Willett, Joseph H. 1962. "The Recent Record in Agricultural Production," in U.S. Joint Economic Committee, *Dimension of Soviet Economic Power*, pp. 91-113. Washington: U.S. Government Printing Office.

World Bank. 1992. *Development and the Environment—World Development Report 1992.* Washington: Oxford University Press.

Wotzkow, Carlos. 1998. *Natumaleza Cubana.* Miami: Ediciones Universal.

Yablokov, Andrei V. 1990. "The Current State of the Soviet Environment." *Environmental Policy Review* 4(1):1-14.

Ziegler, Charles E. 1991. "Environmental Protection in Soviet-East European Relations." In Joan De-Bardeleben, editor, *To Breath Free: Eastern Europe's Environmental Crisis*, pp. 83-100. Baltimore: The Johns Hopkins University Press.

Zoerb, Carl. 1965. "The Virgin Land Territory: Plans, Performance, Prospects," in Roy D. Laird and Edward L. Crowley, editors, *Soviet Agriculture: The Permanent Crisis*, pp. 29-44. New York: Praeger Publishers.

INVESTMENT AND INTERNATIONAL COOPERATION IN CUBA'S ENERGY SECTOR

Jonathan Benjamin-Alvarado

This paper investigates the external factors of influence on Cuba's efforts to develop nuclear energy. This discussion will center on the bilateral, multilateral and international aspects of Cuba's cooperation and interaction in the nuclear and energy fields. This is presented in three sections. The first section on bilateral cooperation reviews Cuba's relations with its primary development partner as well as its burgeoning relations with partners in Europe, Canada and Latin America. The section on multilateral and international cooperation focuses on Cuba's membership, role and interaction with the myriad international organizations, nuclear and energy related associations, in which it has participated in the period since the inception of the nuclear program. The following section will investigate the impact of the United States opprobrium to Cuban efforts in the energy sector with a specific emphasis on U.S. law and policy initiatives directed at undermining Cuba's nuclear ambition.

The modernization literature suggests that the source of the modernizing ideal will have a significant impact on the success and appropriateness of modernization schemes in developing states. Moreover, these schemes whether internal or external in nature will also carry significant implications for the trajectory of development within these states. On one hand, modernization schemes that take into consideration states' human, technological and scientific resource bases are more likely to be sustainable. This has been a major challenge to the proponents of modernization theory, where things solely western are construed to be modern and vice versa, without consideration for their appropriateness to the society to which they are being applied. On the other hand, development may be nearly impossible without the involvement of external forces, both positive and negative. From this paradox it becomes necessary to review and analyze the impact of these forces. This is an especially important component in the analysis of Cuba's nuclear ambition. This paper seeks to specifically identify and explain the key external variables and influences that potentially impact and influence Cuban decision-making in the energy sector.

With the demise of the Soviet Union and the ending of the Cold War in the early 1990s much attention was focused on the resulting impact of the Russian Federation's withdrawal of significant elements of assistance that it had been sending to Cuba. Moreover, the emerging "New World Order" now appeared to be democratically centered and market oriented. The Soviet denouement, the "democratic" renewal in Latin America, and the growing global economic interdependence were signals that Cold War posturing and centrally planned economies would become a thing of the past. The overly dependent Cuban economy seemed ill equipped to manage this dramatic shift in world power, and for some, the days of the Castro regime certainly appeared numbered.[1]

Within this new environment analysts sought to predict, as it were, the future of Cuba and what this period of transition would mean for Cuba's foreign relations. They were especially concerned with identifying the key external variables of influence that would most significantly influence Cuba's foreign relations. In the first place, there was a concern of how the evolution of Russian approaches to its Cuban partner would impact the old order of relations with the island nation. Would Russia, perhaps under nationalist pressure, expand its support of Cuba, particularly through economic assistance and the provision of military equipment? Or on the contrary, would Russia, experiencing serious economic difficulties, prefer to curtail its relations with Cuba even further, this resulting in the "Cuban lobby" in the Russian Foreign and Defense Ministries being purged or ostracized?[2] Despite the problems that had arisen in the immediate aftermath of the ending of the Cold War and in the economic relations between Russia and Cuba, cooperation between the two countries held the promise of potentially large benefits.[3]

In broadening this inquiry, the attitudes of other Latin American states toward Cuba would also play a significant role in the future. This included both trade and political relations, the readmission of Cuba in international organizations of the region, and the increased pressure on the United States to change its policies toward Cuba. Other external factors of influence could impact future Cuban development. The changing attitudes of Western Europe (especially Spain) and Canada; in more general terms, changing positions of the "non-U.S." developed world could under certain circumstances mitigate or undermine American policies.[4] Interestingly, Western European positions on Cuba have significantly deviated from the U.S. position, especially since the passage of the Helms-Burton Law of 1996. It was thought that there would be more rhetorical than practical opposi-

tion by the European Union countries to U.S. efforts.[5]

It is with these ideas in mind that we detail these relationships for the way in which they have influenced Cuban nuclear energy development policy, both positively and negatively. These relationships have evolved significantly in the period since 1991 and they continue to change in ways unforeseen by even the most keen observers and analysts of Cuban foreign relations.

BILATERAL NUCLEAR COOPERATION
Russian-Cuban Relations

The consideration of nuclear energy exploitation in Cuba would have been all but impossible for Cuba without the Soviet Union (or another similarly equipped and willing benefactor). The case history suggests that Cuba's nuclear ambitions owe much credit to its relationship with the former Soviet Union. It is clear that in the initial stages of development, the nuclear program could be viewed as a "satellite" project of the overall program of nuclear energy expansion in the Soviet Union and Eastern Europe.

During this period Cuba relied heavily on the Soviet Union for financing and assistance, the training of personnel, the provision of materials and equipment, and construction of facilities. An integral part of the relationship between the Soviet Union and Cuba was the designing and implementation of a program for nuclear infrastructural development. This would include the creation of myriad support bureaucracies and the training of the personnel to work within these organizations. From 1982, when construction at the Juraguá site began, until 1992 when the suc-

---

1. Among the most audacious of these tomes is Andres Oppenheimer, *Castro's Final Hour: The Secret Story behind the Coming Downfall of Communist Cuba* (New York: Simon and Schuster, 1992).

2. See Andrei V. Kortunov, "The Role of External Factors in the Cuban Transition," in *The Military and Transition in Cuba: A Reference Guide for Policy and Crisis Management*, Néstor Sánchez, editor (Leesburg, VA: International Research 2000, March 17, 1995), p. III-13-2.

3. Vladimir A. Borodaev, "Economic and Political Relations: Issues and Trends in the 1990s," in *The Military and Transition in Cuba*, p. III-10-4.

4. Kortunov, "The Role of External Factors in the Cuban Transition," p. III-13-2.

5. Ibid.

cessor state, the Russian Federation stopped providing assistance for the project, the Soviet Union poured over $1 billion into the construction at the site alone. Because the figures are unavailable one can only conjecture as to how much assistance was provided to Cuba in the formation and operation of this bureaucracy.[6] This assistance, in addition to the capital outlays, included the provision of construction and training personnel, and technical support in the design, construction and operation of the research centers, facilities and agencies within the nuclear energy sector.

This is not to say that the Cubans were completely satisfied with the terms of this relationship. They were certainly grateful for the assistance but were not always in agreement with the accounting practices, the schedule of delivery for key equipment and components, the chronic lack of spare parts, and the poor quality of those materials when finally delivered. Cuba's client status and its reliance on the Soviet Union made pursuit of the nuclear energy capability possible but it also provided it with obstacles. These obstacles included debates over safety practices in the construction process, questions on reactor design, and the delays in the construction of the Juraguá Unit-1.

Nonetheless, by 1992, Cuba together with the Soviet Union and then the Russian Federation had between 75 and 80 percent of the base construction at Juraguá Unit-1 completed, in addition to the creation of a vibrant nuclear scientific-technological infrastructure. This was a significant accomplishment for a developing state such as Cuba and by the early 1990s was suggestive of a bright future in the nuclear energy sector. Cuban officials, in part because of Russian patronage, enjoyed an elevated status among developing states. This elevated status was by virtue of its participation in international nuclear organizations,

the renown of its nuclear medicine sector and the treatment of the victims of the Chernobyl accident, and the creation of highly trained cadres of nuclear engineers, specialists and technicians.

The collapse of the Soviet empire in 1991 significantly impacted the terms of the relationship between the now Russian Federation and the Republic of Cuba. It presented challenges of the kind that could relegate much of the Cuban economy to pre-Revolutionary levels. In a short time this did come to pass. At the closing session of the Cuban National Assembly in 1993, Fidel Castro stated, "we are facing a very, very great challenge. We have to be ready for greater difficulties than we can imagine."[7] This stark assessment was based on the fact that in 1993 oil imports and international trade had declined by over half their previous levels, resulting in a severe energy crisis.

In April 1992, Russia and Cuba concluded an agreement to continue funding for the Juraguá plant. With the project more than three-fourths complete, Cuba only needed to install the instrumentation and control systems for the reactor. Russian nuclear officials had contracted Siemens AG of Germany to install the systems. Unfortunately, Russia's own precarious economic situation precluded that they pay for these services in hard currency as demanded by Siemens. Cuba, left to negotiate the $21 million payment with the German firm, was unable to generate the hard currency to complete the deal.

In September 1992, Fidel Castro proclaimed that Cuba was placing the nuclear project into a state of "temporary suspension" because of Russia's demand of $200 million to continue work. Yet, in November 1992, Russian and Cuban officials jointly announced that construction would resume with French assistance. Contrary to the announcement in 1993, Rus-

---

6. In 1998, this includes 9 major agencies under the Agencia de Energía Nuclear (AEN) within the Ministerio de Ciencia, Tecnología y Medio Ambiente (CITMA). For details of the bureaucratic structure and functions see, Darío Gandarias Cruz and Daniel Codorniú Pujals, "El Programa Nuclear Cubano y Su Infraestructura Científico-Técnica," a paper prepared for the Regional Seminar on Public Information, Havana, Cuba (May 19, 1995).

7. Quoted in José de Córdoba, "Survival Tactics: Its Economy Dying, Cuba Seeks Salvation in Dollars," *The Wall Street Journal* (July 19, 1993), p. A1.

sia advanced Cuba $30 million to mothball the construction. A letter from Secretary of State Warren Christopher to Senator Connie Mack of Florida stated: "The Russian government ... has concluded that the completion of the project is not feasible under present circumstances."[8]

This began a cycle of announcements of the resumption of construction between Russia and Cuba and the search for a joint venture partner willing to underwrite the project. Since 1992, Cuba has concluded four major trade and economic agreements with Russia containing reference to the Juraguá project and the resumption of activities at the construction site with no positive changes actually having occurred.[9] Little has come of these announcements and it raises questions as to whether or not Russia maintains a legitimate interest in completing it Cuban venture.

Russia's Ministry of Atomic Energy (MINATOM) plans to export nuclear materials and technologies worth $3.5 to 4 billion by the year 2000. It currently has eight nuclear power units at different stages of construction in Iran, Slovakia, Ukraine, the Czech Republic and Cuba.[10] In the post-Cold War period, MINATOM has emerged as one of Russia's major currency earning exporters along with Gazprom and Rosvooruzheniye. With a work force of 2 million Russia's MINATOM-run empire earned $4.25 billion in exports in 1995 and 1996 with the annual projected growth of $3.5 billion by the year 2010.[11] Talks are underway for the construction of plants in India, Indonesia and China.

With Russia's announcement calling for the resumption of construction of the Cuban project in February 1998, the plans clearly illustrate the instrumental nature of its involvement in the Cuban project. Russia still needs to demonstrate to its potential suitors that it can successfully undertake and complete a nuclear reactor construction project far outside its borders. Moreover, this is one of the few instances where Russian work is being subjected to international scrutiny during the entire construction process. With the legacy of the Chernobyl accident and other nuclear incidents, the Cuban project has been vilified for poorly designed systems, safety practices, and the lack of adequate nuclear waste storage and disposal. Russians counter this claim with the "fact" that "foreigners are attracted by (sic) Russia's plants because, although cheap, their safety standards are comparatively high."[12] The safe and successful completion of a reactor in Cuba would go far in assuaging the suspicions of critics of the Russian nuclear industry. It would also present potential buyers of Russian nuclear reactors with an example of its ability to deliver the goods. This is the most important factor in attracting new buyers for Russian nuclear technology.

In 1997 the Russian Federation made no secret of its 'desire' to return to Cold War period trading levels with the Republic of Cuba. After a series of high-level meetings on trade Russia and Cuba are once again seeking to increase trade and economic cooperation. This culminated in the negotiation of an oil-for-sugar swap and the expansion of Russian cooperation in the fields of nickel mining and once again on nuclear energy. Evgeniy Reshetnikov, MINATOM Deputy Minister announced that both countries needed this

8. Wilson Dizard III, "Christopher Says Moscow to Pay Juragua's $30-million Mothball Tab," *Nucleonics Week* (September 30, 1993), p. 7.

9. This includes the concluding of these types of agreements in July 1993, October 1995, June 1997 and most recently February 1998. See Sergei Batchikov, "The Cuba that We are Losing Everyone Else is Finding: Russian Departments Are Hampering Trade with that Country," *Current Digest of the Post-Soviet Press* (December 17, 1997), p. 21; see also "Cuba, Russia promise to reach deal soon on US-feared nuclear plant," Agence France-Presse,(February 21, 1998) via Clari.Net.

10. There is also a mothballed reactor in Slovenia. It is uncertain given the hostilities in the region if the project will ever by resurrected. See Alexei Zayko, "Cabinet Gives the Green Light to Nuclear Power Engineering Development Program," *Russkiy Telegraf*, No. 65 (December 19, 1997), p. 4.

11. Ibid.

12. Vladimir Teslenko, "Russia's Nuclear Power Reactors for Sale," *Moscow News* (December 25, 1997), p. 52.

special agreement on the nuclear plant: "On the one hand Cuba is in desperate need of self-sufficiency in electrical supply, and on the other, the operation of the reactor will be the only way for Russia to get back from Cuba the enormous debts it owes our country."[13]

All reactor market considerations aside, the current status of the trade between the two countries belies these optimistic announcements and Russian critics of the post-Cold War Cuba policy paint an unflattering picture of the Russian Federation's "ignominiously squandering (of) the legacy built by the selfless labor of several generations of our fellow countrymen."[14] The criticism is directed at the diminished arsenal of Russia's foreign policy assets and the blame lies with the leaders of the "young democratic Russia" and their decisions to reduce commercial contacts with the "ideologically foreign regime."[15] Bilateral trade between Russia and Cuba has steadily declined from $3.3 billion in 1991 to $550 million in 1996. The once wide assortment of goods exchanged has shrunk to a bare minimum. In effect, bilateral trade has been reduced to a single barter transaction, the exchange of raw Cuban sugar for Russian oil. For these critics, this state of affairs in bilateral trade relations' results mainly from the actions of the Russian side, which abruptly altered its foreign economic orientation, to the detriment of not only its foreign partners, but also itself.[16] In defense of the Russian position, nuclear officials with MINATOM maintain that the only reason for their withdrawal from the nuclear program is economic considerations. The return on Russia's investment looks hardly profitable given the over $1 billion dollars spent and the additional estimated $1 billion more that would have to be invested before construction in completed.[17]

As both countries enter the 21st century they are attempting to re-kindle their trade relations and mutual cooperation. Together they have built an impressive nuclear program in Cuba that includes the cadres of highly trained personnel devoted to the peaceful exploitation of nuclear energy. Their failure to complete construction of the nuclear reactors at Juraguá points to the now feeble economic foundation of the over 20-year nuclear cooperation relationship. It appears that the willingness remains firmly intact, it is just now that the limited economic capability of both states prohibits any significant advancement on the project. This has forced the Russian-Cuban partnership to look outside to attract potential partners to engage in a joint venture to complete the Juraguá project. The next section will detail Cuba's relations with other countries in the energy sector. It will include a discussion of the efforts to elicit support from "tercer socios" in the nuclear project, but also with its relative success in attracting partners and investors for the conventional energy generation sector.

Initially, while both countries could "disregard" the economic elements of the decision to develop a nuclear energy capability in Cuba, it has become apparent that the Russian Federation could not afford to support Cuban ambitions in the post-Cold War period. Moreover, the terms of trade are now cast in strictly economic terms eschewing any notion of the now moribund "socialist brotherhood." These factors indicate that Cuba's nuclear program is now mostly likely conforms to the expectations of the economic and technological modernization model of energy development. The evidence supports the contention of this model that would promote the nuclear program as long as it corresponds to the promotion of economic self-sufficiency. Given the overwhelming changes since 1991, it is hardly surprising that Russia has curtailed its activities because it could hardly jus-

13. Sergey Rybak, "Russians to Resume Juragua Construction Alone, Minatom Says." *Nucleonics Week*, Vol. 38, No. 7 (1997), p. 2.

14. Batchikov, "The Cuba that We Are Losing," p. 21.

15. Ibid.

16. Ibid.

17. Interview by author with Russian Ministry of Atomic Energy officials, Athens, Georgia, October 6, 1997 and November 15, 1997.

tify the Cuban drain on its resources. Nor could the Cubans in an even more precarious economic state justify the expense of such a grandiose project when its ability to meet the basic needs of its population has been seriously compromised.

Cooperation with Other Countries

Until 1992, Cuba sought and received assistance for its nuclear program from the Soviet Union. The demise of the USSR and the COMECON[18] states left Cuba, as well as those states in a severe economic crisis. Russia attempted to continue providing support for the Juraguá construction but its own economic travails at home left it with little recourse but to search out a partner to assist it in finishing construction at the Juraguá site. Russia had successfully constructed a nuclear reactor through a joint venture in Finland. In constructing the VVER-1000 model reactor at Loviisa, the Russians were responsible for a majority of civil construction at the site and contracted the installation of the instrumentation and control (I&C) systems to the German engineering firm Siemens-Kraftwerk Union (KWU). This partnership was successful and as a result the Loviisa plant has been among the most efficiently operating facilities in the world.

The Russians felt strongly that this success could be replicated in Cuba and contacted the German firm. Siemens officials visited the Juraguá site in early 1992 and agreed to move forward on the planned joint venture. Cuba only needed to pay the $21 million that Siemens was asking. It was $21 million dollars that the Cubans did not have. The project was soon scuttled and Cuba with little prospect for continuing work on the project without external support decided to place the project in a "temporary state of suspension."

This was not the first instance in which Cuba had engaged in nuclear cooperation efforts with countries other than the Soviet Union. Dating back to 1986, Cuba has actively engaged other countries on two fronts. Initially, it sought nuclear cooperation agreements with other governments. After the fall of the Soviet Union the rationale for seeking cooperation in this area became more instrumental: to find willing partners (international commercial nuclear enterprises) to invest in the Juraguá project.

In 1986 Cuba and Argentina signed a nuclear cooperation agreement under which both states would exchange technical information in a number of nuclear areas, including radiological safety, technical information, regulatory procedures and safety practices. One suggestion for this cooperation would be that Argentina could somehow assist the Cubans with the construction of the reactors at Juraguá. At that time the Cubans were reportedly short of funds to meet payments to the Russian contractor, Atomoenergoexport. Cuba was seeking assistance from Argentina on projects related to fuel fabrication and equipment supply.[19] On the heels of this agreement Argentina sought to expand its nuclear cooperation to land potential reactor contracts in Cuba for four VVER-440 model pressurized water reactors planned for 1995 to 2003. Brazil was also expanding its cooperation by training Cuban nuclear specialists and high-level technicians.[20]

At this time all three states were not signatories to the regional nuclear-free zone accord, the Treaty of Tlatelolco. In addition, all three were perceived to have nuclear weapons development programs and were the subject of much scrutiny from the international nonproliferation community. Shortly thereafter both Argentina and Brazil began to investigate the development of bilateral nuclear confidence building measures. This began with exchanges and information sharing, ending with a comprehensive regional nuclear cooperation organization linking both Argentina and Brazil with the International Atomic En-

---

18. This is the acronym of the Council for Mutual Economic Assistance, the organization that managed trade among the socialist countries. Prior to 1991, over 80 percent of Cuba's export and import trade was with this group of states.

19. Richard Kessler, "Argentina and Cuba Signed A Nuclear Cooperation Agreement," *Nucleonics Week* (November 13, 1986), pp. 12-13.

20. Richard Kessler, "Argentina Confirms It Plans Deeper Nuclear Ties With Cuba," *Nucleonics Week* (February 11, 1988), pp. 3-4.

ergy Agency (IAEA) and a new bilateral organization, the Agencia Brasiliero-Argentino de Contabilidad y Control (ABACC). This cooperation culminated with both countries signing the Treaty of Tlatelolco in the early 1990s.

In the immediate aftermath of the fall of the Berlin Wall, Cuba began to investigate alternate means of completing the Juraguá project. By May 1991, at the behest of the Russian Federation, Siemens-KWU of Germany was nearing the end of negotiations to supply the I&C equipment for the Juraguá units. Cuba was also discussing the I&C upgrade with two other nuclear firms, Cegelec of France and Skoda Works of Czechoslovakia. The work was valued at about $40 million. Cegelec and Siemens held discussions with the Cuban and Russian officials about the extent of work needed to upgrade required to improve the safety of the reactors. This bid was similar to the contract that Siemens won to upgrade the I&C systems at Mochovce-1 and -2 in Czechoslovakia. After consultations with the United States Nuclear Regulatory Commission about the adequacy of I&C technology at the Cuban plants, Cuba approached Skoda. Skoda together with the Russians had supplied these systems for reactors throughout Eastern Europe. It told the Cubans that the work would cost around $300 million. It was then that Cuba sought more economical bids from Siemens and Cegelec. At that time the United States Departments of State encouraged countries with advanced nuclear sectors such as France and Germany to become involved in improving the safety of the Cuban reactors. The United States Departments of Defense and Energy, however, were wary of any steps, which would allow the reactors to go on-line.[21] Even with this flurry of activity the inability of the Cubans to provide the required financing for continued construction on the reactors

effectively relegated these potential deals to the trash heap.

In 1995, after three years of inactivity and little interest in the nuclear program under the "temporary state of suspension" rumors started coming out of Havana that the Russians were prepared to begin construction once again. To revitalize the program, Cuba sought the assistance from Ansaldo SpA of Italy; National Nuclear Corporation (NNC) of the U.K., Furnas of Brazil, and an unnamed British firm to conduct an economic and technological feasibility study. The long-term goal of this study was to establish a private multinational consortium to operate the plant and then sell the electricity to Cuba.[22] The cost to complete the project was estimated at $800 million.[23]

The proposed multinational joint venture sought to attract a third partner (tercer socio) to join the Russians and the Cubans. This vaunted partner would invest $500 million and would receive a return on the investment before the Russians and the Cubans. During the period after these figures were released there was much speculation as to which the third partner might be. The Russians and Cubans concluded yet another inter-governmental agreement in June 1997 but as the year closed, there was no indication that any of the firms mentioned was interested in investing the $500 million or anything remotely near that figure. A site visit by a group of American nuclear specialists to Juraguá in October 1997 provided no indication that any work had been done at the site other than the installation of pressure vessels already at the site, structural reinforcement and the painting of exposed piping. Rudimentary storage structures had been constructed to preserve material

---

21. Mark Hibbs, "Siemens Looking For Contracts to Upgrade I&C for Cuban PWR's," *Nucleonics Week* (May 16, 1991), pp. 1, 10-11.

22. See "Cuban N-Plant: Completion Study Ready Soon," *NucNet News* (August 9, 1995); Mark Hibbs, "Havana Says Juragua Feasibility Study Will Be Ready by August," *Nucleonics Week* (June 29, 1995), pp. 3-4; "Minister Enlists Russia's Help To Complete Nuclear Power Plant," Radio Rebelde (Havana), May 6, 1995 in *Latin American Developments*, FBIS-LAT-95-090 (May 6, 1995).

23. Interview by author with Miguel Serradet Acosta, Director of Nuclear Energy Facilities, Ministry of Basic Industry, Havana, Cuba, January 26, 1996.

and equipment that had been in part exposed to the tropical elements.[24]

The efforts of Cuba to involve other states or multinational nuclear firms in the Juraguá project have been largely unsuccessful. A number of these firms have visited the Juraguá site and then opted not to participate in the venture. The reasons remain undisclosed and one can only conjecture to why there has been reluctance for involvement in this venture. Certainly, the economic difficulties that Cuba has experienced since the early 1990s have mitigated interest in the nuclear program. The potential for U.S. opprobrium to the Cuban venture has potentially lessened the desire of these firms to conclude any type of agreement with the Cubans but this remains only as speculation. The impact of the "temporary state of suspension" has significantly effected Cuba, and because of its continuing reliance on a deteriorating energy infrastructure the energy sector was near collapse. Many of the existing thermoelectric generating facilities were old and in immediate need of major repair or outright replacement.

To address this chronic problem Fidel Castro announced in January 1997 that Cuba would seek alternative sources of energy to stave off the collapse of the energy sector and to maintain the economic growth trend of the mid 1990s. Remarkably, the response to this initiative was well received within and outside of Cuba. At the start of 1998, Cuba was negotiating or had concluded a number of deals to upgrade its existing thermoelectric facilities and to construct new facilities on the island. All of these projects were joint ventures between Cuban and foreign firms. Moreover, all of these projects were concluded with guaranteed sources of funding.

The Cuban government also announced a two-pronged strategy for boosting the cash-short energy sector that seeks to upgrade existing facilities while at the same time reducing domestic demand. One component of this effort involves the upgrading of five 100MW of Czech and Soviet manufacture (two plants at the Antonio Maceo-Renté complex in Santiago de Cuba, two units at the Mariel facility near Havana, and one unit at Nuevitas facility in Camagüey province) with foreign capital. French engineering companies Babcock and Gemco International have agreed to supply the equipment for one of the facilities (the Antonio Maceo plant) under a deal that is unwritten by a $15 million short-term credit from the French export insurance agency Coface. The French government also reportedly has given the Cuban government a $5.7 million grant to help improve efficiency at the island's heavy oil burning units near the Varadero-Boca oilfields.[25]

Cuba by 1999 also plans to build a 250MW thermal unit in Holguín province to serve its vibrant nickel-mining sector. It has not been revealed where the $250 million in needed for financing the projects will come from.

The government is also planning an ambitious plan to increase overall generating capacity through a $500 million program to upgrade three 100MW units at the Santa Cruz del Norte generating complex and build an additional 350MW unit over the next three years. The Canadian firm First Key Project Technologies will carry out the work. The project will involve the creation of a joint venture between First Key, the Chilean firm Santa Ana, and the Cuban state power company Unión Eléctrica. The venture will sell the power for hard currency to mining interests and other companies doing business in Cuba. It is also expected to be the first project to date in Cuba to be run by an external enterprise. The leading candidates for the project are Spain's Endesa and Electricite de France (EdF). Funding for this venture is expected to come from the Canadian Export Development Corporation and other lenders.

Additionally, the Canadian firm Sherritt International has completed talks with the Cuban state oil company, CUPET regarding a joint venture to build

---

24. The author was a part of a delegation from the Center for Defense Information investigating the Cuban nuclear program. The delegation visited the Juraguá nuclear plant construction site October 25-31, 1997.

25. "Foreign Capital to Fund Expansion of Cuban Capacity," *Latin American Power Watch*, Vol. 4, No. 4 (February 1, 1998).

135MW of new thermal generating capacity that will be fired by the natural gas from the CUPET wells in the Varadero-Boca de Jaruco oilfields. Sherritt established a new subsidiary Sherritt Power Corporation to hold its electricity generating business in Cuba. As things currently stand the joint venture, Energas, plans to have two 50MW units running by mid-1999 and a 33MW unit running by the end of 1998.[26] The total generating output of the units will amount to 206MW. The cost of the planned works has been pegged at $150 million and the Canadian company is expected to earn 100 percent of the generated cash flow until the capital costs are repaid. Sherritt Power is using proceeds from an initial public stock offering to finance the Varadero-Boca de Jaruco gas and electricity project.[27] The project will upgrade the existing Antonio Guiteras Thermoelectric Plant and the José Martí Thermoelectric Plant, and once the Energogas project (150MW) starts to operate, electricity production will increase to more than 500MW.[28] The new facility will de-sulphurize petroleum gas from the Varadero oilfields for energy. These projects are not solely limited to thermoelectric generation. Cuba's hydroelectric potential is also being investigated. Boralex, a Canadian firm has conducted a pre-feasibility study to construct three hydroelectric stations with a generating capability of 85 Mw on the Toa River near Baracoa. The price for the project will be approximately $59 million. The financing is to be provided by the Canadian International Development Agency for a joint venture between the Cuban firm, Cuba's state electricity firm Unión Eléctrica, and Cuba's state oil firm, CUPET. Construction is expected to begin by early 2000.[29]

All told, the rapid expansion of projects in the thermoelectric generation sector is remarkable given the static nature of investment and activity in the nuclear energy sector over the past six years. As of early 1998 plans are underway to upgrade the generating capacity of eight existing units with the potential of 800MW. The investment for these units totals $315 million completely underwritten by foreign firms. Meanwhile, Cuba has plans to expand this sector by 600MW generating capacity over the next three years; $350 million of the $600 million required for the projects has already been secured. The additional 600MW generating capacity will in increase Cuba's total capacity by 16 percent. This will be bolstered by Cuba's efforts to conserve and reduce domestic energy demand and increase the efficiency of existing facilities.

The decision to deemphasize the nuclear program has opened the possibility of expanding the thermoelectric sector. Foreign firms have wasted little time in seeking out investments in this area and for the time being it appears that these projects will help Cuba to address it chronic energy problem. But the movement toward this type of energy generation raises other questions. Will Cuba's oil imports increase as a result of this expansion? Will this consume an even larger portion of Cuba's export earnings in the short-term period? And does this signal a return to the foreign dominated concerns to Cuba?

The terms and conditions of these projects seek to reward the investor first and the Cubans last. Moreover, these projects are directed at supplying energy and services for firms doing business in Cuba. It appears outwardly, at least in the short-term, that the lot of the Cuban society will improve little as a result of these projects. Moreover, it appears that the focus of Cuba's foreign relations in the energy sector has shifted from government-to-government nuclear cooperation and development agreements, to joint venture projects involving Cuban state firms and foreign

26. Ibid.

27. "Cuba: Construction Plans for Proposed $150,000,000 Build-Operate (BO) Power Plant Project, Sherritt Power Corp., Canada – Order # 0331198," *Export Sales Prospector: ESP–Business Opportunities in Latin America & the Caribbean*, Vol. 7, No. 3 (March 1, 1998).

28. "Project Planned to Increase Power Generation in Matanzas," Radio Rebelde, Havana, in Spanish, January 27, 1998; British Broadcasting Corporation, February 3, 1998.

29. Economist Intelligence Unit, *EIU Country Report: Cuba, Dominican Republic, Haiti, Puerto Rico*, 2nd Quarter (1998), pp. 6-10.

energy concerns. This shift also reflects the movement away from a reliance on a single source of materials, assistance, equipment and financing for Cuban energy ventures. Unfortunately, for Cuba this has not included participation by these firms in the nuclear energy development program.

As mentioned, numerous foreign firms have exhibited an interest in the Cuban project and have visited the facility at Juraguá. In each instance the prospective suitor has declined to invest or participate in the venture. This surely prompted the shift in policy by the Castro regime. A cursory examination of the change in policy orientation has been moderately successful and lessens the disappointment of maintaining the "temporary state of suspension" for Cuba's nuclear ambitions.

As with the previous section on Cuban relations with the Russian Federation, this section offers evidence supporting the economic and technological modernization model. All of the bilateral activities are consistent with this approach by seeking to expand Cuba's technical and scientific capability, as well as corresponding to the expectation of promoting economic self-sufficiency. The bilateral energy initiatives selected have been oriented toward the modernization of the existing energy infrastructure or expansion of the energy sector's generating capacity. Moreover, investment by external actors in Cuba's energy sector is indicative of the economic viability of these projects.

Unlike the previous analyses offered where the evidence presented supported the economic and technological modernization model as well as the economic and energy security model, Cuba's efforts to increase its thermoelectric capability significantly deviates from the expectations of the economic and energy security model. Whereas the model focuses on the maintenance of access to secure sources of energy, the Cuban bilateral activities indicate a shift away from this priority. Cuba by increasing its thermoelectric capability also increases its dependence on external sources of fossil fuel. In addition this increases Cuba's exposure to the vagaries of the world energy markets, of which the implications are the increased possibility of an imbalance between economic growth and security planning. From this point forward the economic and energy security modernization model loses much of its explanatory value because it can no longer account for the priorities or the trajectory of the Cuban energy sector.

MULTILATERAL NUCLEAR COOPERATION

This section of the paper looks at the cooperative efforts by the Cubans with multilateral organizations in the field of nuclear energy development. This includes a discussion of Cuba's relations and involvement with the International Atomic Energy Agency (IAEA), the United Nations Development Programme and the Organización por la Proscripción de Armas Nucleares en América Latina (OPANAL). In addition it will touch upon the other nuclear related international organizations of which Cuba is a member or participant. Moreover, this section will detail how these efforts have assisted Cuba in advancing its nuclear energy policy.

International Atomic Energy Agency

Cuba has been a member of the IAEA since its inception in the 1960s. From that period through the present, Cuba has maintained a positive relationship with the multilateral organization. It has received assistance in the forms of training of personnel in specialized fields of nuclear science and technology, laboratory equipment, grants and fellowships for study and training abroad, and consultation on aspects of nuclear safety, materials handling, quality assurance and regulatory and licensing procedures. In addition, Cuban representatives have served the IAEA in a number of capacities, including safeguards inspection team members, resident technicians, international civil servants and as a member of the Agency's Board of Governors. Cuba for its part has had an active role in the IAEA. In 1983, it was elected for the first time to the Board of Governors, this was repeated in 1987. Fidel Castro Díaz-Balart, the Executive Director of Cuba's Atomic Energy Commission (CEAC), served as the Cuban representative to the Board. The relationship has been fruitful and beneficial for Cuba and until recently was viewed as a means of monitoring the development of the nuclear program and of proliferation risks. There is presently debate over the nature of assistance be provided from the IAEA to Cuba by the U.S. Congress, yet the positive relationship continues. Supporters of this relationship between the IAEA and Cuba contend that it serves the interests of all parties, directly and indirectly, involved.

During the 1970s Cuba signed, at the insistence of the Soviet Union, three safeguards agreements with the IAEA, which currently apply to all nuclear facilities on the island, including the nuclear facilities, a nuclear research reactor, and a zero power reactor.[30] The IAEA spent about $12 million on nuclear technical assistance projects for Cuba since 1963—when Cuba began receiving nuclear technical assistance from the international agency—though 1996. About three fourths of this assistance Cuba received through these projects consisted of equipment such as computer systems, and radiation monitoring and laboratory equipment (See Table 1).

Table 1. Dollar Value and Type of all Nuclear Technical Assistance Projects Provided by the IAEA to Cuba, 1963-996

Type	Assistance (Million U.S.$)	Percentage
Equipment	8.72	73
Fellowships/Scientific visits	1.92	16
Expert Services	1.25	10
Subcontracts	0.11	1
Total	12.0	100

Source: International Atomic Energy Agency.

The IAEA's nuclear technical assistance was given primarily in the areas of general atomic energy development and in the application of isotopes and radiation in agriculture. In 1997, the IAEA approved an additional $1.7 million for nuclear technical assistance for projects in Cuba for 1997 through 1999.[31] In addition the IAEA spent about $2.8 million on training for Cubans and research contracts for Cuba that were not part of the specific nuclear technical assistance projects.[32] Of the total dollar value of all nuclear technical assistance that the IAEA has provided to Cuba, about $680,000 was approved for nuclear safety assistance for the nuclear reactors under construction at Juraguá for 1991 through 1998, of which about $313,000 has been spent. The IAEA is assisting Cuba in developing the ability to conduct a safety assessment of the nuclear power reactors, and in preserving, or "mothballing" the reactors while construction remains suspended. The IAEA is also implementing a training program for personnel involved in the operational safety and maintenance of all nuclear installations in Cuba, including the reactors.[33] The Agency's technical cooperation fund has been the primary source of funding for the nuclear assistance projects provided for Cuba (see Table 2).

Specifically, the IAEA has provided four major nuclear assistance programs for Cuba; of the $680,000 that has been approved, $313,364 had been spent on

30. The three INFCIRC.66 model agreements are: INFCIRC.281 (signed May 5, 1980); INFCIRC.298 (signed September 25, 1980); and INFCIRC.311 (signed October 7, 1983). INFCIRC/66 model agreements relate to "item-only" safeguards, particular technologies or materials. Any new projects that Cuba might consider in the future will have to be based on the INFCIRC/153 model. These agreements cover "full-scope" safeguards, all nuclear material in the peaceful activities of a nation. As Cuba has signed but not yet ratified the Treaty of Tlatelolco, it will have to re-negotiate full-scope safeguards agreements for all of its existing facilities and technologies.

31. See United States General Accounting Office, *Nuclear Safety: International Atomic Energy Agency's Nuclear Technical Assistance for Cuba*, GAO/RCED-97-72 (March 1997), p. 2.

32. These projects include the contracting of translation services of official IAEA documents and technical reports into Spanish by Cuban nuclear agencies. Interview by author with senior Cuban nuclear official, Havana, Cuba, May 25, 1997.

33. This training consisted of courses in radiation protection and nuclear safety, probabilistic safety assessment, safety analysis and assessment techniques for operational safety of nuclear power plants, and quality assurance for nuclear plants. In addition, from 1989 through 1996, the IAEA spent $433,000 on research contracts for Cuba. Under the IAEA's research program, the agency places contracts and cost-free agreements with research centers, laboratories, universities, and other institutions in member states to conduct research projects supporting its scientific programs. See United States General Accounting Office, *Nuclear Safety: International Atomic Energy Agency's Nuclear Technical Assistance for Cuba*, pp. 3, 5.

Table 2. Sources of Funding for IAEA Nuclear Technical Assistance Projects in Cuba, 1963-1996

Source	Assistance (Million U.S. $)	Percentage
Technical cooperation fund	9.38	78
UNDP	2.26	19
In-kind	0.20	2
Member states	0.15	1
Total	12.0	100

Source: International Atomic Energy Agency.

two of these projects as of January 1997. The IAEA assistance programs currently underway in Cuba are:

- Since 1991, the IAEA has assisted Cuba in undertaking a safety assessment of the reactor's ability to respond to accidents and in conserving the nuclear reactors under construction. The Agency has spent three-fourths of the $396,000 approved for the project. Spain has provided about $159,000 in extra-budgetary funds. This project is designed to develop proper safety and emergency systems and to preserve the plant's emergency work and infrastructure in order to facilitate the resumption of the plant's activities.[34]

- Since 1995, the IAEA has assisted Cuba in designing and implementing a training program for personnel involved in the operational safety and maintenance of nuclear facilities and installations. The IAEA has spent $31,000 of the $74,000 allotted for these activities.

- For 1997 and 1998, the technical assistance program will focus on two new projects to assist in licensing the reactors and establishing quality assurance programs for them. The purpose of these activities is to strengthen the ability of the Cuban nuclear regulatory body, CNSN, to carry out the process of licensing the reactors.[35] The quality assurance project will assist the Cuban nuclear officials at the nuclear power plant in developing an effective program that will improve safety practices and lower construction costs.[36]

Cuba has also served as a regional actor on behalf of the IAEA by hosting various conferences and meetings in Havana. Most notable, have been meetings held in 1995 and 1997. In May 1995, Cuba hosted a regional seminar on public information in Havana where there were representatives from the Caribbean basin states, Mexico and Central America. The purpose of this meeting was to disseminate information regarding the exploitation of nuclear energy in the region and the social and environmental implications of those actions. In October 1997, Cuba again was the host for two IAEA sponsored meetings. The meetings focused on the practical applications of nuclear technologies in fields of agriculture, industry, health, environment and science. These meetings were organized by a committee of representatives from the IAEA, Cuba and other Latin American countries, and were part of Cuba's commemorative activities marking the IAEA's 40th anniversary.[37]

---

34. Ibid., p. 8.

35. This is consistent with Cuban legislative measures to bolster the legal basis of nuclear activities in Cuba. See Jonathan Benjamin-Alvarado, "The New Cuban Nuclear Law Project: Commentary on Cuba's Decreto No. 208," *The Monitor: Arms Control, Nonproliferation and Demilitarization* Vol. 3, No. 3 (Summer 1997), pp. 40-45.

36. United States General Accounting Office, *Nuclear Safety: International Atomic Energy Agency's Nuclear Technical Assistance for Cuba*, p. 9.

37. The author attended these two joint meetings in Havana. The "International Symposium on Nuclear and Related Techniques in Agriculture, Industry, Health and Environment (NURT-97)," focused on the wide spectrum of nuclear techniques being applied in the region. They included those related to pest control; crop production; plant breeding; water resources; non-destructive testing in industry; radiation processing techniques; nuclear medicine; radiotherapy, radiopharmaceuticals; and nuclear analytical techniques in environmental studies. The "Workshop on Nuclear Physics (WONP-97)" covered topics on fast neutron physics and activation analysis; software on nuclear applications; development and design of nuclear instrumentation for spectroscopy and experimental physics; and advanced semiconductor detectors and related electronic research and developments. These meetings were attended by over 400 scientists and technicians from thirty countries.

Cuba's thirty five-year history of participation and cooperation with the IAEA has been impressive. As a developing country, Cuba has served as a leader in the advancement of nuclear science and technology, and has played a significant role in the administration and leadership of the IAEA. It has relied heavily on the agency for financial and technical support in areas of nuclear science.

In the period since the end of the Cold War, the IAEA has become one of the few reliable supporters of Cuba's nuclear program. The IAEA's dual objectives of promoting the peaceful exploitation of nuclear energy and monitoring proliferation threats in the world has served the Cubans' own ambitions well. Cuba enjoys an elevated status in the region because of its involvement with the IAEA and in turn continues to be an ardent supporter of the agency and its objectives. Cuba's President of the Agencia de Energía Nuclear, Daniel Codorniú Pujals coherently summarized the impact of the relationship between Cuba and the IAEA was in a speech by before the 38th Session of the General Conference of the IAEA:

> In this manner, we have worked intensely with the regulating agency in the perfection of a legal and standardized system, as well as in the preparation of personnel to guarantee that the evaluation of security of the nuclear energy facility is correct and integrated in all stages of licensing. It is necessary to recognize the understanding and support of the Secretariat of the IAEA of our determination to complete the nuclear energy facility and to guarantee the on-going preparation of our nuclear security system, which has contributed to the development of experts and support in other countries.[38]

OPANAL and the Treaty of Tlatelolco

In December 1995, Cuba formally signed the Latin American nuclear weapon-free-zone accord, the Treaty of Tlatelolco, in Mexico City. Cuba was the last country in Latin America to sign the Tlatelolco accord.[39] A preliminary assessment of the proliferation risks emanating from Cuba suggests that the Cuban government, by virtue of its "positive" movement in nonproliferation matters, has embarked on a course favorable to the international community that would be difficult if not impossible to reverse. Cuba, upon ratification of this regional accord by its National Assembly, agrees not to introduce nuclear weapons of any kind into the region. It also agrees that the IAEA, with which it already has favorable relations, will be allowed to inspect all Cuban nuclear facilities. Upon ratification Cuba must submit a full inventory of all nuclear materials and technologies to the accord's organizing body, the Organización por la Proscripción de Armas Nucleares en América Latina (OPANAL), and also conclude full-scope safeguards agreements for all these materials with the IAEA.

Given the growing cooperation in nuclear affairs and sense of unity in Latin American relations, the Castro government has astutely engaged its Latin American partners in regional and bilateral security and nuclear cooperation arrangements to garner much needed closer economic ties. The signing of the Tlatelolco accord attests to this aspect of Cuba's burgeoning cooperative resolve. The present regime has placed its credibility in the post-Cold War period on being a "good neighbor," one that is willing to engage in international cooperative efforts. This activity may also serve an instrumental function. It is possible that Cuba is using this movement to attract a potential investor for its moribund nuclear reactors at Juraguá. Be that as it may, Cuba has taken a significant step away from its Cold War posture in relation to such nuclear nonproliferation and security arrangements.

---

38. Speech by Daniel Codorniu Pujals, President, Agencia de Energía Nuclear, before the 38th Session of the General Conference of the International Atomic Energy Agency, Vienna, Austria, September 22, 1995. Translated by the author.

39. Six months after the Cuban Missile Crisis of October 1962, the Presidents of Bolivia, Chile, Ecuador and Mexico, all deeply affected by the crisis, announced their intention to develop a multilateral accord with the objective of prohibiting the production. importation, storage and testing of nuclear weapons in their territories. After two years of intensive efforts, on February 14, 1967 the Treaty for the Prohibition of Nuclear Arms in Latin America was signed at the Mexican Ministry of Foreign Relations in the Tlatelolco district of Mexico City. The treaty entered into force on April 22, 1968. For a detailed history of the Treaty, see Monica Serrano, *Common Security in Latin America: The 1967 Treaty of Tlatelolco* (London: Institute of Latin American Studies, 1992).

Throughout the Cold War period it maintained that the nuclear nonproliferation regime discriminated against those states that did not possess nuclear weapons and favored those that did. Cuba also maintained that it was no going to sign any such accord until all other states in the region did so as well. With the accession of both Argentina and Brazil into the Tlatelolco regime in the early 1990s, Cuba remained the only hold out. Cuba's intransigence in this area was also inconsistent with its participation in other similar non-nuclear arrangements.

As of the time of writing, Cuba has not ratified the Tlatelolco accord, and it remains a non-voting observer in the proceedings of OPANAL. Cuba also has not signed, nor has it expressed in interest in signing, the Nuclear Nonproliferation Treaty.

Other International Organizations

Cuba has not limited its international cooperation to the IAEA alone. Cuba received financing and support from the United Nations Development Program (UNDP) in the initial development stages of the nuclear program. In the period from 1980 until 1988, Cuba received approximately $1.66 million in assistance from the UNDP. Most of this aid was in the form of equipment for research laboratories and facilities employing nuclear applications. The total figure of UNDP assistance to the Cuban nuclear program from 1963 through 1997 is $2.26 million. Almost all of these funds have been channeled to Cuba in the form of grants to the IAEA.

Seeking to expand its cooperation in the nuclear sphere with other countries in the region, Cuba in 1988 began to cooperate in the Arreglos Regionales Cooperativos para la Promoción de la Ciencia y Tecnología Nucleares (ARCAL). Cuba is involved in a majority of the projects which the group undertakes.

As Cuba's close nuclear cooperation with the Russians has waned, its international cooperation and participation in multilateral organizations have increased appreciably. Cuban nuclear agencies now have established cooperative arrangements with the

following international and regional nuclear related organizations: the World Association of Nuclear Operators (WANO); World Health Organization (WHO); Food and Agriculture Organization (FAO); Pan-American Health Organization (PAHO); Organización Latino Americana de Energía (OLADE); Agencia Brasileiro-Argentino de Contabilidad y Control (ABACC); and the American Nuclear Society (ANS).[40]

Involvement in these organizations further enhances Cuba's ties within the epistemic communities they serve. But it is difficult to assess the benefits that would accrue directly to the nuclear program through these organizations. With the exception of UNDP assistance, Cuba is not likely to receive assistance significant enough to assist it in advancing the nuclear program. As the focus of these organizations is the promotion and dissemination of information and research to their constituent members, these activities can be viewed as contributing positively to the scientific development in Cuba and elsewhere.

Cuba's cooperation with multilateral organizations has ostensibly served two purposes. First, they have garnered Cuba with a modicum of international political support in its effort to develop a nuclear energy capability. Second, and more importantly, they have provided Cuban nuclear officials with a means of advancing their scientific and technical base through involvement with specialized multilateral organizations, and in particular, the IAEA. This evidence coincides with the expectations of the economic and technological modernization model. Moreover, Cuba's specific efforts to expand the scientific an technological base through IAEA-sponsored training programs in such critical areas as licensing and regulatory procedures, nuclear safety controls and quality assurance can be viewed as a part of its program to expand its knowledge in technical matters. This factor, coupled with the overarching objective of modernization through advanced technological capability, clearly supports the expected behavior of

---

40. Interview by author with Antonio Bolufe Gutiérrez, Director, Consultoría Delfos, Havana, Cuba, January 9, 1996.

actors pursuing modernization under the economic and technological model.

U.S. RESPONSES TO CUBAN INTERNATIONAL NUCLEAR COOPERATION

Prominently displayed in the Helms-Burton legislation are provisions that set out to limit Cuba's ability to complete its nuclear policy objectives of completing construction of the nuclear reactors at Juraguá. Specifically, these provisions aim to reduce the desire of Cuba's would-be nuclear trading partners, most notably the Russian Federation, from engaging the Cubans in any meaningful way. The Helms-Burton Act calls for the "withholding from assistance allocated for any country an amount equal to the sum of assistance or credits … in support of the completion of the Cuban nuclear facility at Juraguá" (Title 1, Sec.111). One could argue that the mostly symbolic nature of Cuban-Russian nuclear cooperation in the post-Cold War period is indicative of the success of this approach.

A much more reasonable appraisal would point to the chronic shortages of hard currency for both partners that have brought this project to a standstill. Yet, these provisions aim to limit the possibilities of this cooperation with the threat of a reduction in foreign aid to Russia. Ironically, this law contains exemptions for the most significant area of assistance effecting Russia's nuclear industry, that pertaining to the stabilization of its nuclear arsenal. Under the 1993 Comprehensive Threat Reduction Act or "Nunn-Lugar Act" (Public Law 103-160), Russia's nuclear infrastructure has been earmarked to receive assistance to stabilize its nuclear assets. Moreover, assistance to Russia and other states of the former Soviet Union are exempted from these sanctions in the areas of political, economic and humanitarian aid. This has the effect of allowing Russia's MINATOM a free hand to continue cooperating with Cuba and pursue reactor sales in the international nuclear markets. Furthermore, under the provisions of interna-

tional nuclear accords and as a member of the IAEA, Cuba is entitled to pursue a nuclear energy capability so long as it adheres to provisions of full safeguards and nuclear safety protocols.

In February 1997, NBC Nightly News reported that funds contributed by the United States to the IAEA were being used to fund training programs for Cuba's nuclear program. A subsequent GAO study of the issue indicated that indeed that a portion of the voluntary contribution by the United States was earmarked for technical assistance programs for the Cubans.[41] But a closer inspection of the figures indicates that there is more smoke than substance in the story.

In 1996, the United States contributed $16 million (about 30 percent) to the IAEA's technical cooperation fund. Cuba for its part contributed $45,150 (or 0.7 percent). The IAEA has approved $1.7 million in technical assistance for projects for Cuba for 1997 through 1999. By extrapolation, the United States contribution to the fund over this same period of time would be around $48 million of the $159 million total. The amount of technical assistance for Cuba—$1.7 million—is 3.5 percent of the total U.S. contribution. That assistance from the IAEA coffers to Cuba represents 1.06 percent of the total contributions to the fund for 1997 through 1999. The reduction of the 3.5 percent that goes to Cuba from the U.S. contribution to the fund would only amount to a paltry $59,500. This would not disable Cuban cooperation with the IAEA, nor could it be conceived as an impediment to the provision of assistance to Cuba from the agency. Symbolically, opponents of the Cuban program could point to the non-involvement of the US for assistance programs from the IAEA. Whether it is $59,500 or $1.7 million matters little. The IAEA will most likely push forward with the assistance and training programs that ultimately benefit the United States as well as Cuba.

This has not gone unnoticed by Cuban official representatives for the IAEA in Vienna. This excerpt of an official protest to the IAEA from Cuba regarding ac-

---

41. See United States General Accounting Office, *International Atomic Energy Agency's Nuclear Technical Assistance for Cuba*, GAO/RCED-97-72 (March 1997).

tions set in motion by the Congress of the United States makes the following direct reference to the Helms-Burton Law:

> These arrogant statements raise a number of questions, all of which necessarily ask what right the United States, as a Member State of the IAEA and a leading nuclear power, has to try to crush the Cuban nuclear program and thus prevent access to the benefits of the peaceful applications of nuclear energy in the country's socio-economic development programs, which are of considerable importance to the well-being to the Cuban people.[42]

Yet in July 1997 a bill was introduced in the House of Representatives by Congressman Robert Menéndez to withhold U.S. assistance for programs and projects of the IAEA in Cuba. H.R. 2092, known as the IAEA Accountability and Safety Act of 1997, is clearly designed to wash American hands clean of any involvement in Cuba's nuclear program. A similarly worded amendment was included in the 1997 Foreign Relations Authorization Act for 1998 and 1999. But short of painting a self-congratulatory and triumphalist picture of uncompromising opposition to the Castro regime these bills are essentially toothless and clawless tigers and would violate the spirit of international nonproliferation cooperation. Like the Helms-Burton law these proposed pieces of legislation, render themselves moot by the nature of the exceptions to their provisions. Sec. 2 (2)(B)(I) states that the law would not apply to IAEA programs for "safety inspection of nuclear facilities or related materials, or for inspections and similar activities designed to prevent the development of nuclear weapons" by Cuba. This sounds very much like the mission of the international organization under which all these activities would take place.

The restrictions specific to the Juraguá facility and the nuclear research center at Pedro Pi would be lifted by the United States if Cuba: (1) ratifies the Treaty of Tlatelolco or the Nuclear Nonproliferation Treaty; (2) negotiates full-scope safeguards with the IAEA not later than two years after ratification of the accord; and (3) incorporates internationally accepted nuclear safety standard into practice. Interestingly enough the latter has been the focus of Cuba's nuclear activities for well over the past year.

In 1996, the Cubans embarked on a new nuclear law project to complement the passage of "Decreto-Ley No. 208—Regarding the National System of Accounting and Control of Nuclear Materials." Cuban nuclear officials have indicated that the reason for delay in the ratification stems from the need to alter the existing legal basis of nuclear law so that it will more easily comply with the provisions of agreements with which they fully intend to comply. Decreto-Ley No. 208 represents part of that effort. Cuban nuclear officials are clearly cognizant of the shortcomings of the Soviet-based systems of accounting, control and materials handling. They have sought to design legislation that conforms to internationally recognized standards and norms of nuclear materials handling and storage. They have modeled the system in spirit on the scope and objectives contained in U.S. Nuclear Regulatory Commission standards. Reaching that standard is another question altogether. But they have sought to make this system amenable to the requirements of the full-scope safeguards agreements that Cuba intends to sign when the treaty comes into force. On a larger scale, the new nuclear law project, under the direction of the Agencia de Energía Nuclear and the Centro Nacional de Seguridad Nuclear, seeks to place all of Cuba's nuclear activities under a system of laws and practices that correspond to existing and future international nuclear standards.[43] Should this come to pass, and by all indications it appears that it will, there will be very little that the United States can do to impede the progress of the Cuban nuclear project.

---

42. See "Text of a Circular Letter of June 16, 1997 from the Permanent Mission of the Republic of Cuba to the International Atomic Energy Agency," Attachment, INFCIRC/537 (July 30, 1997).

43. Jonathan Benjamin-Alvarado, "The Cuban New Nuclear Law Project," *The Monitor: Nonproliferation, Demilitarization, and Arms Control*, Vol. 3, No.3 (Summer 1997), p.41.

SUMMARY DISCUSSION

This paper sought to detail Cuba's external nuclear cooperative efforts, and the impact of these efforts on the Cuban nuclear energy development policy. The impact has been overwhelmingly favorable during the Cold War period and in the face of Cuba's economic troubles during the period since the end of the Cold War. The first section focused on Cuba's bilateral relations with the Russian Federation, and then with Cuba's Western European and Latin American partners. The second section was a review of Cuba's participation and cooperative projects in multilateral, international and regional nuclear-related organizations. This section focused on nuclear assistance agreements established by Cuba and the IAEA. The section also touched on the participation by Cuba in other regional nonproliferation and nuclear cooperation regimes. The last section dealt with the United States' policy to close down or limit nuclear assistance to Cuba from states in the international system.

The purpose of this analysis centers on the impact and influence of these international interactions of the choice, implementation and successful accomplishment of Cuban nuclear policy objectives. The modernization literature has suggested that the impact of these influences is highly determinate of the appropriateness and success of modernization schemes in developing states. Moreover these influences will carry significant implications for the trajectory of development within these states. In relation to these influences, developing states find themselves in a paradoxical situation. For development to be sustainable, the development scheme must take into consideration that country's resource base. Unfortunately, states often disregard the appropriateness of an advanced technology such as nuclear energy for a developing state. But development may be nearly impossible without the involvement and assistance from external sources and their imperatives.

Foreign policy and development analysts have tried to forecast what Cuba's external trade policies would look like in the aftermath of the Soviet demise. How would Cuba respond to the new nature of relations with the former Soviet Union? What role would the

Western Europeans and Latin Americans play in Cuba's attempt to keep the nuclear program alive? And, would the IAEA continue to be willing to simultaneously promote and assist Cuba in the peaceful exploitation of nuclear energy, especially now with intense pressure being applied by the United States to terminate these activities?

The following discussion addresses those questions and other issues germane to the Cuban attempts to keep its nuclear aspirations afloat.

The loss of Cuba's primary nuclear trade partner has devastated the nuclear program. While the Russian Federation has attempted to keep the Juraguá project alive, the fact remains that the numerous trade agreements concluded between Cuba and Russia to complete construction have been mostly symbolic in nature. The search for the third partner in the joint venture to complete the reactors has been fruitless. The Soviet Union made Cuba's nuclear ambition a reality. The Soviet-successor state has had neither the desire or wherewithal to support such a venture so far from home. The suspect investment prospects for the project have limited Russian and Cuban efforts to maintaining a mothballed program until the time when the interest and financing for completing the reactors become tangible. Some critics in Russia now blame the short-sighted leaders of the newly democratic state for losing the Cuba that everyone else in the world is now finding. But to limit the discussion to the failures of post-Cold War policy between Russia and Cuba would minimize the significant advances made in the creation and development of a well-conceived and vibrant nuclear infrastructure. While it is true that Cuba's nuclear reactors is moribund, there now exists a resource base that enables Cuba to easily tackle the nuclear option when the circumstances warrant it. Russia must still demonstrate to its potential nuclear clients throughout the world that it can successfully complete a nuclear reactor outside of its borders and under international scrutiny. For this reason, there is little reason to suggest that either Cuba or Russia will terminate their nuclear cooperation relationship anytime soon.

While a number of other countries have expressed an interest in the Cuban nuclear program, not one has concluded an agreement to work on the program. In the early 1990s representatives from Germany, Spain, Brazil, Italy, and Argentina visited the Juraguá site and walked away. This inability to attract a project partner has been disheartening to the Cubans. Yet the nature of relationships between Cuba and other countries in the energy sector have evolved appreciably since 1991. The change has been especially significant since Fidel Castro announced in 1997 that the nuclear program would no longer be the sole focus of Cuba's energy development program. In fact, it has opened the door to a flurry of joint venture activity to upgrade and construct new thermoelectric facilities throughout the island. The promotion of a national energy efficiency program has accompanied these overtures and promise to more than compensate for the inability to complete the Juraguá project. One issue is raised by the nature of these activities. Cuba has concluded these deals with guaranteed financing from external sources. In one case, the foreign firm will receive all proceeds from the operation of this new facility until such time as it receives it capital investment in full. Moreover, the joint venture with the Cuban state will be seeking to sell electricity to foreign firms for hard currency payments. The arrangement potentially could dampen the investment environment in Cuba, and it eerily resembles the economic arrangements of the pre-Revolutionary period. While states other than the Russian Federation have not stepped up to assume the mantle of primary nuclear trading partners, their activities in the non-nuclear energy generation sector has revitalized Cuban energy policy.

Cuba's nuclear infrastructure has prospered because of its participation in international and multilateral organizations. The interaction between Cuba and the IAEA has been an essential component in the development of the Cuba's nuclear infrastructure. Since 1963, Cuba has received technical assistance from the IAEA to develop nuclear technical capabilities in a number of sectors across the Cuban economy. While Cuba has not received any direct funding from the agency in the construction of the nuclear reactors at Juraguá, IAEA assistance has helped Cuba to expand its nuclear program capabilities in the areas of quality assurance, nuclear safety, materials han-

dling, command and control. The assistance has also provided the Cuban nuclear infrastructure with a model for the creation and development of the requisite agencies to carry out these tasks. Cuba has also benefited from its participation in the administration of the agency's activities by serving on the IAEA Board of Governors, as well as placing Cubans on the nuclear safeguards inspection teams. In other instances, states' have used the placement of their nationals on these inspection teams to later circumvent IAEA safeguards from revealing elements of nuclear weapons development programs. Cuba's active participation and mostly transparent activities suggest that the trajectory of its nuclear program is entirely peaceful in nature. Cuba has concluded safeguards agreements with the IAEA, and by all indications it appears that it will continue to follow through with its commitments to these agreements for the foreseeable future. Cuba has recently signed the Treaty of Tlatelolco, and upon ratification it will more fully integrate its nuclear related activities to international accountability and scrutiny. This dispels any suggestion of a nefarious rationale to Cuba's nuclear ambition. Cuba's participation in the myriad international organizations devoted to the advancement of nuclear applications bolsters its own technical capacity, but also enhances it ties outside of the island. All told the cooperative activities undertaken by Cuba have greatly increased its nuclear capabilities, as well as, positively influencing the direction of nuclear energy development. Rather than constructing impassable obstacles to its nuclear ascendancy Cuba has astutely utilized its participation to support and advance its nuclear program.

The United States opposition to the Cuban nuclear program has had little effect on its prosperity or privations. A majority of the legislative and policy positions taken by the United States has done little other than mollify criticism from the Cuban-American and anti-Castroites who regularly decry the looming Cuban Chernobyl. Moreover, the attempts to halt assistance to the Cuban program from the IAEA and other sources has verged on meddling in matters that are in reality of little concern, and are certainly not national security interests. The best that can be said about the United States position on the issue is that it serves no one's interest to lambaste the Cuban nuclear program from afar when the means of assessing such a threat exists. The United States can and has cooperated with the Cubans on the nuclear issue. When scientific and technical analysis replaces the casting of aspersions across the Straits of Florida, then the United States may be able to construct a policy regarding Cuba's nuclear program that conforms to reality and not to myth. The impact of the U.S. opposition limits legitimate and desirable contact between the American and Cuban scientific communities. Moreover, it places U.S. commercial interests at a disadvantage in investing in the Cuban energy sector while the rest of the world is engaging in successful joint ventures with Cuban state enterprises in Cuba's energy sector.

The survival of Cuba's nuclear aspiration remains assured for the short-term. The influence of external forces in the nuclear program has been overwhelmingly positive. Cuba has advanced its nuclear potential in all areas because of the interaction with foreign states, international organizations and multinational firms. Cuba's nuclear program has floundered primarily because of one reason, the lack of financing. For the Cubans and Russians the loss of the financial wherewithal to construct the reactors was as the ending of the Cold War, completely unforeseen.

Frankly, no one could have predicted that the Soviets or the Russians would not have completed the venture in Cuba. Yet, as this came to pass, Cuba has found it difficult if not impossible to continue its pursuit of nuclear power. The failure to attract project partners stems from both Russia's and Cuba's inefficient scheme to build the reactors. No prudent investor would entertain participating in the nuclear construction venture as long as there is no tangible means to recoup the investment. The attraction of investment in the thermoelectric sector reflects a fundamental shift in the creation of joint ventures that favors the foreign enterprise.

This examination demonstrated that Cuba was cognizant of its domestic energy resource constraints and logically sought and secured external assistance to advance its energy policy. It has been successful in the creation and development of a vibrant nuclear energy sector, short of completing the construction on the nuclear reactors. This is a remarkable accomplishment for any developing state, but especially for one such as Cuba, that has promoted the creation of knowledge and expertise matched by few countries in the developing world.

MEXICO-CUBA COMMERCIAL RELATIONS IN THE 1990s

Demetria Tsoutouras[1] and Julia Sagebien

Cuba and Mexico share many characteristics. Historically, both were Spanish colonies and are now both post-revolutionary countries. Geographically, the countries are close neighbours within Latin America and they are situated next to the United States. While Mexico and the United States maintain friendly relations, relations between Cuba and the United States are severely strained. This fact alone exerts the greatest deal of influence on Mexico-Cuba commercial and diplomatic relations.

The core principle of Mexico's foreign policy is "non-intervention" in the affairs of other states. Mexico has stood by this principle regarding Cuba (Covarrubias, 1996). For instance, Mexico was the only Organization of American States (OAS) member not to break diplomatic ties with Cuba after the 1964 resolution to isolate Cuba. Mexico has also strongly protested the use of the Helms-Burton law to deter commercial relations with Cuba. By basing its relationship with Cuba on the principle of non-intervention, Mexico has maintained an amicable commercial and diplomatic involvement with the island, throughout the Castro regime. Although Cuba-Mexico bilateral trade has never been strong, it increased in the 1990s, until 1995. However, in 1996 and 1997, the value of Mexico's exports to the island, especially in oil and related products, dropped significantly. Likewise, although Mexican companies participated in some important joint ventures on the

island in the early 1990s, they are not currently playing a large investment role in Cuba.

The first section of this study will review Mexican-Cuban relations from the Cuban revolution to the end of the 1980s. It will include an overview of the limited commercial history between Mexico and Cuba, until the breakup of the Soviet Bloc, an event which shook the economy of Cuba and forced the government to search for non-traditional commercial partners. The second section of the study will examine the impact on Mexico of Cuba's re-orientation in the international sector. This section will also put into perspective the influence of the U.S. government on this relationship by examining negotiations between Mexico and the United States regarding the North American Free Trade Agreement (NAFTA), as well as the Mexican Peso Crisis and the implementation of the Helms-Burton Law. The third section of the study will document Mexican investment in Cuba, which reached a peak in the early 1990s. Finally, the paper will review the strategic advantages and disadvantages of Mexican companies exporting to the Cuban market.

The research for this study included both secondary and primary sources. An extensive literature review of Mexican, Cuban and U.S. sources was conducted. This research was complemented by interviews conducted with Mexican government officials, academics and business professionals, during the Spring of 1998. Due to the sensitive nature of trade and invest-

---

1. Tsoutouras would like to thank St. Mary's University for generous financial support to be able to present this paper at the Eighth Annual meeting of the Association for the Study of the Cuban Economy.

ment with Cuba, very little statistical information was made available by either government or private sources. Although interviewed company names have been kept confidential, a list of government agencies interviewed is provided in the Appendix.

EARLY RELATIONS (1959-1988)

Mexico and Castro's Cuba have shared the last 39 years of economic and diplomatic relations based on a single principle: non-intervention. As succinctly put by the Mexican Ministry of Foreign Affairs (SRE):

> The guidelines of international policy are few, clear and simple. They only proclaim: That all countries are equal; they should mutually and scrupulously respect institutions, their laws and their sovereignty; that no country should interfere in any manner and under any motive in the internal affairs of another. All should strictly and with no exception submit themselves to the universal principle of non-intervention (Mexico, SRE in Covarrubias, 1994 p. 51).

Mexico and Canada were the only countries in the Americas that never broke relations with the Castro government. In return, Cuba adopted a similar non-interventionist policy regarding Mexico. While Castro has supported revolutionary movements in other parts of the world, he has never directly supported movements in Mexico, though he may have had opportunities to do so.[2]

Another factor which facilitated relations between both countries immediately following the Cuban revolution was that Mexico, itself, was a post-revolutionary country. Thus Mexican officials and the general public, tended to sympathize with Cuba's position (Covarrubias,1994). Although this sympathy generally dried up after Castro confirmed his communist intentions for the island, the Mexican government continued to disagree with the use of force against Cuba, as well as the imposition of economic and political sanctions and diplomatic isola-

tion used and promoted by the United States (CEPAL, 1995). While Mexico has not supported these U.S. policies against Cuba, it has been careful to state that Mexico's policy on Cuba is based more on principle than on actual support for the Castro regime.[3]

In terms of commercial relations, there was little Mexico-Cuba bilateral trade between 1959 and 1973. Cuba's involvement with the Soviet Bloc and its COMECON market meant that most of Cuba's trading needs were fulfilled through special relations with these countries. A turn around in economic relations between Mexico and Cuba began during the government of Mexican president Echeverría (1970-1976), which corresponded with an increase in interest between Mexico and Cuba for improved trade and cultural co-operation. For example, in 1974, two important joint agreements were signed, one regarding culture and education and the other regarding scientific and technical co-operation (Cornelis & Sierra, 1989 in Covarrubias,1994). During a visit to Cuba, in 1975, and throughout that year, the Echeverría and Castro governments signed several additional cultural and commercial treaties. These treaties covered areas as diverse as industrial and economical collaboration, collaboration in the sugar industry, and exchanges in television and radio broadcasting. Although trade began to increase in the 1970s, the numbers were still low in comparison with each country's respective total trade figures. In other words, economic relations were not significant because both countries had more important trading partners in industrialized countries (Covarrubias, 1994).

It was during the presidency of López Portillo (1976-1982) that Cuba and Mexico shared their closest political relations (Covarrubias, 1994). Collaboration during this period was very strong and marked by rumors of unofficial loans to Cuba and trade in oil (Covarrubias, 1994), which had been strongly dis-

---

2. Mexican Presidents Echeverría and López Portillo strongly and openly supported diplomatic relations with Cuba (Covarrubias, 1994 p. 327).

3. There have been reports of Cuba's involvement in the 1968 clash between student and police, which began on July 26th at a rally celebrating the Cuban Revolution in Mexico City.

couraged by the United States since the 1960s.[4] Among the points of collaboration between Mexico and Cuba during the López Portillo presidency was the establishment of the General Intergovernmental Joint Commission in 1978. The Commission's aim was to review work on all other commissions, treaties and groups and to propose methods or projects for the continued development of relations between Mexico and Cuba.

De la Madrid's presidency (1982- 1988) coincided with the collapse of the Soviet Bloc and a change in Mexico's trade strategy to one of export promotion. During this presidency, the economic relationship between Mexico and Cuba continued to grow, but diplomatic relations began to cool. Two important factors under the de la Madrid presidency helped to streamline the trading process between Mexico and Cuba. First, a Limited Scope Agreement was signed in 1985, which finally allowed Mexico and Cuba to trade basic and manufactured products with reduced or zero tariffs (Covarrubias,1994). Second, lines of credit were established between the Mexican Bank for Foreign Trade (Bancomext) and the Cuban National Bank.

RELATIONS IN THE 1990s

By 1989, the collapse of the Soviet Bloc was almost complete and Cuba was once again alone and isolated without the traditional trade partners it had become accustomed to. While the countries of Eastern Europe changed their economies from within, Cuba was forced to reform its economy in response to external factors (ECLAC, 1997). The breakdown of the Soviet Bloc put an end to the Cuban system of guaranteed full-time employment and lack of concern over productivity. This period of 1989 to 1993 marked a decrease in Cuban GDP of more than 30% (ECLAC, 1997). The Cuban government's response to this crisis included a search for alternative sources of trade and investment.

The Salinas government (1988-1994) witnessed very complicated relations between Mexico and Cuba.

While both countries were interested in Mexican investment in Cuba, Salinas was also strengthening ties to the United States. Although publicly stating that Mexico would help however possible to improve the situation in Cuba, in 1992 Salinas began meeting with members of the Cuban exile community in Miami (Covarrubias,1994). Around the same time, Salinas also received additional pressure during the NAFTA negotiations from members of the U.S. Senate, who sent him a letter expressing their concern about Mexico's policy on Cuba (Epoca, 1992 in Covarrubias,1994). Both actions were seen as pressure tactics to force the Salinas government into adopting a harder line on Cuba.

The Zedillo government (1994-2000?) has weathered even more strain. His government was compelled to accept an aid package (with a series of political demands, reportedly, attached to it), from the U.S. government following the 1994 Peso Crisis. Not long afterwards, the Mexican government was once again forced to re-examine the importance of its commercial relationship with Cuba under the threat of the Helms-Burton legislation.

The implementation of the Helms-Burton law by the United States government has been strongly opposed by Mexico. Like most other countries, the Mexican government is of the opinion that the extraterritorial nature of the Helms-Burton Law violates the basic principles of international law. The two main groups within the Mexican government opposing the Helms-Burton law—the Ministry of Foreign Affairs and the Ministry of Trade and Industrial Promotion—point out that the law violates NAFTA, as well as, Mexico's foreign policy of non-intervention (Covarrubias, 1997). The Mexican Congress has also stated its opposition to the law and its solidarity with the people of Cuba (Covarrubias, 1997). During the August 1996 visit to Mexico of Stuart Einzenstat, U.S. Special Envoy for Cuba, the Mexican government stated that Mexico supports basic human rights, as well as the policies of passive rela-

---

4. Since there was extensive U.S.-Mexican trade in oil products, there was a threat for the Mexican government if they exported oil to Cuba.

tions between states, self-determination and non-intervention. In addition, at the 28th General Assembly of the OAS in June 1997, Mexico reaffirmed its position that open dialogue and communication with Cuba were better alternatives for change than isolation, embargoes and sanctions (SRE, 1998).

In October of 1996, in expressing its intention to use all legal means possible to limit the effect of the Helms-Burton Law, the Mexican government enacted a foreign extraterritorial measures law. The law prohibits Mexican companies from obeying foreign legislation and may impose fines of up to $ 300,000 USD on Mexican companies or citizens. In addition, the law states that Mexican courts will not recognize any U.S. claims under Title III of the Helms-Burton Law. If a Mexican company is sued, it can counter sue the U.S. company in a Mexican court for the same amount of damages. If the U.S. company refuses to pay, the Mexican company could have a legal claim to the U.S. company's assets in Mexico.

Overall, the Zedillo government's stance on Cuba has been a very divided one. While continuing its non-intervention policy in regards to Cuba, the PRI government has distanced itself from Castro. This cooling in diplomatic relations has been best illustrated in the cancellation of Castro's proposed visit to Mexico in 1996 and statements made by President Zedillo that he will not defend antidemocratic governments (Covarrubias, 1997).

Nonetheless, Mexico continues to support Cuba's reintegration into the Americas and continues to work with Cuba on several joint economic commissions (CEPAL, 1997). For instance, in June 1998, the 10th session of the Joint Commission of the Intergovernmental Working Group on Economic and Industrial Collaboration met once again to review the general state of economic relations between the two countries. Mexican officials stated that considering the process of economic transformation occurring within Cuba, it was important that Mexico continue to strengthen economic and commercial relations with the island (SRE, 1998).

INVESTMENT IN THE 1990s

The growth of Mexican foreign investment in Cuba was facilitated by a 1991 agreement between Bancomext (Mexican Bank for Foreign Trade) and the government of Cuba which allowed for non-traditional restructuring of Cuba's debt. This agreement paved the way for Mexico-Cuba debt for equity swaps which financed several Mexican investments on the island. In these swaps, Bancomext gave credits to Mexican companies to invest in or trade with Cuba as a form of repaying Cuba's debt to Mexico (CEPAL, 1995).

One of the first Mexico-Cuba joint ventures initiatives joined Cubanacán (a Cuban tourism parastatal) and Mexican company DSC (Desarollo de Servicios Constructivos) to construct a 4-star hotel in Varadero, Cuba. The project was completed in 1991. DSC contributed $15 million USD with approved financing through Bancomext in a debt for equity swap (CEPAL, 1995).

Shortly thereafter, in 1993, Grupo Danta of Monterrey formed a joint venture with Unión Textil of Cuba. The two entered into a 20-year contract and became partners in a new company, the International Textile Corporation. In this deal, Danta contributed capital for buying the raw materials and financing repairs while Unión Textil contributed the industrial capacity and qualified labour force. The Unión Textil had the use of 33 plants valued at $2.5 billion USD and 37, 000 workers (CEPAL, 1995).

In another debt-equity swap, Cemex of Monterrey, the world's third largest cement producer, joined with Unión de Empresas de Cemento to create Empresa Mixta Cementos Curazao NV (EMCC). The project was a 50-50 joint venture which allowed for the sale of a cement plant in Mariel, Cuba, to EMCC (Babún, 1997). Cemex was able to export cement from the Mariel plant and from Cuba's other 5 plants. A victim of the Helms-Burton legislation, Cemex decided to sacrifice its operations in Cuba to protect larger interests (including 4 plants) in the United States. In May 1996, Cemex notified the U.S. government that it had withdrawn from its operations in Cuba. The notice was given just before Cemex's top executive was to receive a warning from the U.S. government that he might be violating Helms-Burton (Cuba Net, 1996a). The Helms-Burton claim against Cemex was based, in part, on the fact that one of the plants Cemex was using in Cuba was believed to have been confiscated by the Cuban government from Lone Star Industries of Stamford, Connecticut (Cuba Net, 1996b).

Perhaps one of the best known (and largest) joint ventures to this point between a Mexican company and Cuba began in 1994. Grupo Domos entered into a joint venture deal through a 55-year contract with EmtelCuba, the Cuban state enterprise that operates the telephone service. For $750 million USD, Domos bought a 49% stake in the newly formed company, ETECSA. Domos did not have substantial assets going into the deal but secured the transaction through help from Bancomext in the form of an equity swap of $300 million USD of Cuban debt (CEPAL, 1995).

ETECSA planned to spend about $1.4 billion USD to modernize Cuba's telecommunications infrastructure, with both partners contributing half the expenses. ETECSA's goal was to expand Cuba's telephone system from 2.5 lines/100 inhabitants to 20/100 by the year 2000. However, after the peso crisis in December of 1994, Domos began having problems contributing to its share of the investment (de Córdoba, 1996). In 1995, Domos was forced to divest 25% of its stock in ETECSA at lower than market value.

The stock was sold to STET of Italy for $291 million USD (de Córdoba, 1996). Domos contributed $320 million USD of the planned investment and was left with 37% of ETECSA. By the end of 1996, ETECSA had installed 37,000 digital lines and 900 international output circuits. International calls skyrocketed from 400 calls to 60,000 a day (Tamayo, 1996).

In August of 1996, Domos received a letter from the U.S. State Department giving it 45 days to end operations in Cuba (Moore, 1996). The president of Domos, Javier Garza Calderón, and several top executives were told to resign or to break off ties with Cuba or they and their families would not be allowed to enter the United States. Although Domos did not leave the island in response to Helms-Burton, the law

did make it difficult for the company, which was already having financial difficulties, to secure the financing required to continue their Cuban operations. Late in 1996, Domos was forced to leave Cuba after it was unable to secure continued financing for the project. Interestingly, Domos was singled out by the Helms-Burton legislation even though ITT, which ran the phone system before repatriation, had never given any indication that it planned to sue Domos (Moore, 1996). In 1997, within the provisions of Helms-Burton, STET finalized an agreement with ITT to use its properties in Cuba for 10 years. The agreement released STET from Helms-Burton sanctions.

In sum, planned joint ventures in the mid 1990s faced many challenges, especially in strategic areas, such as oil and gas. Any planned joint venture would, of course, face pressure from the U.S. government and would, to some degree, need Mexican government backing (at least financially) to be secure. As mentioned before, 1992 brought about new pressures for the Salinas government from the U.S. Senate and the Cuban exile community, both of which were strongly against foreign investment in Cuba. Additionally, Mexican companies received a harsh blow with the fall out from the 1994 Peso Crisis, which caused severe financing problems and sent interest rates in Mexico soaring. It is rumored that some members of the U.S. Congress tried to link the U.S. financial aid package after the peso crisis for a stricter policy on Cuba (La Jornada, 1995 in Covarrubias, 1997). So although many other countries found investing in Cuba "risky," U.S. pressure on Mexico's government combined with high interest rates, made continued or new investing in Cuba nearly impossible for Mexican companies.

The barriers were even greater for Mexican state-owned companies, such as Telmex and Pemex. These companies would have been natural complements to Cuban state-owned agencies attempting to remedy Cuba's deficiencies in communications and petroleum. For a state-owned company, such as to Pemex, to form a joint venture in a strategic area such as petroleum, would surely have had a profound impact on Mexico-U.S. relations.

While Mexican investment in Cuba came on strong in the early 1990s, supported by debt-equity swaps from Bancomext, Mexican investors now play a significantly smaller role in Cuba. Mexican investment has dropped noticeably from 1995, when Mexican companies made up, arguably, the largest share of investments (dollar-wise) in Cuba, reportedly approximately $1.5 billion USD (Enfoque, 1996). [5]

A few Mexican companies are still involved in joint ventures on the island. For instance, Telecomunicaciones Internacionales de Mexico (TIMSA), is a partner, along with Cuban government operated UTISA and Sherritt International Communications, in Cubacel. Cubacel provides analog and digital cellular service on the island. TIMSA originally held 50% of Cubacel but in 1998, it sold 75% of its shares in Cubacel to Sherritt (Economic Eye on Cuba, 1998b).

In addition, Mexico's Banamex is involved in a project to process receivables and issue consumer credit and charge cards within Cuba (Economic Eye on Cuba, 1997). While strong financing is a great concern for most Mexican companies (interest rates above 20% are common in Mexico), as Mexico's largest bank, Banamex has a definite advantage. Banamex has also signed an agreement with Banco Popular de Cuba (Popular Bank of Cuba) to facilitate wire transfers, and letters of credit between Mexico and Cuba (Wall Street Journal, 1998).

Although Banamex appears to be enjoying its position in Cuba, most Mexican companies have found the barriers to investment in Cuba too great. By examining the survival of Banamex's joint venture in Cuba, and the demise of those of Domos (due to financing complication) and Cemex (a large company with important interests in the U.S.), it can be surmised that Mexican companies can succeed in Cuban joint ventures if they are large, independent of the United States and have strong financing.

TRADE IN THE 1990s

Although investment has weakened, many Mexican companies are continuing to export to Cuba, filling the void for imported, and in some instances American-made, products. With its close location and historical ties and common language, Mexico is a natural trading partner for Cuba. Exports to Cuba have grown to the point that by 1997, Cuba had become the 6th most important destination for Mexican exports (CubaNews, 1997). Attracted by the largest population in the Caribbean and a steady stream of tourists, Mexican exporters have tapped into the growth markets within Cuba of telecommunication, construction, petroleum and consumer goods. Mexicans are exporting products such as souvenirs, spare parts for telephones, food, tourism inputs, primary materials, materials for specialized construction and petroleum. The top five product groups exported from Mexico to Cuba in 1997 were: (1) mineral fuels and oil, (2) soaps, (3) plastics, (4) machines and apparatus and (5) nuclear reactor components (see Table 1). Interestingly, exports of mineral fuels and oil, which were significant in 1995, dropped in 1996 and 1997, from exports of $141 million USD in 1995 to $31 million USD in 1997 (see Table 1). Another interesting fact is that nuclear reactor components have been among the top exports to Cuba for the last 3 years.

Many Mexican exporters began trading with Cuba after being contacted by the Cuban government, through Bancomext. In some cases, Bancomext introduced exporters to Cuban representatives in Mexico, such as MERCO (Cuban trade officials). In the early 1990s, if a company was interested in exporting to Cuba, they would receive strong support from MERCO. MERCO was staffed by Cubans who promoted Cuban trading interests in Mexico. They would buy Mexican products from Mexican companies who were not ready to export and over time, they would teach companies how to export for them-

---

5. In the early 1990s Mexico was listed as a main investor in Cuba (CEPAL, 1995) but by 1998 (Economic Eye on Cuba, 1998a) Mexico was listed as a minor investor. Although actual foreign investment figures in Cuba are difficult to obtain, the June 15-21, 1998 edition of *Economic Eye on Cuba,* reports that France, Spain, UK and Italy make up 50% of investment in Cuba, Canada makes up 20% and Mexico, Venezuela, Argentina and Chile make up 18%.

Table 1. Mexican Exports ($US) to Cuba by Product, 1995-1997

	1995	1996	1997
Mineral Fuels and Oil	141 674 970	45 437 528	31 416 334
Soap and Related Products	22 342 293	17 884 864	21 747 947
Plastic and Related Products	10 043 700	16 934 432	20 468 358
Fertilizer	17 909 273	6 983 732	11 387 460
Nuclear Reactors	11 736 515	13 833 672	13 190 143
Chemicals and Inorganic Products	11 702 017	9 742 898	8 732 5603
Rubber and Related Products	11 279 168	18 509 932	10 810 208
Autos, Tractors	11 074 762	11 426 718	2 670 736
Animal and Vegetable Oils and Fats	10 708 406	7 988 859	8 656 139
Cotton	10 547 732	15 731 394	10 491 192
Machines and Apparatus	9 100567	22 145 919	17 932 808
Manufactured Metals	7 910 599	12 677 540	11 738 901
Steel and Iron Work	6 914 567	11 263 090	3 606 373
Paper and Carton	4 215 340	9 194 476	9 372 192

Source: Bancomext.

selves. Unfortunately for Mexican exporters, MERCO stopped operations in Mexico shortly after the peso crisis.

Mexican exporters to Cuba interviewed for this study mention that another commercial challenge for them has been the change in Bancomext's attitude toward trading with Cuba. Once very helpful, Bancomext now shows little interest in promoting trade and investment with Cuba, most likely due to its ties with the United States. Bancomext's about-face *vis-a-vis* Cuba may explain, in part, the decrease in both investment and trade since 1995. For instance, while exports to the United States have increased over 40% and exports to Spain have risen 18% between 1995 and 1997, exports to Cuba have dropped over 26% during the same period (see Table 2). Despite the fact that Mexico has become one of Cuba's top trading partners, exports to the island dropped in 1996 and 1997, as compared to 1995 (see Table 3).

Another factor in Mexico's diminished presence in the Cuban market is that competition in Cuba is fierce, especially in Mexico's weakest area, financing. Several countries, including Italy, Spain and Panama, offer very attractive financing to Cuban importers, which the Mexicans cannot match. Mexican companies find it difficult to provide long term financing due to high interest rates in Mexico. Additionally, most Mexican companies do not have the capital necessary to wait 60 days for payment from the Cubans.

Table 2. Mexican Exports (Thousand $US) by Country, 1995-1997

	1995	1996	1997
Cuba	394 505	318 227	290 121
United States	66 272 736	80 343 750	93 979 183
Costa Rica	141 898	187 974	225 134
Spain	796 876	919 507	941 313

Source: Bancomext.

Table 3. Mexico-Cuba Bilateral Trade (Thousands $US), 1994-1997

	1994	1995	1996	1997
Mexican Exports to Cuba	173 742	355 096	318 227	290 120
Mexican Exports (minus Oil)	144 853	279 671	278 418	NA
Mexican Imports from Cuba	11 716	6 234	22 850	34 223
Trade Balance for Mexico	162 026	348 862	295 337	255 897

Source: Bancomext.

Note: Bancomext officials were unable to explain the discrepancies between the data in Tables 2 and 3.

While Mexican exporters find it difficult to compete on the basis of financing, Mexico's competitive advantage is speed of delivery. Located only three days away by sea, Mexico can deliver a shipment to Cuba five times faster than European countries can. When a Cuban importer needs a product immediately, Mexico is the best option. Mexican companies, especially manufacturers who export to Cuba, can also compete on price. The Cuban market is still very price sensitive, so Mexican manufacturers that can offer a low price usually have an advantage. The lower cost of labour and shipping can also be factored into Mexican prices.

Of course, the advantages for Mexican companies mentioned above are based on the fact that the U.S, embargo against Cuba provides Mexicans with a window of opportunity that will not exist if the embargo is lifted. Mexico has benefited greatly from the inability of Americans to service the Cuban market. However, many Mexican exporters mention that they will not be able to compete against American products and financing or the pull of Cuba's closest market and potentially largest trading partner, the United States.

CONCLUSION

While Mexico's relationship with Cuba has been based on non-intervention, there has been great pressure on Mexico from the United States to limit diplomatic and economic relations with the island. Mexico has had to walk a tightrope with regards to its policy on Cuba: maintaining its anti-interventionist principles and defending its commercial sovereignty, while not endangering its relationship with the United States. It is in Mexico's best interests to assert its support for non-intervention[6] since its human rights records are also subject to assessment by the US and international organizations (Covarrubias, 1994).

Prior to 1989, Mexico and Cuba favored industrialized countries as trading partners. However, trade and investment between Cuba and Mexico became significant after the fall of the Soviet Bloc, when Cuba began looking at alternative commercial partners. In the early 1990s, several Mexican companies began trading and investing in Cuba with the aid of Bancomext. This was Mexico's "Golden Age" of investment in Cuba, with ventures in tourism, construction and telecommunications. However, the United States was able to exert pressure on the Mexican government during negotiation of NAFTA and, more importantly, with the relief package that followed the peso crisis. Sometime between the peso crisis and the enactment of the Helms-Burton law, Bancomext gave up much of its interest in Cuba, with detrimental consequences for Mexican interests in Cuba.

Interest in trade with Cuba is continuing to grow. Many manufacturers, agents and other exporters have taken advantage of Mexico's proximity to the Cuban market, low wages and their similar climates and common language. While export figures have dropped since 1995, the basket of products exported to Cuba has diversified. Mexicans face disadvantages in the Cuban market such as high domestic interest rates, unavailability of financing and lack of support from Bancomext. Nevertheless, Mexican companies continue to benefit from the absence of Americans in Cuba. The best opportunities for trade with Cuba belong to Mexican low cost manufacturers that can export directly to Cuba. These companies can tap Cuba's cost-sensitive market and take advantage of relatively low transportation costs.

With the lifting of the U.S. embargo, Mexican companies would lose some of their competitive edge in the Cuban market. While no one is certain what could be the outcome of open U.S. trade with Cuba, one thing is sure: there will be a sharp increase in competition. Future prospects for Mexican companies interested in investing in Cuba, after the lifting of the embargo, could include using their knowledge of the Cuban market and low cost manufacturing capabilities to form strategic alliances with American companies. Mexican service providers could also leverage their knowledge of the Cuban market in post-embargo bidding for international aid projects. Of course, for Mexican exporters, any future improvement in the Cuban economy will increase potential exports to the country. In conclusion, Mexican companies interested in Cuba are faced with a difficult decision: either make their move now while they still maintain their competitive advantage or wait and plan a way to integrate their strategies with those of powerful U.S. companies once the embargo is lifted.

---

6. A recent example of Mexico itself being a victim of U.S. intervention is the recent banking scandal, where the U.S. government conducted an undercover investigation of Mexico's banks and money laundering without the Mexican government's consent or knowledge.

Appendix
LIST OF MEETINGS (ACADEMIC AND GOVERNMENT)

1. El Colegio de México

   Dr. Ana Covarrubias, Professor. Specialist in the area of Mexico-Cuba political relations

   Miguel García Reyes, Researcher in the area of Mexico's petroleum industry (phone discussion)

2. Secretaría de Relaciones Exteriores (Ministry of Foreign Affairs)

   Lic. Ricardo Domínguez Guadarrama, Head of Caribbean Department

3. CEPAL (Comisión Económica para América Latina y el Caribe)

   Dr. Jesús M. García Molina, Economic Affairs

4. Bancomext (Mexican Bank for Foreign Trade)

   Lourdes Jiménez, Advisor in Caribbean and Central America Department

   Veronica Marina, Head of Caribbean and Central America Department (phone discussion)

REFERENCES

Babún, Teo A. Jr. (1997) "Cuba's Cement Industry," *Cuba in Transition—Volume 7*, pp. 374-381.

Comisión Económica para América Latina y el Caribe (CEPAL) (1995) *La inversión extranjera en Cuba: Aspectos Recientes*, pp. 9-17.

Comisión Económica para América Latina y el Caribe (CEPAL) (1997) *The Cuban Economy: Structural Reform and Performance in the Nineties.*

Comisión Económica para América Latina y el Caribe (CEPAL) (1997) *Rasgos generales de la evolucion reciente.* Unpublished report.

Cornelis Silva, Oscar and Rogelio Sierra Díaz (1989) "Cronología Cuba-México (1959-1988), *Cuadernos de Nuestra América*, Vol. 6 # 12 (January-June) pp. 186-192.

Covarrubias, Ana (1994) *Mexican-Cuban Relations, 1959-1988,* PhD thesis, University Oxford.

Covarrubias, Ana (1996) "Cuba and Mexico: A Case for Nonintervention," *Cuban Studies*, Vol. 26, pp.121-139.

Covarrubias, Ana (1997), *Mexico's Reaction to the Helms-Burton Law,* notes presented at the conference "Helms-Burton: A Loose Canon?"

Cuba News from Havana (September 1997) #100.

Cuba Net News (May 29, 1996a) "Cemex Leaves Cuba to Avoid US Sanctions."

CubaNet News (August 23, 1996b) "Who Will Do Business in Cuba and Who Won't?."

de Córdoba, José (1996) "Mexico's Domos Catches US-Cuba Heat," *Wall Street Journal* (August 19, 1996), p. A9.

Economic Eye on Cuba (October 27-November 2, 1997) "Fincimex Update."

Economic Eye on Cuba (June 15-21, 1998a) "Foreign Investment Update."

Economic Eye on Cuba (February 25-March 1, 1998b) "Sherritt Acquires 37.5% Interest in Cubacel for US$38 Million."

Enfoque (Reforma supplement) (April 21, 1996) p.4.

Epoca (May 18, 1992) p.16.

La Journada (January 20, 1995), p.40 and (January 25, 1995), p.50.

Moore, Molly (1996) "Tighter Cuban Embargo Snares Mexican, Despite US Ties," *Cuba Net News* (September 9, 1996).

Secretaría de Relaciones Exteriores (SRE) "Historia Documental," *Política Exterior de México*, vol. 1, p. 248.

Secretaría de Relaciones Exteriores (1998), *Carpeta Informativa: República de Cuba.*

Tamayo, Juan O. (1996) "Cuba Selling Off Firms but 'Privatization' Still a Dirty Word," *Cuba Net News* (October 10, 1996).

Wall Street Journal (Interactive Edition) (February 25, 1998) "Mexico's Banamex in Pact with Cuban Bank."

UPDATE ON FOREIGN INVESTMENT IN CUBA 1997-98 AND FOCUS ON THE ENERGY SECTOR

Maria C. Werlau[1]

FOREIGN INVESTMENT TO DATE

Compared to the previous year, "opportunities" for business in Cuba seem to have experienced renewed international attention. This is the likely result of a redoubling of public relations' efforts by the Cuban government together with the Pope's January 1998 visit, several high-profile visits and events held in Cuba and considerable media coverage of certain joint venture investments. But, despite reports of many business and diplomatic delegations visiting Cuba, a scarcity of actual or materialized deals seems to have been the rule.

We might attempt to decipher what has transpired in the area of foreign investment by looking at figures provided by the U.S.-Cuba Trade and Economic Council (USCTEC) in Table 1. The Council obtains most of its data from Cuban government sources and has the official support of Cuban authorities.[2] But, problems with its table of foreign investment illustrate the chronic difficulty of working with data provided by Cuba and attempting to uncover how much is actually being invested. Let's look at just a few of many gaps and discrepancies.

1. To begin with, the Council's unique terminology — "committed/delivered investment" — is highly unusual. It certainly doesn't meet industry standards of foreign direct investment or net foreign direct investment. All efforts to clarify exactly what this means or to obtain from the Council a breakdown of what is included have been unsuccessful.

2. Canadian investment: "Announced" Canadian investment of US$1.3 billion and "committed/ delivered" investment US$600 million are cited (on a cumulative basis) for June 1998. Yet, the table itself notes that Canada's ambassador to Cuba had reported that Canada-based companies had delivered investment in Cuba of US$200 million. Accordingly, committed/delivered investment would drop to $1.35 billion (from the reported $1.7 billion).

Meanwhile, the *Economist Intelligence Unit* reports US$404 million in Canadian foreign direct investment (FDI) by 1997, twice as much as the figure cited by the Canadian Ambassador to Cuba.[3] Complicating matters further, another re-

---

1. Discussion of the papers by Demetria Tsoutouras and Julia Sagebien, "Mexico-Cuba Commercial Relations in the 1990s" and Jonathan Benjamin-Alvarado, "Investment and International Cooperation in Cuba's Energy Sector," both included in this volume.

2. For more on the Council, see María C. Werlau, "Foreign Investment in Cuba: The Limits of Commercial Engagement," *Cuba in Transition—Volume 6* (Washington: Association for the Study of the Cuban Economy, 1996), p. 458, footnote 9.

3. Economist Intelligence Unit, *Business Latin America* (June 29, 1998). This figure of $404 million is reported as an increase of 13.2% from the previous year. This would mean that Canadian FDI rose $53.3 million during 1997 (implying a rise from an accumulated total of $350.7 million in 1996). The annual report of Canada's most visible investor—Sherritt Corporation—rules out this high level of investment from this source.

Table 1. Foreign Investment in Cuba (in U.S. dollars)

Country	Announced	Committed/delivered
Australia	500,000,000	—
Austria	500,000	100,000
Brazil	150,000,000	20,000,000
Canada	1,341,000,000	600,000,000
Chile	69,000,000	30,000,000
China	10,000,000	5,000,000
Dominican Republic	5,000,000	1,000,000
France	100,000,000	50,000,000
Germany	10,000,000	2,000,000
Greece	2,000,000	500,000
Honduras	7,000,000	1,000,000
Israel	22,000,000	7,000,000
Italy	397,000,000	387,000,000
Jamaica	2,000,000	1,000,000
Japan	2,000,000	500,000
Mexico	1,806,000,000	450,000,000
The Netherlands	300,000,000	40,000,000
Panama	2,000,000	500,000
Russia	25,000,000	2,000,000
South Africa	400,000,000	5,000,000
Spain	350,000,000	100,000,000
Sweden	10,000,000	1,000,000
United Kingdom	75,000,000	50,000,000
Uruguay	500,000	300,000
Venezuela	50,000,000	3,000,000
TOTAL	5,636,000,000	1,756,900,000

Notes: At the end of June 1998, H.E. Keith Christie, Ambassador of Canada to the Republic of Cuba, reported that Canada-based companies had *delivered* investment of US$200 million to the Republic of Cuba. Figures in the table represent the amounts of announced, committed, and delivered investments since 1990 by private sector companies and government companies from various countries to enterprises within the Republic of Cuba *as of June 29, 1998.* Information complied through the media, other public sources, individual discussions with company representatives, non-Republic of Cuba government officials, and Republic of Cuba-based enterprise managers and government officials.

Source: U.S.-Cuba Trade and Economic Council, Inc.

puted source which provides financial analysis to the international financial markets reports US$430 million in Canadian investment in Cuba at the end of 1997.[4] For its part, Sherritt International Corporation's audited financial

statement of 12/31/97 states the value of its assets in Cuba at CA$406 million, equivalent to approximately US$282 million. Although this doesn't specify how much capital has actually been invested in Cuba (FDI), it does give an indication of the generally low level of investment involved, given that Sherritt is reported to be the largest foreign investor on the island.

3. Mexican investments: Committed/delivered Mexican investment of US$450 million, as cited in the table, seems highly exaggerated given the nature of existing Mexican operations reported in Cuba. Bancomext, for example, is understood to be involved mainly in financing. Swaps were reportedly behind many of the Mexican "investments" announced in recent years. For example, Grupo Domos' joint venture with Cuba's telephone company, the island's first privatization, was from inception based on a debt-equity swap, which does not involve fresh capital. (See Appendix for a more detailed account of Domos' failed investment in Cuba. This case provides a unique example of the pros and cons to investors of doing business in Cuba.)

Tsoutouras and Sagebien do not provide an estimate of what Mexican FDI in Cuba could be. They do, however, indicate that most companies from Mexico have found the barriers to investment too great. This would explain the noticeable drop from 1996 levels, when Mexican companies are said to have made up "arguably the largest share of investments in Cuba." Tsoutouras and Sagebien do refer to Mexican investments, seemingly at their highest level, of US$1.5 billion. But, a table previously provided by the USCTEC cites committed/delivered Mexican investments as $250 million as of August 1, 1996. The wide discrepancy is puzzling.

---

4. Business Monitor International Ltd., *Caribbean*, Vol. II, No. 6 (June 1998). This report also cites French investment at $100 million, which is the figure cited in the Council's table for announced investment; committed/delivered being half of that amount.

4. Cuba's Ministry of Basic Industry reported that, during the last 5 years, foreign companies have invested approximately US$185 million in oil exploration and US$100 million in oil production.[5] Additionally, US$60 million had been spent on mining prospecting through April 1998.[6] Given capital-intensive nature of theses industries and that investments in these sectors are said to be the highest, a sum total of $345 million seems very low. This might be indicative of the overall low rate of investment in Cuba.

5. Committed/delivered investments are merely 30% of announced investments. This wide disparity (committed/delivered investment hovering around 20 to 30% of announced investment) has prevailed since the Council began publishing tables on foreign investment in Cuba.

Number of Joint Ventures

• The total number of joint ventures and economic associations at the end of September 1998, was said to be 317; of this only 154 were actual joint ventures.[7]

• Official reports are, as usual, vague and contradictory. In January 1998, Cuba's Minister of Foreign Investment and Economic Cooperation reported more than 300 joint ventures[8] with ownership levels from less than 50% to more than 80% and with most the capital originating in Canada, Spain, Italy, France, Holland, Mexico, and the United Kingdom. Additionally, he stated that of the 190 companies operating within the Free Trade Zones, 57 were engaged in

manufacturing, while the remainder were service-related.[9] This does not clarify if the 190 businesses operating in the Free Trade Zones (FTZs) are included in the 300. Most, as I explained in an earlier paper, do not represent FDI.[10] The following month, the same Minister reported 17 more joint ventures, for a total of 317. The same total of 190 foreign companies operating in three FTZs, 140 service-related.[11] This number would leave 50 companies engaged in non-service related activities, the ones which could be assumed to represent more direct capital invested. Nonetheless, from the Minister's report of the previous month, 133, not 140, were implied to be service-related. The discrepancies with the data, thus, render it unreliable.

In June of 1998 the Vice Minister of Foreign Investment and Economic Cooperation reported that 340 joint ventures *and economic associations* were currently operating, compared to approximately 300 at the beginning of 1998. In addition, she stated, another sixty projects near signing and an additional 100 were in their initial stages of negotiation. Most foreign investment was concentrated in basic industry, tourism, light industry, food processing, agriculture, and construction. Companies from Italy, France, Spain, and United Kingdom accounted for 50% of existing foreign investment, companies from Canada for 20%, and companies from Mexico, Argentina, Venezuela, and Chile for 18%. Companies from Canada, however, accounted for nearly 25% of all foreign capital invested within the Republic of Cu-

---

5. The U.S.-Cuba Trade and Economic Council's *Economic Eye on Cuba* (23-29 March 1998). A total of fifteen companies from Canada, Spain, France, Germany, Sweden, and the United Kingdom have operations within the Republic of Cuba. Toronto, Canada-based Sherritt International Corporation is the largest of the companies operating within the Republic of Cuba, producing oil and natural gas, along with investments in nickel plus cobalt production, power generation, agriculture, and tourism.

6. 52 contracts are in place with foreign companies to prospect for nickel, gold, silver, copper, lead, zinc and other minerals. Nickel plus cobalt production was also reported to have increased by more than 100% since 1994 thanks to foreign investment and foreign commercial bank credits of US$200 million, *Economic Eye on Cuba* (13-19 April 1998).

7. Data provided confidentially by a reliable source.

8. This is 40 more than the 260 reported by the end of 1996.

9. *Economic Eye on Cuba* (12-18 January 1998).

10. For more detail on Free Trade Zones, see Maria C. Werlau, "Update on Foreign Investment in Cuba, 1996-97," *Cuba In Transition—Volume 7* (Washington: Association for the Study of the Cuban Economy, 1997), pp. 82-85.

11. *Economic Eye on Cuba* (16-22 February 1998).

ba.[12] This would allow us to derive some interesting calculations from the Council's table, but, since we have no time to do this here, I urge you to do this on your own.

The Minister of Foreign Investment and Economic Cooperation reports that at the end of 1996 foreign companies—260 approved joint ventures *and economic associations*—"had committed capital of" (or "had invested") US$2.2 billion.[13] Both the vague terminology employed and the inclusion of economic associations are peculiar, as these are said to represent management contracts instead of FDI. [14]

Amount of Foreign Investment

At the end of 1997, Cuba's Minister of Economy and Planning[15] reported that foreign investment had increased 7% in 1997, 3% below government estimates, and was expected to increase 22% in 1998 (as a number of joint ventures "moved from the announced/committed to the delivered/operational stages"). With this information we have some indication of the maximum level of foreign investment that could have taken place. Using the figure provided by Cuba of US$2.2. billion, despite the belief that it is highly overstated, a 7% rise in foreign investment would represent investment of US$154 million during 1997. If we use the Council's figures as of April 1997 ($705 million in committed/delivered investment), the 7% rise would represent a rise of $87.3

million from April to December 1997 and an accumulated total of merely US$792 million.

According to the International Monetary Fund (IMF), net direct investment in developing countries, which grew at a steady pace throughout the decade, amounted to US$106.2 billion in 1997 and totaled $441.8 billion in the period 1992-96, averaging US$54.6 billion annually.[16] If we calculate the annual average of Cuba's *official* number for accumulated foreign investment, $2.2 billion, overstated as it is, over the 9 year period 1988 to 1997, this $314 million average annual investment would equal 0.6% of the average annual FDI going into the developing world during the shorter period 1990-96. In turn, if we used the 1996-97 annual average of $103.9 billion[17] reported for developing countries, Cuba's proportion would decrease to 0.03%. This is hardly exciting for what some have reported to be a "hot" new emerging market.

Cuba's Minister of Foreign Investment declared in February 1998 that since the first joint venture was established in 1988, a total of 380 joint ventures had been established, but sixty-three had been dissolved for various reasons (the failure rate would be 16.6%).[18] This is the first reference ever to be found to a number of failed joint ventures and could be indicative of an effort to prepare public opinion for less enthusiastic reports than has been the norm up to now. [19]

---

12. *Economic Eye on Cuba* (15-21 June 1998).

13. *Economic Eye on Cuba* (11–17 August 1997). This number has been fairly consistently repeated by Cuban authorities for some time

14. The Council itself reported that actual "committed-delivered" foreign investment as of 1 April 1997 was estimated to be US$705 million. In August, just a few months later, the numbers rise significantly, to announced: US$5,401,000,000; and committed /delivered: US$1,246,900,000. No reason is given for the steep rise in investment and no deals of significance are reported for that period. *Economic Eye on Cuba* (21-27 April 1997).

15. *Economic Eye on Cuba* (15-21 December 1997).

16. International Monetary Fund, *Interim Assessment* (December 1997), p. 32.

17. Net direct investment in developing countries amounted to US$101.6 billion in 1996 and US$106.2 billion in 1997.

18. *Economic Eye on Cuba* (16-22 February 1998).

19. Cuban defector Jesús Marzo Fernández, a former high-ranking official of the Ministry of the Economy, has reported that new foreign investment for 1997 was a mere US$8 million and that US$60 million have left the island in recent times. Reported during taping of Radio Martí's "Mesa Redonda" Economic Roundtable, August 11, 1998 and in conversations with the author.

Table 2. Cuban Energy Statistics

	Petroleum Availability Thousands of tons				Generation of GWH	
Year	Imports	Crude Extraction	Total Availability	% change from previous year	Electricity	% change from previous year
1985	13.3	0.9	14.2	-	12199	—
1986	12.9	0.9	13.8	-2.8%	13176	8%
1987	13.3	0.9	14.2	2.9%	13594	3.2%
1988	13.1	0.7	13.8	-2.8%	14542	7%
1989	13.1	0.7	13.8	-	15240	4.8%
1990	9.9	0.7	10.6	-23.2%	15025	-1.4%
1991	7.8	0.5	8.3	-21.7%	13247	-11.8%
1992	5.4	0.9	6.3	-24.1%	11538	-12.9%
1993	5.3	1.1	6.4	1.6%	11004	-4.6%
1994	5.6	1.3	6.9	7.8%	11967	8.8%
1995	6.0	1.5	7.5	8.6%	12458	4.1%
1996	6.6	1.6	8.2	9.3%	13000[a]	4.4%

Source: 1998 paper by Jesús Marzo Fernández, based on statistical information from Cuba's Energy Department, Ministry of the Economy; Mining Regulation, Ministry of Basic Industry, and personal experience. Percentages calculated by the author.

a. U.N.'s CEPAL report cites 13, 236 (est.).

Tourism

In 1997, tourism generated gross revenues of US$1.54 billion from 1,170,000 tourists. As of 31 December 1997 there were 23 joint ventures in tourism, "of which 21 had been established."[20] It is generally presumed, however, that most are economic associations based on management contracts which earn the foreign firms 3 to 4% of earnings. FDI in tourism is said to be around 10% of the total investment in tourism.[21]

To help put Cuba's possible tourism investment into perspective, it should be noted that between 1989 and 1997 foreign investment in Mexico's tourist sector alone amounted to US$5.4 billion.[22] On the other hand, Cuba's total accumulated investment for all sectors of the economy is overstated at US$2.2 billion.

References to net revenues from tourism for 1997 are notably absent. This figure is crucial in analyzing the impact of tourism on the economy. My guess is that,

given the high cost of inputs and the inefficiencies of the industry, net revenues would be around 20%, if that much. Officially, net revenues are said to range between 26 to 35%.

Employment in Foreign Joint Ventures

The Ministry of Culture reported[23] that the tourism sector directly employed approximately 71,000 workers; the number employed in the foreign sector was not clarified. At the beginning of 1998 the Vice Minister of Labor and Social Security reported that 3% of the island's 4.5 million workforce worked under the auspices of joint ventures and economic associations (135,000 workers).[24] Workers employed in the foreign sector remain surprisingly unchanged from last year's figures, which is puzzling given the steep rise in the number of joint ventures (80) reported by the Cuban government since the end of 1996.

CUBA'S ENERGY SECTOR[25]

By the end of 1997, Cuba's energy consumption was increasing at a 6% annual rate. Residential use was

20. *Economic Eye on Cuba* (23 February-1 March 1998). In February 1998, the Ministry of Culture reported 179 hotels of varying quality (most two and three-star) with 27,400 rooms.

21. Data provided confidentially by a high-placed source.

22. Nicolás Crespo, "Back to the future, Cuban tourism in the year 200: An analysis of economic, social and cultural impact of tourism in Cuba," Presented at the VIII annual Meeting of the Association for the Study of the Cuban Economy (Miami, August 6-9, 1998).

23. *Economic Eye on Cuba* (23 February-1 March 1998).

24. *Economic Eye on Cuba* (5-11 January 1998).

25. The information herein contained is cited by USCTEC as provided by Cuba's Ministry of Basic Industry.

35% to 40% of total consumption and 95% of Cuba's residents had electricity.[26] Total oil consumption in 1997 was 8.23 million tons.[27] (See Table 2.)

Oil Imports

In 1997, the island spent approximately US$1.2 billion to import oil and oil byproducts.[28] In June 1998 the Minister of the Economy reported that international oil prices in the six months to June 1998 had averaged approximately 60% to 75% of their 1997 levels. If this trend continues, oil import savings would be between US$250 million and US$350 million in 1998.[29] This, however, fails to account for energy consumption said to be increasing at a 6% annual rate.

Non-Oil/Alternative Energy Sources

The President of the Cuban Society for the Promotion of Renewable Energy Sources (CUBASOLAR), reported that non-fossil fuels, hydro, and solar, accounted for 30% of the energy produced within the country in 1997. Non-fossil fuels are expected to continue to gain importance, especially from such sources as sugar cane biomass. Many farm cooperatives are using windmills to power irrigation and other equipment and solar panels are increasingly being used in tourism facilities. There are approximately 200 small hydro-powered generators located throughout the country, 65 of which, including the largest, are located in the Guantánamo Province. In this province, 57% of the energy consumed is generated by small hydroelectric plants and by solar panels.[30] It should be noted, however, that a serious drought affecting especially the western part of the country should have a negative impact in the area alternative energy generation.

Domestic Oil Production

Most of Cuba's crude oil is extremely heavy with a high sulfur content, mainly used as fuel for electricity-producing plants and as fuel at nickel and cement plants. Domestic oil production has increased from 526,800 tons in 1991 to 1.45 million tons in 1997,[31] when 17% of the country's total oil consumption was produced domestically.[32] During the six months to May 1998, Cuba produced approximately 32,000 to 33,000 barrels of oil per day—said to be around 25% of current daily consumption.

Foreign Participation in Domestic Oil Production: Cuba reports 40 contracts with fifteen companies from Canada, Spain, France, Germany, Sweden, and the United Kingdom to explore and produce oil and natural gas: 22 exploration agreements and 18 production agreements.[33] In the last five years, approximately US$185 million has been invested in oil exploration and US$100 million in oil production.[34]

Twenty oil wells are currently producing. Oil exploration is being conducted in 32 different tracts located throughout the country—10 offshore and 22 onshore. 90% of the oil wells drilled to date are located in Havana and Matanzas Provinces.[35] 23 blocks onshore and offshore are still available for exploration.[36]

In 1997, Cuban enterprise Cupet began to engage foreign companies to develop plans to use an estimated 200 million cubic meters of natural gas burned off each year from existing oil wells. Currently, only ap-

---

26. *Economic Eye on Cuba* (15-21 December 1997).

27. *Economic Eye on Cuba* (23-29 March 1998).

28. *Economic Eye on Cuba* (23-29 March 1998) and (15-21 June 1998).

29. *Economic Eye on Cuba* (15-21 June 1998).

30. *Economic Eye on Cuba* (13-19 April 1998).

31. *Economic Eye on Cuba* (18-24 May 1998) and (23-29 March 1998).

32. *Economic Eye on Cuba* (18-24 May 1998) and (23-29 March 1998).

33. This number is contradicted by another report from Cuban authorities that 20 foreign companies had permits to explore for oil in Cuba. *Economic Eye on Cuba* (18-24 May 1998).

34. Economic Eye on Cuba *(23-29 March 1998).*

35. *Economic Eye on Cuba* (18-24 May 1998).

36. *Economic Eye on Cuba* (23-29 March 1998).

proximately 100,000 cubic meters of natural gas are being delivered to the city of Havana for use by residential consumers. Plans include the following:

- A joint venture was established in 1997 with Canada's Sherritt International Corporation to use natural gas in Matanzas Province. The project is to be completed in the year 2000 and would replace the need for approximately 350,000 tons of oil per year. (See more on Sherritt in the Appendix.)

- A joint venture was established with France's Elf Acquitaine to supply gas in Santiago de Cuba, the island's second-largest city. 80% of the residents in Santiago de Cuba currently use kerosene as fuel for cooking.

- An unnamed United Kingdom-based company is negotiating an agreement similar to that of Elf Acquitaine to supply gas to Havana residents.[37]

Jonathan Benjamin-Alvarado has noted that in 1998, Cuba was upgrading generating capacity at eight existing thermoelectric units with the potential of 800MW. This required investments of $315 million, which were allegedly "completely underwritten by foreign firms." A look at each individual deal, however, offers a telling story of how Cuba is actually generating the financial resources so vaguely described. According to existing reports, Cuba is not, as could be interpreted by the uncanny observer, obtaining foreign investment for this purpose. For example, the five plants in Santiago, Nuevitas, and Mariel are being upgraded with equipment purchased from France using US$15 million in short-term credits. (It should be noted that short term financing for a capital intensive investment is highly undesirable.) Post-1998, Cuba plans to boost generating capacity by 16%, or 600 MW, and is reported to have secured US$350 million of the $600 million required for the projects. The source of the funds is not identified,

but no foreign investment deals have been announced. Moreover, the remaining funds—almost half of what is needed for the project—are still unavailable.

An issue of importance in assessing the economic feasibility of energy-sector investments is to look at revenues in the mining industry, which allegedly most of the new capacity is to serve. Nickel prices, for example, experienced a worldwide drop in 1997, which contributed to Sherritt Corporation's inability to turn in an operating profit for 1997.

Cuba's Nuclear Energy Generation Program: The Juraguá Nuclear Plant

In 1983 Cuba began construction of Cuba's first nuclear power plant in Juraguá, Cienfuegos, 250 kilometers southeast of Havana. But the project was suspended in September 1992 allegedly when the former USSR, which had invested most of the US$1.1 billion in the construction, demanded a $200 million payment to continue the project. The two 440 megawatt nuclear reactors are 75% and 30% complete, respectively. According to the director of the plant, US$750 million would be required to complete the first VVER-440 reactor. In the meantime, the plant is being maintained with an annual US$30 million Russian Federation grant.

Beginning in 1997, Cuba renewed efforts to complete the project. In mid-1997 the Russian Federation's Minister of Nuclear Energy said that construction would resume in 1998 through a Russian Federation-controlled consortium of companies from various countries. Companies in Germany, United Kingdom, and Brazil had reportedly expressed interest and financing "was being sought" for the project. Interested parties were to recoup their investment plus interest in eight years. Nonetheless, nothing seems to have come of these plans. In fact, it seems that nothing will happen with the nuclear plant.

---

37. *Economic Eye on Cuba* (23-29 March 1998).

The Russian Federation's support for the Juraguá project is highly questionable. It holds Cuba's U.S.S.R.-issued ruble based debt, estimated at US$17 billion, a figure which is challenged by the Cuban government. Additionally, there are 12 major development projects in Cuba stalled since the 1991 collapse of the former U.S.S.R.[38] Furthermore, the Soviet-designed reactors are said to be deficient even by Soviet standards; evidence of defects and faulty instrumentation has been documented. Equipment has been improperly stored for four years in the corrosive sea air. Containment domes are too weak to withstand pressure levels that might be reached in an accident. Cuba lacks a well-trained cadre of nuclear technicians and the site is located in a seismically active zone.[39]

Experts have pointed out that the cost component of the project was huge and that the plant is already "tremendously redundant."[40] Hence, from its inception, it seems to have been economically irrational. This lack of financial feasibility is not surprising given the non-competitive socialist economy, in which the project was conceived and carried out. Economic/financial feasibility has been typically divorced of the decision-making process of centrally planned economies. Economic indicators and concepts such as pricing, demand, supply, cost allocation, efficien-cy, and competition are absent. The plant is a sad reminder of an endemic problem of the Cuban economy.

In conclusion, the plant appears destined to become a white elephant—and a hugely expensive one at that. It is doubtful that Cuba will find willing partners for this apparent aberration.

The Energy Sector in the Future

Cuba faces tremendous challenges in the area of energy generation and distribution—today and in the future. While the island's energy infrastructure is in appalling decay and already direly deficient for the needs of the country, the energy sector requires very heavy capital investments with a typically long-term return. Russia, for example, is estimated to have only been able to collect 1.5 cents on the dollar of energy generated and sold to domestic customers.[41] Due to the economics of the business and Cuba's pitiful economic condition, the private sector will, in my opinion, only play a secondary role for some time to come. For this reason, actual development in the energy sector might be accomplished only once a transition to a rational economic system is in place and with considerable official, multilateral, financial support in the way of loans and assistance.

Annex
UPDATE ON SHERRITT AND DOMOS

Sherritt's Investments

As is widely reported and confirmed by Cuban authorities, Canada-based Sherritt International Corporation is the largest of the foreign companies operating within Cuba. It produces oil and natural gas, and has made investments in nickel plus cobalt pro-duction, power generation, agriculture, and tourism.[42]

During 1997 Sherritt continued diversifying into different sectors of the Cuban economy and solidifying its privileged position within the island. At fiscal year end 1997 (12/31/97) Sherritt valued its assets in Cuba at CA$406 million (approximately US$282

---

38. *Economic Eye on Cuba* (2-8 June 1997).

39. See Maria C. Werlau, "The state of the Cuban environment," Coalition for a Green and Free Cuba, June 1997.

40. Confidential source.

41. Jonathan Benjamin-Alvarado, "Non-issue: Cuba's mothballed nuclear power plant," International Policy Report (July 1998).

42. Ibid.

million). In April 1997, Sherritt Power was formed in order to enter into a three-way joint venture with Cuba's Cupet (Unión Cubana del Petróleo) and UNE (Unión Eléctrica). The aggregate purchase price of CA$53.3 million entitled Sherritt Power to ownership of a third of the joint venture. In March of 1998, Sherritt Power issued a CA$105 million (approximately US$73 million) debt-equity offering to finance the project, consisting of 2 gas processing plants and power generating facilities in the Varadero area of the Matanzas province, near Havana. The project, to be built in four phases, is calculated to involve an investment of $215 million; Sherritt is responsible for financing three of the four phases. The offer's prospectus appears to visibly downplay the high-risk nature of specific aspects of investing in Cuba. This is notable given the typically overly cautious tone of investment prospectus issued by reputable underwriters worldwide.

For fiscal year 1997, Sherritt International's Cuba operation generated a 20.6% operating return, down from the 27.2% of the previous year. Cuba, accounted for 92.1% of the corporation's consolidated operating earnings.[43] Sherritt's nickel-cobalt joint venture, which includes the Moa plant in Cuba, increased its average daily production by 13%, but earnings were affected by lower international nickel prices. Sherritt's new role as lender to the Republic of Cuba—rather, to unnamed parties within Cuba—explains its avoidance of losses for fiscal year 1997: 84.4% of its consolidated operating earnings resulted from very high financing income, derived from short term high-interest loans to "a third party in Cuba." The company continues to hold a significant portion of its debenture issue of CA$675 million, which were originally earmarked for investment opportunities in Cuba.

On a consolidated basis, however, Sherritt's return on equity was a mere 4.1%, down from an already disappointing 5.5% in 1996. Given this discouraging performance, which is particularly unfavorable in a high-risk scenario, it remains to be seen if investors will continue to support Sherritt's operations with the enthusiasm reported by the media.

In February 1998 Sherritt acquired a 37.5% interest in Teléfonos Celulares de Cuba, S.A. (Cubacel), the sole provider of both digital and analog communications within the 800 MHZ band throughout Cuba. The US$38.3 million purchase gave Sherritt a 75% interest in "a corporation whose primary asset is 50% of the outstanding shares of Cubacel."[44] Curiously, both Sherritt's Annual Report and press release announcing the purchase fail to name this holding company and instead refer to its unidentified owners as "private investors." This is remarkable given that Cuban citizens are not allowed to own property or engage in joint ventures with foreign interests There are however, many reports of businesses operated by members of the Cuban political and military elite, some involved in joint ventures with foreigners. The nature of the capital or ownership structure of these ventures remains shrouded in secrecy.[45] Sherritt's Cubacel investment thus, is illustrative of the degree of influence the company enjoys in Cuba as well as the unusual nature and lack of transparency of its investment arrangements with the Cuban government and/or its representatives.

Domos' Failed Telecommunications Investment [46]

Cuba has offered lucrative telecommunications possibilities for foreign investors since the Cuban Democracy Act of 1992, which authorized gateway-to-gateway service to Cuba and laid the groundwork for guidelines that allow a 50/50 split of telecommunica-

---

43. Sherritt has operations in metals and oil/gas in Canada, Spain and Italy.

44. Sherritt International Corporation, *1997 Annual Report*, p. 40.

45. For more on this, refer to Maria C. Werlau, "Foreign Investment in Cuba: The Limits of Commercial Engagement," *Cuba In Transition—Volume 6* (Washington: Association for the Study of the Cuban Economy, 1996), pp. 488-490.

46. Ibid, p. 463 and footnote 45 for more detail on the Domos' deal and sources of information.

tions revenues from traffic between the U.S. and Cuba.[47]

In June 1994, Mexican Grupo Domos, a Monterrey-based family enterprise focused on real estate development and waste management, entered into a joint venture with Cuba's Empresa de Telecomunicaciones de Cuba (ETECSA) to modernize its service and equipment. The deal, announced with much media hype, became Cuba's largest privatization. Then-Mexican President Carlos Salinas de Gortari was said to have been directly involved in the investment negotiations and flew to Havana to celebrate the signing the of the agreement. Domos reportedly formed a subsidiary, CITEL (Compañía Interamericana de Telecomunicaciones) to run the Cuban operation.

Accounts of the deal have been widely divergent. It appears that an initial $200 million was to be used to buy $300 million in face value Cuban debt from the Mexican National Development Bank; the debt bonds were to be delivered to the Cuban government. As part of the deal the Development Bank was to grant Cuba a $300 million credit line for purchases from Mexico during 1995.

Aside from agreeing to invest via the described debt-equity swap, Domos reportedly promised to invest an additional $500 million in coming years in exchange for 49% of ETECSA. But different sources cited investment amounts ranging from US$734 million to US$1,442 million. In mid-1997 Domos sources reported it had agreed to pay US$706 million for its stake in ETECSA, pledging to invest US$750 million over the next seven years to expand

services. The Dutch subsidiary of the Italian state telecommunications company STET—now privatized—was reported to have promptly entered into the deal by acquiring 25% of Domos' share, equal to a 12.25% share of ETECSA.[48]

By 1996 Domos was looking to sell and it was obvious the deal was falling apart. The Mexican government allegedly refused to extend the loan for the US$300 debt-equity swap that was part of the original deal and Domos was unable to obtain alternative financing. When Domos' debt came due in October 1996, Cuba's Ministry of Communications filed suit in Cuban courts against Domos, with the Court ruling in favor of the government in January 1997. The unpaid amount is said to have totaled $296-320 million. One report states that Domos was ordered by the Cuban government to return US$300 million worth of ETECSA stock for failure to pay around $350 million to Cuba for the 1994 deal. The Cuban government offered to take back Domos' share in ETECSA in order to satisfy the debt, but fixed the price of the shares at the original value, rather than the market value calculated by Domos. In early 1997, the STET -soon to be privatized- purchased Domos' participation of 49% at a cost of US$300 million, increasing its 12.25% share in ETECSA to 29.9%.

The actual amount of the first installment Domos had actually paid is not clear, but in July 1997 Domos' chief counsel claimed that the company had invested US$450 million and had been unable to come up with the remainder. Also, he declared that the company might claim compensation from STET for a minimum of $900 million and was studying its op-

---

47. A US$1.20 per minute accounting rate is split 50/50, while Cuba is allowed a US$1.50 surcharge for each collect call made from Cuba to a party in the United States. (*U.S.-Cuba Policy Report*, Vol. 3, No.10, October 31, 1996, p. 2.) Since 1994 telecom traffic has been increasing steadily, and is estimated at 125 million minutes in 1996 (up from 20 million minutes in 1994. Eight U.S. telecommunications companies paid Cuba $32.6 million for the period July1 thru December 31, 1996. (*U.S.-Cuba Policy Report*, Vol. 4, No. 4, April 30, 1997.) The President of Grupo Domos has said that ETECSA netted a profit of US$1230 million in 1996, with Cuba earning $53.8 million just from calls from the U.S. See "Domos out, but questions linger," *CubaNews* (July 1997), p. 8.

48. Domos was said by one source to have invested $734 million of the $1.442 billion purchase price, with a promise to invest $700 million more in seven years to modernize the system. Another source described the deal as follows: Domos would pay $500 million for its share in Emtel Cuba, of which at least half was said to be expected from a technological partner. $200 million would be obtained through a swap of Cuban debt with the Mexican government. In a period of 7 years, $800 million would be invested, of which half would have to be provided by the Cuban government as partner in the venture. (For details and sources see Werlau, "Foreign Investment in Cuba," footnote 45, p.463, and "Domos out," p. 8.)

tions to reclaim the $450 million it paid for the original investment.[49] It appears that Domos indeed sued STET, apparently due to the forced relinquishment of its shares to the Cuban government, which were then sold to STET at an enhanced value.

Currently ETECSA is reportedly owned by STET's successor—a recently privatized company- (29.9%) and the Cuban government, with the Ministry of Communications holding 51% and UTISA, a wholly-owned subsidiary of the same ministry, holding 19.1%.[50]

---

49. "Domos out," p. 8.

50. *U.S.- Cuba Policy Report*, Vol. 4, No.3 (March 31, 1997), p. 8 and Larry Rohter, "Mexican conglomerate abandons Cuban phone venture," *The New York Times* (June 30, 1997).

THE IMPACT OF THE U.S. EMBARGO ON HEALTH AND NUTRITION IN CUBA

Peter G. Bourne

To appreciate the current state of U.S.-Cuba relations it must be seen in the context of more than two hundred years of history during which the United States has been consistently unwilling to accept Cuban accomplishments and the nation's right to sovereignty and independence. Cuba, while a Spanish possession, was for a hundred years the pre-eminent intellectual and cultural center of the New World at a time when the American colonies remained a primitive frontier. The University of Havana, founded in 1728, was well established by the time comparable institutions were developed in this country.

The Founding Fathers believed that Cuba was inevitably destined to become part of the United States. John Quincy Adams observed that Cuba was "an apple that had to fall by gravity into the hands of the United States." Thomas Jefferson, attracted by the economic possibilities for Southern farmers if, through annexation they could gain access to Cuba's slave population (the largest in the hemisphere) noted "I candidly confess, that I have ever looked on Cuba as the most interesting addition which could ever be made to our system of states." President Polk offered Spain $100 million for the island which was declined. Franklin Pierce upped the offer to $130 million. Both ignored the desperate struggle for independence from Spain being waged by the people of Cuba. Eventually as the struggle was reaching a successful climax the United States entered the war against Spain nominally on the side of those seeking their freedom, but as President McKinley announced on December 6, 1897: "God himself has favored me

with a divine revelation to take over Cuba and the Philippines." The intent was to allow the Cuban forces to become depleted and exhausted fighting Spain so that the United States could then easily move in and take control. General Nelson A. Miles the commander of U.S. forces said in a cable to Washington, "We must destroy everything in range of our guns—we must concentrate the blockade so that hunger and disease, its constant companion, may sap the civilians and cut down their army." These were supposedly our allies to whom he wished to do this.

Subsequently at the Treaty of Paris, signed on December 10, 1898, only the eloquent pleas of the Cuban leader, Calixto García, allowed Cuba to remain nominally independent while the Philippines, Guam and Puerto Rico were ceded to the United States. U.S. troops remained in the country for four years and the U.S.-drafted constitution imposed on Cuba allowed the United States the right to intercede with force in Cuban affairs any time they were dissatisfied with Cuban policies. For fifty years the United States exerted complete economic and political control over the island through a series of corrupt and puppet regimes.

The ascendancy to power of Fidel Castro in 1959 tapped into deep nationalistic yearnings and a continuing desire for independence and self-determination on the part of the Cuban people. U.S. opposition to true Cuban independence, and the right sovereignty remained strong. The imposition of the trade embargo in 1961 was, as much as anything, a reaction to Cuba's assertion of its right to independence. Food and medicine were added to the embargo in 1964 as a way of tightening the noose in the misconceived notion that it would bring down the regime. The inclusion of food and medicine is a clear violation of Article IV of the Geneva Convention and Article 25 of the UN Universal Charter on Human Rights. In no other instance including against Viet Nam, Iran, Iraq, South Africa or Bosnia was food and medicine included in trade embargoes. The objective could only be to inflict death and suffering on the most vulnerable elements in society: women, children and the elderly. Article 2 of the International Convention on the Prevention of the Crime of Genocide states that if a public official or private person engages in acts intended to place the civilian population "on starvation diet" or "engage in the withholding of minimal medical services" such acts qualify as a form of genocide. For physicians it poses a serious problem, as to support a policy that denies access to medicine clearly violates the Hippocratic oath they have sworn to uphold.

Initially Cuba faired reasonably well despite the embargo, obtaining drugs medical equipment and food either from the Soviet Union or through purchases made in Europe or elsewhere, often from U.S. subsidiaries. Initially there were only about thirty drugs that could only be obtained from the United States and to which they had no access. In 1978 I first became involved with this issue when the then Minister of Health, Dr. Gutiérrez Muñiz came to see me at the White House to seek my help in obtaining supplies of these drugs.

The Cuban revolution made the provision of quality health care a high priority, enshrining it as a right in the constitution. Their health care system eventually became the best in the Third World, admired and copied by many other nations. In many respects it has become the standard by which the systems of other nations are judged. By 1990 the infant mortality rate in Cuba was half that in Washington, D.C.

The success of the revolution in providing equitable access to health care, especially to the poorer black citizens who make up the majority of Cuba's population, angered those determined to show that every aspect of the revolution was a failure. Efforts to destroy this accomplishment even if it meant sacrificing the lives of innocent Cubans became a priority on the political agenda of opponents of the regime. Large amounts of money were shoveled into the pockets of U.S. politicians to achieve a policy that was entirely at odds with fundamental American values.

Problems began to develop with the collapse of the Soviet Union. Cuba no longer had access to the hard currency to buy drugs on the open market and could not obtain medical equipment and drugs from Eastern European sources. The situation was dramatically worsened with the passage of the paradoxically-named Cuban Democracy Act, which prevented U.S. subsidiaries from trading with Cuba. The passage of this legislation in 1992 coincided with a surge in takeovers of European companies by U.S. pharmaceutical giants thereby aggravating the situation for Cuba. Although it was increasingly apparent that the health and nutrition of Cubans was suffering due to the embargo, precise data on the situation was lacking.

In 1995, the American Association for World Health undertook, at the request of several foundations, a comprehensive study of the effects of the embargo. Two researchers, one a physician, worked in Cuba for a year. Human rights lawyers conducted detailed research here in Washington on the legal aspects of the embargo. At the end of a year, a 300-page draft report was prepared. A team of a dozen distinguished physicians then went to Cuba for a week to review and validate the findings of the study. Among the findings of the study:[1]

- The health and nutrition of the Cuban people had been adversely affected in many ways by the embargo.

---

1. American Association for World Health, *Denial of Food and Medicine: The Impact of the U.S. Embargo on Health and Nutrition in Cuba* (Washington: AAWH, 1997).

- Of 1,297 drugs available in 1991, Cubans now had access to only 889. Cutting edge drugs come overwhelmingly from the United States. Patented for 17 years, they can not be obtained elsewhere. Cubans can not obtain the latest antibiotics, anti-fungal drugs, anti-nausea drugs for children undergoing chemotherapy for cancer, protease inhibitors for AIDs, or various cardiac drugs.

- Cardiac pacemakers, parts for infant incubators, x-ray film for mammography, sophisticated surgical equipment all are blocked by the embargo.

- Laboratory supplies for carrying out routine tests are unobtainable.

- Spare parts for the water supply system built in the 1940s and 1950s with U.S. components can no longer be obtained.

- Obtaining medical literature, especially textbooks, is almost impossible.

Only the extraordinary dedication of Cuban physicians to their patients and the willingness of the Cuban government to reallocate scarce budgetary resources to the healthcare system has averted a catastrophe of major proportions. While humanitarian aid has helped, it meets only 12% of Cuba's needs and frequently the drugs donated do not match the needs in Cuba. Cuban Cardinal Jaime Ortega says that while any donations are deeply appreciated, they are only a palliative and no substitute for commercial trade in pharmaceuticals.

Advocates for the inclusion of food and medicine in the embargo make a number of arguments. First, despite the embargo Cuba can, through various loopholes, obtain any medicine and food it wants on the international market. An argument that is patently absurd on its face. If the embargo does not succeed in its goal of denying Cubans access to food and medicine, then what is the point of the legislation when the level of condemnation it generates is so overwhelming? It is true that for many drugs that are available on the international market, Cuba can buy without restriction. But these must be clearly distinguished from those they can not. It is secondly argued that embargoed drugs can be obtained for Cuba's elite or for foreigners coming to Cuba to take advantage of the excellence of their healthcare. Small quantities of some drugs can be obtained on the international market for a price, but this is a hopeless prospect for trying to meet the pharmaceutical needs for a population of 12 million.

While the embargo as a whole has been thoroughly condemned by the world community for years, it is the inclusion of food and medicine, flagrantly violating international human rights accords, that have generated most anger towards the United States. It was long argued that these sanctions only served to weaken efforts to improve human rights violations within Cuba. This year we saw this concretely in the UN's rejection of the report condemning Cuba's human rights record. It was more than anything an effort to express utter frustration with U.S. policy. Every major moral authority to which the world looks for guidance, from Nelson Mandela to the Pope, condemns the embargo. In private even President Clinton condemns the inclusion of food and medicine.

There has been a profound change in the attitude towards the embargo and to U.S.-Cuban relations in general in the last eighteen months. Much can be attributed to the visit of the Pope. However, the changes were underway long before last January. It is in retrospect the food and medicine issue that has done most to galvanize public attitudes against the embargo as a whole. The indefensibility of the policy and relative safety of the issue for those who oppose the embargo on other grounds has produced a groundswell across the political spectrum that now suggests that the days of this anachronistic policy are at an end.

215

COMMENTS ON

"The Impact of the U. S. Embargo on Health and Nutrition in Cuba" by Bourne

Sergio Díaz-Briquets

The American Association for World Health report, *The Impact of the U.S. Embargo on Health & Nutrition in Cuba,* is very important. It paints a vivid portrait of how precarious is the health situation in the country today. Readers of the report are sure to view it with awe, both for its breath and comprehensiveness. Seldom do researchers working on Cuba have access to the amount of information needed to produce a report of this nature. Even more remarkable—in the context of socialist Cuba's closed society—is the unfettered access the report's authors had to professionals at all levels of the Cuban medical and political establishment.

Shortages of the most basic medical inputs are described and documented, as are the deteriorated condition of most of Cuba's medical facilities, from primary health posts to the most specialized tertiary hospitals in Havana. The report highlights the collapse of nutritional levels in Cuba between 1989 and 1996, a period in which average intake of calories and essential nutrients declined dramatically. The sequel of these developments is a worsening morbidity and mortality profile evidenced by rising percentages of low birth weight infants, malnourished mothers, and increasing death rates among the elderly. From an information perspective, the report is invaluable. Until its publication, we did not have such a detailed and compelling description of the enormity of the Cuban health crisis.

The main conclusion of the report is that the U.S. economic embargo is responsible for Cuba's current health and nutrition predicament. In fact, the report's principal conclusion was the *a priori* reason why it was prepared. Thus, not surprisingly, the evidence presented in the report simply serves to validate a pre-determined conclusion. The report offers an apocalyptic vision of the embargo's impact on practically every dimension of health care in Cuba. It blames, for example, crippling medicine and medical equipment shortages and the inability of Cuban doctors to obtain medical information, including the latest scientific research, on the embargo.

Cuba's shortages are traced to several embargo measures that impede the free flow of U.S. imports or that increase the costs of imports from other countries. Among these are limitations on subsidiary trade by U.S. corporations and the limited number of licenses issued by the U.S. Treasury and Commerce Departments to permit the export of medicines and medical supplies produced in the United States to Cuba. The report also identifies shipping costs increases arising from the U.S. decision of not permitting ships delivering merchandise to Cuba to unload or pickup cargo in American ports for 180 days after visiting Cuba.

The report is as remarkable for what it says, as much as for what it does not say. It brushes over the fact that the crisis in the Cuban health system is essentially the result of resource scarcity. Even if Cuba had unfettered access to the U.S. market, it could not afford to buy at standard commercial prices the medical supplies the country needs simply because the country is bankrupt. Other countries would be more than happy to supply Cuba with the majority, if not all, of the medications and medical equipment not currently available from the United States. The problem is that the government in Havana does not have the money to pay for these imports. There are few new modern household appliances in Cuba. Yet, no analyst is likely to blame the shortage of consumer goods on the embargo. It is well known that there are many willing sellers in Europe, Asia, and Latin America ready to supply these goods—at prices comparable to or lower than those charged by U. S. companies—if only Cuba had the money to pay for them.

Cuba's bankruptcy has nothing to do with the embargo. It is the direct result of failed economic policies pursued by Cuba's socialist government for over four decades, compounded by the end of Soviet subsidies. These subsidies allowed the Cuban economy to flounder along while mismanaging billions of pesos. This waste was evident in the prohibitively expensive health care system promoted by the authorities, including Fidel Castro, a system that Cuba can no longer sustain. Although the health care system gave great emphasis to prevention, it was and continues to be burdened by high costs associated with heavy dependence on physicians and hospitals.

Castro likes to boast of Cuba's low population-to-physician and population-to-hospital bed ratios, but these low ratios are indicative of the excessive cost associate with the Cuban health system. Cuba was able to bear these costs as long as the national economy was subsidized, but this option is no longer viable. And this was known many years ago. They are the reason why the Cuban health system model was never endorsed by any international health organization, including the Pan American Health Organization, since it was recognized that no other country at Cuba's development level could afford it. The collapse of the national health care system was unavoidable once Soviet subsidies were no longer available.

The report also fails to note that medical health systems all over the world are facing major financial pressures. This is true in the United States, where managed care is a response to rising health care costs. But is also true in practically every Latin American country, where profound reforms are being introduced to make national health care delivery systems more efficient and affordable, even though few of these countries provided health care packages as generous as Cuba's.

It is not necessary to waste many words in addressing the report's allegation that the deteriorated nutritional situation in Cuba is the result of the U.S. embargo. Food shortages have been a part of Cuban life for four decades, for reasons well documented by a plethora of authors going back to the early 1960s. These problems persist and are not likely to end as long as economic policies continue to be designed within the framework of discredited socialist notions of resource allocation and market controls. Not even the most ardent supporters of the socialist government have ever been able to come to terms with why privately-owned small farms in Cuba are considerably more productive than larger and considerably better endowed agricultural units in the state sector (in one guise or another). An equally interesting question is how the embargo impacts on the production of root tubers (e.g., yuca and malanga), domestic traditional foodstuffs that are as rare today in Cuban tables as is imported wheat.

In summary, the American Association for World Health report follows a well-established tradition of manipulating information to serve political ends. While it claims to be a candid, scientific report, it fails to live to standard cannons of objectivity. *The Impact of the U. S. Embargo on Health & Nutrition in Cuba* uses data selectively, conveniently distorting or ignoring information when it fails to support its pre-ordained conclusion. Within the context of the current U.S. policy debate regarding what to do about Cuba, this report is simply one more round of ammunition—developed by sympathizers of Cuban socialism in collaboration with the authorities in Havana—aimed at weakening U.S. resolve to maintain sanctions against Cuba. The end objective of this strategy is to grant Castro's Cuba access to the resources of international financial institutions and, why not, to U.S. economic assistance if it is ever offered with no political strings (a transition to democratic rule) attached.

Perhaps the best course of action for the United States to follow would be to remove all restrictions on the sale of medicines and food to Cuba. By removing these sanctions, the Havana government would be deprived of an effective propaganda tool. The leadership would then be forced to offer the people a more realistic explanation of why, after forty years of "revolution" and endless promises of prosperity, scarcity (material as well as in terms of basic human freedom) continues to be the dominant quality of Cuban life.

THE EFFECTS OF THE U.S. EMBARGO ON HEALTH AND NUTRITION IN CUBA: A CRITICAL ANALYSIS

María C. Werlau

The U.S. embargo on food and medicine exports to Cuba are, in my opinion, critical to the Castro government's ability to manipulate internal and international public opinion by placing the blame for Cuba's grave problems on external factors. It is also key to understanding the bitter international outcry against the Cuba policy of the United States, which lends a certain legitimacy to the Castro government and shields it from stronger demands for a democratic rule of law in Cuba.

The alleged impact of U.S. policy on health and nutrition in Cuba has been the specific target of an intense and effective public relations campaign directed at weakening the embargo. Its success is evidenced by a proliferation of media reports—both in the United States and internationally—claiming that it causes severe harm to the Cuban people. This issue has gained increasing notoriety since the publication in March of 1997 of the American Association for World Health (AAWH) (henceforth "the report").[1]

The report itself has received considerable media attention, fueling interest in an issue plagued by alarming allegations. The Cuban government's relentless accusations against the United States for its policy play to a worldwide audience and have been validated by increasing number of governments and public figures. Castro, while portraying Cuba's health system as an example to the world, has recently blasted the embargo in international forums blaming the U.S. government for "trying to kill" Cuba's children "by starvation"[2] and for committing "genocide" against the Cuban people.[3]

Four foundations[4] provided the funding for the report. To my knowledge, at least three have committed considerable efforts to oppose the embargo and foster engagement and exchanges with Cuba. The dedication of resources and the credentials of many of the individuals involved seem unquestionable. Regrettably, I found the end result to fall way short of its purported goal—which is, as expressly stated, to "assess whether the U.S. embargo jeopardizes the health of the Cuban population." This is due to serious methodological faults which inevitably taint its findings and severely weaken its overall credibility.

The report amasses considerable data on *selected aspects* of health and nutrition on the island—in par-

---

1. American Association for World Health, *Denial of Food and Medicine: The Impact of the U.S. Embargo on Health and Nutrition in Cuba* (Washington: AAWH, 1997).

2. Castro, on a late July 1998 visit to Jamaica. Michelle Faul, "Castro reconciles with Jamaican foe," Associated Press, Montego Bay (July 31, 1998) in CubaNet News (July 31, 1998).

3. Castro in Geneva, speaking before an assembly of the World Health Organization. "Castro says U.S. followed "genocide" policy on Cuba," Reuters, Geneva (May 14, 1998) in CubaNet News (May 14, 1998).

4. The Arca Foundation, The General Services Foundation, the Christopher Reynolds Foundation and the John D. and Catherine T. MacArthur Foundation.

ticular the lacks and limitations currently endured by the Cuban population—and exposes many examples of the embargo's actual or/and alleged costs to Cuba. But I was left with the impression that, more than anything else, it merely adds to the prevailing tendency to confuse fact with myth instead of helping to uncover the truths surrounding this issue. In fact, by failing to offer solid and reliable evidence on what exactly the actual cost of the embargo is or might be in the overall context of health and nutrition, it altogether misses its pivotal objective.

Consequently, it wastes a golden opportunity to put talented brains and substantial financial resources to work for a goal which I believe is ultimately well-intentioned. We are left to speculate whether overzealous opposition to the sanctions on food and medicines on the part of the authors, collaborators, and supporters of the report might have prevailed over reason, objectivity, critical analysis and, perhaps, even academic integrity. Conceivably, a lack of skills on the part of the authors in specific areas such as economic analysis, inadequate research, improper historical focus, gullibility, language and cultural obstacles, or a combination of all of the above, could explain the report's startling flaws. Or, maybe, in essence or in part, there was a greater need to dismiss, ignore or diminish the failures of Cuba's socio-political and economic model, in response to biases—intentional or not—on which we would not even speculate to avoid being unfair or simply wrong.

In the end, whatever the reasons, all of which matter less than the noble goal I believe we all seek in advancing Cuba's interests, the report, I fear, does an injustice to the truth. As a result, it weakens the very cause it advances of ending the embargo on food and medical products. And, more importantly, it does a disservice to the people of Cuba—those who most concern the authors and collaborators of the report and, I believe, everyone who shares a commitment to the well-being of the Cuban people.

From the very beginning of this 302-page long document, its objectivity is suspect. Unqualified praise for the Cuban health care system and the Cuban government's continued efforts to provide for the population in the face of dire economic straits contrast with

consistent and unrestricted blame on the U.S. embargo for the serious problems of health and nutrition in Cuba. This remains an underlying theme of the whole document. In essence, it absolves the Cuban government, at times directly, others more tacitly, of pretty much any responsibility in respect to most, if not all, of the deficiencies described in great detail. Passing references to the reasons for the collapse of the economy are clearly wanting, but they are the norm throughout the whole text. For example, the following passage from the Introduction:

After a year-long investigation, the American Association of World Health has determined that the U.S. embargo of Cuba has dramatically harmed the health and nutrition of large numbers of ordinary Cuban citizens. … It is our expert medical opinion that the U.S. embargo has caused a significant rise in the suffering—and even deaths—in Cuba. … A humanitarian catastrophe has been averted only because the Cuban government has maintained a high level of budgetary support for a health care system designed to deliver primary and preventive health care to all of its citizens. Cuba still has an infant mortality rate half that of the city of Washington, D.C. … The U.S. embargo … has wreaked havoc with the island's model primary health care system. The crisis has been compounded by the country's generally weak economic resources and by the loss of trade with the Soviet bloc.

Repeated references to the achievements of Cuba's health care system appear, first, in an historical vacuum. In addition, the uncritically favorable depiction of healthcare in particular, contrasts with many reports of independent sources in Cuba and many testimonials which I have personally witnessed over the years.

Take, for example, a Cuban Communist Party confidential report prepared in 1988 (notice it was prepared before the elimination of Soviet assistance) to assess the quality of health care in the province of Holguín.[5] According to the report, 87.6% of the 10,756 opinions surveyed were unfavorable—this, taking into account that fear is endemic to totalitarian regimes and is likely to have influenced the degree of candor of respondents. This detailed survey documents all sorts of outrageous complaints regarding the behavior, availability, and qualifications of health care professionals, deplorable conditions in health care facilities, especially in emergency rooms, mistreatment of patients, delays of up to four months in obtaining appointments with specialists, lack of basic medical supplies such as X-rays required for surgeries, contamination in operating rooms, lack of water, prescription of medications unavailable in pharmacies (this, before the Cuban Democracy Act was passed banning subsidiary sales), personal use of ambulances and facilities by health care workers, etc.

Glaring methodological deficiencies compound the compromised credibility of the report. Let me enumerate just a few of many I found dumbfounding:

1. The entire report provides no account nor research of alternative sources or opinions other than official government sources or international institutional sources which validate the overall conclusion that the embargo is to blame for any of the issues addressed in each section.

Despite an impressive list of visits to patient care facilities and institutions and 170 interviews, not one was conducted with Cuban professionals not employed by state-controlled institutions. No effort seems to have been made to contact nor interview people who have left the state establishment or who live in exile. Yet, there is an ample supply of professionals, both in Cuba and in the United States, with a wealth of experience and knowledge of the fields of health and nutrition not dependent on state employment. Growing internet resources, reports of independent journalists in Cuba, dissident medical professionals in Cuba, recent émigrés/exiles, and defectors, point to the easy availability of these sources.

Furthermore, it is not clear which interviews and visits were conducted by the two authors and which were conducted by the 9-person delegation which paid a seven day visit to Cuba in October of 1996. It is also unknown if members of the delegation and/or the authors speak fluent Spanish and if Cuban interpreters were used.

We do not have time here to detail the many deficiencies in the delivery of health and nutrition in Cuba which have nothing to do with external factors and the report failed to identify. Any analyst with some superficial interest in looking into these topics would easily find information about them.

In sum, the report provides no mention of any eloquent arguments or analyses—of which there is overabundance—which contradict the basic premise that the U.S. embargo explains many or most of Cuba's problems. There is no consideration of numerous claims that the root cause of the deterioration in the living standards of the Cuban population might be the combination of a failed economic model with a shameful misallocation of resources and flagrant economic mismanagement, brought to the fore by the cessation of massive Soviet subsidies. Anyone who takes a quick look at ASCE's seven annual volumes will find numerous papers with staggering and documented evidence to support this line of argumentation. Just one of these, a paper submitted by Manuel Madrid-Aris last year, provides some light on how food production has declined consistently during the Revolutionary period due to a chronic mismanagement of resources. These issues are even validated—albeit discreetly—by academics still currently working in Cuba, I suppose at some peril at the very least to their careers.[6]

The report leaves the causes of Cuba's economic problems virtually unexplored despite the obvious repercussions these have on health and nutrition. The following statement illustrates the report's simplistic explanation of Cuba's economic collapse: "The U.S. embargo has seriously impeded Cuba's ability to find

5. "A Public Survey on the quality of health care in the province of Holguín, a confidential report by the Cuban Communist Party." Translated by the Cuban American Foundation, Washington, D.C. 1988. Its publication by the Cuban American National Foundation has not been challenged. The original document was published as "Boletín especial: Equipo de opinión del pueblo, DOR PCC, Provincia de Holguín."

6. For this reason, I have chosen to withhold making specific references to the work of academics currently employed in Cuba.

substitute markets and sources of essential goods and has severely limited access to financing and commercial credit, critical for recovery." The section "Roots and Extent of Cuba's Current Economic Crisis" is a mere seven short paragraphs—two pages long—of a 302-page long report (excluding Appendices). This section essentially summarizes Cuba's loss of trading relationships with the Soviet bloc and the elimination of the oil-for-sugar barter agreement with the Soviet Union. There is no mention of Soviet subsidies[7] nor of Cuba's evident economic decline before the end of massive Soviet assistance.

A four-paragraph section on foreign debt merely provides an itemization of Cuba's external hard currency debt and refers to recent debt-equity swaps (a mechanism to reduce the debt). The Cuban government arguments uncritically repeated, as is standard practice in most of the report. Let me quote: "The Cuban government argues that external factors, principally the 35-year U.S. trade embargo, are largely to blame for the country's debt problems, including the fact that Cuba canceled principal and interest payments in 1986 and broke off formal talks with creditors three years later." The export fails to address the reasons behind Cuba's default on its external debt in 1986, several years before the dissolution of the Soviet bloc and the elimination of Soviet aid. Plus, the issue of how, with the embargo in place, Cuba gained access to billions of dollars in external credits— namely from Western banks—is not mentioned. In addition, there is nothing on how Cuba used this large inflow of capital, not to mention additional billions it now owes the former Soviet Union, China, Vietnam and North Korea.

In contrast to the two pages devoted to the causes of the economic crisis, four-plus pages are devoted to Cuba's "Recovery Plan." No analyses or critique are provided of the adequacy or inadequacy of Cuba's limited reforms, which many specialists describe as grossly insufficient. Again, the embargo is blamed for the island's hard currency shortfalls—for denying credits to Cuba. There is no mention that Cuba indeed has access to international credit markets for financing, but, due to its undeniable lack of creditworthiness, is only able to obtain short-term loans at very high rates and mostly with export receivables as collateral.

After that, the authors proceed to describe the problems in the area of health and nutrition in great detail, assuming that the cause-effect issue has been effectively solved.[8]

2. A second important methodological fault: Despite consistent problems with statistics reported by Cuba, there are no caveats on the reliability of data and information furnished by Cuban authorities, on which the report relies almost solely. Time and time again, the verbatim assertions of interviewees are cited as evidence, without any reference to efforts to corroborate their veracity or put them into any type of context.

Let me cite just one example. On page 112 of the report we find a table which illustrates one of the few efforts to provide a price comparison of the costs to

---

7. The Castro regime has been calculated to have received an estimated $100 to $150 billion in aid from the Soviet bloc over three decades—up to $6.7 billion a year during the last years of Soviet Communism, plus another $1.2 billion or more a year in military assistance. Adolfo Leyva, *Propaganda and Reality: A Look at the U.S. Embargo and Castro's Cuba* (Miami: The Endowment for Cuban American Studies of the Cuban American National Foundation, July 1994).

8. In fact, external financing currently is reported by Minister of the Economy José Luis Rodríguez to total about US$500 million in medium and long-term credits and approximately US$2 billion in short term credits at 14 to 22%. In addition, the Minister reports Cuba requires between US$2-3 billion in low interest, medium-term, credits to implement and sustain a recovery strategy. As a result of Cuba's inability to obtain external financing, "purchases were being made on a day-to-day and week-to-week basis, limiting the ability to take full advantage of volume discounts and lower international commodity prices" *Economic Eye on Cuba* (15-21 June 1998). This publication reports that foreign companies continue to report increases in delays of payments for products and services sold to Republic of Cuba companies. It should be noted that in 1997 private financing to emerging markets (bond and equity issues and loans) totaled $319.8 billion, according to International Monetary Fund, *Global Repercussions of the Asian Crisis and Other Issues* (Washington, 1998), p. 42.

Cuba of importing active ingredients for pharmaceuticals from European countries instead of from the United States. This reflects costs for Cuba as being 40% higher than if these inputs were purchased from a company in Miami—Tilgrex International Export, Inc. The cost of import was provided by MEDICUBA for purchases from European countries and comparative prices were then quoted, presumably by the authors, from the aforementioned company in Miami.[9] The following—which seem crucial to determining if this jeopardizes or not the health of the Cuban population—is left unexplained: a) How much would this added cost, for a seemingly large volume of active ingredients, raise the cost of the finished product?; b) What is the net cost of the embargo on Cuba's growing pharmaceutical export industry, reported to have exported US$125 million in 1996?; c) Was the information provided by Cuba corroborated by quoting the price of the active ingredients on the open market?; d) Are these active ingredients available from other countries—say Latin American countries active in the pharmaceutical market, such as Mexico, Venezuela, Colombia, Chile or Brazil – from where the cost of shipping would be lower? And if so, at what cost?

3. A third fault, which I have already referred to, is the lack of the simplest critical analysis, a failure to dig deeper—this in respect to even uncomplicated issues. Let me illustrate this with respect to just the simple issue of access to medicines and medical products.

The report basically states that current licensing procedures in effect block sale of medicine from the United States, which is allowed under current laws with a license from the Office of Foreign Assets Control (OFAC) of the U.S. Treasury Department. As a result, Cuba allegedly has no access to U.S.-patented medicines or is forced to purchase medicines at higher prices in other countries. The key issue here, in my opinion, is to try to arrive at the actual cost of the embargo by taking a sample list of the medical products most in demand and compare their international prices in alternative markets vis-à-vis their U.S. prices. Then, the cost of shipping should be factored in, adding any extra costs the embargo might impose in this area. The report failed to provide such a list or any table of comparative costs.

Among other aspects the report fails to mention in regards to access to medicines, is Cuba's senseless and inefficient system for distribution of medicines, which has a documented effect on the access of the general population to even the most basic medicines.[10] In addition, there is no mention of incidences in which basic medicines, such as oral penicillin, have been requested to relatives outside of Cuba as unavailable on the island, which have been found for

---

9. A total of 92,909 kilograms in active pharmaceutical ingredients imported from Europe was quoted to have been $786,000 higher (40%) than the price Cuba would have had to pay the company in Miami (US$1.96 million). See table on page 112 of the AAPH report.

10. Most drugs must be prescribed by specialists; family doctors can only prescribe a limited scope of analgesic, antibiotics and vitamins. But specialists only see patients at local clinics ("consultorios") once or twice a month, so a family doctor must examine the patient and refer him/her to a specialist, after which certification must be obtained for that purpose. A six-month wait is common to see a specialist at a specialized clinic ("Policlínico de Especialidades"). If a specialist finally prescribes a medicine, if the medication belongs to a certain group, a certificate must be issued describing the pathology, dose, duration of treatment as well as information on the patient. This document must be signed by the specialist, the head of the department and the Director of the Policlinic before the patient can go the pharmacy to fill the prescription. Oftentimes, if the information on the certificate is not to the full satisfaction of the pharmacist, the medicine is not dispensed and the error or omission must be corrected in the certification. If the pharmacy does not have it, a long and complicated process begins to request it. If a family doctor prescribes a medicine between 8AM and 4PM and the pharmacy only has that medicine for emergency room patients, after 4PM, the prescription must be re-issued. Furthermore, pharmacies are supplied once or twice a month in small quantities, and because each pharmacy is assigned to a certain area and hospital, pharmacies only accept prescriptions from doctors assigned to that jurisdiction. So patients' illnesses must match the pharmacy's particular supply. Many cases of high blood pressure or psychiatric disorders are thrown into crisis due to the impossibility of obtaining the required medication. Described in Emily Rodríguez, "Métodos y mecansimo de distribución de los medicamentos en Cuba," Agencia de Prensa Libre Oriental (APLO), January 12, 1998 in CubaNet News.

sale in Latin American countries at much lower prices than in the U.S. and *produced by Cuba*.[11]

It was my personal experience, after having lived ten years in Latin America—mostly during the profound debt crisis of the eighties—that access of medicines not produced by the U.S. was never a problem. Both Venezuela and Chile, countries where I lived with young children, whom, on occasion, required common as well as more sophisticated medications, had readily available locally-produced prescription and non-prescription drugs and all sorts of medical products. Not one single medicine had to be imported from the U.S. by my family in ten years. And, the prices of the locally-produced products were considerably lower than U.S. equivalents in every single case I can recall.

I further understand that U.S. government officials have in several occasions requested from Cuban authorities a list of products Cuba has stated it is unable to purchase either in third countries or from U.S. companies. In each occasion, a list was not forthcoming,[12] and is also unavailable in the report. Instead, examples of medicines either unavailable or more expensive are offered, but I have not had the chance to research each case.

U.S. Commerce Department officials assert there has been not a single request for a license to sell medicines which are said to be available only from U.S. suppliers. Naturally, if there have been no requests for licenses, none have been denied. In fact, the Department of Commerce reports that license requests for the sale of medical products to Cuba have been extremely limited in number and amount of exports. Of the seven license requests for the sale of medicine,

medical supplies or equipment received since 1992, all have been granted and these total under US$300,000. In addition, the Commerce Department reports never having received a license request to take samples to Cuba for the purpose of commercializing medical products.[13] (I have found reports of two recent requests for licenses to commercialize medical products on the island, made after my interview at the Commerce Department.)

I have not found any evidence of unfulfilled orders by Cuban institutions to U.S. pharmaceutical companies and, furthermore, understand that many Cuban health professionals are not informed of the embargo exception for the licensed sale of medicine to Cuba.[14] Many US. pharmaceutical company executives share this ignorance, partly due to never having received an order of purchase from Cuba. If Cuba were in such desperate need for medicines obtainable only from U.S. companies, why doesn't it place orders of purchase?

It has been widely reported that there is adequate supply of all types of medications generally unavailable to the average Cuban in dollar stores and in health facilities catering to hard currency paying patients—tourists, diplomats or foreign residents. The report altogether fail to mention this. In fact, with the same U.S. embargo in place, health tourism is a growing industry which generates considerable hard currency revenues for Cuba and offers very high standards, quality, and access to all sorts of medicines and medical supplies, all unavailable to the general population.

Let me make just a few comments on the issue of nutrition. In regards to the cause of nutritional deficien-

11. Jesús Hernández Cuellar, "Castro exporta medicinas, pese a la escasez en Cuba," *Contacto* (Abril 7, 1998) in CubaNet News (April 7, 1998).

12. Michael Ranneberger, Coordinator, Office of Cuban Affairs, U.S. Department of State, presentation at conference "U.S. Policy on the Supply of Food and Medicine to Cuba," Capitol Hill, Washington, D.C., April 15, 1998. Roger Noriega, senior staff member for Senator Jesse Helms (R-NC), related a similar account to the author in early 1998. Mr. Noriega went on an official visit to Cuba during the Pope's trip to the island in January 1998 and toured health facilities.

13. The author met with Joan Roberts, Director, and John Bolstein, Cuba Officer, on March 30, 1998 at the Department of Commerce in Washington, D.C. They manage licensing for Cuba from the Foreign Policy Division, Office of Strategic Trade and Foreign Policy Controls, one of five departments of the Bureau of Export Administration.

14. Personally related by Roger Noriega, senior staff member for Senator Jesse Helms, April 1998.

cies, the report cites the Cuban government's allegations[15] in a superficial, two-page, exposition. Selected data are used to show that the domestic food industry experienced considerable growth in the period 1963-89 as a result of government priorities and that agricultural production experienced substantial growth in the 20-year period between 1969 and 1989 (Report, pp. 123-125). To explain the subsequent economic crisis and the declines in agriculture and food production, the report cites the reduction in hard currency for purchases abroad as well as the higher costs and inaccessibility imposed by the Cuban Democracy Act (CDA).[16] This U.S. law is said to have affected purchases for food processing equipment, pesticides, fertilizers, animal feed and fuel. Even the country's severe lack of fuel—amply available in world markets—is blamed on the U.S. embargo, allegedly for raising the cost of other required inputs, which diminishes the availability of hard currency to import oil (Report, p. 128). A short section follows on Cuba's dedicated efforts to develop biotechnology to boost food supplies and many pages describe the effect of deteriorating nutrition in several areas related to health.

According to the report, before the passage of the CDA, three fourths of Cuban imports from U.S. subsidiaries were food and medicines (Report, p. 283). The embargo, particularly since the passage of the CDA in 1992, is said to have cost the Cuban government $196.3 million from 1992 to 1994 in higher shipping costs and prices (Report, pp. 129, 122). It is not clear where this figure comes from, as several numbers provided for specific food imports do not add up to this total. In addition, Cuban government calculations are cited of an additional $8.3 million paid in chemicals used in agriculture in 1994 (Report, p. 127).

With regard to higher shipping costs, the report cites Cuban economists (government employees, one might add) as having calculated that each U.S. ship replacing a European freighter would save $215,800 and $516,700 replacing an Asian freighter (Report, p. 12). These figures had been provided by Cuba's Ministry of Foreign Relations in a letter sent to the United Nations' General Secretary dated June 9, 1995 (Report, footnote 2, p. 135). No effort was seemingly made to corroborate these numbers and no comparison with cost for freighters from Latin American countries or Canada were provided. The U.S. State Department, in turn, has reported that shipping costs for Cuba are 2-3% higher due to the embargo.[17] The report makes no reference of attempts to contact U.S. government representatives regarding this issue nor cites State Department estimates.

Moreover, the report does not take into account the value of donations and assistance for food in assessing the potential cost of the embargo. More importantly, the causes of the pitiful state of nutrition and food supply of the Cuban population remain unexplored. There is an implicit assumption that any cost overruns created by the embargo are to blame for the critical situation of food security and nutrition in Cuba.

I refer you to the tables in the Appendix,[18] which have a brief explanation of which part of their respective contents are relevant to this presentation. They:

1. Demonstrate how, by 1986, Cuba was behind in production of all the selected fool staples when compared with other Latin American countries, including those of similar or lower population and or land mass.

2. Show the steep relative decline in rural population and in employment in agricultural produc-

---

15. For example that in 1989 57% of the proteins and 50% of the calories came from imported foodstuffs. Report, p. 121.

16. U.S. law passed in October of 1992 (also known as the Torricelli Law). Among its provisions, it abolished subsidiary trade with Cuba and prohibited ships from docking in U.S. ports for 180 days after docking in Cuba.

17. "Fact sheet: The Embargo and Healthcare in Cuba: Myth versus reality," Bureau of Inter-American Affairs, U.S. Department of State (August 5, 1997).

18. The tables are not included here because of space considerations. They are available from the author. Many of them originate from Manuel Sánchez Herrero and Arnaldo Ramos Lauzurique, "El sector agropecuario cubano bajo el socialismo de estado," in this volume. Ed.

tion as well as the sharp drop in agricultural production/yields much before 1989.

3. Reveal the descent in Cuba's livestock ("masa ganadera"), in real terms and, even more sharply, in per capita terms. Obviously, this is evidenced by the steady and sharp decline in the per capita consumption of beef of the population. (Cuba, in the meantime is reported to be exporting cattle to Vietnam, with which it is involved in a joint venture!)

What is more puzzling is that the Cuban government, purportedly with the intention of gaining political influence internationally, provides economic assistance to other countries. This is hardly justifiable for a country said to be enduring "genocide by starvation." At the end of 1997, the Cuban government was reported to have made a US$100,000 donation to Vietnam in the aftermath of typhoon Linda.[19] And there are a number of other examples. Around 250 students from Caribbean countries have been granted full scholarships to study at Cuban universities. An undetermined number of Grenadians have been flown to Cuba for medical care and, Cuba sent farmers in St. Kitts and Nevis seeds and tons of fertilizers after they suffered a hurricane.[20]

I am personally aware of Castro's involvement in offering and providing dedicated medical care in Cuba for the son of a right-wing Chilean politician, who suffered severe neurological effects from a near drowning experience.[21] This incident took place during the time that Cuba was lobbying for the reestablishment of diplomatic relations with Chile, which soon followed.

Please refer to the Appendix for a calculation which, given the pervasive unreliability of data provided by Cuba, may seem more an exercise in voodoo economics than anything else. It is a hypothetical calculation based on a number of arbitrary assumptions constructed on data provided mostly by Cuban authorities. I caution that it might be missing unknown factors which might impact each selected caption and might not reflect all the figures that should be or could be estimated or calculated. Nevertheless, instead of a loss, it reflects a considerable gain to Cuba from the embargo in the areas of health and nutrition. At the very least, it could provide for a focused debate and more extensive analysis of the particulars, which I have found to be seriously lacking in addressing this issue.

To end, I would like to briefly address the question of costs/benefits of maintaining the embargo on food and medicine. Regardless of my opinion of the report, I am compelled to state that I believe the embargo poses some inevitable costs to Cuba in the areas of health and nutrition, the extent of which remain unclear. Whatever that cost may be, be them monetary or not, I find it morally unjustifiable and strategically/politically counterproductive. I believe the current ban is not an effective policy tool and, in fact, that it actually acts in our detriment. At the very least, the current impasse with respect to Cuba calls for a serious and high-quality debate in which the overriding concern for the promotion of a peaceful change in Cuba outweighs less transcendental political considerations.[22]

---

19. "Cuba donará 100.00 dólares para damnificados por tifón Linda," EFE/Hanoi (18 November 1997) in CubaNet News (November 11, 1998).

20. Larry Rohter, "Cool to U.S., Caribbean hails Castro all the more warmly," *The New York Times* (August 2, 1997).

21. It is said that at the urging of the Cuban government, Cuban specialists were sent to Chile to evaluate and treat the young son of center-right Congressman Andrés Allamand, of the Partido Renovación Nacional. The child and members of his family were subsequently flown to Cuba, where he was treated for some time, returning to Chile with a staff of dedicated Cuban medical personnel to continue treatment. Allegedly, most if not all, of the expenses related to this case were covered by the Cuban government. This account was related to the author by several close friends of the Allamand family.

22. For more on this see remarks by María C. Werlau at a conference "U.S. Policy on the Supply of Food and Medicine to Cuba: What is the appropriate U.S. response?, sponsored by The Georgetown University Caribbean Project, Capitol Hill, Washington, D.C., April 15, 1998.

Appendix
NET ESTIMATED ANNUAL EFFECT OF THE
U.S. EMBARGO ON NUTRITION AND HEALTH IN CUBA (U.S. DOLLARS)

$ - 30.0 million		Higher cost of imported medicines attributed to the embargo (1996).1
- 10.0 million		Possible higher costs paid by Cuba for other medical imports.2
+ 8.1 million		Export of health professionals (1997).3
+ 7.2 million		Net profit of 15% on health tourism (1996).4
+ 12.5 million		Net profit of 10% on medical exports (1995).5
+ 14.0 million		Estimates of non-U.S. donations reported by Cuba for the health sector (1995, 1996).6
1.8 million		**ESTIMATED NET GAIN TO CUBA'S STATE BUDGET IN THE HEALTH SECTOR EXCLUDING U.S. DONATIONS**
+ 6.1 million		U.S. donations for the health sector reported by the Cuban government (1996).7
7.9 million		**ESTIMATED NET GAIN TO CUBA'S STATE BUDGET IN THE HEALTH SECTOR INCLUDING U.S. DONATIONS**
+ 25.3 million		50% of remaining average annual health-sector donations reported as approved by the U.S. government (1997) -net of U.S. medical donations reported by the Cuban government (1996).8
+ 125.0 million		If 50% of U.S. remittances of US$500 million (lower range of current estimates) were devoted to health).9
158.2 million	(A)	**ESTIMATED NET GAIN TO CUBA IN THE HEALTH SECTOR – INCLUDING U.S. DONATIONS PRESUMABLY IMPACTING STATE BUDGET PLUS DIRECT TO POPULATION / NGOs**
- 204.6 million		Cost of the embargo in the area of food/agriculture as per Cuban authorities (1996).10
+ 67.2 million		Non-health sector, non-U.S., humanitarian donations reported by Cuba (1996).11
20. 8 million		**ESTIMATED NET LOSS TO CUBA'S FOOD BUDGET EXCLUDING U.S. DONATIONS**
+ 225.2 million		50% of approved non-medical U.S. donations.12
246.0 million		**ESTIMATED NET GAIN TO CUBA'S FOOD BUDGET INCLUDING U.S. DONATIONS**
+ 250.0 million		If 50% of U.S. remittances of $500 million were devoted to nutrition (lowest current estimate).13
496.0 million	(B)	**ESTIMATED NET GAIN TO CUBA IN FOOD SECURITY – INCLUDING U.S. DONATIONS DIRECT TO THE POPULATION / NGOs. 14**
654.2 million	(A+B)	**ESTIMATED TOTAL NET GAIN TO CUBA AFTER ACCOUNTING FOR EFFECT OF THE U.S. EMBARGO ON HEALTH AND NUTRITION**
+ 60.0 million		75% of assumed net return for long distance telephone service payments from U.S. carriers to the Republic of Cuba (1997).15
+ 6.0 million		Overflight payments to the Republic of Cuban by U.S. carriers (1997).16
+ 2.0 million		75% of assumed net return for air charter companies' payments to the Rep. Cuba.17
+ 10.5 million		15% net return from authorized daily expenditures in Cuba by individuals subject to U.S. law paying licensed visits to Cuba.18
+ 1.0 million		50% of departure taxes of visitors from Cuba to the U.S. and fees ofemigrating Cuban nationals(1997).19
79.5 million	(C)	**ESTIMATED NET GAIN TO CUBA FROM TRAVEL AND OTHER COMMERCIAL EXCHANGES WITH THE UNITED STATES**
$ 733.7 million		**ANNUAL GRAND TOTAL (A+B+C)**

Note: The Cuban government claims that the U.S. embargo (which it terms "blockade") has cost Cuba $60 billion dollars. The author is not aware of any itemized calculation of how this figure was obtained.

SOURCES

1. Lázaro Barredo Medina, "Es imaginario el bloqueo de medicinas?," *Trabajadores* (16 de mayo de 1997). This article was faxed to the author by the Cuban Interest Section in Washington, first quarter 1998.

2. Rough estimate – no data have been found to indicate there is an additional cost of other medical imports.

3. This calculation assumes that health professionals generated 50% of the $18 million reported by Cuba, minus 10% in costs. At the end of 1997 there were 2,808 Cubans working in more than 80 countries (34 countries of the Americas, 21 African countries, 14 European countries and 13 Asian countries). In 1997 Cuba reported to have received revenues of US$18 million for the export of services via professionals and technicians. "Exportación del trabajo produce $18 millones," *El Nuevo Herald* (March 5, 1998) in Cuba-Net News. The U.S.-Cuba Trade and Economic Council, citing Cuban Minister of Foreign Investment reported that many of these 18,000 workers are said to be health professionals. "Doctors from Cuba said to be working in more than 40 countries." *Economic Eye on Cuba* (16-22 February 1998).

4. In the mid 1980s the government began promoting and in recent years has stepped up what has been labeled "health tourism" (*turismo de salud*), which has attracted many foreigners, generating needed foreign currency. In 1995 health tourism reportedly brought in 3,500 tourists and generated hard currency revenues of US$24 million. "One thing Cuba does right," *The Economist* (September 7, 1996), p. 42. 24 medical centers in Havana and 12 in the interior are reported to be dedicated to health tourism, developed through agreements with more than 200 travel agencies in more than 60 countries. It appears that the comparatively low cost of good quality care in Cuba with respect to medical centers in North America and Europe, is particularly attractive especially to Latin Americans. The State company SERVIMED was formed as a division of Cubanacán, S. A. to offer "sun and medical attention" to foreigners thru programs which includes medical treatment, airfare and accommodations. Dr. Sergio Beltrán, "Cuba: turismo contra salud," *Boletín del Instituto Cubano de Economistas Independientes*, Vol. 1, No. 1 (enero/febrero 1996), pp. 35-36. Cuba is reported to have received 7,000 health tourists in 1996. Eloy Rodríguez, "Por la salud de los turistas," *Granma Internacional* (30 de abril de 1997). The State Department cites press reports that these left Cuba US$25 million. "Fact sheet: The Embargo and Healthcare in Cuba: Myth versus Reality," Bureau of Inter-American Affairs, U.S. Department of State (August 5, 1997). If the 1995 rate of revenue is applied to the 7,000 reported tourists in 1996, Cuba will have generated US$48 million in 1997. The above calculation is assumes gross revenues of $48 million at a net return of 15%, which is much lower than the 32% net return on tourism reported by Cuba for 1996. See Maria C. Werlau, "Foreign Investment: The Limits of Commercial Engagement," *Cuba in Transition—Volume 6* (Washington: Association for the Study of the Cuban Economy, 1996), p. 482, for an explanation on net earnings for tourism.

5. Cuba exported US$125 million in medical products in 1996. Directorate of Intelligence, CIA, *Cuba: Handbook of Trade Statistics, 1996* (Washington, November 1996).

6. The American Association for World Health report cites Cuban government sources indicating that $20 million in donations went to the health sector in 1995. See American Association for World Health, *Denial of Food and Medicine: The Impact of the U.S. Embargo on Health and Nutrition in Cuba* (Washington, March 1997), p. 287. This calculation takes medical donations reported by Cuba minus reported U.S. donations in the health sector of US$6,097,088. "Donativos recibidos por Cuba provenientes de Estados Unidos como ayuda al desarrollo y humanitaria en 1996," undated, Faxed by Cuban Interest Section in Washington, D.C., First quarter 1998.

7. Cuba reported US$6,097,088 in donations originating in the U.S. for the health sector for 1996. The presumption is that this amount went to state-controlled institutions. "Donativos recibidos."

8. The U.S. Department of State reported in August 1997 that $227 million were approved in humanitarian donations of medicines and medical supplies over the last four years. "Fact Sheet," op. cit. For the purposes of the above calculation, a yearly average of $56.75 million was used, from which the Cuban government's reported 1996 figure for medical donations ($6.1 million) was subtracted. For the purpose of erring on the side of caution, only 50% of U.S. donations reported as approved are presumed to reach Cuba.

9. Remittances to Cuba have been estimated as follows: For 1997 the U.S. Cuba Trade and Economic Council cites a total of $575 million -$275 million in remittances from individuals subject to U.S. law (from 1.5 million individuals or 375 thousand families of Cuban descent) plus $300 million from outside the U.S. *Economic Eye on Cuba* (5-11 January 1998).

10. The AAWH report cites a cost to Cuba of $204.6 million just in food and agriculture-related imports. *Denial of Food and Medicine*, p. 129.

11. This calculation takes into account total donations reported by Cuba of $87,535,152, less total U.S. donations of $6,340,562 ("Donativos recibidos," op. cit.) minus non-U.S. donations for the health sector of $14 million, as reported above (see note 4, above).

12. A total of US$2,148,524,744 was approved from 10/23/92 to 7/31/97 by the U.S. government for donations to Cuba in the following categories: gift parcels, clothes, food/agriculture, education, shelter and misc. For the reported period 4.7 years, the annual average is US$450.4 million. "Humanitarian Donations to Cuba Approved by the Dept. of Commerce, Bureau of Export Administration, after the passage of the Cuban Democracy Act: 10/23/92 – 7/31/97," Table dated August 4, 1997, provided by the U.S. Department of State, Office of Cuban Affairs.

13. See note 9, above.

14. Total estimated donations for food, as per above conservative figures, equal $542.4 million, equivalent to 90.4% of Cuba's total expenditures on imported food of $600 million in 1996. As per figures cited by Cuba's Minister of the Economy, *Economic Eye on Cuba* (17-23 February 1997).

15. Companies providing the payments are ATT, WilTel, global One, MCI, IDB Worldcom, ATT Puerto Rico, Sprint and Telefónica Larga Distancia de Puerto Rico. *Economic Eye on Cuba* (5-11 January 1998).

16. Ibid.

17. Approximately 48,653 passengers traveled in air charter flights to Cuba in 1997. Ibid.

18. The U.S. Treasury Department authorizes up to $100 to be spent in Cuba by individuals subject to U.S., although it is estimated they spend an average of $150 to $200 daily. The average visit is 10 days. Estimated travel Visa payments in Cuba were $3.5 million form 70,000 individuals subject to U.S. law. U.S. visitors were estimated to have imported into the U.S. $7.5 million -the estimated $100 quota for personal use of authorized products from Cuba. Ibid.

19. Departure taxes of 70,000 visitors to the U.S. totaled $1,050,000 ($15 per person). Emigration fees were estimated at US$1 million. Ibid. (Departure taxes for relatives and emigration fees required for departure from Cuba are presumed to be mostly paid by family and friends residing in the United States.)

THE UNITED STATES EMBARGO AGAINST CUBA: LEGAL ASPECTS OF THE RESTRICTIONS ON SALES OF PHARMACEUTICAL PRODUCTS, AS SET FORTH IN THE CUBAN DEMOCRACY ACT OF 1992

Wallie Mason and Stephen J. Kimmerling[1]

BRIEF OVERVIEW
OF THE U.S. EMBARGO AGAINST CUBA

The Cuban Democracy Act of 1992[2] (hereinafter "the CDA") is but one of several measures adopted over the last three decades that exert economic pressure to effect political change in Cuba. Economic sanctions against the island were adopted in 1962 and, other than the ebb and flow of their severity brought on by various gestures towards Castro by intervening administrations, the embargo has intensified in its severity and scope. The bulk of U.S. prohibitions against trade with Cuba are set forth in the U.S. Department of the Treasury's Cuban Assets Control Regulations, 31 C.F.R. §§ 515.502-515.574, and the Commerce Department's Export Administration Regulations (notably 15 C.F.R. § 746.2, governing exports to Cuba). Federal law provides that civil penalties may be imposed for any violation of these regulations and that knowing violations are also punishable as criminal offenses, incurring substantial fines and possible prison terms of up to ten years. Property involved in such violations of the U.S. embargo regulations is subject to forfeiture.[3]

Since its formalized institution in 1962, the U.S. embargo against Cuba has become ever more comprehensive. The key elements of the embargo, as it now stands, include the following general prohibitions:

- **Imports:** U.S. law prohibits any imports from Cuba into the United States.

- **Exports:** U.S. law prohibits any exports to Cuba from the United States.

- **Travel:** U.S. law severely restricts the freedom of U.S. citizens and residents from traveling to Cuba. This is achieved by regulations which prohibit U.S. persons from paying Cuba or Cuban nationals for travel-related expenses such as hotels. There are exceptions for certain persons such as those visiting close relatives in Cuba (permitted only in cases of extreme humanitarian need), journalists, academics, and persons traveling on official business for the U.S. government, foreign governments, or international organizations. Even those in these excepted categories are subject to severe restrictions including a $100 per day limit on travel expenses in Cuba.

---

1. This is a revised and edited version of a report prepared in October 1996 by the International Human Rights Consulting Group for the American Association of World Health.

2. Cuban Democracy Act of 1992, Title XVII, Pub. L. No. 102-484, §§ 1701 et seq.; 106 Stat. 2575.

3. 50 U.S.C. app. § 16.

- **Transfer of money or property:** The United States prohibits any U.S. person from transferring money or property of any nature to Cuban nationals. There are exceptions for family remittances, but these are limited to $300 every three months to the household of a close relative in Cuba.

- **Receiving property:** U.S. law prohibits any U.S. person from receiving property from Cuba or a Cuban national.

- **Technical data:** The prohibition on transfers of property also includes the transfer of technical data.

- **Aircraft:** U.S. law prohibits any aircraft, other than those with the necessary licensure, from departing from the U.S. for Cuba and any aircraft owned or controlled by U.S. persons from departing for Cuba, regardless of departure point, unless such travel is licensed by the federal government.

- **Vessels:** U.S. law prohibits any third-country vessel from entering a U.S. port for a 180-day period following the vessel's entry into Cuba. This provision was included in the CDA and has been one of the most objectionable aspects of the embargo to other nations as it dramatically impacts foreign nations' freedom of trade.[4]

- **Penalties against other nations:** The United States may cut off aid and credits to countries which give preferential treatment to Cuba. The United States also maintains veto power within several international financial institutions over loans and credits to Cuba and nations that trade with Cuba.

Following the collapse of the Soviet Union in 1989 and the resulting loss of Soviet subsidies, Cuban trade with U.S. corporate subsidiaries rose dramatically. In the year prior to the October 1992 passage of the CDA, subsidiary sales to Cuba totaled between $400-700 million.[5] With the CDA's tightening of the embargo to include subsidiary sales (which had been licensed on a liberal basis prior to 1992) this growing trade was cut off almost overnight.

Perhaps the most onerous of the CDA's provisions, and that which is the focus of this report, are those restricting the sale of medicines and medical equipment to Cuba. The CDA provides, in relevant part:

Section 1705 (c) Exports of Medicines and Medical Supplies. — Exports of medicines or medical supplies, instruments, or equipment to Cuba shall not be restricted —

(1) except to the extent such restrictions would be permitted under section 5(m) of the Export Administration Act of 1979 or section 203(b)(2) of the International Emergency Economic Powers Act;

(2) except in a case in which there is a reasonable likelihood that the item to be exported will be used for purposes of torture or other human rights abuses;

(3) except in a case in which there is a reasonable likelihood that the item to be exported will be re-exported; and

(4) except in a case in which the item to be exported could be used in the production of any biotechnological product.

(d) Requirements for Certain Exports. –

(1) On Site Verifications. –

(A) Subject to subparagraph (B), an export may be made under subsection (C) only if the President determines that the United States

---

4. This provision also causes grave impact on the price of any goods imported into Cuba, as ships from as far away as Europe and Asia are prohibited from visiting the U.S., and thus, the increased shipping costs are passed on to Cuban consumers.

5. U.S. Government officials have cited various figures. In a Special Report, An Analysis of Licensed Trade with Cuba by Foreign Subsidiaries of U.S. Companies, July 1993, published by the Office of Foreign Assets Control, U.S. Dept. of the Treasury, the figure of $407 million in subsidiary trade for 1992 is cited. Peter Tarnoff, Undersecretary for Political Affairs, has cited the amount as over $700 million in 1992. See testimony before the Foreign Relations Committee, Western Hemisphere Subcommittee, U.S. Senate, May 22, 1995. Richard Newcomb, Director of the Office of Foreign Assets Control, Dept. of the Treasury, has put the 1992 figure at $336 million. See testimony before the Committee on Foreign Affairs, U.S. House of Representatives, November 18, 1993.

Government is able to verify, by on site inspections and other appropriate means, that the exported item is to be used for the purposes for which it was intended and only for the use and benefit of the Cuban people.

(B) Subparagraph (A) does not apply to donations to non-governmental organizations in Cuba of medicines for humanitarian purposes.

(2) Licenses. – Exports permitted under subsection (C) shall be made pursuant to specific licenses issued by the United States Government.

THE CDA'S RESTRICTIONS ON THE SALE OF MEDICINES

On its face, the language of the CDA regarding exports of medicines and medical supplies to Cuba seems to create a liberal policy of granting licenses for such sales. The Cuban Democracy Act's literal wording grants exceptions for commercial and humanitarian exports of medically related goods and for donative (i.e., noncommercial) exports of food. Section 1705 of the CDA exempts "donations of food to nongovernmental organizations [NGOs] ... [and] individuals in Cuba." Section 1705 further exempts "exports of medicines or medical supplies, instruments, or equipment," except where "restrictions would be permitted" under the Export Administration Act of 1979 or the International Emergency Economic Powers Act. The Act restricts the export of medical materials, however, where there is a "reasonable likelihood" of the Cuban government's use of such aid for reexport, human rights violations, or biotechnology.

The restrictions the CDA imposes on the delivery of medicines, however, subvert the spirit of such excep-

tions by making Cuba's access to such materials nearly impossible. The result is a de facto ban on critical medical and other assistance. For example, the medical goods exemption does not seem so generous when one reads that commercial export of such goods is subject to the issuance of specific licenses. Such licenses must issue from either the Department of the Treasury or the Department of Commerce, depending on the provider of the goods and the nature of the goods to be exported.

A Treasury license is required when a foreign U.S. subsidiary seeks to export medically related goods that are not of U.S. origin or that do not contain U.S.-origin matter. A Commerce license, however, is required for all exports of medically related U.S.-origin goods and medically related goods containing "U.S.-origin materials, parts, or components"[6] to be exported from a U.S. entity (whether in the United States or abroad), from a foreign U.S. subsidiary, or from an independent overseas entity.[7] Where foreign firms seek to export foreign-made goods composed of some amount of U.S.-origin matter, the Commerce Department will favorably consider these firms' export license requests if the goods contain only "an insubstantial proportion"[8] of such matter and if the goods are "nonstrategic"[9] in nature. To qualify as insubstantial, U.S.-origin matter incorporated into a foreign-made product can amount to no more than "20 percent of the value of the product to be exported from the third country."[10]

Even when a license does issue, exported goods are subject to the CDA's burdensome verification and on-site inspection procedures.[11] Under the CDA, permission for commercial (i.e., nonhumanitarian)

---

6. 15 C.F.R. § 746.2 (b) (3) (1997).

7. It is not clear whether a Treasury license is *also* required for export of medically related, U.S.-origin goods and medically related, U.S.-origin materials, parts, or components by foreign U.S. subsidiaries and foreign non-U.S.-related entities. Caution would suggest forwarding Treasury a photocopy of the Commerce license application along with a letter requesting that both the photocopy and the letter be deemed a Treasury license request should a Treasury license be required.

8. 15 C.F.R., *supra* note 6, at § 746.2 (b) (3).

9. *Id.*

10. *Id.* at § 746.2 (b) (3) (ii).

11. Cuban Democracy Act of 1992, *supra* note 2, at § 1705 (d) (1) (A); 31 C.F.R. § 515.559 (a) (2) (v) (1993); *see also* 15 C.F.R., *supra* note 6, at § 746.2 (b) (1) (v).

export of medical materials hinges on the President's determination "that the United States Government is able to verify by on site inspections"[12] that the items will be put to their intended use to benefit Cuban citizens. Treasury and Commerce regulations reword this requirement by restricting export of medically related goods "where it is determined that the United States Government is *un*able to verify"[13] the goods' end use. The result is that Cuban citizens must wait and languish while U.S. companies and/or their subsidiaries endure the lengthy (and often fruitless) license application process, await word as to whether the U.S. government can verify that the exported medical items will be put to their intended use, and then submit to on-site inspection procedures.

On-site verification provides the U.S. Treasury and Commerce Departments with an effective weapon in discouraging and denying requests for licenses. In fact, the departments involved both openly state that it is their general policy to deny all applications. For example, in its 1994-1995 Annual Report, the Bureau of Export Administration (BXA) states that "[A]pplications for validated licenses will generally be denied, except on a case-by-case basis for ... exports to Cuba of medicines and medical items that satisfy the requirements of the CDA.[14]

Like Commerce, the Treasury Department also uses the authority and discretion granted it by the CDA to discourage and deny foreign U.S. subsidiaries' requests for licenses to sell to Cuba. Testifying before Congress in 1993 on the one-year anniversary of the passage of the CDA, Richard Newcomb, Director of the Office of Foreign Assets Control, boasted as to how the CDA had virtually cut off all sales to Cuba and stated that it was the agency's intention to see the number of licenses issued fall to zero:

The CDA prohibits the issuance of licenses pursuant to section 559 of our regulations allowing offshore transactions by Cuba with foreign subsidiaries of U.S. firms. The prohibition against issuing licenses was softened slightly, however, in that the CDA provides that the provision shall not affect contracts entered into before the enactment of the CDA ... In 1993 ... [Cuban trade with U.S. subsidiaries] ... was down to $1.6 million. The $1.6 million is accounted for by approximately 15 or 16 licenses which were pre-CDA contracts. We go over these [license applications] very, very carefully and only grant those that absolutely qualify. Frankly, I anticipate the number next year to be even less, falling ultimately to zero.[15]

In his statement before Congress, Mr. Newcomb wrongly stated that the CDA prohibits the issuance of licenses and only allows for the completion of pre-CDA contracts. His statement that the number of licenses would ultimately fall to zero either indicated his mistaken belief that once pre-CDA contracts had been completed no further licenses could be issued, or his intention that, notwithstanding the CDA's provisions for the future licensing of medical sales, the agency would not approve any additional licenses. His confusing comments with regard to the CDA's provisions are echoed throughout his agency and in his counterpart agency within the Department of Commerce, the BXA.

A phone call to the Department of Commerce, Bureau of Export Administration, sums up the similar confusion encountered in trying to obtain a license from that agency to sell medicine to Cuba. In a telephone interview conducted by the authors of this report, we asked a BXA information officer to provide us with an overview of the licensing procedures for sales of medicine to Cuba. The officer responded, incorrectly, that the BXA does not license sales to Cu-

---

12. Cuban Democracy Act of 1992, *supra* note 2, at § 1705 (d) (1) (A).

13. 31 C.F.R., *supra* note 11, at § 515.559 (a) (2) (v) (emphasis added); 15 C.F.R., *supra* note 5, at § 746.2 (b) (1) (v) (emphasis added).

14. Bureau of Export Administration, U.S. Dep't Com., 1994 Export Administration Annual Report and 1995 Report on Foreign Policy Export Controls III-18.

15. Richard Newcomb, Director, Off. of Foreign Assets Control, U.S. Dep't of the Treasury, testimony of November 18, 1993, before a joint hearing of the Subcomm. on Econ. Pol'y, Trade and Env't, W. Hemisphere Aff. and Int'l Cooperation of the Comm. on Foreign Aff., U.S. House of Representatives, at 21, 37.

ba, only donations. We responded that the CDA provides for licensing procedures for sales. The officer then consulted an agency manual and responded that this was indeed correct, but that the requesting company must list on the application "how it will provide for on-site inspection, and also that the goods would be for the benefit of the Cuban people." She then commented, after reading these requirements, "I doubt very seriously that a license to sell medicines to Cuba would be approved; it would be very difficult to satisfy those two criteria."[16] When asked what the term "on-site inspection" meant, she was unable to offer an explanation. In short, the reply we received appears quite typical of the responses pharmaceutical companies encounter in seeking to obtain licenses from BXA or OFAC.

In the course of preparing this report, the authors conducted an informal survey of U.S. pharmaceutical companies to inquire as to their efforts in obtaining licenses for the sale of medicines to Cuba. In addition, the authors contacted the Office of Foreign Assets Control (OFAC) within the Department of the Treasury and the Bureau of Export Administration (BXA) within the Commerce Department, the two offices responsible for the processing of applications for licenses to sell medicines to Cuba.

In our interviews with pharmaceutical company representatives, we were told the same thing over and over: all inquiries to the U.S. government regarding the possibility of obtaining licenses to sell medicine to Cuba are met with confusing, sometimes hostile replies, all designed to discourage the company from even initiating the licensing process. Of the seven companies who agreed to participate in our survey, only one stated that it had successfully obtained licenses to sell to Cuba since 1992 and then only for a few specific items. In short, this company indicated

that it continued to seek to sell medicines to Cuba due to humanitarian concerns, though applying for licenses "is more trouble than it is worth."[17]

We also filed requests with both the BXA and OFAC under the Freedom of Information Act (FOIA) seeking "all applications submitted to and approved licenses from" each agency regarding "subsidiary trade and/or sales of medicines, pharmaceuticals and medical supplies to Cuba" during the period 1990-1995.[18] The request for information from the Commerce Department was denied for "national security reasons." The FOIA request to Treasury was also denied, but information was obtained from the Department through other channels.[19]

According to the information provided by the Treasury Department, in the period 1992-1995, only eight licenses were granted by their agency for sales of medicines to Cuba; two licenses were denied. Considering the high volume of such sales pre-CDA enactment, one wonders why these total figures are so low. Based solely on these figures, it would appear that only ten applications were filed with OFAC between 1992 and 1995. Pharmaceutical industry members explained to us the reason why so few companies actually file applications for licenses. As one drug company representative put it, when a company calls to informally discuss the possibility of a license with OFAC, they are given confusing information and are generally discouraged from filing a request. Similarly, a representative of OFAC confirmed the same, stating that "companies hate to get a denial from the government for any kind of license. When they phone and are told how difficult it is to comply with the licensing procedures, and are generally discouraged from applying, they usually don't follow up with filing a written application."[20]

---

16. Telephone interview with Tracy O'Donald, Dept. of Commerce, Bureau of Export Admin., Feb. 20, 1996.

17. At the request of those interviewed, we are not providing names of individuals quoted.

18. The FOIA requests were filed by the National Security Archives, an independent nongovernmental institute and library located in Washington, D.C.

19. The department provided information regarding licenses it had granted for medical sales in the 1992-1995 period to the office of Rep. Charles Rangel (D-NY) upon his request.

20. Telephone interview with Clara David, Off. of Foreign Assets Control, Apr. 18, 1996.

Of the licensing requirements described to would-be applicants, perhaps the most discouraging is that of on-site verification. Several of the pharmaceutical representatives interviewed mentioned this as an "untenable" requirement. As the CDA states in § 1705 (d) (1) (A), sales of medical supplies to Cuba may be licensed only if "the President determines that the United States Government is able to verify, by on site inspections and other appropriate means, that the exported item is to be used for the purposes for which it was intended and only for the use and benefit of the Cuban people." Besides being an unprecedented requirement in the history of trade embargoes, neither Treasury nor Commerce has published any regulations making it clear what the exact meaning of this requirement is or how it is to be carried out. As some authors have commented, "[t]hrough the plain language of the Act, the United States is taking upon itself the authority to monitor delivery of medical care [in Cuba]. Carried to its logical extreme, authorities could follow shipments of medicines and medical supplies into the offices of physicians, hospitals and clinics to observe their actual use."[21]

Of the copies of the OFAC licenses that we obtained, three were able to satisfy the on-site verification requirements by making special arrangements with U.N. agencies, three with the Belgian embassy in Cuba and one with the assistance of the Red Cross. Pharmaceutical company representatives interviewed indicated that the U.S. licensing agencies offer no guidance to them in interpreting the on-site verification requirement. Further, the ad hoc arrangements with the above-listed bodies were made out of humanitarian concern but were not satisfactory to those involved since international agencies and foreign embassies do not want to get involved in carrying out actions on behalf of the U.S. government or to appear to approve of U.S. policies under the CDA.

Clearly, the lack of clarity in the term "on-site inspection," its political offensiveness to the Cuban government and its undesirability to those bodies which may be able to assist in carrying out the inspection all serve as a strong deterrent to pharmaceutical companies interested in selling medicine to Cuba.

THE REAL INTENT OF THE CDA'S RESTRICTIONS ON MEDICINES

The inclusion of medicines in an economic embargo violates international law principles on numerous grounds, which are discussed below. In general, the international community has declared that the embargo of medicines is incompatible with fundamental human rights guarantees and can only serve to cause needless suffering among the civilian population of the target states. Nevertheless, despite international outcry, including four U.N. resolutions denouncing the embargo, the U.S. has continued to effectively prohibit sales of medicines to Cuba.

An examination of the intent of the key architects of the CDA reveals a desire to dismantle the Cuban health care system. While the creation of its world-class medical capabilities has been called the "prize of the revolution" and Cuba's leaders have been noted as viewing "health indicators as measures of government efficacy,"[22] Cuba's advances in medical care have caused Castro's critics to view the system as a political target which must be destroyed. During a speech in South Florida in 1995, Richard Nuccio,[23] then Special Advisor to the President on Cuba stated: "During the heyday of its $6 billion annual subsidies from the Soviet Union, the Cuban regime was able to establish a completely government-run, command economy, and provide free, universal education and health care. The Government, then, was the only

---

21. Anthony F. Kirkpatrick, M.D., Ph.D., et al., *The Time Has Come to Lift the Economic Embargo Against Cuba*, 81 J. Fla. Med. Ass'n 681 (1994).

22. Julie Feinsilver, Healing the Masses: Cuban Health Politics at Home and Abroad 1 (1993).

23. During the same 1995 address, Nuccio, one of the drafters of the CDA, stated, "Immodestly, I believe that the most effective role for the United States in promoting a democratic transition in Cuba is outlined in the Cuban Democracy Act, legislation I helped draft as an advisor to Congressman Bob Torricelli in 1992 and which President Clinton endorsed when he was still a candidate for office."

source of everything for the individual, from his job to his home to medicine for his family."[24]

The United States' contempt for the accomplishments of the Castro government in creating a viable, universal health care system is clear. The inclusion of medicines in the embargo, which has had devastating effects in Cuba, has been coupled with an increase in support for humanitarian donations of medicine. In explaining how the CDA has cut off trade with Cuba, CDA supporters are usually quick to point out that the amount of donations to Cuba from groups within the U.S. has increased. Richard Nuccio has commented: "Since the enactment of the CDA three years ago, the U.S. government has licensed over $90 million in private humanitarian aid to Cuba, mostly food and medicine from nongovernmental groups in the U.S. distributed through nongovernmental organizations on the island.[25]

No nation, however, can provide adequate medical care for its population through reliance on donations. The quantity of U.S.-donated medical supplies to Cuba falls far below the need of Cuba's residents. Further, the instability and unpredictability of products donated make it impossible for doctors to properly manage the treatment of certain patients, such as diabetics whose treatment necessitates precise potencies of insulin or other medicine.

THE UNITED STATES' ROLE AS LEADER IN WORLD PHARMACEUTICAL DEVELOPMENT AND ITS IMPACT ON CUBA

U.S. pharmaceutical corporations' large-scale acquisitions of foreign drug companies, which are taking place at an unprecedented rate, are worsening Cuba's inability to obtain critical pharmaceuticals and medical equipment. These acquisitions trigger a broadening of the reach of U.S. patent protection and the 1992 Cuban Democracy Act's preemptive embargo provisions.

Cuba's ongoing shortage of certain medical materials is linked to the much-heralded globalization of the world economy. Yet in terms of Cuba's access to world-class drugs and high-end medical technology, such globalization is less a result of neighborly cooperation than it is a byproduct of U.S. pharmaceutical companies' mergers and acquisitions and the resulting international reach of U.S. patent and trade law.

For Cuba, pharmaceutical megamergers and the correspondingly broadened scope of U.S. patent law provisions combine with the 1992 Cuban Democracy Act to place top-tier, often unique, medical products out of Cubans' reach. The results are obvious: critical shortages of even the most basic medicines and medical hardware and a serious threat to ordinary Cuban citizens' health and medical care.

Analyzing just how Cuba's medical supply crisis stems from the interrelationship between U.S. patent law, the Cuban Democracy Act, and pharmaceutical industry mergers requires a brief overview.

U.S. Patent Law: An Overview

U.S. patent law, codified by the 1952 Patent Act (the Act),[26] provides this country's highest level of intellectual property protection. It grants the patentee and his or her successors in title[27] a 17-year exclusive right over a patented invention's or process's[28] manufacture, use, and sale.[29] The Act also bars nonpatentees from actively inducing patent infringement;[30] engaging in contributory infringement;[31] selling es-

---

24. Richard A. Nuccio, Prospects for a Peaceful, Democratic Transition in Cuba: A U.S. Perspective, Remarks to the West Point Society of South Florida (Sept. 8, 1995) [hereinafter Nuccio].

25. *Id.*

26. 35 U.S.C. §§ 1-376 (1952).

27. *Id.* at § 100 (d).

28. *See id.* at § 100 (a), (b).

29. *Id.* at § 271 (a).

30. *Id.* at § 271 (b).

31. *Id.* at § 271 (c).

sential components to induce foreign production of a patented invention;[32] and importing into the United States, or selling or using within this country, any product created through a patented process.[33]

In the pharmaceutical arena, an ingenious chemical composition devised to produce a salutary medical result would be patentable, as would the process or processes invented to created such composition.[34] The underlying chemicals themselves may or may not be patentable: man-made chemicals contained in the composition might receive patents, while naturally occurring substances such as oxygen could not.

Of course, different people may hold the respective patents involved in pharmaceuticals. Theoretically, a lone scientist could hold a patent for the process by which a drug is created. Someone else may hold the patent on the drug's actual composition, while a third person may hold a patent for an improved version of the drug's production process, use, or composition.

Drug patents are valid for 17 years. Yet drug manufacturers must get FDA approval after patent issuance and before full-scale marketing. Because FDA approval can take seven to ten years, a manufacturer may only have ten to seven years left on the patent term. Driven to recoup investments and realize maximum profits, the manufacturer must adjust supplies and prices accordingly to compensate for the marketing and sales opportunities lost to the shortening of the patent's useful life. To address this, Congress used Patent Act § 156 to permit patent term extensions for certain products requiring FDA approval before sale.[35]

The Megamerger Trend among U.S. and Foreign Pharmaceutical Companies

Worldwide mergers among large-scale pharmaceutical companies, particularly between U.S. and foreign corporations, make first-rate drugs and medical technology progressively less accessible to Cuba's needy population. U.S. drug companies' acquisitions of foreign counterparts extend the reach of U.S. patent protection and bring acquired companies under the CDA's discouraging, time-consuming, and often bewildering licensing requirements.

In medicine, time is critical where lives are at stake. For Cuba's medical establishment, such precious time is lost trying to identify a shrinking number of sources for alternatives to the drugs and technology made increasingly out of reach due to megamergers that only lengthen the shadow cast by U.S. patent protection and CDA restrictions.

The past few years have witnessed large-scale pharmaceutical industry mergers and acquisitions. These include drug company purchases of competitors as well as strategic pharmaceutical buys of key drug distributors.

- In 1993, for example, Merck & Co., an industry giant, acquired distributor Medco Containment Services, Inc.[36]

- On May 2, 1994, Roche Holding Ltd., another main industry player, agreed to pay $5.3 billion for Syntex Corp., a commercial counterpart.[37] Just four years earlier, Roche purchased 60% of Genentech, Inc., a leading biotechnology concern.[38] Around the time of the Syntex acquisition, SmithKline Beecham PLC outlined an agreement to buy distributor Diversified Phar-

---

32. *Id.* at § 271 (f).

33. *Id.* at § 271 (g).

34. This assumes the Patent and Trademark Office determines that the product or process meets the statutory standards for novelty, utility, nonobviousness, and originality.

35. R. Dreyfuss & R. Kwall, Intellectual Property 247 (Foundation Press 1994); *see also* 35 U.S.C., *supra* note 26, at § 156.

36. Joseph Weber et al., *Drug-Merger Mania*, Bus. Wk., May 16, 1994 [hereinafter *Drug-Merger Mania*].

37. *Id.*

38. *Id.*

maceutical Services, Inc. for $2.3 billion "and to ally with Diversified's parent, powerhouse health maintenance organization United HealthCare Corp."[39]

- In 1995, Upjohn Co. and Swedish firm Pharmacia, two respected pharmaceutical entities, engaged in a 7 billion-dollar stock-swap merger.[40]

- That same year, Britain's Glaxo Holdings PLC paid $14 billion for Burroughs Wellcome, and Hoechst acquired Marion Merrell Dow for $7.1 billion.[41]

- In February 1996, Johnson & Johnson acquired cardio-technology manufacturer Cordis Corp. for $1.8 billion.[42]

- Finally, St. Jude Medical, Inc., looked forward to a 1996 finalized acquisition of Daig Corporation and Cyberonics, Inc., companies that will "provide St. Jude Medical entry into two additional therapeutic markets—interventional cardiology and interventional neurology."[43]

- Early in 1996, speculation regarding future acquisitions included Bristol-Myers Squibb Co. and Eli Lilly & Co. as possible buyers of such companies as Searle & Co. and Warner-Lambert Co.[44]

Industry mergers and acquisitions are radically reshaping the medical product landscape "as giant multinational producers search for new products and wider distribution."[45] In time, "the way pharmaceuticals are invented, made, and sold will bear little resemblance to the methods of a decade ago."[46] While industry consolidation will slow in pace, "the merger trend among drug companies ... [is not] over. ... [C]ombinations ... [will] continue until only 10 or 15 giants are left."[47]

U.S. pharmaceutical companies are rapidly growing in their percentages of global market share. For example, Merck, one of the industry's largest members, "controls about 5% of the worldwide market."[48] Glaxo Wellcome, the largest pharmaceutical manufacturer formed by the merger of Glaxo Holdings and Burroughs Wellcome, held 6% of the world market as of January 1996.[49] Yet during 1975-1989, 47 of 97 world-class drugs originated in the United States.[50] And in 1994 alone, U.S. patents accounted for 78%—109 out of 140—of "new genetic engineering patents for health-care products issued by the U.S. Patent and Trademark Office."[51]

U.S. pharmaceutical megamergers give U.S. corporations and their exclusive patents greater control of global market share. Roche's acquisitions, for example, "will give ... [the company] a broader product line to sell [to] big customers in the U.S."[52] and pre-

39. *Id.*

40. Joseph Weber, *Robust and Ready to Brawl*, Bus. Wk., Jan. 8, 1996 [hereinafter *Robust and Ready to Brawl*].

41. *Id.*; *see also* Joan Warner & Heidi Dawley, *Drug Stocks to Watch in '96*, Bus. Wk., Jan. 22, 1996.

42. Richard Jacobson, Reuters, Apr. 16, 1996.

43. PRNewswire, Apr. 17, 1996.

44. *Robust and Ready to Brawl, supra* note 39.

45. *Drug-Merger Mania, supra* note 35.

46. *Id.*

47. Warner & Dawley, *supra* note 41.

48. *Drug-Merger Mania, supra* note 36.

49. Warner & Dawley, *supra* note 41.

50. Pharmaceutical Research and Manufacturers of America, World Class Drugs: Origin of 97 "Globalized" Drugs 1975-1989 (citing P. E. Barral, *Fifteen Years of Results of Pharmaceutical Research in the World*, Perspective et Santé Publique (Paris: 1985; updated 1990)).

51. Pharmaceutical Research and Manufacturers of America, 1994 Patent Analysis Results: U.S. Pharmaceutical Industry Continues Leadership in Biotechnology Research (Mar. 1995).

52. *Drug-Merger Mania, supra* note 36.

sumably abroad. Johnson & Johnson's purchase of Cordis has already yielded J&J "about one-third of the worldwide market for heart intervention products."[53]

To secure global market control and increase revenue, "the big [pharmaceutical] producers are scrambling to build market share by selling more products. To fight the growing might of [pharmaceutical] distributors, they're buying the distributors."[54] The acquisition of distributors will eliminate "the middlemen that have forced ... [drug companies' profit] margins down."[55] That will affect pricing, market distribution, gross sales, and even health-care plan administration, including insured individuals' drug choices.[56]

Joining Forces: Megamergers, U.S. Patents, and the CDA

Megamergers mean the global marketplace features fewer, bigger, and more powerful providers of world-class drugs and technology. Fewer competitors may mean higher prices, less consumer freedom of choice, and less industry scrutiny or accountability. More importantly, because many of these commercial titans are U.S. companies, the extraterritorial reach of U.S. patent protection and CDA trade restrictions removes the best medicines and medical equipment from Cuba's reach.

The reasons are clear: as foreign pharmaceutical firms and distributors become part of U.S. entities, they fall under the Cuban Democracy Act's burdensome licensing provisions. Prospective acquisition targets thus face a difficult choice. They can pursue sales contracts with Cuba and forgo a potentially lucrative merger with a U.S. company, or they can complete a merger and sever possibly profitable ties with Cuba. Once acquired by a U.S. firm, the foreign, formerly independent corporation must avoid, cancel, or decline to renew commercial sales contracts with Cuba. Megamergers are therefore quickly shutting off Cuba's access to non-U.S. sources of important drugs and medical technology.

As importantly, acquired companies are likely to work with the patented drugs and technology of their U.S. parent company. Respecting the parent company's U.S. patents would mean not competing with or illicitly pirating such patents. Additionally, powerful U.S. pharmaceutical companies, made even larger through mergers and acquisitions, would have the resources to seek patent protection in as many countries as possible. Because U.S.-patented items fall under the Cuban Democracy Act's licensing provisions, the effect is to cut Cuba off—company by acquired company—from its non-U.S. medical suppliers.

Goods under exclusive U.S. patents are only available from U.S.-owned or -controlled sources and thus are inaccessible to Cuba. Alternative, parallel products available from third countries are often inferior or (in the case of drugs) inflict undesirable side effects.[57] Finally, because some Cuban medical professionals deem other countries' pharmaceutical testing standards to be lower than those of the U.S. Food and Drug Administration, Cuban doctors have less confidence in the quality, safety, and effectiveness of third-country drugs and other goods.[58]

Lack of drugs of guaranteed reliability may ultimately degrade patient care and damage the Cuban medi-

---

53. Jacobson, *supra* note 42.

54. *Drug-Merger Mania, supra* note 36.

55. *Id.*

56. *Id.*

57. Aff. of Anthony F. Kirkpatrick, M.D., Ph.D., at 2-3, 4, 8, in Anthony F. Kirkpatrick, M.D., Ph.D., Adverse Effects of the U.S. Economic Embargo on the Health of Cuba's Children (Feb. 3, 1995) (presented before the Inter-Am. C.H.R.); *see also* Emergency Petition Requesting a Declaration that the U.S. Trade Embargo against Cuba Has Resulted in a Medical Crisis in Cuba and Requesting a Declaration that Said Embargo Violates International Human Rights Laws 6-7 (Oct. 4, 1994) (filed with the Inter-Am. C.H.R.); interview with Senovio González de León, Director of Public Relations, Hospital Nacional Hermanos Ameijeiras, Centro Habana, Havana, Cuba (Mar. 27, 1995).

58. Interview with Senovio González de León, *supra* note 57.

cal system's world-renowned reputation. It may also erode Cuban citizens' faith in the adequacy of their country's health care, prompting both ill and healthy Cubans to forgo preventive and diagnostic care by shying away from a medical system the competence of which they may have come to doubt.[59]

With fewer options and sources for the best medical goods, Cuba must resort to non-U.S. products, whether under foreign patents or pirated abroad. Resorting to pirated products (inexpensive copies of patented drugs, produced without patentees' permission), however, would only compromise already strained political relations between the United States and Cuba, making political and economic rapprochement less likely.

INTERNATIONAL LAW RAMIFICATIONS OF THE CUBAN DEMOCRACY ACT

Extraterritoriality

Since its enactment in 1992, the CDA has provoked an outpouring of protests from various nations around the world as well as official denouncements by international and regional bodies such as the United Nations and the Organization of American States. The objections of many major U.S. trading partners have been made known through various demarches which criticize the extraterritorial aspects of the CDA, particularly those which place prohibitions on third-country ships from entering the U.S. within a six-month period of having docked in Cuba. These provisions, which seek to coerce and control the trade practices of other nations by penalizing them for continuing to do business with Cuba are an affront to the sovereign right of each nation to determine its own foreign commerce practices. On October 7, 1992, one day after Congress passed the CDA, the European Community made a formal demarche to the U.S. government warning that the law would be met with strong opposition and disapproval. The EC stated:

The European Community and its member states are seriously concerned about the reinforcement by the U.S. Congress of the trade embargo against Cuba. Furthermore, the Act's proposed sanctions for vessels that enter a port in Cuba would be in conflict with longstanding rules on comity and international law, and adversely affect international shipping as well as the European Community's trade with the United States. ... Although the EC is fully supportive of a peaceful transition to democracy in Cuba, it cannot accept that the U.S. unilaterally determines and restricts EC economic and commercial relations with any foreign nation which has not been collectively determined by the United Nations Security Council as a threat to peace or order in the world of nations.[60]

The Canadian government made similar complaints, stating that the extraterritorial aspects of the CDA are an affront to the sovereignty of Canada and other nations that have the right to determine their own policies with regard to Cuba.

When the CDA's extraterritorial provisions went into effect in 1992, it signaled a reversal of the United States' earlier-stated policy that it would not seek to penalize third-country trade relations with Cuba. In fact, the inclusion once again of third-country penalties in the embargo against Cuba specifically contradicted actions taken by the United States in 1975 when the government acknowledged the impropriety of such provisions and removed them from earlier laws setting forth the terms of the embargo against Cuba.

In 1962, the Organization of American States adopted stringent resolutions mandating that all member states cut diplomatic ties with Cuba. The OAS also imposed a collective embargo against Cuba at that time. In 1962, the terms of the U.S. embargo against Cuba, the strongest of any of the nations in the hemisphere, included sanctions against other nations which continued to deal with Cuba, similar to those

---

59. *Id.*

60. European Community Press Release (Oct. 8, 1995), *reprinted in* United States Economic Measures Against Cuba: Proceedings in the United Nations and International Law Issues 195 (Michael Krinsky & David Golove eds., 1993) [hereinafter United States Economic Measures Against Cuba].

found in the CDA today which prohibit the entry into the United States of vessels having visited Cuba.

By 1975, a change in sentiment had taken place within the OAS as various member states asserted their right to determine their own polices with Cuba and some reestablished relations with the island nation. On July 29, 1975, the OAS adopted a resolution rescinding its mandatory embargo on Cuba. Based on the principle of nonintervention, a fundamental cornerstone of the OAS which is mentioned throughout the organization's Charter, the regional body called on each member state to freely determine its own policies with regard to trade and other relations with Cuba.[61]

In direct response to the 1975 OAS resolution, the U.S. modified its policies, removing those provisions of U.S. law which sought to penalize or control third countries' relations with Cuba. In a September 1975 official State Department Bulletin, the U.S. announced:

> In keeping with the action by the OAS, the United States is modifying the aspects of our Cuban denial policy which affect other countries. Effective today, August 21, 1975, it will be U.S. policy to grant licenses permitting transactions between U.S. subsidiaries and Cuba for trade in foreign-made goods when those subsidiaries are operating in countries where local law or policy favors trade with Cuba ... In order to conform further with the OAS action, we are taking appropriate steps so that effective immediately countries which allow their ships or aircraft to carry goods to and from Cuba are not penalized by loss of U.S. bilateral assistance. We are initiating steps to modify regulations which deny bunkering in the United States to third-country ships engaged in the Cuba Trade.[62]

Echoing this recognition of the inappropriateness of third-country penalties, William Rogers, then Assistant Secretary for Inter-American Affairs, testified be-

fore the U.S. Congress as to why the third-country constraints were being lifted:

> As a logical and practical corollary to the termination of mandatory OAS sanctions, the U.S. government, on August 21, announced modifications of those aspects of our Cuban denial policy which affect other countries ... This was basically a measure to remove a recurrent source of friction between the United States and friendly countries both in this hemisphere and overseas which, for reasons of their own, have engaged in or never ceased to trade with Cuba.[63]

The CDA restored the third-country constraint provisions in 1992 which had been specifically denounced by the U.S. government in 1975 as unacceptable to other nations and incompatible with the 1975 OAS resolution affirming the right of each member state to freely determine its own polices toward Cuba. The current U.S.-imposed embargo which punishes those who trade with Cuba patently violates the OAS resolution and runs counter to the OAS Charter, which upholds nonintervention as one of the fundamental principles upon which the organization is founded.

In addition to the individual protests of foreign trading partners prompted by the CDA's passage, the law has also brought about formal denouncements from the United Nations. In four consecutive sessions of the United Nations General Assembly, that body has passed resolutions condemning the U.S. embargo against Cuba and calling on the United States to rescind those aspects of its law which are violative of international law principles as well as of the U.N. Charter. In a resolution passed on November 15, 1995, entitled "Necessity of ending the economic, commercial and financial embargo imposed by the United States of America against Cuba," the U.N. General Assembly held, inter alia:

---

61. *See* Final Act, Sixteenth Meeting of Consultation of Ministers of Foreign Affairs, Serving as Organ of Consultation in Application of the Inter-American Treaty of Reciprocal Assistance, July 29, 1975, OEA/Ser.F/II.Doc.9/75, Rev. 2 (1975).

62. Dep't St. Bull., Sept. 15, 1975, at 404, *reprinted in* United States Economic Measures Against Cuba, *supra* note 60, at 215.

63. *U.S. Trade Embargo of Cuba: Hearings Before the Subcomm. on Int'l Trade & Com. & Int'l Organizations of House Comm. on Int'l Rel.*, 94th Cong., 1st Sess. 360 (1975), *quoted in* United States Economic Measures Against Cuba, *supra* note 60, at 217, 218.

Reaffirming, among other principles, the sovereign equality of States, non-intervention and non-interference in their internal affairs and freedom of international trade and navigation, which are also enshrined in many international legal instruments ...

Concerned about the continued promulgation and application by Member States of laws and regulations whose extraterritorial effects affect the sovereignty of other States and the legitimate interests of entities or persons under their jurisdiction, as well as the freedom of trade and navigation ...

Concerned that, since the adoption of its resolutions 47/19, 48/16 and 49/9[64] further measures of that nature aimed at strengthening and extending the economic, commercial and financial embargo against Cuba continue to be promulgated and applied, and concerned also about the adverse effects of such measures on the Cuban people and on Cuban nationals living in other countries ...

[The U.N. General Assembly] reiterates its call to all States to refrain from promulgating and applying laws and measures of the kind referred to in the preamble to the present resolution in conformity with their obligations under the Charter of the United Nations and international law which, inter alia, reaffirm the freedom of trade and navigation ..."[65]

Notwithstanding repeated U.N. resolutions calling for the rescinding of practices against Cuba and against nations that trade with Cuba which violate international law, the U.S. has defiantly maintained and even reinforced its policies.

International Law Violations Precipitated by the U.S. Embargo on Sales of Medicines to Cuba

The Cuban Democracy Act of 1992 violates the Charter of the Organization of American States (hereinafter "the OAS Charter" or "the Charter") by imposing a ban in fact (though not in law) on the sale (and, under some circumstances, the nonhumanitarian donation) of food, medicines, and medically related materials.

Extraterritoriality of Human Rights Obligations in the Americas: The OAS Charter's language and history imply an intent to create a regional, extraterritorial human rights system for the Americas. Drafted in the spirit "of American solidarity and good neighborliness,"[66] the OAS Charter aspires to forge a hemispheric, American "order of peace and justice"[67] that promotes solidarity and collaboration and that defends American states' "sovereignty, ... territorial integrity, ... and independence."[68] Understood more broadly, the Charter establishes an inter-American, hemispheric matrix of reciprocal human rights obligations protecting people from rights violations by their own or another American government.

It should hardly be news that the Americas intentionally established such a hemispheric web of reciprocal rights and duties for international protection of human rights. In fact, the records of international discussion culminating in the Charter show that human rights and regional responsibility have always been central to the inter-American sensibility. The Charter's history reveals that an intent to create a regional rights system has "been manifest since the very origin of the inter-American system. The Treaty of Perpetual Union, League and Confederation ... [a Charter precursor] ... recognized the principle of juridical equality of nationals of a state and foreigners."[69]

---

64. These numbers refer to the three previous resolutions passed by the U.N. General Assembly calling for the elimination of policies against Cuba which violate these principles.

65. G.A. Res. , U.N. GAOR, U.N. Doc. A/RES/50/10 (1995).

66. Charter of the Organization of American States, May 2, 1948, U.S.T. 2, Doc. 2394, T.I.A.S. no. 2361 (1948); U.S.T. 21, Doc. 607, T.I.A.S. no. 6847 (*as amended* 1970) (at introductory text).

67. *Id.* at art. 1; *see also id.* at art. 29, which seeks a hemispheric approach to rights ("The Member States, inspired by the principles of inter-American solidarity and co-operation, pledge themselves to a united effort to ensure social justice in the Hemisphere and dynamic and balanced economic development for their peoples.").

68. *Id.* at art. 1.

69. Thomas Buergenthal et al., Protecting Human Rights in the Americas: Selected Problems 2 (N. P. Engel 1982).

While this speaks directly to equal treatment for foreigners and citizens living in the same country, it seems clear that the Charter's evolution involved the application of the same protection to peoples living in *different* (i.e., their respective) countries. Deliberations leading to the OAS Charter's creation suggest the creators envisioned extraterritorial human rights obligations that would hold nations accountable for those of their actions that violated the human rights of member states' citizens. Under this interpretation, a member state would therefore violate the spirit of the Charter and the inter-American system's codified norms if that state's law and/or administrative actions conflicted with "the exercise or enjoyment of rights protected by the [inter-American] system."[70]

Bound by the OAS Charter: A full-fledged OAS Member State, the United States is bound to the spirit and word of the Charter. Obligated to adhere to Charter standards "in good faith,"[71] the United States should "not invoke the provisions of its internal law as justification for its failure to perform a treaty."[72]

As importantly, U.S. obligations under the Charter apply to Cuba. Contentions that Cuba's nebulous status within the OAS obviates the United States' international law duties toward Cuba under the Charter are arguably unsound. Though the OAS excluded Cuba from the organization in 1962[73] and directed member states to sever diplomatic and commercial

ties to the island,[74] the OAS later withdrew these sanctions and left "to each member state the right to determine its diplomatic and trade relations with Cuba."[75] Most importantly, the OAS, through the Inter-American Commission on Human Rights, recognizes the "Cuban State [rather than the Government of Cuba] ... [as] ... a party to ... the Charter of the Organization of American States."[76] Asserting that "Government and State are two juridical and institutionally differentiable concepts,"[77] the Commission has unequivocally stated that "[i]t was the Cuban Government—not the State—that was excluded from the inter-American system"[78] in 1962 and that such exclusion "was not [intended] to leave the Cuban people unprotected."[79] Thus the United States' human rights obligations within the inter-American system apply to Cuba.

Violating OAS Charter Provisions: By denying Cuba access to critical medical supplies, the Cuban Democracy Act directly endangers Cuban lives, denies Cubans' right to protection of life, and cripples the Cuban government's ability to meet the international human rights obligations it owes its people. The Act therefore violates the OAS Charter's spirit and purpose.

The Cuban Democracy Act violates the OAS Charter's prohibition on the use of "coercive measures ... to force the sovereign will of another State and obtain from it advantages of any kind."[80] Yet the CDA

---

70. *Id.* at 28.

71. Vienna Convention on the Law of Treaties, May 23, 1969, U.N. Doc. A/CONF. 39/27, art. 26.

72. *Id.* at art. 27.

73. Final Act, Eighth Meeting of Consultation of Ministers of Foreign Affairs, Serving as Organ of Consultation in Application of the Inter-American Treaty of Reciprocal Assistance, Punta del Este, Uruguay, January 22-31, 1962, OEA/ser. C/II.8 (1962).

74. Final Act, Ninth Meeting of Consultation of Ministers of Foreign Affairs, Serving as Organ of Consultation in Application of the Inter-American Treaty of Reciprocal Assistance, OEA/ser. C/II.9, doc. 48 rev. 2 (1964).

75. United States Economic Measures Against Cuba, *supra* note 59, at 213, *citing* Final Act, Sixteenth Meeting of Consultation of Ministers of Foreign Affairs, Serving as Organ of Consultation in Application of the Inter-American Treaty of Reciprocal Assistance, July 29, 1975, OEA/ser. F/II., doc. 9/75 rev. 2 (1975).

76. Inter-Am. C.H.R. 671, OEA/ser. L/V/II.95, doc. 7 rev. (1997) [hereinafter Inter-Am. C.H.R.].

77. *Id.* at 672.

78. *Id.* at 673.

79. Id.

80. Charter of the Organization of American States, *supra* note 65, at art. 19.

arguably violates other pertinent Charter provisions as well. These provisions are worded broadly enough to suggest that Charter obligations apply when one state's acts adversely affect another state and/or its people.

OAS Charter Article 10, for example, states that "[e]very American State has the duty to respect the rights enjoyed by every other State[81] in accordance with international law."[82] Article 11 asserts that "[t]he fundamental rights of States may not be impaired in any manner whatsoever."[83] Finally, Article 14 claims that "[t]he right of each State to protect itself and to live its own life does not authorize it to commit unjust acts against another State."[84] Article 16 proclaims each state's "right to develop its cultural, political, and economic life freely and naturally."[85]

The Cuban Democracy Act violates these provisions individually and as they interrelate. The Act impairs (Article 11)—indeed, denies respect for (Article 10)—Cuban citizens' peremptory rights to life and health by denying them critical pharmaceuticals and equipment *solely* available from the United States. The CDA also violates Cuba's Article 16 "right to develop its ... economic life freely and naturally"[86] by closing off Cuba's access to U.S. and U.S. subsidiaries' products, alternatives to which either do not exist or are prohibitively expensive to procure. Foodstuffs, medicines, and medically related materials and equipment are just some of commodities denied Cuba. Without them, and without items from countries fearful of damaging their *own* commercial ties with the United States, Cuba can hardly enjoy "free and natural" economic development. Nor can it realize its Article 14 right "to live its own life"[87] unimpaired "in any manner whatsoever."[88] Under these conditions, Cuba cannot meet its duty to guarantee its citizens' *jus cogens*[89] *rights to life and health. In its impact, therefore, the CDA represents an "unjust act[] against another State"*[90] in direct violation of Article 14.

Article 18 denies any state "the right to intervene, directly or indirectly, ... in the internal or external affairs"[91] of another state. This prohibition applies to *any* form of interference against another State. Article 19 prohibits "the use of coercive measures of an economic or political character ... to force"[92] another state's "sovereign will."[93] Finally, Article 20 confirms that "[t]he territory of a State is inviolable"[94] and that such territory cannot be the object of direct or indirect force.[95]

---

81. Given the Inter-American Commission's statements regarding the Cuban State's inclusion in the inter-American system and its status as a party to the OAS Charter, Cuba qualifies as a "state" for Charter purposes and thus participates in the Charter's system of reciprocal rights and duties; *see* Inter-Am. C.H.R., *supra* note 75, at 671-673.

82. Charter of the Organization of American States, *supra* note 65, at art. 10.

83. *Id.* at art. 11.

84. *Id.* at art. 14.

85. *Id.* at art. 16.

86. Id.

87. Charter of the Organization of American States, *supra* note 65, at art. 14.

88. *Id.* at art. 11.

89. According to the Restatement (Third) of the Foreign Relations Law of the United States, *jus cogens* norms are "rules of international law ... recognized by the international community of states as peremptory, permitting no derogation. These rules prevail over and invalidate international agreements and other rules of international law in conflict with them." See Restatement (Third) of the Foreign Relations Law of the United States sec. 102 cmt. k (1986).

90. Charter of the Organization of American States, *supra* note 65, at art. 14.

91. *Id.* at art. 18.

92. *Id.* at art. 19.

93. Id.

94. *Id.* at art. 20.

95. Id.

The CDA provisions effect both direct and indirect intervention in Cuba's internal affairs. The law is an economically coercive measure designed to force Cuba to "move toward democratization and greater respect for human rights."[96] No one doubts the Castro regime's historic brutality and denial of human rights. But legislatively endangering innocent lives represents a violative force that hardly jibes with the CDA's stated goal of promoting "a resumption of economic growth in Cuba through ... support for the Cuban people."[97]

Affirmatively neglecting the human rights of another state's people seems a curious way to "vigorously ... oppose the human rights violations of the Castro regime."[98]

The Humanitarian Exception of All Embargoes

The use of economic embargoes as a political sanction is not new. However, over the course of time, various standards have come to be recognized by the international community as to what is the proper scope of a permissible embargo. In short, international practice has come to include an exception for medicines, medical supplies and certain basic foodstuffs in any embargo in order to prevent unnecessary suffering among civilian populations.

Humanitarian exceptions permitting the free flow of medicines and food were features of multilateral embargoes imposed against North Korea, Vietnam, South Africa, Chile, El Salvador, the Soviet Union and Haiti. In the recent U.N.-supported embargoes against Iraq and the territories of the former Yugoslavia, the U.N. upheld the principle that food and medicines must be allowed through in order to serve the basic needs of the civilian population. In the case of Iraq, a special Sanctions Committee was established within the U.N. to ensure that shipments of food and medicines were permitted to get through to Iraqi civilians. In explaining the rationale for allowing these exceptions to the embargo, U.N. Security Council officials stated that it is internationally "unacceptable to cause wide-spread suffering among civilians through impeding the shipment of food and medicines" in order to punish a country's leaders.[99]

In addition to the U.N. General Assembly resolutions denouncing the U.S. embargo against Cuba for its extraterritorial aspects, the United Nations Commission on Human Rights has decried the embargo for its direct impact on the human rights of Cuban citizens who are harmed by its restrictions on food and medicine shipments. In Resolution 1994/47 entitled "Human Rights and Unilateral Coercive Economic Measures," the U.N. Commission on Human Rights particularly singled out the practice of large, developed nations such as the United States in targeting smaller, less-developed nations for unilateral embargoes. The U.N. Commission stated that such unilateral coercive measures against developing countries are in "clear contradiction of international law" and that "such unilateral coercive economic measures create obstacles to trade relations among States, adversely affect the socio-humanitarian activities of developing countries, and hinder the full realization of human rights by the people subject to those measures."

It should be noted that the purposeful impeding of food and medicines to civilians in time of war is expressly prohibited under customary international law and is codified in the Geneva Conventions. If international law requires a humanitarian exception for food and medicine even in times of war, then certainly the U.S. must achieve the same result in times of peace. Through the CDA, the U.S. creates a de facto blockade of Cuba which prevents the country's civilian population from obtaining adequate medicines, medical supplies and foodstuffs.

---

96. Cuban Democracy Act of 1992, *supra* note 2, at § 1703 (6).

97. *Id.* at § 1703 (1).

98. Cuban Democracy Act of 1992, *supra* note 2, at § 1703 (5).

99. *United Nations Eases Rules on Food and Fuel for Iraqis*, N.Y. Times, Mar. 23, 1991.

The Geneva Convention,[100] to which some 165 countries including the United States are parties, requires "free passage" of all medical supplies intended for civilians.[101] This duty is placed on states even in times of war. Surely the recognition of the fundamental human right to medicines must be applied with equal diligence and vigor in the arena of peacetime international relations and trade sanctions. U.S. restrictions on sales by U.S. companies and their subsidiaries of medicines to Cuba and the penalties against third countries who continue to trade with Cuba (including through the sale of medicines) serve to severely restrict the flow of medicines to Cuba's civilian population.

Lastly, it should be noted that the 1962 multilateral embargo against Cuba, mandated by the OAS at the height of tensions with that nation, allowed for the sale of medicines to Cuba, noting that such a humanitarian exception is mandated by international law and practice. Indeed, the OAS's Inter-American Commission on Human Rights, in a February 1995 letter to the United States with regard to the de facto embargo on the sale of medicines to Cuba, stated:

> [The Inter-American Commission on Human Rights] requests that the United States of America

faithfully observe the traditional exemption from an embargo under customary international law, of medicine, medical supplies and basic food items, for humanitarian reasons.

The Commission further stated:

> [I]t is aware that the Cuban Democracy Act contains such exemptions, however the Inter-American Commission Human Rights has been informed that the bureaucratic and other requirements which have to be met in relation to those exemptions [i.e. on-site verification] render them virtually unattainable. Accordingly, the Inter-American Commission on Human Rights requests that the United States of America put in place mechanisms to ensure that the necessary steps are taken for exemption from the trade embargo in respect of medicine, medical supplies and basic food items, capable of effective and speedy implementation.[102]

As it has ignored the resolutions of the U.N. General Assembly and the U.N. Commission on Human Rights calling for an end to the embargo against Cuba, so also has the U.S. ignored the pleas of the Organization of American States. The United States' de facto embargo on medicines remains in place unabated.

---

100. Convention Relative to the Protection of Civilian Persons in Time of War, Geneva Convention, No. IV, Aug. 12, 1949, Int'l Comm. of the Red Cross.

101. *Id.* at art. XXIII.

102. The Commission sent a copy of this letter to the petitioners as a means of notifying them that the letter had been sent to the U.S. Department of State.

RENAISSSANCE AND DECAY: A COMPARISON OF SOCIOECONOMIC INDICATORS IN PRE-CASTRO AND CURRENT-DAY CUBA[1]

Kirby Smith and Hugo Llorens

"The choice is between capitalism and chaos."

— Ludwig von Mises

An enduring myth is that Cuba in the 1950s was a socially and economically backward country whose development, especially in the areas of health and education, was made possible by the socialist nature of the Castro government. Despite the widespread acceptance of this view, readily available data show that Cuba was already a relatively well-advanced country in 1958, certainly by Latin American standards, and in some cases by world standards. The data show that Cuba has at best maintained what were already high levels of development in health and education, but that in other areas, Cubans have borne extraordinary costs as a result of Castro-style totalitarianism and misguided economic policies. Indeed, with the possible exception of health and education, Cuba's relative position among Latin American countries is lower today than in it was in 1958 for virtually every socioeconomic measure for which reliable data are available.

SOURCES AND ANALYTICAL APPROACH

This paper draws a comparison between the socioeconomic development of Cuba prior to Castro's taking power and the Cuba of today, after 40 years of revolutionary socialist government, and compares Cuba's development in each of these periods with that of all other countries in Latin America for which data are available.[2] We have relied most extensively on United Nations (UN) data, particularly from the *Statistical Yearbook* and *Demographic Yearbook*, which we consider among the most extensive data compendiums in the development field. Other trade and macroeconomic data are derived from the International Monetary Fund's *Direction of Trade Statistics*, which provides a consistent data series dating back to the pre-revolutionary period.

For the various international comparisons and rankings given below, only those countries acquiring independence prior to 1958 and having relatively consistent data available for the period 1955-present have been included. The former stipulation excludes many highly developed Caribbean countries from consideration. In some cases, this noticeably affects our results. For example, The Bahamas, Guyana, and Barbados all would rank ahead of Argentina and Cuba as the most literate countries in Latin America and the Caribbean, according to the UN's latest *Statistical Yearbook* published in 1997 (pp. 85-86).

---

1.   A previous version of this paper was released by the State Department's Bureau of Inter-American Affairs (State 1998). The present version has been revised and expanded and as such, reflects only the personal views of the authors.

2.   For a study of the changes in Cuba's socioeconomic indicators relative to Chile, Costa Rica, and Mexico during the period 1920-1990, see Romeu (1995).

HEALTH CARE GAINS EXAGGERATED

The health care system is often touted by many observers as one of the Castro government's greatest achievements. One Latin American head of state, for example, recently called Cuba's health care system "spectacular," adding that Cuba "proved the dialectic truth that revolutions produce healthy children" (Cawthorne 1998). What this and other similar analyses ignore is that the revolutionary government inherited an already advanced health sector when it took power in 1959. In the early 1950s, a World Bank-organized mission declared that for a tropical country, Cuba enjoyed "remarkable freedom from disease" (1951, p. 4).

Indeed, the 25 years prior to Castro's takeover constituted a period of rapid growth in the number of healthcare facilities on the island. A 1977 article in the *Journal of the Florida Medical Association* (Navarro) lists 72 large hospitals operating in Cuba in 1958—double the number that existed just 25 years earlier—with more than 21,000 beds among them. These numbers exclude municipal centers, which provided emergency clinical and surgical assistance in large cities, and the 250 privately-run medical centers, most of which were structured on a "mutual aid" basis that gave patients access to medical and surgical care for less than five pesos per month. At least a half million Cubans were enrolled in such programs as of 1958. Including governmental, municipal, and private hospitals and clinics, Cuba had about 35,000 beds for 6.6 million inhabitants—an impressive one bed per every 190 inhabitants.

Cuba's infant mortality rate of 32 per 1,000 live births in 1957 was the lowest in Latin America and the 13th lowest in the world, according to UN data. Cuba ranked ahead of France, Belgium, West Germany, Israel, Japan, Austria, Italy, Spain, and Portugal, all of which would eventually overtake Cuba in this indicator during the following decades (UN 1979, pp. 67-188).

Today, Cuba remains the most advanced country in the region in this measure, but its world ranking has fallen from 13th to 25th during the Castro era, according to UN Data (1997b, pp. 93-100). Also missing from the conventional analysis of Cuba's infant

mortality rates is its staggering abortion rate—0.71 abortions per live birth in 1991, according to the latest UN data—which, because of selective termination of "high-risk" pregnancies, yields lower numbers for infant mortality. Cuba's abortion rate is at least twice the rate for the other countries listed in Table 1 for which data are available (UN 1997a, pp. 322-326, 369-370).

Table 1. World: Infant Mortality
(Deaths per 1,000 live births)

	1957	1990-95
Japan	40	4
Iceland	16	5
Sweden	18	5
Norway	21	5
Switzerland	23	5
Finland	28	5
Netherlands	18	6
Canada	31	6
Germany[a]	36	6
Luxembourg	39	6
Australia	21	7
United Kingdom	24	7
Ireland	33	7
France	34	7
Austria	44	7
Denmark	23	8
Belgium	36	8
Italy	50	8
Spain	53	8
New Zealand	24	9
United States	26	9
Israel	39	9
Greece	44	9
Portugal	88	9
Cuba	32	10

Source: UN 1979, pp. 67-188; UN 1997b, pp. 93-100.

a. For 1957, includes only the Federal Republic of Germany,

In terms of physicians and dentists per capita, Cuba ranked third in Latin America in 1957, behind only Uruguay and Argentina—both of which were more advanced than the United States in this measure. Cuba's 128 physicians and dentists per 100,000 people in 1957 placed Cuba at the same level as the Netherlands, and ahead of the United Kingdom (122 per 100,000 people) and Finland (96) (UN 1960, pp. 569-573; UN 1979, pp. 67-188). Unfortunately, the UN *Statistical Yearbook* no longer publishes these statistics, so more recent comparisons are not possible, but it is completely erroneous to characterize pre-revolutionary Cuba as backward in terms of healthcare.

LITERACY IMPROVES WITH THE REST OF LATIN AMERICA

Cuba has had one of the most literate populations in Latin America since well before the Castro revolution, when its literacy rate ranked fourth in the region (UN 1957, pp. 600-602). Its relatively advanced educational system produced a highly skilled workforce. The World Bank's *Report on Cuba* stated in 1951,

Cuba's people are intelligent, able and quick to absorb modern knowledge; her business men are shrewd and capable, her doctors and surgeons among the best in the world, her architects bold and imaginative. In other fields, many Cubans are already alert to modern methods and technology and there is no insurmountable obstacle to training as many more as may be required or, in the meanwhile, to obtaining technical advice from abroad. (p. 5)

One should not overstate pre-Castro Cuba's reliance on imported human capital, however. Baklanoff (1975, p. 25), citing U.S. government data, shows that fewer than one-fourth of the 2,000 supervisory, professional, and technical personnel employed by U.S. subsidiaries in 1957 were sent from the United States.

Since the 1950s, Cuba has increased its literacy rate from 76 to 96 percent, which today places it second only to Argentina among those 11 Latin American countries for which comparable 1950s UN data are available (UN 1957, pp. 600-602; UN 1997b, pp. 85-86).[3] This improvement is impressive, but not unique, among Latin American countries. Panama—which ranked just behind Cuba in this indicator during the 1950s—has matched Cuba's improvement when measured in percentage point terms. In fact, a review of the UN statistics below reveals that the

whole hemisphere has made enormous strides in literacy over the past 40 years (see Table 2). We will show that these other countries making significant progress in this area have done so with far less degradation to other measures of human welfare than socialist Cuba has.

Table 2. Latin America: Literacy Rates[a] *(Percent)*

	Latest avail. data for 1950-53	1995	Pct. pt increase
Argentina	87[b]	96	10
Cuba	76	96	19
Chile	81	95	15
Costa Rica	79	95	16
Paraguay	68	92	24
Colombia	62	91	30
Panama	72	91	19
Ecuador	56	90	34
Brazil	49	83	35
Dominican Republic	43	82	39
El Salvador	42	72	29
Guatemala	30	56	26
Haiti	11	45	34

Source: UN 1957, pp. 600-602; UN 1997b, pp. 85-86.

a. Data for 1950-53 are age 10 and over. Data for 1995 are age 15 and over, reflecting a change in common usage over this period.
b. 1947 data, the latest available, are for age 14 and over

Teaching children to read, of course, is but one aspect of primary and secondary education, albeit an important one. We suspect, however, that in other areas, Cuba's government-run schools fall short because of the strong ideological content present in the instruction and the lack of alternatives available to parents. The Cuban government forbids religious or private schools. Pope John Paul II, during his first mass in Cuba in January, strongly criticized the Cuban state's "substitution of the role of parents" in education. He noted that the state's boarding schools in the countryside feed a host of social ills such as sexual promiscuity and have a "traumatic" and "profoundly negative" impact on students (Moore 1998).

---

3. Uruguay's 97-percent literacy rate ranked ahead of Argentina's in 1995, but comparable data for the 1950s are not available. We already have noted that the literacy rates of several former Caribbean colonies also ranked ahead of Argentina's in 1995.

CONSUMPTION COLLAPSE: THE IMPOVERISHMENT OF THE CUBAN PEOPLE

The Cuban people have been deprived not only of luxuries now increasingly enjoyed by the middle classes in other Latin American countries but also of basic commodities such as food.

Food

Rationing has been a feature of Cuban life since the early 1960s. During the early 1990s, the variety and amount of food consumption deteriorated sharply, when massive amounts of Soviet aid were withdrawn and food imports plummeted. On its own without Soviet largesse and abundant food imports, Cuban agriculture was paralyzed by a scarcity of inputs and poor production incentives resulting from collectivism and the lack of appropriate price signals.

In pre-Castro Cuba, by contrast, food supplies were abundant, and its people were among the best fed in the hemisphere. The UN's *Statistical Yearbook, 1960* (pp. 312-316) ranked pre-revolutionary Cuba third out of 11 Latin American countries in per capita daily caloric consumption. This was in spite of the fact that the latest available food consumption data for Cuba at the time were from 1948-49, almost *a decade before* the other Latin American countries' data being used in the comparison. Looking at the same group of 11 countries today (see Table 3), Cuba ranks last in per capita daily caloric consumption, according to the most recent data available from the UN Food and Agricultural Organization. Indeed, the data show Cuba with a food situation slightly worse than that of Honduras (UNFAO 1998).

A closer look at some basic food groups reveals that Cubans now have less access to cereals, tubers, and meats than they had in the late 1940s. According to the latest UN data (UNFAO 1998), Cuba's per capita supply of cereals has fallen from 106 kg per year in the late 1940s to 103 kg today, half a century later. Per capita supply of root crops shows an even steeper decline, from 91 kg per year to 63 kg. Meat supplies have fallen from 33 kg per year to 23 kg per year, measured on a per capita basis.

Table 3. Latin America: Per Capita Food Consumption (*Calories per day*)

	Latest data available for 1954-57	1996
Mexico	2,420	3,137
Argentina	3,100	3,136
Brazil	2,540	2,938
Uruguay	2,960	2,830
Chile	2,330	2,810
Colombia	2,050	2,800
Ecuador	2,130	2,592
Paraguay	2,690	2,485
Venezuela	1,960	2,398
Honduras	2,260	2,368
Cuba	2,730[a]	2,357

Source: UN 1960, pp. 312-316; UNFAO 1998.
a For 1948-49.

The Cuban leadership's claim that the country's food problems are due to the U.S. embargo does not hold up to scrutiny. The food shortages are a function of an inefficient collectivized agricultural system and a scarcity of foreign exchange resulting from Castro's unwillingness to liberalize Cuba's economy, diversify its export base, and pay off debts owed to its Japanese, European, and Latin American trading partners during the years of abundant Soviet aid. This foreign exchange shortage, not the U.S. embargo, has severely limited Cuba's ability to purchase readily-available food supplies from Canada, Latin America, and Europe. We believe that the U.S. embargo has added, at most, relatively small increases in transportation costs by forcing Cuba to import food from non-U.S. sources elsewhere in the hemisphere.

The statistics on the consumption of nonfood items tell a similar story of economic deprivation.

Automobiles

The number of automobiles in Cuba per capita has actually fallen since the 1950s, the only country in the hemisphere for which this is the case. Indeed, the latest available UN data for Cuba used in this comparison are for the late 1980s, a period when Soviet aid to Cuba was at its peak and the rest of Latin America was in the midst of the "lost decade," a period characterized throughout the region by economic stagnation.

These data show that the number of automobiles per capita in Cuba declined slightly between 1958 and 1988, whereas virtually every other country in the region—with the possible exception of Nicaragua—experienced very significant increases in this indicator (see Table 4). Within Latin America, Cuba ranked second only to Venezuela in 1958, but by 1988 had dropped to ninth. We strongly suspect that Cuba's position relative to other Latin American countries has deteriorated even further over the past 10 years, as U.S.-manufactured cars from the 1950s and Soviet Ladas have reached the end of their mechanical lives without replacement.[4]

Table 4. Latin America: Passenger Cars per Capita[a]
(Cars per 1,000 inhabitants)

	1958	1988	Avg. Annual Increase (Pct.)
Argentina	19	129	6.6
Uruguay	22[b]	114	5.3
Venezuela	27	94	4.3
Brazil	7	73	8.1
Mexico	11[c]	70	6.4
Panama	16[d]	56	4.3
Chile	7	52	6.9
Costa Rica	13	47[c]	4.4
Cuba	24	23	-0.1
Dominican Republic	3[d]	23[e]	7.3
Colombia	6	21[f]	4.3
Paraguay	3[c]	20	6.5
Peru	7[g]	18	3.1
Ecuador	2	15	7.0
Bolivia	3[c]	12	4.7
Guatemala	6	11	2.0
El Salvador	7	10	1.2
Nicaragua	7[d]	8	0.5
Honduras	3	6	2.3

Source: UN 1960, pp. 332-339; UN 1979, pp. 67-188; UN 1996a, pp. 534-549; UN 1997a, pp. 152-159.

a. For most countries, excludes police and military cars.
b. 1956.
c. Includes police cars.
d. Excludes all government cars.
e. 1987.
f. Includes cars no longer in use.
g. 1957.

The 1988 data on automobiles also reveal that countries in Asia and Europe that once ranked far behind Cuba in this measure have since surpassed it by a wide margin. Japan, with four cars per 1,000 inhabitants in 1958, was far behind Cuba (24 per 1,000 inhabitants) then, but by 1988, Japan's number had grown to 251, whereas the figure for Cuba—even at the height of Soviet aid!—remained frozen at its 1958 level. Similar comments could be made for Portugal (increased from 15 in 1958 to 216 in 1988), Spain (increased from 6 to 278), and Greece (increased from 4 to 150). Indeed, Italy's 29 cars per capita was not far ahead of Cuba's 24 in 1958, but by 1988, Italy boasted 440 cars per capita, whereas the figure for Cuba was unchanged from the 1950s.

Telecommunications

Telephones are another case in point. While every other country in the region has seen its teledensity increase at least two fold—and most have seen even greater improvements—Cuba's has remained frozen at 1958 levels. As of 1995, the latest year for which UN data are available, Cuba had only three telephone lines per 100 people, placing it 16th out of 20 Latin American countries surveyed and far behind countries that were less advanced than Cuba in this measure in 1958, such as Costa Rica (16 lines per 100 people in 1995), Argentina (16), Chile (13), Panama (11), Venezuela (11), and several others (UN 1997b, pp. 147-149).

Radios

Cuba also has not kept pace with the rest of Latin America in terms of radios per capita. During the period 1956-1958, Cuba ranked second only to Uruguay in Latin America, with 169 radios per 1,000 people (UN 1958, pp. 576-578; UN 1960, pp. 608-609). Worldwide, this put Cuba just ahead of Japan. At that time, Argentina and Cuba were very similar in terms of this measure. Since then, the number of radios per capita in Argentina has grown three times as fast as in Cuba (UN 1997b, pp. 132-134). Cuba also has been surpassed by Bolivia, Venezuela, El Sal-

---

4. Since 1988, the 10 Latin American countries for which the most recent UN data are available, grew by an average of 33 percent in this measure over the 7-year period ending in 1995. Growth was strongest in El Salvador, where the number of passenger cars per capita increased by 97 percent, and Costa Rica, where it rose 61 percent (UN 1997b; UN 1998b, pp.155-156).

vador, Honduras, and Brazil in this indicator. Today, Cuba ranks just above average for Latin American countries.

Television Receivers

In terms of television receivers per capita, Cuba in the 1950s was far ahead of the rest of Latin America and was among the world's leaders. Cuba had 45 television sets per 1,000 inhabitants in 1957, by far the most in Latin America and, amazingly, fifth *in the world*, behind only Monaco, the United States, Canada, and the United Kingdom (UN 1958, p. 580). In fact, its closest competitor in Latin America was Venezuela, which had only 16 television sets per 1,000 people. Today, Cuba has 170 television receivers per thousand, behind Uruguay (232 per capita), Argentina (219), and Brazil (209) (UN 1997b, pp. 132-134). It should be noted that of these three countries, Uruguay in 1957 had fewer than one television set per 1,000 people, and Argentina and Brazil each had only five per 1,000 people—numbers far inferior at the time to Cuba's 45 sets per 1,000 inhabitants.

A WORD ON NATIONAL PRODUCTION STATISTICS

Historically, the most widely cited economic development indicators are per capita national production measures. Unfortunately, due to the prevalence of exchange rate distortions and vast differences in inflation rates among Latin American countries, as well as the lack of continuity in data sources and methods, we are wary of drawing any firm conclusions from these measures alone about the relative progress or lack thereof made by Cuba in economic development during the past 40 years. However, for the sake of completeness, we venture a few comments on the indicators here.

Cuba in 1958, with a per capita gross domestic product (GDP) of $370, ranked fifth out of 20 Latin American countries, according to UN estimates based on commercial exchange rate conversions

(1964, p. 322).[5] Cuba ranked behind only oil-rich Venezuela ($975), Argentina ($474), Uruguay ($450), and Chile ($409). In 1995, also according to the commercial exchange-rate based, per capita GDP statistics published in the national accounts database of the Statistics Division of the UN (1998a), Cuba ranked 11th. Keeping in mind the difficulties inherent in comparing per capita GDP statistics across decades and countries, it is nonetheless interesting to note that the two countries in the region suffering the greatest declines in terms of ranking among Latin American countries in this indicator are the only two countries in the region to have significantly embraced Marxism: Nicaragua fell from 11th to 19th place, and Cuba, as we have already noted, slid from fifth to 11th place.

PRODUCTION PLUMMETS IN KEY SECTORS

We can gain additional insight into Cuba's economic performance today *vis-à-vis* 1958 by looking at specific subsectors of the national economy.

Sugar

The erosion of Cuba's productivity in the sugar sector—by far its top export commodity—has been well documented elsewhere and does not require lengthy elaboration here. Suffice it to say that in 1958, Cuba ranked just ahead of the Soviet Union as the largest sugar producer in the world (UNFAO 1961, pp. 71-73). Today, it barely ranks among the top 10 producers. Indeed, Cuba is the only one among the top 25 world producers whose production of sugar today is lower than it was in 1958 (UNFAO 1997, pp. 157-58). This decline has taken place despite the fact that Cuba's installed milling capacity today is more than 10-percent greater than it was in 1958 (Pérez-López 1991, pp. 39, 42).

Tourism

Cuban government officials are fond of making estimates of the "costs" of the U.S. embargo, but they carefully avoid mention of the enormous costs in-

---

5. U.N. estimates (1964, p. 328) based on purchasing power parity exchange rates (1964, p. 328) put Cuba in seventh place among 20 Latin American countries in 1958. Unfortunately, the U.N. no longer publishes this purchasing power parity exchange rate-based data series.

volved in their own neglect of tourism facilities, infrastructure, and promotion during the first three decades of revolutionary government. Only in the past 10 years have they allowed foreign investment and management in hotels and other tourism facilities on the island—and even then only under restrictive conditions. Of the six countries in Latin America and the Caribbean for which comparable 1958 and 1995 data are available (Cuba, Costa Rica, Dominican Republic, Haiti, Mexico, and Peru), Cuba ranked a comfortable second in 1958, behind only Mexico, in terms of tourist arrivals. By 1995, Cuba's ranking had fallen to fourth, as it was surpassed by the Dominican Republic and Costa Rica (UN 1997b, pp. 797-799). When one considers that in 1958, the Dominican Republic received a mere one-fifth of the number of tourists that Cuba did, and that 37 years later tourist arrivals in the Dominican Republic were twice those received by Cuba, Cuba's foregone opportunities in this sector of the economy become apparent.

Energy

Cuba's difficulties in the provision of basic public utilities such as water and electricity have been well documented by its own state-run media. In electricity production, UN data show that Cuba's relative ranking among 20 Latin American countries has fallen from eighth to 11th during the Castro era (UN 1960, pp. 294-296; UN 1979, pp. 67-188; UN 1997c, pp. 432-441; UN 1998b, pp. 155-156). In fact, in terms of the rate of growth for electricity production over the past 40 years, Cuba ranks 19th of 20 countries in the region, with only Haiti showing less accelerated development.

Agriculture

Turning to agricultural production, Cuba is the only country in Latin America whose production of rice is lower today than it was four decades ago, when it ranked fourth in the region in production of this staple (UNFAO 1961, p. 50; UNFAO 1997, p. 70). Two of the countries in the region ranking ahead of Cuba in rice production in 1958—Colombia and Peru—have since seen their rice production grow by more than three-fold (see Table 5). Cuba's Caribbean neighbor, the Dominican Republic, has increased

Table 5. Latin America: Rice Production
(1,000 metric tons)

	1958	1996	Avg. Annual Increase (Pct.)
Brazil	3,829	10,035	2.6
Colombia	378	1,787	4.2
Ecuador	176	1,346	5.5
Peru	285	1,203	3.9
Argentina	217	974	4.0
Uruguay	58	868	7.4
Venezuela	22	733	9.7
Dominican Republic	99	555	4.6
Mexico	240	455	1.7
Bolivia	11	296	9.1
Panama	86	230	2.6
Cuba	261	223	-0.4
Nicaragua	33	219	5.1
Costa Rica	34	186	4.6
Chile	102	154	1.1
Paraguay	20	119	4.8
Haiti	42[a]	96	2.3
El Salvador	27	51	1.7
Honduras	21	41	1.8
Guatemala	11	33	2.9

Source: UNFAO 1961, p. 50; UNFAO 1997b, p. 70.

a. 1959.

Perhaps even more telling are Cuba's yields per hectare in rice production. Whereas the Dominican Republic has increased rice yields from 2,100 kg per hectare in 1958 to 5,400 kg per hectare in 1996, Cuba's yields today are only 2,500 kg per hectare, a negligible increase from the 2,400 kg per hectare registered in 1958, according to the Food and Agriculture Organization of the United Nations.

Cuba's milk production in 1996 was only 11 percent higher than it was 38 years previously, by far the smallest increase in all of Latin America and the Caribbean (see Table 6). In 1958, Cuba ranked fifth in the region in milk production, producing 828,000 tons (UN 1966). By 1996, Cuba's position in Latin America had fallen to ninth, according to UNFAO data (1997b), as Cuban production stagnated while production in Ecuador, Venezuela, Chile, and Uruguay took off.

Construction materials

In 1958, Cuba ranked sixth among the 17 Latin American and Caribbean countries surveyed by the United Nations in the production of cement, but by

Table 6. **Latin America: Milk Production[a]**
(1,000 metric tons)

	1958	1996	Increase
Brazil	4,603	19,845	331%
Argentina	4,481	9,176	105%
Mexico	4,206[b]	8,059	92%
Colombia	2,085[c]	5,000	140%
Chile	764	1,873	145%
Ecuador	375	1,848	393%
Venezuela	387[b]	1,417	266%
Uruguay	627	1,342	114%
Cuba	**828**	**920**	**11%**
Peru	372	905	143%
CostaRica	76[c]	536	605%
Honduras	111	529	377%
Guatemala	128	321	151%
Paraguay	132	300	127%
Panama	51	155	204%

Source: UN 1966, p. 136; UNFAO 1997b, pp. 216-217.

a. Cows Milk Only
b. 1959
c. 1957

1994, its regional ranking had fallen to 11th (UN 1997b, pp. 488-493). In the intervening years, Cuba's production was surpassed by Peru, Chile, Ecuador, the Dominican Republic, and Guatemala.

CUBA'S EXTERNAL ACCOUNTS: FROM PLENTY TO POVERTY

By virtually any measure, Cuba's external accounts were in far better shape in 1958 than they are today. The economic reforms which have swept the region have literally transformed the region's economies, resulting in massive increases in exports and foreign investment inflows. To date, Castro has refused to implement even what other Latin American leaders would regard as basic, "first generation" economic reforms. As a result, Cuba is falling further behind its neighbors with each passing year.

Cuba's exports have not kept pace with other countries of the region. Of the 20 countries in the region for which comparable IMF data are available, Cuba ranks last in terms of export growth—below even Haiti (IMF 1964, 1997). A startling fact is that Mexico and Cuba had virtually identical export levels in 1958—while Mexico's population was five times Cuba's. Since then, Mexico's exports have increased by almost 130-fold, according to IMF statistics. Cuba's export earnings, on the other hand, are merely

twice as high as they were 40 years ago. Looking at other countries, one finds that Cuba's exports in 1958 far exceeded those of Chile, Colombia, and Peru, countries which have since left Cuba behind (see Table 7).

Table 7. **Latin America: Total Exports**
(Million US $)

	1958	1996	Average Annual Growth (Pct.)
Mexico	736	95,991	14
Panama	23	2,722	13
Ecuador	95	5,243	11
CostaRica	92	3,826	10
Chile	389	15,396	10
Brazil	1,243	47,747	10
Paraguay	34	1,282	10
Honduras	70	2,469	10
Argentina	994	23,794	9
Colombia	461	10,437	9
Guatemala	103	2,330	9
Peru	291	5,854	8
Bolivia	65	1,216	8
Uruguay	139	2,397	8
Venezuela	2,319	23,149	6
El Salvador	116	1,020	6
Nicaragua	71	621	6
Dominican Republic	136	886	5
Haiti	48	181	4
Cuba	**732**	**1,831**	**2**

Source: IMF 1964; IMF 1997.

The comparison between Cuban and Chilean export earnings is particularly striking. Much of the divergence in export performance between the two countries in recent years can be traced to differences in economic policy. Both countries in 1958 were similar in terms of population, each having about 7 million inhabitants. Cuba's exports in 1958, however, were twice those of Chile (IMF 1964), reflecting pre-socialist Cuba's relatively pro-market, pro-export policy stance. Beginning in the late 1970s, Chile began implementing bold economic and trade reforms, closing its export gap with Cuba until the Latin American debt crisis of the 1980s hit Chile's economy hard, resulting in a severe depression. Chile weathered the massive external shock and began a very strong expansion in 1988. In fact, Chile declined to participate in the U.S.-sponsored Brady Plan; officials in Santiago argued that their economic

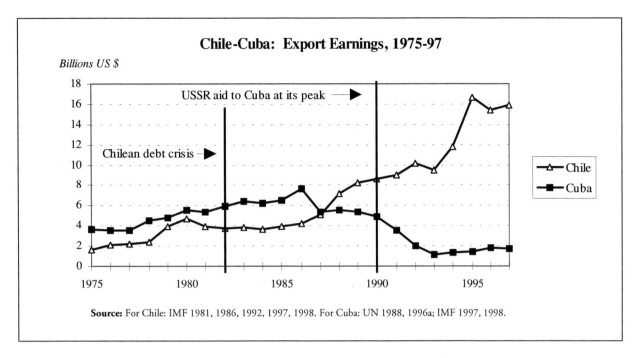

Chile-Cuba: Export Earnings, 1975-97

Billions US $

USSR aid to Cuba at its peak →

Chilean debt crisis →

Chile
Cuba

Source: For Chile: IMF 1981, 1986, 1992, 1997, 1998. For Cuba: UN 1988, 1996a; IMF 1997, 1998.

reforms and market-based debt reduction schemes were sufficient. Indeed, Chilean exports rebounded strongly from the crisis and have since grown by an average 13 percent per year during the last 10 years. The critical elements of Chile's reform plan identified by Edwards (1995, pp. 135-36)—the liberalization of foreign trade, pursuit of stable macroeconomic policies to spur investor confidence, and the strict respect for property rights—were all absent in Cuba as it faced its own external shock when Soviet assistance was withdrawn beginning in 1990-91. The divergence in the export performances of the two countries in the face of external shocks is quite significant, as is demonstrated by the chart above for the period 1975-97.[6]

Cuba's enviable productive base during the 1950s was strengthened by sizable inflows of foreign direct investment. Although foreign investment figures by source country during the 1950s are scarce, Cuba's attractive foreign investment climate at that time is apparent from U.S. data. As of 1958, the value of

U.S. foreign direct investment alone in Cuba was $861 million, according to U.S. government figures published in 1959 (Commerce 1959, p. 30). Adjusting for inflation, that foreign investment number amounts to more than $4.3 billion in today's dollars. The value of U.S. foreign direct investment in Cuba as of 1958 was greater than U.S. direct investment in Mexico, Argentina, or Chile. Among European countries, only the United Kingdom received more U.S. direct investment than did Cuba, while world economic powers such as France and Germany received less.

Contrary to popular perception, these U.S. investments were not limited to raw materials such as sugar. U.S. firms began to gradually sell their Cuban sugar holdings to Cuban firms beginning in 1935. By 1958, U.S. firms owned fewer than 40 of Cuba's 161 mills (Schroeder 1982, p. 258). While U.S. firms were moving away from sugar, they were rapidly investing in a range of other ventures, especially in infrastructure development. According to U.S. gov-

---

6. IMF trade statistics are issued on a more timely basis than those from the United Nations. When possible, we have used IMF trade statistics in this study. However, prior to 1993, IMF data for Cuba excluded Cuba's trade with the former Soviet Union. This situation was remedied in 1993, when Russia, Cuba's most important trade partner, began reporting to the IMF. For Cuba's trade, we use UN statistics for the period 1975-1992 and IMF statistics for 1993-present. Despite the discontinuity, we believe that this usage provides the best picture of Cuba's exports during this period.

ernment statistics (Commerce 1959, p. 30), 41 percent of US direct investments in Cuba were in utilities as of 1958. U.S. investments also were significant in manufacturing, petroleum processing, chemicals and pharmaceuticals, and food processing. In fact, during the decade of the 1950s, U.S. investments in non-sugar sectors of the economy doubled. (Franco and Ventura 1996, pp. 7, 18).

Franco and Ventura (1996) describe the wave of diverse American firms that launched operations in Cuba during the 1950s. Proctor & Gamble chose Cuba as the site of its first detergent plant in all of Latin America. In retail business, Sears Roebuck & Co., F.W. Woolworth, and others launched operations throughout the island. Also in the 1950s, Goodyear and Firestone Tire & Rubber made large-scale investments, following on the success of B.F. Goodrich Co., which built the island's first tube and tire factory in the 1940s. Finally, by the 1950s, Coca-Cola, which had previously imported inputs such as concentrate and bottles, was conducting nearly all of its manufacturing, processing, and bottling on the island.

Today, figures on foreign investment in Cuba are obscured in government secrecy in an attempt to protect investors who may be trafficking in confiscated U.S. properties from possible U.S. government sanctions. Cuba has occasionally released data on the number of joint ventures contracted with foreign enterprises, but statistics on the value of these investments are hard to find. One official claimed in December 1995 that Cuba had received about $1 billion in paid-in foreign investment (Lage 1995), but the statement was not clear as to whether this figure represented a stock value or a flow value, and if the latter, for what period. Reliable intertemporal or intercountry comparisons, therefore, are not possible at this time.

As the numbers above imply, Cuba had a very favorable overall balance of payments situation during the 1950s, contrasted with the tenuous situation today.

In 1958, Cuba had gold and foreign exchange reserves—a key measure of a healthy balance of payments—totaling $387 million in 1958 dollars, according to IMF statistics (1960, p. 90). (That level of reserves would be worth more than $1.9 billion in today's dollars.) Cuba's reserves were third in Latin America, just ahead of Mexico and behind only Venezuela and Brazil, which was impressive for a small economy with a population of fewer than 7 million people. Unfortunately, Cuba no longer publishes information on its foreign exchange and gold reserves. However, we suspect that if Cuba had $1.9 billion in reserves today, its much-publicized balance-of-payments problems would be solved.

MASS MEDIA FALLS VICTIM TO SOCIALIST CENSORSHIP

It is no exaggeration to state that during the 1950s, the Cuban people were among the most informed in the world, living in an uncharacteristically large media market for such a small country. Cubans had a choice of 58 daily newspapers during the late 1950s, according to the *UN Statistical Yearbook*. Despite its small size, this placed Cuba behind only Brazil, Argentina, and Mexico in the region (UN 1960, p. 602). By 1994, government controls had reduced the number of dailies to only 17 (UN 1997b, p. 120).[7]

We suspect that similar comments could be made about the number of radio and television broadcasting stations, although the UN no longer reports these statistics. However, it should be noted that in 1957, Cuba had more television stations (23) than any other country in Latin America, easily outdistancing larger countries such as Mexico (12 television stations) and Venezuela (10) (UN 1960, p. 610). Cuba also was the first Latin American country to broadcast television programs in color (Franco and Ventura 1996, p. 14). It also led Latin America and ranked eighth in the world in number of radio stations (160), ahead of such countries as Austria (83 radio stations), United Kingdom (62), and France (50), ac-

---

7. Totalitarianism, rather than the economic depression of the 1990s, is to blame for the decline in daily newspapers in Cuba. Indeed, the number of dailies in Cuba in 1994 was unchanged from the number in 1980, according to UN statistics (1997b, p. 120).

cording to the *UN Statistical Yearbook* (1960, p. 607).

CONCLUSION

Not long after the previous version of this paper was published (State 1998), the *Washington Times* quoted the Cuban Interests Section's objections to the statistical presentation found in the study (Carter 1998). It did not dispute the statistics themselves, the majority of which are reported by the Cuban government itself to multilateral institutions discussed earlier. Rather, a spokesman asserted that the statistics did not take into account the social achievements of the revolution in relation to the distribution of wealth. For example, he said, "[B]efore the revolution, the rich had more food and the poor had less." This statement is, of course, indisputable, but it leaves unanswered how a society in which virtually *everyone* is poor is preferable to one in which *some* people are poor, others are middle class, and still others are rich.

In fact, the Cuban government's focus on the relative *fairness* of Cuban society today reminds us of socialist claims during the post-World War II period, as reported by the great Austrian economist Ludwig von Mises:

The Marxians used to recommend socialism on the ground that it would multiply productivity and bring unprecedented material wealth to everybody. Only lately have they changed their tactics. They declare that the Russian worker is happier than the American worker in spite of the fact that his standard of living is much lower; the knowledge that he lives under a fair social system compensates by far for all his material hardships (1966, p. 679n).

Mises goes on to note that "this haughty indifference with regard to material well-being is a privilege reserved to ivory-tower intellectuals, secluded from reality..." Most Cubans, if given the choice, would prefer the opportunity at a better life under capitalism over the "fairness" in poverty guaranteed by the Castro government. Perhaps that is why Fidel Castro steadfastly refuses to hold fair and free democratic elections. He realizes that if he were to do so, he would lose, just as his Nicaraguan *compañero* Daniel Ortega was defeated in 1990 and again in 1996.

As we have already stated, the chances that the living standards of Cubans will improve under the current regime relative to living standards elsewhere in the hemisphere are remote. This bleak outlook contrasts strongly with the optimism of the 1950s. The opening paragraphs of the 1,000-plus-page study of Cuba by the economic mission organized by the World Bank (1951, p. 3) read:

Cuba today faces both a problem and an opportunity. Her problem is to reduce her dependence on sugar, not by producing less sugar but by developing additional enterprises. Her opportunity is that her present prosperity offers her the means to do so by further diversifying her economy. Ample, unused human and material resources are available in Cuba with which her people might increase the nation's output, broaden its economic base and create a better standard of living for the population as a whole. Also, at the present time, Cuba has a financial potential of her own, which—if it can be effectively tapped—is adequate for her development.

That such optimistic words would open a publication dedicated to a discussion of the socioeconomic *problems* in a country is striking. Today, by contrast, sound economic policies have been eschewed in favor of anti-U.S. diatribes, which government and party functionaries have repeated with sufficient frequency to divert the world's attention from the degree to which their own actions are responsible for the material deprivation suffered by the Cuban people. That the government continues to show such indifference to the material poverty outlined in this study, steadfastly holding to a completely discredited economic model—and at the same time calling capitalism unsustainable!—constitutes the saddest chapter in the history of the once great Cuban nation.

REFERENCES

Baklanoff, Eric N. 1975. *Expropriation of US Investments in Cuba, Mexico, and Chile.* New York: Praeger Publishers.

Carter, Tom. 1998. "Report Doubts Cuba Better Under Castro." *Washington Times* (March 18) A13.

Cawthorne, Andrew. 1998. "Revolutions Make Healthy Kids—Colombia's Samper." *Reuters Library Service* (June 25).

Commerce, U.S. Department of. 1959. *Survey of Current Business* (August).

Edwards, Sebastián. 1995. *Crisis and Reform in Latin America: From Despair to Hope.* New York: Oxford University Press.

Franco, Alexander and Enrique J. Ventura. 1996. *The Cuban Economy and Legal Environment in the 1950s.* Miami: Renaissance Publishing Group.

International Monetary Fund (IMF). 1960. *International Financial Statistics* (March).

_____. 1964. *Direction of Trade Annual, 1958-62.* Washington: International Monetary Fund and International Bank for Reconstruction and Development.

_____. 1981-97. *Direction of Trade Statistics Yearbook.* Washington: International Monetary Fund.

_____. 1998. *Direction of Trade Statistics Quarterly* (June). Washington: International Monetary Fund.

Lage, Carlos. 1995. "Vice President Lage Interviewed on Economy." Tele Rebelde and Cuba Vision broadcast, December 21. Reproduced and translated in Foreign Broadcast Information Service, *Daily Report* (December 26).

Mises, Ludwig von. 1966. *Human Action: A Treatise on Economics.* 3rd edition. San Francisco: Fox & Wilkes.

Moore, Molly. 1998. "John Paul Calls Island's Schools Anti-Family." *Washington Post* (January 23) A32.

Navarro, Eduardo Borrell. 1977. "Brief Resume of the Hospitals and Numbers of Hospital Beds and an Outline of Social Legislation in Cuba." *Journal of the Florida Medical Association* 64 (August) 554-558.

Pérez-López, Jorge. 1991. *The Economics of Cuban Sugar.* Pittsburgh: University of Pittsburgh Press.

Romeu, Jorge Luis. 1995. "More on the Statistical Comparison of Cuban Socioeconomic Development." *Cuba in Transition—Volume 5* . Washington: Association for the Study of the Cuban Economy, pp.293-301.

Schroeder, Susan. 1982. *Cuba: A Handbook of Historical Statistics.* Boston: G.K. Hall & Co.

State, U.S. Department of. 1998. "Zenith and Eclipse: A Comparative Look at Socio-Economic Conditions in Pre-Castro and Present Day Cuba" (rev. February 9, 1998). Bureau of Inter-American Affairs. www.state.gov/www/regions/ara/economic_conditions.html.

UN (United Nations). 1957-1995. *Statistical Yearbook.* New York: United Nations.

_____. 1964. *Yearbook of National Accounts Statistics, 1963.* New York: United Nations.

_____. 1979. *Demographic Yearbook: Historical Supplement.* New York: United Nations.

_____. 1996. *Energy Statistics Yearbook, 1994.* New York: United Nations.

_____. 1997a. *Demographic Yearbook, 1995.* New York: United Nations.

_____. 1997b. *Statistical Yearbook, 1995* (42). New York: United Nations.

_____. 1997c. *Energy Statistics Yearbook, 1995.* New York: United Nations.

_____. 1998a. "Indicators on Income and Economic Activity."www.un.org/Depts/unsd/social/inc-eco.htm (2 Jan 1998).

_____. 1998b. *Demographic Yearbook, 1996* (48). New York: United Nations.

UNFAO (Food and Agriculture Organization of the United Nations). 1961. *Production Yearbook, 1960.* Rome: Food and Agriculture Organization.

_____. 1997. *FAO Yearbook: Production, 1996.* Rome: Food and Agriculture Organization of the United Nations.

_____. 1998. *Food Balance Sheet.* http://apps.fao.org.

World Bank (International Bank for Reconstruction and Development). 1951. *Report on Cuba.* Washington: IBRD.

CUBA ON THE EVE OF THE SOCIALIST TRANSITION: A REASSESSMENT OF THE BACKWARDNESS-STAGNATION THESIS

Eric N. Baklanoff

A major thesis advanced to explain Cuba's transition into a Marxist-Leninist state centers on that country's presumed economic backwardness and immobilism. In the "received wisdom" pervading academic circles and the media, prerevolutionary Cuba is perceived as a kind of Hispanic-American Haiti. The backwardness-stagnation thesis is often supported by a corollary: the alleged exploitative grip by which U.S. investors held the Cuban economy.

It is not surprising that distortions and inaccuracies regarding Cuba's prerevolutionary economic condition should appear in neo-Marxist publications outside of Cuba nor that Cuban authorities deliberately falsify statistics on their country's social condition—before and since the revolution. What is surprising, as well as disturbing, is that these distortions have unwittingly been accepted by reputable economists and political scientists, members of Congress, and as well as by editors and journalists of the Western press.

In an important monograph published five years after Batista's fall, Dudley Seers, the volume's editor, describes prerevolutionary Cuba as "a somewhat backward tropical country."[1] Benjamin Higgins, whose work in economic development is generally highly regarded for its theoretical rigor and thorough

documentation, appears to have partially accepted the "backwardness thesis." Thus, in a chapter entitled, "Cuba: The Anatomy of Revolution," he writes that Cuba's relatively high per capita income "does not properly indicate the extent of poverty, ignorance, and ill health that prevailed in Cuba in 1958."[2] His statement that Cuba's illiteracy "was about equal to the Latin American average, about 40 percent" is contradicted by United Nations and Cuban statistics which show the island's illiteracy rate to be only about half that figure.

In her comprehensive treatment of the revolution, entitled *Back from the Future: Cuba Under Castro*, Susan Eckstein writes that, on some measures, Cuba fared well relative to other countries in the region. Following this generalization, however, she erroneously ranks Cuba tenth in per capita income, the median for Latin America.[3]

Michael P. Todaro's 1997 edition of *Economic Development* includes a brief "Case Study: The Economy of Cuba" prepared for the author by Professor Frank Thompson which claims that American-based firms dominated every major sector of the Cuban economy, including sugar, until the revolution. Describing Cuba in the 1950s, Thompson writes: "Regulations modeled on southern U.S. Jim Crow laws were im-

---

1. Dudley Seers, "Editor's Preface," in *Cuba: The Economic and Social Revolution*, edited by Dudley Seers (Chapel Hill: The University of North Carolina Press, 1964), p. V.

2. Benjamin Higgins, *Economic Development* (New York: W. W. Norton and Company, 1968), p. 806.

3. Susan Eva Eckstein, *Back from the Future: Cuba Under Castro* (Princeton: Princeton University Press, 1994), p. 18.

posed, and Havana, the Cuban capital, became known as 'the Bordelo' for U.S. vacationers seeking pleasures forbidden at home."[4] Writing glowingly of the transformation in health and education systems under the Castro regime, the author is silent on Cuban health and literacy indicators on the eve of the revolution.

In an insightful article titled "A Look at Castro's Statistics," Professor Norman Luxenburg exposes the Castro regime's propaganda which systematically belittles the country's prerevolutionary achievements in medicine, public health, and literacy. He refers to a Congressional House committee headed by Representative Jonathan Bingham of New York which visited Cuba in 1977. Apparently impressed by talks with Cuban officials, the committee stated in its official report that before Castro there were 187,000 students in Cuba and that the literacy rate under Castro had risen from 25 to 99 percent.[5] However, as Luxenburg points out, on the eve of the revolution there were not 187,000 students, but about one million and the literacy rate was not 25 percent but 78 percent. When Senator George McGovern made his fact-finding trip to Cuba in the spring of 1975, he was apparently unaware of the prerevolutionary origin of the island's steel plant. In his report to the Senate Foreign Relations Committee he writes:

> We toured Cuba's one steel mill, which, with technical and financial assistance from the Soviet Union, is being expanded to raise output toward self-sufficiency in steel . . . The mill looks, sounds and smells like

steel mills in the United States - down to the posters urging safety on the job.[6]

In his edited volume entitled *Foreign Investment in Latin America*, Marvin Bernstein concludes:

> If private capital ever had the chance, through its economic and political influence, to demonstrate its ability to improve the lot of people while still earning profits, American private capital did in Cuba. Castro is a chicken come home to roost.[7]

Writing in *Cuban Studies/Estudios Cubanos*, William M. LeoGrande contends that the advent of socialism in Cuba, including the establishment of a centrally planned economy, brought about a sharp and substantial decline in Cuban dependency. He furthermore states that by "expropriating U.S. holdings, Cuba was able to regain control over economic decision-making in these critical economic sectors, and at the same time halt a capital drain in the form of remitted profits."[8] Zeitlin and Scheer contend that the U.S. firms, "from their secure economic and political position in Cuba, could have initiated new ventures but failed to do so."[9]

Taking a journalistic perspective, my Alabama colleague Frank Deaver believes that pre-Castro Cuba "represented the culmination of more than a half-century of exploitation, largely by American business interests."[10] He predicts that when Castro is gone, "external business interests will likely descend on Cuba like vultures on a road kill. Their motives will be dominated by profit and renewed exploitation is a possibility."

---

4. Michael P. Todaro, *Economic Development* (Reading, Massachusetts: Addison-Wesley Publishing Co., sixth edition, 1997), p. 97.

5. Norman Luxenburg, "A Look at Castro's Statistics," *Encounter* 67:3 (March 1984), p. 58.

6. *Cuban Realities: May 1975*, A report by Senator George S. McGovern, to the Committee on Foreign Relations, United States Senate (Washington: U.S. Government Printing Office, 1975), p. 6.

7. From the editor's introduction to Robert F. Smith, "The United States and Cuba," in *Foreign Investment in Latin America*, edited by Marvin Bernstein (New York: Alfred A. Knopf, 1966), p. 145.

8. William M. LeoGrande, "Cuban Dependency: A Comparison of Pre-Revolutionary and Post-Revolutionary International Economic Relations," *Cuban Studies/Estudios Cubanos* 9:2 (July 1979) p. 22.

9. Maurice Zeitlin and Robert Scheer, *Cuba: Tragedy in our Hemisphere* (New York: Grove Press, 1963), p. 29.

10. Frank Deaver, "Cuba's Outlook: More of Same," in the Ideas and Issues section of *The Tuscaloosa News* (November 5, 1995), p. 5E. Until his recent retirement, Deaver was professor of journalism at the University of Alabama. In 1990, he directed an international journalism project for the Alabama Press Association and in that capacity led a delegation of reporters and editors on a reporting mission to Cuba.

"High level stagnation," writes James O'Connor, "is an appropriate description of the old Cuban social economy . . ."[11] Finally, according to Seers, the existing state of affairs on the eve of the revolution, "in which people were short of food and work but land lay idle and factories were not built—could not continue."[12]

The purpose of this paper is to reassess Cuba's economic condition on the eve of the 1959 revolution. Four decades following Fidel Castro's rise to power, this assessment can now be considered in the perspective of the "New Thinking" in Latin America that came in the aftermath of the region's 1982 debt crisis. The first section previews Cuba's sugar-dependent "export economy." The second section analyzes the country's resource endowment and living standard, including social indicators, on the eve of the revolution. The third section focuses on Cuba's successful diversification drive during the 1950s.[13] The fourth section considers the changing sectoral profile and economic impact of U.S. direct investment in the host country from 1946 to 1959. The paper closes with a summary and some observations on the "backwardness-stagnation-exploitation" allegations.

AN "EXPORT ECONOMY" IN TRANSITION

In organization and structure, Cuba, until the latter 1950s, typified what economists have come to call an "export economy."[14] Such an economy exhibits the following properties: a high ratio of export production to total output in the cash sector of the economy; a concentrated export structure; substantial inflow of long-term capital, including the presence of foreign-owned enterprises; and a high marginal propensity to import. Commonly, in such an economy, government revenues are tied closely to the oscilla-

tions of export income. The export sector constitutes the dynamic, autonomous variable that powers the nation's development; it is also the short-run disturber. The sheer weight of exports in relation to total economic activity dictates that the external market rather than private investment or government expenditure exercise predominant influence on aggregate demand. Because of its specialized structure, the export economy is heavily dependent on foreign sources for many kinds of consumer and capital goods.

In the immediate postwar period, Cuba's sugar "sector"—including cane growing and the industrial and commercial income from the milling and marketing of raw sugar—contributed directly about one-third of the national income and accounted for 90 percent of Cuba's external receipts from exports and thereby constituted the great independent variable," the "master beam," of the island's economy.

Because of the central position of sugar in Cuba's exports and national product, the nation suffered from chronic seasonal unemployment. Economic activity oscillated between the *zafra*, the grinding period, (February-April) and the dead season, August through October, when unemployment normally reached a level of 20 percent and much capital equipment remained idle.[15] The unemployment problem for sugar workers in the latter 1950s was mitigated to some degree by the availability of alternative job opportunities. During 1958, for example, one-fourth of the cane labor worked for two or three months in the coffee harvest, which preceded the *zafra*; other off-season jobs were available in rice farming, construction, and in the maintenance of sugar mills. However, as O'Connor observes, the "vast majority of seasonally employed workers returned to the family

---

11. James O'Connor, "Cuba: Its Political Economy," in *Cuba in Revolution*, edited by Rolando E. Bonachea and Nelson P. Valdés (Garden City, New York: Doubleday and Co., Inc., 1972), p. 80.

12. Seers, "The Economic and Social Background," in *Cuba: The Economic and Social Revolution*, p. 19.

13. This section and the next draw liberally from Eric N. Baklanoff, *Expropriation of U.S. Investments in Cuba, Mexico, and Chile* (New York: Praeger Publishers, 1975), chapter 2, and Baklanoff, "The Structure of Cuba's Dependency Preceding the Revolution," *SECOLAS Annals*, vol. 11 (March 1980).

14. See, for example, Gerald M. Meier, *International Trade and Development* (New York and Evanston: Harper and Row, 1963), pp. 5-6.

15. See Consejo Nacional de Economía, *El empleo, el subempleo y el desempleo en Cuba* (La Habana, January 1959), Tables 2 and 6.

farms, grew subsistence crops on plots furnished by the sugar mills, or eked out a bare subsistence on credits furnished by local stores."[16]

During the 1958 crop year, there were 471,420 workers employed in sugar production, and nearly 18,000 earned their wages in related industries such as sugar refineries, distilleries, and 12 bagasse pulp and paper plants.[17] Of the total number of workers in raw sugar production, approximately 350,000 were engaged in cane cutting and related agricultural activities and the remainder were employed in the sugar mills. Cuba had 161 mills in 1958 with a productive capacity of 8.2 million metric tons of sugar. This capacity could easily be increased to 10 million tons provided there were sufficient cane for grinding. The capital investment in the sugar mills and related industries was estimated at $1,158,850,000 at the end of 1957, or about 45 percent of Cuba's accumulated industrial investment.[18]

In 1958, on the eve of the Cuban Revolution, the United States was purchasing two-thirds of the island's exports and was supplying 70 percent of its imports. Next to Brazil, Cuba was the most important Latin American source of agricultural imports of the United States. During the five-year period, 1954-1958, the United States purchased three-fourths of Cuba's tobacco and 60 percent of its sugar. Raw Cuban sugar was sold to the U.S. under a quota system at prices that in most years were substantially above the world price.[19] Both the quota and the more stable U.S. premium price helped to curb the annual fluctuations of Cuban sugar sales abroad. Prior to 1959, the framework of Cuba's commercial policy was the

General Agreement on Tariffs and Trade (GATT). Negotiated preferences under this agreement gave the United States and Cuba lower tariff rates on most products imported from each other than were obtained on imports from other countries.

Some 30 percent of Cuba's trade turnover in 1958 was carried on with non-Communist nations other than the United States, while only 3 percent of the island's exports went to the Soviet bloc. The Communist nations in that year were an insignificant source of imports for Cuba. Next to the United States, Western Europe was Cuba's most important geographical trading area, purchasing 15 percent of its exports and supplying 14 percent of its purchases abroad. The composition, by commodities, of Cuba's exports in 1957-58 revealed the following value shares: sugar and related products, 79 percent; tobacco and products, 6 percent; mineral products, 6 percent; and other products, 9 percent.

Cuban sugar output reached a prerevolutionary record of 7.2 million metric tons in 1952. In succeeding years during that decade, with sugar production restricted by Cuba and the diversification policy, the country's dependence on world sugar markets declined: exports declined as a share of national output and sugar played a somewhat diminished role in Cuba's export list. As the third section makes clear, Cuba's economic policymakers heeded the recommendation of the World Bank Mission which visited the island in 1950:

The choice before the people of Cuba is clear-cut. They may take advantage of their present opportunities to start to substitute a growing, dynamic and di-

---

16. James O'Connor, *The Origins of Socialism in Cuba* (Ithaca, N.Y.: Cornell University Press, 1970), p. 182.

17. José R. Alvarez Díaz, et al., *Cuba: Agriculture and Planning* (Coral Gables: University of Miami, Cuban Economic Research Project, 1965), pp. 121-2.

18. Cuban Economic Research Project, *A Study on Cuba* (Coral Gables: University of Miami Press, 1965), p. 555, Table 409. I have subtracted from the total given in the table the sum of $645.4 million which corresponds to "transportation and communication," activities normally excluded from the industrial or secondary sector.

19. For example, in the five-year period 1955-59, the U.S. price averaged 5.2¢ per pound compared with the average world price of 3.7¢. (International Monetary Fund, *International Financial Statistics*, various issues.)

versified economy for their present static one, with its single crop dependence.[20]

CUBA'S RESOURCE ENDOWMENT AND STANDARD OF LIVING

Cuba, in the latter 1950s, had already evolved important professional, technical and managerial middle groups and a substantial pool of skilled workers. Many of the country's energetic and competent administrators were "schooled in large-scale operations through the great development of the sugar industry and other enterprises."[21] Spanish immigrants, particularly those who came to Cuba during the first quarter of the twentieth century, contributed disproportionately to the island's stock of high-level manpower resources.

About 80 percent of the Cuban land mass was under cultivation or used for grazing in the 1950s. The top soil is exceedingly fertile, deep, rich and well-watered, and the topography favorable to widespread use of farm machinery. An absence of climatic variation, however, limits the island to the cultivation of tropical and semi-tropical crops and to livestock raising. Domestic production supplied about 70 percent of Cuba's food consumption. The island also contains important nickel mineral reserves and useful deposits of manganese, chrome, copper and limestone. It is favored with several large, well-protected natural harbors. The energy resources constitute the island's major deficiency, for Cuba has no coal and very little oil had thus far been discovered.

Cuba was one the most capitalized nations in Latin America. The World Bank Mission observed that:

> In the 161 sugar centrales, in the excellent central highway, in the extensive system of public and private railroads, in the harbor installations, in the cities, and their utilities, Cuba has the basis of exceptionally fine equipment for modern economic activity and further development.[22]

An extensive, well-integrated system of highways provided the basis for rapid postwar advance in the island's motorized transport industry.

In 1957, Cuba's real income per capita (national income divided by population) was $378, or fourth, in Latin America.[23] Only Venezuela, Argentina, and Uruguay ranked above Cuba and even Spain ($324) and Portugal ($212), failed to reach Cuba's level. Except for Venezuela, Cuba probably enjoyed the highest per capita income among all countries in the wet tropical zone, extending from the Tropic of Cancer to the Tropic of Capricorn.[24] Other measures provide a better approximation of the degree to which real income was shared among the population. Cuba ranked third in Latin America on a per capita basis in daily calorie consumption, steel consumption, paper consumption and radios per 1,000 persons. In 1959, Cuba had one million radios and the highest ratio of television sets per 1,000 inhabitants.[25]

Compared with the other Latin American and Caribbean countries, Cuba's health advances were impressive. As Luxenburg observed,[26] there were sharp reductions in mortality from gastroenteritis, bronchial

---

20. International Bank for Reconstruction and Development (World Bank), *Report on Cuba* (Baltimore: Johns Hopkins Press, 1951), p. 12.

21. Henry C. Wallich, *Monetary Problems of an Export Economy: The Cuban Experience, 1914-1947* (Cambridge: Harvard University Press, 1950), pp. 5-6.

22. International Bank for Reconstruction and Development, *Report on Cuba*, p. 72.

23. United Nations, *Yearbook of National Accounts Statistics* (New York: United Nations, 1962).

24. Paul Hoffman, former administrator of the Marshall Plan, classified 100 underdeveloped countries of the world into four categories by average per capita income. Fifty-two fell in the under $100 a year category, 23 in the $100-199 category, 16 in the $200-299 category and 9 in the $300-699 category. Cuba was one of the top nine. P.G. Hoffman, *One Hundred Countries, One and One Quarter Billion People* (Washington: Committee for International Economic Growth, 1960).

25. See United Nations, *Statistical Yearbook* (New York: United Nations, 1960) and Center for Latin American Studies, *Statistical Abstract of Latin America* (Los Angeles: University of California at Los Angeles, 1961).

26. Norman Luxenburg, "A Look at Castro's Statistics," p. 59.

pneumonia, chronic bronchitis, typhoid fever, and pulmonary TB every decade after 1933. In 1958, the 6.6 million Cubans had twice as many physicians as the 19 million residents of the other Caribbean countries combined. The number of medical doctors in Cuba had grown from 3,100 in 1948 to 6,500 in 1958. The ratio in that 10-year period had increased from one physician for every 1,650 persons to one per 1,021—which compared favorably with many First World countries. Significantly, in 1957, Cuba's death rate (6.3 per 1,000) and infant mortality rate (32 per 1,000 live births) were the lowest in Latin America.[27]

With an organized labor force of over 1.5 million workers, Cuba ranked with Uruguay and Argentina in the degree of unionization. The island's unionized workers enjoyed the protection of what was probably the most comprehensive labor code in Latin America. Ernest Schwarz, the executive secretary of the CIO's Committee on Latin American Affairs gave his impressions of the achievements of Cuba's labor federation , the Confederation of Cuban Workers (CTC):

> The CTC has enabled the Cuban workers to set an example to others of what can be achieved by labor unity and strength. Wages are far above those paid in many other parts of the Caribbean or, for that matter, Latin America.[28]

The level of wages in Cuban manufacturing contributed significantly to the nation's relatively high living standards. In 1957, wages averaged $6 for an eight-hour day in manufacturing as a whole and ranged from over $4 for unskilled workers to $11 for skilled

employees in Cuba's sugar mills.[29] Real wages in Cuba were higher than any country in the Western Hemisphere, excepting the United States and Canada.

Between 1949-58, the average annual share of national income paid in workers' remuneration (wages, fringe benefits, pensions) was 65 percent, and it showed a noticeable tendency to rise. Surprisingly by 1958, as Mesa-Lago notes, Cuba's percentage was surpassed by only three developed Western countries: Great Britain, the United States, and Canada.[30]

As was true of the other countries in the region in the 1950s, in Cuba there existed a substantial disparity in the levels of social and economic development between the more prosperous capital province and some of the more rural provinces. A survey taken in 1956-1957 by Agrupación Católica Universitaria showed that the position of the Cuban peasant in regard to caloric intake, diet, health, medical attention, housing, and income was very much below the national averages for 1953. The privileged status of the unionized workers as reflected in the high remuneration/national income index cited above was, in Mesa-Lago's words, "obtained in large measure at the cost of the unemployed and the peasants."[31]

THE DIVERSIFICATION DRIVE, 1953-58

Given the nature of the international sugar market and Cuba's substantial share as a world exporter,[32] the nation's policy makers perceived that the sugar sector no longer could provide the growing edge for the economy. After the record sugar crop in 1952, the Cuban government reinstituted restrictions on sugar production in the following year and, with the

27. Carmelo Mesa-Lago, "Economic Policies and Growth," in *Revolutionary Change in Cuba*, edited by Carmelo Mesa-Lago (University of Pittsburgh Press, 1971), p. 295.

28. Ernest Schwarz, "Some Observations on Labor Organizations in the Caribbean" in *The Caribbean: Its Economy*, edited by A. Curtis Wilgus (Gainesville: University of Florida Press, 1954), p. 167.

29. Alice Shurcliff, *Labor in Cuba* (Washington: U.S. Bureau of Labor Statistics, 1958), p. 21 cited in O'Connor, *The Origin of Socialism in Cuba*, pp. 185-6.

30. Mesa-Lago, "Economic Policies and Growth," pp. 279-80.

31. Mesa-Lago, "Economic Policies and Growth," pp. 280.

32. The island produced approximately 15 percent of the global production and supplied one-third of the sugar sold in the international market. Further, sugar is characterized by very low income elasticity, i.e., a rise in world income has little effect on the demand for the commodity.

financial backing of the National Bank of Cuba, established a Stabilization Reserve.

Thus, Cuba's new development strategy aimed at reducing the economy's dependence on its traditional export staple while stimulating industrial and agricultural diversification. Several measures were taken by the government to give substance to this diversification strategy.[33] In 1952, Cuba negotiated a new trade agreement with the United States, superseding the one in force since 1934. This agreement, notes Antonio Jorge,[34] was favorable to Cuba for it allowed the country moderate protection for its infant industries while simultaneously promoting diversification of exports to old and new markets. Unlike, e.g., Chile, Argentina, and Uruguay which—following the so-called ECLA (CEPAL) Doctrine—pursued strongly inward-looking trade strategies, Cuba in the late 1950s chose the more prudent middle course. An Industrial Promotion Law was enacted in 1953 that granted, among other things, tax incentives to new industries. Finally, credit was mobilized through official development banks set up during the early fifties. These included the Banco de Fomento Agrícola e Industrial de Cuba (1951); the Financiera Nacional de Cuba, organized in 1953 mainly to provide credits for public works; the Banco Cubano de Comercio Exterior, founded in 1954 to encourage nontraditional exports; and the Banco de Desarrollo Económico y Social, established in 1955 to administer the government's development program.[35] The public works projects included the construction of a good water system for Havana, a toll road and the tunnel under Havana Bay, and a new highway, the Vía Blanca.

Cuba's balance of payments position was strengthened in the 1950s by the development of the island's tourist industry and the growth of export earnings for products other than sugar. The expanded operations of the U.S. government-constructed Nicaro Nickel Co. and the Moa Bay Mining Co., a subsidiary of Freeport Sulphur Company, assured Cuba a position as a major supplier of nickel in the world. Hotel construction from 1952 to 1958 almost doubled the existing hotel existing hotel capacity in Havana and other major cities. In addition, numerous hotels and motels were under construction in 1958, involving a total investment in excess of $90 million and a projected capacity of 6,066 rooms.[36] Foreign tourist expenditures in Cuba increased from $19 million in 1952 to a yearly average of $60 million in 1957-58. Four large hotels, the Habana Hilton, the Capri, the Habana Riviera, and the Nacional—owned by U.S. citizens or corporations—figured importantly in the island's expanded capacity to accommodate tourists seeking first class service.[37]

Cuban agricultural diversification gained momentum after 1952 and was reflected in gains in exports of farm and livestock products other than sugar. Rice production, advancing from 118,000 tons in 1951 to 261,000 tons in 1957, was a notable case of foreign exchange savings. The livestock industry, second only to sugar as a source of farm income, prospered during the fifties; Cuba's cattle herd was built up rapidly from about 4 million head in 1952 to 5.8 million head in 1959.[38] Starting from a small base, Cuba's fish catch grew notably, from an annual average of 8,300 metric tons (MT) in 1948-52 to 22,600 MT in 1957.

---

33. See Banco Nacional de Cuba, *La Economia Cubana en 1956-57* (La Habana, 1958).

34. Antonio Jorge, "Cuba's Economic Model(s) and Economic Rationality," in *The Cuban Economy: Dependency and Development,* edited by Antonio Jorge and Jaime Suchlicki (Coral Gables: University of Miami North-South Center for the Research Institute for Cuban Studies, 1989).

35. United Nations, Economic Commission for Latin America, *Economic Survey of Latin America, 1957* (New York: United Nations, 1959), p. 182.

36. Cuban Economic Research Project, *A Study on Cuba,* derived from Table 428, p. 569.

37. Cole Blasier, "The Elimination of United States Influence," in *Revolutionary Change in Cuba,* p. 62.

38. U.S. Department of Agriculture, *A Survey of Agriculture in Cuba* (Washington, 1958), p. 22, Table 6.

Industrial diversification gained momentum in the 1950s with particularly sharp increases registered from 1952 to 1957 in the output of cement (56 percent), rubber tires (66 percent), and chemical fertilizers (46 percent).[39] Production of electric energy grew at a cumulative annual rate of 10.6 percent from 1952 to 1957. Rapid advances also were made in the manufacture of paper from bagasse, in flour milling, and the dairy products industry. Cuba achieved self-sufficiency in petroleum refining with a capacity at the end of 1959 of 83,000 barrels per day supplied exclusively by two U.S. affiliates, Texaco and Exxon, and the Royal Dutch-Shell group.[40]

According to the Banco Nacional, investment in Cuban industrial installations exceeded $600 million from 1952 to 1956.[41] Of this amount, $324 million was invested in 154 new plants and $288 million in the expansion of existing plants. The magnitude of these industrial undertakings can better be appreciated by comparing the $600 million investment increment with the accumulated industrial capital stock in the sugar sector of $1,159 million (cited earlier): the new investment in diversification equaled over half the capital in the sugar industry. In its review of Cuba's economy, the U.N. Economic Commission for Latin America observed that a significant number of projects were underway in 1957:

> The purpose of these investment programs in the manufacturing sector is to make Cuba completely self-sufficient at an early date in cement, tires and tubes, glass containers, aluminum sheet and copper wire and cables, and relatively self-sufficient in light steel products . . .[42]

During the latter 1950s Cuba's steel mill, Antillana de Acero, was mounted and operated by a Cuban entrepreneurial group with the technical assistance of

Table 1.   Cuba: Gross Investment in Fixed Capital, 1953-57 *(millions of pesos at 1950 prices and percentages of the gross product)*

Year	Public Investment		Private Investment		Total	
	Value	%	Value	%	Value	%
1953	26	1.3	194	9.5	220	10.8
1954	39	1.8	209	9.7	248	11.6
1955	109	4.8	266	11.7	374	16.5
1956	171	6.8	309	12.5	480	19.4
1957	151	5.6	334	12.4	485	18.1

Source: United Nations, Economic Commission for Latin America, *Economic Survey of Latin America, 1957* (New York, 1959), p. 182.

With 1953 as a base year, the index of manufacturing production (excluding sugar) rose from 133 percent in 1958 to 145 in 1959.[43] This robust growth rate during the first year of the revolutionary regime suggests that many of these investment projects were still in their gestation phase when Batista fell from power. Examples include the Moa Bay plant which started operations in 1959 and the Cuban Telephone Co. which, in 1957, began a five-year development program.

From 1953 to 1957, the Cuban economy experienced a sharp upward trend in real capital formation, both private and public, signifying growing autonomy of this key variable from the exigencies of international trade. As Table 1 indicates, real gross investment increased from 220 million pesos in 1953 (about 11 percent of Cuba's GDP) to an average annual level exceeding 480 million pesos in 1956-57 (nearly 19 percent of GDP). The accelerated capitalization of the Cuban economy in sectors other than sugar production is also reflected in the changing composition of imports. The purchase abroad of

---

39. United Nations, Economic Commission for Latin America, *Economic Survey of Latin America, 1957* (New York: United Nations, 1959), pp. 190-93.

40. *The New York Times* (August 21, 1960), sec. 3F.

41. Banco Nacional de Cuba, *Programa de Desarrollo Económico*, Informe No. 2 (La Habana, 1957), p. 19.

42. United Nations, Economic Commission for Latin America, *Economic Survey of Latin America, 1957*, p. 192.

43. Jorge Pérez-López, *An Index of Cuban Industrial Output, 1930-1958*, Ph.D. dissertation, State University of New York at Albany, 1974. Cited in Claes Brundenius, *Revolutionary Cuba: The Challenge of Economic Growth and Equity* (Boulder: Westview Press, 1984), pp. 34-35, Table 2.2.

Table 2. Cuba: Composition of Imports by Economic Categories, 1953-58
(million U.S. dollars)

Economic Category	Consumer Goods		Raw Materiala and Fuels		Fixed Capital Goods		Total	
	Value	Percent	Value	Percent	Value	Percent	Value	Percent
1953	221.9	46.2	160.7	32.8	96.9	20.0	480.7	100.0
1954	226.4	46.5	163.7	33.5	977	20.0	487.9	100.0
1955	224.5	39.0	210.7	36.6	139.8	24.4	575.1	100.0
1956	234.4	36.1	244.5	37.5	169.9	26.4	649.0	100.0
1957	287.8	37.1	278.6	36.2	206.4	26.7	772.8	100.0
1958	303.5	39.0	265.3	34.0	208.2	27.0	777.1	100.0

Source: Banco Nacional de Cuba, *Memoria 1956-57*, p. 162, Table 6.16, and Cuban Ecnonomic Research Project, *A Study on Cuba*, p. 618, Table 464.

fixed capital goods (Table 2) climbed steeply from less than $100 million (20 percent of total imports) in 1953 to an average of $207 million annually (27 percent of imports) during the two years 1957-58. Of the fixed capital goods purchased abroad in 1957-58, 63 percent was invested in industry, 10 percent in diversified agriculture, 13 percent in motorized transport, and an equal share represented construction equipment.[44] The share of consumer goods, mainly foodstuffs, in total imports fell from 46 percent to 1953-54 to 38 percent in 1957-58. These data and the preceding discussion indicate that Cuba, in the 1950s, made important gains in diminishing its dependency on the sugar sector.

U.S. DIRECT INVESTMENTS: THE CHANGING STRUCTURE OF DEPENDENCY, 1946-59

Following World War II, Cuba's investment climate was one of the most favorable in Latin America. The Constitution of 1940 guaranteed the protection of property and established the judicial procedure for special cases involving expropriation. Property could be expropriated only for just cause involving a public utility or social interest and, then, only through prior indemnification of the owner in cash as determined by the courts.

In sharp contrast to the more general postwar experience in Latin America, Cuba enjoyed financial stability through the period analyzed. The cost of living re-

mained relatively stable, the peso continued at par with the U.S. dollar, and foreign exchange operations were free of control. The magnitude of the nation's external public debt[45] and the debt-service ratio were of minor importance throughout the 1947-1958 period. Profits, interest, and other factor payments could be freely remitted abroad and the risk of currency devaluation was negligible.

From 1946 on, new U.S. investments in Cuba (see Table 3) assumed a highly diversified pattern and flowed into a spectrum of Cuba's economic activities: infrastructure, manufacturing and commerce, petroleum refining, diversified agriculture, mining, and the tourist industry. The augmented production capabilities represented by U.S. subsidiaries and branches in Cuba were primarily directed to meet the requirements of the local market. Of the $403 million increment in U.S. direct investments in 1946-59, petroleum refining accounted for $129 million, manufacturing for $75 million, public services for $60 million, and commerce for $32 million. New investments in diversified agriculture, mining, and hotels account for the remaining $107 million. These U.S. business investments in Cuba were decisive in the growth of electric power and telephone service, in the rapid advance of petroleum refining, and the mining of nickel, and helped support the diversification and growth of manufacturing.

---

44. Banco Nacional de Cuba, *Memoria 1957-58*, p. 192, Table 6.16.

45. Cuba's total long-term foreign debt was only $48.2 million at the end of 1958. Ministerio de Hacienda data, cited in José M. Illán, *Cuba* (Miami: Editorial AIP, 1964), p. 75, Table 31.

Table 3. U.S. Direct Investment Position[a] in Cuba, by Sector, 1946 and 1959
    (million U.S. dollars)

Industry	1946		1959		Value Change 1946-1959
	Value	%	Value	%	
Agriculture	227	41.0	[b]	—	a
Public Utilities	253	45.8	313	32.7	60
Manufacturing	40	72	115	12.0	75
Commerce	12	2.2	44	4.6	32
Petroleum[c]	14	2.5	143	15.0	129
Other	8	1.4	341	35.7	333
Total	553	100.0	956	100.0	403

Source: U.S. Department of Commerce, *Investment in Cuba* (1956), p. 10, Table 5; *U.S. Investment in the Latin American Economy* (1957), p. 175, Table 96; and *Survey of Current Business* 40:9 (September 1960), p. 20, Table 1.

a. Does not include the U.S. Government-operated Nicaro Nickel Co. or the business holdings of the more than 5,000 U.S. citizens residing in Cuba.
b. Included in "other."
c. Mainly refining only.

LeoGrande's "capital drain" allegation is contradicted by his own data which shows that (except for the year 1951) the stock of U.S. direct investment in Cuba increased every year from 1943 to 1960.[46] As with other "dependency theorists," he fails to appreciate that profit remittances have their origin not in the capital account but in the income or production generated by multinational firms operating within the host country.

A comprehensive survey of the impact of U.S. business investments on foreign countries was issued by the U.S. Department of Commerce in 1960. Among other things, the survey revealed the extent to which U.S. firms participated in the Cuba economy through production of their subsidiaries and branches for the island's market and exports. The survey, however, does not include the export operations of the U.S. Government-operated Nicaro Nickel plant, tourism services provided by U.S.-owned hotels in Cuba, or the sales of more than 5,000 businesses owned by U.S. citizens residing in Cuba. As Table 4 shows, total sales of Cuban subsidiaries and branches of U.S. firms were about $730 million in 1957, of which $456 million (63 percent) were directed to the local market and $273 million (37 percent) to foreign markets. Of the $310 million agricultural sales, 80 percent were exported (principally sugar), and the

balance reflected U.S. operations in cattle ranching, rice and tobacco growing. The preponderant share of the $150 million of manufactures sold by the U.S. affiliates (86 percent) was absorbed by the Cuban market, as were also the sales of petroleum products (98 percent). Exports of manufactured goods ($21 million) comprised mainly processed nickel. The services provided by U.S. affiliates—electric power, telecommunications, and public service railroads—were sold exclusively to Cuban customers ($118 million).

U.S. firms operating in Cuba also made critical contributions to the nation's balance of payments position in 1957[47] through export earnings ($273 million), net capital inflows ($88 million), and foreign exchange saved through import substitution ($130 million). Offsetting these contributions were income remittances plus fees and royalties (totaling $56 million) and imports (other than imports of trading companies or of petroleum to be processed in Cuba) amounting to roughly $100 million. By this calculation, U.S. companies accounted for a direct net foreign exchange gain or saving to Cuba on the order of $335 million. (Analytically, one should deduct from this value an allowance for net production which would be yielded by total resources operating without the capital and organization provided by the U.S.

46. William M. LeoGrande, "Cuban Dependency."

47. "U.S. Business Investments in the Cuban Economy," Release of November 14, 1960 (OBE 60-83).

Table 4.   Sales by U.S. Affiliates and Brances in Cuba, by Industry and Destination, 1957 (million U.S. dollars)

Industry	Local		Export		Total	
	Value	Percent	Value	Percent	Value	Percent
Agriculture	61	19.7	249	80.3	310	100.0
Manufacturing	128	86.0	21	14.0	149	100.0
Public Services	128	100.0	—	0.0	128	1000
Petroleum[a]	115	97.5	3	2.5	118	100.0
Other	24	100.0	—	0.0	24	100.0
Total	456	62.6	273	37.4	729	100.0

Source: U.S. Department of Commerce, *U.S. Business Investments in Foreign Countries* (Washington: U.S. Government Printing Office, 1960), pp. 110-111, Table 22-23.

a. Mainly refining.

subsidiaries. Considering the (a) existence of substantial slack in the Cuban economy and (b) the unlikelyhood of Cuban entrepreneurs to engage in large-scale mineral development, one can conclude that the above-noted adjustment would not significantly alter the value added to Cuba's real national income.)

The U.S. subsidiaries in Cuba employed an estimated 160,000 persons in 1957 and of 2,000 supervisory, professional, and technical personnel, less than 500 were sent from the United States.[48] Foreign subsidiaries were cited by the World Bank Mission as "among those employers who pay the highest wages and who, for the most part, scrupulously observe Cuba's labor legislation."[49] While employing only seven percent of Cuba's labor force, the U.S. companies in 1957 accounted for one-third of the island's merchandise export earnings and a little under one-fifth of total government revenues.

The economic cost to Cuba of U.S. business holdings, measured by the rate of return (profit) on equity investment, appeared to be quite low when compared with U.S. direct investments in the rest of Latin America, in other parts of the world, and at

home. Annual earnings for the 1950-1959 decade averaged $47 million, or 6.3 percent of equity investment, 7 percent of exports, and 2 percent of the GNP, not a price too high to have paid for foreign venture capital.[50] Most profits did not leave the island, but were reinvested.

The participation of U.S. direct investments in the structure of the Cuban economy in the latter 1950s was considerable, as indicated by the following approximate shares: electric power and telephone service (90 percent), raw sugar production (37 percent), commercial banking (30 percent), public service railways (50 percent), petroleum refining (66 percent), insurance (20 percent), and nickel mining (100 percent).[51]

Notwithstanding these large U.S. equity holdings in Cuba, it is very important to observe that private Cuban groups succeeded in winning ownership and control over economic activities formerly dominated by U.S. and other foreign investors. The outstanding cases are sugar, banking and insurance, and air transportation. A majority of the stock in the leading airline, Compañía Cubana de Aviación, originally a

48. U.S. Department of Commerce, *United States Business Investments in Foreign Countries* (Washington, 1960), p. 122, Table 34.

49. International Bank for Reconstruction and Development, *Report on Cuba*, p. 734

50. Derived from *Survey of Current Business*, 1956-1961, August and September issues.

51. See Eric N. Baklanoff, *Expropriation of U.S. Investments in Cuba, Mexico, and Chile* (New York: Praeger Publishers, Inc., 1975), chapters 2 and 6, and Leland L. Johnson, "U.S. Business Interests in Cuba and the Rise of Castro," *World Politics* 18:2 (April 1965).

wholly-owned U.S. subsidiary, passed eventually into Cuban hands.[52]

Table 5. Cuba: Sugar Mills and Production According to Nationality of Ownership or Control

Nationality	1935		1958	
	Number of Mills	Output (%)	Number of Mills	Output (%)
Cuba	50	13	121	62
United States	70	62	36	37
Other Foreigners	59	25	4	1
Total	179	100	161	100

Note: A number of the corporations classified as U.S. owned had Cuban stockholders.

Source: *Anuario Azucarero de Cuba* (La Habana,: Editorial Mercantil, 1959)

From the 1930s on, Cubans purchased a large number of sugar mills from U.S., Canadian, Spanish, Dutch, and French interests.[53] As Table 5 shows, the U.S. share of Cuban sugar production declined from 62 percent in 1935 to 37 percent in 1958. Other foreign investors, whose sugar mills produced 25 percent of Cuba's sugar in 1935, had sold virtually all of their holdings by 1958. The divestiture of sugar mills by foreign enterprises was accompanied by the transfer of cane land to Cuban ownership. Significantly, the small farmers grew only nine percent of Cuba's cane in 1932, but by 1958 their share was well over 50 percent.[54] In consequence, Cuban capital controlled three-fourths of the sugar mills; and these, in turn, accounted for 62 percent of the island's sugar production in 1958. Local business interests, whose share of Cuba's sugar production had been reduced to a mere 13 percent in 1935, thus regained their position of dominance after the Second World War.

Transfer of these foreign assets into Cuban ownership proceeded through normal commercial channels and procedures—a manifestation of the progressive maturation of the island's business community and postwar prosperity.

CONCLUDING OBSERVATIONS

On the eve of the Cuban Revolution, the island had an essentially semi-industrialized market economy with a strong orientation toward the United States— its predominant trading partner and external source of direct investment. Cuba's relatively small population (6.5 million in 1958), its location on the threshold of the United States, the largest "common market" in the world with which it had concluded preferential trade agreements; its tropical climate; and specialized resource endowment—these and other factors conditioned the island's intimate commercial and financial ties with the United States.[55]

In the early 1950s, Cuba's policymakers adopted a new development strategy aimed at rapid economic diversification. Official measures in support of this strategy included the mobilization of new credit facilities, investment tax incentives, a moderate degree of protection from external competition of selected industries, and the construction of public infrastructure projects. This period saw a dramatic rise in the country's investment coefficient, and the accelerated capitalization of the Cuban economy in activities other than sugar production also was reflected in the rapidly-expanding share of machinery and equipment in total imports. Industrial capacity advanced substantially in a number of branches, particularly electric power, glass containers, cement, oil refining, chemicals, nickel mining and processing, paper, and light copper and steel products. In addition to sugar

---

52. United Nations, Department of Economic and Social Affairs, *Foreign Capital in Latin America* (New York: United Nations, 1955), p. 80.

53. From 1934-51, Cubans purchased 32 mills from U.S. interests for about $35 million; nine from Canadians for $7,750,000 and two each from Spanish, Dutch, and French interests for a total of about $5 million. During the period of 1952-55, inclusive, five mills came under Cuban control. U.S. Department of Commerce, *Investment in Cuba* (Washington: Government Printing Office, 1956), p. 37, footnote 16.

54. O'Connor, *The Origins of Socialism*, pp. 27-28.

55. Before Cuban independence, and despite tariff preferences favoring Spain, the value of U.S.-Cuban trade by 1881 was over six times that of the island's commerce with Spain. See Jules Robert Benjamin, *The United States and Cuba: Hegemony and Dependent Development, 1880-1934* (Pittsburgh: University of Pittsburgh Press, 1977), p. 5.

mills and many traditional industries, Cuba had in 1958 an impressive complex of intermediate capital goods industries. American enterprise and technology played an important role in the development of intermediate capital goods production industries in the fifties.

Contrary to the "decapitalization" allegation, U.S. direct investment in Cuba from 1946 to 1959 supported the country's economic growth and diversification drive. The augmented production capabilities of U.S. subsidiaries operating in Cuba made important contributions to the country's balance of payments position through new export earnings (tourism and nickel), and foreign exchange saved through import substitution (manufacturing, oil refining, commerce, the pastoral industry). The economic cost to Cuba of U.S. business holdings, measured by the rate of return on equity investment, appeared to be modest when compared with U.S. direct investments in the rest of Latin America, in other parts of the world, and at home.

Through normal business channels, Cuban entrepreneurs gained ownership and control over economic activities formerly dominated by U.S. and other foreign investors. Most importantly, Cuban private capital owned three-fourths of the sugar mills and these in turn accounted for 62 percent of the island's sugar production in 1958.

The backwardness-stagnation thesis cannot be supported by the preponderance of empirical evidence. In comparison with other Latin American countries, Cuba on the eve of the revolution was not only well off, as measured by per capita income, but also quite advanced in terms of such social indicators as literacy and health.[56] Significantly, the tropical island economy had the lowest mortality and infant mortality rates in Latin America in 1958.

Those who wish to arrive at a fair assessment of the Cuban revolution's achievement, e.g., in literacy and public health, would be well advised, as Luxenburg recommends, to go back to the sources for prerevolutionary figures and then draw their own conclusions. As I have illustrated, numerous academicians, members of Congress, as well as practitioners of the media elite, have failed to follow his sensible advice. On the Cuban experiment, they have engaged in a good deal of self-deception. "It is unfortunate," concludes Luxenburg, "that our Western press lends itself so ignorantly to mendacious handouts."[57]

The newly-installed Castro regime inherited an economy undergoing robust investment in the nonsugar sector. Several industrial projects were still in their development phase and continued into 1959. Domestic and U.S. enterprises clearly were mobilizing their capital resources in preparation for the anticipated Caribbean tourism boom of the 1960s of which Cuba could have been the principal beneficiary.

Problems of high unemployment and rural poverty were negative legacies bestowed by the old regime. On the other hand, Cuba in the late 1950s was not burdened by external debt dependency or an inefficient parastatal sector. Guided by the 1940 Constitution, a new democratic government enjoying widespread popular support could have addressed the negative legacies cited above. Cuba's economic policy makers on the eve of the revolution were more in conformity with the "New Thinking" of the 1990s than the then fashionable (and now somewhat quaint) doctrines that influenced many of their Latin American counterparts.

Four decades after the Marxist-Leninist revolution, Cuba shares with North Korea and Laos the dubious distinction of being classified the most "unfree-repressed" among the world's 150 economies.[58] It is ironic that in Latin America and the Caribbean, only Haiti shares with Cuba the "unfree-repressed" designation.

---

56. On this point see also Robert A. Packenham, "Capitalist Dependency and Socialist Dependency: The Case of Cuba," *Journal of Interamerican Studies and World Affairs* 28:1 (Spring 1986), pp. 59-89.

57. Luxenburg, "A Look at Castro's Statistics," p. 62.

58. Kim R. Holmes, Bryan T. Johnson and Lena Melanie Kirkpatrick, editors, *1997 Index of Economic Freedom* (Washington and New York: The Heritage Foundation and Dow Jones and Co., 1997).

THE STRENGTHS AND WEAKNESSES OF
FACTOR ANALYSIS IN PREDICTING CUBAN GDP

Nicolás Sánchez and Miles Cahill[1]

This paper has a dual purpose. At the technical level, it updates the work of Gitanjali Joglekar and Andrew Zimbalist (1989) on the use of factor analysis to estimate per capita Gross Domestic Product (GDP) for Cuba. At the analytical level, it questions the validity of this approach when the underlying economic structure of factor analysis is based on the data of relatively unregulated economies such as those of other Latin American countries.

The main conclusion of the paper is that while factor analysis is indeed a powerful predictor of the economic performance of market economies, it tends to overestimate the level of economic activity of command economies, and it fails to take into account subjective (i.e., utility-related) values which are assumed to be an intrinsic part of any measure of economic well being. If this criticism stands, then it follows that other similar studies of Cuban GDP are failing to provide a good measure of economic performance and well being in this island nation.

This study is part of a more comprehensive attempt to compare individual Latin American economies, as of 1989-1990, with those of the various states of the United States for prior decades. This has dictated the type of data that has and has not been used: on the one hand, it has been necessary to find comparable statistics for the Latin American countries and the various states of the United States; on the other, it has been impossible to use easily accessible, standard data for international transactions and monetary variables. As a result, the data used in this study are not identical to those used by Joglekar and Zimbalist (1989).

Although the authors found some other per capita GDP estimates for Cuba, these presented at least one of the following problems: (a) the methodologies used in the calculations were not made explicit; (b) the numbers were inconsistent, over time, with well known trends; and (c) the validity of the figures were questioned by the scholars reporting them.

Central Intelligence Agency estimates (CIA, 1990-present) fall under (a) above. For both 1989 and 1990, per capita GNP for Cuba was given at $2,000, a figure that is about 10% below the figure for Argentina for 1989 ($2,217) and close to 20% below the figure for 1990 ($2,560). In contrast, per capita GNP for Haiti was $380 for 1989 and $440 for 1990. In those two years the Cuban figures fell between the two estimates for Chile: $1,970 for 1989 and $2,130 for 1990.[2] Years later, the CIA reported a 1996 per capita GDP figure for Cuba of $1,480; for

---

1. This is a revised version of a longer paper presented at the 1998 ASCE Annual Meetings. The authors thank Roger R. Betancourt and John F. O'Connell for useful comments and criticisms.

2. This is quite significant, as the subsequent analysis will show; however, the comparison has to be qualified by the fact that the Chilean figures were for GDP while the Cuban figures were for GNP. The significance of Chilean statistics to evaluate Cuban performance had been noted by Romeu (1995).

Argentina, $8,600; for Chile, $8,400; and for Haiti, $1,000.

These figures are not entirely comparable over time, since the earlier estimates referred to GNP and the later ones to GDP, and the earlier estimates used market prices while the later ones used purchasing power parity (PPP) prices for the foreign exchange rates. However, the CIA figures suggest that Cuba in 1990 had some catching up to do relative to Argentina, but was very close to Chile; then Cuba experienced a catastrophic drop in economic activity during the 1990s. The first two inferences require confirmation, while the third one is widely agreed to in the economics literature (Betancourt, 1996). Those who have carefully studied the history of the Castro regime have argued that the apparent health of the Cuban economy during the 1980s could be attributed to the massive Soviet subsidies during that period (Pérez, Jr., 1988); this contention will be addressed later in the paper.

United Nations estimates for Cuban GDP,[3] as reported in the various issues of *Human Development Report*, are inconsistent. According to this publication (UNDP, 1991-present), real per capita GDP for Cuba, using PPP$, was $2,500 in 1989, $2,200 in 1990, $2,000 in 1991, and then surprisingly $3,412 for 1992 and $3,000 for 1993. Caveats to the 1992 and 1993 figures state that these new estimates made use of the Penn World Tables, which began to be used widely in the literature in the 1990s.

The figures for 1992 and 1993 present some serious problems of interpretation. Since most scholars consider 1993 the trough of economic performance in Cuba (Mesa-Lago, 1996), would it be appropriate to assume that per capita GDP in 1989 was, say, 35%[4] above the 1993 figure? In other words, was Cuban per capita GDP in 1989 at the $4,050 level, close to that of Argentina ($4,310) for that year? The *Human Development Report* is not supportive of this assertion, since earlier issues noted a much wider disparity between the Cuban and Argentinean economic performances. The puzzle that the newer figures create makes it appropriate to try to find an independent, and hopefully transparent, estimate for Cuban GDP at the end of the 1980s.

A third set of figures for Cuban GDP comes from the *Banco Nacional de Cuba,* and this set has been widely reported by serious scholars interested in Cuban affairs. In addition to being reported in pesos, creating the need to argue about the appropriate exchange rate, their reliability have been seriously questioned. Pérez-López (1997) pointed out that the 34.8% contraction that the Cubans reported between 1989 and 1993 "still is not as large as the one which the Cuban media had reported earlier, one that was presumably also based on official statistics." Carranza Valdés (1993) estimated a cumulative decline of about 38% for the Global Social Product (which presumably would track GDP) for the shorter 1989-92 period. Ritter (1997) estimated a decline of "perhaps" 45% for per capita GDP between 1989 and 1993, while Pastor and Zimbalist (1998) estimated a cumulative decline of 35% to 45% for GDP between 1989 and 1993.

In light of these problems, then, the authors of this study searched for earlier estimates of Cuban economic performance in order to update them to the 1989-1990 period, which was the one of interest to them. This they found in the Joglekar and Zimbalist (1989) article, which had the added advantage of using the same methodology that was being used by the authors to compare the Latin American economies to those of the states within the United States. This methodology had also been used before to find per capita GDP estimates for the Eastern European command economies (Szilágyi, 1978).

THE STRENGTHS OF FACTOR ANALYSIS

Factor analysis is an extension of multiple regression analysis, including some modifications that make the approach less likely to be influenced by the personal biases of the researcher, and less dependent on the assumption of independence among variables. Techni-

---

3. Based on a wide variety of sources, including the World Bank.

4. This figure was chosen to match the estimates of the Cuban National Bank.

cal explanations of factor analysis at various levels of difficulty can be found in the books by Norušis (1994), Kline (1994), Yotopoulos and Nugent (1976), and Mulaik (1974).

Ideally, in multiple regression analysis, one would observe a dependent variable on the left hand side of an equation that is "explained" by a set of independent variables on the right hand side. The problem, however, is that the connecting link between dependent and independent variables needs a strong theoretical basis. Furthermore, many of the so called "independent" variables may not really be independent at all, but rather change or move together in response to some other unknown variables or "factors." Hence the researcher usually encounters criticism of both the proposed theoretical framework and the method of untangling the mutual dependence among the presumably independent variables.

In contrast, factor analysis is used to determine the underlying determinants of many variables, without the need to postulate causality. This is especially useful because economic and social indicators are closely intertwined, making it nearly impossible to find a set of economic and social variables that are not correlated in some way. This interdependence makes normal regression analysis problematic but, surprisingly, does not adversely affect factor analysis.

Factor analysis, then, is a formal mathematical procedure that estimates the unobserved independent factors (or components) that characterize the various so-called independent variables. Because they can be constructed to be independent, the factor estimates (called factor scores) can be used in regression analysis to find the correlation between the factors and the dependent variable. The dependent variable may or may not be incorporated directly into the procedure that estimates the independent factors. If one is looking to estimate a missing observation for a dependent variable, such as per capita GDP for a particular country (as is the goal of this study) then this variable is not made part of the procedure.

The mathematical procedure is less likely to be influenced by the personal biases of the researcher because he or she is supposed to include as many variables as possible, allowing it to dictate how the variables are grouped together into factors. It is also usually found that a much smaller number of factors than variables is able to explain most of the variance of any of the variables included in the procedure, or later used as a dependent variable.

Critics of factor analysis point out that in reducing the original variables into a smaller number of factors, some information is lost. Specifically, when the number of extracted factors is less than the original number of variables, the factors do not explain all the variance of the original variables. Further, it is suggested that the regression coefficients obtained by factor analysis are biased (Green, 1997).

However, when the variables are closely related, simple regressions are not possible. Multicollinearity (as this problem is called) results in high standard errors and low t-statistics despite high R^2 values. This makes it difficult to determine which of the explanatory variables do in fact significantly affect the dependent variable. Factor analysis, by extracting a few linearly independent factors, provides a method to allow the information in the correlated variables to be included in the regression (Green, 1997). Furthermore, this statistical method determines the importance of each of the variables in making up factors, rather than leaving it to the personal biases of the researcher. Thus, factor analysis is an acceptable method with which to address the multicollinearity problem.

Regrettably, the number of factor *sets* that may be constructed is infinite: this follows from the fact that the number of factors is usually less than the number of variables used to construct or discover the factors. Hence, it is customary to follow a small number of standard approaches, and then consider which set of factors provides the better economic interpretation of what has been found. Since this study was mainly interested in finding a set of factors that correlated well with GDP, it allowed the most common procedure, called principal components, to dictate the construction of the factors.

As an indication of the usefulness of factor analysis, this study will first apply it to 1990 social and eco-

275

nomic data of the Latin American economies.[5] The approach will extract underlying factors, and use these factors to estimate 1990 per capita GDP for each market economy (but not Cuba). Later the same approach will be used to estimate the per capita GDP for Cuba.

Per capita GDP is the most often used indicator of economic development and welfare for an economy. GDP measures the market value of all final goods and services produced within the borders of a nation in one year. It is a measure of national income because income is earned from the sale of goods produced. When divided by the population, GDP measures how much income each man, woman and child would receive if all income was distributed equally.

Since higher incomes lead to higher levels of consumption, per capita GDP is also used as an indicator of economic welfare. However, per capita GDP is by no means a flawless yardstick to compare the welfare of nations. One reason is that not all goods are sold on organized markets. Another is that exchange rates for the local currency must be chosen, and these may not be market rates. A third reason is that it does not take into account the actual distribution of income. Yet, despite these faults, it has become the standard with which to measure and compare the level of development and welfare.

A basic hypothesis of this study is that the level of per capita GDP is strongly correlated with, and thus may be predicted by, the combination of 37 social and economic indicators that relate to demographics, labor market, infrastructure, education, health, energy use, the agricultural sector, and the relative importance of other sectors in the economy.[6] The analysis employs the commonly used principal components method of factor analysis to extract seven (independent) factors from these observed indicators, and then uses a linear regression to determine the correlation between these extracted factors and per capita

GDP.[7] Since about 84% of the variance of the sample can be accounted for by the factors, it is appropriate to conclude that the regression equation is a good fit; this is confirmed by an F test, which is statistically significant at the 99.9% level. The formal procedure is detailed below. See now Figure 1.

The figure above compares actual and predicted levels of per capita GDP for 1990, where the countries are sorted by the actual level of per capita GDP for each country. As can be seen, factor analysis is indeed a good method of predicting the level of per capita GDP, despite the fact that it does not use production data.

Few students of the Latin American countries would dispute that *actual* per capita GDP is a good measure of economic development of these countries, yet the *predicted* per capita GDP values of factor analysis may offer an even more accurate ranking of development for the Latin American economies. The *predicted* values place the Southern-cone countries of Argentina, Uruguay and Chile (together with oil-rich Venezuela) ahead of Mexico and Brazil in terms of economic performance and possibly development. The *predicted* values for the poorest countries may also provide a more accurate ranking of economic performance than those based on *actual* GDP.

Given these results, then, it appears that factor analysis is a natural tool to estimate the per capita GDP of relatively unregulated market economies, and that it could conceivably be used to estimate the market value of per capita GDP in command economies, as others have done (e.g. Szilágyi, 1978). This conclusion will be seriously questioned in a subsequent section, after the study reports on the main findings for Cuba.

ESTIMATING CUBAN PER CAPITA GDP

This section gives an explanation of the factor analysis procedure used in this paper, and specifically how

---

5. The countries include Argentina, Bolivia, Brazil, Chile, Colombia, Costa Rica, Cuba, the Dominican Republic, Ecuador, El Salvador, Guatemala, Haiti, Honduras, Mexico, Nicaragua, Panama, Paraguay, Peru, Uruguay, and Venezuela.

6. The list of variables is presented in the Appendix, which also includes a brief explanation of their computation.

7. Cuban data, excluding GDP estimates by other organizations, were used to extract the original seven factors.

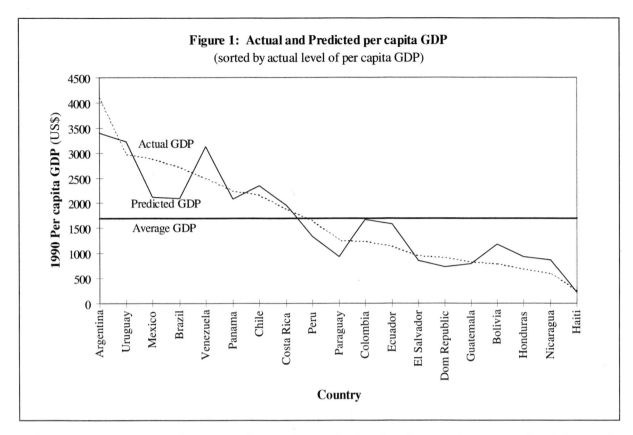

Figure 1: Actual and Predicted per capita GDP
(sorted by actual level of per capita GDP)

Cuban per capita GDP may be estimated using this method. Readers who are more interested in the final results, rather than in the details of the work, should move on to Table 3 and the relevant text at the end of this section.

Factor analysis was used, first, to reduce the 1990 data for 37 variables (not including per capita GDP) to seven factors in the sample of all 20 Latin American economies (including Cuba).[8] Principal components was used to extract these factors. The number of factors was chosen using a commonly accepted rule: use each factor with an eigenvalue of one or greater (for otherwise individual variables would have greater predictive power than the estimated factor). The seventh factor had an eigenvalue of 1.096, and the eighth of 0.968. A screen plot, also traditional in the literature of this procedure, confirmed that seven factors were an appropriate number. Corroboration of the effectiveness of the factor analysis was given by

the fact that the seven factors reproduced the correlation between the 37 variables well. In particular, only 18% of the residuals had absolute values greater than 0.05.

The extraction phase of factor analysis produced a component matrix, which essentially displayed the correlation coefficients of each of the seven factors for each of the 37 variables. These correlation coefficients are equivalent to regression coefficients for each of the factors regressed on the 37 variables, and are called factor loadings.

The component matrix was rotated to allow for an interpretation of the factors. Factor rotation recomputes the factor loadings by shifting the amount of variance accounted for by each individual factor. It does not change the total variance accounted for by all of the factors combined. The Varimax technique with Kaiser Normalization was used for the rotation (Norušis, 1994). This method minimized the num-

---

8. As a side note, the data was converted to standardized (z-score) form. This was done by subtracting each data point by the mean of the sample and dividing the remainder by the sample standard deviation.

Table 1. Total Variance Explained by Rotated Factors

Component (factor)	Eigenvalue	% of Variance explained by factor	Cumulative % explained by factors
1	11.12	30.06	30.06
2	6.64	17.93	47.99
3	5.45	14.73	62.72
4	2.94	7.95	70.67
5	2.43	6.56	77.22
6	2.33	6.30	83.53
7	1.40	3.78	87.30

ber of variables that have high loadings for each factor. The rotated component matrix appears in a separate appendix which is not reported here, but is available directly from the authors upon request.

The factors appear to measure different aspects of modernity. In particular, the values of factors 1, 3, 5 and 7 are negatively associated with modernity, while the rest of the factors are positively associated with it. The variables most strongly correlated with factor 1 are demographic and health variables; factor 2 relates mainly to energy consumption; factor 3 (except for the death rate) accounts both directly and indirectly for certain inputs; factor 4 addresses population density considerations; factor 5 is correlated mainly with the construction sector; and factors 6 and 7 closely track education. Table 1 shows the percent of the variance of the sample that is accounted for by each of the factors after rotation.

Next, values for the seven factors were estimated for each of the 20 Latin American countries using a linear regression technique. The component score coefficient matrix (available in the separate appendix, not included here) displays a vector of coefficients for each factor that, when multiplied against the vector of data (for all 37 variables) for each country, produces factor scores for each country. These factor scores essentially constitute seven new variables, which are estimates of the underlying factors (or components) that explain 87.3% of the variance of the 37 original variables.

To estimate an equation that relates per capita GDP to these seven factors, a linear regression was per-

formed using data from the 19 market economies (but not Cuba). Specifically, 1990 per capita GDP was regressed on a constant and the seven series of factor scores. Since the Varimax method is an orthogonal rotation method, the factor scores are truly independent and hence not correlated with one another.

The regression results show how per capita GDP is correlated with the seven factors in market economies. The results of the regression are presented below, in Table 2. Table 2 also reports results for GDP adjusted for terms of trade (GDPTT) (from the Penn World Tables). This latter measure uses international prices for domestic absorption but current prices for exports and imports.

The predicted values derived from these regression results were those plotted in Figure 1 of the previous section. It was also from this regression that the estimate of per capita GDP for Cuba was obtained. Specifically, the regression coefficients in Table 2 were used in conjunction with the factor scores for Cuba (obtained from the original factor analysis). It should be noted that because the Penn World Tables does not report data for Haiti, those estimates were obtained without Haitian data.

Table 3, below, reports the predicted values for each of the 19 original countries and Cuba. Actual values for the 19 other Latin American countries are also provided for reference. All data has been converted to dollar values from the standardized (z-score) form.

The predicted level of 1990 per capita GDP for Cuba, nearly $2,600, is fourth highest, between Venezuela and Chile. It is almost $900 higher than the average of the countries (almost $1,700). This estimate is consistent with other estimates, including those of the CIA ($2,000 for per capita GNP) and the original estimate reported in the Human Development Report ($2,200 for per capita GDP). When GDPTT data from the Penn World Tables are used, the estimates for Cuban per capita GDPTT are even higher. Estimates using 1990 real per capita GDP in 1985 prices adjusted for changes in terms of trade (GDPTT) is $5,420, second only to Venezuela. These higher estimates are consistent with the revised

Table 2. Regression results

Dependent variable	Per capita GDP (z-score)			Per capita GDPTT (z-score)		
Independent Variable	Regression Coefficient	t-statistic	Significance level	Regression Coefficient	t-statistic	Significance level
Constant	0.000	0.000	1.00	0.002	0.154	0.88
Factor 1	-0.593	-5.170	0.00	-0.546	-3.620	0.01
Factor 2	0.563	4.907	0.00	0.739	7.017	0.00
Factor 3	-0.220	-1.915	0.08	-0.134	-0.486	0.64
Factor 4	-0.246	-2.141	0.05	0.004	-0.239	0.82
Factor 5	0.076	0.660	0.52	-0.144	-0.953	0.36
Factor 6	0.233	2.033	0.06	0.250	1.682	0.12
Factor 7	-0.063	-0.549	0.59	-0.221	-2.239	0.05
R^2	0.842			0.893		
Adjusted R^2	0.750			0.818		
Std. Error of estimate	0.500			0.426		
F	9.135			11.928		

Table 3. Actual and Predicted per capita GDP

Country	Predicted GDP	Actual GDP	Predicted GDPTT	Actual GDPTT
Argentina	3403	4081	5076	4663
Bolivia	1176	796	1485	1591
Brazil	2094	2715	3529	4029
Chile	2338	2170	4778	4399
Colombia	1662	1236	3122	3287
Costa Rica	1957	1881	3536	3447
Cuba	2578	—	5420	—
Dom Republic	726	912	2233	2233
Ecuador	1583	1137	2600	2669
El Salvador	847	954	2101	1760
Guatemala	787	832	1363	2138
Haiti	212	254	N/A	N/A
Honduras	933	686	1691	1401
Mexico	2125	2888	4492	5793
Nicaragua	864	599	1593	1207
Panama	2079	2249	3371	2785
Paraguay	926	1248	2315	2093
Peru	1334	1656	2448	2185
Uruguay	3222	2975	4304	4663
Venezuela	3120	2495	6172	5867

figures found in Human Development Report when the Penn World Tables were used. The use of chain-weight real GDP results in similar findings.[9]

THE WEAKNESSES OF FACTOR ANALYSIS

The GDP estimates of the previous section are remarkable in that they match the previous *relative rankings* obtained by Joglekar and Zimbalist (1989) in their study of per capita GDP for Cuba in 1980, although in their study Venezuela had come out on top among Latin American countries, at $3,621.

9. Specifically, estimates for Penn World Tables 1990 chain weight real per capita GDP (at 1990 prices) is $5,233 (second in the region only to Venezuela). These estimates are consistent with the revised figures found in *Human Development Report* when the Penn World Tables were used.

This country was followed by Argentina, Uruguay, Cuba, Chile, Brazil and Mexico (at $3,265, $2,815, $2,691, $2469, $2,427 and $2,224, respectively).[10] Hence, the Joglekar and Zimbalist study, together with the results of the previous section, lead to the conclusion that Cuba, at least for the decade of the 1980s, had a per capita GDP that approximated that of Chile. Or else, one has to draw the conclusion that the methodology of factor analysis is somehow in error. It should be noted that the estimates of economic output are even higher when GDPTT statistics are used, an issue that will be addressed below.

Using other "rudimentary" methods (according to their own terminology), Joglekar and Zimbalist (1989) estimated that the per capita GDP of the Cuban economy in 1980 was between the Venezuelan and Chilean figures, matching the estimates obtained in this paper. These results, then, must be confronted head on by those who have been critical of the economic performance of the Castro regime. What could possibly be wrong with consistent estimates across independent studies?

Critics of the regime have argued that Cuba did relatively well prior to the 1990s economic collapse due to massive Soviet subsidies—and these subsidies cannot be denied. They have also argued that the regime has been lax or deceitful in calculating economic and social data—and again there is some evidence to support this contention (Aguirre and Vichot, 1996). Yet even most critics of the Cuban regime accept the notion that it achieved significant goals in some fields, such as health, education and basic income security (Romeu, 1995).

With the collapse of the Cuban economy, the focus of attention among Cuban scholars has shifted to *what should be done under present circumstances*.[11] But an important question remains: is it worthwhile to save some of the characteristics of the pre-1990 economic regime, or should Cuba discard its command structure and become a market economy? To answer this question it is necessary to understand as well as possible what was *really* happening in the previous decades.

This study will not dispute the important role of subsidies in propping up the old Cuban economy or the general weakness of Cuban statistics. Rather, it will focus on the fact that (a) the GDP estimates from regression or factor analysis will generally overestimate economic performance; and, even if they do not, (b) the GDP figure is an ambiguous measure of economic welfare.

As noted earlier, the procedure used to estimate per capita GDP essentially found the correlation between the factors and per capita GDP. The seven factors did not contain output data; instead, they consisted of data relating the structure of demographics, health care, education, infrastructure, agriculture, energy, and the relative importance of different economic sectors. The implicit assumption is that countries with a given level of GDP tend to have the same demographic characteristics, level of health care, education, etc. In market economies, it is generally understood that greater levels of income lead to the demand for more public goods or goods with important public goods characteristics, higher energy use, lower birth rates, and certain shifts in economic structure (from agricultural-based to manufacturing and service-based economies).

Public goods have two major characteristics: (a) the consumption of the good by one individual does not subtract from that of others, and (b) it is costly to exclude any individual from enjoying its benefits. National defense is a pure public good, as is the legal framework within a country. A public good may be thought of as providing significant positive externalities or indirect benefits to consumers. A sewer or water system, for example, will tend to improve the overall health of the population, even when some

---

10. Given that Joglekar and Zimbalist had placed more emphasis on output measures (including steel and cement production) and that Venezuela had a strong economy in 1980 as a result of its oil production, the top ranking for Venezuela among the Latin American countries is not surprising.

11. Although many examples could be given, the article by Castañeda and Montalván (1997) is typical of this shift in interest.

people may not have direct access to it. Measures to decrease inequality may tend to reduce social conflict, and potentially make everyone better off. The success of national sports teams makes every citizen proud and hence better off. An educated citizenship will hopefully make better collective choices, which is a positive benefit even to those with limited education.

In contrast, private goods benefit only those consuming them, and it is relatively cheap to acquire exclusive rights to them. Some goods and services produced by governments are purely private in nature, such as mail delivery, but others, like education, have some significant public-goods characteristics. Although in practice it is impossible to find an exact method of dividing goods into two mutually exclusive categories, such categories are commonly used as theoretical constructs within the economics literature; for an example, see Stiglitz (1988, p. 11).

In command economies, many of the socioeconomic behaviors of people (which are associated with modernity in market economies) are not necessarily linked to the income level that the economies have achieved. For example, higher per capita GDP in market economies are associated with lower population growth and fertility rates, as families do not have to rely on children for household labor and elder care. These elements of development are contained in the regression equation of Table 2; factor 1, which is negatively correlated with these health and demographic factors, has a negative regression coefficient when used to estimate per capita GDP. In command economies, elder care and household income is determined and provided by the state, reducing the incentive to have children. Thus, the link between these demographic variables and per capita GDP in the regression equation should not apply—The regression equation is not an appropriate tool for estimating the GDP of command economies. Because command economies with low incomes generally have demographic characteristics similar to countries with high incomes, the factor analysis model is likely to overestimate the per capita GDP of command economies.

In general, in command economies, the quantities of many public goods are not necessarily correlated with

per capita GDP in the same way that they are in market economies. At any output level, the government may choose to limit or restrict the provision of private goods to emphasize the provision of either public goods or goods with important public-goods characteristics. Consider the following example. Marshall (1998, p. 287) notes that in Cuba, "one is struck by the lack of automobiles…[and] a massive six lane super-highway…is normally empty." Apparently, in Cuba, the number of road miles is not related to the number of vehicles. Generally, however, road mileage is related to GDP directly (as commerce increases, so do the number of vehicles and consequently the demand for roads) and indirectly (as the number of roads increases, commerce becomes less costly, raising GDP). In the regression results for the Latin American market economies, GDP indeed increases as road mileage increases. The large number of roads (per capita) in Cuba, then, leads to a spuriously high prediction of per capita GDP. Similar arguments can be made about health care, education, and many other variables whose proportion to GDP in Cuba is greater than in market economies.

The conclusion that must be drawn is that regression or factor analyses, based on the characteristics of market economies, cannot properly estimate the per capita GDP of a command economy. The proportion of public goods—or goods with important public goods characteristics—to private goods, and the relationship between demographic characteristics and GDP will differ significantly between market and command economies. Yet, the factor analysis technique estimated the relationship between the quantities of public goods and GDP, and demographic characteristics and GDP (among other correlations) in market economies to estimate the per capita GDP of Cuba. Since command economies provide public goods at high rates (regardless of GDP) resulting in demographic characteristics similar to higher income market countries, it is likely that GDP is overestimated in command economies.

However, even if that was not the case, one other question remains: does per capita GDP in a command economy reflect the true level of economic welfare? Economic theory is quite clear that to calculate consumer surplus, a measure of economic welfare, one needs to take into account the subjective valuation that consumers place on goods. This is done by considering utility maps and the compensation that consumers must receive to freely move from one consumption bundle to another. The value of commodities to consumers depends on how well the commodities satisfy the consumers' tastes; in fact, it is impossible to derive the demand for goods without acknowledging that these functions depend on the utility or subjective values that consumers derive from commodities.

Suppose that a country produces only two types of goods: private and public goods. In a market economy of a developing nation, or at least in those that are lightly regulated, one is likely to observe a preponderance of private goods benefiting the citizens directly. This is so because the production of public goods requires some degree of centralization, which is costly to achieve, and because it is difficult to prevent anyone from consuming the public goods, giving the citizens an incentive to avoid paying for them (thereby creating the need for a coercive tax mechanism which is resented by the population). It has been observed, however, that as a society becomes more productive and wealthier, market economies produce more public goods, or at least goods with important public-goods characteristics.[12] This is not surprising, for the relative abundance of private goods that accompany development, and the relative dearth of public goods, makes the former less valuable than the latter at the margin, and the citizens are willing to trade off private for public goods. Also, the process of development itself lowers the cost of organizing a central authority. Thus, as countries develop, consumers demand and receive more public goods.

It is now possible to represent the normal growth process of a developing economy with the assistance of Graph 1. It will be assumed that consumers (but

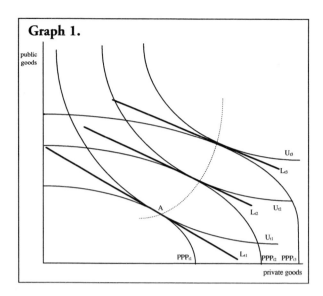

Graph 1.

not the central planner, oligarchy or "ruling class"[13]) have identical and homothetic indifference maps, which are then aggregated in the form of community indifference curves.

The first production possibility frontier PPP_{t1} represents the productive capacity of the economy at the initial period t1, while the community indifference curve U_{t1} represents the aggregate preferences of consumers in that economy. The tangent line L_{t1} represents the price ratio between private and public goods. Initially, consumers desire a large number of private goods, making them relatively expensive.

As the growth process takes place in real time, the productive capacity of the economy is enhanced, and consumers reach higher levels of satisfaction as they move to the tangency of U_{t3} and PPP_{t3}. The broken line shows the expected relative growth of public goods, and tangent line L_{t3} (which is flatter than L_{t1}) demonstrates that private goods are becoming cheaper to obtain while public goods are becoming more expensive.

It is now possible to hypothesize a set of events that will characterize the development process of a command economy, such as has occurred in Cuba since

---

12. This has been the experience throughout most of this century, although there is now evidence that the growth of the government sector is slowing down. See Saunders (1993) and Lin (1993).

13. More on this point below.

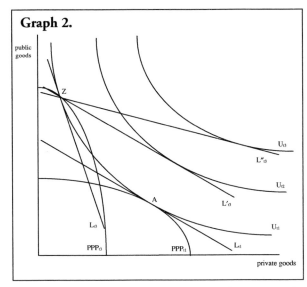

Graph 2.

1960. Starting out from the same set of initial conditions depicted in Graph 1 (with PPP_{t1} and U_{t1}), the adoption of a command economy will bring forth a dramatic restructuring of the economy in real time, leading to greater production of public goods.[14] This will happen both for ideological reasons (since the leaders will prefer public to private goods) and for economic reasons (since it will be easier to maintain the production efficiency of public goods, which are normally produced by national or regional monopolies even in market economies, than the production efficiency of private goods, which normally thrive under market competition).

This restructuring can now be observed in Graph 2, where it is represented by the shift of the production frontier to PPP_{t3}. For analytical purposes, the utility map remains the same, although it is recognized that those in control of the economy may try to influence the preferences of consumers to get them to desire a greater consumption of public goods.

Although prices are not determined in the market in a command economy, that does not mean that it is not possible to calculate the valuation that consumers place on goods when the utility map is known. Assume that A represents the initial consumption level of consumers, and that Z represents the final bundle of goods available to them (as prescribed by the authorities). In this case line L_{t3} is tangent to U_{t1}, representing the subjective value to consumers of the goods that they purchase; but note that consumer welfare, by construction, has not improved at all, since consumers remain on the initial utility line U_{t1}. However, if bundle Z is evaluated at the old market prices, using L'_{t3}, or at market prices that prevail at other economies where public goods have naturally become more expensive, using line L''_{t3}, an outside evaluator will reach the conclusion that the level of output of this economy as measured by GDP has increased or kept up with that of other countries, and then infer that consumer welfare has increased. This conclusion, however, is an illusion.

It is not surprising, then, that when GDPTT statistics are used (which make corrections for the terms of trade—equivalent in developing countries to using line L''_{t3}) one will obtain even higher estimates for the value of economic output.

The typical economic and social variables that are used to compare economies at the macro level contribute to this illusion. Better education, better health and basic income security are perceived by most political leaders as goals that, if attained, provide many benefits to all citizens; but when those economic activities that lead to the achievement of these goals are emphasized, the provision of private goods will have to be neglected, for the simple reason that any society has limited resources. The absence of private markets, including those that contribute to a vigorous financial sector that helps direct the allocation of resources, will destroy the efficient production of private goods.

Neither production statistics, nor variables normally associated with development, allow the researcher to draw unambiguous inferences about consumer welfare in a command economy. It could be argued, of course, that *no one* is in the condition of making welfare comparisons: using identical and homothetic indifference maps for consumers, as is done in this paper, is a very restrictive assumption indeed. While

---

14. With one significant exception: the maintenance of environmental quality. See Sáez (1998).

there is some validity to this argument, it should be noted that (a) the use of this assumption is widespread in the literature; (b) introducing interpersonal comparability without cardinality resolves the theoretical problems associated with social welfare functions and aggregation, making social welfare comparisons possible (Sen, 1987); and (c) dividing the Cuban population between the vast majority of consumers, who may have, if not identical, at least very similar preferences, from a central planner, dictator, oligarchy or a "ruling class" that imposes its own preferences on the rest of the population, is not unrealistic.

Consumers in Cuba are not free to make their choices known, and those in control of the economy do not know what the consumers want. A quote from Moreno Fraginals (1997, pp. 213-214) goes to the heart of this observation: "But when a regime is created in the image of a few people, these few believe it to be their duty to direct others' lives from the cradle to the grave… When the capacity to direct one's own life is reduced, people either reach a point of desperation or become utterly ambivalent about their own lives." This problem becomes particularly acute when the citizens are not even given the opportunity to choose their leaders through a democratic process. The construction industry, for instance, may produce public buildings rather than private houses highly desired by consumers. Hospitals may increase their ability to admit patients, but the consumers will not have access to over-the-counter medicines that would have been sold in private markets. Schools may engage more people in the educational process, but the citizens will be limited as to the choice of books that they can purchase and the career choices open to them. New highways are built which consumers cannot use, for lack of cars and gasoline.

The emphasis on the provision of public goods can be sustained for a long time under two sets of circumstances: if the economy is subsidized from abroad, or if the capital which used to sustain the production of private goods is neglected—and there is no doubt that the capital stock for private good production has been neglected in Cuba (Pastor and Zimbalist, 1998). This has been best observed in Cuba's most important industry, sugar (Sanguinetty, 1997), but it has also affected other industries that are very important for consumer welfare: private transportation and housing (Pérez, Jr., 1988).

When individuals are free to choose their trading opportunities, including those in the labor market, they will choose those occupations that will maximize their utility. It is for this reason that few people will engage in "voluntary" (unpaid) labor for significant amounts of time, unless they are coerced to do so. When coercion is applied, the individual suffers great disutility, even if the outcome of the effort is some measured output. Measures of GDP for command economies fail to account for this disutility, whereas one can assume that labor in a market economy will be engaged in production only if the effort leads to a net gain in personal satisfaction.

The Cuban population has been restricted in its human capital investment plans. By destroying, or at the very least minimizing the size of the private goods economy, the population has failed to develop the skills that allow most populations to engage in foreign transactions, which normally involve trade in private goods. Trading itself will help increase the human capital of the population (Pissarides, 1997). This may explain the inability of the Cuban economy to adapt to producing for the global market. The one exception to this is the tourist trade, which occurs within national borders; not surprisingly, the Cuban government has turned to this industry for its economic survival.[15]

CONCLUSIONS

This study has updated estimates of per capita GDP for Cuba, for the year 1990. In relative terms, the per capita figure for Cuba is similar to that of Chile, confirming the estimates of the Central Intelligence

---

15. Another possible exception might be the biotechnology sector. This industry, however, received support from the government because of its symbolic significance (Feinselver, 1992). It is difficult to believe that these firms will be able to compete in global markets over the long run, since they disregard the patents of other companies and are bound to find legal difficulties in various nations.

Agency for that year. In absolute terms, the estimated $2,578 figure of this study is close to the original United Nations estimate of $2,200 for 1990 and $2,500 for 1989. The consistency of all three estimates cannot be ignored.

In 1960, Cuba was one of the most economically advanced countries of Latin America, matching the per capita consumption of electricity that was observed in Chile for that year (UN, 1961). Thirty years later, if one is to believe the estimates of this study, the CIA, and the United Nations, the Cuban and Chilean economies had similar levels of economic performance; their income growth would presumably indicate an improvement in consumer welfare.

This optimistic picture has been changed with the collapse of the Soviet Union. Chile's per capita GDP continues to be among the highest in Latin America, while the Cuban economic performance is beginning to match that of the poorest country of the hemisphere. This paper has argued, however, that the Cuban performance in the first thirty years of the revolution cannot be interpreted unambiguously as an improvement in economic welfare, regardless of what the GDP estimates say. This is so because once consumer preferences are taken into account, the restructuring of the economy prevents us from concluding that an improvement in economic welfare took place; Cuba was producing more public goods *but* fewer private goods.

There are also reasons to believe that indirect estimates of per capita GDP for a command economy, including Cuba, tend to overestimate economic activity because these estimates are biased by the greater availability of public goods. Market economies produce more public goods as they become wealthier, within a natural development process; command economies, on the other hand, artificially *force* the production of public goods.

It has also been noted that the restructuring of the Cuban economy has made it dramatically vulnerable to global competition: the Cuban people simply do not produce enough private goods for the international market. This may explain why, once Soviet subsidies ended, Cuba's economic performance began to approach that of Haiti.

To repeat, since Cuban authorities do not have access to their countrymen's preference maps, which are normally revealed and acted upon in market economies, it is not possible to conclude that the Cuban people were better off after the first thirty years of the revolution: relatively high GDP figures for 1990 may mean little in terms of economic welfare. Although one cannot strictly argue that the Cuban people are worse off, either, since no one else has access to those preference maps, one must reach the conclusion that any argument about economic welfare based on per capita GDP for a command economy is not compelling.

BIBLIOGRAPHY

Aguirre, Benigno E. and Vichot, Roberto. "Are Cuba's Educational Statistics Reliable?" in *Cuba in Transition* 6 (1996), pp. 371-386.

Betancourt, Roger R. "Growth Capabilities and Development; Implications for Transition Process in Cuba, " in *Economic Development and Cultural Change* 44 (1996), pp.315-31.

Carranza Valdés, Julio. "Cuba: Los Retos de la Economía," in *Cuadernos de Nuestra América* 19 (1993), pp. 131-159.

Castañeda, R. H. and Montalván, G. P. "Cuba: Una Plena Reinserción Internacional, Comercial y Financiera con Estabilización Rápida, sin Recesión y con Crecimiento Alto, Estable y Sustentable," in *Cuba in Transition* 7 (1997), pp. 99-122.

Central Intelligence Agency. *World Fact Book*. Washington: Government Printing Office, (1990-present).

Feinsilver, Julie. "Will Cuba's Wonder Drugs Lead to Political and Economic Wonders? Capitalizing on Biotechnology and Medical Exports," in *Cuban Studies* 22 (1992), pp. 79-111.

Green, William H. *Econometric Analysis*, 3rd ed. Upper Saddle River, NJ: Prentice-Hall, 1997.

Joglekar, Gitanjali and Zimbalist, Andrew. "Dollar GDP per Capita in Cuba," in *Journal of Comparative Economics* 13 (1989), pp.85-114.

Kline, Paul. *An Easy Guide to Factor Analysis*. New York: Routledge, 1994.

Lin, David. "Recent Trends in the Size and Growth of Government in Developing Countries, in *The Growth of the Public Sector*, ed. By Norman Gemmell. Brookfield, VT.: Edward Elgar, 1993.

Marshall, Jeffery H. "The Political Viability of Free Market Experimentation in Cuba: Evidence from *Los Mercados Agropecuarios*," in *World Development* 26 (1998), pp. 277-288.

Mesa-Lago, Carmelo. "The State of the Cuban Economy: 1995-96" in *Cuba in Transition* 6 (1996), pp. 4-7.

Moreno Fraginals, Manuel. "Transition to What?" in *Toward a New Cuba? Legacies of a* Revolution, ed. by M. A. Centeno and M. Font. Boulder, CO: Lynne Reinner Publishers, 1997.

Mulaik, Stanley A. The *Foundations of Factor Analysis*. New York: McGraw Hill, 1972.

National Bureau of Economic Research, *Penn World Table*, <http://www.nber.org/pwt56.doc.html> 1998.

Norušis, Marija J. *SPSS, SPSS Professional Statistics 6.1*. Chicago, IL: SPSS Inc., 1994, pp. 47-82.

Pastor, Jr., Manuel and Zimbalist, Andrew. "Has Cuba Turned the Corner? Macroeconomic Stabilization and Reform in Contemporary Cuba," in *Cuban Studies* 27 (1997), pp. 1-20.

Pérez, Jr., Louis. *Cuba, Between Reform and Revolution*. New York: Oxford University Press, 1988.

Pérez-López, Jorge F. "The Cuban Economy in the Age of Hemispheric Integration," in *Journal of Interamerican Studies and World Affairs* 39 (1997), pp. 3-47.

Pissarides, C. A. "Learning by Trading and the Returns to Human Capital in Developing Countries," in *The World Bank Economic Review* 11 (1997), pp.17-32.

Ritter, Archibald R. "The Cuban Economy in the Mid-1990s: Structural/Monetary Pathology and Public Policy, in *Toward a New Cuba? Legacies of a Revolution*, ed. by M. A. Centeno and M. Font. Boulder, CO: Lynne Reinner Publishers, 1997.

Romeu, Jorge Luís. "More on the Statistical Comparison of Cuban Socioeconomic Development," in *Cuba in Transition* 5 (1995), pp.293-301.

Sáez, Hector. "Resource Degradation, Agricultural Policies, and Conservation in Cuba," in *Cuban Studies* 27 (1997), pp.40-67.

Sanguinetty, Jorge A. "The Structural Transformation of the Cuban Economy: A Report of the Last Twelve Months," in *Cuba in Transition* 7, 1997, pp. 8-12.

Saunders, Peter. "Recent Trends in the Size and Growth of Government in OECD Countries," in *The Growth of the Public Sector*, ed. by Norman Gemmell. Brookfield, VT: Edward Elgar, 1993.

Sen, Amartya. "Social Choice," in *The New Palgrave Dictionary of Economics* IV, ed. by John Eatwell *et. al.* London: Macmillan Press, 1987, pp.382-393.

Stiglitz, Joseph E. *Economics of the Public Sector*. New York: W. W. Norton and Company, 1988.

Szilágyi, G. Y. "Factor-Analytical Comparison of Economic Level and Structure," in *Acta Oeconomica* 21 (1978), pp.379-403.

United Nations. Economic Commission for Latin America and the Caribbean. *Anuario Estadístico de América Latina y el Caribe*. Chile (1990-present).

United Nations Development Programme, *Human Development Report*. New York: Oxford University Press (1991-present).

United Nations. *Statistical Yearbook*. New York: United Nations, 1961.

Wilkie, James W. (Ed). *Statistical Abstract of Latin America*. Los Angeles: UCLA Latin American Center Publications (1995-present).

World Bank, *Social Indicators of Development*. <http://www.ciesin.org/charlotte> 1998.

Yotopoulos, Pan A. and Nugent, Jeffrey B. *Economics of Development; Empirical Investigations*. New York: Harper and Row, 1976.

Appendix
DESCRIPTION OF DATA

AgeDependency—age dependence ratio:(pop. age 0-14 + pop. age 65-)/(pop. age 15-64)

Autos—number of automobiles per 1000 population (1991)

Births—births per 1000 persons, average for 1985-1990

Deaths—deaths per 1000 persons, average for 1985-1990

Dentists—number of dentists per 1000 persons (1993)

LaborParticipationFemale—percent of females age 10+ in labor force (employed or unemployed)

LaborParticipation—percent of total persons age 10+ in labor force

Electricity—electrical energy consumption in kilowatt hours per person

ConstructionEmploy—number of workers in construction sector as a % of total labor force (1994)

FinanceEmploy—number of workers in financial sector as a % of total labor force (1994)

AgEmploy—number of workers in agricultural sector as a % of total labor force (1994)

TradeEmploy—number of workers in trade sector as a % of total labor force (1994)

Energy—total energy consumption in kg of oil equivalent per person

AgSector—% of output produced by agricultural sector

ConstructionSector—% of output produced by construction sector

ManufactureSector—% of output produced by manufacturing sector

TradeSector—% of output produced by trade sector

HospitalBeds—number of hospital beds per 100,000 persons (1993)

Hydrocarbon—hydrocarbon (oil and natural gas) consumption in kg of oil equivalent per person

InfantMort—infant mortality rate: (children age 0-1 deaths/1,000 live births) (1985-90)

Irrigate—% of lands irrigated (1989-94)

Tractors—hectares of land per tractor

Newspapers—newspaper circulation per 1000 persons

Physicians—physicians per 1000 persons (1993)

PopAgeUnder15—population 0-14 as a percent of total population

ChildFemaleRatio—population 0-4 as a percent of female population aged 15-44

PopAgeOver65—population 65- as a percent of total population

PopDensity—population density (persons per square mile)

PopGrowth—average population growth rate (1985-90)

Railroads—1000 persons per mile of rail (1991)

Telephones—persons per telephone lines

Vehicles—persons per vehicle (autos, trucks, busses) (1991)

Roads—road miles per 1000 persons (1991)

St/TeacherPrimary—student teacher ratio at primary level of schooling (1991)

St/TeacherSecondary—student teacher ratio at secondary level of schooling (1991)

CollegeStudents—students in tertiary level of education per 100,000 persons (1992)

Fertility—total fertility rate

Source: NBER, 1998; UN, 1990-present; Wilkie, 1990-present; World Bank, 1998. Unless otherwise noted, all data is for 1990.

COMMENTS ON

"The Strengths and Weaknesses of Factor Analysis in Predicting Cuba's GDP," by Nicolás Sánchez and Miles Cahill

Roger R. Betancourt

This paper is interesting, well written, and for the most part insightful. Nonetheless, it fails to appreciate the main weakness of factor analysis for predicting Cuba's GDP, or that of any other command economy.

The essence of the technique, as the authors clearly explain, is to gather data on a number of socioeconomic indicators (37 of them in this case) for various countries (19 Latin American ones plus Cuba in this case) and to perform a factor analysis on these indicators that generates orthogonal components or factors and corresponding factor scores. These factor scores become (in this case the analysis generated seven factors) seven explanatory variables in a regression through the origin with GDP per capita as the dependent variable for the 19 Latin American countries that have data on GDP per capita. Cuba's GDP per capita can then be predicted by using the coefficients of this regression for each of the seven factors and Cuba's factor scores, based on the 37 underlying indicators for which Cuba does have data.

The results of this exercise are reported in Table 3 of the paper. If one uses GDP per capita in nominal or official exchange rates for the 19 Latin American countries, then Cuba's GDP will also be in terms of these units; if one uses GDP per capita in terms of purchasing power parity exchange rates or ICP$, then Cuba's GDP prediction would be in terms of these rates. Table 3 is in terms of official or nominal exchange rates and it predicts a GDP per capita of $2,578 for Cuba in 1990. One of the figures cited in the text for comparison, however, is from a United Nations *Human Development Report* that gives a figure for Cuba of $2,200 *in terms of purchasing power parity rates or ICP$* in 1990. The prediction for Cuba if one uses factor analysis to predict Cuba's GDP per capita in ICP $ is given by the authors in footnote 8, namely $5,223. This brings out that the prediction is way out of line, in contrast to the authors' assertion in the paper. The latter results from emphasizing the comparison with GDP's per capita in nominal exchange rates and ignoring that at least one of the estimates they use for comparison, namely the one from the *Human Development Report*, refers to ICP$.

This raises two related issues: first, which is the relevant magnitude to predict? and second, why is the difference so great when using ICP$? It is now well accepted in the economics literature that GDP per capita in ICP$ is the proper measure of welfare for international comparisons, because it incorporates both traded goods and nontraded goods and their prices. The difference is so large when using ICP$ precisely because command economies are even more distorted when it comes to nontraded goods and their prices than with respect to other sectors. The GDPs in ICP$ of the Latin American countries used as the dependent variables contained sizable nontraded sectors, for example retail and wholesale trade or banking and financial services. In 1990 Cuba these sectors barely existed (for example banking and insurance) or existed at a low level (for example retail and wholesale trade). This is an important if not the most important reason why it makes no sense to use factor analysis to predict Cuba's GDP per capita in ICP$, which is what one wants to measure in terms of welfare. The authors' own numbers indicate how far the prediction is from other **comparable** estimates—100% overprediction!

CONSUMER PRICES, MONEY SUPPLY AND LIBERALIZATION IN POST-COMMUNIST ECONOMIES

Ernesto Hernández-Catá[1]

The paper examines the behavior of consumer prices during the transition from plan to market in the countries of Central and Eastern Europe and the former Soviet Union from 1990 to 1996. It focuses on the influence of two key explanatory variables: economic liberalization and monetary growth, both across countries of the region and over time. This topic has been a controversial one. During the early stages of the transition in Eastern Europe and the former Soviet Union many who opposed reforms, and some who favored a gradual approach to reform, objected to rapid decontrol of prices on the grounds that it would be disruptive and would trigger an inflationary process. Critics of price liberalization were particularly vocal following the freeing of most prices in Russia by the government of Egor Gaidar in January 1992. The issue also has been a controversial one in the current debate about future reform in Cuba.[2]

On the basis of a simple model estimated for 26 countries over the period 1990–96, the paper concludes that:

- price decontrol had a substantial, albeit temporary effect on the price level, particularly in those countries where the inflation had been severely repressed towards the end of the period of central planning;

- while the initial jump in prices associated with decontrol was quite large in some countries, price liberalization had no *lasting* effect on inflation. Indeed, there are indications that economic liberalization broadly defined has tended to reduce inflation below what it otherwise would have been;

- there is strong evidence that monetary expansion has been the fundamental determinant of inflation in the region in transition countries.[3]

The final section of the paper seeks to explain the behavior of several indicators of liberalization in the former centrally planned economies. It presents empirical results that suggest that, in general, the degree of political freedom, the proximity to a thriving market economy, and the size of the underground economy tend to be associated with a rapid process of liberalization.

PRICES, MONEY AND LIBERALIZATION DURING THE TRANSITION

A number of recent studies have examined the behavior of inflation during the transition, but very few have analyzed the effects of both economic liberalization and monetary growth. The early—and essentially empirical—studies by Åslund, Boone, and Johnson (1996) and de Melo, Denizer, and Gelb

---

1. The views expressed are those of the author and not necessarily those of the International Monetary Fund.

2. See Carranza, Gutiérrez, and Monreal (1997) and Hernández-Catá (1997) for two different views on this issue.

3. This also has been controversial at times. For example, echoing a common view, Petrakov (1994) claimed that inflation in Russia was due not to monetary factors but to "structural deficiencies."

(1996b) found a cross-sectional *negative* correlation between inflation and a cumulative index of liberalization.[4] However, a subsequent study by de Melo and Gelb (1997) also found that there was a *positive* relation between inflation and liberalization in the early stages of transition, a result they correctly attributed to the initial effects of price decontrol. Finally, the important paper by de Melo, Denizer, Gelb, and Tenev (1998) detected a shift in the relationship between price liberalization and inflation from positive in the short run (one year) to negative in the longer run, although no theoretical explanation was provided for this empirical result.[5]

None of the studies cited above examined the link between prices and money—or between inflation and money supply growth—in the transition process.[6] Fischer, Sahay, and Vegh (1996) did include the fiscal deficit in their panel regressions and found that it was positively related to the rate of inflation in transition countries. Cottarelli, Griffiths, and Moghadam (1998) report a similar result in a larger sample including both transition and industrial countries. There is no doubt that fiscal deficits have been an important determinant of monetary expansion—and therefore of inflation—in transition countries as well as in many other economies. For various reasons, however, the fiscal deficit has not been a good proxy for the rate of monetary expansion in the transition countries: first, because at various times the governments' financing requirements were satisfied not only by resorting to the printing press, but also by selling assets, by borrowing from abroad, or by issuing domestic interest-bearing securities; and second, because in many countries, particularly in the former Soviet Union, support for a number of key regions, sectors and enterprises in the early stages

of transition was provided not through the budget, but via central bank credits, often at heavily subsidized interest rates.[7]

The model estimated in this paper provides a simple explanation for the fact that, in most transition countries, inflation appears to be *positively* related to price liberalization in the early stages of the transition, particularly in those countries where the liberalization effort was early and strong, while over the medium term the correlation between inflation and liberalization is negative and statistically significant. The paper differs from previous studies in that (1) it introduces explicitly the money supply as a key variable rather than relying on its proximate determinants such as the fiscal deficit; and (2) it examines separately the role of price decontrol and other aspects of economic liberalization such as privatization and trade liberalization.

THE MODEL

The model combines two basic equations: (1) a demand for *money* function; and (2) a definition of price liberalization:

$$M = (P)*Q/V \tag{1}$$

$$D = P/P* \tag{2}$$

where M = money supply
Q = output
V = velocity
D = an indicator of price decontrol $0 < D \leq 1$
P = actual level of consumer prices, and
$P*$ = equilibrium level of consumer prices.

If prices are fully decontrolled, P is equal to $P*$ and D takes on its maximum value of 1. If prices are fully controlled at a level $\overline{P}$, then $D = \overline{P}/P* > 0$. In words,

---

4. Unless otherwise noted, the index of liberalization used in this paper is the one constructed by a team of World Bank economists and explained in de Melo, Denizer, and Gelb (1996a). See also section on the model below.

5. That paper also contains an extensive investigation of the role of initial conditions in explaining growth and inflation in the transition countries.

6. A few studies have focused on this angle of the problem, but they are unconcerned with the link between inflation and liberalization. See De Broeck, Krajnyak and Lorie (1997), and, in the Russian context, Koen and Marrese (1995).

7. Examples are the support provided by the Central Bank of Russia to the far North and to the agricultural sector in 1992–93. See Hernández-Catá (1995).

D is inversely related to the gap between controlled and equilibrium prices, and therefore to the monetary overhang.[8] The equilibrium price level of P^*—i.e., the hypothetical price level at which the existing money supply would be willingly held—is unobservable, except in the limiting case where prices are fully decontrolled. However, since measures of price liberalization are available for all the countries covered in this paper, a quantifiable relation between the actual level of prices, the demand for money and the degree of price liberalization can be derived by combining equations (1) and (2):

$$P = DMV/Q \qquad (3)$$

The interpretation of equation (3) is straightforward. If prices are fully liberalized $(D=1)$ the actual price level is equal to the equilibrium price level and is therefore fully determined by the money supply, income and the determinants of velocity. If prices are fully controlled, these variables become irrelevant and equation (3) takes on the limiting form $P = \overline{P}$. As the economy is liberalized and D takes on values between zero and one, the money stock and other determinants of the demand for money play an increasingly important role in explaining the behavior of prices.

In quantifying equation (3), the price decontrol variable can be approximated by the de Melo-Denizer-Gelb price liberalization variable (L_{price}).[9] However, that variable is allowed to take zero values (indeed, it is equal to zero for most of the countries of the former Soviet Union in the pre-transition period 1989-90). This raises two problems: first, it makes it impossible to rely on a logarithmic transformation of

equation (3); and second, it is inconsistent with the definition of the price decontrol variable D used in this paper, which must always be positive, even when all prices are fully controlled. To circumvent these difficulties, we define the variable D' as a linear transformation of the de Melo-Denizer-Gelb price liberalization variable:

$$D = \beta + (1 - \beta)L_{price} \qquad (4)$$

where β must be positive but smaller than one, and D takes on a fractional positive value when $L_{price}=0$; both variables take on a maximum value of 1 when all prices are fully decontrolled.

Substituting for D in equation (3) and taking natural logarithms on both sides of the equation yields an expression that can be estimated by linear least squares on the basis of observable variables:

$$p_{it} = m_{it} - q_{it} + d_{it} + v_{it}^0 + \lambda L_{it} \qquad (5)$$

where i and t are subscripts referring to countries and years, respectively, and all other lower-case Latin letters refer to the natural logarithm of the corresponding variables.[10] Equation (5) assumes that velocity has an exogenous component v^0 that reflects the influence of starting conditions and other structural characteristics that may differ from country to country and possibly over time. These are captured by a number of dummy variable explained below. Furthermore, it is assumed that, other things equal, the higher the degree of economic liberalization (abstracting from price decontrol) the lower the price level, because factors such as freedom of entry in domestic markets, including financial markets, and openness

---

8. Consider an economy where a fraction w of all goods is sold at market-clearing prices (P^*) and a fraction $(1-w)$ is sold at controlled prices $(\overline{P})$. The ratio of actual to equilibrium prices will be proportional to the ratio of controlled to equilibrium prices, i.e.: $P/P^* = (\overline{P}/P^*)^w$. The ratio $\overline{P}/P^*$ itself is inversely related to the gap between actual and desired levels of the money stock—i.e., to the excess supply of money, or 'monetary overhang.' It may be noted that the variable V is the *structural* velocity of circulation of money and is *not* equal to the ratio of nominal GDP to money except when prices are fully liberalized, as is clear from equation (3).

9. This is one of the three sub-components of the aggregate liberalization variable constructed by the authors. The other two are for *external markets* (liberalization of foreign trade, including elimination of export controls and taxes, and substitution of low to moderate import duties for import quotas and high import tariffs; and currency convertibility);and for *private sector entry* (including privatization of small scale and large scale enterprises and banking sector reform).

10. In estimating the equations, the value of the parameter β was set arbitrarily at 0.1. Experimentation with alternative values in the range of 0.05 to 0.5 resulted in higher standard errors.

to external trade should be expected to enhance price competition. The more general liberalization variable L was approximated by a simple arithmetic average of the de Melo-Denizer-Gelb sub-indexes for non-price internal and external liberalization.

EMPIRICAL RESULTS

Equation (5) was estimated using data for 26 transition countries in Eastern Europe, the Baltic Region, Russia and other countries of the former Soviet Union, and Mongolia during the period 1990–96 (182 observations). The regression results are presented in Table 1 and detailed definitions and sources of variables are provided in Annex 1.

Equation 1.1 shows the results of estimating equation (5). All the estimated coefficients have the expected sign and are significantly different from zero.[11] Moreover, the estimated elasticities of consumer prices with respect to the money/output ratio $(m - q)$ and the price decontrol variable (d) are not significantly different form unity, which is in line with the model's basic specification. The coefficient of the non-price liberalization variable is significantly negative as expected, implying that liberalization in general tends to act as a restraining force on prices through enhanced competition and efficiency gains.

Equation 1.2. adds a set of four regional dummy variables: for the Baltics, Russia and other countries of the former Soviet Union; for three of the former Yugoslav Republics (Croatia, Macedonia and Slovenia); for the Visegrad countries (the Czech and Slovak Republics, Hungary and Poland); and for the other countries of Central and Eastern Europe. The results suggest that, other things equal, prices tend to be significantly higher in the countries of the former Soviet Union, and significantly lower in the former Yugoslav Republics. However, other results, discussed below suggests these regional coefficients lack robustness. Compared with equation 1.1, the coefficients of $m - q$ and d are virtually unchanged.

Table 1. Regression Results for Consumer Prices in 26 Transition Countries, 1990-96

	1.1	1.2	1.3	1.4
Constant	2.5*	1.91*	0.76	1.71*
	(5.4)	(4.4)	(1.4)	(3.8)
Broad money/real GDP (m - q)	1.05*	1.02*	0.86*	1.06*
	(34.1)	(27.8)	(16.9)	(23.0)
Price decontrol variable (d)	1.09*	1.10*	1.26*	0.95*
	(5.4)	(5.5)	(5.6)	(4.1)
Non-price liberalization variable (L)	-2.97*	-1.91*	-3.16*	-1.68*
	(5.0)	(3.6)	(5.1)	(3.0)
Dummy variables:				
Former Soviet Union	—	0.64*	1.03*	—
		(4.4)	(5.0)	
Former Yougoslav Republics	—	-1.30*	-6.89*	—
		(4.9)	(3.5)	
Visegrad countries	—	-0.02	0.33	—
		(0.2)	(1.2)	
Other Central & Eastern Europe	—	0.07	0.4	—
		(0.3)	(1.6)	
Location	—	—	-0.32	—
			(1.9)	
Age of communist regime	—	—	0.02*	—
			(2.6)	
Age of reform process	—	—	-0.27*	—
			(3.2)	
Fixed exchange rate	—	—	0.18	-0.04
			(0.7)	(0.2)
Adjusted R2	0.920	0.941	0.948	0.969

* The dependent variable in all equations is the natural logarithm of the consumer price index. Stars indicate that the coefficient is significantly larger or smaller than zero, as appropriate, at the 1 percent confidence level. Equation 1.4 is estimated using 25 individual country dummies (results not shown). Numbers in parenthesis are t-ratios based on heteroskedasticity-adjusted standard errors.

Equation 1.3 adds a number of dummy variables. *Location*—a variable proposed by de Melo, Denizer and Gelb and Tenev (1997)—has a value of 1 when the country is located in the proximity of a "thriving" market economy; and a value of zero otherwise. Its coefficient is expected to be negative, as the existence of efficient markets and institutions in neighboring countries should help to improve competition and put downward pressure on profit margins and prices. The *age of the communist regime* is defined for each transition country as the number of years from the beginning of communist rule to the beginning of the

---

11. Tests about whether a coefficient differs significantly from zero in the expected direction are based on one tailed t-tests and a 1 percent confidence interval which, for an infinite number of degrees of freedom, involves an absolute value of t greater than 2.33.

sample period (1990). It is expected to have positive sign because the longer the period, the more ingrained are command and control mechanisms likely to be, and therefore the longer it would take for formal price liberalization to affect behavior. The *age of the reform process* is defined as the current year minus the assumed first year of substantial liberalization (as defined in Annex 1). In this case, the expected sign is negative because the longer the period, the greater the confidence of market participants that reform and liberalization will not be reversed, and therefore the lower velocity is likely to be. Finally, the variable *fixed exchange rate* has a value of one when a country is under a fixed exchange rate system and a value of zero otherwise. This variable, proposed by Fischer, Sahay and Vegh (1996 and 1998), is intended to capture the favorable confidence effects of nominal exchange rate anchors on velocity, and its coefficient is therefore expected to be negative. In equation 1.3, all these dummy variables have the expected sign, except for the fixed exchange rate variable.[12] The variables measuring the length of the communist and reform periods are significantly different from zero. Finally, equation 1.4 provides a test of the fixed effects model by introducing a set of 25 individual country dummies.[13]

An examination of the four equations in Table 1 suggests that in general the results are fairly robust. In particular, the elasticities with respect to the money/output ratio and the price decontrol variable are insignificantly different from one in most equations. The coefficient of the non-price liberalization variable L is always negative, as expected, although its range of variation across equations is wider. Moreover, the coefficients of the regional dummy variables are quite sensitive to changes in specification, although they do suggest that velocity tends to be relatively low in the former Yugoslav republics, and relatively high in the countries of the former Soviet Union.

The role of monetary expansion and price liberalization in explaining price movements during the transition is illustrated by Figures 1 and 2. Each chart shows the actual level of consumer price inflation and the level predicted using a first difference form of equation (5) together with the estimated coefficients of equation 1.1. It also disaggregates predicted inflation into three components that reflect the impact of: (a) monetary expansion; (b) price decontrol; and (c) changes in non-price liberalization.

The left panels of Figure 1 illustrate the case of two countries that adopted a bold approach to liberalization and also succeeded in bringing down inflation rapidly. In Poland, the liberalization of most prices was achieved in 1990 which, coupled with the impact of relatively rapid monetary expansion in that year, caused inflation to rise into triple digit range. However, as the effect of price decontrol tapered off in the next few years and the growth of money was gradually reduced, inflation declined steadily to relatively low levels. Throughout the period, non-price liberalization had a significant dampening effect on inflation. Price liberalization in Lithuania also occurred at an early stage, and its initial effect on prices was even stronger than in Poland—partly because in 1990 prices were more rigidly controlled in Lithuania than in Poland, where some liberalization had already taken place. In Lithuania, however, both the surge of inflation in 1992 and its sharp decline subsequently reflected mostly the evolution of money growth.

The right panels of Figure 1 compare developments in two countries that allowed inflation to reach high levels but differed sharply in their approach to liberalization: Russia decontrolled most prices in early 1992 while in Turkmenistan prices were liberalized very gradually. In both countries inflation surged in 1992, mainly because of a sharp increase in money growth, although price decontrol also played a significant role, particularly in Russia. After that, however,

---

12. This result differs from the earlier results of Fischer, Sahay and Vegh (1996).

13. Most of the other dummy variables had to be removed from the equation because their interaction with the set of country dummies resulted in a quasi-singular matrix.

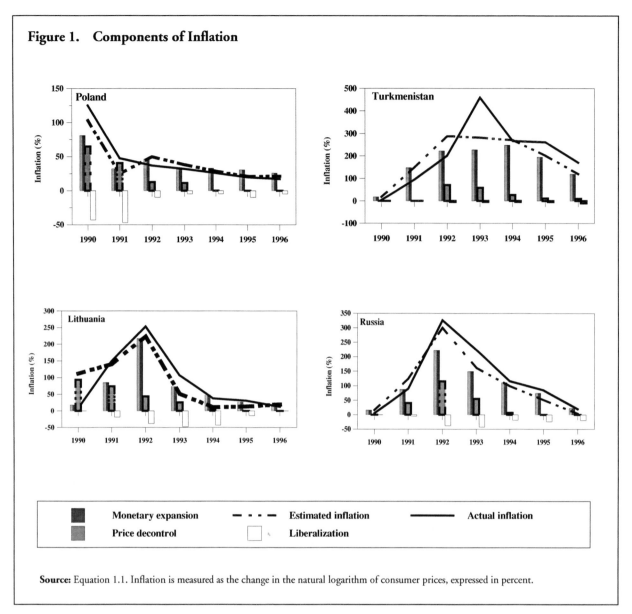

Figure 1.   Components of Inflation

Monetary expansion ■   Estimated inflation - - - -   Actual inflation ——
Price decontrol ▒   Liberalization ☐

Source: Equation 1.1. Inflation is measured as the change in the natural logarithm of consumer prices, expressed in percent.

inflation declined steadily in Russia while it remained at a very high level in Turkmenistan, reflecting a fundamental difference in the stance of monetary policy and, to a lesser extent, a faster pace of liberalization in Russia.

ACCOUNTING FOR LIBERALIZATION

The previous sections have examined the impact of economic liberalization, including price decontrol, on the behavior of prices during the transition. This section asks a different question: why have the speed and intensity of liberalization differed so markedly among transition countries? Table 2 shows the main results of an attempt to answer this question by relating the de Melo-Denizer-Gelb price and non-price liberalization[14] indexes to a number of economic, political and regional variables.

Separate equations were estimated for the price and non-price liberalization variables, although most of the explanatory variables are included in both sets of equations. These variables include the *age of the com-*

---

14. Separate equations were also estimated for the *external* and *market entry* components of the non-price liberalization variables; the results were very similar to those obtained using the average of those two components.

munist regime and the *location* dummies, both defined in the previous section. The longer the period of communist rule the more ingrained the institutions of a command economy and thus the greater the resistance to liberalization. In contrast, proximity to a free market economy should favor privatization and liberalization in general, by increasing familiarity with markets and markets-related institutions and by providing a demonstration effect. In addition, both sets of equations include a *political freedom index*, defined to range between -6 for a highly repressive political system to +7 for a free society with the guarantees for individual rights and the institutions normally associated with a modern democracy. It is assumed that the higher the political freedom index the greater the popular pressure for reform.

In addition to these political variables, the equations include a proxy for the share of the *underground economy*, defined as one minus the ratio of officially measured real GDP to electrical power consumption.[15] It is expected that a large underground economy should be associated with a relatively low resistance to price decontrol—and to economic liberalization more generally—because it indicates that a large share of the economy *de facto* has already been liberalized and, correspondingly, that a sizeable fraction of the labor force is interested in the ultimate success of a free economy. Finally, all the equations in Table 2 include a *Ruble area* dummy equal to one in those years in which a country was a member of the ruble area. The coefficient of this variable was expected to be negative inasmuch as membership in the ruble area often was associated with political interest groups that wished to retain some of the interrepublican ties that existed under the Union and that often opposed reforms.

The equations for price liberalization also include the *price liberalization gap with Russia*, i.e. the difference between the levels of price liberalization indexes in Russia and in transition country i. The larger this difference, the wider (and more widespread) the differentials between relatively free prices in Russia and

Table 2. Regressions for Liberalization Variables in 26 Transition Countries, 1990–96

Explanatory variables:	2.1	2.2	2.3	2.4
	Dependent variable:			
	price liberalization variable:		non-price liberalization	
Constant	36.7*	37.0*	17.9*	27.9*
	(3.5)	(2.5)	(2.5)	(2.4)
Political freedom index	1.33*	3.68*	1.34*	4.37*
	(3.1)	(7.2)	(4.2)	(10.3)
Age of communist regime	-0.34*	-0.20	-0.01	0.04
	(2.5)	(1.1)	(0.1)	(0.3)
Location	8.76*	12.3*	7.51*	13.1*
	(2.8)	(2.9)	(3.5)	(3.8)
Ruble area	-13.3*	-36.1*	-14.6*	-32.9*
	(4.0)	(10.1)	(6.8)	(11.2)
Undeground economy proxy	0.32*	0.69*	0.14*	0.24*
	(3.9)	(6.6)	(2.6)	(2.8)
Price liberalization gap with Russia	28.6*	2.65	—	—
	(5.0)	(0.4)		
Lagged dependent variable	0.58*	—	0.64*	—
	(11.7)		(16.4)	
Former Soviet Union	3.34	18.6*	2.47	9.16
	(0.6)	(2.7)	(0.7)	(1.6)
Former Yugoslav Republics	6.10	22.1*	0.20	15.0
	(0.9)	(2.6)	(0.1)	(2.2)
Visegrad countries	1.17	7.02	-0.20	3.24
	(0.2)	(0.9)	(0.1)	(0.5)
Other Central & Eastern Europe	2.17	13.1	-1.54	2.94
	(0.3)	(1.6)	(0.4)	(0.4)
Adjusted R²	0.838	0.710	0.913	0.776

Source: Numbers in parenthesis are t-ratios based on heteroskedasticity-adjusted standard errors. Stars indicate that the coefficient is significantly greater or smaller than zero, as appropriate, at the 1 percent confidence level.

controlled prices in country i (particularly if that country borders on Russia). Therefore a large price liberalization gap is expected to be associated with intense pressures for price decontrol in that country, so

---

15. Power consumption is used as a proxy for *true* GDP, and the difference between real GDP (as imperfectly measured in the national accounts) and power consumption is therefore interpreted as a measure of unrecorded output.

as to eliminate shortages resulting from arbitrage through either legal exports or smuggling. Finally, equations 2.1 and 2.3 report estimation results including lagged dependent variables as regressors to capture the adjustment costs associated with liberalization.

Turning to Table 2, all the estimated coefficients have the right signs and are significantly different from zero, except for most of the regional dummies and for the variable measuring the length of the communist period. Also, the price liberalization gap with Russia was vulnerable to the omission of the lagged dependent variable from the regression. The estimated coefficients for the latter variable are roughly 0.6, suggesting a speed of adjustment of approximately 40 percent in the first year. The long-term coefficients in the equations with lagged dependent variables (2.1 and 2.3) can be obtained by dividing the reported (short-run) coefficients by the speed of adjustment, i.e, by 0.4. On that basis, and with the exceptions noted above, the estimated parameters in Table 2 appear to be reasonably robust with respect to changes in specification.

Some of the key implications of the analysis are illustrated in Figure 2.[16] Figure 2 includes two countries that have achieved a high degree of liberalization. The Czech Republic benefitted from favorable location—outside the former Soviet Union and in the proximity of free market economies like Austria—and therefore the value of its (non-price) liberalization index was already relatively high in 1990, at the beginning of the sample period. Moreover, an already high degree of political freedom in 1990 increased further during the 1990s, and by 1996 the Czech Republic had attained the highest level of liberalization among the 26 former communist countries included in this study (95). By contrast, in 1990 Latvia still belonged to the ruble area—and, under duress, to the USSR—fared poorly in terms of political freedom, and scored only 5 in the liberalization scale. Over the next six years, however, Latvia's liberalization index increased rapidly (to 85 in 1996) as the country left the ruble area in 1992, its degree of political freedom increased considerably, and the underground economy expanded.

Figure 2 also illustrates the case of two economies where liberalization has made little progress. In the early 1990s, both Belarus and Turkmenistan belonged to the Soviet Union and to the ruble area, they were not geographically close to market economies, and they ranked poorly in terms of political freedom. Not surprisingly, they recorded a low level of liberalization (5, like Latvia) in 1990. Unlike Latvia, however, the indicator of political freedom in Belarus and Turkmenistan remained very low (actually it improved a little in the early years of the transition and then deteriorated) and the underground economy remained very small. By 1996, the non-price liberalization indexes in these two countries reached only 40 and 35, respectively.

* * *

On the basis of the results reported in this paper, the fear that price liberalization could lead to an inflationary process appear to be unjustified. Price decontrol will push up the average price level, but it will not have a lasting effect on inflation. In the transition countries, as anywhere else, high inflation results essentially from excessive monetary expansion. The once-and-for-all adjustment in prices associated with decontrol can be very large, particularly if prices had been severely repressed below their equilibrium levels—but that is the unavoidable cost of past distortions. Thus, there are no good reasons not to liberalize quickly, and there are very good reasons to do so: to do away with rationing and queues, and to allow relative prices to provide undistorted signals to market participants, and thus to allocate resources efficiently. But good reasons do not seem to trigger good policies unless there is enough political freedom to allow reason to prevail.

---

16. In Figures 3 and 4 (as well as in the equations reported in Table 2) the liberalization variables have been multiplied by 100 for ease of interpretation. These variables thus range between zero and 100 while the original de Melo-Denizer-Gelb indexes range between 0 and 1. The estimates underlying the figures relate to the evolution of non-price liberalization and are based on equation 2.4.

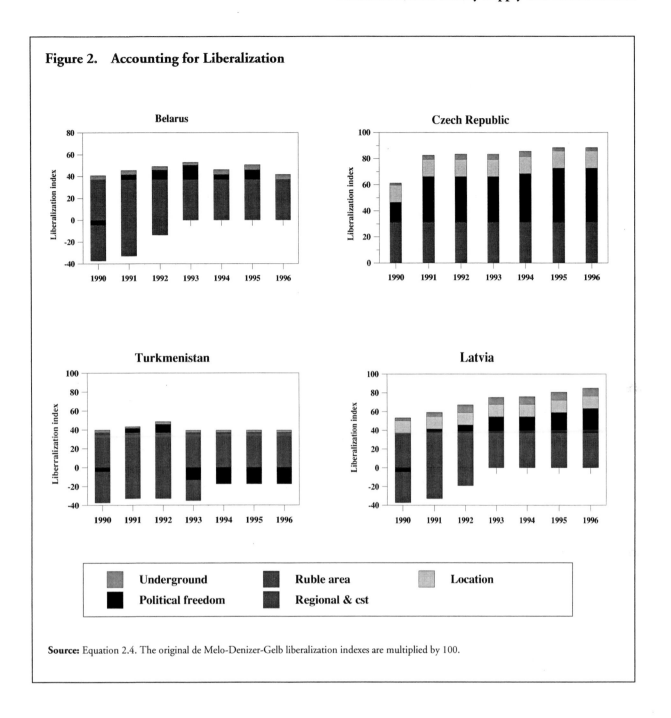

Figure 2. Accounting for Liberalization

Source: Equation 2.4. The original de Melo-Denizer-Gelb liberalization indexes are multiplied by 100.

Annex 1
DEFINITIONS AND SOURCES OF VARIABLES

D = price decontrol variable; linear transformation of L_{price} (two year moving average).

F = index of political freedom; from Raymond D. Gastil, *Freedom in the World, Political Rights and Civil Liberties*, various years (Freedom House). The author provides two scales for each country, one for *political rights*, the other for *civil liberties*. For each scale, a rating of (1) is freest, a rating of (7) is least free. Adding the two scales provides a *combined freedom rating* which ranges between 1 and 14. The freedom variable used in this paper is obtained by subtracting Gastil's combined freedom rating from seven. It thus ranges between -6 (least free) to +7 (freest).

L_{price}, L_{int}, L_{ext} = indexes for domestic price, non-price internal and external liberalization, respectively. From de Melo, Denizer and Gelb (1996a). Updated variables through 1996 were kindly provided by Stoyan Tenev.

L = non-price liberalization index; two year moving average of a simple arithmetic average of L_{int} and L_{ext}.

M = broad money (local currency M2). Derived from end of year percentage changes, from IMF, World Economic Outlook database.

P = consumer price index, end of period. Derived form end of year percentage changes from EBRD, *Transition Report*, 1997.

Q = real GDP index, 1989=1. Derived from growth rates published in IMF, *World Economic Outlook*, 1998; and EBRD, *Transition Report*, various issues.

U = proxy for the size of the underground economy. Calculated as 1 minus the ratio of official real GDP to power consumption.

Dummy variables:

Fixed rate = equal to one when a country is on a fixed exchange rate regime, and to zero otherwise (prorated by the number of months in which the country is on a fixed rate.) Based on information provided by Fischer, Sahay and Vegh (1998), Table 4.

Location = equal to one when a country borders on a thriving market economy, to zero otherwise. From de Melo, Denizer, Gelb, and Tenev (1997).

Ruble area = equal to one when a country uses the Russian ruble as a legal tender, to zero otherwise, i.e., when it uses a national currency or a generalized coupon (prorated by the number of months in which the country used the ruble.)

Age of communism = number of years during which a country was under communist rule. Equal to the difference between 1990 and the following years: 1948 for Bulgaria, the Czech and Slovak Republics, Hungary, Poland and Romania; 1946 for Albania; 1945 for the former Yugoslav republics, Moldova and the Baltic countries; 1924 for Mongolia; and 1918 for the other countries of the former Soviet Union.

Age of reform = equal to the current year minus the first year of substantive reform, the latter being defined as the first year in which the de Melo-Denizer-Gelb aggregate liberalization index reached 0.1 or more.

Price liberalization Gap with Russia = For each country, the difference between the price liberalization variable for Russia and the price liberalization variable for that country.

Former Yugoslav Republics = Croatia, Slovenia and Macedonia

Visegard countries = the Czech and Slovak Republics, Hungary and Poland.

Other Central and Eastern Europe = Albania, Bulgaria and Romania.

REFERENCES

Åslund, Anders, Peter Boone, and Simon Johnson, 1996, "How to Stabilize: Lessons from Post-Communist Countries," *Brookings Papers on Economic Activity 1,* pp. 217–313.

Carranza Valdés, Julio, Luis Gutiérrez Urdaneta and Pedro Monreal Gonzalez, 1998, "Reforming the Cuban Economy: A Proposal," in *Perspectives on Cuban Economic Reform,* (Jorge F. Pérez-López and Matías F. Travieso-Díaz, editors.) Center for Latin American Studies, Arizona State University Press.

Cottarelli, Carlo, Mark Griffiths and Reza Moghadam, 1998, "The Nonmonetary Determinants of Inflation: A Panel Study," IMF *Working Paper* 98/23, March.

De Broeck, Mark, Kornelia Krajnyak and Henri Lorie, 1997, "Explaining and Forecasting the Velocity of Money in Transition Economies, with Special Reference to the Baltics, Russia and other Countries of the Former Soviet Union," IMF *Working Paper* 97/108, September.

Koen, Vincent and Michael Marrese, 1995, "Stabilization and Structural Change in Russia, 1992-1994," IMF *Working Paper* 95/13, January.

de Melo, Martha, Cevdet Denizer, and Alan Gelb, 1996a, " From Plan to Market. Patterns of Transition," *Policy Research Working Paper* 1564. The World Bank: April 1996.

de Melo, Martha, Cevdet Denizer, and Alan Gelb, 1996b, "Patterns of Transition from Plan to Market," *World Bank Economic Review*, Vol. 10 (September), pp. 397–424.

de Melo, Martha, and Alan Gelb, 1997, "Transition to Date: A Comparative Overview,"Chapter 3 in *Lessons from the Economic Transition: Central and Eastern Europe in the 1990s,* ed. By Salvatore Zecchini (Boston: Kluwer Academic Publishers).

de Melo, Martha, Cevdet Denizer, Alan Gelb, and Stoyan Tenev, 1997, unpublished. (The World Bank, Washington, D.C., October.)

Fischer, Stanley, Ratna Sahay and Carlos A. Vegh, 1996, "Stabilization and Growth in Transition Economies: The Early Experience," *Journal of Economic Perspectives*, Vol 10 (Spring), pp. 45-66.

Fischer, Stanley, Ratna Sahay and Carlos A. Vegh, 1996, "From Transition to Market: Evidence and Growth Prospects," *IMF Working Paper* 98/52, April 1998.

Hernández-Catá, Ernesto, 1995, "Russia and the IMF: The Political Economy of Macro-Stabilization," *Problems of Post-Communism*, May.

Hernández-Catá, Ernesto, 1998. "Adjustment and Reform in Cuba: A Critical Assessment", in *Perspectives on Cuban Economic Reform* (Jorge F. Pérez-López and Matías F. Travieso-Díaz, editors.) Center for Latin American Studies, Arizona State University Press.

Petrakov, Nikolai, 1994, "Macroeconomic Regulation of the Market in Russia: Intermediate Results and New Possibilities," Seminar on Economic Reform In Russia and Other Economies in Transition: Issues and Prospects. Moscow, October 15-16.

LA CRISIS FINANCIERA EN MÉXICO: LECCIONES PARA CUBA

Roberto Orro Fernández

Además de los ya conocidos y estudiados procesos de reformas en los países de Europa Oriental, reviste gran importancia para Cuba el estudio de las transformaciones que han experimentado las economías de Latinoamérica. En este sentido, creemos que el caso mexicano constituye una experiencia digna de ser considerada. Pretendemos mediante este trabajo analizar brevemente los errores en la política económica de México que provocaron a finales de 1994 una nueva crisis en ese país, así como exponer nuestro punto de vista sobre las enseñanzas que Cuba pudiese extraer de dicha crisis.

¿Por qué podría ser de interés para Cuba el estudio de la crisis del peso mexicano? Un primer elemento a señalar es el interés que desde el punto de vista teórico la crisis despertó en el ámbito académico. El estudio de la crisis del peso mexicano permite corroborar ciertos postulados de la literatura macroeconómica sobre los procesos de apertura económica y al mismo tiempo enriquecer la misma. Recordemos que la teoría aún tiene mucho que decir en lo referente a los mecanismos macroeconómicos que los países inmersos en procesos de liberalización deben adoptar. Por otra parte, la crisis de 1994 en México, debido a su dimensión internacional, nos revela detalles y características importantes del actual panorama económico internacional. Griffith Jones (1996) sintetiza la importancia del estudio del colapso del peso en 1994: "la crisis financiera mexicana que estalló a fines de 1994 no fue única, si bien tuvo características especiales. De allí la posibilidad de que vuelva a repetirse y la necesidad de entenderla a fondo."

Un segundo elemento que justifica no sólo el estudio de la crisis del peso sino de las reformas en México en general, es que la sociedad mexicana exhibe rasgos característicos de los países que conformaban el antiguo bloque soviético. Una de las peculiaridades importantes del sistema político mexicano es la existencia de un partido de Estado, el Partido Revolucionario Institucional (PRI), que ha conservado el monopolio del poder por más de seis décadas. El poder detentado por el PRI se basa, tal como sucedió en los países socialistas, en el manejo de los sectores de menor nivel cultural, en la creación de ataduras económicas que aseguren la lealtad política de obreros y campesinos, en el control de los medios de información masiva y en la capacidad de conculcar la ley con el objeto de reprimir y controlar a la oposición. En este mismo contexto, hay que destacar la existencia en México de un gigantesco aparato económico estatal, que, además de regular la actividad del sector privado, participa activamente como productor e inversor en sectores claves de la economía. Por otra parte, cabe señalar que la reforma económica mexicana se inició a finales de la pasada década, en los mismos años que marcaron el fin del sistema socialista europeo, lo cual no es una mera coincidencia, sino el resultado del auge que las ideas del libre mercado cobraron en los años ochenta. Por último, quisiéramos mencionar una característica muy importante de México, que inexorablemente estará presente en la Cuba del futuro: su estrecho vínculo económico con los Estados Unidos.

Las reformas económicas en México reflejan el agotamiento del modelo de desarrollo cepalino en el que el gobierno desempeña un rol primordial. La crisis económica de 1982 y la amenaza de total colapso que se cernió sobre el sistema en general, obligaron al gobierno mexicano a desprenderse de parte del enorme poder político y económico acaparado durante años. El gobierno cubano enfrentó en 1993 una situación similar. Ante el grave deterioro de la economía y la posibilidad de que estallase un conflicto social de imprevisibles consecuencias, el gobierno cubano decidió otorgarle a la iniciativa privada algunos derechos que por años le había negado. Claro está, existen sustanciales diferencias entre las reformas económicas de México y Cuba, debido a que en el México priista el sector privado ha tenido mucho mayor peso que en la Cuba socialista. Pudiera argumentarse también que en México se han efectuado cambios que parecen ser irreversibles, mientras que en Cuba no ha ocurrido así, e incluso se ha experimentado cierto retroceso con respecto a 1993. En realidad, puesto que los exiguos cambios que se han dado en la economía cubana no persiguen transformarla radicalmente, las enseñanzas de la crisis mexicana no tendrían gran relevancia para la Cuba de hoy. El estudio de las reformas en México sólo revestiría interés dentro de los marcos de un proceso dirigido a instaurar en Cuba un régimen de economía de mercado.

De los éxitos y fracasos de México en su proceso de reformas se derivan múltiples vertientes de análisis, pero ahondar en cada una de ellas exigiría un esfuerzo que rebasaría los límites de este trabajo. No obstante, creemos que el análisis de la crisis del peso mexicano es la forma idónea de entender los graves errores en los que México incurrió en el diseño y conducción de la política económica. Como veremos más adelante, el estallido de esta crisis se explica en gran medida por la forma desacertada en que se condujo la liberalización de la cuenta de capitales y la falta de una clara regla que asegurase la disciplina monetaria. Cuba, en un futuro no lejano, también deberá encarar el reto de construir un entorno macroeconómico que garantice la transformación exitosa de su economía, así como su plena inserción en el nuevo y dinámico sistema económico mundial. Sobre este último aspecto hay que destacar que la apertura económica no sólo ofrece ventajas; son múltiples los riesgos y externalidades negativas a los que se expone un país que abre sus fronteras económicas.

El trabajo está estructurado como sigue. Destinamos un primer capítulo a describir someramente la evolución de la economía mexicana a partir de la segunda mitad del presente siglo. En un segundo capítulo examinamos el período salinista, mismo en el que se enmarca la crisis del peso mexicano. En el capítulo tres se analiza la conveniencia de implantar en Cuba un consejo monetario en una primera etapa de economía de mercado. Finalmente presentamos las conclusiones.

LA ECONOMÍA MEXICANA 1950-1988

Para una mejor descripción de la evolución de la economía mexicana durante la segunda mitad de este siglo, consideramos conveniente distinguir tres grandes períodos.

1950-1970

A partir de la década de 1950, México adoptó una estrategia de desarrollo hacia adentro sustentada en el proteccionismo comercial y en una significativa presencia del sector estatal en la economía. Durante estos años la economía mexicana creció sostenidamente a una tasa promedio de 6 % mientras que la inflación osciló entre el 5 y 6%. Ahora bien, pese a que las cifras macroeconómicas mostraban una economía sólida y floreciente, paulatinamente se fueron acentuando las deformaciones y distorsiones que conducirían a la crisis de los años 80. El incremento de la producción y el empleo se dan en los marcos de una estructura monopólica e ineficiente, que favoreció una alta concentración del ingreso y fomentó una nociva alianza entre los grandes grupos empresariales y la clase política gobernante.

1970-1982

Durante el sexenio de Luis Echeverría (1970-1976) el modelo de sustitución de importaciones comienza a dar claros signos de agotamiento y sólo elementos de carácter coyuntural permitieron postergar el estallido de la crisis económica. El comportamiento de la tasa de crecimiento es similar al del período anterior, pero la inflación llegó a registrar cifras de dos dígitos. Ello se debió en gran medida a que los recursos crediticios provenientes del exterior no bastaban para financiar las ambiciosas metas industriales que México se había trazado, por lo que las autoridades recurrieron a la emisión de dinero como vía de financiamiento del déficit presupuestario. La consiguiente presión sobre el tipo de cambio no se hizo esperar y, en 1972, el gobierno de Echeverría se vio forzado a ponerle fin a más de 20 años de estabilidad cambiaria en los cuales el dólar se cotizó a 12.50 pesos. Durante 1976-1982, la inflación promedio anual fue muy similar a la del anterior sexenio. Gracias al descubrimiento de importantes yacimientos petrolíferos en Campeche y a las facilidades para la obtención de créditos en el exterior, el presidente José López Portillo pudo sostener la política de desarrollo industrial, pero fue incapaz de controlar la inflación. Este último aspecto, aunado a una coyuntura internacional adversa, provocó que en 1982 se desatara una de las peores crisis económicas en la historia de México.

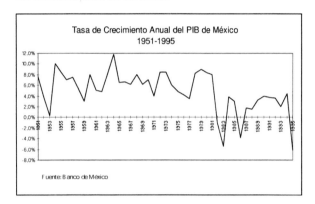

1982-1988

En este sexenio, en el cual la presidencia de la república fue ocupada por Miguel de la Madrid, se inició el proceso de transformación de la economía mexicana. La necesidad perentoria de restablecer los principales equilibrios macroeconómicos relegó a un segundo plano las políticas de desarrollo a mediano y largo plazo, destacando el significativo recorte al gasto público y el inicio de la eliminación de las tarifas arancelarias. Sin embargo, estas medidas no llegaron a conformar un verdadero plan de reformas económicas; más bien constituían una especie de paliativo a la crítica situación que el país vivía. Durante este período la sociedad mexicana hubo de sufrir la coexistencia de la recesión y la inflación, siendo esta última retroalimentada por la continua revisión de los contratos laborales. A lo largo de todo este sexenio persistió la lucha entre los grupos élites de la sociedad mexicana en torno al rumbo que la economía y el país en general deberían tomar. Finalmente, la balan-

za a se inclinó a favor de los partidarios de la apertura económica y la privatización a gran escala. Es así como, en 1988, Miguel de la Madrid designó como su sucesor en la presidencia a un joven de apenas 39 años, miembro de la pujante tecnocracia educada en universidades norteamericanas: Carlos Salinas de Gortari.

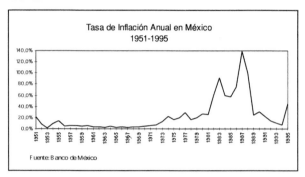

REFORMAS ECONÓMICAS Y CRISIS EN MÉXICO

Con la llegada de Carlos Salinas de Gortari a la presidencia de México en 1988 el país le enviaba al mundo una clara señal de que una radical reforma económica se pondría inmediatamente en marcha. Una de las primeras medidas del nuevo gobierno fue la renegociación de la deuda externa, condición indispensable para oxigenar la maltrecha economía mexicana y garantizar el retorno del país a los mercados de crédito internacionales. En efecto, México logró posponer una parte considerable de los pagos de su deuda externa y disminuir el monto global de la misma, dando así un importante paso en la creación de un clima de estabilidad económica que sirviese de base para una reforma a gran escala. Por otra parte, la privatización de importantes empresas como Teléfonos de México, Mexicana de Aviación y de la banca, nacionalizada por el gobierno de López Portillo en 1982, dotaron al gobierno de Salinas de Gortari de un monto de recursos considerable con el que asegurar el equilibrio de las finanzas públicas.

Otro de los puntos singulares del programa económico de Salinas era la firma de un tratado de libre comercio (TLC) con Estados Unidos y Canadá. Esto era sin lugar a dudas un paso trascendental en la historia de México, pues se pretendía enlazar la economía mexicana a la del país que no sólo es la primera potencia económica mundial y el principal socio económico de México, sino también su añejo antagonista. Pese a los reservas con que no pocos mexicanos acogieron la idea del TLC, Salinas y su gabinete desarrollaron un intenso cabildeo en Estados Unidos con el fin de asegurar el apoyo político necesario para la firma de dicho tratado. Finalmente, el tratado fue aprobado por el Congreso de los Estados Unidos a finales de 1993, generando una verdadera euforia en los círculos gobernantes mexicanos. Sin embargo, pese a las indiscutibles ventajas que el libre comercio con Estados Unidos pudiera brindarle a México, el TLC no ha sido el poderoso motor de desarrollo y apertura que muchos esperaban. De hecho, el TLC fomentó en los círculos financieros internacionales erróneas expectativas acerca de las posibilidades de la economía mexicana, expectativas que contribuyeron a que en 1994 estallara otra nueva crisis del peso mexicano.

En lo que atañe a la política monetaria, ésta se mantuvo dentro de las pautas establecidas a finales del gobierno de Miguel de la Madrid. En 1987, los líderes empresariales y del sector obrero habían acordado con el gobierno—mediante lo que se denominó Pacto de Solidaridad Económica—trabajar mancomunadamente con el propósito de abatir la inflación. Entre los puntos principales de este acuerdo se encontraban: el establecimiento por parte del Banco de México de una política monetaria restrictiva, la creación de contratos salariales basados en las expectativas inflacionarias y no en la inflación pasada y el establecimiento de un mecanismo de revisión y control de precios dirigido dirigido a evitar el alza en el costo de los insumos primarios. En efecto, en un corto lapso se logró contener la inflación, lo cual coadyuvó a crear las condiciones para que el gobierno de Salinas pusiera en marcha su trascendental plan de reformas.

El mantener bajos niveles de inflación fue uno de los objetivos primordiales del gobierno de Salinas y para ello se decidió establecer un régimen cambiario de deslizamiento controlado, que brindase la posibilidad de utilizar el tipo de cambio como ancla nominal. Como es característico en estos casos, la moneda mexicana experimentó una progresiva apreciación

real. Dicha apreciación se agudizó debido a las voluminosas entradas de capital extranjero, factor que permitió financiar el sostenido déficit en cuenta corriente durante el sexenio. En lo tocante a este último aspecto, el gobierno sostenía la idea de que el déficit no era otra cosa que el resultado del flujo positivo de capital extranjero. Si los inversionistas acudían a México era porque el país brindaba condiciones reales para la obtención de jugosos márgenes de ganancia; el gobierno no puede disponer de mejor información que la que los inversionistas poseen y por ende carecía de sentido cualquier intento de intervención estatal en el mercado de capitales. Esta percepción dogmática e ingenua de la realidad omitía el hecho de que los mercados de capitales, como cualquier otro mercado, adolecen de fallas e imperfecciones que demandan la acción interventora del estado.

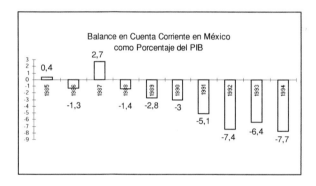

La literatura macroeconómica moderna ha abordado el problema de las imperfecciones en los mercados financieros internacionales. Como resultado de estas fallas se produce una asignación ineficiente de recursos, que, en la mayoría de los casos, perjudica principalmente al país receptor de capitales foráneos. Así, de no tomarse ciertas medidas regulativas que incentiven a los inversionistas a evaluar correctamente los *fundamentos económicos,* es muy probable que se revierta bruscamente la tendencia positiva en los flujos provenientes del exterior.

Uno de los elementos que explica el auge y la caída en los mercados de capitales modernos es que los inversionistas se lanzan a los mercados emergentes movidos por el afán de no quedarse "rezagados," relegando a un segundo plano los fundamentos económicos que deberían justificar la inversión.

Cuando un inversionista observa que una importante cantidad de recursos fluye hacia determinado país, lo más normal es que desee incorporarse al colectivo de inversores. De no hacerlo, el mercado podría castigarlo por haber desechado una gran oportunidad, mientras que de producirse algún acontecimiento que ponga en peligro su inversión, es altamente probable que alguna operación de rescate se lleve a cabo.[1] Por otra parte, los inversionistas suelen reaccionar ante cualquier mala noticia, por pequeña que ésta sea, retirando inmediatamente su capital para reubicarlo en algún mercado más seguro. Como la información detallada puede ser extremadamente cara, la mejor opción para el inversionista es *escapar*. Algunos especialistas señalan que existe una especie de *trade-off* entre diversificación e información; es decir, mientras más diversificado sea un inversionista se sentirá menos estimulado a obtener información de calidad.

La retirada repentina de capitales no sería tan peligrosa si la economía pudiese desplazarse rápidamente hacia el nuevo punto de equilibrio, aunque éste fuese inferior desde todo punto de vista. La reversión brusca en el flujo de capitales genera una secuela de incertidumbre y volatilidad que conduce a la economía a un punto de equilibrio inferior al que sus fundamentos económicos le permitirían alcanzar, todo esto luego de un costosísimo período de ajuste. En México, las autoridades económicas soslayaron el hecho de que la transición de la economía de un alto déficit en cuenta corriente a un bajo déficit, luego de revertirse el flujo de capitales, va acompañada de altos costos económicos.

El cierre de un gran número de fábricas durante el gobierno de Salinas fue motivo de preocupación para muchos economistas, mas el gobierno siempre defendió su postura argumentando que sólo habían quebrado las empresas ineficientes, aquéllas incapaces de resistir la competencia externa. La crisis del 94 de-

mostró que la mencionada ineficiencia era en gran medida el resultado de una moneda altamente sobrevaluada. Una simple interpretación de la teoría del equilibrio general sugeriría que las plantas cerradas podrían otra vez reiniciar su producción, pues la devaluación desestimula el consumo de productos importados. Sin embargo, la realidad es muy distinta. Una vez que una fábrica cierra deberá enfrentar costos y barreras de reentrada que obstaculizarán enormemente su reinserción en el mercado.

Otro gran problema de la transición hacia un nuevo equilibrio consiste en que parte de los proyectos de inversión no se ha completado al desatarse el éxodo de capitales. Algunos de estos proyectos quedarán definitivamente interrumpidos, ya sea porque no pueden acomodarse al alza en las tasas de interés o porque descansan en altos niveles de consumo, típicos de períodos de bonanza económica.

En el caso particular de México, la liberalización de la cuenta de capitales coincidió con el proceso de reprivatización de los bancos y con la abrogación de algunos de los controles que regulaban la actividad financiera.[2] Es conveniente recordar que las fuertes restricciones financieras que enfrentó México a lo largo de la década de los ochenta le impidieron al país acceder a las nuevas tecnologías financieras desarrolladas en esa misma década. 1990 marcó el retorno de México a los mercados financieros internacionales, y pese al optimismo que este acontecimiento despertó en los círculos empresariales y financieros tanto en México como en el exterior, debió haber quedado claro que México distaba enormemente de contar con las condiciones necesarias para acometer una radical reforma financiera.

La labor de la banca mexicana como intermediador financiero fue lamentable. Los bancos comerciales no supieron canalizar correctamente los considerables

---

1. Los hechos le dieron la razón a todos aquellos inversionistas que actuaron bajo la creencia de que en caso de crisis alguna operación de rescate sería llevada a cabo. El "generoso" paquete de ayuda organizado por los Estados Unidos estuvo destinado a asegurar el pago de la deuda contraída por el gobierno mexicano con inversionistas norteamericanos.

2. El proceso de liberalización bancaria se inició en 1989 con la eliminación gradual del encaje legal, continuó a finales de ese mismo año con la autorización a los bancos de determinar libremente las tasas de interés y concluyó en 1991 con la venta de los bancos al sector privado.

montos de recursos provenientes del exterior ni los excedentes que la desregulación bancaria les reportó. Durante el período 1990-1993 el sector privado mexicano recibió créditos del extranjero por un monto de 22,000 millones de dólares (Griffith Jones, 1996), de los cuales dos tercios representaron transacciones interbancarias que incluían depósitos denominados en dólares. Les correspondía a los bancos la tarea de colocar eficientemente tales recursos, mas la falta de personal calificado y de organización les impidió evaluar correctamente los créditos y otros riesgos de mercado. Así, lejos de estimular la inversión productiva, los bancos invirtieron grandes sumas de dinero en el otorgamiento de créditos destinados a la compra de bienes de consumo. Durante el período 1987-1994 el crecimiento en términos reales del crédito para consumo fue de 457.7 %, mientras que el crédito para la compra de casas creció en 966.4 %. En contraste, los créditos otorgados a la industria manufacturera sólo crecieron en un 130.6 % (Ramírez de la O, 1996). Esta expansión desenfrenada del crédito explica en gran medida la drástica caída del ahorro interno en México durante el sexenio anterior.

El gobierno, por su parte, no tomó las medidas pertinentes para supervisar la gestión de los bancos, pues este tipo de controles se consideraba ajeno al esquema neoliberal implantado en México. También se pasó por alto el hecho de que una elevada proporción del capital que entraba a México venía como inversión de cartera, lo cual entraña mayores riesgos para el sistema de intermediación financiera. En 1994, cuando en el ámbito económico mexicano aparecieron alarmantes indicios de crisis, los bancos continuaron invirtiendo principalmente en créditos de baja calidad dirigidos a financiar el consumo privado. Para empeorar las cosas, al estallar la crisis, los bancos intentaron traspasar íntegramente a sus deudores los incrementos en sus pasivos por concepto de deuda con instituciones extranjeras. Empero, este comportamiento abusivo y miope sólo logró retrasar la salida de México de la crisis y colocó a la banca al borde de la quiebra generalizada, situación de la cual sólo se ha salvado gracias a una muy controvertida y cuestionada ayuda gubernamental.

1994: SE DESATA UNA NUEVA CRISIS ECONÓMICA EN MÉXICO

En febrero de 1994 el nivel de las reservas en divisas del Banco de México había llegado a la cifra de 29,200 millones de dólares. Pese al levantamiento armado ocurrido en Chiapas en la víspera de año nuevo, México seguía siendo considerado por los inversionistas como un lugar atractivo donde invertir. Además, la firma del Tratado de Libre Comercio había generado expectativas muy positivas sobre el futuro de la economía mexicana.

Sin embargo, al igual que en 1982, una nefasta combinación de factores de diversa índole provocó que el interés de los inversionistas extranjeros por México decreciera ostensiblemente. En febrero de 1994, la Reserva Federal de los Estados Unidos optó por elevar las tasas de interés de los instrumentos del tesoro estadounidense, disminuyendo así el diferencial entre los pagarés del tesoro estadounidense y mexicano. Aunque la política de la Reserva Federal norteamericana ejerció cierto impacto negativo en la economía mexicana, lo peor estaba por llegar. El 23 de Marzo de 1994 el mundo recibió con estupor la noticia del asesinato de Luis Donaldo Colosio, candidato a la presidencia de México por el PRI. Fue tal la incertidumbre ocasionada por este dramático acontecimiento que en menos de un mes las reservas en divisas cayeron en casi 11,000 millones de dólares. De esta forma, México, el país elogiado por el Fondo Monetario Internacional y considerado por muchos como el paradigma de las reformas económicas, comenzaba a perder su atractivo para los inversionistas extranjeros y las ilusiones de muchos mexicanos empezaron a desvanecerse.

La fuerte caída en las reservas en divisas entrañó un serio dilema para el gobierno mexicano. Era evidente a todas luces la necesidad de reorientar, al menos parcialmente, la actual política económica, pues de lo contrario el país se encaminaría indefectiblemente hacia una nueva crisis. El problema principal estribaba en qué medidas adoptar y cómo llevarlas a cabo. Cabe mencionar que desde antes del asesinato de Colosio existían ya algunas fisuras en el gabinete económico mexicano, fisuras que hacían más difícil la toma de decisiones cruciales. Algunos de los miembros del gabinete abogaban por restringir la oferta monetaria, con la finalidad de elevar la tasas de interés, desalentar el éxodo de capitales y frenar las especulaciones en contra del peso. Otros miembros consideraban que era inadmisible seguir sacrificando el crecimiento del país, y proponían una devaluación con miras a incrementar la competitividad del peso y a estimular las exportaciones.

Al margen del grado de validez de cada una de estas posturas, lo relevante es que el gobierno mexicano optó finalmente por una política plagada de incongruencias. Indudablemente, el gobierno de Salinas sucumbió ante la presión que significaba la proximidad de las elecciones presidenciales, y en 1994 decidió ampliar el crédito gubernamental a los bancos privados,[3] manteniendo a su vez intacta la banda cambiaria. Las autoridades mexicanas consideraban que la salida de capitales era un problema temporal motivado por una incertidumbre política que desaparecería con un nuevo triunfo del PRI en las elecciones presidenciales de agosto de ese mismo año. De hecho, las autoridades monetarias mexicanas optaron por esterilizar el impacto monetario de las salidas de reservas del país, provocando que la base monetaria y el crédito interno se elevasen a la par que disminuían las reservas en divisas. Obviamente, una medida de esta índole era incompatible con el objetivo de mantener el valor del peso dentro de los límites anunciados para la banda cambiaria.

El deterioro en la cuenta de capitales se mantuvo durante casi todo el resto de 1994, con la excepción del ligero repunte observado luego de las elecciones de agosto, en las que el candidato del PRI, Ernesto Zedillo, resultó vencedor. En septiembre, un nuevo asesinato ensombreció el panorama político mexicano. Esta vez la víctima fue José Francisco Ruiz Massieu, secretario general del PRI. A partir de ese instante se aceleró la fuga de capitales hasta que finalmente, el 20 de Diciembre de 1994, las autoridades mexicanas se vieron forzadas a ampliar la banda cambiaria en un 15 %.

Lo que siguió después es una historia bastante conocida. La ampliación de la banda provocó una masiva salida de capitales y el gobierno tuvo que dejar flotar el peso. No queremos detenernos a evaluar el desempeño de las autoridades durante los críticos días de diciembre, mismo que ha sido objeto de críticas tanto dentro como fuera de México. Lo relevante en este caso es la incongruencia entre sí de los objetivos perseguidos por el gobierno mexicano. Si el objetivo primario era el mantenimiento de la paridad cambiaria, ¿por qué se decidió entonces expandir la base monetaria ? ¿ por qué, luego del asesinato de Colosio, el Banco de México no restringió la oferta monetaria?

La respuesta a las anteriores preguntas se encuentra en móviles de tipo político e incluso personal. A la reducción de la oferta monetaria siempre le sucede un período de recesión y desempleo, aunque la duración del mismo es variable (en dependencia de ciertos factores estructurales). El gobierno de Salinas no podía darse el lujo de poner en riesgo el triunfo de su partido en las elecciones de agosto, máxime cuando todo indicaba que la contienda electoral sería extremadamente reñida.[4] Por otra parte, Salinas, al igual que otros miembros de su gabinete, tampoco quería comprometer su imagen de moderno político neoliberal, y por ello no quiso llevar a cabo una devaluación que rememorase las épocas " revolucionarias" de Echeverría y López Portillo.

Con el fin de frenar los ataques al peso e infundir confianza en los inversionistas, el gobierno de Zedillo decidió restringir la oferta monetaria y mantuvo la flotación del peso; pero el nerviosismo y la incertidumbre estuvieron presentes en los mercados financieros mexicanos a lo largo de todo 1995. Aun en oc-

---

3. Este flujo alcanzó el 4 % del PIB, más no fue contabilizado en el déficit fiscal porque los préstamos fueron clasificados como adquisición de activos por el gobierno (Barro, 1996).

4. En anteriores sexenios las devaluaciones solían ocurrir al final de los mismos, pues el presidente saliente sabía que nada podía obstaculizar el camino a la presidencia de la persona que él mismo había elegido como su sucesor . En 1994, el panorama político de México había cambiado notablemente y resultaba prácticamente imposible imponer un presidente. De haberse producido una devaluación antes de agosto de 1994, es muy probable que Zedillo no hubiese ganado las elecciones.

tubre de ese mismo año, cuando daba la impresión de que la calma ya había retornado a los mercados, el peso experimentó una brusca depreciación de más de un 20 %. Bastó el simple rumor de que el ejército asumiría el control de la nación para que el pánico cundiese en los mercados financieros.

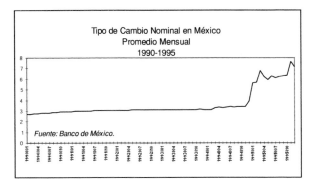

El comportamiento de los principales indicadores financieros en México durante 1995 puso de manifiesto cuán costosa puede ser la falta de credibilidad. La ayuda otorgada por los Estados Unidos y la restricción de la oferta monetaria, con la consiguiente elevación de la tasa de interés, no bastaron para recuperar la credibilidad perdida en diciembre del 94 y los mexicanos tuvieron que afrontar un largo y costoso período de ajuste. Pedro Aspe (1993) señaló: "La credibilidad no es un regalo, hay que hay que ganarla, hay que construirla paso a paso, apoyada por los hechos y la consistencia." Las palabras de Aspe son ciertas; pero habría que agregar que la credibilidad no puede cimentarse en el hecho de que un egresado del MIT ocupe la cartera de Hacienda. La credibilidad ha de alcanzarse mediante leyes e instituciones sólidas que garanticen la disciplina monetaria y la irreversibilidad del proceso de reformas. Argentina brinda un buen ejemplo al respecto. La economía argentina resistió exitosamente en 1995 el "efecto tequila" generado por la crisis mexicana. Ello se debió en gran medida a que en ese país funciona un consejo monetario, que garantiza que la base monetaria esté plenamente respaldada por las reservas en divisas.

FACTORES QUE SUGIEREN LA IMPLANTACIÓN DE UN CONSEJO MONETARIO EN CUBA

La política monetaria sigue siendo una de las áreas más fascinantes y controvertidas de la macroeconomía. Para muchos economistas el dinero es uno de los más útiles instrumentos de los cuales disponen los gobiernos para impulsar el crecimiento económico y atenuar el impacto sobre la economía de los fenómenos aleatorios adversos. Otros economistas defienden con vehemencia la idea de que la principal misión de los bancos centrales es controlar las variables nominales y asegurar así un ambiente estable en el cual el sector privado pueda actuar eficientemente. Nuestro punto de vista personal es que si bien una política monetaria activa puede rendir frutos, sobre todo en el corto plazo, sus costos superan con creces las ventajas que la misma pueda acarrear.

Un consejo monetario constituye una vía eficaz para dotar a la economía de un sano entorno en el cual el sector privado pueda desenvolverse eficientemente. El consejo monetario es una institución independiente del gobierno que tiene a su cargo la emisión de la moneda nacional, cuya convertibilidad en una moneda extranjera específica a un tipo de cambio fijo está plenamente garantizada. Para hacer este compromiso creíble, la base monetaria del país en cuestión ha de ser igual al monto de reservas en moneda extranjera. De este modo, la cantidad de dinero doméstico crece (decrece) en la misma medida en que aumentan (disminuyen) las reservas en moneda extranjera. El consejo monetario ha sido implantado con éxito en Argentina, Singapur, Hong Kong y Estonia, y somos del criterio que Cuba debería adoptar un sistema similar durante su etapa de transición a una economía de mercado. A continuación, abundaremos en los factores que soportan nuestra afirmación.

La urgente necesidad de ganar credibilidad

Luego de casi cuatro décadas de economía planificada y de autoritarismo político la imagen de Cuba ante la comunidad internacional ha quedado seriamente dañada. Cuba sigue siendo considerado un país de alto riesgo para invertir y no le será fácil rebasar esta condición. Incluso, elecciones limpias y democráticas no conllevarán automáticamente una ganancia sustancial en credibilidad y el fantasma de la incertidumbre seguirá gravitando sobre la sociedad cubana. Para obtener credibilidad se requiere de medidas radicales y de la conformación de instituciones que garanticen la irreversibilidad del proceso de reformas.

Como demuestra la experiencia mexicana, mientras el gobierno conserve poderes discrecionales sobre la emisión de dinero, la economía seguirá siendo un rehén de los intereses políticos. En contraste, un consejo monetario constituye una eficaz vía para ganar credibilidad. Un consejo monetario estimularía la disciplina fiscal y coadyuvaría a la formación de un clima político de respeto y tolerancia. Desaparecería la posibilidad de que ciertas personas o grupos manipulen la emisión de dinero para beneficio propio y se le enviaría al mundo una clara señal de que en Cuba no habrá espacio para las engañosas políticas inflacionarias que tanto daño han hecho a las economías latinoamericanas.

El dualismo monetario existente en Cuba

A partir de la despenalización de la tenencia de divisas, ocurrida en 1993, el dólar se ha convertido en un importante medio de pago y en la principal unidad de cuenta de la economía cubana. Existe en Cuba una red comercial estatal totalmente dolarizada y el uso de la moneda estadounidense se ha expandido considerablemente en el ámbito de las economías familiares y los pequeños negocios privados. La mayor parte de estos negocios vende su productos directamente en dólares, pero todos, *sin excepción alguna*, emplean el dólar como unidad de cuenta. Los alquileres de casas y autos, la venta de servicios y productos derivados del trabajo por cuenta propia e incluso la venta de productos robados o malversados—algo muy común en Cuba—son transacciones en las que se utiliza el dólar como unidad de cuenta, al margen de que en no pocas ocasiones el peso cubano funge como medio de pago. Así, de implantarse en Cuba un consejo monetario, no se estaría dolarizando la economía, sólo se aseguraría la continuidad de un proceso nacido hace tiempo.

Cuba es un país de economía abierta

Desde la época colonial, Cuba se ha caracterizado por contar con una economía abierta, y su crecimiento se ha sustentado en el desarrollo de determinados renglones de exportación. Hay que reconocer que la reorientación de la economía cubana le ha concedido un mayor peso a los sectores en los que Cuba tiene

mayores ventajas comparativas. Desde 1991 Cuba ha fortalecido sus lazos económicos con los países de Europa Occidental, y, en la actualidad, el gobierno cubano basa gran parte de sus decisiones en señales provenientes del mercado mundial capitalista y no, como ocurría anteriormente, en arcaicos criterios de industrialización procedentes de Moscú.

El hecho de que el motor impulsor de la economía cubana se localice en los sectores exportables contrarrestaría algunas de las desventajas derivadas de un consejo monetario. En una pequeña economía abierta, en la cual el precio de gran parte de los bienes producidos está determinado en el mercado mundial, resulta mucho más difícil que la elevación del precio de los bienes no comerciables (fenómeno típico de los períodos de auge económico) provoque una apreciación de la moneda en términos reales.

Cuba debe y puede basar su desarrollo futuro en el avance tecnológico

Cuba cuenta sin lugar a dudas con un gran capital humano y es por ello que debe alcanzar la competitividad mediante la innovación y el cambio tecnológico y no a través de salarios deprimidos y miserables. Existe en Cuba un numeroso y capacitado grupo de profesionales, muchos de ellos formados en universidades del extinto bloque soviético; el nivel medio educacional del cubano es de los más altos en el continente y los obreros cubanos, pese a la baja calidad del capital que emplean en el proceso productivo, tienen un buen nivel de capacitación. A todo esto habría que sumarle la gran cantidad de profesionales que viven y laboran fuera del país, cuya capacidad y talento han sido puestos a prueba exitosamente.

¿Qué ventajas podría acarrearle a Cuba, sobre todo en el largo plazo, el sustentar su crecimiento en una competitividad erigida sobre el bajo costo de la fuerza de trabajo? Es común escuchar el argumento de que mediante una devaluación se le puede imprimir mayor competitividad a la moneda, lo cual a su vez redunda en el crecimiento de las exportaciones, la producción y el empleo. En realidad, la devaluación es un instrumento al servicio de ciertos grupos de poder, destinado a perpetuar su hegemonía social, política y económica.

La colocación de productos baratos en los mercados mundiales, basada en los bajos salarios pagados, difícilmente puede sostenerse en el largo plazo. Los empresarios pierden el estímulo para desarrollar nuevos y mejores productos y su única preocupación consiste en presionar al gobierno para que mantenga los salarios deprimidos. Claro está, ninguna economía puede tolerar por mucho tiempo continuas devaluaciones. Por otro lado, existe importante evidencia empírica de que los países que gozan de economías sanas y sistemas políticos democráticos han cimentado su crecimiento económico en la innovación, en el constante desplazamiento de su función de producción. El crecimiento basado en espectaculares superávits comerciales no es sostenible por mucho tiempo y es causa de desequilibrios y distorsiones que más tarde o más temprano emergerán, con su consecuente impacto negativo en la economía y en la sociedad en general.

La no existencia en Cuba de organizaciones sindicales autónomas

No existen actualmente en Cuba sindicatos libres y autónomos y es poco probable que durante los primeros años de transición económica germinen y se desarrollen genuinas organizaciones sindicales. Este es un elemento que los gestores de la política económica habrán de tener en cuenta, pues las revisiones salariales promovidas por los sindicatos y algunas rigideces que les son inherentes son factores que tienden a estimular la inercia inflacionaria. Como se ha observado en México, y también en Argentina, uno de los mayores obstáculos que enfrenta una política monetaria restrictiva es la resistencia de los sindicatos a adaptarse a la misma, lo cual tiende a estimular la recesión y el desempleo.

En el caso de Cuba, durante su verdadera transición hacia una economía de mercado, no existirán sindicatos organizados, capaces de ejercer presiones significativas sobre los salarios. Esto tiene dos importantes implicaciones. En primer lugar, una disminución de la oferta monetaria no tendría por qué afectar fuertemente el empleo, tal como ha ocurrido en otros países. Ahora bien, de quedar abierta la posibilidad de que las autoridades manejen la emisión de dinero discrecionalmente, los sectores políticos y empresariales más poderosos estarían en una posición francamente ventajosa con respecto al resto de la sociedad, pues contarían con la capacidad de presionar y asegurar que la política económica tome el curso más conveniente a sus propios intereses. Este último aspecto pudiera dañar seriamente los intentos de Cuba de crear las bases de una sociedad democrática.

CONCLUSIONES

La crisis del peso mexicano demostró la validez de los postulados teóricos que alertan sobre la necesidad de regular el mercado de capitales. La vulnerabilidad mostrada por la economía mexicana ante la caída significativa en los flujos de capital foráneo puso en tela de juicio el punto de vista de que la economía puede transitar suavemente de una situación de alto déficit externo a una situación de bajo déficit. Cuba, como todo país que intenta dejar atrás el subdesarrollo, tendrá que depender también del ahorro externo y, por ende, convivir con déficits en la cuenta corriente. En este sentido, una de los retos que habrán de encarar los gestores de la política económica en Cuba, será el de diseñar un adecuado mecanismo de control sobre la entrada de capitales foráneos, con miras a asegurar la colocación eficiente de los capitales y a minimizar la probabilidad de que se produzca una retirada masiva de éstos. Sería interesante estudiar la experiencia chilena en materia de regulación de los flujos de capital extranjero. La economía chilena es una de las más vigorosas del continente y parte de este éxito se debe a la existencia de un eficaz mecanismo de control a la entrada de capitales.

Con respecto a la política monetaria, reiteramos la idea de que el sistema monetario cubano debería funcionar como un consejo monetario. Creemos que esta sería la vía más apropiada para garantizar una transición exitosa de Cuba tanto en el plano político como económico. Una de las lecciones de la crisis mexicana es que la política monetaria discrecional puede concederle demasiado espacio a la intervención del gobierno. Debido a ciertas especificidades de la economía cubana, las desventajas asociadas a la implantación de un consejo monetario en Cuba serían mínimas, y es por ello que el país no debería desperdiciar la oportunidad de sentar las bases de un crecimiento económico estable y equilibrado.

BIBLIOGRAFÍA

Aninat, Eduardo; Larraín, Christian. 1996; "Flujos de capitales: lecciones a partir de la experiencia chilena," *Revista de la Cepal*, Nº 60.

Aspe, Pedro. 1993; *Economic Transformation the Mexican Way*, Cambridge, MIT Press.

Barro, Robert. 1996; *Getting It Right*, Cambridge, MIT Press.

Cabarrouy, Evaldo. 1995; *Crisis y reformas económicas en Cuba*, Serie de temas diversos de Economía, Nº 26, Unidad de Investigaciones Económicas, Universidad de Puerto Rico.

Calderón, Angel. 1996; *Determinantes de la caída del ahorro privado en México*, Centro de Estudios Económicos del Colegio de México.

Carranza, J. 1993; "Cuba: los retos de la economía," *Cuadernos de Nuestra América*, vol IX, Nº 19.

Casanova, A. 1994; "The Cuban economy: Reality and perspectives," *Granma International* (4 de enero).

Castañeda, Gonzalo. 1994; *La economía mexicana: un enfoque analítico*, Limusa, 1994.

Griffith-Jones, Stephanie. 1996; "La crisis del peso mexicano," *Revista de la Cepal*, Nº 60.

Huerta, Arturo. 1995; *Causas y remedios de la crisis mexicana*, México, D.F., Diana.

Mansell, Catherine. 1992; *Las nuevas finanzas en México*, México, Editorial Milenio.

Osband, Kent; Villanueva, Delano.1993; *Independent Currency Authorities*, Washington, International Monetary Fund.

Ramírez de la O, Rogelio. 1996; "The mexican peso crisis and recession of 1994-1995: preventable then, avoidable in the future?," en *The mexican peso crisis* por Riordan Rioett, Boulder, Lynne Rienner Publishers.

Ritter, Archibald. 1995; "La dualidad del tipo de cambio en la economía cubana de los noventa," *Revista de la CEPAL*, Nº 57.

Villarreal, René. 1988; *México 2010, de la industrialización tardía a la reestructuración industrial*, México, Diana.

ECONOMIC DEVELOPMENT IN THE TROPICS: FICTION OR POSSIBILITY[1]

Roger R. Betancourt and Carlos Seiglie

The Asian crisis and the problems in many transition economies, especially Russia, have brought to the surface a number of issues that implicitly or explicitly involve addressing one of these two questions: Is economic development feasible for some countries? Or its variant: Under what circumstances is economic development feasible for some countries?

Over the last thirty years the rapid growth of Asian countries has played a critical role in shaping thinking about development by academicians as well as policy makers. For, they have provided real world examples that can be used to argue that development is feasible regardless of initial conditions. Small countries can look at Hong Kong and Singapore; resource poor countries can look at South Korea; resource rich countries with corrupt governments can look at Indonesia, and so on. With the advent of the Asian crisis, these real world examples become less convincing and a wave of pessimism seems to be setting in about the possibilities for development. Hence, the importance of the questions raised above is heightened by the current economic circumstances.

In this essay we examine the underlying rationale for various arguments about the possibilities or lack of possibilities for development put forth in the literature. Anticipating somewhat, one of our conclusions will be that the rosy view before the crisis was as un-

founded in logic as the more pessimistic view emerging from the current crisis. Finally, we will draw the implications of our arguments for Cuba's economic prospects.

THE MEANING OF DEVELOPMENT AND THE CONSISTENCY OF GROWTH PATTERNS

Answering either of the questions raised above requires a clear statement of what one views as economic development. We use as our point of departure the following view, Betancourt (1996): economic development is a process or set of processes whereby a society *consistently* increases the *standard of living* of the majority of its population. The two italicized items stress key features of the definition which can be the source of differences in evaluations of any real world experience.

A restrictive definition of the standard of living would be the level of material well being of an individual viewed as his or her capability to acquire material goods, measured for example by the level of income. This definition seems to be the one most widely used by economists and policy makers in governments and international organizations such as the IMF or the World Bank, Anand and Ravallion (1993). An encompassing definition of the standard of living would be one that would include, in addi-

---

1. An earlier version of this paper was presented at the Eighth Annual Meetings of ASCE in Miami, August 1998. We would like to thank Ricardo Martínez and Francisco Rodríguez for insightful comments, while claiming responsibility for any errors. Betancourt would like to acknowledge summer support from the IRIS Center, under Cooperative Agreement No. DUR-0015-0031-00 with the U.S. Agency for International Development.

tion to material well being, an individual's capabilities in three other dimensions: education, health, and control over one's life through the ability to participate in civic and political activities. This encompassing view of the standard of living has been advanced, for example, by Sen (1987) and Dasgupta (1993). It provides the intellectual basis for measures such as the human development index put out by the United Nations, although it does not justify the particular form adopted in that index.

While the encompassing definition is more attractive, it is also more difficult to conceptualize and measure accurately and reliably. This hinders its use in formal models and in empirical analyses. We will keep the more encompassing definition of the standard of living in the background but we will follow the literature and focus on the restrictive definition unless stated otherwise.

Incidentally, notice that by the mere use of the more encompassing definition of the standard of living the accomplishments of the Asian economies over the last thirty or forty years look less appealing as signs of development, because their record on the enjoyment of civic and political liberties by their citizens is far less stellar than in the other dimensions. Since in our view this is one of the reasons why the East Asian growth experience was overrated as a sign of development, we are biasing the argument against one of our conclusions by choosing the more restrictive definition of the standard of living.[2]

A second source of potential differences in view attaches to the meaning of the word consistently. It has long been recognized that any country can experience rapid growth in per capita income for some period of time without experiencing development in the sense of acquiring the capability for self-sustaining growth. Rostow's (1960) definition based on the choice of a ten year period for his take-off into self sustained growth was not successful. By his definition, there are too many crash landings after take-off.

One aspect of consistency is duration. The longer a growth episode continues the more likely we have development rather than just growth. By choosing a long period, for example half centuries, we have a better proxy for self-sustaining growth. This allows for countries, for example Argentina in the late nineteenth century and early twentieth century, that crash landed after a considerably longer period of growth than ten years. Other examples of several decades of growth followed by similar crash landings are Cuba in the late eighteenth century and early nineteenth century and Venezuela in this century. These historical experiences would suggests that duration of growth over a number of decades is necessary for duration to be a good proxy for sel-sustaining growth—in the sense that the processes determining the operation of a particular society allow it to increase consistently the per capita income level of the majority of its population.

Another complementary dimension of consistency is instability or variability. A recent paper by Pritchett (1998) allows us to look at this dimension somewhat systematically. He classifies countries into developed and less developed by using membership in the OECD (prior to the recent additions), adding Malta and Cyprus to the developed category and subtracting Turkey from this category. Starting in 1960 and using all the data available since then until the most recently available year, he calculates growth rates in GDP per capita in terms of (1985) purchasing power for 111 countries. He discusses three dimensions of these growth rates for the two groups of countries: trend, instability and volatility. For our purposes, it will suffice to consider just the first two dimensions.[3] Table 1 summarizes his results in these two dimensions.

The mean and standard deviation (S.D.) of the trend growth rate is the result of estimating the trend growth rate for each country by regressing the logarithm of income on a linear time trend via ordinary

---

2. A similar argument would apply to China's recent growth experience except that in the initial stages of that process an improvement in civic and political liberties accompanied economic liberalization.

3. Volatility is difficult to measure across countries in a reasonable manner when growth rates are unstable.

Table 1. Consistency of Growth Performance

	Trend Growth Rate	R-Squared of Trend
Developing Countries	Mean = 1.64; S.D. = 1.98	Mean = .58; S.D. = .32
Developed Countries	Mean = 2.90; S.D. = 1.05	Mean = .94; S.D. = .03

least squares and then obtaining the average and standard deviation of this estimate for the countries in the group. The mean and S.D. of the R-Squared of trend is obtained by calculating the average and standard deviations of the R-Squared in the regression estimating the trend growth rate for each country over the countries in the group. The trend growth rate results require little explanation; they suggest that the average growth rate is higher (and has a lower standard deviation) in developed countries. The R-Squared of trend results would be less familiar. The R-Squared of trend is a measure of how well a time trend explains the growth experience of a country. For developed countries, fitting an exponential time trend explains most of the variation in per capita income; all R-Squared's are between .9 and 1. For developing countries, however, the time trend is not as powerful in explaining the variations in per capita income; the R-Squared ranges from 0 to 1. Thus growth rates in developing countries are far less stable than in developed ones, which is one of the main points Pritchett (1998) emphasizes.

In order to increase consistently the standard of living of the majority of the population, a country must not only experience growth over several decades but do so with a limited amount of instability. Circumstances can change dramatically and the ability to adjust to these changes in circumstances without jeopardizing the standard of living of the majority of its population is what characterizes the processes at work in a developed society. With any degree of risk aversion, welfare is decreased by this instability in growth rates, other things equal. Note the perspective this provides on the Asian crisis. Since some countries in Asia that have grown over thirty years may resume growth quickly and others may not, the former could be viewed as having entered a period of development in the precrisis years and the others as having enjoyed a period of growth in the precrisis years (just as the historical examples cited above). Note also that this view of development allows for

societies to move between categories in both directions, depending on their performance.

One of the two main conclusions of Pritchett's analysis is that growth regressions have exhausted their usefulness, but they have taught us that there are three antigrowth syndromes: severe economic imbalances or macroeconomic instability, excessive inward orientation, and state led development by a nondevelopmental state. The other main conclusion is that to make further progress one needs to analyze: what leads to initiation or cessation of growth episodes; how the determinants of growth evolve in particular circumstances; and, finally, the determinants of changes in growth rates over time. In other words, we need to understand the characteristics of development processes that lead to inconsistent increases in per capita income for developing countries (and consistent increases in developed ones) in order to answer the question of under what conditions is development feasible. To this task we now turn.

EXPORT-LED PROCESSES

Perhaps the earliest development literature addressing these issues is the literature on export-led development. Part of it focused on the successful entry into the developed group of the so-called newly settled regions while part of it focused on the reasons why many developing countries did not follow suit despite similar export booms during the same historical period, namely the nineteenth century and early twentieth century. The nature of production processes and the linkages they generated to other industries in terms of inputs and outputs, including social overhead capital and entrepreneurship, were viewed as critical determinants of whether an export boom led to development or not. By now these views have filtered down to the undergraduate textbook level, e.g., Gillis, Perkins, Roemer and Snodgrass (1996), where they are usually accompanied by an optimistic outlook. That is, even in the worst of cases in terms of poor linkages of the industry experiencing the boom, it is argued that government policy via fiscal linkages can be used to address the perceived problems and promote development over the long-term. Since in the nineteenth and early twentieth century governments did not act as developmental states (in fact some of the developing countries experiencing the export boom were colonies), one can explain why countries with unfavorable linkages due to the nature of their production processes failed to develop then but need not fail to develop now.

A similar view arises from the more recent literature on export-led growth focusing on Dutch Disease, or the inflationary boom and real appreciation of the exchange rate that afflicts natural resource based export-led booms. In these cases, which have also reached the undergraduate textbook level, it is argued that economic policy can prevent the undesirable consequences of the boom. Ironically, prior to the recent crisis Indonesia was cited as an example of a country that had ben able to avoid Dutch Disease through their judicious macroeconomic policy. Recent events in Indonesia show that a judicious macroeconomic policy, while it may be able to avoid Dutch Disease, is not a sufficient condition for development in terms of consistently increasing the standard of living of the majority of its population.

A new more pessimistic view of export-led development in resource-rich countries is now emerging from the most recent literature. This literature starts from a negative correlation between the share of exports of primary products in 1970 and the average growth rate of GDP between 1970 and 1989, Sachs and Warner (1995). Since this correlation seems robust to the inclusion of additional variables as well as to the use of alternative measures of resource endowments, the search for explanations is gathering steam.

Rodríguez and Sachs (1998), for example, argue that resource rich economies have lower growth rates because they are likely to be living beyond their means. To support their argument empirically, they point out that if one tries to explain the level of income rather than its rate of growth the share of exports of primary products comes up with a positive coefficient rather than a negative one. To support their argument theoretically, they put forth a growth model in which the output of one sector (the natural resource sector) is fixed to capture the fact that the natural resource is depleted over time. In the steady state, production of the natural resource tends to zero. During the transition state, however, the natural resource allows the economy unusual consumption opportunities, which lead to overshooting or approaching the steady state from above.[4] In their view, the development of the Venezuelan economy since the beginning of the oil industry take-off in 1914 led to a situation in which by 1970 this country was already overshooting its steady state in terms of both production and consumption, and it is quite consistent with the lower growth rates observed since 1970 and the implications of their model.

This explanation, however, requires the inability of the natural resource economy to invest its resource windfall in international assets. They provide three reasons why this restriction may apply: internal political restrictions, lower or declining expected rates of return in international capital markets, or a preference for holding home assets. The second reason seems contrary to fact and there is little evidence for the third one in case of Venezuela. While the first one may have had some validity in the past, it is certainly not immutable. If correct, this explanation does suggest that one of the characteristics of the development process entails directing the collective will of the society toward the pursuit of economic betterment for the majority of its citizens. Moreover, it also suggests that having the outward trappings of a democracy for forty years is neither necessary nor sufficient to guarantee that a society is indeed pursuing this goal, since Venezuela would rank high among developing countries in standard measures of democracy such as the holding of elections.

An alternative explanation of the negative correlation between natural resources and growth is put forth by

---

4. The authors also developed a more complex dynamic general equilibrium model which is calibrated to the Venezuelan economy and derive the same dynamic implications through simulation of this model.

Asea and Lahiri (1998). They develop a two-sector endogenous growth model in which human capital is the engine of growth. One sector produces output essentially with a fixed endowment of a natural resource and unskilled labor. The other produces output with a fixed factor, the accumulated stock of human capital, and the average per capita human capital stock. If unskilled labor and the natural resource are complementary factors of production, then the steady state growth rate of the economy is decreasing in the level of the natural resource and the price of the natural resource. The mechanism bringing this about is that these two exogenous factors increase the opportunity cost of human capital accumulation and this decreases the level of schooling which is the engine of growth in the model. A simple empirical test shows that human capital, measured in terms of secondary school enrollment, loses its power in explaining growth rates between 1970 and 1989 when the share of natural resources is added to the regression as an explanatory variable. It is worth noting that the theoretical result depends on two key assumptions: a low intertemporal elasticity of substitution, which is standard, and the inability to invest abroad, which is not.

IMPORT SUBSTITUTION PROCESSES

A subsequent strand of development literature that sheds light on the nature of development processes is associated with the strategy of import substituting industrialization. Early arguments were based on the notion of externalities, or unpaid benefits and costs of various types accruing to third parties uninvolved in an exchange, or increasing returns at the level of the firm to argue in favor of import substitution. Underlying these arguments was the positive empirical association between the level of per capita income and the share of industry in GDP. Recent and more formal literature has stressed one form of externalities, namely complementarities so that the ranking of benefits of an agent's action depend on the actions of other agents in the economy. Models with comple-

mentarities can generate multiple equilibria, including configurations in which every one would be better off in one equilibrium than in another but history and expectations trap the economy in the less desirable equilibrium.[5] Government intervention can in principle provide a coordination mechanism that moves the economy from one equilibrium to another.

In this case the issue arises of what particular form should the intervention take. With respect to complementarities and in the presence of limited resources, interventions need to account for the characteristics of backward and forward linkages affecting the structure of a particular society. Either perfect competition or an open economy, however, undermine the logic of these arguments. Thus, the role of complementarities in creating development traps has to rely on its application to the nontradable sector of the economy.

Increasing returns at the firm level have been used as the basis for infant industry protection arguments for many years. In the absence of learning to produce effects, however, the logic for government intervention in the form of temporary protection is flawed. Not surprisingly, Bruton (1998) posits learning and the accumulation of knowledge as the main sources of development in his recent essay on why import substitution should be reconsidered. Increasing returns, however, have been given a new interpretation in more recent literature which views development as specialization.

In particular, it is argued that the development process requires the introduction of roundabout methods of production, especially the use of specialized inputs such as producer services. Rodríguez-Clare (1966), for example, mentions banking, auditing, consulting, wholesale services, among others, and argues that these services are nontradable and produced under conditions of decreasing average costs or increasing returns. Under these circumstances, devel-

---

5. See Debraj Ray (1998, Ch.5), for example, for a discussion of these issues from a modern perspective.

opment traps such as those generated by complementarities arise, Ray (1998).[6]

Since technology and globalization are changing the nature of these producer services, the assumption that they are nontradable needs very close scrutiny. Many firms provide international auditing and consulting services. The same is true for banks. The 1990s saw the move of some American retail formats (Wal-Mart) into Mexico, perhaps as a result of NAFTA.

The importance of these developments is enhanced because the often intangible and intertemporal nature of the benefits to some of the parties involved in the exchange of producer services requires the presence of one of the factors Olson (IRIS Newsletter, 1998) calls market augmenting government, namely contract enforcement mechanisms. Yet, internationalization of services to circumvent the lack of existence of these contract enforcement mechanisms in some developing countries takes place with the aid of technology. The introduction of the Tran$card debit card in Cuba by a Canadian firm and its endorsement by the Association of Independent Journalists, a dissident group, is an ironically appropriate example of this possibility. Without nontradability, the development trap due to this type of increasing returns disappears.

Another aspect of this type of increasing returns argument that seems overlooked is best understood by considering the reduced form production function for the increasing returns sector that emerges usually from these models: namely, $S = n^{(1/\alpha)}h$. S is the output of producer services; h is the amount of resources allocated to the production of any one type of producer services; and n is the number of different types of producer services. α is a parameter that measures the degree of substitutability between the different types of services and lies between zero and unity. The higher is α, the higher the degree of substitutability. One might argue that the higher the level of development, the higher is α. In this case, the increasing re-

turns process gets exhausted at some point in the course of development and we would be back to a situation such as the one in the Rodríguez and Sachs model of the previous section.

To conclude, both export-led processes and import substitution processes can generate growth, but their ability to generate development can be hampered by a number of circumstances. In particular if the ability to invest abroad or to draw investments from abroad is substantially limited, by whatever factors, development traps or steady states with low rates of growth can arise through a variety of different mechanisms ranging from complementarities to increasing returns to the usual diminishing returns.

TECHNOLOGICAL CHANGE PROCESSES

Until the last decade modern growth theory was based primarily on the neoclassical model of economic growth, which emphasized the importance of exogenous technological change in determining growth rates and the limits of capital accumulation in affecting growth due to diminishing returns. This raised doubts about the ability of policy to alter long-run outcomes. Moreover, growth accounting exercises based on this view provided quantitative empirical evidence confirming the importance of technological change, measured as a residual, as a determinant of growth rates and they also provided evidence that this factor was far more important in accounting for growth in developed economies than in developing ones.

Extensions of the analysis to optimal growth generates similar results as long as the intertemporal utility function of the representative consumer exhibits no temporal dependence. We show in an Appendix, available from the authors on request, that a simple introduction of temporal dependence in the utility function leads to a substantial modification of the results for one of the simplest growth models that can be constructed. In particular we assume a form for the utility function that introduces what Deaton (1992) calls "habits" in the utility function. The ra-

---

6. The April 1996 issue of the *Journal of Development Economics* is devoted to increasing returns models which highlight these features in a variety of contexts.

tionale for the form is that the minimum standard of living that the representative individual perceives is a function of per capita income, more specifically it is proportional to per capita income.

With this modification alone, we can generate the conclusion that the steady state level of the capital stock is inversely related to the proportionality constant; hence, so is the steady state level of per capita income. This proportionality constant would be influenced, for example, by the expectations that political leaders generate among their citizens. Thus, demagoguery by increasing this proportionality constant leads to a higher expected minimum standard of living and, thus, lowers the long-run level of per capita income in this model. Introducing exogenous technical change in the model results in this parameter affecting the steady state growth rate.

In the last decade the advent of endogenous growth theory has led to a substantial stream of theoretical and empirical research on growth and its determinants, for example Barro and Sala-I-Martin (1995). We shall focus on the part of this recent literature that emphasizes the so-called Schumpeterian view of endogenous growth (Aghion and Howitt, 1998). It is of special interest for our purposes for two reasons. First, it addresses head on the nature of technological processes. It emphasizes the rather sensible point that there are economic costs and benefits to technological change and that this process is endogenous or determined by economic considerations just as any other economic activity. Second, it tries to relate this view of technological change to the main issues addressed in the rest of the modern growth literature. This effort includes showing how a particular type of endogenous growth model of the Schumpeterian variety generates Young's (1995) results with respect to the East Asian experience without the interpretation

that technological change is unimportant or unaffected by policy.[7]

One characteristic of technological change processes is what has been called creative destruction. That is, some innovations are drastic in that they eliminate completely the previous way of doing things by making them economically unattractive whereas others are nondrastic in that the old technology can survive, although at a lower level of profits than the new one. What this implies in either case is that the possibility of appropriating monopoly rents for some time is one of the driving economic forces of innovative activity and that those who may end up on the wrong side of the innovative activity at a particular point in time may have an incentive to prevent the innovation, especially in the case of drastic innovations. Incidentally, if this is one of the foundations of economic development, we should not be surprised that some individuals oppose the process although it would be surprising if they were to admit it openly.

A second characteristic of technological change processes emerging from growth accounting exercises as well as historical evidence is that they seem to influence growth at varying rates across space, time and economic sectors. This suggests that technological change processes may be of more than one type, which Schumpeter argued. The more recent literature captures this feature to some extent by differentiating between processes based on horizontal differentiation or imitations, for example the increasing returns process described at the end of the previous section, and processes based on vertical differentiation (quality improvements).[8] Increasing returns in the former case work by adding more sectors to the economy and any given amount of resources must be spread over more sectors, which leads to the eventual exhaustion of the process. Increasing returns in the

---

7. This influential piece on the empirical side of the literature shows that most of the recent and rapid growth in East Asia was due to the growth of labor and capital, including human capital, rather than to productivity improvements or technological change measured as a residual.

8. Incidentally, it was in the context of this type of distinction that Schumpeter argued in favor of innovations appearing in cycles and the recent literature is in the process of trying to formalize this idea in various ways. For example Aghion and Howitt (1998, Ch. 8) emphasize general purpose technologies, and Evans, Honkapohja and Romer (1998) emphasize expectations in the face of complementarity between the capital goods required by each producing sector.

latter case, however, allow for an economy to grow at a constant rate when the research sector uses capital as an input. In this model capital accumulation and innovations (technological change) are complementary factors in generating a steady state rate of growth of the economy, Aghion and Howitt (1998, Ch. 3). This provides a point of departure for explaining why this constant rate is higher in some countries than in others as well as why it is more stable in some countries than in others, which in turn coincides with the main features of the variations in the growth rate of output per capita identified above.

A third characteristic of technological change processes is that they require resources to produce innovations. These resources take the form of physical capital and human capital. The latter in particular can also take various forms. For example, some forms of skilled labor do not require higher education but skilled workers engaged in research and development activities usually have training beyond high school.[9] Thus, the complementarity between physical capital accumulation and technological change extends easily to the accumulation of human capital and is consistent with the importance of secondary school enrollments in explaining growth rates typically found in growth regressions, for example the one cited earlier when discussing export-led growth.

What is different between the role of education as a characteristic of technological change processes and its role in models such as the Asea and Lahiri (1998) model discussed earlier is that human capital is an input into the production of innovations. This Schumpeterian view implies that the accumulated stock of human capital can affect the growth rate of output. Since human capital also requires human capital in its production and its acquisition is the outcome of individual choices, the incentives societies provide for its acquisition in terms of costs and benefits will be particularly important in determining its accumulation and the technological change processes that are feasible in a society.

A fourth characteristic of technological change processes is that the accumulation of knowledge has both public goods and private goods characteristics. At the simplest level one can think of existing designs as public goods costlessly available and of new designs as private goods which require resources to produce and generate appropriate economic benefits. Some reflection suggests rather quickly, however, that in both cases additional considerations arise. Old designs may require adaptation to remain economically attractive. The adoption of old designs with or without adaptation may not be costless if part of the knowledge base of the design is tacit knowledge, North (1990), which requires learning by doing. The appropriability of benefits in new designs is a strong assumption, since the innovation process for any individual agent is highly uncertain because the pay-offs are in the future whereas the costs are in the present. An immediate implication of these characteristics is that institutions can play an important role in determining the technological change processes that a society adopts.

One aspect of institutions is the so-called market augmenting role of government in providing contract-enforcement mechanisms mentioned earlier. In certain types of markets where transactions are highly uncertain because costs and benefits to a transaction are separate intertemporally, the nonperformance of this function can lead to the absence of the market or to much lower levels of transactions in these markets, Clague, et al. (1994) When governments do not fulfill this function, Betancourt (1998) argues that alternative institutional arrangements may arise, in particular corruption, but that these alternatives do not fulfill this function as effectively as an impartial judiciary, especially in the presence of competitive pressures. This role is nowhere more important than in markets and transactions associated with innovations. In addition to this fundamental role, the public good nature of innovations and learning by doing provide additional reasons for government interventions with subsidies or patent protection, for example. Nonetheless the capacity of governments to in-

---

9. Some stress the importance of entrepreneurial labor at some stages of development, e.g., Iyigun and Owen (1998).

tervene wisely varies considerably. Hence, the quality of governance in a society will be an important factor in determining the technological processes that are feasible.

A second implication of this characteristic is that the role of the international economy in the development process will be quite complex. Two effects are easy to see. In so far as participation in the international economy acts as a transmission mechanism for the diffusion of technological change processes, directly through the transmission of ideas or indirectly through the generation of spillovers, it would influence growth positively. On the other hand, if comparative advantage leads to specialization in economic activities where knowledge accumulation is not a driving force, the influence on growth will be negative. More generally, Aghion and Howitt (1998, Ch. 11) show that the rate of technological change and participation in the international economy are jointly determined. In this setting, openness need not always be beneficial to growth and they conclude their discussion by reviewing the empirical evidence, which is not overwhelmingly convincing but shows a positive association.

Part of the current conventional wisdom is that the beneficial effects of participating in the international economy take place because openness increases competition. If this is the case, then the effect of participating in the international economy on growth will be influenced by the effect of competition on technological change processes. Aghion and Howitt (1998, Ch. 7) analyze the role of market structure in technological change processes. They develop a series of models that show how competition in the innovations sector as well as product market competition can increase growth. The latter effects would be particularly important for developing countries with limited or nonexistent research sectors. Aghion and Howitt identify two basic channels: If managers are agents engaging in nonprofit maximizing behavior, then competition can increase growth by forcing managers to speed-up the rate of innovation; it can also increase growth by providing incentives for resources to move toward research activities within firms operating in product markets, including intermediate product markets.

Summing up, economic development in the tropics or elsewhere is feasible, but it is not easy. It requires the participation of most citizens in a country on both the production side and the consumption side. The effectiveness of this participation on the production side depends on a number of factors that are not trivial to bring about, because they depend on what human beings do and want as both individuals and members of a society. Among the most important of these factors are: high levels of education, broadly defined, among the citizenry, i.e., including business and entrepreneurial skills; institutions that provide incentives to innovative activity (in the innovations sector as well as in product markets); and, institutions that provide incentives for the body politic to focus on the betterment of the economic condition of most of its citizens in terms of actions rather than words.

While the above factors may not be all that controversial as a strategy to pursue, their tactical application in any one setting can generate more debate. For instance, Rodrik (1998) argues that some countries may be better off by slowing down their participation in the globalization process. Why? Because the world market is as much a source of disruption and upheaval as of opportunity for profit and growth and, according to him, having the "right" institutions at home is necessary to take advantage of the latter while mitigating the consequences of the former. To illustrate his point, Russia over the last few years has had a government with minimal ability to collect taxes, pay its debts or even provide money as a medium of exchange for the productive activities of its economic agents. The concurrent globalization of Russia's capital market in such an inhospitable institutional setting seems a less attractive idea currently (at the time of the Summit) than it did at the beginning of this process.

IMPLICATIONS

If the above views have any merit, what are their implications for the development of a country such as Cuba? According to Reynolds (1983) Cuba started the process of intensive growth, where per capita income begins to increase systematically despite a positive rate of population growth, at the turn of this century. Since then the growth rate has exhibited considerable variations. Early in the century the country experienced the "vacas gordas" of the twenties and the "vacas flacas" of the thirties. Late in the century, the country has experienced the ups and downs of revolutionary growth, including the current "special period in time of peace."[10] Thus, Cuba is a developing country that has failed to increase consistently the material well being of the majority of its population during this century.

During this century Cuba has experienced growth episodes through participation in export-led processes as well as in import substitution processes, but neither has resulted in development. While a detailed analysis of these historical episodes from a modern perspective is a useful endeavor, it would take us too far afield in this paper. Instead, we merely note that the limits to development in export-led processes or import substitution processes discussed in earlier sections can be overcome through openness of the economy and the quality of governance. It would be difficult to find a five-year period since 1898 where any Cuban government could be described as an effective developmental state regardless of political label, i.e., dictatorship, totalitarian or democratic. Unless the quality of governance changes with whatever regime comes in the future, development in Cuba is a fiction not a possibility and this conclusion has little to do with the island's location in the "tropics."

We will justify this conclusion by pointing out how it relates to the characteristics of technological processes identified earlier. One of the main driving forces of innovative activities are the incentives provided by the temporary appropriation of monopoly rents that accompany economic innovation. Societies where improving the material well-being of the ma-

jority of their population is not an important outcome of their collective choice processes or goal of their leadership structures tend to create a variety of impediments to the appropriation of these monopoly rents and, thus, lower the incentives for innovative activities.

In Cuba the present government does not even pay lip service to this goal of development through the provision of incentives in economic activities, perhaps due to their fear of the power that unaffected segmenst of the population could acquire as a result of successful entrepreneurship. For instance, their limits on self-employment activities, such as 12 chairs for restaurants, are grotesque from an economic point of view and lead to noncompliance. Similarly, workers in joint ventures get paid in pesos by the government at the official one peso to one U.S. dollar exchange rate while the government receives foreign currency for their wages from the foreign investors. With a black market rate of 1$ for 20 pesos, the disincentive effects for these workers to undertake initiatives within their organizations is strong. Of course, under the table payments mitigate the problem from the point of view of the enterprise. In both cases, however, a culture of corruption is created with negative externalities for society.

In a relatively small country, which Cuba is, size can limit the development of horizontal innovations associated with the division of labor. One mechanism that allows small countries to avoid this limitation is openness or outward orientation. In Cuba, there are formal governmental restrictions on foreign investment, for example limits on the sectors open to joint ventures and on the selection of workers by these enterprises (they have to hire them through a government enterprise). In addition, there are informal restrictions associated with the corruption of a regime that requires the use of certain government enterpris-

---

10. A Cuban economist describes growth from 1972 to 1984 as having exhausted the Soviet model of socialist growth, the rectification process of 1984-1989 as a search for a Cuban national economic model, and 1990-1993 as a special period in time of peace or the first stage of management and adjustment to the crisis, Pérez Villanueva (1998). His estimate of the contraction in GDP during this last period is 33% of the 1990 level.

es controlled by Fidel Castro.[11] Except for unusual circumstances, such as the Tran$card debit card mentioned earlier, this contributor to growth is seriously hampered. Hence, Cuba has to rely mainly on vertical or quality improvement innovations as a source of technological change.

Quality improvement innovations require devoting a significant amount of resources to research and development activities. The Cuban government has actually done that in some areas, of which biotechnology is the most prominent one. There have been successes on the technical side but the outputs of these activities have not yet generated significant economic returns, judging by their limited contribution to export earnings.[12]

Research and development activities require human capital and physical capital. Cuba has invested an enormous amount in the education of its population during the Revolution. In terms of its endowment of human capital, it is in an enviable position among developing countries. It even exports human capital services to other countries (mainly in the form of dentists, doctors and teachers nowadays, and well trained soldiers in earlier decades). Indeed, some of them are going to countries that have substantially higher levels of material well being, for example Chile. Yet, the return to this educational investment has been recently evaluated as nil, Madrid-Aris (1997). Why?

The ability to engage in learning by doing and participate in technological change processes is affected not only by the available stock of human capital but by the incentives provided for its application. In Cuba these incentives are lacking. For instance, there are anecdotes of female doctors in Cuba engaging in prostitution a couple of nights a week, because they earn a much higher standard of living in this activity than in their government paid jobs due to the dis-

torted economy. More systematic evidence from UNESCO was recently reported by Montalván (1998): Namely, a decrease in secondary school enrollments from 89% to 75% and a decrease in University enrollments from 21% to 14%. Finally, human capital has several dimensions. Besides technical knowledge and skills there is also entrepreneurial knowledge and skills. This latter type of education has been nonexistent in Cuba until very recently. Indeed, the new programs in this area have been provided by foreign institutions.

Whether it is in the adaptation of old designs or in the production of new designs, the institutions of a society play a critical role in providing an environment conducive to the development of technological change processes. Governments as part of this institutional matrix play an important role both directly, facilitating the transmission of knowledge, and indirectly, providing contract enforcement mechanisms that facilitate appropriability. Cuba's government by its totalitarian nature acts as a hindrance in the performance of both functions. Ironically, its decay in terms of legitimacy and effectiveness and the availability of new technology has allowed a considerable increase in the amount of information available to the population, as a result of access to the Internet, and an increased ability to appropriate the benefits of private activities, due to the inability or unwillingness of the repressive apparatus to enforce restrictions. One wonders, however, about the ability of a new regime to perform the legitimate functions of government as a result of the attitudes generated by this one, especially considering that good government is not a home grown tradition in this century.

Finally, an important factor that dissipates eventually the necessary monopoly rents associated with technological development and also spurs the continuation of the growth process is competition in innovative activities and in products. A necessary mechanism for

---

11. For an insightful account of this subsystem see "The Comandante's Reserves," *Cuba: Monthly Economic Report* (August 1997) or Sanguinetty (1997).

12. Incidentally, the same report cited in the previous footnote identifies Medicuba as one of the enterprises controlled by Castro with an unknown amount of revenues, but estimated as several million dollars. It adds (p. 3) "Fidel castro is the principal investor in the biotechnology sector."

small countries to ensure competition is openness of their economy. This mechanism is not available in Cuba. While some successful developing economies, such as South Korea, have had considerable government intervention in their participation in international trade, these interventions have had to satisfy eventually two hard budget constraints: their ability to export their products and the need to operate at an economic profit. Indeed, the current crisis in Korea may be due in no small amounts to the suddenness with which the soft credit constraint for favored enterprises was hardened by the international economy. Given the structure of the current Cuban economy, these constraints are considerably softer for the government-controlled enterprises where Castro is a major stakeholder and the result is unlikely to be long-term development sustained by technological progress. With luck this socialist version of crony-capitalism may generate some growth, but it does not have a future as a source of development

REFERENCES

Aghion, P. and P. Howitt, 1998, *Endogenous Growth Theory* (Cambridge: MIT Press).

Anand, S. and M. Ravallion, 1993, "Human Development in Poor Countries: On the Role of Private Incomes and Public Services," *Journal of Economic Perspectives*, 7, 133-50.

Asea, P. and A. Lahiri, 1998, "The Precious Bane," mimeo, Economics Department, UCLA.

Barro, R. and X. Sala-i-Martin, 1995, *Economic Growth* (New York: MacGraw-Hill, Inc.).

Betancourt, R., 1996, "Growth, Capabilities and Development: Implications for Transition Processes in Cuba," *Economic Development and Cultural Change*, 44, 315-31.

_____, 1998, "Cuba's Reforms: A New Institutional Economics Perspective," Ch. 7 in J. Pérez-López and M. Travieso-Díaz (eds.) *Perspectives on Cuban Economic Reforms*, Special Studies No. 30 (Tempe: Arizona State University Press).

Bruton, H., 1998, "A Reconsideration of Import Substitution," *Journal of Economic Literature*, 36, 903-36.

Clague, C., P. Keefer, S. Knack and M. Olson, 1994, "Contract Intensive Money: Contract Enforcement, Property Rights, and Economic Performance," mimeo, University of Maryland.

Dasgupta, P., 1993, *An Inquiry into Well-Being and Destitution* (Oxford: Clarendon Press).

Deaton, A., 1992, *Understanding Consumption* (Oxford: Clarendon Press).

Devtech Systems, 1997, "The Comandante's Reserves," *Cuba: Monthly Economic Report* (August).

Evans, G., S. Honkapohja and P. Romer, 1998, "Growth Cycles," *American Economic Review*, 88, 495-515.

Gillis, M., D. Perkins, M. Roemer and D. Snodgrass, 1996, *Economics of Development*, 4th edition (New York: W. W. Norton & Company).

IRIS, 1998, "Future Research Themes," *Spring Newsletter*, 8, No.1.

Iyigun, M. and A. Owens, 1998, "Risk, Entrepreneurship, and Development, *American Economic Review*, 88, 454-7.

Madrid-Aris, M., 1997, "Growth and Technological Change in Cuba," in *Cuba in Transition--Volume 7* (Washington: Association for the Study of the Cuban Economy).

Montalván, G., 1998, " The Cuban Economy: Reform or Continued Decay," *Cuban Affairs*, 4, 5.

North, D., 1990, *Institutions, Institutional Change and Economic Performance*(London: Cambridge University Press).

Pérez Villanueva, O. E., 1998, "Cuba's Economic Reforms: An Overview," in J. Pérez-López and M. Travieso-Díaz (eds.) *Perspectives on Cuban Economic Reforms*, Special Studies No. 30 (Tempe: Arizona State University Press).

Pritchett, L., 1998,"Patterns of Economic Growth: Hills, Platteaus, Mountains and Plains," mimeo, World Bank.

Ray, D., 1998, *Development Economics* (Princeton: Princeton University Press).

Reynolds, L., 1983, "The Spread of Economic Growth to the Third World," *Journal of Economic Literature*, 31, 941-80.

Rodríguez, F. and J. Sachs, 1998, "Low Growth in Resource Rich Countries: A New Approach and an Application to Venezuela," mimeo, Harvard University.

Rodríguez-Clare, A, 1996, "The Division of Labor and Economic Development," *Journal of Development Economics*, 49, 3-32.

Rodrik, D., 1998, "Globalization, Social Conflict and Economic Growth," *The World Economy*, 21, 143-58.

Rostow, W., 1960, *Stages of Economic Growth* (London: Cambridge University Press).

Sachs, J. and A. Warner, 1995, " Natural Resource Abundance and Economic Growth," NBER Working Paper 5398.

Sanguinetty, J., 1997, "The Structural Transformation of the Cuban Economy,"in *Cuba in Transition--Volume 7* (Washington: Association for the Study of the Cuban Economy).

Sen, A., "The Standard of Living: Lectures I, II," in G. Hawthorn (ed.), *The Standard of Living* (Cambridge: Cambridge University Press, Cambridge).

Young, A., "The Tyranny of Numbers: Confronting the Statistical Realities of the East Asian Growth Experience," *Quarterly Journal of Economics*, 110, 641-80.

CULTURE OF OPPOSITION IN CUBA

Benigno E. Aguirre

The recent attention in the social sciences to social movement organizations as actors in the drama of social change, needs to be modified to make cultures of opposition the more inclusive topic of analysis and theorizing in comparative studies of change in political systems. The paper identifies ten attributes of cultures of opposition (CO) in state polities and illustrates, with information on Cuba, the value of the conceptualization for understanding the forms of collective action that occur in these polities.

The paper identifies the characteristics, context and conditions of Cuba's culture of opposition generating collective action in the island. It concludes that its counterideologies are undeveloped and relatively unknown by the Cuban people. Its extent of appropriation of the constitutive myths and symbols of the Cuban nation is incomplete, contested by the nationalist ideology of the state and its organs of social control. Modally, the CO has been embodied by subcommunities whose ideological voice has not been sufficiently articulated and broadcast inside Cuba. Nor have iconic dissident leaders been able to operate for long in the island. Voluntary organizations and institutions independent of the state that could provide support to it are mostly absent. Organized collectivities have until recently lacked systematic, ongoing cooperative contacts with organizational affiliates outside Cuba. It is a culture of opposition that facilitates the occurrence of loosely structured, uninstitutionalized collective action.

PRELIMINARIES

Cultures of opposition, often devoid of the actions of social movement organizations facilitate and struc-

ture channels for the expression of political dissent. This paper uses the Cuban case to illustrate one such occurrence. Rapid change in national political systems throughout the world, commonly studied nowadays by political scientists and sociologists under the general rubric of the "politics of transition" (Centeno, 1994; Pagnucco, 1996) causes difficulties for existing theory of social movements and social change. The obdurate facts of the recent past force us to question dominant theoretical preconceptions, such as the importance of the actions of social movement organizations (SMO) as producers of these political transformations. Events in Eastern Europe and elsewhere show that the presence of SMOs is not a necessary condition for the occurrence of antihegemonic collective action. It is partly for this reason that scholars (Steven, 1996; Johnston and Klandermans, 1995; Oberschall, 1993) advance theories of culture to understand rapid social change of political systems.

The concept of a culture of opposition (CO), most fully developed by Scott (1990), alerts us to the importance of generalized cultural change, particularly in language and other collective symbols. Such changes facilitate and enrich the occurrence of collective action. Examples of works using the CO concept abound (Johnston, 1991; Fantasia and Hirsch, 1995). The CO gives expression to and facilitates the creation of an imagined, antihegemonic viewpoint of oppressed people. It represents a set of socially restricted collective reactions to shared indignities. Actions of "heroes" dramatize the grievances of collectivities. It is fueled by the elaboration of alternative ideologies and the occurrence of shared experiences of domination. It is located in social spaces to the extent that these are insulated from the control of the state or dominant caste or category of people and inhabited by trusted, known others. The participation of people in the activities and shared experiences of the CO creates individual and collective alternative identities. The CO creates and sustains antihegemonic interpretations of events and standards of rights. It affects their daily activities and social organization. It creates and preserves a collective memory of their experience with prior collective actions. It teaches participants how to deal with the system of repression to which they are exposed (Tilly, 1978: 156).

COs are different from general political cultures, cultures of social movements, and civil society. Analytically, the first three of these dynamically interrelated concepts tap levels of diminishing analytical inclusiveness. The political culture of a nation state impacts the characteristics of its CO. The CO of a nation state shapes the cultures of social movements that are often parts of it (Fine, 1995; Lofland, 1995). Obversely, social movement cultures create and transform COs which in turn bring about changes in the general political culture (Fantasia and Hirsch, 1995; Lofland, 1993: 84-133). The strategic emphasis in this paper is on cultures of opposition, but very fruitful research is done at the other two levels of analysis. Finally, the concept of civil society connotes the relative degree of autonomy of society from the state and its political instrumentalities. It identifies a dimension of the concept of CO (see below).

The concept of CO is analogous to M. Weber's concept of political parties in situations of political repression. Empirically, COs are composed of people who may or may not be members of organized collectivities but who would like to exert control of the bureaucracy of the state to bring about social change. They cannot act openly as political parties do ideotypically, without fear of state repression. Members of COs are opposed to varying degrees to the government, to the political party or parties represented by the government, and to its policies and programs.

The CO is composed of the explicit, often organized political dissidence of a nation state. It is also made up of the countercultures and subcultures in the society to the extent that significant proportions of these communities have an oppositional *political* consensus regarding the desirability of social change. Not all subcultures and countercultures have such preponderance of opinion. To wit, in Cuba this is the case for the various African-religious associational subcultures.

Counterculture communities, including deviant and criminal communities, which by their very nature are persecuted by state authorities, often do not have a consensus regarding desirable political change. Thus, despite the homophobic nature of Cuba's culture and the long history of discrimination against gay people (Arenas, 1992), there has not been a gay movement in the island. COs are social organizations, with cultural codes and patterned structures of social relationships.

Ten attributes of the COs of national political systems are implicated in the forms of political collective action in these national political systems. These attributes are the proportion of the population of a nation-state that participates in the CO; relative ease of communication among members of the CO; strength and viability of the collective memories of heroes, heroic acts and instances of collective suffering in the CO; number and variety of places in a society in which the CO is practiced; degree of connectedness of the CO with institutions and organizations in the society which are independent of the control of the state; extent to which groups and organizations in the CO are involved in international cooperative projects and activities with other national and international associations and movements; presence in the CO of iconic leaders with wide followings in the society; degree of conceptual sophistication of the ideologies of resistance articulating the values and goals of the CO; average degree of knowledge of these ideologies among participants; and degree of connectedness of the CO to the central constitutive historical experiences, beliefs, values and myths of the nation. It is useful to think of these dimensions as forming a multidimensional space. In one of its regions are COs with high loadings in these variables. A historic example would be Poland's CO and the centrality in it of the Catholic Church and the Solidarity Movement immediately prior to the collapse of the communist government. Cuba's CO belongs to a different set with comparatively low scores in many of these variables and in which strong, significant social movement organizations do not occur.

CUBA'S CULTURE OF OPPOSITION: A WEAK CIVIL SOCIETY AND THE ABSENCE OF POLITICAL OPPORTUNITIES

The activities of dissident social movement organizations in Cuba are hindered by the absence of voluntary organizations autonomous from the state and of constitutionally protected citizenship rights (Appendix 1 documents the methods used in this research). The unequaled present day economic crisis and state repression are paired by the absence of opportunities to change the political system through nonviolent legal means and access to political institutions. The crisis has not been accompanied by significant political transformation, the emergence of successful, dominant autonomous associations and dissident social movement organizations akin to Poland's Solidarity, the creation of a new repertoire of collective protest activities (Oberschall, 1994), a weakening of the state's repressive apparatus and the ideological opening of the Castro regime (Gras, 1994). The extent of appropriation by the CO of the constitutive myths and symbols of the Cuban nation is incomplete, contested by the nationalist ideology of the state and its organs of social control. Modally, it has been a CO embodied by subcommunities whose ideological voice has not been sufficiently articulated and broadcast inside Cuba. Until very recently, they have failed to appropriate the history, myths and symbols of the nation from a state that jealously claims exclusive possession of them.

The top leadership of the government remains stable while iconic dissident leaders have not been able to operate for long in the island. Near-absent are the signs of important transformations of the political system such as the legalization and acceptance by the state of new political parties, independent mass media, environmental associations and others concerned with the public good, special interest associations such as labor unions, professional organizations of lawyers, journalists, physicians, artists, and consumer cooperatives. Mostly absent are voluntary organizations and institutions independent of the state that could provide support to a culture of opposition. Existing institutions such as mass organizations and workers' collectives have not gained their autonomy (Gras, 1994; on the repression of the state-directed "Fundación Pablo Milanés," see Puerta, 1996, 21-22). Nearly absent are organizations concerned with specific class or group interests. Moreover, associations concerned with solidary global interests are also persecuted by the state (Puerta, 1995). The exceptions are quasi religious organizations. The most important of these are two Catholic church associations, "Caritas," the service organization of the Conference of Cuban Catholic Bishops, and the "Centro Félix Varela," "Consejo Ecuménico de Cuba" (Cuban Ecumenical Council) an African religion association, "Asociación Cultural Yoruba de Cuba" (Cuban Yoruba Association), a Jewish association, "Casa de la Comunidad Hebrea de Cuba" (House of the Hebrew Community), and the Masons, or "Gran Logia de Cuba de A.L.Y.A.M." (Puerta, 1995; compare to Gunn, 1995).

Reforms carried out in 1993 allowed people to establish businesses independently of the state. Approximately 400,000 Cubans, or 10 percent of the labor force, are now legally or illegally self employed. These reforms were not carried out completely, however, and the government is increasingly opposed to the new class. Indeed, the activities of self employed small entrepreneurs, an important segment of the CO, are under constant scrutiny by the police. They face important difficulties caused by the legal stipulation that they cannot hire workers outside their own family, their lack of legal credits, housing, transportation, supply of materials and intermediaries, and very high taxes. The majority of the self employed (cuentapropistas) use the black market as the source of supply of materials for their businesses (Jatar-Haussmann, 1997, 12).

While laws are passed to sanction perceived problems brought about by the special period (Cubanet #1; henceforth CN—see Appendix 2 for full citations), there have been no advances in the rights of categories of persons. Changes in criminal laws used by the security system to justify its activities have not occurred (Alfonso, 1994; Hidalgo, 1994, 292-299; Murray, 1994). In the aftermath of the 1991 Fourth Party Congress the Cuban Communist Party (CCP) became more homogeneous and pliable to the policy dictates of Fidel Castro (Bengelsdorf, 1994, 169-173; Domínguez, 1994; del Aguila, 1994). In a comparative international context, Cuba is in a pre-transitional stage in which civil society is undeveloped (O'Donnell et al., 1986; Munck, 1994; Puerta, 1996). Cuba's political dynamics are very different from those of East Germany and Czechoslovakia in 1989. In their cases, the worker brigades refused to back the police against the demonstrators (A. Oberschall, personal correspondence) They are quite dissimilar to events in Central Europe in 1989 and similar to the case of Bulgaria and Romania before the disappearance of the USSR (Chilton, 1994; Linden, 1995) and to contemporary events in China in which the state attempts (with mixed success, see Locay, 1995; Centeno, 1994) to keep political power while managing economic and social change.. Absent in them are the political opportunities that come with the end of state repression, as in Hungary and Poland during most of the communist period. The CCP continues to oppose political change (Granma, 1996; Amuchástegui, 1997; Darling, 1997a; CN #2) and leads mobilized supporters and members of the secret police in very effective acts of repression.

INSTITUTIONAL SHADOWS AND IMPLOSIONS

The relative small number of people who participate in dissident organizations even as the CO grows is a function of the social organization of Cuban society, more specifically of its institutional arrangements. The long-standing and unresolvable systemic contradictions of socialist Cuban society, the lack of isomorphism between its institutional practices and the rhetorical fantasy of the state (Bormann, 1985; Staniszkis, 1984) help us understand the present-day institutional implosion and the resulting discontent (on the present day economic crisis see Cuban Council of Ministers, 1993; Fernández and Duyos, 1996; Tejada, 1994; for a personal account of its effects on daily life see Doriga, 1996, 39ff., Mesa-Lago, 1997).

In Cuba, officially sanctioned institutions commingle with their dual deviant shadows. These shadows are not supposed to exist even as they facilitate the operation of the legal institutions. Although unsanctioned by the established institutions, shadow institutions do not exist independently of the institutions that they complement. Parts of the CO, they offer opportunities for covert and surreptitious activities rather than explicit, open to the public acts presenting demands to the authorities. The dynamics of forced deviance caused by the failure of official institutions and the resulting cynicism it engenders in the population has been documented in the Eastern European countries (Sztompka, 1994, 246-258; Dahrendorf, 1990). They also apply to Cuba (Fernández, 1993; Puerta, 1996; Valdés, 1996; CN #3).

As in the former USSR, in Cuba there is a socialist economy and a shadow secondary economy; dollar and peso currencies (currently exchanged at one for one official parity and at 21 to the dollar in the black market; the differential between the two rates of exchange creates opportunities for illegal profit for persons with access to dollars); a socialist constitution and an officially approved, state organized shadow system of illegal and criminal practices violating the former; until very recently official atheism and the persistence of the sacred; a one-party national political system with centralized and stratified power and a micro, local, Machiavelian-like plurality of political arenas and practices (e.g., "sociolismo"), a state program that was designed in the 1960s to provide homes to people and an extraordinary housing crisis and illegal housing market resulting from its failure, or another state program designed to maximize the equal social and economic development of all provinces of the country and an unprecedented in-migration to the City of Havana, especially of people from the province of Oriente searching for a better way of life (CN #4; *Cubanews*, May 1997, 10; July 1997, 9). In these and many other instances, the failure of "official" institutions explain the presence of these shadow.

Shadow institutions impact the civic education and socialization of the citizenry into a deviant culture and social practice that inform the CO and challenge the legitimacy of state authority. They provide institutional spaces in which people create and enact a culture of opposition. Participants in these illegal activities are always faced with risk, for the official acquiescence that usually makes their activities possible is typically an unstable negotiated outcome. Their criminality obtains meaning and justification from an antihegemonic collective definition in which the powerless offer and share alternative interpretation of their motivation, its historical antecedents and the society in which they find themselves. Two good examples are prostitution and illegal economic activities (Alonso and Lago, 1995; Fogel and Rosenthal, 1994, 396-403; Puerta, 1996, 29). Participants in them engage in collective deviant acts in awareness of others and in protected spaces in which surveillance and repression by the state is temporarily suspended.

Prostitution is very often the only way young people have to frequent places such as restaurants and stores that demand dollars and are thus for the use of foreigners and their guests. Prostitutes' services in Varadero Beach and elsewhere could not occur without the authorities' cooperation (Fisher, 1997). These and similar practices show an unresolved contradiction between de jure public morality and de facto public practice (see below). The contradiction is partly resolved through the redefinition of deviance practices in the CO, such as the ongoing transformation of the social meaning of the occupation of "jineteras," as female prostitutes are known. Segments of Cuba's CO show empathy towards these young women. Their deviance is redefined as a "natural" adjustment to the national crisis (Fernández Martínez, 1996; Cifuentes 1996). López (1996) describes the anger and consternation of the neighbors of Zuleidi, a 19 year old jinetera, after she received a prison sentence of two years. Zuleidi is a nice girl. She is a college student, from a good revolutionary family, and prior to her arrest was an important source of material support for her family and neighbors. This ongoing redefinition of prostitution is an example of how the institutional implosion has brought about changes in the value and normative system of Cuban society. What was once for many people orthodox political revolutionary praxis is abandoned.

Illegal economic activities proliferate in Cuba. One of the most important of these involves subterranean exchanges among the economic production units of the state, what in Cuba is known as *cambalache*. As in China, it represents a way used by the administrators of these legal economic enterprises to resolve the rigidities inherent in the centrally planned economy. It involves top managers keeping multiple accounts of the enterprise and reserving a percentage of production for illegal barter exchanges with other state enterprises. Often these exchanges benefit the workers in the enterprises. They secure for them commodities and services that otherwise would not be generally available to them.

The unprecedented post-1989 national economic crisis probably increased the occurrence of illegal economic activities. It rendered individualistic economic adaptations increasingly ineffective as ways of adjusting and surviving in Cuba, even for people who had been active supporters of the regime. It has encouraged and facilitated the development of an explicit collective opposition stance among Cubans. It increased their participation in protests and in dissident organizations. Cuba's CO is energized by the economic deprivations the Cuban people have experienced since 1989 (Alonso, 1995; Rivera, 1995; Valdés and Felipe, 1996; Tejada, 1994). Many people who until recently still believed in the message of Fidel Castro cannot continue to do so, for it is much harder to deny the increasing ruin of the country (Fogel and Rosenthal, 1994, 248). Many who until recently supported the government and were members of its leading cadres can no longer offer rhetorical defense to their revolutionary selves (Bormann, 1985). Nor can they continue to profit from the system. The contemporary economic crisis has meant the destruction of the operational capability of institutions throughout Cuban society that were the source of livelihood for people and provided services to the public. Thus, for example, Popular Power, the nationwide system of political representation at the local level, is widely discredited (Bengelsdorf, 1994; Domínguez, 1994, 9-10; CN #5). The crisis has also brought about the onset of widespread unemployment and underemployment throughout the society (Betancourt, 1995; Alonso, 1995, 20, estimates that between 18 and 25 percent of Cuba's labor force is unemployed). It has brought a nationwide breakdown in the routines of daily life that regulated people's schedules. Unsurprisingly, this institutional implosion has produced unprecedented large numbers of antihegemonic activities of members of highly placed strata in the state apparatus as well as important changes in its repressive strategy and tactics.

The government encourages limited business dealings with capitalist firms (Puchala, 1992). These joint economic enterprises create a great deal of resentment among the Cuban people. They generate profits for the regime and foreign investors. However, the majority of the native population is devoid of hard currencies and is systematically excluded from these profitable economic activities and from the use of the facilities and services generated by them (Betancourt, 1995; Doriga, 1996, 61ff). Simultaneously, this policy created a new class of privileged people with access to dollars. It is made up of small farmers, for reportedly the recently allowed free agricultural markets produced a "massive transfer of income from the cities to the countryside (Betancourt, 1995, p. 2);" Cuban officials who derive illicit profit from their offices' monopolistic control of business relationships with international capital (*El Nuevo Herald*, 12 Feb. 1995, 14A); they profit from the continuation of the Castro regime even as this very state frustrates their illegal behavior through sporadic arrests and harassment; a minority of Cubans with access to the dollar economy generated by family transfers, tourism-related business activities and services and foreign business activities. Their counterparts, accounting for the majority of the population, are losers. They include not only most Blacks but also "retirees, many in the military and police, as well as doctors, teachers and engineers who are specifically forbidden to trade in dollars" (Betancourt, 1995, p. 2). Particularly hard hit by the effects of the present crisis are the poor and blacks, many of who are without social relations outside Cuba who would provide them with aid (Fernández and Duyos, 1996, 112-113; Bobes, 1996, 132). Ironically, they constituted the strongest source of support for the government and are now increasingly alienated from it. Poor neighborhoods in Havana and elsewhere (Darling,

1997b) increasingly become places in which disorder and protests occur. The plight of the poor and their neighborhoods is now the plight of the nation. Their protests now find widespread support among members of other social classes (Fogel and Rosenthal, 1994, 488-497).

The CO is also informed by a second type of institutional failure in which the official institutions achieve goals that are contrary to the seminal rhetorical fantasy of the socialist state (Bormann, 1985). The best example is Cuban education, one of the often claimed achievements of the post 1958 regime (Aguirre and Vichot, 1996). Despite the claim, the educational system has been one of the most important instrumentalities in the reproduction of systems of social inequality in the island. Meritocratic educational policies and programs are very important means for upward social mobility even though they conflict with a rhetorical fantasy that stressed universal access, equality of educational results and abandonment of the distinction between manual and intellectual work (Jiménez, 1991; Castro, 1991). The unresolved conflict between the rhetorical fantasy and the educational practices undermined the legitimacy of the socialist project and created socialization experiences that forced people to participate in the CO.

The generalized existence of shadow and subversive official institutions such as formal education force people to live in two worlds, the world "as is" and the world as "it should be" as outlined by the dominant rhetorical fantasy of the social system. People adapt to this duality by developing an indifference to politics, to issues affecting the public good, and an acceptance of deviance and criminality. Instead, their primary orientation is towards their own private affairs. This duality must be understood as an important factor increasing the resistance of people to cooperate with others and participate in the organized dissidence that is part of Cuba's CO. Multiplied many times in many different contexts, the CO gradually becomes an accepted part of life of people, typified by emergent definitions of right and wrong and by grays of moral meanings.

Institutional arrangements in Cuba prior to 1989 allowed people to use this passive, alienated individualistic orientation towards the political system. It was an orientation that made them members of the CO and unwilling to participate in protests and dissident organizations. The comparatively much more serious economic difficulties of the special period makes such individualist adaptation increasingly untenable. They create discontent in all strata of the society, both former elite and the poor. The economic crisis and its resulting social effects facilitate the occurrence of antihegemonic collective action. It increases the size and activism of what was, prior to 1989, a much more passive and probably smaller national CO.

STRUGGLE FOR
AN ALTERNATIVE IDEOLOGY

The development of an alternative ideology by Cuba's CO is rendered difficult by the vigilance of the government and its aggressive insistence that it has a monopoly on legitimate interpretations of the nation's past, present and future. This claim justifies the political hegemony of the CCP. The contemporary emergence of a nationwide dissidence has produced conflict over control of the constitutive symbols of the nation that are part of the ideology of the government. This struggle over control of symbols includes many of the symbols created during the founding of the nation, the Republican period (1902-1958), and the post 1958 revolutionary culture. It also includes struggle over the definition of objectionable symbols. An example is the recurrent concern expressed in *Granma*, the official newspaper of the government, over the lack of patriotism of some Cuban youngsters presumably shown by their use of the US flag to adorn their clothes (CN #6; Arocha, 1997). Nowhere is this symbolic struggle better exemplified than in the controversy over control of arguably the most important symbol of the Cuban nation, its most exalted founder, José Martí y Pérez.

The government emphasizes Martí's antiimperialist writings to justify its own fears of the US. It justifies the lack of a multiparty political system in Cuba by pointing out that Martí created **one** revolutionary party as he organized Cuba's war of independence

against Spain. On the other hand, the dissidence points to Martí's magnanimous humanism and his emphasis on human rights and freedoms (CN #7; Piñera Llera, 1981). While both emphases are reflected in Martí's writings and revolutionary praxis, the real political issue of social conflict is whether the dissidents' view will find wide resonance among the Cuban people. At stake is the granting of legitimacy for an alternative vision of the history and destiny of the nation. Government repression tries to stop dissidents from celebrating Martí's birthday (CN #8), commemorate his death (CN #9), and quote from some of his writings. And in an unusual twist, the government conducts mass rallies for its army and security personnel in which officers sign declarations reaffirming the validity of the government's interpretation of Martí (CN #10).

Attempts at repressing people from using Jose Martí as a symbol, however, have failed. Martí is the rallying point of all dissidents. Thus it is that independent journalists claim Martí's approval of their duty to inform the nation (CN #11). The most important effort to organize the dissidence "Concilio Cubano" (Cuban Council), scheduled its first national conference in 1996 for 24 February, in remembrance of the date in 1895 of the initiation of the war of independence organized and led by José Martí. Masses are conducted throughout the country to celebrate his birthday (CN #13). Affinity dissident groups incorporate his name in theirs, for example, the "Liga Civica Martiana" and the "Organizacion Juvenil Martiana por la Democracia." Other organizations are founded on his birthday, as is the "Ex Club Cautivo" (Club of Ex Prisoners). Then annually, on the anniversary, they celebrate their founding while venerating Martí's memory (CN #14).

Increasingly, attempts are made to establish alternative, coherent, comprehensive ideologies. So far their success is unclear. One of the most celebrated of these efforts was a document entitled "The Homeland Belongs to Us All." A working group of the internal dissidence wrote it. They criticized the platform of the most recent V Congress of the CCP. They challenged and offered alternative interpretations to every aspect of the CCP's document. Their criticism included the CCP's interpretation of the historical origins and experiences of the nation; the nature of the dissident movement; and the government's view of Jose Martí, the Batista dictatorship, the republican period (1902-1958) and the missile crisis of October of 1962, among others. They reminded the people of the disastrous effects on their liberties of the CCP's emphasis on unity, the chronic mismanagement by the government of foreign assistance and the public good, the need for a multiparty political system, the present national economic impoverishment and the lack of freedoms and legal protections (CN #15). Characteristically, all four members of this working group were arrested almost immediately after the press conference in which they expressed their opinions, prompting a worldwide alert by Amnesty International (CN #16). The other effort is by a group representing a surviving faction of the Concilio. As others have done before, they asked the Council of State for a national plebiscite in which the Cuban people would vote on whether to establish a multiparty political system and constitutionally protected civil rights for minorities (CN #17). The quickness and effectiveness of government security in repressing these (and all other attempts to voice well thought out) alternative visions of Cuba make it very doubtful that a significant proportion of the people of Cuba learned about the details of these documents.

The result is that an alternative ideology to the ideology of the government that is widely understood and acccepted by the Cuban people is missing. The two most likely options for the dissident movement are Christian ethics and the adoption of some version of the liberal democratic ideology that informed the Cuban Constitution of 1940. However, it has been difficult for former Marxists in the dissident movement to accept these alternatives. During almost four decades, the government taught people that this was the constitution of the US-dominated Republic and of the exiled *gusanos*, or worms, as the presumed class enemies of the people were once labeled. Government's laws and policies were militantly anti religious, stressing the old Marxist dictum that religion is the "opium" of the people. It has proven difficult to counter the well-established secularism of the cul-

ture or to escape the effects of this ideological war against the ideals of the Republic. Instead what is taking place is the gradual gaining of legitimacy of the dissident movement and a CO as a social formation providing alternative interpretive schemes to that proffered by the government but **without** a clear coherent ideology (Thompson, 1990). This emergent interpretive scheme comes from the failures of the institutions created by the government and their shadows, the increasing misery of the people, the unintended consequences of government repression, the presence of a dissident movement enriched by former elite members and transnational resources, and the work of an independent press reporting on events in Cuba.

NEW COMMUNICATION LINKS AND THE EMERGENCE OF A TRANSNATIONAL OPPOSITION

Telephone, radio, and electronic communication links now available have eroded the government's control over the information the Cuban people receive about events in Cuba and elsewhere. This in turn has facilitated their collective action. Approximately 15 percent of Cubans listen to the radio daily; 17 percent of daily users listen to US-source radio stations, primarily to Radio Martí (*Cubanews*, 1995, p. 11). In 1989, there were 86 television sets per 100 inhabitants. People spend approximately 40 percent of their daily free time watching television programs (Aróstegui and Fernández, 1991). In 1997 CNN opened a news bureau in Havana (*Cubanews*, February 1997, 7). Also serving Cuba is an international courier mail service. Telephones are widely available in the island.

Average daily international telephone calls increased from 500 in 1995 to 50,000 in 1997 with the lifting of the telecommunication embargo by the U.S. government (*Cubanews*, July 1997, 8). Partly with the assistance of Mexican and Canadian investors (López, 1993, see also *Cubanews*, November 1996; 2; July 1996, 4), international telephone communications were significantly improved after decades of decline in services. It is an important source of income for the Cuban government. During 1995 it received $54 millions in revenue from approximately ten million calls between the United States and Cuba. This revenue exceeded gains from important crops like tobacco (*Cubanews*, 1996a). Reportedly, telephone services inside Cuba are much worse off, although apparently improving (Press, 1996). In contrast to the recent past, it is much easier today to have telephone communications with people in the island.

The economic crisis weakened the government-controlled mass media. The scarcity of paper and ink brought about by the crisis curtailed publication of a number of newspapers and journals. A similar problem with energy affected Cuban radio and television stations. Thirty radio stations continued to operate in 1995 (Editor, 1995, p. 11). Even as the government curtailed their operation, however, established and new electronic means of mass communication operated against it from outside the country. Among the former, the most important is Radio Martí, funded by the U.S. government. Other smaller radio stations operate as parts of specific transnational movement organizations. Examples are "El CID" and the "Voz de la Fundación," the radio station of the Cuban American National Foundation (CANF), with headquarters in Washington, D.C. Despite official attempts to curtail the practice (CN #9) some people also have access to CNN and other major U.S. television stations (El Nuevo Herald, 25 September 1994, p. 3E).

Private citizens' use of electronic mail is curtailed by the government. This is done avowedly to protect them against pornography and to insure national security (Keating and Hecker, 1994). With the possible exception of the Catholic Church and other religious denominations, nongovernmental organizations and private citizens do not usually have access to it. The use of electronic mail and the internet is also restricted to the personnel of foreign governments and corporations doing business in the island (Klee, 1996), and to a limited number of officials, ministries, scientific institutes and other organs of the Cuban government (López, 1996; CN #18). The newly established web page Cubaweb (www.cubaweb.cu) serves many of these entities.

While the Internet (and e-mail) is effectively censored inside Cuba, it is playing a key part in energiz-

ing and transforming the organizations and affinity groups that are part of Cuba's CO. They do not have access to the Internet but have access to the recently improved international telephone services. Increasingly, they also have organizational representatives and cooperating organizational affiliates and representatives outside Cuba that have access to the Internet. These are key sources of organizational resources. Examples of this pattern abound: "Movimiento Humanista Evolucionario Cubano" (Cuban Evolutionary Humanist Movement) circulates its telephone, e-mail address (MHEC@compuserve.com) and home page in the Web (http://ourworld.compuserve.com/homepages/mhec), as does "Hermanos al Rescate" (Brothers to the Rescue; http://www.hermanos.org) and "Partido Demócrata Cristiano de Cuba" (Christian Democratic Party of Cuba, http://www.pdc-cuba.org), to mention three well-known organizations operating in Cuba and elsewhere. A number of organized members of the CO act as clearing houses of information on the action of government security and other events in the island. Among them are the Cuban Information Center (CN #14), the Bureau of Independent Journalists, and the Information Bureau of the Human Right Movement in Cuba. Once contacted via telephone, these transnational organizational resources broadcast the problems of people in the island to other Cubans in Cuba via radio as well as to members of the international community. Using this simple communication system, citizens can report events and government actions (CN# 19), and independent journalists in Cuba devoid of access to the Internet, facsimile machines or office equipment other than antiquated typewriters can practice their profession (Rivero, 1997; Ackerman, 1996).

News about events affecting a community, group, or person in Cuba is more likely to be known nowadays. An excellent example is the convocation by the "Comité Cubano Pro Derechos Humanos" (Committee for Human Rights) of the population in the municipalities of Guines, Nueva Paz, Nicolás de Bari, Güira de Melena, and others in the Mayabeque region in the Province of Havana, to attend a religious rally in the Chapel of Santa Barbara, in the City of Güines, on December 4, 1991, to pray for the democratization of the country. Cuban activists sent the invitation to Cuban Catholic priests in Miami, Florida. The priests were asked to broadcast it to Cuba through "Radio Martí," "El CID," and the "Voz de la Fundación." The system also makes it possible, for example, for interested persons outside Cuba to double-check with their contacts in Havana about the truthfulness of reports circulating outside Cuba of bombings of public buildings and have the information divulged worldwide in a matter of hours after the initiation of the request (CN #20). Government actions are known that in the past were unknown by most people. This includes rumors of political infighting in the CCP and among the highest authorities of the government as well as knowledge of political mobilizations (*LAT 92-188*; *LAT 92-146*). Recently, at least one independent journalist advertised his services to the public (CN #21); and in an unusual case, an underground activist actively being searched for by government security used the system to ask for international protection before his capture (CN #22).

The dependence of organized members of Cuba's CO on transnational organizational partners existed prior to 1989. What is new in the post 1989 period is the enormous power of the Internet to broadcast their appeal and to mobilize their constituencies outside Cuba. Its impact on Cuba's CO and on the Diaspora community in Europe and the US is hard to overestimate. The new electronic system neutralizes governmental secrecy, improves the accuracy and timeliness of the ongoing monitoring of the Cuban government and helps people evaluate their interpretations of events and coordinate their actions. This is the case even thought the Cuban government retains the power to effectively block the distribution in Cuba of hard copies of important works of contemporary literature it finds objectionable, for example, the anathematized work of Cuban writer Reinaldo Arenas (CN #23).

Increasingly, antihegemonic political collective action by Cubans in and out of Cuba is not a national but an international process. As is the case in other social movements in the United States and elsewhere, events in Cuba and South Florida often coincide

with political sensitivities and agendas of agencies and organizations that are distant from the place of action. Distal political participatory events occur as reflections of events elsewhere (McCarthy and Zald, 1977). The transnational nature of the politics of Cuba's CO is shown by instances in which social movement organizations (SMO) contact their organizational counterparts outside Cuba. In a prototypical fashion, the "Cuban Workers Coordinate," an independent labor union organization, sends its greetings to labor unions throughout the world on the occasion of International Workers' Day (CN #24). "Movimiento Cristiano de Liberación" (Movement of Christian Liberation) sends congratulations to the Venezuelan political party COPEI on its 50 anniversary (CN #25). The proscribed youth association "José de la Luz y Caballero" expressed its thanks to Hungarian youth organizations who refused to participate in the 1997 XIII Festival of Youth in Havana as a way of protesting the exclusions of the Cuban youth group from the festival (CN #26).

The transnational nature of politics is also shown by the attention that members of Cuba's CO give to political events in the United States and elsewhere. Again, examples of this are plentiful: Mr. Gustavo Arcos Bergnes, General Secretary of "Comité Cubano Pro Derechos Humanos" (Cuban Committee for Human Rights), expressed his views from Havana about the "Torricelli" Law after hearing the opinions about the law of a well known Miami Cuban lawyer and a Cuban American professor. Independent journalists and dissidents object to the opinions on Cuba expressed by US members of Congress who visited the country for a few days (CN #27). The "Partido Pro Derechos Humanos" objects to the United Nations General Secretary's decision to exclude it from the four organizations in the dissident movement inside Cuba that would be accredited to address the UN Commisssion on Human Rights (CN #28).

The new system of communication facilitates the mobilization of international organizations on behalf of members of the CO. Thus, the Cuban National Jurist Union in cooperation with the Inter American Commission on Human Rights (IACHR) with headquarters in San José, Costa Rica, conducted a "Seminar On Human Rights" in Havana in May of 1994 (IACHR, 1997). Dissidents attend international conferences on the topic of Cuba and are at times successful in eliciting declarations of support from them. An example is an international conference on Cuba sponsored by the government of Holland. It was attended by Representatives of "Plataforma Democrática Cubana" (Cuban Democratic Platform). Participants condemned violations of human rights by the Cuban government (Alfonso, 1997a). In another case, dissidents sent an open letter to government representatives attending the Ibero American Summit in Madrid in July of 1992. Fidel Castro participated in the Summit. The letter asked them to promote peaceful change in Cuba and to request from Castro greater political freedoms (*LAT 92-132*). Prompted by Cuban independent worker organizations, the International Labor Organization continues to speak on behalf of the Cuban labor movement and the right of workers to unionize. The AFL-CIO gave the George Meany Award for Human Rights to 30-year political prisoner Mario Chanes de Armas (Alfonso, 1994c). Human Rights Watch asked the Cuban government for the freedom from imprisonment of Cuban political prisoners (CN #29). Appeals are made to foreign politicians and other personalities to intervene with the Cuban government on behalf of political prisoners (LAT 92 193). Newspapers and other mass media outlets throughout the world often voice support of Cuba's CO (for example, Fisher, 1997; Editorial, 1996); to facilitate their work news items are translated into English and French (CN #30).

The new means of communication facilitate the occurrence and spread of collective behavior throughout the society and the integration of organizations in the Diaspora community into the political dynamics in the island. For example, in June of 1995, the leader of "Cambio Cubano" (Cuban Change), a movement active in Miami and Cuba spoke with Fidel Castro about the future of the island. Cuban exile writers in Paris denounced police brutality against Cuban journalists (CN #31). Exile organizations in Puerto Rico, in cooperation with clandestine organizations in Cuba, called for a campaign of civil disobedience for December 4, the feast day of "Santa Bár-

bara," the patron saint of Cuba (CN #32). The Cuban American Foundation called for a demonstration for September 6, 1991, in front of the notorious prison facility known as "Villa Marista," in Havana, to demand the freedom of political prisoners (*FBIS LAT 91-175*, 9 September, 1991). Members of "Vigilia Mambisa" rallied in Miami to ask for a massive demonstration in support of dissidents in Cuba (*El Nuevo Herald*, 20 de Julio, 12a). The Cuban Human Rights Committee in Mexico protested the repression of the Cuban Democratic Coalition (*LAT 91-175*). In Cuba, leaders of the "Movimiento 13 de Julio" (13 July Movement) advised members of "Movimiento Democracia" (Democracy Movement) in Miami who were forming a flotilla of boats to protest in international waters off Cuba on the anniversary of Cuba's independence day, May 20, 1997 (CN #33; Corzo, 1997). The boat heading this flotilla was bought two years earlier with public donations of Cubans from Miami and it made its maiden voyage to Cuba in June 13, 1995, as part of elaborate ceremonies in Miami protesting the sinking by the Cuban authorities of the tugboat "13 of March" in Havana Bay (see below) (CN #34).

The new communication links also energize voluntary associations of Cubans out of Cuba for which I could not document a clear organizational representation in Cuba. Thus, more than 12 organizations of Cuban exiles in Spain protested the downing of civilian airplanes by the Cuban air force in February of 1996. "Cambio Cubano" (Cuban Change), an organization of Cuban exiles in Stockholm, Sweden, was received in an act of solidarity by the members of three Swedish political parties (CN #35). Cubans in Tampa, Florida, conducted elections in 1994 to select officials to represent them **in Cuba** after the fall of Castro's government. Dissident artists in the City of Santiago de Cuba requested financial support from interested persons in the U.S. Diaspora in order to practice their art (CN #36). Similarly, hospitals and other Cuban institutions on their own initiative use their e-mail capabilities to request aid from individuals and institutions outside Cuba.

These examples argue for the existence of a transnational political dynamic affecting Cuba's CO. The collective actions that occur in Cuba and among Cubans in South Florida, Puerto Rico, and other communities of the Cuban Diaspora must be understood in light of this recently emerged transnational political reality that is facilitated in large part by the new means of mass communication. The new means of communication and the strengthening of its transnational organizational links encourage the occurrence of organized, institutionalized collective action. The Cuban people have a long-standing tradition of opposition to the Castro government mostly enacted in muted acts of defiance that occur in shadow institutions. Increasingly, however, these muted acts are transformed into nonsecretive, open-to-the public antihegemonic acts.

Cuba's weak civil society and the absence of political opportunities, its institutional shadows and implosions, and the lack of alternative ideologies, determine that the most common forms of collective action occurring exemplify loosely structured, uninstitutionalized collective action (Oberschall, 1993: 187-212). These forms are the heroic actions of protest by individuals, prison and food riots, brutality generated protests, mass behavior, and rumors. While there are a number of social movement organizations in Cuba, most have small number of members, are restricted to a city or region, and are the targets of very effective system of state repression. They sponsor a pacifist ideological stance, petitioning the government to allow for peaceful change to take place, trying to convince members of the ruling elite about the need for a multiparty political system and respect for human rights. This strategy has failed to have any measurable effect in bringing about significant changes to the political system of Cuba (Aguirre, manuscript in progress).

CONCLUSION

This paper has documented the more important characteristics of Cuba's culture of opposition and briefly identified the modal forms of collective action occurring in the island. Cuba's political system is inhospitable to social movement organizations. Comparatively, the collective action forms that take place are much less institutionalized. These protests are not usually planned by movement organizers or entrepre-

neurs, nor can these activities be accurately described as carried out by transitory teams led by the staff of social movements. The collective action of dissident organizations in Cuba and among Cubans in South Florida, Puerto Rico, and other communities of the Cuban Diaspora is very much impacted by the recently emerged transnational political system. It is facilitated by the new means of mass communication. This change in connectivity with the outside may precede a more important role for social movement organizations. The Cuban case documents the importance for social movement organizations of **both** distant and indigenous sources of resources.

Models of political opportunity are not fully applicable. Cuba is in a pre-transitional stage in which civil society is undeveloped and in which there has not been increases in legal rights. Likewise, explanatory schemes such as new social movement theory (Johnston, Larana, Gusfield, 1994, 3-10) that do not put emphasis on people's master social statuses and central socioeconomic grievances are also not very useful to help us understand the dominant forms of collective action taking place. The same is true of frame analysis. It assumes the existence of an organization creating a symbolic system or "interpretive schemata" to mobilize constituencies. Undoubtedly such framing efforts take place. However, in Cuba the frames fail to mobilize people **not** because they would not respond to the messages but because government security destroys the organizations and blocks the broadcasting of their frames (Hart, 1996, 95). The consequence is the creation of a tradition of protest without a clear ideology. The Cuban case also shows that there is no necessary correspondence between the extent of people's grievances and their tendency to participate in collective action.

A sociology of culture gives the most useful understanding of antihegemonic collective political participation in Cuba. It is both the result and the means through which a shared symbolic understanding of selves and collectivities occur. Counterculture activities and shared experiences create individual and collective identities that fuel the antihegemonic collective viewpoint in Cuba. People's participation in the CO as well as the organized government reaction the

CO engenders generates instances of relatively unorganized forms of protest which in turn help the CO grow. In the face of an inauspicious political opportunity structure, these collective actions reflect and help form enduring traditions of resistance to the government.

Appendix 1
METHODS

This paper concentrates on the more recent post 1989 period. It uses information from the archives of the Miami-based Information Bureau of the Human Rights Movement in Cuba (www.netpoint.net/~infoburo). The Bureau is an important source on post-1989 collective behavior events and social movements (and social movement-like) organizations and activities. The Bureau is a good source of information on human rights, but it underrepresents unplanned street actions, emergent collective behavior, and unorthodox and sudden transformations of complex organizations.

A second source of more general information is news items distributed electronically by Cubanet, identified in the text with the initials CN (see Appendix 2; cubanet@netpoint.net; www.cubanet.entorno). It includes articles from Cuba authored by independent journalists (also available at ella.netpoint.net/cubanet/bpic/index.html and at www.cubafreepress.org). The information in the archives of the Bureau and in Cubanet appears to be both reliable and valid. It was cross-checked and augmented with information from other sources, if available.

For this purpose, I conducted:

- a systematic review of all post-1988 articles on Cuba published by *El Nuevo Herald* (Miami, Florida; www.elherald.com/cuba/cuba_top.shtml) and *Diario Las Americas* (Miami, Florida; www.diariolasamericas.com);

- in-depth cultural analyses of articles published by *Cubanews*, a newsletter on Cuba published by the Miami Herald (mhinternat@aol.com);

- a search of all post-1988 news items on Cuba included in the *National Newspaper Index*;

- content analysis of Amnesty International USA's reports on Cuba (1988; 1990; 1992; for the AI's 1997 report on Cuba see Freedom House; 1997) and the sections devoted to Cuba in Amnesty International's (AI) *Annual Reports* (1981, 135-138; 1982, 128-130; 1983, 128-130; 1984, 145-147; 1985, 140-142; 1986, 143-146; 1987, 150-154; 1988, 106-108; 1989, 117-119; 1990, 75-78; 1991, 73-75; 1992, 97-100; 1993, 108-111; 1994, 111-114);

- occasional hearings and reports on Cuba from the United Nations Commission on Human Rights (The Endowment for Cuban American Studies, 1993), the U.S. Congress (House and Senate), and U.S. Department of State (1994; its reports on human rights are in the U.S. State Department web site, www.state.gov);

- other information on human rights available from Of Human Rights (www.ofhumanrights.org; see also www.freecuba.org;

- electronic news items selected from CubaWorld (www.cubaworld.com) and Habaguanex Ciboney (ciboney@netside.net which includes home pages with news and information on various social movement organizations); and

- papers in the annual proceedings of the Association for the Study of the Cuban Economy (www.lanic.utexas.edu/la/ca/cuba/asce)

All of the experiences of citizens and communities presented in this paper (as well as many other similar cases not included here) are documented repeatedly by AI and these other sources. Due to space limitations, the paper identifies (but excludes) extended treatment of the modal forms of dissent in Cuba (manuscript available upon request).

Limitations

The paper has important limitations. It lacks information on individual level variables such as perceived grievance that is customarily ascertained in research on protest. It also lacks information on the likely causes for many of the social patterns described below. Also lacking are longitudinal studies and information about individual and collective acts of protests such as boycotts, strikes, refusals, withdrawals, civil disobedience and blockades for which literally nothing is known at present. At time unknown by me, many of the organizations and patterns described below no longer exist while others have taken their place. Prison, police, and court records and the archives of social movement organizations and the organs of state security contain invaluable but unavailable information on instances of social protest and movement activities, strategies and tactics. When and if they become available, this archival material in conjunction with personal narratives and life histories will undoubtedly allow more nuance understandings than are possible at present. Perhaps most crucially, the study is limited by the present day inability to conduct in Cuba interviews with participants and field observations of antihegemonic political individual and collective action. Researchers cannot make good-faith guarantees to respondents regarding their protection as human subjects. Moreover, they are vulnerable to the actions of state security.

Appendix 2
ISSUES OF CUBANET

#1: "Preparan nueva ley para preservar garantias procesales." AFP, 27 Diciembre 1995; #2: "Depuis Cuba." APIC, 29 Abril 1997; #3: "Cuba, the look from within." 28 January 1997; #4: ")Quiénes son los culpables?" 9 Mayo 1997; #5: ")Podría alguien explicarme que es el poder popular?" 1 octubre 1996; #6: "Preocupa a las autoridades el uso de símbolos norteamericanos." 11 Febrero 1997; #7: "Por la reivindicación de la dignidad martiana." 27 Diciembre 1995; #8: "Detenciones y represiones en vísperas del natalicio de Martí." 19 Febrero 1997; #9: "Between tensions and threats." 21 September 1995; #10: "Declaración de los mambises del siglo XX." 18 Marzo 1997; #11: "Truth, once awakened, will not be dormant again." 19 February 1997; #12: "Puja por José Martí entre gobierno y oposición en Cuba." 6 Febrero 1997; #13: "Tensión el 24 de febrero." 25 Febrero 1997; #14: "El Ex Club Cautivo cumplió su primer aniversario." 30 Enero 1997; #15: "La patria es de todos." 6 Julio 1997; #16: "Amnesty International Urgent Action Appeal." 22 July 1997; #17: "Piden opositores cubanos celebración de un plebiscito nacional." 17 Julio 1997; #18: "Cuba Plans Blockade of the Internet." Radio Martí, 6 February 1996; #19: "Declaraciones del padre de Yndamiro Restano hechas desde Cuba via telefónica a la oficina en Miami del Buró de Periodistas Independientes." 11 Enero 1996; #20: "Bomb in Havana." Larry Daley, 17, 22 April 1997; "Rumors from Havana." Larry Daley, Cuba-L, 10 April 1997; #21: "Aviso de Manuel David Orrio." 20 Junio 1997; #22: "Reinaldo Cozano Alen Asks for International Protection." Radio Martí, 24 Febrero 1996; #23: "La Habana Para Su Amante Difunto." 28 Mayo 1995; #24: "Declaration from the opposition Cuban Workers' Coordinate." 2 Mayo 1997; #25: "Mensaje de Paya Sardinas al COPEI." 15 Enero 1996; #26: "Agradecen jóvenes cubanos a Húngaros rechazo a participar en festival." 2 Mayo 1997; #27: "Mensaje de periodistas independientes al congresista norteamericano Esteban Torres." 22 enero 1997; "Dissidents criticize congressman's visit." 27 January 1996; #28: "Carta abierta del Partido Pro Derechos Humanos al Secretario General de la ONU." 23 mayo 1997; #29: "Human Rights Watch pide liberación presos políticos." EFE, 22 Febrero 1996; #30: "Falsos debates de documento partidista en Cuba." 5 Julio 1997; #31: "Protestan escritores por agresiones en Cuba." 19 febrero 1997; "Declaración de organizaciones en España." Cubapress, 5 Marzo 1996; #32: "Exilio cubano apoyará actos de desobediencia civil." 22 noviembre 1995; #33: "Llama el Movimiento 13 de Julio a la cordura de los integrantes de la flotilla Democracia." BPCI, 16 Mayo 1997; #34: "Flotilla de exiliados recordara hundimiento." 27 Junio 1997;

#35: "Encuentro en Suecia." 14 agosto 1995; #36: "Libertad para las musas." 27 enero 1997.

REFERENCES

Ackerman, E. 1996. "Desde Cuba con valor." *El Nuevo Herald* (8 diciembre) 1A.

Aguirre, B. E. and R. Vichot. 1996. "Are Cuba's Educational Statistics Reliable?" in *Cuba in Transition—Volume 6.* Washington: Association for the Study of the Cuban Economy, pp. 371-386.

Alfonso, Pablo. 1994. *Cuba: El diálogo ignorado.* Miami: Ediciones Cambio.

Alfonso, Pablo. 1994c. "AFL-CIO galardona a ex preso Chanes." *El Nuevo Herald,* (8 abril).

Alfonso, Pablo. 1997a. "Conferencia condena el regimen de Castro." *El Nuevo Herald* (20 Abril), 7A.

Alonso, José F. 1995. "The Path of Cuba's Economy Today." *Newsletter of the Association for the Study of the Cuban Economy.* Spring Issue (June), pp. 18-23.

Alonso, José F. and A. Lago. 1995. "A First Approximation Model of Money, Prices and Exchange Rates in Revolutionary Cuba" in *Cuba in Transition—Volume 5.* Washington: Association for the Study of the Cuban Economy, pp. 101-143.

Amnesty International. 1996. Cuba. *Dissidents Imprisoned or Forced into Exile* (July). AI Index: AMR 25/29/96.

Amnesty International. 1996. *Cuba. Crackdown on Dissent.* London: Amnesty International..

Amuchastegui, Domingo. 1994. "Rioting on the Malecon: Castro's Response." *Cubanews,* vol. 2 (September): 9.

Arenas, R. 1992. *Antes que anochezca.* Barcelona: Fabula TusQuets Editores.

Arocha, M. 1997. "Desatan polemica jóvenes que visten de barras y estrellas." *El Nuevo Herald* (16 de Junio).

Arostegui, M. and R. Z. Fernández. 1991. "La televisión en la estructura de actividades recreativas de la población cubana." *Ciencias Sociales,* vol. 26: 89-99.

Bengelsdorf, Carollee. 1994. *The Problem of Democracy in Cuba.* New York: Oxford University Press.

Betancourt, E. F. 1995. "Backgrounder on the Potential Impact of the Helms/Burton Act on Castro's Rule over Cuba." Unpublished manuscript.

Betancourt, E. F. 1997. *Cuba: Bringing the Background to the Foreground.* Washington: Freedom House, The Free Cuba Center.

Bobes, V.C. "Cuba y la cuestión racial." *Perfiles Latinoamericanos,* 8 (Enero/Julio): 115-139.

Bormann, E. G. 1985. *The Force of Fantasy: Restoring the American Dream.* Carbondale: Southern Illinois University Press.

Burawoy, M. and J. Lukacs. 1992. *The Radiant Past: Ideology and Reality in Hungary's Road to Capitalism.* Chicago: The University of Chicago Press.

Castro, F. 1991. "President Castro SNTAF Speech." *FBIS-LAT 91-230* (November 29): 7-21.

Centeno, M. A. 1994. "Between Rocky Democracies and Hard Markets: Dilemmas of the Double Transition." *Annual Review of Sociology,* 20: 125-147.

Chilton, P. 1994. "Mechanics of Change: Social Movements, Transnational Coalitions and the

Transformation Process in Eastern Europe." *Democratization*, 1 (Spring): 151-181.

Cifuentes, A. B. 1996. "La historia de una niña prostituta." *Cubanet* (4 octubre).

Corzo, Cynthia. 1997. "Movimiento Democracia llega hasta 14 millas de las costas cubanas." *El Nuevo Herald* (18 Mayo), 1A.

Cuban Council of Ministers. 1993. *The Inexorable Collapse of the Cuban Economy: A Classified Report of the Castro Regime to its Council of Ministers*. Washington: The Cuban American National Foundation. The Endowment for Cuban American Studies, Paper #2.

Dahrendorf, R. 1990. *Reflections on the Revolution in Europe*. New York: Random House.

Darling, J. 1997a. "Documento del PCC mantiene modelo estalinista." *El Nuevo Herald* (25 de Mayo).

del Aguila, J. M. 1994. "The Party, the Fourth Congress, and the Process of Counterreform" in Jorge F. Pérez-López, editor, *Cuba at a Crossroads*. Gainesville: University Press of Florida, pp. 19-40.

Domínguez, J. I. 1994. "Leadership Strategies and Mass Support" in Jorge F. Pérez-López, editor, *Cuba at a Crossroads*. Gainesville: University Press of Florida, pp.1-18.

Doriga, E. L. 1996. *Cuba 1995: vivencias personales*. Lima: Universidad del Pacífico, Centro de Investigación.

Editor. 1995. "Radio Stations in Cuba." *Cubanews*, vol. 3 (January 15): 11.

Fantasia, R. and E. L. Hirsch. 1995. "Culture in Rebellion: The Appropriation and Transformation of the Veil in the Algerian Revolution" in H. Johnston and B. Klandermans, editors, *Social Movements and Culture*. Minneapolis: University of Minnesota Press, pp. 144-159.

Fernández, D. J. 1993. "Youth in Cuba: Resistance and Accomodation" in E. A. Baloyra and J. A. Morris, editors, *Conflict and Change in Cuba*. Al-

buquerque: University of New Mexico Press, pp. 189-214.

Fernández Martínez, M. 1996. "Rameras por la dignidad." *Carta de Cuba*, verano, p. 4.

Fine, G. 1995. "Public Narration and Group Culture" in H. Johnston and B. Klandermans, editors, *Social Movements and Culture*. Minneapolis: University of Minnesota Press, pp. 127-143.

Fisher, M. 1997. "Where time stands still." *The Toronto Sun* (February 17).

Granma. 1996. "El trabajo del Partido en la actual coyuntura" (15 Agosto).

Gras, C. M. circa 1994. "El Sistema de Gobierno Cubano: Control vs Autonomía." La Habana: Universidad de la Habana, Grupo de Ciencia Política, Facultad de Filosofía e Historia. Unpublished manuscript.

Gunn, G. 1995. *Cuba's NGOs: Government Puppets or Seeds of Civil Society?* Washington: Georgetown University, Cuba Briefing Papers, Number 7.

Hart, S. 1996. "The Cultural Dimension of Social Movements: A Theoretical Reasessment and Literature Review." *Sociology of Religion*, Vol. 57 (spring): 87-100.

Hidalgo, Ariel. 1994. *Disidencia:)Segunda Revolucion Cubana?* Miami: Ediciones Universal.

Interamerican Commission on Human Rights. 1997. *Annual Report, 1996*. Washington: General Secretariat, Organization of American States.

Jatar-Hausmann, Ana Julia. 1997. "The Cuban Self Employed: Emerging Capitalists or Land Rafters." Miami, Florida (unpublished manuscript).

Jiménez, G. 1991. "Podemos desarrollarnos sin Obreros?" *Granma* (Junio 23): 3.

Johnston, H. 1991. *Tales of Nationalism: Catalonia, 1939-1979*. New Brunswick: Rutgers University Press.

Johnston, H., E. Larana, J. Gusfield. "Identities, Grievances and New Social Movements" in H. Johnston, E. Larana and J. Gusfield, editors, *New Social Movements*. Philadelphia, Temple University Press, pp. 3-35.

Johnston, H. and B. Klandermans, editors. 1995. *Social Movements and Culture*. Minneapolis: University of Minnesota Press.

Johnson, P. T. 1993. "The Nuanced Lives of the Intelligentsia" in E. A. Baloyra and J. A. Morris, editors, *Conflict and Change in Cuba*. Albuquerque: University of New Mexico Press, pp. 137-163.

Keating, D. and C. E. Hecker. 1994. "Red de computadoras permite a usuarios 'hablar' con Cuba." *El Nuevo Herald* (29 de Abril): 1A, 10A.

Klee, Peter. 1996. "Cuba Networking Update." *OnTheInternet* (January): 46-49.

LAT 91-175. 1991. "Rights groups demand information on dissidents" (September 10).

LAT 92-193. 1992. "Spanish official urges release of dissident" (October 5).

LAT 92-146. 1992. "Reports of anti government mobilization denied" (July 28).

LAT 92-188. 1992. "Aldana's future to be decided shortly" (September 28).

LAT 92-132. 1992. "Dissidents send letters to summit participants" (July 9).

Linden, R. H. 1995. "Analogies and the Loss of Community: Cuba and East Europe in the 1990s" in C. Mesa-Lago, editor, *Cuba After the Cold War*. Pittsburgh: University of Pittsburgh Press, pp. 17- 58.

Locay, Luis. 1995. "Institutional Requirements for Successful Market Reforms" in *Cuba in Transition—Volume 5*. Washington: Association for the Study of the Cuban Economy, pp. 6-10.

Lofland, J. 1993. *Polite Protesters: The American Peace Movement of the 1980s*. Syracuse: Syracuse University Press.

Lofland, J. 1995. "Charting Degrees of Movement Culture: Tasks of the Cultural Cartographer" in H. Johnston and B. Klandermans, editors, *Social Movements and Culture*. Minneapolis: University of Minnesota Press, pp. 188-216.

López, Ana L. 1996. "A su manera." *Cubanet* (24 January).

López, Enrique. 1996. "El Internet en Cuba." *CubaWorld* (August 20).

López, Enrique. 1993. "Cuba's Telecommunication Needs." *Cubanews* (October): 5.

McCarthy, J. D. and M. N. Zald. 1977. "Resource Mobilization and Social Movements: A Partial Theory." *American Sociological Review*, Vol. 82 (6): 1212-1241.

Mesa-Lago, C. 1997. "Is there economic recovery in Cuba?" *Cuba 1997: The Year in Review. Cuba Brief* (Winter): 7-12 (Washington: Center for a Free Cuba).

Munck, G. L. 1994. "Democratic Transitions in Comparative Perspective." *Comparative Politics*, Vol. 26 (3): 355-375.

Murray, Mary. 1994. "Cuba revisa su situacion de DDHH." Noticias Aliadas (Mayo 19), pp. 4-5.

Pagnucco, R. "The Comparative Study of Social Movements and Democratization: Political Interaction and Political Process Approaches." *Research in Social Movements, Conflict and Change*, Vol. 18: 145-183.

Piñera Llera, Humberto. 1981. *Idea, sentimiento y sensibilidad de Jose Martí*. Miami: Ediciones Universal.

Press, Larry. 1996. "Cuban Telecommunications Infrastructure and Investment" in *Cuba in Transition—Volume 6*. Washington: Association for the Study of the Cuban Economy, pp.145-154.

Puchala, Al. 1992. "The Privatization Process" in Adolfo Leyva, editor, *Cuba's Transition to Democracy: Lessons from the Former Soviet Bloc*. Washington: Cuban American National Foundation, The Endowment for Cuban American Studies, pp. 81-91.

Puerta, Ricardo. 1995. "Sociedad Civil y el Futuro de Cuba." Coral Gables, Florida: Coordinadora Social Demócrata de Cuba.

Puerta, Ricardo, 1996. "Sociedad civil en Cuba" in R. Puerta and M. Donate Armada, *Ensayos Políticos*. Coral Gables, Florida: Coordinadora Demócrata de Cuba, pp. 1-57.

Rivera, Mario Antonio. 1995. "Issues of Legitimacy and Constitutionalism in the Cuban Transition" in *Cuba in Transition—Volume 5*. Washington: Association for the Study of the Cuban Economy, pp. 458-464.

Rivero, José. 1997. "Los periodistas independientes cubanos en el periodo especial." *FYI* (Mayo 1997). Freedom House pamphlet.

Steven, H. 1996. "The Cultural Dimension of Social Movements: A Theoretical Reassessment and Literature Review." *Sociology of Religion*, Vol. 57 (spring): 87-100.

Thompson, John B. 1990. *Ideology and Modern Culture*. Stanford: Stanford University Press.

Oberschall, A. 1994. "Protest Demonstrations and the End of Communist Regimes in 1989." *Research in Social Movements, Conflict and Change*, Vol. 17: 1-2.

Oberschall, A. 1993. *Social Movements: Ideologies, Interests, and Identities*. New Brunswick: Transaction Publishers.

O'Donnell, Guillermo and P. C. Schmitter. 1986. *Transitions from Authoritarian Rule: Tentative Conclusions about Uncertain Democracies*. Baltimore: The John Hopkins University Press.

Scott, J. C. 1990. *Domination and the Arts of Resistance*. New Haven: Yale University Press

Staniszkis, Jadwiga. 1984. *Poland's Self Limiting Revolution*. Princeton: Princeton University Press..

Sztompka, Piotr. 1994. *The Sociology of Social Change*. Cambridge: Blackwell.

Tejada, A. A. 1994. "Cuba: Efectos sociales de la introducción de la lógica del mercado." *Estudios Latinoamericanos*, vol. 1 (2): 131-141.

Tilly, C. 1978. *From Mobilization to Revolution*. Reading, Massachusetts: Addison-Wesley.

Valdes, Nelson. 1996. "Cuba delictuosa, Cuba delictual." *Catálogo de Letras*, Vol. 7-8: 6

Valdés, Teresa and E. Felipe. 1996. "La crisis y el ajuste Cubano en los noventas: Apuntes en torno a lo social." *Perfiles Latinoamericanos*, Vol. 8 (Enero-Junio): 97-114.

POLITICAL CULTURE AND DEMOCRACY IN CUBA: COMPARATIVE REFLECTIONS

Mauricio Solaún

As I saw the portentous events of almost forty years ago unfold in Cuba — the flight of a dictator, the collapse of the state's army, the accession of a savior prophet of the new order — I considered certain the determinant role of culture in them.

For in about sixty years of independence, twice, almost at midpoint, core political institutions of the nation collapsed — in 1933 the breakdown of pre-existing organizations was less extensive, yet still in this first case: the army was reconstituted by a rebellion led by a sergeant; a new generation of revolutionaries abruptly acquired the political upper hand; and given the factionalism that prevailed then, it took seven years to establish elected constitutional rule (under the guidance of the Constitution of 1940).

Why such weak political institutions?

It seemed to me at first that the phenomenon was traceable to what Cubans call *choteo*, a variant of the picaresque Hispanic cultural theme, an ethos central to Cuban national character.[1]

Choteo, says the Spanish Academy dictionary, is Cuban term for *burla*: which in turn is mockery, jest, fun, among other meanings. Choteo in part is *relajo*: to have fun, to kid around, an element of a carnivalistic spirit of life.

It looked to me that choteo was an explanation for the evident weaknesses of political formal organizations, that it contributed to their corruption and subversion, to an undisciplined, highly disorganized — *relajo* ridden — political system, to the recurrent *desprestigio* — widespread loss of prestige — of the dominant political class, hence, to the institutional dissolution that had taken place.

In the consolidation of the 1959 revolutionary regime, it was clear that socioeconomic factors — that is, the poor sectors of the population that existed — played a role. The Revolution with its credibility — it had just defeated a much larger, better equipped army — promised to improve their condition, so why not back it even if dictatorial, these deprived sectors must have thought.

But the revolution had not consisted of a rebellion of the lower classes.[2] The leaders, the critical mass of participants, belonged to Cuba's better off social classes, starting with Fidel Castro himself, who when he organized the rebellion, was married into the family of a prominent member of Fulgencio Batista's team.

This brought me back to general culture — to view in its values, predispositions leading to the convulsive repeated patterns.

---

1. The classic statement is Jorge Mañach, *Indagación del Choteo*, which is critical of this cultural subethos.

2. The better Marxist literature recognized the low participation of the masses in gaining power, and the initial weak ideological ferment and organizational underdevelopment of the revolutionary groups, when compared with major revolutions; for instance, Robin Blackburn, "Prologue to the Cuban Revolution," *New Left Review* (1963).

Yet in Cuba politics could not be reduced to carnival. Heroes or Martyrs Fidel Castro had proclaimed. People died to make a revolution, there was a strong current for serious, honest government in the nation.

In fact, *choteo* was ambivalently held in Cuba. For, after all, people hold some things sacred. It is not fun to be subjected to mockery. The local literature on folkways registered not only the *jodedor* prototype — that is, the carnivalistic picaresque actor — but also the *guapo*, the *macho* descendant of traditional Hispanic chivalry, always prone to fight to maintain status.[3]

In short, culture is a complex construction or entity, not perfectly integrated, rather with subethoses or themes in conflict and subject to dynamic change.

An example. In Cuba there was a weekly called *Zig-Zag* that ridiculed the nation's leaders and politics, which was especially popular during the democratic period. After the Revolution's victory — loyal to its tradition — it started to satirize the revolution. Fidel Castro would not tolerate this: his revolution and him were too sacred to become subjected publicly to *choteo*. And *Zig-Zag* was the first publication that was repressed by the regime.

There is another trait of culture, however: plasticity, malleability. Consider the just cited case: the revolution projecting messianic, millenarian, apocalyptic quasi-religious themes and opposing and suppressing a carnivalistic cultural element. Yet Cuban analysts with different backgrounds have noted how the revolution itself has used the carnivalistic component to rally support for itself in the festive rallies and crowd fiestas that it organizes.[4]

Thus the carnivalistic cultural ethos can be seen as dysfunctional to totalitarian rule — tending to erode it — as well as an instrument to rally support by the totalitarian regime.

It can be argued as well that Ramón Grau San Martín, the most prominent democratic leader in post-1933 years, used the picaresque cultural component to further his in this case democratic cause.

Carlos Márquez Sterling considered him a *pícaro*, a *burlón*, at least an active *bromista* (a joker, one who makes fun of, deceives).[5] Listen to Márquez Sterling:

> [Grau] gave never ending speeches. In them, constantly the phrase '*porque no decirlo, amigos*' bloomed. His long paragraphs, without periods or commas, despaired stenographers [but got] the enthusiasm of the masses, who in those harangues found or deducted what [Grau] had not even sought to say.

Certainly, in Grau's basic decalogue, considered to have framed his political and social thought by Antonio Lancís, his loyal follower, there is an inescapable picaresque presence: among other items, *las mujeres mandan* (women command); *dulce para todos* (candy for everybody); etc.[6]

Indeed, a society's general culture is as if "out there," waiting to be used by history-making political man, who can mold its themes both into democratic and authoritarian politics.

This is why prominent anthropologist Clifford Geertz considers culture as a cognitive science, a discipline of meanings and interpretations rather than one of fixed, inevitable laws of causation.[7] There is both repetition or reproduction and innovation in history.

* * *

While the carnivalistic-*choteo* cultural subethos was relatively very prominent in Cuba there are two other general cultural configurations that have been used to

---

3. A pertinent construction of folk prototypes can be found in Eladio Secades, *Estampas*.

4. Contrast Benigno Aguirre, "The Conventionalization of Collective Behavior in Cuba," *American Journal of Sociology* (1984), and Carlos Franqui, *Vida, Aventuras y Desastres de un Hombre Llamado Fidel*.

5. Carlos Márquez Sterling, *Historia de Cuba*, p.343.

6. Antonio Lancís, *Grau, Estadista y Político*, p. 149.

7. Clifford Geertz, *After the Fact: Two Countries, Four Decades, One Anthropologist*.

interpret democratic pathologies in Latin America that are applicable.

The first, the personalismo/machismo/familismo-amiguismo/clientelismo syndrome or matrix.

Introductory texts have noted the importance given throughout Latin America to family-friendship ties; the role of an extended familism-friendism, of *compadrazgo*, the "co-parenthood" system; the modality of hierarchical patron-client relationships based on paternalism and interpersonal loyalty; etc.[8]

These orientations typically have been seen to stress what sociologists call primary relations, as opposed to secondary, more impersonal social ties. As such the emphasis is on personalistic, personalized solidarity, and distrust of, and weak support for, impersonal institutions and organizations.

Subsequently these cultural values are mentally correlated by observers with political culture, that is, to strictly political objects and concretely ultimately to weak impersonal political organization.

Under this assumption, the state, for one, will be captured by a leader and his group of friends and followers to be personally used, unconstrained by the impersonalities of the rule of law: caudillismo, old-fashion personal rulership, subverted democracy, ruling group partisan privileges, and so on. Political parties are viewed as undermined as well: incapable of transcending a leader, ephemeral, etc.

The second syndrome or matrix, grounded in folk religiosity, can be called the miraculous/manicheanism/salvationism/messianism.

The importance given to miracles; the intervention of, and confrontation between saints and demons; hopes or expectations of salvation from dire reality, are also noted in introductory texts. And have political applications.

Allow me first to parenthetically stress that the phenomenon is not unique to Latin America. In his towering work Max Weber labeled as patrimonial organization a core of these patterns — he knew little about Latin America.

More recently, influenced by Talcott Parsons, Gabriel Almond and his associates defined political development in terms of the secularization of political culture and organizational development ("structural differentiation").[9] Obviously, the two mentioned syndromes define low cultural secularization and organizational development.

* * *

Here are a few political applications of the two cultural constellations.

At the time that Fidel Castro's revolutionary career began to ascend Juan Domingo Perón ruled Argentina. Evita codified the Peronist political doctrine in her memoir *La Razón de Mi Vida*.

It is readily seen in it how general cultural values are used to define the doctrine's key principles. Perón is *un Gran Patrón*. Exulting familism-friendism Perón is "father" and the *amigo* (friend). Protector, godfather: hence paternalism, his *cariño*, and the loyalty owed to him. The regime is defined as an extended family: ruler/the people (especially the poor). Evita glorifies clientelistic relations of dependency in the context of the primary-group ideal dear to Argentines. Accepting as fact that Argentines do not like impersonal organizations and institutions, she says that this is why her social program for the poor is personally run by her — not as in Europe impersonally so, rather with her personalized—*cariño*—contact with the beneficiaries. The doctrine is of a Peronist community led by the Big Father: strong, protective, but loving and a friend; and by her loving wife: the mother figure always there to love, help and

---

8. To cite only one introductory text, Eric Wolf and Edward Hansen, *The Human Condition in Latin America*.

9. Max Weber, *Economy and Society, II*, Chapters 12, 13, and 14; Gabriel A. Almond and G. Bingham Powell, *Comparative Politics: A Developmental Approach*. Feudalistic social organization is of the family of patrimonialism but it is, especially, a more decentralized form than the latter.

sacrifice herself for the "good" Argentines (i.e., the Peronists, not the opposition).

The quasi-religious syndrome also finds expression in her remarkable document, to define doctrine and obtain legitimacy and support. "San Perón" has and makes "miracles" literally. In several Latin American countries the term *maniqueanismo* is used to define a politics perceived as a confrontation between all good-all evil actors or forces, as if saints versus demons. Evita excels in this categorization, hence, the extreme partisanship (*sectarismo* Latins call it), and need to repress the despicable, diabolic opposition: it deserves destruction, one can not "persecute" (i.e., ill-treat) criminals — their suppression is legitimate and needed! During this first phase, when Evita was a principal actor, Peronism is a messianic doctrine, salvationist, apocalyptic, full of popular religious imagery.

In short, Eva Perón shows us how drawing from general culture's ethoses or themes, these can be transformed into political doctrine and a legitimacy formula, in this case of a dictatorship that was high in originality despite its foreign Fascist influence.

I should clarify that what I have in mind when referring to the quasi-religious syndrome is folk religious patterns, not to philosophical doctrines of the clergy.

Concretely, I am not referring to Pope Leo XIII's undemocratic doctrine taught still in the 1950s in Cuba (which Fidel Castro had to learn) that, for example, played an important role in Colombia's civil war and Conservative dictatorship starting in the 1940s.[10] Nor to post-Vatican II dissident political doctrines of sectors of the Catholic clergy known as Liberation Theology, that dismissed elected government — that is representative democracy — as only a "formal" democracy. In this view competitive elections are un-

important; such views played also a role in Central America's long wars that escalated in the 1970s.

I must note also that the two general cultural syndromes are intellectual constructs that should not necessarily be viewed as totally independent of each other; they can interact and reinforce each other.

* * *

My space is very limited. A very brief reference to Cuba: the personalistic, low secularization of its politics prior to the revolution's success.

"Personal" means one's own; private interest or domain. Also, it refers (especially in a hostile way) to an individual's private character, as in the phrase "no need to be personal."

Let us first focus on Batista's 1952 regime. He justified his military coup d'état to avoid a different, planned coup; on the grounds of the immorality/criminality of those he overthrew; and to restore and guarantee the Constitution of 1940. Those whom he ousted and the emergent violent forces that eventually prevailed seven years later accused Batista of even worse immorality/criminality; and claimed that they had to use violence to restore the same Constitution of 1940.[11] (The Constitution had been reestablished to "elect" General Batista president in November 1954.)

Thus a revolution was fought so that the same Constitution that was formally upheld by all the parties become operative(!), guided by mutual accusations of lawbreaking, in a personalized struggle in which the personal character of opponents is stigmatized as totally evil—"criminal."

Such politics in which force is employed by leaders in conflict, in which, to judge by their formal positions, the basic interest involved is their political advantage

---

10. The Jesuits taught us Leo XIII's political doctrine contained in *Libertas Proestantissimum Encyclical Letter*. For the role of Catholic philosophy in Colombia's early *violencia*, see my essay in R. Albert Berry et al., *Politics of Compromise: Coalition Government in Colombia*, chapter l. Again, now ultimately in dissidence from the Vatican, so-called "theologies of liberation" played a role in the civil wars of Central America decades later. See, for example, the undemocratic position from El Salvador, in Universidad Centroamericana José Simeón Cañas, *Estudios Centroamericanos ECA*, "Estados Unidos y la Democratización de Centroamérica," XLI, 1986.

11. These formal positions are well documented: Fulgencio Batista, *Respuesta*; and Fidel Castro, "Condenadme, No Importa: La Historia Me Absolverá," in *Pensamiento Político, Económico y Social de Fidel Castro*, published in 1959.

(the control of the state), is branded (extremely) personalistic, "of personalities."

This is not to say that only personal interest was at stake: issues were involved, not all leaders were democratically acting.[12] In fact — you know — soon after victory Fidel Castro repudiated the democratic Constitution, from his abandonment of the need for elections to his proclamation in December 1961 that he had been Marxist-Leninist all along, what he had hidden to be able to gain power. Indeed, there is no end of ideology.

Technically, to understand pseudo-democratic politics — that is, in Latin America groups as those of Batista, Somoza, Stroessner, among others — it is useful to distinguish "ideologies" from "mentalities." The latter refer to mental outlook, attitude, thought in action or operational concepts; as opposed to the former: a developed, elaborated philosophy. This facilitates engaging in undemocratic behavior (e.g., rig elections, etc.) while claiming ideological or philosophical adherence to democracy.[13]

But let us move to a little bit earlier, the democratic period in Cuba prior to 1952.

Central to the then prevailing culture of opposition was the use given to democratic freedoms to engage in a type of opposition that has been called "primitive radicalism."[14] It is characterized by a prolonged campaign of an opposition leader who accuses the government — especially its head — of immorality and criminality. The participants in such a conflict, which is not unique to Cuban history, label their opponents' personal character thoroughly evil, and the political arena is defined in manichean nonsecular terms — notice the intersection between our two cultural syndromes, the personalistic and the quasireligious — as a stage where personalities Good and Evil, Saints and Demons, are locked in a furious battle in which no quarter is given. Typically, the tone of the accusations involving moral character is vitriolic and populistic: the actions of the president and his associates are designed to injure the people. The attacks that fall under this type are not "ideological" in a proper sense: what is condemned is not that opponents are, say Fascists or Communists, and one is a democrat. Yet this type of radicalism is not conservative: it tends to undermine the position of established authority. And at times, its emotional content can surpass all bounds and take on the air of a dramatic theatrical piece.

Eduardo Chibás was the most prominent exponent of this political style, especially during the Carlos Prío Socarrás administration (1948-52), the last Cuban democratically-elected president half a century ago. Every Sunday, Chibás would subject the government to his accusations until, unable to present the proofs he had promised to make public in a case against the Minister of Education, perceiving losing popularity, he shot himself at the end of his transmission "dramatically shouting that this was his final 'knocking,' and that with his sacrifice he left the accusations proved."[15]

Whether Prio's government was run by indecent Cubans and Chibás' group formed by holy, decent Cubans is not at issue. Regardless of the case's merits (that transcends legal procedure and resolution, and again other nations also witness strong doses of melodramatic politics) these styles of opposition are conducive to democratic ungovernability. Indeed, their

---

12. In fact, Batista had reconstituted himself as leader of the state's armed forces turned into an armed political movement or party with its own flag — the 4 September movement.

13. I first became acquainted with the Weberian concept of mentality through Juan Linz in his essay on Spain in Erik Allardt and Yrjo Littunen eds., *Cleavages, Ideologies and Party Systems: Contributions to Comparative Sociology.*

14. I elaborated the two concepts — primitive and ideological radicalism — based on the Cuban experience. But soon found out its presence in some other countries. See my *Sinners and Heretics: The Politics of Military Intervention in Latin America.*

15. Carlos Márquez Sterling, *op. cit.*, p. 355.

existence has been used by authoritarians to justify their imposition of dictatorship.[16]

The point is that before Fidel Castro became a national figure, uncivil political forms were operative in the country indicative of democratic pathology. And these have been given cultural interpretations.

And the rise of Castro's career was accompanied by increased polarization: the exacerbation of manichean, messianic/salvationist, still personalistic politics, calling for violence/repression before and after the Revolution's success.

To begin with, democracy's overthrow in 1952 ideologized per se the conflict: the ruler was not only allegedly corrupt, but a murderous *tyrant* and not a *democrat*. A civilized, workable consensus among Cubans became further elusive. Increasingly, Cubans became dichotomized: the Good vs. the Bad Cubans; Saints vs. Sinners; Salvation vs. Damnation; as if an apocalyptic confrontation against "heresy."

Suffice these post-revolutionary victory recollections. Early in 1959, Fidel Castro's portrait, as if with a halo of saint/savior, appeared on the cover of *Bohemia*, the weekly with the largest circulation.

The deification of the unconventional supreme-ruler, whose will has been to generate charismatic mystique, total loyalty, subordination and control, continued for decades. Consider this reported conversation with one of the official ruling party gurus: "Cuba's socialism sprang from ... above all ... Fidel. 'We have always had Fidel. His existence is Cuba's special merit,' I was told ... hands folded in benison: 'he is one of the great [men] of the century.' [The collapse of Communism in Europe] 'happened to them because they don't have a Fidel.' And after Fidel? 'People don't think of a successor. They don't want to believe he could die' ..."[17]

Castro continued to exude messianic-millenarian themes, his discourse is salvationist and apocalyptic, dissent is apostasy. Listen to him: "Before the Revolution ceases to be, not one single counterrevolutionary will remain with his head on his shoulders in this country." "Capitalism will never return to Cuba as long as there remains one Communist, one Revolutionary, one patriot ..." "If the Soviet Union disintegrates or disappears we will continue to build socialism in Cuba." "If we are to remain here alone, then so be it." "We prefer the destiny of death to surrender to the Yanquis." "Socialism or Death! *Venceremos!*" (We will triumph).

* * *

In sum, we can conceptualize that political systems are embedded in nations with societal cultural and socioeconomic systems. Naturally, we are to expect in these differentiated societies relationships between politics and these other subsystems or parts. However, so-called "social systems" in fact are not that well integrated. Hence, *political* culture, structure or organization, and behavior show an independence of their own.

Take, for example, the case of Colombia. To be sure the *general* cultural syndrome that we have addressed as of familistic-friendistic orientations with its patron-client social organization (although distinct, cultural values orient social behavior and organization, hence they are related) has been potent in the country throughout the 20th century. As we saw, this cultural configuration has been considered to result in small, weak, highly perishable political parties. But Colombia's political history has been dominated (not without challenge) by two parties, Conservative and Liberal, which have usually controlled the government. Since 1901 Colombia only experienced two military coups d'état (1953 and 1957), and four years of military rule (1953-57 with its aftermath until full devolution to civilians in 1958); no caudillo

---

16. E.g., in his memoir Fulgencio Batista alludes to this type of "pathological" opposition among other reasons to justify his March 10 coup d'état.

17. The quoted statements are taken from David Selbourne, "Rebel Without a Cause: Crisis in Cuba," *The Sunday Times News Review* (London), October 21, 1990, and Michael Frayn, "In Cuba," *The Observer Review* (London), January 26, 1969.

ruled Colombia for more than five years. Contrast this experience with, say, Cuba's or Argentina's.

Latin American nations are unique in that they exhibit cultural and socioeconomic differences and also have particular political institutions and traditions.

Consider the cases of England and Japan. Feudal social organization in both coexisted with important political differences. In Japan with Emperor God/ Shogun (great general). In England with Magna Carta/Parliament, precisely the precursors of representative constitutional government or modern elected rule by consent.

Does this mean that representative democracy can function in an *infinite* variety of societies? The answer is no, but history shows that it has operated in a wide variety of them, from Denmark to India.

My own view is that the society's general culture and socioeconomic organization provide environments that "facilitate" democratic institutionalization or pose "hurdles" to it.

For instance, patron-client social relations — which have been facilitated by a lesser developed money economy — have been also associated with political machines that subverted democratic elections in the United States.[18] And historians show how the birth of the United States as an independent nation took place in a society in which patrimonial social organization, with its culture of personalistic-friendistic-clientelistic dependencies, had a hold.

This had *coexisted*, however, with the beginnings of democratic political institutions in the form of elected assemblies in colonial United States, a reflection in turn of the remarkable traditionalization of parlia-

mentary institutions in Great Britain. Recall the American slogan for independence: "no taxation without representation," that is, the right of subjects of the Mother Country to representation in Parliament. For at the time of the American independence, already a rudimentary form of "elected" government, the descendant also of the Magna Carta/Parliament, existed in Britain.[19]

The conclusion is that personalistic-familistic-clientelistic orientations can and have posed hurdles to representative democracy, from the United States to say Argentina. Yet given the plasticity of culture they can and have been overcome — they can and have coexisted with democracy.

Indeed, because of the relative autonomy of the political system, such cultural orientations can coexist with the prevalence of elected governments that acknowledge the opposition's victory. To wit, in stark contrast with Latin America, by the third president of the United States (Thomas Jefferson, 1801-9) the pattern had been established of accepting electoral defeat by governments. Not even during the Civil War, were elections suspended and the possibility that the President not be reelected contemplated.[20]

What makes the difference — regardless of other social patterns with their dysfunctionalities — is that a critical mass develop in the nation, which supports representative democracy. The greater its numbers, the more sacred the commitment to democracy, the greater the probability of its institutionalization, of course.

You might consider my statement axiomatic and trivial. The first it is; the second unfortunately no. Several types of authoritarian regimes have been jus-

---

18. See the case made by Jimmy Carter about the fraud organized against his election to Georgia's Senate at the beginning of his political career, in *Turning Point*, his early memoir. And on the predominance of cultural and social organizational patrimonial forms at the birth of the United States, Gordon S. Wood, *The Radicalism of the American Revolution*.

19. A feel for this complex representative system can be obtained from Sir Lewis Nemier, *The Structure of Politics at the Accession of George III*.

20. On the importance given to electing the nation's government see Joshua Kleinfeld, "The Union Lincoln Made," *History Today* (1997). Historians have argued that during certain periods, messianic themes have been used in support of democracy in the United States, a rebuttal of their link with only authoritarian or totalitarian regimes. See Paul Boyer, *When Time Shall Be No More: Prophesy Belief in Modern American Culture*. Again, the malleability of culture, its application to democratic and undemocratic politics.

tified in Latin America with allegations that extant social conditions do not permit democracy to function; moreover, that the dictatorship had to be established precisely to cure these national (international also at times) social problems. Of paramount importance in recent years — you will remember — was the issue of poverty to be solved by authoritarian or totalitarian rule. Thus, in fact, sociological "laws" (e.g., the causes of poverty) were used to discard political democracy, even in countries in which it had never taken hold before, the poverty therefor not explainable by it!

To provide a colorful example, when Juan Bosch — the Dominican ex-president 1962-63 — was advocating for his country a "Dictatorship with Popular Backing" no democratic regime had lasted any length of time in the Dominican Republic. Yet he wrote: "The Dictatorship with Popular Backing will not be … a representative democracy, the political system natural to bourgeois society, which has been failing in Latin America for more than a century and a half. It won't be because … in the best of cases, [it] cannot guarantee work, health and education [etc.]"[21] This was not the Dominican case.

In effect, the principal "cause" for not institutionalizing democracies is its insufficient support by political actors (often based on wrong or spurious reasons).

Parsimoniously, these are the axiomatic factors of the problem: insufficient commitment to representative form of government (competitive elections); insufficient support for constitutionality and the rule of law; inadequate levels of political tolerance (of opposition).

* * *

I will conclude with another brief reference to Colombia. Cultural interpretations should be grounded sociologically to overcome their anecdotal propensity. Within a given nation, some individuals and groups hold certain values more than others. Survey research allows to explore these issues.

Despite the historical pluses in terms of its resilient party system and virtual absence of military rule, Colombia's democratic record has not been good. Roughly, during the first half of the twenty century the modality was what I have called protodemocratic rule — that is, a system of the family popularized by the Mexican Partido Revolucionario Institucional (PRI). Its character: a party hegemony — the belief that the ruling party does not submit itself to authentic elections; that democratic electoral institutions do not work; fraud according to need to remain in power is part of the system. For although in 1930, a divided ruling party allowed the electoral victory of the opposition, this resulted in a change from a Conservative hegemony to a Liberal party one. In 1946, again a divided ruling party recognized the victory of an opposition, that all along had not participated in presidential elections on grounds of fraud and suddenly changed tactics. But democracy was not the result. Three years later the Conservatives established their party's dictatorship to be changed subsequently to a military authoritarian regime. From this time, Colombia has never been pacified, though levels of political violence have fluctuated.

In the late 1950s, power was devolved in Colombia to the civilians, and a new full-blown coalition regime of the two parties was established. Many democracies operate under these premises known as "consociational" democracies.[22] Yet the Colombian was not firmly established: it has been subjected from its initiation to serious revolutionary threats and violence. At best, in the last part of the twentieth century Colombia's democracy was an unstable one, though no government was actually overthrown.

What was the profile of such inadequately supported, unconsensual regime?

In the late 1970s, we conducted a survey of political opinion and behavior in Colombia.[23] As we expected significant differences among social classes, the sample was stratified into five social class segments: an upper class — wealthy businessmen and profession-

---

21. Juan Bosch, *Dictadura Con Respaldo Popular: El Próximo Paso*, p. 52.

22. An extensive discussion of consociational regimes can be found in Robert A. Dahl, *Democracy and Its Critics*.

Table 1. Conceptualization of Violence in Colombia

Basic Characteristics	Upper Class %	Middle Class %	Working Class %	Lower Class %	Peasants %
1. Free elections	55.3	49.8	31.2	29.7	30.8
2. Government limited by the law (or Constitution)	22.8	12.0	10.5	7.4	11.1
3. Right to freely criticize and oppose the government	54.9	55.8	49.1	18.3	14.3
4. Right to organize any political, religious, social group	23.6	26.9	20.0	20.7	28.5
5. That everybody has a minimum of material well-being	28.8	21.5	21.8	43.4	46.0
6. Equal economic opportunity for all	35.8	39.2	54.6	59.3	50.6
7. Citizens' opportunity to directly participate in the important decisions	31.8	47.0	36.6	21.3	22.6
8. That people seriously work and the government supervise them so that the citizens fulfill their obligations	29.4	24.5	38.5	56.4	55.2

als; a middle class — smaller business and less prosperous professionals, white collar employees; a working class — skilled urban workers; a lower class — urban unskilled poorer individuals; and peasants — economically marginal, poor rural people.

I do not claim that it is possible to generalize our results to all of Latin America, nor even that they could hold through time in Colombia. Opinions and attitudes are subject to change. All that I will do is report temporarily limited findings for a particular country because of their potential comparative interest.

Most important was to explore the views of democracy held by the population. To this effect we asked: "There are different conceptions of democracy. I will present a list of eight elements that can be characteristic of a democratic system. Please, select among them the three traits that in your opinion better characterize democracy."[24] Table 1 presents the results.

Our premise was that political democracy is defined by the just mentioned three basic elements. The first four items (1, 2, 3, 4) directly covered these aspects (free elections; government under the rule of law; and political tolerance: the right to criticize government, the right to organize various kinds of political and social groups). We added two economic dimensions: equal economic opportunity (item 6) and a guaranteed minimum economic well-being (item 5),

to explore the salience of concepts of socioeconomic democracy. Item 7 — the opportunity to directly participate in important government decisions — was included as a measure of more participatory, direct conceptions of democracy rather than its representative form. Finally, item 8 provided a definition of traditional authoritarianism, a political system composed of duty bound citizens, not very politicized, working under government tutelage (or a Gran Patrón?).

Observe in the table the important differences in the conceptualization of democracy by social class. But first, our publics (as opposed to active politicians whom we did not have the resources to also directly survey) did not give priority to constitutional rule (item 2), a central concept of the descendants of the English cultural tradition and a conceptualization stressed in legal training in Latin America. Secondly, you can observe the relative low importance given to free elections as a component of democracy — only *small* majorities of the upper and middle class considered it to best characterize democracy. We might view in this light the appeal that some leaders questioning the importance of elections and constitutionality might have in populations with similar distribution of preferences. The depreciation of elections can result not only from formalized ideologies — say Marxism-Leninism — it can be also affected by the

23. The study was conducted with two Colombian colleagues, Rodrigo Losada and Eduardo Vélez. The findings discussed here are unpublished. Parts of the project's results appeared in Rodrigo Losada and Eduardo Vélez, *Identificación y Participación Política en Colombia*, and Eduardo Vélez, *Political Participation in an Unstable Democracy* (Ph.D. Dissertation, University of Illinois, 1981).

24. The order in which the questions in the table actually appeared on the questionnaire was: 3, 5, 2, 6, 1, 8, 7, 4.

absence of a deep-rooted conviction in them in the traditions of folk political culture.

In the table, two different conceptualizations of democracy clearly appear: one held by the upper and middle classes, the other by the lower classes, urban and rural. (The working class fell between these two conceptualizations.) The first one is closer to the classical liberal political conception of democracy, with elections (item 1) and the right to criticize and oppose the government (item 3), i.e., political freedoms, as part of them. But notice that the two highest strata included other aspects — the upper class added a "modern" economic dimension to its conceptualization: its third choice was item 6 (equal economic opportunity for all); while the middle class emphasized (direct) political participation with its third choice, opportunity to directly participate in important decisions.

The second conceptualization, held by our lower class and peasant samples, was markedly different. Focusing again on the three top choices, these poorer respondents stressed economic rights: equal economic opportunities (item 6) and a minimum material well-being (item 5). At the same time, however, they also *defined* democracy in traditional autocratic terms (item 8, "that people seriously work and the government supervise them so that the citizens fulfill their obligations"). The data suggested that democratic political ideas had not penetrated much, especially in the poorer segments of the population.

This importance given to economic issues by the lower strata is not surprising, of course. This is precisely the opinion of publics in wealthier countries, that the Third World's downtrodden are not interested in elections but in food, clothing, shelter, I had often heard in lecture tours. Notice that among all social class respondents a preference was shown for equal economic opportunity over a guaranteed minimum material well-being. I construed the pattern as consonant with the spirit of enterprise and attachment to private property that we had found among the Colombian lower classes — a priority on opportunity as opposed to equality of economic result or outcome.

Indeed, while there were disagreements among our samples in preferred socioeconomic policies and the wealthy were more sensitive toward maintaining extant private property arrangements, there was a relatively high consensus among all in having a mixed economy, with both privately and publicly owned industries, and government assisting areas and those in need of economic help — one of the bases of the welfare state. There was broad support for a state promoting development. At the same time, there was wide opposition to a statist socialist economy, in which the state owned the means of production. Colombians held both that individual achievement should be recognized and a fundamental egalitarian conception of man with sympathy for working people.

In conclusion, our exploration suggested the absence of a national coherent consensus about the basic institutions of democracy related to social class differences. There was a political conceptualization and an economic one, with the better off emphasizing relatively more the first. However, at the same time, among the poor sectors, there was a remarkable identification with a traditional authoritarian concept of government. And among all social class groups there was dissent on the fundamentals of democracy. Even among the prosperous classes where its liberal traditional conceptualization was strongest, there was disagreement, for example, on the importance of free elections and constitutional government.

We found a society with a significant cleavage about the ideal political order. Only minorities explicitly preferred authoritarian military rule: the range, from 14 percent of the upper class to 40 percent of the peasants. And substantial majorities of all social classes did not support the use of violence to obtain the political and social change that they desired: the "no violence" pattern per social class was 72, 69, 65, 69, 72 percent. The latter suggests that only minorities backed the violent revolutionaries, an important reason why they were unable to get the momentum necessary to triumph.

But the profile of the masses described in the table, combining a preference for an economic form of democracy with an authoritarian conceptualization of the political order was suggestive of the potential support for authoritarian or totalitarian populism: the exchange of an intense emotional adherence to a ruler (Gran Patrón) for the state's handing out of wealth. That populistic strongmen caudillos — a Juan Perón, Fidel Castro — had never kept power in Colombia for any considerable time is suggestive of the importance of other political factors in the outcome (i.e., the resilience of party traditions supporting plural leadership among the political elites of the largest parties, who had constituted the nation's principal political power structure).

Actually, receptivity to traditional authoritarianism — in the spirit of item 8 — by the lower classes was part of Cuban folklore. In the 1950s, one still heard a poetical musical composition popularized four decades earlier around the political campaigns of General Mario García Menocal, one of the earlier towering national caudillos. The populace danced singing:

> Tumba la caña, anda ligero,
> mira que ahí viene el Mayoral
> sonando el cuero,
> mira que ahí viene Menocal
> sonando el cuero.

Tumba la caña refers to the manual harvesting with machetes of sugar cane, Cuba's principal crop. *Anda ligero*, to the order imposed on sugar workers reluctant to accept work discipline (or arbitrariness) established by the managers and foremen of the sugar mills. *Sonando el cuero*, to the whip used to ensure worker discipline. And Menocal, the *Mayoral* (boss), was precisely who would impose the discipline on the (Cuban) people "cracking the whip." The song had other verses, one full of the earlier discussed picaresque choteo ethos approvingly involving sinecures (*botellas*).

Poverty fosters conditions of dependence and this can take the form of a folk culture of patron-client mentalities. There is an immemorial thesis about the inclinations of the populace to support (some) dictators. However, the traditional paternalistic conception of government — the ruler "Father of the Fatherland," to be "loyally and obediently" obeyed in his "firmly grounded" authority — has not been the exclusive domain of the lower classes, and incoherences and cracks in democratic ideas among the better off also contribute to the success of authoritarianism.

Two final considerations. Continued adherence by popular sectors to socialistic leaders claiming to represent the lower class is not guaranteed. Remember, in recent years two governments close to Fidel Castro eventually were voted out — Jamaica's Michael Manley 1980 and Nicaragua's Sandinista 1990. Poor majorities can also view governments too intrusive in one's personal life, impeding one's economic fulfillment; there can be popular dissatisfaction with "over-regulation" by the state.

And our respondents showed a motley profile. The presence of the traditional patron-client archetype did not simply portray a humble, modest lower class accustomed to obey and equate the ruler a protector. Our interviewees were neither fatalistic nor social revolutionaries. A peculiarity of Colombia was the early penetration of party politics among the masses, to the point that peasants came to identify themselves and traditionalize identification with the parties. But we could not depict the bottom of the class stratification pyramid in strictly "traditional" terms. For example, the sample was asked about qualifications for high office: very substantial proportions chose having high levels of education and specialized knowledge over traditional, so-called ascribed characteristics, i.e., to belong to a family with high social position or follow traditional ways. (The social class pattern that chose the latter two options consisted of only: 8, 10, 6, 13, 11 percent.)

LECCIONES DE LA PAZ EN CENTROAMERICA: UN INTENTO DE APLICACIÓN A CUBA

Nelson Amaro

Este trabajo quiere examinar las similitudes y diferencias entre diferentes conflictos que lograron culminar en firmas de paz o procesos electorales en el área centroamericana. Ello ofrece la base para escoger el caso guatemalteco como aquél que teniendo aspectos comunes con los demás conflictos en el área tales como el nicaragüense y el salvadoreño, se acerca más a la situación que prevalece en Cuba comparativamente. Estas condiciones en Guatemala y El Salvador culminan con la firma de la paz mientras en Nicaragua se acuerda entre gobierno y oposición un proceso electoral.

Esta selección anticipada de Guatemala como un caso paradigmático, será justificada en las secciones que siguen para desprender de aquí lecciones que pudieran trasladarse a la experiencia cubana si se logran reproducir determinadas condiciones que precipitaron el proceso de paz que hoy vive Guatemala. El caso guatemalteco en particular y las condiciones que propiciaron el proceso de paz en Centroamérica puede servir entonces como un paradigma con el cual podemos contrastar los eventos cubanos cuyas particularidades muchas veces resisten generalizaciones esquemáticas.[1] Por ello calificamos este ejercicio como un modesto "intento" enmarcado entre la objetividad de las ciencias sociales y políticas educadas que derivan de valores eternos.

NICARAGUA: UN CASO ESPECIAL EN CENTROAMIRICA Y UNA SOLA LECCI[N

En toda Centroamérica se ha desencadenado un proceso de paz después un largo tiempo de lucha armada y desavenencias intransigentes. Tanto en El Salvador como Guatemala se trató de movimientos armados dentro del concepto de "guerras de baja intensidad" contra agrupaciones políticas, fuerzas armadas y elites oligárquicas. El caso nicaragüense constituyó un caso especial. Si bien en un principio, estas características eran llenadas aquí, fuerzas desalojadas del poder disputaron su hegemonía a una guerrilla devenida en poder. Este desenlace acerca esta toma del poder a una situación similar a la de Cuba en el año 1959. Las orientaciones marxistas de sus dirigentes y las medidas internas y externas que propugnaron en los inicios profundiza la similaridad. Tanto sus orientaciones, como los sectores internos de apoyo como sus enemigos pasaban por los mismos meridianos.[2]

Este marco pudiera ser suficiente para extraer las similitudes con la situación cubana. Sin embargo, el arribo a la solución del conflicto bélico hace que la si-

---

1. Se trata de usar el mismo término que Kuhn pero para un caso. El paradigma dentro de esos términos es una serie de conceptos interrelacionados en los cuales concurre la comunidad científica para crear un "rompecabezas" o una serie de enigmas, que guían posteriormente la investigación. El caso guatemalteco es usado en este trabajo de esa manera pero referido a un caso que alumbra en mejor manera una serie de campos y conceptos alrededor de la paz que de esa forma son mejor aclarados. Al mismo tiempo, alumbra áreas de investigación susceptibles de ser esclarecidas. Ver Kuhn (1971).

2. Este marco de análisis fue usado en mi artículo "Mass and Class in the Origins of the Cuban Revolution" (Amaro 1987). Las fases de instauración del poder total bien pudieran aplicarse al Frente Sandinista en Nicaragua.

tuación nicaragüense se aparte de la cubana. Cabría preguntarse...¿no fue éste el escenario en un principio de los primeros años triunfantes de la elite de poder cubana? ¿Cuál hubiera sido el desenlace si en vez de jugarse todo el futuro a una "invasión" incierta, se hubiera alimentado la tesis de muchos grupos insurgentes en aquel momento que confiaban en la infiltración y los alzamientos lo cual estaba más a tono con los últimos 100 años de historia cubana y con la realidad nicaragüense antes de instalarse el proceso de paz?

No obstante, un proceso electoral puso punto final a los intentos continuistas a la cubana. El viejo adagio tuvo completa aplicación: "Nunca segundas partes fueron buenas." ¿Por qué el resultado sandinista ha sido diferente al cubano? ¿Faltó el elemento carismático personalizado en Fidel Castro? ¿Estuvo ausente el entusiasmo de una Unión Soviética ya decepcionada de los subsidios permanentes que negaba a su población necesitada? ¿Estuvo presente acaso un grupo que bebía intelectualmente en la Teología de la Liberación y por tanto había mayores restricciones al haber alianzas más amplias?[3] ¿O acaso hubo menos de esas mismas restricciones en la Administración Reagan para hacer la guerra frontal a Nicaragua cuando se compara con las políticas cautelosas de Kennedy respecto a Cuba en el pasado? Las respuestas a estas preguntas ya nos indican las particularidades del proceso de paz nicaragüense. Por tanto, su desenlace no puede ser comparado a lo que pudiera aplicarse a Cuba.[4]

La polarización en la isla es de tal naturaleza que elude en estos momentos la posibilidad que una situación multipartidaria conduzca a un proceso electoral; que existan contingentes armados en lugares inhóspitos que cuenten con equipamiento y financiamientos directamente suministrados por USA y apoyados por países limítrofes; tampoco se observa una joven guerrilla en el poder; con un oposición con capacidad de reclutamiento militar de jóvenes capaces de plantear un reto en vez de una asimilación al país que la acogió en la emigración. No se cuenta con factores de posiciones de "centro" dentro de Cuba como los que se alinearon alrededor de Violeta Chamorro que sin mirar el pasado somocista con nolstalgia, eran capaces de plantear un régimen democrático de cara al futuro. Por tanto, ese proceso de paz no puede arrojar las lecciones necesarias para el caso cubano.

No obstante, lo ocurrido en Nicaragua pudiera colocarse en la ola de desalojo del poder de gobiernos marxistas en el mundo entero. Aquel axioma político que preconizaba que ningún gobierno marxista, una vez instalado en el poder, había sido derrocado, aludía a países de Asia, la Unión Soviética y Europa Oriental. Este axioma ha pasado a la historia. Nicaragua es también un ejemplo de ello y por tanto añade mayor peso a la vulnerabilidad de la permanencia del régimen cubano.

COMPARACIONES ÚTILES ENTRE GUATEMALA Y EL SALVADOR

Una vez desechado el caso nicaragüense como paradigmático es necesario establecer que también hay diferencias cruciales entre el proceso armado de El Salvador y Guatemala. Esta condición es imprescindible para obtener cualquier conclusión comparativa respecto al caso cubano. Mientras en el caso guatemalteco la guerrilla en su momento cumbre llegó a controlar un 10% del territorio nacional, en el caso salvadoreño dicho control llegó a establecerse en un tercio del territorio nacional.[5] No obstante, en el caso de Guatemala esta fuerza se evapora y en el momento

---

3. En apoyo de esta aserción se encuentra que con el triunfo del sandinismo no ocurrieron fusilamientos masivos como en Cuba y los comité populares a nivel de manzana fueron bastante tímidos a diferencia de los Comités de Defensa de la Revolución (CDR), en la isla. En parte esto último puede deberse a la mayor urbanización de Cuba, donde los CDRs y la reforma urbana, su base, constituyeron un elemento de aglutinación importante.

4. Las informaciones de la época en que se gestaba una salida electoral, dan cuenta que el régimen cubano presidido por Fidel Castro vió con escepticismo esa posibilidad ante la consulta de la elite de poder nicaragüense.

5. Estas cifras tienen su fuente en un alto oficial de los mandos militares guatemaltecos que merece la más alta credibilidad y eran los números que se manejaban en las altas esferas del gobierno cuando fungí como Viceministro de Desarrollo Urbano y Rural en los años 1987-89 durante la Administración de Cerezo en Guatemala.

que se firma la paz en diciembre de 1996, la guerrilla opera en territorios marginales del país.

Realmente su capacidad de acción era muy limitada. La retirada fue de tal magnitud que hizo imposible al alto mando guerrillero convocar de nuevo a una guerra generalizada. Tanto en el caso guatemalteco como el cubano, desde frentes ideológicos opuestos, hubo una carencia de convocatoria para una nueva guerra, después de haberse frustrado una primera convocatoria (para el caso cubano fueron cruciales los años 1959-61 y para el caso guatemalteco 1979-83).[6]

La guerrilla salvadoreña llegó a contar con un contingente de alrededor de 10 mil hombres armados mientras que la guatemalteca coquetea con ese número a principios de 1982, para luego después de firmado el proceso de paz presentar como tropas para su desmovilización alrededor de 3,000 hombres.[7] Incluso esa cifra se estima inflada debido a incorporaciones a última hora de población civil cercana a la guerrilla.[8]

Después de principios de 1982, la insurgencia guatemalteca fue abatida y operaba en zonas marginales del territorio guatemalteco. No constituían una amenaza militar. La principal causa de su derrota fue que el ejército hizo un idéntico llamado para combatir a los insurgentes a la población. Esta estrategia le quitó "el agua al pez" para parafrasear la famosa frase de Mao-Tse-Tung respecto a la necesidad de la guerrilla de contar con el apoyo de la población en los territorios donde operaba.[9]

Mientras, en el caso salvadoreño existía un "impasse" en donde ninguno de los dos ejércitos, el insurgente y el oficial podían derrotarse. Esta característica aleja el caso salvadoreño del guatemalteco. En este sentido, en Nicaragua, los "contras" disfrutaban de igual estatus ya que era difícil su eliminación por parte del Sandinismo. No obstante aquí la relación de poder es inversa: la guerrilla en el poder y las fuerzas más tradicionales eran contestarias. El caso cubano es más parecido al guatemalteco ya que las fuerzas de oposición no constituyeron después del fin de la "invasión" y mucho más tímidamente después de los brotes del Escambray a mediados de los sesenta, una fuerza bélica capaz de desafiar al régimen cubano. Brotes de oposición permanente, sin embargo, pueden ser encontrados en Cuba como nos enseña Benigno Aguirre (1988).

Por otra parte, basta ver las listas de presos políticos adelantadas por países con los cuales Cuba mantiene relaciones para darse cuenta que esta oposición está lejos de ser pasiva. No deja de llamar la atención las incursiones invasoras de personas de edades avanzadas como la ocurrida hace poco tiempo en la Provincia de Pinar del Río. Si a lo anterior se añade la oposición de aquellos que han votado con los pies en forma masiva y que se congregan mayormente en USA, la presencia de un contingente guerrillero es circunstancial y es un problema de grado. Tan efectivo es el "lobby" cubano ante Washington para impedir la eliminación del embargo, como cualquier brote guerrillero que haya cortado las comunicaciones en un lugar alejado de Guatemala, Nicaragua o El Salvador en el momento más álgido del conflicto. Más todavía, la economía de escalas que representa el "em-

---

6. Se pudiera desafiar esta afirmación diciendo que hubo una convocatoria anterior por parte de la guerrilla en la etapa guevarista a finales de los 60. La realidad fue que los centros geográficos de rebelión fueron distintos. En los 60 fue en el Oriente del país, en los 80 en el Altiplano. En los sesentas la guerrilla no pasó de ser un "foco guerrillero" molesto, mientras en los 80 hubo participación amplia de uno y otro lado de la población.

7. Estas cifras se infieren de los programas que han reicorporado la población combatiente de la Unidad Nacional Revolucionaria Guatemalteca (URNG). Lo mismo puede decirse del Frente Farabundo Martí de Liberación Nacional (FMLN) de 29,266 beneficiarios del Programa de Transferencia de Tierras (al 10 de mayo de 1995), dirigidos a la reincorporación de ex-combatientes, 21,542 eran "tenedores" de tierra sin propiedad residiendo en tierras ocupadas bajo control guerrillero, el resto era ex-combatiente. Ver Reyes Illescas (1997, pp. 87-94).

8. Estas cifras han sido dadas a la publicidad en los principales periódicos de Guatemala y son los números que manejan las agencias de desarrollo que apoyan el proceso de incorporación de los combatientes.

9. El ejército organizó las llamadas Patrullas de Autodefensa Civil (PAC) que llegaron a alcanzar 900,000 hombres en casi todas las comunidades del altiplano. Al ocurrir ello, otra máxima proclamada por Fidel Castro cayó cuando retaba a los gobiernos del continente latinoamericano a armar al pueblo como se hacía en Cuba. En Guatemala, el pueblo fue armado por los militares, con una ideología inversa a la preconizada por la revolución cubana.

bargo" es superior a la acción limitada de cualquier grupo insurgente armado.

De todas maneras este escenario aleja el caso guatemalteco del salvadoreño ya que en el primero no hay control territorial ni tampoco contingente armado de envergadura. Esto último, sin embargo acerca el caso cubano al guatemalteco. Por otra parte, no puede descartarse tampoco el "lobby" internacional de la URNG y otras fuerzas de oposición que supieron mantener activo el tema de los derechos humanos en Guatemala, a pesar de la baja intensidad del conflicto bélico.

Por otra parte, tanto el caso salvadoreño como el guatemalteco, son conflictos entre oposición y gobierno que tienen su origen hace un largo número de años al igual que el caso cubano. Las desavenencias que dieron lugar a los procesos de paz pueden trazarse en Guatemala hasta 1954, cuando el Presidente Arbenz fue derrocado por una fuerza insurgente apoyada por la Central de Inteligencia Americana (CIA). Desde ese punto de vista, al lado de los 38 años de permanencia del régimen instaurado por Fidel Castro pueden colocarse los 44 ó 36 años que ha durado el conflicto guatemalteco.[10] Tanto en El Salvador como en Guatemala, los procesos de paz tomaron largo tiempo. Para Guatemala el Acuerdo Básico fue suscrito en Oslo, Noruega en 1990, y la paz se firma 7 años después. El inicio de estas pláticas se produce de manera informal con una visita del Presidente Vinicio Cerezo a Costa Rica en 1986. Diez años y medio después se produce la firma de la paz. La implementación de estos acuerdos tienen 1 año y algunos meses de implementación.

El fruto de estas negociaciones graduales está a la vista. En 1991 se celebró un acuerdo; en 1994-95 se llegó a 4; y en 1996 se llegó a 6 acuerdos firmados.

Estas negociaciones han tenido lugar a lo largo de 4 administraciones: Cerezo, Serrano, De León Carpio y actualmente Alvaro Arzú. Ello constituye un ejemplo de continuidad de gobierno por encima de banderas políticas. Estos acuerdos han llevado a más de 400 compromisos y se estima que su implementación completa pueda tomar más de dos generaciones. La concertación en Guatemala ha culminado en el diseño de un modelo de desarrollo, más que una paz momentánea.

Existe otra característica que acerca el caso guatemalteco al cubano y lo diferencia del salvadoreño. La agenda que necesitan los cubanos de la oposición debe ser amplia y profunda. En el caso salvadoreño no alcanzó tal perfil. Los acuerdos militares y políticos tomaron precedencia sobre los aspectos económico-sociales en El Salvador. Por esa razón Miguel Angel Reyes Illescas (1997, p. 103) dice:

> en El Salvador el corto y eficaz periodo de negociación demostró que se "resolvió" el conflicto militar, pero que en el postconflicto no se produjeron los acontecimientos necesarios y suficientes para establecer las bases económico-sociales que garantizaran la paz "justa" y "duradera" que demandaba la población menos favorecida. La "sostenibilidad" de la paz, la democracia y el desarrollo dependerán en proporción considerable de la solución de los problemas sociales que estuvieron en el origen del conflicto.

La anterior información olvida que en El Salvador hubo tres reformas similares a las que había dictado el gobierno sandinista en Nicaragua: la reforma agraria, la nacionalización del comercio exterior y la de la banca.[11] Uno de los elementos contribuyentes a la finalización del proceso violento en El Salvador, sin duda se debe a que las "banderas" de la izquierda insurgente fueron asumidas por los militares y el Parti-

---

10. La primera fecha denota la salida del poder de Arbenz en 1954. La segunda que es aceptada por muchos autores y actores marca el inicio de la guerra civil en noviembre de 1960 cuando ocurre una rebelión militar que tenía como queja, entre otras, el entrenamiento de exiliados cubanos en territorio guatemalteco. Esta rebelión fue más que una asonada. Hoy sabemos que los oficiales involucrados alcanzaban la cifra de 150 oficiales aunque en el momento de la rebelión sólo 45 respondieron realmente al llamado. Véase Gabriel Aguilera (1989, p. 21) y Lawrence A. Yates (1988, p. 50).

11. Tuve la oportunidad de observar la expropiación física de una hacienda extensa en el Departamento de La Unión después de dictada la Ley de Reforma Agraria. Los mismos militares acompañaron a las autoridades civiles para proceder a la expropiación. Al menos para las fincas de gran tamaño, este proceso fue en serio, provocando la brecha entre el Partido Democracia Cristiana y la cúpula del poder militar por una parte y la oligarquía terrateniente por otra parte. La Derecha ilustrada representada por Cristiani, sin embargo, da un paso al frente y hace la paz.

do Democracia Cristiana en alianza. Probablemente había menos necesidad que en Guatemala que ello formara parte de las conversaciones de paz.

Al omitir estas dimensiones que son necesarias en cualquier arreglo hacia la paz en Cuba, el proceso de paz salvadoreño se aleja como caso paradigmático y en este sentido se rebela con mayor visibilidad el caso guatemalteco. De esta manera, el caso guatemalteco, al no representar una amenaza militar, al haber un conflicto de tan larga duración como el cubano y al presentar una larga secuela de negociaciones alrededor de temas cruciales para la estructura social, económica y política de carácter amplio y profundo, se convierte en el caso a estudiar. En las secciones que siguen se derivarán de aquí las lecciones apropiadas.

EL CASO GUATEMALTECO: UN PARADIGMA DE POSIBLE APLICACIÓN AL CASO CUBANO

En esta sección extraeremos los elementos singulares del caso guatemalteco que pudieran ofrecer un marco orientador para el caso cubano y estableceremos comparaciones de las influencias de diversos actores en los dos procesos. Para ello estableceremos las dimensiones más relevantes y alrededor de ellas construiremos la comparación entre Guatemala y Cuba cuando sea apropiado.

En el caso guatemalteco, al menos en los Acuerdos de Paz firmados, hay una extensa y compleja red de gamas económicas y sociales que apuntan a desmantelar en base a consensos, las causas de la guerra civil. Los Acuerdos, por ejemplo, fijan tasas de crecimiento económico, porcentajes de cargas fiscales, aumentos de las coberturas educativas y de salud, etc. Este elemento particular es expresado así por Aguilera:

> Si bien en otras experiencias se ha buscado poner fin al confrontamiento armado mediante la apertura de canales apropiados para la reincorporación de las insurgencias a la vida legal (todos los procesos mencionados anteriormente, o bien se han incorporado disposiciones de reforma política (Colombia, Nicaragua, El Salvador), o de reforma económica y social (principalmente El Salvador) o bien de reconocimiento de

derechos locales (Surinam) o se ha intentado un reparto del poder político (Africa), el proceso guatemalteco, con diversa intensidad, recoge todos esos elementos en una agenda amplísima, profunda y ambiciosa.[12]

La agendas en el caso guatemalteco contiene elementos que pudieran servir para una reflexión. Si uno ve esta lista encuentra los siguientes puntos: (1) Democratización, derechos humanos; (2) Fortalecimiento del poder civil y función del ejército en una sociedad democrática; (3) Identidad y derechos de los pueblos indígenas; (4) Reformas constitucionales y régimen electoral; (5) Aspectos socioeconómicos; (6) Situación agraria; (7) Reasentamiento de poblaciones desarraigadas por el enfrentamiento armado; (8) Bases para la incorporación de la URNG a la vida política del país; (9) Arreglos para el definitivo cese del fuego; (10) Cronograma para la implementación, cumplimiento y verificación de los acuerdos; y (11) Firma de los Acuerdos de Paz Firme y Duradera, y Desmovilización (Reyes Illescas 1997, p. 60).

Una revisión a estos temas indica que ellos no son ajenos a la situación cubana. En este sentido, y sobre la base de las experiencias anteriores, los siguientes temas deben merecer la atención de una experiencia que partiendo del proceso de paz centroamericano, pudiera extenderse a los desacuerdos que han prevalecido en la isla durante los últimos años. Una dimensión importante es que esta agenda sea discutida en su conjunto al principio de cualquier reunión. Los puntos que esa agenda contiene deben recoger las aspiraciones de la oposición cubana. No obstante desde un principio debe evitarse el "maximalismo." Si se quiere hacer una negociación, necesariamente ambas partes tienen que hacer concesiones. La agenda a discutir pudiera contener los siguientes puntos:

El embargo económico. Este tema es controversial. El Gobierno Cubano coloca este tema en la categoría de "inmoral" y por tanto no está sujeto a negociaciones. No obstante, el espíritu de la Ley Helms-Burton recoge un espacio de negociación según los cambios democráticos se produzcan en la isla. Se coloca en el

---

12. Torres-Rivas y Aguilera Peralta (1998, p. 123).

primer lugar de la agenda porque el régimen cubano ha demostrado su deseo que dicha medida sea levantada. El Papa en su visita también expresó su desaprobación. No obstante, para cualquier negociación, la capacidad de infringir daño al enemigo, forma parte de una estrategia de concesiones. Al no haber dentro de la isla insurgencia armada, este tema se convierte en un mecanismo poderoso para la oposición. En el caso guatemalteco se negociaba y al mismo tiempo las operaciones de guerra continuaron. Por el contrario, los ascensos en el clima bélico y sus bajas dependieron de los resultados en la mesa negociadora. Por último, el cese al fuego se produce cuando ya todos los acuerdos sustantivos están firmados. Desde esta perspectiva y dentro de un horizonte temporal mediano, esta temática puede ser un arma poderosa de negociación para cualquier oposición cubana. De hecho es la única, aparte de una oposición colectiva dentro de la isla que no logra cristalizar sus esfuerzos en una escala suficiente para provocar cambios. Se coloca en el primer lugar de la lista porque sería una buena demostración de buena voluntad el poder comenzar a levantar el embargo, conforme haya buena voluntad por parte del gobierno cubano de conversar sobre temas cruciales en relación al destino del pueblo cubano.

Elecciones en forma de plebiscito dentro de un clima de libertad de información y con certificaciones válidas confiables dentro de un nuevo régimen constitucional. Se debe convocar a una Constituyente y ello debe ser sometido al consenso de la población cubana.

Democratización y derechos humanos. Un punto crucial es la aceptación de un sistema político multipartidario. En el caso guatemalteco si bien normativamente existía la posibilidad de organizarse en partidos políticos, en la práctica se permitían éstos siempre y cuando su alineamiento no pusiera en peligro el marco de la "guerra fría." El Acuerdo de Paz implicó la posibilidad de organización política de la antigua guerrilla. No se trata de hacer ello de la noche a la mañana en Cuba, pero debe haber un horizonte temporal en que esta aspiración finalmente se plasme. Otro es la libre asociación y expresión otorgando una

carta de legitimidad a los grupos disidentes dentro de Cuba.

La reunificación familiar. Este punto recoge una necesidad sentida por la población fuera y dentro de Cuba. La ampliación de los vuelos aéreos; la normalización de los permisos de entrada y salida; y la desregulación de todo lo que envuelve las transacciones entre los cubanos de afuera y de adentro, debe ser un tema relevante de negociación. Esta aspiración es un rasgo totalmente perteneciente al proceso cubano.

Anmistía para los delitos políticos y marco institucional de acogida para la población cubana en el exterior. Este punto debe ser un gesto de buena voluntad por parte del régimen existente en Cuba.

Fortalecimiento de la sociedad civil y función del ejército en una sociedad democrática. El tema de organizaciones no gubernamentales, de una universidad libre, un sindicato autónomo, agrupaciones económicas libre de la tutela estatal y política, debe figurar en la agenda. Al mismo tiempo se debe desvincular los cuerpos militares de la actividad económica y social hacia un profesionalismo. En el caso de Guatemala, el ejército aceptó su reducción hasta en un 33% de su gasto y admitió la creación de la Policía Nacional Civil que agrupa en la actualidad a diversos cuerpos encargados del orden interno fuertemente influenciados en el pasado por los militares.

Desvinculación de los aparatos de seguridad del estado de la vida ciudadana. La pesada carga de los organismos de vigilancia y de la estructura de un Ministerio del Interior moviendo los hilos de los Comités de Defensa de la Revolución debe ser desmantelado. La politización de toda la vida de los ciudadanos sin dar margen a la propia privacidad y produciendo una hipocresía como norma de sobrevivencia debe terminar.

Descentralización, gobierno local y participación ciudadana. Todos los países en transición hacia la democracia que estaban bajo la tutela ideológica marxista, han orientado sus acciones hacia el fortalecimiento de los niveles locales en oposición a la centralización que ahogaba todas las iniciativas.[13] Este tema figuró en la agenda de Guatemala concertándose compromisos de fortalecimiento municipal y de participación ciudadana a través del Sistema de Consejos de Desarrollo Urbano y Rural que forma parte de la Constitución guatemalteca. Curiosamente este punto que formó parte de la "izquierda" guatemalteca coloca al gobierno cubano a la "derecha" debido a su poca sensibilidad en estos temas.

Bases para el libre juego de fuerzas políticas e incorporación de la disidencia y población en el exterior a este proceso. Esta negociación supone acuerdos en todos los puntos anteriores y las normas que se desprendan estarán dirigidas a normalizar el proceso político en el corto plazo. En el caso guatemalteco ello se ha producido con éxito. La URNG respeto los comicios de noviembre de 1995 haciendo un alto al fuego cuando se producían y en la actualidad se encuentran participando en alianzas electorales.

Firma de acuerdos de paz. Cada uno de los puntos señalados arriba debe ser fruto de un planteamiento realista y que busque consensos entre las partes. En este sentido esta primera aproximación al tema quiere hacer un llamado para ir fortaleciendo esta agenda o para irla modificando. La experiencia del caso guatemalteco fue que en muchos de los puntos discutidos como fueron las concesiones del ejército, las posiciones de la URNG lucían más brillantes, mientras que en otros como los "Acuerdos Socio-Económicos," las posiciones del gobierno parecieron prevalecer y la URNG aparece concediendo en mayor grado.

La agenda de los cubanos en el exterior y dentro de Cuba aparece en total desarraigo. No hay acuerdos respecto a los temas a discutir. Siempre las alianzas han sido precarias y en la actualidad aparecen grupúsculos cuyos nombres y propósitos se pierden en la diversidad y heterogeneidad de sus planteamientos. Más éxito han demostrado personalidades individuales que encarnan la oposición como Elizardo Sánchez o Gustavo y Sebastián Arcos o Ricardo Bofill. En el caso guatemalteco fue definida desde 1991.

La necesidad de una unidad de los cubanos. Este tema ha sido constante a lo largo de más de 38 años

de existencia del régimen cubano. Ni siquiera el entusiasmo de la desaparición de los regímenes socialistas y de la Unión Soviética ha tenido el imán para unir las voluntades. Sin embargo, si se quiere llegar a una mesa para hablar del futuro de la isla con aquellos que hoy la manejan, es necesario plantearse esta dimensión. En Guatemala, El Salvador y Nicaragua, hubo alianzas estratégicas que permitieron ya sea presentarse a un diálogo con el gobierno con una voz o presentar al electorado una alternativa. Si ello no se produce en la situación cubana nunca se avanzará en esta agenda.

Este nuevo diálogo no puede ser como aquél de finales de los setentas, mirado con desdén desde las alturas del poder y manejado por actores de tercera fila. Ni tampoco con francotiradores o "turistas" escogidos por el propio régimen que está acostumbrado a seleccionar su propia oposición. Tampoco se trata desde afuera de excluir a nadie de adentro. Se deben discutir puntos concretos y temas que forman parte de una agenda y no personas.

La participación de la sociedad civil. Esta incorporación es relevante ya que saca de la esfera política y militar las conversaciones. Los empresarios en Canadá, el sector religioso en Quito y en México los sectores sindicalistas y populares fueron al diálogo con la URNG mediante acuerdos celebrados con el gobierno guatemalteco para el efecto. En el exilio todavía hay mucho pueblo organizado activo como los médicos, los municipios y otros que pueden también contribuir desde su perspectiva. Por cierto que fueron las organizaciones de empresarios los más recalcitrantes en incorporarse al proceso de paz. Sólo en el último año, con el triunfo electoral de Alvaro Arzú, estas entidades se incorporan al proceso de paz.

Los terceros. En una situación en que la oposición no representa una amenaza militar como en Guatemala y Cuba, existe la necesidad de incorporar países amigos y organizaciones internacionales y multinacionales. Para los conflictos centroamericanos, el Grupo de Contadora jugó un papel relevante que apuntaba a concluir las luchas internas. Ello fue se-

---

13. En este sentido véase Amaro (1998).

guido por las reuniones de los presidentes centroamericanos después del Acuerdo de Esquipulas en mayo de 1986 dirigidas a hacer intervenir la moderación de las partes y normalizar las secuelas de esos conflictos en otros países. La Iglesia Católica jugó un papel relevante en la Comisión Nacional de Reconciliación, cuyo Presidente (1988-93) fue Monseñor Rodolfo Quezada Toruño. Posteriormente, en su etapa final, dicha comisión fue mediada por Naciones Unidas (1994-96).

Numerosos países de Europa y América Latina comparten para sus propios países la agenda enunciada preliminarmente que pudiera representar las aspiraciones de la oposición cubana, recogiendo las demandas generadas del pueblo cubano a lo largo de 38 años. A ellos corresponde el acompañamiento del proceso junto con la Iglesia, y las organizaciones internacionales. Incluso fuerzas insospechadas pudieran tener contradicciones si no se apoya a un proceso de paz en Cuba similar al ocurrido en Guatemala. ¿Por qué negar a la oposición cubana las mismas plataformas que la izquierda insurgente, aliada táctica de la elite de poder cubana, ha conseguido especialmente en Guatemala y El Salvador mediante un proceso de diálogo?

El examen de la oposición cubana en este sentido deja mucho que desear. Las sugerencias de los cónclaves internacionales no han tenido eco en la isla. El régimen cubano sigue persiguiendo su propia agenda a contrapelo de casi el mundo entero. Sin embargo, el curso sensato es estructurar más estas aspiraciones de gobiernos amigos. Es difícil hacer ello si la agenda es dispersa y la unidad precaria. La visita del Papa, la visita reciente del Cánciller de Brasil quien se acercó a la disidencia cubana e incluso la apertura reciente de la Embajada de Guatemala en Cuba son ventanas de oportunidades para fijar las definiciones de la agenda y calendarizar las mesas de conversaciones.

La voluntad de la más alta magistratura. En todos los conflictos centroamericanos los que detentaban el poder decidieron abrazar las soluciones pacíficas. Tanto Daniel Ortega en Nicaragua, como Cristiani en El Salvador como Alvaro Arzú en Guatemala, decidieron apoyar el proceso de paz aunque las alternativas fueron diferentes en cada país. En el caso de

Guatemala, Alvaro Arzú fue quien verdaderamente dió impulso a las negociaciones de paz. Después de su elección en primera vuelta en noviembre de 1995 se fue a México a conversar directamente con la URNG y una vez electo propició todo el andamiaje que hizo posible la firma de la paz a finales de 1996.

No nos engañemos. La alta voluntad exhibida por la alta magistratura guatemalteca no existe en la élite de poder cubana. Sería un proceso increíble ver a la figura de Fidel Castro, asentar estas bases de solución. Para que este proceso culminara con éxito y sin derramamiento de sangre, se necesitaría un liderazgo de futuro que definitivamente diera alternativas graduales al pueblo cubano, aún después de la muerte del "líder máximo." Se necesita un alto grado de patriotismo para esa renuncia. No obstante la articulación de una agenda de discusión, la unidad de la oposición cubana, la participación de la sociedad civil en el exilio y dentro de Cuba, el apoyo de coaliciones de terceros, pudiera ir creando las condiciones necesarias para el tránsito que tarde o temprano tiene que ocurrir.

CONCLUSIONES

Esta ponencia ha sido un ejercicio comparativo intentando colocar el caso guatemalteco como un ejemplo paradigmático que permitiría extraer lecciones si se quiere un proceso de paz en la isla. Las conclusiones de este ejercicio arrojan las lecciones que pueden inferirse de la exposición anterior.

El caso guatemalteco se acerca más al cubano respecto al perfil situacional que presenta en el periodo que antecede a la paz. La amenaza militar de los "contras" y el FMLN, era de tal magnitud que creaba "impasses" cada vez más costosos hacia el futuro. Al igual que la situación cubana, la guerrilla guatemalteca no representaba una verdadera amenaza militar. Su desenlace tiene que ver más con condiciones externas relacionadas con el descongelamiento de la "guerra fría" y la voluntad política de un nuevo grupo en el poder, que con avances militares. No obstante, la fuerza guerrillera guatemalteca, podía infligir ataques aislados al sistema; pero esta fuerza pudiera compararse con la "oposición colectiva" y la capacidad de "lobby" del exilio cubano en el exterior. Por otra parte, los temas de la agenda guatemalteca con su amplitud y profundidad y la duración tanto del conflicto como del proceso de paz hacen paradigmático el caso guatemalteco respecto al cubano.

La experiencia guatemalteca nos alerta respecto a la necesidad de definir una agenda que recoja las aspiraciones del pueblo cubano por espacio de 38 años. La instauración de una democracia, la reunificación familiar, el embargo, anmistía política y creación de condiciones para el regreso de la comunidad cubana en el exterior, modernización del estado y medidas de corto plazo para asegurar todo ello constituye una primera agenda tentativa e los temas que habría que comenzar a discutir en caso que el gobierno cubano acepte un proceso de paz.

Otra lección apunta a la necesidad de comenzar las conversaciones con la aprobación del más alto nivel de decisión por parte las fuerzas opuestas. En este sentido, la necesidad de una unidad de las fuerzas de oposición para tener la capacidad de hablar con una sola voz se hace imperativo.

El factor temporal en las diversas conversaciones apunta a ser relativo. Lo importante es el inicio de una mesa de conversaciones donde las partes puedan llevar sus agendas y al mismo tiempo tener la capacidad para hacer concesiones dependiendo del tema que se trate. No caben los "maximalismos" si se emprende este camino.

Poner a bordo a "los terceros" es una condición prioritaria. Las buenas voluntades conseguidas con la visita del Papa, deben llevarse al plano de los espacios de la vida diaria y a las articulaciones políticas que permitan que "Cuba se abra al mundo y que el mundo se abra a Cuba." Estas invitaciones deben ser extendidas y articuladas para incorporar en forma coherente también a los países que puedan servir de intermediarios.

Los cubanos debemos empezar a pensar en términos de la "sociedad civil" y no tanto en sólo alcances políticos. En la sociedad cubana, la sociedad civil, aquella definida como partiendo de los intereses de la sociedad y que no necesariamente están de acuerdo con los intereses del gobierno, se encuentra aplastada por un régimen que confunde "la cultura con la ideología" de un partido político. No obstante, los grupos religiosos, los trabajadores por cuenta propia, las organizaciones locales y municipales, los profesionales y otros grupos, pudieran ser interlocutores válidos de contrapartes en la oposición cubana. Esto equivaldría a un aire de oxígeno en las discusiones demasiado politizadas de afuera y de adentro.

Los temas de la agenda son los que mandan. No se puede excluir a nadie de la posibilidad de contribuir a la paz. Las más altas magistraturas han jugado un papel positivo en las experiencias centroamericanas. Actitudes semejantes son difíciles de concebir en la elite cubana que ha gobernado sin discusión por espacio de 38 años. Las estrategias de francotiradores o los "oposicionistas" legitimados por el régimen no pueden llegar a ninguna parte. Tampoco las conversaciones sostenidas a un tercer nivel llegan a tener desenlances éxitosos. Al ocurrir de esta manera, las conversaciones hace resaltar la necesidad de incorporar a sectores de la sociedad civil al proceso. El riesgo es quedarse demasiado a nivel de cúpula que es la crítica que se ha hecho al proceso de paz guatemalteco.

Una última lección, sin embargo, apunta a que todos los procesos de paz en Centroamérica tuvieron un comienzo. Si se quiere hacer la paz, entonces hay que comenzarla mañana.

BIBLIOGRAFIA

Aguirre, B. E. "Culture of Opposition and Collective Action in Cuba," Department of Sociology, Texas A&M University. Ponencia presentada en la VIII Conferencia de la Asociación de Economistas Cubanos celebrada en Miami, en agosto 6-8 de 1998.

Aguilera, Gabriel. *El Fusil y el Olivo*. Costa Rica: DEI-FLACSO, 1989.

Amaro, Nelson. "Decentralization, Local Government and Citizen Participation in Cuba," in Irving L. Horowitz, Ed., *Cuban Communism*. New Brunswick : Transaction Books, 1998.

_____. "Mass and Class in the Origins of the Cuban Revolution," in Irving L. Horowitz, Ed., *Cuban Communism*. New Brunswick: Trasnsaction Books, 1987.

Kuhn, Thomas S. *The Structure of Scientific Revolutions*. Chicago: The University of Chicago Press, 1971.

Reyes Illescas, Miguel Angel. *Los Complejos Senderos de la Paz. Un análisis comparado de las negociaciones de paz en El Salvador, Guatemala y México*. Guatemala: INCEP, 1997.

Torres Rivas, Edelberto y Aguilera Peralta, Gabriel. *Del Autoritarismo a la Paz*. Guatemala: FLACSO, 1998.

Yates, Lawrence A. "The United States and Rural Insurgency in Guatemala 1960-70: An Inter-American 'Success Story,'" in Ralph L. Woodward, Ed., *Central America: Historical Perspectives on the Contemporary Crisis*. Westport, Connecticut: Greenwood Press, 1988.

CUBAN PUBLIC OPINION DYNAMICS (1997-1998) AND THE POTENTIAL FOR BUILDING A CIVIL SOCIETY

Ernesto Betancourt

This paper is written as a policy paper to discuss the dynamics of public opinion in Cuba in terms of the impact of selected events on different groups of the population and the potential it provides for building a civil society in Cuba. It is a follow-up of a previous analysis published by Freedom House in 1997 under the title *Cuba: Bringing the Background to the Foreground.* It contains three sections designed to address various levels of interest of potential readers.

The first section, "Analysis of Impact of Selected Events on Public Opinion Dynamics" provides a summary of events that took place between the Spring of 1997 and June 1998. It summarizes in a chart the resulting dynamics of Cuban public opinion in response to these selected events. If you just want to get an idea of the trends in public opinion and do not have an interest in further elaboration, this will be all you need to read.

The second section, entitled "Summary of Selected 1997-98 Events," provides a brief description of the events selected and the resulting dynamics of Cuban public opinion, with the exception of the Pope's visit which is covered at some length because the magnitude and intensity of its historical impact. If you are interested in learning more about the selected events included in the Analysis, then this section will be useful to you.

Finally, an Appendix provides the description of the various sectors into which Cuban public opinion is grouped for purposes of this analysis. In essence, this grouping of the population is an application to the current Cuban situation of the methodology developed in my book *Revolutionary Strategy: a Handbook for Practitioners*, which was published by Transaction Books in 1991. If you are interested in learning more about the methodology, or you do not agree with the criteria I use, this is the section for you to read. Any comments or suggestions are welcomed.

ANALYSIS AND IMPACT OF SELECTED EVENTS ON PUBLIC OPINION DYNAMICS

First, we will discuss briefly how Castro stays in power and then we will analyze the events of the last year.

How Castro Stays in Power

Over the years, Castro has developed a very effective scheme to stay in power. He understands very well revolutionary dynamics, since he learned the strategy of how to play that game during the struggle against Batista. Only this time he is following the strategy of the leadership of the *status quo.*

In essence, the strategy is simple. The first asset in favor of perpetuating his rule is his charismatic leadership. Many of Castro's international initiatives are undertaken to preserve his image as a symbol of Cuban nationalism and as an internationally respected statesman. Domestically, Castro shifts blame to others for failures and takes credit for successes. At the same time, he prevents the emergence of alternative ideologies and of an opposition leadership. That is why freedom of expression is not allowed in any local mass media and the rights of association and assembly are repressed. This is complemented by overwhelming repression.

The regime, aware of the inevitability of the displacement of population groups along the spectrum of positions, from support to indifference to opposition, has tried to prevent the final stage of the process that will force the transition from a totalitarian to an authoritarian situation which will inevitably end in a democratic and free Cuba. To do that it has resorted to relentless but controlled repression, sending people to prison or exile, whether internal or external, unleashing gangs of thugs to intimidate dissenters, preventing the publication of their positions, refusing legality to their organizations and forbidding their meetings. It has also deprived them of their livelihood, confiscated their equipment, papers, and so on, and engaged in other means of repression, including occasional resort to killings. The resulting Pavlovian response is what Marta Beatriz Roque refers to when she says that "every Cuban carries his own internal policeman."

Despite all this, more and more people are losing their fear and crossing the threshold of enduring violent repression. Once that happens, a totalitarian regime has either to crush the opposition or go down the slope of a transition away from authoritarian rule, at which point it becomes extremely vulnerable. Instead, in Cuba Castro is trying to attain an indefinite continuation of his rule. But the need for international support limits his repressive options.

Resorting to open violence is not feasible for the opposition in view of the overwhelming repressive capacity of the regime and the effectiveness of the intelligence apparatus. But eventually, overt manifestations of opposition and willingness to endure repression, combined with the inability of the regime to satisfy the needs and aspirations of those on whom it depends for support under groups A and B (see definitions below and the Appendix), are eroding its repressive capacity. In Cuba, this process is not easy to observe through outward manifestations; as is possible in freer societies, even in the traditional Latin American dictatorships.

In an authoritarian situation, those willing to resort to violence in opposition gain support slowly in the face of hesitant repression until eventually they are able to challenge successfully the forces supporting the regime under group A. The overthrow of Batista and Somoza are good examples of this case of revolutionary dynamics.

However, in totalitarian situations, the overwhelming repressive capacity of the regime, and its willingness to use it mercilessly, prevents the emergence of such a violent challenge. That is, until the dissatisfaction of the population reaches such a level that there is a sudden popular explosion and/or a division among group A forces leading to a coup d'etat or a civil war. The collapse of the Soviet Bloc provides various examples of such revolutionary dynamics.

Impact of Events Since February 1997

By the middle of 1998, although no clear challenge has emerged to Castro's perpetuation in power, the cumulative impact of the events analyzed in this document continues the negative drift in public opinion that was commented in the previous analysis published by Freedom House in 1997.

The analysis of the impact of selected events since that publication is presented in summary form in the following Public Opinion Dynamics Chart. The totalitarian nature of the regime has precluded so far any open measurement of public opinion changes through polls, demonstrations or elections. In our summary, we consider the potential changes of direction of attitude of the various groups under each sector of national public opinion in response to some selected events during the period. The direction signifies that the sector is decreasing regime support (>) or increasing regime support (<). Since adequate public opinion measurement is not available at this time, only a judgmental degree of the intensity of the change and its direction during the period is given in accordance with the following criteria: little (-> or <-), some (--> or <--), moderate (---> or <---), significant (----> or <----), high (-----> or <-----), and, no relevant impact (<=>).

According to the methodology used, the population is grouped under five sectors or groups:

A. Those willing to resort to violence to support the status quo;

Chart 1.   Summary of Public Opinion Dynamics

| Events | Public Opinion SectorsEvents | | | | |
	Group A	Group B	Group C	Group D	Group E
La Patria es de Todos	More Divided reduced threat ->	More Divided reduced threat ->	Does not care remains neutral <=>	+ Fear, reassured by world support -->	Action example likely to imitate ---->
Struggle for Succession	More Divided power ambitions -->	More Divided ambitions-reform -->	Does not care has no ambitions <=>	More active reforms likely -->	Raises hope more reforms, less fear --->
Bombings of tourist hotels	More Divided reform pressure -->	Fear leads to repressive stance <-	Rejects terrorism supports police <-	Rejects terrorism inept police a plus <=>	Rejects terrorism causes repression <=>
Death of Jorge Mas Canosa	Reduces threat --->	Reduces threat --->	*Does not care <=>	Reduced threat, loss US support - <=>	Reduces threat, potential rival -->
Economy reforms reversal	Hardliners vs Corrupt <=>	Hardliners vs corrupt <=>	Threat to profits drift to oppose -->	Possible hurt, will be critical -->	Possible hurt, highly critical -->
Failure to restore growth	Weaker charisma more repression ------>	Weaker charisma repression-reform ----->	Threat to profits Drift to sector D ---->	More hardships, less passive, drift to E ----->	Feels vindicated, more opposition ----->
Failure to prevent US/EU agreement	weaker charisma need for reforms -->	weaker charisma need for reform -->	Ignorant, if aware will drift to D <=>	Castro setback encourages sector -->	Castro setback encourages sector -->
Congressional finding and US aid initiatives	National dignity vs meeting needs <=>	National dignity vs meeting needs <=>	Very receptive refusal leads to D ->	Very receptive, refusal leads to E -->	Highly receptive, more resistance -->
Latin American hesitation	Legits rights violations, raises charisma appeal <---	Legits rights violations, raises charisma appeal <--	Does not care results not relevant to them <=>	Human rights vote most discouraging <--	Human rights vote seen as betrayal +danger <---
Pope's visit	weaker charisma more resistance ----->	weaker charisma more local defiance ----->	Losing fear more likely drift to D ----->	Losing fear and dissent legitimacy ----->	Great morale boost, Poland 2 ------>

B. Those willing to support the status quo peacefully;

C. Those unwilling to take sides;

D. Those opposing the regime but unwilling to take risks; and,

E. Those opposing the regime willing to endure or resort to violence.

For a more elaborate discussion of the composition of these sectors in the case of Cuba please refer to the Appendix.

As to the events selected for the analysis of this period, they include events in the political, economic and international spheres. The political events selected are: the issuance of "La Patria es de Todos" by the Working Group of the Dissidence in response to the Party Congress of October, 1997 and the new Popular Power Assembly installed in February 1998; the struggle for succession; bombs in tourist facilities; and, the death of Jorge Mas Canosa. As to economic events, those selected are: the slow reversal of economic reform and the failure to restore economic growth. With regard to international affairs, the selected events are: the agreement between the United States and the European Union; Congressional findings and new U.S. initiatives; and, the hesitation of Latin America. Finally, as an event by itself, with multiple ramifications, the Pope's visit. For a more elaborate description and analysis of the selected events, please refer to the next section. The event's impact is determined by how it may affect the various sectors of public opinion, either when they find about it or its consequences affect the interests of the groups involved.

During this period, the central force supporting the regime, which is Castro's charismatic appeal, was weakened by three events. The first is the failure of Castro's efforts overseas to consolidate the isolation of the United States on the Helms-Burton issue. On the contrary, the success of the Clinton Administration in making some progress in the negotiations with the Europeans has broadened the international questioning of Castro's rule. The second, is his failure to restore economic growth and the third the Pope's visit. The hesitation of Latin America provides him with some successes and some failures but, in the end, is still the most favorable international factor enhancing Castro's charisma.

Besides weakening his charismatic standing and, consequently, his personal authority internally, the events of the period have reduced the appeal of nationalism and fear of exile return to power. This encourages divisions and ambitions among his followers. This is particularly so as a result of the death of Jorge Mas Canosa. The immobility reflected in the Party Congress and the National Assembly of Popular Power is persuading the people and, according to some reports, even those within his inner circle, that Castro offers no hope of leading Cuba into the solution of its problems. That is why there seems to be some jockeying for his succession among the upper ranks of the regime and reformists' and dissidents' hopes are raised.

Of special interest in relation to the military and repressive forces is the impact of the bombings of tourist installations. First, it must be pointed that Castro did not get involved at all in this matter, as is his usual practice. On the contrary, he let lower ranking security officers handle this threatening event. Second, if the hypothesis of this being the work of disaffected former military and security staffers turns out to be true, the implications of this being the beginning of a potential split under Sector A, must be very worrisome for Castro. No wonder, he has remained silent on this event. On the other hand, this tactic is rejected by the dissidents.

In contrast, Castro furiously attacked the movie *Guantanamera*—a satire of life and death, including a funeral, in today's Cuba—during his marathon seven and one-half hour speech before the National Assembly of Popular Power. An attack that met a strong rejection among intellectual circles, not only of the dissidence, but also among regime loyalists hoping for an opening.

True, Concilio Cubano has been repressed but what it was doing is being continued by others. Dissidence survives, and, its support keeps growing as the ability to meet the most basic needs continues shrinking, the door of emigration remains closed definitively and pressure increases for an internal solution. And, although repression has intensified, the regime has been forced to act with restraint to avoid closing the door to any international support. That Castro is forced to rely on hesitant repression. Under this modality, the repressive monolith is less effective as a deterrent, as more and more people dare to defy the regime.

The failure to restore sugar production and the regression in economic reforms, particularly the slow elimination of self-employment, practically dooms any hope of economic recovery. The possibility of any success in reversing the U.S. embargo is remote. On the contrary, the European Union is pressuring for the kind of opening Castro cannot tolerate. Once the population realizes that with Castro there is no solution, the mood of public opinion is going to increasingly turn against the regime. More so, now that the door of leaving Cuba is very narrow due to the immigration agreement with the United States.

In the long run, the impact of the Pope's visit will depend on whether Castro is able to force the Church to maintain a discreet silence or make only moderate criticisms of human rights violations, as it has done so far, while taking at the same time an aggressive stance against Helms-Burton. The meeting called in the Vatican with the Cuban Bishops early in June 1998, indicates this option is not acceptable to the Pope. His Holiness realizes this is not the way to replicate the Poland experience.

The Pope's message during the visit—to say the truth and not to be afraid—must have worried Castro a lot, not to mention the demand that rights of freedom of expression, association and assembly be restored. Castro's regime is based on people being afraid and not saying the truth and their being unable to articulate an opposition to his regime. Now, the Pope is telling the Cuban hierarchy he really meant to replicate the Polish experience. The scene for a conflict between Castro and the Vatican is set.

Actions that May be Required to Build a Civil Society

The action side of this policy analysis is predicated on the nature of human behavior. Once a person starts losing fear in one realm, he is likely to start behaving without fear in other aspects of his life. Acting freely and without fear tends to become a universal style of behavior. True, the Catholic Church has made it clear that their actions are limited to the religious and spiritual sphere of life, although they are not indifferent to what happens in other realms of the life of its followers. It is this broadening base of people willing to assert their basic rights that opens the opportunity for developing a civil society movement inside Cuba. But in these matters nothing happens by accident, there is need for deliberate actions.

With the increase of dissidence in Cuba, the time has come for those overseas to take advantage of the new mood created by the Pope, and parallel to the efforts of the Church to expand the exercise of civil rights in the spiritual realm, promote and support civil society building efforts in other realms of social interaction.

Internally, it is more evident every day that Castro's charismatic hold on the Cuban population is fast losing ground. Although the residual magnitude of this charismatic hold should not be underestimated, there are many signals that his stubborn refusal to allow a transition, combined with his inability to produce workable solutions to the increasing daily life problems faced by the Cuban people, is weakening his hold over average Cubans.

There are reports that even many around Castro are convinced that he has no future solution to offer but feel trapped in the situation because they are also convinced that, without Castro, the regime will collapse and their own positions will be imperiled. Externally, Castro is faced for the first time with not only the United States, but also the European Union, demanding that he open the system economically and politically. The Church is subtly supporting this demand. Only, Latin America continues to stubbornly support him through a misdirected anti-Americanism reinforced by the negative image that prevails of the exile community.

What the cause of Cuba's freedom needs now is a totally new approach, based on a movement and an organization that could overcome the present negative image of Castro's opposition that prevails, both internally as well as externally. It is urgent that overseas Cubans mobilize themselves for this dual goal: i) to promote the growth a civil society inside Cuba from overseas; and ii) to promote international support for a transition to a really free Cuba, based on a civil society as vibrant as the one that existed before Castro came to power. That civil society, under the banner of the Civic Resistance Movement, played a key role in overthrowing Batista.

SUMMARY OF SELECTED 1997-98 EVENTS
La Patria es de Todos

Two political events, the Party Congress and the first meeting of the new National Assembly of Popular Power, took place in October, 1997 and in February, 1998 respectively, with the Pope's visit in between. Since in Cuba the electoral system is rigged to ensure perpetuation of Castro and his chosen collaborators in power, neither changes in the party, nor changes in the legislature, have any great significance for Cuban public opinion. They are merely changes in the Castro's coterie of collaborators. Nevertheless, there are some significant issues related to these events worth commenting.

In terms of the emerging opposition, the most important development was the challenge by the Dissidence Working Group both to the electoral process and to the document submitted as a draft for consideration of the Party Congress. The Working Group included, among others, Marta Beatriz Roque, Vladimiro Roca, René Gómez Manzano and Félix

Table 1.   La Patria es de Todos

Event impact on public opinion dynamics		Direction/Intensity
Sector A:	Weakens sector cohesion, Vladimiro Roca is a former MIG pilot, reduces image opposition is threat to them, international response damaging to Castro's charismatic appeal	(->)
Sector B:	Same as above, Roca is the son of Blas Roca, who chaired the Communist Constitutional Convention in 1975	(->)
Sector C:	Reinforces wisdom of staying neutral to avoid repression	(<=>)
Sector D:	Threatened by repressive response, encouraged by courage of authors and reassured by persistence of international response	(-->)
Sector E:	Highly encouraged by daring action and international response, motivated by articulation of ideological challenge and example of willingness to endure repression	(--->)

Bonné Carcassés. Their statement, entitled *La Patria es de Todos* (The Fatherland Belongs to All) constitutes the first formal ideological challenge, released internally during a press conference with foreign reporters accredited in Havana, against the official ideological position (see Table 1).

Shortly after, the four authors were arrested on July 16, 1997 and remain imprisoned as of the date of this writing. Their release has been requested by *The Wall Street Journal*, *The New York Times* and *The Washington Post*, among others. It has been also requested by prominent visitors, including His Holiness and Canadian Prime Minister Jean Chretien. More recently, the European Union, to the annoyance of Foreign Minister Roberto Robaina, made their release one of the token actions to meet the standards of political openness expected before Cuba could attain full membership in the Lomé Convention.

Why is Castro so afraid of these dissidents? Their document challenges his interpretation of Cuban history, in particular the use of the writings of Martí to justify the single party system he has imposed on Cuban society, as well as of many other recent events. It reminds the people of many of the foolish Castro initiatives, like creating a new variety of cow, draining the Zapata Swamp or internationalist adventures, in which substantial national financial and human resources were wasted. It points that "the main purpose of the regime is not to serve the people but to be its dictator." After criticizing the official reaction to the January 28, 1997 message from President Clinton offering U.S. assistance for a transition, the document asks for a Constitutional Assembly and free

elections to allow an economic and political opening that will avoid the violent end towards which the present paralysis and stagnation is leading the nation.

This document has had a world-wide impact like no other statement issued by Castro's opposition and it has the legitimacy of its authors being willing to endure repression for their ideas. The more the regime delays their release, the higher the interest it generates.

The Struggle for Succession

One of the frequently destabilizing issues in caudillista and communist governments is the matter of succession. Cuba has a government that incorporates the outer trappings of Communism, while being in essence another Caribbean dictatorship a la Trujillo. This comparison offends the leftist intellectuals who, out of their hostility to the United States, embraced Castro as their guru. But, the longer Castro stays in power, the more socialist ideological trappings continue falling, as in a dance of the seven veils, and we are exposed to the naked truth of a traditional Latin caudillista dictatorship.

At the Party Congress, Fidel anointed his brother Raúl with the mantle of succession, shall the Maximun Leader disappear. This is nothing new because Raúl is number two in all political positions and number one in the MINFAR, with his loyal henchman General Abelardo Colomé controlling the MININT since the Ochoa crisis in 1989. However, there is an interesting manifestation of two things: 1) the fact that the end of Castro's rule is within sight; and 2) that there is already a struggle for power within the Party (see Table 2).

Table 2.   Struggle for Succession

Event impact on public opinion dynamics	Direction/Intensity
Sector A: Sector cohesion weakened, encourages ambitions among middle level officers, raises specter of potential civil war	(-->)
Sector B: Similar to above but with more emphasis on ambitions, closet reformers encouraged to push their agenda	(-->)
Sector C: Little impact, they are out of the power game	(<= >)
Sector D: Encouraged to be more active, expectation of potential opening due to division within regime increased	(-->)
Sector E: Very encouraged, any regime division generates doubt and reduces legitimacy and willingness to repress	(-->)

There are many reports that Castro's health is failing. It is hard to verify them and we should not place too much hope on that solution, because there is contradictory evidence in front of our eyes all the time. Sometimes Castro seems to be worn out and slow and other times he is back to his long speaking feats. However, the fact is that he was the one who raised the issue of the succession at the Party Congress, not anyone in Miami or in the overseas Cuban community. Shortly after, Ricardo Alarcón, President of the Popular Power Assembly, an internationally well known former Foreign Minister, granted an interview to a reporter from the San Juan, Puerto Rico newspaper *El Nuevo Día,* during which he answered in the affirmative the question of whether he would accept an offer to be Castro's successor. This was a clear challenge to Fidel's appointment of his brother, Raúl, as the chosen successor.

This would have been a passing incident, subject to diverse interpretations, were it not for the fact that in his more than seven hours' speech to the new Popular Power Assembly after he was reelected President of the Council of State in February 1998, Castro reversed his position and made the surprising comment that Cuba was not a monarchy and wondered where people got the idea that Raúl was to inherit power automatically. Nobody dared tell him it was he in his October speech to the Party Congress. In this case, *Gramma* never published Castro's long oratorical exercise as is the usual practice. There could be two explanations: 1) lack of paper to print the newspaper; and 2) that this reversal of Castro's support for his brother was a reflection of a power struggle that

could not be resolved, so it was better to remove the issue from any printed text.

Bombs in Tourist Installations

During this period, Cuba experienced for the first time in many years the type of terrorism to which it subjected the rest of the Americas during the years when exporting the revolution was a priority tool of Cuban foreign policy. Some links to support for kidnaping people and terrorism, revealed by isolated events, indicates that this type of actions are still in Castro's arsenal, although in a more discreet way.

When bombs started exploding in Cuban hotels in the Spring of 1997, there was some speculation as to the potential culprits. The speculation centered on Cuban exile community groups which from time to time organize pinprick actions against Castro's regime. Then, two bombs exploded within a short period of time at the hotels Nacional and Capri in the former Rampa section of Havana's Vedado neighborhood. And finally, there were four more bombs in early September at three hotels and the popular "Bodeguita del Medio" restaurant in Old Havana. Regime spokesmen accused the U.S. government without providing any evidence despite demands by the U.S. Department of State to provide proof. Then, out of the blue sky, appeared a young Salvadorean terrorist, Raúl Ernesto Cruz León, whom State Security accused of being the author of the bombings. The initial versions of the story disseminated by Cuban intelligence painted Cruz León as a kind of Central American Rambo from the Salvadorean military, trained at The School of the Americas in Georgia, who was part of a right-wing military

Table 3. Bombings of Tourist Hotels

Event impact on public opinion dynamics		Direction/Intensity
Sector A:	Definitely weakens cohesion if it comes from their ranks, reinforces fears of potential internal conflict among them, increases pressure for concessions from hardliners	(-->)
Sector B:	Most worrisome development, raises fear that comfortable position of peaceful political support is not tenable, likely to encourage support for stronger repression	(<-)
Sector C:	Repudiates terrorism, likely to support increased repression	(<-)
Sector D:	Ambivalent, encouraged by signal of repressive incompetence and increased opposition, repudiates terrorism, a draw	(<=>)
Sector E:	Most determined may support, most idealistic repudiate terrorism as unacceptable instrument, fear it will be used by regime to justify increased repression	(<=>)

conclave motivated by revenge for Cuba's support of the Salvadorean guerrillas.

However, the Salvadorean's family pointed out that the young man had dropped out of the military academy, had never visited the United States, and his links to Cuba were the result of his work as a personal bodyguard for visiting artists. Not a very ideological chap, this Raúl. These clarifications weakened the most juicy aspects of U.S. involvement in the bombings. Nevertheless, State Security maintains the external link accusation, but focusing now on Cuban exiles. So far, only *The Miami Herald* seems to have given credibility to the version advanced by Cuban intelligence. That version has a great gap: Cruz León was not in Cuba in April, when the first three bombs exploded.

A hypothesis which could provide a potential explanation is that the bombs—which used Cuban training explosives aimed at not causing injuries—were actually placed by demobilized members of the armed forces and the security services. There are thousands of these individuals, many of whom were sympathizers of Generals Arnaldo Ochoa (executed), Patricio de la Guardia (imprisoned) and Minister of Interior General José Abrantes (died in prison). It is these followers of disgraced leaders of the military and security services who are most likely to have access to the explosive materials and intelligence information required to undertake such terrorists actions in the face of the effective Cuban repressive system.

As to motivation, besides revenge for the fate of people with whom they shared many military operations overseas, many of these individuals are surviving on the income they get from self-employment, mostly related to tourism, such as room renting and paladares restaurants. When Castro taxed many of these people out of their profitable dollar activities (as will be discussed under the next event) they may have decided: if we cannot get the tourist dollars neither will you. Once the regime discovered the real culprits, they could not afford to make this public. Instead, they decided to railroad the young Salvadorean, who most likely was a "mule" using television sets to smuggle drugs into Cuba, as a scapegoat. Instead of drugs, Cuban intelligence services said he was using the TV sets to smuggle explosives to make the bombs he allegedly placed in the hotels. This is only a hypothesis. It certainly meets the usual police criteria in crime investigations of opportunity, means and motivation better than the official Cuban version (see Table 3).

The Death of Jorge Mas Canosa

With the passing of Jorge Mas Canosa, fear has been expressed among Castro's opponents that U.S. policy will revert to a possible accommodation with Castro. The notion is that, without his dynamic and effective leadership, the exile community will lose its influence over U.S. policy. This is not an imaginary fear, but a real possibility. Shortly after Mr. Mas passed away, Castro's friends among the U.S. liberal community and some sympathizers within the exile community mounted a full-fledged offensive to lift the embargo. These efforts have been based on a total distortion of the meaning of the Pope's visit to Cuba.

Castro used Jorge Mas as the symbol of a two-fold threat: 1) against Cuban nationalism as a leader to be imposed by an American invasion; and 2) against his

Table 4.   Death of Jorge Mas Canosa

Event impact on public opinion dynamics	Direction/Intensity
Sector A: Weaken cohesion due to less fear of a U.S. invasion and a threat to their personal positions and interests, reduces need to coalesce around Fidel	(--->)
Sector B: Same as above	(--->)
Sector C: Does not care one way or the other	(<=>)
Sector D: Will be encouraged because opposition is freed from stigma successfully planted by Fidel but may be discouraged by fear U.S. opposition to Castro may weaken	(<=>)
Sector E: Likely to be encouraged by disappearance of negative force used by Castro to give cohesion to his followers, as well as a potential political rival force in post-Castro's Cuba, may be less concerned than Sector D with U.S. reaction	(--->)

collaborators as the leader of a movement to restore the past and deprive them of their positions and houses, if not their freedom and lives. Castro also tagged the exile community, particularly in Europe and Latin America, with the image of a reactionary ideology based on revenge and restoration of the old Batista regime. That negative image has been exploited by those whose motivation is really anti-Americanism to mount impressive campaigns against U.S. policy, in particular the Helms-Burton Law and the embargo.

Internationally, such an image has been a great obstacle to gain support for the anti-Castro cause, as well as to focus attention on the repressive nature of the Castro regime, not to mention its colossal failure. Internally, this image of the exile community has allowed Castro to rally his followers around his leadership. So, contrary to what many people in the exile community think, the passing of Jorge Mas is a setback for Castro (see Table 4).

The Slow Reversal of the Economic Opening

The economic opening advanced by Castro sympathizers all over the world has been predicated mostly on allowing people to engage in self-employment. True, there are other initiatives, particularly the opening of the country to foreign investors in the export sector. But the focus on internal sector reform has been on self-employment. Thousands of words and even substantial studies have been written on this issue. In fact, at one time, one of the spokesmen for the economic reformers predicted that the 800,000 to 1,000,000 subsidized Cuban workers in non-productive enterprises were going to be ab-

sorbed by this expanding private sector of the Cuban economy.

The fact that Cubans are not allowed to hire other Cubans to do any paid work, except members of their families, and that the *paladares* restaurants were limited to twelve chairs reveal the weak economic grounds for the claims of those researchers who were telling us that these moves represented the beginnings of economic reform in Cuba. To absorb such large numbers of workers would have required that the internal economy be allowed to work under free market rules and Castro has reiterated time and again his adamant opposition to accept such an opening.

For all practical purposes, the push for even these meager reforms came to an end sometime late in 1996. And the Castro brothers wiped it out, through taxes and repressive measures, in the Spring of 1997, not to mention Raúl's ominous criticism of those who advocated these modest measures in the think tanks attached to the Central Committee. This occurred around the same time that Castro ordered the downing over international waters of U.S. civilian planes piloted by members of Hermanos al Rescate, triggering the approval of the Helms-Burton Law. We have now additional evidence of this slow demise of the economic reform movement.

The classification of the economically active population in Table A-28 of the Statistical Annex to the recent report by the Comisión Económica para América Latina y el Cariba, *La economía cubana: Reformas estructurales y desempeño en los noventa* reveals that the total number of self-employed workers grew from only 25,200 in 1989, the year the Soviet system start-

Table 5. Reversal of Economic Reforms

Event impact on public opinion dynamics	Direction/Intensity
Sector A: Probably weakens cohesion. Hardliners support austerity and resent corruption and privileges, while opportunist beneficiaries within this sector resent being deprived of access to dollars	(<=>)
Sector B: Same as above	(<=>)
Sector C: This group is likely to be greatly irritated since these measures reduce their profiteering opportunities, may move to D	(-->)
Sector D: Since group is against regime, it is likely to join critics of lack of opening and may also be beneficiaries of private sector activities	(-->)
Sector E: Similar to sector D	(-->)

ed imploding, to 225,000 in 1995 and 340,000 in 1996, the years Cuba claimed it was recovering. This is the data used by those who claim that the economic reform is represented by this growing number of self-employed Cubans. However, Table A-35 of the same report states that in February 1997, there were only 171,861 persons authorized for self-employed work by the Labor Ministry. That is almost exactly 50 percent of the statistic reported at the end of 1996 in Table A-28.

In a June 22, 1998 Agence France Presse dispatch from Havana, it is reported that the Labor Ministry official responsible for registering the self-employed reports that their number is decreasing at the rate of three to four thousand per month. The official added that "nobody who works legally can enrich himself." Thus reiterating Fidel Castro's contribution to improve economic thought by amending the thinking of great economists, such as Adam Smith, Maynard Keynes, Joseph Schumpeter or Milton Friedman, with the oxymoron concept of "not-for-profit capitalism" (see Table 5).

The Failure to Restore Economic Growth

The most serious setback the regime has suffered in the economic arena has been the double hit of a decrease in the sugar crop, combined with the decline in the price of sugar. This is offset to some extent by the decline in oil prices. As a symptom of the disarray in the upper echelons of the regime, there were diverse estimates given by different ministers and Carlos Lage, the Vice-President and economic czar.

Unofficial estimates place this year's sugar output at the level of 2.7 million tons. The most optimistic official figures reach only 3.2 million tons. In any case, these are sugar output volumes attained by Cuba after the First World War, when it had one fourth the present population. Combined with prices hovering below ten cents per pound and even down to eight cents, Cuba is going to suffer a severe decrease in its financial capability to import. This could be offset by declines in oil prices and the growth in other exports and in tourism revenues. However, prices of other exports, such as nickel, have also been affected by the Asian crisis. As to tourism, the problem is that the value added in Cuba is very low due to the lack of production of tourist-quality goods. The recently released ECLAC report on the Cuban economy provides the example of Cuban chickens and eggs being of such poor quality that hotels have to import them. As a consequence, the tourist industry is reported to have fallen to only 29 cents out of every dollar in value added.

The analysis of the economy as a whole is outside the scope of this paper. Besides, there will be many papers at this ASCE meeting discussing various aspects of the Cuban economy. Therefore, the topic is relevant only in terms of its impact on the dynamics of public opinion. There are already warnings of further electric power cuts and shortages of all kinds. As a result, there is already an increase in the flow of illegal immigrants to the United States. Young people are reported to be convinced that there is no hope of any future in Cuba and, therefore, it is increasingly more attractive to apply for the U.S. visa lottery or to take any risks in order to escape an island that is seen as a big prison (see Table 6).

Table 6. Failure to Restore Growth

Event impact on public opinion dynamics	Direction/Intensity
Sector A: Seriously weakens cohesion, undermines Fidel's charismatic leadership, raises specter of having to recur to more repression, brings material adversities that affect even the middle and lower ranks, thus making upper echelon privileges more offensive, may encourage support for reformist positions, legitimacy of repression seriously reduced	(----->)
Sector B: Same as above	(----->)
Sector C: Increased shortages and discomforts reduces benefit of indifference, may shift to Sector D	(---->)
Sector D: Increased shortages and discomforts reduces attractiveness of passivity, may shift to Sector E	(---->)
Sector E: Feels vindicated in frontal opposition, determination to endure repression is reinforced, may perceive possibility of end of regime intransigence, reform if not outright collapse becomes feasible	(---->)

The Failure to Prevent Agreement between Europe and the United States

During this period Castro continued his campaign of trying to isolate the United States internationally on the issue of Helms-Burton and the embargo. The last such ostentatious effort was his May 1998, visit to Geneva to attend the 50th anniversary of the World Health Organization and the meeting of the World Trade Organization. A secondary benefit to Castro of these travels is that he is the object of protocol attentions from his hosts and, as a celebrity, receives enormous media attention. This helps maintain his charismatic image in Cuba. However, in this case the results were extremely negative.

In the first place, Pablo Alfonso, the *Nuevo Herald* reporter sent to Geneva to cover his visit was able to obtain a scoop that the real purpose of the visit was for treatment of a rare heart condition at the Genolier Clinic. This explained his long stay and the secrecy surrounding his official activities while in Geneva. Poor health is never associated with charismatic leadership, since followers expect their charismatic leaders to have superhuman traits and being sick is proof of human frailty. To further damage his image while there, the official session at the Legislative Palace had to be moved to a private residence because the legislators considered hosting a notorious dictator a blemish on their democratic image.

Moving to the goal of isolating the United States in relation to the embargo, during Castro's visit the European Union and the United States reached an agreement by which in exchange for offering to request some changes in Helms-Burton, which are un-

likely to be approved by the U.S. Congress, the Europeans agreed to multilateral restrictions on investments in confiscated properties. Castro realized immediately that this was a setback for his propaganda efforts, voicing his concern that an agreement was being made at Cuba's expense, and Ricardo Alarcón, the President of the Cuban legislature, who was attending an Ibero-American Parliaments meeting in Montevideo, also expressed his disapproval of the US-EU agreement. The Europeans have agreed to withdraw any credit or insurance support for investments by their companies in confiscated properties subject to claims from their previous owners. This will further discourage investors to go to Cuba.

To crown the negatives of this trip, the Cubans were trying to be admitted as observers to the Lomé Convention, a system of special treatment regarding customs and financing the Europeans offer to their former colonies. Cuba sought this door as a way to bypass the European Union Common Position on Cuba that was agreed on December 2, 1996. This Common Position requires Cuba to open politically and economically before it can sign a Cooperative Agreement to provide a framework for granting economic assistance to the island. Eventually, the observer status was granted but, in response to objections from Germany and Sweden, full status was made formally contingent on Cuba meeting the criteria of the Common Position and among other actions freeing the jailed members of the Working Group of the Dissidence. Conditions that irritated Mr. Robaina, who said "that Cuba placed no conditions for joining." Mr. Robaina does not seem to

Table 7. Failure to Prevent US-EU Agreement

Event impact on public opinion dynamics	Direction/Intensity
Sector A: Those familiar with the situation realize that Cuba is losing the isolation battle against the U.S. Despite the posturing of Latin leaders and the overt cordiality and politeness shown to their leader, Cuba continues to be a financial and economic pariah, with no solution in sight. This weakens cohesion and reduces patience with Castro's intransigence, thus giving legitimacy to the opposition and the reformists	(-->)
Sector B: Same as above	(-->.)
Sector C: Most are not even aware of these events, so it is a draw. However, once they become aware, are likely to shift to D	(<=>)
Sector D: The failure to isolate the U.S. moderately encourages this group	(->)
Sector E: Same as Sector D	(->)

Table 8. Congressional Findings and U.S. Initiatives

Event impact on public opinion dynamics	Direction/Intensity
Sector A: Offer of humanitarian aid weakens cohesion, rejection on national dignity grounds has high acceptance in this group, facing more shortages middle and lower ranks are likely to be more receptive	(<=>)
Sector B: Same as above	(<=>)
Sector C: Very receptive, will resent assistance refusal, likely to drift to D	(-->)
Sector D: Similar to C, but more likely to increase opposition	(-->)
Sector E: Likely to exploit against regime, will reinforce commitment to resist, sector most receptive to a U.S. initiative on this matter	(--->)

understand that, when one wants to join a club or an organization, the organization, and not the aspiring member, has the right to set conditions for admission (see Table 7).

Congressional Findings and New U.S. Initiatives

One of the most damaging consequences for Castro of the Pope' visit is the opportunity it offered to U.S. Congressional staffers to visit Cuba and travel at length throughout the island. Up to this time, most staffers of the Republican controlled U.S. Congress were at a disadvantage when dealing with pro-Castro advocates who claimed first-hand knowledge of the situation and viewpoints of the Cuban people. Three key Republican staffers visited Cuba for ten days during and after the Pope's visit: Roger Noriega and Marc Thiessen of the Senate Foreign Relations Committee and Caleb McCarry of the House International Relations Committee.

Among the many findings in their report, perhaps the most outstanding one is that while they were in the Plaza de la Revolución during the last Papal mass, the audience kept their hands in their pockets rather than applaud Fidel Castro. They report that the same happened in Santiago de Cuba in response to the presence of Raúl Castro at the Papal mass there. Quite correctly, they interpret this hand passivity as a discreet "acto de repudio" against Castro and his brother. Since they were able to get an in-depth view of the real situation, beyond tame foreign press coverage, they now have a solid basis of facts to oppose any accommodation with Castro.

The findings of the staffers not only made it less likely they will accept any weakening changes in the Helms-Burton legislation, this visit also encouraged them to come out with a series of additional ideas to provide direct humanitarian support to Cubans and to the growing civil society that is emerging. Castro's rejected humanitarian aid as offensive to national dignity (see Table 8).

The Hesitation of Latin America

Latin America and the Caribbean continue their contradictory policies of advocating the strengthening of democracy in the Hemisphere while sending ambiguous messages on their position towards Castro and his regime. There are two basic factors determining this ambiguity: one, confusing the interests of Cuba and its people with those of Castro and his regime; the other, using the Cuba issue as a proxy for their anti-Americanism. A position which, a recent survey financed by the *Wall Street Journal* and sixteen Latin newspapers shows, is not shared by the people of the region, only 27 per cent of whom have a good opinion of Castro, with only 18 percent of Mexicans sharing their government's admiration for Castro.

The Mexican government is the most outspoken in its support of Cuba against the United States. At the recently held meeting of the OAS General Assembly in Caracas, the Mexican Foreign Minister, Mrs. Rosario Green, spoke in favor of creating a Group of Friends of the Secretary General to start conversations on the reintegration of Cuba to the OAS. This is extremely important because Cuba cannot have access to any financing from the Inter-American Development Bank unless it is a member of the OAS. The proposal was not on the agenda and was dropped when the U.S. objected to it. Several governments agreed that this was premature in view that Cuba had not expressed any interest in meeting the democratic standards that have been agreed by the OAS at the suggestion of Canada, precisely one of the countries that now wants to look the other way in relation to Cuba's undemocratic behavior.

One disappointing experience, very favorable to Castro, was the rejection of the resolution of the UN Human Rights Commission on Cuba at its last session in Geneva. This rejection was caused by the abstention of six Latin American delegations, Brazil, Chile, Ecuador, Guatemala, Uruguay and Venezuela. Did these governments realize that their diplomatic game of showing their displeasure with the United States was being played at the expense of the most helpless participants in this matter: the oppressed, the mistreated and the imprisoned by Castro? No doubt Castro and his hardline followers must have been extremely pleased, while the dissidents and other regime opponents must have been dismayed by this callous vote.

Interestingly, upon his return from a visit to Cuba, the Foreign Minister of Brazil restated Brazilian for-

eign policy on Cuba as conditioned on expressions of willingness by Cuba to meet some minimal conditions of democratic opening and human rights respect. As an indication of the seriousness with which Castro and his friends see this change in policy, shortly after, a group of prominent Brazilian left-wing Castro sympathizers, led by Celso Furtado and Oscar Niemeyer, issued a statement criticizing this shift in Brazilian foreign policy.

Finally, comes the election of Daniel Pastrana in Colombia. One would think that a Conservative and democrat faced with a guerrilla insurrection supported by Castro for decades, would be an ally of democracy and freedom for Cuba. But a June 25, 1998 dispatch by Andrés Oppenheimer in *The Miami Herald,* based on conversations with President-elect Pastrana, reveals such hopes perhaps are unfounded. According to Oppenheimer, Pastrana is anxious to negotiate with the guerrillas to bring peace to his country. A most worthy goal.

However, this requires making concessions to the Cuban supported guerrillas. Already, departing and discredited President Samper, in a visit to Havana, announced Castro's willingness to mediate the Colombian conflict. Of course, the price for such a mediation will be paid at the expense of Cuba's freedom. Oppenheimer's report hints that the United States will be pressured in exchange to loosen up its position on Castro.

Is Pastrana ready to join Mexico in sacrificing the victims of Castro's tyranny for the sake of getting his cooperation in solving internal problems and posturing against the United States? The fact that writer Gabriel García Márquez, a rabid Castro supporter, was one of those who campaigned for Pastrana, despite his conservative ideological orientation, gives Castro another card to play. And, to those who wish Cuba to be free, this gives another reason for concern.

There are some recent examples of events in which Castro used his terrorist connections to gain diplomatic influence. One is the kidnaping of the brother of OAS Secretary General, César Gaviria, by pro-Castro guerrillas in Colombia. The guerrillas stated

Table 9. Latin American Hesitation

Event impact on public opinion dynamics		Direction/Intensity
Sector A:	In the short run, success in getting support reinforces Castro's charismatic image and his stranglehold over the sector, it also legitimizes human rights violations, lack of tangible economic results in the end reduces its impact	(<--)
Sector B:	Same as above	(<--)
Sector C:	Does not care one way or the other due to lack of visible results	(<=>)
Sector D:	Discouraged by diplomatic support given to Castro, particularly in matters such as the vote on human rights in Geneva	(<--)
Sector E:	Very demoralized by loss of international support on human rights; this is a serious betrayal, international support is the only source of protection this sector can count on against regime repression	(<---)

that they would release Gaviria's brother only at Castro's request. He made the request and gained a spokesman, who even refuses to call him a dictator, while pretending to use his OAS position as a mediator. During the hijacking of the Japanese embassy in Lima by the Castro supported MRTA, Castro played the role of the reluctant mediator with his followers, thus enhancing his standing with the governments involved, in particular, the Japanese from whom he expected financial concessions. In this case, however, President Fujimori fooled Castro and wiped out his sympathizers without giving even a hint to Castro of what he was about to do. Nevertheless, Japan agreed to refinance its debt of more than 700 million dollars (see Table 9).

Impact of the Pope's Visit

The ultimate step in Castro's efforts to gain international support against the U.S. and the Helms-Burton Law was the Pope's visit to Cuba. This visit was a reluctant concession to exploit photo opportunities to boost his charismatic image and call attention to the Pope's rejection of embargoes in general and the Cuban one in particular.

Castro's agreement to accept the Pope's visit to Cuba ended a negotiation that went for a decade. Having attained his goal of being invited to the Vatican, Castro started hedging on the conditions set by the Vatican. The main reason for his hedging is that Castro did not want to strengthen the Cuban Catholic Church. It is the only independent national organization parallel to his government, it has its own ideology based on a religion that is basically consistent

with the spiritual needs of many Cubans and it can mobilize worldwide support through the Vatican.

Besides, Castro is very aware of the impact of the Pope's visit to Poland. When the Pope undertook that visit to his native land and unleashed the Solidarity movement, Castro ordered that country out of bounds for training Cubans within the Soviet Bloc. Not only that, any Cuban official or student stationed in other Soviet Bloc countries had to obtain a special authorization from Cuban security services before visiting Poland on vacation.

The initial negotiations over a Papal visit in 1987 stalled over Castro's refusal to allow the Pope to move from one end of the island to the other over land holding public masses, as well as other conditions loosening limitations to the Church in access to mass media, publication capabilities and immigration of priests. The Castro regime wanted a mere stopover in Rancho Boyeros airport or at the most holding masses in Havana and Santiago within the limited spaces of churches.

It must be pointed that at that time there was a serious division inside the Cuban Church between the so-called "collaborationist" hierarchy, who advocated a passive stance merely to be allowed to survive, and some more defiant members of the hierarchy who advocated a more aggressive stance. This last group had the support of Catholic lay members who were being persecuted by the regime. Among this group of laymen, one of the most prominent figures was Oswaldo Payá, who is now a dissident leader.

Much of the hope being placed on the impact of the Pope's visit stems from comparisons with the impact of the Pope's visits to Poland. But it is important to consider the differences. In the first place, Castro is more a Stalinist style ruler than either Gierek or Jaruselski. It is doubtful that a Pope visit to Moscow under Stalin would have been allowed the space the Pope enjoyed in Poland or even that it would have taken place. Furthermore, while the Polish Catholic Church is closely identified with the nation, the Cuban Church has been historically identified with support of Spain in the War of Independence.

The Spanish Church hierarchy during the last century clashed with Martí and other leaders of independence who were Free Masons. It also persecuted Cuban priests who sympathized with independence. The best known being Father Félix Varela, who is considered the intellectual father of Cuban nationality, although he was forced to live most of his life as a parish priest in the United States and died in Saint Augustine, Florida. After independence, the Church continued to be dominated by the Spanish provinces of the various religious orders. It also had little presence in the countryside or among the poorest segments of society.

By the time Castro reached power, the Church was rapidly broadening its appeal to Cubans and Catholic leaders were very active in the opposition to Batista. When Castro turned to Communism, Catholics were among the earliest opponents. However, the Church had too weak a hold on the masses and Castro dealt with their challenge by expelling several hundred priests and nuns to Spain. At that point, the Vatican very wisely decided to keep a low profile and quietly attempt to build the bases for a rebirth of the Church in spite of tremendous limitations and outright regime persecution.

The fact is that, despite those efforts, in today's Cuba, Santería is the religion with the largest following. The Catholic Church has the second largest following. The regime has encouraged some Protestant denominations which have supported it, not only in Cuba but also abroad. The exception being the Jehovah Witnesses, which is the most persecuted religious denomination in Cuba today.

Therefore, it is understandable, and beneficial in the long run for the ethical reconstruction of Cuba, for the Catholic Church to try to gain more space for its purely religious and humanitarian activities. However, the hierarchy will have to balance that goal with the danger of use of the Church by Castro for his own ends. This is not easy when the Church hierarchy itself is divided. The most outspoken member of the collaborationist faction is Monsignor Carlos Manuel de Céspedes. The most outspoken member of the rebellious hierarchy is the Bishop of Santiago de Cuba, Pedro Meurice. If the collaborationists prevail, the Church will pay the same price it paid for the behavior of the Spanish hierarchy in colonial times.

So far, the price for strengthening the Church in the spiritual realm has been to make meek protests against Castro's repression while providing arguments to effectively support him in opposing the Helms-Burton law. This means that building the Church is being done at the expense of the rights and freedoms of the Cuban people at large, the majority of whom are not practicing Catholics at present. Most Cubans will consider this as too big a price to pay and may resent the Church as a discreet collaborating agent of Castro's repression. The Vatican and the Cuban hierarchy will have to ponder very carefully the course to follow.

Castro agreed to provide the support required to facilitate the visit but, as he always does in these situations, he tried to wear out the Vatican in the details. Initially, Cuba refused to provide support for the events related to the visit unless the Church paid for them to the tune of US$10 million. In addition, there were all kinds of logistical questions that a Vatican delegation had to settle well in advance of the visit. Even the provision of cars for Church officials was a point of contention, with Cuban authorities refusing to allow the importation of cars and forcing the Church to buy them locally for dollars in a Cuban Government dealership.

And there were more serious obstacles. Castro had abolished Christmas as an official holiday in 1969. One would expect the restoration of such a holiday to be a prerequisite for a Pope's visit. This was an elementary friendly gesture to the head of the Church. To make the point more offensive, in 1996, right after Castro returned from his visit to the Vatican, the Cuban legislature scheduled its two-day session for December 24 and 25. To make matters even more offensive to the Church and all Christians, among its decisions during that session, the Legislature gave Cubans an extended holiday over New Year's day. This issue was not settled until mid-December 1997 when there were leaks from the Vatican on this matter being a stumbling block and Castro finally relented. But, the restoration of Christmas as a holiday was granted for only one year. In view of this behavior, on a matter so central to the Church, it is hard to understand the basis for Cardinal Law, of Boston, claiming that Fidel has never persecuted the Church.

Regardless of all these obstacles, which were finally overcome, the fact is that the Pope's visit has been a turning point in the Cuban situation. To the surprise of Castro, it revealed that there are millions of Cubans who crave the spiritual guidance and comfort offered by religion. When Castro realized the mistake he had made, it was too late to cancel the visit. With three thousand journalists already accredited, he could not afford the negative image of a cancellation.

Instead, he shifted gears. That is why, in his speech the weekend before the visit, he encouraged Party cadres to attend the various events and tried to claim credit for the visit by allowing television coverage and all the other logistical requests made by the Vatican delegation during the long and tortuous negotiating period. Alarmed by this attempt to hijack the Pope's visit, Cardinal Ortega immediately challenged Castro's assertions and clarified that the Pope was coming as a guest of the Church and the Cuban people and not of the regime.

Furthermore, that explains Castro's very discourteous welcoming speech upon the Pope's arrival. The Pope has nothing to do with Spanish colonization, during which, according to Castro, 70 million Indians and 12 million Africans had been killed. Neither could the Pope or the Catholic Church be blamed for the 300 hundred thousand Cubans who died during the last decade of the Spanish colonial administration or

the fact that at Belén, the Jesuit school he attended, there were no black students.

Castro raised those issues as a warning to the Pope that he was prepared to unleash Cuban nationalism against the Catholic Church. This was not too subtle a reminder that all he needed to do was to call attention to the role, commented above, of the Catholic hierarchy, at the time dominated by Spaniards, in supporting the Spanish colonial system. That was his way of threatening the Pope to stay away from mobilizing the population in any way against the regime.

Ignoring Castro's threatening remarks, during the visit, the Pope raised the issue of losing *fear* and saying the *truth*, of the need to *strengthen the family* and allow *religious education*, of the need to respect the *rights of organization, assembly and free speech*, as well as of *reconciliation among all Cubans* no matter where they lived. He even told Cubans, restating a Martí phrase, that *"rights are demanded, not begged."* In all, a most subversive message to a long passive and submissive population. True, as he has done previously, His Holiness also expressed his opposition to embargoes of all kinds. But only once. He refused to provide Castro the unconditional support Castro was expecting against the United States. On balance, the positions taken by the Pope challenged the roots of Castro's system of holding power.

That is why, in his farewell speech to the Pope, being again discourteous although respectful, Castro said that "in Cuba nobody was afraid." A week later, he went back to TV again and tried to coopt the Pope's position to his view of the world and international relations, while ignoring all other issues raised by the Pope during his visit. On that occasion, as was to be expected, Castro also rejected the initiative advanced by the Cuban American National Foundation (CANF), later on proposed as legislation by Senator Helms, for the United States to finance provision of humanitarian food and medical supplies to Cuba. Castro labeled such assistance as offensive to Cuba's national dignity. Unfortunately, Cardinal Ortega supported him.

In conclusion, the Pope surprised Castro and, once back in the Vatican, stated publicly his hope that the

Table 10. Pope's Visit

Event impact on public opinion dynamics	Direction/Intensity
Sector A: Weakens Castro's charismatic hold and ideological monopoly, encourages many closet Catholics within the sector, increases support for opening and reforms, rather than more repression, appeal for religious rights likely to increase resistance to regime	(----->)
Sector B: Same as above, more outspoken in resenting Castro' decision to invite Pope because it encouraged opponents at their level	(----->)
Sector C: Encouragement to lose fear and speak the truth likely to cause drift towards opposition, particularly among those repressing their spiritual needs, legitimizes dissenting with the regime	(----->)
Sector D: Great encouragement to dissenting views, particularly to lay Catholics feeling legitimized by regime's acceptance of the Pope, despite posterior regime efforts to dissuade them, more likely to move to sector E	(----->)
Sector E: Got a boost in their morale despite timid position of hierarchy in refusing to let the Pope even give Communion to dissidents like Oswaldo Payá, Pope's message will reinforce willingness to endure repression and legitimizes their position, in the end, they, more than the timid members of the hierarchy, are likely to make true the Pope's hope of this visit leading to another Poland.	(----->)

visit would trigger in the long run an outcome similar to that of his visit to Poland. Naturally, Castro has other ideas. The question now is how the visit impacts on the attitude of many Cubans who, encouraged and inspired by the Pope's message, will be determined to cross the threshold of fear that has ruled their life and assert their rights. When they do so in the religious realm, Castro is likely to make albeit reluctant concessions. At this point, he does not want, or can afford, worldwide hostility from the Catholic Church. But, beyond the religious realm, no way.

To nip such a possibility in the bud, Castro started what Pax Christy, a Dutch Catholic NGO which has been denouncing human rights violations in Cuba all over Europe, has properly labeled a campaign of "de-popefication." That is, an increased repressive campaign to dispel any hopes among Cuban citizens that the Pope visit was going to lead to any opening. Castro and his friends were emboldened further by the already commented unfortunate vote at the UN Human Rights Commission in Geneva. A vote, incidentally, that pro-Castro advocates interpreted as a response to the Pope's hope that "the world open itself to Cuba."

Obviously displeased with this turn of events, the Pope convoked the Cuban bishops to the Vatican for a full week session starting on June 8. The session expressed the Church's displeasure with lack of progress in "opening Cuba to the world," the other

hope expressed by the Pope. What is really needed is for Castro to open Cuba to the Cuban people.

In his speech to the bishops, the Pope expressed his confidence that Cuba will evolve peacefully towards development of all rights, advocating the promotion of freedom of expression, association and assembly "without arbitrary limitations." Bishop Meurice of Santiago de Cuba informed the Italian press that "although the Church requires some space to be able to satisfy the spiritual needs of the people inside and outside Cuba," those spaces should be open to all. Finally, the Pope exhorted the bishops, upon their return to Cuba, to be prepared to "face all the challenges" derived from his pastoral visit to Cuba.

The threat this represents for Castro is predicated on the nature of human behavior. Once a person starts losing fear in one realm, he is likely to start behaving without fear in other aspects of his life. Acting freely and without fear tends to become a universal style of behavior. True, the Catholic Church has made it clear that their actions are limited to the religious and spiritual sphere of life, although they are not indifferent to what happens in other realms of the life of its followers. This broadening base of people willing to assert their basic rights opens the opportunity for developing a civil society movement inside Cuba. Precisely what Castro is determined to prevent. The clash of wills between the Pope and Castro has just started (see Table 10).

Appendix
DEFINITION OF SECTORS GROUPING THE POPULATION

Under the methodology developed to analyze revolutionary propensity, the population is grouped according to the degree of support or opposition they are prepared to offer the status quo. Although many will disagree with this decision, for our purposes the population to be grouped will include those in the island and in exile. Regardless of the traditional division between those living in a country and the overseas communities from the same nation, the irreversible fact is that as a result of the Cuban revolution, Cuba has now a permanent overseas population. The majority of these people, spread throughout the world, are unlikely to ever return to Cuba, but are also an integral part of Cuban society with many economic, emotional, affective and cultural links that impact internal political dynamics in many ways. Even the Castro regime has recognized this fact and tries to infiltrate and manipulate the overseas community to serve its purposes.

On the extreme right side are those under *Group A* who are committed to resort to violence in order to support the status quo, either because it is their duty as members of the army or police or because their ideological commitment makes them willing to do so as paramilitay forces. In the current situation in Cuba, Group A includes MINFAR and MININT members, as well as the brigades of "Patria o Muerte" civilian hoodlums the regime unleashes at will, with guaranteed impunity, against any opponent. Most members of these brigades are also members of the Party and the Committees for the Defense of the Revolution.

In terms of age, at the senior officer level this group includes a heavy proportion of those who shared the initial period of revolutionary success and/or uplifted their class status. Despite the end of "internationalism" and the resulting shrinking career opportunities it entails, members of this group are offered access to privileges and employment, upon retirement, in joint enterprises dealing in the dollar market. Younger middle and junior level officers do not necessarily share the privileges and interests of the leadership

and their careers opportunities are very limited. However, for all of them a return of exiles to power is a dreadful threat to their interests and nationalism is a powerful motivating force.

Despite the apparent loyalty of this group, it is not a monolith and there are serious divisions within their ranks. The armed forces are unwilling to face a popular revolt and have pressed Castro to make concessions to avoid such a situation. Draftees do not necessarily share the interests of the professionals and in a crisis are likely to share the feelings of the average citizen and not those of the institution.

MINFAR members pride themselves on being military professionals and not a repressive force and share popular contempt for MININT members. Within the MININT there is resentment of the MINFAR takeover in 1989 and the massive purge of its senior and middle ranks that followed the arrest of its Minister, General José Abrantes, at the time of the Ochoa trial.

During General Ochoa's trial, more than twenty of the Generals forced to make public statements supporting his sentence praised him while stating that, if the accusation was true, he deserved the death sentence. Today, few believe that the accusation was true. There are more than forty prisons for members of the military and before Castro visits a garrison all side weapons are removed. Obviously, there are some cracks in the monolith.

Those in *Group B*, who are willing to support the regime only peacefully, act out of ideological sympathy or in response to some economic or status interest. In the present situation in Cuba, this group includes a hard core of members of the Party and the so-called mass organizations who are still committed to the revolution and its leadership. It also includes the so-called reformists, who advocate moderate reforms to facilitate a peaceful transition, as well as those who are pretending to be committed just in order to protect their positions or to avoid retribution for disaffection.

In terms of age, this group includes many older people who shared the initial period of revolutionary successes. The level of commitment is weaker among many who became adults after Castro reached power who, although sharing the initial benefits of the revolution, do not necessarily feel their future is irrevocably linked to Castro. And, finally, this group includes a minority of younger people who although not sharing the initial period of revolutionary euphoria are still sympathetic to the revolution for a variety of reasons. Nationalism ranks high among this group, as does fear of the return of the exiles to power.

Within overseas communities, the most recent addition to this group is that of the so-called "quedaditos" or "ni-nis"—neither against nor in favor—who live and work abroad as medical doctors, artists, professors, writers or performers, while paying ideological and financial tribute to the regime in exchange for being allowed to visit Cuba. Close to the "ni-nis," and preceding them by several years, are those associated with the regime in businesses which profit overseas from travel to Cuba and remittances of food, medicines and money. Despite the lip service they pay to the regime, neither nationalism nor fear of the exiles return to power are seriously felt by this people. They are opportunists willing to make the best out of an unpleasant situation.

Then there are those under *Group C*, who are in the center unwilling to take sides either because their interests are not affected or because they believe whatever they do is irrelevant or out of fear of an even worse future in a post revolutionary Cuba. This is perhaps the largest group within today's Cuba and continues growing after each promise of a turnaround turns to be only a mirage, while Cuba's standard of living continues to sink into Haiti's level.

This group today includes perhaps the largest proportion of young people who did not enjoy the glorious initial moments of the revolutionary experience and have lived only the period of adversities and shortages, having a much higher level of educational attainment than previous generations. It also includes many among the first revolutionary generation who are disenchanted and some of the older pre-Castro revolutionaries who disagree with Castro but think the odds make any attempt at opposition unrealistic.

In the face of little hope for any change, the frustration of Group C in some cases leads to escape or anomie. In the case of escape, even in facing the risks and dangers involved in "rafting". The escape option has been closed by the US/Cuba migration agreements. In its most dramatic manifestation, the hopelessness of anomie is reflected in those youngsters who injected themselves with the HIV virus in order to at least have access to a shorter but better life in the hospitals for HIV infected.

On the other hand, many of the profiteers from the dollar trade, whether from agricultural cooperatives, joint enterprises with foreign investors, self-employment, prostitution, overseas remittances, etc. are members of this group. Although they have given up hope of any change in the regime, to the extent they are allowed a way to improve their personal situation, the profiteers are unwilling to take any risks to oppose the regime in any way. This is the essence of the "resolver" attitude: to survive. These are very pragmatic and cynical people who have decided to take care of themselves and nothing else.

The more successful among them, including privileged members of the *nomenklatura*, generate strong resentment among "Patria o Muerte" Party cadres under groups A and B, that is those who are totally committed to Castro and the Revolution. That leads to Castro's occasional verbal outbursts of hostility and even harassment of some of them through taxation and control measures. True, he is doing it to placate the hardliners in Groups A and B but, as long as they can "resolver", they are no threat to his rule. And, may even pay lip service to it. Nationalism and fear of exile return is less of a motivation for them, wheeler dealers are confident they can "resolver" under any post-Castro regime.

Group D gathers those who are openly in disagreement with the regime and for a variety of reasons stay in the island as well as many in the exile community who still have close family links with them. Over the years, starting with listening to Radio Martí in 1985 to legalizing the holding of dollars in 1993, as well as verbalizing frustration by openly criticizing the regime and even its leadership, the regime has been forced to reluctantly grant some space to this group. Under present circumstances, however, this group is unable to articulate itself into an effective opposition force due to the severe limitations on the exercise of the rights of association and assembly that prevail in today's Cuba.

With the closing of the migration option, this group is likely to increase as a potential source for members of a formal opposition. While the annual 20,000 U.S. visas, including the lottery for 5,000, makes hundreds of thousands of them abstain from any activity that may clash with the regime and could jeopardize their exit permits. One perverse twist is that fake dissidence is resorted to by some in this group as a means to be expelled from Cuba and obtain U.S. visas.

Agewise, this group includes many young people and those who were adolescents at the time of the revolution, as well as a minority among the older people who shared the initial revolutionary experience and are now disenchanted. Most of the latter group who rejected the regime earlier constitute the bulk of the overseas community. Up to now Castro has been able to export his opposition, but not any longer. Since they are free to express themselves, meet and organize, those in the exile community are the most vocal and articulate manifestation of opposition to Castro, although highly ineffective internally and even counterproductive due to their impact on other groups, in particular A and B, who see them as threats to their interests. Nationalism fluctuates widely as a motivational force among group D.

Finally, *Group E* includes those who are willing to endure or resort to violence in opposing the status quo. In the present Cuba situation, this group is constituted by diverse dissident organizations, based on human rights defense, on professional associations such as lawyers, journalists, doctors, economists, etc. and political affiliations such as Social democrats or Christian democrats. The first dissident organization emerged in 1976 to defend human rights and the process has accelerated in the last few years in response to two factors: the collapse of communism

with its traumatic economic and ideological impact and the availability of Radio Martí as a national means of public opinion awareness.

Agewise, this group includes old revolutionaries associated with Castro, children of old Communist Party leaders, former military officers and younger professionals from many fields. A common characteristic is that these dissidents were supportive of and associated with the Revolution in its initial phase but became disenchanted along the way for a variety of reasons. The collapse of the Soviet Bloc and the abysmal failure of Communism as a system has encouraged them to come out into the open with misgivings they had on the basis of their diverse personal experiences and even risking regime repression.

Nationalism is a strong motivational force among these groups. In contrast with the cynical and pragmatic approach of those in the center or the passivity of those in the peaceful opposition, those who cross the threshold of enduring violent repression do so out of deeply felt principles and for them nationalism is as central a motivational force as it is with many in groups A and B. As to the exile community, these groups have ambivalent feelings. They fear the revenge that may accompany the access to power of exile leaders, or even the competition for power with them in a post-Castro era. At the same time, their comments on overseas Cubans are usually conciliatory and inclusive, which indicates that besides the open arms and forgiving philosophy that guides them, they realize that an effective opposition to Castro, their survival and the reconstruction of Cuba requires the support of the exile community.

Ideologically, they represent the whole range of positions in the political spectrum. That is one of the reasons they are so fragmented, the other being that small closely knit groups are the only possible organizational level that can be attained without being infiltrated by repressive forces. The patterns of behavior developed by these groups to cope with the extremely effective regime repressive apparatus, have been discussed at great length by Dr. Benigno Aguirre in an excellent paper entitled, "The Culture of Political Opposition in Cuba.

Open resort to violence has been an unworkable and futile alternative for internal dissenters throughout the years and is still a futile undertaking today. Isolated incidents take place from time to time but it is unlikely that there will be a repetition of the revolutionary process against Batista. The case of the bombs that exploded in several hotels in Varadero and Havana during 1997 provided a good lesson. Although the explanation provided by the government is not internally consistent and lacks credibility, the fact is that the bombings stopped. Overseas Cubans try to mimic revolutionary historical experiences from time to time, in some cases out of sheer ignorance not realizing they are doomed to failure, in other cases for ego or even monetary reasons. At the extreme of resorting to violence in the overseas community there are those who think violence can be used to provoke a U.S./Cuba conflict, thus escalating to the final outcome or intervention option.

THE CUBAN ECONOMIC CRISIS
OF THE 1990s AND THE EXTERNAL SECTOR

Jorge F. Pérez-López[1]

In late September 1990, speaking at a ceremony marking the 30th anniversary of the creation of the Committees for the Defense of the Revolution (CDRs), President Fidel Castro announced that the country had entered a "special period in time of peace."[2] He likened the prevailing economic situation—sharply reduced levels of imports of fuel, food, raw materials, machinery and spare parts—to what would have ensued from the imposition of an air and naval blockade in a war situation. Surviving this "special period in time of peace" would require emergency measures similar to those called for in a war setting.

The economic crisis of the 1990s has been the most severe to beset the country in the 20th century. Between 1989 and 1993, Cuba's economy contracted by a third to a half. The positive economic growth during 1994-97 has made a very modest contribution to the population standard of living, which plummeted since the second half of the 1980s. Minister of the Economy and Planning José Luis Rodríguez told journalists in April 1997 that "the special period has not been overcome yet" and predicted that "in a reasonable time period, which may be a matter of a few years, Cuba will again reach [economic] levels achieved prior to the special period."[3]

The events that triggered Cuba's economic crisis of the 1990s are undoubtedly related to the shift in trade and economic relations with the former socialist countries that began in 1989 as these economic partners abandoned central planning and began to transition toward market economies. In the late 1980s, Eastern European countries and the former Soviet Union purchased 85 percent of Cuba's exports, provided a like share of imports, and were the main source of the island's development financing. The disappearance of socialist regimes in Eastern Europe and the former Soviet Union, and these countries' demand that henceforth trade relations be conducted using convertible currencies and following normal commercial practices, meant that the economic support Cuba had received from the socialist community for nearly three decades vanished almost overnight.

While external sector shocks triggered the economic crisis of the 1990s, they alone are not responsible for its occurrence, severity or length. The underlying causes of the crisis are the well-known inefficiencies of centrally planned economies, compounded by distortions created by massive inflows of resources from the socialist bloc and the obstinacy of the leadership to undertake the political and economic reforms necessary to overcome the crisis. Under the current political and economic scenario, the external sector ap-

---

1. An earlier version of this paper was presented at the Workshop on U.S.-Latin American Economic Relations, Institute of Latin American Studies, University of London. The paper expresses exclusively the personal views of the author.

2. Fidel Castro, "Speech during the ceremony marking the 30th Anniversary of the Committees for the Defense of the Revolution, on 28 September 1990," in *FBIS-LAT-90-190* (1 October 1990), p. 5.

3. "Estamos aún en 'período especial,' dice Ministro," *El Nuevo Herald* (25 April 1997), 6A.

pears unlikely to be capable of being the engine that pulls the economy out of the crisis.

The purpose of the paper is to analyze Cuba's external sector during the economic crisis, policies adopted by the government to improve its performance, results and prospects. It begins with a summary of Cuban economic performance in the 1990s. This is followed by a brief description of the external sector situation at the end of the 1980s. The next two sections look, respectively, at policies that have been implemented to address foreign sector imbalances and their results. The paper closes with some observations on the prospects for the external sector and for the Cuban economy in the next few years.

RECENT CUBAN ECONOMIC PERFORMANCE

There is very little official information on the structure and performance of the Cuban economy during the 1990s. The most recent comprehensive statistical yearbook available is for 1989.[4] In August 1995, the Cuban National Bank (Banco Nacional de Cuba, BNC) issued a report that for the first time contained selected official economic statistics though 1994 and some estimates for 1995;[5] a similar report—but with fewer statistics—was released a year later.[6] The national product statistics in the BNC reports follow a different methodology than was used through the early 1990s, disallowing long term comparisons.[7] With regard to the external sector, the BNC reports

do not contain disaggregated data on merchandise trade, investment or foreign debt. A report released by the Ministry of Economy and Planning for 1997 provides macroeconomic results and a few statistics related to the performance of the external sector.[8]

In mid-1997, the U.N. Economic Commission for Latin America and the Caribbean (Comisión Económica para la América Latina y el Caribe, CEPAL) released a comprehensive study of the Cuban economy prepared with the cooperation of the Cuban government; a statistical annex to the study— reportedly based on information provided by Cuban official statistical sources—provides a great deal of economic data not published directly by the Cuban authorities.[9] Using information contained in the BNC and CEPAL reports, together with fragmentary information from other sources, it is possible to gain an appreciation for the severity of the economic crisis of the 1990s.

National Product

After falling freely since 1989—by 3.0 percent in 1990, 10.7 percent in 1991, 11.6 percent in 1992 and 14.9 percent in 1993, according to BNC statistics (Table 1)—the Cuban economy apparently hit bottom around mid-1994. The gross domestic product (GDP) at constant prices of 1981 was about 12.8 billion pesos in 1993, 34.8 percent lower than in 1989.[10] Although extremely significant, this contrac-

---

4. Comité Estatal de Estadísticas, *Anuario Estadístico de Cuba 1989* (La Habana, 1991).

5. Banco Nacional de Cuba, *Economic Report 1994* (La Habana: Banco Nacional de Cuba, August 1995).

6. Banco Nacional de Cuba, *Economic Report 1995* (La Habana: Banco Nacional de Cuba, May 1996).

7. Beginning in the early 1960s and through about 1992, Cuban economic statistics followed the Material Product System (MPS) of National Accounts, the economic accounting system used by countries with centrally planned economies. With the disappearance of socialist, centrally planned regimes, the MPS has become disused and most countries of the world—including Cuba—have turned to the System of National Accounts (SNA), the economic accounting system used by market economies. The Global Social Product (GSP) is the broadest measure of an economy's output under the MPS; the corresponding measures under the SNA are Gross National Product (GNP) or Gross Domestic Product (GDP). GSP and GNP/GDP are not comparable. GSP consists of the value of goods and "material" services generated by the productive sphere of the economy in a given time frame. Moreover, GSP is a gross output concept, subject to double-counting because the cost of inputs is not deducted from final output, as is done in GNP/GDP. Also unlike GNP/GDP, GSP *does not* include the value of production of "nonmaterial" services such as education, housing, health services, culture and art, and defense and administration. For additional information on the two national product accounting system see Carmelo Mesa-Lago and Jorge Pérez-López, *A Study of Cuba's Material Product System, Its Conversion to the System of National Accounts, and Estimation of Gross Domestic Product per Capita and Growth Rates*, Staff Working Paper 770 (Washington: World Bank, 1985), Appendix A.

8. Ministerio de Economía y Planificación, *Cuba: Informe económico, año 1997*, undated.

9. Comisión Económica para América Latina y el Caribe, *La economía cubana: Reformas estructurales y desempeño en los noventa* (México: Fondo de Cultura Económica, 1997).

10. The GDP series published in CEPAL, *La economía cubana*, p. 352, yields a decline in GDP during 1989-93 of 31.6 percent.

Table 1. Gross Domestic Product (GDP), by Economic Activity
(in million pesos at 1981 prices)

	1989	1990	1991	1992	1993	1994	1995
Gross domestic product	19586	19008	16976	15010	12777	12868	13185
Agriculture, hunting, forestry, and fishing	1925	1756	1335	1197	925	879	916
Mining and quarrying	123	92	82	106	96	98	152
Manufacturing industries	4887	4640	4200	3507	3104	3341	3555
Electricity, gas, and water	452	455	427	378	335	350	384
Construction	1350	1508	1085	604	386	384	412
Trade, restaurants, and hotels	5151	4936	4396	4050	2936	2935	2985
Transport, warehousing, and communications	1353	1202	1059	912	733	709	748
Finance, real estate, and business services	585	603	639	544	513	492	484
Community, social, and personal services	3762	3816	3753	3713	3748	3681	3548

Source: Banco Nacional de Cuba, *Economic Report 1994* (La Habana, August 1995), Appendix A and Banco Nacional de Cuba, *Informe económico 1995* (La Habana, May 1996), Appendix A.

tion in GDP is smaller than the 48 percent decline reported earlier by the Cuban media, presumably also based on official statistics.[11] The larger contraction is also consistent with estimates of reductions in GSP or in GDP over the period 1989-93 estimated by economists inside and outside the island.[12]

According to official statistics, GDP grew by 0.7 percent in 1994, 2.5 percent in 1995, 7.8 percent in 1996 and 2.5 percent in 1997. As has become the practice in the 1990s, Cuba has not provided detailed statistics to support the growth rates reported for 1996 or 1997. Experts on the Cuban economy have raised fundamental questions about the reliability of Cuban economic statistics for 1996 and, by extension, about those for other recent years and about the Cuban system of national accounts at large.[13] Taking the official statistics at face value, the cumulative growth rate over the period 1993-97 is 14.1 percent, following a contraction of GDP of at least one-third and perhaps even one-half between 1989 and 1993.

Economic growth had slowed down during the 1980s, before the external sector shocks took their toll in 1990-91, consistent with the "exhaustion" of the central planning model experienced by other socialist countries. While growth rates averaged 7.2 percent per annum during 1981-85, they fell sharply in the second half of the 1980s, during the so-called "rectification process,"[14] when growth rates of 1.2

11. Ariel Terrero, "Tendencias de un ajuste," *Bohemia* (28 October 1994). According to this source, GDP in 1993 was 10 billion pesos, 48 percent lower than the 19.3 billion pesos recorded in 1989.

12. For example, Cuban economist Carranza estimated that GSP fell by 3.6 percent in 1990, 24 percent in 1991, and 15 percent in 1992, for a cumulative decline of about 38 percent over the three-year period 1989-92. See Julio Carranza, "Cuba: Los retos de la economía," *Cuadernos de Nuestra América* 9:19 (July-December 1992), p. 142. Relying on different sources of information, Pastor and Zimbalist have estimated that GDP fell in 1990 by 3.1 percent, in 1991 by 25.0 percent, in 1992 by 14 percent, and in 1993 by 20 percent, for a cumulative fall over the four-year period 1989-93 of 50.2 percent. See Manuel Pastor and Andrew Zimbalist, "Waiting for Change: Adjustment and Reform in Cuba," *World Development* 23:5 (May 1995), p. 708.

13. See, e.g., Marta Beatriz Roque Cabello and Arnaldo Ramos Lauzurique, "PIB (Producto Interno Bruto)," in *Documentos del Instituto de Economistas Independientes* (Miami: Cuban Studies Association, 1997), pp. 1-5; and Carmelo Mesa-Lago, ¿Recuperación económica en Cuba?, *Encuentro de la Cultura Cubana*, no. 3 (Winter 1996/97), pp. 54-61.

14. The "rectification process" (*proceso de rectificación de errores y tendencias negativas*) was an ideological campaign launched by President Castro in mid-1986 which resulted in the elimination of incipient market-oriented mechanisms (e.g., farmers' free markets) and greater centralization of economic decisionmaking in the hands of the state. See, e.g., Carmelo Mesa-Lago, "Cuba's Economic Counterreform (*rectificación*): Causes, Policies and Effects," *Journal of Communist Studies* 5:4 (December 1989); Jorge F. Pérez-López, "Rectification at Three: Impact on the Cuban Economy," *Studies in Comparative International Development* 25 (Fall 1990); and Pérez-López, "The Cuban Economy: Rectification in a Changing World," *Cambridge Journal of Economics* 16:1 (March 1992).

percent in 1986, -3.9 percent in 1987, 2.2 percent in 1988, and 1.1 percent in 1989 were recorded.[15]

State Budget

During the crisis, the nation's budget deficit nearly tripled, rising from 1.4 billion pesos in 1989 to nearly 5.1 billion pesos in 1993.[16] In the latter year, the budget deficit amounted to over 30 percent of GDP. Shortages of consumer products in the state distribution system, coupled with low (officially set) prices for basic consumption goods, the lack of a tax system, and government policy of continuing to pay a portion (60 percent) of salaries to idle workers, led to a sharp rise of monetary balances in the hands of the population. These balances grew from about 4 billion pesos in 1989 to 11.4 billion pesos in 1993.[17]

As part of a stabilization program instituted in 1993, government revenues were increased and expenditures cut, sharply reducing the government budget deficit to the pre-crisis level of about 1.0 billion pesos in 1994, 480 million pesos in 1995, and 360 million pesos in 1996;[18] in 1997, the deficit climbed to about 450 million pesos.[19] Meanwhile, monetary balances in the hands of the population declined to 9.9 billion pesos in 1994 and 9.3 billion pesos in 1995, rose to 9.5 billion pesos in 1996 and fell to 9.4 billion pesos in 1997.

Key Economic Sectors

The economic crisis of the 1990s affected nearly all sectors of the economy. While overall GDP fell by 34.8 percent during 1989-93 according to official statistics, the performance of several key sectors of the economy was worse: output of the construction sector fell by 71.4 percent, agriculture by 51.9 percent, transportation by 45.8 percent, commerce by 43.0 percent, and manufacturing by 36.5 percent. The downturn of the construction industry was attributed to a sharp contraction in domestic investment and shortages of construction materials, while non-sugar agriculture was adversely affected by the lack of imported inputs (e.g., fertilizers, pesticides, spare parts for machinery) and of manpower to cultivate the land and harvest crops. Sugar production, still the mainstay of the economy and the most significant source of export revenue in the early 1990s, fell from 7.3 million tons in 1989 to 4.1 million tons in 1993, or by 43.8 percent, contributing to the decline in the manufacturing sector, while nickel production declined by 35.2 percent.

Two bright spots for the Cuban economy during the gloomy 1989-93 period were the oil and tourism industries. Domestic oil production for the first time exceeded 1 million metric tons in 1993.[20] Between 1989 and 1993, the number of international tourists visiting the island doubled (from 300,000 to 600,000 persons) and gross income increased more than four-fold (from 166 to 720 million pesos).

The slight recovery registered in 1994 was reportedly fueled by sharp growth in the manufacturing sector (7.6 percent) and in the electricity industry (4.4 percent). For 1995, Cuba reported a growth rate of 2.5 percent, led by increases in the mining (56 percent), construction (7.7 percent) and manufacturing (6.4 percent) sectors. Unfortunately, the requisite data

---

15. Calculated from Cuban official statistics in *Anuario Estadístico de Cuba 1989*, p. 85. Growth rates calculated on the basis of GSP at constant prices of 1981.

16. Banco Nacional de Cuba, *Economic Report 1994*, p. 16.

17. Banco Nacional de Cuba, *Economic Report 1994*, p. 14.

18. CEPAL, *La economía cubana*, Table A-9.

19. *Cuba: Informe económico, año 1997*, p. 7.

20. Banco Nacional de Cuba, *Economic Report 1994*, p. 8. Despite this increase, domestically-produced oil still accounted for less than one-fifth of the depressed oil consumption level of about 5 million metric tons. Apparent consumption of oil and oil products was in the range of 10-12 million metric tons per annum in the late 1980s. See Jorge F. Pérez-López, "Cuba's Transition to Market-Based Energy Prices," *The Energy Journal* 13:4 (1992).

and information on methodology to confirm aggregate growth trends are not available.[21] Fragmentary data that are available raise some questions. For example, the strong growth of the manufacturing sector in 1994 and 1995 suggested by the official statistics is incongruent with the poor performance of the sugar industry, an industry with a very large weight within the manufacturing sector: in 1994, sugar production was 3.9 million tons, 4.9 percent lower than in 1993, and in 1995 it reached only 3.3 million tons, the lowest output in 50 years.[22]

Thus far, Cuba has officially released only a handful of economic statistics for 1996 and 1997. Minister of Economy and Planning José Luis Rodríguez informed the National Assembly in December 1996 that the national product had grown by 7.8 percent in that year, highlighting a recovery in sugar production (to 4.45 million tons, a 35 percent increase over the disastrous 1995 level), an all-time-high production level of nickel, nearly 1 million foreign tourists who generated 1 billion pesos in tourist receipts, and sizable gains in output in agriculture (17.3 percent), manufacturing (7 percent) and construction (30.8 percent). Sugar production in 1997 (actually, the 1996-97 *zafra*) has been reported at 4.2 million metric tons, a 6.7 decline from a year earlier, the number of foreign tourists at 1.1 million and tourism receipts at 850 million. Manufacturing output in 1997 reportedly rose by 7.7 percent, construction by 4.8 percent, forestry by 13.6 percent and transportation by 4.6 percent.[23]

THE EXTERNAL SECTOR IN THE 1980s[24]

Beginning in the early 1960s, and through around 1990, Cuba's external sector was segmented into two parts: economic relations with the socialist world, conducted within the framework of the Council for Mutual Economic Assistance (CMEA), and economic relations with market economies, mainly Western European nations, Canada and Japan and some key developing countries, conducted on commercial terms. Economic relations with the socialist countries were by far the more significant quantitatively; relations with market economies, although quantitatively small, were strategically significant as they afforded Cuba the possibility to import goods and services and obtain technology not available from the socialist camp.

Socialist Cuba began to publish balance of payments (BOP) statistics in the 1990s. During the 1980s, Cuba published BOP statistics for its hard currency accounts in a series of reports that were issued from 1982 forward by the Cuban National Bank to support renegotiation of the hard currency debt.[25] These partial BOP statistics are of very limited value since hard currency transactions accounted for a small share of overall economic activity in Cuba during the 1980s. The lack of comprehensive BOP statistics means that there are no data on important components of the external sector, such as trade in services, transfers and capital flows.

Economic Relations with Socialist Nations

Cuba's economic relations with the Soviet Union and the socialist countries were based on a web of bilateral agreements covering merchandise trade, payments, credits and technical assistance. During the period 1961-69 alone, Cuba concluded over 400 bilateral agreements with socialist countries. To coordinate the burgeoning economic and scientific-techni-

21. For example, detailed physical output data, product prices adjusted for inflation, relative importance of each product within a sector and within the economy at large, methodology for incorporating non-state sector activities into national product aggregates are not available.

22. "Zafra de Cuba es la más baja en 50 años, según cifra oficial," *El Nuevo Herald* (19 June 1995), p. 1B.

23. *Cuba: Informe económico, año 1997*, p. 2.

24. This section of the paper draws liberally from Jorge F. Pérez-López, "Cuba's Foreign Economic Relationships," pp. 311-352 in Georges Fauriol and Eva Loser, editors, *Cuba: The International Dimension* (New Brunswick: Transaction Publishers 1990).

25. Banco Nacional de Cuba, *Economic Report* (La Habana, February 1982) and similar reports issued in March 1984 and February 1985. Beginning in December 1982 and lasting through about mid-1990, the BNC also issued a *Quarterly Economic Report* and its Spanish version, *Informe económico trimestral*.

cal assistance relationship, several government-to-government commissions were established in the 1960s and 1970s with East Germany (in 1964), Bulgaria and Czechoslovakia (1965), Hungary (1966), Romania (1967), North Korea (1968), Poland (1969) and the Soviet Union (1970). Economic relations with the socialist countries deepened after 1972, when Cuba became a member of the CMEA, the organization that coordinated trade and economic relations among the socialist countries.

The bulk of Cuba's trade with the socialist countries was conducted through bilateral balancing agreements—tantamount to barter arrangements—in which individual transactions were made, and accounts settled, using either the currency of one of the two trading partners or "transferable rubles," an artificial currency whose sole role was to serve as the unit of account in transactions among socialist countries. Because neither the currencies of the socialist countries nor the transferable ruble could be freely converted into "hard" currencies (e.g., dollars, Swiss francs, deutsche marks) to purchase goods and services in international markets, socialist nations endeavored to balance trade bilaterally each year. To the extent that bilateral trade was not balanced annually, the gap was covered by "soft" currency (transferable ruble) credits.

In the 1960s, the Soviet Union began to purchase Cuban sugar at prices that were fixed for several years (typically five years). Because world market prices for sugar fluctuated—sometimes exceeding, but more often falling below the contracted price—the arrangement on the whole favored Cuba. In December 1972, Cuba and the Soviet Union signed two agreements that formalized a system of preferential (i.e., higher than world market) prices for Cuban sugar and nickel exports. In the aftermath of very high world market prices for sugar in 1974 and 1975, the contract price for Cuban sugar exports to the Soviet Union and other CMEA nations was renegotiated and adjusted upward. In 1975, Cuba and the Soviet Union agreed to a mechanism whereby sugar export prices were adjusted annually, above a very high floor, in proportion to changes in the prices of a basket of commodities Cuba imported from the Soviet

Union. As a result of this indexing scheme, henceforth the price of Cuban sugar exports to the Soviet Union consistently exceeded the world market price by a considerable margin. Cuba also negotiated agreements with East Germany, Bulgaria, Czechoslovakia, Hungary, Poland and Romania which granted preferential prices to Cuban sugar exports.

In addition, Cuba benefitted in the 1970s and first half of the 1980s from pricing arrangements in intra-CMEA trade that held down the price of oil below the world market price. Because the Soviet Union relied first on fixed prices and later on a five-year moving average of world market prices to set the price of oil it exported to its CMEA partners, world market price increases were passed on to importers—including to Cuba—with a significant time lag. These pricing schemes insulated Cuba from the sharp increases in the world market price of oil that affected importing countries throughout the 1970s and early 1980s. The moving average mechanism turned against Cuba in the second half of the 1980s as world market prices for oil fell while intra-CMEA oil prices—which reflected earlier price increases—continued to climb.

Economic Relations with Market Economies

Cuban trade with developed market economies and with many developing countries was conducted following common commercial practices and using hard currencies. Cuba earned hard currencies through the sale of its exports (especially sugar) and used such earnings to finance imports from hard currency areas. On occasion, Western governments, financial institutions or suppliers provided hard currency credits to Cuba to finance imports; these interest-bearing credits were repayable in hard currencies subject to a predetermined schedule. Because of currency inconvertibility, Cuba could not apply surpluses in trade with the socialist countries to offset deficits with developed market economies or to service debt with these nations.

In conclusion, Cuba's external accounts were segmented: soft currency accounts which covered most of the commercial and financial relations with the socialist nations, and hard currency accounts which ap-

Table 2. **Distribution of Cuban Merchandise Trade by Groups of Partner Countries**
(Percentages)

	1983	1984	1985	1986	1987	1988	1989
Exports	100.0	100.0	100.0	100.0	100.0	100.0	100.0
Soviet Union and Eastern Europe	81.6	85.4	86.0	86.9	83.4	81.8	75.3
Other socialist countries	4.5	4.2	3.0	1.4	5.4	4.5	4.4
Capitalist countries	8.8	6.9	8.2	8.7	8.4	10.5	13.5
Developing countries	5.1	3.5	2.8	3.0	2.8	3.2	6.8
Imports	100.0	100.0	100.0	100.0	100.0	100.0	100.0
Soviet Union and Eastern Europe	83.9	79.9	80.5	82.5	86.8	84.6	80.9
Other socialist countries	3.1	4.1	3.8	2.3	1.0	2.8	4.5
Capitalist countries	10.1	12.1	11.3	11.7	8.3	7.9	8.2
Developing countries	2.9	3.9	4.4	3.5	3.9	4.7	6.5

Eastern Europe: Bulgaria, Czechoslovakia, East Germany, Hungary, Poland and Romania. Other socialist countries: China, North Korea, Vietnam, Mongolia, Yugoslavia, Albania.

Source: 1987-89—*Anuario Estadístico de Cuba 1989*; 1986--*Anuario Estadístico de Cuba 1986*; 1983-85—*Anuario Estadístico de Cuba 1985*.

plied to economic relations with the rest of the world. The soft currency accounts dominated: over the period 1978-85, for example, Cuba sold 76 percent of its exports and purchased 83 percent of its imports using soft currencies.

Merchandise Trade

From 1962 to 1974, Cuba's merchandise trade turnover—the sum of merchandise exports and imports—averaged 24 percent of GSP; in 1985-89 it averaged 50 percent,[26] evidencing greater openness of the economy and a greater influence of trade. Since the early 1960s, the Soviet Union and the other socialist countries accounted for the bulk of Cuba's trade, far outstripping trade with capitalist countries and with developing countries. Over the period 1983-89, the socialist countries members of the CMEA (the Soviet Union, Bulgaria, Czechoslovakia, East Germany, Hungary, Poland and Romania) accounted on average for 82.9 percent of Cuba's exports and absorbed 82.7 percent of Cuba's imports; other socialist countries (China, North Korea, Vietnam, Mongolia, Yugoslavia, Albania) for 3.9 percent of exports and 3.1 percent of imports; capitalist countries for 9.3 percent of exports and 9.9 percent of imports; and developing countries for 6.8 percent of exports and 6.5 percent of imports (Table 2).

Merchandise trade deficits set records in the 1980s, as Cuba's imports rose at a much faster rate than exports. The deficit rose from 660 million pesos in 1980 to 2.0 billion in 1985; in 1989, the deficit recorded an all-time record high when it reached over 2.7 billion pesos. Table 3 shows data on merchandise exports and imports and deficits for selected years over the period 1965-89. Also shown in the table are corresponding data for Cuban-Soviet bilateral trade. The two series show similar trends for growth of the deficit, with the exception of 1975, when Cuba actually recorded a positive merchandise trade balance with the Soviet Union. The percentage of the overall trade deficit incurred with the Soviet Union rose steadily in the second half of the 1980s, from about 50 percent in 1984-85 to over 80 percent in 1988-89. These huge deficits in bilateral trade were routinely financed through transferable ruble credits issued by the Soviet Union.

Price Subsidies

The large trade deficits with the Soviet Union are the more remarkable given the very favorable terms of trade for Cuba's main exports (sugar and nickel) and imports (oil). The socialist practice of fixing commodity prices for multiyear periods (typically the five-year period covered by a plan) eliminated international commodity price fluctuations. They also re-

---

26. Carmelo Mesa-Lago, "The Economic Effects on Cuba of the Downfall of Socialism in the USSR and Eastern Europe," in Mesa-Lago, editor, *Cuba After the Cold War* (Pittsburgh: University of Pittsburgh Press, 1993), p. 138.

Table 3. Cuban Merchandise Trade: Soviet Union and All Countries
(In million pesos)

	1965	1970	1975	1980	1984	1985	1986	1987	1988	1989
Soviet Union										
Exports	332.5	529.0	1661.9	2253.5	3952.2	4481.6	3935.9	3868.7	3683.1	3231.2
Imports	428.4	690.6	1250.2	2903.7	4782.4	5418.9	5337.7	5446.0	5364.4	5522.4
Deficit	-95.9	-161.6	411.7	-650.2	-830.2	-937.3	-1401.8	-1577.3	-1681.3	-2291.3
All Countries										
Exports	690.6	1049.5	2952.2	3966.7	5476.5	5991.5	5321.5	5402.1	5518.3	5342.0
Imports	866.2	1311.0	3113.1	4627.0	7227.5	8035.0	7596.1	7583.6	7579.8	8124.2
Deficit	-175.6	-261.5	-160.9	-660.3	-1751.0	-2043.5	-2274.6	-2181.5	-2061.5	-2732.2
% Deficit with Soviet Union / Overall Deficit	54.6	61.8	--	98.5	47.4	45.9	61.6	72.3	81.6	83.9

Source: Comité Estatal de Estadísticas, *Anuario Estadístico de Cuba 1989*.

sulted in transfers from one country to the other (nonrepayable subsidies) whenever intra-CMEA prices diverged from world market prices.

For sugar, the agreement reached with the Soviet Union in 1975 that set a very high minimum price for Cuban sugar exports (500 rubles/ton or about 30.4 cents/pound), adjusted upward annually in step with changes in the prices of Cuban imports from the Soviet Union, resulted in huge gains for Cuba. In 1986, for example, the contract price for Cuban sugar exports to the Soviet Union was reported as 50.6 cents/pound; Cuban official statistics show an average export price (unit value) of 47.56 cents/pound, while Soviet official statistics show an average import price (unit value) of 51.57 cents/pound. In that same year, the world market price for sugar was 6.05 cents/pound, and the average price (unit value) of Cuban sugar exports to market economies was 6.77 cents/pound.[27] Cuba also benefitted from preferential prices for nickel exports: beginning in the 1970s, the price of nickel was set for five-year intervals, but it was raised whenever the world market price exceeded by a substantial margin this threshold. In 1981-84, for example, Cuba greatly benefitted from the Soviet concessionary prices for nickel imports, which were more than twice the world market price.[28]

The Soviet Union became revolutionary Cuba's virtual sole supplier of oil and oil products in 1960, on the heels of the Cuban government's takeover of the refineries operated by the multinational oil companies. The price of Soviet oil exports, like the prices of other basic commodities traded by the socialist countries among themselves, was fixed for a five-year period, purportedly to avoid fluctuations in capitalist world markets. Because of this arrangement, Cuba was spared the shock associated with the quadrupling of world oil market prices that occurred in 1973 and additional price increases in 1974. In 1975, however, the Soviet Union began to adjust prices of oil exports to its CMEA allies annually, based on a moving average of world market prices in the previous five years. Throughout the 1970s and early 1980s, as oil world market prices rose, Cuba benefitted from this arrangement. However, as oil world market prices fell in the mid-1980s, the arrangement worked to Cuba's disadvantage, with the island paying prices in the late 1980s for Soviet oil that were above the world market price.[29] Over the entire period 1960-90, however, the oil price supply arrangements with the Soviet Union resulted in net gains for Cuba.

Another oil trade arrangement between the Soviet Union and Cuba that benefitted Cuba was the ability to reexport Soviet oil to buyers willing to pay with

---

27. For full information on the sources of these data see Jorge F. Pérez-López, *The Economics of Cuban Sugar* (Pittsburgh: University of Pittsburgh Press, 1991), pp. 140-141.

28. Carmelo Mesa-Lago and Fernando Gil, "Soviet Economic Relations with Cuba," in Eusebio Mujal-León, editor, *The USSR and Latin America: A Developing Relationship* (Boston: Unwin Hyman, Inc., 1989), p. 201.

29. Pérez-López, "Cuba's Transition to Market-Based Energy Prices," p. 22.

Table 4. Soviet Economic Aid to Cuba, 1960-90
(In million U.S. dollars)

| | Repayable Loans (Debt) | | | Nonrepayable | |
	Trade Deficit	Development	Total	Price Subsidies	Total Aid
1960-70	2083	344	2427	1131	3558
1971-75	1649	749	2398	1143	3541
1976-80	1115	1872	2987	11228	14215
1981-85	4046	2266	6312	15760	22072
1986-90	8205	3400	11605	10128	21733
Total (1960-90)	17098	8631	25729	39390	65119

Source: Carmelo Mesa-Lago, "The Economic Effects on Cuba of the Downfall of Socialism in the USSR and Eastern Europe," in Mesa-Lago, editor, *Cuba After the Cold War* (Pittsburgh: University of Pittsburgh Press, 1993), p. 148.

hard currency. In 1977, Cuba reexported over 900,000 metric tons of oil obtained from the Soviet Union; volume of reexported oil rose to 2 million tons in 1982 and peaked at 3.7 million tons in 1986. The significance of these exports for the Cuban economy should not be underestimated. In 1986 and 1987, oil reexports overtook sugar as Cuba's most significant hard currency export earner, contributing 27 and 30 percent, respectively, of hard currency earnings in those two years.[30]

Development Assistance

The socialist countries were the source of nearly all of the development finance received by revolutionary Cuba. There are no systematic data on development assistance to Cuba, but scattered information suggests that such aid was substantial, originated primarily from the Soviet Union, covered a wide swath of economic activities and took mostly the form of repayable loans at very low interest rates.[31]

According to Cuban sources, during the period 1981-85, the Soviet Union provided the island with 1.8 billion rubles in development assistance (mostly loans), while the Eastern European socialist countries granted about 1 billion rubles and the CMEA another 1 billion rubles in multilateral assistance.[32] Up through 1986, the Soviet Union had assisted Cuba in completing 360 development projects, and 289 others were in progress.[33] Enterprises built with Soviet assistance were responsible for 15 percent of the nation's gross industrial output, 100 percent of steel plates, 90 percent of steel products, 50 percent of mixed fertilizers, 70 percent of nitrogen fertilizers, 70 percent of electricity, 50 percent of the products of the metalworking industry, 100 percent of the repair of Soviet vehicles, and 65 percent of textiles.[34]

According to Mesa-Lago's estimates (Table 4), the Soviet Union extended to Cuba assistance amounting to more than $65 billion during the period 1960-90; about 67 percent of this aid was extended in the 1980s. Approximately 40 percent of the assistance (about $25.7 billion) took the form of repayable loans—credits to finance trade deficits (27 percent) and development credits (13 percent)—and about 60 percent ($39.4 billion) was in the form of nonrepayable price subsidies.

Hard Currency Debt

During the first two decades of revolutionary government, Cuba banned foreign investment. In 1982,

30. See Jorge F. Pérez-López, "Cuban Oil Reexports: Significance and Prospects," *The Energy Journal* 8 (1987) and Pérez-López, "Cuba's Transition to Market-Based Energy Prices," p. 27.

31. For further elaboration on this subject see Jorge F. Pérez-López, "Swimming Against the Tide: Implications for Cuba of Soviet and Eastern European Reforms in Foreign Relations," *Journal of Interamerican Studies and World Affairs* 33:2 (Summer 1991), pp. 98-100.

32. Ernesto Meléndez Bachs, "Relaciones económicas de Cuba con el CAME," *América Latina* (Moscow), no. 7 (1987), pp. 95-96.

33. José Luis Rodríguez, "Las relaciones económicas entre Cuba y los países socialistas: Situación actual y perspectivas," mimeo (1989).

34. A. Bekarevich, "Cuba y el CAME: El camino de la integración," in Academia de Ciencias de la URSS, *Cuba: 25 años de construcción del socialismo* (Moscú: Redacción Ciencias Sociales Contemporáneas, 1986), p. 98.

however, Cuba passed a law that for the first time allowed foreign investors from capitalist countries to operate in the island by joint venturing with domestic entities. Foreign investors evidently did not find the Cuban investment climate to be conducive to their activities, as the law attracted only one foreign investor during the 1980s.[35]

Thus, hard currency capital flows into the island during the period 1960-90 consisted primarily of loans from private and public institutions and supplier credits. In 1969, Cuba's hard currency debt was small, amounting to $291 million; it grew rapidly in the 1970s, reaching over $1.3 billion in 1975 and nearly $3.3 billion in 1979 as Cuba borrowed heavily from commercial banks flush with "petrodollars" and official lenders willing to back sales of machinery and equipment to the island.[36] In 1982, a sharp reduction in short term loans and deposits prompted Cuba to seek to reschedule its hard currency debt due in 1982-85. Cuba was successful in getting some short term relief, but a sharp deterioration in the balance of payments in 1985 led to Cuba's decision to suspend payment on the hard currency effective July 1, 1986. The unpaid debt and accrued service payments amounted to nearly $6.1 billion in 1987, $6.5 billion in 1988 and $6.2 billion in 1989.[37]

EXTERNAL SECTOR POLICIES

In the second half of the 1980s, while the Soviet Union under Gorbachev and Eastern European countries accelerated the pace of market-oriented reforms to their economies and to their systems of foreign economic relations, Cuba was engaged in a national campaign to dismantle its few market-oriented mechanisms and enhance the role of the state in the economy through the "rectification process." Thus,

Cuba was ill prepared to react to the economic crisis of the 1990s. Moreover, the Cuban leadership was slow to react to the crisis and, when it did, it mustered mostly defensive measures.

Even after the communist regime in Poland had collapsed and been replaced by Solidarity and East Germany had disappeared by virtue of its reunification with West Germany, Cuba continued to argue for maintaining the preferential trade relations it had enjoyed with CMEA nations. At the January 1990 meeting of the CMEA, the Soviet Union proposed that, effective 1 January 1991, trade among member countries be conducted on the basis of market prices and hard currencies. The Cuban representative (then-Vice President Carlos Rafael Rodríguez) took issue with the proposal, arguing that the proposed changes would (1) restore the "production anarchy" associated with markets; and (2) result in unfair terms of trade for developing countries. Rodríguez demanded the continuation of special and differential trade treatment (via preferential prices) for Mongolia, Cuba and Vietnam, so that these countries could reach the same level of development of the Soviet Union and Eastern Europe.[38] Not only were Cuba's arguments ignored, but the CMEA itself was dissolved a few months later.

The Cuban leadership's initial approach to deal with the economic crisis was reactive. In August 1990, facing a severe energy shortage prompted by a slowdown of shipments of Soviet oil, the Cuban government announced the first of several austerity measures, decreeing drastic cutbacks in energy consumption, reallocation of resources from idle sectors into agriculture and a shift to labor-intensive agricultural techniques. In September, President Castro for-

---

35. For a description of the law and the investment climate in the 1980s see Jorge F. Pérez-López, *The 1982 Cuban Joint Venture Law: Context, Assessment and Prospects* (Coral Gables: North-South Center, University of Miami, July 1985).

36. The discussion on hard currency debt draws heavily from A.R.M. Ritter, "Cuba's convertible currency debt problem," *CEPAL Review* 36 (December 1988).

37. This information originates from various issues of the Banco Nacional de Cuba, *Quarterly Economic Report*. It should be noted that some of the year to year fluctuation in the value of the debt is a function of changes in the exchange rates between the U.S. dollar and other hard currencies.

38. Carlos Rafael Rodríguez, "Discurso pronunciado en la sesión XLV del CAME, Sofía, Bulgaria, 9 de enero de 1990," *Granma* (10 January 1990), p. 4.

mally announced that the "special period" had begun as shortages of imported raw materials, spare parts and foodstuffs took their toll on all areas of the economy. Cuba also attempted to negotiate follow-up trade arrangements with the former CMEA countries in order to restore basic levels of imports and sought new markets in Europe and Latin America for its exports and sources of supply for imports.

IV Communist Party Congress

In the midst of a deteriorating economic situation and uncertainty about the future of international socialism, Cuba postponed the IV Congress of the Cuban Communist Party, scheduled to be held at the end of 1990. By the time the Party met in October 1991, the international outlook had changed significantly—and for the worse—for Cuba: the international socialist community had virtually disappeared and there was no longer a socialist bloc to turn to for moral and material support. Even the fraternal and all-powerful Communist Party of the Soviet Union had ceased to exist for all practical purposes: in March 1990 it had lost its "leading role" in Soviet society and its activities had been suspended in the aftermath of the August 1991 coup.

The hope of reformists that the IV Congress of the Cuban Communist Party would adopt concrete steps to begin a genuine process of democratization and economic liberalization on the island were dashed by the hard-line stance taken by President Castro and the Party leadership. The rhetoric and substance of President Fidel Castro's central report and conclusions at the Party Congress were unyielding: Cuba would hold the line and remain a bastion of socialism regardless of the economic sacrifices that this would require.[39] As he stated in his concluding remarks, "only within socialism can there be democracy, and only within socialism can democracy be perfected. We have worked for these objectives, and we will

continue to do so without the most minimal concession of principles either by the Party or by the State."[40]

In the same remarks, President Castro admitted that the Party did not have a blueprint to overcome the economic crisis. He stated:

> Under the direction of the revolution and the socialist government, we will adopt the necessary measures to ensure that our factories operate, our workers work, and we overcome the present difficult conditions, following the principle of protecting everyone, so that not a single citizen is unprotected in our country. We will distribute [to the population] all that we have. We will search for formulas to save the homeland, to save the revolution, to save socialism.[41]

The economic strategy adopted by the Congress in its "Resolution on Economic Development" had several strands:

- a program of import substitution, centered on a food production program *(programa alimentario)* aimed at achieving self-sufficiency in foodstuffs;

- across-the-board energy substitution measures, including replacing oil-consuming machinery and equipment with animal (oxen) and human (bicycles) power, as well as cutting back output in oil-intensive lines of production (e.g., nickel, cement);

- a major effort at export promotion, including seeking new markets for traditional exports (especially sugar), and the development of new lines of exports that would generate hard currency, in particular biotechnology products and tourism;

- greater efforts to attract foreign investment;

- some management reforms to increase efficiency and productivity; and

---

39. The two addresses were published for mass distribution under the title *Independientes hasta siempre*. See Fidel Castro, *Independientes hasta siempre: Discursos de inauguración y en el acto de masas, IV Congreso del Partido Comunista de Cuba, Santiago de Cuba, 10 y 14 de octubre de 1991* (La Habana: Editora Política, 1991).

40. Castro, *Independientes hasta siempre*, p. 67.

41. Castro, *Independientes hasta siempre*, p. 69.

• toleration of a higher degree of decentralization, autonomy and improvisation in enterprise management.[42]

The shortcomings of the development strategy, which avoided structural changes to the economy, were most evident with regard to the food program. Despite the importance attached to it by the leadership—for example, Vice President Carlos Lage stated in November 1992 that "the food program is the fundamental priority because the basic objective of the Party and Government during the Special Period is to guarantee food to the population at present levels"—results were disappointing, in large part because the program was grafted onto an economic model that did not promote efficiency.[43] Moreover, the continuing deterioration of import capacity prevented the assignment of adequate resources to the food program. Several of its crucial elements—construction of new dams and irrigation systems, formation of worker brigades, creation of new towns—were halted and essential imported inputs, such as fertilizers, herbicides and fungicides, fuel and spare parts for agricultural machinery, were not delivered, dooming it.[44]

Economic Reforms

In the summer of 1993, as the economic situation worsened, the Cuban government instituted a number of economic reform measures that sought to revitalize the economy and introduce some macroeconomic stability. Additional measures were introduced in the summer of 1994 and a few others 1995-97. Arguably, every reform measure instituted by the Cuban government has some effect on the external sector. This is not the place to describe or analyze the full complement of reforms, particularly since there is already a fairly extensive literature on the subject.[45] The following measures implemented during 1993-97 tend to affect the external sector more directly than others:

Dollarization: In the summer of 1993, Cuba decriminalized the holding and use of hard currency by Cuban citizens.[46] The government also created special stores at which individuals holding hard currencies could shop for items not available to Cubans holding pesos and liberalized travel to the island by relatives and friends of Cuban citizens. The objective of these actions was to stimulate hard currency remittances from family and friends living abroad, mostly in the United States, and to provide a legal alternative to the very active black market.

Other complementary steps have been taken to accommodate the needs of citizens holding hard currencies. In September 1995, the Cuban National Bank for the first time began to accept hard currency

---

42. The "Resolution on Economic Development" adopted by the IV Congress is reproduced, e.g., in Gail Reed, editor, *Island in the Storm: The Cuban Communist Party's Fourth Congress* (Melbourne: Ocean Press, 1992), pp. 132-141. The articulation of the priority elements of the strategy given here is from Archibald R.M. Ritter, "Cuba's Economic Strategy and Alternative Futures," in Jorge Pérez-López, editor, *Cuba at a Crossroads: Politics and Economics After the Fourth Party Congress* (Gainesville: University Press of Florida, 1994), pp. 75-76. To some extent, the IV Congress merely ratified policies that had already been implemented since the beginning of the "special period."

43. Sergio Roca, "Reflections on Economic Policy: Cuba's Food Program," in Pérez-López, editor, *Cuba at a Crossroads: Politics and Economics After the Fourth Party Congress*, pp. 94-117. Lage is cited on p. 94.

44. Carmelo Mesa-Lago, *Are Economic Reforms Propelling Cuba to the Market?* (Coral Gables: North-South Center, University of Miami, 1994), p. 24.

45. For descriptions and/or analysis of reform measures in the 1990s see, e.g., Mesa-Lago, *Are Economic Reforms Propelling Cuba to the Market?*, especially pp. 13-56; Bert Hoffmann, editor, *Cuba: Apertura y reforma económica* (Caracas: Editorial Nueva Sociedad, 1995); Jorge Pérez-López, "Cuba's Socialist Economy Toward the Mid-1990s," *The Journal of Communist Studies and Transition Politics* 11:5 (June 1995); Rubén Berríos, "Cuba's Economic Restructuring, 1990-1995," *Communist Economies & Economic Transformation* 9:1 (1997); and Omar Everleny Pérez Villanueva, "Cuba's Economic Reforms: An Overview," in Jorge Pérez-López and Matías Travieso-Díaz, editors, *Perspectives on Cuban Economic Reforms* (Tempe: Center for Latin American Studies Press, Arizona State University, 1998).

46. "Decreto-Ley No. 140," *Gaceta Oficial* (August 13, 1993) and "Informa Banco Nacional de Cuba sobre uso de las monedas libremente convertibles," *Trabajadores* (August 15, 1993).

deposits from individuals and to pay interest on such deposits. And in mid-October 1995, the government created foreign currency exchange houses (*Casas de Cambio*, CADECA) at which Cuban citizens could exchange (buy and sell) hard currencies in exchange for pesos at rates close to those prevailing in the hard currency black market.[47]

Convertible Peso: In December 1994, Cuba announced the creation of a new currency, the convertible peso, that would gradually replace the U.S. dollar and other foreign currencies within the island.[48] The convertible peso, valued at par with the U.S. dollar, would eventually be the currency used in the tourism sector and in outlets authorized since mid-1993 to sell goods for foreign currencies. Incentive payments to workers of certain key industries that generate hard currency—e.g., tourism, oil extraction and tobacco—would henceforth be made in convertible pesos rather than in hard currencies, as had been the practice.

Foreign Investment: As mentioned above, Cuba first passed legislation allowing foreign investment in the island in 1982. This initiative generated very little interest among Western investors until the 1990s, when Cuba began an aggressive campaign to attract foreign investment. In 1992, Cuba's National Assembly passed several amendments to the 1976 Constitution clarifying the concept of private property and providing a legal basis for transferring state property to joint ventures established with foreign partners.[49]

One of the areas in which Cuba has been particularly active in seeking foreign investment has been mining. A new mining law, aimed at facilitating foreign investment in exploration and production of oil and minerals, was passed by the National Assembly in December 1994 and became effective in January 1995.[50]

In September 1995, the National Assembly adopted a new foreign investment law that codified the *de facto* rules under which joint ventures had been operating and introduced some minor innovations to the legal framework for foreign investment.[51] For example, pursuant to the new law, 100 percent foreign ownership of investments would be permitted, up from the 49 percent generally allowed by the earlier statute. The new law also simplified the process for screening incoming foreign investment, explicitly allowed foreign investments in real estate, and authorized the establishment of export processing zones.

Export Processing Zones: Complementing the September 1995 foreign investment law, in June 1996 the Council of State passed legislation creating export processing zones (*zonas francas y parques industriales*).[52] Regulations establishing an official registry of export processing zone operators and investors and issuing special customs regulations applicable to foreign investments locating in the zones were issued in October 1996.[53]

---

47. Larry Rohter, "Cuba Allowing Citizens to Buy and Sell Foreign Currencies," *The New York Times* (November 9, 1995), p. 3A; and "Casas de cambio aumentan compra de dólares," *El Nuevo Herald* (November 28, 1995), p. 1B.

48. "New Convertible Peso Announced," Havana Radio Reloj Network (December 20, 1994), as reproduced in *FBIS-LAT-94-245* (December 21, 1994), p. 5.

49. On changes to the 1982 foreign investment law in the area of property rights see Jorge F. Pérez-López, "Islands of Capitalism in an Ocean of Socialism: Joint Ventures in Cuba's Development Strategy," in Pérez-López, editor, *Cuba at a Crossroads*, pp. 193-4.

50. "Ley No. 76—Ley de Minas," *Gaceta Oficial* (January 23, 1995).

51. "Ley No. 77—Ley de Inversión Extranjera," *Gaceta Oficial* (September 6, 1995).

52. "Decreto-ley No. 165—Ley sobre Zonas Francas y Parques Industriales" (3 June 1996), www.prensa-latina.org.

53. Ministerio para la Inversión Extranjera y la Colaboración Económica, "Resolución No. 66/96—Sobre el Registro Oficial de Concesionarios y Operadores de Zona Franca" (24 October 1996), www.tips.cu; and Aduana General de la República, "Resolución No. 34/96—Sobre el Régimen Especial Aduanero en las Zonas Francas y Parques Industriales" (18 October 1996), www.tips.cu.

Financial Sector Reforms:[54] Since 1960, when the private banks were nationalized, the Cuban National Bank (*Banco Nacional de Cuba*, BNC) operated as both a central bank and a commercial bank. Under a centrally planned system, the BNC's main function was financing the implementation of the national economic plan as reflected in the national budget. In 1978, the BNC created a People's Savings Bank (*Banco Popular de Ahorro*, BPA) that for the first time allowed interest-bearing savings accounts, and in 1984, an International Financing Bank (*Banco Financiero Internacional, S.A.*, BFI) that operated solely with hard currencies; the BFI was the institution with which foreign investors interacted regarding their activities.

In response to the perception by foreign investors that the financial sector was not sufficiently developed and incapable of supporting their activities, in the 1990s Cuba has taken a number of steps. In 1994, Cuba granted a license to ING Bank of Holland to operate in the island, the first foreign bank to be so permitted since 1960. In 1995, similar licenses were issued to the Société Generále de France and to Banco Sabadell from Spain. Other foreign banks have also been allowed to establish representative offices in Cuba.

In order to expand the number of financial services available to foreign investors and semi-autonomous enterprises, the BNC created the New Banking Group (*Grupo Nueva Banca, S.A.*, GNB), a holding company for a network of new financial institutions which include an International Bank of Commerce (*Banco Internacional de Comercio, S.A.*, BICSA) similar to BFI, an export-import bank by the name of National Financier (*Financiera Nacional, S.A.*, FINSA), the already-mentioned CADEDA foreign exchange houses and an Investment Bank (*Banco de Inversiones, S.A.*).

Long-expected legislation to reform the banking system was finally passed by the Council of State in May 1997. Decree-Law 172 established the Cuban Central Bank (*Banco Central de Cuba*, BCC) as an autonomous and independent entity and assigned to it traditional central banking functions. The BNC, which as mentioned above had performed central and commercial banking functions since 1960, remained in existence, but its role was relegated to commercial banking. Decree-Law 173, passed at the same time, set out the legal framework for registration and operation of commercial banks and financial institutions under the supervision of the BCC.[55]

Decentralization of Foreign Trade: Cuba has decentralized some of its foreign trade activities. Prior to the 1990s, foreign trade was a state monopoly; Cuban foreign trade institutions mirrored those of the Soviet Union and Eastern European socialist nations. Export trade was conducted by specialized enterprises of the Ministry of Foreign Trade (*Ministerio del Comercio Exterior*); import trade was primarily the responsibility of the State Committee on Technical-Material Supply (*Comité Estatal de Abastecimiento Técnico-Material*).[56] Currently, organizations that produce goods and services are also permitted to import and export, with many working on the basis of hard-currency self-financing schemes.

V Communist Party Congress

Held in October 1997, coinciding with the 30th anniversary of the death of Ernesto Guevara in Bolivia, the V Congress of the Cuban Communist Party concentrated on ideology, short shrifting the gamut of other subjects that were normally discussed at these gatherings of the Party leadership. The "call" issued in April 1997 announcing the Congress presaged that no policy departures would be forthcoming. With regard to economic matters, the "call" stated:

---

54. This section relies heavily on Yosem E. Companys, "Institution-Building: Financial Sector Reform in Cuba," in *Cuba in Transition—Volume 7* (Washington: Association for the Study of the Cuban Economy, 1997), pp. 430-444.

55. "Central Bank of Cuba established," *Granma International Electronic Edition*, no. 25 (1977).

56. The State Committee on Technical-Material Supply was abolished by the reorganization of government functions of April 1994. See "Decreto-Ley No. 47—De la Reorganización de los Organismos de la Administración del Estado," *Gaceta Oficial* (21 April 1994).

The focus of our attention will continue to be economic efficiency, social justice and defense, which are inseparable parts of a whole and necessary for victory in the political battle and struggle of ideas. As our best salute to the 5th Congress, let us struggle for the development of the food program, lowering costs, achieving profitability in production and services, the best possible results in the current sugar harvest despite the difficult conditions which have emerged, optimum work in the planting and growing of sugarcane, construction and exploitation of tourist facilities, energy savings and generation, decreasing the amount of exports [sic] and substituting them with domestic products, an increase in exports, the application of a tax system and the improvement of internal finances.[57]

Meanwhile, the draft Party Platform, issued in May, stated that:

In the midst of innumerable difficulties, the country has managed in recent years to halt its economy's free-fall and has adopted the necessary measures for initiating its recovery and finding new markets and economic and trading partners. ... Today there will be no restoration of capitalism in Cuba because the revolution was never defeated. The country will continue intact and will continue to be socialist.[58]

Indeed, neither President Castro's kilometric central report[59] nor his closing remarks to the Congress[60] broke any new ground in terms of economic policy. In the closing remarks Castro did highlight the importance of overcoming the economic crisis:

Today, we must continue to be committed to the principle of "Homeland or Death." But in addition, we must become managers, good managers. A Party cadre at the level of a municipality, in addition to disseminating political doctrine, being in contact with the masses and other duties, must have sufficient knowledge to be able to ensure that all matters for which he is responsible are going well. This means that beans are more important than cannons. Today the economy is number one in importance, more so than ever during the special period, more so now that the blockade against the country has hardened, more so since we have to pay an additional 42 cents for each dollar that is loaned to us to buy fuel...[61]

EXTERNAL SECTOR PERFORMANCE DURING THE 1990s

How has the external sector performed during the economic crisis of the 1990s? Have the policy initiatives of the Cuban government—described in the previous section—been successful in improving the unbalances that characterized the external sector in the 1980s?

As mentioned above, Cuba published statistics for the hard currency portion of the BOP in the 1980s, but did not publish overall BOP statistics. The shift in Cuban external economic relations in the 1990s did away with the dichotomy in external accounts, eliminating the soft currency accounts. The BNC has recently published BOP statistics (in pesos, at the official rate of 1 peso=$1 U.S dollar) for 1993-95 that purport to cover all external economic relations (Table 5); CEPAL has done the same (in U.S. dollars)

---

57. "Call to the 5th Congress of the Communist Party of Cuba," *Granma International Electronic Edition*, no. 16 (April 1997).

58. "The Party of unity, democracy and the human rights we defend," *Granma International Electronic Edition*, no. 21 (June 1997).

59. The speech, which lasted more than 6 hours, was reportedly delivered extemporaneously by Castro, who chose not to present a written report, as had been done in the first three Party Congresses. According to observers, Castro had not delivered an extemporaneous speech of such length since the 1960s. See Pablo Alfonso, "Castro habla 6 horas al inaugurar congreso," *El Nuevo Herald* (9 October 1997), p. 6A. The text of the central report, as issued by the Cuban government, appears, e.g., as "Informe Central al V Congreso del Partido Comunista de Cuba, presentado por el Comandante en Jefe Fidel Castro Ruz, Primer Secretario del Comité Central del Partido Comunista de Cuba y Presidente de los Consejos de Estado y de Ministros, en el Palacio de las Convenciones, el día 8 de octubre de 1997," *Granma International Edición Digital*, no. 43 (November 1997).

60. "Discurso Pronunciado por el Comandante en Jefe Fidel Castro Ruz, Primer Secretario del Comité Central del Partido Comunista de Cuba y Presidente de los Consejos de Estado y de Ministros, en la Clausura del V Congreso del Partido Comunista de Cuba, efectuada en el Palacio de las Convenciones, el día 10 de octubre de 1997," *Granma International Edición Digital*, no. 43 (November 1997).

61. "Discurso ... en la Clausura del V Congreso del Partido Comunista de Cuba," *Granma International Edición Digital*, no. 43 (November 1997).

Table 5. Balance of Payments *(In million pesos)*

	1993	1994	1995ᵃ
Current account balance	-371.6	-260.2	-418.2
Exports of goods and services	1990.3	2552.8	2956.8
Exports (FOB)	1136.6	1381.4	1528.5
Nonfactor services	831.6	1160.4	1418.9
Factor services	22.1	11.0	9.4
Imports of goods and services	2624.8	3283.2	4021.2
Imports	1984.0	2352.8	2865.4
Nonfactor services	354.9	496.6	621.6
Factor services	285.9	433.8	534.2
Current transfers (net)	262.9	470.2	646.2
Capital account balance	356.1	262.4	496.7
Long-term capital (net)	118.4	817.4	24.2
Direct investment	54.0	563.4	4.7
Others	64.4	254.0	19.5
Other capital (net)	237.7	-555.0	472.5
Variation in reserves	15.5	-2.2	-78.5

Source: Banco Nacional de Cuba, *Economic Report 1994* (La Habana, August 1995), p. 20 and Banco Nacional de Cuba, *Informe económico 1995* (La Habana, May 1996), p. 22.

a. Preliminary

Table 6. Balance of Payments *(In million U.S. dollars)*

	1989	1990	1991	1992	1993	1994	1995	1996ᵃ
Current account balance	-3001	-2545	-1454	-420	-388	-242	-515	-520
Trade balance	-2615	-2076	-1138	-215	-382	-211	-500	-1082
Exports of goods and services	5993	5940	3563	2522	1992	2197	2687	3380
Goods	5392	5415	2980	1779	1137	1315	1479	1967
Services	601	525	583	743	855	882	1208	1413
Imports of goods and services	8608	8017	4702	2737	2373	2408	3187	4462
Goods	8124	7417	4233	2315	2037	2111	2772	3695
Services	484	600	469	422	336	297	415	767
Current transfers (net)	-48	-13	18	43	255	310	532	1112
Factor services	-338	-456	-334	-248	-262	-340	-547	-550
Capital account balance	4122	2621	1421	419	404	240	435	510
Global balance	1121	76	-33	-1	16	-2	-80	-10

Source: CEPAL, *La economía cubana: Reformas estructurales y desempeño en los noventa*, Table A-15, based on official statistics of the Oficina Nacional de Estadísticas, the Banco Nacional de Cuba and unofficial statistics.

a. Estimate

for each of the years during the period 1989-96 (Table 6).[62] The review of the performance of the external sector in the 1990s in this section of the paper relies heavily on these two series of BOP statistics.

Merchandise Trade

Cuban merchandise exports in 1993 amounted to slightly over $1.1 billion, 79 percent lower than the $5.4 billion recorded in 1989 (Table 6). Over the

same period, merchandise imports fell from $8.1 to just over $2.0 billion pesos, or by 75 percent. In 1994, exports recovered slightly, increasing by about 18 percent to about $1.3 billion, while imports grew by about 5 percent to $2.1 billion pesos. In 1995 and 1996, exports increased again to nearly $1.5 and $2.0 billion, respectively, but imports grew at a much faster rate, rising by 31 percent in 1995 and 33

---

62. Although the statistics for the three years for which there is overlap in the two sources of data are not identical, they are sufficiently close to justify their use to assess the performance of the external sector during the 1990s.

Table 7.   Top Ten Destination of Cuban Merchandise Exports and Sources of Cuban Merchandise Imports, 1996 *(Million US $)*

	1991	1992	1993	1994	1995	1996
Top 10 Destinations of Merchandise Exports						
Russia	NA	632	436	301	225	523
Canada	133	212	132	142	234	294
Netherlands	118	131	89	101	172	230
China	202	183	74	121	214	138
Spain	91	85	65	78	96	131
Japan	142	115	51	63	89	67
France	61	44	39	44	57	48
Italy	48	51	33	50	54	38
United Kingdom	32	23	13	16	13	30
Germany	19	21	14	25	31	22
Top 10 as a % of total exports	NA	71.8	71.4	64.2	72.9	75.4
Top 10 Sources of Merchandise Imports						
Spain	285	199	191	289	396	465
Russia	NA	NA	NA	249	237	465
Mexico	107	120	189	271	355	318
Canada	114	100	107	84	200	197
France	63	90	127	133	148	197
Argentina	99	63	72	48	65	125
Italy	163	104	64	63	81	114
China	224	200	177	147	146	101
Germany	123	59	40	41	70	70
Netherlands	36	42	55	50	71	54
Top 10 as a % of total imports	NA	NA	NA	66.9	63.1	65.7

Source: Central Intelligence Agency, *Cuba: Handbook of Trade Statistics, 1997*, APLA 97-10006 (Washington: Central Intelligence Agency, November 1997).

percent in 1996, to nearly $2.8 and $3.7 billion, respectively. Reportedly, exports in 1997 grew by 0.6 percent and imports by 19.9 percent.[63]

Prior to the changes in international economic relations that occurred in the 1990s, Cuba routinely ran a very large merchandise trade deficit, financed mainly by bilateral credits from the Soviet Union. The disappearance of the Soviet Union as a source of trade financing meant that Cuba had to reduce its imports drastically in order to bring them closer to exports. Absent financing from the former Soviet Union, the trade deficit fell sharply in 1992, to $535 million, but grew thereafter to $900 million in 1993, $800 million in 1994, $1.3 billion in 1995, $1.7 billion in 1996, and nearly $2.5 billion in 1997.

Disaggregated merchandise trade statistics—either by country or by commodity—are not available from official sources. Using statistics published by partner countries, the U.S. Central Intelligence Agency (CIA) has constructed Cuban merchandise trade accounts by country and commodity for the period 1985-96.[64] These estimates are the foundation for the discussion that follows.

Merchandise trade by country: Table 7 shows Cuba's top ten destinations of merchandise exports and sources of merchandise imports in 1996. Interestingly, Russia tops the list of destinations of Cuban exports and occupies the same position with regard to sources of imports. With the exception of Canada, China and Japan, the remaining six top destinations of Cuban exports in 1996 were Western European

63. *Cuba: Informe económico, año 1997*, p. 4.

64. Central Intelligence Agency, *Cuba: Handbook of Trade Statistics, 1997*, APLA 97-10006 (Washington: Central Intelligence Agency, November 1997) and earlier issues.

Table 8.   Composition of Cuban Merchandise Trade *(In million US $)*

	1985	1986	1987	1988	1989	1990	1991	1992	1993	1994	1995	1996
Exports	6531	6439	5402	5518	5392	4910	3565	2085	1325	1465	1625	2015
Sugar, molasses and honey	4873	4698	4020	4124	3959	3690	2670	1300	820	785	855	1095
Fuels	677	326	365	197	221	52	25	0	0	0	0	0
Nickel	323	365	317	440	485	400	260	235	170	190	345	450
Fish	129	149	141	146	127	125	115	120	90	110	115	125
Tobacco	100	94	91	98	85	95	100	95	75	80	90	90
Medical products	11	12	11	8	55	130	50	50	20	110	40	85
Fruit	157	182	163	171	139	150	100	50	50	80	45	50
Other	262	342	556	335	320	268	245	235	100	110	135	120
Imports	8758	9191	7584	7579	8124	6745	3690	2235	1990	2055	2805	3205
Fuels	2871	3038	2600	2569	2598	1950	1240	835	750	750	835	1060
Food	1067	961	794	816	1011	840	720	450	490	430	560	610
Machinery	2023	2183	1752	1780	1922	1790	615	350	235	240	405	510
Semifinished goods	1078	1116	821	816	838	700	425	195	180	220	385	410
Chemical products	447	525	447	434	530	390	270	170	150	180	280	230
Consumer goods	281	325	245	234	277	225	90	50	50	80	130	160
Trsnsport equipment	614	645	601	629	609	590	170	125	80	110	100	120
Raw materials	353	371	302	281	307	240	140	40	35	25	85	90
Other	23	27	22	19	33	20	20	20	20	20	25	15
Trade deficit	2227	2752	2182	2061	2732	1835	125	150	665	590	1180	1190

Source: Same as Table 7.

nations: Netherlands, Spain, France, Italy, the United Kingdom and Germany. As a group, the top ten destinations accounted for 75.4 percent of Cuba's total exports in 1996; for previous years, these countries accounted for between 64 and 73 percent of exports.

Spain and Russia shipped about the same value of merchandise to Cuba in 1996. Rounding up the list of top ten suppliers to Cuba in 1996 were Canada, Mexico and Argentina in the Americas; China; and four Western European countries: France, Italy, Germany and Netherlands. The top ten Cuban suppliers in 1996 accounted for 65.7 percent of imports in that year, 63.1 percent in 1995 and 66.9 percent in 1994.

Merchandise trade by commodity: Table 8 shows estimates of Cuban exports and imports by broad commodity groups. With regard to merchandise exports, several trends are worth noting:

- Fuel exports, which were a significant source of exports in the mid-1980s, disappeared altogether by the end of the decade; this is not surprising since these were actually reexports of Soviet oil sold by Cuba in the world market in order to obtain hard currency.

- Sugar and related products remained as the most significant hard currency earner. Even in the 1990s, when Soviet price subsidies no longer existed, sugar and associated products accounted for over 50 percent of the value of Cuban merchandise exports in every year.

- After slumping in the early 1990s, nickel exports recovered in 1995-96, contributing about one-fifth of total export revenue in these years.

- Exports of medical products—a proxy for exports of products of the biotechnology industry—performed erratically. Starting from a very low level in the mid-1980s, they peaked at $130 million in 1990, fell to $20 million by 1993, recovered in 1994 to $110 million, and fell again in the next two years.

- Exports of fruits—an indicator of the performance of the food program—also behaved erratically in the 1990s, failing to reach the levels recorded in the mid-1980s and falling from $100 million in 1990 to about half that amount during 1991-96.

Throughout the 1990s, fuels continued to be the most significant import category, accounting for 33-

Table 9. **Top Ten Destinations of Cuban Sugar Exports** *(Million U.S. $)*

	1991	1992	1993	1994	1995	1996
Russia	NA	535	NA	255	223	503
China	182	181	65	114	213	136
Morocco	0	7	0	0	27	57
Romania	0	4	8	17	30	54
Canada	69	95	32	36	42	43
Algeria	51	54	49	31	34	36
Japan	88	61	20	34	58	35
Egypt	8	23	13	25	40	28
Syria	29	12	6	15	14	24
Tunisia	0	8	0	82	39	16
Top Ten as a % of total exports	NA	75.3	NA	77.6	84.2	85.1

Source: Same as Table 7.

Table 10. **Top Five Destinations of Cuban Nickel Exports** *(Million U.S. $)*

	1991	1992	1993	1994	1995	1996
Canada	47	102	84	82	173	232
Netherlands[a]	78	105	64	77	132	191
Italy	22	20	11	21	29	10
China	0	0	2	0	0	1
Japan	2	0	0	0	0	0
Top Five as a % of total exports	57.3	96.6	94.7	94.7	96.8	96.4

Source: Same as Table 7.

a. Primarily nickel for reexport.

Table 11. **Top Ten Sources of Cuban Fuels Imports** *(Million U.S. $)*

	1991	1992	1993	1994	1995	1996
Russia[a]	NA	NA	NA	210	131	335
Mexico	25	53	103	158	102	46
Venezuela	0	47	87	58	75	NA
Colombia	9	2	15	26	3	NA
Netherlands	8	3	2	2	2	5
Spain	0	11	12	14	9	2
Trinidad & Tobago	5	6	4	NA	NA	NA
Ecuador	0	1	4	5	NA	NA
China	1	1	0	0	0	2
Germany	0	2	3	1	1	1

Source: Same as Table 7.

a May include oil shipped under triangular trade agreements.

exports in 1995-96. Russia remained the top importer of Cuban sugar, accounting for 46 percent of the value of exports in 1996. Middle Eastern countries were also significant purchasers of Cuban sugar.

Exports of nickel (Table 10) were very heavily concentrated in two countries: Canada and the Netherlands.[65] In 1996, Canada alone absorbed 52 percent of Cuban nickel exports by value, and the Netherlands 42 percent. Exports to Canada were almost entirely comprised of intermediate products (nickel-cobalt sulfide) for further refining, while exports to the Netherlands were predominantly charge nickel (nickel-cobalt oxide and nickel-cobalt sinter).

Russia topped Cuba's suppliers of fuels in 1996 (Table 11), providing about 32 percent of the value of such imports. Several Latin American countries—Mexico, Venezuela, Colombia and Ecuador—provided significant amounts of fuels in some years during the early 1990s, but sales from these countries fluctuated severely from year to year.

Services Trade

Cuba recorded surpluses in services trade in every year in 1989-96, with the exception of 1990 (Table 6). There is no additional information on specific traded services, but presumably the favorable balance in the services export account reflects the performance of the tourism industry. As is discussed below,

35 percent of the total value of merchandise imports. Meanwhile, imports of machinery, semifinished goods, raw materials and consumer goods were slashed: in 1993, imports of machinery amounted to 13 percent of their level in 1989, raw materials to 15 percent, consumer goods to 22 percent and semifinished goods to 26 percent. In 1995-96, imports in all four of these categories rose, contributing to the doubling the trade deficit that occurred between 1994 and 1995.

Key export and import commodities: Tables 9-11 present statistics on the value of Cuban exports or imports to the leading purchasers or sellers of sugar, nickel and fuels. With regard to sugar exports (Table 9), the top ten destinations listed in the table accounted for about 85 percent of the value of sugar

---

65. Reportedly, exports to the Netherlands were for reexport through the Rotterdam spot market.

Table 12. Tourism Industry Indicators

	1990	1991	1992	1993	1994	1995	1996
Number of visitors (thousands)	340	424	461	546	619	742	1004
Length of average stay (days)	8.7	8.7	9.1	9.6	9.1	8.7	7.3
Stock of hotel rooms (thousands)	NA	31.8	32.9	35.5	34.5	37.5	NA
Stock of hotel rooms suitable for international tourism (thousands)	12.9	16.6	18.7	22.1	23.3	24.2	26.9
Occupancy rate of hotel rooms (percent)	NA	69.8	60.4	57.9	59.1	62.6	60.0
Occupancy rate of hotel rooms suitable for international tourism (percent)	39.7	43.0	42.0	43.8	46.0	52.6	55.9
Gross income (million U.S. dollars)	243.4	387.4	567.0	720.0	850.0	1100.0	1380.0
Average income per vistor (U.S. dollars)	82.5	105.3	135.6	137.9	150.3	170.3	187.8

Source: CEPAL, *La economía cubana: Reformans estructurales y desempeño en los noventa*, Table A-23.

foreign investment has played an important role in the development of this industry.

Table 12 shows several indicators of capacity and performance of the tourism industry in the 1990s. With regard to capacity to accommodate tourists, the stock of hotel rooms suitable for international tourism more than doubled between 1990 and 1996, from 12,900 to 26,900 rooms. During this period, the number of foreign visitors nearly tripled, from 340,000 in 1990 to over 1 million in 1996. The number of tourists arriving in 1997 has been reported at 1.169 million.[66]

With regard to efficiency indicators, the occupancy rate of hotel rooms was nearly 70 percent in 1991; it fell to about 60 percent in subsequent years. The average length of stay was 8.7 days in 1990-91, rose to 9.6 days in 1993, and then fell to 9.1 days in 1994, 8.7 days in 1995 and 7.3 days in 1996.

Income generated by tourism rose by 467 percent between 1990 and 1996; it first exceeded the $1 billion mark in 1995 and reached nearly $1.4 billion in 1996. It reportedly rose by 12 percent in 1997.[67] A comparison of tourism income (Table 12) and revenues generated by sugar and nickel exports (Table 8) shows that tourism surpassed nickel to become the

second largest source of revenue in 1991 and overtook sugar exports in 1994.

Income per visitor per day increased steadily over the period 1990-96, from $82.50 in 1990 to $187.60 in 1996. According to an industry expert, Cuba continues to be regarded as an inexpensive "package" destination, reflecting the strategy of quickly penetrating source markets by offering low, all-inclusive packages. Moreover, the ability to increase prices is hindered by the lack of quality of products and services in other associated industries: food and beverage operations, retail facilities, recreation and entertainment activities, and other tourism infrastructure.[68]

The figures given above refer to gross income and include the value of imported goods and services consumed by visitors; the foreign exchange cost of capital investment; payments that leave Cuba in the form of profits, interest payments, royalties, management fees, payments to foreign travel agents and so on; the cost of advertising and promoting travel to Cuba; and the overseas cost of training service personnel.[69] Unlike other nations, Cuba also reports aviation receipts from its airlines and airport fees as part of gross tourism income.[70] A better measure of tourism's contribution to the BOP would be net receipts, i.e.,

---

66. *Cuba: Informe económico, año 1997*, p. 5.

67. *Cuba: Informe económico, año 1997*, p. 5.

68. Charles Suddaby, "Cuba's Tourism Industry," in *Cuba in Transition—Volume 7* (Washington: Association for the Study of the Cuban Economy, 1997), p. 129.

69. María Dolores Espino, "Tourism in Cuba: A Development Strategy for the 1990s?," in Pérez-López, editor, *Cuba at a Crossroads*, pp. 158-159.

70. Francoise L. Simon, "Tourism Development and Transition Economies: The Cuba Case," *Columbia Journal of World Business* 30:1 (Spring 1995), p. 30.

gross receipts minus the associated hard-currency imports and other expenditures. For the Cuban tourism industry, net receipts are a fraction of gross income: in the range of 30-38 percent, according to one expert[71] and about 33 percent according to another.[72] Reports on the performance of the Cuban tourism industry often do not distinguish between gross and net receipts, with Cuban officials tending to report only gross receipts, which are, of course, larger.[73]

Transfers

In the BOP methodology, unrequited transfers are defined as "transactions stemming from the noncommercial considerations, such as family ties or legal obligations, that induce a producer or owner of real resources and financial items to part with them without any return in those same forms."[74] That is, they represent flows of resources from one economy to another for which there is no *quid pro quo*. Unrequited transfers could be of an official nature (e.g., foreign grants or aid-in-kind for which no repayment is required) or of a private nature (e.g., remittances from persons who have migrated to relatives or friends who have remained at home) either in cash or in the form of goods.

According to data in Table 6, net transfers were negative in 1989-90, meaning that resources actually flowed out of the Cuban economy in those two years in the form of transfers. They turned positive beginning in 1991, however, and boomed thereafter, rising from $18 million in 1991 to over $1.1 billion in 1996. Transfers were Cuba's most significant source of hard currency in 1996, exceeding gross revenues from sugar or nickel and *net* revenues from tourism. Transfers quadrupled between 1993—when the government legalized holding and using dollars by the population—and 1996. The two mentioned Cuban National Bank reports identify transfers as "the most dynamic element of the balance of payments, mainly due to the income from donations and remittances"[75] and "an important source in generating hard currency for the nation."[76]

Cuban BOP statistics (Tables 5 and 6) do not distinguish between official and private transfers. According to CEPAL, transfers received by Cuba are predominantly private and take the form of cash remittances.[77] CEPAL estimates that private transfers amounted to $600 million in 1995[78] and $800 million in 1996. These estimates are in line with those of Díaz-Briquets, who estimated remittances in the

---

71. Espino, "Tourism in Cuba: A Development Strategy for the 1990s?," p. 159, based on studies conducted by the Cuban Ministry of Tourism.

72. Simon, "Tourism in Transition Economies: The Cuba Case," p. 30.

73. As an example of the difficulties in dealing with statistical information on Cuba, a news item carried in *El Nuevo Herald* in January 1998 based on a Spanish news agency EFE report from La Habana cites a story published in *Granma* in which an official of the Ministry of Tourism states that *gross* tourism revenues in 1997 were $850 million when 1,171,000 foreign tourists visited the island. The same official predicts that revenue from tourism will exceed $1 billion in 1998, when 1.4 million tourists are expected to visit the island. While the statistics on the number of visitors does match the series in Table 12 and in a recent report by the Ministry of the Economy and Planning cited above, the revenue figures do not, putting into question whether they refer to the same concept, i.e., gross revenue v. net revenue, or whether the series include or exclude certain expenditures such as aviation and telecommunications costs. See "Turismo reportó ingresos de $850 millones en 1997," *El Nuevo Herald* (7 January 1998), p. 6A.

74. International Monetary Fund, *Balance of Payments Manual*, Fourth Edition (Washington: International Monetary Fund, 1977), p. 71.

75. Banco Nacional de Cuba, *Economic Report 1994*, p. 21.

76. Banco Nacional de Cuba, *Informe económico 1995*, p. 23.

77. CEPAL, *La economía cubana: Reformas estructurales y desempeño en los noventa*, p. 172.

78. BOP statistics (Table 6) show net transfers of $532 million in 1995; this means that sizable outgoing transfers must have occurred in this year to offset the estimated $600 million in private transfers.

range of $300 to $400 million annually in the early 1990s.[79]

Cuba is making use of the latest technology to maximize remittances by making it easier for individuals to send remittances to family and friends in the island:

- The official World Wide Web page of the Government of Cuba, www.cubaweb.cu, prominently advertises "Quick Cash," a service provided by Canadian firm Careebe Consolidated Management and Cuban entity American International Service, S.A., whereby remittances can be sent to Cuba by charging the amount on-line to either a VISA or MasterCharge credit card. The service claims delivery within to 5 working days at a banking institution in Cuba; nearly 130 outlets (primarily offices of the Banco Popular de Ahorro) located in all 14 provinces and the Isle of Youth can receive the transfers and make them available to recipients. The advertisement states that the transfers comply with all Cuban laws and, to conform with U.S. laws, must be made in Canadian dollars (although the sender may pay for the transfers in U.S. dollars).

- In June 1998, Canadian firm Tran$card and the Cuban enterprise Simex, S.A., launched a debit card which would be issued to Cuban residents for free; the debit card reportedly contains a 16-digit code and a password to ensure confidentiality and safety of the funds. Convertible currency transfers (deposits) made into the account from abroad are available to Cuban residents to use almost as soon as they are received.[80]

Current Account

The current account records transactions between residents and foreigners such as two-way flows of merchandise and services and transfers. A surplus in the current account generally denotes that a country is gaining net claims on the rest of the world. Con-versely, current account deficits are associated with insufficient domestic savings relative to investment and the net inflow of foreign capital. Neither the level of the current account nor its direction (credit or deficit) are important in and of themselves. Developing countries generally experience current account deficits financed by inflows of foreign savings (in the form of foreign investment and loans). However, persistent and escalating current account deficits may indicate structural problems in the external sector.

Data in Tables 5 and 6 show that Cuba's current account was in a deficit position throughout the period 1989-96. The deficit was very large during 1989-91, a period when the Soviet Union was still financing the bulk of Cuba's trade deficit and offering other forms of assistance. With the disappearance of special economic relations with the Soviet Union, beginning in 1992 Cuba was forced to limit imports to what it could finance through exports and the current account deficit fell to $242 million in 1994; in 1995-96, the current account deficit grew to about twice as high as in 1994.

Capital Account

Cuba has released publicly so very little information on its capital account that analysis is tantamount to a guessing game. The BOP statistics provided by the Cuban government to CEPAL (Table 6) group together all elements of the capital account into a single datum; the statistics released in the Cuban National Bank reports (Table 5) are somewhat more revealing in that they break out direct investment and (presumably) long- and short-term loans, but these data are only available for 1993-95.

Debt

As was discussed above, Cuba suspended service on its hard currency debt effective on July 1, 1986. While this action had a favorable impact on the BOP—since debt service payments were mooted—it seriously impaired Cuba's ability to turn to foreign

79. Sergio Díaz-Briquets, "Emigrant Remittances in the Cuban Economy: Their Significance During and After the Castro Regime," in *Cuba in Transition—Volume 5* (Washington: Association for the Study of the Cuban Economy, 1995), pp. 218-227.

80. David Orrio, "Tran$card: 'mulas' y disidencias," www.cubanet.org (June 21, 1998) and "Tarjeta de crédito para enviar dólares," *El Nuevo Herald Digital* (June 24, 1998).

Table 13. Foreign Debt in Convertible Currency *(In million U.S. dollars)*

	1993	1994	1995
Total debt	8785	9083	10504
Official bilateral	4067	3992	4550
Intergovernmental loans	40	44	47
Credits for development aid	151	164	181
Export credits with government guarantee	3855	3784	4321
Official multilateral	438	503	601
Suppliers	1867	2058	2403
Financial institutions	2406	2501	2919
Bank loans and deposits	2156	2254	2602
Medium and long-term bilateral and consortium loans	1027	1135	1222
Short-term deposits	1130	1119	1380
Credits for current imports	249	248	317
Other credits	27	29	31

Source: Banco Nacional de Cuba, *Economic Report 1994* (La Habana, August 1995), p. 25, and Banco Nacional de Cuba, *Informe económico 1995* (La Habana, May 1996), p. 24.

markets to obtain new financing. As a result, since the mid-1980s, Cuba has had to rely primarily on short-term loans at very high interest rates.[81] According to BOP data in Table 5, Cuba had inflows of long-term loans of $64 million in 1993, $254 million in 1994 and $20 million in 1995, while short-term loans were $238 million in 1993, outflows of $555 million in 1994 and loans of $473 million in 1995.

Table 13 shows statistics on Cuban hard currency debt in 1993-95. Outstanding debt grew from $8.8 billion in 1993 to $9.1 billion in 1994 and $10.5 billion in 1995. The fact that the outstanding debt grew does not mean that Cuba actually obtained fresh loans: the year-to-year value of the outstanding debt is affected by several factors, among them the accumulation of unpaid interest and relative changes in the value of currencies in which the debt was contracted. The hard currency debt at the end of 1996 has also been reported at $10.5 billion.[82]

Investment

BOP statistics (Table 5) report that direct investment in the island amounted to $54 million in 1993, $564 million in 1994 and under $5 million in 1995. These data are significant for at least two reasons: (1) they are the first official statistics on actual investment

flows reported by the Cuban government; and (2) they suggest lower investment flows than have been reported by Cuban officials and in Cuban investment promotion literature.

The foreign investment decision is a complex one, with investors considering a variety of factors, economic and political. In the case of investment in Cuba, investors face significant economic and political obstacles. Among the economic obstacles are the poor condition of the economy and infrastructure and the lack of institutions to support foreign investment; a positive economic factor might be the above-average quality of human resources in Cuba. The numerous political obstacles include the statist outlook of the Cuban government, the discriminatory treatment accorded foreign investors, and uncertainty associated with government assurances regarding the sanctity of investments, the likelihood of changes in economic policy, the risk of sanctions by the United States and the possibility of expropriation by a future Cuban government.

Cuban officials have justified the secrecy with which they treat investment data on concerns about possible action by the United States Government against potential or actual investors. The rationale behind the policy of "minimum reporting," as articulated by

---

81. CEPAL, *La economía cubana: Reformas estructurales y desempeño en los noventa*, p. 123.

82. *Cuba: Informe económico, año 1997*, p. 5.

Vice President Carlos Lage, is "the pressure which everyone who comes to invest in Cuba is subjected by the United States."[83] While this may be so, the lack of transparency in reporting foreign investment information may also be a deliberate ploy by Cuban officials to influence the investment climate by giving the impression that larger investments have occurred, or are under negotiation, than is actually the case.

Flows of foreign investment reported by Cuban officials appear too high in the light of other information and the BOP data mentioned above. For example, in October 1991, Julio García Oliveras, chairman of the Cuban Chamber of Commerce, reported that negotiations were ongoing with investors representing investments of $1.2 billion.[84] Vice President Carlos Lage stated in November 1994 that by the end of 1994, joint ventures would have provided Cuba with $1.5 billion in investments.[85] By the end of 1995, according to official sources, foreign investment had reached more than $2.1 billion.[86] There are good reasons to believe that the estimates of foreign investment provided by official sources overstate actual equity capital flows into the island: (1) multi-year disbursements may be involved; (2) some investments may be contingent on performance; (3) some investments may take the form of assets rather than cash; (4) some of the investments may be management contracts, production partnership agreements

(particularly in mining and oil exploration) or debt-equity swaps, where funds invested are minimal; and (5) others may actually be supplier contracts rather than equity investments.[87] At best, the figures reported by Cuban government officials might represent *intentions* of foreign investors, but they significantly overstate—by a factor of 3 or even higher—actual capital that has flowed into the island.

The U.S.-Cuba Trade and Economic Council (USTEC), an organization with collaborative relations with Cuban government entities—the Chamber of Commerce of the Republic of Cuba, the Cuban Ministries of Foreign Trade, Foreign Investment and Economic Cooperation, Tourism, Public Health, Steel-Mechanical and Electronic Industry and Foreign Affairs and the National Assembly of People's Power[88]—has compiled statistics on foreign investment in Cuba from a variety of sources, including discussions with individual company representatives and government officials in Cuba and abroad. The latest such compilation (Table 14), covering the period from 1990 to May 1998, lends credence to the cleavage between investment intentions and realizations. Thus, according to USTEC, while investments amounting to nearly $5.6 billion had been "announced" through May 1998, the volume "committed/delivered" was a more modest $1.8 billion, or 31.2 percent of the announced amount.

---

83. "Carlos Lage Comments on Economy," Havana Tele Rebelde and Cuba Vision (November 7, 1992), as reproduced in *FBIS-LAT-92-219* (November 12, 1992), p. 9.

84. Cited in Business International Corporation, *Developing Business Strategies for Cuba* (New York: Business International Corporation, 1992), p. 24.

85. "Carlos Lage Addresses Conference 21 November," Havana Tele Rebelde Network (November 23, 1994), as reproduced in *FBIS-LAT-94-229-S* (November 29, 1994).

86. "Support for Economic Changes," Havana Radio Havana Cuba (July 12, 1995), as reproduced in *FBIS-LAT-95-137* (July 18, 1995).

87. For further elaboration see, e.g., Jorge F. Pérez-López, "Foreign Investment in Socialist Cuba: Significance and Prospects," *Studies in Comparative International Development* 31:4 (Winter 1996/97); Pérez-López, *Odd Couples: Joint Ventures Between Foreign Capitalists and Cuban Socialists*, North-South Agenda Paper No. 16 (Coral Gables: North-South Center, University of Miami, November 1995); Maria C. Werlau, "Foreign Investment in Cuba: The Limits of Commercial Engagement," in *Cuba in Transition—Volume 6* (Washington: Association for the Study of the Cuban Economy, 1996); and Werlau, "Update on Foreign Investment in Cuba: 1996-97," in *Cuba in Transition—Volume 7* (Washington: Association for the Study of the Cuban Economy, 1997).

88. The objective of USTEC, an organization created in the United States in 1994, is to "provide an efficient and sustainable educational structure in which the United States business community may access accurate, consistent and timely information and analysis on matters and issues of interest regarding Unites States-Republic of Cuba commercial, economic, and political relations." See "About the U.S.-Cuba Trade and Economic Council," www.cubatrade.org.

Table 15 shows the number of foreign joint ventures established in Cuba in each of the years 1988-95. As was discussed earlier, Cuba was unsuccessful in attracting investment during the 1980s despite the passage of the legal framework for foreign joint ventures in 1982. This is reflected in Table 15, which shows that only one joint venture was established in 1988 and 2 in 1990. Foreign investment activity picked up in 1992-94, with 33 joint ventures established in 1992, 60 in 1993 and 74 in 1994, but slowed in 1995, when only 31 joint ventures were created.

In all, Cuban government statistics indicate that 212 joint ventures with foreign investors had been established through the end of 1995; Spanish investors were responsible for the largest number of joint ventures (47 or 22 percent) followed by Canada (26 or 12 percent), Italy (17 or 8 percent) and France and Mexico (13 or 6 percent each) (Table 15). The largest concentration of joint ventures was in the industrial sector (56 or 26 percent), followed by tourism (34 or 16 percent), mining (28 or 13 percent) and the oil sector (25 or 12 percent) (Table 16).

In the aftermath of the tragic February 24, 1996 incident in which Cuban military planes shot down two civilian planes piloted by Cuban-Americans, the United States adopted the Cuban Liberty and Solidarity Act (the so-called Helms-Burton Act). Title III of the Act gives U.S. citizens who hold valid claims a right of action in U.S. courts against those who knowingly "traffic" in their confiscated properties. Title IV allows the exclusion of traffickers and their immediate families from the United States. Under the terms of the Helms-Burton Act, the U.S. State Department reportedly issued letters in late 1996 warning several companies that they were suspected of trafficking in confiscated property.[89]

Several countries—among them Canada, Mexico and the members of the European Union—have vigorously protested the enactment of Helms-Burton,

Table 14. Foreign Investment in Cuba (As of 2 May 1998; in million U.S. dollars)

Country of Origin of Investment	Amount of Investment		(2)/(1) percent
	Announced (1)	Committed/ Delivered (2)	
Australia	500.0	NA	NA
Austria	0.5	0.1	20.0
Brazil	150.0	20.0	13.3
Canada	1341.0	600.0	44.7
Chile	69.0	30.0	43.5
China	10.0	5.0	50.0
Dominican Republic	5.0	1.0	20.0
France	100.0	50.0	50.0
Germany	10.0	2.0	20.0
Greece	2.0	0.5	25.0
Honduras	7.0	1.0	14.3
Israel	22.0	7.0	31.8
Italy	397.0	387.0	97.5
Jamaica	2.0	1.0	50.0
Japan	2.0	0.5	25.0
Mexico	1806.0	500.0	27.7
Netherlands	300.0	40.0	13.3
Panama	2.0	0.5	25.0
Russia	25.0	2.0	8.0
South Africa	400.0	5.0	1.3
Spain	350.0	100.0	28.6
Sweden	10.0	1.0	10.0
United Kingdom	75.0	50.0	66.6
Uruguay	0.5	0.3	60.0
Venezuela	50.0	3.0	6.0
Total	5636.0	1756.9	31.2

Note to the source table: The above figures represent amounts of announced, committed, and delivered investments since 1990 by private sector companies and government-controlled companies from various countries to enterprises within the Republic of Cuba as of 2 May 1998. Information, which may or may not be in the public domain, compiled through the media, other public sources, individual discussions with company representatives, non-Republic of Cuba government officials, and Republic of Cuba-based enterprise managers and government officials.

Source: U.S. Trade and Economic Council, www.cubatrade.org.

claiming that it impinges on their sovereignty and its extraterritorial reach is inconsistent with international obligations the United States has assumed in the World Trade Organization (WTO) and the North American Free Trade Agreement (NAFTA). Cuban official reaction to the legislation has been mixed:

---

89. Christopher Marquis, "Two Firms Face Helms-Burton Sanctions," *The Miami Herald* (January 22, 1997). The companies include Canada's Sherritt, Israel's Group BM and a Panamanian company selling automobiles in Cuba. Mexico's Grupo Domos and CEMEX reportedly withdrew from Cuba before being formally warned.

Table 15. Foreign Joint Ventures in Cuba, by Country of Origin

	1988	1990	1991	1992	1993	1994	1995	Total
Spain	1		3	9	10	14	10	47
Mexico			2	3	3	4	1	13
Canada				2	8	16		26
Italy				1	5	4	7	17
France		1		3	5	2	2	13
Netherlands				1	2	3	3	9
Tax havens		1	3	10	5	12		31
Rest of Latin America			2	3	11	9	4	29
Rest of the World			1	1	11	10	4	27
Total	1	2	11	33	60	74	31	212

Source: Consultores Asociados, S.A. (CONAS), *Cuba: Inversiones y Negocios, 1995-1996* (La Habana, 1995), p. 18.

Table 16. Foreign Joint Ventures in Cuba, by Economic Sector

	1988	1990	1991	1992	1993	1994	1995	Total
Agriculture			1	1	3	3	2	10
Mining			1		10	17		28
Oil		1	1	11	8	4		25
Industry			5	9	17	12	13	56
Tourism	1			4	9	16	4	34
Transportation						1	4	5
Construction/construction materials			2	3	6	10	1	22
Communications		1		1		1		3
Other			1	4	7	10	7	29
Total	1	2	11	33	60	74	31	212

Source: Consultores Asociados, S.A. (CONAS), *Cuba: Inversiones y Negocios, 1995-1996* (La Habana, 1995), p. 18.

- Vice Minister of Tourism Eduardo Rodríguez de la Vega told a visiting group of Catalonian tourism writers and journalists in late June 1996 that "surprisingly, the Helms-Burton law benefits the marketing and ranking of Cuban tourism because it stirs interest in the island in places where it was not known before.[90]

- At about the same time, Minister of Foreign Investment and Economic Cooperation Ferradaz described the reaction of foreign investors to the enactment of Helms-Burton as follows: "The 230 investors from 50 countries present in Cuba knew beforehand what could happen. I do not doubt that some partners will be frightened off and will delay their plans. Some have announced this even though we have not yet received official notification. We do not reproach the victims of an unjust law but rather those who have promulgated this law. The vast majority of companies have opted to stay and are seeking, with us and their countries of origin, legal formulas to defend themselves and thus reduce the risk."[91]

- On the other hand, Vice President Lage told journalists in La Habana in July 1996 that the Helms-Burton Law had "negative effects" on the Cuban economy: "The effects [of the Helms-Burton Law] are negative not because of the practical application of the law itself, but because of its objective of intimidation and the concerns

90. "Helms-Burton Law Said to Benefit Tourist Trade," Havana Prensa Latina (June 24, 1996), as reproduced in *FBIS-LAT-96-126* (June 18, 1996), p. 4.

91. "Foreign Investment Minister on Helms-Burton Law," *El País* (Madrid) (June 15, 1996), as reproduced in *FBIS-LAT-96-119* (June 19, 1996), pp. 2-3.

that it raises with a significant number of entrepreneurs."[92]

- At its December 1996 session, Cuba's Asamblea Nacional approved an "antidote" to Helms-Burton, which declares the U.S. legislation "null, invalid and without merit," gives Cuban citizens the right to claim compensation from the United States for damages incurred as a result of U.S. actions (which includes the trade embargo and military actions conducted from U.S. territory) and proclaims measures to protect foreign companies investing or trading with Cuba, including maintaining such operations in secret.[93]

According to Minister of Foreign Investment and Economic Cooperation Ferradaz, by the end of 1996, 260 joint ventures with foreign capital had been established in the island—an increase of 48 joint ventures or 23 percent over the 212 at the end of 1995—in 34 sectors of the economy.[94] By the end of 1997, the number of joint ventures had reportedly increased to 317.[95]

Finally, the first two Export Processing Zones (EPZs), created pursuant to Decree-Law 165 of 1996, opened in May 1997 in Berroa and Wajay, near the city of La Habana. Two other EPZs in the ports of Mariel and Cienfuegos were ready to follow suit.[96]

CONCLUDING OBSERVATIONS

The economic crisis that has enveloped Cuba during the 1990s has affected every aspect of Cuban society. The standard of living of the Cuban population has dropped significantly and even their access to public services has been curtailed. The bottom of the crisis seems to have been reached in 1994. Modest growth since then has made a very small contribution to the average Cuban's standard of living but has stabilized the domestic political situation.

The external sector of the Cuban economy was heavily unbalanced during the 1980s. Despite very large price subsidies and other aid from the Soviet Union and the socialist countries, Cuba routinely incurred very large trade deficits, which were financed by these same nations. The Cuban merchandise export basket remained composed primarily of traditional products and concentrated in a few markets. Cuba imported nearly all the oil it demanded and also imported significant quantities of food despite being an exceptionally well-endowed agricultural country.

The economic crisis of the 1990s manifested itself through the external sector. Cuba was forced to adjust import levels to match—more or less—what it could afford to pay for through exports. This meant drastic cutbacks in imports across the board, sharp reductions in economic activity, idled workers, and inability to provide basic services (such as transportation) to the population. The initial response from the Cuban leadership was "special period" austerity. Economic reforms implemented during the summer of 1993 and 1994 and subsequently in very small doses, have been quite successful at macro stabilization, but less so at promoting economic growth. This is not surprising since the Cuban government has been reluctant to make meaningful changes (for example, enterprise reform, privatization, permitting the creation of factor markets) in order to avoid losing political control. Some of the policy initiatives taken in the 1990s have had a salutary effect on the external sector, particularly those that have stimulated tourism, foreign investment and remittances from abroad.

---

92. Pablo Alfonso, "Lage: Ley tiene 'efectos negativos' en Cuba," *El Nuevo Herald* (July 24, 1996), p. 1B.

93. Juan O. Tamayo, "'Antídoto' contra la Ley Helms intenta socavar presión de Estados Unidos," *El Nuevo Herald* (January 2, 1997), pp. 1B, 2B.

94. "Hay empresas de 40 países en la isla, dice Ministro," *El Nuevo Herald* (October 17, 1997), p. 6A.

95. *Cuba: Informe económico, año 1997*, p. 6.

96. Werlau, "Update on Foreign Investment in Cuba: 1996-97," p. 83.

The disappearance of the soft currency accounts—and the myriad special conditions and quid pro quos they entailed—will make it easier in the future to analyze the structure and performance of the Cuban external sector once the adequate statistical information is made available. At the present time, only minimal information is available, and its reliability is untested.

Structurally, the Cuban external sector accounts in the 1990s differ significantly from the 1980s: regarding the current account, exports of services (tourism) and remittances play a much more significant role, as does also investment in the capital account. In the absence of economic assistance and financing of trade deficits from the Soviet Union, Cuba's ability to attract foreign capital (via foreign investment or loans) is key to financing the necessary imports of goods and services the economy requires in order to grow. Cuba continues to be have very little access to international credit markets and those loans that are available are short term and carry extremely high interest rates. It is puzzling that Cuba has not made debt renegotiation a higher priority. In fact, Cuban Central Bank President Francisco Soberón told journalists in October 1997 that although Cuba has maintained a dialogue with creditors, it "does not feel pressured" to enter into a multilateral agreement that would potentially restore its access to international capital markets.[97] Very little is known about Cuba's debt with the former Soviet Union—taken over by Russia—and what arrangements, if any, are being made to determine its current dollar value and terms of repayment.[98]

In 1995 and 1996, the merchandise trade deficit rose significantly, as Cuba began to increase imports—particularly of raw materials, semimanufactured products and machinery, which had been severely cut back in earlier years and virtually shot down significant portions of the productive sector—in the expectation that exports would also rise. The disappointing performance of the sugar sector and of the food program thwarted the expected recovery of exports. In 1997, exports rose only by 0.6 percent, while imports grew by 19.9 percent, resulting in a marked widening of the trade deficit.

Economic growth in 1997 has been reported officially as 2.5 percent, about half the 5 percent rate of growth predicted at the beginning of the year. For 1998, Minister of the Economy and Planning José Luis Rodríguez has predicted a growth rate of 2.5 to 3.5 percent and a *zafra* of under 4 million tons of sugar, lower than the 4.25 million tons reached in 1997; the prospects for 1998 thus are modest economic growth, a smaller sugar crop and continuation of austerity measures.[99] Early results of the 1998 *zafra* suggest that sugar production may be around, or even below, the 3 million ton mark, which would represent the lowest sugar output in 50 years.[100] Under this scenario, it is difficult to be optimistic about the external sector. It is likely to perform as it has in the most recent years, providing enough foreign resources for the economy to continue to operate at very low levels of capacity and efficiency but not incapable of pulling the economy out of its depressed state.

---

97. "Cuba 'no se siente presionada' para solucionar deuda externa," *El Nuevo Herald* (October 26, 1997), p. 6A.

98. According to a report by the Russian press agency ITAR-TASS issued in May 1998, Cuba was Russia's largest debtor, responsible for $18.3 billion or 15.2 percent of the overall debt of $120.2 billion owed to Russia. "Cuba es el principal deudor," *El Nuevo Herald* (May 26, 1998), p. 6A.

99. "Lage pide optimismo y confianza en el futuro," *El Nuevo Herald* (December 27, 1997), p. 4A.

100. Andrew Cawthorne, "Una economía de corcho sobre un mar de desastres," *El Nuevo Herald Digital* (June 15, 1998).

THE CUBAN CIGAR INDUSTRY AS THE TRANSITION APPROACHES

Joseph M. Perry, Louis A. Woods, Stephen L. Shapiro, and Jeffrey W. Steagall

For many decades, premium Cuban cigars have served as the world standard against which other cigars are judged. The story is told that, immediately before President John F. Kennedy approved the embargo against Cuba in 1962, he sent an assistant to Washington tobacco shops to buy up the available supply of the hand-made Cuban cigars that he preferred. Since that time, Cuban cigars have been conspicuously absent from the shelves of retailers in the United States. The Cuban tobacco and cigar industries, however, have adjusted to changing market conditions, and now serve as an expanding source of foreign exchange at a time when the Cuban sugar industry has fallen on hard times.

World-wide cigar production and consumption declined from a relative peak in the mid-1960s until the early 1990s. At that time, consumers rediscovered large, premium cigars. The demand for these high-priced products began to increase, and has yet to reach a peak, according to some industry analysts.

The Cuban hand-made cigar industry has responded to this burgeoning demand by training new rollers and expanding its production for export. Cuba's position in the international cigar market is complicated by the fact that U. S. citizens may not normally buy or possess cigars produced in Cuba. Cigar output from Cuba therefore affects the worldwide cigar market, but impinges on U. S. production and consumption primarily through smuggling.

This paper briefly delineates the international cigar market, examines Cuba's position in the premium segment of that market, considers thecigar boom in the United States, and makes some suggestions concerning near-term trends, especially if some transitional changes occur in the Cuban economy.

THE INTERNATIONAL CIGAR MARKET

Cigars are tobacco products that originated in the New World. First identified by Columbus in 1492, they were adopted, along with pipe smoking, by consumers around the world (Ortiz, 1947, pp. 72-73). Cigars are rolls of tobacco wrapped within a tobacco leaf, all of which is consumed as the cigar is smoked. Cigars that are produced today fall into three categories: cigarillos, which are small, slender cylinders of tobacco (cigarettes in a tobacco wrapper are often included in this group); cheroots, which are cigars cut square at both ends; and cigars proper, which are usually cut square on one end. From the point of view of the U.S. Federal government, which taxes their production and sale, cigars are classified as small (weighing no more than three pounds per thousand) and large (weighing more than three pounds per thousand) (USCFR, 1998).

Within the large cigar category are found almost all of the premium, hand-rolled cigars that are so favored by smokers today. These cigars consist of a filler of one or more types of tobacco, held together and shaped by a binder of tobacco, and wrapped in a carefully-chosen tobacco leaf. At retail, premium cigars today will typically sell for $7.50 to more than $25.00 each. Although concrete sales data are not available, it is likely that some premium Cuban cigars smuggled intothe United States sell for substantially higher prices (Morrow, 1996).

The size of the international cigar market is not known exactly. Various tobacco trade organizations collect data on production and consumption, but do not have a complete accounting from all countries and all producers. Data from the Tobacco Merchants Association, the primary data-collecting organization in the United States, suggest that the world production of cigars in all sizes is about 14 billion pieces per year.

The major cigar producing countries around the globe generally keep close track of cigar production and estimate levels of consumption, since tobacco growing is often regulated, and tobacco products are frequently taxed. In the United States, for example, the Bureau of Alcohol, Tobacco, and Firearms, in the Department of the Treasury, maintains monthly running balances of the production of tobacco products, removals, imports, and exports. Since the major producing countries account for a large percentage of total cigar output, the only figures really in doubt are those from smaller countries.

Table 1. Top Ten Producers of Cigars (All Sizes), 1994-1996, Millions

Country	1996	1995	1994
United States	4,048	3,488	3,327
Belgium	2,246	2,146	2,052
Netherlands	1,801	1,713	1,835
Germany	1,364	1,173	1,300
United Kingdom	975	977	978
Spain	704	675	851
Denmark	334	349	n/a
Switzerland	178	177	n/a
Dominican Rep.	150	101	n/a
Finland	55	53	n/a
Totals:	11,855	10,852	10,143

Source: Cigar Association of America, June, 1998

Table 1 presents data showing the output of the world's top ten producers of cigars over the 1994-1996 period. As the figures indicate, world production is dominated by a handful of countries. Given that world production is about 14 billion cigars, the top six countries in the table account for 80 percent of that total.

Table 2 shows the top ten countries, ranked by the consumption of cigars over the 1994-1996 period. Consumption levels are the net result of domestic production (or removals from storage) minus exports plus imports. The list includes almost the same countries as in Table 1, except that Sweden replaces the Dominican Republic.

Table 2. Top Ten Consumers of Cigars (All Sizes), 1994-1996, Millions

Country	1996	1995	1994
United States	4,303	3,642	3,428
Germany	1,469	1,298	1,377
United Kingdom	1,150	1,158	1,165
Spain	755	738	706
Belgium	591	608	827
Netherlands	316	248	471
Switzerland	210	211	213
Denmark	180	202	n/a
Sweden	81	90	n/a
Finland	65	64	n/a
Totals:	9,129	8,259	8,187

Source: Cigar Association of America, June, 1998

A comparison of the figures in Tables 1 and 2 shows that the largest producers of cigars are also major international cigar traders. The United States market, for example, consumed 255 million more cigars than it produced in 1996. It both exported and imported large quantities of cigars. This pattern reflects a broad market, with diverse tastes, and a preference for variety. Germany, theUnited Kingdom, and Spain were also net importers of cigars. In contrast, Belgium and the Netherlands, long-time producers of tobacco products, were net exporters of cigars.

The data also confirm the dominance of the United States market for cigars. Both production and consumption figures for the U.S. are currently estimated to be between 4 and 5 billion cigars annually, which constitutes between 29 and 36 percent of the world market.

Worldwide cigar production and consumption showed a marked decline for at least three decades, before turning up again in the mid-1990's. In the major producing countries, output reached a peak in the mid-1960's. The 1964 *Surgeon General's Report on Smoking and Health* produced a momentary cigar

Table 3. **Sales of Cigars and Cigarillos in U. S. And Main European Union Markets, 1970-1996, Millions of Units**

Country	1996	1995	1990	1985	1980	1975	1970
United States	4,587	4,040	3,554	4,335	5,374	8,645	8,881
France	1,531	1,460	1,475	1,749	1,927	1,543	972
Germany	1,424	1,314	1,291	1,639	2,155	2,553	3,213
United Kingdom	1,095	1,070	1,490	1,420	1,715	1,800	1,190
Spain	709	693	729	824	904	1,098	561
Belgium/Luxembourg	591	608	673	839	1,013	1,168	1,014
Holland	n/a	455	487	677	902	1,200	1,112
Denmark	190	202	328	474	733	909	1,074
Italy	174	180	210	185	178	200	234
Sweden	81	90	134	111	155	250	326

Source: Cigar Association of America, Inc., June, 1998.

boom in the United States, with U. S. cigar production alone reaching a peak of 8.7 billion units in that landmark year. Thereafter, the decline in output becomes pronounced.

World production, which was down to about 14.3 billion units in 1988, continued trending downward until 1993, when it dropped below 14 billion cigars. Incomplete data from the Tobacco Merchants Association suggest a low of 13.7 billion. From that time until the present, however, both cigar production and consumption have enjoyed a moderate upsurge.

The data in Table 3 verify the rise in cigar usage in the major consuming countries. U. S. cigar sales, including imports, reached a peak of 8.9 billion in 1970, then fell by more than 50 percent through 1990. 1996 sales levels were 29 percent higher. Germany showed essentially the same pattern, while France and the United Kingdom experienced a slightly later peak in consumption.

The reasons for the expansion are still not fully analyzed. A strongly increased demand for premium cigars, especially in countries such as the United States, is clearly one of the forces at work. Advertisements in the popular press in this country show celebrities such as Bruce Willis, Arnold Schwarzenegger, Jack Nicholson, and even Demi Moore enjoying expensive, hand-rolled cigars. Cigar rooms have been established at major restaurants. And specialty shops have installed walk-in humidors to satisfy the demand.

Importers of premium cigars have placed pressure upon producers in countries such as the Dominican Republic and Honduras to meet the growing demand. One may speculate that several years of very strong economic growth, with rising disposable income, may have contributed to the U. S. increase through a wealth effect.

A stronger international market has also stimulated some recent structural changes in cigar production. For example, Tabacalera S.A., Spain's most important manufacturer and distributor of tobacco products, has moved to expand its share of the international cigar market. In late 1997, the firm purchased Tabacalera San Cristóbal de Honduras S.A., and Tabacalera San Cristóbal de Nicaragua S.A., two key Central American tobacco firms which together produce 24 million premium cigars annually. It also acquired the assets of the cigar division of long-established Havatampa, Inc., of Tampa, Florida. The total acquisition bring Tabacalera's share of the world cigar market from an estimated 3.5 percent to a much healthier 10.8 percent. The Havatampa acquisition is especially significant, since that company's two factories produce 1.3 billion cigars per year (Escarey, 1997).

The United States embargo against Cuba has exerted a significant effect on the cigar production in the Caribbean. When Castro came to power, the Dominican Republic produced and exported tobacco, but had only an embryonic cigar industry. Today, the Dominican Republic is one of the world's largest producers of premium, hand-rolled cigars. Cuban expatriates and other entrepreneurs, losing access to Cuba's prime growing regions, sawthe opportunity to relocate tobacco production to the nearby island. The Cibao River valley, near Santiago, offered suitable soil and climate. Using Cuban seed in many instances, growers produced tobacco that was similar to the same varieties grown in Cuba. Cigar factories were built, rollers were trained, and the industry was under way. Familiar brands such as Cohiba and Montecristo began to appear with Dominican provenance. Exports to the United States rose from 5 million in 1976, to 33 million in 1981, and to 52 million in 1990, when Dominican cigars enjoyed about 47 percent of the U. S. premium market.

Cigar exports from the Dominican Republic were expected to reach 162 million in 1997, with a value of US$210 million. 1996 revenues were US$130 million. The bulk of the exports were premium cigars. Hendrik Kelner, president of Tabacos Dominicanos S. A., indicated that the high rate of growth in the Dominican cigar industry could not last, and would slow to 10 to 15 percent in 1998, as the international market stabilized (DR Economic News, November 13-18, 1997).

The embargo has stimulated cigar production in Honduras, Nicaragua, and Jamaica, which also enjoy the lack of Cuban competition in the United States. Honduran cigar output has remained fairly stable over the past decade, and has now been surpassed by that of the Dominican Republic. Mexico and Costa Rica also produce cigars in this hemisphere.

TOBACCO AND CIGARS IN CUBA

As Fernando Ortiz (1947, p. 7) pointed out in rather emphatic prose, tobacco and sugar "bothflourish in Cuba and are both perfectly adapted, climatically and ecologically, to the country. . . Cuba has in its different zones the best land for the cultivation of both plants. And the same happens in the combinations of the climate with the chemistry of the soil."

The Vuelta Abajo region, in particular, has the ideal combination of light, gravelly soil, humidity, and rainfall to grow the world's finest cigar wrapper leaf (Lestina, 1940b; Dambaugh, 1956).

Tobacco production in Cuba takes place in about 25 named districts (distritos tabacaleros), located within four major geographic zones: Vuelta Abajo and Semivuelta, located in Pinar del Río province; Partido, located primarily in Havana, but crossing over into Pinar del Río; the Remedios, located in Santa Clara and Camagüey provinces; and Oriente, in Oriente province. The latter two zones are often collectively termed the Vuelta Arriba (Stout, 1997, pp. 30-31).

Tobacco culture and cigar usage in Cuba go back to pre-Columbian times when the native Americans in many parts of Latin America smoked rolled-up tobacco leaves. Once European settlements became common on the island, first sugar, and then tobacco were institutionalized as cash crops.

As Ortiz points out (1947, pp. 286-289), the tobacco trade in Cuba was taken over by the Spanish government 1557. As would be expected, government intervention resulted in a vigorous trade in smuggled tobacco. The illicit sales of Cuban tobacco and cigars became so troublesome that the Spanish crown forbade the growing of tobacco in Cuba between 1606 and 1614. The royal proscription was ignored by the Cuban tobacco growers, who continued to sendtheir leaf and products abroad. By the 1760's, the Havana type of cigar was being used in England. German production of cigars using Havana leaf began in 1788. And it is said that U. S. production of Havana leaf cigars started between 1801 and 1810. By 1797, large-scale commercial production of cigars was occurring in and around the city of Havana itself. (Ortiz, 1947, p. 286-289, 301-309; Baer, 1933, p. 63).

For many years, the tobacco trade remained a royal monopoly. Following the mercantilistic reasoning of the time, tobacco sales and resales were manipulated by the government for its own benefit. In 1820, the crown finally permitted Cuba to export cigars to countries other than Spain, thus creating the international market for Cuban cigars (Stout, 1997, pp. 12-13).

Over the years, premium Havana cigars established a worldwide reputation for excellence. They dominated the high-quality markets during the nineteenth

Table 4. **Exports of Cigars and Cheroots from Cuba, 1975-1989, in Pounds and in Thousands of US Dollars**

Year	Weight (Lbs.)	Value (US$K)
1989	61,130	45,260
1988	69,403	53,700
1987	67,583	47,770
1986	59,870	44,987
1985	n/a	51,152
1984	54,512	41,226
1983	n/a	72,241
1982	n/a	63,377
1981	n/a	45,849
1980	n/a	40,552
1979	n/a	41,598
1978	n/a	40,350
1977	n/a	37,707
1976	n/a	43,819
1975	n/a	28,000

Source: United Nations, *Yearbook of Inter-national Trade Statistics*, various issues.

Table 5. **Cuban Unmanufactured Tobacco Exports and Imports, 1990-1996, Metric Tons**

Year	Exports	Imports
1996	5,000	300
1995	5,000	300
1994	4,000	300
1993	3,000	300
1992	7,900	3,201
1991	13,500	300
1990	13,000	1,500
1989	14,491	3,000

Source: USDA, *Agricultural Statistics*, various issues.

century, before cigarettes became accepted socially. They remained the benchmark against which other cigars were measured, even as cigar consumption began to decline after 1920.

When President Kennedy established the trade embargo with Cuba in 1962, smokers in the United States were enjoying about 190 million premium cigars per year. Cuba produced 15 million of that total, or about 9 percent of the market. It also exported almost all of the tobacco that was used to roll the other premium cigars, which were produced in U. S. factories. At that time, the Dominican Republic, Honduras, Jamaica, and Nicaragua produced few cigars (Mendoza, 1997).

Table 4 presents a picture of Cuban cigar exports from 1975 to 1989, before the current cigar boom began. Over a decade and a half,the value of cigar exports fluctuated around an average level of US$46.5 million. Good harvest years buoyed the figures, while bad harvest years reduced them. It is clear that, while cigar exports generated foreign exchange during this period, they were not a major decision variable in the eyes of the Castro government. While support from the Soviet Union and other Communist Bloc countries continued, and as along as the sugar harvests and nickel prices remained at acceptable levels, cigars

did not enter importantly into a foreign exchange equation.

After 1990, the breakup of the Soviet Union caused severe economic dislocations in Cuba. The supply of fertilizer, pesticides, and other crop supplies dwindled. The U. S. embargo continued in effect. To top it all off, Hurricane Lili hit Cuba in October 1996, doing damage tocash crops across the island, including tobacco. The figures in Table 5 show how the exports of unmanufactured tobacco were slowed by this complex of factors. Exports dropped by about two-thirds from their 1989 peak. Imports also dropped drastically, at least in part because of the lack of adequate foreign exchange.

In spite of this pessimistic picture, some positive changes have taken place. Tabacalera S.A. came to the rescue of the Cuban cigar industry after the breakup of the Soviet Union generated widespread shortages of fertilizer and pesticides. The Spanish tobacco giant set up a system of credit advances to Cuban cigar producers, in essence lending them the funds to produce cigars, based upon a guaranteed level of cigar exports to Spain ("Cuba on course," 1997). This financial help has made it possible for cigar production to recover somewhat, and to respond to the burgeoning worldwide demand for premium cigars.

Manuel García, vice president of Habanos S. A., the Cuban cigar agency, asserts that the current world demand for premium Cuban cigars lies between 115 and 120 million pieces per year, still greater than the current level of Cubanproduction (Darnberger, 1997).

Cuba's current major markets for its premium cigars are located in Europe. Figures from Habanos S. A., indicate that, during 1997, 63 million cigars were exported to Europe. Of this total, 35 million went to Spain, 12 million to France, and 5.5 million to the United Kingdom. Switzerland and Germany are also important markets. About 4.3 million cigars were also exported to the Middle East and to the Pacific region, as those markets began to develop (Darnberger, 1997).

Table 6. Tobacco Exports from Cuba, by Country of Destination, 1990-1995, Millions of U.S. Dollars

Country of Destination	1990	1991	1992	1993	1994	1995
France	14	8	6	8	9	10
Germany	4	4	3	3	3	
Netherlands	2	4	5	2	1	1
Spain	42	54	54	40	46	51
Switzerland	8	6	7	6	7	10
United Kingdom	7	6	5	3	3	5
Others	18	18	15	13	11	13
Totals	95	100	95	75	80	90

Source: *Cuba: Handbook of Trade Statistics, 1996.* CIA, Directorate of Intelligence.

The data in Table 6 confirm both post-Soviet decline in tobacco exports and their recent recovery. The figures reflect exports of both unmanufactured and manufactured tobacco, and so are indicative of general conditions in the industry. The value of exports hit an estimated US$100 million in 1991, then dropped by 25 percent by 1993. 1994 and 1995 show some recovery, but not to the previous peak level.

Very recent trends have been more favorable. According to Manuel García, vice president of Habanos S. A., exports of Cuban cigars reached102 million units in 1997, exceeding the 100 million goal previously set. Previous reported export levels were 50 to 55 million in 1994, and 60 to 70 million in 1995. Foreign exchange revenue from this level of exports was US$179 million. Production plans are to produce 160 million cigars in 1998, 175 million in 1999, and 200 million in the year 2000, almost all for export. At this point in time, cigars are the fourth most important generator of hard currencies, exceeded only by tourism, sugar, and nickel. Francisco Linares, president of Habanos S. A., speculates that Cuba may be able to produce as many as 400 million premium cigars in the new millennium ("Havanas ready," 1998; Suckling, 1995; Martínez, 1998).

THE UNITED STATES CIGAR BOOM

As the figures presented above clearly indicate, the United States dominates the internationalcigar market in both production and consumption. U. S. smokers consume more cigars annually than smokers in Germany, France, and the United Kingdom combined. Tobacco-use trends in the United States therefore both influence and are reflective of conditions in other major producing countries.

Cigar production and consumption in the United States have shown long cyclical fluctuations. From a low of less than 2 million cigars consumed in 1870, U. S. usage increased to a peak of 8.5 million cigars in 1920. From that point, consumption gradually dropped to 4.6 million in 1933, the trough year of the Great Depression. Once the recovery began, consumption rose above 5 million per year, and, with few exceptions, stayed in the 5 to 6 million range until 1957, when a short, sharp growth trend developed.

The postwar consumption of domestically-produced cigars reached a peak level of 9.1 billion in 1964, and then gradually declined to 2.1 billion in 1993. Since that time, the recent cigar craze has helped to pull both production and consumption up to higher levels (Johnson, 1984, Table 2.1; data from the Cigar Association of America).

The number of U. S. companies producing cigars has shown similar fluctuations. Historical data show that the number of cigar factories in the United States was 15,732 in 1915. From that point until 1982, the number of factories gradually dropped, on an almost straight-line trend. In 1982, only 112 factories produced cigars. Note that these numbers do not accurately reflect the number of cigar companies, since multi-factory companies were becoming more common (Cigar Association of America data). In 1977, 94 U. S. cigar companies were producing, with 7,700 employees. By 1987, the number of domestic cigar producers was down to 16, with 2,500 employees. In 1992, the last available Census data show 25 cigar companies with 2,600 employees (Bureau of the Census, 1992, Table 1a).

Table 7 shows the production, removal, and estimated consumption of domestic cigars over the 1987-1997 period in the United States. The difference between the production and removal figures is explained by the fact that cigars are usually aged in warehouses for some months after production and that some cigars are exported. The consumption figure reflects the net effect of removals, exports, and imports for each year. Since the last low point in 1991, cigar production in the United States has increased by two-thirds. And since 1993, total cigar consumption has also risen by two-thirds.

Table 7. Output and Consumption of Cigars, United States, 1987-1997, in Millions of Cigars

Year	Output	Removals	Consumption
1997	2,900	2,960	3,589
1996	2,430	2,720	3,031
1995	2,040	2,320	2,518
1994	1,916	2,145	2,294
1993	1,795	2,010	2,138
1992	1,741	2,106	2,219
1991	1,740	2,134	2,246
1990	1,896	2,232	2,345
1989	2,010	2,365	2,470
1988	1,980	2,426	2,531
1987	2,133	2,674	2,728

Source: BATF Annual Data

Cigar imports and exports for the same period of time are presented in Table 8. Note that all sizes and types of cigars are included in this accounting. It appears that the worldwide increased taste for cigars affected both the level of cigar imports into the United States, which increased more than fivefold between 1991 and 1997, and exports of U. S. cigars, which rose by more than 30 percent between 1993 and 1997. These figures also underscore a point that was made earlier in the paper: the world's largest economy is also an economy of varied tastes, so that it not

only produces more cigars than any other country on earth, it also exports much of its output, and imports cigars for those consumers who favor foreign brands.

Table 8. Cigar Imports and Exports, United States, 1987-1997, Millions of Cigars

Year	Imports	Exports
1997	609	90
1996	320	105
1995	195	94
1994	146	74
1993	127	67
1992	111	76
1991	109	70
1990	111	72
1989	103	78
1988	112	87
1987	113	145

Source: BATF Annual Data.

Cigar and cheroot imports into the United States from the leading Latin American producers, excluding Cuba, for the period 1980-1991, are shown in Table 9. Note that the Dominican Republic gradually moved into a position of dominance, unseating Honduras from first place. According to the Cigar Association of America, the consumption of premium cigars was 97 million in 1991 (Morrow, 1996).

Table 9. U.S. Imports of Cigars and Cheroots for Consumption, 1980-1991, By Producing Country, Millions of Units

Country	1980	1985	1991
Dom. Republic	19.8	40.5	49.8
Honduras	31.1	27.2	35.0
Nicaragua	6.2	4.6	1.6
Jamaica	17.6	18.0	7.5
Mexico	12.3	8.0	6.8

Source: USDA, Foreign Agricultural Service

Table 10 provides more detail on patterns of individual cigar consumption in the United States. As data from the Cigar Association of America show, the per capita consumption of large cigars among the total U. S. population dropped to a low of 8 in 1993, then rose to 13 by 1997. By all popular accounts, the figure will be higher in 1998. Among male smokers only, consumption fell to 25 per capita in 1993, then recovered to 40, a 60 percent increase over a four-year period. Note that the category of "large cigars" includes the premium, hand-rolled types.s

Table 10. U.S. Total and Per Capita Consumption of Large Cigars, 1980-1997

Year	Annual Consumption (000)	Per Capita Total Population	Consumption Male Population
1997	3,542,161	13	40
1996	3,097,910	12	35
1995	2,631,987	10	30
1994	2,334,870	9	27
1993	2,136,720	8	25
1992	2,211,364	9	26
1991	2,234,204	9	26
1990	2,334,858	9	28
1985	3,110,311	13	40
1980	3,952,478	17	55

Source: Cigar Association of America, June, 1998

Over the past decade, American consumers haveannually spent about 2 percent of disposable personal income on cigars. Recorded dollar expenditures on cigars rose from US$620 million in 1987 to US$979 million in 1996, an increase of 57.9 percent (USDA, 1997b, Table 29). In 1987, 5.3 percent of adult males in the United States smoked cigars. Those in the 45-64 age group were more likely to be cigar smokers (7 percent). Interestingly, more women are becoming cigar smokers, but in relatively small numbers (CDC, October 13, 1989).

The market for premium cigars has been the driving force behind the overall increase in cigar consumption in the United States. As Table 11 shows, the 1995-1996 increase was substantial.

As the figures in the table also show, the top five producing countries listed dominate the premium cigar market in the United States, accounting for 92.1 percent of sales. The Dominican Republic, alone, provided almost half of the premium cigars sold. Based upon these figures, the imports of premium cigars increased by two thirds between 1995 and 1996. Other analysts suggest a more moderate, butstill substantial increase of 32 percent in premium cigar imports, and

Table 11. Premium Cigars Imported into the United States, By Country of Origin, in Millions of Cigars

Source	1995	1996	Percent Change	Market Share
Dom. Rep	81.1	138.6	70.9%	47.2%
Honduras	53.5	83.7	56.6	28.5
Nicaragua	3.5	18.0	411.7	6.1
Jamaica	15.3	15.5	1.3	5.3
Mexico	9.7	14.5	49.5	4.9
Total, Top 5	163.1	270.4	65.8	92.1
Others	13.2	23.4	77.0	7.9
Grand total	176.3	293.7	66.6	100.0

Source: Cigar Insider, Cigar Aficionado.

a rise of 42 percent in large cigars in general (Mendoza, 1997).

The U. S. Department of Agriculture (USDA) tracks general trends in tobacco production and use. According to USDA data, the consumption of cigars of all kinds in the United States rose by 16 percent in 1997. Government analysts predicted a continuation of the growth trend through 1998 (USDA, 1998).

CIGARS AND THE CUBAN ECONOMY TODAY

The Reuters news agency reported on June 13, 1998, that Cuba is once again facing a very tense economic situation because of adverse conditions in three of its key export industries. The 1997-1998 sugar *zafra* is reported to be at a low of 3.2 million metric tons, 20 percent below the meager harvest of last year. In addition, sugar prices have dropped on international markets. Nickel prices have also moderated, reducing the foreign exchange yield from that important export. Government policy-makers appear to be pinning their hopes on a growing tourist sector, expanding cigar exports, and higher seafood exports ("Cuba's economic situation," 1998). There must also be some unexpressed hope that remittances from Cuban expatriates will continue at a high level.

Vice President Carlos Lage puts a brave face on the situation, arguing that Gross Domestic Product will show an increase in 1998 in the 2.5 to 3 percent range, perhaps exceeding the 2.5 percent growth rate of 1997. On balance, the increase in tourist expenditures and the higher level of cigar exports seem to be two major factors keeping the Cuban economy out of decline. (Tamayo, 1998).

In 1996, an English distributor estimated that the world-wide demand for Cuban cigars was at an annual level of 100 million, causing spot shortages and higher prices in many countries. Ana López, head of marketing for Habanos S.A., stated recently that world demand for Cuban cigars has risen from 125 million to 130 million per year, and that the cigars are now sold in over 80 countries. Smuggled Cuban cigars do reach smokers in the United States. The number is still uncertain, but American cigar manufacturers estimate that they lose from US$50 to US$75 million in revenues each year from lost sales. The number of smuggled cigars is variously estimated at 4 to 10 million per year (Morrow, 1996; Oramas, 1997).

NEAR TERM PROSPECTS

From a world wide point of view, the recent expansion of the Cuban cigar industry has not had overwhelming impacts upon the market. The worldwide consumption of all cigars is now about 14 billion. An increase in output from 100 million to 167 million *habanos* — or even 200 million — is therefore a minuscule change, about seven-tenths of one percent of the total market supply. It would exert no perceptible influence on average cigar prices worldwide, particularly since the international market has been experiencing an expansion.

Any price effects would be found in the sub market for premium cigars. In the United States, prices for smuggled Cuban cigars would continue to be higher than open-market prices in other countries as long as the demand for them remains strong. In other markets, where *habanos* are sold legally, prices will remain strong as long as Cuban supply lags increases in demand, and as long as demand does not peak and begin to fall.

According to available data and observations by Cuban cigar industry officials, the demand for premium Cuban cigars in other countries apparently has not peaked. In the 80 countries now importing Cuban cigars, more could be sold than are now placed on the market. Cuban officials are also looking at other markets, including the Near East and the Pacific region, where Cuban cigars now have a foothold. Expansion is possible up to some limiting level, where natural resources in Cuba and conditions in the market place dictate a ceiling.

Resource constraints in Cuba are obvious. Although the island is the largest in the Caribbean, good tobacco land is limited. There is only one Pinar del Río area, and it is being intensively exploited. Other tobacco-growing areas can be pushed only so far. At the point where leaf production is maximized (or optimized), cigar production also reaches a maximum. The only alternative would then be to import leaf to make cigars, thus violating one of the five legal characteristics of an *habano*: that all of the tobacco in the cigar must be grown in Cuba (Stout, 1997, pp. 9-10).

Following this line of reasoning, it may be said that prime tobacco land in the Dominican Republic is similarly limited. Once the suitable areas in the Cibao River Valley and around Santiago are placed in cultivation, a ceiling on output is effectively reached. In both Cuba and the Dominican Republic, moving to less desirable lands will lower the quality of the tobacco, dropping its quality to a level with that of less desirable tobaccos grown in other countries. In other words, the uniqueness of the soil endowment limits premium cigar production.

Pre-transition then, a continuation of present output trends seems likely, with both Cuban andnon-Cuban premium cigars enjoying an expanding market for at least one or two more years, perhaps longer.

Interestingly, the recent cigar boom has followed a pattern similar to that of the life cycle of a product. There was an initial strong surge of interest in and consumption of premium cigars, much like the initial introduction of a successful product, when output increases at an increasing rate. After hitting an inflection point, cigar consumption rose more slowly, at a decreasing rate. As far as may be determined, the submarket for top-end cigars is still expanding. The critical question is: When will it reach a peak (essentially a market saturation point), and perhaps be poised for a decline?

As noted above, a booming U. S. economy, low levels of unemployment, and high levels of disposable personal income may be necessary, but not sufficient, factors behind the cigar boom. Since 1993, real disposable personal income has followed a clearly upward trend, spiking once in 1995. U.S. real Gross Domestic Product has also grown at healthy annual rates: 3.5 percent in 1994, 2.5 percent in 1995, 2.0 percent in 1996, and 3.8 percent in 1997. Estimated real growth during the first quarter of 1998 exceeds 4 percent. (FRB St. Louis, June, 1998). Such robust growth has pushed the national unemployment rate to around 4.5 percent, well below the "natural rate" level identified by many economists.

In addition to the robust economic growth that has buoyed disposable income, there have been substantial wealth effects at the same time. Over the past four years, stock values on U. S. markets have risen by about 28 percent per year. At the same time, stock values in European markets have been rising at about 5 to 6 percent per year. Given an upward trend in both wealth and income, higher levels of luxury good consumption, such as premium cigars, is to be expected. Note, too, that cigar consumption in the United States is most common among males who are 45 to 64 years old, or who are normally in their highest earning years.

If the U.S. embargo continues, it is likely that the current trends in premium cigar production will continue until the boom peaks, or until there is an economic downturn. Continuing strong economic growth in the United States could encourage further expansion in Caribbean cigar production, particularly in the Dominican Republic. Recent efforts by the U. S. Customs Service to reduce the smuggling of Cuban cigars into the United States suggest that illicit *habanos* might decline in numbers.

If the transition to a market economy takes place, with the consequent elimination of the U.S. trade embargo, or if the embargo is dropped for other reasons while the Castro administration is still in power, then other changes may be expected.

One critical question has to do with trade policy in a more liberal international environment. Will the Castro government (or its successor) encourage the immediate development of the U.S. market for cigars? Cuban cigar producers cannot now satisfy the world demand for their products. If the world demand remains strong, or expands, then entry into the U.S. market would take place at the expense of other markets that are now being serviced around the world. Habanos S.A. officials articulate the position that they will continue to supply the markets in which they now have a strong position., even if the U.S. embargo is lifted.

If U.S. smokers could legally buy Cuban cigars, but they were not directly supplied from Cuba, then the expression of their demand could result in re-exports from countries other than Cuba, and a rise in premium cigar prices.

The opening of the U.S. market to Cuban cigars would also jeopardize the position of the cigar industries in the Dominican Republic and Honduras, which depend critically upon U.S. demand for their growth. As pointed out above, the U.S trade embargo has been a primary reason behind the expansion of the Dominican industry, which has a protected market in the United States. The extent to which Dominican or Honduran cigars would substitute for Cuban premium cigars is impossible to determine, without some kind of market test. There would clearly be a substitution effect, once Cuban cigars were available from standard retail establishments.

One post-transition possibility is that not only Cuban cigars, but also Cuban tobacco could once more be exported to the United States. If appropriate fillers, binders, and wrappers could be put together, then cigar factories in the United States could produce cigars that would be competitive with those coming from Cuba, similar to the situation that existed in 1959. Cuban trade policies would clearly influence such a trend.

And what about the future consumption of cigars? Since the mid-1960s, the world-wide use of cigars has followed a generally declining trend. How long will the current boom last? Since both Cuba and the Dominican Republic are continuing to expand their productive capacity for premium cigars, is overproduction a near-term possibility?

It is clear that the future of the Cuban cigar industry depends upon a complex of factors, many of them impossible to assess at themoment. The near-term expansion of the industry will be largely determined by world economic conditions, in particular the strength of the U.S. economy. Given current economic indicators, a continuation of existing trends for Cuban cigars appears likely.

A longer-term analysis will require more detailed information, and needs to be based upon more rigorous analysis. As additional data are collected, this initial essay will be extended through some formal modeling of the international and U.S. cigar markets, to generate results that are technically more satisfactory.

REFERENCES

Baer, Willis N. (1933). *The Economic Development of the Cigar Industry in the United States.* Lancaster, Pa.: The Art Printing Co.

Collins, John. (1997). "Special Report: Cigar Industry Booming in the Dominican Republic." *Dominican Republic Economic News.* Electronic edition (November 13-18). www.dr1.com/news/EB/Cigars1373.html.

"Cuba on course to produce 100 million cigars in '97." (1997). *CubaNet News.* Electronic version (August 21) www.cubanet.org.

"Cuba's economic situation 'tense' minister says." (1998). *CubaNet News* (June).

Dambaugh, Luella N. (1956). "Tobacco Production: Vuelta Abajo Region, Cuba." *The Journal of Geography*, 55 (December) 442-446.

Darnberger, Alfred. (1997). "Havanas: Same Quality, Larger Quantities." *Tobacco Journal International* (March), p. 83.

Escarey, Sharman. (1997) "Spain's Tabacalera buys cigar firms in Americas." *CubaNet News* (September 12).

Federal Reserve Bank of St. Louis. (1998). *National Economic Trends* (June).

"Havanas ready for all markets." (1998). *Granma International.* Electronic edition (January 1).

Heimann, Robert K. (1960). *Tobacco and Americans.* New York: McGraw-Hill Book Company.

Cabrera Infante, G. (1985). *Holy Smoke.* New York: Harper and Row Publishers.

Johnson, Paul R. (1984). *The Economics of the Tobacco Industry.* New York: Praeger Publishers.

Lestina, Mildred Letitia. (1940a). "Tobacco Production: San Juan-San Luis, Cuba." *The Journal of Geography* XXXIX (May) 173-182.

Lestina, Mildred Letitia. (1940b). "Vuelta Abajo, Cuba: A Study of Its Tobacco Industry." *The Journal of Geography* XXXIX (February), 45-55.

Madrid-Aris, Manuel. (1997). "Growth and Technological Change in Cuba." In *Cuba in Transition—Volume 7.* Washington: Association for the Study of the Cuban Economy, pp. 216-228.

Martínez, Silvia. (1998). "Cuba exporta habanos de calidad a todo el mundo." *Granma Diario*, electronic edition (June 6).

Mendoza, Zindar. (1997). "Netting Cuban Cigars." *Boardwatch Magazine*, Electronic edition, XI:1 (January). www.boardwatch.com cigar.htm.

Messina, William A., Jr., Richard N. Brown, James E. Ross, and José Alvarez. (1997). "Cuban Non-Sugarcane Agricultural Trade Patterns: Historical Perspectives and Future Prospects." In *Cuba in Transition—Volume 7.* Washington: Association for the Study of the Cuban Economy, pp. 13-20.

Morrow, David J. (1996). "Black Market Prices for Cuban Cigars Skyrocket." LatinoLink, from the N. Y. Time News Service (April 16). www.latinolink.com.

Oramas, Joaquín. (1997). "80 million Havana cigars exported as of October." *Granma International*, electronic edition (November 5). www.cubaweb.cu/granma.

Ortiz, Fernando. (1947). *Cuban Counterpoint: Tobacco and Sugar*. New York: Alfred A. Knopf.

Ross, James E. "Agribusiness Investment in Cuba's Post Embargo Period." In *Cuba in Transition—Volume 6*. Washington: Association for the Study of the Cuban Economy, pp. 163-168.

Stout, Nancy. (1997). *Habanos: The Story of the Havana Cigar*. New York: Rizzoli International Publications, Inc.

Stubbs, Jean. (1985). *Tobacco on the Periphery: A Case Study in Cuban Labour History, 1860-1958*. Cambridge: Cambridge University Press.

Suckling, James. (1995). "Francisco Linares." *Cigar Aficionado*. Electronic edition (February). www.cigaraficionado.com.

Tamayo, Juan A. (1998). "An Island of Insecurity." *Miami Herald*. Electronic edition (April 13).

United States. (1998). *Code of Federal Regulations*. Title 27, Volume I, Part 27, Section 270.11.

United States. Centers for Disease Control. (1989). "Tobacco Use by Adults—United States, 1987." *Morbidity and Mortality Weekly Report*, 38:40 (October 13) 685-687.

United States. Department of Agriculture. Economic Research Service. (1998). *Tobacco Summary* (April 17). Publication TBS-238.www.usda.mannlib. cornell.edu/reports.

United States. Department of Agriculture. National Agricultural Statistics Service. (1997a). *Agricultural Statistics: 1997*. Washington: U.S. Government Printing Office.

United States. Department of Agriculture. (1997b). *Tobacco Summary Tables: 1997*. Washington: U.S. Government Printing Office.

United States. Department of Commerce. Bureau of the Census. (1992). *Census of Manufactures: Industry Series*. Tobacco Products, Section 21A. Washington: U.S. Government Printing Office.

Westfall, L. Glenn. (1977). "Don Vicente Martínez Ybor, the Man and His Empire: Development of the Clear Havana Industry in Cuba and Florida in the Nineteenth Century." (Doctoral dissertation, University of Florida, 1977).

COMMENTS ON

"The Cuban Cigar Industry as the Transition Approaches" by Joseph M. Perry, Louis A. Woods, Stephen L. Shapiro and Jeffrey W. Steagall

José Alvarez

This is a well structured and written paper. The topic could not be more important this year since tobacco is now among Cuba's top four earners of foreign exchange. The paper starts by discussing the international cigar market, followed by a section on tobacco and cigars in Cuba, then the quantification of the U.S. cigar boom. The paper ends with two sections on cigars and the Cuban economy today, and its near term prospects, which includes different pre- and post-transition scenarios.

The paper, however, does not include what is happening in Cuba's agricultural tobacco sector. The title would not require this inclusion, but the current trends in Cuba's cigar exports that the paper quantifies originate at the farm level. These comments are intended to fill that gap.

The agricultural tobacco sector is showing signs of recovery. To this discussant, three reforms are responsible for the improvement:

Land distribution to families: This program started after Resolution 357 of 1993 established the distribution, in usufruct, of idle lands to families with experience in growing several crops, including tobacco ("Crece," 1995). From September 1993 to December 1996, 27,700 hectares were turned over to about 13,000 tobacco farmers. According to the Ministry of Agriculture, only 3% of this land has had to be reclaimed on account of contract shortfalls ("More land," 1997). An interesting and important point is

the fact that *campesinos* (small farmers) are responsible for 92% of the country's tobacco production (Paneque Brizuelas, 1997). The latter figure must reflect the agricultural reorganization that came about after the break-up of the state monopoly on land in September 1993.

Foreign currency incentives system: This system covers the entire productive chain: from seed production to exports. When a worker has fulfilled the production norms, s(he) receives a certificate that can be used to purchase goods in the so-called dollar stores ("Estímulo," 1995). This type of foreign exchange (convertible currency) incentive reaches around 5% of workers' wages (Mondelo, 1995). In 1996, about 60,000 tobacco workers received this form of incentive (Tobacco, 1997). The payment of foreign currency incentives is strictly enforced and seems to be working. For example, in order to increase yields, the number of new plants actually planted are counted; if a farmer does not reach the specified number in the contract, s(he) does not receive the portion of the incentive payment corresponding to that phase of production (Pagés, 1996).

Foreign financing: Starting in 1994, and mentioned by Perry et al. in their paper, the Spanish tobacco firm Tabacalera, S.A. signed an agreement with Cuba aimed at financing the necessary inputs for tobacco production in the farms at Vuelta Abajo, on the western part of the island. In return, Cuban producers must guarantee certain levels of cigar production for the Spanish market (Mondelo, 1995). The $25 million financing was mainly arranged by Pedro Pérez, president of Tabacalera, for which he received the title of "Cigar Man of the Year" in Havana (Oramas, 1995). In addition to Tabacalera, S.A., other entities involved in similar deals include the French monopoly Seita, and other exclusive cigar distributors (Opup, 1995).

As mentioned by Perry et al., the Cuban cigar industry has shown some recovery in the last few years, but not to the previous peak level. In that regard, the authors make an interesting point: expansion is possible up to some limiting level, where natural resources in Cuba and conditions in the market place dictate a ceiling. This statement challenged the discussant's curiosity, who found the necessary base figures for the analysis in an article by Pagés (1996).

Cuba's maximum land potential for tobacco production appears to be 5,000 caballerías (70,000 ha), which was reached in seven campaigns (two before and five after the 1959 revolution), according to a study covering 61 years. The same study concluded that the maximum average yield potential for the country of 30,000 lb/cab (1mt/ha) was never achieved during the study period, although some individual producers may have surpassed that figure (Pagés, 1996). Thus, total potential production of the country is about 70,000 metric tons per season. Cuban tobacco exports in 1989 were approximately 14,520 mt,[1] or about 21% of the maximum potential production. As Perry et al. recognize, that was before the current cigar boom, at a time when tobacco exports were not a high priority of the Cuban government. In contrast with the current situation, it was also the era of a heavily subsidized Cuban economy.

The modest advances that the Cuban tobacco industry has made in recent years, when compared with 1989, have been primarily the result of the three re-

forms taking place in its agricultural sector. The tobacco sector, as opposed to a stagnant and even declining sugar sector, appears to be moving forward. After producing 100 million cigars in 1997, the goal for 1998 was set at 160 million, 175 million for 1999, and 200 million for the year 2000. These figures, however, do not obtain the high foreign exchange earnings that the Cuban leadership is attributing to them. For example, it has been reported that the 160 million cigars expected to be produced by Cuba in 1998 would represent between $170 and $180 million[2] (*El Nuevo Herald*, June 18, 1998, p. 8A). Furthermore, the 21% of potential capacity achieved in 1989 resulted in exports of about $85.2 million; at 1989 prices, total capacity utilization would have resulted in exports of $405 million. That figure is about half of the $800 million per year that CEPAL has recently reported as the value of remittances to Cuba. An additional difference is that the latter are net while the former are gross figures. Thus, even at today's prices, total potential foreign exchange earnings from the exports of tobacco products would not be as high as many people would like to believe.

For those thinking about a booming future U.S.-Cuba cigar trade, data in Perry et al. show U.S. imports of 176 and 294 million cigars in 1995 and 1996, respectively. It is going to be very hard for Cuba to capture a substantial share of the U.S. market. Perhaps anticipating that situation, The Pacific Cigar Company Ltd., based in Hong Kong, has been given the responsibility by the Cuban government of marketing Cuban cigars in Asia and the Pacific. There are great expectations for selling Cuban cigars to almost half of the world's population in a growing market (Campos, 1995). The world market appears to be a realistic potential market to expand Cuba's foreign exchange earnings from tobacco exports.

---

1. Calculated on the basis of data in CEE (1989, p. 267) for 1989.

2. Based on a price per cigar between $1.06 and $1.12. A simple computation made with the data for 1989 in CEE (1989, p. 267) yields an average export price of $0.74 per cigar.

REFERENCES

Campos, Roberto F. "La leyenda asiática de un buen habano," *Business TIPS on Cuba*, Vol. 2, No. 1 (January 1995), pp. 17-18.

Comité Estatal de Estadísticas (CEE). *Anuario Estadístico de Cuba, 1989*. La Habana: Editorial Estadística.

"Crece vinculación familiar a la tierra," *Business TIPS on Cuba*, Vol. 2, No. 1 (January 1995), p. 11.

"Estímulo económico a tabacaleros," *Business TIPS on Cuba*, Vol. 2, No. 1 (January 1995), p. 11.

Mondelo, Raúl. "Favorable campaña tabacalera," *Business TIPS on Cuba*, Vol. 2, No. 6 (June 1995), p. 6.

"More land to usufructuaries," *Business TIPS on Cuba*, Vol. 4, No. 3 (March 1997), p. 8.

Opup, Syren. "Entre los habanos, Partagás," *Business TIPS on Cuba*, Vol. 2, No. 9 (September 1995), p. 16.

Oramas, Joaquín. "Habanos, S.A." *Business TIPS on Cuba*, Vol. 2, No. 12 (December 1995), p. 17.

Pagés, Raisa. "Despejar las cortinas de humo," *Granma* (April 2, 1996), p. 4.

Paneque Brizuelas, Antonio. "Campesinos and food production," *Granma International* (July 13, 1997).

"Tobacco production grows," *Business TIPS on Cuba*, Vol. 4, No. 8 (August 1997), p. 4.

EXPERIENCIAS AGROCLIMATOLÓGICAS DE REPÚBLICA DOMINICANA Y EL CARIBE ADAPTABLES A CUBA: LA AGRICULTURA DESDE UNA PERSPECTIVA CARIBEÑA

Hipólito Mejía Domínguez

Es un honor para mí tener la oportunidad de reunirme con ustedes aquí en esta hermosa ciudad de Miami, para compartir ideas en torno a los avances de la agricultura de nuestros países y exponerles mi visión sobre el futuro de ésta en el Caribe. Recuerdo que cuando aún no se hablaba de globalización o de integración regional, Miami se perfilaba como un lugar de encuentro de la cultura, el comercio, las finanzas y los sueños de muchos de nuestros conciudadanos que dejan sus tierras de origen en busca de oportunidades.

Permítanme agradecerles a los organizadores de este evento la amable invitación que nos hicieron para participar en el mismo, y tener la ocasión de presentarles mi experiencia en materia de desarrollo, y hablarles de las perspectivas de la agricultura en el Caribe.

EL CARIBE: POBLACIÓN Y CULTURA

La región del Caribe está conformada por 32 Estados y posesiones de ultramar de las potencias que colonizaron esta parte del mundo en los umbrales del siglo XVI. Su población se estima en 33.6 millones de habitantes, de los cuales alrededor de 29 millones corresponden a cinco países con más de un millón de personas: Cuba, República Dominicana (R.D.), Haití, Jamaica y Trinidad y Tobago. Es bueno significar que de la población total del Caribe, Cuba y R.D. tienen el 60%.

La posición geográfica que ocupa la región la convierte en privilegiada desde la perspectiva del comercio internacional. No sólo por su cercanía a uno de los principales mercados del mundo como lo es Estados Unidos, sino por su localización estratégica para el tráfico del comercio entre los océanos Pacífico y Atlántico.

Cuba y República Dominicana: Una misma geografía

No cabe duda que de todos los países en el área, Cuba y República Dominicana son las naciones que presentan mayor grado de similitud. Son las de mayor territorio y población, y fueron los países donde la cultura española se asentó con mayor fuerza, dejando no sólo sus huellas arquitectónicas, sino también una profunda influencia de la cultura latina.

En lo que respecta al clima y a la biodiversidad, ambas naciones son muy similares. Esta similitud se observa no sólo en la belleza de sus playas y su caliente sol, sino en la riqueza genética de su flora y de su fauna. El relieve topográfico de ambas islas es de una gran complejidad y diversidad, compuesto por montañas, llanuras y alturas de las cuales sobresalen el Pico Real del Turquino en Cuba, con 1,972 metros de altura, y el Pico Duarte en la República Dominicana con 3,175 metros de altura, el más alto de las Antillas. Basta analizar los regímenes de lluvias, vientos, distribución de temperaturas, divisiones ecológicas y su patrón de cultivos, para hacernos pensar que nos encontramos en la continuación de un territorio que alguna vez perteneció a la misma porción terrestre.

Cuba y R.D. presentan sistemas de producción agrícola muy parecidos, basados en los cultivos de caña de azúcar, tabaco, café, cacao, arroz, vegetales, flores y frutas tropicales. Es evidente que ambas naciones pueden emprender acciones de desarrollo de manera conjuntas, así como extrapolar experiencias sin verse expuestas a grandes costos de ajuste, para garantizar su éxito.

LA ECONOMÍA DEL CARIBE

El sistema de producción organizado en el Caribe desde sus inicios, respondió fundamentalmente a los objetivos económicos de determinados países más que a una estrategia de desarrollo local. El primer ingenio azucarero en el nuevo mundo fue establecido en el año 1516, en la República Dominicana. Antes de finalizar el siglo XVI, Cuba, Jamaica, Puerto Rico y otras de las Antillas Mayores también estaban integradas a la producción de azúcar, todas bajo el control de España. En el curso del siglo siguiente Gran Bretaña, Holanda, Francia y Dinamarca también se integraron a la producción de azúcar en las Pequeñas Antillas. Y fue tanta la significación del Caribe en la producción de azúcar para Europa, que el eminente economista inglés Adams Smith, en su clásico libro *Las Riquezas de las Naciones*, se refería a esta región como "nuestras colonias del azúcar o islas del azúcar," de la misma manera que se refería a Maryland y Virginia en los Estados Unidos, como "nuestras provincias del tabaco."

Se puede afirmar que las sociedades del Caribe, en cuanto a su organización económica, social, política y crecimiento demográfico, fueron notablemente diferentes, dependiendo del país que las colonizó. El resultado de ese fenómeno histórico repercute hasta nuestros días. Así encontramos variaciones tan notables en el PIB per cápita de la región: en Haití es de 250 dólares y en Bahamas, 11,940 dólares. Las economías del Caribe son relativamente abiertas, ya que sus importaciones y exportaciones representan proporciones considerables de su producto interno bruto. Este nivel de apertura de las economías caribeñas pone a la región en buenas condiciones para tomar ventaja de los procesos de globalización y apertura comercial que caracterizan los intercambios comerciales hoy día.

No obstante, debemos tener en cuenta las diferencias entre países, antes de proceder a una generalización de las medidas de apertura. Este es el caso de mi país, el cual está obligado a ajustar los tiempos de la apertura al proceso de creación y construcción en nuestra economía, de instrumentos que eleven la competitividad del sector productivo. Ahora bien, esta necesidad de proceder con cautela no debe usarse como excusa para obstaculizar el proceso de apertura y modernización de nuestras economías.

EE.UU.: Principal Socio Comercial del Caribe

Si observamos el comportamiento del comercio de la región con los Estados Unidos, principal socio comercial del Caribe, se notará que mientras en 1983 el 77% de las exportaciones eran de productos tradicionales, en su mayoría de origen agrícola, hoy día está constituído por un 73% de productos *no tradicionales,* principalmente producidos en zonas francas. Para 1994, el 86% de las exportaciones de zonas francas estaban destinadas al mercado de los EE.UU., y de éstas, alrededor de la mitad las constituían las exportaciones de ropas. A este respecto, me refiero a la solicitud que están haciendo un grupo de países caribeños, incluyendo la República Dominicana, para que EE.UU. beneficie al Caribe con un programa que otorgue a la región el mismo tratamiento arancelario que recibe México bajo el acuerdo NAFTA.

Gran parte de los avances que se han logrado en la diversificación de la economía regional, se debe a los incentivos y programas que los EE.UU. ha ofrecido a través de acuerdos preferenciales como el de la Iniciativa para la Cuenca del Caribe (CBI). Para impedir que se pierdan los cientos de miles de empleos que se han creado en la zona con la industria textil, es muy importante que el Congreso norteamericano acceda a otorgar la *paridad textil* con México a los países caribeños. Esta medida contribuiría significativamente a la paz social y estabilidad política de la región.

El Turismo

Es interesante hacer notar que el mismo sol que hizo del Caribe una potencia en la producción de azúcar, con el cultivo de caña como el más eficiente convertidor de la energía solar, a través de un intrincado proceso de fotosíntesis, en materia orgánica utilizable. Ese mismo sol está sirviendo para transformar la economía del Caribe, apoyada en el turismo como sector dinámico de la región. El turismo ha sido la industria líder de la región en los últimos 15 años, con una tasa de crecimiento anual de 5% y una contribución aproximada de 25% al Producto Interno Bruto (PIB). Se estima que uno de cada 6 trabajadores de la región, lo hace en el sector turístico. Es decir que alrededor de un millón de personas trabajan en esta actividad. Anualmente 25 millones de personas visitan el Caribe, de los cuales una parte son turistas de cruceros. El impacto de esta industria turística en la economía de los diferentes países se estima en unos 60,000 millones de dólares anuales. El turismo hace un innegable aporte al mejoramiento de la balanza de pago, a la expansión del sector servicio, a la generación de empleos y a la atracción de capitales para la inversión en el desarrollo de obras de infraestructura de la región.

Por su parte, el ecoturismo presenta la oportunidad de un nuevo impulso a la industria turística. Muchos de los gobiernos del Caribe están empezando a reconocer el potencial de la región para ofrecer productos turísticos basados en la diversidad natural. Esto significa que las naciones del Caribe incrementen las áreas dedicadas a parques naturales, marinos y terrestres y tomen medidas destinadas a proteger sus recursos naturales. Investigaciones realizadas en los Estados Unidos muestran que 43 millones de norteamericanos prefieren el ecoturismo en lugar del turismo tradicional. Según una encuesta del Centro Nacional de Viajes de los EE.UU., los turistas norteamericanos están dispuestos a pagar precios 8.5% más elevados por servicios provistos de sensibilidad ecológica. Y un porcentaje muy elevado dijo preferir hoteles que implementen programas medioambientales.

La belleza que caracteriza la riqueza natural del Caribe y que atrae a millones de personas a disfrutar de sus encantos, también presenta grandes retos para la conservación de sus recursos naturales por los impactos que tiene la intervención humana sobre sistemas ecológicos frágiles. A este respecto, el Programa Ambiental de las Naciones Unidas advierte que el turismo más que ninguna otra industria puede causar daños irreversibles a los recursos sobre los cuales se desarrolla, si no tomamos las medidas preventivas de

lugar. Existe la necesidad de actuar coordinadamente en la defensa y uso de nuestros recursos naturales. Acciones conjuntas en la región pueden expresarse en dos direcciones: a) por medio de programas de conservación y protección medioambientalistas, incluyendo la disposición de desechos, y b) a través de programas de explotación y desarrollo tecnológico para el aprovechamiento de los recursos marinos.

LA GLOBALIZACIÓN Y SU IMPACTO EN LAS NACIONES CARIBEÑAS

Cada día es más difícil determinar el origen de un producto, debido a que la materia prima, los componentes y la transformación industrial provienen de y se ensamblan en diferentes partes del mundo. Esto significa no sólo diversos movimientos de bienes y servicios a través de nuestras fronteras, sino también traslados de capitales e inversiones así como de mano de obra. El Caribe debe ver este proceso de globalización como una oportunidad y no como una amenaza. Este proceso puede ser beneficioso para la región sólo sí desarrolla la capacidad técnica, y si los gobiernos y sus líderes diseñan políticas de estímulos al progreso y esfuerzo creativo de hombres y mujeres de ésta región que han demostrado su amor al trabajo a través de los años.

El proceso de globalización, el cual en gran medida ha sido concebido a partir de las grandes economías, obliga a las pequeñas economías de la región a fomentar procesos de integración dirigidos a elevar la capacidad negociadora de cada país, en particular a través de la fuerza en bloque. ¿Cómo pueden los países del Caribe sacar ventajas al proceso de globalización? Creando el ambiente adecuado para atraer la inversión, explotar nuestras ventajas comparativas y educar a nuestra población.

Esto se logra teniendo un Estado de Derecho en el que se respeten y cumplan las leyes, y las personas tengan las mismas oportunidades sin importar ciudadanía, color, religión o sexo. Aquellas sociedades apoyadas en el imperio de la ley, son las que mayores perspectivas tienen para alcanzar el crecimiento sostenido y la eliminación gradual de la pobreza. El Estado debe jugar un papel regulador que garantice un ambiente de libre competencia y proteja al sector privado contra prácticas desleales de comercio, y al consumidor y a los productores contra prácticas mono-pólicas. También procurando que los países disfruten de una adecuada infraestructura que sirva de apoyo a los procesos de producción y fortalecimiento de las ventajas competitivas de los sistemas productivos nacionales.

Cuando hablo de infraestructura, me refiero a tener carreteras, puertos y aeropuertos adecuados y en buen estado; tener procesos administrativos ágiles y eficientes; y disponer de servicios permanentes de electricidad, acueducto, tratamiento de aguas residuales y teléfonos modernos. ¿Qué deseo significar con la expresión, políticas económicas adecuadas? Políticas que proporcionen estabilidad relativa en los precios, que estimulen el crecimiento económico y no discriminen entre sectores y productos. ¿Qué es una política económica transparente? Aquellas políticas adoptadas mediante un proceso democrático y de consulta con todos los sectores interesados, y divulgadas para que la ciudadanía las conozca antes de entrar en efecto y durante su ejecución.

Y me refiero a políticas económicas estables para precisar que no se cambian de la noche a la mañana y cuando se cambian, se debería dar un tiempo prudente antes de su adopción. La prudencia del tiempo depende de la industria afectada. Una industria con altos costos de instalación y de cierre necesitará más tiempo que una industria con bajos costos de entrar y salir.

La importancia de adecuar los tiempos es porque el país necesita de la inversión, y los inversionistas necesitan un horizonte lo suficientemente amplio para garantizar el retorno de su inversión, bajo los supuestos que asumieron al hacer el estudio de factibilidad.

LA COMPETITIVIDAD: IMPRESCINDIBLE PUNTO DE PARTIDA

La competitividad es un concepto que se basa en el posicionamiento de un producto en el mercado. Ésta tiene dos dimensiones: bajos costos de producción, y transformación para dotar al producto de las cualidades y atributos requeridos por el mercado. El desafío para nuestras naciones está en diseñar y trabajar en el desarrollo de una estrategia que conlleve a lograr ambas dimensiones. La experiencia acumulada nos indi-

ca que los principales componentes de esa estrategia deben ser los siguientes:

- **Impulsar el desarrollo tecnológico.** En un ambiente de libre competencia, aquellos países con amplio desarrollo tecnológico llevarán ventajas comparativas sobre aquéllos que, por una razón u otra, no renuevan sus tecnologías para producir y mercadear sus productos.

  El aumento de la productividad y de la competitividad se logran mediante la utilización de tecnologías que sean más eficientes en el uso de los recursos, por lo que el sector público necesita trabajar con el sector privado para mejorar los sistemas de generación y transferencia de tecnología.

- **Disponer de recursos financieros.** En la generalidad de los casos, las tasas de interés en los países caribeños está muy por encima del promedio de países desarrollados, por ejemplo Estados Unidos de Norteamérica, y ligeramente por encima del de los países de América del Sur y la zona Andina.

  El sector público debe unir fuerzas al sector privado para lograr flujos de capitales locales e internacionales, que aseguren disponibilidad suficiente en el momento requerido y a tasas competitivas.

- **Promover la participación del sector empresarial.** La competitividad difícilmente se logra o se hace sostenible en un sistema estatal, donde el Estado tiene que asumir todo el costo del desarrollo.

  En las economías modernas, el Estado tiene un papel normativo y facilitador, dejando al sector privado el papel operativo o de ejecución. Sin embargo, toca al Estado orientar y promover la participación del sector privado en los diferentes aspectos de la cadena agroalimentaria e industrial.

- **Capacitar los recursos humanos.** La capacitación de los recursos humanos en los diferentes niveles productivos es imprescindible para lograr la competitividad. Para lograr ser competitivo debemos contar con una gerencia efectiva y mano de obra especializada. En el mundo de hoy es más importante el cómo hacer las cosas, que el con qué hacerlas. Hoy día, más importante que tener recursos naturales abundantes, es tener la capacidad de agregarles valor.

- **Desarrollar un sistema eficiente de información.** En el nuevo orden mundial el cambio es ya parte del diario vivir. De aquí la importancia de contar con un buen sistema de información para ser competitivo.

La información, junto a la capacitación de los recursos humanos, se ha convertido en uno de los parámetros imprescindibles para el desarrollo sostenible. El mercado nos exige que cambiemos de la mentalidad de producir y vender productos básicos, o "commodities," a productos más diferenciados.

- **Promover políticas balanceadas para todos.** La responsabilidad del Estado es proteger a todos los sectores que componen la nación. Para ello deberá adoptar una política que proteja a la mayoría de sus ciudadanos. Sin embargo, no basta contemplar el bienestar a corto plazo; de aquí que las políticas deberán ser balanceadas para no perjudicar a ninguno de los sectores productivos.

Bajos salarios no son sinónimos de bajos costos. La clave para ser competitivos en costos es productividad, y la alta productividad de la mano de obra es lo que nos permite pagar mayores salarios, contribuyendo así a la equidad.

Esta mayor productividad de la mano de obra se logra a través de la educación, una adecuada alimentación y buena salud del trabajador. Es por esto que necesitamos educar nuestra población y ser diligentes en llevarles los servicios de salud, así como mejorar los sistemas de comercialización, para que nuestros productores reciban un mejor precio por sus productos, mejorando así su acceso al disfrute de los bienes materiales y espirituales.

- **Promover la equidad.** El tema de la equidad es un tema sumamente delicado y a la vez muy importante. Del nivel de equidad que tengamos dependerá el nivel de paz y seguridad social de la que disfrutaremos todos en el Caribe.

La pobreza se diferencia por países. Observamos las grandes diferencias del producto per cápita que existe entre los países del Caribe; así es también en los índices de pobreza.

Mientras muchos países concentran la mayor parte de su pobreza en las zonas urbanas, unos cuantos la tienen mayormente en la zona rural.

Esto requiere estrategias diferenciadas para atacar el fenómeno desde el punto de vista agroindustrial. Aunque en ambos casos se precisa de alimentos relativamente baratos, lo cual es un reto para la agricultura, cuando la pobreza se concentra en la zona rural y entre los más pobres se encuentran los pequeños productores, los mismos necesitan mejorar sus ingresos mediante la obtención de mayores precios.

¿Cómo conjugamos estos objetivos? Aumentando la productividad, principalmente de la mano de obra, del mejoramiento de la eficiencia de la comercialización, de la diferenciación del producto, de la formación de alianzas estratégicas, y de la solidaridad entre los más grandes y los más pequeños.

UNA NUEVA INSTITUCIONALIDAD: UN MARCO NORMATIVO

Para poder aprovechar las oportunidades que los nuevos escenarios nos presentan, necesitamos hacer cambios en nuestras instituciones públicas y privadas. La institucionalidad que es urgente construir en nuestros países debe sustentarse en un ambiente de cooperación y de convergencias en las relaciones entre el Estado y la sociedad civil, en el marco de una economía de mercado con reglas iguales para todos. Este nuevo enfoque supone por un lado la creación de consensos entre intereses opuestos y, por otro lado, el liderazgo del Estado para que sean respetados. Un Estado que actúe efectivamente como promotor de un desarrollo con mayor equidad, como un eficiente prestador de servicios y garante de los derechos sociales.

Los cambios institucionales se proponen como mecanismos para resolver problemas de asignación de recursos, de cambios tecnológicos y eficiencia económica. Pero también con el objetivo de maximizar el bienestar, mejorar la equidad y promover la justicia social. Esta institucionalidad debe construirse a partir de objetivos claros, que contribuyan a mejorar los niveles de competitividad en una forma tal que también alivie la pobreza, e impulse el manejo racional e integrado de los recursos naturales.

Hoy día no pueden ignorarse las presiones que imponen la apertura comercial y los equilibrios macroeconómicos sobre las políticas públicas y los sectores productivos locales, pero tampoco puede dejarse de lado el riesgo que representa para la sociedad, su gobernabilidad y la democracia, el deterioro que podrían crear las tensiones sociales. El gobierno está obligado a defender esas medidas y proveer los instrumentos que requiere el sector productivo para insertarse en las nuevas reglas del comercio internacional. De igual manera, los productores de la región tendremos que propiciar las transformaciones que requieren las empresas para ser eficientes. Hoy son los países los que tienen que ser competitivos. Es muy difícil a las empresas lograr niveles altos de eficiencia en un país que no lo sea.

LA AGRICULTURA: NUEVOS ESCENARIOS Y POSIBILIDADES AGROTECNOLÓGICAS

El nuevo ordenamiento mundial nos plantea un ambiente de cambios en el cual la agricultura ha dejado de ser una excepción. Hemos pasado de los centros de decisiones nacionales a los mundiales, con una mayor integración de los mercados financieros y una mayor concentración del mercado mundial en las empresas multinacionales. Los avances logrados en el campo de la cibernética, la microelectrónica, biotecnología y la ingeniería genética han permitido incrementar la eficiencia y la productividad en toda la cadena agroalimentaria. Por ejemplo, el uso de computadoras en la fertirrigación, permite controlar con exactitud la cantidad de agua y fertilizantes de acuerdo a las necesidades de cada planta de manera individual. Imaginémonos el impacto que ya está teniendo la manipulación del DNA en plantas y animales. Esta realidad se ha puesto en evidencia en Inglaterra con *Dolly*, la primera oveja clonada.

En términos prácticos, estos hechos rompen las barreras para la solución de innumerables problemas de producción, tales como el control de plagas y enfermedades, la adaptabilidad de un cultivo a diversos tipos de suelos y climas, y el incremento de la productividad más allá de lo que pudiéramos imaginarnos hace sólo una década. La producción de híbridos interespecíficos, la producción de embriones somáticos y la misma posibilidad de clonar animales, aves y peces ya son parte del presente, en la producción de semillas y animales de alta producción y resistencia a plagas y enfermedades diversas. La oportunidad de manipular los genes de especies como la soya para permitir el uso de herbicidas que anteriormente no se podían usar en determinadas plantas, o el lograr cruces interespecíficos entre especies no compatible, seleccionadas por ejemplo, por su sabor, productividad, resistencia al transporte o a la temperatura. También puede usarse para producir frutas libres de semillas. Estos ejemplos son sólo algunas de la infinidad de campos que nos abre el nivel actual de conocimiento de la ciencia. Un pequeño empresario agrícola con algunos acres de tierra, usando materiales genéticos de alto potencial puede producir toneladas de tomates o pimientos. Unas cuantas matas de guayabas cultivadas apropiadamente pueden generar ingresos suficientes para una familia.

Desafortunadamente, la realidad que he descrito anteriormente no es la que caracteriza la mayoría de nuestros productores en la región. En la generalidad de los casos y, a pesar de los ejemplos de éxitos, nuestros países se caracterizan por el uso de una tecnología inapropiada, deficiente y en ocasiones obsoleta. Esto es así porque la inversión en desarrollo tecnológico es muy poca comparado con el resto del mundo, incluyendo los países del Cono Sur.

En su gran mayoría, la agricultura regional está en crisis. Contrario a los países desarrollados, las políticas agrícolas en la región han penalizados los ingresos de los productores rurales, mientras los países ricos compensan a sus productores para lograr paridad de ingresos con los sectores urbanos. No podemos dejar de mencionar que la presión de las importaciones desde países con altos subsidios y apoyo a sus productores está sacando del mercado a los productores locales, debido, no a que nuestros productores son ineficientes, sino a las diferencias en los sistemas de apoyo a la agricultura de una región a otra.

El resultado de las políticas expuestas ha significado un proceso de empobrecimiento del mundo rural, más acentuado que en el del resto de los sectores sociales. Y esto debe preocuparnos porque si bien es cierto que la pobreza es el mayor flagelo de nuestros países, es en el campo donde ésta es más agobiante. Por esta razón, no son casuales las frecuentes manifestaciones de agitación social que se presentan en los medios rurales centroamericano, sudamericano y caribeño. Como tampoco lo son en las áreas marginadas de las zonas urbanas cubiertas cada vez más rápido por los pobres que llegan del campo.

Es por esto que el nuevo enfoque de la agricultura, no sólo debe incluir los principios de la competitividad, sino también de la sostenibilidad y la equidad. Tan malo para nuestros países es la equidad sin crecimiento como el crecimiento sin equidad. La sostenibilidad debe ofrecernos las herramientas para seguir un desarrollo productivo, consistente con la obligación creciente de producir conservando y conservar produciendo. En la medida que la población envejece y los ingresos de la población aumentan, los hábitos alimenticios cambian a un mayor consumo de frutas y vegetales que tienen un mayor valor que los productos tradicionales.

Se estima que para el año 2015 alrededor del 25% del total de la demanda de productos agropecuarios en los países desarrollados, responderá a preferencias de productos cosechados atendiendo a criterios ecológicos. En R.D., por ejemplo, es significativo el número de proyectos dedicados a la producción para la exportación de frutas tales como bananas, naranjas, café, cacao y hasta azúcar de caña bajo condiciones libre de pesticidas. Este mercado está en crecimiento y si nuestros países apoyan su desarrollo, puede convertirse en un mercado de importancia para los pequeños productores de la región.

El producir cultivos exóticos para nichos de mercados ofrece grandes oportunidades para los países del Caribe por el predominio de pequeños productores en modelos familiares. Esta ventaja comparativa nos permite competir en cultivos con pequeñas demandas localizadas, las cuales no ofrecen un atractivo para los países grandes, reduciéndose así la posibilidad de competencia. Así mismo, podemos mencionar el gran potencial de la región para productos diferenciados y autóctonos o aquellos cultivos que por condiciones agroclimáticas sólo pueden producirse en pocas regiones del mundo. Algunos ejemplos de lo anterior es la producción y comercialización de la manzana de oro (Golden Apple) en Granada. Dada que la demanda mundial de esta fruta es muy pequeña, países como los EE.UU., el cual además no tiene condiciones para producirla, no se han interesado en cultivarla. Sin embargo, en Granada, este cultivo ha llegado a representar uno de los lugares preferenciales en la gama de cultivos exportables. El potencial genético de Cuba es reconocido mundialmente. Sus aguacates, nísperos, anónaceas como la guanábana y la chirimoya, sus mangos y otros exóticos, ofrecen un amplio potencial latente para la exportación en fresco y como productos procesados.

Con la apertura de los mercados, en la agricultura tenemos un reto adicional, que es el relacionado con los asuntos fitosanitarios. Los representantes del sector público agrícola tienen la gran responsabilidad de salvaguardar la producción de la entrada, establecimiento y propagación de plagas y enfermedades exóticas sin restringir el comercio. Sin embago, necesitamos que los países no utilicen las medidas fitosanitarias como barreras al comercio y que se reduzca el tiempo para hacer los análisis requeridos para que un nuevo producto sea admitido en el país importador, que en algunos casos el proceso toma un mínimos de tres a cinco años. En el control fitosanitario, las islas del Caribe tienen la gran ventaja de estar aisladas por el agua, lo que hace menos difícil el control de las plagas y enfermedades, facilitando así la declaratoria del país entero como área libre. Esto facilita la exportación de productos agrícolas frescos.

Modelos y Ejemplos Exitosos en el Caribe

En el Caribe tenemos ejemplos muy exitosos de cómo mejorar la eficiencia y expandir los mercados. Un ejemplo es lo que ha estado haciendo Jamaica en la promoción y desarrollo de sus exportaciones de productos agrícolas a través de JAMPRO. Otro ejemplo es lo que está haciendo la Organización de Estados del Caribe del Este (OECS), cuyos miembros, a través de la Unidad Coordinadora de Diversificación Agrícola, han hecho estudios de competitividad, probando cultivos alternos, desarrollando el mercado de frutas, vegetales y flores frescas y promoviendo su siembra.

El ejemplo de la Junta Agroempresarial Dominicana (JAD), la cual aglutina productores, procesadores, comerciantes importadores y exportadores, es otra muestra de la comprensión que han estado adquiriendo los empresarios de la región en el proceso de impulsar la transformación productiva del sector agroalimentario. El caso del Central Romana es uno de los más exitosos en la República Dominicana. Aparte de ser uno de los mayores y más eficientes productores de azúcar de caña, el Central Romana, desde la década de los setentas, inició un proceso de diversificación de sus operaciones agrícolas en el Caribe. Sus aportes a la economía, hoy día, incluyen impulso a la industria de carne con la crianza de ganado estabulado y mejoramiento de razas, zona franca, el turismo, promoción de la cultura del país con el patrocinio de una escuela de diseño y arte y un sinnúmero de actividades que han enriquecido la vida económica y social de la nación dominicana.

Otros renglones donde nuestro país ha mostrado grandes habilidades en los últimos años son en la producción de puros, producción de bananas para el mercado de Europa, cítricos y vegetales frescos para el mercado norteamericano. En este último campo, al igual que en la producción de ornamentales, donde la Florida es un productor líder, la R.D. tiene grandes oportunidades para la inversión.

No quiero terminar sin mencionar la maricultura como un renglón de gran potencial productivo en la región. Tenemos el mercado de los turistas y existe la tecnología para la producción controlada de especies marinas. Sólo hace falta que el empresariado y los gobiernos emprendan el desarrollo de este sector.

Finalmente, vivimos bajo el calor de un mismo sol y la brisa fresca de un mismo mar en esta región, multirracial por obra del destino, pero enriquecida por la fuerza de diferentes culturas. Es justamente su diversidad la que encierra un inmenso potencial de esperanza para sus habitantes. Un potencial que se incrementa por nuestro origen y nuestra tradición de hombres y mujeres incansablemente trabajadores. Razón suficiente para pensar como una vez lo hicieron los japoneses, de que su recurso más importe es su gente.

Los recursos que abundan a todo lo ancho y largo de nuestras islas están ahí, esperando ser explotados. Y ese potencial sólo podrá ser puesto al servicios del bienestar de nuestros pueblos si hacemos realidad los sueños de *unidad* de nuestros padres fundadores entre quienes sobresalen Juan Pablo Duarte y José Martí.

COMENTARIOS A

"Experiencias Agroclimatológicas de República Dominicana y el Caribe Adaptables a Cuba" de Hipólito Mejía

Raúl Fernández García

Pocas veces el ejercicio del deber profesional se presenta asociado a un país al cual, como la República Dominicana, me unen años de trabajos fecundos compartidos con distinguidos dominicanos como Don Hipólito Mejía. En esos años, tuve la suerte de acompañar el renacimiento de la República Dominicana, tras una de las tiranías más obscuras de América. Tanto para mi distinguido amigo Ingeniero Mejía como para mí, estoy seguro que Cuba y la República Dominicana constituyen un contínuo, donde las diferencias de las banderas se atenúan ante la multitud de elementos similares.

El trabajo de Mejía abarca un extenso escenario agrotécnico y agroeconómico. Con toda propiedad se refiere a cómo, en los últimos años, nuevas tecnologías se han desarrollado en diversos países. El reloj de la civilización se aceleró cuando el hombre, hace apenas medio siglo, aprendió a escribir programas para que las computadoras ejecutaran las más complejas operaciones. Pocos entonces imaginaron que otra computadora, una que ha venido perfeccionándose durante cuatro mil millones de años, sería pronto objeto de manipulaciones capaces de generar resultados biológicos insospechados. Nos referimos a los programas genéticos codificados por el DNA, sujetos ahora a adaptaciones útiles en la agricultura, la medicina y otros campos.

Pese a esas prometedoras hazañas de la ciencia, no debemos perder de vista que el hombre no sólo está limitado por la capacidad de sus máquinas, sino tam-

bién, y de manera muy importante, por el entorno de la naturaleza, dentro del cual surgió como especie y al cual se adaptó so pena de perecer. En este contexto, no debemos olvidarnos de la debida atención a los recursos naturales como el suelo. Nuestras experiencias en Cuba, la República Dominicana, Jamaica y Haití nos indican que graves problemas en el desempeño ordenado y próspero de esos pueblos, inevitablemente se presentarán si no se otorga al suelo la jerarquía que merece como uno de los recursos más preciosos del hombre.

Destaca Don Hipólito la importancia de la competitividad, que a nosotros nos parece algo así como el nudo gordiano que el Tercer Mundo tiene que deshacer. Porque en la competitividad vienen a incidir, como señala Mejía, diversas causas. Dice él: "En el mundo de hoy son los países los que tienen que ser competitivos. Es muy difícil a las empresas lograr niveles altos de eficiencia en un país que **no** lo sea."

O sea, un país no será eficiente, a menos que entre los valores de su sociedad se incorporen, destacadamente, aquellos que contribuyen a la eficiencia del individuo, de la familia y de las empresas. En otras palabras, lo que concluímos del trabajo de Mejía en este aspecto es que un país que quiera ser competitivo requiere, ni más ni menos, crear en su pueblo una cultura de la eficiencia.

Compartimos las indicaciones hechas sobre los componentes que deberían incluirse en una estrategia para desarrollar la competitividad. Inpulsar el desarrollo tecnológico figura, merecidamente, en el primer lugar. ¡Cuán frecuentemente, cuando abrimos el periódico nos sorprenden noticias, casi de ciencia ficción, relativas a descubrimientos o inventos en la biotecnología, la medicina, la electrónica, la cosmología, etc! ¿Es posible para algún país dejar de impulsar el desarrollo tecnológico?

Disponer de los recursos financieros es otro requisito destacado por Mejía. No podemos extendernos, pero conviene señalar respecto de los altas tasas de interés en el Caribe, que dichas tasas, entre otros factores, reflejan el nivel de riesgos. En la medida en que nuestros países sean estables y que la comunidad de prestatarios honre fielmente sus compromisos de pagos, por leyes naturales de economía y de finanzas, esas tasas de interés deben descender.

Otros componentes de la estrategia para alcanzar la competitividad son señalados en el trabajo. Entre ellos quisiéramos destacar la promoción de políticas balanceadas para todos. La falta de políticas balanceadas es usualmente el producto de prácticas corruptas. Al repecto valdría decir que si a la corrupción se le considera un obstáculo al desarrollo, por los recursos que directamente succiona, yo creo que la corrupción, por el desaliento que genera en el seno de la sociedad y la pérdida de estímulo consiguiente, posiblemente constituye un gravamen mayor para los países que la propia malversación directa de recursos.

UNA MISMA GEOGRAFIA

Subrayando la existencia de una misma geografía, Mejía sugiere la oportunidad de que la República Dominicana y Cuba puedan emprender acciones de desarrollo de manera conjunta. Compartimos esa sugerencia para que, en el momento apropiado, se explore la factibilidad de proyectos como el siguiente.

La República Dominicana y Cuba, con dinamismo y sentido común, deberían procurar acuerdos de cooperación técnica y científica con los centros internacionales de investigación, y otros centros públicos y privados. Países como la India e Israel, con áreas que comparten condiciones ecológicas del Caribe y que disfrutan de un alto nivel tecnológico, podrían brindar una asistencia muy efectiva. La captación inmediata de informaciones y material genético ya disponibles daría un gran impulso a las dos naciones antillanas. Ello permitiría a ambas, como señala Don Hipólito "interpolar aquellas experiencias positivas que tengan lugar en sus países o en la región, sin verse expuestas a grandes costos de ajuste, para garantizar su éxito."

Deseo terminar expresando mi satisfacción por haberme correspodido el privilegio de comentar un trabajo que revela la capacidad del Ingeniero Hipólito Mejía para ver y comprender, en su complejidad, los retos a los que deberá dar adecuada respuesta la República Dominicana.

EL SECTOR AGROPECUARIO CUBANO BAJO EL SOCIALISMO DE ESTADO

Manuel Sánchez Herrero y Arnaldo Ramos Lauzurique[1]

En los primeros años de la década de los 90 se desató la crisis económica que por su complejidad y alcance ha sido considerada una de las más graves ocurridas en nuestro país, afectando profundamente a todos los sectores de la economía nacional, incluyendo al que en la actualidad integran la agricultura, la actividad forestal y la pesca. Con su estallido, a causa fundamentalmente del derrumbe del campo socialista, se puso en evidencia que la producción agropecuaria y alimentaria cubana no garantiza por sí misma las necesidades nutricionales de la población, pues ésta dependía básicamente de las importaciones de alimentos recibidas de esos países. Aunque la crisis de este importante sector no es reciente, ha venido presentando en los últimos años una tendencia a agravarse cada vez más.

Hay que señalar que el presente estudio se circunscribe al plano del otrora denominado sector agropecuario solamente, englobado ahora en el de agricultura, caza, silvicultura y pesca, por cuanto la silvicultura y la pesca constituyen, en interés de los objetivos de este análisis, tema de una reflexión posterior y más abarcadora por la relevancia que tienen las mismas dentro de la economía de la nación.

En términos generales se puede afirmar que, a pesar de tener un elevado nivel de calificación los numerosos técnicos ocupados en las actividades agropecuarias y considerables recursos agrícolas naturales, así como equipos, implementos y sistemas de riego en cantidades substanciales para un país subdesarrollado económicamente, la agricultura cubana ha progresado poco en sus niveles productivos, caracterizados a lo largo de todos estos años por modestos crecimientos y en ocasiones abruptas caídas. La inestabilidad es el rasgo predominante que afecta a la agricultura de nuestro país. Estos resultados decepcionantes se analizan en apretada síntesis a continuación.

ASPECTOS GENERALES
Indicadores de Eficiencia
Al examinar en el período estadístico 1975-88 el comportamiento de los principales indicadores de eficiencia del que fuera hasta hace algunos años atrás el sector agropecuario, los resultados que muestran los mismos son de total deterioro. Debemos señalar, en primer lugar, la tendencia descendente que registró en la etapa analizada el rendimiento de los fondos básicos asignados[2] a este conjunto de actividades (agrícolas y pecuarias), el cual disminuyó a un ritmo promedio anual del 7.32% (Ver Tabla No. 1 y Gráfico No. 1).

Por otro lado, el stock de fondos básicos creció más deprisa que el promedio de trabajadores. En conse-

---

1. Este trabajo apareció originalmente como un suplemento especial del Boletín No. 8 del Grupo de Trabajo de la Disidencia Interna para el Análisis de la Situación Económica Cubana, Diciembre de 1997. Fue leído en la reunión de ASCE por Ricardo A. Puerta.

2. Este indicador era el utilizado antes de la crisis actual en las estadísticas oficiales: Rf=Producción bruta/Fondos básicos productivos. Es equivalente a la relación Producción bruta/Capital fijo.

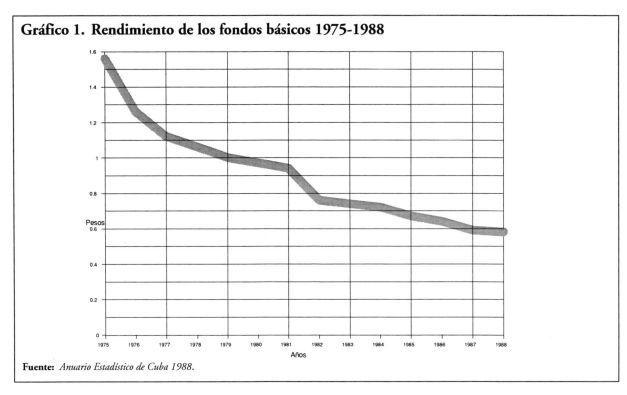

Gráfico 1. Rendimiento de los fondos básicos 1975-1988

Fuente: *Anuario Estadístico de Cuba 1988.*

Gráfico 2. Dotación de fondos básicos por trabajador y productividad

Tabla 1.   Rendimiento de los fondos básicos

Años	Pesos	Años	Pesos
1975	1.56	1982	0.76
1976	1.26	1983	0.74
1977	1.12	1984	0.72
1978	1.06	1985	0.67
1979	1.00	1986	0.64
1980	0.97	1987	0.59
1981	0.94	1988	0.58

Fuente: *Anuario Estadístico de Cuba 1988.*

Tabla 2.   Dotación de fondos básicos por trabajador y productividad del trabajo

Año	Dotación	Product.	Año	Dotación	Product.
1975	2,480	3,039	1982	6,773	4,318
1976	3,282	3,250	1983	7,553	4,452
1977	3,842	3,446	1984	8,336	5,027
1978	4,262	3,634	1985	9,514	5,185
1979	4,772	3,824	1986	9,927	5,124
1980	5,097	3,865	1987	10,115	4,805
1981	6,024	4,414	1988	9,743	4,565

Fuente: *Anuario Estadístico de Cuba 1986* y *1988.*

Table 3. Indice del volumen físico de la producción agropecuaria Año base: promedio anual 1989-1991=100

Año	Indice
1970	90
1980	84
1982	95
1988	100
1989	102
1990	100
1991	98
1992	83
1993	68
1994	68
1995	64

Fuente: *Anuario Estadístico de la CEPAL 1996*, pp. 594-595.

Table 4. Participación de la agricultura el el PIB en las diferentes regiones (%)

Regiones	1960	1970	1980	1985
Países subdesarrollados	31.6	23.9	15.9	15.8
Africa	39.6	31.2	20.9	22.8
Asia	38.0	34.6	18.1	18.1
America Latina	16.5	12.8	11.1	11.1

Fuente: UNCTAD, *Handbook of International Trade and Development Statistics 1987*, p. 340.

cuencia, éstos tuvieron una cantidad creciente de medios con la que trabajar y, sin embargo, la productividad del trabajo quedó muy por debajo de ese incremento (Ver Tabla No. 2 y Gráfico No. 2).

La dotación de fondos básicos por trabajador se incrementó a una tasa promedio anual del 11.1%, mientras que la productividad del trabajo creció a un ritmo medio anual del 3.2% en igual período. En 1984-88 la productividad del trabajo descendió en un 2.45% como promedio anual.

Ahora conviene analizar un indicador que combina ambos factores (los fondos básicos y la fuerza laboral), conocido como "eficiencia conjunta de los recursos productivos." Este es favorable cuando registra valores superiores a uno (Ec>1), siendo desfavorable cuando es menos de uno (Ec<1). Entre 1980 y 1988 este índice sólo alcanzó el valor de 0.79 en el sector agropecuario.

Como resultado de la crisis económica y del mal endémico del sistema—la ineficiencia—el índice de volumen físico de la producción agropecuaria declinó entre 1989 y 1995 en un 37.3%. Y 1989 no se caracterizó precisamente por ser un año de plétora en la producción agrícola y pecuaria (Ver Tabla No. 3). En 1996 el sector agropecuario registró un decrecimiento del 2.8% con relación al año anterior.

Rasgos Más Sobresalientes del Sector Agropecuario Cubano

El sector agropecuario se caracterizó antes de la crisis actual por presentar una pérdida de importancia rela-

tiva expresada en la tendencia decreciente de su participación en el Producto Material Total (PMT) con un incremento en casi la misma magnitud de las construcciones y un aumento muy ligero en algunos años de la industria (Ver Anexo No. 1). Entre 1962 y 1988 su participación en el PMT descendió del 23.1 al 14%.

En términos generales esta misma situación se produjo en los países subdesarrollados respecto a 1968. La parte de la agricultura en el PIB bajó en las tres regiones subdesarrolladas (Africa, Asia y América Latina) y fue en esta última donde el sector agropecuario hizo menor aporte en la generación del producto en 1985, con un 11.1%, mientras que en Africa representó alrededor de la quinta parte en el mismo año (Ver Tabla No. 4).

Otra de las características más sobresalientes del sector agropecuario en nuestro país es la disminución relativa de la población rural. Entre 1931 y 1988 la población rural cubana disminuyó en términos relativos en un 21%, aunque en términos absolutos se incrementó en más del 47% (Ver Tabla No. 5).

El papel desempeñado en la agricultura en la mayoría de los países subdesarrollados se reafirma al analizar el porcentaje que la población rural representa de la población total en las tres regiones señaladas anteriormente. Si bien en las tres desde 1975 a 1988, la tendencia presentada ha sido descendente—en concordancia con el lugar que ocupa el sector agropecuario respecto a los otros sectores—en 1988 todavía era muy elevada la población agrícola en Asia y Africa, donde representaba más de la mitad de la población total, mientras que en América Latina la relación era casi igual a la de Cuba en 1988 (27.6 frente a 27.2 Cuba). Ver Tabla No. 6.

Table 5. Disminución relativa de la población rural cubana, 1931-1988

Año del Censo	Población total (u)	Población rural residente (u)	% de la población rural del total de la población	Tasa anual de crecimiento de la población total (%)
1931	3,962,344	1,927,310	48.6	2.6
1942	4,778,583	2,171,093	45.4	1.6
1953	5,829,029	2,504,401	43.0	2.0
1970	8,569,121	3,381,272	39.5	2.3
1981	9,706,369	3,007,798	31.0	1.2
1988	10,468,661	2,849,609	27.2	1.1

Fuente: Periódico *Granma*, La Habana, 30 de octubre de 1981, p. 3, *Anuario Estadístico de Cuba 1988*, La Habana, 1989, p. 61.

Table 6. Población agrícola respecto a la población total (%)

Región	1975	1980	1985	1988
Africa	73.7	70.9	68.4	66.9
Asia	64.4	62.2	59.8	58.3
América Latina	36.4	32.2	29.3	27.6

Fuente: Elaborado a partir de "Cuadro por países," FAO 1989.

Toda la información disponible sobre la distribución de la fuerza laboral cubana por actividad económica se presenta en la Tabla No. 7. Ahora bien, si nos llevamos exclusivamente por los datos estadísticos vemos que la participación relativa de la fuerza laboral en el sector agropecuario disminuye de un 41.5% en 1953 al 20.4% en 1989. Sin embargo, este no es realmente así, pues cada año han sido movilizadas decenas de miles de personas de las zonas urbanas hacia las áreas rurales del país—trabajadores de diferentes sectores de la economía nacional, estudiantes de secundaria básica, preuniversitarios, universitarios—con el objetivo de que realicen labores agrícolas como siembras, cultivos y recolección de cosechas. Estos trabajadores son reportados estadísticamente por otros sectores, no por el agropecuario, mientras que los estudiantes son registrados por las estadísticas de educación. No obstante, tanto los trabajadores como los estudiantes laboran una buena parte del año en actividades agrícolas, de forma permanente o individual. Por tanto, esta información está distorsionada y no es representativa de la realidad cubana.

Las Reformas Agrarias en Cuba

Las dos reformas agrarias realizadas en Cuba repartieron determinadas tierras a los campesinos, pero la mayor parte—los grandes latifundios ganaderos, arroceros y cañeros—los convirtieron primero en cooperativas de trabajadores que al poco tiempo fue-

Table 7. Estructura del empleo en Cuba *(por esferas y sectores, porcentajes)*

Sectores	1953	1970	1975	1980	1989
Industria	17.5	20.3	19.7	20.0	21.8
Agropecuario	41.5	30.0	28.6	22.8	20.4[a]
Construcción	3.3	6.0	8.7	10.0	9.8
Transporte	5.3	5.5	6.9	6.3	5.8
Comunicaciones	—	0.6	1.0	0.8	0.9
Comercio	11.8	11.6	7.5	11.1	11.2
Otros productivos	—	—	—	—	0.7
Sub-total	79.4	74.0	72.4	71.0	70.6
Servicios sociales	20.4	23.6	22.5	21.9	23.7
Otros sectores	0.5	2.4	5.1	7.1	5.7
Total	100.0	100.0	100.0	100.0	100.0

Fuente: Jose Luis Rodríguez, *Erradicación de la pbreza en Cuba*, La Habana, 1987, p. 65; *Anuario Estadístico de Cuba 1985 y 1989*.

a. Incluye silvicultura

ron convertidas en granjas estatales. Es decir, el mismo proceso de colectivización de la agricultura que se llevó a cabo anteriormente en las desaparecida Unión Soviética y en otros ex socialistas.

En la primera (17 de mayo de 1959) se expropiaron las tierras con más de 30 caballerías (402 hectáreas) absorbiendo el Estado el 40% de las mismas. La segunda reforma agraria (3 de octubre de 1963) limitó la propiedad individual a 67 hectáreas, con lo que el Estado se convirtió en el poseedor del 70% de las tierras del país. En 31 de diciembre de 1989 la propiedad estatal ascendía al 82.3% (Ver Tabla No. 8).

Además, el Estado estableció el monopolio más absoluto sobre la producción agropecuaria, la comercialización mayorista y la distribución minorista de esos productos. El gobierno central le exige aún a las unidades de producción agropecuaria, tanto estatales como no estatales, que le entreguen la mayor parte de su producción a sus empresas de acopio, a los precios

**Table 8. Estructura por forma de tenencia del uso de la tierra del país
En diciembre 31 de 1989**

Concepto	Total	Sector Socialista			Sector Privado		
		Total	Estatal	CPA	Total	CCS	Disperso
Superficie total	100.0	90.2	82.3	7.9	9.8	7.6	2.2
Agrícola	100.0	85.7	74.3	11.4	14.3	10.9	3.4
Cultivada	100.0	88.2	78.0	10.2	11.8	8.5	3.3
Cultivos permanentes	100.0	63.9	50.2	13.7	36.1	23.4	12.7
Cultivos temporales	100.0	63.9	50.2	13.7	36.1	23.4	12.7
Viveros y semilleros	100.0	93.0	75.4	17.6	7.0	7.0	1.0
No cultivada	100.0	80.9	67.4	13.5	19.1	15.5	3.6
Pastos naturales	100.0	80.1	65.7	14.4	19.1	16.4	3.5
Ociosas	100.0	84.5	74.2	10.3	15.5	12.0	3.5
No agrícolas	100.0	97.3	95.0	2.3	2.7	2.2	0.5
Forestal	100.0	98.1	96.5	1.6	1.9	1.5	0.4
No aptas para la agricultura y la silvicultura	100.0	92.6	87.2	5.4	7.4	6.4	1.0
Acuosa	100.0	97.8	95.5	8.3	2.2	1.9	0.3
Poblacional y const.	100.0	98.4	96.0	2.4	1.6	1.2	0.4

Fuente: *Anuario Estadístico de Cuba 1989*, p. 186.

fijados por él. Todos los recursos productivos que utilizan las entidades agropecuarias en sus actividades se los distribuyen las empresas estatales, de acuerdo con sus criterios y a los precios establecidos por ellas.

División Organizativa del Sector Agropecuario Cubano antes de la Crisis Económica

Antes de la crisis económica actual, el sector agropecuario se dividía en dos grandes sectores sociales: el estatal y el no estatal.

En el primero se incluían las empresas agropecuarias y silvícolas estatales, así como las de servicios agropecuarios—excepto la aviación agrícola—las cuales estaban adscriptas al Ministerio de la Agricultura. Las empresas cañeras, subordinadas al Ministerio de la Industria Azucarera, también estaban incluidas en este sector, conformando los complejos agroindustriales.

En el sector no estatal se incluyen las Cooperativas de Producción Agropecuaria (CPA), las Cooperativas de Créditos y Servicios (CCS) y finalmente los pequeños productores privados dispersos que establecen compromisos con el Estado en cuanto a la venta de productos agropecuarios.

Las CPA son agrupaciones de campesinos para producir colectivamente, en las cuales se unen las tierras y demás medios de producción fundamentales. Las CCS son organizaciones primarias de carácter colecti-

vo, que posibilitan el uso del riego, de algunas instalaciones, servicios y otros medios, así como el trámite global de sus créditos, aunque la propiedad de cada finca, sus equipos y la producción resultante sigue siendo privada. En 1988, la situación de las empresas agropecuarias estatales y de las cooperativas de producción agropecuarias se presentan en las Tablas No. 9 y 10.

Table 9. Indicadores seleccionados del sector agropecuario estatal

Concepto	1988
Número de empresas (U)	185
Agricultura cañera	146
Agricultura no cañera	106
Ganadería	130
Servicios agropecuarios	3
Promedio de trabajadores (M)	653.2
Agricultura cañera	235.1
Agricultura no cañera	209.7
Ganadería	106.7
Servicios agropecuarios	12.3

Fuente: *Anuario Estadístico de Cuba 1988*, p. 304.

Evolución del Sector Agropecuario en el Período 1966-70

Si le preguntásemos a un estudioso de la economía cubana y en particular del sector agropecuario cuál ha sido su etapa más difícil antes de la crisis actual, la mejor respuesta escueta que podría darnos sería: el período 1966-70.

Table 10. Indicadores seleccionados de las cooperativas de producción agropecuaria

Concepto	1988
Cantidad de cooperativas (U)	1398
Supercie existente (M ha)	907.7
Cooperativistas (U)	66014
Superficie promedio por CPA (ha)	649.29
De ello:	
Cooperativas cañeras	
Cantidad de cooperativas (U)	429
Superficie existente (M ha)	385.5
Cooperativistas (U)	28607
Superficie promedio por CPA (ha)	898.58
Cooperativistas por CPA (U)	67
Cooperativas tabacaleras	
Cantidad de cooperativas (U)	200
Superficie existente (M ha)	88.4
Cooperativistas (U)	10538
Superficie promedio por CPA (ha)	442.22
Cooperativistas por CPA (U)	53
Cooperativas cafetaleras	
Cantidad de cooperativas (U)	279
Superficie existente (M ha)	156.9
Cooperativistas (U)	9222
Superficie promedio por CPA (ha)	562.36
Cooperativistas por CPA (U)	33

Fuente: *Anuario Estadístico de Cuba 1988*, p. 304.

En el plano nacional: Se inició en 1965 en todo el país el proceso de lucha contra el burocratismo. El Instituto Nacional de Reforma Agraria (INRA) fue reducido de acuerdo con la opinión del jefe del régimen de que "con 100 hombres se controlaba toda la agricultura." El aparato central de planificación (la Junta Central de Planificación, JUCEPLAN) se torna en una función meramente operativa. En 1966 el plan anual pierde toda su vigencia práctica, no obstante se continuó elaborando para los fines internos de la Junta, pues fue reemplazado por instrucciones del partido a los centros de producción.

Entre 1967 y 1968 se estableció una forma de dirección que se apartaba tanto del cálculo económico, que era generalmente aplicado en los países socialistas, como del sistema de financiamiento presupuestario que había comenzado a ensayarse en Cuba. El riguroso y moderno sistema de contabilidad heredado

de las empresas capitalistas fue desmantelado y en su lugar se estableció un nuevo sistema de registro económico, con mediciones físicas de la actividad empresarial, el cual nunca llegó a concretarse en la práctica, siendo precedido por la erradicación de las formas mercantiles y la supresión de los cobros y pagos entre las unidades del sector estatal. De facto fue eliminado el presupuesto del Estado.

La escala salarial introducida en 1961 en todos los sectores de la economía nacional fue abolida, así como el sistema de normas de trabajo; se introduce el horario de conciencia y las horas extras voluntarias gratuitas. La desvinculación del salario y la norma y la distribución sin tener en cuenta el aporte laboral realizado, actuaron como un factor desestimulante de la productividad del trabajo en todos los sectores, creando condiciones para la indisciplina y el ausentismo. Según René Dumont, ingeniero agrónomo francés, que fue asesor económico del régimen en aquella época. "No había nada que comprar, por cuya razón no existía ningún estímulo para trabajar."[3]

En el sector agropecuario: La colectivización fue ampliada mediante la eliminación de las pequeñas áreas destinadas al cultivo familiar de las que disfrutaban los trabajadores de las granjas estatales. En abril de 1968 se le prohibe a los campesinos la venta de la producción excedente, con la obligación de entregársela al Estado.

Se multiplicaron en la agricultura los planes especiales (en el argot popular planes de Fidel) y los planes integrales. La administración de estos planes se le encomendaba por lo general a personas leales al régimen, mientras que la asignación de recursos para los mismos se realizaba bajo ordenes superiores, al margen de la JUCEPLAN.

Los planes especiales eran agrupaciones productivas de fincas privadas y estatales. Los planes integrales representaban una empresa productiva territorial en que la tierra y demás medios de producción de los pequeños agricultores se integraban en la granja estatal. Los propietarios privados en este caso cobraban un

---

3. René Dumont, *Cuba ¿es socialista?* Editorial Tiempo Nuevo, 1970, pp. 70-71.

salario por el trabajo realizado y una renta de la tierra por la granja estatal. Sin embargo, el sector privado campesino no se resistió a la tentativa de englobarlo en estos planes, pues solo el 15% de las familias campesinas habían sido absorbidas por aquello que René Dumont definiera como la tercera reforma agraria.

El resultado de estos planes lo podemos obtener del propio Dumont: "La historia de los planes de Fidel, que fueron muy costosos con resultado realmente desastrosos." El plan especial más importante fue el "Cordón de la Habana," cuya intención era circundar la ciudad con frutales, café y hortalizas. En este plan "como en muchos otros, la operación de plantación era acompañada de presas de agua, calles, casas, etc.," más el resultado fue el señalado por el francés Dumont: "¡desastroso!"

El primer año de la década de 1970 llamado de los "Diez Millones" no llegó a serlo. Todo el país se movilizó en función de alcanzar esa cifra en la producción azucarera, limitando a su más mínima expresión todas las demás actividades, entre ellas la agropecuaria.

Esta situación fue el resultado de la tendencia a establecer metas sin tenerse la menor idea de poderlas mantener e incluso cumplir. Así, por ejemplo, con motivo del décimo aniversario del "Triunfo de la Insurrección," se aseguró que la producción agrícola de Cuba aumentaría a un ritmo promedio anual de un 15% durante los doce años siguientes, lo que representaba la mayor tasa de crecimiento en toda la historia mundial; sin embargo, a la luz de la realidad esta promesa era irrealizable, pues durante la primera década de régimen revolucionario lo que en verdad hubo fue un brusco ascenso de la producción agrícola en general. En diciembre de 1968 se plateó que la producción de leche se duplicaría en dos años; sin embargo en 1970 esta disminuyó un 25% con respecto a 1969.

Al final del experimento la situación de este sector fue el indicado en la Tabla No.11. Como se puede observar en ésta, un producto tan importante como el maíz inició un descenso vertical después de 1962; la producción de yuca, boniato, papa, ñame y malanga—alimentos relevantes en la dieta tradicional del pueblo cubano—disminuyeron considerablemente sus niveles productivos entre 1960 y 1970. La situación de crecimientos que presentaron otras producciones agrícolas puede verse en la Tabla No. 12.

Table 11. Producción de los principales productos agrícolas (en miles de toneladas)

Año	Maíz	Yuca	Boniato	Papa	Áame	Malanga
1960	213,9	255.1	230.5	101.2	11.3	256.7
1961	197.8	154.5	117.0	89.6	25.0	77.0
1962	158.7	162.5	181.0	100.2	20.2	60.2
1963	88.2	90.4	81.7	85.7	8.8	45.0
1964	35.5	73.2	89.3	75.3	8.4	43.2
1965	21.6	62.4	80.7	83.5	8.4	46.0
1966	17.8	94.0	153.0	104.0	11.5	69.3
1967	0	49.2	88.2	104.2	5.9	42.3
1968	0	53.4	99.2	119.6	2.3	42.5
1969	0	37.2	45.9	95.3	3.1	35.0
1970	0	22.0	22.0	77.3	2.3	42.0

Fuente: A.R.M. Ritter (1974), *The Economic Development of Revolutionary Cuba. Strategy and Performance*, Praeger Publishers

Table 12. Otras producciones agrícolas (en miles de toneladas)

Año	Ajo	Piña	Plátano
1960	6.5	58.0	—
1961	1.3	—	—
1962	0.2	55.0	76.5
1963	0.6	41.2	42.7
1964	0.4	31.8	32.7
1965	0.1	15.8	36.3
1966	0.0	9.6	29.0
1967	0.0	6.7	26.9
1968	0.1	7.2	25.0
1969	0.1	10.5	28.5
1970	0.3	14.2	47.2

Fuente: A.R.M. Ritter (1974), *The Economic Development of Revolutionary Cuba: Strategy and Performance*, Praeger Publishers.

Además, se produjo una baja considerable en la producción de leche. Según datos de la FAO disminuyó en un 25% entre 1969 y 1970. En la ganadería vacuna el descenso fue de 1.4 millones de cabezas en el período 1967-70.

Todo esto, no obstante, las grandes inversiones realizadas en el sector: "... la superficie agrícola cultivada pasó de 2371.4 miles de hectáreas en 1965 a 3059 en 1970; se desarrolló grandemente la mecanización de la cosecha cañera, elevándose la proporción de corte manual y alza mecanizada del 18% en 1964 al 83% en 1970; aumentó la aplicación de fertilizantes en la

Table 13. Producciones agrícolas seleccionadas *(per capita) (Kg)*

Conceptos	1958	Promedio 1975-79	Promedio 1986-89	1995	1996	1997
Maíz	31.50	1.75	3.80	7.36	9.46	—
Frijoles	5.68	0.35	1.31	1.04	1.27	4.82
Tubérculos y raíces	114.40	45.93	63.45	56.8	67.70	—
Tabaco	7.41	4.39	3.97	2.26	2.93	—
Café	6.43	2.12	2.60	2.40	—	—
Plátanos	37.09	22.84	29.89	36.4	48.90	—
Otras frutas*	58.90	39.40	21.91	10.20	9.30	—
Arroz	33.00	46.68	49.40	20.30	32.50	29.40
Tomate	15.70	18.62	25.40	12.60	14.70	—

Fuente: Para la producción de 1958: (CEE) *Cuba: Desarrollo Económico y Social durante el período 1958-80*, diciembre de 1981, p. 194, Informe de la FAO. Para los promedios 1975-79 and 1986-89: *Anuarios Estadísticos de Cuba*, 1981, 1988 and 1989. Para 1995 y 1996: *Estadísticas Seleccionadas de Cuba 1986*, Oficina Nacional de Estadísticas, abril de 1997, p. 6. Para 1997: Informe de José Luis Rodríguez a la Asamblea Nacional, periódico *Trabajadores*, 15 de diciembre de 1997.

agricultura a 360 mil tm en 1970 en términos de materia nutriente; y la cantidad de tractores subió de 26.8 mil en 1968 a 51.6 mil en 1970."[4]

En realidad, el país se precipitó en el más completo caos, muchas inversiones fueron paralizadas. La producción de la agricultura no cañera volvió a los niveles de 1965. La producción de la mayor parte de las ramas industriales, a excepción de la azucarera, sufrió un significativo deterioro. En 1966 por cada peso pagado por salarios (sin considerar otros costos en los cálculos) se recibía una producción de 1.58 pesos; en 1970 se reducía a 1.38. En muchos centros de trabajo se redujo en un 20% el uso de la jornada y no se superaba el 60% del nivel de eficiencia. En esa etapa el mercado negro se desarrolló considerablemente, a pesar de las restricciones gubernamentales.

ANALISIS RAMAL
Agricultura No Cañera

La producción agrícola no cañera, compuesta por la producción alimentaria y no alimentaria, se ha caracterizado por sus bajos niveles per cápita con relación a 1958. Así tenemos que cultivos como el maíz, los frijoles, los tubérculos y las raíces (boniato, yuca, papa y otros), los plátanos, el tabaco, el café, etc., han registrado disminuciones—en algunos casos extremas —con respecto a ese año (ver Tabla No. 13).

Los resultados de la agricultura no cañera han sido bajos, dado el desarrollo alcanzado en la mecaniza-

ción, la fertilización y el riego, sobre todo los del sector estatal. El sector privado, no obstante poseen instrumentos de trabajo inferiores a los de las granjas del Estado y no haber disfrutado de las grandes inversiones que tuvieron éstas, ha presentado siempre un nivel de eficiencia superior. El papel del sector privado ha sido importante en la producción agrícola nacional: en algunos cultivos especializados, difíciles de mecanizar, su participación ha sido determinante (ver Tabla No. 14). En otros productos agrícolas ha sobresalido también, incluso por encima del socialista (ver Tabla No. 15).

La producción de tabaco alcanzó una cifra récord en 1961 (57,600 toneladas). Sin embargo, declinó gradualmente a menos de la mitad diez años después. En 1978 se planteó públicamente "la necesidad de recuperar y elevar los récord históricos del tabaco alcanzados bajo el capitalismo." Los niveles de actividad llegaron a su mínima expresión en 1980 (8,239 toneladas) al ser afectado el cultivo por el moho azul. En 1959-60 se registró la mayor cosecha de café (55,200 toneladas), manteniéndose después de 1980—en términos generales—sobre las 20 mil toneladas hasta 1989. La producción de tubérculos y raíces tubo su pico en 1958 (780,700 toneladas), después sus niveles han sido variados, llegando en 1970 a solo 122840 toneladas. La producción de otras frutas, excluyendo los cítricos, fue alta en 1958 (402,500 toneladas), descendiendo durante las déca-

---

4. José Luis Rodríguez, *Estrategia del desarrollo económico en Cuba*, La Habana, 1990, p. 128.

Table 14. Acopio de productos agrícolas seleccionados por sector de origen *(toneladas)*

Concepto	Promedio 1976-80	Promedio 1984-85
Tabaco total	84,602.6	38,663.8
Socialista	7,527.0	12,791.9
Privado	27,075.5	25,871.9
Rama negra	30,149.5	39,566.8
Socialista	5,740.1	15,479.9
Privado	24,409.4	24,086.9
Rama rubio	4,453.0	5,097.0
Socialista	1,786.9	3,311.9
Privado	2,666.2	1,785.0
Café total	17,923.9	19,625.4
Socialista	9,637.2	12,493.2
Privado	8,286.6	7,132.2
Cacao total	1,450.0	1,650.3
Socialista	389.6	577.8
Privado	1,060.4	1,072.5

Fuente: *Anuario Estadístico de Cuba 1988*, pp. 327-328.

Table 15. Acopio de productos agrícolas seleccionados, por sector de origen *(toneladas)*

Concepto	Promedio 1976-80	Promedio 1981-85
Tubérculos y raíces	436,255.4	546,786.7
Socialista	277,548.2	445,031.9
Privado	158,707.2	101,754.3
Maíz seco	2,484.9	1,848.4
Socialista	1,085.2	796.5
Privado	1,399.7	1,051.9
Maíz tierno	11,549.1	15,074.3
Socialista	7,400.8	10,236.4
Privado	4,148.6	4,838.0
Frijoles total	3,006.6	4,291.8
Socialista	1,385.8	2,545.2
Privado	1,620.7	1,746.6
Negro	2,299.3	3,544.6
Socialista	1,177.5	2,265.2
Privado	1,121.8	1,279.5
Colorado	121.5	464.4
Socialista	22.0	212.4
Privado	99.5	252.0
Hortalizas	362,250.0	490,821.6
Socialista	137,385.5	245,774.0
Privado	224,864.5	245,047.6
Tomates	169,268.6	227,463.6
Socialista	76,775.9	111,824.1
Privado	92,492.7	115,639.5
Pimiento	31,105.1	29,981.1
Socialista	2,796.1	7,923.4
Privado	28,309.0	22,057.6
Cebolla	10,101.0	15,721.4
Socialista	3,596.1	10,169.2
Privado	6,504.9	5,553.2
Calabaza	31,677.8	54,018.5
Socialista	16,354.5	28,605.9
Privado	15,323.3	25,412.6

Fuente: *Anuario Estadístico de Cuba 1988*, pp. 324-325.

das de los 70 y los 80. La producción de arroz, el artículo principal de la dieta cubana, alcanzó su máximo en 1986 (570,517 toneladas). En 1958 la cosecha de maíz registró las 215,200 toneladas, cayendo posteriormente en picada. Este resumen de la producción agrícola de Cuba puede verse en la Tabla No. 16.

De acuerdo con la FAO, el desempeño de la agricultura cubana en 1959-76 fue el peor (empatado con Chile) de América Latina.[5] En 1974, 1986 y 1995, Cuba quedó por debajo de varios países latinoamericanos en la producción per cápita de importantes productos agrícolas (ver Anexos No. 2, No. 3, y No. 4).

En el período 1981-89, en los umbrales de la crisis, los rendimientos de los principales cultivos del país registraron fuertes decrecimientos alcanzando en algunos casos más del 50% (Ver Tabla No. 17). Con la crisis económica la producción agrícola en general registro un descenso considerable, lo cual puede verse en la Tabla No. 18. El cuadro es aún más lóbrego en términos per cápita, pues la producción de cereales en 1994 fue de dos tercios de la correspondiente a 1986 (Ver Anexo No. 5).

La agricultura cubana ha venido presentando en los últimos años una disminución notable en las superficies cosechadas de varios cultivos de gran importancia para el país, entre los que se encuentran los consignados en la Tabla No. 19. Entre los cultivos más afectados se encuentra el arroz, el cual constituye uno de los alimentos básicos más importantes para el pueblo cubano, pues de su consumo depende en gran medida su alimentación o simplemente su subsistencia (Ver Tabla No. 20).

---

5. FAO, *Anuario de Producción 1976*, Roma, 1977, pp. 74-75.

Table 16. Producción de cultivos seleccionados *(miles de toneladas)*

Cultivos	1958	1960	1961	1977	1978	1979	1980	1986	1988	1989	1995	1996
Tabaco	50.6	45.3	57.6	43.3	41.0	32.2	8.2	45.6	39.4	41.6	24.9	32.3
Café	43.6	55.2	38.5	16.8	14.8	28.6	19.9	24.5	28.8	28.9	—	—
Tubérculos y raíces	780.7	—	—	402.3	580.3	581.5	736,8	675.4	653,1	681.2	624.2	746.8
Otras frutas	402.5	—	—	188.2	160.4	178.5	199.2	201.1	269.4	218.9	112.3	102.5
Arroz	225.7	304.2	345.7	455.7	457.4	425.1	477.8	570.5	488.8	536.4	222.8	358.6
Maíz	215.2	213.9	197.8	16.3	16.2	16.5	23.6	34.5	35.5	47.1	80.9	104.3

Fuente: (CEE): *Cuba: Desarrollo económico y social durante el período 1958-1980.* Jacques Chonchol: "Análisis crítico de la Reforma Agraria cubana," Revista *El Trimestre Económico,* No. 177, 1963. *Anuarios Estadísticos de Cuba 1988* y *1989. Estadísticas Seleccionadas de Cuba 1996,* ONE, p. 6.

Table 17. Rendimientos agrícolas: Sector estatal *(toneladas por hectarea)*

Concepto	1981	1987	1988	1989	% 1989/1981
Tubérculos y raíces	8.50	7.64	7.10	6.75	79.4
De ello:					
Papa	20.10	17.54	17.86	16.72	83.2
Malanga	11.30	8.36	7.86	5.49	48.2
Hortalizas	9.11	4.81	5.00	3.76	41.2
De ello:					
Tomate	12.76	8.77	8.01	6.44	50.5
Cebolla	8.10	6.25	6.77	3.69	45.5
Cereales	3.00	2.61	2.79	2.79	93.0
De ello:					
Arroz	3.41	3.11	3.22	3.28	96.2
Maíz	0.83	0.61	0.71	0.78	94.0
Tabaco	0.83	0.71	0.82	0.81	97.6
Plátano (vianda fruta)	10.89	7.80	9.89	8.10	81.1

Fuente: *Anuario Estadístico de Cuba 1989,* p. 203.

Table 18. Indice de volumen físico de cultivos agrícolas Año base: promedio anual trienio 1989-1991=100

Años	Indice
1970	87
1980	81
1982	94
1988	101
1989	105
1990	101
1991	94
1992	81
1993	66
1994	62
1995	58

Fuente: *Anuario Estadístico de la CEPAL 1996,* pp. 596-597.

Table 19. Superficie cosechada de cultivos seleccionados *(miles de hectáreas)*

Cultivos	1970	1988	1989	1990	1991	1992	1993	1994	1995
Arroz	195	151	167	142	137	130	45	60	55
Café	130	109	100	99	90	82	82	85	95
Maíz	105	77	77	77	77	77	77	77	74

Fuente: *Anuario Estadístico de la CEPAL 1996,* pp. 616-617, 618-619 and 624-625.

Table 20. Producción de arroz

Años	Producción total (Mt)	% con relación al año anterior
1989	536.4	109.7
1995	222.8	41.6
1996	358.6	160.9
1997	325,9	90.6

Fuente: *Anuario Estadístico de la CEPAL 1996. Estadísticas Seleccionadas de Cuba 1996,* Oficina Nacional de Estadísticas, p. 6. Informe de José Luis Rodríguez a la Asamblea Nacional.

Agricultura Cañera

La caña de azúcar es el principal cultivo agrícola de Cuba, tanto desde el punto de vista de su extensión territorial, la cual abarcaba en 1989 el 45% de la superficie cultivada del país *(Anuario Estadístico de Cuba 1989*, p. 186), que como suministrador de materia prima a la industria azucarera, principal renglón de exportación de la economía cubana.

En los primeros años de la década de los 60 el régimen no pudo llegar a una decisión sobre el papel del azúcar en la futura economía del país. Aunque la industria azucarera era hasta ese momento la base fundamental del desarrollo de Cuba, se puso en práctica la osada idea de que la Isla debía poner punto final a su dependencia de ese producto.

Fue así que "en agosto de 1961 surge la decisión de reducir en más de 130,000 hectáreas las áreas cultivadas de caña de azúcar, que se encontraban entonces en el sector cooperativo (después sector estatal). De este modo se trataba de diversificar la agricultura."[6] A esto se agrega que se demolieron en la mayoría de los casos las áreas de mayor rendimiento cañero, las que quedaban más cerca de los centrales. Las áreas cañeras fueron reducidas para dar paso a nuevos cultivos, lo que significó un descenso general de la producción agrícola. Serían necesarios varios años para poder restaurar la capacidad productiva de caña de azúcar por parte del sector de la agricultura.

A la vez, mientras que la demolición de las áreas cañeras provocaba una disminución de la producción bruta agropecuaria, las tierras que iban quedando libre no podían ser sembradas, simultaneamente, con los cultivos que debían llevar a la diversificación. En este sentido contra tal pretensión jugaba la inexperiencia para introducir económicamente estos nuevos cultivos, así como la escasez de equipos, semillas, etc., que garantizaran rendimientos suficientemente atractivos. No hubo pues compensación.

La falta de un aparato de control adecuado hizo que no fuera posible determinar, con exactitud, el monto real de las áreas cañeras demolidas, que posiblemente superaron las 10,000 caballerías (134,200 ha.). El resultado fue indudablemente catastrófico. La disminución de la superficie de caña trajo como consecuencia una baja vertiginosa de la producción de azúcar, la que cayó de 6.8 millones de toneladas en 1961, a 4.8 en 1962 y a 3.9 en 1963, repercutiendo este hecho en toda la economía nacional. Veamos lo que dijo posteriormente el dirigente comunista Carlos Rafael Rodriguez, presidente del INRA entre 1963 y 1965:

El error cometido en la agricultura cubana durante los años 1960 y 1961 consistió de una parte, en relegar la caña como si ello fuera indispensable para diversificar la agricultura, y en segundo lugar llevar la diversificación al plano local, es decir, convertir cada granja en un mosaico de cultivos.[7]

Después las realidades económicas obligaron a abandonar la idea de que la industrialización pudiera convertirse rápidamente en la nueva fuente de riquezas de Cuba. Por consiguiente se le devolvió al azúcar y a la agricultura cañera la prioridad productiva, pasando después al otro extremo de conseguir zafras record, lo cual sería otro lamentable error. La de 1970 es un buen ejemplo de esta cuestión.

En esos primeros años, de 1962-1969, la producción promedio de caña de azúcar (40.8 millones de toneladas) permaneció más o menos a los mismos niveles del período 1953-58 (40.4 millones de toneladas como promedio anual). En 1962-69 los rendimientos por hectárea oscilaron entre 30 y 40 toneladas, mientras que en el período 1970-88 no alcanzaron las 60 toneladas/hectárea (la cifra más alta del período se registro en 1979—58.94 toneladas/hectárea). Estos niveles de rendimiento resultan bajos cuando se los compara con otros países productores de caña de azúcar. En cuanto a sus rendimientos en términos de azúcar, éstos muestran una tendencia decreciente,

---

6. Charles Bettelheim, "Cuba en 1965: Resultados y perspectivas económicas," *Revista Nuestra Industria Económica*, No. 18 (1966), pp. 8-9.

7. Carlos Rafael Rodríguez, "El nuevo camino de la agricultura cubana," *Cuba Socialista*, No. 27 (1963), p. 71.

disminuyendo de más de 12% entre 1959 y 1968 hasta 10.85% en 1988.

También el sector no estatal superó al estatal en el rendimiento de caña de azúcar por hectárea cosechada. En la Tabla No. 21 se comparan ambos sectores sociales en este importante indicador de la agricultura cañera en 1962-89. En 1962-67 los rendimientos del sector estatal eran ligeramente superiores a los rendimientos del no estatal. Sin embargo, este último logró cerrar la brecha y, a partir de 1968 mostraron rendimientos constantemente más altos que los del sector estatal.

Table 21. Rendimiento de la caña de azúcar en el sector estatal y no estatal (*toneladas/hectárea*)

Años	Estatal	Privado	Años	Estatal	Privado
1962	35.3	30.8	1976	42.7	50.3
1963	30.8	28.6	1977	51.1	62.8
1964	38.5	34.4	1978	55.3	61.2
1965	48.2	47.3	1979	57.8	64.6
1966	38.5	39.4	1980	45.2	50.5
1967	49.3	45.8	1981	53.8	61.3
1968	41.2	44.2	1982	53.9	61.0
1969	42.8	48.2	1983	56.7	63.6
1970	54.7	59.9	1984	57.3	57.6
1971	41.1	44.1	1985	49.8	50.7
1972	37.1	39.1	1986	51.3	52.7
1973	44.4	47.1	1987	51.7	54.5
1974	45.0	48.7	1988	55.9	61.3
1975	43.6	48.0	1989	59.4	62.8

Fuente: *Anuario Estadístico de Cuba*, 1972, 1975, 1988 y 1989.

En el pasado la producción promedio de caña era de 45,000 arrobas por caballería, con un rendimiento del 12 al 13% de azúcar. Este promedio agrícola también era bajo en comparación con el logrado por otros países, lo que se debía al sistema de cultivo extensivo que predominaba en Cuba. (En Hawaii, mediante cultivos intensivos se obtenía hasta 400 mil arrobas por caballería, con un rendimiento industrial del 8 al 12% de azúcar.) Pero en Cuba se podían obtener numerosas cosechas con una sola siembra (como promedio 10 años existiendo en esa época campos donde se daban cortes durante 20 años), el costo de producción de la caña era mucho más bajo que en otros países donde el mayor rendimiento se obtenía por un costoso cultivo intensivo, a base de regadíos y

fertilizantes. Las excelentes condiciones ecológicas de Cuba para el cultivo de la caña lo permitían.

La crisis económica ha agravado considerablemente la situación de la agricultura cañera, pues la producción cayó de 81.0 millones de toneladas en 1989 a 36.0 millones en 1995, mientras que el rendimiento descendió de 59.9 toneladas por héctarea a sólo 34.3 toneladas en igual período. En la Tabla No. 22 se comparan estos indicadores con el total para América Latina y el Caribe.

Rama Pecuaria

La rama pecuaria, no obstante ser una de las de mayor importancia porque constituye fuente de suministro de proteínas de orígen animal para la alimentación de la población, ya estaba en crisis antes del derrumbe total. Desde finales de los años 70, Cuba viene confrontando graves problemas con el ganado vacuno. Según los datos de la Tabla No. 23, en 1989 el país contaba con un rebaño de 4,919.7 miles de cabezas, cifra que es muy inferior a la registrada en 1970 (5,738.1 miles de cabezas), inferior en un 12.5% con relación a 1975 y en un 31.4% respecto a 1967, año en que las existencias vacunas alcanzaron, según el censo de ese año, la mayor cantidad registrada en el país (7,172.0 miles de cabezas).

Las existencias promedio de vacas en ordeño se mantuvieron prácticamente estancadas entre 1966 y 1969 (378.4 y 369.2 miles de cabezas, respectivamente), aunque se incrementó la producción por vaca en ordeño, pasando de 2.8 Kg. diarios en 1966 a 6.8 Kg. en 1988. Esta producción se redujo en 1994 a 4.7 Kg.

Cuba es uno de los países latinoamericanos donde más recursos se han invertido en el "mejoramiento" de las razas de ganado vacuno. Entre los factores que propiciaron este esfuerzo de "mejoramiento" genético cabe mencionar la importación de reproductores de alto pedigree, los cruzamientos mediante inseminación artificial, los programas de extensión, investigación, etc. Un ambicioso plan en la segunda mitad de la década del 60 trató de desarrollar un nuevo tipo de ganado, apareando cepa cubana (principalmente cebú, un deficiente productor de leche) con ganado

Table 22. Resumen estadístico de la agricultura cañera

Concepto	1989	1990	1991	1992	1993	1994	1995
América Latina y el Caribe							
Superficie cosechada (M ha)	7670	7852	7948	8005	7266	7773	7959
Producción (M t)	482294	488646	487426	484684	445819	487156	496198
Rendimiento (t/ha)	62.9	62.2	61.3	60.5	61.3	62.7	62.3
Cuba							
Superficie cosechada (M ha)	1351	1350	1435	1550	1150	1100	1050
Producción (M t)	81003	76230	71000	58000	44000	39000	36000
Rendimiento (t/ha)	59.9	56.4	49.5	37.4	38.2	35.4	34.3

Fuente: *Anuario Estadístico de la CEPAL 1996*, pp. 620-624 y 642-643.

Holstein y Brown Swiss directamente o a través de la inseminación artificial.

Sin embargo, a pesar de todos estos "avances" genéticos, a la producción de medicamentos, etc., los rendimientos en general de la ganadería vacuna se han mantenido a nivel bajo, con un descenso constante de la masa. El mejoramiento zootécnico es un requisito indispensable aunque no suficiente, pues requiere complementarse con buena alimentación, control sanitario y administración adecuada. Y en este último campo hay mucho que hacer en Cuba.

Ahora bien, la información sobre el comportamiento de la masa vacuna en Cuba, en términos absolutos, no aporta toda la información requerida. Se necesita para realizar una evaluación más completa compararla con el crecimiento poblacional, cuestión que se expone en la Tabla No. 24. Esta cuestión se repite cuando se compara la ganadería vacuna de Cuba con otros países de América Latina (Ver Tabla No. 25). Sin embargo, con motivo del IV aniversario del triunfo de la insurrección, el jefe del régimen afirmó que: "Nuestra ganadería se desarrolla y no tenemos dudas que será en el curso de pocos años una de las mejores ganaderías del mundo."

Las entregas a sacrificio de ganado vacuno descendieron en el decenio de 1980 con relación a las cifras alcanzadas en 1968 y los primeros años de la década del 70 (Ver Tabla No. 26). En el fondo, esta situación debe atribuirse a la reducción de las existencias. Entre 1989 y 1994 las entregas a sacrificio cayeron de 885.7 miles de cabezas a solo 437.1 miles, respectivamente.

Table 23. Existencia de ganado en años seleccionados *(miles de cabezas)*

Concepto	Vacuno	Porcino	Avícola	Ovino	Caprino
Censos					
1946	4,115.7	—	—	—	
1947	4,042.1	1,285.8	—	193.9	161.6
Años					
1957	5,325.0	—	—	—	—
1958	5,700.0	1,780.0	—	—	—
Censos					
1961	5,776.0	—	—	—	—
1967	7,172.0	342.7	—	—	—
1973	5,486.5	—	—	—	—
1978	5,273.6	—	—	62.9	16.6
Años					
1970	5,738.1	276.6	13,500.3	49.2	12.6
1975	5,621.8	581.1	17,857.3	401.2	23.8
1980	5,057.2	765.4	24,608.0	208.8	20.8
1981	5,095.1	840.2	23,988.7	259.1	22.3
1982	5,112.3	853.1	23,052.4	317.0	24.8
1983	5,101.0	910.6	25.744.1	352.0	24.2
1984	5,115.2	1,009.4	26,734.5	440.8	29.6
1985	5,019.5	1,038.0	25,859.3	494.6	29.7
1986	5,007.1	1,100.8	25.677.9	618.2	33.4
1987	4,984.0	1,093.2	25.959.3	739.9	37.0
1988	4,926.8	1,168.7	27.307.8	804.2	33.2
1989	4,919.7	1,292.2	27,904.0	839.3	34.2

Fuente: *Anuario Estadístico de Cuba, 1957. Geografía de Cuba* de Leví Marrero, 1957, p. 251. Las cifras de ganado para 1958 fueron estimadas por Raúl Cepero Bonilla: "Los problemas de la agricultura en América Latina, y la reforma agraria cubana." *Cuba Socialista*, 13 de enero de 1968. *Anuarios Estadísticos de Cuba, 1985, 1988 y 1989.*

El consumo de carne de res per cápita era muy alto en Cuba. En 1956 el consumo promedio anual fue de 62.5 Kg. per cápita. En La Habana, ese mismo año, se elevaba el consumo per cápita anual a 97.9 Kg. (*Geografía de Cuba* de Leví Marrero, p. 258). En 1961 el consumo de carne de res bajó a 55.2 Kg. En La Habana y el área urbana circundante el consumo era de 69 Kg. per cápita anual (*Panorama Económico*

Table 24. Existencia de ganado vacuno *(per cápita)*

Años	Cabezas/habitante (U)	Años	Cabezas/habitante (U)
1957	0.84	1984	0.51
1958	0.83	1985	0.49
1961	0.80	1986	0.48
1967	0.87	1987	0.48
1970	0.67	1988	0.47
1975	0.60	1989	0.46
1980	0.52	1990	0.45
1981	0.52	1991	0.44
1982	0.51	1992	0.42
1983	0.51	1993	0.41

Fuente: Leví Marrero, *Geografía de Cuba*, p. 251. *Anuarios Estadísticos de Cuba, 1985, 1988 y 1989;* Raúl Cepero Bonilla, "Los problemas de la agricultura en América Latina y la reforma agraria cubana," *Cuba Socialista*, 13 de enero de 1963. Revista *Bohemia*, 24 de octubre de 1994.

Table 25. Existencias de ganado vacuno, 1986 *(cabezas por mil habitantes)*

Países	Cantidad
Uruguay	3,342.6
Paraguay	1,876.9
Argentina	1,852.6
Brasil	930.9
Costa Rica	904.5
Bolivia	809.2
Colombia	808.3
Venezuela	693.1
Panamá	641.5
Honduras	621.5
Nicaragua	620.4
Cuba	490.9

Fuente: *Anuario Estadístico de Cuba 1988*. Estadísticas Internacionales.

Latinoamericano, 26 de diciembre de 1961, p. 34). En cuanto a la carne de res deshuesada, limpia, el consumo per cápita en 1955 fue de 11.9 Kg. (*Anuario Estadístico de Cuba 1957*, p. 114), disminuyendo progresivamente a partir de la década de 1960 (Ver Tabla No. 27).

El desarrollo del ganado porcino también ha sido pobre después de 1958. Como lo muestra la Tabla No. 23, el número de cabezas porcinas descendió en 1967 en más del 80% con relación a 1958 y un 73% con respecto a 1952 (las cifras se refieren sólo al sector estatal). En 1970 la masa porcina declina aún más debido principalmente a una epidemia de cólera porcina o fiebre africana. A partir de 1975 se produjo una

recuperación sobrepasando el millón de cabezas a partir de 1984. En 1989 alcanza 1,292.2 miles de cabezas (0.12 cabezas por habitante, menos de la mitad de las 0.26 cabezas por habitante registradas en 1958).

La carne de cerdo desapareció del escenario nacional desde los primeros años de la década del 60, a causa fundamentalmente de las fuertes caídas en las existencias de ganado porcino, comentadas en el párrafo anterior, reapareciendo a partir de abril de 1980 con la apertura de los mercados libres campesinos hasta su cierre en 1986. En octubre de 1994 aparece de nuevo a la venta con el establecimiento de los mercados agropecuarios, al astronómico precio de 40-45 pesos la libra. En la actualidad el precio oscila entre 22-23 pesos la libra. Sobre estos dos mercados comentaremos más adelante. La carne de pollo en moneda nacional está prácticamente desaparecida, pues sólo se puede adquirir en las tiendas en divisas.

En cuanto a la producción de leche de vaca, veamos a continuación como se comportó ésta en términos absolutos y per cápita, antes y después de 1959. "La producción en 1945 se estima en el orden de las 337,000 T, nivel éste que no evolucionó significativamente en los años posteriores" (Enrique Pérez Marín, *Agropecuaria, Desarrollo Económico*, La Habana, 1990, p. 43). Sin embargo, considerando incluso que esta situación se hubiera mantenido hasta 1958, la producción per cápita de ese año sólo hubiera sido superada en 1972.

En 1945, según la *Geografía de Cuba* de Leví Marrero, p. 259, al realizarse el último censo agrícola, la producción anual de leche de vaca era de 400 millones de litros (412 mil toneladas aproximadamente), mientras que en 1957 la producción anual fue calculada en más de 700 millones de litros (más de 721 mil toneladas). Entre 1989 y 1997 la producción anual de leche descendió de 924.1 miles de toneladas a 570.6 miles de toneladas, lo que representa un decrecimiento de un 38.3% en ese período (Ver Tablas No. 28 y 29).

Con la crisis económica la producción pecuaria ha disminuido considerablemente, lo cual puede observarse en las Tablas No. 30 y 31. En 1995, el índice a

Table 26. Entregas a sacrificio de ganado vacuno por el sector estatal
(incluye animales comprados al sector no estatal)

Concepto	1968	1970	1972	1980	1983	1984	1985	1988	1989
Cabezas (M)	1354.1	1190.1	1013.2	987.9	919.1	899.4	916.4	896.4	885.7
Peso en pie (M t)	429.7	381.5	338.1	293.0	302.8	301.8	298.9	291.7	289.1
Peso promedio (Kg)	317	321	334	326	329	336	326	325	326

Fuente: *Anuarios Estadísticos de Cuba 1985 y 1989.*

Table 27. Consumo per cápita de carne de res deshuesada

Años	Kilogramos
1965	11.7
1971	11.5
1974	7.5
1977	8.7
1980	7.8
1982	7.6
1983	7.5
1988	7.4
1989	6.8
1993	menos de 1

Fuente: José Luis Rodríguez: *Erradicación de la pobreza en Cuba*, La Habana, 1990, Tabla 31, p. 57. *Anuarios Estadísticos de Cuba 1988 y 1989.* Estimado.

nivel de América Latina y el Caribe fue de 116, mientras que en Cuba fue de 74 (*Anuario Estadístico de la CEPAL 1996*). En términos de per cápita, el índice de producción pecuaria cayó de 106.36 en 1989 a 68.46 en 1994.

ORGANIZACION ACTUAL DE LA AGRICULTURA CUBANA

El 15 de septiembre de 1993, el Gobierno Cubano anunció una reestructuración de las propiedades agrícolas estatales, con el fin de aumentar la productividad en el sector agroecuario. La medida establecía la subdivisión de las granjas estatales en las llamadas Unidades Básicas de Producción Cooperativa (UBPC) que por tiempo indefinido tendrán el derecho al "usufructo de la tierra." Pequeñas parcelas fueron distribuidas a trabajadores permanentes de las mismas para el cultivo individual. De este modo se pretendía estimular la producción y fomentar la autosuficiencia alimentaria del país. En febrero de 1995, se habían creado 1,440 UBPC, la mayoría en la agricultura cañera, de un total previsto de 2,000.

Sin embargo, las UBPC no han dado una respuesta positiva a los objetivos para las cuales fueron creadas. Su falta de autonomía les impide el buen desenvolvimiento del proceso productivo que llevan a cabo, destacándose los problemas siguientes:

- Lo que deben producir es determinado por la empresa estatal, manteniéndose un estrecho cordón umbilical con la misma.

- El destino de la producción lo fija la empresa estatal.

Table 28. Producción de leche, total y per cápita

Años	Producción total (Mt)	Producción per cápita (Kg)	Años	Producción total (Mt)	Producción per cápita (Kg)
1958	337.0 [a]	49.8	1967	368.7	45.3
1962	187.0	25.7	1968	356.3	43.0
1963	212.8	28.7	1969	356.8	42.3
1964	336.7	44.2	1970	379.5 [b]	44.3
1965	306.8	39.2	1971	384.6	44.2
1966	362.7	46.0	1972	476.4	53.7

Fuente: Obra citada anteriormente y *Anuarios Estadísticos de Cuba 1971 y 1973.*

a. En el supuesto que se haya mantenido el mismo nivel de 1945.
b. Según la FAO descendió en un 2.5% con relación a 1969.

- Los precios de venta de los productos son fijados por las empresas de acopio estatal, excluyendo sólo la parte de la producción que las UBPC comercializan en el Mercado Agropecuario.

Table 29. Producción de leche de vaca

Años	Producción total (Mt)	% con relación al año anterior
1989	924.1	100.6
1994	436.0	47.2
1995	608.3	139.5
1996	640.0	105.2
1997	570.6	89.1

Fuente: *Anuario Estadístico de Cuba 1989*. Revista *Economía y Desarrollo*, No. 1, 1995. *Estadísticas Seleccionadas de Cuba 1996*, Oficina Nacional de Estadísticas, p. 6. Informe de José Luis Rodríguez a la Asamblea Nacional, periódico *Trabajadores*, 15 de diciembre de 1997.

Table 30. Indice de volumen físico de la producción pecuaria (Año base: promedio anual trienio 1989-1991 = 100)

Años	Indice
1970	85
1980	90
1982	92
1988	101
1989	101
1990	101
1991	98
1992	80
1993	74
1994	74
1995	74

Fuente: *Anuario Estadístico de la CEPAL 1996*, pp. 598-599.

- Todos los suministros para realizar las actividades productivas—fertilizantes, herbicidas, plaguicidas, combustible, etc.—lo recibe a través de la empresa estatal, la cual les fija los precios.

- Todos los servicios de reparación de equipos, preparación de tierra, entre otros, se los proporciona la empresa estatal, los cuales son cobrados de acuerdo con las tarifas fijadas por ella.

Lo anterior demuestra plenamente que se mantiene el mismo grado de subordinación a la empresa estatal, lo que trae aparejado que se reproduzcan las viejas relaciones de producción y se mantengan categorías del sistema de propiedad centralizada. Es por ello que los

Table 31. Productos pecuarios: Indices de producción per cápita (1979-1981 = 100)

Años	Indice
1983	104.85
1984	107.93
1985	108.62
1986	108.83
1987	106.68
1988	106.00
1989	106.36
1990	104.35
1991	102.74
1992	81.54
1993	70.25
1994	68.46

Fuente: *Anuario FAO de Producción 1994*.

productores no se sientan estimulados, lo cual incide indudablemente en sus resultados productivos.

Además, a las Unidades Básicas de Producción Cooperativa cañeras se les prohibe participar en el mercado agropecuario con los excedentes resultantes de las áreas dedicadas al autoconsumo; las ganaderas, arroceras y cafetaleras no pueden comercializar sus producciones principales allí. A las UBPC de cultivos varios se les prohibe ofertar papa en ese mercado.

Las Cooperativas de Producción Agropecuaria (CPA) y las Cooperativas de Crédito y Servicios (CCS) siguen produciendo, en términos generales, con su misma estructura organizativa, estando obligadas por el Decreto 125 a venderle la mayor parte de su producción al Estado. "Los artículos 8 y 9 de ese decreto ley establecen que todo agricultor ... está en obligación de explotar la tierra en interés del desarrollo económico y social del país. En ellos se sanciona entre otras figuras, la no venta al Estado de los productos que deben ser acopiados, la comercialización ilícita y el incumplimiento de las producciones principales a que están obligados los campesinos."[8]

Aplicando este Decreto Ley se le han quitado las tierras a los campesinos por no cumplir sus contratos de entregar al Estado y vender sus productos directa-

---

8. Entrevista a Orlando Lugo Fonte, presidente de la oficialista Asociación Nacional de Agricultores Pequeños (ANAP), *Trabajadores* (11 de julio de 1994).

mente a la población. Mediate el Decreto Ley 149 se ha hecho lo mismo, a pesar de que en "La historia me absolverá" se dice: "La segunda ley revolucionaria concedía la propiedad inembargable...a todos los colonos, sub-colonos, arrendatarios." "Si ha habido casos..... Hay un grupo de campesinos al cual se les ha aplicado el Decreto Ley 125 y existen otros 35 casos que se encuentran sujetos a expendiente por enriquecimiento ilícito, según el Decreto Ley 149."[9]

Hoy es más evidente que nunca el rotundo fracaso del llamado "Plan Alimentario" para alcanzar incrementos de la producción agropecuaria. Sin embargo, la falta de alimentos en Cuba no es un fenómeno correspondiente a los últimos años, aunque la crisis ha contribuido a acentuarlo considerablemente. En rigor, la escasez de alimentos ha sido después de 1960 un componente básico del "sistema económico cubano."

ESTADO NUTRICIONAL DE LA POBLACION CUBANA

Abastecimiento de Productos Agropecuarios a la Población Antes del Llamado Período Especial

En marzo de 1962 se decretó el racionamiento de los bienes de consumo, vigente hasta la fecha, como resultado de los grandes desniveles entre la oferta estatal y la demanda solvente de la población. La Tabla No. 32 presenta las cuotas de racionamiento de varios productos alimenticios, entre los cuales se incluyen algunos agropecuarios, en cuatro momentos del período 1962-1979.

De acuerdo con varios estimados oficiales, el racionamiento aseguró un minimo de 2,100-2,846 calorías diarias en 1977, pero Dudley Sears informó que el racionamiento en 1962 (cuando las cuotas eran más altas) permitió solamente 1,307 calorías a los mayores de 7 años y 2,155 a los menores de 7. En cualquier caso las cifras que corresponden a los últimos años de la década del 70 se encuentran por debajo de

la disponibilidad nacional promedio per cápita para 1951-1958, la que se reportara en 2,740-2,870.[10]

El éxodo de más de 120 mil cubanos por el puerto de Mariel hacia los Estados Unidos en 1980 obligó practicamente al régimen cubano a aflojar la mano en el consumo. En 1980 y hasta 1986 en el país se establecieron los mercados libres campesinos (MLC), en donde se vendió la producción excedente de los agricultores privados y cooperativistas, luego de cumplir sus entregas al Estado. En estos mercados los precios se formaron libremente de acuerdo con la oferta y la demanda. La introducción del MLC trajo como resultado una apreciable diversificación de la oferta, vendiéndose en el mismo productos que no se veían desde los primeros años de la década del 60. Además, su calidad era muy superior a la de los que se podían adquirir en el mercado estatal.

Table 32. Cuotas per cápita mensuales de bienes de consumo racionados seleccionados en La Habana, 1962-1979 (en libras)

Concepto	1962	1969	1971-72	1978-79[a]
Carne de res[b]	3	3	3	2.5
Pescado	1	2	4	Libre
Arroz	6	4	3 - 6	5
Frijoles	1.5	1.5	1.5 - 3	1.25
Tubérculos y raíces	14	9		
Grasas	2	1	2	1.5
Huevos (unidades)	5	15	15 - 24	Libre
Mantequilla	0.125	0.125	Libre	Libre
Café	1	0.375	0.375	0.125
Leche (enlatada) [c]	6	2	3	3
Azúcar	Libre	6	6 - 4	4
Pan	Libre	15		15

Fuente: Carmelo Mesa Lago: *La Economía de Cuba Socialista*, Editorial Playor, Cuadro 41, p. 236.

a.   También en 1978 se vendían por la libre macarrones, spaghetis y yogurt, tortas y vegetales (de acuerdo a la estación) y pan (después de las 4:00 PM).

b.   Carne, si no estaba disponible, se suministraba pollo, únicamente por esta vía.

c.   Los niños menores de 7 años tenían una ración diaria de medio litro de leche fresca y los adultos de mas de 65 años recibían seis latas mensuales de leche condensada y evaporada.

---

9. Ibid.

10. Carmelo Mesa Lago, "La economía en Cuba socialista," p. 238.

A la par del MLC se crearon los mercados paralelos estatales con ofertas diversas, a precios muy superiores a los del mercado racionado. La mayor parte de los productos que se vendían allí eran importados de los países ex socialistas.

En 1986 fue clausurado el MLC, sobre él se dijo lo siguiente: "Creo que el mercado libre campesino va a pasar sin gloria y habiéndonos dejado una gran lección y no pocos daños, no se cuantos millonarios por ahí. Rectificaremos lo que incuestionablemente fue una decisión equivocada."[11]

La gran ayuda económica recibida del desaparecido campo socialista, fundamentalmente de la ex Unión Soviética, durante la década del 80 creó la imagen de un país bien alimentado y con "virtual pleno empleo." Las grandes cantidades de alimentos recibidos de ese país—tanto para la alimentación humana como animal—redundaron en un aporte diario de calorías superior al de muchas naciones de América Latina y en algunos productos el consumo fue superior al de otros con ingresos más o menos similares al de Cuba, ya que en el mismo influían precios al por menor relativamente bajos y fuertemente subvencionados (Ver Tabla No. 33).

Table 33. Participación promedio de la URSS en las importaciones cubanas de alimentos, 1980–1988

Concepto	% de participación de la URSS
Carne en conserva	59.5
Leche condensada	100.0
Mantequilla	91.6
Queso	65.5
Pescados y mariscos	97.5
Trigo en grano	85.3
Arros consumo	44.6
Maíz grano	54.1
Harina de trigo	100.0
Frijoles	51.1
Materia destinada a la alimentación de animales	13.7
Manteca de cerdo	61.5
Aceites vegetales crudos	77.7

Fuente: *Anuarios Estadísticos de Cuba 1985 y 1988.*

Situación Actual

Con el derrumbe del socialismo en los países de Europa Oriental y la desparición de la Unión Soviética, Cuba quedó prácticamente sin ningun fuente de abastecimiento del exterior. Además, según datos de la CEPAL, la producción de alimentos registró fuertes decrecimientos a partir de 1990 (Ver Tabla No. 34). Estos decrecimientos produjeron a su vez un considerable descenso en el índice de volumen físico de la producción de alimentos por habitante (Ver Tabla No. 35).

Table 34. Crecimiento de la producción de alimentos

Años	Tasas anuales medias
1970-1980	-0.6
1980-1982	4.5
1985-1990	0.6
1980-1990	1.5
1990	-2.0
1991	-2.0
1992	-15.3
1993	-19.3
1994	0.0
1995	-6.0

Fuente: *Anuario Estadístico de la CEPAL 1996*, p. 85.

Table 35. Indice de volumen físico de la producción de alimentos por habitante (Año base: promedio trienio 1989-1991 = 100)

Año	Indice	Año	Indice
1970	113	1991	97
1980	93	1992	81
1982	102	1993	66
1988	102	1994	65
1989	103	1995	60
1990	100		

Fuente: *Anuario Estadístico de la CEPAL 1996*, pp. 602-603.

Considerando los datos más recientes sobre la disponibilidad de alimentos, calculada con arreglo al suministro de energía alimentaria (SEA) per cápita diario, vemos que esta cayó abruptamente en los primeros años de la década del 90 (Ver Tabla No. 36). En

---

11. F. Castro, en el Encuentro Nacional de Cooperativas de Producción Agropecuaria, Ciudad de La Habana, 18 de mayo de 1986, *Cuba Socialista*, septiembre-octubre 1986.

1992, Cuba quedó por debajo de varios países de América Latina y el Caribe en el consumo de proteínas y grasas per cápita diario (Ver Tabla No. 37).

Table 36. Suministro alimentario per cápita diario

Concepto	1970	1980	1990	1992
Calorías (No.)	2,638	2,998	3,104	2,833
Proteínas (g)	67.8	72.9	68.9	61.7
Grasas (g)	67.8	79.8	84.8	65.4

Fuente: *Anuario FAO de* Producción 1994.

Table 37. Suministro alimentario per cápita diario, 1992

Países	Calorías (No.)	Proteínas (g)	Grasas (g)
Argentina	2,990	99.3	100.1
Barbados	3,207	89.0	120.4
Brasil	2,824	65.9	82.8
Chile	2,582	71.7	68.8
Costa Rica	2,883	67.3	77.6
Cuba	2,833	61.7	65.4
Dominica	2,778	66.4	71.6
México	3,146	78.7	55.8
Paraguay	2,670	69.7	104.9
Uruguay	2,750	87.3	101.4
Venezuela	2,638	66.1	77.2

Fuente: Anuario FAO de Producción 1994.

Del análisis del SEA per cápita diario en Cuba queda un saldo poco alentador, pues cuando se comparan los registrados en los últimos años con los resultados promedio alcanzados por los países desarrollados más de diez años atrás, se observa que el consumo calórico per cápita diario de los mismos fue de 3,299 calorías, 97.6 gramos de proteínas y 136 gramos de grasa. Ello deja en evidencia el rezago en materia nutricional que actualmente tiene nuestro país, partiendo de que estos datos no hayan sido alterados por el régimen cubano. La crisis de los años 90 ha provocado efectos muy negativos en la utilización de los medios productivos agrícolas, y en la productividad del otrora sector agropecuario, lo que ha repercutido en el empeoramiento de sus niveles de producción.

El 1 de octubre de 1994, después de varios años de restricciones entró en vigor el "Mercado Agropecuario." Se trata de la reaparición del antiguo "Mercado Libre Campesino." A diferencia de este último, en el Agropecuario se autoriza la participación de entida-

des estatales: Unidades Básicas de Producción Agropecuaria (UBPC), Ejército Juvenil del Trabajo (EJT) y otras.

El Mercado Agropecuario, la medida más popular de todas las implantadas con motivo de la crisis económica (Ver Anexo No. 6), inició sus operaciones en medio de un agudo descenso de la producción agrícola y pecuaria, impulsada su creación por la situación imperante en ese momento y no por el deseo oficial de establecerlo. Sin embargo, en la actualidad existen un grupo de factores que impiden su expansión. Enfrentando una de las peores crisis alimentarias que ha padecido el país, el Estado mantiene la prohibición de comercializar una serie de productos en este mercado. Entre estos se encuentran la papa, la leche, la carne vacuna y de caballo, el café y otras.

Además, existen un grupo de problemas que inciden sobre la participación de las entidades estatales y los productores privados autorizados a participar en este mercado, entre los que se pueden enumerar los siguientes:

- El alto compromiso de venta al acopio estatal.

- Los altos costos de transportación de los productos (alquiler de vehículos automotores).

- Los gastos de comercialización de los productos (alquiler de la tarima en el mercado y un segundo alquiler por el espacio—almacenamiento—si se dejan los productos para el siguiente día, por el alquiler de las pesas, por los altos impuestos).

La apertura del Mercado Agropecuario desflacionó los precios a que se vendían los productos agropecuarios en la llamada economía sumergida o mercado negro. Sin embargo, éstos se han mantenido altos, fuera del alcance de las posibilidades de las personas de bajo ingreso. Por otra parte, lo exíguo del abastecimiento racionado estatal obliga a la gran mayoría de la población a acudir a esos mercados, aumentando considerablemente la participación de la alimentación en el presupuesto familiar.

En realidad, el descenso de los precios en el Mercado Agropecuario—una vez sobrepasada la baja inicial—sólo será posible mediante el incremento de la producción agropecuaria. Los factores antes señalados imposibilitan este descenso.

En sus inicios, en C. La Habana solamente, las ventas realizadas en este mercado entre octubre de 1994 y abril de 1995 generaron ingresos estimados de 903.8 millones de pesos. Sin embargo, entre 1995 y 1996 descendieron en un 21.9%, descendiendo de 1,848.5 millones de pesos en 1995 a 1,158.9 millones en 1996 (*Estadísticas Seleccionadas de Cuba 1996*, Oficina Nacional de Estadísticas, abril de 1997, p. 7). Y esto no se debió a que aumentarán las entregas racionadas a la población.

MEDIOS DE PRODUCCION Y RENDIMIENTOS

Las actividades agrícolas y pecuarias constituyen la laguna más visible del ineficiente "sistema económico" cubano. No obstante, han sido en su conjunto las mejores dotadas de recursos en toda la economía nacional. Entre 1960 y 1969, Cuba invirtió 15,856.3 millones de pesos en las mismas. En 1989 nuestro país contaba con 76,783 tractores de diferentes tipos (*Anuario Estadístico de la CEPAL 1996*, p. 658), registrando uno de los más bajos índices de América Latina y el Caribe en el indicador hectáreas de tierra cultivable/tractor (Ver Anexo No. 7).

Para los países subdesarrollados el consumo de fertilizantes adquiere una importancia particular, porque de su acción depende en gran medida la autosuficiencia alimentaria. Si se analiza el consumo de fertilizantes en los países latinoamericanos durante la década de los 80, se observa que Cuba registró el mayor consumo por hectarea cultivable, pasando su consumo total de 73,500 toneladas en 1980 a 107,000 toneladas en 1989. En 1995 el consumo total ascendió a 137,000 toneladas, a pesar de haber descendido la producción en el país de 161 mil toneladas en 1989 a sólo 15 mil en 1994 (*Anuario Estadístico de la CEPAL 1996*, p. 682).

Otro elemento de gran importancia en la agricultura cubana es el riego, que permite bajo condiciones normales de organización la elevación de los rendimientos y la recuperación de tierras, con lo que se puede ampliar la superficie cultivada. Cuba, en cuanto al indicador de tierras irrigadas del total de tierras en cul-

tivos, ocupaba un lugar destacado en el mundo. En 1980 tenía 729.4 ha. bajo riego por cada 1000 de superficie agrícola, pasando en 1989 a 879.6 ha. A lo anterior se agregan los miles de técnicos de diferentes niveles de calificación y especialidades que trabajan en las actividades agrícolas y pecuarias.

Sin embargo, como hemos visto anteriormente, los resultados del otrora sector agropecuario han sido bastante decepcionantes. ¿Cuáles han sido las causas de esta situación?

El sistema de dirección basado en la rígida centralización de toda la actividad económica en el Estado, con la ausencia total en determinados períodos de estímulos materiales a los productores, sustentado fundamentalmente en la ayuda económica recibida del exterior, ha sido una de las causas principales de las ineficiencias presentadas no sólo por el sector agropecuario, sino también por los demás sectores de la economía nacional.

Todos los que han trabajado en las actividades económicas en Cuba, saben que hasta hace muy poco timepo las cuestiones de la eficiencia, tan pregonadas en la actualidad, se consideraban exclusivamente como un problema consistente en conseguir aumentos de la producción sin tener en cuenta para nada el gasto productivo. Sin embargo, eficiencia significa que no hay despilfarro de recursos, o sea, todo lo contrario de lo que ha ocurrido en la economía cubana, caracterizada por el derroche.

En verdad, la dirección del país nunca ha asumido plenamente la responsabilidad de lo que ella misma ha mandado a hacer, manteniendo una gran inestabilidad en la conducción de la economía. La mala administración existente en todo momento y en todos los sectores de la economía nacional ha afectado negativamente el trabajo y la producción, y las carencias resultantes de todo ello han agravado el problema de la baja productividad, el elevado ausentismo y el despilfarro de recursos en los centros de producción y servicios del país. El robo continuado en entidades estatales, así como el mercado negro, constituyen constantes en el panorama económico nacional. Sin embargo, se rechaza de que el gran culpable de todo eso sea el supercentralizado e ineficiente "sistema económico."

PROBLEMAS ECOLOGICOS

Un aspecto adicional que influye sobre la crisis agrícola y alimentaria en Cuba es la constante degradación del medio ambiente. Este fenómeno universal para todos los países subdesarrollados, tiene rasgos propios y resultados singularmente desvastadores para la agricultura cubana.

Cuba, con una extensión de 11086,1 miles de hectáreas y unos 8,8 millones de hectáreas cultivables presenta hoy:[12]

- Un millón de hectáreas afectadas por la erosión.

- Un millón de hectáreas afectadas por la salinidad y de ellas medio millón en grado extremo.

- Un millón de hectáreas en peligro de salinizarse.

- Veinte por ciento del territorio afectado por la erosión y un sesenta por ciento con algún tipo de daño al respecto.

- Acidez en el 25% del territorio.

- Los centrales azucareros y destilerías arrojan más de 60 millones de m^3 de aguas residuales no tratadas a ríos, lagunas y bahías.

- Las cuencas hidrográficas, con unos 6,7 millones de hectáreas están afectadas en gran medida por todos los males anteriormente apuntados.

- Creciente deforestación para atender necesidades de industrias, como la azucarera que consume 600 mil m^3 de leña anualmente; así como para sustituir combustible doméstico.

- Disminución de los manglares por la contaminación y para sustituir combustible doméstico.

- Tala indiscriminada de frutales.

---

12. Basado en información en *Gramma, Juventud Rebelde, Trabajadores* y *Anuarios Estadísticos*.

Anexo 1:
PARTICIPACIÓN DE LA INDUSTRIA, EL SECTOR AGROPECUARIO Y LAS CONSTRUCCIONES EN EL PRODUCTO MATERIAL TOTAL (PMT)
(A PRECIOS CONSTANTES DE 1965; EN POR CIENTOS)

Años	Total	Industria	Sector Agropecuario	Construcciones
1962	100.0	67.7	23.2	9.1
1963	100.0	68.3	22.8	8.9
1964	100.0	67.0	22.8	10.2
1965	100.0	64.2	23.7	12.1
1966	100.0	57.6	23.5	18.9
1967	100.0	65.0	22.8	12.2
1968	100.0	64.5	27.0	8.5
1969	100.0	64.6	26.2	9.2
1970	100.0	70.6	21.7	7.7
1971	100.0	70.7	19.5	9.8
1972	100.0	68.8	18.7	12.5
1973	100.0	68.4	17.4	14.2
1974	100.0	68.3	16.7	15.0
1975	100.0	66.6	17.6	15.8
1976	100.0	66.3	17.6	16.1
1977	100.0	65.1	17.7	17.2
1978	100.0	65.6	17.4	17.0
1979	100.0	65.8	17.3	16.9
1980	100.0	66.5	16.8	16.7
1981	100.0	66.0	16.8	17.2
1982	100.0	67.4	15.7	16.9
1983	100.0	67.1	14.8	18.1
1984	100.0	66.4	14.3	19.3
1985	100.0	68.0	13.5	18.5
1986	100.0	67.7	13.6	18.7
1987	100.0	68.0	13.9	18.1
1988	100.0	67.7	14.0	18.3

Fuente: Cálculos realizados en base a los datos de la Tabla 11, p. 279 del libro de José Luis Rodríguez, *La estrategia del desarrollo económico en Cuba*, La Habana, 1990.

Anexo 2:
PRODUCCIÓN PER CÁPITA DE PRODUCTOS
AGROPECUARIOS EN AMÉRICA LATINA, 1974 (KG)

Producción de carne de res		Producción de carne de cerdo		Producción de arroz		Producción de maíz	
Uruguay	115	Paraguay	10	Panamá	110	Argentina	395
Argentina	89	Uruguay	9	Brasil	62	Brasil	166
Paraguay	48	Argentina	9	Colombia	60	México	134
Costa Rica	30	México	7	Costa Rica	56	Honduras	118
Brasil	26	Brasil	7	Uruguay	49	Paraguay	113
Panamá	25	Ecuador	6	Cuba	48	El Salvador	102
Nicaragua	25	Haití	5			Nicaragua	93
Chile	17	Puerto Rico	5			Haití	55
Honduras	16	Santo Domingo	5			Bolivia	51
Bolivia	11	Chile	5			Venezuela	48
México	9	Venezuela	5			Ecuador	37
Santo Domingo	9	Costa Rica	4			Panamá	36
Cuba	8	Panamá	3			Colombia	32
		Colombia	3			Costa Rica	29
		Cuba	2			Cuba	10

Fuente: Fuente: *Anuario Estadístico de Cuba 1976.* Estadísticas Internacionales.

Anexo 3:
PRODUCCIONES AGRÍCOLAS PER CÁPITA EN AMÉRICA LATINA, 1986 (KG)

Países	Tubérculos y raíces	Tomates	Hortalizas	Cítricos	Tabaco	Arroz	Papa
Cuba	66.2	20.7	54.0	76.5	4.5	56.0	31.0
Bolivia	108.9	—	46.3	—	—	28.9	106.4
Brazil	205.0	13.3	34.3	102.7	3.0	75.1	13.2
Colombia	126.2	10.4	55.1	—	—	59.3	78.1
Ecuador	54.3	—	35.3	—	—	53.8	40.3
Paraguay	779.9	13.1	63.5	133.0	6.8	16.3	—
Uruguay	62.4	22.1	64.4	48.7	—	132.2	42.5

Fuente: Fuente: *Anuario Estadístico de Cuba 1988.* Estadísticas Internacionales.

Anexo 4:
PRODUCCIÓN PER CÁPITA DE PRODUCTOS AGRÍCOLAS
SELECCIONADOS EN AMÉRICA LATINA, 1995 *(KG)*

Country	Maíz	Plátano	Café	Frijoles secos
Argentina	26.6	4.92	—	6.90
Bolivia	35.5	57.0	2.69	1.75
Brazil	70.6	35.6	5.84	18.3
Chile	9.57	—	—	3.94
Colombia	48.8	150.5	22.6	4.46
Costa Rica	35.6	613.0	44.7	13.1
Cuba	8.66	23.7	2.46	2.0
Ecuador	122.6	557.8	17.2	2.88
El Salvador	8.83	13.8	26.6	9.0
Guatemala	4.89	55.0	19.8	10.2
Haití	11.1	69.6	4.73	6.96
Honduras	6.19	181.8	22.2	6.72
México	4.98	23.5	4.47	14.0
Nicaragua	57.0	25.7	13.3	19.4
Panama	76.0	385.8	4.56	2.28
Paraguay	25.9	15.7	1.03	9.53
Peru	48.5	45.3	4.12	2.55
República Dominicana	66.8	120.4	5.36	4.72
Uruguay	198.0	—	—	0.94
Venezuela	29.4	80.4	3.80	1.92

Fuente: Fuente: *Anuario Estadístico de la CEPAL 1996.*

Anexo 5:
INDICES DE PRODUCCIÓN PER CAPITA (1979-81=100)

Concepto	1983	1984	1985	1986	1987	1988	1989	1990	1991	1992	1993	1994
Productos alimenticios	103.11	108.34	103.63	106.12	99.85	102.87	102.80	98.82	101.08	89.33	67.24	65.19
Cultivos		100.53	110.17	103.73	103.87	100.38	106.38	109.76	101.66	94.31	80.71	64.90	61.36
Cereales		110.12	116.55	109.45	117.63	96.49	99.66	107.96	88.50	74.69	58.06	40.97	40.60

Concepto	Cosechado (1000 ha)				Rendimiento (kg/ha)				Producción (M t)			
	1979-81	1992	1993	1994	1979-81	1992	1993	1994	1979-81	1992	1993	1994
Cereales totales	224	208	156	156	2458	1784	1776	1776	551	371	277	277
Arroz en cáscara	146	130	78	78	3106	2115	2325	2325	455	275	186	188
Raíces y tubérculos	164	156	151	151	6092	5228	4944	4914	813	813	744	744
Papa	14	15	14	14	16509	16333	15429	15319	238	245	216	216
Tomate	29	31	28	28	7758	8323	7143	7143	228	258	200	200

Fuente: *Anuario FAO de Producción 1994.*

Anexo 6
PRINCIPALES MEDIDAS

En 1990, el Gobierno cubano implanta una serie de medidas que introducen algunos mecanismos de mercado en el modelo de economía planificada. Estas medidas afectaron en un primer momento al sector externo y a la promoción de las inversiones extranjeras y el turismo. A partir de 1993, las medidas afectaron directamente al funcionamiento interno de la economía cubana.

Medidas
26 de julio de 1993: El Decreto Ley No. 140 legaliza la tenencia de divisas.

8 de septiembre de 1993: El Consejo de Ministros aprueba el Decreto Ley No. 141 que regula el trabajo por cuenta propia para 135 actividades laborales privadas, excepto aquellas definidas como "en beneficio de toda la sociedad," tales como la medicina y la enseñanza. Los trabajadores por cuenta propia no pueden contratar empleados. En 1995 existían unos 203000 trabajadores por cuenta propia. En la actualidad no llegan a 160 mil.

15 de septiembre de 1993: Se crean los Mercados Agropecuarios.

24 de abril de 1994: El Decreto Ley No. 147 establece la reestructuración de la organización del Estado con la creación de cinco nuevos ministerios, que sustituyen a varios anteriores "Comités Estatales." Entre los nuevos ministerios están los de Economía y Planificación, Inversión Extranjera y Colaboración Económica, Finanzas y Precios y el Ministerio del Turismo, creado por primera vez.

2 de mayo de 1994: En sesión extraordinaria, la Asamblea Nacional anuncia otro paquete de medidas destinadas a absorber el exceso de liquidez y tendentes a reducir el déficit público, entre las cuales se encuentran:

- el establecimiento de un sistema de impuestos sobre la renta, aplicables a los trabajadores por cuenta propia y a las actividades pagadas con divisas extranjeras;

- la reducción o eliminación de las subvenciones a empresas y organismos estatales, el cobro de algunas gratuities como los cursos de idiomas opcionales o las entradas a los museos, espectáculos y exposiciones;

- la confiscación de bienes e ingresos obtenidos por enriquecimiento indebido con el fin de restringir el enriquecimiento en el mercado negro y recoger una parte del esceso de moneda en circulación;

- la subida drástica de los precios de electricidad, agua y transporte, así como de varios productos no considerados básicos, tales como el tabaco, el ron y la gasolina.

4 de agosto de 1994: La Asamblea Nacional aprueba una nueva Ley de impuestos que entrará en vigor el próximo año y gravará los beneficios de las empresas, los ingresos personales, las ventas y algunas propiedades como la vivienda.

1 de octubre de 1994: Entra en vigor el Mercado Agropecuario, regido por la ley de oferta y demanda.

1 de diciembre de 1994: Entra en vigor el Mercado Libre Industrial y Artesanal, regido por la ley de oferta y demanda.

3 de enero de 1995: El Banco Nacional de Cuba (BNC) empieza a cambiar las divisas extranjeras por un peso convertible. El cambio oficial equipara el peso cubano con el dólar (un dólar=un peso). El peso convertible no puede ser, sin embargo, adquirido por la moneda oficial cubana sino sólo con divisas y funciona como medio de pago en establecimientos turísticos y tiendas diferenciadas en coexistencia con el dólar.

marzo de 1995: El Gobierno anuncia la liberalización de las regulaciones aduaneras, lo que supondría la posibilidad de introducir hasta 1000 dólares en efectivo o en mercancías tanto para los cubanos como para los extranjeros.

julio de 1995: El Gobierno decide autorizar la apertura de cinco oficinas de cambio en La Ciudad de La Habana de forma experimental.

5 de septiembre de 1995: La Asamblea Nacional aprueba una nueva Ley de Inversiones que establece que todos los sectores de la economía quedan abiertos a la inversión extranjera con excepción de la defensa,

la salud y la educación. La nueva Ley autoriza, por otra parte, la participación mayoritaria o del 100% de compañías extranjeras en inversiones previamente autorizadas por el Gobierno.

9 de septiembre de 1995: El diario *Granma* anuncia que el Gobierno autoríza a partir de entonces a los cubanos residentes en la isla o en el exterior a abrir cuentas de ahorros en pesos convertibles, dólares u otras divisas y percibir intereses de dichas cuentas. Hasta entonces, el Banco Nacional de Cuba (BNC) sólo había autorizado a empresas extranjeras o a ciu-

dadanos extranjeros abrir cuentas en una moneda distinta a la moneda oficial.

23 de octubre de 1995: Abre sus puertas la nueva agencia estatal de cambio "Cadeca," que ofrecerá pesos por dólares.

25 de noviembre de 1995: El diario *Granma* anuncia que a partir del 1 de enero de 1996, el Gobierno cubano gravará los ingresos personales en dólares con la excepción de las remesas del exterior.

Anexo 7:
MECANIZACIÓN: HECTÁREAS DE TIERRA CULTIVADA POR TRACTOR, AMÉRICA LATINA Y EL CARIBE

País	1989	1991	1992	1993	1994	1995
Antigua y Barbuda	34	34	34	33	33	33
Argentina	101	101	97	97	77	97
Bahamas	130	128	128	125	125	125
Barbados	28	27	27	26	26	26
Belice	52	51	52	50	50	50
Bolivia	452	446	445	445	445	445
Brasil	79	73	70	70	67	69
Colombia	153	152	151	150	150	148
Costa Rica	83	83	81	76	76	76
Cuba	44	43	43	43	43	43
Chile	124	120	117	106	102	103
Dominica	189	189	189	189	189	189
Ecuador	332	336	340	339	334	341
El Salvador	215	214	214	213	213	213
Granada	464	464	414	367	367	367
Guatemala	427	425	423	415	437	444
Guyana	138	138	137	137	137	137
Haiti	4114	4114	4022	3957	3957	3957
Honduras	525	524	528	546	413	414
Jamaica	72	72	71	71	71	71
Mexico	147	145	144	144	144	144
Nicaragua	499	490	480	471	470	470
Panamá	125	128	130	132	132	133
Paraguay	151	146	141	138	138	138
Perú	294	294	297	291	264	318
Rep. Dominicana	623	621	618	617	617	630
San Vicente	141	141	141	138	138	138
Suriname	54	53	52	51	51	51
Trinidad y Tobago	46	46	46	46	46	46
Uruguay	39	40	40	40	40	40
Venezuela	82	81	81	80	80	80
Total	101	98	98	95	93	95

Fuente: *Anuario Estadístico de la CEPAL 1996*, p. 80.

INVESTMENT, HUMAN CAPITAL, AND TECHNOLOGICAL CHANGE: EVIDENCE FROM CUBA AND ITS IMPLICATIONS FOR GROWTH MODELS

Manuel E. Madrid-Aris[1]

This paper is a follow up to, and complements, my paper published last year in *Cuba in Transition—Volume 7* (Madrid-Aris, 1997), in the sense that better data have been collected, and some tests have been performed to find some explanations for the Cuban decreasing total factor productivity (TFP) growth. In addition, Cuban TFP results are used to draw some implications for growth models.

This paper has four main goals. The first one is to provide a descriptive analysis of the historical pattern of Cuban factor accumulation (physical investment and human capital creation), social investment, and labor force structure. The second is to discuss the validity of TFP growth, estimated by using the traditional methodology (Solow, 1957), and to show that in the case of Cuba, those estimates are consistent with econometric estimations. The third goal is to find a theoretical explanation for decreasing TFP, through performing an analysis of technological change embodiment in capital and economies of scale analysis. The final goal is to analyze the applicability of linear growth models to the Cuban case.

It is widely known that the importance of TFP changes over time. TFP growth measures the economic and technical efficiency of the process of transforming inputs or resources into products or final goods. The growth of an economy, or of a sector of an economy, is determined mainly by the rate of growth of its productive resources (especially labor and capital) and the rate of technological change or TFP growth. Thus, TFPs are important in explaining why some countries grow more rapidly than others, or why some specific industries or sectors grow faster than others for a given period of time.[2] In addition, TFP is useful for the design of a country's "catching up" process, which involves economic policies directed to exploit some industries' or economic sectors' comparative advantage, and to keep the country competitive internationally (Nishimizu and Robinson, 1984). Therefore, the differential rate of sectoral TFP growth is a crucial determinant of the comparative advantage that could help growth and define structural economic adjustments in the medium- to long-run for a specific country.

The empirical literature on growth and technological change has accumulated a large body of "stylized

---

1. I would like to express my deepest appreciation to the people who helped me in Cuba to find and collect some of the data which were used in this research. The author wishes to acknowledge the helpful comments received from Jeffrey Nugent, Caroline Betts, Ernesto Hernández-Catá, Matt Nussbaum and Borislav Arabajiev. The views expressed, opinions, and conclusions reached in this paper are those of the author, and do not necessarily reflect those of the institutions with which the author is affiliated.

2. For an interesting comparative cross-country research on total factor productivity (TFP), which includes Korea, Japan, Turkey, and Yugoslavia, see Nishimizu and Robinson, 1984.

facts" about the contribution of TFP and factors input (labor and capital) to economic performance.[3] Most of the empirical studies of TFP show that increased investment and human capital are directly related with higher level of TFP.[4] Theoretical linear endogenous growth models emphasize this relationship. Madrid-Aris (1997) showed that this relationship goes in the opposite way in Cuba. He also showed that Cuban economic growth during the period 1962-1988 was much like the Russian growth (Krugman, 1994)—it was mainly won by massive, often wasteful capital accumulation, rather than productivity growth. Cuba's increased investment was possible thanks to the Soviet assistance/subsidies. Also, in the Cuban economy there were no positive correlations between investment in human capital (better-educated labor force) and TFP growth performance. Cuba had decreasing TFP while human and physical investment increased considerably over the same period.

This paper is organized as follows. The first section provides a brief review of the historical patterns of Cuban growth, factor accumulation, and human capital for the period 1962-1988. The second section contains estimations of Cuba's aggregate and sectoral rate of technical progress or total factor productivity (TFP) growth during the period 1962-1988, using two different methodologies—traditional methodology (Solow, 1957) and econometric methodology. The third section contains theoretical explanations of Cuban TFP growth results, such as technological change, embodiment in capital, and economies of scale analysis. The fourth section contains an endogenity analysis of Cuban investment using linear growth models, for the purpose of drawing some implications for their applicability to the Cuban case. The final section contains the conclusions.

REVIEW OF CUBAN FACTOR ACCUMULATION AND LABOR FORCE STRUCTURE

Cuban Growth and Investment Indicators

Table 1 shows a summary of Cuban main macroeconomic indicators and the Soviet assistance received by Cuba during the period 1960-1988. Cuba's gross material product (GMP)[5] was able to grow at a steady rate of 4.4% and per capita income increased at an average rate of 3.2% during this period. Cuba greatly increased the rate of investment, which went from 15% in 1960 to 30% in 1988. As the data in Table 1 show, between 1960 and 1964, there was no increase in income per capita. On the other hand, during the period 1965-1988 income per capita increased at a considerable rate. Data show that Soviet assistance increased considerably over time. During the period 1960-64, Soviet assistance was on average only 7% of GMP, but it increased to a level of 33% of GMP for the period 1980-1984. The amount of Soviet assistance was larger than the investments realized by the Cuban government for the period 1980-1984. In other words, during this period, it could be assumed that most of the investments realized by the Cuban government were realized by using capital coming from the Soviet Union.[6] Therefore, it could be inferred that the Cuban economy was losing its saving capacity.

Note that the highest rate of economic growth (10%) was achieved in the period 1970-1974. Ironically, during this period, the Cuban investment rate was low (17%) and even decreased, from 19% to 17%. Additionally, the lowest rate of economic growth (1.3%) was during the period 1985-1988, when the

---

3. For a critical survey about TFP, see Nelson (1981). For case studies applied to less developed countries (LDCs), see Teitel and Westphal (1984) and Solimano (1996).

4. Singapore is an exception (Young, 1992).

5. The Cuban accounting system is different from the western concept of Gross National Product (GNP). Cuba uses the Soviet system of Global Social Product (GSP) and Gross Material Product (GMP), which is also called "gross product." For further explanation of the Cuban Accounting System, see Brundenius (1984), pp. 19-40, Mesa-Lago and Pérez-López (1985), Madrid-Aris (1998).

6. Note that in a centrally planned economy like Cuba, the investment is mainly realized by the government since there are no opportunities for private enterprises or for private investment. Therefore, private income is spent mostly in consumption.

Table 1.   Macroeconomic Indicators

Period	Economic Growth (%)	Income Per capita Growth	Investment as share of GMP	Total Soviet Assistance as share of GMP[a]	Exports as share of GMP	Imports as share of GMP
1960-1964	1.9	-0.2	0.14	0.08	0.15	0.19
1965-1969	3.6	1.7	0.19	0.07	0.14	0.21
1970-1974	10.0	8.2	0.17	0.07	0.18	0.23
1975-1979	3.4	2.2	0.28	0.18	0.34	0.40
1980-1984	5.7	5.1	0.30	0.33	0.44	0.52
1985-1988	1.3	0.3	0.31	n.a.	0.40	0.60
AVERAGE	4.4	3.2	0.23	0.15	0.28	0.36

Notes: Economic growth has been estimated with Gross Material Product (GMP) since statistics of Gross Social Product (GSP) are not as accurate as GMP (See Mesa-Lago and Pérez-López, 1985).

Source: Rodríguez (1990), Brundenius (1984), Mesa-Lago and Pérez-López (1985), Central Intelligence Agency, Directorate of Intelligence (1984, 1989), Comité Estatal de Estadísticas (CEE)-*Anuario Estadístico de Cuba*, several years, and author's estimations.

a.   Total Soviet Assistance includes Soviet trade subsidies (sugar, petroleum and nickel) plus development aid (for further details, see, Central Intelligence Agency, Directorate of Intelligence, 1984, p. 40 and 1989, p. 39).

Table 2.   National Income and Social Investment *(Education and Health)*

	(In millions of Current Cuban Pesos)			Ratios in Percentage	
Year	Value of National Income	Investment in Education	Investment in Health	Investment in Education as % of National Income	Investment in Health as % of National Income
1960	2,625.5	83.7	51.3	3.2	2.0
1965	3,888.2	260.4	148.9	6.7	3.8
1970	3,517.6	351.1	216.4	10.0	6.2
1975	8,112.6	808.5	304.2	10.0	3.8
1980	9,853.1	1,340.8	440.2	13.6	4.5
1987	12,202.2	1,600.0	810.2	13.1	6.6

Source: Rodriguez, José Luis. *Estrategia del Desarollo Económico de Cuba.* La Habana, 1990, p. 218 and p. 293.

highest rate of investment (31%) was observed. Looking at these figures, it seems that the Cuban economy was not able to absorb in an efficient way such a high level of investment.[7] If the rate of investment exceeds the country's technical, human and institutional capacity to allocate it in an efficient way, most of the investment goes to poorly-managed projects. Hence, investment is not very productive and depreciates. In sum, it can be concluded that during the 1980s, investment was not allocated as efficiently as during the 1970s.

National Income and Social Investment

Table 2 summarizes Cuban investment in education and health, and its percentage of total income. It shows that investment in education increased considerably. In 1960, it was only 3.2% of total national income, and increased to a level of 13.1% in 1987. Investment in health also increased considerably during this period. In 1990, investment in health represented only 2.0% of national income, and it increased to a level of 6.6% of national income by 1987.

Population Growth and Human Capital[8]

Table 3 summarizes Cuban infant mortality and population growth during the period 1960-1989.

7. Miguel Figueras, the former Director of Planning of the Cuban Ministry of Industry, supports this view. For further details, see Figueras, 1994.

8. Human capital investment is a concept widely used by economists, meaning the process of improving of the quality of the labor force. Thus, human capital is referred to as the level of education of the labor force. This improvement of the labor force quality is basically achieved by education and training (Becker, 1963).

Cuban average rate of population growth in the 60s is 1.9%, in the 70s is 1.4%, and in the 80s is only 0.9%. These figures show the decreasing tendency of population growth in Cuba. At the same time that infant mortality was reduced considerable. The low rate of population growth could be explained by two factors: (1) the emigration of Cuban people to other countries; and (2) the reduction in the birth rate. Both elements indicate that Cuba presents the lowest population growth rate in Latin America.

Table 3. Infant Mortality and Population Growth (%)

Period	Infant Mortality (per 1,000)	Population growth (percentage)
1960-1969	38.5	1.9 %
1970-1979	27.0	1.4 %
1980-1989	15.4	0.9 %

Source: Madrid-Aris (1998).

Table 4 shows data on enrollment per 1,000 habitants by educational levels in Cuba between 1958 and 1985. Since there is no accurate data concerning the rate of change of education of the Cuban labor force, for purposes of discussion in this study, it is assumed that human capital changes at the same rate as enrollment rates changes.[9]

Cuba considerably increased the rate of enrollment during the period 1959-1988. Data from Table 4 show that human capital accumulation has been quite rapid in Cuba during the last 35 years. Without looking at economic variables such as the amount invested in education and the return on human capital creation, it could be concluded that the Cuban government was successful in achieving a very high rate of enrollment during this period.

Table 4. Student Enrollment by Level of Education (per 1,000 habitants)

Year	Primary Education	Secondary Education	Higher Education	Other Education	Total Enrollment
1958	104.9	11.8	3.8	0	120.5
1970	193.4	24.9	4.1	32.4	254.8
1975	205.2	57.1	9.0	31.3	302.6
1980	164.2	110.0	15.7	6.8	296.7
1985	116.8	110.0	23.2	2.0	252.0

Notes: For Cuba, secondary education includes technical schools. Other types of education include the worker farm educational program developed after the revolution.

Source: Madrid-Aris (1998).

Labor Force Structure

Centrally planned economies have an astonishing power to mobilize resources, especially labor. Hence, to understand growth in a centrally planned economy, it is essential to understand how the labor structure changes through time under this type of regime. Empirical evidence shows that in the Soviet Union, the rapid rate of economic growth achieved under communism, especially during the 1950s and 1960s,[10] was mainly the result of the increased labor force and capital accumulation rather than of technological change.[11] Table 5 shows the change in the labor force structure in Cuba from 1962 through 1988.

Data in Table 5 show that the labor force increased considerably after the revolution. The labor force as percentage of total population surged from 15% in 1962 to 33% in 1988. Thus, over the past generation, the percentage of people entering the labor force doubled, but it obviously can not double again in the future.[12] Large portions of this new labor force were women, which more than doubled from 1962 to 1988. The analysis of TFP presented in the coming section clearly shows that increased labor inputs

---

9. This approximation is assumed due to the lack of accurate and reliable data about graduation rates and their relation to the labor force.

10. The average growth rate of the Soviet Union during 1950-1964 was 4.3%. The growth rate of the U.S. was only 2.2% for this period. For further details, see Bergson (1968).

11. For further detail, see Krugman (1994) and Poznanski (1985).

12. Labor force as percentage of total population can not double again because today the labor force is already 33% of the total population. Doubling this figure means that 66% of the population would be part of the labor force. In reality this is not feasible, because to achieve that rate, it would mean that most of the women, old men, and children would have to be a part of the labor force.

Table 5. Total and Sectoral Labor Force Structure *(in percentage)*

Year	Total Labor Force (as % of Total Population)	Productive Labor Force (as % of Total Population)	Industrial Labor Force (as % of Total Population)	Agriculture Labor Force (as % of Total Population)	Female Share of Total Labor Force (%)
1962	15	12	3.6	4.1	14
1970	23	18	4.9	7.6	18
1975	26	20	5.6	7.3	26
1982	28	21	6.1	6.5	35
1988	33	23	7.1	6.8	38

Notes: Under GMP accounting system, the total labor is broken onto two categories, productive and unproductive labor force.

Source: Comité Estatal de Estadísticas (CEE), *Anuario Estadístico de Cuba*, several years, and Brundenius (1984).

are directly correlated with the Cuban economic growth.

CUBAN TECHNOLOGICAL CHANGE

Review of Different TFP Growth Methodologies and their Applicability to a Centrally Planned Economy

Krugman's (1994) publication in *Foreign Affairs*, where he mentioned Kim and Lau's (1994) and Young's (1992, 1994) works, encouraged a debate regarding the validity of the TFP obtained under the application of different methodologies (indirect method—Solow, 1957—or econometric method). Subsequently, Harberger (1996) criticized the validity of some econometric estimation of TFPs due to multicollinearity problems. Lately, he proposed a third methodology to estimate TFP which is the "two-deflator method."[13]

Harberger (1996, p.2) shows his preference for TFP estimates by using either the traditional growth-accounting methodology (Solow, 1957) or his two-deflator method instead of econometric estimation. It is clear that Harberger's preference toward traditional methodology could not be extrapolated when estimating TFP growth for a centrally planned economy, since traditional methodology assumptions,[14] especially perfect competition, is not be suitable to a centrally planned economy like Cuba. Thus, the va-

lidity (or lack) of each of these traditional assumptions affects the measurement of technical progress, and, therefore, its contribution to economic growth. Hence, under the absence of a multicollinearity problem, an econometric estimation of TFP could be a better way to estimate TFP growth as opposed to using traditional methodology.

In this section, TFP using traditional methodology is estimated, and verified with econometric estimations. Results show that the TFP estimations using traditional methodology results are consistent with econometric results. Unfortunately, due to the lack of accurate and reliable data, it was not feasible to apply the two-deflator method to estimate TFP growth for Cuba

Total Factor Productivity (TFP) Using Traditional Methodology

The starting point of growth accounting is the following aggregated production function.

$$Y_t = F(K_t, L_t, t) \qquad (1)$$

$$Y_t = A(t)G(K_t, L_t) \qquad (1')$$

Here Yt, Kt, and Lt are the quantities of aggregate real output, physical capital and labor, respectively, at time t, and t is an index of chronological time. The second equation (1') is the traditional neoclassical

---

13. For further details about Harberger's criticism of econometric estimation of TFP, see Harberger (1990, 1996). For an explanation of his two-deflator method, see Harberger (1998). For an application of the two-deflator method to Mexico's manufacturing sector, see Torres (1997).

14. The traditional assumptions are profit maximization with competitive labor and output markets (perfect competition), and constant returns to scale (CRTS), which implies that firms will set the return on capital equal to marginal product of the capital.

growth model, which is a specific case of the first one, since $A(t)$ varies with time and independently of K and L. Technological change is by assumption disembodied, where a Hicks neutral technological change is assumed. This is the basic neoclassical Solow (1957) model for TFP growth estimation.[15] By totally differentiating the production function (1'), and completing elasticities, equation (1') can be written as follows:

$$\hat{Y} = \hat{A} + \alpha_k \cdot \hat{K} + \beta_l \cdot \hat{L} \tag{2}$$

In equation (2) the sign (^) denotes the rate of growth of the variable, and parameters α_k, β_l, are the elasticities of capital and labor with respect to output respectively. Finally, the term $\hat{A}$ is the residual, or the well-known neoclassical expression for exogenous technological change or total factor productivity growth (TFP).

Then, discrete approximations of equation (2) can be written as,

$$\frac{\Delta Y}{Y} = \frac{\Delta A}{A} + \alpha \frac{\Delta K}{K} + \beta \frac{\Delta L}{L} \tag{3}$$

Thus, equation (3) is used to estimate Cuban TFP growth at aggregated and sectoral levels.

Total Factor Productivity (TFP) Growth and Investment for the Cuban Economy.

Applying equation (3), and using the aggregate rate of growth of productive factors (labor and capital), the sectoral factor shares, and the stock of capital time series,[16] TFP growth estimates are computed and presented in Table 6. Thus, the Cuban rate of technological change (TFPs) decreased over time, achieving negative values after 1980. On the other hand, Table 1 shows that investment increased considerably from 18% of GMP in the period 1963-1970 to a level of 31% in the period 1981-1988. These results are contrary to what any economist would expect and to what endogenous growth models would predict. Empirical estimations of TFP from capitalist economies show that an increase of investment, human capital, and a lower rate of population growth leads to higher TFP growth (Barro, 1991).[17] Hence, economists would have expected a higher rate of TFP growth for Cuban economy given the increasing investment in physical and human capital creation, but the Cuban economy shows opposite results.

Table 6. TFP Growth Estimates and Investment for the Cuban Economy

	TFP (%)	Output Rate of Growth (%)	Investment Rate of Growth (%)	Investment /GMP
1963-1970	1.0	4.4	3.2	0.18
1971-1980	0.8	5.9	18.3	0.26
1981-1988	-1.2	3.8	4.9	0.31
AVERAGE (63-88)	0.2	4.5	9.3	0.25

Notes: For references about output and investment figures, see Table 1.

Based on previous work estimating TFP, the factors contributing to the aggregate economic growth are given in Table 7. Cuba's average TFP contribution to economic growth for the period 1963-1988, is very low (only 2%). The average contribution of capital to economic growth is very high (70%). From these results, it could be concluded that Cuba's economic growth has been basically driven by increased investment. In addition, Cuba's economic growth during the period 1975-1988 is directly linked to the increased level of Soviet subsidies, which allowed the Cuban economy to achieve the high rate of investment observed during this period. In sum, the TFP growth results show that Cuba was not able to take advantage of the investment in human capital to gain some economic efficiency, especially during the 1980s.

Results from Table 7 suggest that Cuban central planning policy, and especially the New System of

---

15. For a detailed review of neoclassical growth models, see Sala-i-Martin (1990).

16. For further explanation about the methodology used to built the stock of capital time series, see, Madrid-Aris (1997, 1998).

17. An exception is Young (1992, 1994). Young found similar productivity patterns for Singapore.

Table 7. Factors Contributing to Growth for the Whole Economy

	Labor Contribution to Growth (%)	Capital Contribution to Growth (%)	TFP Contribution to Growth (%)	Investment as % of GMP	Subsidies as % of GMP[a]
1963-1970	30	57	13	18	7
1971-1980	22	70	8	26	15
1981-1988	35	81	-16	31	33[b]
AVERAGE (63-88)	28	70	2	25	

a. Subsidies figures from Madrid-Aris (1998).

b. This figure represents the 1981-1984 average.

Economic Management and Planning (SDPE),[18] failed to achieve technological change. Note that the implementation of SDPE could have led to an even lower rate of growth of technological change. This failure is even confirmed by Cuban officials who recognized the inefficiency of this plan (Zimbalist and Eckstein, 1987).

It seems that Cuba's low rate of technical progress may simply be due to over-investment and to the absence of competitive pressure and economic incentives that provides motivation to maximize profits. The Cuban case of low contribution of TFP to economic growth seems to be a common pattern of the ex-socialist economies. Nishimizu and Robinson (1984) found that in Yugoslavia, almost all the industries derived their growth from increases in factors inputs, with zero or negative contribution from TFP growth. Bergson (1983) found that most of the Soviet growth was based on rapid growth in inputs (labor and capital). Reality shows that Stalinist planners—as Castro's planners also did—moved millions of workers, especially women, into the labor force. These research results confirm Krugman's statement, in that the special strength of Soviet economies (centrally planned economies) was their ability to mobilize resources (especially labor), not their ability to use them efficiently (Krugman, 1994, p. 69).

Sectoral Total Factor Productivity Growth (TFP) and Investment

The sectoral analysis included only agriculture and industry, since under the Soviet national accounting system, the total output of productive sectors is only aggregated into six categories (industry, agriculture, construction, transportation, communications, and commerce). Note that these two sectors represented more than two thirds of the total GMP.

Total Factor Productivity and Investment for the Agricultural Sector: Applying equation (3) and using the rate of growth of agricultural productive factors (labor and capital) and the sectoral factor shares, yields TFP estimates in Table 8. They show that the agricultural sector experienced negative growth of TFP for the period 1963-1988. Therefore, it could be assumed that resources invested (especially capital) were not used efficiently in this economic sector. In sum, Cuban agricultural output growth was basically driven by expansion of inputs, especially investment, during the period 1963-1988. Note that the average investment rate (1963-1988) in the agricultural sector was extremely high (37%). It was three times higher than the industrial average investment rate (12%).

Again, the only possible explanation is that most of the agricultural output was the result of increased investment, as result of increased Soviet subsidies given to Cuba during this period. It seems fair to say that the negative agricultural TFP reflects the low level of

---

18. The New System of Economic Management and Planning (SDPE) was introduced in the second half of the 1970s. It was modeled on Soviet economic reforms. This management system had different goals, among those: (1) to force enterprises on a self-financing basis; (2) to increase incentives to achieve a better rate of growth of productivity; and (3) to promote decentralization, organizational coherence, and efficiency (Zimbalist and Eckstein, 1987).

Table 8.   TFP Growth and Investment for the Agricultural Sector

	Agricultural TFP	Agriculture Output Rate of Growth (%)	Agricultural Investment Rate of Growth (%)	Agricultural Investment as Share of Agric. GMP
1963-1970	-1.9	3.8	8.0	0.28
1971-1980	-1.2	2.7	10.3	0.35
1981-1988	-1.5	1.7	5.6	0.48
AVERAGE	-1.5	2.7	8.1	0.37

Table 9.   TFP Growth Estimations for the Industrial Sector

	Industrial TFP	Industry Output Rate of Growth (%)	Industry Investment Rate of Growth (%)	Industry Investment as Share of Indus. GMP
1963-1970	1.4	5.2	13.2	0.06
1971-1980	0.7	4.6	25.6	0.11
1981-1988	-0.3	4.3	6.0	0.19
AVERAGE	0.6	4.7	15.0	0.12

yields of Cuban agriculture.[19] It is also possible to conclude that the Cuban centrally planned agricultural economic policies were inefficient in their attempt to force some technological change during the period 1963-1988. In sum, Cuba was not able to take advantage of the large amount of resources invested, especially in human capital creation. The large investment destined to human capital creation, complemented with the high level of investment in physical capital, could have led to an increase in TFP growth, thus leading to an increase of agricultural output, but the results are opposite.

Total Factor Productivity Growth and Investment for the Industrial Sector: It is important to note that under the Cuban accounting system, the industrial sector includes several industries[20] (e.g., mining, electrical energy, oil, fuels, electrical machinery, chemicals, paper products, wood products, construction products, food, textiles, glass, etc.) which under the Western accounting system are classified by different SIC codes under many subcategories (e.g., light manufacturing, heavy manufacturing, mining, and services such as utilities).

Applying equation (3) and using the rate of growth of industrial productive factors (labor and capital), the sectoral factor shares, and the stock of capital of the industrial sector, the industrial TFP growth estimates are given in Table 9. Industrial TFP growth achieved was moderate (0.6%) for the period of 1963-1980, but negative (-0.4%) for the period 1981-1988.

Evidence provided in this paper shows that the average ratio of investment to output in the industrial sector was very low (12%) compared with the agricultural sector (37%). Industrial and agricultural TFP results from this research and investment data suggest that the right level of investment, and avoiding over-investment, could make people more productive, thus achieving higher rates of technological change.

Summary of Factors Contributing to Economic Growth: Previous results show that the industrial sector, which had a lower rate of investment, had the higher TFP growth. Thus, for a better understanding of Cuban economic growth and its linkage with input factors (labor and capital), the factors contribut-

---

19.   During the last 40 years, the Cuban agricultural yields increased at a lower rate than the world average. Today, Cuba's average yields are less than 50% of those of developed economies. For further details, see Figueras (1994) and Food and Agriculture Organization (1969, 1990).

20.   For further details, see *Anuario Estadístico de Cuba* (industrial production).

Table 10. Aggregated and Sectoral Factors Rate of Growth

| | Rate of Growth (%) | | | | | | | | |
| | All Economy (%) | | | Agriculture (%) | | | Industry (%) | | |
PERIOD	Labor	Capital	TFP	Labor	Capital	TFP	Labor	Capital	TFP
1963-1970	2.4	4.5	1.0	2.4	8.8	-1.9	2.3	5.1	1.4
1971-1980	2.1	6.8	0.8	0.7	6.9	-1.2	2.3	5.5	0.7
1981-1988	2.6	6.1	-1.2	0.9	5.6	-1.5	3.9	4.1	-0.3
AVERAGE	2.3	5.8	0.2	1.3	6.7	-1.5	2.9	4.9	0.6

Table 11. Factors' Contribution to Aggregated and Sectoral Economic Growth

| | Contribution of Factors (as % of total economic growth) | | | | | | | | |
| | All Economy (%) | | | Agriculture (%) | | | Industry (%) | | |
PERIOD	Labor	Capital	TFP	Labor	Capital	TFP	Labor	Capital	TFP
1963-1970	30	57	13	25	95	-20	26	58	16
1971-1980	22	70	8	11	108	-19	27	65	8
1981-1988	35	81	-16	18	112	-30	51	53	-4
AVERAGE	28	70	2	20	103	-23	35	59	7

ing to economic growth have been estimated in Tables 10 and 11.

Previous tables show that for the agricultural sector, the average TFP growth is negative (-1.5), and its contribution of TFP to output is negative (-23%) during the period of 1963-1988. In the industrial sector, at least the average TFP growth positive, but it was moderate (0.6), and its contribution to economic growth was very low (7%).

In sum, the Cuban governments' interventionist policy during 1975-1988 was accompanied by very low TFP performance, especially in agriculture. Thus, the creation by governments of institutional mechanisms to deal with inefficiencies may not always be an efficient way to force technological change. It seems very difficult to understand why the massive investments in physical and human capital led to such a low TFP in the 1970s and 1980s, but it seems a common pattern of centrally planned economies

Econometric Estimation of Cuba's Rate of Technological Change

With the purpose of avoiding the criticism about the use of traditional growth accounting methodology to estimate TFP growth in a centrally planned economy, where the strong assumption of perfect competition does not hold, TFP was estimated using econometric methodology, and compared with previous results. Results obtained in this section show that results obtained under the two methodologies are consistent.

Growth accounting can be conducted by subtracting from the residual the contribution stemming from increases of inputs (especially human capital), as well as the contribution from research and development. For the purpose of comparison with previous TFP estimates where human capital adjustment was not considered, in this section TFP was estimated without considering human capital quality adjustment. In other words, quality of labor is considered constant through time.

In general, when TFPs are estimated econometrically, it is convenient to keep the assumption of constant returns to scale (CRTS) because it reduces the number of independent parameters to be estimated, and thereby, mitigates the possible multicollinearity among the data on capital and labor inputs and time (Boskin and Lau, 1992). From this paper analysis of economies of scale, it seems reasonable to keep the assumption of CRTS, especially for the Cuban economy and industrial sector.

The right way of estimating technical progress econometrically is by including in the production function a term (terms) to capture the effect of technical progress through time, in order to allow technical progress to be non-linear over time. Thus, the Hicks neutral equation (11) was estimated econometrically.

$$Y_t = A(t)f(K_t, L_t) = A_0 \cdot e^{rt} \cdot K_t^{\alpha} \cdot L_t^{(1-\alpha)} \quad (4)$$

Then, in equation (4) the rate of technical progress or TFP is equal to:

$$\frac{\dot{A}(t)}{A} = \frac{e^{rt} \cdot r}{e^{rt}} = r \quad (5)$$

Applying natural log to equation (4), leads to equation (6).

$$\ln Y_t = \ln A + r \cdot t + \alpha \ln K_t + (1-\alpha)\ln L_t + \varepsilon \quad (6)$$

Thus, the linear equation to estimate TFP growth econometrically is,

$$\ln(Y_t / L_t) = \ln A + r \cdot t + \alpha \ln(K_t / L_t) + \varepsilon \quad (6')$$

Econometric estimation of equation (6') leads to the results in Table 12.

The capital elasticity with respect to output obtained (0.47) for the Cuban economy, as a whole, is very close to that obtained indirectly using national accounts (0.51) and used in the indirect estimation of the TFP. The average rate of technical progress during the period 1962-1988, obtained econometrically for the Cuban economy as a whole, is equal to 0.4, which is very close to that obtained using indirect methodology (0.2). Therefore, results in Table 12

confirm the validity of TFP obtained in the previous section for the Cuban economy as a whole.

Econometric estimations of TFP for the agricultural sector over the period 1962-1988 are much lower (-4.2%) than those obtained indirectly (-1.5%). This difference could be explained by the fact that the agricultural sector does not present constant return to scale. But, the main issue is that in both cases, agriculture presented a negative growth of TFP during the period 1962-1988.

THEORETICAL EXPLANATIONS OF CUBAN TECHNOLOGICAL CHANGE

Technological Change Embodiment in Capital Analysis

In a case of capital embodied technical change, the depreciation rate is endogenous, because the appearance of newer technologies can eliminate rents on older assets.[21] In the case of Cuba, it makes sense to analyze the effect of endogenous depreciation because Cuba received a large amount of machinery and equipment from the Soviet Union, which created a structural transformation in the economy, especially in the industrial sector.[22]

The aggregated rates of depreciation used to determine the stock of capital time series, and therefore the TFP previously determined, was equal to 4.5%, which could be low. Thus, there could exist the possibility that Cuban depreciation estimates are inappropriate for an economy which experienced structural change. A higher depreciation rate implies that the capital stock accumulates more slowly, thus higher technological change can be observed.

Table 12. Econometric TFP Results (1962-1987)

	Ln A	r	α	N	R2	TFP (%)
Yt- Agriculture	-0.748	-0.0423	1.00	27	0.86	-4.2
Yt Industry	0.589	0.00418	0.67	27	0.74	0.4
Yt-Cuban Economy	0.394	0.00427	0.47	27	0.84	0.4

21. For examples, see Solow (1959, 1962). For a formal model of technical progress embodied in capital, see Hulten (1992).

22. After the revolution, a large amount of equipment and investment was mainly destined to mechanize the agricultural sector and to create an industrial base. Investment went to the development of new industries and expansion of existing industries, such as cement, fertilizers, electrical, and mining among others, which created a structural transformation of the Cuban economy, especially in the industrial sector. For further details, see Figueras (1994), pp. 96-111 and Madrid-Aris (1998).

Table 13. Rates of Growth of Factors for Different Depreciation Rates

| DEPRECIATION | Rate of Growth (%) | | | | | | | | |
| | All Economy (%) | | | Agriculture (%) | | | Industry (%) | | |
	Labor	Capital	TFP	Labor	Capital	TFP	Labor	Capital	TFP
Previous Results (4.5%)	2.3	5.8	0.20	1.3	6.7	-1.50	2.9	4.9	0.60
Depreciation 10%	2.3	5.5	0.58	1.3	5.8	-0.97	2.9	3.7	1.26
Depreciation 20%	2.3	4.9	0.70	1.3	5.0	-0.66	2.9	2.6	1.65

Table 14. Factors Contributing to Economic Growth for Different Depreciation Rates

| DEPRECIATION | Contribution of Factors (as % of total economic growth) | | | | | | | | |
| | All Economy (%) | | | Agriculture (%) | | | Industry (%) | | |
	Labor	Capital	TFP	Labor	Capital	TFP	Labor	Capital	TFP
Previous Results (4.5%)	28	70	2	20	103	-23	35	58	7
Depreciation 10%	27	66	7	21	95	-16	37	47	16
Depreciation 20%	29	62	9	23	89	-12	41	36	23

To test the effect of endogenous depreciation, TFPs were estimated using the methodology previously explained (equation 3), but using new stock of capital time series, which were constructed by increasing the depreciation rate to a level of 10% and 20%, respectively. Tables 13 and 14 show the new TFPs estimated and their contribution to economic growth.

The results show that increasing the rate of depreciation does not change the TFP patterns much or TFPs' contribution to economic growth as a whole. It seems that depreciation has some effect in the industrial sectors, since TFP contribution to economic growth increased from 7% to 23%. It is difficult to believe that depreciation rates could be higher than 20%. Hence, the upper bound or "best scenario" would be that Cuban technological change contributed only 9% to the total output (Table 14). In sum, an endogenous rate of depreciation does not provide explanation about the low-level TFP growth during the period of 1963-1988 in Cuba.

ECONOMIES OF SCALE ANALYSIS

In this section, a Cobb-Douglas production function will be used to analyze economies of scales. Therefore, this analysis helps us to dispel whether the low TFP could be a result of the existence of decreasing return to scale. Thus,

$$Y_t = A \cdot K_t^{\alpha} \cdot L_t^{\beta} \tag{4}$$

Applying natural log to equation (4), we obtain a linear equation equal to:

$$\ln Y_t = \ln A + \alpha \ln K_t + \beta \ln L_t + \varepsilon \tag{5}$$

Applying ordinary least square (OLS) to equation (5) and using time series data for the period 1962-1988, the results in Table 15 are obtained. Note that econometric estimation of equation (5) could lead to a multicollinearity problem (Boskin and Lau, 1992; Harberger 1996). Our data base was tested for multicollinearity problems without finding serious problems.[23] On the other hand, the null hypothesis of the existence of CRTS for the industrial sector, and the Cuban economy as a whole, would not be rejected.[24] Previous results show the presence of CRTS in the whole economy and industrial sector.

It is important to note that the agricultural sector, where most of the investment was allocated, shows decreasing return to scale. Therefore, diminishing re-

---

23. A Belsley, Kuh, and Welch (1980) test of multicollinearity was conducted. In the Cuban economy as a whole, and the agricultural sector, there are no multicollinearity problems at all. The only regression that presents some multicollinearity problems is the agricultural sector.

24. Hypotheses is not rejected at 95% confidence level.

turns could be explained by the clear over-investment in this sector. Investment in agriculture was 48% of GMP in the period 1981-1988 (see Table 8).

In sum, economies of scale results obtained in this section provide at best, a partial explanation for the decreasing and low TFP growth found in the agricultural sector. Economies of scale analysis do not provide many answers to the decreasing TFP found in the Cuban industrial sector and in the economy as a whole.

Table 15. Economies of Scale Analysis— Regression Results (1962-1988)

	Ln A	a	b	$\alpha+\beta$	N	R2
Yt-Agriculture	2.56	0.37	0.11	0.48	27	0.94
Yt- Industry	-2.64	0.71	0.38	1.09	27	0.98
Yt-Cuban Economy	-3.89	0.52	0.54	1.06	27	0.97

CUBAN INVESTMENT ANALYSIS AND LINEAR GROWTH MODELS

This section follows closely the methodology applied by Alwyn Young (1992) to Singapore. I follow closely Young's methodology, with the purpose of analyzing Cuban results and to draw some conclusions for linear growth models. Table 16 presents time series regressions at aggregated and sectoral levels of log output per worker on a constant and the natural log of capital per worker.[25]

As Young (1992, p. 47) notes, "the large coefficient on capital (coefficient B), well in excess of capital share, can represent strong evidence in favor of linear growth models. However, if one believes in a concave neoclassical production function, then the large coefficient in the regression (coefficient B) could represent its correlation with the error term of the TFP, therefore, in that case investment is considered endogenous."

Regression results from Table 16 provides mixed results. Obviously, reality suggests that Cuban investment was realized exogenously in all economic sec-

Table 16. Regression of Ln (Y/L) on Ln (K/L)

COUNTRY	Coefficient (B)	Standard Error	Grade	R2
Hong-Kong	0.81	0.035	B	
Taiwan	0.57	0.012	D	
Cuba (62-88)	0.56	0.050		0.83
China	0.53	0.050	D	
Korea	0.50	0.017	B	
Yugoslavia	0.50	0.044	B	
Singapore	0.39	0.035	C	
Chile	0.36	0.087	C	
Costa Rica	0.36	0.040	C	
Cuba Industry (62-88)	0.92	0.110		0.74
Cuba Agriculture (62-88)	0.28	0.062		0.44

Notes: Coefficient B refers to the regression: ln (Y/L) = C + B*ln (K/L). Grades refer to the Summers and Heston quality rating.

Source: Young (1992, pp. 48-49), and Cuban estimations from Madrid-Aris (1998).

tors, since Cuban capital accumulation was mainly forced by governmental interventionist policies. There is doubt about Cuban investment exogenity, since Young (1992) argues that in Singapore, with a less interventionist government, the capital stock is considered to be increased exogenously.

Results from Table 16 show that only the agricultural sector presents a lower coefficient (0.28) than the income share coefficient, which is equal to 0.5. Thus, this results would not favor linear growth models. One can argue that capital stock increased exogenously in this economic sector. Obviously, exogenity in capital accumulation in the agricultural sector could have been a consequence of government interventionist policies which can be considered as exogenous. But, on the other hand, it is important to note that agricultural data presents some multicollinearity problems, and also the regression correlation factor is low (0.44), therefore, the agricultural coefficient should be taken with caution.

The high coefficient of the industrial sector (0.92) is evidence in favor of linear models. Thus, in the industrial sector, capital stock could have increased en-

---

25. Cuban results were obtained using the author's database.

dogenously. In this case, Cuban interventionist policies should be lower in this sector compared with the agricultural sector. Reality seems to validate this result, because investment in the industrial sector was much lower than that of the agricultural sector, therefore, it could assume there were less interventionist policies in this sector. On the other hand, the industrial sector was able to achieve positive TFP growth under a presence of a much lower level of investment. This suggests that industrial less exogenous investment was more efficiently allocated than the exogenous agricultural investment. The industrial sector regression result complemented with the agricultural sector results seems to suggest that linear models could explain level of endogenity of capital accumulation across sectoral levels within the country context.

The result for Cuba, as a whole, makes even more difficult to draw some conclusions regarding linear growth models, since regression results does not favor linear growth models because the coefficient on capital (0.56) is very close to the capital share of national income (0.51). These results seem to support Young's conclusions.

From Singapore's evidence and cross-countries analysis, Young concludes that the constancy of capital-output ratio and large coefficient on capital in cross-national and country-specific regressions (Young, 1992, p. 48-49), are due to endogenous response to capital accumulation to technical change, within the context of an otherwise concave production function. Then, he concludes that simple linear endogenous growth models is not a useful means of thinking about the growth process (Young, 1992, p. 50 and p.60).

Looking at Young's results and from the present study results, the question to be addressed should be: Do the Cuban aggregated and sectoral results support or not Young's conclusions about linear growth models? Since results from the present research are mixed, there is not a unique answer. Some feasible explanation from this study and Young's (1992) research is that the use of "linear models" is not a very good tool for explaining growth in economies with a very high rate of investment. Therefore, maybe linear

models should be limited to non-interventionist economies, and where investment is not force by governmental interventionist policies. However, from this analysis, it seems that linear models can provide some insight at sectoral levels regarding level of endogenity investment within the country. Obviously, much more empirical research is needed to support this conclusion.

CONCLUSIONS

TFP analysis results show that Cuba's growth during 1963-1988 was almost entirely the result of capital accumulation rather than productivity gains. Decreasing TFP growth through the 1970s and 1980s, with increasing amount of subsidies received from Soviet Union during the same period, seem to suggest that Soviet dependency created inefficiency in Cuba.

Conclusions from the theoretical analysis of TFP could be summarized as follows: (1) Increasing the rate of depreciation does not change the TFP patterns much or TFPs' contribution to economic growth as a whole. In sum, an endogenous rate of depreciation or technological change embodiment in capital does not provide an explanation for the low-level TFP growth during the period of 1963-1988 in Cuba; (2) The agricultural sector where most of the investment was allocated shows decreasing return to scale. Diminishing return could be explained by the over-investment in this sector, which was forced by poor investment planning policies. Therefore, economies of scale results provide at best, a partial explanation for the decreasing and low TFP growth found in the agricultural sector. Economies of scale do not provide answers to the decreasing TFP found in the Cuban industrial sector and in the economy as a whole.

Results show that Cuba's case is very different from that of most economies. The results show that theoretical endogenous growth models could not easily explain Cuba's economic performance. In Cuba's case, an increase of capital stock and human capital occurred at the same time as a decrease in the rate of technological change. Cuba's unique case could be partially explained by several factors, principal among them is the extreme inefficiency of the centrally planned investment policy in allocating resources (especially in human capital creation), which led to an overinvestment and decreasing TFP. The overinvestment in agricultural sector led to decreasing returns to scale. From this research, it seems that the use of linear growth models for explaining the process of economic growth under an exogenous investment may be limited. Hence, in cases where there is over-investment, such as the Cuban case, linear growth models may not be an appropriate tool to explain the process of economic growth.

TFP and investment evidence from industrial and agricultural analysis, seems to suggest that there is an optimal level of investment that maximizes technological change. It seems that the optimal level should be directly related to the country's technical capacity (infrastructure, level of technology, research capacity, etc.), human capital, the efficiency of its institutions and markets. Investment over the optimal level, lead to inefficiency in investment allocation, and to a reduction in the rate of technological change.

In sum, one important conclusion resulting from this study is that under a centrally planning resource allocation system (as the Cuban case), more investment does not lead to an increase in the capital efficiency factor, and could actually lead to diminishing returns to scale. Thus, under an over-investment condition, such as the Cuban case, linear growth models should be used with caution, since they may not be an appropriate tool for explaining the process of economic growth. In addition, sectoral results from this research seems to suggest that linear growth models can provide some insight at sectoral levels regarding different levels of endogenity investment within the country. Further studies of economies with high rate of investment, and contrasting similar pattern and institutions could help to our understanding of the role of overinvestment, human capital accumulation and economic growth, in centrally planned economies and the applicability of linear growth models.

REFERENCES

Amann, R., J. Cooper and R Davies. *The Technological Level of Soviet Industry*. New Haven: Yale University Press, 1978.

Barro, Robert, "Government Spending in a Simple Model of Endogenous Growth," *Journal of Political Economy*, S103-S125, 1990.

Barro, Robert, "Economic Growth in a Cross Section of Countries," *Quarterly Journal of Economics,* 407-444, 1991.

Barro, R., and Xavier Sala-i-Martin. *Economic Growth*. New York: McGraw Hill Press, 1995.

Becker, Gary. *Human Capital: A Theoretical and Empirical Analysis With Special Reference to Education*. NBER: The University of Chicago Press, 1963.

Belsley, D.A., E. Kuh, and R.E. Welsch. *Regression Diagnostics: Identifying Influential Data and Sources of Collinearity*. New York: Willey Press, 1980.

Bergson, A. *Planing and Production Under Soviet Socialism*. Pittsburgh: Carnegie Mellon University, 1968.

Bergson, A. "Technological Progress," in *The Soviet Union Toward 2000*, eds. A. Bergson and H. Levine. New York: Columbia University Press, 1983.

Boskin, B., and Lawrence Lau. "Capital, Technology and Economic Growth," in *Technology and the Wealth of the Nations*, eds. Ralph Landau, Nathan Rosemberg and David Mowery. Stanford: Stanford University Press, 1992.

Brundenius, Claes. Revolutionary Cuba: The Challenge of Economic Growth with Equity. Boulder: Westview Press, 1984.

Central Intelligence Agency (CIA), Directorate of Intelligence. *The Cuban Economy: A Statistical Review*. Washington, D.C., 1984, 1989.

Comité Estatal de Estadísticas (CEE), *Anuario Estadístico de Cuba*, several years

Denison, E. *Trends in American Economic Growth, 1929-1982*. Washington, D.C.: Brookings Institution Press, 1985.

Figueras, Miguel. *Aspectos Estructurales de la Economía Cubana*. Editorial de Ciencias Sociales, La Habana, Cuba, 1994.

Figueras, Miguel. "Structural Changes in the Cuban Economy," in *Latin American Perspectives* 69, Spring 1991, Volume 18, No. 2.

Food and Agriculture Organization, *Annual Reports*, Geneva, 1969, 1990.

Harberger, Arnold. "Reflections on the Growth Process," manuscript, UCLA, 1990.

Harberger, Arnold. "Reflections on Economic Growth in Asia and the Pacific," manuscript, UCLA, August 1996.

Harberger, Arnold. "A Vision of the Growth Process," *American Economic Review*, Vol 88, No 1, pp. 1-31, March 1998.

Hulten, Charles, "Growth Accounting When Technical Progress is Embodied in Capital." *The American Economic Review*, Vol 82, No 4, pp. 964-980, 1992.

Jimenez, Georgina. *Hablemos de Educación, Recopilación de Artículos, Comentarios y Reportajes sobre Educación*. La Habana: Editorial Pueblo y Educación, 1985.

Jones, Larry E., and Rodolfo Manuelli. "A Convex Model of Equilibrium Growth," *Journal of Political Economy*, 98, 1008-1038, 1990.

Jorgenson, Dale, Frank M. Gollop, and Barbara M. Fraumeni. *Productivity and U.S. Economic Growth*. Cambridge: Harvard University Press, 1987.

Kim, J.I., and Lawrence Lau. "Economic Growth of the East Asian Newly Industrializing Countries," *Journal of the Japanese and International Economics*, 235-271, 1994.

Krugman, Paul. "The Myth of Asia's Miracle," *Foreign Affairs*, November/December, pp. 62-78, 1994.

Landau Ralph, Natham Rosemberg, and David Mowery. *Technology and the Wealth of the Nations*. Stanford: Stanford University Press, 1992.

Lucas, Robert. "Why Can't Capital Flow From Rich to Poor Countries?," *American Economic Review*, Papers and Proceeding, 1990.

Madrid-Aris, Manuel, "Growth and Technological Change in Cuba," in *Cuba in Transition—Volume 7*. Washington: Association for the Study of the Cuban Economy, 1997.

Madrid-Aris, Manuel. *Economic Policies, Human Capital, Growth and Technological Change in a Centrally Planned Economy: Evidence from Cuba*. Forthcoming 1998.

Mesa-Lago, Carmelo. *The Economy of Socialist Cuba: A Two Decade Appraisal*. Albuquerque: University of New Mexico Press, 1981.

Mesa-Lago, Carmelo and Jorge Pérez-López, "A Study of Cuba's Material Product System, its Conversion to the System of National Accounts, and Estimation of GDP per Capita and Growth Rates," *World Bank Staff Working Papers*, Number 770, 1985.

Mincer, Jacob. *Schooling, Experience and Earnings*. New York: Columbia University Press, 1974.

Nelson, R.R., "Research on Productivity Grwoth and Differences," *Journal of Economic Literature*, no 19, pp. 1029-1064, 1981.

Nishimizu, M. and S. Robinson. "Trade Policies and Productivity Change in Semi-Industrialized Countries," *Journal of Development Economics*, 16, 177-206, 1984.

Pérez-López, Jorge. *Measuring Cuban Economic Performance*. Austin: University of Texas Press, 1987.

Poznanski, K. "The Environment for Technological Change in Centrally Planned Economies," *World Bank Staff Working Papers*, #718, Washington D.C., 1985.

Psacharopoulos, George, "Returns to Investment in Education: A Global Update," *World Development*, 22(9):1325-134, 1994.

Rodríguez, José Luis, "Agricultural Policy and Development in Cuba," *World Development*, Vol 15, No 1, pp. 23-39, 1987.

Rodríguez, José Luis. *Estrategia del Desarrollo Económico en Cuba*. Editorial de Ciencias Sociales, Habana, Cuba, 1990.

Rodríguez, José Luis. "Cuba en la Economía Internacional: Nuevos Mercados y Desafíos de los Años Noventa," in *Estudios Internacionales*, Universidad de Chile, #103, Julio-Septiembre 1993.

Romer, Paul. "Increasing Returns and Long-Run Growth," *Journal of Political Economy*, 94, pp.1002-1037, 1986.

Romer, Paul. "Human Capital and Growth: Theory and Evidence," *NBER Working Paper #3173*, 1989.

Romer, Paul. "Endogenous Technical Change," *Journal of Political Economy*, 98, S71-S102, 1990.

Sala-i-Martin, "Lecture Notes on Economic Growth (I): Introduction to the Literature and Neoclassical Models," *NBER*, Working Paper #3563, December, 1990.

Solimano, Andrés. *Road Maps to Prosperity: Essays on Growth and Development*. Michigan: The University of Michigan Press, 1996.

Solow, Robert. "A Contribution to the Theory of Economic Growth," *Quarterly Journal of Economics*, 70, 65-94, 1956.

Solow, Robert. "Technical Change and the Aggregate Production Function," *Review of Economic and Statistics*, 39, 312-320, 1957.

Solow, Robert. "Investment and Technical Progress." In *Mathematical Methods in the Social Sciences*. Edited by Kenneth J. Arrow, Samuel Karbin and Patrick Suppes. Stanford University Press, 1959.

Summers, Lawrence, and Braford J. De Long. "Equipment Investment and Economic Growth," *The Quarterly Journal of Economics*, 445-501, 1992

Teitel, S. and L. Westphal. "Editors' Introduction," *Journal of Development Economics*, 16, 1-11, 1984.

Torres, Leonardo, "Concentration Patterns of the Contribution of TFP to Output Growth: Evidence from the Mexican Manufacturing Sector." Paper presented at the Western Economic Association, 1997.

University of Chile, Departamento de Economía. *Special Issue on Economic Growth*. Santiago, Chile, 1993.

World Bank. *World Development Report*. Oxford University Press, 1990

Young, Alwyn. "Learning by Doing and the Dynamic Effects of International Trade," *The Quarterly Journal of Economics*, 369- 405, 1991.

Young, Alwyn. "A Tale of Two Cities: Factor Accumulation and Technical Change in Hong Kong and Singapore," in *NBER Macroeconomics Annual*, Cambridge MA: MIT Press, pp. 13-63, 1992.

Young, Alwyn. "The Tyranny of Numbers: Confronting the Statistical Realities of the East Asian Growth Experience," *Quarterly Journal of Economics*, 641-680, 1994.

Zimbalist, Andrew. *Cuba's Socialist Economy Toward the 1990s*. Boulder: Lynne Rienner Publishers, 1987a.

Zimbalist, Andrew. "Cuban Industrial Growth, 1965-1984," *World Development*, Vol 15, No 1, 83-93, 1987b.

Zimbalist, Andrew and Susan Eckstein. "Patterns of Cuban Development: The First Twenty-Five Years," *World Development*, Vol 15, No 1, pp. 5-22, 1987.

THE IMPACT OF POPE JOHN PAUL II's VISIT TO CUBA

Silvia Pedraza

More than any other Pope before him, John Paul II has traveled far and wide. Few of his visits, however, have captured the imagination as much as his visit to Cuba, a country that when he visited in January 1998 had been under the communist rule of Fidel Castro for 38 years. This international drama was played out alongside many personal dramas, such as my own. The Cuban revolution deeply divided both sides of my family—the Pedrazas and the Lubiáns. Like many families in Cuba, my family split between those who left, rejecting it, and remade their lives in exile, and those who remained, became integrated, and ascended in social status within it. (See Carol Morello, "A Family Divided: Reunion, Reconciliation, as Pope Arrives Today," *USA Today*, January 21, 1998.)

A child of the Cuban exodus myself, I had long committed myself to helping my aunts, uncles, and cousins who remained. In recent years, as my understanding of the Cuban reality matured, my efforts also turned to promoting peaceful, democratic change in Cuba. Many Cubans who left the island as exiles, or the children of exiles, returned to Cuba—some for the first time—to share this dramatic event on Cuban soil. Prior to the Pope's visit, I had made eight trips to Cuba since 1979, the first year that Cubans in exile were allowed to return to their homeland for family reunification purposes. But no other trip was as thrilling as this last one, as it showed the most change in Cuba.

THE SPECIAL PERIOD

Even before he arrived, Cubans prepared a warm welcome for the Pope. All over the city posters of the Pope against a true blue sky were pasted on the walls. They said: John Paul II, *¡Bendícenos!* (Bless Us!). When he arrived, the response of the Cuban people was nothing less than joyful, as was evident even on television. Thousands and thousands of people on the streets and at the masses waved flags, chanted their support for the Pope in unison, and expressed their sense of happiness. Even young men from the Rapid Response Brigades, who were in charge of keeping order on the streets while the Pope passed by on the "papamobil" shouted and jumped with joy when they saw him.

To really understand this response one has to realize the enormity of the changes that have taken place in Cuba with respect to religion over the course of the Cuban revolution, and especially in this decade during the period that Castro euphemistically called "the special period."

With the collapse of communism in Eastern Europe and the former Soviet Union, the heavy subsidy which Cuba received from those countries came to an end. Now Cuba had to rely on itself, and the result was a steep decline in economic conditions and a society that was devastated. The real impact of the U.S. trade embargo was finally felt when these subsidies evaporated. Hunger, malnutrition, disease, and poverty became the daily lot of people. The talents of the well-educated Cubans are also going to waste. For example, Cuba has many well-trained doctors, and due to its advances in public health during the early years of the revolution, Cuban medicine was once a model for other Third World countries. But in recent years, the medical infrastructure has decayed to the point where doctors work with no medicine, not even over the counter drugs. Hence, doctors can diagnose, but they can not cure. The Cuban economy has remained stagnant, even with some foreign investment from Canada, Spain, and France.

Professionals not only can not find employment in their fields, but take other jobs that are more likely to be paid in dollars, such as cab drivers. The "dollar economy" dominates and many Cubans invest considerable energy in developing ingenious schemes and crafts that will earn them dollars so they can feed their families. With the sugar harvest at the lowest point in this century, tourism has become the mainstay of the economy, and Canadian, European, and Spanish visitors predominate. However, the luxuries afforded to tourists—good accommodations, meals, and medicines—are not available for average Cuban citizens, who oftentimes are not even allowed to enter the hotels. Side by side with the tourist industry have grown other social problems, such as that of the *jineteras* (teenage prostitutes) that promote a sexual tourism.

A NEW CHURCH

In the early years of the revolution when Castro, due to his immense charisma and popularity with the people, was able to redirect the revolution along the road to communism, the church and the government collided with each other. Many of the institutions run by the Catholic church—schools, Universities, seminaries, hospitals—were taken over by Castro's government. Most priests and nuns were also expelled from the island. Cuba then defined itself as an atheist state. Thereafter, the churches were nearly empty, except for the many old ladies that, rosary in hand, never ceased attending. For many years, religious affiliation and participation entailed very serious social costs, such as a promotion at work, or a fellowship to the University, or the award of a major consumer goods, such as a television or refrigerator. But the "special period" constituted not only an economic crisis but also a crisis of disbelief. Cubans on the island began to feel that their leaders were less than capable and the promise of a future communist society with a decent life for all faded. Little by little, they began going to churches—not only the Catho-

lic church but also the many Protestant churches, the Afro-Cuban *santería* cults, the Jewish synagogues. And Cuba changed its self-definition to that of a secular state. Today the churches are full. And along with this change came a new generation of young Cuban priests, rather than priests from Spain and other countries. The Pope's visit affirmed and strengthened this new church.

In this period of scarcity, today the church is also a source for tangible help. While the religiously-based social services are not fully developed, informal help is available. Through the international organization *Caritas*, the church is able to offer some food, some medicine, when there is something to share. More important, however, the church presents an alternative vision of society, one where social classes and races are not pitted against one another, but where the social message is about justice with mercy—helping others through compassion.

THE POPE'S VISIT

The Pope offered four masses while in Cuba, two of which I attended—the first one in Santa Clara, in the middle of the country (where both sides of my family, the Rodríguez de Arciniega and the Lubiáns, were among the founding families in the early 1700s) and the last one at the Plaza of the Revolution in Havana. The other two—in the Eastern part of the country, Camagüey and Oriente provinces—I watched on television, along with millions of Cubans in the island. People really came out for these masses, something no one could have predicted. Posters, banners, and flags welcoming the Pope went up everywhere. And Cubans who came out to the masses in support of the Pope were of all social classes, all races, all ages—truly *el pueblo* (the people).

At the masses, people waved the Vatican and Cuban flags together with enormous joy, a sight I never thought I would see. In Cuba, there is a culture of mobilization—where people come out on the streets and plazas and express themselves in chants and songs. Like much else in Cuban culture, it has both Spanish and African origins. It is the culture of people who for centuries would go out on the streets, *arroyando*—singing and dancing in unison—during Carnival, as well as during religious processions.

During the revolution, Castro used this same culture of mobilization for political purposes, as during his speeches he would elicit this same response from the masses of people around him. During the Pope's visit, Cubans used this same culture of mobilization to express themselves. The crowds chanted, rhythmically, their support for the Pope and his message, with rhymes such as:

> *Juan Pablo, amigo,*   Juan Pablo, our friend,
> *el pueblo está contigo.*   the people are with you.

and

> *Se ve,*   We can see it,
> *Se siente,*   we can feel it,
> *el Papa está presente.*   the Pope is with us.

While in the first mass, in Santa Clara, people were still hesitant in their behavior, after the masses in Camagüey and Santiago de Cuba they had lost all reticence. The mass in Santiago de Cuba was particularly moving in a number of ways. The Archbishop of Santiago, Pedro Meurice, spoke loudly and boldly in defense of human rights when he underscored that the Cuban nation lives both in the island and in the diaspora, and Cubans "suffer, live, and hope both here and there." The church's commitment, as affirmed in Puebla, is, indeed, with the poorest of the poor; and, he added, the poorest among us are those who lack liberty.

Moreover, since Santiago de Cuba is very near El Cobre, the shrine where Cuba's patron saint, *la Virgen de la Caridad* (Our Lady of Charity) resides, at the Santiago de Cuba mass the Pope symbolically crowned her. Our Lady of Charity has long been a symbol of identity and nationhood in Cuban society. Like the story of Mexico's Virgin of Guadalupe's appearance to Juan Diego, a poor Indian, shortly after the Spanish conquest, the story of the appearance of Our Lady of Charity symbolizes the origins of the Cuban people. A Spanish Catholic virgin, legend has it that she appeared in the early 1600s to three Cuban fishermen—two Indian brothers that set out with a 10-year old African slave—that were caught in a tempest at sea. In their fear, they fervently prayed for help and protection, which came when an image of the virgin appeared floating on a board as

the sea and sky became calm. Religion and nationalism became deeply in the figure of Our Lady of Charity when Cubans who fought in their long struggle for their independence in the 19th century prayed to her as a symbol of nationhood. Even more, she is also special to followers of *Santería*, the Afro-Cuban religion, who worship her as *Ochún*.

The importance of this devotion in Cuba itself can be seen in the way Cubans express their present plight in Cuba in paintings that depict Our Lady of Charity herself in the traditional manner yet substitute the *balseros* of the nineties—the thousands of Cubans who desperately put out to sea on anything that floats—for the rowing boat with the three fishermen. The paintings sometimes depict the *balsas* as empty, while the seas continue to rage, expressing the tragedy that Cubans in despair live today. Moreover, when real *balseros* finally arrived to the shores of Key West, oftentimes a representation of Our Lady of Charity was found among the few belongings they had with them, evidence that while at sea many fervently prayed for her help and protection.

Hence, the devotion to Our Lady of Charity has many meanings in Cuban society, as she is a symbol of both faith and national identity. And when Pope John Paul II crowned her, the Cuban people accompanied him in song, to the tune of *Virgen Mambisa*—the Lady to whom Cuba's patriots who fought for independence from Spain in the 19th century prayed. The *Virgen*'s crowning, therefore, constituted a deeply moving *rencuentro* of the Cuban people with themselves—a newly found tradition.

By the time the last mass took place in Havana, Cubans came out very massively—running to the Plaza of the Revolution, where it was held. The happiness and joy with which they sang could not be contained. And in the middle of the mass repeated shouts of "liberty" could be heard. The Pope's visit was a meld of religious and political purposes. As he has for many years, the Pope both criticized the U.S. embargo of Cuba as a form of violence against a poor country that hurts the poorest there the most, as well as Castro's human rights violations as a denial of individual human dignity. Throughout, he called for Cubans to assume their protagonist role within their own history—not to seek their liberty elsewhere by leaving the island but to seek it within.

In this "special period" in Cuba's history, something very powerful and special happened, indeed. The Cuban government refuses to engage in any real democratic reforms, such as a plebiscite and elections, or even in a dialogue among the major political actors in the society (the government, the church, the dissident movement, and the exile community) that both the dissident movement and the church have called for. Yet the Pope's visit seems to have changed the personal biographies of many Cubans, and the context in which they live.

The Pope's visit holds various meanings for Cubans. First is that which John Paul II himself intended, as expressed in one of his homilies: to defend a larger space for the church, and along with it a larger space of liberty for all Cubans. The impact of the Pope's visit needs to be understood as part of the process of the return of civil society—a process that is already underway in Cuba and which the experience of other countries tells us constitutes the *sine qua non* of successful democratic transitions. Second, since the Pope himself called "for Cuba to open itself to the world, and for the world to open itself up to Cuba," within the U. S. it has reopened the debate and controversy on whether to continue the U.S. embargo of Cuba and sparked efforts at humanitarian assistance of food and medicine. Third, Cubans in the island came out clearly and massively in support of the alternative values the Pope articulated regarding the central importance of the family, the school, the church, as independent social institutions that need to play leading roles in society not totally usurped by government. And, in so doing, they issued a call for change. And, as if that were not all, for me personally, as for so many other Cubans, his visit prompted a family reunion and reconciliation. A month after I returned, I received a letter from my cousin in Cuba that said, "The best thing about the Pope's visit was that he brought you to us."

IMPRESSIONS ON THE VISIT OF POPE JOHN PAUL II TO CUBA

Maria C. Werlau[1]

Aside from very powerful personal experiences and testimonies of people I met in Cuba, the limited time available forces me to be pragmatic. Following are some of my conclusions regarding the Pope's visit to Cuba.

First, Cuba is not in a process of transition yet. In fact, in the aftermath of the Pope's visit, this has been clearly confirmed by the Cuban leadership. I think it is reasonable to say that a transition is inevitable at some point in the future, but I believe it is likely to be post-Castro and will refer to it accordingly.

What Cuba has today is a selective and distorted opening to aspects of capitalism, because of sheer economic necessity. This cannot, in and of itself, effect meaningful change in the system. Because the Pope has raised concerns regarding the ills of neo-liberalism, it is pertinent to focus attention on Cuba's unique adoption of neo-liberal elements, which is, in many ways, capitalism of the worst kind. Because the privatization of financial resources currently taking place precludes the participation of the population and exclusively favors foreigners and a select few in the nomenklatura, the consequences are very worrisome. This situation will prove very detrimental to achieving a stable and just transition, when that process does begin. The Pope's warning should be centered on this particular aspect; foreign investors and their governments participating in this type of "engagement" ought to be held accountable.

Cuba's peculiar model of enclave capitalism has an additional implication. For free markets and capitalism to work effectively—as per theory and experience—they require a proper value system and institutional framework. The problems of former Soviet bloc countries, especially the former Soviet Union, warn of the need to avoid replicating that disaster in Cuba. Therefore, the various exile political parties, groups, or currents ought to engage in some serious pre-planning regarding what kind of democracy and economic model they favor and what legal and institutional framework is called for. This planning should ideally be done with counterparts in the organized dissident community in Cuba that correspond to the political definitions of each tendency.

I also believe that especially the Cuban community in exile will need to accept that when a transition actually takes place, Cuba will be far from the ideal we have struggled for. Because I'm convinced of a real commitment to contributing to a post-Castro Cuba, I think we need to understand that we'll have to work with people who have lived under the current system all their lives and have idiosyncrasies and ideas very different from those of us who left. This will require that we learn to live with and forgive many gray areas. Unavoidably, the majority has either supported or, at best, acquiesced by participation, believed in or, at least, tolerated the current system. The role of the Catholic Church, as that of other churches, is very important in creating a psyche of reconciliation

---

1. This paper is an abridged version of a longer document published by the Cuban Studies Association of the University of Miami, CSA Documents Series No. 3, March 1, 1998.

and peace. But this is long-term work, not a short-term solution. Because social and moral issues that pose huge challenges will have to be dealt with, turning for guidance to the sobering experiences of the former Soviet bloc countries may prove useful.

Second, people on the island have no point of reference with respect to such things as how different systems of government work. Yes, they recognize that their lives are hard and their cities and dwellings decrepit; they want something better, but they seem to have no clue what that "better" might mean. In fact, the alternatives they are presented with play consistently on fear. Amidst an almost total government control of information, the population is subject to constant propaganda on the ills of Western societies. The vast majority has either been born during or has grown under the present system. Few have traveled abroad and many of those who have, lived or traveled within the former Soviet bloc.

Given the unique space that institutionalized religion has gained in Cuba and the people's eager response to the Pope's visit, the Catholic Church in particular—and other religious denominations to some extent—could play a decisive role in helping shape the ethos of an alternative society and in providing a value system on which to sustain an institutional framework. We should look at working with these religious institutions, as well as with different governments and foundations, in the on-going task of teaching democratic and universal values that have been absent from Cuba. (I understand that some planning is currently being done to this effect, but it seems minimal.) And it is essential to make TV Martí available and boost Radio Martí's signal and to make sure that their programming responds to the needs and the frame of mind of the audience on the island.

Third, the one theme that surfaces loud and clear when contemplating a different system or way of life is that—regardless of the deficiencies of the actual system—Cubans do not want to lose free access to health and education. This plays very prominently in the expectations of the population. And the Pope only consolidated this conviction. We need to prioritize this aspect in both planning for a transition and helping design a proper model of a democratic Cuba

as well as in our contacts with people there. The general failure of former Soviet bloc countries to assure the basic social safety net and the consequent re-emergence of a yearning for a Communist society point to the relevance of this issue.

Fourth, I found the Castro regime nowhere close to falling, at least in the way that the majority of the exile community has expected or wanted it to end. I did not get the impression that there is readiness to revolt or demand change and it looks like the system could survive indefinitely despite the precarious economic condition. The possible exception—which I find improbable as well as hard to assess accurately—would be a revolt at the top. If Castro were to die or become impaired, the system seems institutionalized and strong enough to survive, at least in the short term.

The Pope's visit appeared to have an authentically powerful and highly symbolic impact at the level of the individual. People seem eager to seek meaning for their lives to ease the burden and replace the void left by the failures of a lifetime of sacrifice for "Socialism or Death." The Pope's themes—peace, love, compassion, justice, tolerance, family—are the opposite of what Cubans have been hearing for almost four decades. Yet, I witnessed how most people of all walks of life were deeply touched. They are hungry for this message and welcomed it, which might have very positive effects both in the short and long terms. But, I cannot conclude that it was taken as a call to revolt.

As a result, I wouldn't bank on policies that assume that the abrupt collapse of the Castro regime is near. Rather, in the aftermath of the Pope's visit, I would engage in some very serious reflection concerning the adequacy of existing U.S. policy. Status quo being the order of the day, things may well remain frozen for a very long time unless we take decisive steps to design a pro-active and comprehensive policy that takes advantage of existing opportunities in order to induce certain outcomes. I believe we need to brainstorm, thinking very pragmatically and strategically, in order to design a policy with philosophical grounding and the incorporation of the themes used by the Pope which (1) focuses on de-legitimizing the regime; (2) is composed of a selection of the most effective elements of current policy while eliminating its most detrimental aspects; and (3) is spiced with creative tactical measures designed to break the status quo. This should seek to change the focus from talk about lifting or keeping the embargo to changing strategic aspects of the current policy.

Fifth, the government's propaganda of blaming many of the economic ills of the Special Period on the U.S. embargo—which they all refer to as "blockade"—is almost universally effective. This doesn't mean that there's no recognition of the deficiencies of the system, but, rather that the government's effective manipulations indeed legitimize the regime's failures to a degree I never imagined. Plus, the Pope's words can easily be interpreted as endorsing this notion—misguided in my opinion. He made no specific references to the government's terrible mismanagement of the economy, within the context of an already disastrous model, as the primary source of its problems.

For this reason, I'm more convinced than before my trip that we need to look carefully at loosening trade aspects of the embargo, exclusively with respect to U.S. exports to Cuba (not imports from Cuba). As a tactical move I would recommend the immediate, unilateral and unconditional elimination of all restrictions on the sale of food and health-related products. Instead of conditionality, Cuba could be called to, in good faith, reciprocate by, for example, allowing independent press. (This would be a tactical tool, unlikely to achieve the desired result.) I have long believed that we have pretty much nothing to lose and everything to gain by lifting this aspect of the embargo. I'd love to have the time to expand on this issue, but am forced to leave it here for lack of time. It should be looked at and debated exhaustively.

In addition, propaganda about hostility by the United States and the leadership of the exile community seems generally effective. Therefore, I think it's very important to take into account the perceptions and sensitivities of the people who've lived under the current system and carefully word policy statements and laws, avoiding what sounds most interventionist. Less specific requirements than those in current legislation which spell out the necessary terms of a transition, could generally call for a democratic system respectful of human rights and more effectively convey our essential support of the Cuban people's right to self-determination. Specifics should be carefully weighed so as not to fall prey of propaganda that plays on nationalism, which I found strong despite Cuba's sorry state.

Sixth, I have seen first-hand why people-to-people contacts are of utmost importance. I perceived nothing but good feelings towards the exile community. Just as my understanding was greatly expanded with this visit, the understanding of people on the island widens with these contacts. Family visits and remittances, although they help the regime in an important measure and remain controversial, have at least played a significant part in dispelling the bad propaganda of the past regarding those who have left. These are the type of contacts that reach the people directly, the ones the government finds most difficult to control. As a result, I'd recommend intensifying and increasing people-to-people contacts as per the Cuban Democracy Act's Track II, relaxing travel restrictions for academic and scientific exchanges as well as for visits by Cuban-Americans. I believe that the cost-benefit equation in this area weighs in favor of the benefits for those of us who want to see a free Cuba reconciled as one nation.

At the same time, I would direct efforts and resources to account for the victims of the 38 years of Castro's regime. The Catholic Church might now be in a position to take a more active role in this area, as it has done in other Latin American countries in the past. The Cuban tragedy needs to be personalized—given names and faces—in order to raise awareness in the island and worldwide. It's important to provide the Cuban people of today and of future generations the well-documented evidence of the violent nature of the Castro regime. Up to now, I think we have done a poor job in this area.

What is perhaps the most important lesson I have drawn from my trip is one that the Holy Father has attempted to communicate to Cubans everywhere: that with faith, tolerance and hope we must explore all viable avenues to find a solution to the Cuban predicament and that we must not be afraid. In some ways, those avenues may require compromises we'd rather not contemplate. But reality is dynamic, we must be open to learning along the way and be willing to take action—with caution, but without fear. Because Cuba cannot be today what we desire or expect, we must work with what we have—imperfect as it is—and make the best of it.

Given our terribly painful history, all who have been born Cuban or feel Cuban, wherever we live, can benefit from listening with open minds and practicing more tolerance and pluralism—the values of true democratic behavior. Those of us fortunate enough to live in free societies are called upon to set the example by finding ways to argue and negotiate our differences with respect, honesty, and integrity. Importantly, those of us who hold spiritual beliefs are challenged to do so with compassion and empathy. This may be our greatest challenge in the midst of the pain and ruins this Revolution has left in its wake.

The Pope brought a message to all Cubans, wherever we might be, which implies a commitment, at the heart of each one of us, to seek and defend the values that can nourish our lives and that of those who surround us. We must also do it collectively, as a nation. We are urged to reflect on how that calls on each and every one of us to contribute our part and find a way to work together for a common good. This is the only possible answer to rescuing something from the ashes that injustice, hatred, antagonism, abuse, separation, exclusion, deprivation—indeed, a long trail of sufferings—have left behind. I think that it's not only our duty, but, more importantly, that we have no choice if we are to plant the seeds for the moral, cultural and material restoration of the Cuban nation.

LO QUE FUE Y NO FUE: LA VISITA DEL PAPA A CUBA

José M. Hernández

Antes que nada dejemos constancia de los hechos. La visita de Juan Pablo II a Cuba insufló vida y entusiasmo a la Iglesia cubana. Su tarea evangelizadora cada vez es acogida con mayor entusiasmo por la población; de cada cien casas a cuyas puertas tocan los evangelizadores son invitados a entrar en 97. El gobierno cubano, sin embargo, no ha correspondido al mensaje conciliador de Su Santidad. La situación imperante fué descrita con exactitud en una reciente declaración del Movimiento Cristiano de Liberación que preside el ingeniero Osvaldo Payá Sardiñas: "Lejos de irse logrando un mejor clima de distensión por parte del estado hacia la Iglesia, lo que ha ocurrido en la practica ha sido, desdichadamente, todo lo contrario."

Como han transcurrido escasamente seis meses desde la visita papal, quizá sea muy pronto para derivar conclusiones de lo ocurrido hasta el presente. Mejor será poner la visita en perspectiva analizándola en el contexto de las visitas hechas por el Papa con anterioridad a otros países, especialmente la primera que hizo a Polonia en 1979.

Esto, sin duda, parecerá disparatado a muchos, dadas la profundas diferencias que separan a Cuba de Polonia y las obvias divergencias entre la situación polaca en 1979 y la de Cuba en 1998. Hay sobre todo el hecho de que en 1979 Juan Pable II era un polaco regresando triunfalmente a su país después de haber sido elegido pastor universal de la Iglesia Católica. Regresaba, además, a una nación cuya historia está indisolublemente ligada a la de su Iglesia, razón por la cual ésta tiene una influencia considerable en los asuntos nacionales. No hay comparación entre la Iglesia polaca y la cubana, como no la hay tampoco entre el régimen comunista polaco y el cubano. El comunismo polaco fue impuesto por las bayonetas soviéticas. El comunismo cubano es de origen indígena. El comunismo polaco creció y se desarrolló a la sombra de la Unión Soviética; el cubano lo hizo a la sombra hostil de los Estados Unidos. El comunismo polaco siempre fue menos omnicomprensivo y represivo que el cubano y sus líderes nunca estuvieron tan aferrados al poder como los cubanos. En los momentos más críticos los líderes comunistas polacos demostraron ser mucho más patriotas que Castro y sus seguidores.

El mismo Juan Pablo II ha sido, no obstante, el que al regresar a Roma de La Habana, dijo que el viaje le había recordado el que hizo a Polonia just después de su elección. Los que crean que la comparación de la visita a Cuba con la de Polonia es improcedente, por tanto, están discrepando de lo expresado por el mismo Papa, que es un líder mundial de vastísima experiencia, nada propenso a hacer declaraciones a la ligera.

Vayamos adelante, pues, con la comparación. ¿Hay alguna similitud entre la situación prevaleciente en Polonia en junio 2 de 1979, fecha del arribo del Papa a Varsovia, y la prevaleciente en Cuba en enero de 1998? En aquella época Polonia atravesaba por una aguda crisis política, económica y social, igual que Cuba en 1998. La Iglesia polaca estaba resignada a coexistir con el gobierno comunista, con el cual había cooperado a calmar los disturbios de 1976, causados por la escasez de alimentos. Los obispos polacos dialogaban con los funcionarios comunistas cuanto fuera necesario para mantener buenas relaciones con ellos. Ni anticipaban ni querían que en Polonia se produjera una explosión social. Pensaban que la situación de la Iglesia podía mejorar pero no creían en la proximidad de ningún cambio. Yo no puedo asegurar que los pensamientos de los obispos cubanos hace seis meses hayan sido los mismos de los obispos polacos, pero de su conducta no puede derivarse que hayan sido muy distintos, tampoco. Igual conclusión puede sacarse con relación a la actitud del gobierno. Hoy sabemos que Edward Gierek, jefe del gobierno polaco en aquel entonces, se avino a la visita de Juan Pablo II, entre otras razones, porque creía que serviría para legitimar su régimen en el orden internacional. Podemos estar seguros que semejante consideración entró también en los cálculos de Fidel Castro cuando invitó al Papa a venir a Cuba.

Y ¿por qué el Sumo Pontífice decidió viajar a Cuba? ¿Cúal fue su propósito primero en ir a Polonia y luego ir a Cuba? Cuando descendió del avión en el aeropuerto de Varsovia declaró taxativamente que había ido a Polonia como un peregrino, y que su visita había sido dictada por motivos exclusivamente religiosos. Fue a su tierra nativa sólo para predicar y enseñar, para infundir experanza y levantar los ánimos de la sociedad polaca. Nada más lejos de su mente que derribar el gobierno ni mucho menos precipitar una rebelión. Mientras ejerció su ministerio en su patria como sacerdote y como obispo siempre evitó las confrontaciones con el régimen. Su política como Papa fue la misma, tanto en Polonia como en Cuba. Al llegar a La Habana declaró, refiriéndose a los cubanos, que había ido a "confirmarlos en la fe, animarlos en la esperanza y a alentarlos en la caridad." No se propuso, desde luego, derrocar al gobierno, pero tampoco fue a crear una crisis con sus denuncias. No es ese su estilo, ni su estrategia.

Cuando fue a Polonia Juan Pablo II atrajo las multitudes más grandes de la historia del país. ¿Podía pasar semejante acontecimiento inadvertido y no dejar consecuencia ni huella de clase alguna? Hubo que esperar 14 meses, hasta agosto de 1980, para que estallara en el astillero Lenin de Gdansk la famosa huelga donde nació Solidaridad, y aún después las cosas empeoraron notablemente: sobrevino una intensa pre-

sión por parte de la Unión Soviética para liquidar el sindicalismo independiente en Polonia; el 13 de mayo de 1981 tuvo lugar el atentado contra la vida del Papa en la Plaza de San Pedro en Roma; siete meses después, el 13 de diciembre, el gobierno polaco declaró la ley marcial (o estado de guerra), Solidaridad fue disuelta y sus dirigentes y otros opositores arrestados. Por ese motivo, el gobierno de Reagan en los Estados Unidos dictó una serie de sanciones económicas contra Polonia que los obispos polacos objetaron, alegando que sólo servirían para empeorar la situación del pueblo. Reagan y sus consejeros se quedaron boquiabiertos por la actitud de los obispos, y quizá más que nada por el hecho de que el Papa la aprobó expresamente. En junio de 1983 tuvo efecto una segunda visita papal a Polonia, estando todavía en vigor la ley marcial. Muchos polacos que creyeron que Juan Pablo II iba a conducir al pueblo a las barricadas quedaron desilusionados. En su lugar el Papa continuó sus conversaciones confidenciales con los líderes comunistas polacos, que después de la muerte de Breshnev (1983), el ascenso al poder de Gorbachev (1985), la derogación de la ley marcial en 1986 (con la consiguiente abolición de las sanciones americanas) y un tercer viaje papal a Polonia en 1987 al fin fructificaron en 1989 con el restablecimiento de la democracia en el país. Habían transcurrido en su totalidad diez años desde la primera visita papal en 1979.

¿Hay alguna relación entre la visita del Papa a Polonia y los acontecimientos que acabamos de describir brevemente? La opinión generalizada de los analistas políticos es que no, que no existió tal relación. Y el mismo Papa años después dijo un día que "en cierto sentido, el comunismo, como sistema, cayó por si sólo, víctima de sus propios abusos y errores." Estas opiniones, sin embargo, no pueden explicar hechos tan significativos como el de que, al estallar la huelga en Gdansk en 1980, los obreros del astillero decidieran adornar la entrada con retratos del Papa y banderas papales. ¿Será que los obreros vieron cosas que ni los analistas políticos ni el propio Papa pudieron ver?

Hay hechos históricos y conmociones populares que resisten los análisis más rigurosos, como los que resultan no de lo que está ocurriendo en un momento dado sino de lo que las masas populares **creen** que está ocurriendo, o los que son consecuencia de cambios de actitud más bien que de reacciones específicas ante ciertos acontecimientos. Quizá fue ésto lo que quiso decir un obispo polaco cuando expresó que la primera visita de Juan Pablo II a su patria despertó la sociedad polaca, que estaba desorientada. Quince años después, Marek Skwarnicki, un viejo amigo del Papa que edita su poesía y frecuentemente lo acompaña en sus viajes, expresó el mismo pensamiento, pero mucho más contundentemente. Skwarnicki dijo que el viaje del Papa había sido una "sacudida de libertad" ("freedom shock") para Polonia. Tal fue el resultado de los famosos "nueve días de libertad" por los que atravesó el país en aquella oportunidad.

Uno de los comentarios que los críticos del viaje papal en el exilio citan más frecuentemente es el de Ramón Humberto Colás, católico y disidente. Dijo Colás refiriéndose a las triunfales actividades del Papa en Cuba: "Fueron cinco días de libertad. Pero fueron sólo cinco días en cuarenta años." El comentario, producto de una explicable impaciencia, es ciertamente negativo, pero, paradójicamente, subraya el hecho clave de la visita: fueron cinco días de libertad, el "freedom shock" a que se refirió Skwarnicki en el caso de Polonia. Como dijo una dignísima cubana en la Plaza José Martí el día de la misa papal: "Hoy nos han quitado la mordaza."

¿Queremos decir con lo que antecede que en Cuba va a ocurrir indefectiblemente lo mismo que en Polonia? Afirmar semejante cosa sería tan infantil como decir a solo seis meses de la visita que el viaje del Papa a Cuba fue contraproducente porque "el mundo se ha abierto a Cuba pero Cuba no se ha abierto al mundo." La única conclusión absolutamente lógica que se desprende de lo dicho es que hay que esperar antes de emitir juicio alguno sobre la visita del Papa.

Ya lo dijo hace unas semanas Lech Walesa en Montevideo, Uruguay, donde fue a participar en una conferencia: "Solidaridad tardó un año, y la apertura al mundo otros diez."

La espera no excluye, sin embargo, que se experimente un cierto optimismo. El propio Walesa dejó traslucir el que él siente cuando agregó: "La apertura del régimen comunista cubano vendrá; el comunismo no va a continuar en la isla." Se basa en un hecho incontrovertible: "Cuba es otra después de la visita del Papa Juan Pablo II." Es otro modo de referirse al "freedom shock," que por caminos difíciles de delinear en el mapa de la historia futura infaliblemente contribuirá a acelerar el proceso de transición que desde hace algunos años está atravesando Cuba.

Es posible que haya sido este hecho el que decidió al pontífice a aceptar la invitación de Castro para visitar la isla. Cuando viajó a Polonia en 1979 estaba persuadido de que el país estaba evolucionando lenta, pero inevitablement hacia mayores libertades. Y sabía dos cosas: 1) que la prédica del evangelio es revolucionaria; y 2) que el comunismo no admite reformas. Fue ese el comentario que hizo cuando le hablaron de los planes de Gorbachev. "Es un buen hombre," dijo, "pero fracasará porque quiere algo que es imposible: reformar el comunismo. El comunismo no puede ser reformado." He aquí las dos razones fundamentales por las que es posible que la transición cubana eventualmente culmine en el colapso del comunismo. Tardará, y ésto es lo que desanima a muchos. Pero tiene la ventaja de que el acontecimiento se producirá sin necesidad de disparar un tiro y, además, lo que es más importante, estamos presenciando la utilización de un método probado. ¿Por qué seguir empeñados en los métodos tradicionales del exilio que, además de ser cruentos, solo han producido fracasos?

CUBA Y POLONIA: SEMEJANZAS, DIFERENCIAS

Raúl Fernández García[1]

La noticia de la visita a Cuba que Juan Pablo II llevaría a cabo, constituyó, para muchas personas, un motivo de interés y expectativa durante todo el año de 1997. En lo personal, a mí me estimuló a conocer mejor al Pastor de la Iglesia Católica, su vida y especialmente, el papel que desempeñó en la lucha de los polacos para afirmar sus valores nacionales.

Una vez que empecé a familiarizarme con los detalles del personaje y su escenario histórico, comprendí que la lucha de Polonia contenía importantes lecciones, algunas de las cuales podrían ser aplicables a Cuba. Ello me decidió a escribir el presente ensayo.

La versión original se completó antes del viaje a Cuba de Su Santidad haciéndose necesario, una vez realizado aquel, actualizar el texto e incorporar el importante material generado en la visita. Cuando nosotros considerábamos dar por terminadas las labores de actualización, observamos con satisfacción y asombro que el *Diario Las Américas*, en su edición del 6 de agosto de 1998, publicaba bajo el título "Walesa sugiere que Cuba seguirá el ejemplo polaco," un reportaje originado durante la visita del dirigente obrero a Montevideo, Uruguay. Ello ocurrió al mismo tiempo que en Miami tenía lugar la Octava Reunión de la Asociación para el Estudio de la Economía Cubana celebrada del 6 al 8 de agosto de 1998, evento en el cual tuve el privilegio de ofrecer el presente ensayo.

Fue la noticia sobre la sugerencia de Walesa la razón por la cual se han añadido estos breves comentarios al trabajo original. Creemos que la autorizada opinión del líder de los obreros polacos, fundador de Solidaridad y Premio Nobel de la Paz 1983, quien con tanto éxito y comedimiento combatió el comunismo, debe ser del conocimiento de los lectores.

Cuba y Polonia[2] han jugado, en la segunda mitad del siglo XX, papeles históricos que sobrepasan sus dimensiones. Ambos han carecido de la protección geográfica que benefició a la Gran Bretaña y a los Estados Unidos. Cuba, la república deficiente pero con amplia vocación democrática y uno de los más ricos idearios políticos de las Américas, a sólo las proverbiales "90 millas" de la superpotencia que se declara campeona de la libertad, pronto iniciará el cuadragésimo año de sufrimientos bajo una tiranía clásica. Decimos clásica porque cumple las especificaciones propuestas por los tratadistas que se han ocupado de la tiranía. Y no atenúa su condición el hecho de que por razones de fuerza mayor, tal régimen se vista con ropajes cambiantes, unos pseudo democráticos, otros socialistas o capitalistas. Una tiranía clásica es un organismo político vivo y como tal comprometido, como primera prioridad, con su propia supervivencia. Pese a los sacrificios de héroes y mártires cubanos que la han combatido, esa tiranía parece desafiar con éxito todos los peligros.

1. Este trabajo, realizado en el seno de la familia, fuera del contexto institucional, mucho debe a los valiosos aportes de mi esposa, María, de mi hijo Raúl José, y de mis sobrinas Vilma, Lucy y Joanna Narváez.

2. El análisis de la epopeya polaca se ha basado principalmente en las fuentes bibliográficas que se mencionan al final. Ese análisis se ha enriquecido con el valioso aporte de la experiencia de la Señora Hanna Mitchell, quien participó activamente en las demostraciones estudiantiles en Varsovia, las que tanto contribuyeron al triunfo de la causa del pueblo polaco.

Polonia, que fuera una de las grandes potencias de Europa y que sufriera ataques, invasiones, desmembramientos a manos de sus vecinos poderosos e incontables intervenciones en sus asuntos internos, emergió de la Segunda Guerra Mundial (declarada precisamente con motivo de la invasión nazi a su territorio), como un codiciado estado cuya dependencia de la URSS los Aliados reconocieron. Polonia a pesar de vivir a cero millas de los soviéticos, inició su lucha en afirmación de sus valores nacionales y humanos, y finalmente se liberó del yugo ruso y la tiranía comunista, mediante una serie de eventos donde el heroísmo, la prudencia, la persistencia, la capacidad de los líderes, la efectiva organización y la enunciación de claros objetivos inspirados en los ideales del pueblo polaco, produjeron no sólo el rescate de su propio destino, sino el derrumbe del Imperio Bolchevique. El nacionalismo fue el factor que dió inspiración y sustento a la lucha de los polacos. Ese factor no debe interpretarse simplemente como una repulsa a los rusos. La heróica resistencia de Polonia a la brutal invasión nazi de 1939 confirma la disposición de los polacos de afirmar sus valores nacionales en cualquier circunstancia.

Creemos que un examen cuidadoso de los casos de Cuba y Polonia podría ayudar a cristalizar una estrategia que permita curar la grave dolencia que aflige a Cuba. Dado lo avanzado de la hora histórica, el análisis de la cuestión cubana demanda gran profundidad y honestidad para mirar las verdades de frente, sin intenciones de disimulo, pero tampoco de ofensa; simplemente como se mira un diagnóstico médico, grato o ingrato, pero necesario para sanar una grave enfermedad. Parafraseando al Maestro digamos "para verdades trabajemos y no para sueños." Al tratar de buscar esas verdades en un laberinto de datos a ambos lados del Atlántico, lo haremos siguiendo el método que nos parezca más lógico, claro y efectivo, sin restringir nuestro análisis a un rígido ordenamiento cronológico o de otro tipo. No perderemos de vista que la finalidad es "curar la grave dolencia que aflige a Cuba," y no, llevar a cabo un ejercicio intelectual más o menos interesante, ni tampoco aumentar la bibliografía sobre el tema cubano, la que ya es numerosa y cuenta con excelentes trabajos. Los ejercicios intelectuales se realizarán solamente en la medida necesaria

para aportar ideas frescas para curar un mal que ha sido inmune a los remedios caseros tradicionales.

La visita a Cuba en enero de 1998 de Su Santidad Juan Pablo II, quien como polaco y como Papa jugó un papel estelar en la liquidación del régimen comunista en su patria, ha sembrado prometedoras esperanzas en el suelo cubano. En el texto de este ensayo nos referiremos a la brillante labor de pastor que realizó el Papa en la conducción de sus hermanos polacos y al excepcional papel que jugó la Iglesia Católica. Ha sido un privilegio para Cuba recibir al Pontífice que representa, no sólo el amor cristiano, sino la postura vigilante e inteligente del celoso guardián de los derechos humanos. Y es también una oportunidad, ya sea como resultado de su presencia física o intelectual o moral, para ofrecer ideas nuevas a un auditorio fatigado, tras casi cuarenta años de monótonos discursos, con ecos siempre predecibles a ambos lados del Canal de la Florida.

Sabemos que cada país y cada circunstancia histórica tienen sus propias características y demandan ajustes de las fórmulas generales. Pero creemos también que los casos de Cuba y Polonia tienen elementos comunes importantes, y que su análisis documentado e inteligente, podría ayudar a la búsqueda de una solución cubana.

Además, los resultados diferentes obtenidos por ambos países deben poderse explicar con razones lógicas, el encuentro de las cuales debe ayudar a hallar el camino que conduzca a liquidar la actual tiranía y a establecer, por fin, la república que encarne la substancia misma de la nacionalidad cubana.

BOSQUEJOS HISTORICOS
El caso polaco: La postguerra
Referirse a la compleja historia de Polonia, aún en forma sinóptica, escapa al alcance de este trabajo. Pero como es necesario para el análisis contar con un marco conceptual histórico de referencia, abordaremos oportunamente las cuestiones pertinentes.

Polonia, durante el período que siguió a la terminación de la Segunda Guerra Mundial, fue substancialmente dominada por la Unión Soviética a través de gobiernos controlados por organizaciones comunistas polacas, generalmente (pero no siempre) obedientes a los dictados de Moscú. Sin embargo, es un hecho aceptado por los estudiosos, que los procedimientos típicos del régimen de Stalin no fueron impuestos en Polonia con la rudeza que se practicó en el resto de Europa Oriental.

Los gobiernos comunistas polacos de la postguerra aceleraron la reconstrucción del país procediendo a la reparación de los daños causados por el conflicto. Pero ello se hizo a un alto costo para la ciudadanía. Medidas típicas de las economías centralmente planificadas se pusieron en vigor, haciendo gravitar sobre la población el mayor peso del costo de reactivar la producción. Muerto Stalin en marzo de 1953, a partir de 1954 se empezaban a adoptar tímidas medidas tendientes a aliviar las cargas del pueblo, dentro de un limitado esquema de liberalización que no alcanzaba a satisfacer la población. Al mismo tiempo, comenzaban a soplar vientos diferentes en el Imperio, no pequeña parte de lo cual sería el famoso discurso del 5 de febrero de 1956 de Nikita Khrushchev ante el Vigésimo Congreso del Partido Comunista Soviético, en el que denunció las purgas de Stalin y el culto a la personalidad. Nótese que Polonia fue el único país de Europa Oriental donde no se erigió estatua alguna a Stalin. Por otra parte, aunque la Iglesia Católica era objeto de múltiples presiones, conservaba aún algunas libertades. Por ejemplo, la Universidad Católica de Lublín continuaba funcionando, proporcionando un refugio a profesores y estudiantes que, por motivos sociales o políticos, encontraban dificultades para tener acceso a la educación superior.

A pesar de los paliativos, un poco más tarde se produciría en Polonia el primer estallido de descontento popular ante las presiones que ejercía el aparato gubernamental sobre el pueblo. Así, el 28 de junio 1956 los obreros industriales de Poznan realizaron una huelga general y una demostración en la que participaron 50,000 personas demandando pan, libertad, elecciones libres y la salida de los rusos. El orden fue restaurado sólo mediante el uso de los tanques del ejército. Cincuenta y tres personas murieron y 200 quedaron heridas. Al considerar la situación, la plenaria del Comité Central Comunista, reunida en julio de 1956 mostró la existencia de tres grupos: la línea stalinista (los que habían permanecido en la URSS

durante la Guerra) abogaba por censura estricta y establecimiento de límites a la liberalización; el grupo que había permanecido en la Polonia ocupada por Alemania deseaba la continuación del proceso de liberalización; los Realistas, en el medio de ambos, querían que la liberalización continuara, pero sin anarquía.

En busca de consenso, estos tres grupos convinieron en aceptar el regreso de Wladyslaw Gomulka, antiguo Secretario General del Partido de los Trabajadores Polacos Unidos (Comunistas), y figura de cúpula de gobiernos anteriores, quien en 1948 se había opuesto a la condena de Yugoeslavia y al inicio de la colectivización de la agricultura en Polonia. Gomulka había sido destituído del cargo de Secretario General del Partido; ahora regresaba al poder como el único líder que podía restaurar la unidad comunista y disfrutar amplio apoyo en el país.

En octubre 19 de 1956, mientras se celebraba una asamblea del Comité Central, inesperadamente, la plana mayor rusa encabezada por Khrushchev llegó a Varsovia mientras divisiones soviéticas se movían hacia la capital alegando "maniobras de otoño."

Las reuniones que siguieron entre rusos y polacos los días 19 y 20 de octubre fueron atormentadas, al defender los polacos la tesis de que la democracia polaca debía ocupar un lugar como miembro igual y soberano del campo socialista. Mientras tanto, los obreros y estudiantes, irritados por la presencia rusa hacían demostraciones contra la presión extranjera y en apoyo de Gomulka. A Khrushchev parecía interesarle solamente que el regreso de Gomulka no significara un deterioro de las relaciones soviético polacas. Cuando consideró que ese peligro no existía, regresó a Moscú. Entre tanto Gomulka recibiría un apoyo político aplastante, mientras los "stalinistas" perdían todas las posiciones en los cuerpos decisorios. Por su parte, Gomulka adelantó la liberalización y aflojó en lo que pudo los controles totalitarios. Estabilizada así la situación, no volvió a ocurrir otro estallido violento significativo hasta 1970.

Consideraciones preliminares

¿Fue la carta de triunfo de los polacos en 1956 su indiscutible afirmación de los valores nacionales; en otras palabras, su genuino nacionalismo? Invitamos al lector a no perder de vista los comentarios sobre el tema del nacionalismo polaco en el presente trabajo. Asimismo debe meditarse sobre el nacionalismo en el caso cubano, especialmente su importancia en la estrategia de lucha de las fuerzas anticomunistas de Cuba. No deben ignorarse las ventajas derivadas por la tiranía castrista al adjudicarse, sin mérito pero con poder persuasivo, la auténtica representación de la nacionalidad cubana, y proclamar nada menos que a José Martí como autor intelectual del ataque al Cuartel Moncada.

Cuba ha perdido 40 años de su historia manejada por un personaje comprometido exclusivamente en la búsqueda y mantenimiento del poder político para sí y, en la promoción, además, de un extremado culto a su personalidad. El arribo de ese tipo de personaje al escenario cubano fue previsto desde 1950 por una misión de expertos que estudió la situación de Cuba nueve años antes del ascenso de Castro al poder. Esa misión, la famosa Misión Truslow del Banco Mundial, que fuera invitada por el Gobierno de Carlos Prío Socarrás para ofrecer un dictamen técnico sobre la situación de la Isla, escribió en su *Report on Cuba* (p. 13):

V. LA SELECCION QUE SE PRESENTA ANTE CUBA: La elección es clara; y la Misión cree que dejar de elegir la alternativa dinámica [diversificación] puede traer a Cuba las consecuencias más serias. La prosperidad de la Guerra ha creado nuevos niveles de vida para mucha gente. Si su economía no puede mantenerlos, al menos en un grado razonable, en tiempos menos prósperos, Cuba será sometida a grandes tensiones políticas. Si los líderes descuidan preparar a Cuba para ésto, ellos serán culpados por el pueblo. Y si eso sucediera, **el control bien puede pasar a manos subversivas pero atractivas, como ha sucedido en otros países cuyos líderes han ignorado las tendencias de los tiempos.**[3]

Lo dicho en el *Report* evidencia algo que queremos destacar. Cuando se conocen las reglas del juego político, se cuenta con información adecuada, y se analizan los problemas lógicamente, la política no tiene

muchos misterios. Su comprensión requiere, eso sí, abandonar las ilusiones infantiles y afrontar la realidad y las soluciones a los problemas con total franqueza.

El caso cubano: Raíces nacionalistas

Este bosquejo, como los demás, se limita a proveer un escueto marco conceptual histórico que permita un análisis ilustrado de la situación.

Las guerras de independencia: Para lograr su independencia Cuba pagó el más alto precio que país alguno tuvo que abonar en las Américas para ganar su libertad. El Imperio Español, vencido en los extensos territorios de México, Centro y Sudamérica en los inicios del siglo XIX, concentró sus recursos militares y económicos en la pequeña Isla de Cuba, parte del diminuto residuo del otrora inmenso dominio donde "jamás se ponía el sol." Además, Cuba fue también el símbolo del orgullo peninsular, la que, en las palabras de un líder español sería defendida "hasta el último soldado y hasta la última peseta". Y así fue que, en ese contexto, durante un período de treinta años, a partir de 1868, los cubanos libraron tres guerras devastadoras por su libertad.

Cuba peleó sola. En el país vecino del norte, aunque se veía con simpatías la causa cubana, la posición oficial, la mayor parte del tiempo, fue indiferente u hostil. Cuando convenía a sus relaciones con España, Estados Unidos confiscaba las armas del Ejército Libertador, compradas con los modestos aportes de los tabaqueros cubanos de Tampa. Pero cuando la fruta del Caribe estuvo madura, abonada con torrentes de sangre cubana y de sangre española, el coloso del norte, en una guerra de unos cien días, y contando con la eficaz colaboración de los cubanos, derrotó a España. El famoso "Mensaje a García" no fue otra cosa que la comunicación que sirvió para coordinar los esfuerzos bélicos de los ejércitos estadounidense y cubano. Como resultado de la brevísima guerra, los Estados Unidos se adjudicaron las Filipinas, Guam y Puerto Rico, y ganaron una decisiva influencia en Cuba, la que "legitimaron" con la llamada Enmienda Platt. Esta, insertada bajo presión en la constitución

---

3. Son nuestras la traducción del inglés al español, así como las negritas de la oración final.

cubana, daba a Estados Unidos el derecho de intervenir en Cuba. Pocas veces en la historia, la relación costo beneficio ha sido tan favorable a una tardía y limitada acción bélica.

El alto precio que pagó Cuba por su libertad ha tenido un peso abrumador sobre la historia de la Isla, y desde luego, fertilizó las raíces del nacionalismo cubano. Joaquín Balaguer, con la autoridad de su cultura y experiencia y la objetividad que le permite su condición de dominicano, ha señalado el "destino trágico que desde un principio preside la suerte de la revolución cubana. En la especie de tragedia griega que marca el rumbo de esa gesta sin precedentes en los anales de la humanidad, los sucesos desencadenan bajo un signo de grandeza y horror que no se advierte en ninguna de las otras guerras de independencia de América." La anterior cita se comprueba al constatar que la mayoría de los grandes hombres de Cuba murió en el conflicto. Desde Céspedes y Agramonte hasta Martí y Maceo, Cuba perdió el talento y el amor de muchos de sus mejores hijos. A veces nos preguntamos ¿qué habría sido de los Estados Unidos si hombres como Washington, Jefferson, John Adams o Alexander Hamilton hubieran caído bajo las balas inglesas en los inicios de la Guerra Revolucionaria? ¿O si Lincoln, en vez de ser abatido una vez concluída la Guerra Civil, hubiera sido asesinado al iniciarse ésta?

Pero no especulemos. Anotemos sí, y subrayemos, que el nacionalismo cubano tiene una fuerte raíz histórica y un contenido emocional que sólo puede ignorarse al costo de enajenar el interés y la colaboración de los cubanos. Castro siempre prestó atención al componente nacionalista. Aún cuando los favores de la Unión Soviética y el precio que por ellos se hizo pagar la metrópoli, ensombrecieron la soberanía nacional, el régimen cuidó de que se mantuvieran los símbolos cubanos sintetizados en el lema: "Patria o Muerte." La interpretación textual del lema hacía creer que se luchaba por la patria, no por ninguna otra finalidad subalterna. Claro, en Castro el nacionalismo ha sido un medio más para conquistar y mantener el poder. Hoy, los privilegios otorgados en Cuba a los inversionistas y turistas extranjeros, en detrimento de los derechos de los cubanos, ofrecen una ocasión para demostrar que Castro no es un naciona-

lista sincero sino un oportunista. Ese es un débil talón de Aquiles del régimen que debería ser puesto en evidencia, una y otra vez, ante el pueblo de Cuba. Del otro lado de la ecuación cubana, bien harían las fuerzas que se oponen al régimen castrista, en revisar el fondo y la forma de sus conductas, a fin de trasmitir al pueblo cubano una imagen inequívoca de cubanidad y de indivisible lealtad a Cuba.

El examen de los antecedentes históricos cubano americanos no estaría completo si no se dijera que una vez establecida la República de Cuba en 1902, el flujo hacia Cuba de capital y tecnología estadounidenses, así como la apertura del gran mercado del norte, unido a los recursos naturales de la Isla y al dinamismo de los cubanos, permitieron que Cuba se encontrara pronto en los primeros lugares de América Latina en cuanto a los indicadores económicos y sociales. Además, debe señalarse que cubanos y norteamericanos se mezclaron con facilidad y que elementos importantes de sus culturas se adoptaron recíprocamente a ambos lados del Canal de la Florida. Por ejemplo, la rumba llegó a ser uno de los ritmos favoritos en la Casa Blanca durante la presidencia de Franklin Delano Roosevelt. Más tarde, el actor, músico y empresario cubano Desi Arnaz, con su incomparable esposa y compañera americana Lucille Ball, transformó la técnica de producción de las comedias televisadas. La serie "I love Lucy" realizada por ellos, llegó a alcanzar una teleaudiencia de cuarenta y cuatro millones (28% de la población). Tal vez nadie mejor que Arnaz simbolizó el nacionalismo cubano en sus aspectos más íntegros y constructivos. Su personaje Ricky Ricardo habla un inglés con fuerte acento latino sin pretensión anglosajona alguna. En todo, su personaje refleja y capitaliza lo cubano, incluyendo muy especialmente los ritmos musicales tropicales encabezados por el famoso Babalú. Y así como la cultura cubana triunfaba en el Norte, la influencia del Norte se hacía sentir en todas las actividades en Cuba.

Todo ello demuestra que el nacionalismo cubano, aunque vigoroso y afirmativo, no tuvo elementos agresivos importantes hasta la llegada de Castro al poder. Esto se confirma al notar que Cuba independiente recibió con los brazos abiertos una numerosa inmigración española apenas habían terminado treinta años de guerra con España. Pero asimismo creemos que el hecho de que Castro jugara con énfasis la carta nacionalista, fue un factor que lo favoreció en contraste con la imagen de un nacionalismo a medias que frecuentemente proyectan sectores importantes de la oposición, especialmente en el exilio.

Las revoluciones de los años treinta: La Gran Depresión, con su cosecha de penuria alrededor del globo, desestabilizó al mundo. Mientras en Europa tiranos como Hitler, Stalin y Mussolini preparaban la Segunda Guerra Mundial, en Estados Unidos Franklin Delano Roosevelt ensayaba medidas creativas para contener un malestar social y económico que parecía amenazar la estabilidad del país. Cuba no podía escapar de esa tormenta que derrumbó los precios del azúcar. Y así, sin válvulas políticas e institucionales adecuadas para remediar el descontento, el pueblo cubano se vió sacudido por convulsiones revolucionarias que se extendieron a lo largo de la década de los años treinta.

Esas convulsiones tuvieron un fuerte y diverso contenido doctrinario. La expresión nacionalista se manifestó, entre otros aspectos, en la demanda de que la Enmienda Platt fuera abolida, lo que de hecho ocurrió en 1934. El monocultivo azucarero demostró su incapacidad de proteger el bienestar de los cubanos en tiempos malos, y fue considerado como una característica de la economía que debía corregirse mediante la diversificación. Asimismo, la concentración de tierras en los latifundios fue proscrita y se indicó la limitación restrictiva de la adquisición y posesión de la tierra por personas y compañías extranjeras. Además, se postuló la adopción de medidas para revertir la tierra al cubano, todo lo cual quedaría plasmado en la Constitución de 1940.

A finales de la década, los diversos partidos, y grupos políticos del país convinieron en reordenarlo jurídica y políticamente y se convocaron elecciones para integrar una asamblea constituyente que diera a Cuba una nueva carta magna. El proceso se desarrolló de manera ejemplar. Tal vez ese fue el momento estelar de la democracia cubana. De las deliberaciones de la asamblea salió la famosa Constitución de 1940, la

que recogió lo substancial del ideario político y económico que se había debatido en la década recién terminada. Esa característica incluyente hizo de la Constitución una voluminosa ley fundamental que para algunos escapaba de los límites deseables en un documento constitucional. Por otra parte, los excesivos detalles de la carta le quitarían pronto parte de su aplicabilidad en un mundo en rápida transformación. Decimos ésto a propósito de algunos intentos de proponer la Constitución de 1940 como la base de un gobierno de transición. Creemos que tal cosa crearía serias dificultades. No obstante sus aspectos positivos, no hay que perder de vista que la Constitución del 40 se dictó para un país cuyas características han cambiado totalmente y para una época que hoy es sólo un recuerdo. La alternativa a la vieja constitución sería un estatuto constitucional sencillo que normara las funciones del gobierno provisional mientras, a su debido tiempo, se convoca una nueva asamblea constituyente.

En su momento histórico la Constitución del 40 cumplió su función durante los gobiernos constitucionales del período 1940-52. Fue ésa una época generalmente próspera debido a los altos precios del azúcar generados por la Segunda Guerra Mundial, el Plan Marshall y la Guerra de Corea. Fue también una época de gran corrupción y de ataques vitriólicos contra la misma por parte de algunos voceros de la oposición. Todo ello debilitó la confianza de la ciudadanía en sus líderes e instituciones políticas. El 10 de marzo de 1952, Fulgencio Batista interrumpió un proceso electoral normal en el cual era candidato a la presidencia y en la madrugada, mediante un golpe de estado, se apoderó del gobierno. Si se hiciera una lista de las fechas trágicas de la nación cubana, el 10 de marzo debería figurar entre las primeras. Ese día, destruído el estado de derecho, se abrieron frente a Cuba las más dolorosas alternativas. El carácter sorpresivo del golpe y el respaldo al mismo de las fuerzas armadas, impidió que cristalizara una resistencia efectiva. A ello contribuyó el rápido reconocimiento al gobierno ilegal que otorgaron con diligencia los gobiernos democráticos "amigos" de Cuba. El 10 de marzo de 1952 inició un proceso que conduciría, siete años más tarde, a la ascensión de Fidel Castro al poder.

El caso polaco

Las reformas de Gomulka: La ascensión de Wladyslaw Gomulka al poder a finales de 1956, alentó grandes esperanzas en Polonia. En muchos aspectos Gomulka actuó como un reformador moderado, por ejemplo, al restablecer la agricultura privada. Así, entre octubre y diciembre de 1956, más del 80% de las fincas colectivas existentes se disolvieron, representando las restantes sólo el 1.3% de la producción. Al mismo tiempo se daban otras ventajas a los agricultores. Sin embargo, su gobierno evitó, en general, apartarse de los principios marxista leninistas, y mantuvo estrechos lazos con la Unión Soviética. Recuérdese que 1956 fue también el año del levantamiento anticomunista en Hungría el que fuera brutalmente aplastado. Sin embargo, ésto no comprometería la independencia polaca que Gomulka comentó en los siguientes términos: "La cualidad más característica de la nación polaca, que es consecuencia de su historia, es su sensibilidad respecto de su independencia." Esa cualidad pronto volvería a jugar un papel trascendental.

Respecto a la Iglesia Católica, y por razones tácticas, Gomulka parecía buscar un modus operandi. El Partido, argumentaba él, no puede ignorar la existencia de una gran masa de católicos, y en sus políticas no debe aplicar métodos administrativos a los creyentes, ignorando que la vieja disputa con la Iglesia ha ahuyentado a millones de personas del socialismo. La tiranía castrista no siguió en Cuba el curso conciliatorio sugerido por Gomulka para su país. Adelante, anotamos las duras medidas contra la Iglesia adoptadas en Cuba. En la Isla no ocurrieron los ajustes de política con la Iglesia en el grado y oportunidad en que se practicaron en Polonia. Pero considerando sólo la duración de los gobernantes en el poder, sin tener en cuenta el bienestar del pueblo u otras consideraciones éticas, lo hecho en Cuba, en contraste con lo realizado en Polonia, parece haber favorecido, lamentablemente, la prolongada longevidad del régimen castrista. Desde luego, no debe perderse de vista que las iglesias polaca y cubana eran diferentes en muchos aspectos y que lo que el gobierno hizo en Cuba tal vez no hubiera podido haberse hecho en Polonia.

Los primeros años del gobierno de Gomulka fueron considerados satisfactorios por la mayoría de los polacos. Entre sus logros destacan la redefinición de las relaciones con la Unión Soviética en términos más ventajosos para Polonia y el restablecimiento de la agricultura privada. Como antes se apuntó, la agricultura privada disfrutó de un tratamiento favorable. Ciertamente, las políticas de Gomulka hacia la Iglesia Católica y los agricultores sirvieron para salvaguardar esos centros independientes de poder: espiritual el uno, económico el otro.

Las relaciones con la Iglesia Católica continuaron evolucionando. En octubre de 1956 el Cardenal Wyszynski fue relevado de su confinamiento junto con otros sacerdotes y obispos. A pesar de estas medidas las relaciones entre la Iglesia y el Estado estuvieron lejos de ser armónicas, pero se mantuvieron dentro de límites de "coexistencia pacífica." Recuérdese que la Iglesia se identificó con la causa de la nacionalidad polaca desde muy temprano en su historia, y este hecho le otorgó el prestigio y la protección que disfrutan las instituciones vinculadas a la patria.

El precario equilibrio en el país logrado después de la crisis de 1956 no duró muchos años. A partir de 1964 las cosas empezaron a empeorar seriamente a lo que se unió el deteriorado estado de salud de Gomulka. La situación económica se hizo cada vez más insatisfactoria. Las medidas parciales de reforma económica que habían sido introducidas en 1956 no estimularon un alto grado de crecimiento económico, lo que limitó las oportunidades de empleo de las jóvenes generaciones nacidas en el "baby boom" polaco de los años cincuenta. Por otra parte, las relaciones entre el Gobierno y la Iglesia se deterioraron debido a diferencias sobre cómo celebrar el milésimo aniversario de la introducción del cristianismo en Polonia en el año 966. La Iglesia pudo resistir con éxito las presiones del Gobierno y poco a poco las tensiones comenzaron a desaparecer, persistiendo, sin embargo, una atmósfera de mutua sospecha.

La década de los sesenta fue tumultuosa. La Universidad de Varsovia y amplios sectores de la intelectualidad se convirtieron en centros de oposición. Un nuevo grupo político dentro del Partido Comunista, los "Partidarios," formado por la gente que había pasado los años de la guerra en la resistencia en Polonia, desarrollaron una amarga oposición a aquellos comunistas, muchos de ellos judíos, que habían pasado esos años en la Unión Soviética. Los Partidarios abogaban por una política autoritaria frente a la Iglesia y por un nacionalismo agresivo. De hecho, el grupo logró eliminar a un gran número de oficiales judíos del Partido.

En diciembre de 1967 un nuevo régimen reformador quedó establecido en Checoeslovaquia bajo el liderazgo de Alexander Dubcek, lo cual estimuló demandas por parte de estudiantes e intelectuales polacos en favor de cambios similares. Las tensiones culminaron en el mes de marzo, en grandes demostraciones de los estudiantes, con la consecuente violencia policiaca y el arresto de más de mil personas. Los disturbios dieron a los Partidarios un pretexto para reforzar su posición y desalojar de sus puestos a sus adversarios políticos, especialmente los liberales y los judíos. En total 9,000 personas perdieron sus empleos y la mayoría de los 30,000 judíos de Polonia dejaron el país exilándose en Israel, Europa Occidental y América del Norte. Gomulka nadó a favor de la corriente y logró fortalecer su posición, ayudado además por su lealtad a la Unión Soviética en la crisis checoeslovaca. Así, en el Quinto Congreso del Partido de los Trabajadores Polacos Unidos (Comunistas), Gomulka tenía un firme control sobre el Partido. Toda esa fortaleza política, sin embargo, no le serviría de mucho ante la persistencia de la crisis económica.

La nueva crisis: La crisis fue tipicamente la que se observa en los países regidos por la planificación central. Los resultados adversos de esa planificación se reforzaron por los efectos negativos en la balanza de pagos que ocasionó la importación de maquinaria occidental destinada a aliviar la brecha tecnológica polaca. Para mejorar la disponibilidad de divisas se aumentaron las exportaciones de alimentos, especialmente carne, con resultados devastadores en la oferta y el abastecimiento del mercado interno. Las medidas que se ensayaron en 1970 como soluciones, sirvieron de hecho para desencadenar una revuelta.

Ajustes de política económica se adoptaron a principios de 1970. El 12 de diciembre el gobierno anunció aumentos de precios de alimentos básicos de hasta

30% mientras se rebajaban los de aparatos de televisión, automóviles y otros. Tales medidas constituyeron la gota de agua que desbordó el vaso. Los trabajadores de los astilleros de las tres ciudades del norte (Gdansk, Gdynia y Szczecin) llevaron a cabo huelgas masivas y demostraciones, las que fueron brutalmente reprimidas entre el 14 y el 19 de diciembre. Por lo menos 500 personas perdieron sus vidas mientras el espectro de la guerra civil parecía acercarse. Gomulka no pudo obtener un apoyo soviético significativo y se vió obligado a renunciar tras sufrir una embolia. En su lugar, Edward Gierek asumía el poderoso cargo de Primer Secretario el 20 de diciembre de 1970. Así terminaba una esperanza más en la historia del marxismo leninismo en Polonia.

El gobierno de Gierek: La primera prioridad del Gobierno de Gierek fue restablecer una apariencia de orden, para lo cual consideró necesario anunciar al Parlamento el 23 de diciembre que su Gobierno revisaría drasticamente las políticas económicas de su predecesor, así como el Plan Quinquenal para el período 1971-5. La agricultura, las viviendas y los bienes de consumo serían beneficiados. No habría cancelación de los aumentos de precios pero se darían pequeños aumentos de salarios a los trabajadores más modestos. Esas concesiones, sin embargo, no calmaron a los trabajadores y una ola de huelgas se extendió por el país, acompañada de demandas de que se hicieran cambios en el sistema económico y político y se castigara a los responsables por la pérdida de vidas en los disturbios de diciembre.

Buscando apaciguar los ánimos, el propio Gierek encabezó discusiones con los obreros de los astilleros de Gdansk y Szczecin, a los que persuadió de que volvieran al trabajo previas concesiones. Sin embargo, las huelgas se extendieron a la industria textil, lo que hizo necesario nuevas concesiones. El resultado más importante parecía ser la clara demostración del extraordinario poder de la clase obrera (en eso el marxismo leninisno parecía tener razón). El Politbureau en un informe al Pleno del Comité Central anotaba la moraleja destacando que el Partido "en el futuro debe siempre procurar evitar conflictos con la clase trabajadora."

Dada la precaria situación del Gobierno de Gierek, éste adelantó un programa de reformas económicas, siendo favorecida la producción de alimentos, así como los incentivos a los agricultores privados. Se abolieron limitaciones en relación con la venta y herencia de tierras y se confirmaron derechos de propiedad a un millón de agricultores privados a quienes por primera vez se incorporó al sistema de salud estatal. Además se adoptaron otras medidas en favor de los agricultores.

La crisis aumentó la dependencia de Gierek de la URSS la que proveyó a Polonia de productos agrícolas y préstamos. Gierek, no obstante, aprovechó el compromiso de la Unión Soviética con la política de détente para mejorar sus propias relaciones con países occidentales y adquirir maquinaria en condiciones favorables a fin de modernizar la industria. Ello impulsó el comercio de Polonia con Occidente y redujo el nivel de aquel con la Unión Soviética. También se otorgó alguna autonomía, y acceso a recursos en moneda dura, a ciertas grandes industrias. Los resultados fueron muy satisfactorios y estimularon el talento empresarial polaco. En general Polonia disfrutó de una marcada prosperidad durante los primeros años del Gobierno de Gierek. En esa época las relaciones con la Iglesia Católica mejoraron y el régimen le restituyó unos 7000 edificios eclesiásticos que habían sido confiscados por el Estado. Por otra parte, mediante hábiles maniobras políticas, Gierek se aseguró el total control del Partido recibiendo además el endoso personal de Breznnev.

Como paso siguiente de su hasta ahora exitosa carrera, Gierek intentó apretar los controles ideológicos. Se temía que el mejoramiento del nivel de vida de la población erosionara los principios marxista leninistas. La URSS y otros países del campo socialista compartían esa preocupación. Ello dió lugar a campañas masivas de adiestramiento ideológico de los miembros del Partido. Por otra parte no se perdía de vista a los oponentes. Un prominente integrante del Politbureau, Jan Szydlak, atacó a la Iglesia Católica como el "único centro de fuerzas sociales derechistas que disponen de una visión filosófica coherente, una fuerte organización básica y numerosos activistas." Si se suprime el discutible calificativo "derechistas," esa ca-

racterización de la Iglesia define los atributos que la convirtieron en la poderosa estructura capaz de desafiar al estado comunista. Jan Szydlak tuvo una visión certera del adversario.

Otro importante oponente del régimen era la intelligentsia, la que resentía el aparente servilismo del gobierno polaco ante la URSS, especialmente repecto de restricciones en la vida cultural de un millón de polacos que aún vivían en la Unión Soviética en áreas que habían sido parte de Polonia antes de 1939. La censura y las restricciones a la vida cultural fueron igualmente atacadas por la intelligentsia y la Iglesia.

Lo que provocó una confrontación otra vez fue el intento del régimen de introducir una nueva constitución cuyo texto subrayaba el carácter socialista del Estado Polaco basado en los mismos principios que triunfaron en la "Gran Revolución Socialista de Octubre." La intelligentsia y la Iglesia reaccionaron negativamente. El socialista veterano Edward Lipinski dirigió una carta a Gierek que concluía así: "No hay objetivo mas importante para Polonia que reafirmar su soberanía. Sólo después de recuperar la independencia política será posible acometer reformas económicas sistemáticas y restructurar el sistema político y social a fin de liberar el potencial creativo de la nación." El régimen cedió; el texto se modificó.

En el episodio anterior se pone de manifiesto una vez más la importancia que los sentimientos nacionalistas han tenido en la historia de Polonia. La situación en Cuba no ha sido muy diferente pero la oposición a la tiranía no ha jugado con éxito la carta nacionalista. A ello nos hemos referido antes y nos referiremos adelante, así como a las razones por las cuales los estallidos populares multitudinarios de Polonia no han encontrado homólogos en Cuba.

El caso cubano: Factores que favorecieron a Castro

El gobierno producto del golpe de estado del 10 de marzo de 1952 que encabezó Batista fue corrupto, dilapidador y dictatorial. Para ganar un apoyo popular que nunca obtuvo, creó una prosperidad aparente gastando las reservas que Cuba había acumulado en los años de buenos precios del azúcar, y aumentando la deuda nacional; pero de nada le sirvió ese derroche.

El país jamás aceptó el golpe de estado, el cual se hizo más intolerable por el elevado grado de corrupción en el gobierno y los abusos de poder que cometía. En una afanosa búsqueda de una fórmula que restaurara el orden constitucional, la ciudadanía concentró sus actividades primero en la política y después en la revolución.

Los políticos fueron incapaces de producir una fórmula viable. Por su parte Castro ensayó, en el asalto al cuartel Moncada en 1953, la tesis insurreccional, la que en esa ocasión fracasó. Pero los demás ensayos políticos también fracasaron, y cuando él inició la campaña de la Sierra Maestra en 1956, parte de la población empezó a verlo como posiblemente el único líder que tenía la fórmula capaz de devolver a Cuba a un régimen de derecho. Después de todo, el gobierno de Batista era el resultado de la fuerza y parecía aceptable ponerle fin por medio de la fuerza. Y así creció en progresión geométrica el apoyo a las guerrillas castristas. La extendida corrupción y desmoralización en el ejército de Batista facilitó a Castro los modestos aspectos militares del conflicto, mientras la población aumentaba su apoyo irrestricto al poco conocido líder de la Sierra. Para dolor de Cuba, la traición de un golpe de estado empezaba a engendrar un mito trágico, el mito de Fidel. Por otra parte, en contraste con aquel golpe, a la llegada del nuevo año de 1959, otro mito se deshacía en pedazos: Batista huía de Cuba para acogerse a la protección del tirano de la República Dominicana Rafael Trujillo.

El régimen de Fidel Castro: Castro llegó al poder revestido de una aureola mixta de héroe y mesías que le granjeó el apoyo delirante de muchos cubanos.. Las simpatías que despertó derivaron en gran parte de la profunda antipatía que el régimen de Batista inspiraba, según una lógica simplona del tipo "si Batista es malo, Fidel que lo derrotó debe ser bueno." Además, las promesas del nuevo régimen alimentaban, en una parte de la población, esperanzas de un bienestar extraordinario. A los simpatizantes simplones hay que sumar los patriotas idealistas sinceros que deseaban ver a Cuba transitar mejores caminos que los que había recorrido; también hay que añadir quienes encontraron en la Revolución las explicaciones que justificaban sus propios fracasos personales; igualmente los

que tenían agravios que esperaban vengar o que ya veían vengados en la desventura de los perjudicados por el régimen; los que aspiraban a beneficiarse de los frutos del poder y un número adicional de gente de todo tipo. En contra de la Revolución estaban las clases más acomodadas, los intereses ligados a los Estados Unidos y al gobierno derrotado, y muchos otros cubanos que percibieron desde el principio el carácter autoritario del fidelismo y se negaron a sumarse a la gran comparsa revolucionaria.

El régimen se movió rapidamente hacia la consolidación del poder y el logro de sus objetivos. Desde sus inicios creó una atmósfera psicológica que oscilaba entre la desconfianza, el miedo y el terror, la que le ayudaría, como a otros tiranos, a "ablandar" a los enemigos reales o potenciales. Así, a pocas horas de la huída de Batista, se iniciaron juicios sumarísimos que culminaron en los fusilamientos, supervisados por el Che Guevara, de centenares de ex miembros de los cuerpos de seguridad del gobierno derrotado, a quienes se imputaban crímenes. Las ejecuciones, en algunos casos trasmitidas de día por televisión a todo el país, ayudaron a crear un clima de cautela y temor, especialmente entre quienes ponderaban disentir del régimen. Paralelamente, campañas contra enemigos reales o imaginarios de la "revolución," calificados como "latifundistas," "esbirros," "contrarrevolucionarios," "agentes de la CIA," etc., complementaban aquel clima. Dentro del crescendo histérico que el régimen propiciaba, se hacía cada vez más riesgoso emitir expresiones que no concordaran fielmente con la posición del "líder máximo." Así, como otros tiranos antes que él, Fidel Castro aprovechaba la euforia del triunfo para empezar a establecer los controles dictatoriales sobre el pueblo. Primero, a falta de otros recursos, emplearía los de tipo psicológico. Más tarde, los aparatos represivos del Estado, como los Comités de Defensa de la Revolución, harían un trabajo más profesional. En todo momento el régimen aprovechó las tensiones raciales y de clase (en Cuba relativamente benignas), para fortalecer la Revolución.

Desde el principio se cometieron abusos de varios tipos. Además de las violaciones a los derechos humanos, las relativas a los derechos de propiedad (con vista a debilitar el poder de adversarios y robustecer el del estado) se hicieron pronto presentes; de hecho, aún antes de que se promulgaran las leyes respectivas. Por otra parte, el antagonismo con Estados Unidos se subrayó una y otra vez, aprovechando los sentimientos antiestadounidenses existentes en una parte del pueblo, así como la penosa conducta de ese país en su contubernio con la dictadura de Batista. Es la creencia personal del autor que las motivaciones que inspiraron a Castro en su conducta antinorteamericana se explican dentro de la siguiente hipótesis de trabajo.

Al haber logrado Castro un triunfo político significativo con relativo poco esfuerzo, apenas a los 31 años de edad, y conociendo los problemas que afectaban, y aún afectan, a los países latinoamericanos, una vez asegurado el poder en Cuba, Fidel consideraría la América Latina como su siguiente campo de operaciones y en ella pretendería desarrollar una gran revolución latinoamericana bajo su liderazgo como un nuevo Bolívar. Esto explica que su régimen auspiciara o colaborara desde el principio, con diversas expediciones, conspiraciones e insurrecciones en varios países, entre ellos, República Dominicana, Nicaragua, El Salvador, Chile, Panamá, Venezuela, Uruguay, Argentina y Bolivia, país donde, en ese empeño, fracasaría el Che. En relación con esa violencia se ha dicho que "la guerra fría no fue tan fría en la América Latina." Ahora bien, como las revoluciones, por definición, se hacen contra el statu quo, dados los intereses que vinculan a Estados Unidos con el statu quo en Latinoamérica, una revolución en este subcontinente chocará pronto o tarde con el Coloso del Norte. Siendo así, para subsistir tal revolución tiene que apoyarse en un poder equivalente al estadounidense. La Unión Soviética resultó ser el poder equivalente. Y desde luego, la revolución castrista recibiría la protección económica y militar de la URSS. Por eso creemos que la alianza de dicha revolución con los soviéticos se produjo más por conveniencias estratégicas que por motivos ideológicos.

La dinámica revolucionaria en Cuba no se detendría. Como el poder económico es parte importante del poder, una personalidad como la de Castro, insaciable en busca de poder e influída por la ideología marxista leninista, buscaría todas las razones y pretextos para justificar un despojo casi total de la riqueza pri-

vada cubana en favor del Estado, que como el de Luis XIV, estaría personificado en el propio Fidel: "L'état, c'est mois!" [El estado soy yo.] Nótese que en este caso la riqueza no sería necesariamente, como para otros tiranos, un medio para ostentar lujos y disfrutar placeres. No, en este caso la riqueza sería principalmente una herramienta de poder y tendría la función primaria de ejercer control sobre los demás, o sea, robustecer el propio poder. Además, su confiscación serviría para disminuir o eliminar el poder de los adversarios acaudalados.

El éxodo: Muy pronto después de llegar la Revolución al poder se impulsó el gran éxodo cubano, el que llegaría a alcanzar cifras muy superiores al millón. Los cubanos se exilaron por muchos motivos. Los primeros en irse fueron los partidarios y asociados de Batista que se encontraron en una atmósfera hostil. Le siguieron aquellos cuyas actividades económicas fueron perjudicadas por la Revolución. Siguieron los que imaginaban el futuro en Cuba y sólo veían un Hitler tropical comandando una Isla arruinada. Con el exilio de numerosos tecnócratas algunos pretendían preservar para la futura reconstrucción, gente preparada por su experiencia para realizar esa tarea. Como individuos, muchos cubanos contemplaron la idea de quedarse y oponerse al régimen. Gran parte de los que así lo hicieron, sufrieron persecución, cárcel y frecuentemente la muerte. La mayoría, sin embargo, evaluó la situación y concluyó que dado el apretado control que ejercía el régimen sobre la ciudadanía y la histeria fidelista generalizada entre la población, la única alternativa juiciosa era el exilio, especialmente teniendo en cuenta que si bien el ser humano tiene responsabilidades como ciudadano, además tiene otras responsabilidades. La mayoría pensó que la duración del exilio se mediría en meses o algunos años. Tal vez pocos o ninguno (incluyendo a Castro) consideró que el régimen sobreviviría por largas décadas.

Estados Unidos alentó el éxodo esperando que Castro, al perder la tecnocracia y estar expuesto a las presiones estadounidenses vería derrumbarse su régimen. Obviamente no fue así. Países del Bloque Soviético proveyeron reemplazos para los profesionales ausentes y los subsidios de la URSS compensaron parte de la ineficiencia del sistema. Otro resultado del éxodo fue algo muy distinto de lo esperado. La enorme masa de población que se exiló facilitó a Castro controlar el país con una mínima oposición. Además, creó una división entre "los que se fueron y los que se quedaron," la que la propaganda castrista insinúa como entre los cubanos a medias y los verdaderos cubanos. Peor aún, como la mayoría de los exilados provenían de las clases más acomodadas y educadas, muchos cubanos de la Isla se consideran como los abanderados de una patria que defiende el patrimonio nacional, frente a "enemigos de clase" que pretenden despojarlos. O sea, a la Revolución, que en su origen fué política mas que económica y social, y que, por haber sido patrocinada en gran medida por las clases medias y altas (incluyendo a Castro), excluyó los ataques recíprocos entre las clases, después se la ha presentado precisamente como una lucha de clases. Muchos cubanos, especialmente profesionales universitarios, fueron declarados "traidores a la patria" por el hecho de haber emigrado. El histerismo de las autoridades que evidencia esa declarión parece justificar la conducta de quienes, al irse, evitaron vivir bajo tales jerarcas.

Todo esto plantea un problema importante para los sociólogos, los líderes religiosos, los políticos, y en general, para todos los cubanos de buena voluntad. Tal problema es que una vez que terminen los largos días de la tiranía en Cuba, sólo se logrará una república viable si los cubanos se integran como un pueblo unido en sus raíces esenciales y no se yuxtaponen simplemente como grupos irreconciliables en una isla común. El Papa Juan Pablo II al visitar Polonia en junio de 1997, indicó que él estaba convencido de que su patria era "capaz de unirse alrededor de objetivos comunes y de valores fundamentales para cada hombre y mujer." El Santo Padre no necesita consejos. Su poderoso intelecto y su brillante actuación en la transformación de Polonia y Europa Oriental, lo colocan por encima de cuanto pudiera sugerírsele. Pero si fuera dado expresar un ruego, éste sería el siguiente, inspirado en las propias palabras del Papa: "Rogamos que los cubanos se unan alrededor de objetivos comunes y de valores fundamentales para cada hombre y mujer."

Conflictos: Playa Girón, la crisis de los cohetes: La cuestión cubana ha sido motivo de múltiples conflictos, habiéndose destacado temprano en la cronología del régimen castrista, el relativo a la penosa invasión de Playa Girón. Muchas lecciones enseña ese triste episodio, pero creemos que ninguna es más importante que la siguiente: "los líderes de un pueblo, o los que pretenden serlo, no tienen el derecho de comprometerlo en acciones importantes sobre las cuales esos líderes no ejercen control efectivo alguno." Sin restar importancia a Girón, es obvio que el conflicto de mayor gravedad lo fue la crisis de los cohetes en octubre de 1962. El enfrentamiento se originó por la colocación en Cuba de ojivas nucleares soviéticas situadas en la Isla como un seguro contra cualquier intento estadounidense de suprimir al régimen castrista por la fuerza. El incidente es ampliamente conocido y nosotros nada podríamos añadir sino los breves comentarios que siguen.

El régimen de Castro no sufrió deterioro como resultado de la crisis. Por lo contrario, aparentemente se benefició de inmunidades dadas por EEUU respecto de posibles acciones militares de ese país contra el régimen de la Isla, siempre que Cuba no actuara como una base de armas soviéticas ofensivas. Así, de hecho, el régimen castrista se ha mantenido tan firmemente en el poder, que ha podido contar 36 años de existencia a partir de aquel evento. Tras las confrontaciones de Playa Girón y la crisis de los cohetes, el castrismo no tendría más problemas de esa gravedad hasta el colapso de la Unión Soviética en diciembre de 1991.

El caso polaco: La oposición se estructura

No obstante sus éxitos iniciales, finalmente una crisis económica afectó al gobierno de Gierek. Dicha crisis, generada por múltiples causas, indujo protestas y huelgas de los trabajadores, las que el gobierno trató de dominar mediante arrestos y largas sentencias de cárcel. Esto acercó a los obreros y a los intelectuales descontentos, dando origen, en septiembre de 1976 al Comité de Defensa de los Trabajadores (KOR). En mayo de 1977, después de demostraciones en gran escala en Cracovia, numerosos líderes de KOR fueron arrestados. Sin embargo, junto con la gran mayoría de detenidos en las huelgas de 1976, los nuevos arrestados fueron liberados como parte de una amnistía en gran escala en julio de 1977.

En ese momento, las fuerzas no comunistas polacas comenzaban a ganar un elevado grado de integración y coherencia. La unión de intelectuales y trabajadores dió gran pujanza a la oposición. Pedían, entre otras reformas, establecer sindicatos independientes con derecho a huelga. A medida que se acentuaba la crisis y el descontento se extendía a los propios comunistas, se ponía de manifiesto la impopularidad de los líderes marxistas y la debilidad, insensibilidad e inmovilidad del gobierno. Para mejorar la situación, Gierek intentó poner sus relaciones con la Iglesia en un plano más armónico. La Iglesia reiteró su posición en favor de la libertad de todos los obreros presos, el respeto de los derechos civiles, y la conducción de un verdadero diálogo con la sociedad. La Iglesia también reafirmó su oposición a las protestas violentas.

En octubre de 1978 el Cardenal Karol Wojtyla, Arzobispo de Cracovia, fue elevado a la posición de Sumo Pontífice. Tal designación tuvo un efecto casi mágico entre los polacos a quienes infundió autoconfianza y dió la certeza de que cambios políticos importantes eran ahora inevitables. La crisis económica, cuyos efectos se venían acumulando, indujo al gobierno a adoptar una serie de medidas en favor de los agricultores, las que tuvieron poco efecto. Otras iniciativas tuvieron aún peores resultados debido a extrema incompetencia y corrupción, mientras la deuda nacional crecía geometricamente. En el verano de 1980 la crisis económica era tan grave que a pesar del temor a la reacción popular, el gobierno introdujo un nuevo programa de austeridad. Las huelgas no se hicieron esperar en Varsovia y Lublin extendiéndose a Gdansk y otros lugares. Las demandas, que en un principio no tenían claras tonalidades políticas, culminaron en Gdansk en un pliego de 21 demandas económicas y políticas, las que incluían el establecimiento de sindicatos independientes con derecho a huelga. Claramente, el desarrollo político de los últimos años maduraba ahora en toda su plenitud.

Lech Walesa encabezó las negociaciones con el Gobierno, las que fueron largas y difíciles. La Unión Soviética amenazó con intervenir, mientras la Iglesia Católica recomendaba moderación. Finalmente, el 31 de agosto de 1980 se firmó el acuerdo. En septiembre Gierek perdía su cargo, siendo sustituído como Primer Secretario del Partido Comunista por Stanislaw Kania. El principal negociador del gobierno resumió así los trabajos: "Hemos hablado como polacos a polacos....No hay vencedores ni vencidos." Esta es una clara indicación de cuán profundamente el nacionalismo polaco presidió el proceso.

El panorama político cambió rapidamente. Surgieron sindicatos libres en todo el país y se estructuró Solidaridad como una organización nacional con unos diez millones de miembros, siendo sus lugares más fuertes las grandes concentraciones industriales. [Nótese que señalamos en otra parte, que la falta de similares concentraciones industriales en Cuba había sido un factor adverso a la organización y lucha de los obreros.] Solidaridad agrupaba, logicamente, personas de diversas ideologías, inclusive miembros del Partido Comunista que, cumpliendo instrucciones del gobierno, pretendían sabotear la organización. Entretanto, la crisis económica se agravaba, no obstante lo cual, había sectores de la población que se mantenían esperanzados; después de todo, se pensaba, el comunismo polaco había demostrado que podía desviarse de la ortodoxia marxista al mantener la agricultura privada y reconocer una posición especial a la Iglesia Católica.

El período que siguió se caracterizó por forcejeos entre Solidaridad y el Gobierno, al final de los cuales este último, para desesperación de la línea dura, siempre terminaba haciendo concesiones. Para robustecer su posición, a principios de 1981, Kania designó como Primer Ministro al General Wojciech Jaruzelski. Poco después la línea dura, aprovechando ausencias de Kania y Jaruzelski, provocó una confrontación con Solidaridad. Hábiles intervenciones de Kania y Jaruzelski y la efectiva mediación de la Iglesia evitaron el escalamiento de la crisis. Entre los resultados positivos figuró la autorización para crear un sindicato de agricultores, Solidaridad Rural. Así, los moderados y quienes favorecían las reformas, avanzaban hacia posiciones cada vez más ventajosas. Pero como la línea dura se mantenía firme, una nueva confrontación con la Unión Soviética (apoyando ésta la ortodoxia marxista), parecía inevitable.

Kania superó la crisis pero se sintió inclinado a hacer concesiones, reemplazando funcionarios liberales por personeros de la línea dura. Ahora bien, la falta de capacidad y voluntad del Partido Comunista de atender las presiones de la sociedad en favor de cambios, creó un vacío político. Solidaridad, aunque renuente a jugar un papel político, se vió presionado a llenar ese vacío. Las resultantes propuestas de Solidaridad significaban cambios profundos. Por otra parte la inercia del Partido Comunista se hacía más peligrosa dado el deterioro de la situación económica. El verano de l981 registró demostraciones en las calles y marchas de hambre que el liderazgo de Solidaridad trató infructuosamente de canalizar en una forma constructiva. La muerte, el 28 de mayo, del Cardenal Wyszynski, había apagado una voz en favor de la estabilidad política. El Arzobispo Jósef Glemp, su sucesor, no disfrutaba aún de la influencia de su predecesor.

Dentro de una tensa atmósfera política y económica, Solidaridad celebró su Conferencia Nacional en septiembre, precedida por una misa solemne que oficié el Arzobispo Glemp. Mientras tanto, los soviéticos ejecutarían ejercicios militares de mar y tierra en el occidente de la URSS y en el Báltico. Los planteamientos iniciales en la Conferencia fueron en favor de reformas radicales. Esto condujo a un estado de grave crisis, exacerbando a los soviéticos hasta el límite. Walesa comprendió los peligros y durante la segunda parte de la Conferencia logró derrotar a sus oponentes y proyectar una imagen menos radical. Las tensiones entre las diversas facciones en el Gobierno continuaron y, entre otros resultados, produjeron la destitución de Kania y el ascenso del General Jaruzelski al cargo de Primer Secretario, reteniendo éste además los cargos de Primer Ministro y Ministro de Defensa. Siguió un tenso período en el que el Gobierno y Solidaridad, y dentro de éstos sus diversas facciones, maniobraron para lograr sus objetivos. Pero el 13 de diciembre de 1981 la situación cambió drasticamente al decretarse la ley marcial, la que se impuso con la amplitud, precisión y rigor propios de un gobierno totalitario. La crudeza del invierno, el arresto sorpresivo de miles de líderes disidentes y el corte de las comunicaciones telefónicas y telegráficas internacionales, inhibieron posibles reacciones de la población. La URSS aplaudió la medida; los Estados Unidos impusieron sanciones económicas por el tiempo que durara la ley marcial. Tal vez Jaruzelski había dictado esa ley para prevenir una intervención soviética.

La eficiencia en la implantación de la ley marcial no fue acompañada por éxitos en la política económica. El trauma de la ley había dejado en la población una gran hostilidad hacia el Gobierno. La retórica que acompañó la ley marcial, omitía la fraseología marxista, pero destacaba los méritos del soldado polaco. Este es un ejemplo más de un nacionalismo afirmativo. Entretanto, las huellas del trauma impedían el diálogo nacional entre Solidaridad y el Gobierno, por lo que éste apeló a la intercesión de la Iglesia, la que, bajo el liderazgo del Arzobispo Glemp, exhortó a mantener la calma y "no iniciar una lucha entre polacos."

Las tensiones políticas, aunque a veces agudas, eran manejables. Sin embargo, lo que las hacía peligrosas era la continuación de la crisis económica. Y la economía se mostraba incapaz de superar las incongruencias impuestas por el marxismo. Así, las ventajas de las medidas que se adoptaban para mejorar un aspecto de la situación, eran pronto anuladas por otras medidas incoherentes destinadas a otras finalidades. La falta de convicción ideológica, por otra parte, restaba eficacia a ciertas iniciativas de economía de mercado, cuando éstas se trataban de compensar con medidas típicas del estado de bienestar social. No sorprende, por tanto, que no se lograra que la colunma vertebral de la economía descansara en la disciplina del mercado, sustituyendo ésta a la planificación central. La agricultura volvió a ser escenario del fracaso marxista. A pesar de haberse otorgado estímulos a los agricultores, la producción cayó un 4.5% en 1982. Razón: la falta de artículos de consumo restaba incentivos a los agricultores para producir. Como resultado, el suministro de alimentos a las ciudades era deficiente y constituía una fuente de tensión. El ingreso nacional, a su vez, caía otro 8% en 1982.

La escasez de moneda dura y las dificultades que las sanciones económicas creaban para obtenerla, originaban problemas adicionales. Polonia tenía relaciones estrechas con los países de Occidente, por lo que las sanciones de éstos tuvieron un efecto apreciable. La URSS no pudo compensar el déficit polaco de moneda dura que se estimaba en no menos de dos mil millones de dólares anuales. La prolongada crisis de 1980-82 exacerbada con la promulgación de la ley marcial y el agudo malestar económico, había radicalizado a la sociedad polaca, aproximándola a un violento estallido. Restos de Solidaridad que habían escapado, con el apoyo de la Iglesia, a la redada del Gobierno, resistieron el impulso de confrontar a éste con una huelga general. En su lugar hilvanaron una precaria organización secreta que propuso la resistencia pasiva.

Jaruzelski se encontraba dentro de una pinza que, por un lado, lo apretaba con la crisis económica y por el otro lo presionaba con las sanciones de los países de occidente. El General optó por hacer concesiones graduadas principalmente en los campos del derecho constitucional y la investigación de las crisis en Polonia comunista. A pesar de esas reformas la sociedad permanecía hostil y muchos polacos se exilaron en Europa y Estados Unidos. La Iglesia sirvió de refugio espiritual a quienes buscaban los más genuinos valores nacionales. Además, jugó un papel estabilizador, sirviendo de protectora de los derechos de la población y aconsejando una actitud conciliatoria. Lech Walesa fue liberado de su detención en noviembre de 1982. En junio de 1983 Juan Pablo II visitó a Polonia y en julio la ley marcial fue formalmente derogada. Polonia evolucionaba hacia la pacificación y la estabilidad. Pero la economía seguía en crisis y la población se mantenía escéptica u hostil. Sólo la Iglesia podría mediar entre el gobierno y el pueblo.

La Iglesia, muy particularmente el Papa Juan Pablo II, tenía lazos muy estrechos con Solidaridad, de manera que un importante paso hacia la reconciliación se dió cuando Jaruzelski anunció una amplia amnistía para los líderes y asesores de Solidaridad. Sin embargo, el asesinato del Reverendo Jerzy Popieluszko, conocido por sus sermones antigubernamentales, en octubre de 1984, así como otros hechos pudieron haber aumentado las tensiones si no hubiera sido por el rápido y ejemplar castigo de los culpables. En noviembre de 1985 Jaruzelski pasó a ser Jefe de Estado mientras Zbigniew Messner lo sustituía como Primer Ministro. Algunos destacados miembros de la línea dura perdieron sus posiciones. Pero la economía no reaccionaba y la sociedad permanecía dividida. Parecía validarse el mensaje de Solidaridad de que las reformas políticas eran una precondición para una exitosa reforma económica. Ciertamente, no había habido reformas políticas significativas y la economía yacía en ruinas.

El Partido Comunista polaco pierde el poder: Los males económicos que afectaban a Polonia también se hacían sentir en el resto del Bloque Soviético, especialmente en la URSS. Mikhail Gorbachev ascendía en 1985, en esas adversas circunstancias, al cargo de Secretario General del Partido Comunista de la Unión Soviética y, con vista a superarlas, decidía acometer reformas políticas y económicas similares a las que el General Jaruzelski avanzaba, todavía sin éxito, en Polonia. El parecido enfoque de ambos líderes creó simpatías recíprocas, las que darían amplitud de maniobra al General tal como poder extender, en septiembre de 1986, una amnistía condicional a los restantes 225 prisioneros políticos y tomar otras medidas de liberalización. Los Estados Unidos en febrero de 1987 levantaron las sanciones aún vigentes.

Solidaridad dejaba atrás la lucha sindical y ponía su atención ahora en las reformas al sistema, adoptando una posición a favor de la economía de mercado. En enero de 1987 Jaruzelski hacía una visita oficial a Italia y al Vaticano, donde sostuvo conversaciones con Juan Pablo II. Cinco años antes, el 7 de junio de 1982 el Presidente Ronald Reagan había visitado también al Papa. Al día siguiente Reagan, en Londres, predijo el final del Imperio Soviético acreditando a Polonia el papel de eje del proceso. La reunión del presidente estadounidense y el papa polaco daría muchos frutos en la coordinación de esfuerzos para finalidades deseadas por ambos. Ahora, en 1987, entraba a la Santa Sede el Jefe de Estado de Polonia. Se dice que en la entrevista Jaruzelski informó al Papa que su gobierno estaba derrotado, que no había futuro para el comunismo en Polonia y que él estaba dispuesto a compartir el poder sin derramamiento de sangre. Mas tarde el General diría que le informó a Juan Pablo II sobre el papel que Gorbachev estaba jugando, sus intenciones, las dificultades que afrontaba, cuán importante era apoyarlo y comprenderlo y qué gran oportunidad era ésta para Europa y el mundo.

La turbulencia económica y política en Polonia continuó. Depués de varios intentos por alcanzar un modus faciendi, el Gobierno y Solidaridad, con la participación de un delegado de la Iglesia como observador neutral, iniciaron negociaciones en la histórica "Mesa Redonda," las que determinaron que se celebrarían nuevas elecciones. Pronto el Sejm (parlamento) levantó la prohibición sobre Solidaridad dándole completo reconocimiento legal. Las elecciones tuvieron lugar el 4 de junio de 1989, ganando Solidaridad casi todos los cargos tanto en el Senado como en el Sejm. El 19 de julio, según el acuerdo de la Mesa Redonda, el Sejm eligió como Presidente, así como Comandante en Jefe de las Fuerzas Armadas al General Jaruzelski, quien tendría amplios poderes en política exterior. La designación para la importante posición de primer ministro bajo la presidencia del General, causó tensiones que el 19 de agosto se resolvieron con la nominación de Tadeusz Mazowiecki, asociado de Walesa y periodista católico con estrechos lazos en la jerarquía eclesiástica. Así, un general comunista y un periodista católico asumían el poder juntos, en un esfuerzo por devolver a Polonia estabilidad y bienestar económico. Cuando líderes comunistas polacos expresaron reservas de participar en tal Gobierno, el propio Gorbachev respondió que él estaba dispuesto a aceptar un gobierno polaco con una minoría comunista y sugirió hacer lo mismo a los recalcitrantes. Había ocurrido un milagro: una dictadura totalitaria se había transformado, como resultado de las luchas del pueblo, de la Iglesia Católica y especialmente del proletariado polaco, en una democracia parlamentaria, todo ello a la sombra de la superpotencia campeona de la llamada dictadura del proletariado.

La crisis terminal del comunismo en Europa ocurrió como resultado de las fuerzas históricas, sociales, políticas, económicas, religiosas y éticas que se habían acumulado, unas a través de los siglos, otras como resultado de la ineficiencia económica y pobreza espiritual del marxismo. Aunque el actor principal del drama polaco fue el pueblo con su militancia, su valor, su prudencia y su persistencia, Polonia contó además con un grupo de hombres excepcionales, que dentro y fuera de sus fronteras, inclinaron la balanza de la historia. Wyszynski, Walesa, Wojtyla, Glemp, Jaruzelski, Gorbachev, Reagan y tantos otros, son acreedores a la gratitud de la humanidad por el liderazgo que ejercieron con extraordinario acierto en una situación casi insoluble. Entre esos nombres se incluyen los de dos líderes comunistas, Jaruzelski y Gorbachev, porque a ambos cabe la gloria de haber puesto valores éticos y el bienestar de sus propias naciones, por sobre las pequeñeces de las ideologías, los intereses de los partidos y las tentaciones de la egolatría.

Pronto, los acontecimientos de Polonia inspiraron una avalancha en al resto de Europa Oriental y una increíble transformación continental se puso en marcha.

FACTORES CRÍTICOS

Hemos pasado revista a los acontecimientos ocurridos en Cuba y Polonia que tienen un significado especial a los fines del presente trabajo. Esto nos permite ahora ofrecer un breve análisis de los factores que hicieron una contribución crítica a la liberación de Polonia, comparándolos con el comportamiento de los mismos factores en Cuba. Los subtítulos no deben entenderse como restringidos geograficamente, así por ejemplo, "En Cuba" comprende tanto la Isla como las actividades de las comunidades cubanas fuera de ella. Empecemos.

En Polonia: Los obreros

La capacidad de organización de los obreros y su militancia y voluntad de luchar por el bienestar y los derechos del proletariado y los valores de la nacionalidad, fueron decisivos en la transformación polaca. Nótese el alto precio pagado por los trabajadores de ese país, solamente en los disturbios de 1956 y 1970, el que ascendió a centenares de vidas, sin tener en cuenta los heridos y encarcelados. La formación de Solidaridad, la organización obrera que galvanizó la lucha del proletariado, fue el resultado de una larga maduración, de penalidades y de confrontación con las autoridades. De hecho, la existencia de Solidaridad fue un requisito, sine qua non, para la ulterior transformación de Polonia en un estado democrático. El aporte de líderes de la eficacia de Lech Walesa fue decisivo.

En Cuba: Los obreros

Los obreros cubanos, por largo tiempo antes de la Revolución, habían tenido y ejercido el derecho a organizarse y luchar por sus intereses de clase usando los medios típicos de los conflictos sindicales como la huelga. La Confederación de Trabajadores de Cuba (CTC) fue característica de esa época así como, en su clase, una de las organizaciones más poderosas en América Latina. Todo ello terminó rapidamente cuando, una vez en el poder el régimen castrista, éste cambió la naturaleza de la CTC y estableció un estricto control de los obreros, profesionales, etc., control al que añadió la presión de nuevas organizaciones tales como el Ejército Rebelde, la Milicia, los Comités de Defensa de la Revolución, etc. La CTC de hecho dejó de representar los intereses de los trabajadores para convertirse en parte del aparato de control del régimen. A diferencia de Polonia, en Cuba no existían las concentraciones de industrias tales como las de Gdánsk, Gdynia, Sopot, Tarnów, Katowice y otras, que por aglutinar multitud de obreros en pequeñas áreas, facilitaban organizar la resistencia con efectividad. En la Isla, por lo contrario, en la mayor industria, la azucarera, debido a su dispersión en las zonas rurales, se dificultó organizar movimientos de masa.

En Polonia: Las políticas marxistas

Las políticas marxistas no se implantaron en Polonia de la forma radical en que ocurrió en Cuba, lo que permitió que sobrevivieran estructuras religiosas, sociales y económicas no comunistas, en las cuales pudo apoyarse más tarde la resistencia al régimen. Por ejemplo, la propiedad rural en Polonia quedó en un 75% en poder de dueños privados, mientras que en Cuba ese porcentaje osciló alrededor del 25%. Además, Polonia experimentó cierto libre juego de las fuerzas políticas marxistas y registró cambios de gobierno dentro del marxismo. Los nuevos gobiernos frecuentemente introdujeron variaciones sustantivas en las políticas del estado y produjeron alternancia en el liderazgo, al mismo tiempo que reforzaban importantes cambios ya introducidos.

En Cuba: Las políticas marxistas

Castro aplicó en Cuba, con rigor y fidelidad, los principios en que descansa la autocracia, o sea, la metodología consagrada no solamente por los autores marxistas, sino también por los autores clásicos que han tratado de los medios de conquistar el poder absoluto y retenerlo indefinidamente. Esa aplicación rigurosa por parte de Castro obedeció tal vez menos a convicciones ideológicas que a inclinaciones de su personalidad egocéntrica y a conveniencias tácticas y estratégicas con vista a manipular directamente todos los resortes del poder y privar de su uso a sus adversarios. Además, Castro ha ejercido el poder omnímodo continuamente desde un principio, lo que le ha permitido evitar los cambios de política típicos de las situaciones, como en Polonia, donde se compartió y alternó el poder. Si ha habido cambios en Cuba éstos han sido impuestos por la fuerza de las circunstancias, pero en esos casos a Castro le ha quedado siempre un margen para maniobrar. Además, una vez que las circunstancias lo han vuelto a permitir, Castro ha suprimido los cambios y ha regresado a su propio modelo.

En Polonia: La Iglesia Católica

En Polonia el gobierno comunista no intentó un desmantelamiento de la Iglesia tan agresivo como el que se llevó a cabo en Cuba. Por otra parte la Iglesia polaca, probablemente hubiera podido resistir con mayor éxito cualquier ataque, que la Iglesia cubana, debido a diferencias importantes en la historia de ambas. Esas diferencias contribuyeron a que la Iglesia en Polonia reuniera los requisitos para asumir con éxito el extraordinario papel que asumió, tan pronto las circunstancias lo hicieron aconsejable.

Consecuentemente, a pesar del establecimiento del régimen comunista, la Iglesia polaca logró permanecer robusta y decidida defensora de los valores cristianos y los de la nacionalidad. El prestigio y organización de la Iglesia bajo el liderazgo del Cardenal Stefan Wyszynski primeramente, y más tarde del Cardenal Karol Wojtyla, con su excepcional talento, dedicación y carisma, fueron factores cruciales en la feliz culminación de la lucha del pueblo polaco. La existencia dentro de la jerarquía eclesiástica de hombres de vastísima cultura, inteligencia y capacidad de liderazgo como el Cardenal Jósef Glemp, modeló no sólo la actuación de la propia Iglesia sino que le permitió servir como un andamiaje intelectual, moral y organizativo que dió apoyo al movimiento obrero que finalmente encarnó Solidaridad. En la cúpula eclesiástica el Cardenal Wojtyla, una vez investido como el Sumo Pontífice Juan Pablo II, actuó con excepcional efectividad, destacándose sus advertencias a los soviéticos, con severidad y firmeza pero sin provocación, sobre el costo que tendría para la URSS una intervención o el empleo de la violencia en Polonia. Otras veces coordinó acciones con países que compartían los puntos de vista del Vaticano, particularmente Estados Unidos, nación con la que se iniciaron contactos a través de Zbigniew Brzezinski, asesor de seguridad del gobierno de Jimmy Carter, contactos que se robustecieron durante el gobierno de Ronald Reagan mediante la intervención de William Casey, Director de la Agencia Central de Inteligencia. La realidad política de Polonia y la importancia de la Iglesia en esa realidad es ilustrada por la definición que se ha dado de los tres poderes de la nación polaca en la década de los años ochenta, los que según la misma estaban constituídos por la Iglesia, el Ejército y Solidaridad.

En Cuba: La Iglesia Católica y Juan Pablo II

Por razones cuyo análisis escapa al alcance de este trabajo, la Iglesia Católica en Polonia era más fuerte que su equivalente en Cuba, y estaba históricamente más vinculada a la nacionalidad y a los valores nacionales que la Iglesia de la Isla. Igualmente, por razones obvias, no puede establecerse paralelo con Cuba en lo que respecta a la función que el Papa desempeñó en Polonia. Por tanto, sólo consideraremos esa función con el fin de comprender mejor el proceso polaco y explorar algunos aspectos sobre los cuales el Papa podría formular sugerencias útiles a Cuba. Es de esperar que de la visita a la Isla del Sumo Pontífice a principios de 1998, se proyectará una duradera influencia espiritual constructiva sobre el pueblo cubano. Cuán significativa será esa influencia dependerá de los propios cubanos, muy particularmente de sus líderes (políticos y no políticos). Por todo eso examinaremos adelante brevemente, el papel que el Pontífice desempeñó en su tierra natal. Pero antes, tomemos nota del tratamiento que se dió a la iglesia cubana.

La Iglesia Católica en Cuba sufrió tempranas agresiones del régimen castrista. Según el Documento Final de las Comunidades de Reflexión Eclesial Cubana en la Diáspora (CRECED), "Usando como pretexto el ataque armado contra el régimen ocurrido en Playa Girón, Bahía de Cochinos, en abril de 1961, el gobierno allana iglesias, conventos, colegios católicos, centros de beneficiencia, etc. Al mes siguiente confisca la enseñanza privada, incluídas las universidades católicas de Villanueva y la más reciente Social Católica San Juan Bautista de la Salle y, de paso, los noviciados, las casas de ejercicios espirituales, los centros de Acción Católica, etc. Comienza también la expulsión de sacerdotes, que culminará en septiembre con la del Obispo Boza Masvidal y 131 sacerdotes, en el barco 'Covadonga.' Se determina la prohibición de todo acto católico fuera de los templos."

Fue esa agresión masiva contra la Iglesia un ejemplo de la técnica castrista que yo llamaría el "contragolpe" y que se ha repetido cuantas veces Castro lo ha creído necesario. Consiste en aprovechar una agresión real o ficticia "a la Revolución" para descargar sobre los culpables reales o imaginarios, el peso de una represión desproporcionada. Este procedimiento le ha servido para atemorizar adversarios y despojarlos de los medios que podrían permitirles oponerse al régimen.

Entre los incalculables servicios de Juan Pablo II a la causa de Polonia destaca la defensa firme y responsable de los derechos de ese país y sus ciudadanos. Siendo el jefe de una iglesia universal por propia definición, no olvidó en momento alguno su condición de polaco. Tal vez de ese indudable compromiso con la nación, dependió su éxito al propiciar un final feliz a la grave crisis de su patria terrenal. Tal compromiso con la nación le dió, además, una enorme influencia moral entre los disidentes lo que le permitió moderar, cuando fue necesario, las acciones de éstos y así dejar sin pretextos cualquier intento bolchevique de usar la fuerza en respuesta a probables acciones violentas. La elección de Wojtyla a la silla de San Pedro no tan solo situó en una de las posiciones más importantes del mundo a un ilustre hijo de Polonia, sino que restituyó a la nación polaca el merecido respeto y prestigio que habrían querido negarle los vecinos ambiciosos y brutales que repetidamente ensangrentaron su suelo. Y de esa elección se alegrarían todos los polacos: los católicos y los escépticos. Los comunistas se alegrarían también, porque en lo más profundo de sus sentimientos prevalecería, como prevaleció más tarde, la lealtad a la patria por sobre la lealtad a la ideología marxista.

La capacidad de los polacos de hacer descansar la lucha del pueblo, en aquellos valores que, como una estrella polar, orientan los más genuinos sentimientos de la nación, dió una gran unidad a esa lucha. Especialmente, la libró del desgaste que en el caso de Cuba ha producido la dispersión, el antagonismo ideológico y el desperdicio de fuerzas cuando éstas se han dedicado a tareas periféricas. El 2 de junio de 1979 al aterrizar el avión que traía a Varsovia por primera vez al Papa Juan Pablo II, las campanas de las iglesias comenzaron a tañer en todo el territorio de Polonia. El Papa fue recibido por dos niñas que le ofrecieron ramos de flores de los colores de Polonia (blanco y rojo) y del Vaticano (blanco y amarillo). Ese día a lo largo del país no se habría podido encontrar una sola bandera comunista. Más de un millón y cuarto de fieles atendería, después, a una misa al aire libre en Czestochowa. El viaje del Papa superaba las expectativas. La Iglesia Católica reafirmaba su aptitud para ejercer el papel de pastor del pueblo polaco en las horas difíciles que pronto vendrían. Y ese pueblo concretaba su capacidad de aglutinarse alrededor de instituciones, ideas y valores comunes. Dios quiera que el Papa en su viaje a Cuba, como lo hizo en Polonia, haya infundido en los cubanos la voluntad de exaltar los más bellos ideales que han inspirado históricamente a la nación cubana y de velar por el bienestar de todos los hijos de la Isla. Así, Juan Pablo II habría añadido el nombre de Cuba al de Polonia entre los países que habrían podido vencer las limitaciones materiales y morales impuestas por regímenes opresivos.

En Polonia: El liderazgo, los valores nacionales

Otros importantes factores que favorecieron la victoria del pueblo polaco fueron la exaltación de los valores nacionales con que se impregnó el movimiento disidente, y la competencia de su liderazgo. La lucha se planteó por Polonia, sus valores cristianos, su cultura, sus intereses, su libertad, su dignidad, su integridad, el respeto a sus ciudadanos, la salvaguardia de los intereses de sus trabajadores. ¿Qué polaco habría

podido objetar ese programa? Sobre los máximos dirigentes comunistas del gobierno polaco se dice que, en ocasiones críticas, actuaron más como hijos de Polonia que como miembros del partido de la hoz y el martillo. Pudieron hacerlo, precisamente porque los ideales que inspiraron al pueblo de Polonia apelaban a los más profundos sentimientos polacos y no eran innecesariamente hostiles o agresivos frente a los adversarios. Esto nos lleva a la siguiente reflexión sobre la que volveremos más tarde: es necesario que una transformación nacional profunda y trascendental, costosa en recursos, en dolor o en peligros, se inspire en valores de universal y hondo significado para toda la sociedad, y no en intereses y sentimientos que sólo motivan a una minoría.

En Cuba: El liderazgo, los valores nacionales

El liderazgo de la oposición contra Castro estuvo dividido desde el primer momento. Los partidarios de Batista y los personajes políticos y económicos asociados con ellos constituyeron el primer contingente de la oposición. Pronto le siguieron quienes originalmente colaboraron en el gobierno de Castro pero se desilusionaron y lo abandonaron. Este grupo ha continuado aumentando durante la vida del régimen.

Mientras Castro ha fingido devoción de la Revolución a los valores nacionales, la oposición a su régimen, salvo excepciones, no solamente ha sido descuidada y poco convincente al respecto, sino que a menudo ha demostrado escasa sensibilidad y respeto hacia los más importantes símbolos culturales de la nación. Este es el caso del abandono del idioma español en segmentos de las nuevas generaciones, o del uso del español y el inglés en muchas comunidades cubanas en Estados Unidos, en las que con frecuencia, por razones triviales, se prefiere el idioma de Shakespeare al de Cervantes. ¿Qué mensaje lleva a los cubanos de la Isla esa preferencia? Si queremos comunicarnos con el pueblo cubano, obviamente debemos hacerlo en español que es el idioma de Cuba y el que entienden los cubanos. Sin embargo, lastima la sensibilidad la abundancia innecesaria con que se usa el inglés en conversaciones y diversos documentos. Un documento sobre Cuba escrito en inglés podrá provocar distintas reacciones en el cubano, que como la mayoría, solo conoce el español. La más benigna rección podría ser desechar el documento con un comentario como: "Esto no es para mí," lo cual estaría indicando un grado de marginación indeseable. Ciertamente la oposición a Castro, salvo honrosas excepciones, no ha logrado acreditar su identificación inequívoca con una cubanía íntegra.

En ambos países: La penuria económica y el hambre

Aristóles en *La política* escribió: "¿Cómo se sostienen las tiranías? Manteniendo al pueblo hambriento y ocupado, como hicieron los egipcios cuando construyeron las pirámides." Aristóteles se refiere a condiciones extremas de hambre y trabajo, las que por ser agobiantes no dan a la población el margen de tiempo, recursos y disposición de ánimo como para estructurar una revolución. En todo caso ese estado de penuria puede provocar motines, atentados y actos de terrorismo y sabotaje engendrados por la desesperación, pero no una revolución. La Revolución Americana, la Revolución Francesa y la Revolución Cubana las hicieron las clases acomodadas, porque eran las que tenían los recursos, el tiempo (y la educación) necesarios para llevarlas a cabo. Eso no significa que las clases más humildes no se incorporan a la revolución, porque de hecho lo hacen, pero al principio sólo como seguidores, cuando "el hambre y el exceso de trabajo" de que hablaba Aristóteles se lo permiten.

En Polonia la difícil situación económica contribuyó a la liberación, pero no por sí sola, sino en presencia de otros importantes factores que se analizan en este trabajo. Esos factores incluyen la organización y militancia de los obreros, la presencia de la venerada e influyente Iglesia Católica Polaca, el nacionalismo del pueblo, etc. En Cuba, ante la ausencia de factores equivalentes a los presentes en Polonia y bajo un régimen represivo de gran eficacia como tal, no se ha logrado organizar un movimiento capaz de dar vida a una república sagaz y cordial, sin otro dueño que el pueblo de Cuba. Lograrlo, es el desafío que afrontan los cubanos.

¿QUÉ DEBERÍAMOS HACER?

El estudio precedente de Cuba y Polonia sugiere respuestas probables a muchos de los problemas más apremiantes que plantea la cuestión cubana. Las respuestas, desde luego, deberán traducirse a la realidad

para que se conviertan en soluciones. Llevar a cabo esto último está pendiente y la responsabilidad de hacerlo descansa en los hombros de los cubanos. Ahora bien, conocer las probables soluciones es ya un gran paso adelante, porque lamentablemente con frecuencia hemos preferido ignorarlas.

Salvo una operación militar que no parece factible ni deseable, la liquidación de la tiranía en Cuba requeriría que se materializaran, al menos, los siguientes requisitos:

1. Sería útil que los cubanos contaran con una doctrina para orientar el cambio de la autocracia a la democracia. Esa doctrina debe contemplar todos los aspectos y actores importantes. Ningún sector debería quedar ignorado, marginado o innecesariamente sacrificado. Dada la precariedad de la economía cubana, será imposible satisfacer a plenitud a todos los sectores e individuos. Pero esas limitaciones no deben servir de excusa para justificar el sacrificio indebido de unos grupos en beneficio de otros.

2. Sin renunciar a los principios, deberá procurarse una comprensión de la cuestión cubana que no se apoye en dogmas o intransigencias, sino que se oriente en un afán por derivar de la larga tragedia de Cuba, una síntesis nacional que permita conducir al país en paz y con éxito, hacia la solución de sus problemas.

3. Las ideas básicas que deberían promoverse son aquellas que tienden a unificar, tales como:

   • las que apelan a todos los cubanos, los de la Isla y los de la diáspora, como son los conceptos de patria y bienestar general. Ningún lema sería mejor para inspirar a la ciudadanía que el pensamiento martiano "con todos y para el bien de todos";

   • las que promueven la participación efectiva de la ciudadanía en las decisiones nacionales, mediante la devolución de la soberanía al pueblo de Cuba. ¿Cómo seguir aceptando que una persona (Castro) o que en nombre de una figura retórica (la Revolución) se gobierne al país por décadas sin una consulta substantiva al pueblo?

4. Debería darse a la política cubana y a la subsecuente gestión del gobierno un contenido nacionalista afirmativo (no agresivo), evitando el deslumbramiento ante el poder o la riqueza de otras naciones que, por ser diferentes, no deben ser tomadas como modelos para compararlas con Cuba. El pueblo cubano ha profesado un credo nacionalista a lo largo de su historia y se engañarían los dirigentes que, en busca de ventajas transitorias, trataran de ignorar o menospreciar ese credo.

5. La política exterior y el ordenamiento económico futuro de Cuba deberían tener en cuenta los diversos factores sociológicos, históricos, geopolíticos, etc., que inciden en la cuestión, pero lo determinante debe ser el interés de Cuba y el de los cubanos.

6. A fin de llevar a cabo las tareas conducentes a la reunificación del pueblo de Cuba, es conveniente que los cubanos se organicen en una única estructura operativa. Decimos "estructura operativa" porque no creemos que puede aspirarse a una unidad total. Consideramos ilusorio esperar consenso en la solución del cúmulo de importantes problemas que aguardan, luego de cuatro décadas de un régimen autocrático consagrado al narcisismo. Afortunadamente muchos de esos problemas han sido estudiados en forma reposada por competentes expertos, y los resultados de tales estudios sólo esperan actualizaciones finales, aprobación autorizada y la capacidad ejecutiva para ponerlos en práctica. Además, la democracia tiene mecanismos apropiados para dirimir casos polémicos. Tales mecanismos incluyen la convocatoria a una asamblea constituyente; elecciones generales; consultas vía referéndum o plebiscitos; etc. Ahora sólo se requeriría convenir en la citada estructura operativa y en un programa de trabajo destinado a dar fin al presente statu quo en Cuba. Una estructura operativa existió en la Segunda Guerra Mundial entre líderes tan disímiles como Roosevelt, Churchill y Stalin. También se debería acordar que la resolución de los asuntos

polémicos de interés nacional, se someterían a la decisión del pueblo mediante los mecanismos democráticos antes señalados. Sería ésta una garantía que los dirigentes darían a los cubanos de que los principios democráticos serían efectivamente respetados.

7. Si bien es importante promover las ideas unificadoras, lo es también evitar las ideas disociadoras. A ese fin procedería lo siguiente:

- Desalentar las ideas que fomentan o acentúan la división entre los cubanos, como la llamada ley Helms-Burton. Esa ley responde a los intereses económicos y políticos de los Estados Unidos, no a los de Cuba. Es más, ha habido informes de prensa recientes que atribuyen al gobierno estadounidense, respecto al terreno que ocupa su Embajada en Varsovia, la misma conducta de beneficiario de propiedades confiscadas por el antiguo régimen comunista de Polonia, que la citada ley condena en relación con la misma cuestión en Cuba. Los informes de prensa mencionan otros casos similares en otros países del Este de Europa. No gravemos a Cuba, además de lo mucho que pesa sobre ella, con la carga del servicio a intereses económicos ajenos y a carreras políticas sin raíces cubanas.

- Evitar las acciones que ocupan tiempo y recursos en actividades periféricas que poco o nada tienen que ver con la médula del problema cubano.

- Evitar la tendencia a confiar el destino de Cuba a potencias extranjeras. En el caso de Estados Unidos se ha visto claramente la falta de resultados satisfactorios después de Playa Girón, de la crisis de los cohetes, de la caída de la Unión Soviética y del paso por la Casa Blanca de nueve presidentes en un período de cuarenta años. Cada país tiene sus propios intereses y su particular dinámica política y a ellos sirve, no a los de países ajenos, y así han hecho los Estados Unidos, lo cual no debería sorprender. Ahora bien, la renuncia a confiar el destino de Cuba a otra potencia no debe descartar, como decía Martí "la amistad durable y deseable de los Estados Unidos y de Cuba."

- Suprimir los ataques entre los distintos grupos o personalidades que luchan por el restablecimiento de la democracia en Cuba. Esos ataques han sido un serio obstáculo a la formación de un poderoso movimiento capaz de liberar a Cuba. Obviamente, tal movimiento para ser efectivo deberá contar con líderes creativos que el pueblo de Cuba identifique como suyos.

- Desalentar que se proponga como objetivos nacionales lo que no es sino intereses de grupos, generalmente en conflicto con sectores más numerosos de la población.

8. La tiranía debe ser atacada preferentemente donde es más vulnerable a los ojos del pueblo de Cuba. Pocos hechos ofenden más a los cubanos que los privilegios que disfrutan, en detrimento de los ciudadanos del país, los extranjeros en general y los turistas en particular. Si a muchos habitantes de la Isla les resulta indiferente la "economía de mercado" y otros componentes de la propaganda habitual de los opositores a la tiranía, seguramente se enrojecen de ira cuando son impedidos de entrar en una playa cubana mientras un turista extranjero la disfruta con la protección de la fuerza pública. Ese tipo de situación y otras similares son las que deben constituir una parte substancial del material de divulgación que se dirija a Cuba.

Finalmente, como se señala en otra parte de este trabajo, es necesario que una transformación nacional profunda y trascendental, costosa en recursos, en dolor o en peligros, se inspire en valores de universal y hondo significado para toda la sociedad, y no en intereses y sentimientos que solo motivan a una minoría.

EL MENSAJE DE SU SANTIDAD

Juan Pablo II al besar la tierra cubana el 21 de enero de 1998, traía en sus recuerdos una niñez humilde, el dolor de su propia familia abatida por el reiterado flagelo de la muerte, la vivencia de la brutal ocupación nazi de su tierra natal, el subsiguiente control de su patria por comunistas al servicio de Moscú, las luchas heroicas del pueblo polaco por el respeto a sus derechos individuales y nacionales, el delicado papel jugado por la Iglesia y por el propio Pontífice en defensa de Polonia, al oponerse a los abusos de una superpotencia termonuclear, y tantos otros de esos tipos de recuerdos que dejan profundas huellas en el espíritu. Además, los labios que besaban la tierra cubana, eran labios por los que fluían ocho idiomas del mundo, respaldados por una rica y elaborada cultura que no parecía tener límites. El augusto visitante así iniciaba su jornada en la tierra de Martí, de Varela y de tantos otros hijos amorosos de Cuba.

¿Qué llevaba el Papa a la Isla del Caribe? Además de su presencia y su talento, el Papa llevaba un mensaje a los cubanos, especialmente necesario por la esterilidad de cuarenta años en los que la reconocida inteligencia de los hijos de Cuba parece haber sufrido un prolongado eclipse político. El mensaje se fundamenta en un estado de cosas en Cuba que el Pontífice define con sinceridad.

Tal estado de cosas incluye los grandes problemas que gravitan sobre la sociedad. Entre estos, el Papa analizó los diversos retos y dificultades que agobian a la familia en la Isla, tales como las carencias materiales y el poder adquisitivo muy limitado de los salarios. Adelante señala el Pontífice la separación forzosa de las familias dentro del país y la emigración, lo que ha desgarrado a incontables hogares y ha sembrado dolor en una parte considerable de la población. En éste como en otros aspectos, el discurso del Pontífice es claro y sincero, pero exento de las provocaciones que suelen ganar aplausos fáciles, aunque estériles, de la galería. Ese discurso es por sí mismo una denuncia del régimen, por cuanto la responsabilidad de éste respecto de las deficiencias señaladas por Juan Pablo II, no puede ignorarse después de que los actuales mandatarios han permanecido en el poder durante cuarenta años.

En general, el mensaje apóstolico descansa en la convicción del Santo Padre de que los cubanos "son y deben ser los protagonistas de su propia historia personal y nacional." Señala el Papa que él acompaña sus mejores votos "para que esta tierra pueda ofrecer a todos una atmósfera de libertad, de confianza recíproca, de justicia social y de paz duradera. Que Cuba se abra con todas sus magníficas posibilidades al mundo y que el mundo se abra a Cuba..."

Atmósfera de libertad, confianza recíproca, justicia social, paz duradera. Esas ideas caracterizan un estado de cosas antagónico con la situación que prevalece en Cuba. Estas y otras expresiones del Pontífice lo sitúan en una posición genuinamente revolucionaria respecto del statu quo en la Isla. Revolucionaria, porque pretende cambiar una situación indeseable por otra que satisfaga las aspiraciones de los cubanos. Y es Castro quien, al defender el estado de cosas actual, se hace abanderado de la contrarrevolución.

El arzobispo de Santiago de Cuba, Monseñor Meurice, no dejó dudas sobre la unidad de pensamiento existente entre el Sumo Pontífice y la Iglesia Católica Cubana cuando afirmó: "...este es un pueblo noble y es también un pueblo que sufre. Este es un pueblo que tiene la riqueza de la alegría y la pobreza material que lo entristece y agobia casi hasta no dejarlo ver más allá de la inmediata subsistencia." Luego añadió: "Nuestro pueblo es respetuoso de la autoridad y le gusta el orden, pero necesita aprender a desmitificar los falsos mesianismos."

Juan Pablo II reiteró, significativamente, el pensamiento martiano sobre la construcción del futuro de Cuba "con todos y para el bien de todos." Esta debería ser la piedra angular de la nueva política cubana. Con todos, con los hombres y mujeres de todas las razas, con los pobres, con los ricos, con los que han tenido el privilegio de recibir educación y con los que no lo han tenido. Todos, en el diccionario de la Real Academia Española se define como "cosa íntegra, o que consta de la suma y conjunto de sus partes integrantes, sin que falte ninguna.". Recuérdese, sin que falte ninguna. Porque si alguien propusiera que deben ser todos pero excluyendo algunos que no reunan ciertos requisitos, estaríamos suprimiendo del pensamiento de Martí un concepto básico.

El Papa, al recordar el pensamiento martiano, proyecta sobre Cuba uno de los elementos esenciales que permitieron resolver felizmente en paz la grave crisis de Polonia. No se debe perder de vista que la derrota electoral del Partido Comunista en Polonia en 1989 se produjo dentro de un proceso en el cual participaron pacíficamente los diversos sectores. En la tierra natal del Papa y dentro de su influencia pontificia, se llevó a cabo una solución al problema polaco bajo la inspiracion de un principio equivalente a "con todos y para el bien de todos." Hoy Polonia, disfrutando una paz que le fue negada bajo el comunismo, adelanta en el camino de la prosperidad. Hoy, cuando el obispo de Roma entrega a los cubanos su mensaje, nos corresponde agradecer a la Providencia el poder enriquecernos con los frutos del talento de dos hombres excepcionales, Jose Martí y Juan Pablo II, uno cubano, polaco el otro, coincidiendo ambos en la fórmula que podría devolver a Cuba la paz y la prosperidad con todos y para el bien de todos.

OBRAS CONSULTADAS

Aristotle, *Politics*. New York: Gramercy Books, 1971.

Bernstein, Carl and Politi, Marco. *His Holiness*. New York: Doubleday, 1996.

Comunidades de Reflexión Eclesial Cubana en la Diáspora (CRECED), *Documento Final*. CRECED, 1993.

Foreign Area Studies. *Area Handbook for Cuba*. Washington: The American University, 1971.

Foreign Area Studies, *Cuba a Country Study*. Washington: The American University, 1985.

Halecki, O., et al. *A History of Poland*. New York: Barnes & Noble, 1993.

International Bank for Reconstruction and Development in collaboration with the Government of Cuba, *Report on Cuba* (Washington, 1951).

L'Osservatore Romano, Ciudad del Vaticano, *Crónica y Discursos Pronunciados por Juan Pablo II Durante su Viaje Apostólico a Cuba* (Enero de 1998).

The Polish Americans, Public Television, MPT (Maryland Public Television). Video.

Sienkiewicz, Henryk. *Quo Vadis?* San Francisco: Ignatius Press, 1993.

COMENTARIOS A

"Cuba y Polonia: Semejanzas, Diferencias," de Raúl Fernández

Carlos N. Quijano

Antes que nada quisiera expresar mi agradecimiento a Raúl Fernández por haber enviado su trabajo con bastante anticipación. El trabajo de Raúl es un documento interesante y sin dudas una contribución a esta conferencia. Mis comentarios están enviados en tres partes. Primero: aspectos metodológicos generales. Segundo: algunas sugerencias con respecto a los aspectos analíticos. Y finalmente, algunos comentarios sobre los temas normativos del documento.

Tradicionalmente los tres ejercicios más difíciles en las ciencias sociales han sido:

- hacer análisis históricos comparativos;

- comprender y explicar la lógica generalizable que se encuentra en funcionamiento en los procesos revolucionarios; y

- la formulación de predicciones de cambios sociales, o sea, la búsqueda de un futuro cuyas posibilidades se encuentran en el presente

Recientemente hemos encontrado uno nuevo: la política económica de las transiciones. La transición de las antiguas economías socialistas hacia una economía de mercado y una sociedad democrática.

El análisis histórico comparativo requiere conocimientos acerca de la historia, cultura, estructura social, economía e idioma de ambos países. Comprender y explicar la lógica de una revolución es un reto metodológico, ya que necesariamente tenemos que seguir tres pasos: primero, analizar su historia en las acciones sociales; segundo, explicar esas acciones por una lógica situacional; y por último, comprobar la

explicación mediante evidencia empírica. Muchos han tratado, y hoy en día hay varias escuelas que van desde las explicaciones antropológicas hasta la imaginería volcánica: el cambio convulsiona la sociedad; el descontento hierve, la violencia estalla. La formulación de predicciones de cambios sociales es también fascinante, sobre todo cuando el análisis es ex-post facto. Siempre se encuentra todo tipo de razón y explicación acerca de por qué ocurren los cambios. Desafortunadamente el récord de estas predicciones es pobre. No creo que exista ningún cambio social importante que haya sido pronosticado por los politólogos o economistas. Todas las revoluciones han sido sorpresas, tanto para los vencedores como para los derrotados. En la Revolución Francesa, tanto Luis XV como los que tomaron la Bastilla fueron los más sorprendidos. En el caso de la Revolución Cubana, no hubo nadie que hizo la predicción que el dictador Fulgencio Batista iba a tomar un avión para marcharse fuera del país. Tanto sus seguidores como Fidel Castro, y todos los que participaron en la Revolución, fueron de nuevo sorprendidos el 31 de diciembre de 1958.

Un ejemplo más reciente fue la sorpresa de 1989. La Academia Americana de Artes y Ciencias Sociales reunió a una docena de especialistas de Europa Central y del Este, incluyendo algunos residentes de la región. Se les pedía que intentaran explicar los desarrollos que estaban teniendo lugar en la región. Los trabajos fueron revisados durante 1988 para su publicación en 1990. De más está decir que ninguno de los participantes habían previsto lo que sucedió.

Los cambios dramáticos que han ocurrido y están ocurriendo en los países que fueron economías centralmente planificadas presentaron y presentan retos formidables a todos aquellos que se dedican a estudiar dichos acontecimientos. La realidad es que ninguna de las disciplinas, sea economía, sociología o las ciencias políticas, aún no nos ofrecen individual o conjuntamente una teoría que explique con exactitud los cambios, y menos todavía que nos sirvan de base para hacer predicciones.

Desde luego, estas dificultades no nos impiden, ni deberían impedir, que individuos como todos los aquí presentes persigamos con ahínco nuestros instintos y tratemos de expandir nuestros conocimientos sobre algunos de los problemas específicos de la transición hacia una economía de mercado y una democracia pluripartidista en Cuba. Este es el caso de la monografía acerca de la cual hoy comentamos — "Cuba y Polonia: Semejanzas, diferencias."

Creo que la monografía es una contribución importante para esclarecer algunos de los complejos problemas que podemos hallar, como dice su autor, "en la búsqueda de una solución cubana."

Yo estoy de acuerdo con mucho de lo que este estudio señala, pero quizás para no defraudar al público me gustaría señalar algunos puntos en los cuales se podría quizás reforzar el análisis, sobre todo en aquellos aspectos donde no se definen muy claramente las diferencias entre ambos países.

Primero, las diferencias que existen entre la posición de la Iglesia Católica. En los años 70, la Iglesia Católica en Polonia contaba con 15,544 sacerdotes, 26,586 monjas, 12,213 iglesias, 2,949 conventos, 46 seminarios, cuatro facultades papales, una universidad católica y una academia de teología. La prensa católica publicaba 15 importantes revistas. En resumen, la Iglesia Católica era una fuerza terrenal y espiritual que no se podía ignorar. Hoy día, la Iglesia Católica en Cuba cuenta solamente con 281 sacerdotes. No existen centros de enseñanza ni universidades, y si bien se publican algunas revistas como *Palabra nueva* y *Vitral*, su impacto es limitado.

Segundo, con respecto a la importancia del sector privado. En 1989, el sector privado en Polonia empleaba aproximadamente al 47% de la fuerza laboral.

En Cuba en 1996, si contamos los empleados de las Unidades Básicas de Producción y las Cooperativas, este coeficiente era el 24%; y si no los contamos era solamente 13.5%. Además, en Polonia en 1989 ya existían 15,552 compañías privadas, 429 joint ventures, 813,145 empresas privadas de dueños individuales, y como bien señala el documento, la agricultura estaba prácticamente en manos privadas (73.5%). Las comparaciones con Cuba en estos aspectos son desconsoladoras.

Aunque el documento describe los eventos que antecedieron a lo ocurrido en Polonia antes de 1989, quizás valdría la pena hacer algunas referencias a lo ocurrido en otros países cercanos en el sentido que lo que pasó en Polonia es un ejemplo clásico de cambio gradual y no de Revolución. En resumen, fue un cambio que resultó de una combinación de presión desde abajo pero también cambios desde arriba por una cúpula ilustrada, a diferencia de lo ocurrido en Hungría, Checoslovaquia, Bulgaria y desde luego, Rumania. Fue un movimiento continuo hacia la democracia, con algunas interrupciones a partir del año 1956 cuando el estalinismo fue derrotado, y ya para el año 1976 de los 460 escaños en el parlamento, 261 eran del Partido Comunista, 113 del Partido de los Campesinos, 37 del Partido Demócrata, 36 no asociados con ningún partido, y 13 activistas católicos.

Ese fue el telón de fondo a lo que pasó en 1989. ¿Y qué fue lo que pasó en 1989? Pasaron tres cosas simultáneamente. Primero: el Partido Comunista perdió las elecciones. Segundo: Solidaridad ganó. Tercero: el Partido Comunista aceptó que Solidaridad ganara las elecciones. Eso suena como un silogismo. Pero el hecho real es que se permitió que hubiera elecciones. Además, Solidaridad ganó contra una oposición fuerte, incluyendo contra candidatos demócrata-cristianos apoyados públicamente por la alta jerarquía de la Iglesia Católica. También valdría la pena señalar que las elecciones en Polonia se celebraron el 4 de junio de 1989, o sea, el mismo día en que ocurrió la masacre de Tianamen. Es decir, que hay intentos de cambios que fracasan. En resumen, la transición en Polonia, como bien señala el documento, tiene características especiales. Pero quizás valdría la pena hacer hincapié en aquellos aspectos que no solamente la diferencian del caso de Cuba sino también de otras transformaciones de Europa Central y del Este.

El documento también sugiere una serie de respuestas a muchos de los problemas más acuciantes que plantea la cuestión cubana. Esta es una sección útil, pero quizás valdría la pena aclarar algunas de las premisas sin descartar su tema principal de "todos para el bien de todos." Una de las recomendaciones es organizarse alrededor de una estructura operativa. Como objetivo eso puede ser deseable, pero no creo que, dada la historia de Cuba, la naturaleza del régimen, y la experiencia de otras transformaciones eso sea posible, y mucho menos recomendable. Si examinamos la experiencia de Polonia vemos que Solidaridad, como dice el documento, jugó un papel crucial, pero también es cierto que en el año 1988 la oposición al régimen polaco consistía de más de 60 grupos, movimientos independientes y partidos, además de cientos de organismos pequeños. No tengo cifras de la diáspora polaca, pero no creo que haya sido muy diferente de la cubana, quizás menos organizada.

Además, si examinamos el mensaje principal de todos los grupos y organizaciones que existen en la oposición al régimen en Cuba, vemos que hay unanimidad de criterio con respecto a tres principios fundamentales: Primero, todos respaldan los principios registrados en la Declaración Universal de los Derechos Humanos. Segundo, en materia política todos respaldan el principio de una democracia basada en elecciones libres y un sistema pluripartidista. Tercero, en materia económica todos respaldan el principio de una economía de mercado en todos sus matices.

El documento también hace referencia a la ley Helms-Burton como una ley que responde a los intereses económicos y políticos de los Estados Unidos. Eso es evidente, ya que es una ley emitida por el Congreso norteamericano. Podríamos estar de acuerdo o discutir si algunos de sus aspectos tienen un impacto nega-tivo o positivo para los intereses de Cuba, o si no valdría la pena eliminar los aspectos que tratan acerca de la exportación de alimentos y medicinas. Pero lo que no podemos ignorar es que la presión internacional también jugó un papel importante en lograr los cambios en Polonia. Como respuesta a la implantación de la ley marcial en Polonia en diciembre de 1981, los Estados Unidos y poco más tarde los gobiernos europeos impusieron sanciones severas. El levantamiento de las sanciones fueron condicionadas a la eliminación de la ley marcial, la libertad de presos políticos, y el restablecimiento del diálogo político entre el régimen, Solidaridad y la Iglesia Católica. Las sanciones económicas fueron eliminadas gradualmente después de 1984 en reconocimiento de las acciones por parte del régimen hacia una liberalización política y económica. Las relaciones tanto diplomáticas como económicas no se normalizaron hasta 1987, luego que el régimen de Jaruzelski anunciara en 1986 una amnistía general y reconociera tácitamente la existencia de la oposición política.

El documento también hace referencias a que debería darse un contenido más nacionalista afirmativo al discurso de oposición al régimen. En ese sentido yo sería un poco más cauteloso, ya que el nacionalismo ha sido quizás en Cuba, en algunos de sus aspectos más dogmáticos y arcaicos, un factor negativo en la formación de una sociedad estable y democrática. Quizás para terminar valdría la pena citar al Monseñor Pedro Meurice Estiu en su reciente discurso de bienvenida al Santo Padre:

> Le presento además, a un número creciente de cubanos que han confundido la Patria con un partido, la nación con el proceso histórico que hemos vivido en las últimas décadas y la cultura con una ideología. Son cubanos que al rechazar todo de una vez sin discernir, se sienten desarraigados, rechazan lo de aquí y sobrevaloran todo lo extranjero. Algunos consideran esta como una de las causas más profundas del exilio interno y externo.[1]

---

1. "Discurso de bienvenida al Papa Juan Pablo II pronunciado por el Monseñor Pedro Meurice Estiu en Santiago de Cuba, 24 de enero de 1998," en *Juan Pablo con los cubanos* (Washington: Of Human Rights, 1998), p. 89.

BIBLIOGRAFIA

Daedalus. Journal of the American Academy of Arts and Sciences. Winter 1990. Vol. 119, No. 1.

Dahrendorf, Rolf. *Reflections on the Revolution in Europe.* New York: Random House, Inc., 1990.

Garton Ash, Timothy. *The Magic Lantern: The Revolution of 89.* New York: Random House, 1990.

Rostowski, Sarah. *Macroeconomic Instability in Post-Communist Countries.* Oxford: Clarendon Press, 1998.

Sachs, Jeffrey. *Poland's Jump to the Market Economy.* Cambridge, Massachussetts: M.I.T. Press, 1993.

THE PENSION SYSTEM OF CUBA: THE CURRENT SITUATION AND IMPLICATIONS OF INTERNATIONAL PENSION REFORM EXPERIENCES FOR ADDRESSING CUBA'S PROBLEMS

Lorenzo L. Pérez[1]

Systems of financial support for old people are experiencing serious financial difficulties worldwide and the old-age, disability, and survivors' pension system of Cuba (the pension system from now on) is no exception to this trend. The pension system of Cuba has been extensively discussed in the literature by Mesa-Lago (see below) and it has also been analyzed in the 1994 and 1995 ASCE conferences by Buttari; Alonso, Donate-Armada and Lago; and Donate-Armada.[2] The objective of this paper is to analyze the current situation of Cuba's pension system; to review the proposals that have been advanced in the literature in recent years to strengthen the finances of pension systems throughout the world; to assess the experience of transition economies in reforming their pension systems; and to draw preliminary policy recommendations on how to reform the Cuban pension system.

The first section of the paper presents the main characteristics of Cuba's pension system: how it has evolved over the years, its coverage, the level of benefits, sources of financing, and the financial problems experienced in recent years. The second section reviews the recent literature regarding pension economics and reform proposals to address pension system problems, while the third reports on the pension reform experience of transition economies. The fourth section presents the paper's conclusions about possible reform initiatives for the Cuban pension system.

THE OLD-AGE, DISABILITY, AND SURVIVORS' PENSION SYSTEM OF CUBA

Cuba was one of the first countries to introduce a pension scheme (in the 1920s) and on the eve of the Cuban revolution in 1958 the country had one of the most developed pension systems among countries with similar levels of income.[3] However, there was no

1. The views expressed here of the author's and do not necessarily represent the official views of the International Monetary Fund. The author would like to thank Philip Gerson for useful comments and Jorge Pérez-Lopez for providing reference materials.

2. See Juan Buttari, "The Labor Market and Retirement Pensions in Cuba During the Transition: Reflection on the Social Safety Net Experience of Former Socialist Economies"; J. Alonso, R. Donate-Armada, A. Lago, "A First Approximation Design of the Social Safety Net for a Democratic Cuba"; and Donate-Armada, "Cuban Social Security: A Preliminary Actuarial Analysis of Law 324 of Social Security," all in *Cuba in Transition—Volume 4* (Washington: Association for the Study of the Cuban Economy, 1994). See also R. Donate-Armada, "Preliminary Analysis of Retirement Programs for Personnel in the Ministry of the Armed Forces and Ministry of Interior of the Republic of Cuba," in *Cuba in Transition—Volume 5* (Washington: Association for the Study of the Cuban Economy, 1995).

3. This discussion of the pension system in Cuba owes a great deal to the writings of Professor Carmelo Mesa-Lago. For a more wide-ranging discussion of the social security system of Cuba than contained in this section, see Carmelo Mesa-Lago, "La seguridad social y la pobreza en Cuba," in *La Seguridad Social en America Latina: Seis Experiencias Diferentes* (Buenos Aires/Alemania: Konrad-Adenauer-Stiftung-CIEDLA, 1996).

general pension program and pension coverage was fragmented among 52 autonomous programs that only covered certain groups in urban areas. Each of the programs had its own regulations and financing and there was no coordination among the programs. According to Mesa-Lago, the coverage of the pension programs totaled 55 to 63 percent of the economically active population (the second or third highest coverage in Latin America), but excluded the poorest segments of the population such as rural workers, the self-employed, domestic servants, and the unemployed.[4]

The revolutionary government of Cuba carried out a number of important reforms in the pension field. By 1962 a process of unifying the benefits and contribution rates of existing programs had been completed. A 1963 law widened the coverage of the pension system to all the salaried labor force and made the financing of the system a direct responsibility of the government. Between 1964 and 1983 the coverage was made pretty much universal as other groups of workers were incorporated into the pension program: the self-employed, small entrepreneurs, members of agricultural cooperatives, and small farmers that gave up the titles of their lands to the state. The armed forces and members of the internal security apparatus of the state were the only groups that were outside the general program, enjoying more generous pension benefits.

The retirement age in Cuba is currently 55 years for women and 60 years for men with 25 years of employment (Box 1). If the last 12 years of employment (or 75 percent of the total work period) is in dangerous or arduous work, the retirement age becomes 55 years for men and 50 years for women. There is a reduced pension (at 65 years for men and 60 years for women) with 15 years of employment. The retirement age in Cuba is lower than in most countries in Latin America (Table 1) which, combined with a higher life expectancy than in most Latin American

countries, results in longer retirement periods.[5] The retirement pension is equivalent to 50 percent of average earnings during the highest five of last ten years of employment (the portion of earnings above 3,000 pesos a year is reduced by half for purposes of this calculation), plus 1 percent of earnings for each year of employment beyond 25 years. Pensions increase between 1.5 percent to 4 percent for each year of delayed retirement between the ages of 60 and 65 for men and between the ages 55 and 60 for women and 1 percent a year thereafter. The maximum pension is 90 percent of average earnings. The pensions are not indexed. Members of the armed forces and the internal security personnel have a privileged system. They can retire with 25 years of service, there is no minimum age requirement, and a more generous average salary base is used to calculate pensions. On the other side of the spectrum, the self-employed have a less generous pension system.

Cuba's pension system is a defined-benefit, pay-as-you-go system (PAYG). Employers (i.e., the government, public enterprises, and some limited number of private enterprises) currently pay 14 percent of the wage bill to finance pension benefits. This is significantly lower than what was charged in other centrally planned countries in the early 1990s at the beginning of their transition period. Employees do not have to pay, while the self-employed pay a tax equivalent to 10 percent of their earnings. Given that almost all of the economically active population is employed by the state, in principle there should not be a serious problem of tax evasion. The central government covers the cash deficit of the pension system and the pension tax payments are part of the general tax revenues of the central government.

Cuba's budgetary figures from 1989 to 1997 show the dire financial situation of the pension system. Social security expenditure rose from 1,094 million pesos (equivalent to 5.3 percent of GDP) in 1989 to 1,707 million pesos (6.7 percent of GDP) in 1997.[6]

---

4. Mesa-Lago, "La Seguridad Social y la Pobreza," pp. 52-53.

5. Mesa-Lago, "La Seguridad Social y la Pobreza." Cuba's retirement age, on the other hand, is similar to that of the Baltic and former Soviet Union republics (Table 2).

Box 1. Cuba: Old-Age, Disability, and Survivors' Pension Program

First Laws

Numerous laws and decrees established separate pension systems for over 50 different occupations; superseded and unified by 1963 law. Self-employed, liberal professions, charcoal makers, and members of fishery cooperatives brought into consolidated system in 1964.

Current law

1979

Type of program: Social insurance system.

Coverage

All wage earners.

Special system for members of armed forces, Interior Ministry, self-employed, artists, and agricultural cooperatives.

Source of Funds

Insured person: None. (10 percent of earnings if self-employed.)

Employer contributes an amount equivalent to: 14 percent of payroll.

Government: Makes up deficit and also contributes as employer. Above contributions also finance sickness and maternity and work-injury programs.

Qualifying Conditions

Old-age pension: Age 60 (men) or 55 (women) with 25 years of employment (55 and 50 if last 12 years or 75 percent of employment is dangerous or arduous work).

Reduced pension, age 65 (men) or 60 (women) with 15 years of employment.

Retirement unnecessary, but total current income cannot exceed former income. Not payable abroad.

Disability pension: Full pension, physical or mental inability to work. Partial pension, inability to perform usual work. Employed when incapacity occurs if under age 23. If age 23 or over, number of years of employment needed to qualify increases with age. Partial pension at age 28 or older, requires three years of employment.

Survivor pension: Deceased was employed or pensioner at death, or employed within six months thereof and for three-fourths of adult life.

Old-Age Benefits

Old-age pension: 50 percent of average earnings (that portion of earnings above 3,000 pesos a year is reduced by 50 percent) during highest 5 of last 10 years, plus 1 percent of earnings for each year of employment beyond 25 years (1.5 percent if dangerous or arduous work). Increments of 1.5 percent to 4 percent for each year between the ages 60 and 65 for men and between the ages 55 and 60 for women for each year of deferred pension, 1 percent a year thereafter.

Reduced pension, 40 percent of average earnings, plus 1 percent of earnings for each year of employment beyond 15 years.

Minimum pension varies depending on level of average earnings and number of years of employment.

Minimum pension: 59 pesos per month or 79 pesos per month or 80 percent of wages, depending on average level of earnings and number of years of employment.

Maximum: 90 percent of average earnings.

Permanent Disability Benefits

Disability pension: 40 percent of average earnings (that portion of earnings above 3,000 pesos a year is reduced by 50 percent) during highest 5 of last 10 years, plus 1 percent of earnings per year of employment beyond 15 years.

Minimum and maximum pensions: Same as old-age pension.

Partial disability: 30 percent to 50 percent (40 percent to 60 percent in case of work injury or occupational disease) of lost earnings depending on number of years of employment up to 25 years, increased 1 percent for each year of employment above 25 years. During rehabilitation, 70 percent of former earnings.

If unable to find employment, 50 percent of former earnings in first year, 25 percent thereafter.

Survivor Benefits

Survivor pension: If deceased was employed at the time of death, pension will be 100 percent of earnings the first month and 50 percent for the next two months; if deceased was receiving a pension, then 100 percent of pension of insured for three months. Thereafter, 70 percent, 85 percent, or 100 percent of pension of insured for 1, 2, or 3 or more dependent survivors, respectively (80 percent, 90 percent, or 100 percent if pension of insured is less than 60 pesos a month). Divided equally among eligible dependents. Eligible dependents: Widow or female that had permanent relationship and is single, needy widower or male that had permanent relationship and is single, age 60 or disabled, orphans under age 17 or disabled, and needy parents.

Maximum pension for working widow: 25 percent of survivor pension.

Nonworking widow under age 40 and without dependents receives full pension for two years.

Widows age 40 or above who are unemployed receive complete pension.

Administrative Organization

Ministry of Labor and Social Security, administration of program through its Social Security and Social Assistance Directorate. Municipal social security offices and work centers process applications. Pensions paid through the Popular Savings Bank.

Source: U.S. Social Security Administration, Office of Research, Evaluation, and Statistics, *Social Security Programs Throughout the World—1997*, Research Report No. 65 (August 1997).

Table 1. Selected Latin American Countries: Basic Features of Public Pension Systems

	GNP per Capita (US$,1996)	Coverage	Financing Source	Pension contribution rates (% of earnings) Insured — Wage or Salaried	Insured — Self-employed	Employer	Statutory Pensionable Age — Men	Women	Years of Services	Benefits
Middle income countries										
Argentina	8380	Employed and self-employed persons, except for military personnel	PT,GR	11	27	16	64	59	30	Basic universal benefit(PBU): 2.5 AMPO[a] plus 1% for every year of contribution exceeding 30, up to max. Of 45 years
Brazil	4400	Employed and self-employed persons; separate systems for public employees and military	PT,GR	8-10	20	20	65[b]	60[b]	30	70% of avg. earnings in last 3 years plus 1% of avg. earnings for each year of contrib. Up to 100% of avg. earnings; Minimum.: 100% of minimum wage; Maximum: 956.57 reais (as of April 1997)
Chile-New system	4860	All workers; voluntary coverage for self-employed	PT,GR	13	13	0	65	60	20	Insured's contributions plus accrued interest; Minimum pension guaranteed by government
Uruguay	5760	Employed and self-employed persons; separate systems for bank employees, police, and armed forces	PT,GR	15-16		12.5-15	60	56[c]	35	50% of avg. earnings in last ten years; (822 new pesos/month, as of 1997); Maximum: 6425 new pesos/month (as of 1997)
Lower middle income countries										
Cuba	[d]	All wage earners; special systems for armed forces, self-employed, artists, and agricultural cooperatives.	PT,GR	0	10	14	60[e]	55[e]	25	50% of average earnings during highest 5 of last 10 years; Minimum: depending on avg. level of earnings, 59 pesos/month or 79 pesos/ month or 80% of wage; Maximum: 90% of average earnings
Costa Rica	2640	All workers; voluntary coverage for self-employed	PT,GR	2.5	4.5-7.25	4.75	61-11/12	59-11/12	38-10/12	60% of avg. earnings on highest 48 monthly wage during last 5 years; Minimum: 21000 colones/month; Maximum: 226056 colones/month
Bolivia-New system	830	All workers; voluntary coverage for self-employed	PT,GR	12.5	12.5	0	65	60		Contributions plus accrued interest.
Lower income countries										
Honduras	660	Employed persons, excluding domestic, casual, and agricultural workers (except those employed by employers with more than 10 permanent employees); coverage being extended gradually to different areas.	PT,GR	1		2	65	60	15	-40% of basic monthly earnings, plus increment of 1% of earnings for each 12 months of contrib. Beyond 60 months; Minimum pension: 50% of earnings; Maximum pension: 80% of earnings
Nicaragua	380	All workers (excluding domestic workers); voluntary coverage for self-employed; special system for miners, indigents and those who have performed services for the country	PT, GR	1.75		3.5	60[f]	60[f]	15	40% of avg. earnings during last 5,4, or 3 years plus 1.365% for each 50 weeks of contributions; Minimum: 66-2/3% min. salary plus family allowances; Maximum: 80% of earnings, if more than 2 times the min. salary

Source: Sources: World Bank, *World Bank Atlas*, 1998; and U.S. Social Security Administration. *Social Security Programs Throughout the World-1997.*

Notes: Financing Source, PT indicates Payroll tax, GR indicates General revenues.

a. AMPO is the average mandatory provisional contribution, determined by dividing the total employee's contributions by the total number of contributors. As of April 1997, the AMPO was 80.

b. Refers to urban employees. For rural employees 60(men) and 55(women).

c. Age for women gradually increased to 60 by year 2003.

d. Estimated to be lower middle income. Based on World Bank Atlas, the lower middle income range is US $766-US $3035.

e. Reduced pension, age 65 for men, age 60 for women with 15 years of services.

f. Age 55 for miners, teachers and the physically or mentally impaired.

Table 2. Selected BRO Countries: Basic Features of Public Pension Systems

	GNP per Capita (US$, 1996)	Coverage	Financing Source	Pension contribution rates (% of earnings) Insured — Wage or Salaried	Insured — Self-employed	Employer	Statutory Pensionable Age — Men	Women	Years of Services	Benefits
Armenia	630	All employees	PT	1		35	60	55	25(M),20(F)	60% of wage base[a]
Belarus	2070	All employed permanent residents	PT,GR	1		4.7-35	60	55	25(M),20(F)	55% of wage base[b]; Minimum: 100% minimum wage; Maximum: 75% of wage base
Estonia	3080	residents	PT,GR	0	20	20	60[c]	55[c]	25(M),20(F)	The basic pension sum is equal to national pension: National pension set by legislature and adjusted by CPI, national pension is 410 kroons as of April 1995
Georgia	850	All employed residents; special systems for aged, disabled, and survivors not eligible for employment-related social benefits	PT,GR	1		37	60	55	25(M),20(F)	55% of average earnings[d]; Minimum: 100% of minimum wage
Kazakhstan	1350	All employed residents	PT,GR	1		30	60-1/2	55-1/2	25(M),20(F)	60% of earnings; Minimum: 100% of social minimum established yearly in the Republic budget , 550 tenge as of January 1997
Kyrgyz Republic	550	All employees, special systems for aged disabled, and survivors not eligible for employment-related social benefits	PT, GR	2.5		34	60	55	25(M),20(F)	55% of average monthly wage[e]; Min. 100% of min. wage(75 soms as of January 1997)
Russian Federation	2410	Employed citizens, self-employed, and independent farmers	PT,GR	1	28	28	60	55	25(M),20(F)	55% of wage base[f]; Minimum: 78620 rubles as of March 1997; Maximum: 75% of wage base, not to exceed 3 times the minimum pension
Turkmenistan	940	All employees, special systems for aged disabled, and survivors not eligible for employment-related social benefit	PT,GR	1		37	60	55	25(M),20(F)	55% of assessed wage[g]; Minimum: 100% of minimum wage, minimum wage:1000 manats/month as of December 1994); Maximum: 10 times the minimum wage
Ukraine	1200	All employees	PT	1		37	60	55	25(M),20(F)	55% of wage base[f]; Minimum: 200% of min. wage, (minimum wage: 15 hryvnias/ month as of January 1997); Maximum: 75 % of wage base

Source: World Bank, *World Bank Atlas*, 1998; and U.S. Social Security Administration, *Social Security Programs Throughout the World-1997.*

Note: Financing source, PT indicates Payroll tax, GR indicates General revenues.

a.   Gross average earnings of any 5 consecutive years in last 15 years of covered employed.

b.   Wage base equals percentage of gross earnings in any 5 consecutive years in last 15 years.

c.   As of Jan. 1994, pensionable age has been rising by 6 months per year until reach 65 for men and 60 for women in 2007.

d.   Average wage in last year or last 5 years, whichever is higher.

e.   Average wage of any 60 consecutive months in last 15 years.

f.   Wage base equals gross average earnings in last 2 years or best 5 consecutive years of covered employed.

g.   Assessed wage equals percentage of gross average earnings in best 5 consecutive years in last 15 years.

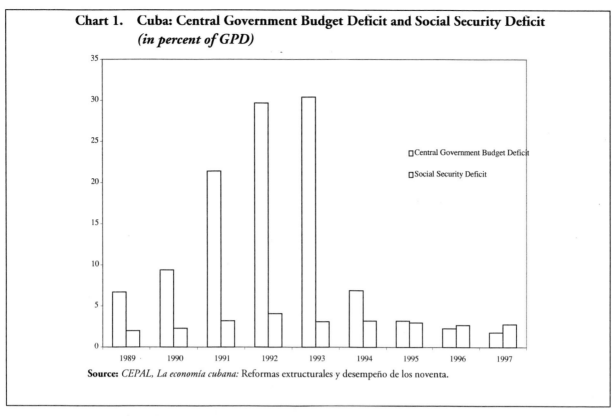

Chart 1. Cuba: Central Government Budget Deficit and Social Security Deficit *(in percent of GPD)*

☐ Central Government Budget Deficit

☐ Social Security Deficit

Source: *CEPAL, La economía cubana:* Reformas extructurales y desempeño de los noventa.

Old-age and survivors' pensions account for over 80 percent of the payments, and disability payments for the rest. At the same time, social security revenues increased from 676 million pesos in 1989 to 985 million pesos. As a result, the cash deficit of the pension system grew from 417 million pesos in 1989 to 712 million pesos in 1997 (equivalent to 2.7 percent of GDP) (Chart 1). In the latter year, the cash deficit of the pension system was greater than the overall budget deficit of 470 million pesos. The large estimated deficit for 1997 is rather surprising because if the contribution rate is 14 percent and the dependency ratio is 1:4 (see below), then in principle, the system should be able to provide an income replacement rate of 56 percent (more than the pension for a person retiring after 25 years). It is true that the replacement rate of the maximum pension is 90 percent and that about 20 percent of the contributions go to pay disability pensions, but still the deficit of 712 million pesos appears to be on the high side unless most of the pensions are closer to the 90 percent replacement rate.

An actuarial evaluation of the pension system also confirms the lack of viability of the pension system under the current rules. Donate-Armada has calculated that contribution rates from current active participants of the pension system need to be increased sharply to finance both existing old-age retirement pensions and their future old-age pensions.[7] With reasonable assumptions about interest rates, salary increases, and the rate of inflation, combined with the assumption that the pension rules will not change, he estimated that the contribution rate would have to increase in 1995 from 10 percent (the rate prevailing at that time) to 36 percent. The contribution rate was calculated as the ratio of the actuarial present value of future old-age pension payments to the actuarial present value of salaries of the current participants

---

6. Official figures reported in CEPAL, *La economía cubana: Reformas estructurales y desempeño en los noventa* (México: Fondo de Cultura Económica, 1997), Tables A-7 and A-8.

7. Donate-Armada, "Cuban Social Security."

of the system. A contribution rate of 20 percent was needed to pay the current pensions with the additional 16 percent being required to accumulate a fund to pay future pensions of current active participants. Based on 1997 data, a contribution rate of 24 per cent (assuming no decline in compliance) would be required simply to eliminate the cash-flow deficit of the system, without accumulating any prefunding.

Another factor that will cause the financial situation of the pension system to worsen is the aging of the population. Mesa-Lago has estimated that the population of retirement age will reach 1.82 million in 2000 and 2.34 million in 2010, compared with 1.45 million in 1990 and 0.68 million in 1960.[8] As a result, the ratio of economically active to economically inactive of the working age population would drop from 4:1 to 3:1. Unless reforms are adopted, these changes will undoubtedly worsen the financial situation of the pension system.

At the same time, it has to be noted that the value of pensions in peso terms is low and that their purchasing power has declined drastically in the 1990s with the collapse of the economy after the elimination of the Soviet subsidy. According to the CEPAL study, the average salary in Cuba was 188 pesos in 1989 and 196 pesos in 1995.[9] Using these salary figures as the base, it can be estimated that the monthly pension for a pensioner after 25 years of service was 94 pesos in 1989 and 98 pesos in 1995 (although these are likely to be low estimates of the pension because the wage profile slopes upward with age), while the maximum monthly pensions were 169 pesos in 1989 and 176 pesos in 1995. In the past, pension income was combined with the availability of rationed foodstuffs and other essential items to provide pensioners with a minimum standard of living (albeit at a fairly low level). As the economic crisis has worsened during the decade, goods have become increasingly less available through the official rationing channels, and

increasingly in the informal market for those who have U.S. dollars. Anecdotal information indicates that prices of goods that are available for sale in pesos have increased sharply, although it is not possible to know with precision because no price statistics are available. For example, Mesa-Lago reports that a typical meal for three persons would have cost 58 pesos in February 1995, or more than half of the average monthly pension in that year.[10]

In these circumstances, as suggested by Mesa-Lago, one can get an idea of the purchasing power of the pensions by converting them to U.S. dollars and comparing them to U.S. dollar prices in the informal market. For the end of 1995, CEPAL reports a black market exchange rate of 25 pesos per U.S. dollar and 7 pesos per U.S. dollar at the end of 1990. Using these exchange rates, the maximum pension declined from US$24 in 1989 to US$7 in 1995.[11] These are very low levels of income compared to reported dollar prices of basic necessities in Cuba, confirming the sad reality that the pension levels cannot provide pensioners with a minimum standard of living.

To sum up, the existing pension system in Cuba fails to provide a minimum level of income for pensioners to buy the basic necessities of life. It is true that medical care, which is one of the largest expenditures categories for the aged is provided essentially free of charge (although the availability and quality of health care also has deteriorated sharply in recent years) and housing is provided at very low rents. Nevertheless, it is clear that the pension system is a meager system, which is already running large cash deficits and is building a large contingent liability for the government. The next sections discuss key issues in pension economics, proposals that have been advanced to reform pension systems, and the experience of the former centrally planned economies in addressing their pension problems.

---

8. Mesa-Lago, "La Seguridad Social y la Pobreza," Table 8.

9. CEPAL, *La economía cubana*, Table A-31.

10. Mesa-Lago, "La Seguridad Social y la Pobreza," p. 91.

11. CEPAL, *La economía cubana*, Table A-14.

PENSION ECONOMICS AND REFORM PROPOSALS TO ADDRESS PENSION SYSTEM PROBLEMS

Pension System Experiences Throughout the World

Income insecurity in old age is a worldwide problem. In industrialized and semi-industrialized countries, this has manifested itself in the difficult financial situation that pension systems have faced in recent years and in the rising amount of resources spent on pensions as the populations grow old, which have been documented in a study by the World Bank.[12] In poor and less urban societies of Africa and Asia, where the old make up a smaller part of the population and are cared for by extended family arrangements, mutual aid societies, and informal mechanisms, it tended to be lesser of a problem for a while. However, as urbanization and mobility increased in these countries the extended family ties and informal systems started feeling the strain. This strain has been felt most in countries where the proportion of the old has been growing rapidly as a result of declining fertility and improved medical care. There is an urgency in these countries to set up formal systems of income maintenance, while helping to maintain informal arrangements of protecting the poor.

Latin America and the former socialist countries of Europe and Central Asia have been forced to reform formal pension systems that had been in operation for a long time. Liberal pension benefits, including early retirement provisions, required high contribution rates which, in turn, have led to large contribution evasion and other distortions in the labor markets. The labor market distortions reduced productivity, pushing contribution rates and evasion still higher, even as limited long-term saving and capital accumulation further dampened economic growth. These countries have not had any alternative but to cut the benefits of their pension programs.

The industrialized countries members of the Organization for Economic Cooperation and Development (OECD) have faced similar problems, as their population has aged and productivity stagnated. These countries experienced several decades of prosperity beginning in the 1960s and large pensions were paid to the old, with the result that poverty declined more rapidly among the older segments of the population. More recently, payroll taxes have risen and will likely need to rise more and benefits fall. The increase in payroll taxes tends to discourage labor supply and productive capital formation, contributing to contain economic growth. As a World Bank study notes, these countries are moving to systems that combine publicly managed pension plans designed to meet basic needs with privately managed occupational pension plans or personal saving accounts to satisfy the higher demand for pension income of middle- and upper-income groups.[13]

Reasons for Government Involvement in Pension Systems

In addressing the problems of providing a retirement income for the old, it is generally recognized that governments need to play an important role, including in countries that until now have relied on informal arrangements to provide old-age security. Governments need to take actions to provide old-age security because people can be shortsighted and may not save enough for their old age, with the result that they could become a burden on the rest of society.

In many countries, there may also be inadequate saving instruments because capital markets are underdeveloped and macroeconomic conditions unstable, justifying government intervention. Insurance market failures are other problems that arise, particularly in poor countries—adverse selection, moral hazard, and correlation among individuals make insurance against many risks (such as the risks of longevity and disability) unavailable. Another important problem is that there might be information gaps regarding the solvency of insurance and other type of financial institutions, or about the relative profitability of alternative types of investment which might result that se-

---

12. See World Bank, *Averting the Old Age Crisis: Policies to Protect the Old and Promote Growth* (1994).

13. World Bank, *Averting the Old Age Crisis.*

rious mistakes are only discovered late in life with dire consequences.

Objectives of Pension Systems

In evaluating alternative policy approaches to address pension system problems, the World Bank study mentioned above notes that pension systems should be both an instrument of growth and social safety nets. The World Bank study stressed that pension systems should help the old by:

- Facilitating people's efforts to shift some of their income from their active working years to old age, by saving or other means;

- Redistributing additional income to the old who are lifetime poor, but avoiding perverse intra generational redistributions and unintended inter-generational redistributions;

- Providing insurance against the many risks to which the old are especially vulnerable;

and help the broader economy by:

- Minimizing hidden costs that impede growth—such as reduced employment and saving, excessive fiscal and administrative burdens, and misallocated capital;

- Being sustainable in the long term by taking into account expected changes in economic and demographic changes;

- Being transparent, to allow decisions to be based on informed choices and insulated from political manipulations that can lead to poor economic outcomes.[14]

Justification for PAYG Systems and Criticisms

Most countries have tried to fulfill the saving, redistribution, and insurance objectives through a publicly managed scheme that pays an earnings-related defined benefit and is financed out of payroll taxes on a pay-as-you-go basis, similar to the Cuban system. In these schemes, some of the contributions of the richer people go to help pay the pensions of the poorer. The system forces the workers to save part of their in-

come and they are protected against disability and other risks.

The combination of functions in one program has been defended on grounds that it keeps administrative costs low through economies of scale and builds political support for the program. However, experience has shown that governments tend to succumb to the temptation of providing too generous benefits to pensioners at the beginning of these programs. Later, governments try to cover the costs with increases in contributions, which result in tax evasion problems and increases in the size of labor market distortions mentioned above, particularly in developing countries that have less efficient tax administration.

The fact that older workers tend to retire earlier than they would do if they had less generous benefits also complicates the situation. Eventually, the costs in terms of higher taxes and their distortionary effects become too large to bear by the countries following these policies. In some developing countries, partially funded defined benefit systems also have a record of misuse. In these countries, the pension funds have been required to invest solely in public securities, which yield very low returns. The availability of this inexpensive financing have led governments to borrow and spend more than they would have otherwise in unproductive ways. This practice results in a hidden tax on labor and deprive the private sector of access to funds and thereby inhibit economic growth.

Moreover, it has been argued that PAYG systems also miss an opportunity for capital market development. In a PAYG system, when the first old generation gets pensions that exceed their savings, national consumption may rise and savings decline. The next generations pay their social security tax instead of saving for their own old age so this loss in saving is never made up. In contrast, a mandatory funded plan could increase capital accumulation if it increases long-term saving beyond the voluntary point and requires that these funds be transferred to financial institutions. This, in turn, stimulates a demand for

---

14. World Bank, *Averting the Old Age Crisis*, pp. 9-10.

financial instruments and eventually the increased availability of these instruments.

In industrial countries, PAYG systems have tended to be regressive contrary to the original intentions. This has been due in part to the way that the systems have been designed, but also because workers with higher income live longer, have a rising age income profile, and join the labor force later, thus having a shorter contributory period. Moreover, there is no equitable distribution of benefits and costs across generations: while the first generation of beneficiaries typically receives considerably more than they contributed, future retired generations typically face lower rates of return on their contributions, particularly in the case of aging populations.[15] The systems have also promoted intra-generational inequities, since different rates of return may apply for contributors within a given population cohort, owing to different life expectancies (e.g., women tend to live longer).

The Multipillar Approach to Pension Reform

To address these problems, the World Bank has proposed a shift from a single pillar approach—characteristic of a PAYG system—to a multipillar approach to provide old-age income security.[16]

A mandatory, publicly-managed first pillar would have the limited object of alleviating old-age poverty and coinsuring against a multitude of risks. With the backing of the government's power of taxation, this first pillar would have the unique ability to pay benefits to people growing old shortly after the plan is introduced, to redistribute income toward the poor, and to coinsure against spells of low investment returns, recession, inflation, and market failures. This pillar could take a number of forms: a universal or employment-related flat benefit, a minimum pension, or means-tested benefits. A main objective of this pillar would be to try to reduce the required contribution rate substantially and, therefore, tax evasion

and misallocation, as well as pressures to overspend. It should also prevent perverse intra- and inter-generational transfers. Benefits should be set at a low level to allow other pillars to grow.

A second mandatory pillar would be fully funded and privately managed, linking benefits actuarially to costs and contributions, and its main purpose would be to carry out the income smoothing or saving function for all income groups within the population. The successful establishment of this pillar (and of the third) requires the existence of a banking system and of, at least, a rudimentary stock and bond market with the capacity to develop further in response to demand from pension funds. Full funding of this pillar is expected to boost capital accumulation and financial market development. A successful second pillar should encourage economic growth that would in turn help finance the first pillar, but it will also reduce the demand for it.

The third pillar would take the form of voluntary occupational or personal saving plans which would provide additional protection for people who want more income and insurance in their old age. Under the multipillar proposal the redistribution and saving functions are separated and the insurance function would be provided jointly by all three pillars.[17]

Skepticism about Widening the Role of the Private Sector

On the other side of the reform literature of pension systems, there are a number of authors who argue that the problems of PAYG systems can be addressed by reforming some of the features causing the problems. Proposals have been made to increase the retirement age and introduce income means testing as a way of reducing benefits and improving the financial conditions of pension systems. This is the approach taken in the past in reforming the United States social security system and the pension systems

---

15. See Marta Castello Branco, *Pension Reform in the Baltics, Russia, and Other Countries in the Former Soviet Union,* IMF Working Paper 98/11 (February 1998).

16. World Bank, *Averting the Old Age Crisis.*

17. For a more thorough discussion of the choices to be made in establishing the three pillars, see World Bank, *Averting the Old Age Crisis,* pp.17-18.

of other countries. In recent literature, there is also the view that some of the benefits of the private funded pillars are overrated.[18]

Shifting from a defined-benefit PAYG system to mandatory defined-contribution schemes managed by the private sector as the dominant pension pillar could be criticized because these schemes could be subject to significant risks, limitations, and complications. Heller has noted that the purported advantages of defined-contribution schemes can be obtained only at the expense of higher underlying risks to the incomes of future pensioners. If policies are introduced to limit such risks, this may result in reinjecting the government into the financing of social insurance, thus raising questions as to the relative merits of defined-contribution over defined-benefit schemes or the desirability of private sector solutions.[19] Similarly, since defined-contribution schemes by themselves do not redistribute income intra-generationally or provide safety nets, income security measures need to be developed to complement a defined-contribution scheme. These will need to be financed and managed by the government which also raises the question whether it is not more efficient and cost effective to build such redistributional/safety net elements directly into the social insurance system, rather than make them a separate pillar. Hemming has pointed out that there is not a strong case for choosing funded public sector pension systems over PAYG systems because the justification that exists for funding pensions in the private sector (possible bankruptcy and the availability of tax advantages) do not carry over to the public sector.[20]

At the same time, the empirical evidence does not permit a generalization about the impact of the public pension system on saving. Replacing a PAYG defined-benefits public sector plan with a defined-contribution private sector plan as done in Chile may increase aggregate saving but, for this to happen, the levels of the contribution rates of the new plan and the means of financing the increase in the public sector deficit that characterizes the period of transition during which the old system is phased out are critically important. To maximize the impact of saving, the public sector deficit created as workers stop paying payroll taxes and start making contributions to the new system should be financed as much as possible through fiscal consolidation and the contribution rate to the new system should be as high as possible.[21] That being said, a fiscal consolidation and an increase in payroll tax rates would raise saving anyway, with or without a switch to a funded system.

Regarding the impact of public pension program on labor supply, public pension programs probably cause people to retire earlier than they would otherwise. But it has to be recognized this is one of the reasons they were created to begin with, and there is also some evidence that the possibility of retiring early increases the number of hours worked before retirement. Thompson argues that there is no evidence to suggest that how a plan is financed (whether pay-as-you-go or funded) will alter the degree of labor supply.[22]

PENSION REFORM IN COUNTRIES IN TRANSITION

It is interesting to review what has been happening to the pension systems in the transition economies because their pension systems and social spending policies were similar to those of Cuba before the demise of central planning. The public pension systems cur-

---

18. See Federal Reserve Bank of St. Louis' *Review* (March/April 1998) for a discussion of current proposals for reform the U.S. social security system which includes provisions for tightening of benefits and setting up individual retirement accounts.

19. Peter S. Heller, *Rethinking Public Pension Reform Initiatives*, IMF Working Paper 98/61 (April 1998).

20. Richard Hemming, *Should Public Pensions be Funded?*, IMF Working Paper 98/35 (March 1998). Hemming argues that a case could be made for the funding of public pension systems if it can be demonstrated that it results in greater inter-generational fairness, if it can better handle demographic and economic risks, if it can more clearly signal future pension costs, or if it is associated with higher saving.

21. G.A. Mackenzie, Philip Gerson, and Alfredo Cuevas, *Pension Regimes and Saving*, IMF Occasional Paper No. 153 (August 1997).

22. Lawrence Thompson, *Older and Wiser: The Economics of Public Pensions* (Washington: The Urban Institute Press, 1997).

Table 3. Public Pension Systems in Countries in Transition *(In percent)*

	System Dependency Ratio[a]			Average Replacement Rate[b]		
	1990	1993	1996	1990	1993	1996
Eastern European countries						
Bulgaria	55.0	80.0	74.4	42.8	40.2	31.4
Croatia	31.0	43.0	54.3	73.0	62.0	35.4
Czech Republic 3/	42.0	51.0	61.0	47.6	43.4	47.8
Hungary	47.0	66.0	76.9	49.7	47.3	41.4
Poland	40.0	53.0	61.3	59.0	76.8	61.3
Romania[c]	34.0	49.0	52.3	41.9	26.0	29.7
Slovak Republic	39.0	53.0	46.1	48.3	44.0	42.0
Baltics, Russia, and other countries of the former Soviet Union						
Armenia	33.8	43.7	44.1	44.6	30.7	24.3
Azerbaijan	38.8	42.9	41.6	42.3	21.2	29.2
Belarus	46.1	54.0	71.0	40.1	38.0	40.9
Estonia	45.3	47.9	55.9	...	—	29.4
Georgia	34.6	37.3	54.9	—	—	36.4
Kazakhstan	31.9	43.7	57.1	38.5	39.3	34.0
Kyrgyz Republic	34.6	38.0	34.0	44.8	38.4	48.5
Latvia	42.7	53.1	54.9	31.2	33.3	38.6
Lithuania	47.4	50.2	53.8	36.3	28.4	30.8
Moldova	34.6	46.9	50.2	38.6	32.1	40.1
Russia	44.9	52.4	57.0	38.0	24.5	28.4
Tajikistan	27.3	32.9	27.0	47.8	45.9	23.7
Turkmenistan	25.4	28.0	25.3	41.1	47.5	53.3
Ukraine	51.4	60.5	65.3	41.6	26.9	32.7
Uzbekistan	29.9	33.1	29.2	45.1	29.9	40.9
Major advanced economies[d]	—	39.2	—	—	—	37.5

Source: *The 1998 World Economic Outlook*; Andrew and Rashid, "The Financing of Pension Systems in Central and Eastern Europe;" Castello Branco, *Pension Reform in the Baltics, Russia, and Other Countries of the Former Soviet Union*; The Vienna Institute for Comparative Economic Studies; and IMF staff estimates.

a. Pensioners as a percent to the number of people employed.

b. The average pension in terms of the average wage.

c. The system dependency ratios for the Czech Republic and Romania reflect data for 1995.

d. Major advanced economies include the United States, Japan, Germany, France, Italy, the United Kingdom, and Canada; for the system dependency ratio, unweighted average of selected OECD countries.

rently in place in the Baltics, Russia, and other countries of the Former Soviet Union (BRO) and in Eastern Europe were introduced originally as contributory pension schemes with universal coverage based on PAYG financing.[23] Castello Branco notes that this scheme was part of a public welfare system designed to provide "cradle-to-grave" protection to the population, including a myriad of social protection arrangements, ranging from the provision of health and education to the delivery of subsidies, cash benefits (including pensions and various allowances) and benefits provided in kind (such as housing) as well as guaranteed employment. Under this system, pension benefits were only loosely linked to contributions, the same way wages were often unrelated to workers' productivity. As the budgetary situation deteriorated in these countries, guaranteed employment and direct subsidies to the population were virtually eliminated, and the provision of the social benefits promised under the old system became increasingly burdensome, especially in light of competing demands from other expenditures necessary to carry forward the transition process.

23. This section is based on Castello Branco, *Pension Reform in the Baltics, Russia and Other Countries of the Former Soviet Union*, and on Box 10 of the 1998 *World Economic Outlook* of the International Monetary Fund.

System dependency ratios — defined as the ratio of pensioners to working population — were already high at the beginning of the transition, and they increased further (Table 3) as employment fell, as the incidence of early retirement increased, and, in a few countries, as populations aged. Some central and eastern European countries have intentionally used early retirement and disability pensions as a safety net to prevent a sharp increase in unemployment, adding to the financial pressures. At the same time, financial weakness of enterprises, a rise in private and informal sector activities, and an inefficient collection system resulted in a decline in contributions.

Most BRO countries responded to the declining number of contributors and the weakening in tax compliance by initially reducing the generosity of the benefits. During the initial, high inflation, phase of the transition period, the lack of formal indexation mechanisms resulted in a significant erosion of the real value of pensions. Subsequently, the use of sporadic indexation and modifications in the benefit formula, in particular changing the way the initial pension was determined, flattened the pension benefit structure in most countries.[24] For example, the average replacement rates — defined as the average pension in terms of the average wage — fell by more than 10 percentage points in Albania, Croatia, and Romania in 1991-93 and benefit levels were also compressed in Russia. In some cases the benefit levels were reduced to just slightly above the poverty line, and in some instances below it. Pensioners in these countries seem to have survived through transfers provided by extended family arrangements, income from informal activities, and sales of personal assets. In these circumstances, Castello Branco points to the fact that these pension systems have become crude social safety nets, providing small amounts of benefits to a large section of the population. In the poorest countries, like Armenia and Georgia, the official safety nets have become largely irrelevant for household income. In recent years, with progress achieved in macroeconomic stabilization there have been at-

tempts to increase the level of benefits but there have been insufficient funds to do this.

Despite the reduced benefits, pension funds began to run cash budget deficits. Moreover, most of these countries, except Albania and some countries in the Caucasus and Central Asia, face the prospect of aging populations which will add to the financial strains of the pension systems. To address the growing financial imbalances in the pension funds, contribution rates were raised significantly. Payroll taxes are now in excess of 30 percent of wages, and they were as high as 52 percent in Ukraine in 1996. However, the increase in contribution rates apparently has discouraged compliance in a significant way. At the same time during the transition period, arrears have accumulated both in contributions and in payments of pension benefits.

In addition to the short-term responses of compressing benefits (but not the number of beneficiaries), increasing contribution rates, and accumulating arrears, several BRO countries have adopted piecemeal reform measures to correct some of the distortions existing in their PAYG system. Notably, they have introduced amendments to the existing legislation to change the benefit structure and eligibility criteria, and made efforts to improve targeting of benefits and strengthen tax collection. A few countries (Armenia, Azerbaijan, Estonia, Kazakhstan, and Lithuania) have actually initiated the process of gradually increasing retirement ages, while in Georgia the retirement age was raised by five years in one go in February 1996. Some countries have reduced or eliminated benefits for working pensioners. BRO countries also are trying to improve the collection of contributions to the pension systems. To try to improve the disappointing collections of contribution rates, some countries (Armenia, Georgia, and Ukraine) have decided to gradually cut contribution rates in an attempt to increase compliance over time. Countries like Ukraine have taken steps to harmonize contribution rates by raising rates for some privileged categories, and others including Russia and Ukraine have

---

24. Castello Branco, *Pension Reform in the Baltics, Russia and Other Countries of the Former Soviet Union*, pp. 28-29.

attempted to broaden the tax base by including some previously untaxed nonwage income.

A number of countries are considering more systemic pension reforms and are in some cases preparing the introduction of private pension funds. Others like Kazakhstan, Latvia, Hungary, and Poland have taken steps to adopt a multipillar system as recommended by the World Bank. The Kazakh reform plan that became operational in January 1998 envisages a transition toward a new system, based on the Chilean model, in which the first pillar will play a minimal role. All current and new workers will immediately participate in the funded system of individual accounts. In Hungary, Latvia, and Poland, the first pillar retains a more important role and continues to provide benefits partially linked to contributions. These three countries are also taking a more gradual approach toward introducing the privately managed pillars and Hungary and Poland offer those currently working and within a certain age range the option to continue participation in the old system.

THE POSSIBLE REFORM OF THE CUBAN PENSION SYSTEM

The shock that the Cuban economy suffered from the elimination of the subsidies of the former Soviet Union in 1989, and the impact of the accumulation of economic distortions as a result of central planning, has had serious negative consequences on the economy and on the fiscal accounts. The discussion above shows that the finances of the pension system of Cuba were also negatively affected and that pensions had fallen to very low levels in U.S. dollar terms at a time when the economy became increasingly dollarized. As in the transition economies, reforming the pension system in Cuba is in many ways a more difficult task than in industrial and developing countries. The difficult situation of the public finances, the large competing expenditure needs, and the lack of financial markets and regulatory frameworks, create very serious constraints to reform. Politically and

on ethical grounds, there is a need to provide a minimum protection to pensioners who may not live to enjoy the eventual benefits from the reform of the pension system and from the improvements in macroeconomic performance, but expect the government to honor their promise of an adequate pension.

To address the pension and other serious economic problems of Cuba, it is clear that a medium- to long-term macroeconomic program would need to be put in place with a strong emphasis in carrying out the needed structural reforms to eliminate the distortions and generate a strong supply response from the economy. Up to now, the adjustment to the economic shock of the 1990s has been essentially from the demand side, and it is imperative to increase economic growth to raise living standards and generate resources to reform the pension system.[25] With higher rates of growth in the future, the PAYG finances would improve significantly.

Concerning the reform of the pension system, Cuba is faced with the double problem that the system is already running a large cash deficit which is likely to increase over time as the population ages, while at the same time the pension system does not redistribute income in an adequate amount to old people who have been poor most of their lives and now face a dismal future at the current levels of pensions. Neither does the current system provide an adequate vehicle to save a share of income of the active population for their old age needs, or provide insurance against disability or protection to survivors. To come up with specific recommendations on how to reform the pension system, more comprehensive information would be needed about the state of public finances and about demographic trends in Cuba. In a country like Cuba, there are likely to be large amounts of off-budgetary transactions that would need to be brought into the budget before one can assess the real fiscal situation and how much leeway the government has in meeting its pension obligations.

---

25. See Lorenzo L. Pérez, "The Implications of Good Governance for the Reconstruction of Cuba," in *Cuba in Transition—Volume 7* (Washington: Association for the Study of the Cuban Economy, 1997), for reforms that need to be implemented to promote an economic recovery in Cuba.

At the outset of the reform of the Cuban pension system, it appears that there is little choice but to try to reform the existing PAYG system and implement piecemeal reforms to correct some of the most obvious distortions, as has been done by transition economies, as well as by industrial and developing countries. It is clear that the retirement age would need to be raised—preferably to 65 years old for both men and women, given that the latter group tends to have a longer life expectancy. Contribution rates will need to be increased, although it would be important to be mindful of the limits that exist before serious evasion problems arise; actuarial calculations will be a key input in determining by how much to increase retirement age and contributions.

The rules for early retirement would need to be tightened and the targeting of the benefits improved by means-testing (except that for some time the introduction of means-testing is unlikely to have strong payoff given how widespread poverty is in the population) and stronger surveillance exercised over disability claims to reduce abuses to the system.

The cost of all noncontributor benefits should be transferred to the budget and the special retirement program of the military and others should be integrated with the general pension program. A decision will have to be made about indexing existing pension benefits. Preferably, changes in pensions rather than in wages will be linked to changes in the consumer price index, given that increases of the latter will tend to reflect increases in productivity in better functioning labor markets.

The more difficult question would have to be what to do about the level of pensions. One possibility would be to have instead of a basic public pension (on a universal or means-tested basis) a minimum flat rate which, while higher than the current level, would still be relatively low, plus a limited earnings related pension scheme. The option of developing private pensions (either mandatory like the World Bank's second pillar or voluntary as in the third pillar) should not be excluded. However, it is evident that significant progress would have to be made in creating a financial system and an appropriate regulatory framework before a serious program of privatization of pensions can be considered. In this context, the reforms being implemented in transition economies, particularly the more ambitious ones of Latvia and Kazakhstan, merit close analysis by Cuban policy makers. Moreover, adopting a privatized system will have little impact in the short run in the circumstances of Cuba because the government would have no way to close the cash-flow deficit. Most, if not all, of the private pension surplus would need to go into the financing of the fiscal deficit through the purchase of government securities.

COMMENTS ON

"The Pension System of Cuba: The Current Situation and Implications of International Pension Reform Experiences for Addressing Cuba's Problems" by Pérez

Carmelo Mesa-Lago

Based on my work for four decades on both Cuba and social security pensions, I can say that Lorenzo Pérez' paper on pension reform in Cuba is very good and that I agree with almost all it says. Especially interesting for me is his comparison of the Cuban pension system with that of nations that were part of the former Soviet Union. His recommendations for pension reform are balanced and very careful as such difficult issue demands. In fact, a recurrent nightmare of mine is that the Castro regime has fallen and I am called to design a new pension reform in the island! The following comments address some minor points in Pérez' paper and provide comparisons with pension reform in eight countries in Latin America.

1. Comparison of Cuba with former Soviet Republics. Cuba's pension system faces a worse financial and actuarial deficit than those of the nine new independent states, because its revenue is proportionally lower and its expenditures higher. On the revenue side, the employer's wage contribution in those countries is 32%, more than twice that of Cuba (14% after 1994), and the employee contribution is 1% compared to zero in Cuba (the 1994 tax law mandated such contribution, but it was postponed at that time and, again, by the V Party Congress in 1997). The total contribution in the former Soviet Republics, therefore, is 33% versus 14% in Cuba. But in Cuba, it had been actuarially estimated in 1995 that the total contribution had to be 36%,

which means, that the employer contribution had to be raised to 18% and a similar percentage charged to the workers. (A few days after our session was held, Cuba's monopoly State Insurance Enterprise offered citizens and residents, between 17 and 65 years of age, disability and survivors insurance—not for old age—for a rather high premium based on their wages; the maximum lump sum to be paid will be 50,000 pesos or less than $4,000. See Raúl Rivero, "Proletarios de Cuba, !aseguráos!" *El Nuevo Herald*, August 21, 1998, p. 17A). On the expenditures side, retirement ages are the same in Cuba and in those nine countries (55 for women and 60 for men), but the longevity of Cuban pensioners is the highest among them (at least until 1989); furthermore, under the Rectification Process (1986-90) there was a relaxation in entitlement conditions, which led to a jump in the number of pensioners. The longer it takes to raise/establish the proper level of contributions, the higher they will have to be (more than 36% combined in 1998, if current entitlement conditions are maintained).

2. Erosion of Pensioners' Living Standards in Cuba. Pérez deals with this issue in his paper but I want to add a couple of things. Based on the inflation index estimated for Cuba, the average *real* pension decreased 42% in 1989-97. Rationing currently covers less than half the minimum food needs monthly. With the dollar equivalent of such average pension

535

(about $5 monthly) it is impossible to buy food for the remaining half of the month. Transportation is a major problem for retired people because the immense majority of them can not ride bikes, and they suffer most from the deterioration of the health care system.

3. Regressiveness of the Pension System in Developing Countries. In most of Latin America, the pension system is even more regressive than in industrialized countries, due to two reasons: in half of those countries less than 25% of the labor force (mostly low income) is covered by pensions, but contribute to the system of those covered (middle income) through state taxes partly used to subsidize it, as well as through transfer of the employers' contribution to prices.

4. Investment Deficiencies. Investment of the pension fund in public securities was not the only reason for negative real yields in the 1980s. In Latin America, a significant part of pension fund investment was of the "social" type (housing, social insurance hospitals and equipment, mortgage and personal loans) which also had negative real yields, thus provoking a drastic reduction in the reserves. Because of the latter, often the first generation of pensioners got a good pension and a cheap (almost free) house due to inflation, but the second or third generations neither received a fair pension nor a house.

5. Multipillar Approaches. Before the World Bank published its famous report on pensions (1994) that included the multipillar model, the International Labor Office had published its own version (1993) but with a second (core) pilar completely different from that of the Bank (both models have almost equal first and third pillars). In my opinion, universal unique models are unfeasible due to the enormous divergence of economic, demographic, social security, labor market and political variables among close to 200 countries in the world. Each one has to adapt the pension reform to its own peculiarities, needs and resources.

6. Pension Privatization Boosts Capital Accumulation and Financial Market Development. Pérez properly questions this assumption in his paper. Let me add that in estimating *net* capital accumulation, one must take into account not only the positive accumulation generated in the new fully-funded pension system, but the triple fiscal cost of the transition too: (I) pension deficit in the old system; (ii) transfer of contributions (adjusted by inflation) from the old to the new system; and (iii) minimum pension guaranteed in the new system (for those who do not accumulate sufficient funds in their individual account). Studies conducted by Robert Holzmann and Alberto Arenas de Mesa prove that pension "privatization" in Chile has had a negative impact on net capital accumulation (at least in the first 14 years of operation), and the first expert has also shown that it has not played a role in the development of the financial market either.

7. Lessons for Cuba from Pension Reforms in Latin America. Eight countries in the region have already implemented a pension reform: Chile (the pioneer, in 1981), and Argentina, Bolivia, Colombia, El Salvador, Mexico, Peru and Uruguay (all since 1993). My own work shows that all the reforms are different, a result of the variety of conditions in those countries. The only country among the eight that has had some type of socialism is Chile (but it did not go too far); the other country in the region that tried socialism was Nicaragua (although far from the level achieved in Cuba), but it has not undertaken a pension reform yet. In Chile, the Allende government was overthrown by the military and pensions did not have enough time to be badly affected by the "Revolution" (as in Cuba and Nicaragua), while the authoritarian government faced no political obstacles to implement a radical pension reform ("privatization"). Conversely, in Nicaragua the economic policies of the Sandinistas led to record-high inflation which liquidated the reserves of the pension system; instead of an authoritarian government, a democracy was installed in Nicaragua, and the pension reform has been obstructed by political and economic obstacles. Cuba is in a worse situation than Nicaragua (there has not been a pension "fund" under the Revolution, because the employers' contributions go to the state and the pension system is financed out of the state budget). The type of pension reform that the island will adopt (e.g., full privatization Chilean style, mixed as in Argentina and Uruguay, or parallel as in Colombia and Peru), will depend on how authoritarian or democratic the transition is.

8. Inclusion of the Armed Forces. They were and are excluded from Cuba's general pension system, something true all over Latin America with the exception of Costa Rica that fortunately lacks armed forces. In Chile, the military government designed and implemented the pension reform, which has been successful so far and a model for the rest of the region and elsewhere, but the reform excluded the armed forces and the police, which kept their separate privileged program. I do agree with Pérez on the need to include the armed forces in an overall pension reform in Cuba, but the feasibility of that action will largely depend on how the transition occurs: if the armed forces take over power and lead the process, it would be extremely difficult that they accept incorporation into a general pension system.

FREE FROM WHAT? WHERE TO?
AND THE ROLE OF THE CUBAN-AMERICANS

Armando Ribas

Let me tell you that I feel rather awkward to address the "Cubans" (Cubans?) in English, but as I am a law abiding man, I accept the rules of the game. Hence, I know that what I am going to say may be a little daring to say the least, so let me start with one of José Martí's poems:

> Do not place me in darkness
> to die as a traitor.
> I am good, and as good
> I will die facing the sun.

What I am going to say today is related not only to Cuba and the United States, but also to Western Civilization, and last but not least, my proposal for that very special breed, the so called Cuban-Americans. And let me point out to you that the denominations of Hispanics is unacceptable from the scientific as well as from the moral point of view. But I do not have time to delve into this subject, so let's get to work (manos a la obra).

FREE FROM WHAT

The first question that I asked in the title of this reflections is free from what? And certainly, I think that if we cannot answer this question it will be rather difficult to find a way for a liberated Cuba. The more I read the Miami press, the more I think that there is a common agreement that as soon as the deity decides to call Fidel Castro into his or her womb, the sun of liberty will shine radiantly in Cuba. If that were the case, then I would be forced to blame God for being so harsh on our compatriots (are they?) as to postpone for such a long time this decision. Cer-

tainly, I do not accept this conclusion, but then I cannot accept the first one either.

The assumption that Cuba is an unlucky country that gave birth to Fidel Castro is as simplistic as to assume that Germany was very unlucky for having Hitler or Italy Mussolini and even more Russia with the "steel man," Stalin. Nothing would be more damaging to the possibility of a new Cuba than to accept that simplistic approach.

And as the purpose of the annual reunion of ASCE is to provide intellectual means for transforming Cuba after Fidel, what you call "Cuba in transition," we should acknowledge which were and are the determining factors which allowed the appearance and continuity of Mr. Castro at the helm. Well, maybe we all have forgotten Mr. Castro's speech, I guess it was on the 7th of January 1959, when the pigeon rested on his shoulder and he asked "¿Voy bien, Camilo?" I remember that he said we are here not thanks to the Pentagon but against the will of the Pentagon and regretted that in 1898 it was not the lone star flag the one that flew at the Morro. I think that that was a political definition which decided the future of revolutionary Cuba. I do remember that since that very day, everyone who dared to disagree with the revolution was anti-revolutionary and *el paredón* was the deserved punishment. I also remember that only those people who were *siquitrillados*— sorry, I don't have a translation for that word— could have a reason for complaining, but the large majority of the Cubans were having the luck of living in the *territorio libre de América* and we believed it.

I do think that if we are going to talk about historical luck, Cuba was a privileged country. Given its insularity it was not possible for the Cubans to have independence until almost the end of the century. And let me tell you, the Spaniards were backward but to some extent it was better to live under the *Leyes de Indias* imposed by them than when they were enforced by the *criollos* as Alberdi very well expressed. So we were spared of all the hazards and civil wars which plagued the rest of the continent led by the caudillos after independence.

Now I know that what I'm going to say may send me right back to the *paredón* but I am going to say it any way. So please, listen; when we finally got the independence from Spain at the end of the historically-called Spanish-American War we did it under the aegis of the greatest civilization ever produced by humankind: the United States of America. As a consequence of this epic luck, of which 100 years have elapsed, Cuba could learn the difference between independence and freedom.

The Americans decided the war against Spain, and when they finally declared the independence of Cuba in 1902, they left their legacy of individual rights, the real meaning of freedom in the Bill of Rights included in the so-called provisional Constitution. Even José Duarte Oropesa, who certainly is not very keen about the Americans in his book *Historiología Cubana*, said with respect to that Constitution: "to the Cubans, for centuries, victims of the Spanish despotism, it seemed incomprehensible because it contained phrases and rights that up to that moment we did not know." Moreover, the great thinker Enrique José Varona in a letter to General Ramos wrote: "The United States have saved Cuba for civilization and humankind: and this is an eternal title to our gratitude, it gives them in the eyes of the world and in the present state of our relations under international law, a title that no power could dispute, to consider themselves a part in the constitution of our definitive government."

Unfortunately, the views of Varona, which I have only partially quoted, were not shared by the majority of the Cubans who then and probably until now were under the spell of the Martian romanticism.

That ethical duality, which has characterized our continent South of Rio Grande in which we apply the Don Quixote morality to judge our neighbors while we keep for ourselves the "wisdom" of Sancho Panza. Hence, instead of appreciating the American influence on our shores, we kept thinking about the Platt Amendment. Once again, in our case forms and words prevailed over substance and Martí's lyrics sounded in our ears but very far from our deeds. "Con los pobres de la tierra quiero yo mi suerte echar" was the life project of *el apóstol*. Hence, we cannot be surprised that in the last visit of Pope Juan Pablo II to La Habana, Fidel could have said that he had accepted his visit now that the Church had changed and was, as he always was, in favor of the poor, the so-called "preferencia por los pobres." In only 25 years after the abolition of the Platt Amendment, with full sovereignty, Fidel Castro brought us all to the communist paradise, at the rhythm of the song "Cuba sí, Yankees no."

I know that anyone could ask me, then, if this ethical duality is common to all Latin America, as it was defined by the Ariel of the Uruguayan Enrique José Rodó, why was it only Cuba that reached that extreme? This is a valid question and my answer, which could be controversial, is that the army put some limits in those countries to the fantasies of socialist utopia. With the full approval of our excellent democratic class, Grau San Martín, Carlos Prío, Carlos Saladrigas, Sergio Carbó and the Directorio Revolucionario, the country was put in the hands of the sergeants. The sergeants turned it back to the revolutionaries and Cuba was the only country in the continent where the guerrillas with majority support won the war.

I would say that the answer to my first question is that the Cubans should be free from the ethical duality in which socialism is based. And this is an important message, because I have to say to my economist colleagues that there are not economic problems but ethical and political ones. Socialism and capitalism are not two different economic systems, but two diametrically different ethical approaches to human nature.

It is obvious that my answer to the first question is that Castro is an accident though a long term one, but what matters is to be free from the rational and/ or sentimental attachment to socialism. The hatred of Castro and the love of socialism may be the recipe for disaster in the future Cuba. It has already been a determining factor in the enactment of the Helms-Burton law and the embargo, whose failure is proven by the very permanence of Castro regime for forty years only ninety miles from the United States. And socialism, in that sense, is not only an ideology as such which people may reject. Socialism is based on the assumption that generosity and solidarity can be the basis of political institutions. Those may be attractive, as Adam Smith very well explained, but can never be the basis on which freedom and justice can be achieved in society.

I think that by now it is very clear that if the Cubans in Cuba – now, I don't know if there are others – thought that Castro betrayed the revolution and that Martí's idyllical concepts of democracy as presented in the program of the Cuban Revolutionary Party prevailed, the tyranny would collapse into chaos in the future. Because as Edward Burke wisely said with respect to the French Revolution: "For having the right to everything they lack everything." And allow me to say that when people believe that they have the right to everything and they lack everything, the only political alternative is dictatorship; witness the majority of the Eastern European countries where the Communist are back in town. That is, if people expect that the so-called capitalist system will deliver the unfulfilled promises of socialism, the communists will be back in the future.

WHERE TO

Then, where to? To answer this question I will have to transcend the Cuban shores to delve into the very meaning of the so called Western Civilization. There is no such thing as Western Civilization, allow me to say without having again to face the *paredón*. The history of the West in terms of freedom has been as poor if not worse than the Oriental counterparts. We do not know very much about the latter, sometimes because of lack of communications and others due to the lack of interest.

But we should remember that the survival of Europe was more luck than wisdom and certainly not because Europe was the land of morality and freedom. There is no doubt, however, that at the end of the century, what we call the West has reached a level of well being and freedom that was completely unknown in history. It is then of the utmost importance to find out the reasons why this is so. Now more than ever, because of what is known as globalization, a kind of historical determinism that projects societies to wealth and freedom regardless of their values and cultures has been almost accepted. I do believe that for better or for worse, history—in spite of Kant, Hegel or Marx—is in the hands of men, and not the other way around.

An unfortunate event has contributed to a large extent to a great misunderstanding on this subject. The French Revolution, produced under the spell of the enlighment, endarkened the world through the absolute of reason. A new absolute took the place of the deity in order to oppress and kill in the name of rationally and goodness. Absolute love and absolute reason became the tools for oppression on behalf of absolute goodness. As Alberdi said "everybody wanted to be a hero and nobody was satisfied to be a man."

Instead of "sapere aude" we should accept "non sapere aude," that is you have to dare not to know; that is that rationality is not a synonym of "truth." Knowledge is contingent precisely because, as Hume wisely observed, we are saved from total skepticism through the non rational aspects of our nature.

The West, then, is not a historical pattern of virtue. After the collapse of the feudal system and what may be called the oppression of the faith, two different ways were open to the West. On one side, the enlightment, with Descartes followed by Rousseau, Kant, Hegel and Marx, developed a mix of rationalism and romanticism which gave rise to the totalitarian systems that appeared in the West during the twentieth century. Despotism had been known throughout history, but only in the West did political philosophy rationalize and revalue the authoritarian state in the name of order as the only alternative to chaos. Hitler, Mussolini and Stalin were the product of that approach, in which the rationality of man deprived him of its complex nature.

As a consequence, an entelechy called sovereignty deprived him of his will and created the state as the very representation of the ethicality of the society against the concupiscence of private interest. In Hegel's words, the state was the divine idea as it was manifested on earth. That is what Alberdi called the Latin freedom. He asked himself what is Latin freedom and responded: "It is the freedom of all, consolidated in one and only collective and solidary liberty, whose exclusive execution is in the hands of a free emperor or a liberator Czar. It is the freedom of the country personalized in its government and its government in its totality personalized in one man."

Sovereignty was the right to arbitrary rule in defense of national interests. Then, war was the name of the game and racism intermingled with tribal passion to build absolute power in the name of national interest. It was Hegel who said in his *Philosophy of Law* that war is the way to keep in equilibrium the ethical health of the people. On the other hand, and coming out from the same way of thinking, Marx, another representative of enlighted Western thought, substituted the war between states for the war between classes in order to suppress the alienation caused by private property as the dialectical dynamic of history. Concentration camps and Gulags were the final development of those utopias as the specter of Rousseau haunted over the head of the incorruptible while other heads ran down the drain under the ethical prevalence of the guillotine, administered by the public health committee.

It was on the other side of the British Channel that a more modest approach to human nature prevailed and political thinking was mainly concerned with human frailty in order to guarantee men rights under proper institutions. In the words of Locke, men had the rights to life, freedom, property and the pursuit of happiness. These rights did not derive from government but it was the duty of government to protect and guarantee them. The entelechy of sovereignty as the absolute power had been replaced by the rule of law which set a limit to political power on the recognition that governments were framed by men.

Locke wrote: "But I shall desire those who make this objection to remember that absolute monarchy is but men: and if government is to be the remedy of those evils which necessarily follow from men being judges of their own cases, and the state of nature is therefore not to be endured, I desire to know what kind of government that is, and how much better it is than the state of nature, where one man commanding a multitude has the liberty to be judge his own case, and may do to all his subjects whatever he pleases without the least question or control of those who execute his pleasure?... Is one to think that men are so foolish that they take care to avoid what mischiefs may be done to them by polecats or foxes but are content to be devoured by lions."

This different approach represented a new covenant between the government and the governed, where private interests were not supposed to be against the general interest but ethically accepted in accordance to general rules to be applied and enforced by governments. That was the underlying reason of the Bill of Rights, and the very foundation of justice as it was well expressed by David Hume in his *Treatise on Human Nature* where he said: "It is only from the selfishness and confined generosity of men, along with the scanty provision that nature has made for his wants, that justice derives its origins"... "Increase to a sufficient degree the benevolence of men or the bounty of nature and you render justice useless by supplanting its place with much nobler virtues and more valuable blessings."

I'm not going to insist further on the ethical aspects of liberalism but let me say that those principles were the ones that were fully recognized on this side of the Atlantic in the construction of the United States. It was Madison who best expressed the concern for human frailty when he said in the *Federalist Papers*: "It may be a reflection on human nature, that such devises should be necessary to control the abuses of government. But what is government itself if not the greatest of all reflection of human nature? If men were angels, no government would be necessary. If angels were to govern men, neither external or internal controls on government would be necessary. In framing a government which is to be administered by men over men, the great difficulty lies in this. You must first enable the government to control the governed; and in the next place oblige it to control itself. A dependence on the people is no doubt the primary control on the government; but experience has taught mankind the necessity of auxiliary precautions."

Those were the same principles that recognized the necessity of insuring private property from the demagoguery of the assemblies, notably the Congress. That is, the protection of minorities from the force of majorities. And that was why he also said: "In a society under the form of which the stronger faction can readily unite and oppress the weaker, anarchy may as truly said to reign, as in the state of nature, where the weaker individual is not secured against the violence of the stronger."

The limitation to majority power in the name of the rule of law through the Supreme Court is undoubtedly the main tenet of the Republican system as developed and implemented by the Americans to protect private interest and individual rights. This ethical approach is at the same time the support of the so called capitalism system. That is why there is no contradiction between American democracy – the dream of individual freedom of Washington, Jefferson, Madison, Lincoln—and Wall Street or Madison Avenue. It was this symbiotic feed back between political freedom and private interest that decided the success of the American society. That universal principle applied to a universal society as against the parochialism of the "Europe de les patries" sustained on the confusion between socialism and democracy that characterized the failures of democracy both in Europe prior to the Second World War and in Latin America up to the present.

Unfortunately, a further confusion has arisen on account of the social-democratic path of the European countries. It was Edward Bernstein who in his *Preconditions of Socialism* stated: "It is indeed true that the great liberal movement of modern times has in the first instance benefited the capitalist bourgeoisie, and that the parties which took the name of liberal were or became in time, nothing but straight forward defenders of capitalism. There can of course, be nothing but enmity between these parties and Social Democracy. But with respect to liberalism as a historical movement, socialism is its legitimate heir not only chronologically, but also intellectually." Definitely, Bernstein's confusion remains up to the present, with the failure to realize that liberalism and socialism, as was said above, are two different perception about human nature and consequently also about political institutions.

That confusion results from a great misunderstanding between continental rationalism cum romanticism and the pragmatic (empiricist) and skeptical philosophical approach of the Anglo-Saxons. In Bernstein own words, his basic confusion was stated as follows: "As a movement opposed to the subjection of nation to institutions which are either imposed from without or which have no justification but tradition, liberalism first sought its realisation as the sovereignty of the age and of the people, both of which principles were endlessly discussed by the political philosophers of the seventeenth and eighteenth centuries until Rousseau, in the Social Contract, established them as the basic conditions of legitimacy of any constitution; and in the democratic constitution of 1793, imbued with the spirit of Rousseau, the French Revolution proclaimed them the inalienable rights of man..." "The constitution of 1793 was the logical expression of the liberal ideas of the epoch, and a cursory glance at its content shows how little it was, or is, an obstacle to socialism."

I would say that Bernstein was right in his conclusion, although not so much on the premises, where he based liberalism in the Social Contract of "the Newton of moral science," as Kant called Rousseau. It should not be surprising then, that continental liberalism through the democratic process misled the Europeans to confuse democracy with socialism, as it had been already done by Montesquieu. It was the Baron de Secondat who in *The Spirit of Laws* wrote: "The love of democracy is the love of equality. To love democracy is to love frugality. If everybody has the same well-being and the same advantages, then all should enjoy the same pleasures and the same hopes: this is something that cannot be attained if frugality in not general." And he continues: "In a democracy, the love of equality sets a limit to ambition, only wishing to do more services to the fatherland, more and greater services than to the other citizens. Just for being born there is a debt to the fatherland that it is never paid."

Here again, we not only perceive that the very idea of democracy is socialism but that citizens should only have duties and of course the fatherland will be always represented by the state. The entelechy is built from the fallacy of the assumptions with respect to human nature, but the power is guaranteed to those very men who will try to force equality on others. The democratic failures in Europe prior to the Second World War should be a lesson. Unfortunately, the Europeans are deeply socialist, nationalist and racist and the present welfare state is the product of those assumptions which, as we have said before, have very little to do with the American capitalism.

Let me now say some words about Latin America, where the French Revolution disease produced the death at birth of republican governments. This dramatic difference between the political conceptions of what we may call liberal rationalism was closely perceived by Alberdi and also by Domingo Faustino Sarmiento. The third President of Argentina (1868-1874) said in his *Commentaries to the Argentine Constitution* with respect to the United States: "in the United States all the parties agree over what in the rest of the world is the cause or ordinary pretext for revolutions and despotism." This is the idea that put Argentina on the way of the universal Anglo-Saxon political project and in only fifty years converted a desert into one of the richest countries of the world at the beginning of twentieth century. But it was more than that: Argentina was actual proof that the universality of the so-called new covenant as expressed in the Bill of Rights is not only a privilege of the Anglo-Saxons who discovered it, but a possibility for any country which accepts and implements it regardless of race or creed.

The rest of the continent did not have so much wisdom. There the French endarkment in collusion with or in opposition to the Spanish one determined the poverty of the continent as well as the resentment of the large majority of our intellectuals with respect

to the success of the United States. Unfortunately as Luis Alberto Herrera, the Uruguayan politician, said in his *La Revolución Francesa y Sud América*: "The French Revolution continues, though from its grave, governing our independent destinies."

Allow me to quote some other thoughts of Mr. Herrera, which I consider as valid at this time of so-called "globalization" as when they were first expressed in 1910: "Whereas the Anglo-Saxon child (the United States), loyal to his tradition, grew with the healthy practice of the law, without doubting that in his own person, and not in the country of origin, dwelled the fate of his own will, the Latin children only understand that same right as a benevolent grant of the semidivine chief of the great colonial machine, and was never able to know how to put in motion that concept, deprived of the opportunity to execute it through suffrage"... "All our tyrants and all organized political calamities have found in that inexhaustible fountain declamation over rights, freedom, sovereignty, royalty, the oppressed people, the social welfare, the universal suffrage, etc. a formidable defensive shield for their assaults".... "It is very sad that South America insists on adoring general ideas, that trying to define too much, define nothing instead of accepting the temperament of the precious political contradictions taught by the masters in the managing of free institutions"... "The French Revolution told us, and we believed with Rousseau, that it was our humanitarian duty to rebuild the society by suppressing hierarchies, conventionalisms and prejudices, and above all it propelled us to the democratic hallucinations with its uncontrollable interpretation of the sovereignty of the people." And last, but not least, he wrote: "No nation has given such a wonderful life to the free institutions as the United States. The humankind has never known such a powerful republican organization."

It was another Latin-American, the Venezuelan Carlos Rangel, who clearly recognized the character of our tragedy and in his *Del Buen Salvaje al Buen Revolucionario*, where the specter of Rousseau and the Jacobins intermingle with the specter of Marx and communism. He wrote: "And the gravest thing of all is that the difference between the two Americas is not only economic and power success, but also public and private morality."

Then, my answer to the second question is that there are two dramatically opposed ethical and political approaches to society: the rationalism of the French Revolution, on the one hand, and what may be called the skepticism of the Anglo-Saxons, on the other. It is through this second approach that we should try to understand the way to freedom and justice.

I think that I have gone longer than I intended on the reasons for my answer to my second question "where to?" The answer seems to be in front of our eyes, but unfortunately we have been able to perceive the results but never understood the reasons. Particularly our *apóstol* experienced this partial knowledge, under the influence of the romantic Rousseau. Then, what is important is to distinguish the abysmal difference between individual rights as the fundamental character of the very concept of freedom, and the socialist approach of social rights and sovereignty.

I'm sorry to say to my friends and economist colleagues: the problems is not the control of the money supply or the budget deficit. The problem is created when the security of individual rights is politically overwhelmed by the majority rule of apparent equal rights enforced by government. The lack of private participation in the production of goods and services is replaced by the very generous function of redistributing wealth, which results in the accumulation of power to satisfy the private interest of the bureaucracy through the very unproductive process of redistributing poverty. The business of virtue substitutes for the business of producing wealth and tyranny arises as the only alternative to chaos.

THE ROLE OF CUBAN-AMERICANS

Now that I think that I have answered my two questions in the sense that we have to be free not from Castro but from socialism and that the process to imitate is the American Republic, let me address what I have called the role of the Cuban-Americans in the continent.

There is something that it is not possible to deny. That is the success of the Cuban-Americans in the United States and in particular in Miami. I am not

going to delve into the description of the history of this successful process of reacommodation to this society, which only ninety miles from Cuban shores was alien in thoughts and feelings to our culture. Then, it is necessary to answer another question: why did you not do it in Cuba?

Allow me not to include myself into the question because I am not a Cuban-American and I have not produced any success anywhere. We may come back to the first simplistic approach and answer: because of Fidel. Well, but Fidel was not there before 1959. Again, we could blame Batista (1933-1944 and 1952-1959), or if we go back in history we could mention Machado. Well, they were all Cubans as far as I know, and although I have to acknowledge that economically we were ahead of the majority of the Latin American countries, that was not certainly true with respect to our political behavior and institutions. I apologize if I have said something that may offend someone, but believe me, I would like it not to be true.

We should acknowledge that to some extent the system that has allowed the success of the Cuban-American has to be confirmed by your political behavior. In that sense, it is of the utmost importance that Miami not be confused with what happened in Washington. Majority rule is not necessarily equal to justice. Your behavior, in that sense, is before the eyes of Latin Americans who, deep in their hearts are closer to Castro than to the United States in spite of the recent democratic changes. Your failure in this area is a success for Mr. Castro.

For sometime we could even think, though it may sound somewhat petulant, that the first Cuban immigration pertained to a sort of elite. That may be, but it is also true that during the last 39 years, Cubans of all classes continued deserting and apparently the majority of them participate in this successful experience. Even more other Latin Americans have come now to participate too, although their countries are not even similar to what you have created in this area.

I know that many Cubans logically still have their soul *in la tierra más fermosa que ojos humanos vieren,* but if they look deep into their soul they know that never in Cuba did they have the opportunity to achieve in their lifetime what they achieved in this land of opportunity. Even more, they know that this would have been impossible in any other country in the world; of course, I am including the other industrial countries. We should also know that in Cuba we would not have accepted this tide of immigration, which still pretends not to assimilate and speak an alien language in the face of the original immigrants. In fact I would say that this has been for the Cubans a lucky misfortune.

Well, I am going to risk an answer. The institutional system. But this institutional system has not been created in a vacuum of values and principles. They are based on respect for private interest and the conscientious acceptance of human frailty as the basic tenet of the institutional structure. We may even say or believe that American society now takes its institutions for granted and has forgotten about the roots. That may be true, but we should not forget that the triumph of the Americans over the Soviets was not due to their inherent talents or their knowledge of mathematics or physics. As Alberdi used to say: "South America has been disorganized by the talented people." It is the system that converts mediocrity into excellence through striving and responsibility instead of assuming excellence to justify mediocrity and irresponsibility.

I know that the purpose of this already well known seminar on "Cuba in Transition" is to provide some sort of knowledgeable assistance to the *Cuba que sufre*. But I am going to propose a more challenging, and at the same time more rewarding, objective to this prosperous and successful community. Like the Argentines in the second half of the nineteenth century, the Cuban-Americans are living within the institutional framework created by the Anglo-Saxons without changing their race, their culture or even their language. And like the Argentines of that time, you are reaping the benefits of this unique environment in freedom and well-being. Like them, you are

now an example to the rest of the continent that it is possible to accept a universal civilization without relinquishing your culture as long as you respect the culture of the other without breaking the rules of the civilization.

The whole continent is in transition and it is possible that such transition will be more accelerated that the one that we may expect in Cuba. And this transition is not an economic transition but an ethical and political transition. I know that Claudio Loser is going to speak about this subject. But I insist that economic efficiency is never a sufficient argument against the utopian aspiration of socialism. As I said before, if people expect that capitalism will deliver the promises of socialism, capitalism is dead before being born.

As you know, Miami has been selected as the site for the negotiations for the ALCA (Free Trade Agreement of the Americas) for the next two years. That is a sort of recognition to the Cuban-Americans' success in converting Miami in the key to Latin America. I propose to open ASCE to the rest of the continent and to provide them with the Cuban-American experience. The Cuban-Americans are still more Cuban that American. That is, you are still Latin, but instead of Martí's experience you know the entrails, and the monster is not a monster. While we attempt this continental project of communication and sharing, we are also helping the future of Cuba: to return to the womb of a continent, in transition to the universal civilization not on account of a technological revolution, but as a result of a different conceptualization of ethics as the only support for the development of free institutions.

And to finish this already long *perorata* allow me to say something in Spanish:

Yo quiero, cuando me muera,
con Patria pero sin amo,
en la tierra que libertad me dio
haber contribuído un poco
a que otros menos afortunados
tengan mejor oportunidad que yo.

Appendix A
AUTHORS AND DISCUSSANTS

BENIGNO E. AGUIRRE is Professor of Sociology at Texas A&M University.

JOSÉ ÁLVAREZ is Professor, Food and Research Economics Department, Institute of Food and Agricultural Sciences, University of Florida, where he works as the Area Economist at the Everglades Research and Education Center, Belle Glade, Florida. He has been traveling to Cuba in the past few years as one of the principal investigators in two grants from the John D. and Catherine T. MacArthur Foundation to study Cuban agriculture and the potential economic impact on the agricultural economies of Florida and Cuba after the lifting of the U.S. economic embargo. He earned a B.A. in Economics (1971) and M.S. (1974) and Ph.D. (1977) in Food and Resource Economics all from the University of Florida.

NELSON AMARO is Dean of the Faculty of Social Sciences at the Universidad del Valle de Guatemala, Guatemala City, where he also directs the Master's Program in Development. He worked for more than ten years for United Nations agencies in El Salvador, Rome and New York and served on missions to Asia, Africa, Latin America and the mid-East. He is the author of *Descentralización y Participación Popular en Guatemala* (1990), *Guatemala: Historia Despierta* (1992) and *Descentralización, Gobierno Local y Participación Ciudadana, América Latina-Honduras* (1994) as well of numerous other professional publications.

ERIC N. BAKLANOFF is Research Professor of Economics, Emeritus, at the University of Alabama, where he also served as Dean for International Studies and Programs (1969-74). Before joining Ala-

bama, he directed Louisiana State University's Latin American Studies Institute (1965-69) and Vanderbilt's Graduate Center for Latin American Studies (1962-65). He is the author of eight books, among them *The Economic Transformation of Spain and Portugal* and *Expropriation of U.S. Investments in Cuba, Mexico and Chile*, as well as of numerous book chapters and articles in professional journals. He received his Ph.D. in Economics from the Ohio State University.

ERNESTO BETANCOURT was representative in Washington of the 26th of July Movement during the insurrection against Batista. He joined the Revolutionary Government in 1959 as Director of the Exchange Stabilization Fund at the National Bank of Cuba and was Governor for Cuba at the International Monetary Fund, positions he resigned with Che Guevara was appointed President of the National Bank. He held positions at the Organization of American States and was the first Director of the Radio Martí Program at the Voice of America. He has also been a consultant in institutional development for the World Bank, IDB and the UNDP. He is currently a senior consultant for public sector reform and Cuban affairs at DevTech Systems.

ROGER R. BETANCOURT is Professor of Economics at the University of Maryland-College Park. He has been a Visiting Professor and Scholar at the University of Washington and at INSEAD (Fountainbleau, France). He received his Ph.D. from the University of Wisconsin-Madison.

JONATHAN BENJAMIN-ALVARADO is a Senior Research Associate at the Center for International Trade and Security, University of Georgia, specializing in Latin American security and economic development issues. Since 1992, he has visited Cuba six times for field research on the nuclear energy development program and has conducted interviews with a number of senior officials in Cuba's nuclear agencies. He has published articles, monographs and commentaries on this subject in both Spanish and English in newspapers, scholarly and policy journals. He received his M.A. in International Policy Studies at the Monterey Institute of International Studies in 1993, and his Ph.D. in Political Science from the University of Georgia in 1998.

FÉLIX BLANCO GODÍNEZ is currently a law student at Case Western Reserve University, School of Law. He received a Master of Philosophy in Politics and Economics of Latin America from the University of Oxford in 1998 and also holds a BA in Political Science (Magna Cum Laude) from Drew University.

PETER G. BOURNE, M.D., M.A., is Chairman of the Board, American Association for World Health, and Vice Chancellor, St. George's University, Grenada.

MILES B. CAHILL received his Ph.D. in Economics from Purdue University in 1995, where he studied Development Economics, International Trade and Finance, Macroeconomics and Labor Economics. He received his B. S. in Economics from Binghamton University in 1991. He is currently an Assistant Professor of Economics at the College of the Holy Cross in Worcester, Massachusetts. He writes mainly in the area of Macroeconomics.

ROLANDO H. CASTAÑEDA is currently Principal Sectorial Specialist in Chile at the Inter-American Development Bank (IDB), where he has held different positions since 1974, mainly in Washington D.C. He is also actively involved in a project evaluating and reviewing sectorial programs supported by the IDB in the 1990s. Before joining the IDB he worked as Senior Economist and Unit Chief at the Organization of American States and Senior Economist at the Puerto Rican Planning Board. He has taught at the University of Puerto Rico in Rio Piedras, at Interamerican University in San Germán, and with the Rockefeller Foundation at the Universi-

ty of Cali, Colombia. He holds an M.A. and Ph.D. candidate at Yale University, concentrating in monetary policy and econometrics.

ALFRED G. CUZÁN is Professor of Political Science in the Department of Government at the University of West Florida. He received his Ph.D. from Indiana University in 1975. His published bibliography includes articles in such journals as *Public Choice, Polity, Behavioral Science, Latin American Research Review, Presidential Studies Quarterly, Western Political Quarterly, Political Research Quarterly*, and *The American Journal of Economics and Sociology*. In 1996, he received The University of West Florida Research and Creative Activities Award.

SERGIO DÍAZ-BRIQUETS is Vice President of Casals and Associates, a Washington-based consulting firm. He was research director of the Congressional Commission for the Study of International Migration and Cooperative Economic Development, and earlier held appointments with the International Development Research Centre, Population Reference Bureau, and Duquesne University. He is the author of numerous articles and books dealing with Cuba. He received his Ph.D. in Demography from the University of Pennsylvania.

JOSÉ M. HERNÁNDEZ is Professor Emeritus from Georgetown University, Washington, D.C., where he was also Associate Dean and Director of Latin American Studies. He is the author of several articles and a book on Cuban history.

ERNESTO HERNÁNDEZ-CATÁ is currently Deputy Director of the African Department, International Monetary Fund (IMF). Previously, he served as Deputy Director of the IMF's Western Hemisphere Department and of the European II Department (in charge of relations with Russia and other states of the former Soviet Union) and held other positions at the IMF and at the Board of Governors of the Federal Reserve System. He received a License from the Graduate Institute of International Studies in Geneva (1967) and M.A. (1970) and Ph.D. (1974) in economics from Yale University.

ARTIMUS KEIFFER is an Assistant Professor of Geography at Indiana University Purdue University at Indianapolis. He focuses on tourism in Cuba and teaches a class on the Geography of Cuba at his institution, where he also heads the Latin America Studies program. He has been to Cuba five times in the last three years and researches land use, architecture, historic preservation and the environmental impact of tourism. He received his Ph.D. in Human Geography from Kent State University in December 1994.

STEPHEN J. KIMMERLING is an attorney actively involved in legal issues surrounding U.S.-Cuban relations. As Cuba Conferences Director at the New York University School of Law, he organized symposia at the Law School on vanguard legal issues in U.S.-Cuban affairs. Mr. Kimmerling was also a principal international law researcher and writer for the American Association for World Health's March 1997 report, *Denial of Food and Medicine: The Impact of the U.S. Embargo on Health and Nutrition in Cuba*. Mr. Kimmerling holds a J.D. from the New York University School of Law and is a member of the New York and Florida Bars and of the Cuban-American Bar Association.

ALDO M. LEIVA is a business litigation and transactional attorney in Miami, Florida. Mr. Leiva earned his J.D. from the University of Arizona College of Law and also holds an M.S. in Biology from the University of Massachusetts, where he focused his research on environmental science and policy. Mr. Leiva has taught environmental issues in Costa Rica and in the United States and has also researched Mexican environmental law for the National Law Center for Inter-American Free Trade in Arizona.

HUGO LLORENS is Deputy Director of the Office of Economic Policy and Summit Coordination, Bureau of Inter-American Affairs, at the U.S. Department of State. He joined the Foreign Service in 1981 and has held diplomatic posts in Manila, La Paz, Asunción, San Salvador, and Tegucigalpa. Following the completion of his undergraduate studies at Georgetown University, he received an M.A. in economics from the University of Kent at Canterbury, England. He received an M.S. in National Security Studies from the National War College in 1997.

MANUEL MADRID-ARIS is Adjunct Professor, Department of Economics, at Florida International University. He is an engineer and economist. He is currently an international economic and environmental consultant specializing in Latin America. He holds a Civil Engineering Degree from Universidad Técnica Federico Santa María de Chile and M.A. in economics and Ph.D. in Political Economy and Public Policy from the University of Southern California.

WALLIE MASON, an experienced international human rights and immigration attorney, has handled several high-profile human rights cases arising out of Central America. She was one of the first lawyers to raise the U.S.-Cuban embargo as a human rights issue before the Inter-American Commission on Human Rights. Ms. Mason was also an originator of the idea behind the American Association for World Health's report, *Denial of Food and Medicine: The Impact of the U.S. Embargo on Health and Nutrition in Cuba*, a project to which she contributed leading research and writing on the embargo's international law aspects.

HIPÓLITO MEJÍA DOMÍNGUEZ is an agricultural engineer, businessman and politician. He served as Secretary of Agriculture of the Dominican Republic during 1978-82. He is currently a pre-candidate for the Presidency of the Dominican Republic for the Partido Revolucionario Dominicano (PRD).

CARMELO MESA-LAGO is Distinguished Service Professor of Economics and Latin American Studies at the University of Pittsburgh. He is the author of numerous books and articles on different aspects of the Cuban economy and on social security issues, among others. His most recent books include *Breve historia económica de la Cuba socialista* (Madrid: Alianza Editorial, 1994) and *Are Economic Reforms Propelling Cuba to the Market?* (Coral Gables: North-South Center, University of Miami, 1995).

ROBERTO ORRO FERNÁNDEZ is a Lecturer-Researcher at the Escuela de Economía, Universidad de Guanajuato, Mexico, a position he has held since 1995. He held a similar position at the Facultad de Economía, Universidad de la Habana, from 1989 to 1993. He received a Master's Degree in Economics from El Colegio de México in 1995 and a degree in economic planning from the Universidad de la Habana in 1986.

SILVIA PEDRAZA is Associate Professor of Sociology at the University of Michigan. She is the author of *Political and Economic Migrants in America: Cubans and Mexicans* (University of Texas Press, 1985) and co-editor with Rubén Rumbaut of *Origins and Destinations: Immigration, Race and Ethnicity in America* (Wadsworth, 1995).

LORENZO L. PÉREZ is Assistant Director of the Fiscal Affairs Department, International Monetary Fund (IMF). Previously, he served in the IMF's Western Hemisphere, Exchange and Trade Relations, and European Departments, and held positions at the U.S. Department of the Treasury and the U.S. Agency for International Development. He received a Ph.D. in economics from the University of Pennsylvania.

JORGE F. PÉREZ-LÓPEZ is an international economist with the Bureau of International Labor Affairs, U.S. Department of Labor. He is the author of *Cuba's Second Economy: From Behind the Scenes to Center Stage* (Transaction Publishers, 1995) and co-editor of *Perspectives on Cuban Economic Reforms* (Arizona State University Center for Latin American Studies Press, 1998). He received his Ph.D. in economics from the State University of New York at Albany.

JOSEPH M. PERRY is Professor of Economics and Chairperson of the Department of Economics and Geography at the University of North Florida, where he has been a faculty member since 1971. He was previously a member of the economics faculty of the University of Florida. Dr. Perry received his Ph. D in Economics from Northwestern University in 1966, after completing undergraduate studies at Emory University and Georgia State University. His recent research has focused on regional economic development, with specific reference to Central American and Caribbean nations, and their trade relationships with the United States.

CARLOS N. QUIJANO is an economic consultant and visiting professor at the Instituto Universitario

Ortega y Gasset in Madrid. He was formerly Senior Advisor to the World Bank.

ARNALDO RAMOS LAUZURIQUE received a Licenciatura in economics from the Universidad de la Habana. He worked at the Ministry of Foreign Trade for 7 years, the Central Planning Board (JUCEPLAN) for 15 years, and the State Committee on Prices. In 1993 he resigned his government position and joined the dissident movement. He has been unemployed since then.

MARIO A. RIVERA is Associate Professor of Public Administration at the University of New Mexico. A consultant and trainer in program evaluation, organizational restructuring, and management systems, he has worked in international projects in Costa Rica, Equatorial Guinea, Mexico and Peru.

JORGE LUIS ROMEU is an Associate Professor of Statistics and Computers with the Department of Mathematics at the State University of New York (SUNY) at Cortland, and a consultant in statistics, operations research and international education. Romeu, who won the 1997 Saaty Award for best applied statistics paper published in the *American Journal of Mathematical and Management Sciences*, has over twenty publications in refereed journals and proceedings. He has taught or consulted at universities in the United States, Mexico, Argentina, Venezuela and Spain and was a Fulbright Senior Lecturer in Mexico in 1994. Romeu will retire from SUNY in December of 1998, after 14 years of teaching, and has accepted a position as Senior Engineer with the Engineering and Business Division of IIT Research Institute, in Rome, NY. He is a Chartered Statistician Fellow of the Royal Statistical Society and member of ASA and INFORMS.

DIEGO R. ROQUÉ is currently Adjunct Professor of Mathematics at Barry University in Miami Springs, Florida. He was Senior Defense Analyst with the U.S. Army Concepts Analysis Agency (1987-94), an Assistant Professor of Operations Research at George Mason University (1982-87), and a Junior Defense Analyst with the Center for Naval Analysis (1974-77). He earned a Doctorate of Science degree from George Washington University, a

Master of Science from the University of California, Berkeley, and a Bachelor of Science in Industrial and Systems Engineering from the University of Miami, Florida.

JOSE MARÍA RUISÁNCHEZ is a consultant on project finance based in Falls Church, Virginia. He is a former Vice President of the IFC (World Bank Group) and a graduate of Georgetown University and the Massachusetts Institute of Technology

JULIA SAGEBIEN is an Associate Professor at the School of Business Administration and an Adjunct Professor in the International Development Studies program at Dalhousie University in Halifax, Nova Scotia, Canada. Her areas of expertise are marketing strategy, international trade and economic policy development. Her articles have appeared in journals such as *Business Quarterly*, *Cuban Studies*, the *International Journal of PublicAdministration* and the *Canadian Journal of Administrative Sciences*. She was selected as "Commerce Professor of the Year" at Saint Mary's University in 1989/1990 and in 1993/1994. Her corporate and consulting experience includes assignments for Fidelity Investments (Boston), Lotus Development Corporation (Cambridge) and Industry Canada (Halifax). She is the Manager of Special Projects for DRM Equities and Advisory, a consulting and investment firm (Halifax). She holds a B.A. (Hampshire College), an M.B.A. (Simmons College Graduate School of Management) and a Ph.D. in Economics/Regional Planning (London School of Economics).

NICOLAS SÁNCHEZ is currently Associate Professor of Economics at the College of the Holy Cross in Worcester, Massachusetts. He received his Ph.D. from the University of Southern California in 1972. His specialties are Property Rights Analysis and Development Economics. His writings have appeared in *The Review of Economics and Statistics*, *Economic Development and Cultural Change*, *Explorations in Economic History*, *American Journal of Agricultural Economics*, *Weltwirtschaftliches Archiv*, and many other journals and books. He has been elected to public office at the local level, enjoys writing popular articles for the local press, and has also lectured in Mexico, Spain and Puerto Rico.

MANUEL SÁNCHEZ HERRERO received Licenciaturas in economics, economic control and accounting from the Universidad de la Habana. He is also a painter and calligrapher. He worked for the Central Planning Board (JUCEPLAN) as an auditor in the area of agriculture and as a specialist in transportation. He was jailed in 1985 for producing political materials and fired from his job. Currently in ill health, he has been unemployed and a member of the dissident movement since 1985.

JORGE A. SANGUINETTY is founder and President of DevTech Systems, Inc. a Washington, D.C.-based international and domestic economic consulting firm. He holds a Ph.D. in economics from City University of New York and has worked as a planner, researcher or teacher of economics at the Central Planning Board and the Ministry of the Sugar Industry in Cuba, and after migrating to the U.S. in 1967, Merrill Lynch, National Bureau of Economic Research, Yale University, Brookings Institution, United Nations, and American University.

CARLOS SEIGLIE is a Professor of Economics at Rutgers University, Newark, New Jersey.

STEPHEN L. SHAPIRO is Professor of Economics at the University of North Florida, where he has been a faculty member since 1972. Dr. Shapiro received his Ph. D. Degree in Economics from the University of South Carolina in 1972, after prior graduate study at the University of Utah. He has published extensively on the impact of state lotteries on education and taxes. His most recent research has been focussed on regional economic development.

KIRBY SMITH is a U.S. government economist whose recent responsibilities at the State Department's Bureau of Inter-American Affairs, Office of Economic Policy and Summit Coordination, included regional services trade, such as aviation and telecommunications, and various other trade and financial issues. Currently, he is completing his graduate studies in economics at George Mason University. He received a B.S. degree in economics from Louisiana State University in 1989.

MAURICIO SOLAUN is a Professor of Latin American social and political institutions at the University of Illinois. He served as U.S. Ambassador to Nicaragua from September 1977 to February 1979, the first Cuban-American to serve as U.S Ambassador. Among his published books are *Sinners and Heretics: The Politics of Military Intervention Latin America*, *Discrimination with Violence: Miscegenation and Racial Conflict in Latin America* and *Politics of Compromise: Coalition Government in Colombia*. He holds degrees in law, economics and sociology from the Universidad de Villanueva, Cuba, Yale University and the University of Chicago, respectively.

JEFFREY W. STEAGALL is Associate Professor of Economics and Director of the International Studies in Business Program at the University of North Florida. Dr. Steagall received his Ph. D. in Economics from the University of Wisconsin at Madison in 1990. His undergraduate studies were completed at St. Norbert College. Dr. Steagall is an international trade and finance specialist, with a particular interest in the trade relationships of developing countries.

DEMETRIA TSOUTOURAS holds an MBA degree with a concentration in International Development Management from St. Mary's University in Nova Scotia, Canada. The subject of her graduate thesis was Mexican-Cuban commercial relations, which she researched while working at the Canadian Embassy in Mexico City in 1997-98. Ms. Tsoutouras also holds a BSc degree, with a major in Biochemistry from Carleton University in Ottawa. She currently works in the area of export development at DayLight Technologies in Halifax, Nova Scotia.

SARAH K. WAGNER, is a Junior Analyst for Geographic Information at the POLIS Center. She is interested in historical perceptions and education and is starting graduate school majoring in Public History. She has a degree in History from Indiana University.

LOUIS A. WOODS is Professor of Geography and Economics at the University of North Florida, where he has been a faculty member since 1972. Dr. Woods received his Ph. D. in Geography from the University of North Carolina at Chapel Hill in 1972, after completing undergraduate studies in Geography at Jacksonville University. He completed postgraduate work in Economics at East Carolina University. His recent research has focussed on the determinants of regional economic development, and the constraints imposed by environmental concerns.

Appendix B
ACKNOWLEDGEMENTS

We want to take this opportunity to acknowledge the continued financial support provided to ASCE's activities by the following sponsoring members.

Acosta, José D.	OAS Retired
Alonso, José F.	USIA Retired
Amaro, Nelson R.	Universidad del Valle de Guatemala
Asón, Elías R.	
Batista-Falla, Víctor	
Betancourt, Ernesto	DevTech Systems
Betancourt, Roger	University of Maryland
Cisneros, Frank G.	
Costales, René	Interamerican Development Bank
Crespo, Nicolás	Cuban Society of Tourism Professionals
Crews, Eduardo T.	Bristol-Myers Squibb
Díaz, Manuel G.	Republic International Bank of New York
Domíguez, Julio P.	Great Eastern Bank
Falk, Pamela	CUNY School of Law
Fernández, Carlos J.	KPMG
Fernández, Matías A..	Caribbean Roofing Consultants
Fernández-Morrell, Andrés	Popular Leasing and Rental
García-Aguilera Hamshaw, Carolina	C&J Investigations
Gayoso, Antonio	World Council of Credit Unions
Hernández-Catá, Ernesto	International Monetary Fund
Lima, José E.	IPS Consultants
Linde, Armando	International Monetary Fund
Locay, Luis	University of Miami
López, Roberto I.	
Laredo, Jorge	
Luis, Luis R.	
Luzárraga, Alberto	
Miranda, José E. ('Gene')	Kelly Tractor Co.
O'Connell, Richard	
Padial, Carlos M.	
Pérez, Lorenzo	International Monetary Fund
Pérez-López, Jorge	U.S. Department of Labor

Perry, Joseph M.	University of North Florida
Pinón, Jorge R.	
Quijano, Carlos N.	
Reich, Ambassador Otto J.	
Roca, Rubén	
Rodríguez, José Luis	Trans-Tech-Ag Corporation
Sánchez, Federico F.	Interlink Group
Sánchez, Nicolás	College of the Holy Cross
Seiglie, Carlos	Rutgers University
Vallejo, Jorge I.	
Villalón, Manuel F.	
Werlau Cañizares, María	Orbis International

ASCE also gratefully acknowledges the generous contribution of the following corporate sponsors of the Eighth Annual Meeting and volume 8 of *Cuba in Transition*:

University of Miami School of International Studies

University of Miami School of Business Administration

Citibank Florida
U.S. Investment Corporation
Casals & Associates
Shaw, Pittman, Potts & Trowbridge